America's Top-Rated Cities: A Statistical Handbook

Volume 1

2023
Thirtieth Edition

America's
Top-Rated Cities:
A Statistical Handbook

Volume 1: Southern Region

Cover image: Charleston, South Carolina

PUBLISHER: Leslie Mackenzie
EDITORIAL DIRECTOR: Stuart Paterson
SENIOR EDITOR: David Garoogian

RESEARCHER & WRITER: Jael Bridgemahon; Laura Mars
MARKETING DIRECTOR: Jessica Moody

Grey House Publishing, Inc.
4919 Route 22
Amenia, NY 12501
518.789.8700 • Fax 845.373.6390
www.greyhouse.com
books@greyhouse.com

While every effort has been made to ensure the reliability of the information presented in this publication, Grey House Publishing neither guarantees the accuracy of the data contained herein nor assumes any responsibility for errors, omissions or discrepancies. Grey House accepts no payment for listing; inclusion in the publication of any organization, agency, institution, publication, service or individual does not imply endorsement of the editors or publisher.

Errors brought to the attention of the publisher and verified to the satisfaction of the publisher will be corrected in future editions.

Except by express prior written permission of the Copyright Proprietor no part of this work may be copied by any means of publication or communication now known or developed hereafter including, but not limited to, use in any directory or compilation or other print publication, in any information storage and retrieval system, in any other electronic device, or in any visual or audio-visual device or product.

This publication is an original and creative work, copyrighted by Grey House Publishing, Inc. and is fully protected by all applicable copyright laws, as well as by laws covering misappropriation, trade secrets and unfair competition.

Grey House has added value to the underlying factual material through one or more of the following efforts: unique and original selection; expression; arrangement; coordination; and classification.

Grey House Publishing, Inc. will defend its rights in this publication.

Copyright © 2023 Grey House Publishing, Inc.
All rights reserved

Thirtieth Edition
Printed in the U.S.A.

Publisher's Cataloging-in-Publication Data
(Prepared by The Donohue Group, Inc.)

America's top-rated cities. Vol. 1, Southern region : a statistical handbook. — 1992-

   v. : ill. ; cm.
   Annual, 1995-
   Irregular, 1992-1993
   ISSN: 1082-7102

1. Cities and towns—Ratings—Southern States—Statistics—Periodicals. 2. Cities and towns—Southern States—Statistics— Periodicals. 3. Social indicators—Southern States—Periodicals. 4. Quality of life—Southern States—Statistics—Periodicals. 5. Southern States—Social conditions—Statistics—Periodicals. I. Title: America's top rated cities. II. Title: Southern region

HT123.5.S6 A44
307.76/0973/05   95644648

4-Volume Set	ISBN: 978-1-63700-534-7
Volume 1	**ISBN: 978-1-63700-536-1**
Volume 2	ISBN: 978-1-63700-537-8
Volume 3	ISBN: 978-1-63700-538-5
Volume 4	ISBN: 978-1-63700-539-2

Table of Contents

Athens, Georgia

Background	1
Rankings	2
Business Environment	3
Demographics	3
Economy	5
Income	5
Employment	6
City Finances	8
Taxes	8
Transportation	9
Businesses	10
Living Environment	11
Cost of Living	11
Housing	11
Health	13
Education	14
Employers	16
Public Safety	16
Politics	17
Sports	17
Climate	17
Hazardous Waste	17
Air Quality	17

Atlanta, Georgia

Background	19
Rankings	20
Business Environment	24
Demographics	24
Economy	26
Income	26
Employment	27
City Finances	29
Taxes	29
Transportation	30
Businesses	31
Living Environment	33
Cost of Living	33
Housing	33
Health	35
Education	37
Employers	38
Public Safety	39
Politics	40
Sports	40
Climate	40
Hazardous Waste	40
Air Quality	41

Austin, Texas

Background	43
Rankings	44
Business Environment	48
Demographics	48
Economy	50
Income	50
Employment	51
City Finances	53
Taxes	53
Transportation	54
Businesses	55
Living Environment	56
Cost of Living	56
Housing	56
Health	58
Education	60
Employers	62
Public Safety	63
Politics	63
Sports	63
Climate	63
Hazardous Waste	64
Air Quality	64

Brownsville, Texas

Background	67
Rankings	68
Business Environment	70
Demographics	70
Economy	72
Income	72
Employment	73
City Finances	75
Taxes	75
Transportation	76
Businesses	77
Living Environment	78
Cost of Living	78
Housing	78
Health	80
Education	81
Employers	83
Public Safety	83
Politics	83
Sports	84
Climate	84
Hazardous Waste	84
Air Quality	84

Cape Coral, Florida

Background 87
Rankings 88
Business Environment 90
   Demographics 90
   Economy 92
   Income 92
   Employment 93
   City Finances 95
   Taxes 95
   Transportation 96
   Businesses 97
Living Environment 98
   Cost of Living 98
   Housing 98
   Health 100
   Education 101
   Employers 102
   Public Safety 103
   Politics 103
   Sports 103
   Climate 103
   Hazardous Waste 104
   Air Quality 104

Charleston, South Carolina

Background 107
Rankings 108
Business Environment 111
   Demographics 111
   Economy 113
   Income 113
   Employment 114
   City Finances 116
   Taxes 116
   Transportation 117
   Businesses 118
Living Environment 119
   Cost of Living 119
   Housing 119
   Health 121
   Education 123
   Employers 124
   Public Safety 124
   Politics 125
   Sports 125
   Climate 125
   Hazardous Waste 125
   Air Quality 125

Clarksville, Tennessee

Background 127
Rankings 128
Business Environment 129
   Demographics 129
   Economy 131
   Income 131
   Employment 132
   City Finances 134
   Taxes 134
   Transportation 135
   Businesses 136
Living Environment 137
   Cost of Living 137
   Housing 137
   Health 139
   Education 140
   Employers 141
   Public Safety 142
   Politics 142
   Sports 142
   Climate 142
   Hazardous Waste 143
   Air Quality 143

College Station, Texas

Background 145
Rankings 146
Business Environment 147
   Demographics 147
   Economy 149
   Income 149
   Employment 150
   City Finances 152
   Taxes 152
   Transportation 153
   Businesses 154
Living Environment 155
   Cost of Living 155
   Housing 155
   Health 157
   Education 158
   Employers 160
   Public Safety 160
   Politics 160
   Sports 161
   Climate 161
   Hazardous Waste 161
   Air Quality 161

Columbia, South Carolina

Background 163
Rankings 164
Business Environment 166
   Demographics 166
   Economy 168
   Income 168
   Employment 169
   City Finances 171
   Taxes 171
   Transportation 172
   Businesses 173
Living Environment 174
   Cost of Living 174
   Housing 174
   Health 176
   Education 178
   Employers 179
   Public Safety 179
   Politics 180
   Sports 180
   Climate 180
   Hazardous Waste 180
   Air Quality 181

Dallas, Texas

Background 183
Rankings 184
Business Environment 187
   Demographics 187
   Economy 189
   Income 189
   Employment 190
   City Finances 192
   Taxes 192
   Transportation 193
   Businesses 194
Living Environment 196
   Cost of Living 196
   Housing 196
   Health 198
   Education 200
   Employers 201
   Public Safety 202
   Politics 203
   Sports 203
   Climate 203
   Hazardous Waste 204
   Air Quality 204

El Paso, Texas

Background 207
Rankings 208
Business Environment 211
   Demographics 211
   Economy 213
   Income 213
   Employment 214
   City Finances 216
   Taxes 216
   Transportation 217
   Businesses 218
Living Environment 219
   Cost of Living 219
   Housing 219
   Health 221
   Education 223
   Employers 224
   Public Safety 224
   Politics 225
   Sports 225
   Climate 225
   Hazardous Waste 225
   Air Quality 225

Fort Worth, Texas

Background 227
Rankings 228
Business Environment 232
   Demographics 232
   Economy 234
   Income 234
   Employment 235
   City Finances 237
   Taxes 237
   Transportation 238
   Businesses 239
Living Environment 240
   Cost of Living 240
   Housing 240
   Health 242
   Education 244
   Employers 245
   Public Safety 245
   Politics 246
   Sports 246
   Climate 246
   Hazardous Waste 246
   Air Quality 247

viii Table of Contents

Houston, Texas

Background 249
Rankings 250
Business Environment 254
    Demographics 254
    Economy 256
    Income 256
    Employment 257
    City Finances 259
    Taxes 259
    Transportation 260
    Businesses 261
Living Environment 263
    Cost of Living 263
    Housing 263
    Health 265
    Education 267
    Employers 269
    Public Safety 270
    Politics 270
    Sports 270
    Climate 271
    Hazardous Waste 271
    Air Quality 271

Huntsville, Alabama

Background 273
Rankings 274
Business Environment 276
    Demographics 276
    Economy 278
    Income 278
    Employment 279
    City Finances 281
    Taxes 281
    Transportation 282
    Businesses 283
Living Environment 284
    Cost of Living 284
    Housing 284
    Health 286
    Education 287
    Employers 288
    Public Safety 289
    Politics 289
    Sports 289
    Climate 289
    Hazardous Waste 290
    Air Quality 290

Jacksonville, Florida

Background 293
Rankings 294
Business Environment 297
    Demographics 297
    Economy 299
    Income 299
    Employment 300
    City Finances 302
    Taxes 302
    Transportation 303
    Businesses 304
Living Environment 305
    Cost of Living 305
    Housing 305
    Health 307
    Education 309
    Employers 310
    Public Safety 310
    Politics 311
    Sports 311
    Climate 311
    Hazardous Waste 311
    Air Quality 312

Lafayette, Louisiana

Background 315
Rankings 316
Business Environment 317
    Demographics 317
    Economy 319
    Income 319
    Employment 320
    City Finances 322
    Taxes 322
    Transportation 323
    Businesses 324
Living Environment 325
    Cost of Living 325
    Housing 325
    Health 327
    Education 328
    Employers 330
    Public Safety 330
    Politics 331
    Sports 331
    Climate 331
    Hazardous Waste 331
    Air Quality 331

Miami, Florida

Background.................................. 333
Rankings.................................... 334
Business Environment....................... 338
   Demographics............................... 338
   Economy.................................... 340
   Income..................................... 340
   Employment................................. 341
   City Finances.............................. 343
   Taxes...................................... 343
   Transportation............................. 344
   Businesses................................. 345
Living Environment......................... 347
   Cost of Living............................. 347
   Housing.................................... 347
   Health..................................... 349
   Education.................................. 351
   Employers.................................. 352
   Public Safety.............................. 353
   Politics................................... 353
   Sports..................................... 353
   Climate.................................... 354
   Hazardous Waste............................ 354
   Air Quality................................ 354

Midland, Texas

Background.................................. 357
Rankings.................................... 358
Business Environment....................... 359
   Demographics............................... 359
   Economy.................................... 361
   Income..................................... 361
   Employment................................. 362
   City Finances.............................. 364
   Taxes...................................... 364
   Transportation............................. 365
   Businesses................................. 366
Living Environment......................... 367
   Cost of Living............................. 367
   Housing.................................... 367
   Health..................................... 369
   Education.................................. 370
   Employers.................................. 372
   Public Safety.............................. 372
   Politics................................... 373
   Sports..................................... 373
   Climate.................................... 373
   Hazardous Waste............................ 373
   Air Quality................................ 373

Nashville, Tennessee

Background.................................. 375
Rankings.................................... 376
Business Environment....................... 380
   Demographics............................... 380
   Economy.................................... 382
   Income..................................... 382
   Employment................................. 383
   City Finances.............................. 385
   Taxes...................................... 385
   Transportation............................. 386
   Businesses................................. 387
Living Environment......................... 388
   Cost of Living............................. 388
   Housing.................................... 388
   Health..................................... 390
   Education.................................. 392
   Employers.................................. 393
   Public Safety.............................. 394
   Politics................................... 395
   Sports..................................... 395
   Climate.................................... 395
   Hazardous Waste............................ 395
   Air Quality................................ 395

New Orleans, Louisiana

Background.................................. 397
Rankings.................................... 398
Business Environment....................... 402
   Demographics............................... 402
   Economy.................................... 404
   Income..................................... 404
   Employment................................. 405
   City Finances.............................. 407
   Taxes...................................... 407
   Transportation............................. 408
   Businesses................................. 409
Living Environment......................... 410
   Cost of Living............................. 410
   Housing.................................... 410
   Health..................................... 412
   Education.................................. 414
   Employers.................................. 415
   Public Safety.............................. 415
   Politics................................... 416
   Sports..................................... 416
   Climate.................................... 416
   Hazardous Waste............................ 417
   Air Quality................................ 417

Table of Contents

Orlando, Florida

Background 419
Rankings 420
Business Environment 424
   Demographics 424
   Economy 426
   Income 426
   Employment 427
   City Finances 429
   Taxes 429
   Transportation 430
   Businesses 431
Living Environment 432
   Cost of Living 432
   Housing 432
   Health 434
   Education 436
   Employers 437
   Public Safety 437
   Politics 438
   Sports 438
   Climate 438
   Hazardous Waste 438
   Air Quality 439

San Antonio, Texas

Background 441
Rankings 442
Business Environment 446
   Demographics 446
   Economy 448
   Income 448
   Employment 449
   City Finances 451
   Taxes 451
   Transportation 452
   Businesses 453
Living Environment 454
   Cost of Living 454
   Housing 454
   Health 456
   Education 458
   Employers 459
   Public Safety 460
   Politics 460
   Sports 460
   Climate 460
   Hazardous Waste 461
   Air Quality 461

Savannah, Georgia

Background 463
Rankings 464
Business Environment 466
   Demographics 466
   Economy 468
   Income 468
   Employment 469
   City Finances 471
   Taxes 471
   Transportation 472
   Businesses 473
Living Environment 474
   Cost of Living 474
   Housing 474
   Health 476
   Education 477
   Employers 479
   Public Safety 479
   Politics 480
   Sports 480
   Climate 480
   Hazardous Waste 480
   Air Quality 480

Tampa, Florida

Background 483
Rankings 484
Business Environment 488
   Demographics 488
   Economy 490
   Income 490
   Employment 491
   City Finances 493
   Taxes 493
   Transportation 494
   Businesses 495
Living Environment 496
   Cost of Living 496
   Housing 496
   Health 498
   Education 500
   Employers 501
   Public Safety 501
   Politics 502
   Sports 502
   Climate 502
   Hazardous Waste 503
   Air Quality 503

Tuscaloosa, Alabama

Background 505
Rankings 506
Business Environment 507
   Demographics 507
   Economy 509
   Income 509
   Employment 510
   City Finances 512
   Taxes 512
   Transportation 513
   Businesses 514
Living Environment 515
   Cost of Living 515
   Housing 515
   Health 517
   Education 518
   Employers 520
   Public Safety 520
   Politics 520
   Sports 520
   Climate 521
   Hazardous Waste 521
   Air Quality 521

Appendixes

Appendix A: Comparative Statistics A-3
Appendix B: Metropolitan Area Definitions A-175
Appendix C: Government Type & Primary County .. A-179
Appendix D: Chambers of Commerce A-181
Appendix E: State Departments of Labor A-187

Introduction

This thirtieth edition of *America's Top-Rated Cities* is a concise, statistical, 4-volume work identifying America's top-rated cities with estimated populations of approximately 100,000 or more. It profiles 100 cities that have received high marks for business and living from prominent sources such as *Forbes, Fortune, U.S. News & World Report, The Brookings Institution, U.S. Conference of Mayors, The Wall Street Journal,* and *CNNMoney.*

Each volume covers a different region of the country—Southern, Western, Central, Eastern—and includes a detailed Table of Contents, City Chapters, Appendices, and Maps. Each city chapter incorporates information from hundreds of resources to create the following major sections:
- **Background**—lively narrative of significant, up-to-date news for both businesses and residents. These combine historical facts with current developments, "known-for" annual events, and climate data.
- **Rankings**—fun-to-read, bulleted survey results from over 221 books, magazines, and online articles, ranging from general (Great Places to Live), to specific (Friendliest Cities), and everything in between.
- **Statistical Tables**—88 tables and detailed topics that offer an unparalleled view of each city's Business and Living Environments. They are carefully organized with data that is easy to read and understand.
- **Appendices**—five in all, appearing at the end of each volume. These range from listings of Metropolitan Statistical Areas to Comparative Statistics for all 100 cities.

This new edition of *America's Top-Rated Cities* includes cities that not only surveyed well, but ranked highest using our unique weighting system. We looked at violent crime, property crime, population growth, median household income, housing affordability, poverty, educational attainment, and unemployment. You'll find that we have included several American cities despite less-than-stellar numbers. New York, Los Angeles, and Miami remain world-class cities despite challenges faced by many large urban centers. Part of the criteria, in most cases, is that it be the "primary" city in a given metropolitan area. For example, if the metro area is Raleigh-Cary, NC, we would consider Raleigh, not Cary. This allows for a more equitable core city comparison. In general, the core city of a metro area is defined as having substantial influence on neighboring cities. A final consideration is location—we strive to include as many states in the country as possible.

New to this edition are:
Volume 1 - Brownsville, TX
Volume 2 - Greeley, CO; Salem, OR
Volume 4 - Greensboro, NC; Worcester, MA

Praise for previous editions:

> "...[ATRC] has...proven its worth to a wide audience...from businesspeople and corporations planning to launch, relocate, or expand their operations to market researchers, real estate professionals, urban planners, job-seekers, students...interested in...reliable, attractively presented statistical information about larger U.S. cities."
> —ARBA

> "...For individuals or businesses looking to relocate, this resource conveniently reports rankings from more than 300 sources for the top 100 US cities. Recommended..."
> —Choice

> "...While patrons are becoming increasingly comfortable locating statistical data online, there is still something to be said for the ease associated with such a compendium of otherwise scattered data. A well-organized and appropriate update...
> —Library Journal

BACKGROUND
Each city begins with an informative Background that combines history with current events. These narratives often reflect changes that have occurred during the past year, and touch on the city's environment, politics, employment, cultural offerings, and climate, and include interesting trivia. For example: Peregrine Falcons were rehabilitated and released into the wild from Boise City's World Center for Birds of Prey; Grand Rapids was the first city to introduce fluoride into its drinking water in 1945; and Thomas Alva Edison discovered the phonograph and the light bulb in the city whose name was changed in 1954 from Raritan Township to Edison in his honor.

RANKINGS

This section has rankings from a possible 221 books, articles, and reports. For easy reference, these Rankings are categorized into 16 topics including Business/Finance, Dating/Romance, and Health/Fitness.

The Rankings are presented in an easy-to-read, bulleted format and include results from both annual surveys and one-shot studies. **Fastest-Growing Economies** . . . **Best Drivers** . . . **Most Well-Read** . . . **Most Wired** . . . **Healthiest for Women** . . . **Best for Minority Entrepreneurs** . . . **Safest** . . . **Best to Retire** . . . **Most Polite** . . . **Best for Moviemakers** . . . **Most Frugal** . . . **Best for Bikes** . . . **Most Cultured** . . . **Least Stressful** . . . **Best for Families** . . . **Most Romantic** . . . **Most Charitable** . . . **Best for Telecommuters** . . . **Best for Singles** . . . **Nerdiest** . . . **Fittest** . . . **Best for Dogs** . . . **Most Tattooed** . . . **Best for Wheelchair Users**, and more.

Sources for these Rankings include both well-known magazines and other media, including *Forbes, Fortune, USA Today, Condé Nast Traveler, Gallup, Kiplinger's Personal Finance, Men's Journal,* and *Travel + Leisure,* as well as *Asthma & Allergy Foundation of America, American Lung Association, League of American Bicyclists, The Advocate, National Civic League, National Alliance to End Homelessness, MovieMaker Magazine, National Insurance Crime Bureau, Center for Digital Government, National Association of Home Builders,* and *Milken Institute.*

Rankings cover a variety of geographic areas; see Appendix B for full geographic definitions.

STATISTICAL TABLES

Each city chapter includes 88 tables and detailed topics—45 in Business and 43 in Living. Over 90% of statistical data has been updated. This edition also includes newly released data from the 2020 Census. A new table on household relationships has also be added, which includes information on same-sex spouses and unmarried partners.

Business Environment includes hard facts and figures on 8 major categories, including Demographics, Income, Economy, Employment, and Taxes. *Living Environment* includes 11 major categories, such as Cost of Living, Housing, Health, Education, Safety, and Climate.

To compile the Statistical Tables, editors have again turned to a wide range of sources, some well known, such as the *U.S. Census Bureau, U.S. Environmental Protection Agency, Bureau of Labor Statistics, Centers for Disease Control and Prevention,* and the *Federal Bureau of Investigation*, plus others like *The Council for Community and Economic Research, Texas A&M Transportation Institute,* and *Federation of Tax Administrators.*

APPENDIXES: Data for all cities appear in all volumes.
- **Appendix A**—*Comparative Statistics*
- **Appendix B**—*Metropolitan Area Definitions*
- **Appendix C**—*Government Type and County*
- **Appendix D**—*Chambers of Commerce and Economic Development Organizations*
- **Appendix E**—*State Departments of Labor and Employment*

Material provided by public and private agencies and organizations was supplemented by original research, numerous library sources and Internet sites. *America's Top-Rated Cities, 2023,* is designed for a wide range of readers: private individuals considering relocating a residence or business; professionals considering expanding their businesses or changing careers; corporations considering relocating, opening up additional offices or creating new divisions; government agencies; general and market researchers; real estate consultants; human resource personnel; urban planners; investors; and urban government students.

Customers who purchase the four-volume set receive free online access to *America's Top-Rated Cities* allowing them to download city reports and sort and rank by 50-plus data points.

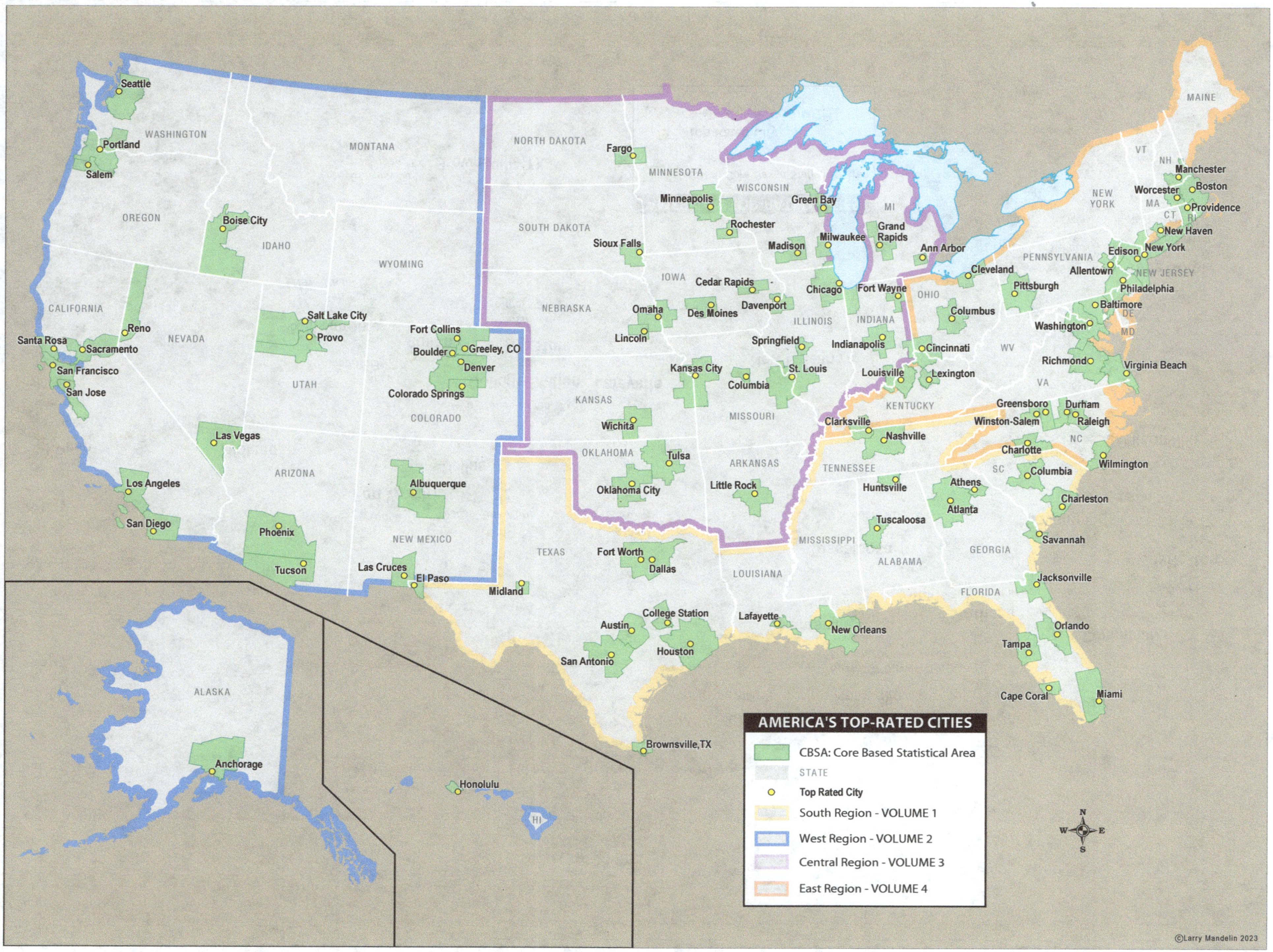

AMERICA'S TOP-RATED CITIES
CBSA: Core Based Statistical Area
STATE
Top Rated City
South Region - VOLUME 1
West Region - VOLUME 2
Central Region - VOLUME 3
East Region - VOLUME 4
WASHINGTON
OREGON
CALIFORNIA
NEVADA
IDAHO
MONTANA
WYOMING
UTAH
ARIZONA
COLORADO
NEW MEXICO
NORTH DAKOTA
SOUTH DAKOTA
NEBRASKA
KANSAS
OKLAHOMA
TEXAS
MINNESOTA
IOWA
MISSOURI
ARKANSAS
LOUISIANA
WISCONSIN
ILLINOIS
MI
INDIANA
OHIO
KENTUCKY
TENNESSEE
MISSISSIPPI
ALABAMA
GEORGIA
FLORIDA
SC
NC
VA
WV
MD
DE
PENNSYLVANIA
NEW JERSEY
NEW YORK
VT
NH
MA
CT
RI
MAINE
ALASKA
HI
Seattle
Portland
Salem
Boise City
Reno
Santa Rosa
Sacramento
San Francisco
San Jose
Los Angeles
San Diego
Las Vegas
Phoenix
Tucson
Salt Lake City
Provo
Fort Collins
Boulder
Greeley, CO
Denver
Colorado Springs
Albuquerque
Las Cruces
El Paso
Midland
Fargo
Minneapolis
Rochester
Sioux Falls
Omaha
Lincoln
Des Moines
Cedar Rapids
Davenport
Madison
Green Bay
Milwaukee
Chicago
Grand Rapids
Ann Arbor
Fort Wayne
Springfield
Indianapolis
Kansas City
Columbia
St. Louis
Wichita
Tulsa
Oklahoma City
Little Rock
Fort Worth
Dallas
College Station
Austin
San Antonio
Houston
Brownsville,TX
Lafayette
New Orleans
Louisville
Lexington
Cincinnati
Columbus
Cleveland
Pittsburgh
Clarksville
Nashville
Huntsville
Tuscaloosa
Athens
Atlanta
Savannah
Jacksonville
Orlando
Tampa
Cape Coral
Miami
Charleston
Columbia
Charlotte
Greensboro
Winston-Salem
Durham
Raleigh
Wilmington
Richmond
Virginia Beach
Washington
Baltimore
Philadelphia
Allentown
Edison
New York
New Haven
Providence
Boston
Worcester
Manchester
Anchorage
Honolulu
N
S
E
W
©Larry Mandelin 2023

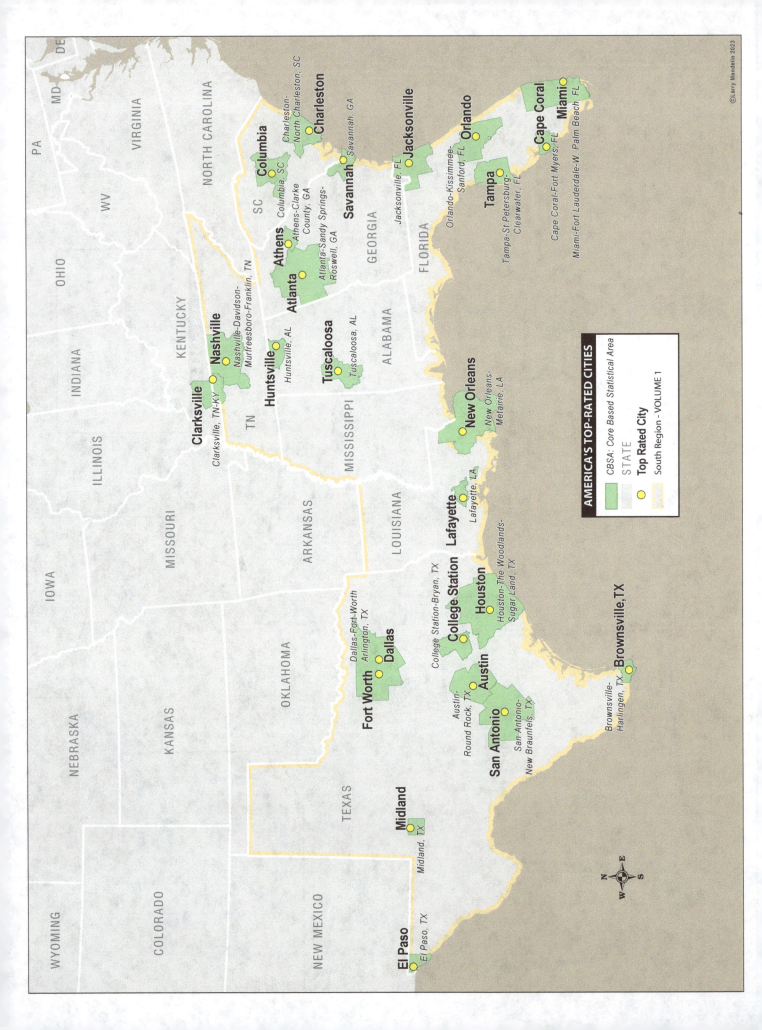

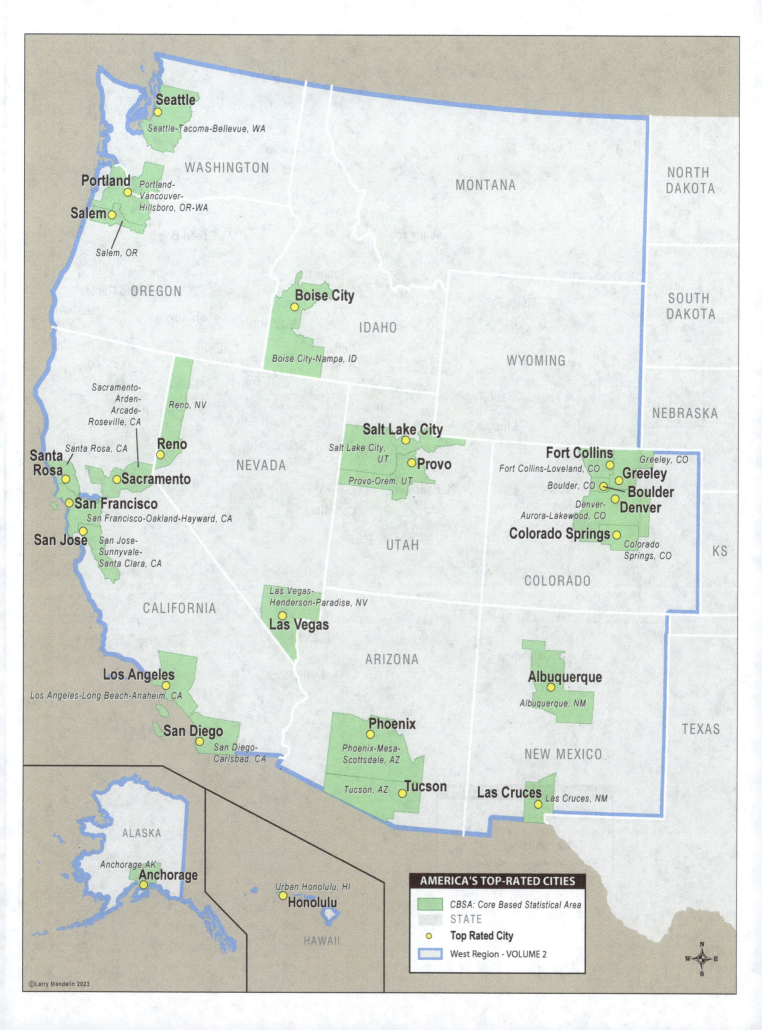

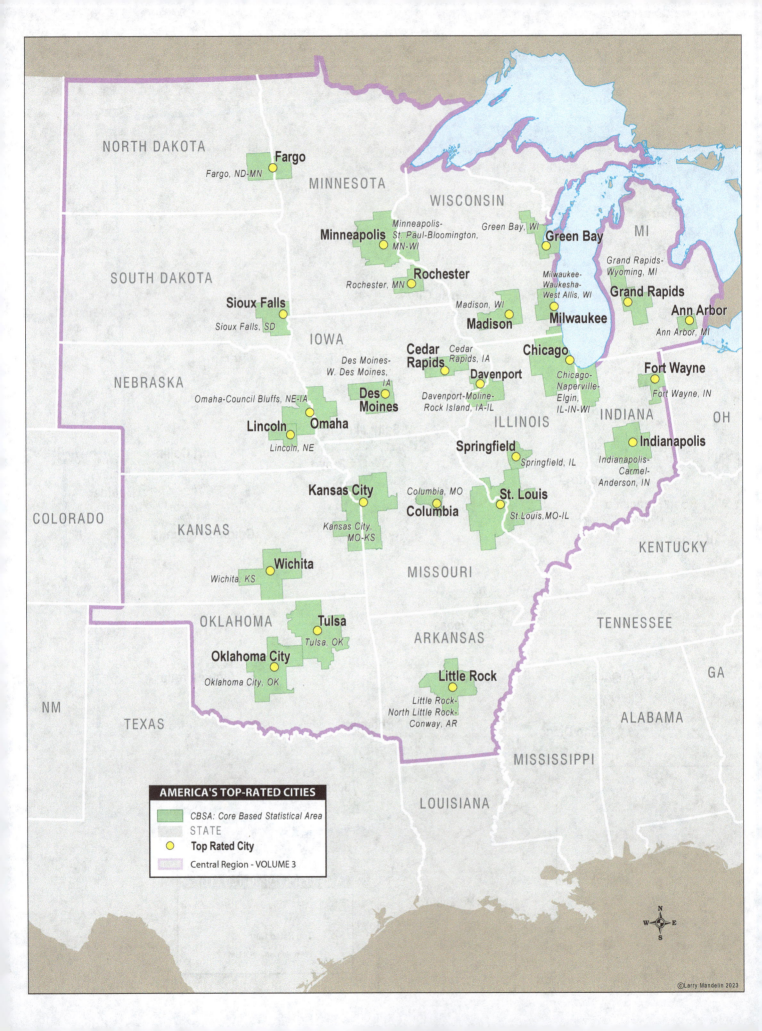

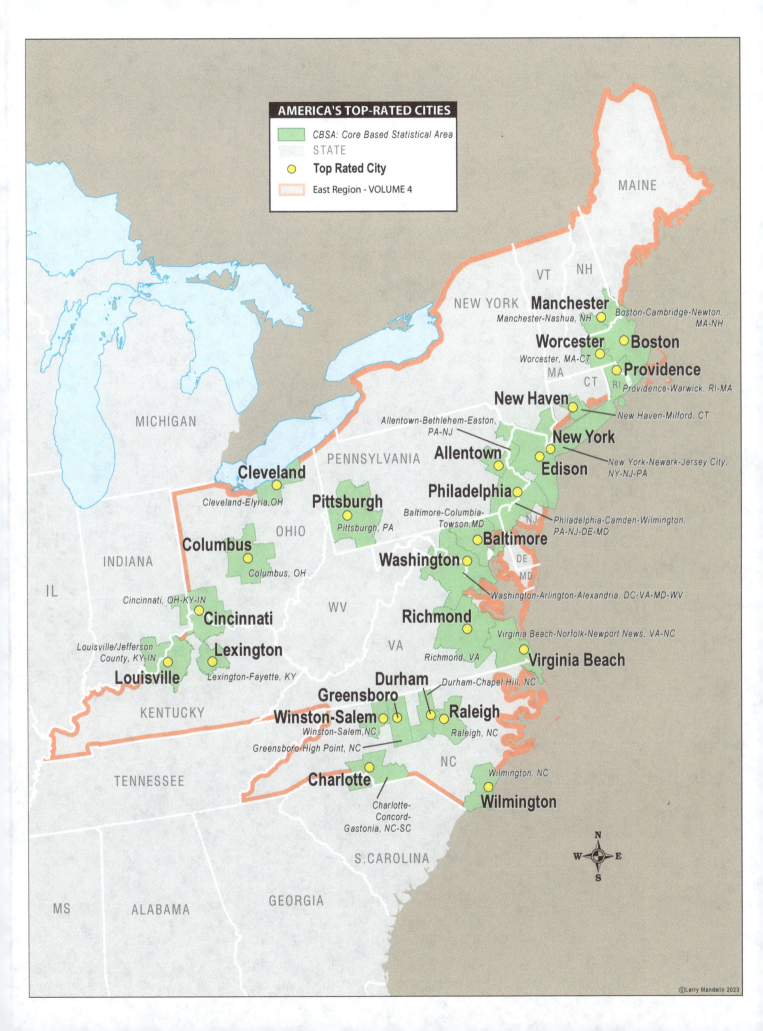

Athens, Georgia

Background

Athens, home to the University of Georgia, retains its old charms while cultivating new ideas. Antebellum homes that grace the city still stand because Gen. William Tecumseh Sherman's March to the Sea took a route that left this northeast Georgia town intact (while burning Atlanta, about 60 miles to the southwest). The Athens Music History Walking Tour, available through the local convention and visitors' bureau, stops at Weaver D's soul food restaurant with the slogan, "Automatic for the People," that went national as the name of locally grown REM's 1992 album. In 2020, the city launched the Athens Music Walk of Fame.

Present-day Athens started as a small settlement where an old Cherokee trail crossed the Oconee River. In 1785 the state's General Assembly chartered the university, which established a campus here in 1801. Three years later, the school held its first graduation ceremony. The city was named for the ancient Greece's center of learning.

Undoubtedly the major influence in the city and surrounding Clarke County, the University of Georgia, is also the area's largest employer. The comprehensive land- and sea-grant institution offers all levels of degree programs in numerous disciplines. Other educational institutions in Athens are the Navy Supply School, Athens Technical College, and branches of Piedmont College and Old Dominion University.

Other major employers are focused on health care, government, and manufacturing. They include Athens Regional Medical Center and St. Mary's Health Care System, which specialize in oncology, pediatrics, heart disease, and other areas. Manufacturing continues to be a major employment sector.

With its shops, boutiques and restaurants, Athens offers plenty to do. The Georgia State Museum of Art, Museum of Natural History, and the State Botanical Garden are affiliated with the university. The restored 1910 Morton Theater once hosted Cab Calloway, Duke Ellington, and Louis Armstrong, and now hosts dramatic and musical performances. Undoubtedly the strong presence of young people in Athens has contributed to its burgeoning artistic scene. The city center is home to bars, galleries, cafes, and music venues that cater to the city's creative climate. The city's annual AthFest, an outdoor celebration of Athen's creative scene, happens June 23-25, 2003. Athens is repeatedly named one of the best places for small business, the best college town for retirees, and the best place to recapture your youth. The city also boasts a bicycle-friendly culture and hosts several annual bicycle races.

The climate is mild, with average temperatures about 20 degrees warmer than the U.S. average. Snowfall is next to nothing, but precipitation is at its highest from January-March. Spring is lovely, with three to four inches of rain, sunshine up to 70 percent of the time starting in April, and temperatures averaging in the 70s.

Rankings

Business/Finance Rankings

- The Athens metro area appeared on the Milken Institute "2022 Best Performing Cities" list. Rank: #121 out of 201 small metro areas (population over 60,000). Criteria: job growth; wage and salary growth; high-tech output growth; housing affordability; household broadband access. *Milken Institute, "Best-Performing Cities 2022," March 28, 2022*

- *Forbes* ranked 203 smaller metro areas (population under 268,000) to determine the nation's "Best Small Places for Business and Careers." The Athens metro area was ranked #6. Criteria: costs (business and living); job growth (past and projected); income growth; quality of life; educational attainment (college and high school); projected economic growth; cultural and leisure opportunities; workplace tolerance laws; net migration patterns. *Forbes, "The Best Small Places for Business and Careers 2019," October 30, 2019*

Safety Rankings

- The National Insurance Crime Bureau ranked 390 metro areas in the U.S. in terms of per capita rates of vehicle theft. The Athens metro area ranked #188 (#1 = highest rate). Criteria: number of vehicle theft offenses per 100,000 inhabitants in 2021. *National Insurance Crime Bureau, "Hot Spots 2021," September 1, 2022*

Seniors/Retirement Rankings

- From its Best Cities for Successful Aging indexes, the Milken Institute generated rankings for metropolitan areas, weighing data in nine categories—health care, wellness, living arrangements, transportation and convenience, financial characteristics, education, employment, community engagement, and overall livability. The Athens metro area was ranked #62 overall in the small metro area category. *Milken Institute, "Best Cities for Successful Aging, 2017" March 14, 2017*

- Athens made the 2022 *Forbes* list of "25 Best Places to Retire." Criteria, focused on overall affordability as well as quality of life indicators, include: housing/living costs compared to the national average and state taxes; air quality; crime rates; home price appreciation; risk associated with climate-change/natural hazards; availability of medical care; bikeability; walkability; healthy living. *Forbes.com, "The Best Places to Retire in 2022," May 13, 2022*

- Athens was identified as #16 of 20 most popular places to retire in the Southeast region by *Topretirements.com*. The site separated its annual "Best Places to Retire" list by major U.S. regions for 2019. The list reflects the 20 cities that visitors to the website are most interested in for retirement, based on the number of times a city's review was viewed on the website. *Topretirements.com, "20 Most Popular Places to Retire in the Southeast: 2019," October 16, 2019*

Business Environment

DEMOGRAPHICS

Population Growth

Area	1990 Census	2000 Census	2010 Census	2020 Census	Population Growth (%) 1990-2020	Population Growth (%) 2010-2020
City	86,561	100,266	115,452	127,315	47.1	10.3
MSA[1]	136,025	166,079	192,541	215,415	58.4	11.9
U.S.	248,709,873	281,421,906	308,745,538	331,449,281	33.3	7.4

Note: (1) Figures cover the Athens-Clarke County, GA Metropolitan Statistical Area
Source: U.S. Census Bureau, 1990 Census, 2000 Census, 2010 Census, 2020 Census

Race

Area	White Alone[2] (%)	Black Alone[2] (%)	Asian Alone[2] (%)	AIAN[3] Alone[2] (%)	NHOPI[4] Alone[2] (%)	Other Race Alone[2] (%)	Two or More Races (%)
City	58.1	24.7	3.9	0.5	0.1	6.1	6.7
MSA[1]	67.0	17.9	3.6	0.4	0.0	4.7	6.3
U.S.	61.6	12.4	6.0	1.1	0.2	8.4	10.2

Note: (1) Figures cover the Athens-Clarke County, GA Metropolitan Statistical Area; (2) Alone is defined as not being in combination with one or more other races; (3) American Indian and Alaska Native; (4) Native Hawaiian and Other Pacific Islander
Source: U.S. Census Bureau, 2020 Census

Hispanic or Latino Origin

Area	Total (%)	Mexican (%)	Puerto Rican (%)	Cuban (%)	Other (%)
City	11.0	5.9	0.4	0.6	4.0
MSA[1]	8.9	4.7	0.8	0.4	2.9
U.S.	18.4	11.2	1.8	0.7	4.7

Note: Persons of Hispanic or Latino origin can be of any race; (1) Figures cover the Athens-Clarke County, GA Metropolitan Statistical Area
Source: U.S. Census Bureau, 2017-2021 American Community Survey 5-Year Estimates

Age

Area	Under Age 5	Age 5–19	Age 20–34	Age 35–44	Age 45–54	Age 55–64	Age 65–74	Age 75–84	Age 85+	Median Age
City	5.1	16.6	38.4	10.7	8.8	8.5	7.3	3.5	1.2	28.2
MSA[1]	5.3	18.8	28.8	11.6	10.9	10.5	8.6	4.2	1.3	32.5
U.S.	5.6	19.2	20.2	12.7	12.4	13.1	10.0	4.9	1.9	38.8

Note: (1) Figures cover the Athens-Clarke County, GA Metropolitan Statistical Area
Source: U.S. Census Bureau, 2020 Census

Disability by Age

Area	All Ages	Under 18 Years Old	18 to 64 Years Old	65 Years and Over
City	11.8	6.1	9.6	35.6
MSA[1]	12.5	5.6	10.2	34.4
U.S.	12.6	4.4	10.3	33.4

Note: Figures show percent of the civilian noninstitutionalized population that reported having a disability. Disability status is determined from six types of difficulty: vision, hearing, cognitive, ambulatory, self-care, and independent living. For children under 5 years old, hearing and vision difficulty are used to determine disability status. For children between the ages of 5 and 14, disability status is determined from hearing, vision, cognitive, ambulatory, and self-care difficulties. For people aged 15 years and older, they are considered to have a disability if they have difficulty with any one of the six difficulty types; Note: (1) Figures cover the Athens-Clarke County, GA Metropolitan Statistical Area
Source: U.S. Census Bureau, 2017-2021 American Community Survey 5-Year Estimates

Ancestry

Area	German	Irish	English	American	Italian	Polish	French[2]	Scottish	Dutch
City	8.4	8.2	9.8	3.5	3.4	1.5	2.0	2.8	0.8
MSA[1]	8.4	10.1	11.7	6.7	2.9	1.1	1.8	2.6	1.0
U.S.	12.8	9.6	8.1	5.7	5.0	2.7	2.2	1.6	1.1

Note: Figures are the percentage of the total population reporting a particular ancestry. The nine most commonly reported ancestries in the U.S. are shown. Figures include multiple ancestries (e.g. if a person reported being Irish and Italian, they were included in both columns); (1) Figures cover the Athens-Clarke County, GA Metropolitan Statistical Area; (2) Excludes Basque
Source: U.S. Census Bureau, 2017-2021 American Community Survey 5-Year Estimates

Foreign-born Population

Area	Any Foreign Country	Asia	Mexico	Europe	Caribbean	Central America[2]	South America	Africa	Canada
City	9.5	2.9	2.4	0.9	0.3	1.0	1.0	1.0	0.2
MSA[1]	7.4	2.5	1.7	0.7	0.2	0.8	0.7	0.6	0.2
U.S.	13.6	4.2	3.3	1.5	1.4	1.1	1.1	0.8	0.2

Note: (1) Figures cover the Athens-Clarke County, GA Metropolitan Statistical Area; (2) Excludes Mexico.
Source: U.S. Census Bureau, 2017-2021 American Community Survey 5-Year Estimates

Household Size

Area	One	Two	Three	Four	Five	Six	Seven or More	Average Household Size
City	34.2	34.5	14.9	11.2	3.5	1.2	0.6	2.20
MSA[1]	28.7	34.6	16.6	13.3	4.5	1.3	1.0	2.50
U.S.	28.1	33.8	15.5	12.9	6.0	2.3	1.4	2.60

Note: (1) Figures cover the Athens-Clarke County, GA Metropolitan Statistical Area
Source: U.S. Census Bureau, 2017-2021 American Community Survey 5-Year Estimates

Household Relationships

Area	Householder	Opposite-sex Spouse	Same-sex Spouse	Opposite-sex Unmarried Partner	Same-sex Unmarried Partner	Child[2]	Grandchild	Other Relatives	Non-relatives
City	40.1	11.6	0.2	2.7	0.2	20.8	2.0	3.7	10.7
MSA[1]	38.6	15.6	0.2	2.3	0.2	25.1	2.3	3.7	7.3
U.S.	38.3	17.5	0.2	2.5	0.2	28.3	2.4	4.8	3.4

Note: Figures are percent of the total population; (1) Figures cover the Athens-Clarke County, GA Metropolitan Statistical Area; (2) Includes biological, adopted, and stepchildren of the householder
Source: U.S. Census Bureau, 2020 Census

Gender

Area	Males	Females	Males per 100 Females
City	59,963	67,352	89.0
MSA[1]	103,235	112,180	92.0
U.S.	162,685,811	168,763,470	96.4

Note: (1) Figures cover the Athens-Clarke County, GA Metropolitan Statistical Area
Source: U.S. Census Bureau, 2020 Census

Marital Status

Area	Never Married	Now Married[2]	Separated	Widowed	Divorced
City	53.8	31.8	1.7	3.7	9.0
MSA[1]	43.0	41.5	1.6	4.4	9.5
U.S.	33.8	48.0	1.8	5.6	10.8

Note: Figures are percentages and cover the population 15 years of age and older; (1) Figures cover the Athens-Clarke County, GA Metropolitan Statistical Area; (2) Excludes separated
Source: U.S. Census Bureau, 2017-2021 American Community Survey 5-Year Estimates

Religious Groups by Family

Area	Catholic	Baptist	Methodist	LDS[2]	Pentecostal	Lutheran	Islam	Adventist	Other
MSA[1]	6.4	12.8	5.7	1.0	2.4	0.3	0.2	1.3	7.9
U.S.	18.7	7.3	3.0	2.0	1.8	1.7	1.3	1.3	11.6

Note: Figures are the number of adherents as a percentage of the total population and cover the eight largest religious groups in the U.S; (1) Figures cover the Athens-Clarke County, GA Metropolitan Statistical Area; (2) Church of Jesus Christ of Latter-day Saints
Sources: 2020 U.S. Religion Census, Association of Statisticians of American Religious Bodies; The Association of Religion Data Archives (ARDA)

Religious Groups by Tradition

Area	Catholic	Evangelical Protestant	Mainline Protestant	Black Protestant	Islam	Judaism	Hinduism	Orthodox	Buddhism
MSA[1]	6.4	19.1	7.2	2.6	0.2	0.2	0.2	0.1	<0.1
U.S.	18.7	16.5	5.2	2.3	1.3	0.6	0.4	0.4	0.3

Note: Figures are the number of adherents as a percentage of the total population; (1) Figures cover the Athens-Clarke County, GA Metropolitan Statistical Area
Sources: 2020 U.S. Religion Census, Association of Statisticians of American Religious Bodies; The Association of Religion Data Archives (ARDA)

ECONOMY

Gross Metropolitan Product

Area	2020	2021	2022	2023	Rank[2]
MSA[1]	10.5	11.5	12.8	13.4	213

Note: Figures are in billions of dollars; (1) Figures cover the Athens-Clarke County, GA Metropolitan Statistical Area; (2) Rank is based on 2021 data and ranges from 1 to 381
Source: U.S. Conference of Mayors, U.S. Metro Economies: U.S. Metros Compared to Global and State Economies, June 2022

Economic Growth

Area	2018-20 (%)	2021 (%)	2022 (%)	2023 (%)	Rank[2]
MSA[1]	-2.1	5.6	6.1	1.6	288
U.S.	-0.6	5.7	3.1	2.9	—

Note: Figures are real gross metropolitan product (GMP) growth rates and represent average annual percent change; (1) Figures cover the Athens-Clarke County, GA Metropolitan Statistical Area; (2) Rank is based on 2020 2-year average annual percent change and ranges from 1 to 381
Source: U.S. Conference of Mayors, U.S. Metro Economies: U.S. Metros Compared to Global and State Economies, June 2022

Metropolitan Area Exports

Area	2016	2017	2018	2019	2020	2021	Rank[2]
MSA[1]	332.1	297.7	378.1	442.1	338.7	448.1	223

Note: Figures are in millions of dollars; (1) Figures cover the Athens-Clarke County, GA Metropolitan Statistical Area; (2) Rank is based on 2021 data and ranges from 1 to 388
Source: U.S. Department of Commerce, International Trade Administration, Office of Trade and Economic Analysis, Industry and Analysis, Exports by Metropolitan Area, data extracted March 16, 2023

Building Permits

Area	Single-Family 2021	Single-Family 2022	Pct. Chg.	Multi-Family 2021	Multi-Family 2022	Pct. Chg.	Total 2021	Total 2022	Pct. Chg.
City	180	227	26.1	986	1,548	57.0	1,166	1,775	52.2
MSA[1]	856	771	-9.9	992	1,574	58.7	1,848	2,345	26.9
U.S.	1,115,400	975,600	-12.5	621,600	689,500	10.9	1,737,000	1,665,100	-4.1

Note: (1) Figures cover the Athens-Clarke County, GA Metropolitan Statistical Area; Figures represent new, privately-owned housing units authorized (unadjusted data); All permit data are based on estimates with imputation
Source: U.S. Census Bureau, Manufacturing, Mining, and Construction Statistics, Building Permits, 2021, 2022

Bankruptcy Filings

Area	Business Filings 2021	Business Filings 2022	% Chg.	Nonbusiness Filings 2021	Nonbusiness Filings 2022	% Chg.
Clarke County	10	4	-60.0	162	212	30.9
U.S.	14,347	13,481	-6.0	399,269	374,240	-6.3

Note: Business filings include Chapter 7, Chapter 9, Chapter 11, Chapter 12, Chapter 13, Chapter 15, and Section 304; Nonbusiness filings include Chapter 7, Chapter 11, and Chapter 13
Source: Administrative Office of the U.S. Courts, Business and Nonbusiness Bankruptcy, County Cases Commenced by Chapter of the Bankruptcy Code, During the 12-Month Period Ending December 31, 2021 and Business and Nonbusiness Bankruptcy, County Cases Commenced by Chapter of the Bankruptcy Code, During the 12-Month Period Ending December 31, 2022

Housing Vacancy Rates

Area	Gross Vacancy Rate[2] (%) 2020	2021	2022	Year-Round Vacancy Rate[3] (%) 2020	2021	2022	Rental Vacancy Rate[4] (%) 2020	2021	2022	Homeowner Vacancy Rate[5] (%) 2020	2021	2022
MSA[1]	n/a	n/a	n/a	n/a	n/a	n/a	n/a	n/a	n/a	n/a	n/a	n/a
U.S.	10.6	10.8	10.5	8.2	8.4	8.2	6.3	6.1	5.8	1.0	0.9	0.8

Note: (1) Figures cover the Athens-Clarke County, GA Metropolitan Statistical Area; (2) The percentage of the total housing inventory that is vacant; (3) The percentage of the housing inventory (excluding seasonal units) that is year-round vacant; (4) The percentage of rental inventory that is vacant for rent; (5) The percentage of homeowner inventory that is vacant for sale; n/a not available
Source: U.S. Census Bureau, Housing Vacancies and Homeownership Annual Statistics: 2020, 2021, 2022

INCOME

Income

Area	Per Capita ($)	Median Household ($)	Average Household ($)
City	27,194	43,466	65,960
MSA[1]	31,392	52,958	80,272
U.S.	37,638	69,021	97,196

Note: (1) Figures cover the Athens-Clarke County, GA Metropolitan Statistical Area
Source: U.S. Census Bureau, 2017-2021 American Community Survey 5-Year Estimates

Household Income Distribution

| Area | Percent of Households Earning ||||||||
	Under $15,000	$15,000 -$24,999	$25,000 -$34,999	$35,000 -$49,999	$50,000 -$74,999	$75,000 -$99,999	$100,000 -$149,999	$150,000 and up
City	17.8	12.2	12.4	12.8	15.4	9.2	11.3	8.8
MSA[1]	14.0	10.2	11.1	12.3	15.9	10.2	13.7	12.5
U.S.	9.4	7.8	8.2	11.4	16.8	12.8	16.3	17.3

Note: (1) Figures cover the Athens-Clarke County, GA Metropolitan Statistical Area
Source: U.S. Census Bureau, 2017-2021 American Community Survey 5-Year Estimates

Poverty Rate

Area	All Ages	Under 18 Years Old	18 to 64 Years Old	65 Years and Over
City	26.6	25.8	29.5	11.1
MSA[1]	20.1	20.5	22.3	9.5
U.S.	12.6	17.0	11.8	9.6

Note: Figures are percentage of people whose income during the past 12 months was below the poverty level; (1) Figures cover the Athens-Clarke County, GA Metropolitan Statistical Area
Source: U.S. Census Bureau, 2017-2021 American Community Survey 5-Year Estimates

EMPLOYMENT

Labor Force and Employment

| Area | Civilian Labor Force ||| Workers Employed |||
	Dec. 2021	Dec. 2022	% Chg.	Dec. 2021	Dec. 2022	% Chg.
City	60,379	61,240	1.4	58,643	59,627	1.7
MSA[1]	102,226	103,727	1.5	99,578	101,194	1.6
U.S.	161,696,000	164,224,000	1.6	155,732,000	158,872,000	2.0

Note: Data is not seasonally adjusted and covers workers 16 years of age and older; (1) Figures cover the Athens-Clarke County, GA Metropolitan Statistical Area
Source: Bureau of Labor Statistics, Local Area Unemployment Statistics

Unemployment Rate

| Area | 2022 ||||||||||||
	Jan.	Feb.	Mar.	Apr.	May	Jun.	Jul.	Aug.	Sep.	Oct.	Nov.	Dec.
City	3.2	3.2	3.2	2.3	2.7	3.5	2.9	3.2	2.5	3.1	2.7	2.6
MSA[1]	2.9	2.9	2.9	2.1	2.5	3.1	2.6	2.9	2.3	2.9	2.5	2.4
U.S.	4.4	4.1	3.8	3.3	3.4	3.8	3.8	3.8	3.3	3.4	3.4	3.3

Note: Data is not seasonally adjusted and covers workers 16 years of age and older; (1) Figures cover the Athens-Clarke County, GA Metropolitan Statistical Area
Source: Bureau of Labor Statistics, Local Area Unemployment Statistics

Average Wages

Occupation	$/Hr.	Occupation	$/Hr.
Accountants and Auditors	35.00	Maintenance and Repair Workers	19.81
Automotive Mechanics	22.03	Marketing Managers	54.36
Bookkeepers	20.51	Network and Computer Systems Admin.	36.48
Carpenters	23.47	Nurses, Licensed Practical	24.20
Cashiers	11.77	Nurses, Registered	38.59
Computer Programmers	29.81	Nursing Assistants	14.53
Computer Systems Analysts	35.56	Office Clerks, General	19.23
Computer User Support Specialists	23.39	Physical Therapists	49.24
Construction Laborers	17.59	Physicians	106.67
Cooks, Restaurant	14.12	Plumbers, Pipefitters and Steamfitters	26.88
Customer Service Representatives	16.00	Police and Sheriff's Patrol Officers	24.49
Dentists	83.95	Postal Service Mail Carriers	25.97
Electricians	25.40	Real Estate Sales Agents	21.38
Engineers, Electrical	51.99	Retail Salespersons	14.84
Fast Food and Counter Workers	11.00	Sales Representatives, Technical/Scientific	41.34
Financial Managers	67.23	Secretaries, Exc. Legal/Medical/Executive	17.79
First-Line Supervisors of Office Workers	27.18	Security Guards	19.33
General and Operations Managers	47.82	Surgeons	n/a
Hairdressers/Cosmetologists	17.24	Teacher Assistants, Exc. Postsecondary*	11.12
Home Health and Personal Care Aides	12.56	Teachers, Secondary School, Exc. Sp. Ed.*	31.25
Janitors and Cleaners	14.99	Telemarketers	n/a
Landscaping/Groundskeeping Workers	15.97	Truck Drivers, Heavy/Tractor-Trailer	26.85
Lawyers	n/a	Truck Drivers, Light/Delivery Services	22.03
Maids and Housekeeping Cleaners	12.50	Waiters and Waitresses	13.09

Note: Wage data covers the Athens-Clarke County, GA Metropolitan Statistical Area; (*) Hourly wages were calculated from annual wage data based on a 40 hour work week; n/a not available.
Source: Bureau of Labor Statistics, Metro Area Occupational Employment & Wage Estimates, May 2022

Employment by Industry

Sector	MSA[1] Number of Employees	MSA[1] Percent of Total	U.S. Percent of Total
Construction, Mining, and Logging	n/a	n/a	5.4
Private Education and Health Services	n/a	n/a	16.1
Financial Activities	n/a	n/a	5.9
Government	27,900	27.8	14.5
Information	n/a	n/a	2.0
Leisure and Hospitality	11,600	11.5	10.3
Manufacturing	n/a	n/a	8.4
Other Services	n/a	n/a	3.7
Professional and Business Services	9,000	9.0	14.7
Retail Trade	11,200	11.1	10.2
Transportation, Warehousing, and Utilities	n/a	n/a	4.9
Wholesale Trade	n/a	n/a	3.9

Note: Figures are non-farm employment as of December 2022. Figures are not seasonally adjusted and include workers 16 years of age and older; (1) Figures cover the Athens-Clarke County, GA Metropolitan Statistical Area; n/a not available
Source: Bureau of Labor Statistics, Current Employment Statistics, Employment, Hours, and Earnings

Employment by Occupation

Occupation Classification	City (%)	MSA[1] (%)	U.S. (%)
Management, Business, Science, and Arts	45.0	44.0	40.3
Natural Resources, Construction, and Maintenance	4.9	6.9	8.7
Production, Transportation, and Material Moving	13.0	13.3	13.1
Sales and Office	17.9	18.7	20.9
Service	19.1	17.1	17.0

Note: Figures cover employed civilians 16 years of age and older; (1) Figures cover the Athens-Clarke County, GA Metropolitan Statistical Area
Source: U.S. Census Bureau, 2017-2021 American Community Survey 5-Year Estimates

Occupations with Greatest Projected Employment Growth: 2022 – 2024

Occupation[1]	2022 Employment	2024 Projected Employment	Numeric Employment Change	Percent Employment Change
Laborers and Freight, Stock, and Material Movers, Hand	124,130	131,700	7,570	6.1
Retail Salespersons	139,030	146,370	7,340	5.3
Industrial Truck and Tractor Operators	48,230	54,230	6,000	12.4
General and Operations Managers	95,580	101,230	5,650	5.9
Fast Food and Counter Workers	116,760	122,340	5,580	4.8
Stockers and Order Fillers	73,270	78,260	4,990	6.8
Software Developers and Software Quality Assurance Analysts and Testers	58,710	63,610	4,900	8.3
Cooks, Restaurant	42,420	47,160	4,740	11.2
Heavy and Tractor-Trailer Truck Drivers	68,660	73,100	4,440	6.5
Project Management Specialists and Business Operations Specialists, All Other	93,000	97,320	4,320	4.6

Note: Projections cover Georgia; (1) Sorted by numeric employment change
Source: www.projectionscentral.com, State Occupational Projections, 2022–2024 Short-Term Projections

Fastest-Growing Occupations: 2022 – 2024

Occupation[1]	2022 Employment	2024 Projected Employment	Numeric Employment Change	Percent Employment Change
Musicians and Singers	710	850	140	19.7
Amusement and Recreation Attendants	6,720	8,030	1,310	19.5
Reservation and Transportation Ticket Agents and Travel Clerks	4,000	4,710	710	17.8
Fitness Trainers and Aerobics Instructors	4,620	5,420	800	17.3
Manicurists and Pedicurists	1,810	2,120	310	17.1
Hotel, Motel, and Resort Desk Clerks	7,700	9,000	1,300	16.9
Machine Feeders and Offbearers	3,020	3,490	470	15.6
Massage Therapists	2,980	3,430	450	15.1
Skincare Specialists	1,730	1,990	260	15.0
Parking Lot Attendants	2,820	3,240	420	14.9

Note: Projections cover Georgia; (1) Sorted by percent employment change and excludes occupations with numeric employment change less than 50
Source: www.projectionscentral.com, State Occupational Projections, 2022–2024 Short-Term Projections

CITY FINANCES

City Government Finances

Component	2020 ($000)	2020 ($ per capita)
Total Revenues	313,257	2,528
Total Expenditures	266,611	2,152
Debt Outstanding	259,820	2,097
Cash and Securities[1]	350,597	2,829

Note: (1) Cash and security holdings of a government at the close of its fiscal year, including those of its dependent agencies, utilities, and liquor stores.
Source: U.S. Census Bureau, State & Local Government Finances 2020

City Government Revenue by Source

Source	2020 ($000)	2020 ($ per capita)	2020 (%)
General Revenue			
From Federal Government	10,334	83	3.3
From State Government	4,375	35	1.4
From Local Governments	84,893	685	27.1
Taxes			
Property	66,764	539	21.3
Sales and Gross Receipts	23,325	188	7.4
Personal Income	0	0	0.0
Corporate Income	0	0	0.0
Motor Vehicle License	0	0	0.0
Other Taxes	5,885	47	1.9
Current Charges	87,311	705	27.9
Liquor Store	0	0	0.0
Utility	20,269	164	6.5

Source: U.S. Census Bureau, State & Local Government Finances 2020

City Government Expenditures by Function

Function	2020 ($000)	2020 ($ per capita)	2020 (%)
General Direct Expenditures			
Air Transportation	2,506	20	0.9
Corrections	16,012	129	6.0
Education	0	0	0.0
Employment Security Administration	0	0	0.0
Financial Administration	9,410	75	3.5
Fire Protection	16,090	129	6.0
General Public Buildings	6,327	51	2.4
Governmental Administration, Other	15,461	124	5.8
Health	2,039	16	0.8
Highways	15,939	128	6.0
Hospitals	0	0	0.0
Housing and Community Development	0	0	0.0
Interest on General Debt	14,829	119	5.6
Judicial and Legal	14,734	118	5.5
Libraries	6,693	54	2.5
Parking	0	0	0.0
Parks and Recreation	22,445	181	8.4
Police Protection	28,016	226	10.5
Public Welfare	753	6	0.3
Sewerage	16,155	130	6.1
Solid Waste Management	7,910	63	3.0
Veterans' Services	0	0	0.0
Liquor Store	0	0	0.0
Utility	21,441	173	8.0

Source: U.S. Census Bureau, State & Local Government Finances 2020

TAXES

State Corporate Income Tax Rates

State	Tax Rate (%)	Income Brackets ($)	Num. of Brackets	Financial Institution Tax Rate (%)[a]	Federal Income Tax Ded.
Georgia	5.75	Flat rate	1	5.75	No

Note: Tax rates as of January 1, 2023; (a) Rates listed are the corporate income tax rate applied to financial institutions or excise taxes based on income. Some states have other taxes based upon the value of deposits or shares.
Source: Federation of Tax Administrators, State Corporate Income Tax Rates, January 1, 2023

State Individual Income Tax Rates

State	Tax Rate (%)	Income Brackets ($)	Personal Exemptions ($) Single	Personal Exemptions ($) Married	Personal Exemptions ($) Depend.	Standard Ded. ($) Single	Standard Ded. ($) Married
Georgia	1.0 - 5.75	750 - 7,001 (i)	2,700	7,400	3,000	5,400	7,100

Note: Tax rates as of January 1, 2023; Local- and county-level taxes are not included; Federal income tax is not deductible on state income tax returns; (i) The Georgia income brackets reported are for single individuals. For married couples filing jointly, the same tax rates apply to income brackets ranging from $1,000, to $10,000.
Source: Federation of Tax Administrators, State Individual Income Tax Rates, January 1, 2023

Various State Sales and Excise Tax Rates

State	State Sales Tax (%)	Gasoline[1] ($/gal.)	Cigarette[2] ($/pack)	Spirits[3] ($/gal.)	Wine[4] ($/gal.)	Beer[5] ($/gal.)	Recreational Marijuana (%)
Georgia	4	0.4005	0.37	3.79	1.51	0.48	Not legal

Note: All tax rates as of January 1, 2023; (1) The American Petroleum Institute has developed a methodology for determining the average tax rate on a gallon of fuel. Rates may include any of the following: excise taxes, environmental fees, storage tank fees, other fees or taxes, general sales tax, and local taxes; (2) The federal excise tax of $1.0066 per pack and local taxes are not included; (3) Rates are those applicable to off-premise sales of 40% alcohol by volume (a.b.v.) distilled spirits in 750ml containers. Local excise taxes are excluded; (4) Rates are those applicable to off-premise sales of 11% a.b.v. non-carbonated wine in 750ml containers; (5) Rates are those applicable to off-premise sales of 4.7% a.b.v. beer in 12 ounce containers.
Source: Tax Foundation, 2023 Facts & Figures: How Does Your State Compare?

State Business Tax Climate Index Rankings

State	Overall Rank	Corporate Tax Rank	Individual Income Tax Rank	Sales Tax Rank	Property Tax Rank	Unemployment Insurance Tax Rank
Georgia	32	8	35	31	28	35

Note: The index is a measure of how each state's tax laws affect economic performance. The lower the rank, the more favorable a state's tax system is for business. States without a given tax are given a ranking of 1. The scores/rankings for the District of Columbia do not affect other states. The 2023 index represents the tax climate as of July 1, 2022.
Source: Tax Foundation, State Business Tax Climate Index 2023

TRANSPORTATION

Means of Transportation to Work

Area	Car/Truck/Van Drove Alone	Car/Truck/Van Carpooled	Public Transportation Bus	Public Transportation Subway	Public Transportation Railroad	Bicycle	Walked	Other Means	Worked at Home
City	72.0	8.0	2.7	0.0	0.0	1.4	4.8	1.0	10.2
MSA[1]	75.1	8.0	1.6	0.0	0.0	0.8	3.4	1.2	9.9
U.S.	73.2	8.6	2.0	1.6	0.5	0.5	2.5	1.5	9.7

Note: Figures are percentages and cover workers 16 years of age and older; (1) Figures cover the Athens-Clarke County, GA Metropolitan Statistical Area
Source: U.S. Census Bureau, 2017-2021 American Community Survey 5-Year Estimates

Travel Time to Work

Area	Less Than 10 Minutes	10 to 19 Minutes	20 to 29 Minutes	30 to 44 Minutes	45 to 59 Minutes	60 to 89 Minutes	90 Minutes or More
City	18.0	45.8	16.6	9.8	3.5	3.5	2.8
MSA[1]	14.2	38.2	21.9	13.5	5.2	4.0	3.0
U.S.	12.4	28.5	21.0	20.9	8.2	6.2	2.9

Note: Note: Figures are percentages and include workers 16 years old and over; (1) Figures cover the Athens-Clarke County, GA Metropolitan Statistical Area
Source: U.S. Census Bureau, 2017-2021 American Community Survey 5-Year Estimates

Key Congestion Measures

Measure	1990	2000	2010	2015	2020
Annual Hours of Delay, Total (000)	n/a	n/a	n/a	3,417	1,707
Annual Hours of Delay, Per Auto Commuter	n/a	n/a	n/a	24	12
Annual Congestion Cost, Per Auto Commuter ($)	n/a	n/a	n/a	496	256

Note: n/a not available
Source: Texas A&M Transportation Institute, 2021 Urban Mobility Report

Freeway Travel Time Index

Measure	1985	1990	1995	2000	2005	2010	2015	2020
Urban Area Index[1]	n/a	n/a	n/a	n/a	n/a	n/a	1.09	1.05
Urban Area Rank[1,2]	n/a	n/a	n/a	n/a	n/a	n/a	n/a	n/a

Note: Freeway Travel Time Index—the ratio of travel time in the peak period to the travel time at free-flow conditions. For example, a value of 1.30 indicates a 20-minute free-flow trip takes 26 minutes in the peak (20 minutes x 1.30 = 26 minutes); (1) Covers the Athens-Clarke County GA urban area; (2) Rank is based on 101 larger urban areas (#1 = highest travel time index); n/a not available
Source: Texas A&M Transportation Institute, 2021 Urban Mobility Report

Public Transportation

Agency Name / Mode of Transportation	Vehicles Operated in Maximum Service[1]	Annual Unlinked Passenger Trips[2] (in thous.)	Annual Passenger Miles[3] (in thous.)
Athens Transit System			
Bus (directly operated)	17	627.8	2,278.0
Demand Response (directly operated)	2	3.8	19.1

Note: (1) Number of revenue vehicles operated by the given mode and type of service to meet the annual maximum service requirement. This is the revenue vehicle count during the peak season of the year; on the week and day that maximum service is provided. Vehicles operated in maximum service (VOMS) exclude atypical days and one-time special events; (2) Number of passengers who boarded public transportation vehicles. Passengers are counted each time they board a vehicle no matter how many vehicles they use to travel from their origin to their destination. (3) Sum of the distances ridden by all passengers during the entire fiscal year.
Source: Federal Transit Administration, National Transit Database, 2021

Air Transportation

Airport Name and Code / Type of Service	Passenger Airlines[1]	Passenger Enplanements	Freight Carriers[2]	Freight (lbs)
Athens Municipal (AHN)				
Domestic service (U.S. carriers - 2022)	8	1,525	1	8,999
International service (U.S. carriers - 2021)	0	0	0	0

Note: (1) Includes all U.S.-based major, minor and commuter airlines that carried at least one passenger during the year; (2) Includes all U.S.-based airlines and freight carriers that transported at least one pound of freight during the year.
Source: Bureau of Transportation Statistics, The Intermodal Transportation Database, Air Carriers: T-100 Domestic Market (U.S. Carriers), 2022; Bureau of Transportation Statistics, The Intermodal Transportation Database, Air Carriers: T-100 International Market (U.S. Carriers), 2021

BUSINESSES

Major Business Headquarters

Company Name	Industry	Rankings Fortune[1]	Forbes[2]
No companies listed	-	-	-

Note: (1) Companies that produce a 10-K are ranked 1 to 500 based on 2021 revenue; (2) All private companies with at least $2 billion in annual revenue through the end of their most current fiscal year are ranked 1 to 246; companies listed are headquartered in the city; dashes indicate no ranking
Source: Fortune, "Fortune 500," 2022; Forbes, "America's Largest Private Companies," 2022

Living Environment

COST OF LIVING

Cost of Living Index

Composite Index	Groceries	Housing	Utilities	Transportation	Health Care	Misc. Goods/Services
n/a	n/a	n/a	n/a	n/a	n/a	n/a

Note: The Cost of Living Index measures regional differences in the cost of consumer goods and services, excluding taxes and non-consumer expenditures, for professional and managerial households in the top income quintile. It is based on more than 50,000 prices covering almost 60 different items for which prices are collected three times a year by chambers of commerce, economic development organizations or university applied economic centers in each participating urban area. The numbers shown should be read as a percentage above or below the national average of 100. For example, a value of 115.4 in the groceries column indicates that grocery prices are 15.4% higher than the national average. Small differences in the index numbers should not be interpreted as significant; n/a not available.
Source: The Council for Community and Economic Research, Cost of Living Index, 2022

Grocery Prices

Area[1]	T-Bone Steak ($/pound)	Frying Chicken ($/pound)	Whole Milk ($/half gal.)	Eggs ($/dozen)	Orange Juice ($/64 oz.)	Coffee ($/11.5 oz.)
City[2]	n/a	n/a	n/a	n/a	n/a	n/a
Avg.	13.81	1.59	2.43	2.25	3.85	4.95
Min.	10.17	0.90	1.51	1.30	2.90	3.46
Max.	19.35	3.30	4.32	4.32	5.31	8.59

Note: (1) Values for the local area are compared with the average, minimum and maximum values for all 286 areas in the Cost of Living Index; (2) Figures cover the Athens GA urban area; n/a not available; **T-Bone Steak** (price per pound); **Frying Chicken** (price per pound, whole fryer); **Whole Milk** (half gallon carton); **Eggs** (price per dozen, Grade A, large); **Orange Juice** (64 oz. Tropicana or Florida Natural); **Coffee** (11.5 oz. can, vacuum-packed, Maxwell House, Hills Bros, or Folgers).
Source: The Council for Community and Economic Research, Cost of Living Index, 2022

Housing and Utility Costs

Area[1]	New Home Price ($)	Apartment Rent ($/month)	All Electric ($/month)	Part Electric ($/month)	Other Energy ($/month)	Telephone ($/month)
City[2]	n/a	n/a	n/a	n/a	n/a	n/a
Avg.	450,913	1,371	176.41	99.93	76.96	190.22
Min.	229,283	546	100.84	31.56	27.15	174.27
Max.	2,434,977	4,569	356.86	249.59	272.24	208.31

Note: (1) Values for the local area are compared with the average, minimum and maximum values for all 286 areas in the Cost of Living Index; (2) Figures cover the Athens GA urban area; n/a not available; **New Home Price** (2,400 sf living area, 8,000 sf lot, in urban area with full utilities); **Apartment Rent** (950 sf 2 bedroom/1.5 or 2 bath, unfurnished, excluding all utilities except water); **All Electric** (average monthly cost for an all-electric home); **Part Electric** (average monthly cost for a part-electric home); **Other Energy** (average monthly cost for natural gas, fuel oil, coal, wood, and any other forms of energy except electricity); **Telephone** (price includes the base monthly rate plus taxes and fees for three lines of mobile phone service).
Source: The Council for Community and Economic Research, Cost of Living Index, 2022

Health Care, Transportation, and Other Costs

Area[1]	Doctor ($/visit)	Dentist ($/visit)	Optometrist ($/visit)	Gasoline ($/gallon)	Beauty Salon ($/visit)	Men's Shirt ($)
City[2]	n/a	n/a	n/a	n/a	n/a	n/a
Avg.	124.91	107.77	117.66	3.86	43.31	34.21
Min.	36.61	58.25	51.79	2.90	22.18	13.05
Max.	250.21	162.58	371.96	5.54	85.61	63.54

Note: (1) Values for the local area are compared with the average, minimum and maximum values for all 286 areas in the Cost of Living Index; (2) Figures cover the Athens GA urban area; n/a not available; **Doctor** (general practitioners routine exam of an established patient); **Dentist** (adult teeth cleaning and periodic oral examination); **Optometrist** (full vision eye exam for established adult patient); **Gasoline** (one gallon regular unleaded, national brand, including all taxes, cash price at self-service pump if available); **Beauty Salon** (woman's shampoo, trim, and blow-dry); **Men's Shirt** (cotton/polyester dress shirt, pinpoint weave, long sleeves).
Source: The Council for Community and Economic Research, Cost of Living Index, 2022

HOUSING

Homeownership Rate

Area	2015 (%)	2016 (%)	2017 (%)	2018 (%)	2019 (%)	2020 (%)	2021 (%)	2022 (%)
MSA[1]	n/a	n/a	n/a	n/a	n/a	n/a	n/a	n/a
U.S.	63.7	63.4	63.9	64.4	64.6	66.6	65.5	65.8

Note: (1) Figures cover the Athens-Clarke County, GA Metropolitan Statistical Area; n/a not available
Source: U.S. Census Bureau, Housing Vacancies and Homeownership Annual Statistics: 2015-2022

House Price Index (HPI)

Area	National Ranking[2]	Quarterly Change (%)	One-Year Change (%)	Five-Year Change (%)	Since 1991Q1 (%)
MSA[1]	33	0.64	16.98	76.16	301.70
U.S.[3]	–	0.34	8.41	58.44	289.08

Note: The HPI is a weighted repeat sales index. It measures average price changes in repeat sales or refinancings on the same properties. This information is obtained by reviewing repeat mortgage transactions on single-family properties whose mortgages have been purchased or securitized by Fannie Mae or Freddie Mac since January 1975; (1) Figures cover the Athens-Clarke County, GA Metropolitan Statistical Area; (2) Rankings are based on annual percentage change for all metro areas containing at least 15,000 transactions over the last 10 years and ranges from 1 to 257; (3) figures based on a weighted average of Census Division estimates using a seasonally adjusted, purchase-only index; all figures are for the period ending December 31, 2022
Source: Federal Housing Finance Agency, Change in FHFA Metropolitan Area House Price Indexes, 2022Q4

Median Single-Family Home Prices

Area	2020	2021	2022p	Percent Change 2021 to 2022
MSA[1]	n/a	n/a	n/a	n/a
U.S. Average	300.2	357.1	392.6	9.9

Note: Figures are median sales prices of existing single-family homes in thousands of dollars; (p) preliminary; n/a not available; (1) Figures cover the Athens-Clarke County, GA Metropolitan Statistical Area
Source: National Association of Realtors, Median Sales Price of Existing Single-Family Homes for Metropolitan Areas, 4th Quarter 2022

Qualifying Income Based on Median Sales Price of Existing Single-Family Homes

Area	With 5% Down ($)	With 10% Down ($)	With 20% Down ($)
MSA[1]	n/a	n/a	n/a
U.S. Average	112,234	106,237	94,513

Note: Figures are preliminary; Qualifying income is based on a mortgage rate of 6.77%. Monthly principal and interest payment is limited to 25% of income; n/a not available; (1) Figures cover the Athens-Clarke County, GA Metropolitan Statistical Area
Source: National Association of Realtors, Qualifying Income Based on Median Sales Price of Existing Single-Family Homes for Metropolitan Areas, 4th Quarter 2022

Home Value

Area	Under $100,000	$100,000 -$199,999	$200,000 -$299,999	$300,000 -$399,999	$400,000 -$499,999	$500,000 -$999,999	$1,000,000 or more	Median ($)
City	16.0	34.3	25.3	10.4	5.8	6.9	1.2	199,300
MSA[1]	16.8	30.0	23.5	12.5	7.6	8.0	1.7	211,500
U.S.	16.2	24.2	20.1	13.6	8.3	13.6	4.1	244,900

Note: Figures are percentages except for median and cover owner-occupied housing units; (1) Figures cover the Athens-Clarke County, GA Metropolitan Statistical Area
Source: U.S. Census Bureau, 2017-2021 American Community Survey 5-Year Estimates

Year Housing Structure Built

Area	2020 or Later	2010 -2019	2000 -2009	1990 -1999	1980 -1989	1970 -1979	1960 -1969	1950 -1959	1940 -1949	Before 1940	Median Year
City	0.1	5.7	17.6	18.6	15.8	15.8	12.5	6.6	2.2	5.1	1985
MSA[1]	0.2	7.5	17.8	20.4	16.4	15.2	10.0	5.3	1.9	5.2	1988
U.S.	0.2	7.3	13.6	13.6	13.2	14.8	10.3	10.0	4.7	12.2	1979

Note: Figures are percentages except for Median Year; Note: (1) Figures cover the Athens-Clarke County, GA Metropolitan Statistical Area
Source: U.S. Census Bureau, 2017-2021 American Community Survey 5-Year Estimates

Gross Monthly Rent

Area	Under $500	$500 -$999	$1,000 -$1,499	$1,500 -$1,999	$2,000 -$2,499	$2,500 -$2,999	$3,000 and up	Median ($)
City	5.4	52.2	29.1	9.4	2.2	0.8	0.8	939
MSA[1]	5.6	51.9	28.9	9.1	2.7	0.9	0.8	939
U.S.	8.1	30.5	30.8	16.8	7.3	3.1	3.5	1,163

Note: Figures are percentages except for median; Gross rent is the contract rent plus the estimated average monthly cost of utilities (electricity, gas, and water and sewer) and fuels (oil, coal, kerosene, wood, etc.) if these are paid by the renter (or paid for the renter by someone else); (1) Figures cover the Athens-Clarke County, GA Metropolitan Statistical Area
Source: U.S. Census Bureau, 2017-2021 American Community Survey 5-Year Estimates

HEALTH

Health Risk Factors

Category	MSA[1] (%)	U.S. (%)
Adults aged 18–64 who have any kind of health care coverage	n/a	90.9
Adults who reported being in good or better health	n/a	85.2
Adults who have been told they have high blood cholesterol	n/a	35.7
Adults who have been told they have high blood pressure	n/a	32.4
Adults who are current smokers	n/a	14.4
Adults who currently use e-cigarettes	n/a	6.7
Adults who currently use chewing tobacco, snuff, or snus	n/a	3.5
Adults who are heavy drinkers[2]	n/a	6.3
Adults who are binge drinkers[3]	n/a	15.4
Adults who are overweight (BMI 25.0 - 29.9)	n/a	34.4
Adults who are obese (BMI 30.0 - 99.8)	n/a	33.9
Adults who participated in any physical activities in the past month	n/a	76.3

Note: (1) Figures for the Athens-Clarke County, GA Metropolitan Statistical Area were not available.
(2) Heavy drinkers are classified as adult men having more than 14 drinks per week and adult women having more than 7 drinks per week; (3) Binge drinkers are classified as males having five or more drinks on one occasion or females having four or more drinks on one occasion
Source: Centers for Disease Control and Prevention, Behavioral Risk Factor Surveillance System, SMART: Selected Metropolitan Area Risk Trends, 2021

Acute and Chronic Health Conditions

Category	MSA[1] (%)	U.S. (%)
Adults who have ever been told they had a heart attack	n/a	4.0
Adults who have ever been told they have angina or coronary heart disease	n/a	3.8
Adults who have ever been told they had a stroke	n/a	3.0
Adults who have ever been told they have asthma	n/a	14.9
Adults who have ever been told they have arthritis	n/a	25.8
Adults who have ever been told they have diabetes[2]	n/a	10.9
Adults who have ever been told they had skin cancer	n/a	6.6
Adults who have ever been told they had any other types of cancer	n/a	7.5
Adults who have ever been told they have COPD	n/a	6.1
Adults who have ever been told they have kidney disease	n/a	3.0
Adults who have ever been told they have a form of depression	n/a	20.5

Note: (1) Figures for the Athens-Clarke County, GA Metropolitan Statistical Area were not available.
(2) Figures do not include pregnancy-related, borderline, or pre-diabetes
Source: Centers for Disease Control and Prevention, Behavioral Risk Factor Surveillance System, SMART: Selected Metropolitan Area Risk Trends, 2021

Health Screening and Vaccination Rates

Category	MSA[1] (%)	U.S. (%)
Adults who have ever been tested for HIV	n/a	34.9
Adults who have had their blood cholesterol checked within the last five years	n/a	85.2
Adults aged 65+ who have had flu shot within the past year	n/a	68.6
Adults aged 65+ who have ever had a pneumonia vaccination	n/a	71.0

Note: (1) Figures for the Athens-Clarke County, GA Metropolitan Statistical Area were not available.
Source: Centers for Disease Control and Prevention, Behavioral Risk Factor Surveillance System, SMART: Selected Metropolitan Area Risk Trends, 2021

Disability Status

Category	MSA[1] (%)	U.S. (%)
Adults who reported being deaf	n/a	7.2
Are you blind or have serious difficulty seeing, even when wearing glasses?	n/a	4.8
Are you limited in any way in any of your usual activities due to arthritis?	n/a	11.1
Do you have difficulty doing errands alone?	n/a	7.0
Do you have difficulty dressing or bathing?	n/a	3.6
Do you have serious difficulty concentrating/remembering/making decisions?	n/a	12.1
Do you have serious difficulty walking or climbing stairs?	n/a	12.8

Note: (1) Figures for the Athens-Clarke County, GA Metropolitan Statistical Area were not available.
Source: Centers for Disease Control and Prevention, Behavioral Risk Factor Surveillance System, SMART: Selected Metropolitan Area Risk Trends, 2021

Mortality Rates for the Top 10 Causes of Death in the U.S.

ICD-10[a] Sub-Chapter	ICD-10[a] Code	Crude Mortality Rate[1] per 100,000 population County[2]	U.S.
Malignant neoplasms	C00-C97	125.5	182.6
Ischaemic heart diseases	I20-I25	48.6	113.1
Other forms of heart disease	I30-I51	68.3	64.4
Other degenerative diseases of the nervous system	G30-G31	49.9	51.0
Cerebrovascular diseases	I60-I69	37.4	47.8
Other external causes of accidental injury	W00-X59	26.2	46.4
Chronic lower respiratory diseases	J40-J47	24.2	45.7
Organic, including symptomatic, mental disorders	F01-F09	12.2	35.9
Hypertensive diseases	I10-I15	29.1	35.0
Diabetes mellitus	E10-E14	14.8	29.6

Note: (a) ICD-10 = International Classification of Diseases 10th Revision; (1) Crude mortality rates are a three-year average covering 2019-2021; (2) Figures cover Clarke County.
Source: Centers for Disease Control and Prevention, National Center for Health Statistics. National Vital Statistics System, Mortality 2018-2021 on CDC WONDER Online Database

Mortality Rates for Selected Causes of Death

ICD-10[a] Sub-Chapter	ICD-10[a] Code	Crude Mortality Rate[1] per 100,000 population County[2]	U.S.
Assault	X85-Y09	6.2	7.0
Diseases of the liver	K70-K76	20.0	19.8
Human immunodeficiency virus (HIV) disease	B20-B24	Suppressed	1.5
Influenza and pneumonia	J09-J18	5.7	14.7
Intentional self-harm	X60-X84	10.1	14.3
Malnutrition	E40-E46	5.2	4.3
Obesity and other hyperalimentation	E65-E68	Suppressed	3.0
Renal failure	N17-N19	13.8	15.7
Transport accidents	V01-V99	11.7	13.6
Viral hepatitis	B15-B19	Suppressed	1.2

Note: (a) ICD-10 = International Classification of Diseases 10th Revision; (1) Crude mortality rates are a three-year average covering 2019-2021; (2) Figures cover Clarke County; Data are suppressed when the data meet the criteria for confidentiality constraints; Crude mortality rates are flagged as unreliable when the rate would be calculated with a numerator of 20 or less.
Source: Centers for Disease Control and Prevention, National Center for Health Statistics. National Vital Statistics System, Mortality 2018-2021 on CDC WONDER Online Database

Health Insurance Coverage

Area	With Health Insurance	With Private Health Insurance	With Public Health Insurance	Without Health Insurance	Population Under Age 19 Without Health Insurance
City	87.5	70.8	25.1	12.5	9.1
MSA[1]	88.1	70.2	27.8	11.9	7.0
U.S.	91.2	67.8	35.4	8.8	5.3

Note: Figures are percentages that cover the civilian noninstitutionalized population; (1) Figures cover the Athens-Clarke County, GA Metropolitan Statistical Area
Source: U.S. Census Bureau, 2017-2021 American Community Survey 5-Year Estimates

Number of Medical Professionals

Area	MDs[3]	DOs[3,4]	Dentists	Podiatrists	Chiropractors	Optometrists
County[1] (number)	419	21	67	6	29	20
County[1] (rate[2])	326.1	16.3	52.1	4.7	22.5	15.5
U.S. (rate[2])	289.3	23.5	72.5	6.2	28.7	17.4

Note: Data as of 2021 unless noted; (1) Data covers Clarke County; (2) Rate per 100,000 population; (3) Data as of 2020 and includes all active, non-federal physicians; (4) Doctor of Osteopathic Medicine
Source: U.S. Department of Health and Human Services, Health Resources and Services Administration, Bureau of Health Professions, Area Resource File (ARF) 2021-2022

EDUCATION

Public School District Statistics

District Name	Schls	Pupils	Pupil/Teacher Ratio	Minority Pupils[1] (%)	LEP/ELL[2] (%)	IEP[3] (%)
Clarke County	21	12,556	10.5	79.3	10.6	14.9

Note: Table includes school districts with 2,000 or more students; (1) Percentage of students that are not non-Hispanic white; (2) Percentage of students that are Limited English Proficient or English Language Learners (2018-19); (3) Percentage of students that have an Individualized Education Program (2019-20).
Source: U.S. Department of Education, National Center for Education Statistics, Common Core of Data, Local Education Agency (School District) Universe Survey: School Year 2021-2022

Athens, Georgia

Highest Level of Education

Area	Less than H.S.	H.S. Diploma	Some College, No Deg.	Associate Degree	Bachelor's Degree	Master's Degree	Prof. School Degree	Doctorate Degree
City	10.3	19.2	17.0	6.4	23.4	14.8	2.7	6.1
MSA[1]	10.6	22.7	17.6	7.4	20.8	13.0	3.2	4.7
U.S.	11.1	26.5	20.0	8.7	20.6	9.3	2.2	1.5

Note: Figures cover persons age 25 and over; (1) Figures cover the Athens-Clarke County, GA Metropolitan Statistical Area
Source: U.S. Census Bureau, 2017-2021 American Community Survey 5-Year Estimates

Educational Attainment by Race

Area	High School Graduate or Higher (%) Total	White	Black	Asian	Hisp.[2]	Bachelor's Degree or Higher (%) Total	White	Black	Asian	Hisp.[2]
City	89.7	94.3	83.2	92.5	67.4	47.1	59.0	23.3	72.4	27.0
MSA[1]	89.4	92.3	82.2	89.7	69.1	41.7	46.6	21.7	67.5	30.6
U.S.	88.9	91.4	87.2	87.6	71.2	33.7	35.5	23.3	55.6	18.4

Note: Figures shown cover persons 25 years old and over; (1) Figures cover the Athens-Clarke County, GA Metropolitan Statistical Area; (2) People of Hispanic origin can be of any race
Source: U.S. Census Bureau, 2017-2021 American Community Survey 5-Year Estimates

School Enrollment by Grade and Control

Area	Preschool (%) Public	Private	Kindergarten (%) Public	Private	Grades 1 - 4 (%) Public	Private	Grades 5 - 8 (%) Public	Private	Grades 9 - 12 (%) Public	Private
City	61.1	38.9	96.2	3.8	91.8	8.2	88.7	11.3	91.8	8.2
MSA[1]	64.9	35.1	93.2	6.8	89.6	10.4	87.0	13.0	88.4	11.6
U.S.	58.8	41.2	86.3	13.7	88.3	11.7	88.6	11.4	89.4	10.6

Note: Figures shown cover persons 3 years old and over; (1) Figures cover the Athens-Clarke County, GA Metropolitan Statistical Area
Source: U.S. Census Bureau, 2017-2021 American Community Survey 5-Year Estimates

Higher Education

Four-Year Colleges Public	Private Non-profit	Private For-profit	Two-Year Colleges Public	Private Non-profit	Private For-profit	Medical Schools[1]	Law Schools[2]	Voc/ Tech[3]
1	0	0	1	0	0	0	1	1

Note: Figures cover institutions located within the Athens-Clarke County, GA Metropolitan Statistical Area and include main campuses only; (1) includes schools accredited by the Liaison Committee on Medical Education and the American Osteopathic Association's Commission on Osteopathic College Accreditation; (2) includes ABA-accredited schools, schools with provisional ABA accreditation, and state accredited schools; (3) includes all schools with programs that are less than 2 years.
Source: National Center for Education Statistics, Integrated Postsecondary Education System (IPEDS), 2021-22; Wikipedia, List of Medical Schools in the United States, accessed April 10, 2023; Wikipedia, List of Law Schools in the United States, accessed April 10, 2023

According to *U.S. News & World Report*, the Athens-Clarke County, GA metro area is home to one of the top 200 national universities in the U.S.: **University of Georgia** (#49 tie). The indicators used to capture academic quality fall into a number of categories: assessment by administrators at peer institutions; retention of students; faculty resources; student selectivity; financial resources; alumni giving; high school counselor ratings of colleges; and graduation rate. *U.S. News & World Report, "America's Best Colleges 2023"*

According to *U.S. News & World Report*, the Athens-Clarke County, GA metro area is home to one of the top 100 law schools in the U.S.: **University of Georgia** (#29). The rankings are based on a weighted average of 12 measures of quality: peer assessment score; assessment score by lawyers/judges; median LSAT scores; median undergrad GPA; acceptance rate; employment rates for graduates; placement success; bar passage rate; faculty resources; expenditures per student; student/faculty ratio; and library resources. *U.S. News & World Report, "America's Best Graduate Schools, Law, 2023"*

According to *U.S. News & World Report*, the Athens-Clarke County, GA metro area is home to one of the top 75 business schools in the U.S.: **University of Georgia (Terry)** (#38). The rankings are based on a weighted average of the following nine measures: quality assessment; peer assessment; recruiter assessment; placement success; mean starting salary and bonus; student selectivity; mean GMAT and GRE scores; mean undergraduate GPA; and acceptance rate. *U.S. News & World Report, "America's Best Graduate Schools, Business, 2023"*

Athens, Georgia

EMPLOYERS

Major Employers

Company Name	Industry
Athens Regional Health Care	Healthcare
Athens-Clarke County	Government
Baldor	Industrial motors
Burton+Burton	Balloons & gifts
Carrier Transicold	Truck refrigeration units
Caterpillar	Excavators
Certainteed	Fiberglass insulation
Clarke County School District	Education
DialAmerica	Telemarketing
McCann	Aerospace products
Merial	Animal health products
Noramco	Medical grade products
Pilgrim's	Food processing
Power Partners	Transformers, chillers, solar panels
Skaps	Non-woven plastics
St. Mary's Healthcare	Healthcare
University of Georgia	Higher education

Note: Companies shown are located within the Athens-Clarke County, GA Metropolitan Statistical Area.
Source: Hoovers.com; Wikipedia

PUBLIC SAFETY

Crime Rate

Area	Total Crime	Murder	Rape[3]	Robbery	Aggrav. Assault	Burglary	Larceny-Theft	Motor Vehicle Theft
City	3,463.9	3.1	81.9	79.6	345.7	465.9	2,213.8	273.9
Suburbs[1]	1,270.6	2.3	20.5	11.4	171.1	219.0	735.7	110.6
Metro[2]	2,572.9	2.8	57.0	51.9	274.8	365.6	1,613.3	207.6
U.S.	2,356.7	6.5	38.4	73.9	279.7	314.2	1,398.0	246.0

Note: Figures are crimes per 100,000 population; (1) All areas within the metro area that are located outside the city limits; (2) Figures cover the Athens-Clarke County, GA Metropolitan Statistical Area; (3) All figures shown were reported using the revised Uniform Crime Reporting (UCR) definition of rape; Due to the transition to the National Incident-Based Reporting System (NIBRS), limited city and metro area data was released for 2021.
Source: FBI Uniform Crime Reports, 2020

Hate Crimes

Area	Number of Quarters Reported	Race/Ethnicity/Ancestry	Religion	Sexual Orientation	Disability	Gender	Gender Identity
City	4	4	1	0	0	0	2
U.S.	4	5,227	1,244	1,110	130	75	266

Note: Due to the transition to the National Incident-Based Reporting System (NIBRS), limited crime data was released for 2021.
Source: Federal Bureau of Investigation, Hate Crime Statistics 2020

Identity Theft Consumer Reports

Area	Reports	Reports per 100,000 Population	Rank[2]
MSA[1]	537	255	100
U.S.	1,108,609	339	-

Note: (1) Figures cover the Athens-Clarke County, GA Metropolitan Statistical Area; (2) Rank ranges from 1 to 391 where 1 indicates greatest number of identity theft reports per 100,000 population
Source: Federal Trade Commission, Consumer Sentinel Network Data Book 2022

Fraud and Other Consumer Reports

Area	Reports	Reports per 100,000 Population	Rank[2]
MSA[1]	1,599	759	250
U.S.	4,064,520	1,245	-

Note: (1) Figures cover the Athens-Clarke County, GA Metropolitan Statistical Area; (2) Rank ranges from 1 to 391 where 1 indicates greatest number of fraud and other consumer reports per 100,000 population
Source: Federal Trade Commission, Consumer Sentinel Network Data Book 2022

POLITICS

2020 Presidential Election Results

Area	Biden	Trump	Jorgensen	Hawkins	Other
Clarke County	70.1	28.1	1.6	0.1	0.1
U.S.	51.3	46.8	1.2	0.3	0.5

Note: Results are percentages and may not add to 100% due to rounding
Source: Dave Leip's Atlas of U.S. Presidential Elections

SPORTS

Professional Sports Teams

Team Name	League	Year Established

No teams are located in the metro area
Source: Wikipedia, Major Professional Sports Teams of the United States and Canada, April 12, 2023

CLIMATE

Average and Extreme Temperatures

Temperature	Jan	Feb	Mar	Apr	May	Jun	Jul	Aug	Sep	Oct	Nov	Dec	Yr.
Extreme High (°F)	79	80	85	93	95	101	105	102	98	95	84	77	105
Average High (°F)	52	56	64	73	80	86	88	88	82	73	63	54	72
Average Temp. (°F)	43	46	53	62	70	77	79	79	73	63	53	45	62
Average Low (°F)	33	36	42	51	59	66	70	69	64	52	42	35	52
Extreme Low (°F)	-8	5	10	26	37	46	53	55	36	28	3	0	-8

Note: Figures cover the years 1945-1990
Source: National Climatic Data Center, International Station Meteorological Climate Summary, 9/96

Average Precipitation/Snowfall/Humidity

Precip./Humidity	Jan	Feb	Mar	Apr	May	Jun	Jul	Aug	Sep	Oct	Nov	Dec	Yr.
Avg. Precip. (in.)	4.7	4.6	5.7	4.3	4.0	3.5	5.1	3.6	3.4	2.8	3.8	4.2	49.8
Avg. Snowfall (in.)	1	1	Tr	Tr	0	0	0	0	0	0	Tr	Tr	2
Avg. Rel. Hum. 7am (%)	79	77	78	78	82	83	88	89	88	84	81	79	82
Avg. Rel. Hum. 4pm (%)	56	50	48	45	49	52	57	56	56	51	52	55	52

Note: Figures cover the years 1945-1990; Tr = Trace amounts (<0.05 in. of rain; <0.5 in. of snow)
Source: National Climatic Data Center, International Station Meteorological Climate Summary, 9/96

Weather Conditions

Temperature			Daytime Sky			Precipitation		
10°F & below	32°F & below	90°F & above	Clear	Partly cloudy	Cloudy	0.01 inch or more precip.	0.1 inch or more snow/ice	Thunder-storms
1	49	38	98	147	120	116	3	48

Note: Figures are average number of days per year and cover the years 1945-1990
Source: National Climatic Data Center, International Station Meteorological Climate Summary, 9/96

HAZARDOUS WASTE

Superfund Sites

The Athens-Clarke County, GA metro area has no sites on the EPA's Superfund Final National Priorities List. There are a total of 1,165 Superfund sites with a status of proposed or final on the list in the U.S. *U.S. Environmental Protection Agency, National Priorities List, April 12, 2023*

AIR QUALITY

Air Quality Trends: Ozone

	1990	1995	2000	2005	2010	2015	2018	2019	2020	2021
MSA[1]	n/a	n/a	n/a	n/a	n/a	n/a	n/a	n/a	n/a	n/a
U.S.	0.087	0.089	0.081	0.080	0.072	0.067	0.069	0.065	0.065	0.067

Note: (1) Data covers the Athens-Clarke County, GA Metropolitan Statistical Area; n/a not available. The values shown are the composite ozone concentration averages among trend sites based on the highest fourth daily maximum 8-hour concentration in parts per million. These trends are based on sites having an adequate record of monitoring data during the trend period. Data from exceptional events are included.
Source: U.S. Environmental Protection Agency, Air Quality Monitoring Information, "Air Quality Trends by City, 1990-2021"

Air Quality Index

Area	Percent of Days when Air Quality was...[2]					AQI Statistics[2]	
	Good	Moderate	Unhealthy for Sensitive Groups	Unhealthy	Very Unhealthy	Maximum	Median
MSA[1]	71.8	27.9	0.3	0.0	0.0	107	41

Note: (1) Data covers the Athens-Clarke County, GA Metropolitan Statistical Area; (2) Based on 365 days with AQI data in 2021. Air Quality Index (AQI) is an index for reporting daily air quality. EPA calculates the AQI for five major air pollutants regulated by the Clean Air Act: ground-level ozone, particle pollution (aka particulate matter), carbon monoxide, sulfur dioxide, and nitrogen dioxide. The AQI runs from 0 to 500. The higher the AQI value, the greater the level of air pollution and the greater the health concern. There are six AQI categories: "Good" AQI is between 0 and 50. Air quality is considered satisfactory; "Moderate" AQI is between 51 and 100. Air quality is acceptable; "Unhealthy for Sensitive Groups" When AQI values are between 101 and 150, members of sensitive groups may experience health effects; "Unhealthy" When AQI values are between 151 and 200 everyone may begin to experience health effects; "Very Unhealthy" AQI values between 201 and 300 trigger a health alert; "Hazardous" AQI values over 300 trigger warnings of emergency conditions (not shown).
Source: U.S. Environmental Protection Agency, Air Quality Index Report, 2021

Air Quality Index Pollutants

Area	Percent of Days when AQI Pollutant was...[2]					
	Carbon Monoxide	Nitrogen Dioxide	Ozone	Sulfur Dioxide	Particulate Matter 2.5	Particulate Matter 10
MSA[1]	0.0	0.0	32.9	(3)	67.1	0.0

Note: (1) Data covers the Athens-Clarke County, GA Metropolitan Statistical Area; (2) Based on 365 days with AQI data in 2021. The Air Quality Index (AQI) is an index for reporting daily air quality. EPA calculates the AQI for five major air pollutants regulated by the Clean Air Act: ground-level ozone, particle pollution (also known as particulate matter), carbon monoxide, sulfur dioxide, and nitrogen dioxide. The AQI runs from 0 to 500. The higher the AQI value, the greater the level of air pollution and the greater the health concern; (3) Sulfur dioxide is no longer included in this table (as of December 8, 2021) because SO_2 concentrations tend to be very localized and not necessarily representative of broad geographical areas like counties and CBSAs.
Source: U.S. Environmental Protection Agency, Air Quality Index Report, 2021

Maximum Air Pollutant Concentrations: Particulate Matter, Ozone, CO and Lead

	Particulate Matter 10 (ug/m^3)	Particulate Matter 2.5 Wtd AM (ug/m^3)	Particulate Matter 2.5 24-Hr (ug/m^3)	Ozone (ppm)	Carbon Monoxide (ppm)	Lead (ug/m^3)
MSA[1] Level	n/a	10.1	25	0.06	n/a	n/a
NAAQS[2]	150	15	35	0.075	9	0.15
Met NAAQS[2]	n/a	Yes	Yes	Yes	n/a	n/a

Note: (1) Data covers the Athens-Clarke County, GA Metropolitan Statistical Area; Data from exceptional events are included; (2) National Ambient Air Quality Standards; ppm = parts per million; ug/m^3 = micrograms per cubic meter; n/a not available.
Concentrations: Particulate Matter 10 (coarse particulate)—highest second maximum 24-hour concentration; Particulate Matter 2.5 Wtd AM (fine particulate)—highest weighted annual mean concentration; Particulate Matter 2.5 24-Hour (fine particulate)—highest 98th percentile 24-hour concentration; Ozone—highest fourth daily maximum 8-hour concentration; Carbon Monoxide—highest second maximum non-overlapping 8-hour concentration; Lead—maximum running 3-month average
Source: U.S. Environmental Protection Agency, Air Quality Monitoring Information, "Air Quality Statistics by City, 2021"

Maximum Air Pollutant Concentrations: Nitrogen Dioxide and Sulfur Dioxide

	Nitrogen Dioxide AM (ppb)	Nitrogen Dioxide 1-Hr (ppb)	Sulfur Dioxide AM (ppb)	Sulfur Dioxide 1-Hr (ppb)	Sulfur Dioxide 24-Hr (ppb)
MSA[1] Level	n/a	n/a	n/a	n/a	n/a
NAAQS[2]	53	100	30	75	140
Met NAAQS[2]	n/a	n/a	n/a	n/a	n/a

Note: (1) Data covers the Athens-Clarke County, GA Metropolitan Statistical Area; Data from exceptional events are included; (2) National Ambient Air Quality Standards; ppm = parts per million; ug/m^3 = micrograms per cubic meter; n/a not available.
Concentrations: Nitrogen Dioxide AM—highest arithmetic mean concentration; Nitrogen Dioxide 1-Hr—highest 98th percentile 1-hour daily maximum concentration; Sulfur Dioxide AM—highest annual mean concentration; Sulfur Dioxide 1-Hr—highest 99th percentile 1-hour daily maximum concentration; Sulfur Dioxide 24-Hr—highest second maximum 24-hour concentration
Source: U.S. Environmental Protection Agency, Air Quality Monitoring Information, "Air Quality Statistics by City, 2021"

Atlanta, Georgia

Background

Atlanta was born of a rough-and-tumble past, first as a natural outgrowth of a thriving railroad network in the 1840s, and second as a resilient go-getter that proudly rose again above the rubble of the Civil War.

Blanketed over the rolling hills of the Piedmont Plateau, at the foot of the Blue Ridge Mountains, Georgia's capital stands 1,000 feet above sea level. Atlanta is located in the northwest corner of Georgia where the terrain is rolling to hilly, and slopes downward to the east, west, and south.

Atlanta proper begins at the "terminus," or zero-mile mark of the now defunct Western and Atlantic Railroad Line. However its metropolitan area comprises 28 counties that include Fulton, DeKalb, Clayton, and Gwinnet, among others. Population-wise, Atlanta is the largest city in the southeast United States and has been growing at a steady rate for the last decade. Within the city itself, Atlanta's has a diversified economy that allows for employment in a variety of sectors such as manufacturing, retail, and government.

The city hosts many of the nation's Fortune 500 company headquarters, including CNN, as well as the nation's Centers for Disease Control and Prevention (CDC). The city boasts an involved city government that seeks to work closely with its business community; the city inaugurated its first black mayor in 1974.

While schools in the city remain predominantly black and schools in its suburbs predominantly white, Atlanta boasts a racially progressive climate. The Martin Luther King, Jr. Historic Site and Preservation District is in the Sweet Auburn neighborhood, which includes King's birth home and the Ebenezer Baptist Church, where both he and his father preached. The city's consortium of black colleges that includes Morehouse College and the Interdenominational Theological Center testifies to the city's appreciation for a people who have always been one-third of Atlanta's population. Atlanta continues to be a major regional center for film and television production, with Tyler Perry Studios, Turner Studios and EVE/ScreenGems Studio in the city.

King is one of Atlanta's two Nobel Peace Prize winners. The second, former President Jimmy Carter, famously of Plains, Georgia, also brings his name to Atlanta via the Carter Center. Devoted to human rights, the center is operated with neighboring Emory University, and sits adjacent to the Jimmy Carter Library and Museum on a hill overlooking the city. Habitat for Humanity, also founded by Carter, is headquartered in Atlanta. The city's largest city park, Westside Park at Bellwood Quarry was completed in August 2020.

MLB's Atlanta Braves won the World Series in 2021, their first since 1995. The franchise has four World Series wins.

Hartsfield-Jackson Atlanta International Airport, the world's busiest passenger airport, underwent significant expansion in recent years. MARTA, the city's public transport system, is the nation's 9th largest and transports on average 500,000 passengers daily on a 48-mile, 38-station rapid rail system with connections to hundreds of bus routes.

The Appalachian chain of mountains, the Gulf of Mexico, and the Atlantic Ocean influence Atlanta's climate. Temperatures are moderate to hot throughout the year, but extended periods of heat are unusual, and the city rarely reaches 100-degrees. Atlanta winters are mild with a few, short-lived cold spells. Summers can be humid.

Rankings

General Rankings

- The Atlanta metro area was identified as one of America's fastest-growing areas in terms of population and business growth by *MagnifyMoney*. The area ranked #32 out of 35. The 100 most populous metro areas in the U.S. were evaluated on their change from 2011 to 2016 in the following categories: people and housing; workforce and employment opportunities; growing industry. *www.businessinsider.com, "The 35 Cities in the US with the Biggest Influx of People, the Most Work Opportunities, and the Hottest Business Growth," August 12, 2018*

- Atlanta was selected as one of the best places to live in America by *Outside Magazine*. Criteria centered on diversity; sustainability; outdoor equity; and affordability. Local experts shared highlights from hands-on experience in each location. *Outside Magazine, "The 20 Most Livable Towns and Cities in America," October 15, 2021*

- Atlanta was selected as one of the best places to live in the United States by *Money* magazine. The city ranked #1 out of 50. This year's list focused on cities that would be welcoming to a broader group of people and with populations of at least 20,000. Beginning with a pool of 1,370 candidates, editors looked at 350 data points, organized into the these nine categories: income and personal finance, cost of living, economic opportunity, housing market, fun and amenities, health and safety, education, diversity, and quality of life. *Money, "The 50 Best Places to Live in the U.S. in 2022-2023" September 29, 2022*

- The human resources consulting firm Mercer ranked 231 major cities worldwide in terms of overall quality of life. Atlanta ranked #64. Criteria: political, social, economic, and socio-cultural factors; medical and health considerations; schools and education; public services and transportation; recreation; consumer goods; housing; and natural environment. *Mercer, "Mercer 2019 Quality of Living Survey," March 13, 2019*

Business/Finance Rankings

- The Brookings Institution ranked the nation's largest cities based on income inequality. Atlanta was ranked #1 (#1 = greatest inequality). Criteria: the "95/20 ratio," a figure representing the income at which a household earns more than 95 percent of all other households, divided by the income at which a household earns more than only 20 percent of all other households. *Brookings Institution, "Household Income Inequality, Largest Cities of 97 Large U.S. Metro Areas, 2014-2016," February 5, 2018*

- The Brookings Institution ranked the 100 largest metro areas in the U.S. based on income inequality. Atlanta was ranked #26 (#1 = greatest inequality). Criteria: the "95/20 ratio," a figure representing the income at which a household earns more than 95 percent of all other households, divided by the income at which a household earns more than only 20 percent of all other households. *Brookings Institution, "Household Income Inequality, 100 Largest U.S. Metro Areas, 2014-2016," February 5, 2018*

- Payscale.com ranked the 32 largest metro areas in terms of wage growth. The Atlanta metro area ranked #9. Criteria: quarterly changes in private industry employee and education professional wage growth from the previous year. *PayScale, "Wage Trends by Metro Area-1st Quarter," April 20, 2023*

- The Atlanta metro area was identified as one of the most debt-ridden places in America by the finance site Credit.com. The metro area was ranked #7. Criteria: residents' average credit card debt as well as median income. *Credit.com, "25 Cities With the Most Credit Card Debt," February 28, 2018*

- Atlanta was identified as one of America's most frugal metro areas by *Coupons.com*. The city ranked #8 out of 25. Criteria: digital coupon usage. *Coupons.com, "America's Most Frugal Cities of 2017," March 22, 2018*

- Atlanta was cited as one of America's top metros for total corporate facility investment in 2022. The area ranked #6 in the large metro area category (population over 1 million). *Site Selection, "Top Metros of 2022," March 2023*

- Atlanta was identified as one of the happiest cities to work in by CareerBliss.com, an online community for career advancement. The city ranked #3 out of 10. Criteria: an employee's relationship with his or her boss and co-workers; daily tasks; general work environment; compensation; opportunities for advancement; company culture and job reputation; and resources. *Businesswire.com, "CareerBliss Happiest Cities to Work 2019," February 12, 2019*

- The Atlanta metro area appeared on the Milken Institute "2022 Best Performing Cities" list. Rank: #47 out of 200 large metro areas (population over 250,000). Criteria: job growth; wage and salary growth; high-tech output growth; housing affordability; household broadband access. *Milken Institute, "Best-Performing Cities 2022," March 28, 2022*

- *Forbes* ranked the 200 most populous metro areas to determine the nation's "Best Places for Business and Careers." The Atlanta metro area was ranked #13. Criteria: costs (business and living); job growth (past and projected); income growth; quality of life; educational attainment (college and high school); projected economic growth; cultural and leisure opportunities; workplace tolerance laws; net migration patterns. *Forbes, "The Best Places for Business and Careers 2019: Seattle Still On Top," October 30, 2019*

- Mercer Human Resources Consulting ranked 227 cities worldwide in terms of cost-of-living. Atlanta ranked #42 (the lower the ranking, the higher the cost-of-living). The survey measured the comparative cost of over 200 items (such as housing, food, clothing, domestic supplies, transportation, and recreation/entertainment) in each location. *Mercer, "2022 Cost of Living City Ranking," June 29, 2022*

Children/Family Rankings

- Atlanta was selected as one of the most playful cities in the U.S. by KaBOOM! The organization's Playful City USA initiative honors cities and towns across the nation that have made their communities more playable. Criteria: pledging to integrate play as a solution to challenges in their communities; making it easy for children to get active and balanced play; creating more family-friendly and innovative communities as a result. *KaBOOM! National Campaign for Play, "2017 Playful City USA Communities"*

Culture/Performing Arts Rankings

- Atlanta was selected as one of the 25 best cities for moviemakers in North America. Great film cities are places where filmmaking dreams can come true, that offer more creative space, lower costs, and great outdoor locations. NYC & LA were intentionally excluded. Criteria: longstanding reputations as film-friendly communities; film community and culture; affordability; and quality of life. The city was ranked #1. *MovieMaker Magazine, "Best Places to Live and Work as a Moviemaker, 2023," January 18, 2023*

Dating/Romance Rankings

- Atlanta was selected as one of the nation's most romantic cities with 100,000 or more residents by Amazon.com. The city ranked #9 of 20. Criteria: per capita sales of romance novels, relationship books, romantic comedy movies, romantic music, and sexual wellness products. *Amazon.com, "Top 20 Most Romantic Cities in the U.S.," February 1, 2017*

Education Rankings

- Personal finance website *WalletHub* analyzed the 150 largest U.S. metropolitan statistical areas to determine where the most educated Americans are putting their degrees to work. Criteria: education levels; percentage of workers with degrees; education quality and attainment gap; public school quality rankings; quality and enrollment of each metro area's universities. Atlanta was ranked #26 (#1 = most educated city). *www.WalletHub.com, "Most & Least Educated Cities in America," July 18, 2022*

- Atlanta was selected as one of America's most literate cities. The city ranked #6 out of the 84 largest U.S. cities. Criteria: number of booksellers; library resources; Internet resources; educational attainment; periodical publishing resources; newspaper circulation. *Central Connecticut State University, "America's Most Literate Cities, 2018," February 2019*

Environmental Rankings

- The U.S. Environmental Protection Agency (EPA) released its list of U.S. metropolitan areas with the most ENERGY STAR certified buildings in 2022. The Atlanta metro area was ranked #3 out of 25. *U.S. Environmental Protection Agency, "2023 Energy Star Top Cities," April 26, 2023*

Health/Fitness Rankings

- For each of the 100 largest cities in the United States, the American Fitness Index®, compiled in partnership between the American College of Sports Medicine and the Elevance Health Foundation, evaluated community infrastructure and 34 health behaviors including preventive health, levels of chronic disease conditions, food insecurity, sleep quality, pedestrian safety, air quality, and community/environment resources that support physical activity. Atlanta ranked #18 for "community fitness." *americanfitnessindex.org, "2022 ACSM American Fitness Index Summary Report," July 12, 2022*

- The Atlanta metro area was identified as one of the worst cities for bed bugs in America by pest control company Orkin. The area ranked #16 out of 50 based on the number of bed bug treatments Orkin performed from December 2021 to November 2022. *Orkin, "The Windy City Can't Blow Bed Bugs Away: Chicago Ranks #1 For Third Consecutive Year On Orkin's Bed Bug Cities List," January 9, 2023*

- Atlanta was identified as a "2022 Spring Allergy Capital." The area ranked #72 out of 100. Three groups of factors were used to identify the most challenging cities for people with allergies during the spring season: annual spring pollen scores; over the counter allergy medicine use; number of board-certified allergy specialists. *Asthma and Allergy Foundation of America, "Spring Allergy Capitals 2022," March 2, 2022*

- Atlanta was identified as a "2022 Fall Allergy Capital." The area ranked #72 out of 100. Three groups of factors were used to identify the most challenging cities for people with allergies during the fall season: annual fall pollen scores; over the counter allergy medicine use; number of board-certified allergy specialists. *Asthma and Allergy Foundation of America, "Fall Allergy Capitals 2022," March 2, 2022*

- Atlanta was identified as a "2022 Asthma Capital." The area ranked #30 out of the nation's 100 largest metropolitan areas. Criteria: estimated asthma prevalence; asthma-related mortality; and ER visits due to asthma. Risk factors analyzed but not factored in the rankings: annual pollen score; annual air quality; public smoking laws; access to board-certified asthma specialists; rescue and controller medication use; uninsured rate; poverty rate. *Asthma and Allergy Foundation of America, "Asthma Capitals 2022: The Most Challenging Places to Live With Asthma," September 14, 2022*

Pet Rankings

- Atlanta appeared on *The Dogington Post* site as one of the top cities for dog lovers, ranking #6 out of 15. The real estate marketplace, Zillow®, and Rover, the largest pet sitter and dog walker network, introduced a new list of "Top Emerging Dog-Friendly Cities" for 2021. Criteria: number of new dog accounts on the Rover platform; and rentals and listings that mention features that attract dog owners (fenced-in yards, dog houses, dog door or proximity to a dog park). *www.dogingtonpost.com, "15 Cities Emerging as Dog-Friendliest in 2021," May 11, 2021*

Real Estate Rankings

- *WalletHub* compared the most populated U.S. cities to determine which had the best markets for real estate agents. Atlanta ranked #18 where demand was high and pay was the best. Criteria: sales per agent; annual median wage for real-estate agents; monthly average starting salary for real estate agents; real estate job density and competition; unemployment rate; home turnover rate; housing-market health index; and other relevant metrics. *www.WalletHub.com, "2021 Best Places to Be a Real Estate Agent," May 12, 2021*

- According to Penske Truck Rental, the Atlanta metro area was named the #5 moving destination in 2022, based on one-way consumer truck rental reservations made through Penske's website, rental locations, and reservations call center. *gopenske.com/blog, "Penske Truck Rental's 2022 Top Moving Destinations," April 27, 2023*

- Atlanta was ranked #117 out of 235 metro areas in terms of housing affordability in 2022 by the National Association of Home Builders (#1 = most affordable). Criteria: the share of homes sold in that area affordable to a family earning the local median income, based on standard mortgage underwriting criteria. *National Association of Home Builders®, NAHB-Wells Fargo Housing Opportunity Index, 4th Quarter 2022*

Safety Rankings

- Allstate ranked the 200 largest cities in America in terms of driver safety. Atlanta ranked #178. Criteria: internal property damage claims over a two-year period from January 2016 to December 2017. The report helps increase the importance of safety and awareness behind the wheel. *Allstate, "Allstate America's Best Drivers Report, 2019" June 24, 2019*

- Atlanta was identified as one of the most dangerous cities in America by NeighborhoodScout. The city ranked #94 out of 100 (#1 = most dangerous). Criteria: number of violent crimes per 1,000 residents. The editors evaluated cities with 25,000 or more residents. *NeighborhoodScout.com, "2023 Top 100 Most Dangerous Cities in the U.S.," January 12, 2023*

- The National Insurance Crime Bureau ranked 390 metro areas in the U.S. in terms of per capita rates of vehicle theft. The Atlanta metro area ranked #118 (#1 = highest rate). Criteria: number of vehicle theft offenses per 100,000 inhabitants in 2021. *National Insurance Crime Bureau, "Hot Spots 2021," September 1, 2022*

Seniors/Retirement Rankings

- From its Best Cities for Successful Aging indexes, the Milken Institute generated rankings for metropolitan areas, weighing data in nine categories—health care, wellness, living arrangements, transportation and convenience, financial characteristics, education, employment, community engagement, and overall livability. The Atlanta metro area was ranked #62 overall in the large metro area category. *Milken Institute, "Best Cities for Successful Aging, 2017" March 14, 2017*

Sports/Recreation Rankings

- Atlanta was chosen as one of America's best cities for bicycling. The city ranked #42 out of 50. Criteria: cycling infrastructure that is safe and friendly for all ages; energy and bike culture. The editors evaluated cities with populations of 100,000 or more. *Bicycling, "The 50 Best Bike Cities in America," October 10, 2018*

Transportation Rankings

- Atlanta was identified as one of the most congested metro areas in the U.S. The area ranked #8 out of 10. Criteria: yearly delay per auto commuter in hours. *Texas A&M Transportation Institute, "2021 Urban Mobility Report," June 2021*

- According to the INRIX "2022 Global Traffic Scorecard," Atlanta was identified as one of the most congested metro areas in the U.S. The area ranked #10 out of 25. Criteria: average annual time spent in traffic and average cost of congestion per motorist. *Inrix.com, "Return to Work, Higher Gas Prices & Inflation Drove Americans to Spend Hundreds More in Time and Money Commuting," January 10, 2023*

Women/Minorities Rankings

- *Travel + Leisure* listed the best cities in and around the U.S. for a memorable and fun girls' trip, even on a budget. Whether it is for a special occasion, to make new memories or just to get away, Atlanta is sure to have something for all the ladies in your tribe. *Travel + Leisure, "25 Affordable Girls Weekend Getaways That Won't Break the Bank," November 25, 2022*

- Atlanta was selected as one of the queerest cities in America by *The Advocate*. The city ranked #6 out of 25. Criteria, among many: Trans Pride parades/festivals; gay rugby teams; lesbian bars; LGBTQ centers; theater screenings of "Moonlight"; LGBTQ-inclusive nondiscrimination ordinances; and gay bowling teams. *The Advocate, "Queerest Cities in America 2017" January 12, 2017*

- Personal finance website *WalletHub* compared more than 180 U.S. cities across two key dimensions, "Hispanic Business-Friendliness" and "Hispanic Purchasing Power," to arrive at the most favorable conditions for Hispanic entrepreneurs. Atlanta was ranked #24 out of 182. Criteria includes: share of Hispanic-Owned Businesses; Hispanic entrepreneurship rate to median annual income of Hispanics; Small Business-Friendliness score; cost of living; and number of Hispanics with at least a bachelor's degree. *WalletHub.com, "2019's Best Cities for Hispanic Entrepreneurs," May 1, 2019*

Miscellaneous Rankings

- *MoveHub* ranked 446 hipster cities across 20 countries, using its new and improved *alternative* Hipster Index and Atlanta came out as #14 among the top 50. Criteria: population over 150,000; number of vintage boutiques; density of tattoo parlors; vegan places to eat; coffee shops; and density of vinyl record stores. *www.movehub.com, "The Hipster Index: Brighton Pips Portland to Global Top Spot," July 28, 2021*

- In its roundup of St. Patrick's Day parades "Gayot" listed the best festivals and parades of all things Irish. The festivities in Atlanta as among the best in North America. *www.gayot.com, "Best St. Patrick's Day Parades," March 2023*

- The watchdog site, Charity Navigator, conducted a study of charities in major markets both to analyze statistical differences in their financial, accountability, and transparency practices and to track year-to-year variations in individual philanthropic communities. The Atlanta metro area was ranked #18 among the 30 metro markets in the rating category of Overall Score. *www.charitynavigator.org, "2017 Metro Market Study," May 1, 2017*

- *WalletHub* compared the 150 most populated U.S. cities to determine their operating efficiency. A "Quality of Services" score was constructed for each city and then divided by the total budget per capita to reveal which were managed the best. Atlanta ranked #125. Criteria: financial stability; economy; education; safety; health; infrastructure and pollution. *www.WalletHub.com, "2022's Best- & Worst-Run Cities in America," June 21, 2022*

- The National Alliance to End Homelessness listed the 25 most populous metro areas with the highest rate of homelessness. The Atlanta metro area had a high rate of homelessness. Criteria: number of homeless people per 10,000 population in 2016. *National Alliance to End Homelessness, "Homelessness in the 25 Most Populous U.S. Metro Areas," September 1, 2017*

Business Environment

DEMOGRAPHICS

Population Growth

Area	1990 Census	2000 Census	2010 Census	2020 Census	Population Growth (%) 1990-2020	2010-2020
City	394,092	416,474	420,003	498,715	26.5	18.7
MSA[1]	3,069,411	4,247,981	5,268,860	6,089,815	98.4	15.6
U.S.	248,709,873	281,421,906	308,745,538	331,449,281	33.3	7.4

Note: (1) Figures cover the Atlanta-Sandy Springs-Alpharetta, GA Metropolitan Statistical Area
Source: U.S. Census Bureau, 1990 Census, 2000 Census, 2010 Census, 2020 Census

Race

Area	White Alone[2] (%)	Black Alone[2] (%)	Asian Alone[2] (%)	AIAN[3] Alone[2] (%)	NHOPI[4] Alone[2] (%)	Other Race Alone[2] (%)	Two or More Races (%)
City	39.8	47.2	4.5	0.3	0.0	2.4	5.8
MSA[1]	45.5	33.6	6.6	0.5	0.0	6.0	7.7
U.S.	61.6	12.4	6.0	1.1	0.2	8.4	10.2

Note: (1) Figures cover the Atlanta-Sandy Springs-Alpharetta, GA Metropolitan Statistical Area; (2) Alone is defined as not being in combination with one or more other races; (3) American Indian and Alaska Native; (4) Native Hawaiian and Other Pacific Islander
Source: U.S. Census Bureau, 2020 Census

Hispanic or Latino Origin

Area	Total (%)	Mexican (%)	Puerto Rican (%)	Cuban (%)	Other (%)
City	5.0	1.9	0.8	0.3	2.0
MSA[1]	11.0	5.5	1.1	0.4	3.9
U.S.	18.4	11.2	1.8	0.7	4.7

Note: Persons of Hispanic or Latino origin can be of any race; (1) Figures cover the Atlanta-Sandy Springs-Alpharetta, GA Metropolitan Statistical Area
Source: U.S. Census Bureau, 2017-2021 American Community Survey 5-Year Estimates

Age

Area	Under Age 5	Age 5–19	Age 20–34	Age 35–44	Age 45–54	Age 55–64	Age 65–74	Age 75–84	Age 85+	Median Age
City	4.9	15.5	33.3	14.3	11.2	9.5	6.8	3.3	1.3	33.1
MSA[1]	5.7	20.6	20.9	13.7	13.8	12.1	8.3	3.7	1.2	36.9
U.S.	5.6	19.2	20.2	12.7	12.4	13.1	10.0	4.9	1.9	38.8

Note: (1) Figures cover the Atlanta-Sandy Springs-Alpharetta, GA Metropolitan Statistical Area
Source: U.S. Census Bureau, 2020 Census

Disability by Age

Area	All Ages	Under 18 Years Old	18 to 64 Years Old	65 Years and Over
City	11.4	4.7	9.3	35.0
MSA[1]	10.3	4.0	8.6	31.5
U.S.	12.6	4.4	10.3	33.4

Note: Figures show percent of the civilian noninstitutionalized population that reported having a disability. Disability status is determined from six types of difficulty: vision, hearing, cognitive, ambulatory, self-care, and independent living. For children under 5 years old, hearing and vision difficulty are used to determine disability status. For children between the ages of 5 and 14, disability status is determined from hearing, vision, cognitive, ambulatory, and self-care difficulties. For people aged 15 years and older, they are considered to have a disability if they have difficulty with any one of the six difficulty types; Note: (1) Figures cover the Atlanta-Sandy Springs-Alpharetta, GA Metropolitan Statistical Area
Source: U.S. Census Bureau, 2017-2021 American Community Survey 5-Year Estimates

Ancestry

Area	German	Irish	English	American	Italian	Polish	French[2]	Scottish	Dutch
City	6.8	5.9	8.1	4.8	2.9	1.4	1.8	1.5	0.5
MSA[1]	6.5	6.4	8.0	8.0	2.6	1.2	1.3	1.6	0.6
U.S.	12.8	9.6	8.1	5.7	5.0	2.7	2.2	1.6	1.1

Note: Figures are the percentage of the total population reporting a particular ancestry. The nine most commonly reported ancestries in the U.S. are shown. Figures include multiple ancestries (e.g. if a person reported being Irish and Italian, they were included in both columns); (1) Figures cover the Atlanta-Sandy Springs-Alpharetta, GA Metropolitan Statistical Area; (2) Excludes Basque
Source: U.S. Census Bureau, 2017-2021 American Community Survey 5-Year Estimates

Foreign-born Population

Area	Any Foreign Country	Asia	Mexico	Europe	Caribbean	Central America[2]	South America	Africa	Canada
City	8.3	3.4	0.7	1.4	0.8	0.2	0.8	0.8	0.3
MSA[1]	14.1	4.7	2.3	1.1	1.6	1.2	1.2	1.7	0.2
U.S.	13.6	4.2	3.3	1.5	1.4	1.1	1.1	0.8	0.2

Note: (1) Figures cover the Atlanta-Sandy Springs-Alpharetta, GA Metropolitan Statistical Area; (2) Excludes Mexico.
Source: U.S. Census Bureau, 2017-2021 American Community Survey 5-Year Estimates

Household Size

Area	One	Two	Three	Four	Five	Six	Seven or More	Average Household Size
City	45.9	31.9	11.0	6.8	2.5	1.2	0.7	2.10
MSA[1]	26.8	31.8	17.1	14.3	6.2	2.4	1.4	2.70
U.S.	28.1	33.8	15.5	12.9	6.0	2.3	1.4	2.60

Note: (1) Figures cover the Atlanta-Sandy Springs-Alpharetta, GA Metropolitan Statistical Area
Source: U.S. Census Bureau, 2017-2021 American Community Survey 5-Year Estimates

Household Relationships

Area	Householder	Opposite-sex Spouse	Same-sex Spouse	Opposite-sex Unmarried Partner	Same-sex Unmarried Partner	Child[2]	Grandchild	Other Relatives	Non-relatives
City	45.7	10.4	0.5	3.1	0.6	20.7	2.1	3.9	5.9
MSA[1]	37.1	16.7	0.2	2.1	0.2	30.4	2.7	5.7	3.5
U.S.	38.3	17.5	0.2	2.5	0.2	28.3	2.4	4.8	3.4

Note: Figures are percent of the total population; (1) Figures cover the Atlanta-Sandy Springs-Alpharetta, GA Metropolitan Statistical Area; (2) Includes biological, adopted, and stepchildren of the householder
Source: U.S. Census Bureau, 2020 Census

Gender

Area	Males	Females	Males per 100 Females
City	245,444	253,271	96.9
MSA[1]	2,933,974	3,155,841	93.0
U.S.	162,685,811	168,763,470	96.4

Note: (1) Figures cover the Atlanta-Sandy Springs-Alpharetta, GA Metropolitan Statistical Area
Source: U.S. Census Bureau, 2020 Census

Marital Status

Area	Never Married	Now Married[2]	Separated	Widowed	Divorced
City	55.1	29.0	1.8	4.0	10.1
MSA[1]	35.7	47.6	1.8	4.4	10.6
U.S.	33.8	48.0	1.8	5.6	10.8

Note: Figures are percentages and cover the population 15 years of age and older; (1) Figures cover the Atlanta-Sandy Springs-Alpharetta, GA Metropolitan Statistical Area; (2) Excludes separated
Source: U.S. Census Bureau, 2017-2021 American Community Survey 5-Year Estimates

Religious Groups by Family

Area	Catholic	Baptist	Methodist	LDS[2]	Pentecostal	Lutheran	Islam	Adventist	Other
MSA[1]	10.7	14.7	6.7	0.8	2.0	0.4	1.9	1.9	12.4
U.S.	18.7	7.3	3.0	2.0	1.8	1.7	1.3	1.3	11.6

Note: Figures are the number of adherents as a percentage of the total population and cover the eight largest religious groups in the U.S; (1) Figures cover the Atlanta-Sandy Springs-Alpharetta, GA Metropolitan Statistical Area; (2) Church of Jesus Christ of Latter-day Saints
Sources: 2020 U.S. Religion Census, Association of Statisticians of American Religious Bodies; The Association of Religion Data Archives (ARDA)

Religious Groups by Tradition

Area	Catholic	Evangelical Protestant	Mainline Protestant	Black Protestant	Islam	Judaism	Hinduism	Orthodox	Buddhism
MSA[1]	10.7	22.3	7.4	5.3	1.9	0.5	0.7	0.3	0.2
U.S.	18.7	16.5	5.2	2.3	1.3	0.6	0.4	0.4	0.3

Note: Figures are the number of adherents as a percentage of the total population; (1) Figures cover the Atlanta-Sandy Springs-Alpharetta, GA Metropolitan Statistical Area
Sources: 2020 U.S. Religion Census, Association of Statisticians of American Religious Bodies; The Association of Religion Data Archives (ARDA)

ECONOMY

Gross Metropolitan Product

Area	2020	2021	2022	2023	Rank[2]
MSA[1]	425.4	465.1	507.9	540.7	11

Note: Figures are in billions of dollars; (1) Figures cover the Atlanta-Sandy Springs-Alpharetta, GA Metropolitan Statistical Area; (2) Rank is based on 2021 data and ranges from 1 to 381
Source: U.S. Conference of Mayors, U.S. Metro Economies: U.S. Metros Compared to Global and State Economies, June 2022

Economic Growth

Area	2018-20 (%)	2021 (%)	2022 (%)	2023 (%)	Rank[2]
MSA[1]	-0.1	5.9	3.3	3.1	151
U.S.	-0.6	5.7	3.1	2.9	—

Note: Figures are real gross metropolitan product (GMP) growth rates and represent average annual percent change; (1) Figures cover the Atlanta-Sandy Springs-Alpharetta, GA Metropolitan Statistical Area; (2) Rank is based on 2020 2-year average annual percent change and ranges from 1 to 381
Source: U.S. Conference of Mayors, U.S. Metro Economies: U.S. Metros Compared to Global and State Economies, June 2022

Metropolitan Area Exports

Area	2016	2017	2018	2019	2020	2021	Rank[2]
MSA[1]	20,480.1	21,748.0	24,091.6	25,800.8	25,791.0	28,116.4	16

Note: Figures are in millions of dollars; (1) Figures cover the Atlanta-Sandy Springs-Alpharetta, GA Metropolitan Statistical Area; (2) Rank is based on 2021 data and ranges from 1 to 388
Source: U.S. Department of Commerce, International Trade Administration, Office of Trade and Economic Analysis, Industry and Analysis, Exports by Metropolitan Area, data extracted March 16, 2023

Building Permits

Area	Single-Family 2021	Single-Family 2022	Pct. Chg.	Multi-Family 2021	Multi-Family 2022	Pct. Chg.	Total 2021	Total 2022	Pct. Chg.
City	855	1,775	107.6	1,558	10,078	546.9	2,413	11,853	391.2
MSA[1]	31,560	26,623	-15.6	7,906	21,484	171.7	39,466	48,107	21.9
U.S.	1,115,400	975,600	-12.5	621,600	689,500	10.9	1,737,000	1,665,100	-4.1

Note: (1) Figures cover the Atlanta-Sandy Springs-Alpharetta, GA Metropolitan Statistical Area; Figures represent new, privately-owned housing units authorized (unadjusted data); All permit data are based on estimates with imputation
Source: U.S. Census Bureau, Manufacturing, Mining, and Construction Statistics, Building Permits, 2021, 2022

Bankruptcy Filings

Area	Business Filings 2021	Business Filings 2022	% Chg.	Nonbusiness Filings 2021	Nonbusiness Filings 2022	% Chg.
Fulton County	87	124	42.5	2,072	2,323	12.1
U.S.	14,347	13,481	-6.0	399,269	374,240	-6.3

Note: Business filings include Chapter 7, Chapter 9, Chapter 11, Chapter 12, Chapter 13, Chapter 15, and Section 304; Nonbusiness filings include Chapter 7, Chapter 11, and Chapter 13
Source: Administrative Office of the U.S. Courts, Business and Nonbusiness Bankruptcy, County Cases Commenced by Chapter of the Bankruptcy Code, During the 12-Month Period Ending December 31, 2021 and Business and Nonbusiness Bankruptcy, County Cases Commenced by Chapter of the Bankruptcy Code, During the 12-Month Period Ending December 31, 2022

Housing Vacancy Rates

Area	Gross Vacancy Rate[2] (%) 2020	2021	2022	Year-Round Vacancy Rate[3] (%) 2020	2021	2022	Rental Vacancy Rate[4] (%) 2020	2021	2022	Homeowner Vacancy Rate[5] (%) 2020	2021	2022
MSA[1]	5.8	6.1	5.9	5.4	5.7	5.7	6.4	5.2	6.7	0.8	1.0	0.8
U.S.	10.6	10.8	10.5	8.2	8.4	8.2	6.3	6.1	5.8	1.0	0.9	0.8

Note: (1) Figures cover the Atlanta-Sandy Springs-Alpharetta, GA Metropolitan Statistical Area; (2) The percentage of the total housing inventory that is vacant; (3) The percentage of the housing inventory (excluding seasonal units) that is year-round vacant; (4) The percentage of rental inventory that is vacant for rent; (5) The percentage of homeowner inventory that is vacant for sale
Source: U.S. Census Bureau, Housing Vacancies and Homeownership Annual Statistics: 2020, 2021, 2022

INCOME

Income

Area	Per Capita ($)	Median Household ($)	Average Household ($)
City	54,466	69,164	118,074
MSA[1]	39,267	75,267	104,478
U.S.	37,638	69,021	97,196

Note: (1) Figures cover the Atlanta-Sandy Springs-Alpharetta, GA Metropolitan Statistical Area
Source: U.S. Census Bureau, 2017-2021 American Community Survey 5-Year Estimates

Atlanta, Georgia

Household Income Distribution

Area	Under $15,000	$15,000 -$24,999	$25,000 -$34,999	$35,000 -$49,999	$50,000 -$74,999	$75,000 -$99,999	$100,000 -$149,999	$150,000 and up
City	14.2	8.1	7.3	9.4	14.5	11.0	13.5	22.0
MSA[1]	7.6	6.5	7.5	11.1	17.2	13.3	17.3	19.5
U.S.	9.4	7.8	8.2	11.4	16.8	12.8	16.3	17.3

Note: (1) Figures cover the Atlanta-Sandy Springs-Alpharetta, GA Metropolitan Statistical Area
Source: U.S. Census Bureau, 2017-2021 American Community Survey 5-Year Estimates

Poverty Rate

Area	All Ages	Under 18 Years Old	18 to 64 Years Old	65 Years and Over
City	18.5	27.1	16.5	16.9
MSA[1]	11.1	15.5	9.9	8.5
U.S.	12.6	17.0	11.8	9.6

Note: Figures are percentage of people whose income during the past 12 months was below the poverty level; (1) Figures cover the Atlanta-Sandy Springs-Alpharetta, GA Metropolitan Statistical Area
Source: U.S. Census Bureau, 2017-2021 American Community Survey 5-Year Estimates

EMPLOYMENT

Labor Force and Employment

Area	Civilian Labor Force Dec. 2021	Civilian Labor Force Dec. 2022	% Chg.	Workers Employed Dec. 2021	Workers Employed Dec. 2022	% Chg.
City	271,164	274,219	1.1	261,888	265,951	1.6
MSA[1]	3,175,581	3,216,104	1.3	3,085,734	3,133,430	1.5
U.S.	161,696,000	164,224,000	1.6	155,732,000	158,872,000	2.0

Note: Data is not seasonally adjusted and covers workers 16 years of age and older; (1) Figures cover the Atlanta-Sandy Springs-Alpharetta, GA Metropolitan Statistical Area
Source: Bureau of Labor Statistics, Local Area Unemployment Statistics

Unemployment Rate

Area	Jan.	Feb.	Mar.	Apr.	May	Jun.	Jul.	Aug.	Sep.	Oct.	Nov.	Dec.
City	4.0	3.8	3.9	2.9	3.1	3.7	3.4	3.5	3.1	3.4	3.2	3.0
MSA[1]	3.3	3.2	3.2	2.4	2.6	3.2	2.8	3.0	2.5	2.9	2.7	2.6
U.S.	4.4	4.1	3.8	3.3	3.4	3.8	3.8	3.8	3.3	3.4	3.4	3.3

Note: Data is not seasonally adjusted and covers workers 16 years of age and older; (1) Figures cover the Atlanta-Sandy Springs-Alpharetta, GA Metropolitan Statistical Area
Source: Bureau of Labor Statistics, Local Area Unemployment Statistics

Average Wages

Occupation	$/Hr.	Occupation	$/Hr.
Accountants and Auditors	42.89	Maintenance and Repair Workers	21.53
Automotive Mechanics	23.34	Marketing Managers	73.79
Bookkeepers	23.13	Network and Computer Systems Admin.	50.54
Carpenters	24.77	Nurses, Licensed Practical	26.03
Cashiers	12.29	Nurses, Registered	43.40
Computer Programmers	47.05	Nursing Assistants	17.12
Computer Systems Analysts	50.28	Office Clerks, General	19.42
Computer User Support Specialists	30.05	Physical Therapists	46.86
Construction Laborers	19.06	Physicians	123.80
Cooks, Restaurant	14.12	Plumbers, Pipefitters and Steamfitters	28.56
Customer Service Representatives	19.35	Police and Sheriff's Patrol Officers	26.02
Dentists	n/a	Postal Service Mail Carriers	26.65
Electricians	27.76	Real Estate Sales Agents	28.00
Engineers, Electrical	56.29	Retail Salespersons	15.55
Fast Food and Counter Workers	11.65	Sales Representatives, Technical/Scientific	52.79
Financial Managers	83.96	Secretaries, Exc. Legal/Medical/Executive	19.44
First-Line Supervisors of Office Workers	31.25	Security Guards	16.02
General and Operations Managers	59.75	Surgeons	212.04
Hairdressers/Cosmetologists	18.59	Teacher Assistants, Exc. Postsecondary*	14.07
Home Health and Personal Care Aides	12.95	Teachers, Secondary School, Exc. Sp. Ed.*	34.25
Janitors and Cleaners	15.06	Telemarketers	15.50
Landscaping/Groundskeeping Workers	17.07	Truck Drivers, Heavy/Tractor-Trailer	26.24
Lawyers	84.73	Truck Drivers, Light/Delivery Services	21.28
Maids and Housekeeping Cleaners	13.58	Waiters and Waitresses	14.52

Note: Wage data covers the Atlanta-Sandy Springs-Alpharetta, GA Metropolitan Statistical Area; (*) Hourly wages were calculated from annual wage data based on a 40 hour work week; n/a not available.
Source: Bureau of Labor Statistics, Metro Area Occupational Employment & Wage Estimates, May 2022

Employment by Industry

Sector	MSA[1] Number of Employees	MSA[1] Percent of Total	U.S. Percent of Total
Construction	141,200	4.6	5.0
Private Education and Health Services	398,500	13.1	16.1
Financial Activities	204,100	6.7	5.9
Government	343,400	11.3	14.5
Information	115,200	3.8	2.0
Leisure and Hospitality	299,400	9.8	10.3
Manufacturing	178,900	5.9	8.4
Mining and Logging	1,800	0.1	0.4
Other Services	106,000	3.5	3.7
Professional and Business Services	590,300	19.4	14.7
Retail Trade	309,000	10.1	10.2
Transportation, Warehousing, and Utilities	199,600	6.5	4.9
Wholesale Trade	160,900	5.3	3.9

Note: Figures are non-farm employment as of December 2022. Figures are not seasonally adjusted and include workers 16 years of age and older; (1) Figures cover the Atlanta-Sandy Springs-Alpharetta, GA Metropolitan Statistical Area
Source: Bureau of Labor Statistics, Current Employment Statistics, Employment, Hours, and Earnings

Employment by Occupation

Occupation Classification	City (%)	MSA[1] (%)	U.S. (%)
Management, Business, Science, and Arts	57.1	43.7	40.3
Natural Resources, Construction, and Maintenance	2.2	7.5	8.7
Production, Transportation, and Material Moving	7.9	12.6	13.1
Sales and Office	19.3	21.8	20.9
Service	13.4	14.5	17.0

Note: Figures cover employed civilians 16 years of age and older; (1) Figures cover the Atlanta-Sandy Springs-Alpharetta, GA Metropolitan Statistical Area
Source: U.S. Census Bureau, 2017-2021 American Community Survey 5-Year Estimates

Occupations with Greatest Projected Employment Growth: 2022 – 2024

Occupation[1]	2022 Employment	2024 Projected Employment	Numeric Employment Change	Percent Employment Change
Laborers and Freight, Stock, and Material Movers, Hand	124,130	131,700	7,570	6.1
Retail Salespersons	139,030	146,370	7,340	5.3
Industrial Truck and Tractor Operators	48,230	54,230	6,000	12.4
General and Operations Managers	95,580	101,230	5,650	5.9
Fast Food and Counter Workers	116,760	122,340	5,580	4.8
Stockers and Order Fillers	73,270	78,260	4,990	6.8
Software Developers and Software Quality Assurance Analysts and Testers	58,710	63,610	4,900	8.3
Cooks, Restaurant	42,420	47,160	4,740	11.2
Heavy and Tractor-Trailer Truck Drivers	68,660	73,100	4,440	6.5
Project Management Specialists and Business Operations Specialists, All Other	93,000	97,320	4,320	4.6

Note: Projections cover Georgia; (1) Sorted by numeric employment change
Source: www.projectionscentral.com, State Occupational Projections, 2022–2024 Short-Term Projections

Fastest-Growing Occupations: 2022 – 2024

Occupation[1]	2022 Employment	2024 Projected Employment	Numeric Employment Change	Percent Employment Change
Musicians and Singers	710	850	140	19.7
Amusement and Recreation Attendants	6,720	8,030	1,310	19.5
Reservation and Transportation Ticket Agents and Travel Clerks	4,000	4,710	710	17.8
Fitness Trainers and Aerobics Instructors	4,620	5,420	800	17.3
Manicurists and Pedicurists	1,810	2,120	310	17.1
Hotel, Motel, and Resort Desk Clerks	7,700	9,000	1,300	16.9
Machine Feeders and Offbearers	3,020	3,490	470	15.6
Massage Therapists	2,980	3,430	450	15.1
Skincare Specialists	1,730	1,990	260	15.0
Parking Lot Attendants	2,820	3,240	420	14.9

Note: Projections cover Georgia; (1) Sorted by percent employment change and excludes occupations with numeric employment change less than 50
Source: www.projectionscentral.com, State Occupational Projections, 2022–2024 Short-Term Projections

CITY FINANCES

City Government Finances

Component	2020 ($000)	2020 ($ per capita)
Total Revenues	2,317,279	4,572
Total Expenditures	2,149,533	4,241
Debt Outstanding	7,935,109	15,657
Cash and Securities[1]	5,126,296	10,115

Note: (1) Cash and security holdings of a government at the close of its fiscal year, including those of its dependent agencies, utilities, and liquor stores.
Source: U.S. Census Bureau, State & Local Government Finances 2020

City Government Revenue by Source

Source	2020 ($000)	2020 ($ per capita)	2020 (%)
General Revenue			
From Federal Government	46,552	92	2.0
From State Government	10,390	21	0.4
From Local Governments	172,085	340	7.4
Taxes			
Property	576,583	1,138	24.9
Sales and Gross Receipts	123,618	244	5.3
Personal Income	0	0	0.0
Corporate Income	0	0	0.0
Motor Vehicle License	0	0	0.0
Other Taxes	120,136	237	5.2
Current Charges	949,234	1,873	41.0
Liquor Store	0	0	0.0
Utility	271,139	535	11.7

Source: U.S. Census Bureau, State & Local Government Finances 2020

City Government Expenditures by Function

Function	2020 ($000)	2020 ($ per capita)	2020 (%)
General Direct Expenditures			
Air Transportation	761,563	1,502	35.4
Corrections	20,449	40	1.0
Education	0	0	0.0
Employment Security Administration	0	0	0.0
Financial Administration	24,171	47	1.1
Fire Protection	96,768	190	4.5
General Public Buildings	13,078	25	0.6
Governmental Administration, Other	41,698	82	1.9
Health	925	1	0.0
Highways	84,554	166	3.9
Hospitals	0	0	0.0
Housing and Community Development	2,148	4	0.1
Interest on General Debt	147,241	290	6.8
Judicial and Legal	36,248	71	1.7
Libraries	0	0	0.0
Parking	0	0	0.0
Parks and Recreation	64,949	128	3.0
Police Protection	221,921	437	10.3
Public Welfare	16,611	32	0.8
Sewerage	18,196	35	0.8
Solid Waste Management	64,712	127	3.0
Veterans' Services	0	0	0.0
Liquor Store	0	0	0.0
Utility	438,206	864	20.4

Source: U.S. Census Bureau, State & Local Government Finances 2020

TAXES

State Corporate Income Tax Rates

State	Tax Rate (%)	Income Brackets ($)	Num. of Brackets	Financial Institution Tax Rate (%)[a]	Federal Income Tax Ded.
Georgia	5.75	Flat rate	1	5.75	No

Note: Tax rates as of January 1, 2023; (a) Rates listed are the corporate income tax rate applied to financial institutions or excise taxes based on income. Some states have other taxes based upon the value of deposits or shares.
Source: Federation of Tax Administrators, State Corporate Income Tax Rates, January 1, 2023

State Individual Income Tax Rates

State	Tax Rate (%)	Income Brackets ($)	Personal Exemptions ($) Single	Personal Exemptions ($) Married	Personal Exemptions ($) Depend.	Standard Ded. ($) Single	Standard Ded. ($) Married
Georgia	1.0 - 5.75	750 - 7,001 (i)	2,700	7,400	3,000	5,400	7,100

Note: Tax rates as of January 1, 2023; Local- and county-level taxes are not included; Federal income tax is not deductible on state income tax returns; (i) The Georgia income brackets reported are for single individuals. For married couples filing jointly, the same tax rates apply to income brackets ranging from $1,000, to $10,000.
Source: Federation of Tax Administrators, State Individual Income Tax Rates, January 1, 2023

Various State Sales and Excise Tax Rates

State	State Sales Tax (%)	Gasoline[1] ($/gal.)	Cigarette[2] ($/pack)	Spirits[3] ($/gal.)	Wine[4] ($/gal.)	Beer[5] ($/gal.)	Recreational Marijuana (%)
Georgia	4	0.4005	0.37	3.79	1.51	0.48	Not legal

Note: All tax rates as of January 1, 2023; (1) The American Petroleum Institute has developed a methodology for determining the average tax rate on a gallon of fuel. Rates may include any of the following: excise taxes, environmental fees, storage tank fees, other fees or taxes, general sales tax, and local taxes; (2) The federal excise tax of $1.0066 per pack and local taxes are not included; (3) Rates are those applicable to off-premise sales of 40% alcohol by volume (a.b.v.) distilled spirits in 750ml containers. Local excise taxes are excluded; (4) Rates are those applicable to off-premise sales of 11% a.b.v. non-carbonated wine in 750ml containers; (5) Rates are those applicable to off-premise sales of 4.7% a.b.v. beer in 12 ounce containers.
Source: Tax Foundation, 2023 Facts & Figures: How Does Your State Compare?

State Business Tax Climate Index Rankings

State	Overall Rank	Corporate Tax Rank	Individual Income Tax Rank	Sales Tax Rank	Property Tax Rank	Unemployment Insurance Tax Rank
Georgia	32	8	35	31	28	35

Note: The index is a measure of how each state's tax laws affect economic performance. The lower the rank, the more favorable a state's tax system is for business. States without a given tax are given a ranking of 1. The scores/rankings for the District of Columbia do not affect other states. The 2023 index represents the tax climate as of July 1, 2022.
Source: Tax Foundation, State Business Tax Climate Index 2023

TRANSPORTATION

Means of Transportation to Work

Area	Car/Truck/Van Drove Alone	Car/Truck/Van Carpooled	Public Transportation Bus	Public Transportation Subway	Public Transportation Railroad	Bicycle	Walked	Other Means	Worked at Home
City	59.8	4.8	4.8	3.6	0.2	1.0	4.4	2.8	18.6
MSA[1]	72.7	8.7	1.5	0.7	0.1	0.2	1.2	1.7	13.2
U.S.	73.2	8.6	2.0	1.6	0.5	0.5	2.5	1.5	9.7

Note: Figures are percentages and cover workers 16 years of age and older; (1) Figures cover the Atlanta-Sandy Springs-Alpharetta, GA Metropolitan Statistical Area
Source: U.S. Census Bureau, 2017-2021 American Community Survey 5-Year Estimates

Travel Time to Work

Area	Less Than 10 Minutes	10 to 19 Minutes	20 to 29 Minutes	30 to 44 Minutes	45 to 59 Minutes	60 to 89 Minutes	90 Minutes or More
City	6.9	29.5	25.6	21.8	7.3	5.4	3.5
MSA[1]	6.9	22.5	19.9	25.2	12.2	9.6	3.5
U.S.	12.4	28.5	21.0	20.9	8.2	6.2	2.9

Note: Note: Figures are percentages and include workers 16 years old and over; (1) Figures cover the Atlanta-Sandy Springs-Alpharetta, GA Metropolitan Statistical Area
Source: U.S. Census Bureau, 2017-2021 American Community Survey 5-Year Estimates

Key Congestion Measures

Measure	1990	2000	2010	2015	2020
Annual Hours of Delay, Total (000)	61,868	146,271	184,962	212,509	109,475
Annual Hours of Delay, Per Auto Commuter	33	53	60	71	37
Annual Congestion Cost, Per Auto Commuter ($)	901	1,598	1,609	1,707	869

Note: Covers the Atlanta GA urban area
Source: Texas A&M Transportation Institute, 2021 Urban Mobility Report

Freeway Travel Time Index

Measure	1985	1990	1995	2000	2005	2010	2015	2020
Urban Area Index[1]	1.11	1.15	1.22	1.24	1.26	1.23	1.27	1.10
Urban Area Rank[1,2]	25	22	13	18	22	28	20	29

Note: Freeway Travel Time Index—the ratio of travel time in the peak period to the travel time at free-flow conditions. For example, a value of 1.30 indicates a 20-minute free-flow trip takes 26 minutes in the peak (20 minutes x 1.30 = 26 minutes); (1) Covers the Atlanta GA urban area; (2) Rank is based on 101 larger urban areas (#1 = highest travel time index)
Source: Texas A&M Transportation Institute, 2021 Urban Mobility Report

Public Transportation

Agency Name / Mode of Transportation	Vehicles Operated in Maximum Service[1]	Annual Unlinked Passenger Trips[2] (in thous.)	Annual Passenger Miles[3] (in thous.)
Metropolitan Atlanta Rapid Transit Authority (MARTA)			
Bus (directly operated)	442	27,346.5	120,638.5
Demand Response (purchased transportation)	188	427.5	4,842.2
Heavy Rail (directly operated)	210	18,533.6	125,036.9
Streetcar Rail (directly operated)	2	86.2	68.6

Note: (1) Number of revenue vehicles operated by the given mode and type of service to meet the annual maximum service requirement. This is the revenue vehicle count during the peak season of the year; on the week and day that maximum service is provided. Vehicles operated in maximum service (VOMS) exclude atypical days and one-time special events; (2) Number of passengers who boarded public transportation vehicles. Passengers are counted each time they board a vehicle no matter how many vehicles they use to travel from their origin to their destination. (3) Sum of the distances ridden by all passengers during the entire fiscal year.
Source: Federal Transit Administration, National Transit Database, 2021

Air Transportation

Airport Name and Code / Type of Service	Passenger Airlines[1]	Passenger Enplanements	Freight Carriers[2]	Freight (lbs)
Hartsfield-Jackson Atlanta International Airport (ATL)				
Domestic service (U.S. carriers - 2022)	30	40,543,215	18	397,839,299
International service (U.S. carriers - 2021)	6	2,428,977	7	69,775,266

Note: (1) Includes all U.S.-based major, minor and commuter airlines that carried at least one passenger during the year; (2) Includes all U.S.-based airlines and freight carriers that transported at least one pound of freight during the year.
Source: Bureau of Transportation Statistics, The Intermodal Transportation Database, Air Carriers: T-100 Domestic Market (U.S. Carriers), 2022; Bureau of Transportation Statistics, The Intermodal Transportation Database, Air Carriers: T-100 International Market (U.S. Carriers), 2021

BUSINESSES

Major Business Headquarters

Company Name	Industry	Fortune[1]	Forbes[2]
Coca-Cola	Beverages	93	-
Cox Enterprises	Media	-	13
Delta Air Lines	Airlines	113	-
Genuine Parts	Wholesalers, diversified	191	-
Global Payments	Financial data services	407	-
Graphic Packaging Holding	Packaging, containers	466	-
Holder Construction	Construction	-	112
Home Depot	Specialty retailers, other	17	-
Intercontinental Exchange	Securities	384	-
Newell Brands	Home equipment, furnishings	348	-
PulteGroup	Homebuilders	267	-
RaceTrac Petroleum	Convenience stores & gas stations	-	22
Southern	Energy, telecom	153	-
UPS	Delivery	34	-
Veritiv	Wholesalers, diversified	477	-

Note: (1) Companies that produce a 10-K are ranked 1 to 500 based on 2021 revenue; (2) All private companies with at least $2 billion in annual revenue through the end of their most current fiscal year are ranked 1 to 246; companies listed are headquartered in the city; dashes indicate no ranking
Source: Fortune, "Fortune 500," 2022; Forbes, "America's Largest Private Companies," 2022

Fastest-Growing Businesses

According to *Inc.*, Atlanta is home to 19 of America's 500 fastest-growing private companies: **SnapNurse** (#2); **RateForce** (#36); **Core Clinical Partners** (#40); **Stord** (#57); **PrizePicks** (#66); **Neighborly Software** (#72); **Steady Platform** (#86); **Polygon.io** (#199); **Flock Safety** (#213); **Apptega** (#234); **Aimpoint Digital** (#242); **Whittley Agency** (#252); **PadSplit** (#290); **Skystone Acquisitions** (#324); **Bitcoin Depot** (#367); **Birdsey Construction Management** (#371); **11TEN Innovation Partners** (#385); **Offbeat Media Group** (#403); **Mile Auto** (#477). Criteria: must be an independent, privately-held, for-profit, U.S. corporation, proprietorship or partnership as of December 31, 2021; revenues must be at least $100,000 in 2018 and $2 million in 2021; must have four-year operating/sales history. *Inc.*, "America's 500 Fastest-Growing Private Companies," 2022

According to *Initiative for a Competitive Inner City (ICIC)*, Atlanta is home to five of America's 100 fastest-growing "inner city" companies: **Aspire Construction & Design** (#6); **Sisters Traveling Solo** (#18); **The Laundry Centers** (#31); **Webmyers Construction** (#53); **Gordon's Automotive Service Center** (#74). Criteria for inclusion: company must be headquartered in or have 51 percent or more of its physical operations in an economically distressed urban area; must be an independent, for-profit corporation, partnership or proprietorship; must have 10 or more employees and have a five-year sales history that includes sales of at least $200,000 in the base year and at least $1 million in the current year with no decrease in sales over the two most recent years. Companies were ranked overall by revenue growth over the five-year period between 2017 and 2021. *Initiative for a Competitive Inner City (ICIC), "Inner City 100 Companies," 2022*

According to Deloitte, Atlanta is home to 15 of North America's 500 fastest-growing high-technology companies: **Flock Safety** (#7); **Kobiton** (#18); **Stord** (#25); **PrizePicks** (#48); **Popmenu** (#57); **Splitit** (#114); **IRONSCALES** (#206); **Florence Healthcare** (#264); **CoreView** (#310); **CENTEGIX** (#321); **FullStory** (#322); **LeaseQuery** (#422); **PlayOn! Sports** (#452); **Salesloft** (#473); **Wahoo Fitness** (#477). Companies are ranked by percentage growth in revenue over a four-year period. Criteria for inclusion: company must be headquartered within North America; must own proprietary intellectual property or technology that is sold to customers in products that contributes to a significant portion of the company's operating revenue; must have been in business for a minumum of four years with 2018 operating revenues of at least $50,000 USD/CD and 2021 operating revenues of at least $5 million USD/CD. *Deloitte, 2022 Technology Fast 500*™

Atlanta, Georgia 33

Living Environment

COST OF LIVING

Cost of Living Index

Composite Index	Groceries	Housing	Utilities	Transportation	Health Care	Misc. Goods/ Services
101.6	92.5	107.6	85.8	102.5	107.0	104.2

Note: The Cost of Living Index measures regional differences in the cost of consumer goods and services, excluding taxes and non-consumer expenditures, for professional and managerial households in the top income quintile. It is based on more than 50,000 prices covering almost 60 different items for which prices are collected three times a year by chambers of commerce, economic development organizations or university applied economic centers in each participating urban area. The numbers shown should be read as a percentage above or below the national average of 100. For example, a value of 115.4 in the groceries column indicates that grocery prices are 15.4% higher than the national average. Small differences in the index numbers should not be interpreted as significant; Figures cover the Atlanta GA urban area.
Source: The Council for Community and Economic Research, Cost of Living Index, 2022

Grocery Prices

Area[1]	T-Bone Steak ($/pound)	Frying Chicken ($/pound)	Whole Milk ($/half gal.)	Eggs ($/dozen)	Orange Juice ($/64 oz.)	Coffee ($/11.5 oz.)
City[2]	12.23	1.21	1.94	1.87	3.63	4.51
Avg.	13.81	1.59	2.43	2.25	3.85	4.95
Min.	10.17	0.90	1.51	1.30	2.90	3.46
Max.	19.35	3.30	4.32	4.32	5.31	8.59

Note: (1) Values for the local area are compared with the average, minimum and maximum values for all 286 areas in the Cost of Living Index; (2) Figures cover the Atlanta GA urban area; **T-Bone Steak** (price per pound); **Frying Chicken** (price per pound, whole fryer); **Whole Milk** (half gallon carton); **Eggs** (price per dozen, Grade A, large); **Orange Juice** (64 oz. Tropicana or Florida Natural); **Coffee** (11.5 oz. can, vacuum-packed, Maxwell House, Hills Bros, or Folgers).
Source: The Council for Community and Economic Research, Cost of Living Index, 2022

Housing and Utility Costs

Area[1]	New Home Price ($)	Apartment Rent ($/month)	All Electric ($/month)	Part Electric ($/month)	Other Energy ($/month)	Telephone ($/month)
City[2]	489,573	1,551	-	90.61	44.15	188.95
Avg.	450,913	1,371	176.41	99.93	76.96	190.22
Min.	229,283	546	100.84	31.56	27.15	174.27
Max.	2,434,977	4,569	356.86	249.59	272.24	208.31

Note: (1) Values for the local area are compared with the average, minimum and maximum values for all 286 areas in the Cost of Living Index; (2) Figures cover the Atlanta GA urban area; **New Home Price** (2,400 sf living area, 8,000 sf lot, in urban area with full utilities); **Apartment Rent** (950 sf 2 bedroom/1.5 or 2 bath, unfurnished, excluding all utilities except water); **All Electric** (average monthly cost for an all-electric home); **Part Electric** (average monthly cost for a part-electric home); **Other Energy** (average monthly cost for natural gas, fuel oil, coal, wood, and any other forms of energy except electricity); **Telephone** (price includes the base monthly rate plus taxes and fees for three lines of mobile phone service).
Source: The Council for Community and Economic Research, Cost of Living Index, 2022

Health Care, Transportation, and Other Costs

Area[1]	Doctor ($/visit)	Dentist ($/visit)	Optometrist ($/visit)	Gasoline ($/gallon)	Beauty Salon ($/visit)	Men's Shirt ($)
City[2]	115.86	132.58	128.60	3.87	51.09	40.24
Avg.	124.91	107.77	117.66	3.86	43.31	34.21
Min.	36.61	58.25	51.79	2.90	22.18	13.05
Max.	250.21	162.58	371.96	5.54	85.61	63.54

Note: (1) Values for the local area are compared with the average, minimum and maximum values for all 286 areas in the Cost of Living Index; (2) Figures cover the Atlanta GA urban area; **Doctor** (general practitioners routine exam of an established patient); **Dentist** (adult teeth cleaning and periodic oral examination); **Optometrist** (full vision eye exam for established adult patient); **Gasoline** (one gallon regular unleaded, national brand, including all taxes, cash price at self-service pump if available); **Beauty Salon** (woman's shampoo, trim, and blow-dry); **Men's Shirt** (cotton/polyester dress shirt, pinpoint weave, long sleeves).
Source: The Council for Community and Economic Research, Cost of Living Index, 2022

HOUSING

Homeownership Rate

Area	2015 (%)	2016 (%)	2017 (%)	2018 (%)	2019 (%)	2020 (%)	2021 (%)	2022 (%)
MSA[1]	61.7	61.5	62.4	64.0	64.2	66.4	64.2	64.4
U.S.	63.7	63.4	63.9	64.4	64.6	66.6	65.5	65.8

Note: (1) Figures cover the Atlanta-Sandy Springs-Alpharetta, GA Metropolitan Statistical Area
Source: U.S. Census Bureau, Housing Vacancies and Homeownership Annual Statistics: 2015-2022

House Price Index (HPI)

Area	National Ranking[2]	Quarterly Change (%)	One-Year Change (%)	Five-Year Change (%)	Since 1991Q1 (%)
MSA[1]	40	-0.35	16.14	73.42	274.52
U.S.[3]	–	0.34	8.41	58.44	289.08

Note: The HPI is a weighted repeat sales index. It measures average price changes in repeat sales or refinancings on the same properties. This information is obtained by reviewing repeat mortgage transactions on single-family properties whose mortgages have been purchased or securitized by Fannie Mae or Freddie Mac since January 1975; (1) Figures cover the Atlanta-Sandy Springs-Roswell, GA Metropolitan Statistical Area; (2) Rankings are based on annual percentage change for all metro areas containing at least 15,000 transactions over the last 10 years and ranges from 1 to 257; (3) figures based on a weighted average of Census Division estimates using a seasonally adjusted, purchase-only index; all figures are for the period ending December 31, 2022
Source: Federal Housing Finance Agency, Change in FHFA Metropolitan Area House Price Indexes, 2022Q4

Median Single-Family Home Prices

Area	2020	2021	2022p	Percent Change 2021 to 2022
MSA[1]	260.8	317.2	365.1	15.1
U.S. Average	300.2	357.1	392.6	9.9

Note: Figures are median sales prices of existing single-family homes in thousands of dollars; (p) preliminary; (1) Figures cover the Atlanta-Sandy Springs-Alpharetta, GA Metropolitan Statistical Area
Source: National Association of Realtors, Median Sales Price of Existing Single-Family Homes for Metropolitan Areas, 4th Quarter 2022

Qualifying Income Based on Median Sales Price of Existing Single-Family Homes

Area	With 5% Down ($)	With 10% Down ($)	With 20% Down ($)
MSA[1]	105,702	100,138	89,012
U.S. Average	112,234	106,237	94,513

Note: Figures are preliminary; Qualifying income is based on a mortgage rate of 6.77%. Monthly principal and interest payment is limited to 25% of income; (1) Figures cover the Atlanta-Sandy Springs-Alpharetta, GA Metropolitan Statistical Area
Source: National Association of Realtors, Qualifying Income Based on Median Sales Price of Existing Single-Family Homes for Metropolitan Areas, 4th Quarter 2022

Home Value

Area	Under $100,000	$100,000 -$199,999	$200,000 -$299,999	$300,000 -$399,999	$400,000 -$499,999	$500,000 -$999,999	$1,000,000 or more	Median ($)
City	8.9	17.3	17.4	13.6	10.3	23.2	9.3	346,600
MSA[1]	8.9	26.9	25.0	16.1	9.3	11.7	2.0	252,100
U.S.	16.2	24.2	20.1	13.6	8.3	13.6	4.1	244,900

Note: Figures are percentages except for median and cover owner-occupied housing units; (1) Figures cover the Atlanta-Sandy Springs-Alpharetta, GA Metropolitan Statistical Area
Source: U.S. Census Bureau, 2017-2021 American Community Survey 5-Year Estimates

Year Housing Structure Built

Area	2020 or Later	2010 -2019	2000 -2009	1990 -1999	1980 -1989	1970 -1979	1960 -1969	1950 -1959	1940 -1949	Before 1940	Median Year
City	0.4	12.7	22.0	10.2	7.6	7.7	11.0	10.6	5.7	12.1	1984
MSA[1]	0.3	9.4	23.6	20.8	17.1	12.4	7.3	4.5	1.7	2.8	1992
U.S.	0.2	7.3	13.6	13.6	13.2	14.8	10.3	10.0	4.7	12.2	1979

Note: Figures are percentages except for Median Year; Note: (1) Figures cover the Atlanta-Sandy Springs-Alpharetta, GA Metropolitan Statistical Area
Source: U.S. Census Bureau, 2017-2021 American Community Survey 5-Year Estimates

Gross Monthly Rent

Area	Under $500	$500 -$999	$1,000 -$1,499	$1,500 -$1,999	$2,000 -$2,499	$2,500 -$2,999	$3,000 and up	Median ($)
City	11.0	18.0	31.3	25.2	9.2	2.9	2.4	1,342
MSA[1]	4.3	19.1	43.9	23.8	6.2	1.5	1.2	1,294
U.S.	8.1	30.5	30.8	16.8	7.3	3.1	3.5	1,163

Note: Figures are percentages except for median; Gross rent is the contract rent plus the estimated average monthly cost of utilities (electricity, gas, and water and sewer) and fuels (oil, coal, kerosene, wood, etc.) if these are paid by the renter (or paid for the renter by someone else); (1) Figures cover the Atlanta-Sandy Springs-Alpharetta, GA Metropolitan Statistical Area
Source: U.S. Census Bureau, 2017-2021 American Community Survey 5-Year Estimates

HEALTH

Health Risk Factors

Category	MSA[1] (%)	U.S. (%)
Adults aged 18–64 who have any kind of health care coverage	83.5	90.9
Adults who reported being in good or better health	84.0	85.2
Adults who have been told they have high blood cholesterol	35.1	35.7
Adults who have been told they have high blood pressure	33.7	32.4
Adults who are current smokers	12.9	14.4
Adults who currently use e-cigarettes	7.4	6.7
Adults who currently use chewing tobacco, snuff, or snus	2.6	3.5
Adults who are heavy drinkers[2]	6.4	6.3
Adults who are binge drinkers[3]	14.6	15.4
Adults who are overweight (BMI 25.0 - 29.9)	34.3	34.4
Adults who are obese (BMI 30.0 - 99.8)	31.8	33.9
Adults who participated in any physical activities in the past month	78.6	76.3

Note: (1) Figures cover the Atlanta-Sandy Springs-Roswell, GA Metropolitan Statistical Area; (2) Heavy drinkers are classified as adult men having more than 14 drinks per week and adult women having more than 7 drinks per week; (3) Binge drinkers are classified as males having five or more drinks on one occasion or females having four or more drinks on one occasion
Source: Centers for Disease Control and Prevention, Behaviorial Risk Factor Surveillance System, SMART: Selected Metropolitan Area Risk Trends, 2021

Acute and Chronic Health Conditions

Category	MSA[1] (%)	U.S. (%)
Adults who have ever been told they had a heart attack	3.5	4.0
Adults who have ever been told they have angina or coronary heart disease	3.1	3.8
Adults who have ever been told they had a stroke	3.2	3.0
Adults who have ever been told they have asthma	14.0	14.9
Adults who have ever been told they have arthritis	21.3	25.8
Adults who have ever been told they have diabetes[2]	10.4	10.9
Adults who have ever been told they had skin cancer	5.7	6.6
Adults who have ever been told they had any other types of cancer	5.1	7.5
Adults who have ever been told they have COPD	5.1	6.1
Adults who have ever been told they have kidney disease	4.0	3.0
Adults who have ever been told they have a form of depression	15.1	20.5

Note: (1) Figures cover the Atlanta-Sandy Springs-Roswell, GA Metropolitan Statistical Area; (2) Figures do not include pregnancy-related, borderline, or pre-diabetes
Source: Centers for Disease Control and Prevention, Behaviorial Risk Factor Surveillance System, SMART: Selected Metropolitan Area Risk Trends, 2021

Health Screening and Vaccination Rates

Category	MSA[1] (%)	U.S. (%)
Adults who have ever been tested for HIV	46.3	34.9
Adults who have had their blood cholesterol checked within the last five years	87.0	85.2
Adults aged 65+ who have had flu shot within the past year	61.3	68.6
Adults aged 65+ who have ever had a pneumonia vaccination	67.4	71.0

Note: (1) Figures cover the Atlanta-Sandy Springs-Roswell, GA Metropolitan Statistical Area.
Source: Centers for Disease Control and Prevention, Behaviorial Risk Factor Surveillance System, SMART: Selected Metropolitan Area Risk Trends, 2021

Disability Status

Category	MSA[1] (%)	U.S. (%)
Adults who reported being deaf	4.1	7.2
Are you blind or have serious difficulty seeing, even when wearing glasses?	4.5	4.8
Are you limited in any way in any of your usual activities due to arthritis?	9.5	11.1
Do you have difficulty doing errands alone?	6.8	7.0
Do you have difficulty dressing or bathing?	3.4	3.6
Do you have serious difficulty concentrating/remembering/making decisions?	11.0	12.1
Do you have serious difficulty walking or climbing stairs?	13.1	12.8

Note: (1) Figures cover the Atlanta-Sandy Springs-Roswell, GA Metropolitan Statistical Area.
Source: Centers for Disease Control and Prevention, Behaviorial Risk Factor Surveillance System, SMART: Selected Metropolitan Area Risk Trends, 2021

Mortality Rates for the Top 10 Causes of Death in the U.S.

ICD-10[a] Sub-Chapter	ICD-10[a] Code	Crude Mortality Rate[1] per 100,000 population County[2]	U.S.
Malignant neoplasms	C00-C97	133.3	182.6
Ischaemic heart diseases	I20-I25	48.2	113.1
Other forms of heart disease	I30-I51	48.6	64.4
Other degenerative diseases of the nervous system	G30-G31	51.0	51.0
Cerebrovascular diseases	I60-I69	40.2	47.8
Other external causes of accidental injury	W00-X59	32.6	46.4
Chronic lower respiratory diseases	J40-J47	21.9	45.7
Organic, including symptomatic, mental disorders	F01-F09	15.8	35.9
Hypertensive diseases	I10-I15	46.2	35.0
Diabetes mellitus	E10-E14	22.7	29.6

Note: (a) ICD-10 = International Classification of Diseases 10th Revision; (1) Crude mortality rates are a three-year average covering 2019-2021; (2) Figures cover Fulton County.
Source: Centers for Disease Control and Prevention, National Center for Health Statistics. National Vital Statistics System, Mortality 2018-2021 on CDC WONDER Online Database

Mortality Rates for Selected Causes of Death

ICD-10[a] Sub-Chapter	ICD-10[a] Code	Crude Mortality Rate[1] per 100,000 population County[2]	U.S.
Assault	X85-Y09	16.7	7.0
Diseases of the liver	K70-K76	13.0	19.8
Human immunodeficiency virus (HIV) disease	B20-B24	5.6	1.5
Influenza and pneumonia	J09-J18	8.7	14.7
Intentional self-harm	X60-X84	11.5	14.3
Malnutrition	E40-E46	5.8	4.3
Obesity and other hyperalimentation	E65-E68	2.8	3.0
Renal failure	N17-N19	16.1	15.7
Transport accidents	V01-V99	13.2	13.6
Viral hepatitis	B15-B19	0.7	1.2

Note: (a) ICD-10 = International Classification of Diseases 10th Revision; (1) Crude mortality rates are a three-year average covering 2019-2021; (2) Figures cover Fulton County; Data are suppressed when the data meet the criteria for confidentiality constraints; Crude mortality rates are flagged as unreliable when the rate would be calculated with a numerator of 20 or less.
Source: Centers for Disease Control and Prevention, National Center for Health Statistics. National Vital Statistics System, Mortality 2018-2021 on CDC WONDER Online Database

Health Insurance Coverage

Area	With Health Insurance	With Private Health Insurance	With Public Health Insurance	Without Health Insurance	Population Under Age 19 Without Health Insurance
City	89.4	70.1	27.0	10.6	6.2
MSA[1]	87.4	69.4	27.2	12.6	7.9
U.S.	91.2	67.8	35.4	8.8	5.3

Note: Figures are percentages that cover the civilian noninstitutionalized population; (1) Figures cover the Atlanta-Sandy Springs-Alpharetta, GA Metropolitan Statistical Area
Source: U.S. Census Bureau, 2017-2021 American Community Survey 5-Year Estimates

Number of Medical Professionals

Area	MDs[3]	DOs[3,4]	Dentists	Podiatrists	Chiropractors	Optometrists
County[1] (number)	5,737	157	794	56	622	211
County[1] (rate[2])	536.7	14.7	74.5	5.3	58.4	19.8
U.S. (rate[2])	289.3	23.5	72.5	6.2	28.7	17.4

Note: Data as of 2021 unless noted; (1) Data covers Fulton County; (2) Rate per 100,000 population; (3) Data as of 2020 and includes all active, non-federal physicians; (4) Doctor of Osteopathic Medicine
Source: U.S. Department of Health and Human Services, Health Resources and Services Administration, Bureau of Health Professions, Area Resource File (ARF) 2021-2022

Best Hospitals

According to *U.S. News,* the Atlanta-Sandy Springs-Alpharetta, GA metro area is home to seven of the best hospitals in the U.S.: **Emory Rehabilitation Hospital** (1 adult specialty); **Emory University Hospital Midtown** (1 adult specialty); **Emory University Hospital at Wesley Woods** (5 adult specialties); **Emory University Hospital** (5 adult specialties); **Northside Hospital Atlanta** (1 adult specialty); **Shepherd Center** (1 adult specialty); **WellStar Kennestone Hospital** (1 adult specialty). The hospitals listed were nationally ranked in at least one of 15 adult or 10 pediatric specialties. The number of specialties shown cover the parent hospital. Only 164 U.S. hospitals performed well enough to be nationally ranked in one or more specialties. Twenty hospitals in the U.S. made the Honor Roll. The Best Hospitals Honor Roll takes both the national rankings and the procedure and condition ratings into account. Hospitals received points if they were nationally ranked in one of the 15 adult specialties—the higher they ranked, the more points they got—and how many ratings of "high performing" they earned in the 17 procedures and conditions. *U.S. News Online, "America's Best Hospitals 2022-23"*

According to *U.S. News,* the Atlanta-Sandy Springs-Alpharetta, GA metro area is home to one of the best children's hospitals in the U.S.: **Children's Healthcare of Atlanta** (10 pediatric specialties). The hospital listed was highly ranked in at least one of 10 pediatric specialties. Eighty-six children's hospitals in the U.S. were nationally ranked in at least one specialty. Hospitals received points for being ranked in a specialty, and the 10 hospitals with the most points across the 10 specialties make up the Honor Roll. *U.S. News Online, "America's Best Children's Hospitals 2022-23"*

EDUCATION

Public School District Statistics

District Name	Schls	Pupils	Pupil/Teacher Ratio	Minority Pupils[1] (%)	LEP/ELL[2] (%)	IEP[3] (%)
Atlanta Public Schools	87	49,994	12.3	84.1	3.8	11.6
Fulton County	110	90,355	14.7	74.3	6.8	10.6
State Charter Schls-GA Cyber Acad.	1	11,878	21.0	71.0	1.1	15.3

Note: Table includes school districts with 2,000 or more students; (1) Percentage of students that are not non-Hispanic white; (2) Percentage of students that are Limited English Proficient or English Language Learners (2018-19); (3) Percentage of students that have an Individualized Education Program (2019-20).
Source: U.S. Department of Education, National Center for Education Statistics, Common Core of Data, Local Education Agency (School District) Universe Survey: School Year 2021-2022

Highest Level of Education

Area	Less than H.S.	H.S. Diploma	Some College, No Deg.	Associate Degree	Bachelor's Degree	Master's Degree	Prof. School Degree	Doctorate Degree
City	7.9	17.5	13.6	5.4	31.6	15.8	5.6	2.7
MSA[1]	9.5	23.3	18.9	7.8	24.9	11.1	2.6	1.6
U.S.	11.1	26.5	20.0	8.7	20.6	9.3	2.2	1.5

Note: Figures cover persons age 25 and over; (1) Figures cover the Atlanta-Sandy Springs-Alpharetta, GA Metropolitan Statistical Area
Source: U.S. Census Bureau, 2017-2021 American Community Survey 5-Year Estimates

Educational Attainment by Race

Area	High School Graduate or Higher (%)					Bachelor's Degree or Higher (%)				
	Total	White	Black	Asian	Hisp.[2]	Total	White	Black	Asian	Hisp.[2]
City	92.1	98.3	86.3	96.7	84.0	55.6	79.9	29.9	86.1	48.0
MSA[1]	90.5	92.5	91.5	87.7	67.2	40.4	44.6	32.6	59.7	22.9
U.S.	88.9	91.4	87.2	87.6	71.2	33.7	35.5	23.3	55.6	18.4

Note: Figures shown cover persons 25 years old and over; (1) Figures cover the Atlanta-Sandy Springs-Alpharetta, GA Metropolitan Statistical Area; (2) People of Hispanic origin can be of any race
Source: U.S. Census Bureau, 2017-2021 American Community Survey 5-Year Estimates

School Enrollment by Grade and Control

Area	Preschool (%)		Kindergarten (%)		Grades 1 - 4 (%)		Grades 5 - 8 (%)		Grades 9 - 12 (%)	
	Public	Private	Public	Private	Public	Private	Public	Private	Public	Private
City	50.7	49.3	75.7	24.3	85.9	14.1	78.5	21.5	79.9	20.1
MSA[1]	54.8	45.2	85.7	14.3	89.8	10.2	88.2	11.8	89.0	11.0
U.S.	58.8	41.2	86.3	13.7	88.3	11.7	88.6	11.4	89.4	10.6

Note: Figures shown cover persons 3 years old and over; (1) Figures cover the Atlanta-Sandy Springs-Alpharetta, GA Metropolitan Statistical Area
Source: U.S. Census Bureau, 2017-2021 American Community Survey 5-Year Estimates

Higher Education

Four-Year Colleges			Two-Year Colleges			Medical Schools[1]	Law Schools[2]	Voc/Tech[3]
Public	Private Non-profit	Private For-profit	Public	Private Non-profit	Private For-profit			
8	15	6	8	3	12	3	3	20

Note: Figures cover institutions located within the Atlanta-Sandy Springs-Alpharetta, GA Metropolitan Statistical Area and include main campuses only; (1) includes schools accredited by the Liaison Committee on Medical Education and the American Osteopathic Association's Commission on Osteopathic College Accreditation; (2) includes ABA-accredited schools, schools with provisional ABA accreditation, and state accredited schools; (3) includes all schools with programs that are less than 2 years.
Source: National Center for Education Statistics, Integrated Postsecondary Education System (IPEDS), 2021-22; Wikipedia, List of Medical Schools in the United States, accessed April 10, 2023; Wikipedia, List of Law Schools in the United States, accessed April 10, 2023

According to *U.S. News & World Report,* the Atlanta-Sandy Springs-Alpharetta, GA metro area is home to two of the top 200 national universities in the U.S.: **Emory University** (#22 tie); **Georgia Institute of Technology** (#44 tie). The indicators used to capture academic quality fall into a number of categories: assessment by administrators at peer institutions; retention of students; faculty resources; student selectivity; financial resources; alumni giving; high school counselor ratings of colleges; and graduation rate. *U.S. News & World Report,* "America's Best Colleges 2023"

According to *U.S. News & World Report,* the Atlanta-Sandy Springs-Alpharetta, GA metro area is home to two of the top 100 liberal arts colleges in the U.S.: **Spelman College** (#51 tie); **Agnes Scott College** (#63 tie). The indicators used to capture academic quality fall into a number of categories: assessment by administrators at peer institutions; retention of students; faculty resources; student selectivity; financial resources; alumni giving; high school counselor ratings of colleges; and graduation rate. *U.S. News & World Report,* "America's Best Colleges 2023"

According to *U.S. News & World Report,* the Atlanta-Sandy Springs-Alpharetta, GA metro area is home to two of the top 100 law schools in the U.S.: **Emory University** (#30 tie); **Georgia State University** (#78 tie). The rankings are based on a weighted average of 12 measures of quality: peer assessment score; assessment score by lawyers/judges; median LSAT scores; median undergrad GPA; acceptance rate; employment rates for graduates; placement success; bar passage rate; faculty resources; expenditures per student; student/faculty ratio; and library resources. *U.S. News & World Report,* "America's Best Graduate Schools, Law, 2023"

According to *U.S. News & World Report,* the Atlanta-Sandy Springs-Alpharetta, GA metro area is home to one of the top 75 medical schools for research in the U.S.: **Emory University** (#22 tie). The rankings are based on a weighted average of 11 measures of quality: quality assessment; peer assessment score; assessment score by residency directors; research activity; total research activity; average research activity per faculty member; student selectivity; median MCAT total score; median undergraduate GPA; acceptance rate; and faculty resources. *U.S. News & World Report,* "America's Best Graduate Schools, Medical, 2023"

According to *U.S. News & World Report,* the Atlanta-Sandy Springs-Alpharetta, GA metro area is home to two of the top 75 business schools in the U.S.: **Emory University (Goizueta)** (#21); **Georgia Institute of Technology (Scheller)** (#28). The rankings are based on a weighted average of the following nine measures: quality assessment; peer assessment; recruiter assessment; placement success; mean starting salary and bonus; student selectivity; mean GMAT and GRE scores; mean undergraduate GPA; and acceptance rate. *U.S. News & World Report,* "America's Best Graduate Schools, Business, 2023"

EMPLOYERS

Major Employers

Company Name	Industry
Apartments.com	Apartment locating service
Aquilex Holdings	Facilities support services
AT&T	Engineering services
Children's Healthcare of Atlanta	Healthcare
Clayton County Board of Education	Public elementary & secondary schools
County of Gwinnett	County government
Delta Air Lines	Air transportation, scheduled
Georgia Department of Behavioral Health	Administration of public health programs
Georgia Department of Human Resoures	Administration of public health programs
Georgia Department of Transportation	Regulation, administration of transportation
IBM	Engineering services
Internal Revenue Service	Taxation department, government
Lockheed Martin Aeronautical Company	Aircraft
NCR Corporation	Calculating and accounting equipment
Northide Hospital	Healthcare
Progressive Logistics Services	Labor organizations
Robert Half International	Employment agencies
Saint Joseph's Hospital	Healthcare
The Coca-Cola Company	Bottled and canned soft drinks
The Fulton-Dekalb Hospital Authority	General medical & surgical hospitals
The Home Depot	Hardware stores
U.S. Army	U.S. military
WellStar Kennestone Hospital	General medical & surgical hospitals
World Travel Partners Group	Travel agencies

Note: Companies shown are located within the Atlanta-Sandy Springs-Alpharetta, GA Metropolitan Statistical Area.
Source: Hoovers.com; Wikipedia

Best Companies to Work For

Alston & Bird; PulteGroup, headquartered in Atlanta, are among "The 100 Best Companies to Work For." To pick the best companies, *Fortune* partnered with the Great Place to Work Institute. Two-thirds of a company's score is based on the results of the Institute's Trust Index survey, which is sent to a random sample of employees from each company. The questions related to attitudes about management's credibility, job satisfaction, and camaraderie. The other third of the scoring is based on the company's responses to the Institute's Culture Audit, which includes detailed questions about pay and benefit programs, and a series of open-ended questions about hiring practices, internal communication, training, recognition programs, and diversity efforts. Any company that is at least five years old with more than 1,000 U.S. employees is eligible. *Fortune, "The 100 Best Companies to Work For," 2023*

BeyondTrust; Insight Global; PulteGroup, headquartered in Atlanta, are among "Fortune's Best Workplaces for Women." To pick the best companies, *Fortune* partnered with the Great Place to Work Institute. To be considered for the list, companies must be Great Place To Work-Certified. Companies must also employ at least 50 women, at least 20% of their non-executive managers must be female, and at least one executive must be female. To determine the Best Workplaces for Women, Great Place To Work measured the differences in women's survey responses to those of their peers and assesses the impact of demographics and roles on the quality and consistency of women's experiences. Great Place To Work also analyzed the gender balance of each workplace, how it compared to each company's industry, and patterns in representation as women rise from front-line positions to the board of directors. *Fortune, "Best Workplaces for Women," 2022*

Alston & Bird; BeyondTrust; PulteGroup, headquartered in Atlanta, are among "Fortune's Best Workplaces for Parents." To pick the best companies, *Fortune* partnered with the Great Place to Work Institute. To be considered for the list, companies must be Great Place To Work-Certified and have at least 50 responses from parents in the US. The survey enables employees to share confidential quantitative and qualitative feedback about their organization's culture by responding to 60 statements on a 5-point scale and answering two open-ended questions. Collectively, these statements describe a great employee experience, defined by high levels of trust, respect, credibility, fairness, pride, and camaraderie. In addition, companies provide organizational data like size, location, industry, demographics, roles, and levels; and provide information about parental leave, adoption, flexible schedule, childcare and dependent health care benefits. *Fortune, "Best Workplaces for Parents," 2022*

Children's Healthcare of Atlanta, headquartered in Atlanta, is among the "100 Best Places to Work in IT." To qualify, companies had to have a minimum of 100 total employees and five IT employees. The best places to work were selected based on DEI (diversity, equity, and inclusion) practices; IT turnover, promotions, and growth; IT retention and engagement programs; remote/hybrid working; benefits and perks (such as elder care and child care, flextime, and reimbursement for college tuition); and training and career development opportunities. *Computerworld, "Best Places to Work in IT," 2023*

PUBLIC SAFETY

Crime Rate

Area	Total Crime	Murder	Rape[3]	Robbery	Aggrav. Assault	Burglary	Larceny-Theft	Motor Vehicle Theft
City	5,423.2	17.7	49.4	221.5	480.1	621.2	3,366.4	666.8
Suburbs[1]	2,666.3	4.6	24.0	82.5	168.8	373.2	1,770.4	242.7
Metro[2]	2,895.7	5.7	26.1	94.1	194.7	393.9	1,903.2	278.0
U.S.	2,593.1	5.0	44.0	86.1	248.2	378.0	1,601.6	230.2

Note: Figures are crimes per 100,000 population; (1) All areas within the metro area that are located outside the city limits; (2) Figures cover the Atlanta-Sandy Springs-Roswell, GA Metropolitan Statistical Area; (3) All figures shown were reported using the revised Uniform Crime Reporting (UCR) definition of rape; Due to the transition to the National Incident-Based Reporting System (NIBRS), limited city and metro area data was released for 2021.
Source: FBI Uniform Crime Reports, 2018 (data for 2020 was not available)

Hate Crimes

Area	Number of Quarters Reported	Race/Ethnicity/Ancestry	Religion	Sexual Orientation	Disability	Gender	Gender Identity
City	1	3	0	1	0	0	0
U.S.	4	5,227	1,244	1,110	130	75	266

Note: Due to the transition to the National Incident-Based Reporting System (NIBRS), limited crime data was released for 2021.
Source: Federal Bureau of Investigation, Hate Crime Statistics 2020

Identity Theft Consumer Reports

Area	Reports	Reports per 100,000 Population	Rank[2]
MSA[1]	46,195	777	5
U.S.	1,108,609	339	-

Note: (1) Figures cover the Atlanta-Sandy Springs-Alpharetta, GA Metropolitan Statistical Area; (2) Rank ranges from 1 to 391 where 1 indicates greatest number of identity theft reports per 100,000 population
Source: Federal Trade Commission, Consumer Sentinel Network Data Book 2022

Fraud and Other Consumer Reports

Area	Reports	Reports per 100,000 Population	Rank[2]
MSA[1]	117,759	1,980	2
U.S.	4,064,520	1,245	-

Note: (1) Figures cover the Atlanta-Sandy Springs-Alpharetta, GA Metropolitan Statistical Area; (2) Rank ranges from 1 to 391 where 1 indicates greatest number of fraud and other consumer reports per 100,000 population
Source: Federal Trade Commission, Consumer Sentinel Network Data Book 2022

POLITICS

2020 Presidential Election Results

Area	Biden	Trump	Jorgensen	Hawkins	Other
Fulton County	72.6	26.2	1.2	0.0	0.0
U.S.	51.3	46.8	1.2	0.3	0.5

Note: Results are percentages and may not add to 100% due to rounding
Source: Dave Leip's Atlas of U.S. Presidential Elections

SPORTS

Professional Sports Teams

Team Name	League	Year Established
Atlanta Braves	Major League Baseball (MLB)	1966
Atlanta Falcons	National Football League (NFL)	1966
Atlanta Hawks	National Basketball Association (NBA)	1968
Atlanta United FC	Major League Soccer (MLS)	2017

Note: Includes teams located in the Atlanta-Sandy Springs-Alpharetta, GA Metropolitan Statistical Area.
Source: Wikipedia, Major Professional Sports Teams of the United States and Canada, April 12, 2023

CLIMATE

Average and Extreme Temperatures

Temperature	Jan	Feb	Mar	Apr	May	Jun	Jul	Aug	Sep	Oct	Nov	Dec	Yr.
Extreme High (°F)	79	80	85	93	95	101	105	102	98	95	84	77	105
Average High (°F)	52	56	64	73	80	86	88	88	82	73	63	54	72
Average Temp. (°F)	43	46	53	62	70	77	79	79	73	63	53	45	62
Average Low (°F)	33	36	42	51	59	66	70	69	64	52	42	35	52
Extreme Low (°F)	-8	5	10	26	37	46	53	55	36	28	3	0	-8

Note: Figures cover the years 1945-1990
Source: National Climatic Data Center, International Station Meteorological Climate Summary, 9/96

Average Precipitation/Snowfall/Humidity

Precip./Humidity	Jan	Feb	Mar	Apr	May	Jun	Jul	Aug	Sep	Oct	Nov	Dec	Yr.
Avg. Precip. (in.)	4.7	4.6	5.7	4.3	4.0	3.5	5.1	3.6	3.4	2.8	3.8	4.2	49.8
Avg. Snowfall (in.)	1	1	Tr	Tr	0	0	0	0	0	0	Tr	Tr	2
Avg. Rel. Hum. 7am (%)	79	77	78	78	82	83	88	89	88	84	81	79	82
Avg. Rel. Hum. 4pm (%)	56	50	48	45	49	52	57	56	56	51	52	55	52

Note: Figures cover the years 1945-1990; Tr = Trace amounts (<0.05 in. of rain; <0.5 in. of snow)
Source: National Climatic Data Center, International Station Meteorological Climate Summary, 9/96

Weather Conditions

Temperature			Daytime Sky			Precipitation		
10°F & below	32°F & below	90°F & above	Clear	Partly cloudy	Cloudy	0.01 inch or more precip.	0.1 inch or more snow/ice	Thunder-storms
1	49	38	98	147	120	116	3	48

Note: Figures are average number of days per year and cover the years 1945-1990
Source: National Climatic Data Center, International Station Meteorological Climate Summary, 9/96

HAZARDOUS WASTE

Superfund Sites

The Atlanta-Sandy Springs-Alpharetta, GA metro area has no sites on the EPA's Superfund Final National Priorities List. There are a total of 1,165 Superfund sites with a status of proposed or final on the list in the U.S. *U.S. Environmental Protection Agency, National Priorities List, April 12, 2023*

AIR QUALITY

Air Quality Trends: Ozone

	1990	1995	2000	2005	2010	2015	2018	2019	2020	2021
MSA[1]	0.088	0.089	0.089	0.077	0.067	0.069	0.068	0.070	0.059	0.064
U.S.	0.087	0.089	0.081	0.080	0.072	0.067	0.069	0.065	0.065	0.067

Note: (1) Data covers the Atlanta-Sandy Springs-Alpharetta, GA Metropolitan Statistical Area. The values shown are the composite ozone concentration averages among trend sites based on the highest fourth daily maximum 8-hour concentration in parts per million. These trends are based on sites having an adequate record of monitoring data during the trend period. Data from exceptional events are included.
Source: U.S. Environmental Protection Agency, Air Quality Monitoring Information, "Air Quality Trends by City, 1990-2021"

Air Quality Index

Area	Percent of Days when Air Quality was...[2]					AQI Statistics[2]	
	Good	Moderate	Unhealthy for Sensitive Groups	Unhealthy	Very Unhealthy	Maximum	Median
MSA[1]	57.3	40.5	2.2	0.0	0.0	150	47

Note: (1) Data covers the Atlanta-Sandy Springs-Alpharetta, GA Metropolitan Statistical Area; (2) Based on 365 days with AQI data in 2021. Air Quality Index (AQI) is an index for reporting daily air quality. EPA calculates the AQI for five major air pollutants regulated by the Clean Air Act: ground-level ozone, particle pollution (aka particulate matter), carbon monoxide, sulfur dioxide, and nitrogen dioxide. The AQI runs from 0 to 500. The higher the AQI value, the greater the level of air pollution and the greater the health concern. There are six AQI categories: "Good" AQI is between 0 and 50. Air quality is considered satisfactory; "Moderate" AQI is between 51 and 100. Air quality is acceptable; "Unhealthy for Sensitive Groups" When AQI values are between 101 and 150, members of sensitive groups may experience health effects; "Unhealthy" When AQI values are between 151 and 200 everyone may begin to experience health effects; "Very Unhealthy" AQI values between 201 and 300 trigger a health alert; "Hazardous" AQI values over 300 trigger warnings of emergency conditions (not shown).
Source: U.S. Environmental Protection Agency, Air Quality Index Report, 2021

Air Quality Index Pollutants

Area	Percent of Days when AQI Pollutant was...[2]					
	Carbon Monoxide	Nitrogen Dioxide	Ozone	Sulfur Dioxide	Particulate Matter 2.5	Particulate Matter 10
MSA[1]	0.0	3.6	40.8	(3)	55.6	0.0

Note: (1) Data covers the Atlanta-Sandy Springs-Alpharetta, GA Metropolitan Statistical Area; (2) Based on 365 days with AQI data in 2021. The Air Quality Index (AQI) is an index for reporting daily air quality. EPA calculates the AQI for five major air pollutants regulated by the Clean Air Act: ground-level ozone, particle pollution (also known as particulate matter), carbon monoxide, sulfur dioxide, and nitrogen dioxide. The AQI runs from 0 to 500. The higher the AQI value, the greater the level of air pollution and the greater the health concern; (3) Sulfur dioxide is no longer included in this table (as of December 8, 2021) because SO_2 concentrations tend to be very localized and not necessarily representative of broad geographical areas like counties and CBSAs.
Source: U.S. Environmental Protection Agency, Air Quality Index Report, 2021

Maximum Air Pollutant Concentrations: Particulate Matter, Ozone, CO and Lead

	Particulate Matter 10 (ug/m³)	Particulate Matter 2.5 Wtd AM (ug/m³)	Particulate Matter 2.5 24-Hr (ug/m³)	Ozone (ppm)	Carbon Monoxide (ppm)	Lead (ug/m³)
MSA[1] Level	44	9.7	22	0.07	2	n/a
NAAQS[2]	150	15	35	0.075	9	0.15
Met NAAQS[2]	Yes	Yes	Yes	Yes	Yes	n/a

Note: (1) Data covers the Atlanta-Sandy Springs-Alpharetta, GA Metropolitan Statistical Area; Data from exceptional events are included; (2) National Ambient Air Quality Standards; ppm = parts per million; ug/m³ = micrograms per cubic meter; n/a not available.
Concentrations: Particulate Matter 10 (coarse particulate)—highest second maximum 24-hour concentration; Particulate Matter 2.5 Wtd AM (fine particulate)—highest weighted annual mean concentration; Particulate Matter 2.5 24-Hour (fine particulate)—highest 98th percentile 24-hour concentration; Ozone—highest fourth daily maximum 8-hour concentration; Carbon Monoxide—highest second maximum non-overlapping 8-hour concentration; Lead—maximum running 3-month average
Source: U.S. Environmental Protection Agency, Air Quality Monitoring Information, "Air Quality Statistics by City, 2021"

Maximum Air Pollutant Concentrations: Nitrogen Dioxide and Sulfur Dioxide

	Nitrogen Dioxide AM (ppb)	Nitrogen Dioxide 1-Hr (ppb)	Sulfur Dioxide AM (ppb)	Sulfur Dioxide 1-Hr (ppb)	Sulfur Dioxide 24-Hr (ppb)
MSA[1] Level	17	50	n/a	4	n/a
NAAQS[2]	53	100	30	75	140
Met NAAQS[2]	Yes	Yes	n/a	Yes	n/a

Note: (1) Data covers the Atlanta-Sandy Springs-Alpharetta, GA Metropolitan Statistical Area; Data from exceptional events are included; (2) National Ambient Air Quality Standards; ppm = parts per million; ug/m³ = micrograms per cubic meter; n/a not available.
Concentrations: Nitrogen Dioxide AM—highest arithmetic mean concentration; Nitrogen Dioxide 1-Hr—highest 98th percentile 1-hour daily maximum concentration; Sulfur Dioxide AM—highest annual mean concentration; Sulfur Dioxide 1-Hr—highest 99th percentile 1-hour daily maximum concentration; Sulfur Dioxide 24-Hr—highest second maximum 24-hour concentration
Source: U.S. Environmental Protection Agency, Air Quality Monitoring Information, "Air Quality Statistics by City, 2021"

Austin, Texas

Background

Starting out in 1730 as a peaceful Spanish mission on the north bank of the Colorado River in south-central Texas, Austin soon engaged in an imbroglio of territorial wars, beginning when the "Father of Texas," Stephen F. Austin, annexed the territory from Mexico in 1833 as his own. Later, the Republic of Texas named the territory Austin in honor of the colonizer and conferred upon it state capital status. Challenges to this decision ensued, ranging from an invasion by the Mexican government to reclaim its land, to Sam Houston's call that the capital ought to move from Austin to Houston.

During peaceful times, however, Austin has been called the "City of the Violet Crown." Coined by the short story writer, William Sydney Porter, or O. Henry, the name refers to the purple mist that circles the surrounding hills of the Colorado River Valley.

This city of technological innovation is home to a strong computer and electronics industry. Austin offers hundreds of free wireless spots, including city parks, and its technology focus has traditionally drawn numerous high-tech companies. A major Samsung Electronics computer chip plant was built in Austin in the late 1990s with several expansions since. Along with this technology growth came increased traffic, especially on Interstate 35, the main highway linking the U.S. and Mexico. An 89-mile bypass has helped to relieve some of the traffic difficulties long associated with I-35, after which Facebook opened a sales and operations facility in the city.

In addition to its traditional business community, Austin is home to the main campus of the University of Texas. The university provides Austin with diverse lifestyles; today there is a solid mix of white-collar workers, students, professors, blue-collar workers, musicians and artists, and members of the booming tech industry who all call themselves Austinites.

The influx of young people centered on university life has contributed to the city's growth as a thriving live music scene. The city maintains the Austin Music Commission to promote the local music industry.

South by Southwest Conference (SXSW) returned in-person to Austin in March of 2022, after a two-year COVID hiatus, showcasing about 2,000 film, interactive media, and music performers at venues throughout the city. It is the highest revenue-producing event, other than athletic events, for the Austin economy.

The civic-minded city operates from a city hall which also houses a public plaza facing Town Lake, and the Long Center for the Performing Arts is one of the town's cultural hubs. The city's first major-league professional sports team, Austin FC, part of the Major League Soccer League, started playing in 2021.

Austinites' pride in their creative and independent culture has spawned a movement to keep the city from too much corporate development. The slogan "Keep Austin Weird" was adopted by the Austin Independent Business Alliance to promote local and alternative business.

Austin's skyline, dominated for years by the Texas State Capitol and the University of Texas, now includes a significant number of large buildings, including The Austonian (2010), Northshore (2016), The Independent (2019), SXSW Center (2019), and 70 Rainy (aka Rainy Historic District) (2019).

Austin consistently gets high marks in best-of city surveys. It sits at a desirable location along the Colorado River, and many recreational activities center on the water. Austin boasts three spring-fed swimming pools, and the city has more than 100 miles of bike paths, including the Lance Armstrong Crosstown Bikeway.

The climate of Austin is subtropical with hot summers. Winters are mild, with below-freezing temperatures occurring on an average of 25 days a year. Cold spells are short, seldom lasting more than two days. Daytime temperatures in summer are hot, while summer nights are usually pleasant. In February 2021, a series of severe winter storms caused record low temperatures in Austin, falling below Anchorage, Alaska, and causing a massive electricity generation failure in the state.

Rankings

General Rankings

- *US News & World Report* conducted a survey of more than 3,600 people and analyzed the 150 largest metropolitan areas to determine what matters most when selecting where to settle down. Austin ranked #13 out of the top 25 as having the best combination of desirable factors. Criteria: cost of living; quality of life and education; net migration; job market; desirability; and other factors. *money.usnews.com, "The 25 Best Places to Live in the U.S. in 2022-2023," May 17, 2022*

- The Austin metro area was identified as one of America's fastest-growing areas in terms of population and business growth by *MagnifyMoney*. The area ranked #1 out of 35. The 100 most populous metro areas in the U.S. were evaluated on their change from 2011 to 2016 in the following categories: people and housing; workforce and employment opportunities; growing industry. *www.businessinsider.com, "The 35 Cities in the US with the Biggest Influx of People, the Most Work Opportunities, and the Hottest Business Growth," August 12, 2018*

- The Austin metro area was identified as one of America's fastest-growing areas in terms of population and economy by *Forbes*. The area ranked #8 out of 25. The 100 most populous metro areas in the U.S. were evaluated on the following criteria: estimated population growth; employment; economic output; wages; home values. *Forbes, "America's Fastest-Growing Cities 2018," February 28, 2018*

- Austin was selected as one of the best places to live in America by *Outside Magazine*. Criteria centered on diversity; sustainability; outdoor equity; and affordability. Local experts shared highlights from hands-on experience in each location. *Outside Magazine, "The 20 Most Livable Towns and Cities in America," October 15, 2021*

- Austin appeared on *Travel + Leisure's* list of "The 15 Best Cities in the United States." The city was ranked #11. Criteria: sights/landmarks; culture; food; friendliness; shopping; and overall value. *Travel + Leisure, "The World's Best Awards 2022" July 12, 2022*

Business/Finance Rankings

- According to *Business Insider*, the Austin metro area is a prime place to run a startup or move an existing business to. The area ranked #7. More than 300 metro areas were analyzed for factors that were of top concern to new business owners. Data was based on the 2019 U.S. Census Bureau American Community Survey, statistics from the CDC, Bureau of Labor Statistics employment report, and University of Chicago analysis. Criteria: business formations; percentage of vaccinated population; percentage of households with internet subscriptions; median household income; and share of work that can be done from home. *www.businessinsider.com, "The 20 Best Cities for Starting a Business in 2022 Include Baltimore, Boulder, and Boston," January 5, 2022*

- *24/7 Wall St.* used metro data from the Bureau of Labor Statistics' Occupational Employment database to identify the cities with the highest percentage of those employed in jobs requiring knowledge in the science, technology, engineering, and math (STEM) fields as well as average wages for STEM jobs. The Austin metro area was #9. *247wallst.com, "15 Cities with the Most High-Tech Jobs," January 11, 2020*

- Based on metro area social media reviews, the employment opinion group Glassdoor surveyed 50 of the most populous U.S. metro areas and equally weighed cost of living, hiring opportunity, and job satisfaction to compose a list of "25 Best Cities for Jobs." Median pay and home value, and number of active job openings were also factored in. The Austin metro area was ranked #24 in overall job satisfaction. *www.glassdoor.com, "Best Cities for Jobs," February 25, 2020*

- The Brookings Institution ranked the nation's largest cities based on income inequality. Austin was ranked #47 (#1 = greatest inequality). Criteria: the "95/20 ratio," a figure representing the income at which a household earns more than 95 percent of all other households, divided by the income at which a household earns more than only 20 percent of all other households. *Brookings Institution, "Household Income Inequality, Largest Cities of 97 Large U.S. Metro Areas, 2014-2016," February 5, 2018*

- The Brookings Institution ranked the 100 largest metro areas in the U.S. based on income inequality. Austin was ranked #37 (#1 = greatest inequality). Criteria: the "95/20 ratio," a figure representing the income at which a household earns more than 95 percent of all other households, divided by the income at which a household earns more than only 20 percent of all other households. *Brookings Institution, "Household Income Inequality, 100 Largest U.S. Metro Areas, 2014-2016," February 5, 2018*

- Payscale.com ranked the 32 largest metro areas in terms of wage growth. The Austin metro area ranked #15. Criteria: quarterly changes in private industry employee and education professional wage growth from the previous year. *PayScale, "Wage Trends by Metro Area-1st Quarter," April 20, 2023*

- Austin was cited as one of America's top metros for total corporate facility investment in 2022. The area ranked #7 in the large metro area category (population over 1 million). *Site Selection, "Top Metros of 2022," March 2023*

- Austin was identified as one of the happiest cities to work in by CareerBliss.com, an online community for career advancement. The city ranked #10 out of 10. Criteria: an employee's relationship with his or her boss and co-workers; daily tasks; general work environment; compensation; opportunities for advancement; company culture and job reputation; and resources. *Businesswire.com, "CareerBliss Happiest Cities to Work 2019," February 12, 2019*

- The Austin metro area appeared on the Milken Institute "2022 Best Performing Cities" list. Rank: #2 out of 200 large metro areas (population over 250,000). Criteria: job growth; wage and salary growth; high-tech output growth; housing affordability; household broadband access. *Milken Institute, "Best-Performing Cities 2022," March 28, 2022*

- *Forbes* ranked the 200 most populous metro areas to determine the nation's "Best Places for Business and Careers." The Austin metro area was ranked #8. Criteria: costs (business and living); job growth (past and projected); income growth; quality of life; educational attainment (college and high school); projected economic growth; cultural and leisure opportunities; workplace tolerance laws; net migration patterns. *Forbes, "The Best Places for Business and Careers 2019: Seattle Still On Top," October 30, 2019*

Culture/Performing Arts Rankings

- Austin was selected as one of the 25 best cities for moviemakers in North America. Great film cities are places where filmmaking dreams can come true, that offer more creative space, lower costs, and great outdoor locations. NYC & LA were intentionally excluded. Criteria: longstanding reputations as film-friendly communities; film community and culture; affordability; and quality of life. The city was ranked #12. *MovieMaker Magazine, "Best Places to Live and Work as a Moviemaker, 2023," January 18, 2023*

Dating/Romance Rankings

- *Apartment List* conducted its Annual Renter Satisfaction Survey and asked renters "how satisfied are you with opportunities for dating in your current city." The cities were ranked from highest to lowest based on their satisfaction scores. Austin ranked #5 out of 85 cities. *Apartment List, "Best Cities for Dating 2022 with Local Dating Insights from Bumble," February 7, 2022*

Education Rankings

- Personal finance website *WalletHub* analyzed the 150 largest U.S. metropolitan statistical areas to determine where the most educated Americans are putting their degrees to work. Criteria: education levels; percentage of workers with degrees; education quality and attainment gap; public school quality rankings; quality and enrollment of each metro area's universities. Austin was ranked #10 (#1 = most educated city). *www.WalletHub.com, "Most & Least Educated Cities in America," July 18, 2022*

- Austin was selected as one of the best cities for post grads by *Rent.com*. The city ranked among the top 10. Criteria: jobs per capita; unemployment rate; mean annual income; cost of living; rental inventory. *Rent.com, "Best Cities for College Grads," December 11, 2018*

- Austin was selected as one of America's most literate cities. The city ranked #15 out of the 84 largest U.S. cities. Criteria: number of booksellers; library resources; Internet resources; educational attainment; periodical publishing resources; newspaper circulation. *Central Connecticut State University, "America's Most Literate Cities, 2018," February 2019*

Environmental Rankings

- Sperling's BestPlaces assessed the 50 largest metropolitan areas of the United States for the likelihood of dangerously extreme weather events or earthquakes. In general the Southeast and South-Central regions have the highest risk of weather extremes and earthquakes, while the Pacific Northwest enjoys the lowest risk. Of the most risky metropolitan areas, the Austin metro area was ranked #2. *www.bestplaces.net, "Avoid Natural Disasters: BestPlaces Reveals The Top 10 Safest Places to Live," October 25, 2017*

- The U.S. Environmental Protection Agency (EPA) released its list of U.S. metropolitan areas with the most ENERGY STAR certified buildings in 2022. The Austin metro area was ranked #15 out of 25. *U.S. Environmental Protection Agency, "2023 Energy Star Top Cities," April 26, 2023*

Food/Drink Rankings

- The U.S. Chamber of Commerce Foundation conducted an in-depth study on local food truck regulations, surveyed 288 food truck owners, and ranked 20 major American cities based on how friendly they are for operating a food truck. The compiled index assessed the following: procedures for obtaining permits and licenses; complying with restrictions; and financial obligations associated with operating a food truck. Austin ranked #7 overall (1 being the best). *www.foodtrucknation.us, "Food Truck Nation," March 20, 2018*

Health/Fitness Rankings

- For each of the 100 largest cities in the United States, the American Fitness Index®, compiled in partnership between the American College of Sports Medicine and the Elevance Health Foundation, evaluated community infrastructure and 34 health behaviors including preventive health, levels of chronic disease conditions, food insecurity, sleep quality, pedestrian safety, air quality, and community/environment resources that support physical activity. Austin ranked #27 for "community fitness." *americanfitnessindex.org, "2022 ACSM American Fitness Index Summary Report," July 12, 2022*

- Austin was identified as a "2022 Spring Allergy Capital." The area ranked #73 out of 100. Three groups of factors were used to identify the most challenging cities for people with allergies during the spring season: annual spring pollen scores; over the counter allergy medicine use; number of board-certified allergy specialists. *Asthma and Allergy Foundation of America, "Spring Allergy Capitals 2022," March 2, 2022*

- Austin was identified as a "2022 Fall Allergy Capital." The area ranked #62 out of 100. Three groups of factors were used to identify the most challenging cities for people with allergies during the fall season: annual fall pollen scores; over the counter allergy medicine use; number of board-certified allergy specialists. *Asthma and Allergy Foundation of America, "Fall Allergy Capitals 2022," March 2, 2022*

- Austin was identified as a "2022 Asthma Capital." The area ranked #66 out of the nation's 100 largest metropolitan areas. Criteria: estimated asthma prevalence; asthma-related mortality; and ER visits due to asthma. Risk factors analyzed but not factored in the rankings: annual pollen score; annual air quality; public smoking laws; access to board-certified asthma specialists; rescue and controller medication use; uninsured rate; poverty rate. *Asthma and Allergy Foundation of America, "Asthma Capitals 2022: The Most Challenging Places to Live With Asthma," September 14, 2022*

Real Estate Rankings

- *WalletHub* compared the most populated U.S. cities to determine which had the best markets for real estate agents. Austin ranked #9 where demand was high and pay was the best. Criteria: sales per agent; annual median wage for real-estate agents; monthly average starting salary for real estate agents; real estate job density and competition; unemployment rate; home turnover rate; housing-market health index; and other relevant metrics. *www.WalletHub.com, "2021 Best Places to Be a Real Estate Agent," May 12, 2021*

- According to Penske Truck Rental, the Austin metro area was named the #10 moving destination in 2022, based on one-way consumer truck rental reservations made through Penske's website, rental locations, and reservations call center. *gopenske.com/blog, "Penske Truck Rental's 2022 Top Moving Destinations," April 27, 2023*

- The Austin metro area was identified as one of the 20 worst housing markets in the U.S. in 2022. The area ranked #173 out of 187 markets. Criteria: year-over-year change of median sales price of existing single-family homes between the 4th quarter of 2021 and the 4th quarter of 2022. *National Association of Realtors®, Median Sales Price of Existing Single-Family Homes for Metropolitan Areas, 4th Quarter 2022*

- Austin was ranked #181 out of 235 metro areas in terms of housing affordability in 2022 by the National Association of Home Builders (#1 = most affordable). Criteria: the share of homes sold in that area affordable to a family earning the local median income, based on standard mortgage underwriting criteria. *National Association of Home Builders®, NAHB-Wells Fargo Housing Opportunity Index, 4th Quarter 2022*

Safety Rankings

- Allstate ranked the 200 largest cities in America in terms of driver safety. Austin ranked #160. Criteria: internal property damage claims over a two-year period from January 2016 to December 2017. The report helps increase the importance of safety and awareness behind the wheel. *Allstate, "Allstate America's Best Drivers Report, 2019" June 24, 2019*

- The National Insurance Crime Bureau ranked 390 metro areas in the U.S. in terms of per capita rates of vehicle theft. The Austin metro area ranked #114 (#1 = highest rate). Criteria: number of vehicle theft offenses per 100,000 inhabitants in 2021. *National Insurance Crime Bureau, "Hot Spots 2021," September 1, 2022*

Seniors/Retirement Rankings

- From its Best Cities for Successful Aging indexes, the Milken Institute generated rankings for metropolitan areas, weighing data in nine categories—health care, wellness, living arrangements, transportation and convenience, financial characteristics, education, employment, community engagement, and overall livability. The Austin metro area was ranked #6 overall in the large metro area category. *Milken Institute, "Best Cities for Successful Aging, 2017" March 14, 2017*

- Austin was identified as #15 of 20 most popular places to retire in the Southwest region by *Topretirements.com*. The site separated its annual "Best Places to Retire" list by major U.S. regions for 2019. The list reflects the 20 cities that visitors to the website are most interested in for retirement, based on the number of times a city's review was viewed on the website. *Topretirements.com, "20 Most Popular Places to Retire in the Southwest for 2019," October 2, 2019*

Sports/Recreation Rankings

- Austin was chosen as one of America's best cities for bicycling. The city ranked #13 out of 50. Criteria: cycling infrastructure that is safe and friendly for all ages; energy and bike culture. The editors evaluated cities with populations of 100,000 or more. *Bicycling, "The 50 Best Bike Cities in America," October 10, 2018*

Transportation Rankings

- According to the INRIX "2022 Global Traffic Scorecard," Austin was identified as one of the most congested metro areas in the U.S. The area ranked #18 out of 25. Criteria: average annual time spent in traffic and average cost of congestion per motorist. *Inrix.com, "Return to Work, Higher Gas Prices & Inflation Drove Americans to Spend Hundreds More in Time and Money Commuting," January 10, 2023*

Women/Minorities Rankings

- *Travel + Leisure* listed the best cities in and around the U.S. for a memorable and fun girls' trip, even on a budget. Whether it is for a special occasion, to make new memories or just to get away, Austin is sure to have something for all the ladies in your tribe. *Travel + Leisure, "25 Affordable Girls Weekend Getaways That Won't Break the Bank," November 25, 2022*

- The *Houston Chronicle* listed the Austin metro area as #2 in top places for young Latinos to live in the U.S. Research was largely based on housing and occupational data from the largest metropolitan areas performed by *Forbes* and NBC Universo. Criteria: percentage of 18-34 year-olds; Latino college grad rates; and diversity. *blog.chron.com, "The 15 Best Big Cities for Latino Millenials," January 26, 2016*

- *Women's Health*, together with the site Yelp, identified the 15 "Wellthiest" spots in the U.S. Austin appeared among the top for happiest, healthiest, outdoorsiest and Zen-iest. *Women's Health, "The 15 Wellthiest Cities in the U.S." July 5, 2017*

- Personal finance website *WalletHub* compared more than 180 U.S. cities across two key dimensions, "Hispanic Business-Friendliness" and "Hispanic Purchasing Power," to arrive at the most favorable conditions for Hispanic entrepreneurs. Austin was ranked #17 out of 182. Criteria includes: share of Hispanic-Owned Businesses; Hispanic entrepreneurship rate to median annual income of Hispanics; Small Business-Friendliness score; cost of living; and number of Hispanics with at least a bachelor's degree. *WalletHub.com, "2019's Best Cities for Hispanic Entrepreneurs," May 1, 2019*

Miscellaneous Rankings

- *WalletHub* compared the 150 most populated U.S. cities to determine their operating efficiency. A "Quality of Services" score was constructed for each city and then divided by the total budget per capita to reveal which were managed the best. Austin ranked #85. Criteria: financial stability; economy; education; safety; health; infrastructure and pollution. *www.WalletHub.com, "2022's Best- & Worst-Run Cities in America," June 21, 2022*

Business Environment

DEMOGRAPHICS

Population Growth

Area	1990 Census	2000 Census	2010 Census	2020 Census	Population Growth (%) 1990-2020	Population Growth (%) 2010-2020
City	499,053	656,562	790,390	961,855	92.7	21.7
MSA[1]	846,217	1,249,763	1,716,289	2,283,371	169.8	33.0
U.S.	248,709,873	281,421,906	308,745,538	331,449,281	33.3	7.4

Note: (1) Figures cover the Austin-Round Rock-Georgetown, TX Metropolitan Statistical Area
Source: U.S. Census Bureau, 1990 Census, 2000 Census, 2010 Census, 2020 Census

Race

Area	White Alone[2] (%)	Black Alone[2] (%)	Asian Alone[2] (%)	AIAN[3] Alone[2] (%)	NHOPI[4] Alone[2] (%)	Other Race Alone[2] (%)	Two or More Races (%)
City	54.7	7.3	9.0	1.0	0.1	11.9	16.1
MSA[1]	57.3	7.0	7.1	0.9	0.1	11.1	16.5
U.S.	61.6	12.4	6.0	1.1	0.2	8.4	10.2

Note: (1) Figures cover the Austin-Round Rock-Georgetown, TX Metropolitan Statistical Area; (2) Alone is defined as not being in combination with one or more other races; (3) American Indian and Alaska Native; (4) Native Hawaiian and Other Pacific Islander
Source: U.S. Census Bureau, 2020 Census

Hispanic or Latino Origin

Area	Total (%)	Mexican (%)	Puerto Rican (%)	Cuban (%)	Other (%)
City	33.1	25.6	1.0	0.7	5.8
MSA[1]	32.7	26.3	1.0	0.5	5.0
U.S.	18.4	11.2	1.8	0.7	4.7

Note: Persons of Hispanic or Latino origin can be of any race; (1) Figures cover the Austin-Round Rock-Georgetown, TX Metropolitan Statistical Area
Source: U.S. Census Bureau, 2017-2021 American Community Survey 5-Year Estimates

Age

Area	Under Age 5	Age 5–19	Age 20–34	Age 35–44	Age 45–54	Age 55–64	Age 65–74	Age 75–84	Age 85+	Median Age
City	5.5	16.7	31.8	16.1	11.4	9.0	6.1	2.5	1.0	33.0
MSA[1]	5.9	20.0	24.8	15.3	12.4	10.3	7.3	3.1	1.1	34.7
U.S.	5.6	19.2	20.2	12.7	12.4	13.1	10.0	4.9	1.9	38.8

Note: (1) Figures cover the Austin-Round Rock-Georgetown, TX Metropolitan Statistical Area
Source: U.S. Census Bureau, 2020 Census

Disability by Age

Area	All Ages	Under 18 Years Old	18 to 64 Years Old	65 Years and Over
City	8.7	4.1	7.4	28.5
MSA[1]	9.3	3.8	7.8	29.4
U.S.	12.6	4.4	10.3	33.4

Note: Figures show percent of the civilian noninstitutionalized population that reported having a disability. Disability status is determined from six types of difficulty: vision, hearing, cognitive, ambulatory, self-care, and independent living. For children under 5 years old, hearing and vision difficulty are used to determine disability status. For children between the ages of 5 and 14, disability status is determined from hearing, vision, cognitive, ambulatory, and self-care difficulties. For people aged 15 years and older, they are considered to have a disability if they have difficulty with any one of the six difficulty types; Note: (1) Figures cover the Austin-Round Rock-Georgetown, TX Metropolitan Statistical Area
Source: U.S. Census Bureau, 2017-2021 American Community Survey 5-Year Estimates

Ancestry

Area	German	Irish	English	American	Italian	Polish	French[2]	Scottish	Dutch
City	10.9	8.3	8.7	2.9	3.0	1.8	2.4	2.1	0.7
MSA[1]	12.3	8.1	9.1	3.7	2.8	1.6	2.3	2.1	0.8
U.S.	12.8	9.6	8.1	5.7	5.0	2.7	2.2	1.6	1.1

Note: Figures are the percentage of the total population reporting a particular ancestry. The nine most commonly reported ancestries in the U.S. are shown. Figures include multiple ancestries (e.g. if a person reported being Irish and Italian, they were included in both columns); (1) Figures cover the Austin-Round Rock-Georgetown, TX Metropolitan Statistical Area; (2) Excludes Basque
Source: U.S. Census Bureau, 2017-2021 American Community Survey 5-Year Estimates

Foreign-born Population

Area	Any Foreign Country	Asia	Mexico	Europe	Caribbean	Central America[2]	South America	Africa	Canada
City	18.5	6.3	6.3	1.5	0.6	1.7	0.8	0.9	0.3
MSA[1]	15.2	4.8	5.8	1.2	0.4	1.2	0.7	0.7	0.3
U.S.	13.6	4.2	3.3	1.5	1.4	1.1	1.1	0.8	0.2

Note: (1) Figures cover the Austin-Round Rock-Georgetown, TX Metropolitan Statistical Area; (2) Excludes Mexico.
Source: U.S. Census Bureau, 2017-2021 American Community Survey 5-Year Estimates

Household Size

Area	One	Two	Three	Four	Five	Six	Seven or More	Average Household Size
City	34.8	33.7	14.4	10.4	4.3	1.5	0.9	2.30
MSA[1]	27.3	33.7	15.9	13.6	6.0	2.3	1.3	2.50
U.S.	28.1	33.8	15.5	12.9	6.0	2.3	1.4	2.60

Note: (1) Figures cover the Austin-Round Rock-Georgetown, TX Metropolitan Statistical Area
Source: U.S. Census Bureau, 2017-2021 American Community Survey 5-Year Estimates

Household Relationships

Area	Householder	Opposite-sex Spouse	Same-sex Spouse	Opposite-sex Unmarried Partner	Same-sex Unmarried Partner	Child[2]	Grandchild	Other Relatives	Non-relatives
City	42.7	14.5	0.4	3.6	0.4	23.2	1.5	4.1	6.4
MSA[1]	38.6	17.3	0.3	2.7	0.3	27.8	1.9	4.4	4.6
U.S.	38.3	17.5	0.2	2.5	0.2	28.3	2.4	4.8	3.4

Note: Figures are percent of the total population; (1) Figures cover the Austin-Round Rock-Georgetown, TX Metropolitan Statistical Area; (2) Includes biological, adopted, and stepchildren of the householder
Source: U.S. Census Bureau, 2020 Census

Gender

Area	Males	Females	Males per 100 Females
City	485,739	476,116	102.0
MSA[1]	1,138,942	1,144,429	99.5
U.S.	162,685,811	168,763,470	96.4

Note: (1) Figures cover the Austin-Round Rock-Georgetown, TX Metropolitan Statistical Area
Source: U.S. Census Bureau, 2020 Census

Marital Status

Area	Never Married	Now Married[2]	Separated	Widowed	Divorced
City	43.0	41.9	1.4	3.0	10.6
MSA[1]	35.5	49.4	1.4	3.5	10.3
U.S.	33.8	48.0	1.8	5.6	10.8

Note: Figures are percentages and cover the population 15 years of age and older; (1) Figures cover the Austin-Round Rock-Georgetown, TX Metropolitan Statistical Area; (2) Excludes separated
Source: U.S. Census Bureau, 2017-2021 American Community Survey 5-Year Estimates

Religious Groups by Family

Area	Catholic	Baptist	Methodist	LDS[2]	Pentecostal	Lutheran	Islam	Adventist	Other
MSA[1]	18.8	6.5	2.2	1.3	0.7	1.1	1.0	1.0	9.9
U.S.	18.7	7.3	3.0	2.0	1.8	1.7	1.3	1.3	11.6

Note: Figures are the number of adherents as a percentage of the total population and cover the eight largest religious groups in the U.S; (1) Figures cover the Austin-Round Rock-Georgetown, TX Metropolitan Statistical Area; (2) Church of Jesus Christ of Latter-day Saints
Sources: 2020 U.S. Religion Census, Association of Statisticians of American Religious Bodies; The Association of Religion Data Archives (ARDA)

Religious Groups by Tradition

Area	Catholic	Evangelical Protestant	Mainline Protestant	Black Protestant	Islam	Judaism	Hinduism	Orthodox	Buddhism
MSA[1]	18.8	13.5	4.0	1.7	1.0	0.2	0.6	0.2	0.3
U.S.	18.7	16.5	5.2	2.3	1.3	0.6	0.4	0.4	0.3

Note: Figures are the number of adherents as a percentage of the total population; (1) Figures cover the Austin-Round Rock-Georgetown, TX Metropolitan Statistical Area
Sources: 2020 U.S. Religion Census, Association of Statisticians of American Religious Bodies; The Association of Religion Data Archives (ARDA)

Austin, Texas

ECONOMY

Gross Metropolitan Product

Area	2020	2021	2022	2023	Rank[2]
MSA[1]	168.4	192.3	215.9	231.0	22

Note: Figures are in billions of dollars; (1) Figures cover the Austin-Round Rock-Georgetown, TX Metropolitan Statistical Area; (2) Rank is based on 2021 data and ranges from 1 to 381
Source: U.S. Conference of Mayors, U.S. Metro Economies: U.S. Metros Compared to Global and State Economies, June 2022

Economic Growth

Area	2018-20 (%)	2021 (%)	2022 (%)	2023 (%)	Rank[2]
MSA[1]	3.2	10.1	5.9	3.8	13
U.S.	-0.6	5.7	3.1	2.9	—

Note: Figures are real gross metropolitan product (GMP) growth rates and represent average annual percent change; (1) Figures cover the Austin-Round Rock-Georgetown, TX Metropolitan Statistical Area; (2) Rank is based on 2020 2-year average annual percent change and ranges from 1 to 381
Source: U.S. Conference of Mayors, U.S. Metro Economies: U.S. Metros Compared to Global and State Economies, June 2022

Metropolitan Area Exports

Area	2016	2017	2018	2019	2020	2021	Rank[2]
MSA[1]	10,682.7	12,451.5	12,929.9	12,509.0	13,041.5	15,621.9	25

Note: Figures are in millions of dollars; (1) Figures cover the Austin-Round Rock-Georgetown, TX Metropolitan Statistical Area; (2) Rank is based on 2021 data and ranges from 1 to 388
Source: U.S. Department of Commerce, International Trade Administration, Office of Trade and Economic Analysis, Industry and Analysis, Exports by Metropolitan Area, data extracted March 16, 2023

Building Permits

Area	Single-Family 2021	Single-Family 2022	Pct. Chg.	Multi-Family 2021	Multi-Family 2022	Pct. Chg.	Total 2021	Total 2022	Pct. Chg.
City	4,180	3,344	-20.0	14,542	15,102	3.9	18,722	18,446	-1.5
MSA[1]	24,486	19,717	-19.5	26,421	22,647	-14.3	50,907	42,364	-16.8
U.S.	1,115,400	975,600	-12.5	621,600	689,500	10.9	1,737,000	1,665,100	-4.1

Note: (1) Figures cover the Austin-Round Rock-Georgetown, TX Metropolitan Statistical Area; Figures represent new, privately-owned housing units authorized (unadjusted data); All permit data are based on estimates with imputation
Source: U.S. Census Bureau, Manufacturing, Mining, and Construction Statistics, Building Permits, 2021, 2022

Bankruptcy Filings

Area	Business Filings 2021	Business Filings 2022	% Chg.	Nonbusiness Filings 2021	Nonbusiness Filings 2022	% Chg.
Travis County	113	76	-32.7	443	372	-16.0
U.S.	14,347	13,481	-6.0	399,269	374,240	-6.3

Note: Business filings include Chapter 7, Chapter 9, Chapter 11, Chapter 12, Chapter 13, Chapter 15, and Section 304; Nonbusiness filings include Chapter 7, Chapter 11, and Chapter 13
Source: Administrative Office of the U.S. Courts, Business and Nonbusiness Bankruptcy, County Cases Commenced by Chapter of the Bankruptcy Code, During the 12-Month Period Ending December 31, 2021 and Business and Nonbusiness Bankruptcy, County Cases Commenced by Chapter of the Bankruptcy Code, During the 12-Month Period Ending December 31, 2022

Housing Vacancy Rates

Area	Gross Vacancy Rate[2] (%) 2020	2021	2022	Year-Round Vacancy Rate[3] (%) 2020	2021	2022	Rental Vacancy Rate[4] (%) 2020	2021	2022	Homeowner Vacancy Rate[5] (%) 2020	2021	2022
MSA[1]	7.0	6.5	5.5	6.8	6.2	4.9	6.6	8.5	5.6	2.0	1.3	0.6
U.S.	10.6	10.8	10.5	8.2	8.4	8.2	6.3	6.1	5.8	1.0	0.9	0.8

Note: (1) Figures cover the Austin-Round Rock-Georgetown, TX Metropolitan Statistical Area; (2) The percentage of the total housing inventory that is vacant; (3) The percentage of the housing inventory (excluding seasonal units) that is year-round vacant; (4) The percentage of rental inventory that is vacant for rent; (5) The percentage of homeowner inventory that is vacant for sale
Source: U.S. Census Bureau, Housing Vacancies and Homeownership Annual Statistics: 2020, 2021, 2022

INCOME

Income

Area	Per Capita ($)	Median Household ($)	Average Household ($)
City	48,550	78,965	111,233
MSA[1]	44,830	85,398	114,103
U.S.	37,638	69,021	97,196

Note: (1) Figures cover the Austin-Round Rock-Georgetown, TX Metropolitan Statistical Area
Source: U.S. Census Bureau, 2017-2021 American Community Survey 5-Year Estimates

Austin, Texas

Household Income Distribution

Area	Under $15,000	$15,000 -$24,999	$25,000 -$34,999	$35,000 -$49,999	$50,000 -$74,999	$75,000 -$99,999	$100,000 -$149,999	$150,000 and up
City	8.3	5.5	6.7	10.4	16.8	12.6	17.7	22.1
MSA[1]	6.8	5.1	6.3	9.7	16.1	13.6	19.1	23.4
U.S.	9.4	7.8	8.2	11.4	16.8	12.8	16.3	17.3

Percent of Households Earning

Note: (1) Figures cover the Austin-Round Rock-Georgetown, TX Metropolitan Statistical Area
Source: U.S. Census Bureau, 2017-2021 American Community Survey 5-Year Estimates

Poverty Rate

Area	All Ages	Under 18 Years Old	18 to 64 Years Old	65 Years and Over
City	12.5	15.9	11.7	11.3
MSA[1]	10.2	12.0	9.9	8.3
U.S.	12.6	17.0	11.8	9.6

Note: Figures are percentage of people whose income during the past 12 months was below the poverty level; (1) Figures cover the Austin-Round Rock-Georgetown, TX Metropolitan Statistical Area
Source: U.S. Census Bureau, 2017-2021 American Community Survey 5-Year Estimates

EMPLOYMENT

Labor Force and Employment

Area	Civilian Labor Force Dec. 2021	Civilian Labor Force Dec. 2022	% Chg.	Workers Employed Dec. 2021	Workers Employed Dec. 2022	% Chg.
City	626,475	642,058	2.5	609,403	625,541	2.6
MSA[1]	1,339,834	1,372,624	2.4	1,301,083	1,335,791	2.7
U.S.	161,696,000	164,224,000	1.6	155,732,000	158,872,000	2.0

Note: Data is not seasonally adjusted and covers workers 16 years of age and older; (1) Figures cover the Austin-Round Rock-Georgetown, TX Metropolitan Statistical Area
Source: Bureau of Labor Statistics, Local Area Unemployment Statistics

Unemployment Rate

2022

Area	Jan.	Feb.	Mar.	Apr.	May	Jun.	Jul.	Aug.	Sep.	Oct.	Nov.	Dec.
City	3.2	3.2	2.6	2.4	2.6	2.9	2.9	2.9	2.7	2.7	2.6	2.6
MSA[1]	3.3	3.3	2.7	2.5	2.7	3.1	3.1	3.0	2.8	2.8	2.8	2.7
U.S.	4.4	4.1	3.8	3.3	3.4	3.8	3.8	3.8	3.3	3.4	3.4	3.3

Note: Data is not seasonally adjusted and covers workers 16 years of age and older; (1) Figures cover the Austin-Round Rock-Georgetown, TX Metropolitan Statistical Area
Source: Bureau of Labor Statistics, Local Area Unemployment Statistics

Average Wages

Occupation	$/Hr.	Occupation	$/Hr.
Accountants and Auditors	41.33	Maintenance and Repair Workers	20.40
Automotive Mechanics	25.45	Marketing Managers	70.73
Bookkeepers	22.37	Network and Computer Systems Admin.	46.20
Carpenters	24.23	Nurses, Licensed Practical	27.17
Cashiers	13.85	Nurses, Registered	41.69
Computer Programmers	46.80	Nursing Assistants	16.17
Computer Systems Analysts	48.67	Office Clerks, General	19.06
Computer User Support Specialists	28.69	Physical Therapists	47.33
Construction Laborers	19.04	Physicians	136.94
Cooks, Restaurant	15.59	Plumbers, Pipefitters and Steamfitters	28.42
Customer Service Representatives	19.39	Police and Sheriff's Patrol Officers	35.58
Dentists	85.63	Postal Service Mail Carriers	27.22
Electricians	27.12	Real Estate Sales Agents	39.51
Engineers, Electrical	62.22	Retail Salespersons	16.52
Fast Food and Counter Workers	12.48	Sales Representatives, Technical/Scientific	44.57
Financial Managers	81.29	Secretaries, Exc. Legal/Medical/Executive	21.45
First-Line Supervisors of Office Workers	32.79	Security Guards	17.41
General and Operations Managers	56.28	Surgeons	n/a
Hairdressers/Cosmetologists	16.04	Teacher Assistants, Exc. Postsecondary*	15.16
Home Health and Personal Care Aides	12.07	Teachers, Secondary School, Exc. Sp. Ed.*	30.16
Janitors and Cleaners	14.63	Telemarketers	16.31
Landscaping/Groundskeeping Workers	16.91	Truck Drivers, Heavy/Tractor-Trailer	23.73
Lawyers	72.31	Truck Drivers, Light/Delivery Services	22.03
Maids and Housekeeping Cleaners	13.88	Waiters and Waitresses	13.42

Note: Wage data covers the Austin-Round Rock-Georgetown, TX Metropolitan Statistical Area; (*) Hourly wages were calculated from annual wage data based on a 40 hour work week; n/a not available.
Source: Bureau of Labor Statistics, Metro Area Occupational Employment & Wage Estimates, May 2022

Employment by Industry

Sector	MSA[1] Number of Employees	MSA[1] Percent of Total	U.S. Percent of Total
Construction, Mining, and Logging	77,500	5.9	5.4
Private Education and Health Services	146,200	11.2	16.1
Financial Activities	78,500	6.0	5.9
Government	188,100	14.3	14.5
Information	53,400	4.1	2.0
Leisure and Hospitality	146,800	11.2	10.3
Manufacturing	72,100	5.5	8.4
Other Services	49,600	3.8	3.7
Professional and Business Services	283,100	21.6	14.7
Retail Trade	120,000	9.2	10.2
Transportation, Warehousing, and Utilities	36,800	2.8	4.9
Wholesale Trade	59,000	4.5	3.9

Note: Figures are non-farm employment as of December 2022. Figures are not seasonally adjusted and include workers 16 years of age and older; (1) Figures cover the Austin-Round Rock-Georgetown, TX Metropolitan Statistical Area
Source: Bureau of Labor Statistics, Current Employment Statistics, Employment, Hours, and Earnings

Employment by Occupation

Occupation Classification	City (%)	MSA[1] (%)	U.S. (%)
Management, Business, Science, and Arts	54.1	49.8	40.3
Natural Resources, Construction, and Maintenance	6.1	7.3	8.7
Production, Transportation, and Material Moving	7.0	8.3	13.1
Sales and Office	19.1	20.6	20.9
Service	13.7	14.0	17.0

Note: Figures cover employed civilians 16 years of age and older; (1) Figures cover the Austin-Round Rock-Georgetown, TX Metropolitan Statistical Area
Source: U.S. Census Bureau, 2017-2021 American Community Survey 5-Year Estimates

Occupations with Greatest Projected Employment Growth: 2022 – 2024

Occupation[1]	2022 Employment	2024 Projected Employment	Numeric Employment Change	Percent Employment Change
Home Health and Personal Care Aides	338,130	364,760	26,630	7.9
General and Operations Managers	395,700	416,100	20,400	5.2
Heavy and Tractor-Trailer Truck Drivers	206,850	222,220	15,370	7.4
Software Developers	119,810	134,060	14,250	11.9
Laborers and Freight, Stock, and Material Movers, Hand	214,680	228,680	14,000	6.5
Farmers, Ranchers, and Other Agricultural Managers	274,740	287,430	12,690	4.6
Stockers and Order Fillers	212,180	224,670	12,490	5.9
Construction Laborers	153,220	164,330	11,110	7.3
Cooks, Restaurant	131,480	141,860	10,380	7.9
Industrial Truck and Tractor Operators	83,270	93,190	9,920	11.9

Note: Projections cover Texas; (1) Sorted by numeric employment change
Source: www.projectionscentral.com, State Occupational Projections, 2022–2024 Short-Term Projections

Fastest-Growing Occupations: 2022 – 2024

Occupation[1]	2022 Employment	2024 Projected Employment	Numeric Employment Change	Percent Employment Change
Wind Turbine Service Technicians	5,240	5,990	750	14.3
Information Security Analysts (SOC 2018)	14,170	16,110	1,940	13.7
Solar Photovoltaic Installers	2,240	2,540	300	13.4
Veterinary Technologists and Technicians	16,140	18,200	2,060	12.8
Actuaries	1,810	2,040	230	12.7
Data Scientists	7,340	8,270	930	12.7
Web Developers	6,920	7,790	870	12.6
Veterinarians	6,830	7,670	840	12.3
Veterinary Assistants and Laboratory Animal Caretakers	5,990	6,720	730	12.2
Ushers, Lobby Attendants, and Ticket Takers	9,100	10,190	1,090	12.0

Note: Projections cover Texas; (1) Sorted by percent employment change and excludes occupations with numeric employment change less than 50
Source: www.projectionscentral.com, State Occupational Projections, 2022–2024 Short-Term Projections

Austin, Texas

CITY FINANCES

City Government Finances

Component	2020 ($000)	2020 ($ per capita)
Total Revenues	4,067,834	4,155
Total Expenditures	4,023,329	4,110
Debt Outstanding	2,220,171	2,268
Cash and Securities[1]	2,790,157	2,850

Note: (1) Cash and security holdings of a government at the close of its fiscal year, including those of its dependent agencies, utilities, and liquor stores.
Source: U.S. Census Bureau, State & Local Government Finances 2020

City Government Revenue by Source

Source	2020 ($000)	2020 ($ per capita)	2020 (%)
General Revenue			
From Federal Government	67,456	69	1.7
From State Government	18,970	19	0.5
From Local Governments	14,313	15	0.4
Taxes			
Property	584,302	597	14.4
Sales and Gross Receipts	412,398	421	10.1
Personal Income	0	0	0.0
Corporate Income	0	0	0.0
Motor Vehicle License	0	0	0.0
Other Taxes	48,993	50	1.2
Current Charges	891,417	911	21.9
Liquor Store	0	0	0.0
Utility	1,769,044	1,807	43.5

Source: U.S. Census Bureau, State & Local Government Finances 2020

City Government Expenditures by Function

Function	2020 ($000)	2020 ($ per capita)	2020 (%)
General Direct Expenditures			
Air Transportation	165,305	168	4.1
Corrections	0	0	0.0
Education	0	0	0.0
Employment Security Administration	0	0	0.0
Financial Administration	45,755	46	1.1
Fire Protection	192,552	196	4.8
General Public Buildings	0	0	0.0
Governmental Administration, Other	58,532	59	1.5
Health	173,077	176	4.3
Highways	196,209	200	4.9
Hospitals	0	0	0.0
Housing and Community Development	78,670	80	2.0
Interest on General Debt	90,305	92	2.2
Judicial and Legal	43,511	44	1.1
Libraries	84,675	86	2.1
Parking	270	< 1	< 0.1
Parks and Recreation	197,438	201	4.9
Police Protection	398,459	407	9.9
Public Welfare	0	0	0.0
Sewerage	184,928	188	4.6
Solid Waste Management	127,318	130	3.2
Veterans' Services	0	0	0.0
Liquor Store	0	0	0.0
Utility	1,734,955	1,772	43.1

Source: U.S. Census Bureau, State & Local Government Finances 2020

TAXES

State Corporate Income Tax Rates

State	Tax Rate (%)	Income Brackets ($)	Num. of Brackets	Financial Institution Tax Rate (%)[a]	Federal Income Tax Ded.
Texas	(u)	–	–	(u)	No

Note: Tax rates as of January 1, 2023; (a) Rates listed are the corporate income tax rate applied to financial institutions or excise taxes based on income. Some states have other taxes based upon the value of deposits or shares; (u) Texas imposes a Franchise Tax, otherwise known as margin tax, imposed on entities with more than $1,230,000 total revenues at rate of 0.75%, or 0.375% for entities primarily engaged in retail or wholesale trade, on lesser of 70% of total revenues or 100% of gross receipts after deductions for either compensation or cost of goods sold.
Source: Federation of Tax Administrators, State Corporate Income Tax Rates, January 1, 2023

State Individual Income Tax Rates

State	Tax Rate (%)	Income Brackets ($)	Personal Exemptions ($) Single	Married	Depend.	Standard Ded. ($) Single	Married
Texas			– No state income tax –				

Note: Tax rates as of January 1, 2023; Local- and county-level taxes are not included
Source: Federation of Tax Administrators, State Individual Income Tax Rates, January 1, 2023

Various State Sales and Excise Tax Rates

State	State Sales Tax (%)	Gasoline[1] ($/gal.)	Cigarette[2] ($/pack)	Spirits[3] ($/gal.)	Wine[4] ($/gal.)	Beer[5] ($/gal.)	Recreational Marijuana (%)
Texas	6.25	0.20	1.41	2.40	0.20	0.19	Not legal

Note: All tax rates as of January 1, 2023; (1) The American Petroleum Institute has developed a methodology for determining the average tax rate on a gallon of fuel. Rates may include any of the following: excise taxes, environmental fees, storage tank fees, other fees or taxes, general sales tax, and local taxes; (2) The federal excise tax of $1.0066 per pack and local taxes are not included; (3) Rates are those applicable to off-premise sales of 40% alcohol by volume (a.b.v.) distilled spirits in 750ml containers. Local excise taxes are excluded; (4) Rates are those applicable to off-premise sales of 11% a.b.v. non-carbonated wine in 750ml containers; (5) Rates are those applicable to off-premise sales of 4.7% a.b.v. beer in 12 ounce containers.
Source: Tax Foundation, 2023 Facts & Figures: How Does Your State Compare?

State Business Tax Climate Index Rankings

State	Overall Rank	Corporate Tax Rank	Individual Income Tax Rank	Sales Tax Rank	Property Tax Rank	Unemployment Insurance Tax Rank
Texas	13	47	7	37	38	12

Note: The index is a measure of how each state's tax laws affect economic performance. The lower the rank, the more favorable a state's tax system is for business. States without a given tax are given a ranking of 1. The scores/rankings for the District of Columbia do not affect other states. The 2023 index represents the tax climate as of July 1, 2022.
Source: Tax Foundation, State Business Tax Climate Index 2023

TRANSPORTATION

Means of Transportation to Work

Area	Car/Truck/Van Drove Alone	Car-pooled	Public Transportation Bus	Subway	Railroad	Bicycle	Walked	Other Means	Worked at Home
City	66.2	7.7	2.5	0.1	0.1	1.0	2.6	1.4	18.4
MSA[1]	69.7	8.4	1.3	0.0	0.1	0.6	1.8	1.3	16.8
U.S.	73.2	8.6	2.0	1.6	0.5	0.5	2.5	1.5	9.7

Note: Figures are percentages and cover workers 16 years of age and older; (1) Figures cover the Austin-Round Rock-Georgetown, TX Metropolitan Statistical Area
Source: U.S. Census Bureau, 2017-2021 American Community Survey 5-Year Estimates

Travel Time to Work

Area	Less Than 10 Minutes	10 to 19 Minutes	20 to 29 Minutes	30 to 44 Minutes	45 to 59 Minutes	60 to 89 Minutes	90 Minutes or More
City	9.7	32.0	24.5	21.7	6.9	3.7	1.5
MSA[1]	9.3	26.6	22.1	23.8	10.1	6.3	1.9
U.S.	12.4	28.5	21.0	20.9	8.2	6.2	2.9

Note: Note: Figures are percentages and include workers 16 years old and over; (1) Figures cover the Austin-Round Rock-Georgetown, TX Metropolitan Statistical Area
Source: U.S. Census Bureau, 2017-2021 American Community Survey 5-Year Estimates

Key Congestion Measures

Measure	1990	2000	2010	2015	2020
Annual Hours of Delay, Total (000)	9,263	25,499	47,034	61,262	48,435
Annual Hours of Delay, Per Auto Commuter	24	42	49	61	41
Annual Congestion Cost, Per Auto Commuter ($)	360	748	1,097	1,320	945

Note: Covers the Austin TX urban area
Source: Texas A&M Transportation Institute, 2021 Urban Mobility Report

Freeway Travel Time Index

Measure	1985	1990	1995	2000	2005	2010	2015	2020
Urban Area Index[1]	1.12	1.15	1.19	1.26	1.31	1.29	1.33	1.13
Urban Area Rank[1,2]	21	22	23	13	12	13	11	6

Note: Freeway Travel Time Index—the ratio of travel time in the peak period to the travel time at free-flow conditions. For example, a value of 1.30 indicates a 20-minute free-flow trip takes 26 minutes in the peak (20 minutes x 1.30 = 26 minutes); (1) Covers the Austin TX urban area; (2) Rank is based on 101 larger urban areas (#1 = highest travel time index)
Source: Texas A&M Transportation Institute, 2021 Urban Mobility Report

Public Transportation

Agency Name / Mode of Transportation	Vehicles Operated in Maximum Service[1]	Annual Unlinked Passenger Trips[2] (in thous.)	Annual Passenger Miles[3] (in thous.)
Capital Metropolitan Transportation Authority (CMTA)			
Bus (purchased transportation)	302	15,789.4	74,122.2
Commuter Bus (purchased transportation)	11	45.9	759.8
Demand Response (purchased transportation)	182	487.9	3,203.8
Hybrid Rail (purchased transportation)	12	257.0	3,044.3
Vanpool (purchased transportation)	98	235.7	11,511.5

Note: (1) Number of revenue vehicles operated by the given mode and type of service to meet the annual maximum service requirement. This is the revenue vehicle count during the peak season of the year; on the week and day that maximum service is provided. Vehicles operated in maximum service (VOMS) exclude atypical days and one-time special events; (2) Number of passengers who boarded public transportation vehicles. Passengers are counted each time they board a vehicle no matter how many vehicles they use to travel from their origin to their destination. (3) Sum of the distances ridden by all passengers during the entire fiscal year.
Source: Federal Transit Administration, National Transit Database, 2021

Air Transportation

Airport Name and Code / Type of Service	Passenger Airlines[1]	Passenger Enplanements	Freight Carriers[2]	Freight (lbs)
Austin-Bergstrom International (AUS)				
Domestic service (U.S. carriers - 2022)	30	9,937,649	20	133,620,313
International service (U.S. carriers - 2021)	9	95,094	2	2,949,674

Note: (1) Includes all U.S.-based major, minor and commuter airlines that carried at least one passenger during the year; (2) Includes all U.S.-based airlines and freight carriers that transported at least one pound of freight during the year.
Source: Bureau of Transportation Statistics, The Intermodal Transportation Database, Air Carriers: T-100 Domestic Market (U.S. Carriers), 2022; Bureau of Transportation Statistics, The Intermodal Transportation Database, Air Carriers: T-100 International Market (U.S. Carriers), 2021

BUSINESSES

Major Business Headquarters

Company Name	Industry	Rankings Fortune[1]	Forbes[2]
No companies listed	-	-	-

Note: (1) Companies that produce a 10-K are ranked 1 to 500 based on 2021 revenue; (2) All private companies with at least $2 billion in annual revenue through the end of their most current fiscal year are ranked 1 to 246; companies listed are headquartered in the city; dashes indicate no ranking
Source: Fortune, "Fortune 500," 2022; Forbes, "America's Largest Private Companies," 2022

Fastest-Growing Businesses

According to *Inc.*, Austin is home to 12 of America's 500 fastest-growing private companies: **AdOutreach** (#60); **Webforce** (#62); **Homestead Brands** (#117); **Digital Thrive** (#168); **Everly Health** (#201); **Element 26** (#285); **Boostlingo** (#312); **Cover Desk** (#317); **Canopy Management** (#325); **OJO** (#355); **Restore Hyper Wellness** (#411); **Action Behavior Centers** (#499). Criteria: must be an independent, privately-held, for-profit, U.S. corporation, proprietorship or partnership as of December 31, 2021; revenues must be at least $100,000 in 2018 and $2 million in 2021; must have four-year operating/sales history. *Inc., "America's 500 Fastest-Growing Private Companies," 2022*

According to Deloitte, Austin is home to 13 of North America's 500 fastest-growing high-technology companies: **OJO Labs** (#93); **L7 Informatics** (#101); **Measured** (#120); **SpyCloud** (#203); **Overhaul** (#236); **CrowdStrike Holdings** (#242); **ActivTrak** (#299); **AlertMedia** (#303); **Molecular Templates** (#327); **Enboarder** (#356); **CrowdStreet** (#385); **NinjaOne** (#397); **Digital Turbine** (#404). Companies are ranked by percentage growth in revenue over a four-year period. Criteria for inclusion: company must be headquartered within North America; must own proprietary intellectual property or technology that is sold to customers in products that contributes to a significant portion of the company's operating revenue; must have been in business for a minumum of four years with 2018 operating revenues of at least $50,000 USD/CD and 2021 operating revenues of at least $5 million USD/CD. *Deloitte, 2022 Technology Fast 500™*

Living Environment

COST OF LIVING

Cost of Living Index

Composite Index	Groceries	Housing	Utilities	Transportation	Health Care	Misc. Goods/Services
101.0	88.4	115.5	93.6	90.9	103.2	99.0

Note: The Cost of Living Index measures regional differences in the cost of consumer goods and services, excluding taxes and non-consumer expenditures, for professional and managerial households in the top income quintile. It is based on more than 50,000 prices covering almost 60 different items for which prices are collected three times a year by chambers of commerce, economic development organizations or university applied economic centers in each participating urban area. The numbers shown should be read as a percentage above or below the national average of 100. For example, a value of 115.4 in the groceries column indicates that grocery prices are 15.4% higher than the national average. Small differences in the index numbers should not be interpreted as significant; Figures cover the Austin TX urban area.
Source: The Council for Community and Economic Research, Cost of Living Index, 2022

Grocery Prices

Area[1]	T-Bone Steak ($/pound)	Frying Chicken ($/pound)	Whole Milk ($/half gal.)	Eggs ($/dozen)	Orange Juice ($/64 oz.)	Coffee ($/11.5 oz.)
City[2]	11.44	1.08	2.14	2.18	3.36	4.26
Avg.	13.81	1.59	2.43	2.25	3.85	4.95
Min.	10.17	0.90	1.51	1.30	2.90	3.46
Max.	19.35	3.30	4.32	4.32	5.31	8.59

*Note: (1) Values for the local area are compared with the average, minimum and maximum values for all 286 areas in the Cost of Living Index; (2) Figures cover the Austin TX urban area; **T-Bone Steak** (price per pound); **Frying Chicken** (price per pound, whole fryer); **Whole Milk** (half gallon carton); **Eggs** (price per dozen, Grade A, large); **Orange Juice** (64 oz. Tropicana or Florida Natural); **Coffee** (11.5 oz. can, vacuum-packed, Maxwell House, Hills Bros, or Folgers).*
Source: The Council for Community and Economic Research, Cost of Living Index, 2022

Housing and Utility Costs

Area[1]	New Home Price ($)	Apartment Rent ($/month)	All Electric ($/month)	Part Electric ($/month)	Other Energy ($/month)	Telephone ($/month)
City[2]	484,044	1,807	-	101.22	51.85	196.79
Avg.	450,913	1,371	176.41	99.93	76.96	190.22
Min.	229,283	546	100.84	31.56	27.15	174.27
Max.	2,434,977	4,569	356.86	249.59	272.24	208.31

*Note: (1) Values for the local area are compared with the average, minimum and maximum values for all 286 areas in the Cost of Living Index; (2) Figures cover the Austin TX urban area; **New Home Price** (2,400 sf living area, 8,000 sf lot, in urban area with full utilities); **Apartment Rent** (950 sf 2 bedroom/1.5 or 2 bath, unfurnished, excluding all utilities except water); **All Electric** (average monthly cost for an all-electric home); **Part Electric** (average monthly cost for a part-electric home); **Other Energy** (average monthly cost for natural gas, fuel oil, coal, wood, and any other forms of energy except electricity); **Telephone** (price includes the base monthly rate plus taxes and fees for three lines of mobile phone service).*
Source: The Council for Community and Economic Research, Cost of Living Index, 2022

Health Care, Transportation, and Other Costs

Area[1]	Doctor ($/visit)	Dentist ($/visit)	Optometrist ($/visit)	Gasoline ($/gallon)	Beauty Salon ($/visit)	Men's Shirt ($)
City[2]	122.17	119.14	118.78	3.47	52.91	34.72
Avg.	124.91	107.77	117.66	3.86	43.31	34.21
Min.	36.61	58.25	51.79	2.90	22.18	13.05
Max.	250.21	162.58	371.96	5.54	85.61	63.54

*Note: (1) Values for the local area are compared with the average, minimum and maximum values for all 286 areas in the Cost of Living Index; (2) Figures cover the Austin TX urban area; **Doctor** (general practitioners routine exam of an established patient); **Dentist** (adult teeth cleaning and periodic oral examination); **Optometrist** (full vision eye exam for established adult patient); **Gasoline** (one gallon regular unleaded, national brand, including all taxes, cash price at self-service pump if available); **Beauty Salon** (woman's shampoo, trim, and blow-dry); **Men's Shirt** (cotton/polyester dress shirt, pinpoint weave, long sleeves).*
Source: The Council for Community and Economic Research, Cost of Living Index, 2022

HOUSING

Homeownership Rate

Area	2015 (%)	2016 (%)	2017 (%)	2018 (%)	2019 (%)	2020 (%)	2021 (%)	2022 (%)
MSA[1]	57.5	56.5	55.6	56.1	59.0	65.4	62.2	62.4
U.S.	63.7	63.4	63.9	64.4	64.6	66.6	65.5	65.8

Note: (1) Figures cover the Austin-Round Rock-Georgetown, TX Metropolitan Statistical Area
Source: U.S. Census Bureau, Housing Vacancies and Homeownership Annual Statistics: 2015-2022

House Price Index (HPI)

Area	National Ranking[2]	Quarterly Change (%)	One-Year Change (%)	Five-Year Change (%)	Since 1991Q1 (%)
MSA[1]	222	-5.35	7.56	75.92	618.91
U.S.[3]	–	0.34	8.41	58.44	289.08

Note: The HPI is a weighted repeat sales index. It measures average price changes in repeat sales or refinancings on the same properties. This information is obtained by reviewing repeat mortgage transactions on single-family properties whose mortgages have been purchased or securitized by Fannie Mae or Freddie Mac since January 1975; (1) Figures cover the Austin-Round Rock, TX Metropolitan Statistical Area; (2) Rankings are based on annual percentage change for all metro areas containing at least 15,000 transactions over the last 10 years and ranges from 1 to 257; (3) figures based on a weighted average of Census Division estimates using a seasonally adjusted, purchase-only index; all figures are for the period ending December 31, 2022
Source: Federal Housing Finance Agency, Change in FHFA Metropolitan Area House Price Indexes, 2022Q4

Median Single-Family Home Prices

Area	2020	2021	2022[p]	Percent Change 2021 to 2022
MSA[1]	367.1	488.6	555.4	13.7
U.S. Average	300.2	357.1	392.6	9.9

Note: Figures are median sales prices of existing single-family homes in thousands of dollars; (p) preliminary; (1) Figures cover the Austin-Round Rock-Georgetown, TX Metropolitan Statistical Area
Source: National Association of Realtors, Median Sales Price of Existing Single-Family Homes for Metropolitan Areas, 4th Quarter 2022

Qualifying Income Based on Median Sales Price of Existing Single-Family Homes

Area	With 5% Down ($)	With 10% Down ($)	With 20% Down ($)
MSA[1]	143,279	135,738	120,656
U.S. Average	112,234	106,237	94,513

Note: Figures are preliminary; Qualifying income is based on a mortgage rate of 6.77%. Monthly principal and interest payment is limited to 25% of income; (1) Figures cover the Austin-Round Rock-Georgetown, TX Metropolitan Statistical Area
Source: National Association of Realtors, Qualifying Income Based on Median Sales Price of Existing Single-Family Homes for Metropolitan Areas, 4th Quarter 2022

Home Value

Area	Under $100,000	$100,000 -$199,999	$200,000 -$299,999	$300,000 -$399,999	$400,000 -$499,999	$500,000 -$999,999	$1,000,000 or more	Median ($)
City	3.6	8.4	20.6	21.5	15.3	24.7	6.0	381,400
MSA[1]	6.2	12.5	25.9	20.6	12.6	18.1	4.1	326,400
U.S.	16.2	24.2	20.1	13.6	8.3	13.6	4.1	244,900

Note: Figures are percentages except for median and cover owner-occupied housing units; (1) Figures cover the Austin-Round Rock-Georgetown, TX Metropolitan Statistical Area
Source: U.S. Census Bureau, 2017-2021 American Community Survey 5-Year Estimates

Year Housing Structure Built

Area	2020 or Later	2010 -2019	2000 -2009	1990 -1999	1980 -1989	1970 -1979	1960 -1969	1950 -1959	1940 -1949	Before 1940	Median Year
City	0.2	17.5	17.1	14.7	18.6	15.0	7.7	4.5	2.1	2.6	1990
MSA[1]	0.6	22.4	22.8	16.7	15.5	10.6	4.9	3.0	1.5	2.1	1997
U.S.	0.2	7.3	13.6	13.6	13.2	14.8	10.3	10.0	4.7	12.2	1979

Note: Figures are percentages except for Median Year; Note: (1) Figures cover the Austin-Round Rock-Georgetown, TX Metropolitan Statistical Area
Source: U.S. Census Bureau, 2017-2021 American Community Survey 5-Year Estimates

Gross Monthly Rent

Area	Under $500	$500 -$999	$1,000 -$1,499	$1,500 -$1,999	$2,000 -$2,499	$2,500 -$2,999	$3,000 and up	Median ($)
City	2.8	10.6	43.9	26.9	10.3	3.0	2.6	1,415
MSA[1]	2.6	12.4	43.5	26.5	9.9	2.7	2.4	1,398
U.S.	8.1	30.5	30.8	16.8	7.3	3.1	3.5	1,163

Note: Figures are percentages except for median; Gross rent is the contract rent plus the estimated average monthly cost of utilities (electricity, gas, and water and sewer) and fuels (oil, coal, kerosene, wood, etc.) if these are paid by the renter (or paid for the renter by someone else); (1) Figures cover the Austin-Round Rock-Georgetown, TX Metropolitan Statistical Area
Source: U.S. Census Bureau, 2017-2021 American Community Survey 5-Year Estimates

HEALTH

Health Risk Factors

Category	MSA[1] (%)	U.S. (%)
Adults aged 18–64 who have any kind of health care coverage	83.7	90.9
Adults who reported being in good or better health	87.2	85.2
Adults who have been told they have high blood cholesterol	35.7	35.7
Adults who have been told they have high blood pressure	26.6	32.4
Adults who are current smokers	7.6	14.4
Adults who currently use e-cigarettes	5.6	6.7
Adults who currently use chewing tobacco, snuff, or snus	1.7	3.5
Adults who are heavy drinkers[2]	6.0	6.3
Adults who are binge drinkers[3]	17.5	15.4
Adults who are overweight (BMI 25.0 - 29.9)	32.5	34.4
Adults who are obese (BMI 30.0 - 99.8)	29.5	33.9
Adults who participated in any physical activities in the past month	81.6	76.3

Note: (1) Figures cover the Austin-Round Rock, TX Metropolitan Statistical Area; (2) Heavy drinkers are classified as adult men having more than 14 drinks per week and adult women having more than 7 drinks per week; (3) Binge drinkers are classified as males having five or more drinks on one occasion or females having four or more drinks on one occasion
Source: Centers for Disease Control and Prevention, Behaviorial Risk Factor Surveillance System, SMART: Selected Metropolitan Area Risk Trends, 2021

Acute and Chronic Health Conditions

Category	MSA[1] (%)	U.S. (%)
Adults who have ever been told they had a heart attack	3.2	4.0
Adults who have ever been told they have angina or coronary heart disease	2.8	3.8
Adults who have ever been told they had a stroke	1.4	3.0
Adults who have ever been told they have asthma	12.2	14.9
Adults who have ever been told they have arthritis	20.9	25.8
Adults who have ever been told they have diabetes[2]	8.7	10.9
Adults who have ever been told they had skin cancer	6.2	6.6
Adults who have ever been told they had any other types of cancer	5.5	7.5
Adults who have ever been told they have COPD	4.0	6.1
Adults who have ever been told they have kidney disease	2.6	3.0
Adults who have ever been told they have a form of depression	20.4	20.5

Note: (1) Figures cover the Austin-Round Rock, TX Metropolitan Statistical Area; (2) Figures do not include pregnancy-related, borderline, or pre-diabetes
Source: Centers for Disease Control and Prevention, Behaviorial Risk Factor Surveillance System, SMART: Selected Metropolitan Area Risk Trends, 2021

Health Screening and Vaccination Rates

Category	MSA[1] (%)	U.S. (%)
Adults who have ever been tested for HIV	38.2	34.9
Adults who have had their blood cholesterol checked within the last five years	86.5	85.2
Adults aged 65+ who have had flu shot within the past year	72.8	68.6
Adults aged 65+ who have ever had a pneumonia vaccination	75.7	71.0

Note: (1) Figures cover the Austin-Round Rock, TX Metropolitan Statistical Area.
Source: Centers for Disease Control and Prevention, Behaviorial Risk Factor Surveillance System, SMART: Selected Metropolitan Area Risk Trends, 2021

Disability Status

Category	MSA[1] (%)	U.S. (%)
Adults who reported being deaf	5.1	7.2
Are you blind or have serious difficulty seeing, even when wearing glasses?	3.1	4.8
Are you limited in any way in any of your usual activities due to arthritis?	8.2	11.1
Do you have difficulty doing errands alone?	5.3	7.0
Do you have difficulty dressing or bathing?	2.5	3.6
Do you have serious difficulty concentrating/remembering/making decisions?	11.6	12.1
Do you have serious difficulty walking or climbing stairs?	8.9	12.8

Note: (1) Figures cover the Austin-Round Rock, TX Metropolitan Statistical Area.
Source: Centers for Disease Control and Prevention, Behaviorial Risk Factor Surveillance System, SMART: Selected Metropolitan Area Risk Trends, 2021

Mortality Rates for the Top 10 Causes of Death in the U.S.

ICD-10[a] Sub-Chapter	ICD-10[a] Code	Crude Mortality Rate[1] per 100,000 population County[2]	U.S.
Malignant neoplasms	C00-C97	96.5	182.6
Ischaemic heart diseases	I20-I25	52.8	113.1
Other forms of heart disease	I30-I51	25.2	64.4
Other degenerative diseases of the nervous system	G30-G31	37.7	51.0
Cerebrovascular diseases	I60-I69	24.0	47.8
Other external causes of accidental injury	W00-X59	33.8	46.4
Chronic lower respiratory diseases	J40-J47	15.3	45.7
Organic, including symptomatic, mental disorders	F01-F09	19.1	35.9
Hypertensive diseases	I10-I15	21.0	35.0
Diabetes mellitus	E10-E14	13.3	29.6

Note: (a) ICD-10 = International Classification of Diseases 10th Revision; (1) Crude mortality rates are a three-year average covering 2019-2021; (2) Figures cover Travis County.
Source: Centers for Disease Control and Prevention, National Center for Health Statistics. National Vital Statistics System, Mortality 2018-2021 on CDC WONDER Online Database

Mortality Rates for Selected Causes of Death

ICD-10[a] Sub-Chapter	ICD-10[a] Code	Crude Mortality Rate[1] per 100,000 population County[2]	U.S.
Assault	X85-Y09	4.6	7.0
Diseases of the liver	K70-K76	12.2	19.8
Human immunodeficiency virus (HIV) disease	B20-B24	1.2	1.5
Influenza and pneumonia	J09-J18	6.4	14.7
Intentional self-harm	X60-X84	13.5	14.3
Malnutrition	E40-E46	1.6	4.3
Obesity and other hyperalimentation	E65-E68	1.7	3.0
Renal failure	N17-N19	6.8	15.7
Transport accidents	V01-V99	11.4	13.6
Viral hepatitis	B15-B19	0.8	1.2

Note: (a) ICD-10 = International Classification of Diseases 10th Revision; (1) Crude mortality rates are a three-year average covering 2019-2021; (2) Figures cover Travis County; Data are suppressed when the data meet the criteria for confidentiality constraints; Crude mortality rates are flagged as unreliable when the rate would be calculated with a numerator of 20 or less.
Source: Centers for Disease Control and Prevention, National Center for Health Statistics. National Vital Statistics System, Mortality 2018-2021 on CDC WONDER Online Database

Health Insurance Coverage

Area	With Health Insurance	With Private Health Insurance	With Public Health Insurance	Without Health Insurance	Population Under Age 19 Without Health Insurance
City	87.2	74.3	20.3	12.8	7.9
MSA[1]	87.7	75.1	21.7	12.3	8.1
U.S.	91.2	67.8	35.4	8.8	5.3

Note: Figures are percentages that cover the civilian noninstitutionalized population; (1) Figures cover the Austin-Round Rock-Georgetown, TX Metropolitan Statistical Area
Source: U.S. Census Bureau, 2017-2021 American Community Survey 5-Year Estimates

Number of Medical Professionals

Area	MDs[3]	DOs[3,4]	Dentists	Podiatrists	Chiropractors	Optometrists
County[1] (number)	4,241	244	972	59	457	233
County[1] (rate[2])	327.2	18.8	74.5	4.5	35.0	17.9
U.S. (rate[2])	289.3	23.5	72.5	6.2	28.7	17.4

Note: Data as of 2021 unless noted; (1) Data covers Travis County; (2) Rate per 100,000 population; (3) Data as of 2020 and includes all active, non-federal physicians; (4) Doctor of Osteopathic Medicine
Source: U.S. Department of Health and Human Services, Health Resources and Services Administration, Bureau of Health Professions, Area Resource File (ARF) 2021-2022

Best Hospitals

According to *U.S. News*, the Austin-Round Rock-Georgetown, TX metro area is home to one of the best hospitals in the U.S.: **St. David's Medical Center** (1 adult specialty). The hospital listed was nationally ranked in at least one of 15 adult or 10 pediatric specialties. The number of specialties shown cover the parent hospital. Only 164 U.S. hospitals performed well enough to be nationally ranked in one or more specialties. Twenty hospitals in the U.S. made the Honor Roll. The Best Hospitals Honor Roll takes both the national rankings and the procedure and condition ratings into account. Hospitals received points if they were nationally ranked in one of the 15 adult specialties—the higher they ranked, the more points they got—and how many ratings of "high performing" they earned in the 17 procedures and conditions. *U.S. News Online, "America's Best Hospitals 2022-23"*

According to *U.S. News,* the Austin-Round Rock-Georgetown, TX metro area is home to one of the best children's hospitals in the U.S.: **Dell Children's Medical Center** (1 pediatric specialty). The hospital listed was highly ranked in at least one of 10 pediatric specialties. Eighty-six children's hospitals in the U.S. were nationally ranked in at least one specialty. Hospitals received points for being ranked in a specialty, and the 10 hospitals with the most points across the 10 specialties make up the Honor Roll. *U.S. News Online, "America's Best Children's Hospitals 2022-23"*

EDUCATION

Public School District Statistics

District Name	Schls	Pupils	Pupil/Teacher Ratio	Minority Pupils[1] (%)	LEP/ELL[2] (%)	IEP[3] (%)
Austin ISD	125	74,602	14.2	69.4	23.9	12.9
Eanes ISD	10	7,834	13.1	35.4	2.2	9.3
Harmony Science Academy (Austin)	7	4,225	13.1	84.8	38.5	7.3
Lake Travis ISD	11	11,345	16.9	34.1	5.7	9.6

Note: Table includes school districts with 2,000 or more students; (1) Percentage of students that are not non-Hispanic white; (2) Percentage of students that are Limited English Proficient or English Language Learners (2018-19); (3) Percentage of students that have an Individualized Education Program (2019-20).
Source: U.S. Department of Education, National Center for Education Statistics, Common Core of Data, Local Education Agency (School District) Universe Survey: School Year 2021-2022

Best High Schools

According to *U.S. News,* Austin is home to six of the top 500 high schools in the U.S.: **Liberal Arts and Science Academy (LASA)** (#34); **Chaparral Star Academy** (#122); **Richards School for Young Women Leaders** (#128); **IDEA Montopolis College Preparatory** (#168); **Westlake High School** (#261); **Westwood High School** (#456). Nearly 18,000 public, magnet and charter schools were ranked based on their performance on state assessments and how well they prepare students for college. *U.S. News & World Report, "Best High Schools 2022"*

Highest Level of Education

Area	Less than H.S.	H.S. Diploma	Some College, No Deg.	Associate Degree	Bachelor's Degree	Master's Degree	Prof. School Degree	Doctorate Degree
City	9.4	14.4	15.7	5.4	34.2	14.9	3.5	2.6
MSA[1]	9.0	18.2	18.9	6.5	30.1	12.7	2.6	2.0
U.S.	11.1	26.5	20.0	8.7	20.6	9.3	2.2	1.5

Note: Figures cover persons age 25 and over; (1) Figures cover the Austin-Round Rock-Georgetown, TX Metropolitan Statistical Area
Source: U.S. Census Bureau, 2017-2021 American Community Survey 5-Year Estimates

Educational Attainment by Race

Area	High School Graduate or Higher (%) Total	White	Black	Asian	Hisp.[2]	Bachelor's Degree or Higher (%) Total	White	Black	Asian	Hisp.[2]
City	90.6	93.2	89.5	92.7	76.2	55.1	59.5	31.6	76.5	30.9
MSA[1]	91.0	93.4	92.3	92.8	77.1	47.4	50.3	33.1	73.7	26.1
U.S.	88.9	91.4	87.2	87.6	71.2	33.7	35.5	23.3	55.6	18.4

Note: Figures shown cover persons 25 years old and over; (1) Figures cover the Austin-Round Rock-Georgetown, TX Metropolitan Statistical Area; (2) People of Hispanic origin can be of any race
Source: U.S. Census Bureau, 2017-2021 American Community Survey 5-Year Estimates

School Enrollment by Grade and Control

Area	Preschool (%) Public	Private	Kindergarten (%) Public	Private	Grades 1 - 4 (%) Public	Private	Grades 5 - 8 (%) Public	Private	Grades 9 - 12 (%) Public	Private
City	52.0	48.0	87.1	12.9	88.8	11.2	87.9	12.1	90.9	9.1
MSA[1]	49.5	50.5	89.5	10.5	90.6	9.4	89.8	10.2	91.7	8.3
U.S.	58.8	41.2	86.3	13.7	88.3	11.7	88.6	11.4	89.4	10.6

Note: Figures shown cover persons 3 years old and over; (1) Figures cover the Austin-Round Rock-Georgetown, TX Metropolitan Statistical Area
Source: U.S. Census Bureau, 2017-2021 American Community Survey 5-Year Estimates

Higher Education

Four-Year Colleges			Two-Year Colleges			Medical Schools[1]	Law Schools[2]	Voc/ Tech[3]
Public	Private Non-profit	Private For-profit	Public	Private Non-profit	Private For-profit			
3	7	7	0	0	5	1	1	11

Note: Figures cover institutions located within the Austin-Round Rock-Georgetown, TX Metropolitan Statistical Area and include main campuses only; (1) includes schools accredited by the Liaison Committee on Medical Education and the American Osteopathic Association's Commission on Osteopathic College Accreditation; (2) includes ABA-accredited schools, schools with provisional ABA accreditation, and state accredited schools; (3) includes all schools with programs that are less than 2 years.
Source: National Center for Education Statistics, Integrated Postsecondary Education System (IPEDS), 2021-22; Wikipedia, List of Medical Schools in the United States, accessed April 10, 2023; Wikipedia, List of Law Schools in the United States, accessed April 10, 2023

According to *U.S. News & World Report,* the Austin-Round Rock-Georgetown, TX metro area is home to one of the top 200 national universities in the U.S.: **University of Texas at Austin** (#38 tie). The indicators used to capture academic quality fall into a number of categories: assessment by administrators at peer institutions; retention of students; faculty resources; student selectivity; financial resources; alumni giving; high school counselor ratings of colleges; and graduation rate. *U.S. News & World Report, "America's Best Colleges 2023"*

According to *U.S. News & World Report,* the Austin-Round Rock-Georgetown, TX metro area is home to one of the top 100 liberal arts colleges in the U.S.: **Southwestern University** (#85 tie). The indicators used to capture academic quality fall into a number of categories: assessment by administrators at peer institutions; retention of students; faculty resources; student selectivity; financial resources; alumni giving; high school counselor ratings of colleges; and graduation rate. *U.S. News & World Report, "America's Best Colleges 2023"*

According to *U.S. News & World Report,* the Austin-Round Rock-Georgetown, TX metro area is home to one of the top 100 law schools in the U.S.: **University of Texas—Austin** (#17 tie). The rankings are based on a weighted average of 12 measures of quality: peer assessment score; assessment score by lawyers/judges; median LSAT scores; median undergrad GPA; acceptance rate; employment rates for graduates; placement success; bar passage rate; faculty resources; expenditures per student; student/faculty ratio; and library resources. *U.S. News & World Report, "America's Best Graduate Schools, Law, 2023"*

According to *U.S. News & World Report,* the Austin-Round Rock-Georgetown, TX metro area is home to one of the top 75 business schools in the U.S.: **University of Texas—Austin (McCombs)** (#18). The rankings are based on a weighted average of the following nine measures: quality assessment; peer assessment; recruiter assessment; placement success; mean starting salary and bonus; student selectivity; mean GMAT and GRE scores; mean undergraduate GPA; and acceptance rate. *U.S. News & World Report, "America's Best Graduate Schools, Business, 2023"*

EMPLOYERS

Major Employers

Company Name	Industry
Accenture	Management consulting & software development center
Apple	Computer maker's tech & admin support center
Applied Materials	Semiconductor manufacturing equip, mfg
AT&T	Telecommunications
Austin Community College	Higher education, public
Austin School Independent District	Public education
City of Austin	Municipal government
Dell	Computer technology solutions & equipment mfg./sales
Federal Government	Government
Flextronics	Contract electronics mfg. & integrated supply chain svcs
Hays Consolidated ISD	Public education
IBM	Computer systems, hardware, software, & chip R&D
Keller Williams Realty	Residential real estate
Leander Independent School District	Public education
National Instruments	Virtual instrumentation software & hardware mfg
NXP Semiconductors	Semiconductor chip design & mfg.
Pflugerville Independent School District	Public education
Round Rock Independent School District	Public education
Samsung Austin Semiconductor	Semiconductor chip mfg., R&D
Seton Healthcare Family	Healthcare
St. David's Healthcare Partnership	Healthcare
State of Texas	State government
Texas State University-San Marcos	Higher education, public
Travis County	Government
U.S. Internal Revenue Service	Government, regional call & processing center
University of Texas at Austin	Higher education, public
Whole Foods Market	Grocery stores

Note: Companies shown are located within the Austin-Round Rock-Georgetown, TX Metropolitan Statistical Area.
Source: Hoovers.com; Wikipedia

Best Companies to Work For

CrowdStrike, headquartered in Austin, is among "The 100 Best Companies to Work For." To pick the best companies, *Fortune* partnered with the Great Place to Work Institute. Two-thirds of a company's score is based on the results of the Institute's Trust Index survey, which is sent to a random sample of employees from each company. The questions related to attitudes about management's credibility, job satisfaction, and camaraderie. The other third of the scoring is based on the company's responses to the Institute's Culture Audit, which includes detailed questions about pay and benefit programs, and a series of open-ended questions about hiring practices, internal communication, training, recognition programs, and diversity efforts. Any company that is at least five years old with more than 1,000 U.S. employees is eligible. *Fortune, "The 100 Best Companies to Work For," 2023*

CrowdStrike, headquartered in Austin, is among "Fortune's Best Workplaces for Women." To pick the best companies, *Fortune* partnered with the Great Place to Work Institute. To be considered for the list, companies must be Great Place To Work-Certified. Companies must also employ at least 50 women, at least 20% of their non-executive managers must be female, and at least one executive must be female. To determine the Best Workplaces for Women, Great Place To Work measured the differences in women's survey responses to those of their peers and assesses the impact of demographics and roles on the quality and consistency of women's experiences. Great Place To Work also analyzed the gender balance of each workplace, how it compared to each company's industry, and patterns in representation as women rise from front-line positions to the board of directors. *Fortune, "Best Workplaces for Women," 2022*

agilon health, headquartered in Austin, is among "Best Workplaces in Health Care." To determine the Best Workplaces in Health Care list, Great Place To Work analyzed the survey responses of over 161,000 employees from Great Place To Work-Certified companies in the health care industry. Survey data analysis and company-provided datapoints are then factored into a combined score to compare and rank the companies that create the most consistently positive experience for all employees in this industry. *Fortune, "Best Workplaces in Health Care," 2022*

CrowdStrike, headquartered in Austin, is among "Fortune's Best Workplaces for Parents." To pick the best companies, *Fortune* partnered with the Great Place to Work Institute. To be considered for the list, companies must be Great Place To Work-Certified and have at least 50 responses from parents in the US. The survey enables employees to share confidential quantitative and qualitative feedback about their organization's culture by responding to 60 statements on a 5-point scale and answering two open-ended questions. Collectively, these statements describe a great employee experience, defined by high levels of trust, respect, credibility, fairness, pride, and camaraderie. In addition, companies provide organizational data like size, location, industry, demographics, roles, and levels; and provide information about parental leave, adoption, flexible schedule, childcare and dependent health care benefits. *Fortune, "Best Workplaces for Parents," 2022*

PUBLIC SAFETY

Crime Rate

Area	Total Crime	Violent Crime Rate				Property Crime Rate		
		Murder	Rape[3]	Robbery	Aggrav. Assault	Burglary	Larceny-Theft	Motor Vehicle Theft
City	4,098.2	4.4	47.8	110.1	304.7	477.3	2,747.3	406.6
Suburbs[1]	1,578.6	2.3	40.3	25.2	129.8	227.0	1,028.7	125.3
Metro[2]	2,682.2	3.2	43.6	62.4	206.4	336.6	1,781.5	248.5
U.S.	2,356.7	6.5	38.4	73.9	279.7	314.2	1,398.0	246.0

Note: Figures are crimes per 100,000 population; (1) All areas within the metro area that are located outside the city limits; (2) Figures cover the Austin-Round Rock, TX Metropolitan Statistical Area; (3) All figures shown were reported using the revised Uniform Crime Reporting (UCR) definition of rape; Due to the transition to the National Incident-Based Reporting System (NIBRS), limited city and metro area data was released for 2021.
Source: FBI Uniform Crime Reports, 2020

Hate Crimes

Area	Number of Quarters Reported	Number of Incidents per Bias Motivation					
		Race/Ethnicity/Ancestry	Religion	Sexual Orientation	Disability	Gender	Gender Identity
City[1]	4	13	2	8	0	0	2
U.S.	4	5,227	1,244	1,110	130	75	266

Note: (1) Figures include one incident reported with more than one bias motivation; Due to the transition to the National Incident-Based Reporting System (NIBRS), limited crime data was released for 2021.
Source: Federal Bureau of Investigation, Hate Crime Statistics 2020

Identity Theft Consumer Reports

Area	Reports	Reports per 100,000 Population	Rank[2]
MSA[1]	6,718	309	64
U.S.	1,108,609	339	-

Note: (1) Figures cover the Austin-Round Rock-Georgetown, TX Metropolitan Statistical Area; (2) Rank ranges from 1 to 391 where 1 indicates greatest number of identity theft reports per 100,000 population
Source: Federal Trade Commission, Consumer Sentinel Network Data Book 2022

Fraud and Other Consumer Reports

Area	Reports	Reports per 100,000 Population	Rank[2]
MSA[1]	24,228	1,115	61
U.S.	4,064,520	1,245	-

Note: (1) Figures cover the Austin-Round Rock-Georgetown, TX Metropolitan Statistical Area; (2) Rank ranges from 1 to 391 where 1 indicates greatest number of fraud and other consumer reports per 100,000 population
Source: Federal Trade Commission, Consumer Sentinel Network Data Book 2022

POLITICS

2020 Presidential Election Results

Area	Biden	Trump	Jorgensen	Hawkins	Other
Travis County	71.4	26.4	1.5	0.3	0.4
U.S.	51.3	46.8	1.2	0.3	0.5

Note: Results are percentages and may not add to 100% due to rounding
Source: Dave Leip's Atlas of U.S. Presidential Elections

SPORTS

Professional Sports Teams

Team Name	League	Year Established
Austin FC	Major League Soccer (MLS)	2021

Note: Includes teams located in the Austin-Round Rock-Georgetown, TX Metropolitan Statistical Area.
Source: Wikipedia, Major Professional Sports Teams of the United States and Canada, April 12, 2023

CLIMATE

Average and Extreme Temperatures

Temperature	Jan	Feb	Mar	Apr	May	Jun	Jul	Aug	Sep	Oct	Nov	Dec	Yr.
Extreme High (°F)	90	97	98	98	100	105	109	106	104	98	91	90	109
Average High (°F)	60	64	72	79	85	91	95	96	90	81	70	63	79
Average Temp. (°F)	50	53	61	69	75	82	85	85	80	70	60	52	69
Average Low (°F)	39	43	50	58	65	72	74	74	69	59	49	41	58
Extreme Low (°F)	-2	7	18	35	43	53	64	61	47	32	20	4	-2

Note: Figures cover the years 1948-1990
Source: National Climatic Data Center, International Station Meteorological Climate Summary, 9/96

Austin, Texas

Average Precipitation/Snowfall/Humidity

Precip./Humidity	Jan	Feb	Mar	Apr	May	Jun	Jul	Aug	Sep	Oct	Nov	Dec	Yr.
Avg. Precip. (in.)	1.6	2.3	1.8	2.9	4.3	3.5	1.9	1.9	3.3	3.5	2.1	1.9	31.1
Avg. Snowfall (in.)	1	Tr	Tr	0	0	0	0	0	0	0	Tr	Tr	1
Avg. Rel. Hum. 6am (%)	79	80	79	83	88	89	88	87	86	84	81	79	84
Avg. Rel. Hum. 3pm (%)	53	51	47	50	53	49	43	42	47	47	49	51	48

Note: Figures cover the years 1948-1990; Tr = Trace amounts (<0.05 in. of rain; <0.5 in. of snow)
Source: National Climatic Data Center, International Station Meteorological Climate Summary, 9/96

Weather Conditions

Temperature			Daytime Sky			Precipitation		
10°F & below	32°F & below	90°F & above	Clear	Partly cloudy	Cloudy	0.01 inch or more precip.	0.1 inch or more snow/ice	Thunder-storms
< 1	20	111	105	148	112	83	1	41

Note: Figures are average number of days per year and cover the years 1948-1990
Source: National Climatic Data Center, International Station Meteorological Climate Summary, 9/96

HAZARDOUS WASTE

Superfund Sites

The Austin-Round Rock-Georgetown, TX metro area has no sites on the EPA's Superfund Final National Priorities List. There are a total of 1,165 Superfund sites with a status of proposed or final on the list in the U.S. *U.S. Environmental Protection Agency, National Priorities List, April 12, 2023*

AIR QUALITY

Air Quality Trends: Ozone

	1990	1995	2000	2005	2010	2015	2018	2019	2020	2021
MSA[1]	0.088	0.089	0.088	0.082	0.074	0.073	0.072	0.065	0.066	0.066
U.S.	0.087	0.089	0.081	0.080	0.072	0.067	0.069	0.065	0.065	0.067

Note: (1) Data covers the Austin-Round Rock-Georgetown, TX Metropolitan Statistical Area. The values shown are the composite ozone concentration averages among trend sites based on the highest fourth daily maximum 8-hour concentration in parts per million. These trends are based on sites having an adequate record of monitoring data during the trend period. Data from exceptional events are included.
Source: U.S. Environmental Protection Agency, Air Quality Monitoring Information, "Air Quality Trends by City, 1990-2021"

Air Quality Index

Area	Percent of Days when Air Quality was...[2]					AQI Statistics[2]	
	Good	Moderate	Unhealthy for Sensitive Groups	Unhealthy	Very Unhealthy	Maximum	Median
MSA[1]	68.2	31.5	0.3	0.0	0.0	101	43

Note: (1) Data covers the Austin-Round Rock-Georgetown, TX Metropolitan Statistical Area; (2) Based on 365 days with AQI data in 2021. Air Quality Index (AQI) is an index for reporting daily air quality. EPA calculates the AQI for five major air pollutants regulated by the Clean Air Act: ground-level ozone, particle pollution (aka particulate matter), carbon monoxide, sulfur dioxide, and nitrogen dioxide. The AQI runs from 0 to 500. The higher the AQI value, the greater the level of air pollution and the greater the health concern. There are six AQI categories: "Good" AQI is between 0 and 50. Air quality is considered satisfactory; "Moderate" AQI is between 51 and 100. Air quality is acceptable; "Unhealthy for Sensitive Groups" When AQI values are between 101 and 150, members of sensitive groups may experience health effects; "Unhealthy" When AQI values are between 151 and 200 everyone may begin to experience health effects; "Very Unhealthy" AQI values between 201 and 300 trigger a health alert; "Hazardous" AQI values over 300 trigger warnings of emergency conditions (not shown).
Source: U.S. Environmental Protection Agency, Air Quality Index Report, 2021

Air Quality Index Pollutants

Area	Percent of Days when AQI Pollutant was...[2]						
	Carbon Monoxide	Nitrogen Dioxide	Ozone	Sulfur Dioxide	Particulate Matter 2.5	Particulate Matter 10
MSA[1]	0.0	1.6	50.7	(3)	46.6	1.1

Note: (1) Data covers the Austin-Round Rock-Georgetown, TX Metropolitan Statistical Area; (2) Based on 365 days with AQI data in 2021. The Air Quality Index (AQI) is an index for reporting daily air quality. EPA calculates the AQI for five major air pollutants regulated by the Clean Air Act: ground-level ozone, particle pollution (also known as particulate matter), carbon monoxide, sulfur dioxide, and nitrogen dioxide. The AQI runs from 0 to 500. The higher the AQI value, the greater the level of air pollution and the greater the health concern; (3) Sulfur dioxide is no longer included in this table (as of December 8, 2021) because SO_2 concentrations tend to be very localized and not necessarily representative of broad geographical areas like counties and CBSAs.
Source: U.S. Environmental Protection Agency, Air Quality Index Report, 2021

Maximum Air Pollutant Concentrations: Particulate Matter, Ozone, CO and Lead

	Particulate Matter 10 (ug/m^3)	Particulate Matter 2.5 Wtd AM (ug/m^3)	Particulate Matter 2.5 24-Hr (ug/m^3)	Ozone (ppm)	Carbon Monoxide (ppm)	Lead (ug/m^3)
MSA[1] Level	91	9.4	21	0.066	1	n/a
NAAQS[2]	150	15	35	0.075	9	0.15
Met NAAQS[2]	Yes	Yes	Yes	Yes	Yes	n/a

Note: (1) Data covers the Austin-Round Rock-Georgetown, TX Metropolitan Statistical Area; Data from exceptional events are included; (2) National Ambient Air Quality Standards; ppm = parts per million; ug/m^3 = micrograms per cubic meter; n/a not available.
Concentrations: Particulate Matter 10 (coarse particulate)—highest second maximum 24-hour concentration; Particulate Matter 2.5 Wtd AM (fine particulate)—highest weighted annual mean concentration; Particulate Matter 2.5 24-Hour (fine particulate)—highest 98th percentile 24-hour concentration; Ozone—highest fourth daily maximum 8-hour concentration; Carbon Monoxide—highest second maximum non-overlapping 8-hour concentration; Lead—maximum running 3-month average
Source: U.S. Environmental Protection Agency, Air Quality Monitoring Information, "Air Quality Statistics by City, 2021"

Maximum Air Pollutant Concentrations: Nitrogen Dioxide and Sulfur Dioxide

	Nitrogen Dioxide AM (ppb)	Nitrogen Dioxide 1-Hr (ppb)	Sulfur Dioxide AM (ppb)	Sulfur Dioxide 1-Hr (ppb)	Sulfur Dioxide 24-Hr (ppb)
MSA[1] Level	13	44	n/a	3	n/a
NAAQS[2]	53	100	30	75	140
Met NAAQS[2]	Yes	Yes	n/a	Yes	n/a

Note: (1) Data covers the Austin-Round Rock-Georgetown, TX Metropolitan Statistical Area; Data from exceptional events are included; (2) National Ambient Air Quality Standards; ppm = parts per million; ug/m^3 = micrograms per cubic meter; n/a not available.
Concentrations: Nitrogen Dioxide AM—highest arithmetic mean concentration; Nitrogen Dioxide 1-Hr—highest 98th percentile 1-hour daily maximum concentration; Sulfur Dioxide AM—highest annual mean concentration; Sulfur Dioxide 1-Hr—highest 99th percentile 1-hour daily maximum concentration; Sulfur Dioxide 24-Hr—highest second maximum 24-hour concentration
Source: U.S. Environmental Protection Agency, Air Quality Monitoring Information, "Air Quality Statistics by City, 2021"

Brownsville, Texas

Background

Brownsville sits on the western Gulf Coast in South Texas, adjacent to the state's border with Mexico. The seeds of Brownsville were planted in 1781, when the Spanish government granted 408 square miles of land to José Salvador de la Garza, who constructed a ranch. In 1836, Texas declared its independence from Mexico and in 1846, General Zachary Taylor and his troops arrived in Brownsville and he built Fort Texas, later renamed Fort Brown in honor of Major Jacob Brown, who died during the siege of Fort Texas. Once Brownsville became part of Texas in 1848, early settlers formed the Brownsville Town Company.

During the American Civil War, Brownsville served as a smuggling point for Confederate goods into Mexico, significantly, cotton. Location of the city, southwest of the Cotton Belt, made facilitated the smuggling of cottom to European ships through the Mexican port of Bagdad to avoid Union blockades. In November 1863, Union troops landed at Port Isabel and marched towards Brownsville to take control of Fort Brown. In the ensuing Battle of Brownsville, Confederate forces abandoned and blew up the fort. In 1864, Confederate forces commanded by Colonel John Salmon Ford reoccupied the town, and he became mayor of Brownsville. Fort Brown was decommissioned at the end of World War II in 1945 and, in 1948, the city acquired the land.

At the turn of the 20th century, Texas passed a new constitution and Jim Crow laws. While Hispanic residents were considered white under the terms of the United States annexation of Texas, legislatures found ways to suppress their participation in politics. Today, Brownsville has the third-highest proportion of Hispanic Americans of any city in the United States outside of Puerto Rico.

In the 21st century, Brownsville has received significant media attention surrounding immigration policies and border-wall funding costs. In 2006, President George W. Bush signed into law the Secure Fence Act of 2006, allowing the construction of a border fence extending from San Diego through to the Port of Brownsville. In 2008, the United States issued a proposal to add 70 miles of border fence, but Federal District Judge Andrew Hanen, rejected the plan. In 2017, President Trump directed construction of a 1,000-mile border wall through executive order. In 2023, Trump's wall remains half built.

Downtown Brownsville has recently undergone several revitalization projects: The Texas Historical Commission named Brownsville as part of its Main Street Program in 2016, and several historic buildings were restored; The Environmental Protection Agency (EPA) selected Brownsville as one of six cities for their "Greening America's Communities" program.

Brownsville's economy is heavily dependent on the service and manufacturing industries, with government and the University of Texas Rio Grande Valley at the top of the list. The Port of Brownsville produces significant revenue for the city, providing a link between the road networks of nearby Mexico and the Gulf Intracoastal Waterway of Texas. The port has become an important economic hub for South Texas, where shipments arrive from other parts of the United States, Mexico, and other foreign countries. It also is home to five of the country's eight ship-recycling companies, and recently received a $1.8 million government grant to support business and infrastructure development.

Entrepreneur Elon Musk put Brownsville on the map when he constructed SpaceX—his 137 billion dollar human space exploration company less than 10 miles from the city limits. The SpaceX South Texas launch site's initial purpose was to support launches of the Falcon 9 and Falcon Heavy launch vehicles. In 2018, SpaceX announced that the launch site would be used exclusively for SpaceX's next-generation launch vehicle, Starship. Musk's endeavors play predominantly into Brownsville economic landscape not only as they relate to space transportation, but he has recently committed to injecting massive dollars to improve the city schools.

The University of Texas at Brownsville and the Brownsville Economic Development Council (BEDC), in collaboration with SpaceX, built radio-frequency (RF) technology facilities for STARGATE (Spacecraft Tracking and Astronomical Research into Gigahertz Astrophysical Transient Emission). The facility provides students and faculty access to radio frequency technologies used in spaceflight operations, and includes satellite and spacecraft tracking.

Brownsville is a wildlife refuge center. Several state parks and historical sites are protected by the Texas Parks and Wildlife Department. Brownsville has 37 parks connected by a 1,200-acre system of parkland and 32 miles of bike lanes.

Brownsville has a humid subtropical climate. Winters are warm, and summers are hot and humid. Due to its proximity to the deserts of Chihuahua and Gulf Coastal Plains, Brownsville's geographic location lies near the boundary of a hot semi-arid climate. Snow is very rare in Brownsville. Its wet season is concentrated during the late summer and early fall, peaking in September, when the threat from tropical cyclones is greatest. November through April is the dry season. Brownsville receives modest annual rainfall, averaging about 26.78 inches.

Rankings

Business/Finance Rankings

- The Brownsville metro area appeared on the Milken Institute "2022 Best Performing Cities" list. Rank: #109 out of 200 large metro areas (population over 250,000). Criteria: job growth; wage and salary growth; high-tech output growth; housing affordability; household broadband access. *Milken Institute, "Best-Performing Cities 2022," March 28, 2022*

- *Forbes* ranked the 200 most populous metro areas to determine the nation's "Best Places for Business and Careers." The Brownsville metro area was ranked #190. Criteria: costs (business and living); job growth (past and projected); income growth; quality of life; educational attainment (college and high school); projected economic growth; cultural and leisure opportunities; workplace tolerance laws; net migration patterns. *Forbes, "The Best Places for Business and Careers 2019: Seattle Still On Top," October 30, 2019*

Children/Family Rankings

- Brownsville was selected as one of the most playful cities in the U.S. by KaBOOM! The organization's Playful City USA initiative honors cities and towns across the nation that have made their communities more playable. Criteria: pledging to integrate play as a solution to challenges in their communities; making it easy for children to get active and balanced play; creating more family-friendly and innovative communities as a result. *KaBOOM! National Campaign for Play, "2017 Playful City USA Communities"*

Education Rankings

- Personal finance website *WalletHub* analyzed the 150 largest U.S. metropolitan statistical areas to determine where the most educated Americans are putting their degrees to work. Criteria: education levels; percentage of workers with degrees; education quality and attainment gap; public school quality rankings; quality and enrollment of each metro area's universities. Brownsville was ranked #149 (#1 = most educated city). *www.WalletHub.com, "Most & Least Educated Cities in America," July 18, 2022*

Environmental Rankings

- Brownsville was highlighted as one of the cleanest metro areas for ozone air pollution in the U.S. during 2019 through 2021. The list represents cities with no monitored ozone air pollution in unhealthful ranges. *American Lung Association, "State of the Air 2023," April 19, 2023*

Health/Fitness Rankings

- The Sharecare Community Well-Being Index evaluates 10 individual and social health factors in order to measure what matters to Americans in the communities in which they live. The Brownsville metro area ranked #376 in the bottom 10 across all 10 domains. Criteria: access to healthcare, food, and community resources; housng and transportation; economic security; feeling of purpose; physical, financial, social, and community well-being. *www.sharecare.com, "Community Well-Being Index: 2020 Metro Area & County Rankings Report," August 30, 2021*

Real Estate Rankings

- *WalletHub* compared the most populated U.S. cities to determine which had the best markets for real estate agents. Brownsville ranked #175 where demand was high and pay was the best. Criteria: sales per agent; annual median wage for real-estate agents; monthly average starting salary for real estate agents; real estate job density and competition; unemployment rate; home turnover rate; housing-market health index; and other relevant metrics. *www.WalletHub.com, "2021 Best Places to Be a Real Estate Agent," May 12, 2021*

- Brownsville was ranked #160 out of 235 metro areas in terms of housing affordability in 2022 by the National Association of Home Builders (#1 = most affordable). Criteria: the share of homes sold in that area affordable to a family earning the local median income, based on standard mortgage underwriting criteria. *National Association of Home Builders®, NAHB-Wells Fargo Housing Opportunity Index, 4th Quarter 2022*

Safety Rankings

- Allstate ranked the 200 largest cities in America in terms of driver safety. Brownsville ranked #1. Criteria: internal property damage claims over a two-year period from January 2016 to December 2017. The report helps increase the importance of safety and awareness behind the wheel. *Allstate, "Allstate America's Best Drivers Report, 2019" June 24, 2019*

- The National Insurance Crime Bureau ranked 390 metro areas in the U.S. in terms of per capita rates of vehicle theft. The Brownsville metro area ranked #262 (#1 = highest rate). Criteria: number of vehicle theft offenses per 100,000 inhabitants in 2021. *National Insurance Crime Bureau, "Hot Spots 2021," September 1, 2022*

Seniors/Retirement Rankings

- From its Best Cities for Successful Aging indexes, the Milken Institute generated rankings for metropolitan areas, weighing data in nine categories—health care, wellness, living arrangements, transportation and convenience, financial characteristics, education, employment, community engagement, and overall livability. The Brownsville metro area was ranked #154 overall in the small metro area category. *Milken Institute, "Best Cities for Successful Aging, 2017" March 14, 2017*

Sports/Recreation Rankings

- Brownsville was chosen as a bicycle friendly community by the League of American Bicyclists. A "Bicycle Friendly Community" welcomes cyclists by providing safe and supportive accommodation for cycling and encouraging people to bike for transportation and recreation. There are five award levels: Diamond; Platinum; Gold; Silver; and Bronze. The community achieved an award level of Bronze. *League of American Bicyclists, "Fall 2022 Awards-New & Renewing Bicycle Friendly Communities List," December 14, 2022*

Women/Minorities Rankings

- Personal finance website *WalletHub* compared more than 180 U.S. cities across two key dimensions, "Hispanic Business-Friendliness" and "Hispanic Purchasing Power," to arrive at the most favorable conditions for Hispanic entrepreneurs. Brownsville was ranked #13 out of 182. Criteria includes: share of Hispanic-Owned Businesses; Hispanic entrepreneurship rate to median annual income of Hispanics; Small Business-Friendliness score; cost of living; and number of Hispanics with at least a bachelor's degree. *WalletHub.com, "2019's Best Cities for Hispanic Entrepreneurs," May 1, 2019*

Miscellaneous Rankings

- The financial planning site SmartAsset has compiled its annual study on the best places for Halloween in the U.S. for 2022. 146 cities were compared to determine that Brownsville ranked #8 out of 35 for still being able to enjoy the festivities despite COVID-19. Metrics included: safety, family-friendliness, percentage of children in the population, concentration of candy and costume shops, weather and COVID infection rates. *www.smartasset.com, "2022 Edition-Best Places to Celebrate Halloween," October 19, 2022*

Business Environment

DEMOGRAPHICS

Population Growth

Area	1990 Census	2000 Census	2010 Census	2020 Census	Population Growth (%) 1990-2020	Population Growth (%) 2010-2020
City	114,025	139,722	175,023	186,738	63.8	6.7
MSA[1]	260,120	335,227	406,220	421,017	61.9	3.6
U.S.	248,709,873	281,421,906	308,745,538	331,449,281	33.3	7.4

Note: (1) Figures cover the Brownsville-Harlingen, TX Metropolitan Statistical Area
Source: U.S. Census Bureau, 1990 Census, 2000 Census, 2010 Census, 2020 Census

Race

Area	White Alone[2] (%)	Black Alone[2] (%)	Asian Alone[2] (%)	AIAN[3] Alone[2] (%)	NHOPI[4] Alone[2] (%)	Other Race Alone[2] (%)	Two or More Races (%)
City	34.9	0.3	0.6	0.7	0.0	20.5	42.9
MSA[1]	38.6	0.5	0.7	0.7	0.0	19.0	40.4
U.S.	61.6	12.4	6.0	1.1	0.2	8.4	10.2

Note: (1) Figures cover the Brownsville-Harlingen, TX Metropolitan Statistical Area; (2) Alone is defined as not being in combination with one or more other races; (3) American Indian and Alaska Native; (4) Native Hawaiian and Other Pacific Islander
Source: U.S. Census Bureau, 2020 Census

Hispanic or Latino Origin

Area	Total (%)	Mexican (%)	Puerto Rican (%)	Cuban (%)	Other (%)
City	94.7	90.5	0.2	0.1	3.8
MSA[1]	90.0	86.0	0.3	0.1	3.6
U.S.	18.4	11.2	1.8	0.7	4.7

Note: Persons of Hispanic or Latino origin can be of any race; (1) Figures cover the Brownsville-Harlingen, TX Metropolitan Statistical Area
Source: U.S. Census Bureau, 2017-2021 American Community Survey 5-Year Estimates

Age

Area	Under Age 5	Age 5–19	Age 20–34	Age 35–44	Age 45–54	Age 55–64	Age 65–74	Age 75–84	Age 85+	Median Age
City	6.6	25.8	20.0	12.3	12.0	10.1	7.9	3.8	1.5	32.9
MSA[1]	6.5	25.3	19.3	12.0	11.9	10.6	8.6	4.3	1.6	34.0
U.S.	5.6	19.2	20.2	12.7	12.4	13.1	10.0	4.9	1.9	38.8

Note: (1) Figures cover the Brownsville-Harlingen, TX Metropolitan Statistical Area
Source: U.S. Census Bureau, 2020 Census

Disability by Age

Area	All Ages	Under 18 Years Old	18 to 64 Years Old	65 Years and Over
City	10.6	4.2	7.8	40.6
MSA[1]	12.2	5.6	9.5	39.0
U.S.	12.6	4.4	10.3	33.4

Note: Figures show percent of the civilian noninstitutionalized population that reported having a disability. Disability status is determined from six types of difficulty: vision, hearing, cognitive, ambulatory, self-care, and independent living. For children under 5 years old, hearing and vision difficulty are used to determine disability status. For children between the ages of 5 and 14, disability status is determined from hearing, vision, cognitive, ambulatory, and self-care difficulties. For people aged 15 years and older, they are considered to have a disability if they have difficulty with any one of the six difficulty types; Note: (1) Figures cover the Brownsville-Harlingen, TX Metropolitan Statistical Area
Source: U.S. Census Bureau, 2017-2021 American Community Survey 5-Year Estimates

Ancestry

Area	German	Irish	English	American	Italian	Polish	French[2]	Scottish	Dutch
City	0.9	0.5	0.6	1.7	0.4	0.1	0.4	0.1	0.2
MSA[1]	1.9	1.1	1.8	1.9	0.5	0.2	0.5	0.3	0.1
U.S.	12.8	9.6	8.1	5.7	5.0	2.7	2.2	1.6	1.1

Note: Figures are the percentage of the total population reporting a particular ancestry. The nine most commonly reported ancestries in the U.S. are shown. Figures include multiple ancestries (e.g. if a person reported being Irish and Italian, they were included in both columns); (1) Figures cover the Brownsville-Harlingen, TX Metropolitan Statistical Area; (2) Excludes Basque
Source: U.S. Census Bureau, 2017-2021 American Community Survey 5-Year Estimates

Brownsville, Texas

Foreign-born Population

Area	Any Foreign Country	Asia	Mexico	Europe	Caribbean	Central America[2]	South America	Africa	Canada
City	27.1	0.5	25.5	0.2	0.0	0.7	0.1	0.0	0.1
MSA[1]	22.8	0.6	20.8	0.2	0.1	0.7	0.1	0.0	0.1
U.S.	13.6	4.2	3.3	1.5	1.4	1.1	1.1	0.8	0.2

Note: (1) Figures cover the Brownsville-Harlingen, TX Metropolitan Statistical Area; (2) Excludes Mexico.
Source: U.S. Census Bureau, 2017-2021 American Community Survey 5-Year Estimates

Household Size

Area	One	Two	Three	Four	Five	Six	Seven or More	Average Household Size
City	19.3	23.7	17.1	19.3	12.5	4.7	3.5	3.30
MSA[1]	20.4	26.8	16.5	17.6	10.4	4.9	3.3	3.20
U.S.	28.1	33.8	15.5	12.9	6.0	2.3	1.4	2.60

Note: (1) Figures cover the Brownsville-Harlingen, TX Metropolitan Statistical Area
Source: U.S. Census Bureau, 2017-2021 American Community Survey 5-Year Estimates

Household Relationships

Area	Householder	Opposite-sex Spouse	Same-sex Spouse	Opposite-sex Unmarried Partner	Same-sex Unmarried Partner	Child[2]	Grandchild	Other Relatives	Non-relatives
City	30.8	15.0	0.1	1.4	0.1	36.7	4.7	8.3	1.6
MSA[1]	31.5	15.3	0.1	1.7	0.1	36.1	5.2	7.4	1.7
U.S.	38.3	17.5	0.2	2.5	0.2	28.3	2.4	4.8	3.4

Note: Figures are percent of the total population; (1) Figures cover the Brownsville-Harlingen, TX Metropolitan Statistical Area; (2) Includes biological, adopted, and stepchildren of the householder
Source: U.S. Census Bureau, 2020 Census

Gender

Area	Males	Females	Males per 100 Females
City	89,293	97,445	91.6
MSA[1]	203,223	217,794	93.3
U.S.	162,685,811	168,763,470	96.4

Note: (1) Figures cover the Brownsville-Harlingen, TX Metropolitan Statistical Area
Source: U.S. Census Bureau, 2020 Census

Marital Status

Area	Never Married	Now Married[2]	Separated	Widowed	Divorced
City	34.2	47.6	4.3	6.2	7.8
MSA[1]	33.6	48.2	3.5	6.3	8.4
U.S.	33.8	48.0	1.8	5.6	10.8

Note: Figures are percentages and cover the population 15 years of age and older; (1) Figures cover the Brownsville-Harlingen, TX Metropolitan Statistical Area; (2) Excludes separated
Source: U.S. Census Bureau, 2017-2021 American Community Survey 5-Year Estimates

Religious Groups by Family

Area	Catholic	Baptist	Methodist	LDS[2]	Pentecostal	Lutheran	Islam	Adventist	Other
MSA[1]	36.8	2.8	0.7	1.2	1.0	0.2	0.1	2.5	9.4
U.S.	18.7	7.3	3.0	2.0	1.8	1.7	1.3	1.3	11.6

Note: Figures are the number of adherents as a percentage of the total population and cover the eight largest religious groups in the U.S; (1) Figures cover the Brownsville-Harlingen, TX Metropolitan Statistical Area; (2) Church of Jesus Christ of Latter-day Saints
Sources: 2020 U.S. Religion Census, Association of Statisticians of American Religious Bodies; The Association of Religion Data Archives (ARDA)

Religious Groups by Tradition

Area	Catholic	Evangelical Protestant	Mainline Protestant	Black Protestant	Islam	Judaism	Hinduism	Orthodox	Buddhism
MSA[1]	36.8	13.1	1.2	0.1	0.1	n/a	n/a	n/a	n/a
U.S.	18.7	16.5	5.2	2.3	1.3	0.6	0.4	0.4	0.3

Note: Figures are the number of adherents as a percentage of the total population; (1) Figures cover the Brownsville-Harlingen, TX Metropolitan Statistical Area
Sources: 2020 U.S. Religion Census, Association of Statisticians of American Religious Bodies; The Association of Religion Data Archives (ARDA)

ECONOMY

Gross Metropolitan Product

Area	2020	2021	2022	2023	Rank[2]
MSA[1]	11.9	13.1	14.8	15.6	195

Note: Figures are in billions of dollars; (1) Figures cover the Brownsville-Harlingen, TX Metropolitan Statistical Area; (2) Rank is based on 2021 data and ranges from 1 to 381
Source: U.S. Conference of Mayors, U.S. Metro Economies: U.S. Metros Compared to Global and State Economies, June 2022

Economic Growth

Area	2018-20 (%)	2021 (%)	2022 (%)	2023 (%)	Rank[2]
MSA[1]	1.3	6.2	4.4	2.9	56
U.S.	-0.6	5.7	3.1	2.9	–

Note: Figures are real gross metropolitan product (GMP) growth rates and represent average annual percent change; (1) Figures cover the Brownsville-Harlingen, TX Metropolitan Statistical Area; (2) Rank is based on 2020 2-year average annual percent change and ranges from 1 to 381
Source: U.S. Conference of Mayors, U.S. Metro Economies: U.S. Metros Compared to Global and State Economies, June 2022

Metropolitan Area Exports

Area	2016	2017	2018	2019	2020	2021	Rank[2]
MSA[1]	5,016.7	n/a	6,293.0	4,741.8	n/a	6,953.0	47

Note: Figures are in millions of dollars; (1) Figures cover the Brownsville-Harlingen, TX Metropolitan Statistical Area; (2) Rank is based on 2021 data and ranges from 1 to 388
Source: U.S. Department of Commerce, International Trade Administration, Office of Trade and Economic Analysis, Industry and Analysis, Exports by Metropolitan Area, data extracted March 16, 2023

Building Permits

Area	Single-Family 2021	Single-Family 2022	Pct. Chg.	Multi-Family 2021	Multi-Family 2022	Pct. Chg.	Total 2021	Total 2022	Pct. Chg.
City	883	817	-7.5	246	353	43.5	1,129	1,170	3.6
MSA[1]	1,573	1,940	23.3	479	569	18.8	2,052	2,509	22.3
U.S.	1,115,400	975,600	-12.5	621,600	689,500	10.9	1,737,000	1,665,100	-4.1

Note: (1) Figures cover the Brownsville-Harlingen, TX Metropolitan Statistical Area; Figures represent new, privately-owned housing units authorized (unadjusted data); All permit data are based on estimates with imputation
Source: U.S. Census Bureau, Manufacturing, Mining, and Construction Statistics, Building Permits, 2021, 2022

Bankruptcy Filings

Area	Business Filings 2021	Business Filings 2022	% Chg.	Nonbusiness Filings 2021	Nonbusiness Filings 2022	% Chg.
Cameron County	0	4	n/a	171	195	14.0
U.S.	14,347	13,481	-6.0	399,269	374,240	-6.3

Note: Business filings include Chapter 7, Chapter 9, Chapter 11, Chapter 12, Chapter 13, Chapter 15, and Section 304; Nonbusiness filings include Chapter 7, Chapter 11, and Chapter 13
Source: Administrative Office of the U.S. Courts, Business and Nonbusiness Bankruptcy, County Cases Commenced by Chapter of the Bankruptcy Code, During the 12-Month Period Ending December 31, 2021 and Business and Nonbusiness Bankruptcy, County Cases Commenced by Chapter of the Bankruptcy Code, During the 12-Month Period Ending December 31, 2022

Housing Vacancy Rates

Area	Gross Vacancy Rate[2] (%) 2020	2021	2022	Year-Round Vacancy Rate[3] (%) 2020	2021	2022	Rental Vacancy Rate[4] (%) 2020	2021	2022	Homeowner Vacancy Rate[5] (%) 2020	2021	2022
MSA[1]	n/a	n/a	n/a	n/a	n/a	n/a	n/a	n/a	n/a	n/a	n/a	n/a
U.S.	10.6	10.8	10.5	8.2	8.4	8.2	6.3	6.1	5.8	1.0	0.9	0.8

Note: (1) Figures cover the Brownsville-Harlingen, TX Metropolitan Statistical Area; (2) The percentage of the total housing inventory that is vacant; (3) The percentage of the housing inventory (excluding seasonal units) that is year-round vacant; (4) The percentage of rental inventory that is vacant for rent; (5) The percentage of homeowner inventory that is vacant for sale; n/a not available
Source: U.S. Census Bureau, Housing Vacancies and Homeownership Annual Statistics: 2020, 2021, 2022

INCOME

Income

Area	Per Capita ($)	Median Household ($)	Average Household ($)
City	18,207	43,174	58,147
MSA[1]	19,371	43,057	60,107
U.S.	37,638	69,021	97,196

Note: (1) Figures cover the Brownsville-Harlingen, TX Metropolitan Statistical Area
Source: U.S. Census Bureau, 2017-2021 American Community Survey 5-Year Estimates

Brownsville, Texas

Household Income Distribution

Area	Under $15,000	$15,000 -$24,999	$25,000 -$34,999	$35,000 -$49,999	$50,000 -$74,999	$75,000 -$99,999	$100,000 -$149,999	$150,000 and up
City	18.6	13.1	10.0	13.0	18.2	10.7	10.6	5.9
MSA[1]	16.8	13.4	11.5	12.9	17.9	10.7	10.6	6.3
U.S.	9.4	7.8	8.2	11.4	16.8	12.8	16.3	17.3

Note: (1) Figures cover the Brownsville-Harlingen, TX Metropolitan Statistical Area
Source: U.S. Census Bureau, 2017-2021 American Community Survey 5-Year Estimates

Poverty Rate

Area	All Ages	Under 18 Years Old	18 to 64 Years Old	65 Years and Over
City	26.5	36.4	21.2	28.2
MSA[1]	26.3	37.9	21.2	21.8
U.S.	12.6	17.0	11.8	9.6

Note: Figures are percentage of people whose income during the past 12 months was below the poverty level; (1) Figures cover the Brownsville-Harlingen, TX Metropolitan Statistical Area
Source: U.S. Census Bureau, 2017-2021 American Community Survey 5-Year Estimates

EMPLOYMENT

Labor Force and Employment

Area	Civilian Labor Force Dec. 2021	Civilian Labor Force Dec. 2022	% Chg.	Workers Employed Dec. 2021	Workers Employed Dec. 2022	% Chg.
City	78,951	79,589	0.8	73,562	74,739	1.6
MSA[1]	175,175	176,374	0.7	163,657	166,276	1.6
U.S.	161,696,000	164,224,000	1.6	155,732,000	158,872,000	2.0

Note: Data is not seasonally adjusted and covers workers 16 years of age and older; (1) Figures cover the Brownsville-Harlingen, TX Metropolitan Statistical Area
Source: Bureau of Labor Statistics, Local Area Unemployment Statistics

Unemployment Rate

Area	Jan.	Feb.	Mar.	Apr.	May	Jun.	Jul.	Aug.	Sep.	Oct.	Nov.	Dec.
City	7.9	7.4	6.1	6.0	6.1	7.1	6.9	6.4	5.9	5.5	5.7	6.1
MSA[1]	7.6	7.3	6.1	5.9	6.0	6.9	6.8	6.4	5.8	5.6	5.7	5.7
U.S.	4.4	4.1	3.8	3.3	3.4	3.8	3.8	3.8	3.3	3.4	3.4	3.3

Note: Data is not seasonally adjusted and covers workers 16 years of age and older; (1) Figures cover the Brownsville-Harlingen, TX Metropolitan Statistical Area
Source: Bureau of Labor Statistics, Local Area Unemployment Statistics

Average Wages

Occupation	$/Hr.	Occupation	$/Hr.
Accountants and Auditors	31.30	Maintenance and Repair Workers	15.45
Automotive Mechanics	20.87	Marketing Managers	56.84
Bookkeepers	17.66	Network and Computer Systems Admin.	36.42
Carpenters	18.88	Nurses, Licensed Practical	22.93
Cashiers	11.54	Nurses, Registered	35.07
Computer Programmers	n/a	Nursing Assistants	13.19
Computer Systems Analysts	40.71	Office Clerks, General	14.88
Computer User Support Specialists	21.36	Physical Therapists	45.71
Construction Laborers	14.98	Physicians	116.21
Cooks, Restaurant	12.36	Plumbers, Pipefitters and Steamfitters	20.29
Customer Service Representatives	16.29	Police and Sheriff's Patrol Officers	26.68
Dentists	n/a	Postal Service Mail Carriers	26.80
Electricians	21.42	Real Estate Sales Agents	24.87
Engineers, Electrical	44.90	Retail Salespersons	14.27
Fast Food and Counter Workers	10.12	Sales Representatives, Technical/Scientific	n/a
Financial Managers	59.69	Secretaries, Exc. Legal/Medical/Executive	16.45
First-Line Supervisors of Office Workers	25.20	Security Guards	15.55
General and Operations Managers	41.63	Surgeons	n/a
Hairdressers/Cosmetologists	12.81	Teacher Assistants, Exc. Postsecondary*	13.50
Home Health and Personal Care Aides	10.33	Teachers, Secondary School, Exc. Sp. Ed.*	26.50
Janitors and Cleaners	12.36	Telemarketers	n/a
Landscaping/Groundskeeping Workers	12.90	Truck Drivers, Heavy/Tractor-Trailer	22.21
Lawyers	56.07	Truck Drivers, Light/Delivery Services	18.91
Maids and Housekeeping Cleaners	10.80	Waiters and Waitresses	10.94

Note: Wage data covers the Brownsville-Harlingen, TX Metropolitan Statistical Area; (*) Hourly wages were calculated from annual wage data based on a 40 hour work week; n/a not available.
Source: Bureau of Labor Statistics, Metro Area Occupational Employment & Wage Estimates, May 2022

Employment by Industry

Sector	MSA[1] Number of Employees	MSA[1] Percent of Total	U.S. Percent of Total
Construction, Mining, and Logging	3,700	2.3	5.4
Private Education and Health Services	48,300	30.2	16.1
Financial Activities	5,100	3.2	5.9
Government	29,800	18.6	14.5
Information	600	0.4	2.0
Leisure and Hospitality	17,600	11.0	10.3
Manufacturing	7,300	4.6	8.4
Other Services	3,500	2.2	3.7
Professional and Business Services	17,100	10.7	14.7
Retail Trade	18,400	11.5	10.2
Transportation, Warehousing, and Utilities	5,500	3.4	4.9
Wholesale Trade	3,200	2.0	3.9

Note: Figures are non-farm employment as of December 2022. Figures are not seasonally adjusted and include workers 16 years of age and older; (1) Figures cover the Brownsville-Harlingen, TX Metropolitan Statistical Area
Source: Bureau of Labor Statistics, Current Employment Statistics, Employment, Hours, and Earnings

Employment by Occupation

Occupation Classification	City (%)	MSA[1] (%)	U.S. (%)
Management, Business, Science, and Arts	29.5	29.1	40.3
Natural Resources, Construction, and Maintenance	9.9	10.6	8.7
Production, Transportation, and Material Moving	12.4	12.3	13.1
Sales and Office	21.8	21.5	20.9
Service	26.4	26.4	17.0

Note: Figures cover employed civilians 16 years of age and older; (1) Figures cover the Brownsville-Harlingen, TX Metropolitan Statistical Area
Source: U.S. Census Bureau, 2017-2021 American Community Survey 5-Year Estimates

Occupations with Greatest Projected Employment Growth: 2022 – 2024

Occupation[1]	2022 Employment	2024 Projected Employment	Numeric Employment Change	Percent Employment Change
Home Health and Personal Care Aides	338,130	364,760	26,630	7.9
General and Operations Managers	395,700	416,100	20,400	5.2
Heavy and Tractor-Trailer Truck Drivers	206,850	222,220	15,370	7.4
Software Developers	119,810	134,060	14,250	11.9
Laborers and Freight, Stock, and Material Movers, Hand	214,680	228,680	14,000	6.5
Farmers, Ranchers, and Other Agricultural Managers	274,740	287,430	12,690	4.6
Stockers and Order Fillers	212,180	224,670	12,490	5.9
Construction Laborers	153,220	164,330	11,110	7.3
Cooks, Restaurant	131,480	141,860	10,380	7.9
Industrial Truck and Tractor Operators	83,270	93,190	9,920	11.9

Note: Projections cover Texas; (1) Sorted by numeric employment change
Source: www.projectionscentral.com, State Occupational Projections, 2022–2024 Short-Term Projections

Fastest-Growing Occupations: 2022 – 2024

Occupation[1]	2022 Employment	2024 Projected Employment	Numeric Employment Change	Percent Employment Change
Wind Turbine Service Technicians	5,240	5,990	750	14.3
Information Security Analysts (SOC 2018)	14,170	16,110	1,940	13.7
Solar Photovoltaic Installers	2,240	2,540	300	13.4
Veterinary Technologists and Technicians	16,140	18,200	2,060	12.8
Actuaries	1,810	2,040	230	12.7
Data Scientists	7,340	8,270	930	12.7
Web Developers	6,920	7,790	870	12.6
Veterinarians	6,830	7,670	840	12.3
Veterinary Assistants and Laboratory Animal Caretakers	5,990	6,720	730	12.2
Ushers, Lobby Attendants, and Ticket Takers	9,100	10,190	1,090	12.0

Note: Projections cover Texas; (1) Sorted by percent employment change and excludes occupations with numeric employment change less than 50
Source: www.projectionscentral.com, State Occupational Projections, 2022–2024 Short-Term Projections

CITY FINANCES

City Government Finances

Component	2020 ($000)	2020 ($ per capita)
Total Revenues	391,459	2,142
Total Expenditures	327,152	1,790
Debt Outstanding	345,623	1,891
Cash and Securities[1]	584,715	3,199

Note: (1) Cash and security holdings of a government at the close of its fiscal year, including those of its dependent agencies, utilities, and liquor stores.
Source: U.S. Census Bureau, State & Local Government Finances 2020

City Government Revenue by Source

Source	2020 ($000)	2020 ($ per capita)	2020 (%)
General Revenue			
From Federal Government	10,913	60	2.8
From State Government	1,567	9	0.4
From Local Governments	624	3	0.2
Taxes			
Property	47,562	260	12.1
Sales and Gross Receipts	36,859	202	9.4
Personal Income	0	0	0.0
Corporate Income	0	0	0.0
Motor Vehicle License	0	0	0.0
Other Taxes	2,179	12	0.6
Current Charges	46,933	257	12.0
Liquor Store	0	0	0.0
Utility	195,762	1,071	50.0

Source: U.S. Census Bureau, State & Local Government Finances 2020

City Government Expenditures by Function

Function	2020 ($000)	2020 ($ per capita)	2020 (%)
General Direct Expenditures			
Air Transportation	5,114	28	1.6
Corrections	777	4	0.2
Education	0	0	0.0
Employment Security Administration	0	0	0.0
Financial Administration	4,199	23	1.3
Fire Protection	22,565	123	6.9
General Public Buildings	156	< 1	< 0.1
Governmental Administration, Other	10,476	57	3.2
Health	2,144	11	0.7
Highways	12,721	69	3.9
Hospitals	0	0	0.0
Housing and Community Development	1,627	8	0.5
Interest on General Debt	6,162	33	1.9
Judicial and Legal	2,941	16	0.9
Libraries	4,125	22	1.3
Parking	456	2	0.1
Parks and Recreation	9,945	54	3.0
Police Protection	38,110	208	11.6
Public Welfare	426	2	0.1
Sewerage	16,146	88	4.9
Solid Waste Management	5,254	28	1.6
Veterans' Services	0	0	0.0
Liquor Store	0	0	0.0
Utility	153,562	840	46.9

Source: U.S. Census Bureau, State & Local Government Finances 2020

TAXES

State Corporate Income Tax Rates

State	Tax Rate (%)	Income Brackets ($)	Num. of Brackets	Financial Institution Tax Rate (%)[a]	Federal Income Tax Ded.
Texas	(u)	–	–	(u)	No

Note: Tax rates as of January 1, 2023; (a) Rates listed are the corporate income tax rate applied to financial institutions or excise taxes based on income. Some states have other taxes based upon the value of deposits or shares; (u) Texas imposes a Franchise Tax, otherwise known as margin tax, imposed on entities with more than $1,230,000 total revenues at rate of 0.75%, or 0.375% for entities primarily engaged in retail or wholesale trade, on lesser of 70% of total revenues or 100% of gross receipts after deductions for either compensation or cost of goods sold.
Source: Federation of Tax Administrators, State Corporate Income Tax Rates, January 1, 2023

State Individual Income Tax Rates

State	Tax Rate (%)	Income Brackets ($)	Personal Exemptions ($) Single	Personal Exemptions ($) Married	Personal Exemptions ($) Depend.	Standard Ded. ($) Single	Standard Ded. ($) Married
Texas				– No state income tax –			

Note: Tax rates as of January 1, 2023; Local- and county-level taxes are not included
Source: Federation of Tax Administrators, State Individual Income Tax Rates, January 1, 2023

Various State Sales and Excise Tax Rates

State	State Sales Tax (%)	Gasoline[1] ($/gal.)	Cigarette[2] ($/pack)	Spirits[3] ($/gal.)	Wine[4] ($/gal.)	Beer[5] ($/gal.)	Recreational Marijuana (%)
Texas	6.25	0.20	1.41	2.40	0.20	0.19	Not legal

Note: All tax rates as of January 1, 2023; (1) The American Petroleum Institute has developed a methodology for determining the average tax rate on a gallon of fuel. Rates may include any of the following: excise taxes, environmental fees, storage tank fees, other fees or taxes, general sales tax, and local taxes; (2) The federal excise tax of $1.0066 per pack and local taxes are not included; (3) Rates are those applicable to off-premise sales of 40% alcohol by volume (a.b.v.) distilled spirits in 750ml containers. Local excise taxes are excluded; (4) Rates are those applicable to off-premise sales of 11% a.b.v. non-carbonated wine in 750ml containers; (5) Rates are those applicable to off-premise sales of 4.7% a.b.v. beer in 12 ounce containers.
Source: Tax Foundation, 2023 Facts & Figures: How Does Your State Compare?

State Business Tax Climate Index Rankings

State	Overall Rank	Corporate Tax Rank	Individual Income Tax Rank	Sales Tax Rank	Property Tax Rank	Unemployment Insurance Tax Rank
Texas	13	47	7	37	38	12

Note: The index is a measure of how each state's tax laws affect economic performance. The lower the rank, the more favorable a state's tax system is for business. States without a given tax are given a ranking of 1. The scores/rankings for the District of Columbia do not affect other states. The 2023 index represents the tax climate as of July 1, 2022.
Source: Tax Foundation, State Business Tax Climate Index 2023

TRANSPORTATION

Means of Transportation to Work

Area	Car/Truck/Van Drove Alone	Car/Truck/Van Carpooled	Public Transportation Bus	Public Transportation Subway	Public Transportation Railroad	Bicycle	Walked	Other Means	Worked at Home
City	80.7	10.2	0.7	0.0	0.0	0.1	1.3	1.2	5.7
MSA[1]	81.3	9.1	0.4	0.0	0.0	0.1	1.6	1.2	6.3
U.S.	73.2	8.6	2.0	1.6	0.5	0.5	2.5	1.5	9.7

Note: Figures are percentages and cover workers 16 years of age and older; (1) Figures cover the Brownsville-Harlingen, TX Metropolitan Statistical Area
Source: U.S. Census Bureau, 2017-2021 American Community Survey 5-Year Estimates

Travel Time to Work

Area	Less Than 10 Minutes	10 to 19 Minutes	20 to 29 Minutes	30 to 44 Minutes	45 to 59 Minutes	60 to 89 Minutes	90 Minutes or More
City	8.7	42.9	28.9	14.3	2.5	1.7	1.0
MSA[1]	12.8	40.5	25.7	15.0	3.4	1.6	1.0
U.S.	12.4	28.5	21.0	20.9	8.2	6.2	2.9

Note: Note: Figures are percentages and include workers 16 years old and over; (1) Figures cover the Brownsville-Harlingen, TX Metropolitan Statistical Area
Source: U.S. Census Bureau, 2017-2021 American Community Survey 5-Year Estimates

Key Congestion Measures

Measure	1990	2000	2010	2015	2020
Annual Hours of Delay, Total (000)	304	1,273	3,121	4,135	3,788
Annual Hours of Delay, Per Auto Commuter	5	12	24	28	23
Annual Congestion Cost, Per Auto Commuter ($)	72	219	436	536	504

Note: Covers the Brownsville TX urban area
Source: Texas A&M Transportation Institute, 2021 Urban Mobility Report

Freeway Travel Time Index

Measure	1985	1990	1995	2000	2005	2010	2015	2020
Urban Area Index[1]	1.02	1.03	1.04	1.08	1.13	1.14	1.13	1.10
Urban Area Rank[1,2]	96	96	99	97	81	71	83	29

Note: Freeway Travel Time Index—the ratio of travel time in the peak period to the travel time at free-flow conditions. For example, a value of 1.30 indicates a 20-minute free-flow trip takes 26 minutes in the peak (20 minutes x 1.30 = 26 minutes); (1) Covers the Brownsville TX urban area; (2) Rank is based on 101 larger urban areas (#1 = highest travel time index)
Source: Texas A&M Transportation Institute, 2021 Urban Mobility Report

Public Transportation

Agency Name / Mode of Transportation	Vehicles Operated in Maximum Service[1]	Annual Unlinked Passenger Trips[2] (in thous.)	Annual Passenger Miles[3] (in thous.)
City of Brownsville dba Brownsville Metro			
Bus (directly operated)	16	603.9	2,737.8
Demand Response (directly operated)	8	18.9	96.4

Note: (1) Number of revenue vehicles operated by the given mode and type of service to meet the annual maximum service requirement. This is the revenue vehicle count during the peak season of the year; on the week and day that maximum service is provided. Vehicles operated in maximum service (VOMS) exclude atypical days and one-time special events; (2) Number of passengers who boarded public transportation vehicles. Passengers are counted each time they board a vehicle no matter how many vehicles they use to travel from their origin to their destination. (3) Sum of the distances ridden by all passengers during the entire fiscal year.
Source: Federal Transit Administration, National Transit Database, 2021

Air Transportation

Airport Name and Code / Type of Service	Passenger Airlines[1]	Passenger Enplanements	Freight Carriers[2]	Freight (lbs)
Brownsville South Padre Island International Airport (BRO)				
Domestic service (U.S. carriers - 2022)	7	127,180	6	757,263
International service (U.S. carriers - 2021)	2	11,703	2	15,335

Note: (1) Includes all U.S.-based major, minor and commuter airlines that carried at least one passenger during the year; (2) Includes all U.S.-based airlines and freight carriers that transported at least one pound of freight during the year.
Source: Bureau of Transportation Statistics, The Intermodal Transportation Database, Air Carriers: T-100 Domestic Market (U.S. Carriers), 2022; Bureau of Transportation Statistics, The Intermodal Transportation Database, Air Carriers: T-100 International Market (U.S. Carriers), 2021

BUSINESSES

Major Business Headquarters

Company Name	Industry	Rankings Fortune[1]	Forbes[2]
No companies listed	-	-	-

Note: (1) Companies that produce a 10-K are ranked 1 to 500 based on 2021 revenue; (2) All private companies with at least $2 billion in annual revenue through the end of their most current fiscal year are ranked 1 to 246; companies listed are headquartered in the city; dashes indicate no ranking
Source: Fortune, "Fortune 500," 2022; Forbes, "America's Largest Private Companies," 2022

Living Environment

COST OF LIVING

Cost of Living Index

Composite Index	Groceries	Housing	Utilities	Transportation	Health Care	Misc. Goods/Services
77.1	78.8	60.6	107.3	87.7	82.3	78.5

Note: The Cost of Living Index measures regional differences in the cost of consumer goods and services, excluding taxes and non-consumer expenditures, for professional and managerial households in the top income quintile. It is based on more than 50,000 prices covering almost 60 different items for which prices are collected three times a year by chambers of commerce, economic development organizations or university applied economic centers in each participating urban area. The numbers shown should be read as a percentage above or below the national average of 100. For example, a value of 115.4 in the groceries column indicates that grocery prices are 15.4% higher than the national average. Small differences in the index numbers should not be interpreted as significant; Figures cover the Harlingen TX urban area.
Source: The Council for Community and Economic Research, Cost of Living Index, 2022

Grocery Prices

Area[1]	T-Bone Steak ($/pound)	Frying Chicken ($/pound)	Whole Milk ($/half gal.)	Eggs ($/dozen)	Orange Juice ($/64 oz.)	Coffee ($/11.5 oz.)
City[2]	10.74	1.02	2.10	2.06	3.34	3.77
Avg.	13.81	1.59	2.43	2.25	3.85	4.95
Min.	10.17	0.90	1.51	1.30	2.90	3.46
Max.	19.35	4.32	3.30	4.32	5.31	8.59

*Note: (1) Values for the local area are compared with the average, minimum and maximum values for all 286 areas in the Cost of Living Index; (2) Figures cover the Harlingen TX urban area; **T-Bone Steak** (price per pound); **Frying Chicken** (price per pound, whole fryer); **Whole Milk** (half gallon carton); **Eggs** (price per dozen, Grade A, large); **Orange Juice** (64 oz. Tropicana or Florida Natural); **Coffee** (11.5 oz. can, vacuum-packed, Maxwell House, Hills Bros, or Folgers).*
Source: The Council for Community and Economic Research, Cost of Living Index, 2022

Housing and Utility Costs

Area[1]	New Home Price ($)	Apartment Rent ($/month)	All Electric ($/month)	Part Electric ($/month)	Other Energy ($/month)	Telephone ($/month)
City[2]	274,631	757	-	139.72	54.99	196.56
Avg.	450,913	1,371	176.41	99.93	76.96	190.22
Min.	229,283	546	100.84	31.56	27.15	174.27
Max.	2,434,977	4,569	356.86	249.59	272.24	208.31

*Note: (1) Values for the local area are compared with the average, minimum and maximum values for all 286 areas in the Cost of Living Index; (2) Figures cover the Harlingen TX urban area; **New Home Price** (2,400 sf living area, 8,000 sf lot, in urban area with full utilities); **Apartment Rent** (950 sf 2 bedroom/1.5 or 2 bath, unfurnished, excluding all utilities except water); **All Electric** (average monthly cost for an all-electric home); **Part Electric** (average monthly cost for a part-electric home); **Other Energy** (average monthly cost for natural gas, fuel oil, coal, wood, and any other forms of energy except electricity); **Telephone** (price includes the base monthly rate plus taxes and fees for three lines of mobile phone service).*
Source: The Council for Community and Economic Research, Cost of Living Index, 2022

Health Care, Transportation, and Other Costs

Area[1]	Doctor ($/visit)	Dentist ($/visit)	Optometrist ($/visit)	Gasoline ($/gallon)	Beauty Salon ($/visit)	Men's Shirt ($)
City[2]	90.00	91.61	73.32	3.46	23.67	13.19
Avg.	124.91	107.77	117.66	3.86	43.31	34.21
Min.	36.61	58.25	51.79	2.90	22.18	13.05
Max.	250.21	162.58	371.96	5.54	85.61	63.54

*Note: (1) Values for the local area are compared with the average, minimum and maximum values for all 286 areas in the Cost of Living Index; (2) Figures cover the Harlingen TX urban area; **Doctor** (general practitioners routine exam of an established patient); **Dentist** (adult teeth cleaning and periodic oral examination); **Optometrist** (full vision eye exam for established adult patient); **Gasoline** (one gallon regular unleaded, national brand, including all taxes, cash price at self-service pump if available); **Beauty Salon** (woman's shampoo, trim, and blow-dry); **Men's Shirt** (cotton/polyester dress shirt, pinpoint weave, long sleeves).*
Source: The Council for Community and Economic Research, Cost of Living Index, 2022

HOUSING

Homeownership Rate

Area	2015 (%)	2016 (%)	2017 (%)	2018 (%)	2019 (%)	2020 (%)	2021 (%)	2022 (%)
MSA[1]	n/a	n/a	n/a	n/a	n/a	n/a	n/a	n/a
U.S.	63.7	63.4	63.9	64.4	64.6	66.6	65.5	65.8

Note: (1) Figures cover the Brownsville-Harlingen, TX Metropolitan Statistical Area; n/a not available
Source: U.S. Census Bureau, Housing Vacancies and Homeownership Annual Statistics: 2015-2022

House Price Index (HPI)

Area	National Ranking[2]	Quarterly Change (%)	One-Year Change (%)	Five-Year Change (%)	Since 1991Q1 (%)
MSA[1]	n/a	n/a	n/a	n/a	n/a
U.S.[3]	–	0.34	8.41	58.44	289.08

Note: The HPI is a weighted repeat sales index. It measures average price changes in repeat sales or refinancings on the same properties. This information is obtained by reviewing repeat mortgage transactions on single-family properties whose mortgages have been purchased or securitized by Fannie Mae or Freddie Mac since January 1975; (1) Figures cover the , Metropolitan Statistical Area; (2) Rankings are based on annual percentage change for all metro areas containing at least 15,000 transactions over the last 10 years and ranges from 1 to 257; (3) figures based on a weighted average of Census Division estimates using a seasonally adjusted, purchase-only index; all figures are for the period ending December 31, 2022; n/a not available
Source: Federal Housing Finance Agency, Change in FHFA Metropolitan Area House Price Indexes, 2022Q4

Median Single-Family Home Prices

Area	2020	2021	2022p	Percent Change 2021 to 2022
MSA[1]	n/a	n/a	n/a	n/a
U.S. Average	300.2	357.1	392.6	9.9

Note: Figures are median sales prices of existing single-family homes in thousands of dollars; (p) preliminary; n/a not available; (1) Figures cover the Brownsville-Harlingen, TX Metropolitan Statistical Area
Source: National Association of Realtors, Median Sales Price of Existing Single-Family Homes for Metropolitan Areas, 4th Quarter 2022

Qualifying Income Based on Median Sales Price of Existing Single-Family Homes

Area	With 5% Down ($)	With 10% Down ($)	With 20% Down ($)
MSA[1]	n/a	n/a	n/a
U.S. Average	112,234	106,237	94,513

Note: Figures are preliminary; Qualifying income is based on a mortgage rate of 6.77%. Monthly principal and interest payment is limited to 25% of income; n/a not available; (1) Figures cover the Brownsville-Harlingen, TX Metropolitan Statistical Area
Source: National Association of Realtors, Qualifying Income Based on Median Sales Price of Existing Single-Family Homes for Metropolitan Areas, 4th Quarter 2022

Home Value

Area	Under $100,000	$100,000 -$199,999	$200,000 -$299,999	$300,000 -$399,999	$400,000 -$499,999	$500,000 -$999,999	$1,000,000 or more	Median ($)
City	53.5	34.4	9.1	1.4	0.6	0.8	0.1	95,700
MSA[1]	53.6	31.8	8.9	2.9	1.1	1.4	0.2	94,200
U.S.	16.2	24.2	20.1	13.6	8.3	13.6	4.1	244,900

Note: Figures are percentages except for median and cover owner-occupied housing units; (1) Figures cover the Brownsville-Harlingen, TX Metropolitan Statistical Area
Source: U.S. Census Bureau, 2017-2021 American Community Survey 5-Year Estimates

Year Housing Structure Built

Area	2020 or Later	2010 -2019	2000 -2009	1990 -1999	1980 -1989	1970 -1979	1960 -1969	1950 -1959	1940 -1949	Before 1940	Median Year
City	0.2	12.9	22.9	18.0	14.8	15.5	6.2	4.4	2.8	2.3	1992
MSA[1]	0.2	11.0	22.2	17.0	17.9	16.0	5.7	5.3	2.6	2.1	1990
U.S.	0.2	7.3	13.6	13.6	13.2	14.8	10.3	10.0	4.7	12.2	1979

Note: Figures are percentages except for Median Year; Note: (1) Figures cover the Brownsville-Harlingen, TX Metropolitan Statistical Area
Source: U.S. Census Bureau, 2017-2021 American Community Survey 5-Year Estimates

Gross Monthly Rent

Area	Under $500	$500 -$999	$1,000 -$1,499	$1,500 -$1,999	$2,000 -$2,499	$2,500 -$2,999	$3,000 and up	Median ($)
City	20.5	54.9	19.9	3.9	0.7	0.2	0.0	794
MSA[1]	18.4	59.0	18.3	3.2	0.7	0.2	0.2	785
U.S.	8.1	30.5	30.8	16.8	7.3	3.1	3.5	1,163

Note: Figures are percentages except for median; Gross rent is the contract rent plus the estimated average monthly cost of utilities (electricity, gas, and water and sewer) and fuels (oil, coal, kerosene, wood, etc.) if these are paid by the renter (or paid for the renter by someone else); (1) Figures cover the Brownsville-Harlingen, TX Metropolitan Statistical Area
Source: U.S. Census Bureau, 2017-2021 American Community Survey 5-Year Estimates

HEALTH

Health Risk Factors

Category	MSA[1] (%)	U.S. (%)
Adults aged 18–64 who have any kind of health care coverage	n/a	90.9
Adults who reported being in good or better health	n/a	85.2
Adults who have been told they have high blood cholesterol	n/a	35.7
Adults who have been told they have high blood pressure	n/a	32.4
Adults who are current smokers	n/a	14.4
Adults who currently use e-cigarettes	n/a	6.7
Adults who currently use chewing tobacco, snuff, or snus	n/a	3.5
Adults who are heavy drinkers[2]	n/a	6.3
Adults who are binge drinkers[3]	n/a	15.4
Adults who are overweight (BMI 25.0 - 29.9)	n/a	34.4
Adults who are obese (BMI 30.0 - 99.8)	n/a	33.9
Adults who participated in any physical activities in the past month	n/a	76.3

Note: (1) Figures for the Brownsville-Harlingen, TX Metropolitan Statistical Area were not available.
(2) Heavy drinkers are classified as adult men having more than 14 drinks per week and adult women having more than 7 drinks per week; (3) Binge drinkers are classified as males having five or more drinks on one occasion or females having four or more drinks on one occasion
Source: Centers for Disease Control and Prevention, Behavioral Risk Factor Surveillance System, SMART: Selected Metropolitan Area Risk Trends, 2021

Acute and Chronic Health Conditions

Category	MSA[1] (%)	U.S. (%)
Adults who have ever been told they had a heart attack	n/a	4.0
Adults who have ever been told they have angina or coronary heart disease	n/a	3.8
Adults who have ever been told they had a stroke	n/a	3.0
Adults who have ever been told they have asthma	n/a	14.9
Adults who have ever been told they have arthritis	n/a	25.8
Adults who have ever been told they have diabetes[2]	n/a	10.9
Adults who have ever been told they had skin cancer	n/a	6.6
Adults who have ever been told they had any other types of cancer	n/a	7.5
Adults who have ever been told they have COPD	n/a	6.1
Adults who have ever been told they have kidney disease	n/a	3.0
Adults who have ever been told they have a form of depression	n/a	20.5

Note: (1) Figures for the Brownsville-Harlingen, TX Metropolitan Statistical Area were not available.
(2) Figures do not include pregnancy-related, borderline, or pre-diabetes
Source: Centers for Disease Control and Prevention, Behavioral Risk Factor Surveillance System, SMART: Selected Metropolitan Area Risk Trends, 2021

Health Screening and Vaccination Rates

Category	MSA[1] (%)	U.S. (%)
Adults who have ever been tested for HIV	n/a	34.9
Adults who have had their blood cholesterol checked within the last five years	n/a	85.2
Adults aged 65+ who have had flu shot within the past year	n/a	68.6
Adults aged 65+ who have ever had a pneumonia vaccination	n/a	71.0

Note: (1) Figures for the Brownsville-Harlingen, TX Metropolitan Statistical Area were not available.
Source: Centers for Disease Control and Prevention, Behavioral Risk Factor Surveillance System, SMART: Selected Metropolitan Area Risk Trends, 2021

Disability Status

Category	MSA[1] (%)	U.S. (%)
Adults who reported being deaf	n/a	7.2
Are you blind or have serious difficulty seeing, even when wearing glasses?	n/a	4.8
Are you limited in any way in any of your usual activities due to arthritis?	n/a	11.1
Do you have difficulty doing errands alone?	n/a	7.0
Do you have difficulty dressing or bathing?	n/a	3.6
Do you have serious difficulty concentrating/remembering/making decisions?	n/a	12.1
Do you have serious difficulty walking or climbing stairs?	n/a	12.8

Note: (1) Figures for the Brownsville-Harlingen, TX Metropolitan Statistical Area were not available.
Source: Centers for Disease Control and Prevention, Behavioral Risk Factor Surveillance System, SMART: Selected Metropolitan Area Risk Trends, 2021

Mortality Rates for the Top 10 Causes of Death in the U.S.

ICD-10[a] Sub-Chapter	ICD-10[a] Code	Crude Mortality Rate[1] per 100,000 population County[2]	U.S.
Malignant neoplasms	C00-C97	123.9	182.6
Ischaemic heart diseases	I20-I25	110.2	113.1
Other forms of heart disease	I30-I51	36.2	64.4
Other degenerative diseases of the nervous system	G30-G31	44.6	51.0
Cerebrovascular diseases	I60-I69	32.9	47.8
Other external causes of accidental injury	W00-X59	14.4	46.4
Chronic lower respiratory diseases	J40-J47	17.7	45.7
Organic, including symptomatic, mental disorders	F01-F09	12.9	35.9
Hypertensive diseases	I10-I15	36.4	35.0
Diabetes mellitus	E10-E14	39.0	29.6

Note: (a) ICD-10 = International Classification of Diseases 10th Revision; (1) Crude mortality rates are a three-year average covering 2019-2021; (2) Figures cover Cameron County.
Source: Centers for Disease Control and Prevention, National Center for Health Statistics. National Vital Statistics System, Mortality 2018-2021 on CDC WONDER Online Database

Mortality Rates for Selected Causes of Death

ICD-10[a] Sub-Chapter	ICD-10[a] Code	Crude Mortality Rate[1] per 100,000 population County[2]	U.S.
Assault	X85-Y09	3.1	7.0
Diseases of the liver	K70-K76	30.2	19.8
Human immunodeficiency virus (HIV) disease	B20-B24	Unreliable	1.5
Influenza and pneumonia	J09-J18	11.7	14.7
Intentional self-harm	X60-X84	7.6	14.3
Malnutrition	E40-E46	6.3	4.3
Obesity and other hyperalimentation	E65-E68	1.9	3.0
Renal failure	N17-N19	21.3	15.7
Transport accidents	V01-V99	10.5	13.6
Viral hepatitis	B15-B19	Unreliable	1.2

Note: (a) ICD-10 = International Classification of Diseases 10th Revision; (1) Crude mortality rates are a three-year average covering 2019-2021; (2) Figures cover Cameron County; Data are suppressed when the data meet the criteria for confidentiality constraints; Crude mortality rates are flagged as unreliable when the rate would be calculated with a numerator of 20 or less.
Source: Centers for Disease Control and Prevention, National Center for Health Statistics. National Vital Statistics System, Mortality 2018-2021 on CDC WONDER Online Database

Health Insurance Coverage

Area	With Health Insurance	With Private Health Insurance	With Public Health Insurance	Without Health Insurance	Population Under Age 19 Without Health Insurance
City	69.2	37.3	35.7	30.8	18.5
MSA[1]	71.5	38.4	38.3	28.5	17.1
U.S.	91.2	67.8	35.4	8.8	5.3

Note: Figures are percentages that cover the civilian noninstitutionalized population; (1) Figures cover the Brownsville-Harlingen, TX Metropolitan Statistical Area
Source: U.S. Census Bureau, 2017-2021 American Community Survey 5-Year Estimates

Number of Medical Professionals

Area	MDs[3]	DOs[3,4]	Dentists	Podiatrists	Chiropractors	Optometrists
County[1] (number)	590	30	133	13	33	28
County[1] (rate[2])	140.1	7.1	31.4	3.1	7.8	6.6
U.S. (rate[2])	289.3	23.5	72.5	6.2	28.7	17.4

Note: Data as of 2021 unless noted; (1) Data covers Cameron County; (2) Rate per 100,000 population; (3) Data as of 2020 and includes all active, non-federal physicians; (4) Doctor of Osteopathic Medicine
Source: U.S. Department of Health and Human Services, Health Resources and Services Administration, Bureau of Health Professions, Area Resource File (ARF) 2021-2022

EDUCATION

Public School District Statistics

District Name	Schls	Pupils	Pupil/Teacher Ratio	Minority Pupils[1] (%)	LEP/ELL[2] (%)	IEP[3] (%)
BROWNSVILLE ISD	56	38,448	14.5	98.9	30.1	13.4

Note: Table includes school districts with 2,000 or more students; (1) Percentage of students that are not non-Hispanic white; (2) Percentage of students that are Limited English Proficient or English Language Learners (2018-19); (3) Percentage of students that have an Individualized Education Program (2019-20).
Source: U.S. Department of Education, National Center for Education Statistics, Common Core of Data, Local Education Agency (School District) Universe Survey: School Year 2021-2022

Best High Schools

According to *U.S. News,* Brownsville is home to three of the top 500 high schools in the U.S.: **IDEA Frontier College Preparatory** (#106); **Brownsville Early College High School** (#163); **IDEA Brownsville College Preparatory** (#260). Nearly 18,000 public, magnet and charter schools were ranked based on their performance on state assessments and how well they prepare students for college. *U.S. News & World Report, "Best High Schools 2022"*

Highest Level of Education

Area	Less than H.S.	H.S. Diploma	Some College, No Deg.	Associate Degree	Bachelor's Degree	Master's Degree	Prof. School Degree	Doctorate Degree
City	32.0	24.2	16.0	7.3	14.6	4.7	0.9	0.3
MSA[1]	30.5	26.1	17.1	7.4	13.2	4.4	0.9	0.5
U.S.	11.1	26.5	20.0	8.7	20.6	9.3	2.2	1.5

Note: Figures cover persons age 25 and over; (1) Figures cover the Brownsville-Harlingen, TX Metropolitan Statistical Area
Source: U.S. Census Bureau, 2017-2021 American Community Survey 5-Year Estimates

Educational Attainment by Race

Area	High School Graduate or Higher (%) Total	White	Black	Asian	Hisp.[2]	Bachelor's Degree or Higher (%) Total	White	Black	Asian	Hisp.[2]
City	68.0	67.8	78.7	92.7	66.5	20.5	20.4	37.3	61.2	19.3
MSA[1]	69.5	70.7	82.1	89.3	66.1	19.0	18.7	26.6	59.8	16.2
U.S.	88.9	91.4	87.2	87.6	71.2	33.7	35.5	23.3	55.6	18.4

Note: Figures shown cover persons 25 years old and over; (1) Figures cover the Brownsville-Harlingen, TX Metropolitan Statistical Area; (2) People of Hispanic origin can be of any race
Source: U.S. Census Bureau, 2017-2021 American Community Survey 5-Year Estimates

School Enrollment by Grade and Control

Area	Preschool (%) Public	Private	Kindergarten (%) Public	Private	Grades 1 - 4 (%) Public	Private	Grades 5 - 8 (%) Public	Private	Grades 9 - 12 (%) Public	Private
City	95.8	4.2	92.3	7.7	95.6	4.4	94.7	5.3	97.5	2.5
MSA[1]	95.5	4.5	95.8	4.2	97.0	3.0	96.5	3.5	96.7	3.3
U.S.	58.8	41.2	86.3	13.7	88.3	11.7	88.6	11.4	89.4	10.6

Note: Figures shown cover persons 3 years old and over; (1) Figures cover the Brownsville-Harlingen, TX Metropolitan Statistical Area
Source: U.S. Census Bureau, 2017-2021 American Community Survey 5-Year Estimates

Higher Education

Four-Year Colleges Public	Private Non-profit	Private For-profit	Two-Year Colleges Public	Private Non-profit	Private For-profit	Medical Schools[1]	Law Schools[2]	Voc/Tech[3]
0	0	0	1	0	0	0	0	7

Note: Figures cover institutions located within the Brownsville-Harlingen, TX Metropolitan Statistical Area and include main campuses only; (1) includes schools accredited by the Liaison Committee on Medical Education and the American Osteopathic Association's Commission on Osteopathic College Accreditation; (2) includes ABA-accredited schools, schools with provisional ABA accreditation, and state accredited schools; (3) includes all schools with programs that are less than 2 years.
Source: National Center for Education Statistics, Integrated Postsecondary Education System (IPEDS), 2021-22; Wikipedia, List of Medical Schools in the United States, accessed April 10, 2023; Wikipedia, List of Law Schools in the United States, accessed April 10, 2023

Brownsville, Texas

EMPLOYERS

Major Employers

Company Name	Industry
Abundant Life Home Health	Home health care
All Star Metals	Ship recycling
Brownsville ISD	School district
Cameron County	Government, county
City of Brownsville	Government, local
ESCO Marine	Marine yard & ship recycling
HEB Food Stores	Grocery stores
Keppel AmFELS	Drilling rigs & platforms
National Electric Coil	High-voltage generator aftermarket services
Rich SeaPak	Food products supplier
Trico Products	Windshield wiper mfg
U.S. Customs & Border Patrol	Government, federal
University of Texas	Colleges & universities
Valley Baptist Medical Center	General medical & surgical hospitals
Valley Regional Medical Center	General medical & surgical hospitals
Walmart	Retail stores

Note: Companies shown are located within the Brownsville-Harlingen, TX Metropolitan Statistical Area.
Source: Hoovers.com; Wikipedia

PUBLIC SAFETY

Crime Rate

Area	Total Crime	Murder	Rape[3]	Robbery	Aggrav. Assault	Burglary	Larceny-Theft	Motor Vehicle Theft
City	2,250.2	3.8	45.2	83.3	269.6	219.5	1,563.0	65.9
Suburbs[1]	2,358.5	2.5	38.8	39.2	248.9	317.7	1,598.9	112.6
Metro[2]	2,311.6	3.1	41.6	58.3	257.9	275.1	1,583.3	92.3
U.S.	2,356.7	6.5	38.4	73.9	279.7	314.2	1,398.0	246.0

Note: Figures are crimes per 100,000 population; (1) All areas within the metro area that are located outside the city limits; (2) Figures cover the Brownsville-Harlingen, TX Metropolitan Statistical Area; (3) All figures shown were reported using the revised Uniform Crime Reporting (UCR) definition of rape; Due to the transition to the National Incident-Based Reporting System (NIBRS), limited city and metro area data was released for 2021.
Source: FBI Uniform Crime Reports, 2020

Hate Crimes

Area	Number of Quarters Reported	Race/Ethnicity/Ancestry	Religion	Sexual Orientation	Disability	Gender	Gender Identity
City	4	0	0	0	0	0	0
U.S.	4	5,227	1,244	1,110	130	75	266

Note: Due to the transition to the National Incident-Based Reporting System (NIBRS), limited crime data was released for 2021.
Source: Federal Bureau of Investigation, Hate Crime Statistics 2020

Identity Theft Consumer Reports

Area	Reports	Reports per 100,000 Population	Rank[2]
MSA[1]	1,131	268	90
U.S.	1,108,609	339	-

Note: (1) Figures cover the Brownsville-Harlingen, TX Metropolitan Statistical Area; (2) Rank ranges from 1 to 391 where 1 indicates greatest number of identity theft reports per 100,000 population
Source: Federal Trade Commission, Consumer Sentinel Network Data Book 2022

Fraud and Other Consumer Reports

Area	Reports	Reports per 100,000 Population	Rank[2]
MSA[1]	1,726	409	384
U.S.	4,064,520	1,245	-

Note: (1) Figures cover the Brownsville-Harlingen, TX Metropolitan Statistical Area; (2) Rank ranges from 1 to 391 where 1 indicates greatest number of fraud and other consumer reports per 100,000 population
Source: Federal Trade Commission, Consumer Sentinel Network Data Book 2022

POLITICS

2020 Presidential Election Results

Area	Biden	Trump	Jorgensen	Hawkins	Other
Cameron County	56.0	42.9	0.6	0.3	0.1
U.S.	51.3	46.8	1.2	0.3	0.5

Note: Results are percentages and may not add to 100% due to rounding
Source: Dave Leip's Atlas of U.S. Presidential Elections

SPORTS

Professional Sports Teams

Team Name	League	Year Established
No teams are located in the metro area		

Source: Wikipedia, Major Professional Sports Teams of the United States and Canada, April 12, 2023

CLIMATE

Average and Extreme Temperatures

Temperature	Jan	Feb	Mar	Apr	May	Jun	Jul	Aug	Sep	Oct	Nov	Dec	Yr.
Extreme High (°F)	93	94	106	102	102	102	101	102	99	96	97	94	106
Average High (°F)	70	73	78	83	87	91	93	93	90	85	78	72	83
Average Temp. (°F)	60	63	69	75	80	83	84	85	82	76	68	63	74
Average Low (°F)	51	53	59	66	72	75	76	76	73	66	59	53	65
Extreme Low (°F)	19	22	32	38	52	60	67	63	56	40	33	16	16

Note: Figures cover the years 1948-1990
Source: National Climatic Data Center, International Station Meteorological Climate Summary, 9/96

Average Precipitation/Snowfall/Humidity

Precip./Humidity	Jan	Feb	Mar	Apr	May	Jun	Jul	Aug	Sep	Oct	Nov	Dec	Yr.
Avg. Precip. (in.)	1.4	1.4	0.6	1.5	2.5	2.8	1.8	2.6	5.6	3.2	1.5	1.1	25.8
Avg. Snowfall (in.)	Tr	Tr	0	0	0	0	0	0	0	0	Tr	Tr	Tr
Avg. Rel. Hum. 6am (%)	88	89	88	89	90	91	92	92	91	89	87	87	89
Avg. Rel. Hum. 3pm (%)	62	60	57	58	60	59	54	55	60	58	59	61	59

Note: Figures cover the years 1948-1990; Tr = Trace amounts (<0.05 in. of rain; <0.5 in. of snow)
Source: National Climatic Data Center, International Station Meteorological Climate Summary, 9/96

Weather Conditions

Temperature			Daytime Sky			Precipitation		
32°F & below	45°F & below	90°F & above	Clear	Partly cloudy	Cloudy	0.01 inch or more precip.	0.1 inch or more snow/ice	Thunder-storms
2	30	116	86	180	99	72	0	27

Note: Figures are average number of days per year and cover the years 1948-1990
Source: National Climatic Data Center, International Station Meteorological Climate Summary, 9/96

HAZARDOUS WASTE

Superfund Sites

The Brownsville-Harlingen, TX metro area has no sites on the EPA's Superfund Final National Priorities List. There are a total of 1,165 Superfund sites with a status of proposed or final on the list in the U.S. *U.S. Environmental Protection Agency, National Priorities List, April 12, 2023*

AIR QUALITY

Air Quality Trends: Ozone

	1990	1995	2000	2005	2010	2015	2018	2019	2020	2021
MSA[1]	n/a	n/a	n/a	n/a	n/a	n/a	n/a	n/a	n/a	n/a
U.S.	0.087	0.089	0.081	0.080	0.072	0.067	0.069	0.065	0.065	0.067

Note: (1) Data covers the Brownsville-Harlingen, TX Metropolitan Statistical Area; n/a not available. The values shown are the composite ozone concentration averages among trend sites based on the highest fourth daily maximum 8-hour concentration in parts per million. These trends are based on sites having an adequate record of monitoring data during the trend period. Data from exceptional events are included.
Source: U.S. Environmental Protection Agency, Air Quality Monitoring Information, "Air Quality Trends by City, 1990-2021"

Air Quality Index

Area	Percent of Days when Air Quality was...[2]					AQI Statistics[2]	
	Good	Moderate	Unhealthy for Sensitive Groups	Unhealthy	Very Unhealthy	Maximum	Median
MSA[1]	64.4	35.6	0.0	0.0	0.0	99	43

Note: (1) Data covers the Brownsville-Harlingen, TX Metropolitan Statistical Area; (2) Based on 365 days with AQI data in 2021. Air Quality Index (AQI) is an index for reporting daily air quality. EPA calculates the AQI for five major air pollutants regulated by the Clean Air Act: ground-level ozone, particle pollution (aka particulate matter), carbon monoxide, sulfur dioxide, and nitrogen dioxide. The AQI runs from 0 to 500. The higher the AQI value, the greater the level of air pollution and the greater the health concern. There are six AQI categories: "Good" AQI is between 0 and 50. Air quality is considered satisfactory; "Moderate" AQI is between 51 and 100. Air quality is acceptable; "Unhealthy for Sensitive Groups" When AQI values are between 101 and 150, members of sensitive groups may experience health effects; "Unhealthy" When AQI values are between 151 and 200 everyone may begin to experience health effects; "Very Unhealthy" AQI values between 201 and 300 trigger a health alert; "Hazardous" AQI values over 300 trigger warnings of emergency conditions (not shown).
Source: U.S. Environmental Protection Agency, Air Quality Index Report, 2021

Brownsville, Texas

Air Quality Index Pollutants

Area	\multicolumn{6}{c	}{Percent of Days when AQI Pollutant was...[2]}
	Carbon Monoxide	Nitrogen Dioxide	Ozone	Sulfur Dioxide	Particulate Matter 2.5	Particulate Matter 10
MSA[1]	0.0	0.0	31.2	(3)	68.8	0.0

Note: (1) Data covers the Brownsville-Harlingen, TX Metropolitan Statistical Area; (2) Based on 365 days with AQI data in 2021. The Air Quality Index (AQI) is an index for reporting daily air quality. EPA calculates the AQI for five major air pollutants regulated by the Clean Air Act: ground-level ozone, particle pollution (also known as particulate matter), carbon monoxide, sulfur dioxide, and nitrogen dioxide. The AQI runs from 0 to 500. The higher the AQI value, the greater the level of air pollution and the greater the health concern; (3) Sulfur dioxide is no longer included in this table (as of December 8, 2021) because SO_2 concentrations tend to be very localized and not necessarily representative of broad geographical areas like counties and CBSAs.
Source: U.S. Environmental Protection Agency, Air Quality Index Report, 2021

Maximum Air Pollutant Concentrations: Particulate Matter, Ozone, CO and Lead

	Particulate Matter 10 (ug/m^3)	Particulate Matter 2.5 Wtd AM (ug/m^3)	Particulate Matter 2.5 24-Hr (ug/m^3)	Ozone (ppm)	Carbon Monoxide (ppm)	Lead (ug/m^3)
MSA[1] Level	n/a	9.2	24	0.056	n/a	n/a
NAAQS[2]	150	15	35	0.075	9	0.15
Met NAAQS[2]	n/a	Yes	Yes	Yes	n/a	n/a

Note: (1) Data covers the Brownsville-Harlingen, TX Metropolitan Statistical Area; Data from exceptional events are included; (2) National Ambient Air Quality Standards; ppm = parts per million; ug/m^3 = micrograms per cubic meter; n/a not available.
Concentrations: Particulate Matter 10 (coarse particulate)—highest second maximum 24-hour concentration; Particulate Matter 2.5 Wtd AM (fine particulate)—highest weighted annual mean concentration; Particulate Matter 2.5 24-Hour (fine particulate)—highest 98th percentile 24-hour concentration; Ozone—highest fourth daily maximum 8-hour concentration; Carbon Monoxide—highest second maximum non-overlapping 8-hour concentration; Lead—maximum running 3-month average
Source: U.S. Environmental Protection Agency, Air Quality Monitoring Information, "Air Quality Statistics by City, 2021"

Maximum Air Pollutant Concentrations: Nitrogen Dioxide and Sulfur Dioxide

	Nitrogen Dioxide AM (ppb)	Nitrogen Dioxide 1-Hr (ppb)	Sulfur Dioxide AM (ppb)	Sulfur Dioxide 1-Hr (ppb)	Sulfur Dioxide 24-Hr (ppb)
MSA[1] Level	n/a	n/a	n/a	n/a	n/a
NAAQS[2]	53	100	30	75	140
Met NAAQS[2]	n/a	n/a	n/a	n/a	n/a

Note: (1) Data covers the Brownsville-Harlingen, TX Metropolitan Statistical Area; Data from exceptional events are included; (2) National Ambient Air Quality Standards; ppm = parts per million; ug/m^3 = micrograms per cubic meter; n/a not available.
Concentrations: Nitrogen Dioxide AM—highest arithmetic mean concentration; Nitrogen Dioxide 1-Hr—highest 98th percentile 1-hour daily maximum concentration; Sulfur Dioxide AM—highest annual mean concentration; Sulfur Dioxide 1-Hr—highest 99th percentile 1-hour daily maximum concentration; Sulfur Dioxide 24-Hr—highest second maximum 24-hour concentration
Source: U.S. Environmental Protection Agency, Air Quality Monitoring Information, "Air Quality Statistics by City, 2021"

Cape Coral, Florida

Background

Tucked along Florida's Gulf Coast 71 miles south of Sarasota, Cape Coral is a mid-twentieth century community grown from a development launched in 1957. Today, at 115 square miles, it is Florida's third-largest city by land mass and the most populous city between Tampa and Miami. To the east across the Caloosahatchee River lies Fort Myers, and to the west across Pine Island and Pine Island sound lie the fabled barrier islands of Captiva and Sanibel.

Baltimore brothers Leonard and Jack Rosen purchased the former Redfish Point for $678,000 in 1957 and renamed the property Cape Coral. By June of the following year "the Cape," as it is known, was receiving its first residents. The city incorporated in 1970 when its population reached 11,470.

Despite the city's relative youth, this self-named "Waterfront Wonderland" has developed an interest in its roots. It fosters a Cape Coral Historical Museum that is housed in the original snack bar from the local country club; one of its oldest historical documents is the Cape's 1961 phone book.

Four hundred precious miles of salt and fresh water canals slice through the city, providing water access to abundant recreational boaters and numerous opportunities for waterfront living.

Following the economic downturn in 2008, Cape Coral has rebounded, named a "most improved" housing market in a recent National Association of Builders report. The Army Reserve purchased a 15-acre Cape Coral site for use as an Army Reserve Training Center for local reservists.

Industry-wise, Cape Coral has Foreign Trade Zones in two of its three industrial parks, the 92.5-acre North Cape Industrial Park—home to light manufacturers, service industry and warehouses—and the Mid Cape Commerce Park which, at 143.37 acres, is comprised of service industries and warehouses.

A VA Clinic was recently built by the U.S. Dept. of Veteran's Affairs at the Hancock Creek Commerce Park and Indian Oaks Trade Centre. It provides a full range of services ranging from mental health and diagnostic radiology to urology and a full complement of imaging services such as CT scans and nuclear medicine. It is the centerpiece of a Veterans Investment Zone initiative designed to draw office, medical parks, assisted living facilities and the like.

Today the U.S. Bureau of Labor Statistics tracks the success of this retirement and tourism destination in conjunction with that of nearby Fort Myers, and the region boasts trade, transportation, and utilities as its largest economic sector.

Significant recreational opportunities in the area include the Four Mile Cove Ecological Preserve with its nature trail, picnic area, and warm weather kayak rentals, and The Cape Coral Yacht Club with a fishing pier, beach, and community pool. The 18-hole public Coral Oaks Golf Course (replete with pro shop and pub), and Soccer Complex show the city's diverse recreational opportunities.

To the east of Cape Coral—on the other side of Fort Myers—is both the Florida Gulf Coast University and Southwest Florida International Airport.

Cape Coral's climate borders on perfect, with an average 335 days per year of sunshine (albeit hot and humid ones in summertime). Annual rainfall is 53.37 inches, with the most rain coming in summer. The city dries out from October into May. In 2022, Hurricane Ian ripped through the city causing massive damage and several fatalities.

Rankings

General Rankings

- The Cape Coral metro area was identified as one of America's fastest-growing areas in terms of population and economy by *Forbes*. The area ranked #9 out of 25. The 100 most populous metro areas in the U.S. were evaluated on the following criteria: estimated population growth; employment; economic output; wages; home values. *Forbes, "America's Fastest-Growing Cities 2018," February 28, 2018*

Business/Finance Rankings

- The Brookings Institution ranked the nation's largest cities based on income inequality. Cape Coral was ranked #93 (#1 = greatest inequality). Criteria: the "95/20 ratio," a figure representing the income at which a household earns more than 95 percent of all other households, divided by the income at which a household earns more than only 20 percent of all other households. *Brookings Institution, "Household Income Inequality, Largest Cities of 97 Large U.S. Metro Areas, 2014-2016," February 5, 2018*

- The Brookings Institution ranked the 100 largest metro areas in the U.S. based on income inequality. Cape Coral was ranked #73 (#1 = greatest inequality). Criteria: the "95/20 ratio," a figure representing the income at which a household earns more than 95 percent of all other households, divided by the income at which a household earns more than only 20 percent of all other households. *Brookings Institution, "Household Income Inequality, 100 Largest U.S. Metro Areas, 2014-2016," February 5, 2018*

- The Cape Coral metro area appeared on the Milken Institute "2022 Best Performing Cities" list. Rank: #27 out of 200 large metro areas (population over 250,000). Criteria: job growth; wage and salary growth; high-tech output growth; housing affordability; household broadband access. *Milken Institute, "Best-Performing Cities 2022," March 28, 2022*

- *Forbes* ranked the 200 most populous metro areas to determine the nation's "Best Places for Business and Careers." The Cape Coral metro area was ranked #63. Criteria: costs (business and living); job growth (past and projected); income growth; quality of life; educational attainment (college and high school); projected economic growth; cultural and leisure opportunities; workplace tolerance laws; net migration patterns. *Forbes, "The Best Places for Business and Careers 2019: Seattle Still On Top," October 30, 2019*

Education Rankings

- Personal finance website *WalletHub* analyzed the 150 largest U.S. metropolitan statistical areas to determine where the most educated Americans are putting their degrees to work. Criteria: education levels; percentage of workers with degrees; education quality and attainment gap; public school quality rankings; quality and enrollment of each metro area's universities. Cape Coral was ranked #106 (#1 = most educated city). *www.WalletHub.com, "Most & Least Educated Cities in America," July 18, 2022*

Environmental Rankings

- Cape Coral was highlighted as one of the top 59 cleanest metro areas for short-term particle pollution (24-hour PM 2.5) in the U.S. during 2019 through 2021. Monitors in these cities reported no days with unhealthful PM 2.5 levels. *American Lung Association, "State of the Air 2023," April 19, 2023*

Health/Fitness Rankings

- Cape Coral was identified as a "2022 Spring Allergy Capital." The area ranked #45 out of 100. Three groups of factors were used to identify the most challenging cities for people with allergies during the spring season: annual spring pollen scores; over the counter allergy medicine use; number of board-certified allergy specialists. *Asthma and Allergy Foundation of America, "Spring Allergy Capitals 2022," March 2, 2022*

- Cape Coral was identified as a "2022 Fall Allergy Capital." The area ranked #46 out of 100. Three groups of factors were used to identify the most challenging cities for people with allergies during the fall season: annual fall pollen scores; over the counter allergy medicine use; number of board-certified allergy specialists. *Asthma and Allergy Foundation of America, "Fall Allergy Capitals 2022," March 2, 2022*

- Cape Coral was identified as a "2022 Asthma Capital." The area ranked #13 out of the nation's 100 largest metropolitan areas. Criteria: estimated asthma prevalence; asthma-related mortality; and ER visits due to asthma. Risk factors analyzed but not factored in the rankings: annual pollen score; annual air quality; public smoking laws; access to board-certified asthma specialists; rescue and controller medication use; uninsured rate; poverty rate. *Asthma and Allergy Foundation of America, "Asthma Capitals 2022: The Most Challenging Places to Live With Asthma," September 14, 2022*

Real Estate Rankings

- *WalletHub* compared the most populated U.S. cities to determine which had the best markets for real estate agents. Cape Coral ranked #88 where demand was high and pay was the best. Criteria: sales per agent; annual median wage for real-estate agents; monthly average starting salary for real estate agents; real estate job density and competition; unemployment rate; home turnover rate; housing-market health index; and other relevant metrics. *www.WalletHub.com, "2021 Best Places to Be a Real Estate Agent," May 12, 2021*

- Cape Coral was ranked #5 in the top 20 out of the 100 largest metro areas in terms of house price appreciation in 2022 (#1 = highest rate). *Federal Housing Finance Agency, House Price Index, 4th Quarter 2022*

- Cape Coral was ranked #161 out of 235 metro areas in terms of housing affordability in 2022 by the National Association of Home Builders (#1 = most affordable). Criteria: the share of homes sold in that area affordable to a family earning the local median income, based on standard mortgage underwriting criteria. *National Association of Home Builders®, NAHB-Wells Fargo Housing Opportunity Index, 4th Quarter 2022*

Safety Rankings

- Allstate ranked the 200 largest cities in America in terms of driver safety. Cape Coral ranked #10. Criteria: internal property damage claims over a two-year period from January 2016 to December 2017. The report helps increase the importance of safety and awareness behind the wheel. *Allstate, "Allstate America's Best Drivers Report, 2019" June 24, 2019*

- The National Insurance Crime Bureau ranked 390 metro areas in the U.S. in terms of per capita rates of vehicle theft. The Cape Coral metro area ranked #303 (#1 = highest rate). Criteria: number of vehicle theft offenses per 100,000 inhabitants in 2021. *National Insurance Crime Bureau, "Hot Spots 2021," September 1, 2022*

Seniors/Retirement Rankings

- From its Best Cities for Successful Aging indexes, the Milken Institute generated rankings for metropolitan areas, weighing data in nine categories—health care, wellness, living arrangements, transportation and convenience, financial characteristics, education, employment, community engagement, and overall livability. The Cape Coral metro area was ranked #93 overall in the large metro area category. *Milken Institute, "Best Cities for Successful Aging, 2017" March 14, 2017*

Women/Minorities Rankings

- Personal finance website *WalletHub* compared more than 180 U.S. cities across two key dimensions, "Hispanic Business-Friendliness" and "Hispanic Purchasing Power," to arrive at the most favorable conditions for Hispanic entrepreneurs. Cape Coral was ranked #53 out of 182. Criteria includes: share of Hispanic-Owned Businesses; Hispanic entrepreneurship rate to median annual income of Hispanics; Small Business-Friendliness score; cost of living; and number of Hispanics with at least a bachelor's degree. *WalletHub.com, "2019's Best Cities for Hispanic Entrepreneurs," May 1, 2019*

Business Environment

DEMOGRAPHICS

Population Growth

Area	1990 Census	2000 Census	2010 Census	2020 Census	Population Growth (%) 1990-2020	Population Growth (%) 2010-2020
City	75,507	102,286	154,305	194,016	157.0	25.7
MSA[1]	335,113	440,888	618,754	760,822	127.0	23.0
U.S.	248,709,873	281,421,906	308,745,538	331,449,281	33.3	7.4

Note: (1) Figures cover the Cape Coral-Fort Myers, FL Metropolitan Statistical Area
Source: U.S. Census Bureau, 1990 Census, 2000 Census, 2010 Census, 2020 Census

Race

Area	White Alone[2] (%)	Black Alone[2] (%)	Asian Alone[2] (%)	AIAN[3] Alone[2] (%)	NHOPI[4] Alone[2] (%)	Other Race Alone[2] (%)	Two or More Races (%)
City	72.3	4.3	1.7	0.3	0.1	5.8	15.6
MSA[1]	69.7	7.7	1.7	0.5	0.0	7.5	12.8
U.S.	61.6	12.4	6.0	1.1	0.2	8.4	10.2

Note: (1) Figures cover the Cape Coral-Fort Myers, FL Metropolitan Statistical Area; (2) Alone is defined as not being in combination with one or more other races; (3) American Indian and Alaska Native; (4) Native Hawaiian and Other Pacific Islander
Source: U.S. Census Bureau, 2020 Census

Hispanic or Latino Origin

Area	Total (%)	Mexican (%)	Puerto Rican (%)	Cuban (%)	Other (%)
City	23.2	1.7	4.9	9.7	7.0
MSA[1]	22.6	5.4	4.6	5.7	6.8
U.S.	18.4	11.2	1.8	0.7	4.7

Note: Persons of Hispanic or Latino origin can be of any race; (1) Figures cover the Cape Coral-Fort Myers, FL Metropolitan Statistical Area
Source: U.S. Census Bureau, 2017-2021 American Community Survey 5-Year Estimates

Age

Area	Under Age 5	Age 5–19	Age 20–34	Age 35–44	Age 45–54	Age 55–64	Age 65–74	Age 75–84	Age 85+	Median Age
City	4.5	16.6	14.9	11.3	13.4	16.0	14.5	6.8	2.1	47.2
MSA[1]	4.3	15.4	15.4	10.1	11.0	14.7	16.4	9.7	3.0	49.7
U.S.	5.6	19.2	20.2	12.7	12.4	13.1	10.0	4.9	1.9	38.8

Note: (1) Figures cover the Cape Coral-Fort Myers, FL Metropolitan Statistical Area
Source: U.S. Census Bureau, 2020 Census

Disability by Age

Area	All Ages	Under 18 Years Old	18 to 64 Years Old	65 Years and Over
City	13.4	3.8	9.7	29.3
MSA[1]	13.6	3.9	9.8	26.9
U.S.	12.6	4.4	10.3	33.4

Note: Figures show percent of the civilian noninstitutionalized population that reported having a disability. Disability status is determined from six types of difficulty: vision, hearing, cognitive, ambulatory, self-care, and independent living. For children under 5 years old, hearing and vision difficulty are used to determine disability status. For children between the ages of 5 and 14, disability status is determined from hearing, vision, cognitive, ambulatory, and self-care difficulties. For people aged 15 years and older, they are considered to have a disability if they have difficulty with any one of the six difficulty types; Note: (1) Figures cover the Cape Coral-Fort Myers, FL Metropolitan Statistical Area
Source: U.S. Census Bureau, 2017-2021 American Community Survey 5-Year Estimates

Ancestry

Area	German	Irish	English	American	Italian	Polish	French[2]	Scottish	Dutch
City	14.2	11.5	7.8	12.3	9.6	3.4	2.0	1.5	0.9
MSA[1]	13.5	10.7	8.4	12.5	7.8	3.1	2.1	1.7	1.1
U.S.	12.8	9.6	8.1	5.7	5.0	2.7	2.2	1.6	1.1

Note: Figures are the percentage of the total population reporting a particular ancestry. The nine most commonly reported ancestries in the U.S. are shown. Figures include multiple ancestries (e.g. if a person reported being Irish and Italian, they were included in both columns); (1) Figures cover the Cape Coral-Fort Myers, FL Metropolitan Statistical Area; (2) Excludes Basque
Source: U.S. Census Bureau, 2017-2021 American Community Survey 5-Year Estimates

Cape Coral, Florida

Foreign-born Population

Area	Any Foreign Country	Asia	Mexico	Europe	Caribbean	Central America[2]	South America	Africa	Canada
City	17.4	1.5	0.6	2.4	8.3	0.9	3.2	0.1	0.5
MSA[1]	17.1	1.3	2.3	2.0	6.3	1.9	2.2	0.1	0.9
U.S.	13.6	4.2	3.3	1.5	1.4	1.1	1.1	0.8	0.2

Percent of Population Born in

Note: (1) Figures cover the Cape Coral-Fort Myers, FL Metropolitan Statistical Area; (2) Excludes Mexico.
Source: U.S. Census Bureau, 2017-2021 American Community Survey 5-Year Estimates

Household Size

Area	One	Two	Three	Four	Five	Six	Seven or More	Average Household Size
City	26.1	42.6	13.7	10.6	5.1	1.1	0.7	2.60
MSA[1]	28.6	44.2	11.5	8.9	4.6	1.4	0.8	2.50
U.S.	28.1	33.8	15.5	12.9	6.0	2.3	1.4	2.60

Note: (1) Figures cover the Cape Coral-Fort Myers, FL Metropolitan Statistical Area
Source: U.S. Census Bureau, 2017-2021 American Community Survey 5-Year Estimates

Household Relationships

Area	House-holder	Opposite-sex Spouse	Same-sex Spouse	Opposite-sex Unmarried Partner	Same-sex Unmarried Partner	Child[2]	Grand-child	Other Relatives	Non-relatives
City	39.5	21.2	0.3	3.2	0.1	25.5	2.1	4.8	2.8
MSA[1]	41.8	20.9	0.3	3.0	0.2	22.4	1.8	4.4	3.3
U.S.	38.3	17.5	0.2	2.5	0.2	28.3	2.4	4.8	3.4

Note: Figures are percent of the total population; (1) Figures cover the Cape Coral-Fort Myers, FL Metropolitan Statistical Area; (2) Includes biological, adopted, and stepchildren of the householder
Source: U.S. Census Bureau, 2020 Census

Gender

Area	Males	Females	Males per 100 Females
City	95,028	98,988	96.0
MSA[1]	371,444	389,378	95.4
U.S.	162,685,811	168,763,470	96.4

Note: (1) Figures cover the Cape Coral-Fort Myers, FL Metropolitan Statistical Area
Source: U.S. Census Bureau, 2020 Census

Marital Status

Area	Never Married	Now Married[2]	Separated	Widowed	Divorced
City	24.4	53.3	1.2	7.3	13.8
MSA[1]	25.9	51.9	1.5	7.9	12.8
U.S.	33.8	48.0	1.8	5.6	10.8

Note: Figures are percentages and cover the population 15 years of age and older; (1) Figures cover the Cape Coral-Fort Myers, FL Metropolitan Statistical Area; (2) Excludes separated
Source: U.S. Census Bureau, 2017-2021 American Community Survey 5-Year Estimates

Religious Groups by Family

Area	Catholic	Baptist	Methodist	LDS[2]	Pentecostal	Lutheran	Islam	Adventist	Other
MSA[1]	18.8	2.5	1.7	0.6	3.0	0.7	0.2	2.0	12.2
U.S.	18.7	7.3	3.0	2.0	1.8	1.7	1.3	1.3	11.6

Note: Figures are the number of adherents as a percentage of the total population and cover the eight largest religious groups in the U.S; (1) Figures cover the Cape Coral-Fort Myers, FL Metropolitan Statistical Area; (2) Church of Jesus Christ of Latter-day Saints
Sources: 2020 U.S. Religion Census, Association of Statisticians of American Religious Bodies; The Association of Religion Data Archives (ARDA)

Religious Groups by Tradition

Area	Catholic	Evangelical Protestant	Mainline Protestant	Black Protestant	Islam	Judaism	Hinduism	Orthodox	Buddhism
MSA[1]	18.8	16.4	3.0	0.6	0.2	0.2	0.2	0.1	0.1
U.S.	18.7	16.5	5.2	2.3	1.3	0.6	0.4	0.4	0.3

Note: Figures are the number of adherents as a percentage of the total population; (1) Figures cover the Cape Coral-Fort Myers, FL Metropolitan Statistical Area
Sources: 2020 U.S. Religion Census, Association of Statisticians of American Religious Bodies; The Association of Religion Data Archives (ARDA)

ECONOMY

Gross Metropolitan Product

Area	2020	2021	2022	2023	Rank[2]
MSA[1]	34.5	38.8	42.7	45.6	85

Note: Figures are in billions of dollars; (1) Figures cover the Cape Coral-Fort Myers, FL Metropolitan Statistical Area; (2) Rank is based on 2021 data and ranges from 1 to 381
Source: U.S. Conference of Mayors, U.S. Metro Economies: U.S. Metros Compared to Global and State Economies, June 2022

Economic Growth

Area	2018-20 (%)	2021 (%)	2022 (%)	2023 (%)	Rank[2]
MSA[1]	-0.4	8.7	5.0	2.9	165
U.S.	-0.6	5.7	3.1	2.9	—

Note: Figures are real gross metropolitan product (GMP) growth rates and represent average annual percent change; (1) Figures cover the Cape Coral-Fort Myers, FL Metropolitan Statistical Area; (2) Rank is based on 2020 2-year average annual percent change and ranges from 1 to 381
Source: U.S. Conference of Mayors, U.S. Metro Economies: U.S. Metros Compared to Global and State Economies, June 2022

Metropolitan Area Exports

Area	2016	2017	2018	2019	2020	2021	Rank[2]
MSA[1]	540.3	592.3	668.0	694.9	654.8	797.5	183

Note: Figures are in millions of dollars; (1) Figures cover the Cape Coral-Fort Myers, FL Metropolitan Statistical Area; (2) Rank is based on 2021 data and ranges from 1 to 388
Source: U.S. Department of Commerce, International Trade Administration, Office of Trade and Economic Analysis, Industry and Analysis, Exports by Metropolitan Area, data extracted March 16, 2023

Building Permits

Area	Single-Family 2021	Single-Family 2022	Pct. Chg.	Multi-Family 2021	Multi-Family 2022	Pct. Chg.	Total 2021	Total 2022	Pct. Chg.
City	4,279	3,813	-10.9	1,133	922	-18.6	5,412	4,735	-12.5
MSA[1]	11,020	9,145	-17.0	2,374	4,476	88.5	13,394	13,621	1.7
U.S.	1,115,400	975,600	-12.5	621,600	689,500	10.9	1,737,000	1,665,100	-4.1

Note: (1) Figures cover the Cape Coral-Fort Myers, FL Metropolitan Statistical Area; Figures represent new, privately-owned housing units authorized (unadjusted data); All permit data are based on estimates with imputation
Source: U.S. Census Bureau, Manufacturing, Mining, and Construction Statistics, Building Permits, 2021, 2022

Bankruptcy Filings

Area	Business Filings 2021	Business Filings 2022	% Chg.	Nonbusiness Filings 2021	Nonbusiness Filings 2022	% Chg.
Lee County	39	31	-20.5	928	711	-23.4
U.S.	14,347	13,481	-6.0	399,269	374,240	-6.3

Note: Business filings include Chapter 7, Chapter 9, Chapter 11, Chapter 12, Chapter 13, Chapter 15, and Section 304; Nonbusiness filings include Chapter 7, Chapter 11, and Chapter 13
Source: Administrative Office of the U.S. Courts, Business and Nonbusiness Bankruptcy, County Cases Commenced by Chapter of the Bankruptcy Code, During the 12-Month Period Ending December 31, 2021 and Business and Nonbusiness Bankruptcy, County Cases Commenced by Chapter of the Bankruptcy Code, During the 12-Month Period Ending December 31, 2022

Housing Vacancy Rates

Area	Gross Vacancy Rate[2] (%) 2020	2021	2022	Year-Round Vacancy Rate[3] (%) 2020	2021	2022	Rental Vacancy Rate[4] (%) 2020	2021	2022	Homeowner Vacancy Rate[5] (%) 2020	2021	2022
MSA[1]	35.1	36.4	38.2	15.8	13.0	16.9	15.5	10.7	11.6	1.9	2.4	3.9
U.S.	10.6	10.8	10.5	8.2	8.4	8.2	6.3	6.1	5.8	1.0	0.9	0.8

Note: (1) Figures cover the Cape Coral-Fort Myers, FL Metropolitan Statistical Area; (2) The percentage of the total housing inventory that is vacant; (3) The percentage of the housing inventory (excluding seasonal units) that is year-round vacant; (4) The percentage of rental inventory that is vacant for rent; (5) The percentage of homeowner inventory that is vacant for sale
Source: U.S. Census Bureau, Housing Vacancies and Homeownership Annual Statistics: 2020, 2021, 2022

INCOME

Income

Area	Per Capita ($)	Median Household ($)	Average Household ($)
City	34,586	65,282	84,169
MSA[1]	37,550	63,235	89,228
U.S.	37,638	69,021	97,196

Note: (1) Figures cover the Cape Coral-Fort Myers, FL Metropolitan Statistical Area
Source: U.S. Census Bureau, 2017-2021 American Community Survey 5-Year Estimates

Cape Coral, Florida

Household Income Distribution

Area	Under $15,000	$15,000 -$24,999	$25,000 -$34,999	$35,000 -$49,999	$50,000 -$74,999	$75,000 -$99,999	$100,000 -$149,999	$150,000 and up
City	7.6	6.2	8.7	13.7	20.5	15.4	17.2	10.6
MSA[1]	9.1	7.9	9.2	13.2	19.0	13.8	14.9	12.8
U.S.	9.4	7.8	8.2	11.4	16.8	12.8	16.3	17.3

Percent of Households Earning

Note: (1) Figures cover the Cape Coral-Fort Myers, FL Metropolitan Statistical Area
Source: U.S. Census Bureau, 2017-2021 American Community Survey 5-Year Estimates

Poverty Rate

Area	All Ages	Under 18 Years Old	18 to 64 Years Old	65 Years and Over
City	9.9	15.4	8.7	8.8
MSA[1]	12.0	18.7	11.5	9.0
U.S.	12.6	17.0	11.8	9.6

Note: Figures are percentage of people whose income during the past 12 months was below the poverty level; (1) Figures cover the Cape Coral-Fort Myers, FL Metropolitan Statistical Area
Source: U.S. Census Bureau, 2017-2021 American Community Survey 5-Year Estimates

EMPLOYMENT

Labor Force and Employment

Area	Civilian Labor Force Dec. 2021	Civilian Labor Force Dec. 2022	% Chg.	Workers Employed Dec. 2021	Workers Employed Dec. 2022	% Chg.
City	96,606	100,709	4.2	93,922	97,833	4.2
MSA[1]	362,039	377,849	4.4	352,239	366,908	4.2
U.S.	161,696,000	164,224,000	1.6	155,732,000	158,872,000	2.0

Note: Data is not seasonally adjusted and covers workers 16 years of age and older; (1) Figures cover the Cape Coral-Fort Myers, FL Metropolitan Statistical Area
Source: Bureau of Labor Statistics, Local Area Unemployment Statistics

Unemployment Rate

Area	Jan.	Feb.	Mar.	Apr.	May	Jun.	Jul.	Aug.	Sep.	Oct.	Nov.	Dec.
City	3.4	2.9	2.6	2.3	2.4	2.8	2.7	2.6	2.5	4.2	3.6	2.9
MSA[1]	3.4	2.9	2.5	2.2	2.4	2.9	2.8	2.7	2.6	4.0	3.6	2.9
U.S.	4.4	4.1	3.8	3.3	3.4	3.8	3.8	3.8	3.3	3.4	3.4	3.3

2022

Note: Data is not seasonally adjusted and covers workers 16 years of age and older; (1) Figures cover the Cape Coral-Fort Myers, FL Metropolitan Statistical Area
Source: Bureau of Labor Statistics, Local Area Unemployment Statistics

Average Wages

Occupation	$/Hr.	Occupation	$/Hr.
Accountants and Auditors	37.19	Maintenance and Repair Workers	20.21
Automotive Mechanics	23.44	Marketing Managers	65.93
Bookkeepers	21.35	Network and Computer Systems Admin.	42.44
Carpenters	21.78	Nurses, Licensed Practical	25.89
Cashiers	12.98	Nurses, Registered	38.04
Computer Programmers	43.01	Nursing Assistants	16.24
Computer Systems Analysts	46.18	Office Clerks, General	19.43
Computer User Support Specialists	27.26	Physical Therapists	43.77
Construction Laborers	18.06	Physicians	177.87
Cooks, Restaurant	16.07	Plumbers, Pipefitters and Steamfitters	24.29
Customer Service Representatives	18.46	Police and Sheriff's Patrol Officers	31.19
Dentists	77.81	Postal Service Mail Carriers	26.49
Electricians	23.54	Real Estate Sales Agents	24.97
Engineers, Electrical	48.44	Retail Salespersons	15.73
Fast Food and Counter Workers	12.56	Sales Representatives, Technical/Scientific	53.67
Financial Managers	69.72	Secretaries, Exc. Legal/Medical/Executive	18.53
First-Line Supervisors of Office Workers	30.29	Security Guards	14.53
General and Operations Managers	51.54	Surgeons	n/a
Hairdressers/Cosmetologists	18.15	Teacher Assistants, Exc. Postsecondary*	14.90
Home Health and Personal Care Aides	15.99	Teachers, Secondary School, Exc. Sp. Ed.*	33.25
Janitors and Cleaners	14.30	Telemarketers	16.95
Landscaping/Groundskeeping Workers	16.34	Truck Drivers, Heavy/Tractor-Trailer	22.84
Lawyers	58.21	Truck Drivers, Light/Delivery Services	20.22
Maids and Housekeeping Cleaners	14.40	Waiters and Waitresses	15.70

Note: Wage data covers the Cape Coral-Fort Myers, FL Metropolitan Statistical Area; (*) Hourly wages were calculated from annual wage data based on a 40 hour work week; n/a not available.
Source: Bureau of Labor Statistics, Metro Area Occupational Employment & Wage Estimates, May 2022

Employment by Industry

Sector	MSA[1] Number of Employees	MSA[1] Percent of Total	U.S. Percent of Total
Construction, Mining, and Logging	38,800	12.5	5.4
Private Education and Health Services	36,400	11.7	16.1
Financial Activities	15,700	5.0	5.9
Government	45,400	14.6	14.5
Information	3,300	1.1	2.0
Leisure and Hospitality	46,300	14.9	10.3
Manufacturing	8,100	2.6	8.4
Other Services	11,600	3.7	3.7
Professional and Business Services	45,300	14.5	14.7
Retail Trade	44,600	14.3	10.2
Transportation, Warehousing, and Utilities	7,400	2.4	4.9
Wholesale Trade	8,700	2.8	3.9

Note: Figures are non-farm employment as of December 2022. Figures are not seasonally adjusted and include workers 16 years of age and older; (1) Figures cover the Cape Coral-Fort Myers, FL Metropolitan Statistical Area
Source: Bureau of Labor Statistics, Current Employment Statistics, Employment, Hours, and Earnings

Employment by Occupation

Occupation Classification	City (%)	MSA[1] (%)	U.S. (%)
Management, Business, Science, and Arts	31.8	33.0	40.3
Natural Resources, Construction, and Maintenance	11.1	12.1	8.7
Production, Transportation, and Material Moving	10.9	9.8	13.1
Sales and Office	26.0	25.1	20.9
Service	20.2	20.0	17.0

Note: Figures cover employed civilians 16 years of age and older; (1) Figures cover the Cape Coral-Fort Myers, FL Metropolitan Statistical Area
Source: U.S. Census Bureau, 2017-2021 American Community Survey 5-Year Estimates

Occupations with Greatest Projected Employment Growth: 2022 – 2024

Occupation[1]	2022 Employment	2024 Projected Employment	Numeric Employment Change	Percent Employment Change
General and Operations Managers	196,430	209,480	13,050	6.6
Cooks, Restaurant	117,090	129,670	12,580	10.7
Registered Nurses	208,620	221,040	12,420	6.0
Waiters and Waitresses	194,570	206,380	11,810	6.1
Retail Salespersons	327,010	338,390	11,380	3.5
Stockers and Order Fillers	192,890	203,920	11,030	5.7
Customer Service Representatives	283,220	293,670	10,450	3.7
Fast Food and Counter Workers	203,420	212,470	9,050	4.4
Laborers and Freight, Stock, and Material Movers, Hand	138,200	146,930	8,730	6.3
Maids and Housekeeping Cleaners	77,330	85,600	8,270	10.7

Note: Projections cover Florida; (1) Sorted by numeric employment change
Source: www.projectionscentral.com, State Occupational Projections, 2022–2024 Short-Term Projections

Fastest-Growing Occupations: 2022 – 2024

Occupation[1]	2022 Employment	2024 Projected Employment	Numeric Employment Change	Percent Employment Change
Hotel, Motel, and Resort Desk Clerks	23,000	26,650	3,650	15.9
First-Line Supervisors of Gambling Services Workers	990	1,140	150	15.2
Baggage Porters and Bellhops	3,310	3,810	500	15.1
Solar Photovoltaic Installers	860	990	130	15.1
Nurse Practitioners	17,490	20,080	2,590	14.8
Motion Picture Projectionists	490	560	70	14.3
Lodging Managers	5,160	5,870	710	13.8
Transportation Workers, All Other	980	1,110	130	13.3
Information Security Analysts (SOC 2018)	11,910	13,480	1,570	13.2
Statisticians	1,370	1,550	180	13.1

Note: Projections cover Florida; (1) Sorted by percent employment change and excludes occupations with numeric employment change less than 50
Source: www.projectionscentral.com, State Occupational Projections, 2022–2024 Short-Term Projections

CITY FINANCES

City Government Finances

Component	2020 ($000)	2020 ($ per capita)
Total Revenues	438,502	2,255
Total Expenditures	414,456	2,131
Debt Outstanding	774,665	3,983
Cash and Securities[1]	340,824	1,752

Note: (1) Cash and security holdings of a government at the close of its fiscal year, including those of its dependent agencies, utilities, and liquor stores.
Source: U.S. Census Bureau, State & Local Government Finances 2020

City Government Revenue by Source

Source	2020 ($000)	2020 ($ per capita)	2020 (%)
General Revenue			
From Federal Government	13,707	70	3.1
From State Government	50,730	261	11.6
From Local Governments	718	4	0.2
Taxes			
Property	95,581	491	21.8
Sales and Gross Receipts	23,546	121	5.4
Personal Income	0	0	0.0
Corporate Income	0	0	0.0
Motor Vehicle License	0	0	0.0
Other Taxes	16,366	84	3.7
Current Charges	90,792	467	20.7
Liquor Store	0	0	0.0
Utility	31,025	160	7.1

Source: U.S. Census Bureau, State & Local Government Finances 2020

City Government Expenditures by Function

Function	2020 ($000)	2020 ($ per capita)	2020 (%)
General Direct Expenditures			
Air Transportation	0	0	0.0
Corrections	0	0	0.0
Education	23,007	118	5.6
Employment Security Administration	0	0	0.0
Financial Administration	26,239	134	6.3
Fire Protection	32,633	167	7.9
General Public Buildings	0	0	0.0
Governmental Administration, Other	4,054	20	1.0
Health	0	0	0.0
Highways	26,632	136	6.4
Hospitals	0	0	0.0
Housing and Community Development	1,490	7	0.4
Interest on General Debt	8,470	43	2.0
Judicial and Legal	1,464	7	0.4
Libraries	0	0	0.0
Parking	20	< 1	< 0.1
Parks and Recreation	24,398	125	5.9
Police Protection	39,772	204	9.6
Public Welfare	0	0	0.0
Sewerage	32,092	165	7.7
Solid Waste Management	0	0	0.0
Veterans' Services	0	0	0.0
Liquor Store	0	0	0.0
Utility	155,298	798	37.5

Source: U.S. Census Bureau, State & Local Government Finances 2020

TAXES

State Corporate Income Tax Rates

State	Tax Rate (%)	Income Brackets ($)	Num. of Brackets	Financial Institution Tax Rate (%)[a]	Federal Income Tax Ded.
Florida	5.5	Flat rate	1	5.5	No

Note: Tax rates as of January 1, 2023; (a) Rates listed are the corporate income tax rate applied to financial institutions or excise taxes based on income. Some states have other taxes based upon the value of deposits or shares.
Source: Federation of Tax Administrators, State Corporate Income Tax Rates, January 1, 2023

State Individual Income Tax Rates

State	Tax Rate (%)	Income Brackets ($)	Personal Exemptions ($) Single	Personal Exemptions ($) Married	Personal Exemptions ($) Depend.	Standard Ded. ($) Single	Standard Ded. ($) Married
Florida				– No state income tax –			

Note: Tax rates as of January 1, 2023; Local- and county-level taxes are not included
Source: Federation of Tax Administrators, State Individual Income Tax Rates, January 1, 2023

Various State Sales and Excise Tax Rates

State	State Sales Tax (%)	Gasoline[1] ($/gal.)	Cigarette[2] ($/pack)	Spirits[3] ($/gal.)	Wine[4] ($/gal.)	Beer[5] ($/gal.)	Recreational Marijuana (%)
Florida	6	0.4123	1.339	6.50	2.25	0.48	Not legal

Note: All tax rates as of January 1, 2023; (1) The American Petroleum Institute has developed a methodology for determining the average tax rate on a gallon of fuel. Rates may include any of the following: excise taxes, environmental fees, storage tank fees, other fees or taxes, general sales tax, and local taxes; (2) The federal excise tax of $1.0066 per pack and local taxes are not included; (3) Rates are those applicable to off-premise sales of 40% alcohol by volume (a.b.v.) distilled spirits in 750ml containers. Local excise taxes are excluded; (4) Rates are those applicable to off-premise sales of 11% a.b.v. non-carbonated wine in 750ml containers; (5) Rates are those applicable to off-premise sales of 4.7% a.b.v. beer in 12 ounce containers.
Source: Tax Foundation, 2023 Facts & Figures: How Does Your State Compare?

State Business Tax Climate Index Rankings

State	Overall Rank	Corporate Tax Rank	Individual Income Tax Rank	Sales Tax Rank	Property Tax Rank	Unemployment Insurance Tax Rank
Florida	4	10	1	21	12	3

Note: The index is a measure of how each state's tax laws affect economic performance. The lower the rank, the more favorable a state's tax system is for business. States without a given tax are given a ranking of 1. The scores/rankings for the District of Columbia do not affect other states. The 2023 index represents the tax climate as of July 1, 2022.
Source: Tax Foundation, State Business Tax Climate Index 2023

TRANSPORTATION

Means of Transportation to Work

Area	Car/Truck/Van Drove Alone	Car/Truck/Van Carpooled	Public Transportation Bus	Public Transportation Subway	Public Transportation Railroad	Bicycle	Walked	Other Means	Worked at Home
City	79.3	7.8	0.1	0.0	0.0	0.2	0.9	1.9	9.8
MSA[1]	76.3	9.6	0.5	0.0	0.0	0.7	1.0	2.3	9.6
U.S.	73.2	8.6	2.0	1.6	0.5	0.5	2.5	1.5	9.7

Note: Figures are percentages and cover workers 16 years of age and older; (1) Figures cover the Cape Coral-Fort Myers, FL Metropolitan Statistical Area
Source: U.S. Census Bureau, 2017-2021 American Community Survey 5-Year Estimates

Travel Time to Work

Area	Less Than 10 Minutes	10 to 19 Minutes	20 to 29 Minutes	30 to 44 Minutes	45 to 59 Minutes	60 to 89 Minutes	90 Minutes or More
City	8.0	25.3	22.2	27.4	9.4	5.4	2.3
MSA[1]	8.6	25.3	22.8	26.0	9.8	5.2	2.3
U.S.	12.4	28.5	21.0	20.9	8.2	6.2	2.9

Note: Note: Figures are percentages and include workers 16 years old and over; (1) Figures cover the Cape Coral-Fort Myers, FL Metropolitan Statistical Area
Source: U.S. Census Bureau, 2017-2021 American Community Survey 5-Year Estimates

Key Congestion Measures

Measure	1990	2000	2010	2015	2020
Annual Hours of Delay, Total (000)	2,677	6,045	12,851	14,679	7,399
Annual Hours of Delay, Per Auto Commuter	17	29	36	36	15
Annual Congestion Cost, Per Auto Commuter ($)	242	409	688	725	337

Note: Covers the Cape Coral FL urban area
Source: Texas A&M Transportation Institute, 2021 Urban Mobility Report

Freeway Travel Time Index

Measure	1985	1990	1995	2000	2005	2010	2015	2020
Urban Area Index[1]	1.07	1.10	1.13	1.16	1.19	1.10	1.17	1.06
Urban Area Rank[1,2]	48	47	47	43	38	98	46	75

Note: Freeway Travel Time Index—the ratio of travel time in the peak period to the travel time at free-flow conditions. For example, a value of 1.30 indicates a 20-minute free-flow trip takes 26 minutes in the peak (20 minutes x 1.30 = 26 minutes); (1) Covers the Cape Coral FL urban area; (2) Rank is based on 101 larger urban areas (#1 = highest travel time index)
Source: Texas A&M Transportation Institute, 2021 Urban Mobility Report

Public Transportation

Agency Name / Mode of Transportation	Vehicles Operated in Maximum Service[1]	Annual Unlinked Passenger Trips[2] (in thous.)	Annual Passenger Miles[3] (in thous.)
Lee County Transit (LeeTran)			
Bus (directly operated)	49	1,685.8	8,923.0
Demand Response (directly operated)	41	134.3	1,484.6
Vanpool (purchased transportation)	10	18.8	542.5

Note: (1) Number of revenue vehicles operated by the given mode and type of service to meet the annual maximum service requirement. This is the revenue vehicle count during the peak season of the year; on the week and day that maximum service is provided. Vehicles operated in maximum service (VOMS) exclude atypical days and one-time special events; (2) Number of passengers who boarded public transportation vehicles. Passengers are counted each time they board a vehicle no matter how many vehicles they use to travel from their origin to their destination. (3) Sum of the distances ridden by all passengers during the entire fiscal year.
Source: Federal Transit Administration, National Transit Database, 2021

Air Transportation

Airport Name and Code / Type of Service	Passenger Airlines[1]	Passenger Enplanements	Freight Carriers[2]	Freight (lbs)
Southwest Florida International Airport (RSW)				
Domestic service (U.S. carriers - 2022)	24	5,010,752	14	15,380,945
International service (U.S. carriers - 2021)	0	0	0	0

Note: (1) Includes all U.S.-based major, minor and commuter airlines that carried at least one passenger during the year; (2) Includes all U.S.-based airlines and freight carriers that transported at least one pound of freight during the year.
Source: Bureau of Transportation Statistics, The Intermodal Transportation Database, Air Carriers: T-100 Domestic Market (U.S. Carriers), 2022; Bureau of Transportation Statistics, The Intermodal Transportation Database, Air Carriers: T-100 International Market (U.S. Carriers), 2021

BUSINESSES

Major Business Headquarters

Company Name	Industry	Rankings Fortune[1]	Forbes[2]
No companies listed	-	-	-

Note: (1) Companies that produce a 10-K are ranked 1 to 500 based on 2021 revenue; (2) All private companies with at least $2 billion in annual revenue through the end of their most current fiscal year are ranked 1 to 246; companies listed are headquartered in the city; dashes indicate no ranking
Source: Fortune, "Fortune 500," 2022; Forbes, "America's Largest Private Companies," 2022

Fastest-Growing Businesses

According to *Inc.*, Cape Coral is home to one of America's 500 fastest-growing private companies: **Douglas Brooke Homes** (#278). Criteria: must be an independent, privately-held, for-profit, U.S. corporation, proprietorship or partnership as of December 31, 2021; revenues must be at least $100,000 in 2018 and $2 million in 2021; must have four-year operating/sales history. *Inc.*, "America's 500 Fastest-Growing Private Companies," 2022

Living Environment

COST OF LIVING

Cost of Living Index

Composite Index	Groceries	Housing	Utilities	Transportation	Health Care	Misc. Goods/Services
108.9	107.7	117.9	103.1	107.5	104.1	104.5

Note: The Cost of Living Index measures regional differences in the cost of consumer goods and services, excluding taxes and non-consumer expenditures, for professional and managerial households in the top income quintile. It is based on more than 50,000 prices covering almost 60 different items for which prices are collected three times a year by chambers of commerce, economic development organizations or university applied economic centers in each participating urban area. The numbers shown should be read as a percentage above or below the national average of 100. For example, a value of 115.4 in the groceries column indicates that grocery prices are 15.4% higher than the national average. Small differences in the index numbers should not be interpreted as significant; Figures cover the Cape Coral-Fort Myers FL urban area.
Source: The Council for Community and Economic Research, Cost of Living Index, 2022

Grocery Prices

Area[1]	T-Bone Steak ($/pound)	Frying Chicken ($/pound)	Whole Milk ($/half gal.)	Eggs ($/dozen)	Orange Juice ($/64 oz.)	Coffee ($/11.5 oz.)
City[2]	14.43	2.34	2.55	1.83	4.28	4.04
Avg.	13.81	1.59	2.43	2.25	3.85	4.95
Min.	10.17	0.90	1.51	1.30	2.90	3.46
Max.	19.35	3.30	4.32	4.32	5.31	8.59

Note: (1) Values for the local area are compared with the average, minimum and maximum values for all 286 areas in the Cost of Living Index; (2) Figures cover the Cape Coral-Fort Myers FL urban area; **T-Bone Steak** (price per pound); **Frying Chicken** (price per pound, whole fryer); **Whole Milk** (half gallon carton); **Eggs** (price per dozen, Grade A, large); **Orange Juice** (64 oz. Tropicana or Florida Natural); **Coffee** (11.5 oz. can, vacuum-packed, Maxwell House, Hills Bros, or Folgers).
Source: The Council for Community and Economic Research, Cost of Living Index, 2022

Housing and Utility Costs

Area[1]	New Home Price ($)	Apartment Rent ($/month)	All Electric ($/month)	Part Electric ($/month)	Other Energy ($/month)	Telephone ($/month)
City[2]	495,794	1,824	182.94	-	-	195.37
Avg.	450,913	1,371	176.41	99.93	76.96	190.22
Min.	229,283	546	100.84	31.56	27.15	174.27
Max.	2,434,977	4,569	356.86	249.59	272.24	208.31

Note: (1) Values for the local area are compared with the average, minimum and maximum values for all 286 areas in the Cost of Living Index; (2) Figures cover the Cape Coral-Fort Myers FL urban area; **New Home Price** (2,400 sf living area, 8,000 sf lot, in urban area with full utilities); **Apartment Rent** (950 sf 2 bedroom/1.5 or 2 bath, unfurnished, excluding all utilities except water); **All Electric** (average monthly cost for an all-electric home); **Part Electric** (average monthly cost for a part-electric home); **Other Energy** (average monthly cost for natural gas, fuel oil, coal, wood, and any other forms of energy except electricity); **Telephone** (price includes the base monthly rate plus taxes and fees for three lines of mobile phone service).
Source: The Council for Community and Economic Research, Cost of Living Index, 2022

Health Care, Transportation, and Other Costs

Area[1]	Doctor ($/visit)	Dentist ($/visit)	Optometrist ($/visit)	Gasoline ($/gallon)	Beauty Salon ($/visit)	Men's Shirt ($)
City[2]	127.67	112.88	96.64	3.86	50.60	29.74
Avg.	124.91	107.77	117.66	3.86	43.31	34.21
Min.	36.61	58.25	51.79	2.90	22.18	13.05
Max.	250.21	162.58	371.96	5.54	85.61	63.54

Note: (1) Values for the local area are compared with the average, minimum and maximum values for all 286 areas in the Cost of Living Index; (2) Figures cover the Cape Coral-Fort Myers FL urban area; **Doctor** (general practitioners routine exam of an established patient); **Dentist** (adult teeth cleaning and periodic oral examination); **Optometrist** (full vision eye exam for established adult patient); **Gasoline** (one gallon regular unleaded, national brand, including all taxes, cash price at self-service pump if available); **Beauty Salon** (woman's shampoo, trim, and blow-dry); **Men's Shirt** (cotton/polyester dress shirt, pinpoint weave, long sleeves).
Source: The Council for Community and Economic Research, Cost of Living Index, 2022

HOUSING

Homeownership Rate

Area	2015 (%)	2016 (%)	2017 (%)	2018 (%)	2019 (%)	2020 (%)	2021 (%)	2022 (%)
MSA[1]	62.9	66.5	65.5	75.1	72.0	77.4	76.1	70.8
U.S.	63.7	63.4	63.9	64.4	64.6	66.6	65.5	65.8

Note: (1) Figures cover the Cape Coral-Fort Myers, FL Metropolitan Statistical Area
Source: U.S. Census Bureau, Housing Vacancies and Homeownership Annual Statistics: 2015-2022

House Price Index (HPI)

Area	National Ranking[2]	Quarterly Change (%)	One-Year Change (%)	Five-Year Change (%)	Since 1991Q1 (%)
MSA[1]	6	-0.47	20.91	83.64	358.39
U.S.[3]	–	0.34	8.41	58.44	289.08

Note: The HPI is a weighted repeat sales index. It measures average price changes in repeat sales or refinancings on the same properties. This information is obtained by reviewing repeat mortgage transactions on single-family properties whose mortgages have been purchased or securitized by Fannie Mae or Freddie Mac since January 1975; (1) Figures cover the Cape Coral-Fort Myers, FL Metropolitan Statistical Area; (2) Rankings are based on annual percentage change for all metro areas containing at least 15,000 transactions over the last 10 years and ranges from 1 to 257; (3) figures based on a weighted average of Census Division estimates using a seasonally adjusted, purchase-only index; all figures are for the period ending December 31, 2022
Source: Federal Housing Finance Agency, Change in FHFA Metropolitan Area House Price Indexes, 2022Q4

Median Single-Family Home Prices

Area	2020	2021	2022p	Percent Change 2021 to 2022
MSA[1]	289.0	360.0	430.0	19.4
U.S. Average	300.2	357.1	392.6	9.9

Note: Figures are median sales prices of existing single-family homes in thousands of dollars; (p) preliminary; (1) Figures cover the Cape Coral-Fort Myers, FL Metropolitan Statistical Area
Source: National Association of Realtors, Median Sales Price of Existing Single-Family Homes for Metropolitan Areas, 4th Quarter 2022

Qualifying Income Based on Median Sales Price of Existing Single-Family Homes

Area	With 5% Down ($)	With 10% Down ($)	With 20% Down ($)
MSA[1]	123,952	117,428	104,381
U.S. Average	112,234	106,237	94,513

Note: Figures are preliminary; Qualifying income is based on a mortgage rate of 6.77%. Monthly principal and interest payment is limited to 25% of income; (1) Figures cover the Cape Coral-Fort Myers, FL Metropolitan Statistical Area
Source: National Association of Realtors, Qualifying Income Based on Median Sales Price of Existing Single-Family Homes for Metropolitan Areas, 4th Quarter 2022

Home Value

Area	Under $100,000	$100,000 -$199,999	$200,000 -$299,999	$300,000 -$399,999	$400,000 -$499,999	$500,000 -$999,999	$1,000,000 or more	Median ($)
City	3.4	25.6	35.3	19.8	6.7	8.1	1.2	255,700
MSA[1]	12.0	23.6	27.5	16.4	7.3	10.5	2.8	248,300
U.S.	16.2	24.2	20.1	13.6	8.3	13.6	4.1	244,900

Note: Figures are percentages except for median and cover owner-occupied housing units; (1) Figures cover the Cape Coral-Fort Myers, FL Metropolitan Statistical Area
Source: U.S. Census Bureau, 2017-2021 American Community Survey 5-Year Estimates

Year Housing Structure Built

Area	2020 or Later	2010 -2019	2000 -2009	1990 -1999	1980 -1989	1970 -1979	1960 -1969	1950 -1959	1940 -1949	Before 1940	Median Year
City	0.1	8.4	34.8	17.6	21.6	11.7	4.6	0.8	0.2	0.1	1996
MSA[1]	0.2	8.9	29.7	17.4	21.0	14.4	5.2	2.2	0.4	0.6	1994
U.S.	0.2	7.3	13.6	13.6	13.2	14.8	10.3	10.0	4.7	12.2	1979

Note: Figures are percentages except for Median Year; Note: (1) Figures cover the Cape Coral-Fort Myers, FL Metropolitan Statistical Area
Source: U.S. Census Bureau, 2017-2021 American Community Survey 5-Year Estimates

Gross Monthly Rent

Area	Under $500	$500 -$999	$1,000 -$1,499	$1,500 -$1,999	$2,000 -$2,499	$2,500 -$2,999	$3,000 and up	Median ($)
City	1.2	11.9	40.8	37.8	5.8	0.9	1.5	1,456
MSA[1]	3.6	19.1	45.6	21.7	5.9	1.8	2.4	1,307
U.S.	8.1	30.5	30.8	16.8	7.3	3.1	3.5	1,163

Note: Figures are percentages except for median; Gross rent is the contract rent plus the estimated average monthly cost of utilities (electricity, gas, and water and sewer) and fuels (oil, coal, kerosene, wood, etc.) if these are paid by the renter (or paid for the renter by someone else); (1) Figures cover the Cape Coral-Fort Myers, FL Metropolitan Statistical Area
Source: U.S. Census Bureau, 2017-2021 American Community Survey 5-Year Estimates

HEALTH

Health Risk Factors

Category	MSA[1] (%)	U.S. (%)
Adults aged 18–64 who have any kind of health care coverage	n/a	90.9
Adults who reported being in good or better health	n/a	85.2
Adults who have been told they have high blood cholesterol	n/a	35.7
Adults who have been told they have high blood pressure	n/a	32.4
Adults who are current smokers	n/a	14.4
Adults who currently use e-cigarettes	n/a	6.7
Adults who currently use chewing tobacco, snuff, or snus	n/a	3.5
Adults who are heavy drinkers[2]	n/a	6.3
Adults who are binge drinkers[3]	n/a	15.4
Adults who are overweight (BMI 25.0 - 29.9)	n/a	34.4
Adults who are obese (BMI 30.0 - 99.8)	n/a	33.9
Adults who participated in any physical activities in the past month	n/a	76.3

Note: (1) Figures for the Cape Coral-Fort Myers, FL Metropolitan Statistical Area were not available.
(2) Heavy drinkers are classified as adult men having more than 14 drinks per week and adult women having more than 7 drinks per week; (3) Binge drinkers are classified as males having five or more drinks on one occasion or females having four or more drinks on one occasion
Source: Centers for Disease Control and Prevention, Behaviorial Risk Factor Surveillance System, SMART: Selected Metropolitan Area Risk Trends, 2021

Acute and Chronic Health Conditions

Category	MSA[1] (%)	U.S. (%)
Adults who have ever been told they had a heart attack	n/a	4.0
Adults who have ever been told they have angina or coronary heart disease	n/a	3.8
Adults who have ever been told they had a stroke	n/a	3.0
Adults who have ever been told they have asthma	n/a	14.9
Adults who have ever been told they have arthritis	n/a	25.8
Adults who have ever been told they have diabetes[2]	n/a	10.9
Adults who have ever been told they had skin cancer	n/a	6.6
Adults who have ever been told they had any other types of cancer	n/a	7.5
Adults who have ever been told they have COPD	n/a	6.1
Adults who have ever been told they have kidney disease	n/a	3.0
Adults who have ever been told they have a form of depression	n/a	20.5

Note: (1) Figures for the Cape Coral-Fort Myers, FL Metropolitan Statistical Area were not available.
(2) Figures do not include pregnancy-related, borderline, or pre-diabetes
Source: Centers for Disease Control and Prevention, Behaviorial Risk Factor Surveillance System, SMART: Selected Metropolitan Area Risk Trends, 2021

Health Screening and Vaccination Rates

Category	MSA[1] (%)	U.S. (%)
Adults who have ever been tested for HIV	n/a	34.9
Adults who have had their blood cholesterol checked within the last five years	n/a	85.2
Adults aged 65+ who have had flu shot within the past year	n/a	68.6
Adults aged 65+ who have ever had a pneumonia vaccination	n/a	71.0

Note: (1) Figures for the Cape Coral-Fort Myers, FL Metropolitan Statistical Area were not available.
Source: Centers for Disease Control and Prevention, Behaviorial Risk Factor Surveillance System, SMART: Selected Metropolitan Area Risk Trends, 2021

Disability Status

Category	MSA[1] (%)	U.S. (%)
Adults who reported being deaf	n/a	7.2
Are you blind or have serious difficulty seeing, even when wearing glasses?	n/a	4.8
Are you limited in any way in any of your usual activities due to arthritis?	n/a	11.1
Do you have difficulty doing errands alone?	n/a	7.0
Do you have difficulty dressing or bathing?	n/a	3.6
Do you have serious difficulty concentrating/remembering/making decisions?	n/a	12.1
Do you have serious difficulty walking or climbing stairs?	n/a	12.8

Note: (1) Figures for the Cape Coral-Fort Myers, FL Metropolitan Statistical Area were not available.
Source: Centers for Disease Control and Prevention, Behaviorial Risk Factor Surveillance System, SMART: Selected Metropolitan Area Risk Trends, 2021

Mortality Rates for the Top 10 Causes of Death in the U.S.

ICD-10[a] Sub-Chapter	ICD-10[a] Code	Crude Mortality Rate[1] per 100,000 population County[2]	U.S.
Malignant neoplasms	C00-C97	235.7	182.6
Ischaemic heart diseases	I20-I25	164.1	113.1
Other forms of heart disease	I30-I51	38.4	64.4
Other degenerative diseases of the nervous system	G30-G31	100.6	51.0
Cerebrovascular diseases	I60-I69	52.4	47.8
Other external causes of accidental injury	W00-X59	63.4	46.4
Chronic lower respiratory diseases	J40-J47	52.4	45.7
Organic, including symptomatic, mental disorders	F01-F09	10.2	35.9
Hypertensive diseases	I10-I15	40.5	35.0
Diabetes mellitus	E10-E14	34.0	29.6

Note: (a) ICD-10 = International Classification of Diseases 10th Revision; (1) Crude mortality rates are a three-year average covering 2019-2021; (2) Figures cover Lee County.
Source: Centers for Disease Control and Prevention, National Center for Health Statistics. National Vital Statistics System, Mortality 2018-2021 on CDC WONDER Online Database

Mortality Rates for Selected Causes of Death

ICD-10[a] Sub-Chapter	ICD-10[a] Code	Crude Mortality Rate[1] per 100,000 population County[2]	U.S.
Assault	X85-Y09	4.7	7.0
Diseases of the liver	K70-K76	22.9	19.8
Human immunodeficiency virus (HIV) disease	B20-B24	1.9	1.5
Influenza and pneumonia	J09-J18	9.7	14.7
Intentional self-harm	X60-X84	16.4	14.3
Malnutrition	E40-E46	1.8	4.3
Obesity and other hyperalimentation	E65-E68	3.6	3.0
Renal failure	N17-N19	9.4	15.7
Transport accidents	V01-V99	16.0	13.6
Viral hepatitis	B15-B19	1.0	1.2

Note: (a) ICD-10 = International Classification of Diseases 10th Revision; (1) Crude mortality rates are a three-year average covering 2019-2021; (2) Figures cover Lee County; Data are suppressed when the data meet the criteria for confidentiality constraints; Crude mortality rates are flagged as unreliable when the rate would be calculated with a numerator of 20 or less.
Source: Centers for Disease Control and Prevention, National Center for Health Statistics. National Vital Statistics System, Mortality 2018-2021 on CDC WONDER Online Database

Health Insurance Coverage

Area	With Health Insurance	With Private Health Insurance	With Public Health Insurance	Without Health Insurance	Population Under Age 19 Without Health Insurance
City	87.2	64.4	38.6	12.8	10.1
MSA[1]	86.9	61.9	43.5	13.1	9.8
U.S.	91.2	67.8	35.4	8.8	5.3

Note: Figures are percentages that cover the civilian noninstitutionalized population; (1) Figures cover the Cape Coral-Fort Myers, FL Metropolitan Statistical Area
Source: U.S. Census Bureau, 2017-2021 American Community Survey 5-Year Estimates

Number of Medical Professionals

Area	MDs[3]	DOs[3,4]	Dentists	Podiatrists	Chiropractors	Optometrists
County[1] (number)	1,553	238	423	64	220	104
County[1] (rate[2])	203.1	31.1	53.7	8.1	27.9	13.2
U.S. (rate[2])	289.3	23.5	72.5	6.2	28.7	17.4

Note: Data as of 2021 unless noted; (1) Data covers Lee County; (2) Rate per 100,000 population; (3) Data as of 2020 and includes all active, non-federal physicians; (4) Doctor of Osteopathic Medicine
Source: U.S. Department of Health and Human Services, Health Resources and Services Administration, Bureau of Health Professions, Area Resource File (ARF) 2021-2022

EDUCATION

Public School District Statistics

District Name	Schls	Pupils	Pupil/Teacher Ratio	Minority Pupils[1] (%)	LEP/ELL[2] (%)	IEP[3] (%)
Lee	118	97,264	18.8	64.3	11.1	12.1

Note: Table includes school districts with 2,000 or more students; (1) Percentage of students that are not non-Hispanic white; (2) Percentage of students that are Limited English Proficient or English Language Learners (2018-19); (3) Percentage of students that have an Individualized Education Program (2019-20).
Source: U.S. Department of Education, National Center for Education Statistics, Common Core of Data, Local Education Agency (School District) Universe Survey: School Year 2021-2022

Highest Level of Education

Area	Less than H.S.	H.S. Diploma	Some College, No Deg.	Associate Degree	Bachelor's Degree	Master's Degree	Prof. School Degree	Doctorate Degree
City	7.1	37.1	23.0	9.2	15.6	5.3	1.5	1.3
MSA[1]	10.2	30.8	20.5	9.4	17.8	7.5	2.3	1.4
U.S.	11.1	26.5	20.0	8.7	20.6	9.3	2.2	1.5

Note: Figures cover persons age 25 and over; (1) Figures cover the Cape Coral-Fort Myers, FL Metropolitan Statistical Area
Source: U.S. Census Bureau, 2017-2021 American Community Survey 5-Year Estimates

Educational Attainment by Race

Area	High School Graduate or Higher (%)					Bachelor's Degree or Higher (%)				
	Total	White	Black	Asian	Hisp.[2]	Total	White	Black	Asian	Hisp.[2]
City	92.9	94.0	84.8	87.3	88.5	23.6	23.9	22.7	44.4	16.4
MSA[1]	89.8	92.0	81.0	91.5	74.4	29.0	30.9	16.7	50.0	14.7
U.S.	88.9	91.4	87.2	87.6	71.2	33.7	35.5	23.3	55.6	18.4

Note: Figures shown cover persons 25 years old and over; (1) Figures cover the Cape Coral-Fort Myers, FL Metropolitan Statistical Area; (2) People of Hispanic origin can be of any race
Source: U.S. Census Bureau, 2017-2021 American Community Survey 5-Year Estimates

School Enrollment by Grade and Control

Area	Preschool (%)		Kindergarten (%)		Grades 1 - 4 (%)		Grades 5 - 8 (%)		Grades 9 - 12 (%)	
	Public	Private	Public	Private	Public	Private	Public	Private	Public	Private
City	73.5	26.5	96.9	3.1	88.6	11.4	94.2	5.8	90.2	9.8
MSA[1]	60.7	39.3	89.9	10.1	90.4	9.6	90.7	9.3	90.5	9.5
U.S.	58.8	41.2	86.3	13.7	88.3	11.7	88.6	11.4	89.4	10.6

Note: Figures shown cover persons 3 years old and over; (1) Figures cover the Cape Coral-Fort Myers, FL Metropolitan Statistical Area
Source: U.S. Census Bureau, 2017-2021 American Community Survey 5-Year Estimates

Higher Education

Four-Year Colleges			Two-Year Colleges			Medical Schools[1]	Law Schools[2]	Voc/ Tech[3]
Public	Private Non-profit	Private For-profit	Public	Private Non-profit	Private For-profit			
2	1	1	1	0	1	0	0	7

Note: Figures cover institutions located within the Cape Coral-Fort Myers, FL Metropolitan Statistical Area and include main campuses only; (1) includes schools accredited by the Liaison Committee on Medical Education and the American Osteopathic Association's Commission on Osteopathic College Accreditation; (2) includes ABA-accredited schools, schools with provisional ABA accreditation, and state accredited schools; (3) includes all schools with programs that are less than 2 years.
Source: National Center for Education Statistics, Integrated Postsecondary Education System (IPEDS), 2021-22; Wikipedia, List of Medical Schools in the United States, accessed April 10, 2023; Wikipedia, List of Law Schools in the United States, accessed April 10, 2023

EMPLOYERS

Major Employers

Company Name	Industry
Arthrex	Medical device manufacturer
Charlotte County School District	Education
Charlotte Regional Medical Center	Healthcare
Chico's Fas	Retail
City of Cape Coral	Municipal government
Collier County Administration	Government
Collier County Public Schools	Education
Florida Gulf Coast University	Education
Home Depot	Retail
Lee County School District	Education
Lee County Sherriff's Office	Government
Lee Memorial Health System	Healthcare
NCH Naples Hospitals	Healthcare
Palm Automotive	Auto sales
Publix Supermarkets	Retail grocery
St. Joseph Preferred Healthcare Inc	Healthcare
U.S. Sugar	Manufacturing
United States Postal Service	U.S. postal service
Wal-Mart Stores	Retail
Winn-Dixie	Grocery stores

Note: Companies shown are located within the Cape Coral-Fort Myers, FL Metropolitan Statistical Area.
Source: Hoovers.com; Wikipedia

PUBLIC SAFETY

Crime Rate

Area	Total Crime	Violent Crime Rate				Property Crime Rate		
		Murder	Rape[3]	Robbery	Aggrav. Assault	Burglary	Larceny-Theft	Motor Vehicle Theft
City	1,195.5	0.5	9.0	10.0	108.3	152.9	848.1	66.7
Suburbs[1]	1,333.2	5.3	37.6	48.3	222.8	148.9	761.7	108.6
Metro[2]	1,298.3	4.1	30.4	38.6	193.8	149.9	783.6	98.0
U.S.	2,356.7	6.5	38.4	73.9	279.7	314.2	1,398.0	246.0

Note: Figures are crimes per 100,000 population; (1) All areas within the metro area that are located outside the city limits; (2) Figures cover the Cape Coral-Fort Myers, FL Metropolitan Statistical Area; (3) All figures shown were reported using the revised Uniform Crime Reporting (UCR) definition of rape; Due to the transition to the National Incident-Based Reporting System (NIBRS), limited city and metro area data was released for 2021.
Source: FBI Uniform Crime Reports, 2020

Hate Crimes

Area	Number of Quarters Reported	Number of Incidents per Bias Motivation					
		Race/Ethnicity/Ancestry	Religion	Sexual Orientation	Disability	Gender	Gender Identity
City	4	0	0	0	0	0	0
U.S.	4	5,227	1,244	1,110	130	75	266

Note: Due to the transition to the National Incident-Based Reporting System (NIBRS), limited crime data was released for 2021.
Source: Federal Bureau of Investigation, Hate Crime Statistics 2020

Identity Theft Consumer Reports

Area	Reports	Reports per 100,000 Population	Rank[2]
MSA[1]	2,308	305	67
U.S.	1,108,609	339	-

Note: (1) Figures cover the Cape Coral-Fort Myers, FL Metropolitan Statistical Area; (2) Rank ranges from 1 to 391 where 1 indicates greatest number of identity theft reports per 100,000 population
Source: Federal Trade Commission, Consumer Sentinel Network Data Book 2022

Fraud and Other Consumer Reports

Area	Reports	Reports per 100,000 Population	Rank[2]
MSA[1]	8,619	1,139	52
U.S.	4,064,520	1,245	-

Note: (1) Figures cover the Cape Coral-Fort Myers, FL Metropolitan Statistical Area; (2) Rank ranges from 1 to 391 where 1 indicates greatest number of fraud and other consumer reports per 100,000 population
Source: Federal Trade Commission, Consumer Sentinel Network Data Book 2022

POLITICS

2020 Presidential Election Results

Area	Biden	Trump	Jorgensen	Hawkins	Other
Lee County	39.9	59.1	0.5	0.1	0.3
U.S.	51.3	46.8	1.2	0.3	0.5

Note: Results are percentages and may not add to 100% due to rounding
Source: Dave Leip's Atlas of U.S. Presidential Elections

SPORTS

Professional Sports Teams

Team Name	League	Year Established

No teams are located in the metro area
Source: Wikipedia, Major Professional Sports Teams of the United States and Canada, April 12, 2023

CLIMATE

Average and Extreme Temperatures

Temperature	Jan	Feb	Mar	Apr	May	Jun	Jul	Aug	Sep	Oct	Nov	Dec	Yr.
Extreme High (°F)	88	91	93	96	99	103	98	98	96	95	95	90	103
Average High (°F)	75	76	80	85	89	91	91	92	90	86	80	76	84
Average Temp. (°F)	65	65	70	74	79	82	83	83	82	77	71	66	75
Average Low (°F)	54	54	59	62	68	73	74	75	74	68	61	55	65
Extreme Low (°F)	28	32	33	39	52	60	66	67	64	48	34	26	26

Note: Figures cover the years 1948-1995
Source: National Climatic Data Center, International Station Meteorological Climate Summary, 9/96

Average Precipitation/Snowfall/Humidity

Precip./Humidity	Jan	Feb	Mar	Apr	May	Jun	Jul	Aug	Sep	Oct	Nov	Dec	Yr.
Avg. Precip. (in.)	2.0	2.2	2.6	1.7	3.6	9.3	8.9	8.9	8.2	3.5	1.4	1.5	53.9
Avg. Snowfall (in.)	0	0	0	0	0	0	0	0	0	0	0	0	0
Avg. Rel. Hum. 7am (%)	90	89	89	88	87	89	90	91	92	90	90	90	90
Avg. Rel. Hum. 4pm (%)	56	54	52	50	53	64	68	67	66	59	58	57	59

Note: Figures cover the years 1948-1995; Tr = Trace amounts (<0.05 in. of rain; <0.5 in. of snow)
Source: National Climatic Data Center, International Station Meteorological Climate Summary, 9/96

Weather Conditions

Temperature			Daytime Sky			Precipitation		
32°F & below	45°F & below	90°F & above	Clear	Partly cloudy	Cloudy	0.01 inch or more precip.	0.1 inch or more snow/ice	Thunder-storms
1	18	115	93	220	52	110	0	92

Note: Figures are average number of days per year and cover the years 1948-1995
Source: National Climatic Data Center, International Station Meteorological Climate Summary, 9/96

HAZARDOUS WASTE

Superfund Sites

The Cape Coral-Fort Myers, FL metro area has no sites on the EPA's Superfund Final National Priorities List. There are a total of 1,165 Superfund sites with a status of proposed or final on the list in the U.S. *U.S. Environmental Protection Agency, National Priorities List, April 12, 2023*

AIR QUALITY

Air Quality Trends: Ozone

	1990	1995	2000	2005	2010	2015	2018	2019	2020	2021
MSA[1]	0.069	0.066	0.073	0.071	0.065	0.058	0.065	0.062	0.061	0.055
U.S.	0.087	0.089	0.081	0.080	0.072	0.067	0.069	0.065	0.065	0.067

Note: (1) Data covers the Cape Coral-Fort Myers, FL Metropolitan Statistical Area. The values shown are the composite ozone concentration averages among trend sites based on the highest fourth daily maximum 8-hour concentration in parts per million. These trends are based on sites having an adequate record of monitoring data during the trend period. Data from exceptional events are included.
Source: U.S. Environmental Protection Agency, Air Quality Monitoring Information, "Air Quality Trends by City, 1990-2021"

Air Quality Index

Area	Percent of Days when Air Quality was...[2]						AQI Statistics[2]	
	Good	Moderate	Unhealthy for Sensitive Groups	Unhealthy	Very Unhealthy	Maximum	Median
MSA[1]	91.0	9.0	0.0	0.0	0.0	97	36

Note: (1) Data covers the Cape Coral-Fort Myers, FL Metropolitan Statistical Area; (2) Based on 365 days with AQI data in 2021. Air Quality Index (AQI) is an index for reporting daily air quality. EPA calculates the AQI for five major air pollutants regulated by the Clean Air Act: ground-level ozone, particle pollution (aka particulate matter), carbon monoxide, sulfur dioxide, and nitrogen dioxide. The AQI runs from 0 to 500. The higher the AQI value, the greater the level of air pollution and the greater the health concern. There are six AQI categories: "Good" AQI is between 0 and 50. Air quality is considered satisfactory; "Moderate" AQI is between 51 and 100. Air quality is acceptable; "Unhealthy for Sensitive Groups" When AQI values are between 101 and 150, members of sensitive groups may experience health effects; "Unhealthy" When AQI values are between 151 and 200 everyone may begin to experience health effects; "Very Unhealthy" AQI values between 201 and 300 trigger a health alert; "Hazardous" AQI values over 300 trigger warnings of emergency conditions (not shown).
Source: U.S. Environmental Protection Agency, Air Quality Index Report, 2021

Air Quality Index Pollutants

Area	Percent of Days when AQI Pollutant was...[2]					
	Carbon Monoxide	Nitrogen Dioxide	Ozone	Sulfur Dioxide	Particulate Matter 2.5	Particulate Matter 10
MSA[1]	0.0	0.0	66.0	(3)	32.9	1.1

Note: (1) Data covers the Cape Coral-Fort Myers, FL Metropolitan Statistical Area; (2) Based on 365 days with AQI data in 2021. The Air Quality Index (AQI) is an index for reporting daily air quality. EPA calculates the AQI for five major air pollutants regulated by the Clean Air Act: ground-level ozone, particle pollution (also known as particulate matter), carbon monoxide, sulfur dioxide, and nitrogen dioxide. The AQI runs from 0 to 500. The higher the AQI value, the greater the level of air pollution and the greater the health concern; (3) Sulfur dioxide is no longer included in this table (as of December 8, 2021) because SO_2 concentrations tend to be very localized and not necessarily representative of broad geographical areas like counties and CBSAs.
Source: U.S. Environmental Protection Agency, Air Quality Index Report, 2021

Maximum Air Pollutant Concentrations: Particulate Matter, Ozone, CO and Lead

	Particulate Matter 10 (ug/m^3)	Particulate Matter 2.5 Wtd AM (ug/m^3)	Particulate Matter 2.5 24-Hr (ug/m^3)	Ozone (ppm)	Carbon Monoxide (ppm)	Lead (ug/m^3)
MSA[1] Level	54	7.3	17	0.055	n/a	n/a
NAAQS[2]	150	15	35	0.075	9	0.15
Met NAAQS[2]	Yes	Yes	Yes	Yes	n/a	n/a

Note: (1) Data covers the Cape Coral-Fort Myers, FL Metropolitan Statistical Area; Data from exceptional events are included; (2) National Ambient Air Quality Standards; ppm = parts per million; ug/m^3 = micrograms per cubic meter; n/a not available.
Concentrations: Particulate Matter 10 (coarse particulate)—highest second maximum 24-hour concentration; Particulate Matter 2.5 Wtd AM (fine particulate)—highest weighted annual mean concentration; Particulate Matter 2.5 24-Hour (fine particulate)—highest 98th percentile 24-hour concentration; Ozone—highest fourth daily maximum 8-hour concentration; Carbon Monoxide—highest second maximum non-overlapping 8-hour concentration; Lead—maximum running 3-month average
Source: U.S. Environmental Protection Agency, Air Quality Monitoring Information, "Air Quality Statistics by City, 2021"

Maximum Air Pollutant Concentrations: Nitrogen Dioxide and Sulfur Dioxide

	Nitrogen Dioxide AM (ppb)	Nitrogen Dioxide 1-Hr (ppb)	Sulfur Dioxide AM (ppb)	Sulfur Dioxide 1-Hr (ppb)	Sulfur Dioxide 24-Hr (ppb)
MSA[1] Level	n/a	n/a	n/a	n/a	n/a
NAAQS[2]	53	100	30	75	140
Met NAAQS[2]	n/a	n/a	n/a	n/a	n/a

Note: (1) Data covers the Cape Coral-Fort Myers, FL Metropolitan Statistical Area; Data from exceptional events are included; (2) National Ambient Air Quality Standards; ppm = parts per million; ug/m^3 = micrograms per cubic meter; n/a not available.
Concentrations: Nitrogen Dioxide AM—highest arithmetic mean concentration; Nitrogen Dioxide 1-Hr—highest 98th percentile 1-hour daily maximum concentration; Sulfur Dioxide AM—highest annual mean concentration; Sulfur Dioxide 1-Hr—highest 99th percentile 1-hour daily maximum concentration; Sulfur Dioxide 24-Hr—highest second maximum 24-hour concentration
Source: U.S. Environmental Protection Agency, Air Quality Monitoring Information, "Air Quality Statistics by City, 2021"

Charleston, South Carolina

Background

Charleston is located on the state's Atlantic coastline, 110 miles southeast of Columbia and 100 miles north of Savannah, Georgia. The city, named for King Charles II of England, is the county seat of Charleston County. Charleston is located on a bay at the end of a peninsula between the Ashley and Cooper rivers. The terrain is low-lying and coastal with nearby islands and inlets.

In 1670, English colonists established a nearby settlement, and subsequently moved to Charleston's present site. Charleston became an early trading center for rice, indigo, cotton, and other goods. As the plantation economy grew, Charleston became a slave-trading center. In 1861, the Confederacy fired the cannon shot that launched the Civil War from the city's Battery, aimed at the Union's Fort Sumter in Charleston Harbor. Charleston was under siege during the Civil War and experienced many difficulties during Reconstruction. Manufacturing industries including textiles and ironwork became important in the nineteenth century.

Charleston is part of a commercial and cultural center and southern transportation hub whose port is among the nation's busiest shipping facilities. Charleston's other economic sectors include manufacturing, health care, business and professional services, defense activity, retail and wholesale trade, tourism, education, and construction.

Charleston is a popular tourist area, based on its scenery, history, and recreation. The city center is well known for its historic neighborhoods with distinctive early southern architecture and ambiance. As one of the first American cities in the early twentieth century to actively encourage historic restoration and preservation, Charleston has undertaken numerous revitalization initiatives, including the Charleston Place Hotel and retail complex, and Waterfront Park.

In 2000, the Confederate submarine the *HL Hunley*, which sank in 1864, was raised, and brought to a conservation laboratory at the old Charleston Naval Base. As preservation efforts continue, tours are offered on Saturdays and Sundays. Best-selling crime author Patricia Cornwell has donated $500,000 to help researchers solve the mystery of the sinking of the sub, which was the first submarine in history to sink an enemy warship

Charleston is a center for health care and medical research. SPAWAR (US Navy Space and Naval Warfare Systems Command) is the area's largest single employer followed by the Medical University of South Carolina. Other area educational institutions include The College of Charleston, The Citadel Military College, Trident Technical College, Charleston Southern University, and a campus of Johnson and Wales University.

The Charleston area has numerous parks, including a skateboard center and public waterfront areas. Coastal recreation activities such as boating, swimming, fishing and beaches are popular, as are golf and other land sports.

The Charleston Museum is the nation's oldest, founded in 1773. In addition to the area's former plantations, attractions include the South Carolina Aquarium, American Military Museum, Drayton Hall Plantation Museum, Gibbes Museum of Art, Karpeles Manuscript Museum, and North Charleston Convention Center and Performing Arts Center. Cultural organizations include the Spoleto Festival and the annual Charleston International Film Festival, CIFF.

In 2015, 21-year-old Dylann Roof entered Charleston's historic Emanuel African Methodist Episcopal Church and opened fire, killing nine people. The attack garnered national attention, and sparked a debate on racism, Confederate symbolism in Southern states, and gun violence. A month after the attack, the Confederate battle flag was removed from the South Carolina State House and in 2020, the city formally apologized for its role in the American slave trade.

The nearby Atlantic Ocean moderates the climate, especially in winter, and keeps summer a bit cooler than expected. Expect extended summers in fall, and a possible hurricane, while spring sharply turns from the cold winds of March to lovely May. Severe storms are possible.

Rankings

General Rankings

- For its "Best for Vets: Places to Live 2019" rankings, *Military Times* evaluated 599 cities (83 large, 234 medium, 282 small) and compared the locations across three broad categories: veteran and military culture/services; economic indicators; and livability factors such as health, crime, traffic, and school quality. Charleston ranked #24 out of the top 50, in the medium-sized city category (population of 100,000-249,999). Data points more specific to veterans and the military weighed more heavily than others. *rebootcamp.militarytimes.com*, "Military Times Best Places to Live 2019," September 10, 2018

- *Insider* listed 23 places in the U.S. that travel industry trends reveal would be popular destinations in 2023. This year the list trends towards cultural and historical happenings, sports events, wellness experiences and invigorating outdoor escapes. According to the website insider.com Charleston is a place to visit in 2023. *Insider,* "23 of the Best Places You Should Travel to in the U.S. in 2023," December 17, 2022

- The Charleston metro area was identified as one of America's fastest-growing areas in terms of population and business growth by *MagnifyMoney*. The area ranked #4 out of 35. The 100 most populous metro areas in the U.S. were evaluated on their change from 2011 to 2016 in the following categories: people and housing; workforce and employment opportunities; growing industry. *www.businessinsider.com*, "The 35 Cities in the US with the Biggest Influx of People, the Most Work Opportunities, and the Hottest Business Growth," August 12, 2018

- Charleston was selected as one of the best places in the world that are "under the radar, ahead of the curve, and ready for exploring" by *National Geographic Travel* editors. The list reflects 25 of the most extraordinary and inspiring destinations that also support local communities and ecosystems. These timeless must-see sites for 2023, are framed by the five categories of Culture, Family, Adventure, Community, and Nature. *www.nationalgeographic.com/travel*, "Best of the World, 25 Breathtaking Places And Experiences for 2023," October 26, 2022

- Charleston appeared on *Travel + Leisure's* list of "The 15 Best Cities in the United States." The city was ranked #1. Criteria: sights/landmarks; culture; food; friendliness; shopping; and overall value. *Travel + Leisure,* "The World's Best Awards 2022" July 12, 2022

- For its 35th annual "Readers' Choice Awards" survey, *Condé Nast Traveler* ranked its readers' favorite cities in the U.S. Whether it be a longed-for visit or a first on the list, these are the places that inspired a return to travel. The list was broken into large cities and cities under 250,000. Charleston ranked #1 in the small city category. *Condé Nast Traveler, Readers' Choice Awards 2022,* "Best Small Cities in the U.S." October 4, 2022

Business/Finance Rankings

- The Brookings Institution ranked the nation's largest cities based on income inequality. Charleston was ranked #11 (#1 = greatest inequality). Criteria: the "95/20 ratio," a figure representing the income at which a household earns more than 95 percent of all other households, divided by the income at which a household earns more than only 20 percent of all other households. *Brookings Institution,* "Household Income Inequality, Largest Cities of 97 Large U.S. Metro Areas, 2014-2016," February 5, 2018

- The Brookings Institution ranked the 100 largest metro areas in the U.S. based on income inequality. Charleston was ranked #27 (#1 = greatest inequality). Criteria: the "95/20 ratio," a figure representing the income at which a household earns more than 95 percent of all other households, divided by the income at which a household earns more than only 20 percent of all other households. *Brookings Institution,* "Household Income Inequality, 100 Largest U.S. Metro Areas, 2014-2016," February 5, 2018

- Charleston was cited as one of America's top metros for total major capital investment facility projects in 2022. The area ranked #7 in the mid-sized metro area category (population 200,000 to 1 million). *Site Selection,* "Top Metros of 2022," March 2023

- The Charleston metro area appeared on the Milken Institute "2022 Best Performing Cities" list. Rank: #54 out of 200 large metro areas (population over 250,000). Criteria: job growth; wage and salary growth; high-tech output growth; housing affordability; household broadband access. *Milken Institute,* "Best-Performing Cities 2022," March 28, 2022

- *Forbes* ranked the 200 most populous metro areas to determine the nation's "Best Places for Business and Careers." The Charleston metro area was ranked #24. Criteria: costs (business and living); job growth (past and projected); income growth; quality of life; educational attainment (college and high school); projected economic growth; cultural and leisure opportunities; workplace tolerance laws; net migration patterns. *Forbes,* "The Best Places for Business and Careers 2019: Seattle Still On Top," October 30, 2019

Culture/Performing Arts Rankings

- Charleston was selected as one of "America's Favorite Cities." The city ranked #5 in the "Architecture" category. Respondents to an online survey were asked to rate their favorite place (population over 100,000) in over 65 categories. *Travelandleisure.com, "America's Favorite Cities for Architecture 2016," March 2, 2017*

Education Rankings

- Personal finance website *WalletHub* analyzed the 150 largest U.S. metropolitan statistical areas to determine where the most educated Americans are putting their degrees to work. Criteria: education levels; percentage of workers with degrees; education quality and attainment gap; public school quality rankings; quality and enrollment of each metro area's universities. Charleston was ranked #54 (#1 = most educated city). *www.WalletHub.com, "Most & Least Educated Cities in America," July 18, 2022*

Health/Fitness Rankings

- Trulia analyzed the 100 largest U.S. metro areas to identify the nation's best cities for weight loss, based on the percentage of adults who bike or walk to work, sporting goods stores, grocery stores, access to outdoor activities, weight-loss centers, gyms, and average space reserved for parks. Charleston ranked #6. *Trulia.com, "Where to Live to Get in Shape in the New Year," January 4, 2018*

- Charleston was identified as a "2022 Spring Allergy Capital." The area ranked #29 out of 100. Three groups of factors were used to identify the most challenging cities for people with allergies during the spring season: annual spring pollen scores; over the counter allergy medicine use; number of board-certified allergy specialists. *Asthma and Allergy Foundation of America, "Spring Allergy Capitals 2022," March 2, 2022*

- Charleston was identified as a "2022 Fall Allergy Capital." The area ranked #31 out of 100. Three groups of factors were used to identify the most challenging cities for people with allergies during the fall season: annual fall pollen scores; over the counter allergy medicine use; number of board-certified allergy specialists. *Asthma and Allergy Foundation of America, "Fall Allergy Capitals 2022," March 2, 2022*

- Charleston was identified as a "2022 Asthma Capital." The area ranked #6 out of the nation's 100 largest metropolitan areas. Criteria: estimated asthma prevalence; asthma-related mortality; and ER visits due to asthma. Risk factors analyzed but not factored in the rankings: annual pollen score; annual air quality; public smoking laws; access to board-certified asthma specialists; rescue and controller medication use; uninsured rate; poverty rate. *Asthma and Allergy Foundation of America, "Asthma Capitals 2022: The Most Challenging Places to Live With Asthma," September 14, 2022*

Real Estate Rankings

- *WalletHub* compared the most populated U.S. cities to determine which had the best markets for real estate agents. Charleston ranked #70 where demand was high and pay was the best. Criteria: sales per agent; annual median wage for real-estate agents; monthly average starting salary for real estate agents; real estate job density and competition; unemployment rate; home turnover rate; housing-market health index; and other relevant metrics. *www.WalletHub.com, "2021 Best Places to Be a Real Estate Agent," May 12, 2021*

- Charleston was ranked #8 in the top 20 out of the 100 largest metro areas in terms of house price appreciation in 2022 (#1 = highest rate). *Federal Housing Finance Agency, House Price Index, 4th Quarter 2022*

- Charleston was ranked #123 out of 235 metro areas in terms of housing affordability in 2022 by the National Association of Home Builders (#1 = most affordable). Criteria: the share of homes sold in that area affordable to a family earning the local median income, based on standard mortgage underwriting criteria. *National Association of Home Builders®, NAHB-Wells Fargo Housing Opportunity Index, 4th Quarter 2022*

Safety Rankings

- Allstate ranked the 200 largest cities in America in terms of driver safety. Charleston ranked #80. Criteria: internal property damage claims over a two-year period from January 2016 to December 2017. The report helps increase the importance of safety and awareness behind the wheel. *Allstate, "Allstate America's Best Drivers Report, 2019" June 24, 2019*

- The National Insurance Crime Bureau ranked 390 metro areas in the U.S. in terms of per capita rates of vehicle theft. The Charleston metro area ranked #84 (#1 = highest rate). Criteria: number of vehicle theft offenses per 100,000 inhabitants in 2021. *National Insurance Crime Bureau, "Hot Spots 2021," September 1, 2022*

Seniors/Retirement Rankings

- From its Best Cities for Successful Aging indexes, the Milken Institute generated rankings for metropolitan areas, weighing data in nine categories—health care, wellness, living arrangements, transportation and convenience, financial characteristics, education, employment, community engagement, and overall livability. The Charleston metro area was ranked #39 overall in the large metro area category. *Milken Institute, "Best Cities for Successful Aging, 2017" March 14, 2017*

- Charleston was identified as #9 of 20 most popular places to retire in the Southeast region by *Topretirements.com*. The site separated its annual "Best Places to Retire" list by major U.S. regions for 2019. The list reflects the 20 cities that visitors to the website are most interested in for retirement, based on the number of times a city's review was viewed on the website. *Topretirements.com, "20 Most Popular Places to Retire in the Southeast: 2019," October 16, 2019*

Women/Minorities Rankings

- *Travel + Leisure* listed the best cities in and around the U.S. for a memorable and fun girls' trip, even on a budget. Whether it is for a special occasion, to make new memories or just to get away, Charleston is sure to have something for all the ladies in your tribe. *Travel + Leisure, "25 Affordable Girls Weekend Getaways That Won't Break the Bank," November 25, 2022*

- Personal finance website *WalletHub* compared more than 180 U.S. cities across two key dimensions, "Hispanic Business-Friendliness" and "Hispanic Purchasing Power," to arrive at the most favorable conditions for Hispanic entrepreneurs. Charleston was ranked #81 out of 182. Criteria includes: share of Hispanic-Owned Businesses; Hispanic entrepreneurship rate to median annual income of Hispanics; Small Business-Friendliness score; cost of living; and number of Hispanics with at least a bachelor's degree. *WalletHub.com, "2019's Best Cities for Hispanic Entrepreneurs," May 1, 2019*

Miscellaneous Rankings

- In *Condé Nast Traveler* magazine's 2022 Readers' Choice Survey, Charleston made the top ten list of friendliest American cities. Charleston ranked #2. *www.cntraveler.com, "The 10 Friendliest Cities in the U.S.," December 20, 2022*

- *WalletHub* compared the 150 most populated U.S. cities to determine their operating efficiency. A "Quality of Services" score was constructed for each city and then divided by the total budget per capita to reveal which were managed the best. Charleston ranked #22. Criteria: financial stability; economy; education; safety; health; infrastructure and pollution. *www.WalletHub.com, "2022's Best- & Worst-Run Cities in America," June 21, 2022*

Business Environment

DEMOGRAPHICS

Population Growth

Area	1990 Census	2000 Census	2010 Census	2020 Census	Population Growth (%) 1990-2020	Population Growth (%) 2010-2020
City	96,102	96,650	120,083	150,227	56.3	25.1
MSA[1]	506,875	549,033	664,607	799,636	57.8	20.3
U.S.	248,709,873	281,421,906	308,745,538	331,449,281	33.3	7.4

Note: (1) Figures cover the Charleston-North Charleston, SC Metropolitan Statistical Area
Source: U.S. Census Bureau, 1990 Census, 2000 Census, 2010 Census, 2020 Census

Race

Area	White Alone[2] (%)	Black Alone[2] (%)	Asian Alone[2] (%)	AIAN[3] Alone[2] (%)	NHOPI[4] Alone[2] (%)	Other Race Alone[2] (%)	Two or More Races (%)
City	73.5	17.0	2.2	0.3	0.1	1.6	5.3
MSA[1]	64.0	23.0	2.0	0.5	0.1	3.9	6.5
U.S.	61.6	12.4	6.0	1.1	0.2	8.4	10.2

Note: (1) Figures cover the Charleston-North Charleston, SC Metropolitan Statistical Area; (2) Alone is defined as not being in combination with one or more other races; (3) American Indian and Alaska Native; (4) Native Hawaiian and Other Pacific Islander
Source: U.S. Census Bureau, 2020 Census

Hispanic or Latino Origin

Area	Total (%)	Mexican (%)	Puerto Rican (%)	Cuban (%)	Other (%)
City	4.2	1.9	0.6	0.1	1.6
MSA[1]	5.9	2.7	0.8	0.1	2.3
U.S.	18.4	11.2	1.8	0.7	4.7

Note: Persons of Hispanic or Latino origin can be of any race; (1) Figures cover the Charleston-North Charleston, SC Metropolitan Statistical Area
Source: U.S. Census Bureau, 2017-2021 American Community Survey 5-Year Estimates

Age

Area	Under Age 5	Age 5–19	Age 20–34	Age 35–44	Age 45–54	Age 55–64	Age 65–74	Age 75–84	Age 85+	Median Age
City	5.6	14.6	28.5	13.9	10.3	11.2	9.7	4.4	1.8	35.7
MSA[1]	5.8	18.6	21.4	13.5	11.8	12.6	10.0	4.6	1.5	37.8
U.S.	5.6	19.2	20.2	12.7	12.4	13.1	10.0	4.9	1.9	38.8

Note: (1) Figures cover the Charleston-North Charleston, SC Metropolitan Statistical Area
Source: U.S. Census Bureau, 2020 Census

Disability by Age

Area	All Ages	Under 18 Years Old	18 to 64 Years Old	65 Years and Over
City	9.3	2.9	6.2	30.5
MSA[1]	11.6	3.9	9.2	32.1
U.S.	12.6	4.4	10.3	33.4

Note: Figures show percent of the civilian noninstitutionalized population that reported having a disability. Disability status is determined from six types of difficulty: vision, hearing, cognitive, ambulatory, self-care, and independent living. For children under 5 years old, hearing and vision difficulty are used to determine disability status. For children between the ages of 5 and 14, disability status is determined from hearing, vision, cognitive, ambulatory, and self-care difficulties. For people aged 15 years and older, they are considered to have a disability if they have difficulty with any one of the six difficulty types; Note: (1) Figures cover the Charleston-North Charleston, SC Metropolitan Statistical Area
Source: U.S. Census Bureau, 2017-2021 American Community Survey 5-Year Estimates

Ancestry

Area	German	Irish	English	American	Italian	Polish	French[2]	Scottish	Dutch
City	10.8	10.5	11.4	21.1	4.2	2.2	2.5	2.3	0.7
MSA[1]	10.1	9.5	10.6	11.8	3.9	1.8	2.1	2.3	0.6
U.S.	12.8	9.6	8.1	5.7	5.0	2.7	2.2	1.6	1.1

Note: Figures are the percentage of the total population reporting a particular ancestry. The nine most commonly reported ancestries in the U.S. are shown. Figures include multiple ancestries (e.g. if a person reported being Irish and Italian, they were included in both columns); (1) Figures cover the Charleston-North Charleston, SC Metropolitan Statistical Area; (2) Excludes Basque
Source: U.S. Census Bureau, 2017-2021 American Community Survey 5-Year Estimates

Foreign-born Population

Area	Any Foreign Country	Asia	Mexico	Europe	Caribbean	Central America[2]	South America	Africa	Canada
City	5.0	1.5	0.6	1.3	0.4	0.1	0.6	0.3	0.1
MSA[1]	5.8	1.5	1.0	1.1	0.3	0.6	0.7	0.2	0.2
U.S.	13.6	4.2	3.3	1.5	1.4	1.1	1.1	0.8	0.2

Note: (1) Figures cover the Charleston-North Charleston, SC Metropolitan Statistical Area; (2) Excludes Mexico.
Source: U.S. Census Bureau, 2017-2021 American Community Survey 5-Year Estimates

Household Size

Area	One	Two	Three	Four	Five	Six	Seven or More	Average Household Size
City	35.0	38.5	13.3	9.6	2.8	0.6	0.2	2.20
MSA[1]	28.7	36.2	16.2	11.8	5.0	1.4	0.7	2.50
U.S.	28.1	33.8	15.5	12.9	6.0	2.3	1.4	2.60

Note: (1) Figures cover the Charleston-North Charleston, SC Metropolitan Statistical Area
Source: U.S. Census Bureau, 2017-2021 American Community Survey 5-Year Estimates

Household Relationships

Area	Householder	Opposite-sex Spouse	Same-sex Spouse	Opposite-sex Unmarried Partner	Same-sex Unmarried Partner	Child[2]	Grandchild	Other Relatives	Non-relatives
City	45.0	17.0	0.3	3.1	0.2	21.8	1.4	2.7	5.3
MSA[1]	39.9	18.1	0.2	2.4	0.1	27.3	2.6	3.8	3.5
U.S.	38.3	17.5	0.2	2.5	0.2	28.3	2.4	4.8	3.4

Note: Figures are percent of the total population; (1) Figures cover the Charleston-North Charleston, SC Metropolitan Statistical Area; (2) Includes biological, adopted, and stepchildren of the householder
Source: U.S. Census Bureau, 2020 Census

Gender

Area	Males	Females	Males per 100 Females
City	71,681	78,546	91.3
MSA[1]	389,850	409,786	95.1
U.S.	162,685,811	168,763,470	96.4

Note: (1) Figures cover the Charleston-North Charleston, SC Metropolitan Statistical Area
Source: U.S. Census Bureau, 2020 Census

Marital Status

Area	Never Married	Now Married[2]	Separated	Widowed	Divorced
City	40.3	43.3	1.6	5.1	9.8
MSA[1]	33.8	48.5	2.1	5.3	10.3
U.S.	33.8	48.0	1.8	5.6	10.8

Note: Figures are percentages and cover the population 15 years of age and older; (1) Figures cover the Charleston-North Charleston, SC Metropolitan Statistical Area; (2) Excludes separated
Source: U.S. Census Bureau, 2017-2021 American Community Survey 5-Year Estimates

Religious Groups by Family

Area	Catholic	Baptist	Methodist	LDS[2]	Pentecostal	Lutheran	Islam	Adventist	Other
MSA[1]	11.5	7.7	8.0	0.8	1.9	0.7	0.2	1.0	12.8
U.S.	18.7	7.3	3.0	2.0	1.8	1.7	1.3	1.3	11.6

Note: Figures are the number of adherents as a percentage of the total population and cover the eight largest religious groups in the U.S; (1) Figures cover the Charleston-North Charleston, SC Metropolitan Statistical Area; (2) Church of Jesus Christ of Latter-day Saints
Sources: 2020 U.S. Religion Census, Association of Statisticians of American Religious Bodies; The Association of Religion Data Archives (ARDA)

Religious Groups by Tradition

Area	Catholic	Evangelical Protestant	Mainline Protestant	Black Protestant	Islam	Judaism	Hinduism	Orthodox	Buddhism
MSA[1]	11.5	17.1	6.8	6.6	0.2	0.4	<0.1	0.2	n/a
U.S.	18.7	16.5	5.2	2.3	1.3	0.6	0.4	0.4	0.3

Note: Figures are the number of adherents as a percentage of the total population; (1) Figures cover the Charleston-North Charleston, SC Metropolitan Statistical Area
Sources: 2020 U.S. Religion Census, Association of Statisticians of American Religious Bodies; The Association of Religion Data Archives (ARDA)

Charleston, South Carolina   113

ECONOMY

Gross Metropolitan Product

Area	2020	2021	2022	2023	Rank[2]
MSA[1]	45.6	50.4	55.3	59.2	69

Note: Figures are in billions of dollars; (1) Figures cover the Charleston-North Charleston, SC Metropolitan Statistical Area; (2) Rank is based on 2021 data and ranges from 1 to 381
Source: U.S. Conference of Mayors, U.S. Metro Economies: U.S. Metros Compared to Global and State Economies, June 2022

Economic Growth

Area	2018-20 (%)	2021 (%)	2022 (%)	2023 (%)	Rank[2]
MSA[1]	0.4	6.3	3.8	3.8	106
U.S.	-0.6	5.7	3.1	2.9	—

Note: Figures are real gross metropolitan product (GMP) growth rates and represent average annual percent change; (1) Figures cover the Charleston-North Charleston, SC Metropolitan Statistical Area; (2) Rank is based on 2020 2-year average annual percent change and ranges from 1 to 381
Source: U.S. Conference of Mayors, U.S. Metro Economies: U.S. Metros Compared to Global and State Economies, June 2022

Metropolitan Area Exports

Area	2016	2017	2018	2019	2020	2021	Rank[2]
MSA[1]	9,508.1	8,845.2	10,943.2	16,337.9	6,110.5	3,381.6	77

Note: Figures are in millions of dollars; (1) Figures cover the Charleston-North Charleston, SC Metropolitan Statistical Area; (2) Rank is based on 2021 data and ranges from 1 to 388
Source: U.S. Department of Commerce, International Trade Administration, Office of Trade and Economic Analysis, Industry and Analysis, Exports by Metropolitan Area, data extracted March 16, 2023

Building Permits

Area	Single-Family 2021	Single-Family 2022	Pct. Chg.	Multi-Family 2021	Multi-Family 2022	Pct. Chg.	Total 2021	Total 2022	Pct. Chg.
City	1,091	942	-13.7	378	459	21.4	1,469	1,401	-4.6
MSA[1]	5,913	6,329	7.0	2,369	2,994	26.4	8,282	9,323	12.6
U.S.	1,115,400	975,600	-12.5	621,600	689,500	10.9	1,737,000	1,665,100	-4.1

Note: (1) Figures cover the Charleston-North Charleston, SC Metropolitan Statistical Area; Figures represent new, privately-owned housing units authorized (unadjusted data); All permit data are based on estimates with imputation
Source: U.S. Census Bureau, Manufacturing, Mining, and Construction Statistics, Building Permits, 2021, 2022

Bankruptcy Filings

Area	Business Filings 2021	Business Filings 2022	% Chg.	Nonbusiness Filings 2021	Nonbusiness Filings 2022	% Chg.
Charleston County	8	5	-37.5	176	228	29.5
U.S.	14,347	13,481	-6.0	399,269	374,240	-6.3

Note: Business filings include Chapter 7, Chapter 9, Chapter 11, Chapter 12, Chapter 13, Chapter 15, and Section 304; Nonbusiness filings include Chapter 7, Chapter 11, and Chapter 13
Source: Administrative Office of the U.S. Courts, Business and Nonbusiness Bankruptcy, County Cases Commenced by Chapter of the Bankruptcy Code, During the 12-Month Period Ending December 31, 2021 and Business and Nonbusiness Bankruptcy, County Cases Commenced by Chapter of the Bankruptcy Code, During the 12-Month Period Ending December 31, 2022

Housing Vacancy Rates

Area	Gross Vacancy Rate[2] (%) 2020	2021	2022	Year-Round Vacancy Rate[3] (%) 2020	2021	2022	Rental Vacancy Rate[4] (%) 2020	2021	2022	Homeowner Vacancy Rate[5] (%) 2020	2021	2022
MSA[1]	18.1	12.9	10.6	16.5	10.5	7.5	27.7	15.4	8.8	2.3	1.3	0.4
U.S.	10.6	10.8	10.5	8.2	8.4	8.2	6.3	6.1	5.8	1.0	0.9	0.8

Note: (1) Figures cover the Charleston-North Charleston, SC Metropolitan Statistical Area; (2) The percentage of the total housing inventory that is vacant; (3) The percentage of the housing inventory (excluding seasonal units) that is year-round vacant; (4) The percentage of rental inventory that is vacant for rent; (5) The percentage of homeowner inventory that is vacant for sale
Source: U.S. Census Bureau, Housing Vacancies and Homeownership Annual Statistics: 2020, 2021, 2022

INCOME

Income

Area	Per Capita ($)	Median Household ($)	Average Household ($)
City	50,240	76,556	111,903
MSA[1]	39,923	70,275	98,682
U.S.	37,638	69,021	97,196

Note: (1) Figures cover the Charleston-North Charleston, SC Metropolitan Statistical Area
Source: U.S. Census Bureau, 2017-2021 American Community Survey 5-Year Estimates

Household Income Distribution

Area	Percent of Households Earning							
	Under $15,000	$15,000 -$24,999	$25,000 -$34,999	$35,000 -$49,999	$50,000 -$74,999	$75,000 -$99,999	$100,000 -$149,999	$150,000 and up
City	9.1	6.5	6.2	11.3	15.8	12.3	18.6	20.3
MSA[1]	8.4	7.7	7.8	11.6	17.3	13.4	17.1	16.7
U.S.	9.4	7.8	8.2	11.4	16.8	12.8	16.3	17.3

Note: (1) Figures cover the Charleston-North Charleston, SC Metropolitan Statistical Area
Source: U.S. Census Bureau, 2017-2021 American Community Survey 5-Year Estimates

Poverty Rate

Area	All Ages	Under 18 Years Old	18 to 64 Years Old	65 Years and Over
City	12.0	14.6	12.6	6.4
MSA[1]	12.1	18.2	10.9	8.1
U.S.	12.6	17.0	11.8	9.6

Note: Figures are percentage of people whose income during the past 12 months was below the poverty level; (1) Figures cover the Charleston-North Charleston, SC Metropolitan Statistical Area
Source: U.S. Census Bureau, 2017-2021 American Community Survey 5-Year Estimates

EMPLOYMENT

Labor Force and Employment

Area	Civilian Labor Force			Workers Employed		
	Dec. 2021	Dec. 2022	% Chg.	Dec. 2021	Dec. 2022	% Chg.
City	75,129	76,762	2.2	73,011	74,897	2.6
MSA[1]	400,171	408,735	2.1	388,529	398,569	2.6
U.S.	161,696,000	164,224,000	1.6	155,732,000	158,872,000	2.0

Note: Data is not seasonally adjusted and covers workers 16 years of age and older; (1) Figures cover the Charleston-North Charleston, SC Metropolitan Statistical Area
Source: Bureau of Labor Statistics, Local Area Unemployment Statistics

Unemployment Rate

Area	2022											
	Jan.	Feb.	Mar.	Apr.	May	Jun.	Jul.	Aug.	Sep.	Oct.	Nov.	Dec.
City	3.1	3.5	2.9	2.1	2.5	2.8	2.6	2.6	2.4	2.8	2.2	2.4
MSA[1]	3.2	3.6	2.9	2.3	2.8	3.0	2.7	2.8	2.7	3.1	2.2	2.5
U.S.	4.4	4.1	3.8	3.3	3.4	3.8	3.8	3.8	3.3	3.4	3.4	3.3

Note: Data is not seasonally adjusted and covers workers 16 years of age and older; (1) Figures cover the Charleston-North Charleston, SC Metropolitan Statistical Area
Source: Bureau of Labor Statistics, Local Area Unemployment Statistics

Average Wages

Occupation	$/Hr.	Occupation	$/Hr.
Accountants and Auditors	38.80	Maintenance and Repair Workers	21.41
Automotive Mechanics	22.64	Marketing Managers	52.80
Bookkeepers	20.63	Network and Computer Systems Admin.	46.31
Carpenters	23.50	Nurses, Licensed Practical	25.74
Cashiers	12.44	Nurses, Registered	36.96
Computer Programmers	n/a	Nursing Assistants	17.18
Computer Systems Analysts	51.58	Office Clerks, General	17.46
Computer User Support Specialists	26.98	Physical Therapists	41.79
Construction Laborers	18.51	Physicians	141.24
Cooks, Restaurant	15.93	Plumbers, Pipefitters and Steamfitters	24.76
Customer Service Representatives	18.41	Police and Sheriff's Patrol Officers	25.12
Dentists	87.52	Postal Service Mail Carriers	26.88
Electricians	25.86	Real Estate Sales Agents	29.27
Engineers, Electrical	46.55	Retail Salespersons	15.26
Fast Food and Counter Workers	11.69	Sales Representatives, Technical/Scientific	37.04
Financial Managers	65.85	Secretaries, Exc. Legal/Medical/Executive	19.15
First-Line Supervisors of Office Workers	29.33	Security Guards	14.67
General and Operations Managers	52.71	Surgeons	n/a
Hairdressers/Cosmetologists	16.62	Teacher Assistants, Exc. Postsecondary*	12.32
Home Health and Personal Care Aides	13.41	Teachers, Secondary School, Exc. Sp. Ed.*	27.85
Janitors and Cleaners	13.93	Telemarketers	n/a
Landscaping/Groundskeeping Workers	16.99	Truck Drivers, Heavy/Tractor-Trailer	25.58
Lawyers	53.48	Truck Drivers, Light/Delivery Services	19.54
Maids and Housekeeping Cleaners	13.47	Waiters and Waitresses	11.64

Note: Wage data covers the Charleston-North Charleston, SC Metropolitan Statistical Area; (*) Hourly wages were calculated from annual wage data based on a 40 hour work week; n/a not available.
Source: Bureau of Labor Statistics, Metro Area Occupational Employment & Wage Estimates, May 2022

Charleston, South Carolina

Employment by Industry

Sector	MSA[1] Number of Employees	MSA[1] Percent of Total	U.S. Percent of Total
Construction, Mining, and Logging	21,800	5.4	5.4
Private Education and Health Services	47,500	11.7	16.1
Financial Activities	19,700	4.9	5.9
Government	67,700	16.7	14.5
Information	8,900	2.2	2.0
Leisure and Hospitality	50,500	12.5	10.3
Manufacturing	30,800	7.6	8.4
Other Services	15,600	3.9	3.7
Professional and Business Services	65,400	16.2	14.7
Retail Trade	44,100	10.9	10.2
Transportation, Warehousing, and Utilities	20,600	5.1	4.9
Wholesale Trade	12,200	3.0	3.9

Note: Figures are non-farm employment as of December 2022. Figures are not seasonally adjusted and include workers 16 years of age and older; (1) Figures cover the Charleston-North Charleston, SC Metropolitan Statistical Area
Source: Bureau of Labor Statistics, Current Employment Statistics, Employment, Hours, and Earnings

Employment by Occupation

Occupation Classification	City (%)	MSA[1] (%)	U.S. (%)
Management, Business, Science, and Arts	51.9	42.1	40.3
Natural Resources, Construction, and Maintenance	5.9	9.4	8.7
Production, Transportation, and Material Moving	7.1	11.5	13.1
Sales and Office	20.7	20.8	20.9
Service	14.5	16.3	17.0

Note: Figures cover employed civilians 16 years of age and older; (1) Figures cover the Charleston-North Charleston, SC Metropolitan Statistical Area
Source: U.S. Census Bureau, 2017-2021 American Community Survey 5-Year Estimates

Occupations with Greatest Projected Employment Growth: 2022 – 2024

Occupation[1]	2022 Employment	2024 Projected Employment	Numeric Employment Change	Percent Employment Change
Laborers and Freight, Stock, and Material Movers, Hand	65,510	67,830	2,320	3.5
Cooks, Restaurant	24,980	26,740	1,760	7.0
Home Health and Personal Care Aides	32,690	34,380	1,690	5.2
Retail Salespersons	71,670	73,260	1,590	2.2
Stockers and Order Fillers	32,230	33,820	1,590	4.9
Fast Food and Counter Workers	68,620	69,700	1,080	1.6
Miscellaneous Assemblers and Fabricators	42,810	43,730	920	2.1
General and Operations Managers	32,800	33,630	830	2.5
Waiters and Waitresses	37,090	37,880	790	2.1
Customer Service Representatives	59,220	59,970	750	1.3

Note: Projections cover South Carolina; (1) Sorted by numeric employment change
Source: www.projectionscentral.com, State Occupational Projections, 2022–2024 Short-Term Projections

Fastest-Growing Occupations: 2022 – 2024

Occupation[1]	2022 Employment	2024 Projected Employment	Numeric Employment Change	Percent Employment Change
Nurse Practitioners	3,070	3,400	330	10.7
Logisticians	3,160	3,440	280	8.9
Chemical Engineers	600	650	50	8.3
Software Developers and Software Quality Assurance Analysts and Testers	8,510	9,190	680	8.0
Physician Assistants	1,660	1,790	130	7.8
Electrical, Electronic, and Electromechanical Assemblers, Except Coil Winders, Tapers, and Fini	4,730	5,100	370	7.8
Information Security Analysts (SOC 2018)	1,700	1,830	130	7.6
Financial Examiners	700	750	50	7.1
Personal Financial Advisors	2,700	2,890	190	7.0
Cooks, Restaurant	24,980	26,740	1,760	7.0

Note: Projections cover South Carolina; (1) Sorted by percent employment change and excludes occupations with numeric employment change less than 50
Source: www.projectionscentral.com, State Occupational Projections, 2022–2024 Short-Term Projections

CITY FINANCES

City Government Finances

Component	2020 ($000)	2020 ($ per capita)
Total Revenues	443,260	3,222
Total Expenditures	481,641	3,501
Debt Outstanding	784,866	5,705
Cash and Securities[1]	680,882	4,949

Note: (1) Cash and security holdings of a government at the close of its fiscal year, including those of its dependent agencies, utilities, and liquor stores.
Source: U.S. Census Bureau, State & Local Government Finances 2020

City Government Revenue by Source

Source	2020 ($000)	2020 ($ per capita)	2020 (%)
General Revenue			
From Federal Government	6,750	49	1.5
From State Government	5,472	40	1.2
From Local Governments	0	0	0.0
Taxes			
Property	100,131	728	22.6
Sales and Gross Receipts	53,394	388	12.0
Personal Income	0	0	0.0
Corporate Income	0	0	0.0
Motor Vehicle License	0	0	0.0
Other Taxes	60,131	437	13.6
Current Charges	34,959	254	7.9
Liquor Store	0	0	0.0
Utility	146,018	1,061	32.9

Source: U.S. Census Bureau, State & Local Government Finances 2020

City Government Expenditures by Function

Function	2020 ($000)	2020 ($ per capita)	2020 (%)
General Direct Expenditures			
Air Transportation	0	0	0.0
Corrections	0	0	0.0
Education	0	0	0.0
Employment Security Administration	0	0	0.0
Financial Administration	21,231	154	4.4
Fire Protection	35,200	255	7.3
General Public Buildings	379	2	0.1
Governmental Administration, Other	10,615	77	2.2
Health	0	0	0.0
Highways	5,961	43	1.2
Hospitals	0	0	0.0
Housing and Community Development	3,014	21	0.6
Interest on General Debt	6,110	44	1.3
Judicial and Legal	5,830	42	1.2
Libraries	0	0	0.0
Parking	36,000	261	7.5
Parks and Recreation	34,980	254	7.3
Police Protection	55,554	403	11.5
Public Welfare	1,339	9	0.3
Sewerage	32,624	237	6.8
Solid Waste Management	7,954	57	1.7
Veterans' Services	0	0	0.0
Liquor Store	0	0	0.0
Utility	168,198	1,222	34.9

Source: U.S. Census Bureau, State & Local Government Finances 2020

TAXES

State Corporate Income Tax Rates

State	Tax Rate (%)	Income Brackets ($)	Num. of Brackets	Financial Institution Tax Rate (%)[a]	Federal Income Tax Ded.
South Carolina	5.0	Flat rate	1	4.5 (t)	No

Note: Tax rates as of January 1, 2023; (a) Rates listed are the corporate income tax rate applied to financial institutions or excise taxes based on income. Some states have other taxes based upon the value of deposits or shares; (t) South Carolina taxes savings and loans at a 6% rate.
Source: Federation of Tax Administrators, State Corporate Income Tax Rates, January 1, 2023

State Individual Income Tax Rates

State	Tax Rate (%)	Income Brackets ($)	Personal Exemptions ($) Single	Personal Exemptions ($) Married	Personal Exemptions ($) Depend.	Standard Ded. ($) Single	Standard Ded. ($) Married
South Carolina (a)	0.0 - 6.4 (bb)	3,200 - 16,040	(d)	(d)	(d)	13,850	27,700 (d)

Note: Tax rates as of January 1, 2023; Local- and county-level taxes are not included; Federal income tax is not deductible on state income tax returns; (a) 16 states have statutory provision for automatically adjusting to the rate of inflation the dollar values of the income tax brackets, standard deductions, and/or personal exemptions. Oregon does not index the income brackets for $125,000 and over; (d) These states use the personal exemption/standard deduction amounts provided in the federal Internal Revenue Code;
(bb) Louisiana tax rates may be adjusted down if revenue trigger is met on April 1st. Iowa is phasing-in a flat rate by 2027, while Nebraska and South Carolina is phasing-in a reduced top rate by 2027.
Source: Federation of Tax Administrators, State Individual Income Tax Rates, January 1, 2023

Various State Sales and Excise Tax Rates

State	State Sales Tax (%)	Gasoline[1] ($/gal.)	Cigarette[2] ($/pack)	Spirits[3] ($/gal.)	Wine[4] ($/gal.)	Beer[5] ($/gal.)	Recreational Marijuana (%)
South Carolina	6	0.2875	0.57	5.42	1.08	0.77	Not legal

Note: All tax rates as of January 1, 2023; (1) The American Petroleum Institute has developed a methodology for determining the average tax rate on a gallon of fuel. Rates may include any of the following: excise taxes, environmental fees, storage tank fees, other fees or taxes, general sales tax, and local taxes; (2) The federal excise tax of $1.0066 per pack and local taxes are not included; (3) Rates are those applicable to off-premise sales of 40% alcohol by volume (a.b.v.) distilled spirits in 750ml containers. Local excise taxes are excluded; (4) Rates are those applicable to off-premise sales of 11% a.b.v. non-carbonated wine in 750ml containers; (5) Rates are those applicable to off-premise sales of 4.7% a.b.v. beer in 12 ounce containers.
Source: Tax Foundation, 2023 Facts & Figures: How Does Your State Compare?

State Business Tax Climate Index Rankings

State	Overall Rank	Corporate Tax Rank	Individual Income Tax Rank	Sales Tax Rank	Property Tax Rank	Unemployment Insurance Tax Rank
South Carolina	31	6	28	32	35	29

Note: The index is a measure of how each state's tax laws affect economic performance. The lower the rank, the more favorable a state's tax system is for business. States without a given tax are given a ranking of 1. The scores/rankings for the District of Columbia do not affect other states. The 2023 index represents the tax climate as of July 1, 2022.
Source: Tax Foundation, State Business Tax Climate Index 2023

TRANSPORTATION

Means of Transportation to Work

Area	Drove Alone	Car-pooled	Bus	Subway	Railroad	Bicycle	Walked	Other Means	Worked at Home
City	74.5	6.2	0.8	0.0	0.0	1.8	3.8	1.3	11.6
MSA[1]	79.1	7.6	0.6	0.0	0.0	0.6	1.8	1.2	9.1
U.S.	73.2	8.6	2.0	1.6	0.5	0.5	2.5	1.5	9.7

Note: Figures are percentages and cover workers 16 years of age and older; (1) Figures cover the Charleston-North Charleston, SC Metropolitan Statistical Area
Source: U.S. Census Bureau, 2017-2021 American Community Survey 5-Year Estimates

Travel Time to Work

Area	Less Than 10 Minutes	10 to 19 Minutes	20 to 29 Minutes	30 to 44 Minutes	45 to 59 Minutes	60 to 89 Minutes	90 Minutes or More
City	11.4	30.7	26.6	20.6	7.6	1.6	1.4
MSA[1]	8.8	26.0	24.1	25.1	9.5	4.8	1.7
U.S.	12.4	28.5	21.0	20.9	8.2	6.2	2.9

Note: Note: Figures are percentages and include workers 16 years old and over; (1) Figures cover the Charleston-North Charleston, SC Metropolitan Statistical Area
Source: U.S. Census Bureau, 2017-2021 American Community Survey 5-Year Estimates

Key Congestion Measures

Measure	1990	2000	2010	2015	2020
Annual Hours of Delay, Total (000)	6,188	11,402	17,149	20,047	10,973
Annual Hours of Delay, Per Auto Commuter	25	37	45	48	26
Annual Congestion Cost, Per Auto Commuter ($)	532	737	881	951	521

Note: Covers the Charleston-North Charleston SC urban area
Source: Texas A&M Transportation Institute, 2021 Urban Mobility Report

Freeway Travel Time Index

Measure	1985	1990	1995	2000	2005	2010	2015	2020
Urban Area Index[1]	1.10	1.14	1.18	1.20	1.22	1.23	1.23	1.07
Urban Area Rank[1,2]	27	26	26	29	32	28	29	57

Note: Freeway Travel Time Index—the ratio of travel time in the peak period to the travel time at free-flow conditions. For example, a value of 1.30 indicates a 20-minute free-flow trip takes 26 minutes in the peak (20 minutes x 1.30 = 26 minutes); (1) Covers the Charleston-North Charleston SC urban area; (2) Rank is based on 101 larger urban areas (#1 = highest travel time index)
Source: Texas A&M Transportation Institute, 2021 Urban Mobility Report

Public Transportation

Agency Name / Mode of Transportation	Vehicles Operated in Maximum Service[1]	Annual Unlinked Passenger Trips[2] (in thous.)	Annual Passenger Miles[3] (in thous.)
Charleston Area Regional Transportation (CARTA)			
Bus (purchased transportation)	52	1,832.5	8,539.5
Commuter Bus (purchased transportation)	6	63.2	952.2
Demand Response (purchased transportation)	19	62.6	578.0

Note: (1) Number of revenue vehicles operated by the given mode and type of service to meet the annual maximum service requirement. This is the revenue vehicle count during the peak season of the year; on the week and day that maximum service is provided. Vehicles operated in maximum service (VOMS) exclude atypical days and one-time special events; (2) Number of passengers who boarded public transportation vehicles. Passengers are counted each time they board a vehicle no matter how many vehicles they use to travel from their origin to their destination. (3) Sum of the distances ridden by all passengers during the entire fiscal year.
Source: Federal Transit Administration, National Transit Database, 2021

Air Transportation

Airport Name and Code / Type of Service	Passenger Airlines[1]	Passenger Enplanements	Freight Carriers[2]	Freight (lbs)
Charleston International Airport (CHS)				
Domestic service (U.S. carriers - 2022)	34	2,607,489	15	5,857,289
International service (U.S. carriers - 2021)	1	3	6	3,489,859

Note: (1) Includes all U.S.-based major, minor and commuter airlines that carried at least one passenger during the year; (2) Includes all U.S.-based airlines and freight carriers that transported at least one pound of freight during the year.
Source: Bureau of Transportation Statistics, The Intermodal Transportation Database, Air Carriers: T-100 Domestic Market (U.S. Carriers), 2022; Bureau of Transportation Statistics, The Intermodal Transportation Database, Air Carriers: T-100 International Market (U.S. Carriers), 2021

BUSINESSES

Major Business Headquarters

Company Name	Industry	Rankings Fortune[1]	Forbes[2]
No companies listed	-	-	-

Note: (1) Companies that produce a 10-K are ranked 1 to 500 based on 2021 revenue; (2) All private companies with at least $2 billion in annual revenue through the end of their most current fiscal year are ranked 1 to 246; companies listed are headquartered in the city; dashes indicate no ranking
Source: Fortune, "Fortune 500," 2022; Forbes, "America's Largest Private Companies," 2022

Fastest-Growing Businesses

According to *Inc.*, Charleston is home to one of America's 500 fastest-growing private companies: **GoodUnited** (#460). Criteria: must be an independent, privately-held, for-profit, U.S. corporation, proprietorship or partnership as of December 31, 2021; revenues must be at least $100,000 in 2018 and $2 million in 2021; must have four-year operating/sales history. *Inc.*, "America's 500 Fastest-Growing Private Companies," 2022

Living Environment

COST OF LIVING

Cost of Living Index

Composite Index	Groceries	Housing	Utilities	Transportation	Health Care	Misc. Goods/Services
97.9	102.5	96.7	116.8	95.0	93.9	93.1

Note: The Cost of Living Index measures regional differences in the cost of consumer goods and services, excluding taxes and non-consumer expenditures, for professional and managerial households in the top income quintile. It is based on more than 50,000 prices covering almost 60 different items for which prices are collected three times a year by chambers of commerce, economic development organizations or university applied economic centers in each participating urban area. The numbers shown should be read as a percentage above or below the national average of 100. For example, a value of 115.4 in the groceries column indicates that grocery prices are 15.4% higher than the national average. Small differences in the index numbers should not be interpreted as significant; Figures cover the Charleston-N Charleston SC urban area.
Source: The Council for Community and Economic Research, Cost of Living Index, 2022

Grocery Prices

Area[1]	T-Bone Steak ($/pound)	Frying Chicken ($/pound)	Whole Milk ($/half gal.)	Eggs ($/dozen)	Orange Juice ($/64 oz.)	Coffee ($/11.5 oz.)
City[2]	12.23	1.63	2.11	2.00	4.07	4.90
Avg.	13.81	1.59	2.43	2.25	3.85	4.95
Min.	10.17	0.90	1.51	1.30	2.90	3.46
Max.	19.35	3.30	4.32	4.32	5.31	8.59

Note: (1) Values for the local area are compared with the average, minimum and maximum values for all 286 areas in the Cost of Living Index; (2) Figures cover the Charleston-N Charleston SC urban area; **T-Bone Steak** (price per pound); **Frying Chicken** (price per pound, whole fryer); **Whole Milk** (half gallon carton); **Eggs** (price per dozen, Grade A, large); **Orange Juice** (64 oz. Tropicana or Florida Natural); **Coffee** (11.5 oz. can, vacuum-packed, Maxwell House, Hills Bros, or Folgers).
Source: The Council for Community and Economic Research, Cost of Living Index, 2022

Housing and Utility Costs

Area[1]	New Home Price ($)	Apartment Rent ($/month)	All Electric ($/month)	Part Electric ($/month)	Other Energy ($/month)	Telephone ($/month)
City[2]	423,780	1,572	224.48	-	-	195.28
Avg.	450,913	1,371	176.41	99.93	76.96	190.22
Min.	229,283	546	100.84	31.56	27.15	174.27
Max.	2,434,977	4,569	356.86	249.59	272.24	208.31

Note: (1) Values for the local area are compared with the average, minimum and maximum values for all 286 areas in the Cost of Living Index; (2) Figures cover the Charleston-N Charleston SC urban area; **New Home Price** (2,400 sf living area, 8,000 sf lot, in urban area with full utilities); **Apartment Rent** (950 sf 2 bedroom/1.5 or 2 bath, unfurnished, excluding all utilities except water); **All Electric** (average monthly cost for an all-electric home); **Part Electric** (average monthly cost for a part-electric home); **Other Energy** (average monthly cost for natural gas, fuel oil, coal, wood, and any other forms of energy except electricity); **Telephone** (price includes the base monthly rate plus taxes and fees for three lines of mobile phone service).
Source: The Council for Community and Economic Research, Cost of Living Index, 2022

Health Care, Transportation, and Other Costs

Area[1]	Doctor ($/visit)	Dentist ($/visit)	Optometrist ($/visit)	Gasoline ($/gallon)	Beauty Salon ($/visit)	Men's Shirt ($)
City[2]	146.94	92.17	71.32	3.61	59.17	37.27
Avg.	124.91	107.77	117.66	3.86	43.31	34.21
Min.	36.61	58.25	51.79	2.90	22.18	13.05
Max.	250.21	162.58	371.96	5.54	85.61	63.54

Note: (1) Values for the local area are compared with the average, minimum and maximum values for all 286 areas in the Cost of Living Index; (2) Figures cover the Charleston-N Charleston SC urban area; **Doctor** (general practitioners routine exam of an established patient); **Dentist** (adult teeth cleaning and periodic oral examination); **Optometrist** (full vision eye exam for established adult patient); **Gasoline** (one gallon regular unleaded, national brand, including all taxes, cash price at self-service pump if available); **Beauty Salon** (woman's shampoo, trim, and blow-dry); **Men's Shirt** (cotton/polyester dress shirt, pinpoint weave, long sleeves).
Source: The Council for Community and Economic Research, Cost of Living Index, 2022

HOUSING

Homeownership Rate

Area	2015 (%)	2016 (%)	2017 (%)	2018 (%)	2019 (%)	2020 (%)	2021 (%)	2022 (%)
MSA[1]	65.8	62.1	67.7	68.8	70.7	75.5	73.2	71.9
U.S.	63.7	63.4	63.9	64.4	64.6	66.6	65.5	65.8

Note: (1) Figures cover the Charleston-North Charleston, SC Metropolitan Statistical Area
Source: U.S. Census Bureau, Housing Vacancies and Homeownership Annual Statistics: 2015-2022

House Price Index (HPI)

Area	National Ranking[2]	Quarterly Change (%)	One-Year Change (%)	Five-Year Change (%)	Since 1991Q1 (%)
MSA[1]	29	-0.34	17.51	66.55	441.52
U.S.[3]	–	0.34	8.41	58.44	289.08

Note: The HPI is a weighted repeat sales index. It measures average price changes in repeat sales or refinancings on the same properties. This information is obtained by reviewing repeat mortgage transactions on single-family properties whose mortgages have been purchased or securitized by Fannie Mae or Freddie Mac since January 1975; (1) Figures cover the Charleston-North Charleston, SC Metropolitan Statistical Area; (2) Rankings are based on annual percentage change for all metro areas containing at least 15,000 transactions over the last 10 years and ranges from 1 to 257; (3) figures based on a weighted average of Census Division estimates using a seasonally adjusted, purchase-only index; all figures are for the period ending December 31, 2022
Source: Federal Housing Finance Agency, Change in FHFA Metropolitan Area House Price Indexes, 2022Q4

Median Single-Family Home Prices

Area	2020	2021	2022p	Percent Change 2021 to 2022
MSA[1]	324.4	375.2	416.1	10.9
U.S. Average	300.2	357.1	392.6	9.9

Note: Figures are median sales prices of existing single-family homes in thousands of dollars; (p) preliminary; (1) Figures cover the Charleston-North Charleston, SC Metropolitan Statistical Area
Source: National Association of Realtors, Median Sales Price of Existing Single-Family Homes for Metropolitan Areas, 4th Quarter 2022

Qualifying Income Based on Median Sales Price of Existing Single-Family Homes

Area	With 5% Down ($)	With 10% Down ($)	With 20% Down ($)
MSA[1]	124,670	118,108	104,985
U.S. Average	112,234	106,237	94,513

Note: Figures are preliminary; Qualifying income is based on a mortgage rate of 6.77%. Monthly principal and interest payment is limited to 25% of income; (1) Figures cover the Charleston-North Charleston, SC Metropolitan Statistical Area
Source: National Association of Realtors, Qualifying Income Based on Median Sales Price of Existing Single-Family Homes for Metropolitan Areas, 4th Quarter 2022

Home Value

Area	Under $100,000	$100,000 -$199,999	$200,000 -$299,999	$300,000 -$399,999	$400,000 -$499,999	$500,000 -$999,999	$1,000,000 or more	Median ($)
City	3.1	7.6	23.0	23.5	11.5	23.2	8.1	369,500
MSA[1]	10.8	21.0	24.9	16.5	8.1	14.0	4.6	270,700
U.S.	16.2	24.2	20.1	13.6	8.3	13.6	4.1	244,900

Note: Figures are percentages except for median and cover owner-occupied housing units; (1) Figures cover the Charleston-North Charleston, SC Metropolitan Statistical Area
Source: U.S. Census Bureau, 2017-2021 American Community Survey 5-Year Estimates

Year Housing Structure Built

Area	2020 or Later	2010 -2019	2000 -2009	1990 -1999	1980 -1989	1970 -1979	1960 -1969	1950 -1959	1940 -1949	Before 1940	Median Year
City	0.3	18.9	20.0	10.6	12.0	8.8	8.5	5.5	3.4	11.9	1990
MSA[1]	0.3	16.4	20.8	15.5	15.4	13.0	7.7	4.8	2.4	3.7	1992
U.S.	0.2	7.3	13.6	13.6	13.2	14.8	10.3	10.0	4.7	12.2	1979

Note: Figures are percentages except for Median Year; Note: (1) Figures cover the Charleston-North Charleston, SC Metropolitan Statistical Area
Source: U.S. Census Bureau, 2017-2021 American Community Survey 5-Year Estimates

Gross Monthly Rent

Area	Under $500	$500 -$999	$1,000 -$1,499	$1,500 -$1,999	$2,000 -$2,499	$2,500 -$2,999	$3,000 and up	Median ($)
City	5.1	13.9	39.7	27.1	8.4	2.8	3.0	1,400
MSA[1]	4.6	20.9	43.3	20.1	6.9	2.0	2.1	1,274
U.S.	8.1	30.5	30.8	16.8	7.3	3.1	3.5	1,163

Note: Figures are percentages except for median; Gross rent is the contract rent plus the estimated average monthly cost of utilities (electricity, gas, and water and sewer) and fuels (oil, coal, kerosene, wood, etc.) if these are paid by the renter (or paid for the renter by someone else); (1) Figures cover the Charleston-North Charleston, SC Metropolitan Statistical Area
Source: U.S. Census Bureau, 2017-2021 American Community Survey 5-Year Estimates

HEALTH

Health Risk Factors

Category	MSA[1] (%)	U.S. (%)
Adults aged 18–64 who have any kind of health care coverage	85.8	90.9
Adults who reported being in good or better health	86.7	85.2
Adults who have been told they have high blood cholesterol	33.3	35.7
Adults who have been told they have high blood pressure	34.4	32.4
Adults who are current smokers	12.1	14.4
Adults who currently use e-cigarettes	8.5	6.7
Adults who currently use chewing tobacco, snuff, or snus	2.4	3.5
Adults who are heavy drinkers[2]	8.0	6.3
Adults who are binge drinkers[3]	20.3	15.4
Adults who are overweight (BMI 25.0 - 29.9)	33.3	34.4
Adults who are obese (BMI 30.0 - 99.8)	39.0	33.9
Adults who participated in any physical activities in the past month	79.7	76.3

Note: (1) Figures cover the Charleston-North Charleston, SC Metropolitan Statistical Area; (2) Heavy drinkers are classified as adult men having more than 14 drinks per week and adult women having more than 7 drinks per week; (3) Binge drinkers are classified as males having five or more drinks on one occasion or females having four or more drinks on one occasion
Source: Centers for Disease Control and Prevention, Behavioral Risk Factor Surveillance System, SMART: Selected Metropolitan Area Risk Trends, 2021

Acute and Chronic Health Conditions

Category	MSA[1] (%)	U.S. (%)
Adults who have ever been told they had a heart attack	2.7	4.0
Adults who have ever been told they have angina or coronary heart disease	3.1	3.8
Adults who have ever been told they had a stroke	2.4	3.0
Adults who have ever been told they have asthma	11.4	14.9
Adults who have ever been told they have arthritis	25.6	25.8
Adults who have ever been told they have diabetes[2]	11.1	10.9
Adults who have ever been told they had skin cancer	8.1	6.6
Adults who have ever been told they had any other types of cancer	6.8	7.5
Adults who have ever been told they have COPD	5.5	6.1
Adults who have ever been told they have kidney disease	2.2	3.0
Adults who have ever been told they have a form of depression	19.1	20.5

Note: (1) Figures cover the Charleston-North Charleston, SC Metropolitan Statistical Area; (2) Figures do not include pregnancy-related, borderline, or pre-diabetes
Source: Centers for Disease Control and Prevention, Behavioral Risk Factor Surveillance System, SMART: Selected Metropolitan Area Risk Trends, 2021

Health Screening and Vaccination Rates

Category	MSA[1] (%)	U.S. (%)
Adults who have ever been tested for HIV	44.6	34.9
Adults who have had their blood cholesterol checked within the last five years	86.3	85.2
Adults aged 65+ who have had flu shot within the past year	65.3	68.6
Adults aged 65+ who have ever had a pneumonia vaccination	70.2	71.0

Note: (1) Figures cover the Charleston-North Charleston, SC Metropolitan Statistical Area.
Source: Centers for Disease Control and Prevention, Behavioral Risk Factor Surveillance System, SMART: Selected Metropolitan Area Risk Trends, 2021

Disability Status

Category	MSA[1] (%)	U.S. (%)
Adults who reported being deaf	6.2	7.2
Are you blind or have serious difficulty seeing, even when wearing glasses?	5.3	4.8
Are you limited in any way in any of your usual activities due to arthritis?	9.9	11.1
Do you have difficulty doing errands alone?	6.6	7.0
Do you have difficulty dressing or bathing?	2.9	3.6
Do you have serious difficulty concentrating/remembering/making decisions?	12.9	12.1
Do you have serious difficulty walking or climbing stairs?	13.1	12.8

Note: (1) Figures cover the Charleston-North Charleston, SC Metropolitan Statistical Area.
Source: Centers for Disease Control and Prevention, Behavioral Risk Factor Surveillance System, SMART: Selected Metropolitan Area Risk Trends, 2021

Mortality Rates for the Top 10 Causes of Death in the U.S.

ICD-10[a] Sub-Chapter	ICD-10[a] Code	Crude Mortality Rate[1] per 100,000 population County[2]	U.S.
Malignant neoplasms	C00-C97	175.3	182.6
Ischaemic heart diseases	I20-I25	79.3	113.1
Other forms of heart disease	I30-I51	57.7	64.4
Other degenerative diseases of the nervous system	G30-G31	59.6	51.0
Cerebrovascular diseases	I60-I69	44.3	47.8
Other external causes of accidental injury	W00-X59	51.4	46.4
Chronic lower respiratory diseases	J40-J47	36.6	45.7
Organic, including symptomatic, mental disorders	F01-F09	35.5	35.9
Hypertensive diseases	I10-I15	24.4	35.0
Diabetes mellitus	E10-E14	26.4	29.6

Note: (a) ICD-10 = International Classification of Diseases 10th Revision; (1) Crude mortality rates are a three-year average covering 2019-2021; (2) Figures cover Charleston County.
Source: Centers for Disease Control and Prevention, National Center for Health Statistics. National Vital Statistics System, Mortality 2018-2021 on CDC WONDER Online Database

Mortality Rates for Selected Causes of Death

ICD-10[a] Sub-Chapter	ICD-10[a] Code	Crude Mortality Rate[1] per 100,000 population County[2]	U.S.
Assault	X85-Y09	14.3	7.0
Diseases of the liver	K70-K76	20.8	19.8
Human immunodeficiency virus (HIV) disease	B20-B24	2.2	1.5
Influenza and pneumonia	J09-J18	9.5	14.7
Intentional self-harm	X60-X84	16.8	14.3
Malnutrition	E40-E46	5.6	4.3
Obesity and other hyperalimentation	E65-E68	2.1	3.0
Renal failure	N17-N19	13.2	15.7
Transport accidents	V01-V99	17.8	13.6
Viral hepatitis	B15-B19	Suppressed	1.2

Note: (a) ICD-10 = International Classification of Diseases 10th Revision; (1) Crude mortality rates are a three-year average covering 2019-2021; (2) Figures cover Charleston County; Data are suppressed when the data meet the criteria for confidentiality constraints; Crude mortality rates are flagged as unreliable when the rate would be calculated with a numerator of 20 or less.
Source: Centers for Disease Control and Prevention, National Center for Health Statistics. National Vital Statistics System, Mortality 2018-2021 on CDC WONDER Online Database

Health Insurance Coverage

Area	With Health Insurance	With Private Health Insurance	With Public Health Insurance	Without Health Insurance	Population Under Age 19 Without Health Insurance
City	93.2	79.8	25.0	6.8	2.4
MSA[1]	89.7	71.5	31.4	10.3	6.7
U.S.	91.2	67.8	35.4	8.8	5.3

Note: Figures are percentages that cover the civilian noninstitutionalized population; (1) Figures cover the Charleston-North Charleston, SC Metropolitan Statistical Area
Source: U.S. Census Bureau, 2017-2021 American Community Survey 5-Year Estimates

Number of Medical Professionals

Area	MDs[3]	DOs[3,4]	Dentists	Podiatrists	Chiropractors	Optometrists
County[1] (number)	3,406	128	468	24	215	101
County[1] (rate[2])	831.9	31.3	113.3	5.8	52.1	24.5
U.S. (rate[2])	289.3	23.5	72.5	6.2	28.7	17.4

Note: Data as of 2021 unless noted; (1) Data covers Charleston County; (2) Rate per 100,000 population; (3) Data as of 2020 and includes all active, non-federal physicians; (4) Doctor of Osteopathic Medicine
Source: U.S. Department of Health and Human Services, Health Resources and Services Administration, Bureau of Health Professions, Area Resource File (ARF) 2021-2022

Best Hospitals

According to *U.S. News*, the Charleston-North Charleston, SC metro area is home to two of the best hospitals in the U.S.: **MUSC Health-University Medical Center** (2 adult specialties and 4 pediatric specialties); **Roper Hospital** (1 adult specialty). The hospitals listed were nationally ranked in at least one of 15 adult or 10 pediatric specialties. The number of specialties shown cover the parent hospital. Only 164 U.S. hospitals performed well enough to be nationally ranked in one or more specialties. Twenty hospitals in the U.S. made the Honor Roll. The Best Hospitals Honor Roll takes both the national rankings and the procedure and condition ratings into account. Hospitals received points if they were nationally ranked in one of the 15 adult specialties—the higher they ranked, the more points they got—and how many ratings of "high performing" they earned in the 17 procedures and conditions. *U.S. News Online, "America's Best Hospitals 2022-23"*

According to *U.S. News*, the Charleston-North Charleston, SC metro area is home to one of the best children's hospitals in the U.S.: **MUSC Shawn Jenkins Children's Hospital** (4 pediatric specialties). The hospital listed was highly ranked in at least one of 10 pediatric specialties. Eighty-six children's hospitals in the U.S. were nationally ranked in at least one specialty. Hospitals received points for being ranked in a specialty, and the 10 hospitals with the most points across the 10 specialties make up the Honor Roll. *U.S. News Online, "America's Best Children's Hospitals 2022-23"*

EDUCATION

Public School District Statistics

District Name	Schls	Pupils	Pupil/Teacher Ratio	Minority Pupils[1] (%)	LEP/ELL[2] (%)	IEP[3] (%)
Charleston 01	82	49,331	12.9	49.8	6.3	10.6

Note: Table includes school districts with 2,000 or more students; (1) Percentage of students that are not non-Hispanic white; (2) Percentage of students that are Limited English Proficient or English Language Learners (2018-19); (3) Percentage of students that have an Individualized Education Program (2019-20).
Source: U.S. Department of Education, National Center for Education Statistics, Common Core of Data, Local Education Agency (School District) Universe Survey: School Year 2021-2022

Highest Level of Education

Area	Less than H.S.	H.S. Diploma	Some College, No Deg.	Associate Degree	Bachelor's Degree	Master's Degree	Prof. School Degree	Doctorate Degree
City	4.2	16.8	16.1	7.3	34.5	13.6	4.8	2.9
MSA[1]	8.5	24.3	19.7	9.5	24.0	10.0	2.6	1.4
U.S.	11.1	26.5	20.0	8.7	20.6	9.3	2.2	1.5

Note: Figures cover persons age 25 and over; (1) Figures cover the Charleston-North Charleston, SC Metropolitan Statistical Area
Source: U.S. Census Bureau, 2017-2021 American Community Survey 5-Year Estimates

Educational Attainment by Race

Area	High School Graduate or Higher (%)					Bachelor's Degree or Higher (%)				
	Total	White	Black	Asian	Hisp.[2]	Total	White	Black	Asian	Hisp.[2]
City	95.8	97.8	89.2	98.6	86.5	55.7	63.7	24.3	66.2	41.3
MSA[1]	91.5	94.6	85.7	89.7	70.2	38.0	45.2	18.5	50.8	23.0
U.S.	88.9	91.4	87.2	87.6	71.2	33.7	35.5	23.3	55.6	18.4

Note: Figures shown cover persons 25 years old and over; (1) Figures cover the Charleston-North Charleston, SC Metropolitan Statistical Area; (2) People of Hispanic origin can be of any race
Source: U.S. Census Bureau, 2017-2021 American Community Survey 5-Year Estimates

School Enrollment by Grade and Control

Area	Preschool (%)		Kindergarten (%)		Grades 1 - 4 (%)		Grades 5 - 8 (%)		Grades 9 - 12 (%)	
	Public	Private	Public	Private	Public	Private	Public	Private	Public	Private
City	42.4	57.6	81.0	19.0	83.5	16.5	83.8	16.2	76.6	23.4
MSA[1]	46.6	53.4	83.0	17.0	86.2	13.8	88.5	11.5	88.5	11.5
U.S.	58.8	41.2	86.3	13.7	88.3	11.7	88.6	11.4	89.4	10.6

Note: Figures shown cover persons 3 years old and over; (1) Figures cover the Charleston-North Charleston, SC Metropolitan Statistical Area
Source: U.S. Census Bureau, 2017-2021 American Community Survey 5-Year Estimates

Higher Education

Four-Year Colleges			Two-Year Colleges			Medical Schools[1]	Law Schools[2]	Voc/Tech[3]
Public	Private Non-profit	Private For-profit	Public	Private Non-profit	Private For-profit			
3	2	1	1	0	2	1	1	5

Note: Figures cover institutions located within the Charleston-North Charleston, SC Metropolitan Statistical Area and include main campuses only; (1) includes schools accredited by the Liaison Committee on Medical Education and the American Osteopathic Association's Commission on Osteopathic College Accreditation; (2) includes ABA-accredited schools, schools with provisional ABA accreditation, and state accredited schools; (3) includes all schools with programs that are less than 2 years.
Source: National Center for Education Statistics, Integrated Postsecondary Education System (IPEDS), 2021-22; Wikipedia, List of Medical Schools in the United States, accessed April 10, 2023; Wikipedia, List of Law Schools in the United States, accessed April 10, 2023

According to *U.S. News & World Report*, the Charleston-North Charleston, SC metro area is home to one of the top 75 medical schools for research in the U.S.: **Medical University of South Carolina** (#56 tie). The rankings are based on a weighted average of 11 measures of quality: quality assessment; peer assessment score; assessment score by residency directors; research activity; total research activity; average research activity per faculty member; student selectivity; median MCAT total score;

median undergraduate GPA; acceptance rate; and faculty resources. *U.S. News & World Report, "America's Best Graduate Schools, Medical, 2023"*

EMPLOYERS

Major Employers

Company Name	Industry
Bi-Lo Stores	Grocery stores
Boeing South Carolina	Commercial aircraft
Charleston County Government	County government
Charleston County School District	Public elementary & secondary schools
City of Charleston	Municipal government
College of Charleston	Higher education
Evening Post Publishing Co.	Newspapers, publishing & printing
Force Protection	Mine-protected vehicle manufacturing
JEM Restaurant Group	Restaurants/hospitality
Joint Base Charleston	U.S. military
Medical University of South Carolina	State's teaching hospital, medical higher education
Piggly Wiggly Carolina Co	Grocery stores
Roper St. Francis Healthcare	Private hospital system
SAIC	Advanced security
Trident Health System	Hospital system
U.S. Postal Service	Federal mail delivery service
Verizon Wireless Call Center	Call center
Wal-Mart Stores	Retail merchandising

Note: Companies shown are located within the Charleston-North Charleston, SC Metropolitan Statistical Area.
Source: Hoovers.com; Wikipedia

PUBLIC SAFETY

Crime Rate

Area	Total Crime	Violent Crime Rate				Property Crime Rate		
		Murder	Rape[3]	Robbery	Aggrav. Assault	Burglary	Larceny-Theft	Motor Vehicle Theft
City	2,771.1	12.2	38.7	71.6	343.2	233.6	1,747.4	324.5
Suburbs[1]	2,958.7	11.2	35.6	81.5	313.9	324.5	1,914.7	277.3
Metro[2]	2,926.8	11.3	36.1	79.8	318.9	309.0	1,886.2	285.4
U.S.	2,356.7	6.5	38.4	73.9	279.7	314.2	1,398.0	246.0

Note: Figures are crimes per 100,000 population; (1) All areas within the metro area that are located outside the city limits; (2) Figures cover the Charleston-North Charleston, SC Metropolitan Statistical Area; (3) All figures shown were reported using the revised Uniform Crime Reporting (UCR) definition of rape; Due to the transition to the National Incident-Based Reporting System (NIBRS), limited city and metro area data was released for 2021.
Source: FBI Uniform Crime Reports, 2020

Hate Crimes

Area	Number of Quarters Reported	Number of Incidents per Bias Motivation					
		Race/Ethnicity/Ancestry	Religion	Sexual Orientation	Disability	Gender	Gender Identity
City	4	5	0	2	0	0	0
U.S.	4	5,227	1,244	1,110	130	75	266

Note: Due to the transition to the National Incident-Based Reporting System (NIBRS), limited crime data was released for 2021.
Source: Federal Bureau of Investigation, Hate Crime Statistics 2020

Identity Theft Consumer Reports

Area	Reports	Reports per 100,000 Population	Rank[2]
MSA[1]	2,738	346	46
U.S.	1,108,609	339	-

Note: (1) Figures cover the Charleston-North Charleston, SC Metropolitan Statistical Area; (2) Rank ranges from 1 to 391 where 1 indicates greatest number of identity theft reports per 100,000 population
Source: Federal Trade Commission, Consumer Sentinel Network Data Book 2022

Fraud and Other Consumer Reports

Area	Reports	Reports per 100,000 Population	Rank[2]
MSA[1]	9,736	1,231	39
U.S.	4,064,520	1,245	-

Note: (1) Figures cover the Charleston-North Charleston, SC Metropolitan Statistical Area; (2) Rank ranges from 1 to 391 where 1 indicates greatest number of fraud and other consumer reports per 100,000 population
Source: Federal Trade Commission, Consumer Sentinel Network Data Book 2022

POLITICS

2020 Presidential Election Results

Area	Biden	Trump	Jorgensen	Hawkins	Other
Charleston County	55.5	42.6	1.5	0.3	0.1
U.S.	51.3	46.8	1.2	0.3	0.5

Note: Results are percentages and may not add to 100% due to rounding
Source: Dave Leip's Atlas of U.S. Presidential Elections

SPORTS

Professional Sports Teams

Team Name	League	Year Established

No teams are located in the metro area
Source: Wikipedia, Major Professional Sports Teams of the United States and Canada, April 12, 2023

CLIMATE

Average and Extreme Temperatures

Temperature	Jan	Feb	Mar	Apr	May	Jun	Jul	Aug	Sep	Oct	Nov	Dec	Yr.
Extreme High (°F)	83	87	90	94	98	101	104	102	97	94	88	83	104
Average High (°F)	59	62	68	76	83	88	90	89	85	77	69	61	76
Average Temp. (°F)	49	51	57	65	73	78	81	81	76	67	58	51	66
Average Low (°F)	38	40	46	53	62	69	72	72	67	56	46	39	55
Extreme Low (°F)	6	12	15	30	36	50	58	56	42	27	15	8	6

Note: Figures cover the years 1945-1995
Source: National Climatic Data Center, International Station Meteorological Climate Summary, 9/96

Average Precipitation/Snowfall/Humidity

Precip./Humidity	Jan	Feb	Mar	Apr	May	Jun	Jul	Aug	Sep	Oct	Nov	Dec	Yr.
Avg. Precip. (in.)	3.5	3.1	4.4	2.8	4.1	6.0	7.2	6.9	5.6	3.1	2.5	3.1	52.1
Avg. Snowfall (in.)	Tr	Tr	Tr	0	0	0	0	0	0	0	Tr	Tr	1
Avg. Rel. Hum. 7am (%)	83	81	83	84	85	86	88	90	91	89	86	83	86
Avg. Rel. Hum. 4pm (%)	55	52	51	51	56	62	66	66	65	58	56	55	58

Note: Figures cover the years 1945-1995; Tr = Trace amounts (<0.05 in. of rain; <0.5 in. of snow)
Source: National Climatic Data Center, International Station Meteorological Climate Summary, 9/96

Weather Conditions

Temperature			Daytime Sky			Precipitation		
10°F & below	32°F & below	90°F & above	Clear	Partly cloudy	Cloudy	0.01 inch or more precip.	0.1 inch or more snow/ice	Thunder-storms
<1	33	53	89	162	114	114	1	59

Note: Figures are average number of days per year and cover the years 1945-1995
Source: National Climatic Data Center, International Station Meteorological Climate Summary, 9/96

HAZARDOUS WASTE

Superfund Sites

The Charleston-North Charleston, SC metro area is home to two sites on the EPA's Superfund National Priorities List: **Koppers Co., Inc. (Charleston Plant)** (final); **Macalloy Corporation** (final). There are a total of 1,165 Superfund sites with a status of proposed or final on the list in the U.S. *U.S. Environmental Protection Agency, National Priorities List, April 12, 2023*

AIR QUALITY

Air Quality Trends: Ozone

	1990	1995	2000	2005	2010	2015	2018	2019	2020	2021
MSA[1]	0.068	0.071	0.078	0.073	0.067	0.054	0.058	0.064	0.059	0.062
U.S.	0.087	0.089	0.081	0.080	0.072	0.067	0.069	0.065	0.065	0.067

Note: (1) Data covers the Charleston-North Charleston, SC Metropolitan Statistical Area. The values shown are the composite ozone concentration averages among trend sites based on the highest fourth daily maximum 8-hour concentration in parts per million. These trends are based on sites having an adequate record of monitoring data during the trend period. Data from exceptional events are included.
Source: U.S. Environmental Protection Agency, Air Quality Monitoring Information, "Air Quality Trends by City, 1990-2021"

Air Quality Index

Area	Percent of Days when Air Quality was...[2]					AQI Statistics[2]	
	Good	Moderate	Unhealthy for Sensitive Groups	Unhealthy	Very Unhealthy	Maximum	Median
MSA[1]	79.5	20.5	0.0	0.0	0.0	93	40

Note: (1) Data covers the Charleston-North Charleston, SC Metropolitan Statistical Area; (2) Based on 365 days with AQI data in 2021. Air Quality Index (AQI) is an index for reporting daily air quality. EPA calculates the AQI for five major air pollutants regulated by the Clean Air Act: ground-level ozone, particle pollution (aka particulate matter), carbon monoxide, sulfur dioxide, and nitrogen dioxide. The AQI runs from 0 to 500. The higher the AQI value, the greater the level of air pollution and the greater the health concern. There are six AQI categories: "Good" AQI is between 0 and 50. Air quality is considered satisfactory; "Moderate" AQI is between 51 and 100. Air quality is acceptable; "Unhealthy for Sensitive Groups" When AQI values are between 101 and 150, members of sensitive groups may experience health effects; "Unhealthy" When AQI values are between 151 and 200 everyone may begin to experience health effects; "Very Unhealthy" AQI values between 201 and 300 trigger a health alert; "Hazardous" AQI values over 300 trigger warnings of emergency conditions (not shown).
Source: U.S. Environmental Protection Agency, Air Quality Index Report, 2021

Air Quality Index Pollutants

Area	Percent of Days when AQI Pollutant was...[2]					
	Carbon Monoxide	Nitrogen Dioxide	Ozone	Sulfur Dioxide	Particulate Matter 2.5	Particulate Matter 10
MSA[1]	0.0	0.0	41.4	(3)	58.6	0.0

Note: (1) Data covers the Charleston-North Charleston, SC Metropolitan Statistical Area; (2) Based on 365 days with AQI data in 2021. The Air Quality Index (AQI) is an index for reporting daily air quality. EPA calculates the AQI for five major air pollutants regulated by the Clean Air Act: ground-level ozone, particle pollution (also known as particulate matter), carbon monoxide, sulfur dioxide, and nitrogen dioxide. The AQI runs from 0 to 500. The higher the AQI value, the greater the level of air pollution and the greater the health concern; (3) Sulfur dioxide is no longer included in this table (as of December 8, 2021) because SO_2 concentrations tend to be very localized and not necessarily representative of broad geographical areas like counties and CBSAs.
Source: U.S. Environmental Protection Agency, Air Quality Index Report, 2021

Maximum Air Pollutant Concentrations: Particulate Matter, Ozone, CO and Lead

	Particulate Matter 10 (ug/m³)	Particulate Matter 2.5 Wtd AM (ug/m³)	Particulate Matter 2.5 24-Hr (ug/m³)	Ozone (ppm)	Carbon Monoxide (ppm)	Lead (ug/m³)
MSA[1] Level	40	9.5	20	0.059	n/a	n/a
NAAQS[2]	150	15	35	0.075	9	0.15
Met NAAQS[2]	Yes	Yes	Yes	Yes	n/a	n/a

Note: (1) Data covers the Charleston-North Charleston, SC Metropolitan Statistical Area; Data from exceptional events are included; (2) National Ambient Air Quality Standards; ppm = parts per million; ug/m³ = micrograms per cubic meter; n/a not available.
Concentrations: Particulate Matter 10 (coarse particulate)—highest second maximum 24-hour concentration; Particulate Matter 2.5 Wtd AM (fine particulate)—highest weighted annual mean concentration; Particulate Matter 2.5 24-Hour (fine particulate)—highest 98th percentile 24-hour concentration; Ozone—highest fourth daily maximum 8-hour concentration; Carbon Monoxide—highest second maximum non-overlapping 8-hour concentration; Lead—maximum running 3-month average
Source: U.S. Environmental Protection Agency, Air Quality Monitoring Information, "Air Quality Statistics by City, 2021"

Maximum Air Pollutant Concentrations: Nitrogen Dioxide and Sulfur Dioxide

	Nitrogen Dioxide AM (ppb)	Nitrogen Dioxide 1-Hr (ppb)	Sulfur Dioxide AM (ppb)	Sulfur Dioxide 1-Hr (ppb)	Sulfur Dioxide 24-Hr (ppb)
MSA[1] Level	n/a	n/a	n/a	9	n/a
NAAQS[2]	53	100	30	75	140
Met NAAQS[2]	n/a	n/a	n/a	Yes	n/a

Note: (1) Data covers the Charleston-North Charleston, SC Metropolitan Statistical Area; Data from exceptional events are included; (2) National Ambient Air Quality Standards; ppm = parts per million; ug/m³ = micrograms per cubic meter; n/a not available.
Concentrations: Nitrogen Dioxide AM—highest arithmetic mean concentration; Nitrogen Dioxide 1-Hr—highest 98th percentile 1-hour daily maximum concentration; Sulfur Dioxide AM—highest annual mean concentration; Sulfur Dioxide 1-Hr—highest 99th percentile 1-hour daily maximum concentration; Sulfur Dioxide 24-Hr—highest second maximum 24-hour concentration
Source: U.S. Environmental Protection Agency, Air Quality Monitoring Information, "Air Quality Statistics by City, 2021"

Clarksville, Tennessee

Background

Located just south of the Kentucky border and 47 miles north of Nashville, Clarksville is Tennessee's fifth-largest town and has seen significant growth in recent years. Named for Gen. George Rogers Clark, a decorated veteran of the Indian and Revolutionary Wars, the city was founded in 1784, and became incorporated by the state of Tennessee when it joined the union in 1796.

Located near the confluence of Red and Cumberland rivers, Clarksville was the site of three Confederate forts that the Union defeated in 1862. Fort Defiance transferred hands and became known as a place where fleeing or freed slaves could find refuge—and jobs. In the 1980s the well-preserved fort passed from the private hands of a local judge to the city itself, and in 2011 an interpretive center and walking trails were unveiled at what is now called Fort Defiance Civil War Park and Interpretive Center. The site features walking trails as well as the 1,500+ square foot center.

Clarksville is home to the 105,000-acre Fort Campbell, established as Camp Campbell in 1942, with nearly two-thirds of its land mass in Tennessee and the rest—including the post office—located in Kentucky. It is home to the world's only air assault division, known as the Screaming Eagles. Two special ops command units, a combat support hospital, and more make this home to the U.S. Army's most-deployed contingency forces and the its fifth-largest military population. With more than 4,000 civilian jobs, it's the area's largest employer with services on the post ranging from bowling to the commissary to the Fort Campbell Credit Union, as well as medical services and childcare.

Austin Peay State University's main campus is in Clarksville, another of the city's major employers, and named for a local son who became governor. The four-year public master's-level university has seen its enrollment climb steadily throughout the last twenty years. Austin Peay also operates a center at Fort Campbell with fifteen associate, bachelor, and master's level programs.

In 2012, Hemlock Semiconductor Corp, a subsidiary of Dow Corning, opened a $1.2 billion plant in the city, and the state funded a new educational center at APSU to train workers.

A 146-acre Liberty Park and Marina redevelopment project was completed in 2012, replete with pavilions, sports fields, picnic shelters, a dog park, and a ten-acre pond with a boardwalk and fishing piers. The Wilma Rudolph Pavilion and Great lawn is named for the great Olympic runner and Clarksville's native daughter. Another recent development was the creation of an Indoor Aquatic Center with an inflatable dome that allows for water sports in winter.

The Clarksville Downtown Market—with produce and arts and crafts—is a popular summer event.

Clarksville is also home to the state's second largest general museum, the Customs House Museum and Cultural Center, which has seen a recent facelift. Model trains, a gallery devoted to sports champions, and a bubble cave are all part of the experience.

The climate in Clarksville offers hot summers and relatively moderate winters with average lows reaching 25 degrees in January. Precipitation stays fairly steady year-round, getting no higher than 5.39 in March and bottoming out at 3.27 inches in October.

Rankings

General Rankings

- For its "Best for Vets: Places to Live 2019" rankings, *Military Times* evaluated 599 cities (83 large, 234 medium, 282 small) and compared the locations across three broad categories: veteran and military culture/services; economic indicators; and livability factors such as health, crime, traffic, and school quality. Clarksville ranked #12 out of the top 50, in the medium-sized city category (population of 100,000-249,999). Data points more specific to veterans and the military weighed more heavily than others. *rebootcamp.militarytimes.com, "Military Times Best Places to Live 2019," September 10, 2018*

Business/Finance Rankings

- The Clarksville metro area appeared on the Milken Institute "2022 Best Performing Cities" list. Rank: #120 out of 200 large metro areas (population over 250,000). Criteria: job growth; wage and salary growth; high-tech output growth; housing affordability; household broadband access. *Milken Institute, "Best-Performing Cities 2022," March 28, 2022*

- *Forbes* ranked the 200 most populous metro areas to determine the nation's "Best Places for Business and Careers." The Clarksville metro area was ranked #130. Criteria: costs (business and living); job growth (past and projected); income growth; quality of life; educational attainment (college and high school); projected economic growth; cultural and leisure opportunities; workplace tolerance laws; net migration patterns. *Forbes, "The Best Places for Business and Careers 2019: Seattle Still On Top," October 30, 2019*

Environmental Rankings

- Clarksville was highlighted as one of the cleanest metro areas for ozone air pollution in the U.S. during 2019 through 2021. The list represents cities with no monitored ozone air pollution in unhealthful ranges. *American Lung Association, "State of the Air 2023," April 19, 2023*

Safety Rankings

- Allstate ranked the 200 largest cities in America in terms of driver safety. Clarksville ranked #47. Criteria: internal property damage claims over a two-year period from January 2016 to December 2017. The report helps increase the importance of safety and awareness behind the wheel. *Allstate, "Allstate America's Best Drivers Report, 2019" June 24, 2019*

Seniors/Retirement Rankings

- From its Best Cities for Successful Aging indexes, the Milken Institute generated rankings for metropolitan areas, weighing data in nine categories—health care, wellness, living arrangements, transportation and convenience, financial characteristics, education, employment, community engagement, and overall livability. The Clarksville metro area was ranked #185 overall in the small metro area category. *Milken Institute, "Best Cities for Successful Aging, 2017" March 14, 2017*

Business Environment

DEMOGRAPHICS

Population Growth

Area	1990 Census	2000 Census	2010 Census	2020 Census	Population Growth (%) 1990-2020	Population Growth (%) 2010-2020
City	78,569	103,455	132,929	166,722	112.2	25.4
MSA[1]	189,277	232,000	273,949	320,535	69.3	17.0
U.S.	248,709,873	281,421,906	308,745,538	331,449,281	33.3	7.4

Note: (1) Figures cover the Clarksville, TN-KY Metropolitan Statistical Area
Source: U.S. Census Bureau, 1990 Census, 2000 Census, 2010 Census, 2020 Census

Race

Area	White Alone[2] (%)	Black Alone[2] (%)	Asian Alone[2] (%)	AIAN[3] Alone[2] (%)	NHOPI[4] Alone[2] (%)	Other Race Alone[2] (%)	Two or More Races (%)
City	57.0	24.4	2.5	0.5	0.5	4.2	10.9
MSA[1]	65.8	19.1	2.0	0.5	0.4	3.2	9.0
U.S.	61.6	12.4	6.0	1.1	0.2	8.4	10.2

Note: (1) Figures cover the Clarksville, TN-KY Metropolitan Statistical Area; (2) Alone is defined as not being in combination with one or more other races; (3) American Indian and Alaska Native; (4) Native Hawaiian and Other Pacific Islander
Source: U.S. Census Bureau, 2020 Census

Hispanic or Latino Origin

Area	Total (%)	Mexican (%)	Puerto Rican (%)	Cuban (%)	Other (%)
City	11.7	5.6	3.0	0.4	2.8
MSA[1]	9.3	4.7	2.4	0.2	2.0
U.S.	18.4	11.2	1.8	0.7	4.7

Note: Persons of Hispanic or Latino origin can be of any race; (1) Figures cover the Clarksville, TN-KY Metropolitan Statistical Area
Source: U.S. Census Bureau, 2017-2021 American Community Survey 5-Year Estimates

Age

Area	Under Age 5	Age 5–19	Age 20–34	Age 35–44	Age 45–54	Age 55–64	Age 65–74	Age 75–84	Age 85+	Median Age
City	8.3	21.9	28.4	13.0	9.9	9.2	5.8	2.5	0.8	29.9
MSA[1]	7.9	21.3	25.4	12.4	10.7	10.6	7.3	3.3	1.1	31.8
U.S.	5.6	19.2	20.2	12.7	12.4	13.1	10.0	4.9	1.9	38.8

Note: (1) Figures cover the Clarksville, TN-KY Metropolitan Statistical Area
Source: U.S. Census Bureau, 2020 Census

Disability by Age

Area	All Ages	Under 18 Years Old	18 to 64 Years Old	65 Years and Over
City	15.7	6.1	16.4	43.8
MSA[1]	16.7	7.1	16.3	42.9
U.S.	12.6	4.4	10.3	33.4

Note: Figures show percent of the civilian noninstitutionalized population that reported having a disability. Disability status is determined from six types of difficulty: vision, hearing, cognitive, ambulatory, self-care, and independent living. For children under 5 years old, hearing and vision difficulty are used to determine disability status. For children between the ages of 5 and 14, disability status is determined from hearing, vision, cognitive, ambulatory, and self-care difficulties. For people aged 15 years and older, they are considered to have a disability if they have difficulty with any one of the six difficulty types; Note: (1) Figures cover the Clarksville, TN-KY Metropolitan Statistical Area
Source: U.S. Census Bureau, 2017-2021 American Community Survey 5-Year Estimates

Ancestry

Area	German	Irish	English	American	Italian	Polish	French[2]	Scottish	Dutch
City	12.2	8.6	7.1	6.1	4.2	1.0	1.4	1.6	1.1
MSA[1]	11.8	8.8	8.3	7.4	3.2	1.1	1.4	1.7	1.0
U.S.	12.8	9.6	8.1	5.7	5.0	2.7	2.2	1.6	1.1

Note: Figures are the percentage of the total population reporting a particular ancestry. The nine most commonly reported ancestries in the U.S. are shown. Figures include multiple ancestries (e.g. if a person reported being Irish and Italian, they were included in both columns); (1) Figures cover the Clarksville, TN-KY Metropolitan Statistical Area; (2) Excludes Basque
Source: U.S. Census Bureau, 2017-2021 American Community Survey 5-Year Estimates

Foreign-born Population

Area	Any Foreign Country	Asia	Mexico	Europe	Caribbean	Central America[2]	South America	Africa	Canada
City	6.3	2.0	1.3	0.8	0.5	0.7	0.4	0.4	0.2
MSA[1]	4.9	1.5	0.9	0.6	0.3	0.4	0.3	0.6	0.2
U.S.	13.6	4.2	3.3	1.5	1.4	1.1	1.1	0.8	0.2

Note: (1) Figures cover the Clarksville, TN-KY Metropolitan Statistical Area; (2) Excludes Mexico.
Source: U.S. Census Bureau, 2017-2021 American Community Survey 5-Year Estimates

Household Size

Area	One	Two	Three	Four	Five	Six	Seven or More	Average Household Size
City	24.5	32.7	17.1	15.9	6.0	2.4	1.4	2.70
MSA[1]	25.2	33.1	17.7	14.0	6.1	2.5	1.4	2.70
U.S.	28.1	33.8	15.5	12.9	6.0	2.3	1.4	2.60

Note: (1) Figures cover the Clarksville, TN-KY Metropolitan Statistical Area
Source: U.S. Census Bureau, 2017-2021 American Community Survey 5-Year Estimates

Household Relationships

Area	Householder	Opposite-sex Spouse	Same-sex Spouse	Opposite-sex Unmarried Partner	Same-sex Unmarried Partner	Child[2]	Grandchild	Other Relatives	Non-relatives
City	36.6	16.9	0.2	2.5	0.1	31.2	2.4	3.9	3.5
MSA[1]	36.7	18.2	0.2	2.2	0.1	30.5	2.5	3.6	3.0
U.S.	38.3	17.5	0.2	2.5	0.2	28.3	2.4	4.8	3.4

Note: Figures are percent of the total population; (1) Figures cover the Clarksville, TN-KY Metropolitan Statistical Area; (2) Includes biological, adopted, and stepchildren of the householder
Source: U.S. Census Bureau, 2020 Census

Gender

Area	Males	Females	Males per 100 Females
City	81,849	84,873	96.4
MSA[1]	159,552	160,983	99.1
U.S.	162,685,811	168,763,470	96.4

Note: (1) Figures cover the Clarksville, TN-KY Metropolitan Statistical Area
Source: U.S. Census Bureau, 2020 Census

Marital Status

Area	Never Married	Now Married[2]	Separated	Widowed	Divorced
City	30.2	50.3	2.1	3.9	13.6
MSA[1]	29.6	51.1	1.9	4.9	12.5
U.S.	33.8	48.0	1.8	5.6	10.8

Note: Figures are percentages and cover the population 15 years of age and older; (1) Figures cover the Clarksville, TN-KY Metropolitan Statistical Area; (2) Excludes separated
Source: U.S. Census Bureau, 2017-2021 American Community Survey 5-Year Estimates

Religious Groups by Family

Area	Catholic	Baptist	Methodist	LDS[2]	Pentecostal	Lutheran	Islam	Adventist	Other
MSA[1]	4.6	23.2	4.4	1.4	3.2	0.5	0.1	0.8	12.4
U.S.	18.7	7.3	3.0	2.0	1.8	1.7	1.3	1.3	11.6

Note: Figures are the number of adherents as a percentage of the total population and cover the eight largest religious groups in the U.S; (1) Figures cover the Clarksville, TN-KY Metropolitan Statistical Area; (2) Church of Jesus Christ of Latter-day Saints
Sources: 2020 U.S. Religion Census, Association of Statisticians of American Religious Bodies; The Association of Religion Data Archives (ARDA)

Religious Groups by Tradition

Area	Catholic	Evangelical Protestant	Mainline Protestant	Black Protestant	Islam	Judaism	Hinduism	Orthodox	Buddhism
MSA[1]	4.6	35.7	4.8	3.4	0.1	n/a	n/a	0.1	n/a
U.S.	18.7	16.5	5.2	2.3	1.3	0.6	0.4	0.4	0.3

Note: Figures are the number of adherents as a percentage of the total population; (1) Figures cover the Clarksville, TN-KY Metropolitan Statistical Area
Sources: 2020 U.S. Religion Census, Association of Statisticians of American Religious Bodies; The Association of Religion Data Archives (ARDA)

ECONOMY

Gross Metropolitan Product

Area	2020	2021	2022	2023	Rank[2]
MSA[1]	12.3	13.7	14.8	15.6	191

Note: Figures are in billions of dollars; (1) Figures cover the Clarksville, TN-KY Metropolitan Statistical Area; (2) Rank is based on 2021 data and ranges from 1 to 381
Source: U.S. Conference of Mayors, U.S. Metro Economies: U.S. Metros Compared to Global and State Economies, June 2022

Economic Growth

Area	2018-20 (%)	2021 (%)	2022 (%)	2023 (%)	Rank[2]
MSA[1]	0.7	7.1	3.0	1.6	91
U.S.	-0.6	5.7	3.1	2.9	—

Note: Figures are real gross metropolitan product (GMP) growth rates and represent average annual percent change; (1) Figures cover the Clarksville, TN-KY Metropolitan Statistical Area; (2) Rank is based on 2020 2-year average annual percent change and ranges from 1 to 381
Source: U.S. Conference of Mayors, U.S. Metro Economies: U.S. Metros Compared to Global and State Economies, June 2022

Metropolitan Area Exports

Area	2016	2017	2018	2019	2020	2021	Rank[2]
MSA[1]	376.1	360.2	435.5	341.8	246.8	288.7	268

Note: Figures are in millions of dollars; (1) Figures cover the Clarksville, TN-KY Metropolitan Statistical Area; (2) Rank is based on 2021 data and ranges from 1 to 388
Source: U.S. Department of Commerce, International Trade Administration, Office of Trade and Economic Analysis, Industry and Analysis, Exports by Metropolitan Area, data extracted March 16, 2023

Building Permits

Area	Single-Family 2021	Single-Family 2022	Pct. Chg.	Multi-Family 2021	Multi-Family 2022	Pct. Chg.	Total 2021	Total 2022	Pct. Chg.
City	1,452	973	-33.0	1,813	2,160	19.1	3,265	3,133	-4.0
MSA[1]	2,217	1,501	-32.3	1,895	2,592	36.8	4,112	4,093	-0.5
U.S.	1,115,400	975,600	-12.5	621,600	689,500	10.9	1,737,000	1,665,100	-4.1

Note: (1) Figures cover the Clarksville, TN-KY Metropolitan Statistical Area; Figures represent new, privately-owned housing units authorized (unadjusted data); All permit data are based on estimates with imputation
Source: U.S. Census Bureau, Manufacturing, Mining, and Construction Statistics, Building Permits, 2021, 2022

Bankruptcy Filings

Area	Business Filings 2021	Business Filings 2022	% Chg.	Nonbusiness Filings 2021	Nonbusiness Filings 2022	% Chg.
Montgomery County	11	6	-45.5	333	352	5.7
U.S.	14,347	13,481	-6.0	399,269	374,240	-6.3

Note: Business filings include Chapter 7, Chapter 9, Chapter 11, Chapter 12, Chapter 13, Chapter 15, and Section 304; Nonbusiness filings include Chapter 7, Chapter 11, and Chapter 13
Source: Administrative Office of the U.S. Courts, Business and Nonbusiness Bankruptcy, County Cases Commenced by Chapter of the Bankruptcy Code, During the 12-Month Period Ending December 31, 2021 and Business and Nonbusiness Bankruptcy, County Cases Commenced by Chapter of the Bankruptcy Code, During the 12-Month Period Ending December 31, 2022

Housing Vacancy Rates

Area	Gross Vacancy Rate[2] (%) 2020	2021	2022	Year-Round Vacancy Rate[3] (%) 2020	2021	2022	Rental Vacancy Rate[4] (%) 2020	2021	2022	Homeowner Vacancy Rate[5] (%) 2020	2021	2022
MSA[1]	n/a	n/a	n/a	n/a	n/a	n/a	n/a	n/a	n/a	n/a	n/a	n/a
U.S.	10.6	10.8	10.5	8.2	8.4	8.2	6.3	6.1	5.8	1.0	0.9	0.8

Note: (1) Figures cover the Clarksville, TN-KY Metropolitan Statistical Area; (2) The percentage of the total housing inventory that is vacant; (3) The percentage of the housing inventory (excluding seasonal units) that is year-round vacant; (4) The percentage of rental inventory that is vacant for rent; (5) The percentage of homeowner inventory that is vacant for sale; n/a not available
Source: U.S. Census Bureau, Housing Vacancies and Homeownership Annual Statistics: 2020, 2021, 2022

INCOME

Income

Area	Per Capita ($)	Median Household ($)	Average Household ($)
City	27,437	58,838	71,824
MSA[1]	28,243	57,963	74,308
U.S.	37,638	69,021	97,196

Note: (1) Figures cover the Clarksville, TN-KY Metropolitan Statistical Area
Source: U.S. Census Bureau, 2017-2021 American Community Survey 5-Year Estimates

Clarksville, Tennessee

Household Income Distribution

Area	Under $15,000	$15,000 -$24,999	$25,000 -$34,999	$35,000 -$49,999	$50,000 -$74,999	$75,000 -$99,999	$100,000 -$149,999	$150,000 and up
City	9.6	6.8	9.9	15.2	20.6	15.3	15.5	7.2
MSA[1]	10.8	7.6	10.3	14.0	19.6	14.5	14.8	8.5
U.S.	9.4	7.8	8.2	11.4	16.8	12.8	16.3	17.3

Percent of Households Earning

Note: (1) Figures cover the Clarksville, TN-KY Metropolitan Statistical Area
Source: U.S. Census Bureau, 2017-2021 American Community Survey 5-Year Estimates

Poverty Rate

Area	All Ages	Under 18 Years Old	18 to 64 Years Old	65 Years and Over
City	13.2	16.9	12.4	7.2
MSA[1]	13.5	17.0	12.6	9.2
U.S.	12.6	17.0	11.8	9.6

Note: Figures are percentage of people whose income during the past 12 months was below the poverty level; (1) Figures cover the Clarksville, TN-KY Metropolitan Statistical Area
Source: U.S. Census Bureau, 2017-2021 American Community Survey 5-Year Estimates

EMPLOYMENT

Labor Force and Employment

Area	Civilian Labor Force Dec. 2021	Dec. 2022	% Chg.	Workers Employed Dec. 2021	Dec. 2022	% Chg.
City	64,581	62,625	-3.0	62,259	60,449	-2.9
MSA[1]	120,311	117,511	-2.3	115,795	113,311	-2.1
U.S.	161,696,000	164,224,000	1.6	155,732,000	158,872,000	2.0

Note: Data is not seasonally adjusted and covers workers 16 years of age and older; (1) Figures cover the Clarksville, TN-KY Metropolitan Statistical Area
Source: Bureau of Labor Statistics, Local Area Unemployment Statistics

Unemployment Rate

Area	Jan.	Feb.	Mar.	Apr.	May	Jun.	Jul.	Aug.	Sep.	Oct.	Nov.	Dec.
City	4.0	3.6	3.4	3.5	3.9	4.8	4.6	4.1	3.6	4.1	3.9	3.5
MSA[1]	4.1	3.7	3.6	3.6	4.0	4.7	4.5	4.1	3.6	4.0	3.9	3.6
U.S.	4.4	4.1	3.8	3.3	3.4	3.8	3.8	3.8	3.3	3.4	3.4	3.3

Note: Data is not seasonally adjusted and covers workers 16 years of age and older; (1) Figures cover the Clarksville, TN-KY Metropolitan Statistical Area
Source: Bureau of Labor Statistics, Local Area Unemployment Statistics

Average Wages

Occupation	$/Hr.	Occupation	$/Hr.
Accountants and Auditors	32.20	Maintenance and Repair Workers	22.30
Automotive Mechanics	21.35	Marketing Managers	50.21
Bookkeepers	19.54	Network and Computer Systems Admin.	34.09
Carpenters	21.38	Nurses, Licensed Practical	22.40
Cashiers	11.96	Nurses, Registered	34.52
Computer Programmers	n/a	Nursing Assistants	14.53
Computer Systems Analysts	39.23	Office Clerks, General	16.20
Computer User Support Specialists	22.21	Physical Therapists	42.52
Construction Laborers	17.54	Physicians	143.21
Cooks, Restaurant	13.67	Plumbers, Pipefitters and Steamfitters	24.18
Customer Service Representatives	17.08	Police and Sheriff's Patrol Officers	23.65
Dentists	n/a	Postal Service Mail Carriers	25.40
Electricians	25.15	Real Estate Sales Agents	28.07
Engineers, Electrical	45.92	Retail Salespersons	15.47
Fast Food and Counter Workers	11.02	Sales Representatives, Technical/Scientific	32.81
Financial Managers	59.25	Secretaries, Exc. Legal/Medical/Executive	18.04
First-Line Supervisors of Office Workers	27.42	Security Guards	18.30
General and Operations Managers	46.82	Surgeons	n/a
Hairdressers/Cosmetologists	16.59	Teacher Assistants, Exc. Postsecondary*	14.59
Home Health and Personal Care Aides	12.82	Teachers, Secondary School, Exc. Sp. Ed.*	26.06
Janitors and Cleaners	13.88	Telemarketers	n/a
Landscaping/Groundskeeping Workers	16.66	Truck Drivers, Heavy/Tractor-Trailer	22.96
Lawyers	51.48	Truck Drivers, Light/Delivery Services	19.13
Maids and Housekeeping Cleaners	11.75	Waiters and Waitresses	11.97

Note: Wage data covers the Clarksville, TN-KY Metropolitan Statistical Area; (*) Hourly wages were calculated from annual wage data based on a 40 hour work week; n/a not available.
Source: Bureau of Labor Statistics, Metro Area Occupational Employment & Wage Estimates, May 2022

Employment by Industry

Sector	MSA[1] Number of Employees	MSA[1] Percent of Total	U.S. Percent of Total
Construction, Mining, and Logging	4,300	4.3	5.4
Private Education and Health Services	13,300	13.2	16.1
Financial Activities	3,400	3.4	5.9
Government	19,500	19.4	14.5
Information	1,200	1.2	2.0
Leisure and Hospitality	12,200	12.1	10.3
Manufacturing	12,100	12.0	8.4
Other Services	3,400	3.4	3.7
Professional and Business Services	10,300	10.2	14.7
Retail Trade	14,300	14.2	10.2
Transportation, Warehousing, and Utilities	3,400	3.4	4.9
Wholesale Trade	n/a	n/a	3.9

Note: Figures are non-farm employment as of December 2022. Figures are not seasonally adjusted and include workers 16 years of age and older; (1) Figures cover the Clarksville, TN-KY Metropolitan Statistical Area; n/a not available
Source: Bureau of Labor Statistics, Current Employment Statistics, Employment, Hours, and Earnings

Employment by Occupation

Occupation Classification	City (%)	MSA[1] (%)	U.S. (%)
Management, Business, Science, and Arts	33.2	33.1	40.3
Natural Resources, Construction, and Maintenance	9.3	10.2	8.7
Production, Transportation, and Material Moving	16.5	17.0	13.1
Sales and Office	21.3	21.1	20.9
Service	19.8	18.6	17.0

Note: Figures cover employed civilians 16 years of age and older; (1) Figures cover the Clarksville, TN-KY Metropolitan Statistical Area
Source: U.S. Census Bureau, 2017-2021 American Community Survey 5-Year Estimates

Occupations with Greatest Projected Employment Growth: 2022 – 2024

Occupation[1]	2022 Employment	2024 Projected Employment	Numeric Employment Change	Percent Employment Change
Fast Food and Counter Workers	53,640	58,010	4,370	8.1
Waiters and Waitresses	49,450	53,640	4,190	8.5
General and Operations Managers	59,210	62,720	3,510	5.9
Cooks, Restaurant	22,120	25,260	3,140	14.2
Customer Service Representatives	71,500	74,270	2,770	3.9
First-Line Supervisors of Food Preparation and Serving Workers	26,470	29,030	2,560	9.7
Insurance Sales Agents	8,560	11,020	2,460	28.7
Managers, All Other	35,110	37,560	2,450	7.0
Construction Laborers	31,580	33,910	2,330	7.4
First-Line Supervisors of Office and Administrative Support Workers	54,390	56,690	2,300	4.2

Note: Projections cover Tennessee; (1) Sorted by numeric employment change
Source: www.projectionscentral.com, State Occupational Projections, 2022–2024 Short-Term Projections

Fastest-Growing Occupations: 2022 – 2024

Occupation[1]	2022 Employment	2024 Projected Employment	Numeric Employment Change	Percent Employment Change
Library Technicians	770	1,000	230	29.9
Insurance Sales Agents	8,560	11,020	2,460	28.7
Insurance Appraisers, Auto Damage	280	360	80	28.6
Athletes and Sports Competitors	1,280	1,630	350	27.3
Insurance Underwriters	2,060	2,560	500	24.3
Nursing Instructors and Teachers, Postsecondary	1,570	1,930	360	22.9
Biological Science Teachers, Postsecondary	1,240	1,510	270	21.8
Law Teachers, Postsecondary	230	280	50	21.7
English Language and Literature Teachers, Postsecondary	1,450	1,760	310	21.4
Mathematical Science Teachers, Postsecondary	900	1,090	190	21.1

Note: Projections cover Tennessee; (1) Sorted by percent employment change and excludes occupations with numeric employment change less than 50
Source: www.projectionscentral.com, State Occupational Projections, 2022–2024 Short-Term Projections

CITY FINANCES

City Government Finances

Component	2020 ($000)	2020 ($ per capita)
Total Revenues	412,802	2,610
Total Expenditures	389,254	2,461
Debt Outstanding	638,788	4,039
Cash and Securities[1]	430,609	2,723

Note: (1) Cash and security holdings of a government at the close of its fiscal year, including those of its dependent agencies, utilities, and liquor stores.
Source: U.S. Census Bureau, State & Local Government Finances 2020

City Government Revenue by Source

Source	2020 ($000)	2020 ($ per capita)	2020 (%)
General Revenue			
From Federal Government	2,454	16	0.6
From State Government	20,759	131	5.0
From Local Governments	0	0	0.0
Taxes			
Property	33,924	215	8.2
Sales and Gross Receipts	29,690	188	7.2
Personal Income	0	0	0.0
Corporate Income	0	0	0.0
Motor Vehicle License	0	0	0.0
Other Taxes	2,627	17	0.6
Current Charges	68,862	435	16.7
Liquor Store	0	0	0.0
Utility	249,076	1,575	60.3

Source: U.S. Census Bureau, State & Local Government Finances 2020

City Government Expenditures by Function

Function	2020 ($000)	2020 ($ per capita)	2020 (%)
General Direct Expenditures			
Air Transportation	0	0	0.0
Corrections	0	0	0.0
Education	0	0	0.0
Employment Security Administration	0	0	0.0
Financial Administration	1,834	11	0.5
Fire Protection	18,436	116	4.7
General Public Buildings	440	2	0.1
Governmental Administration, Other	2,357	14	0.6
Health	0	0	0.0
Highways	14,067	88	3.6
Hospitals	0	0	0.0
Housing and Community Development	1,877	11	0.5
Interest on General Debt	3,097	19	0.8
Judicial and Legal	898	5	0.2
Libraries	0	0	0.0
Parking	436	2	0.1
Parks and Recreation	8,701	55	2.2
Police Protection	29,614	187	7.6
Public Welfare	0	0	0.0
Sewerage	27,333	172	7.0
Solid Waste Management	0	0	0.0
Veterans' Services	0	0	0.0
Liquor Store	0	0	0.0
Utility	248,694	1,572	63.9

Source: U.S. Census Bureau, State & Local Government Finances 2020

TAXES

State Corporate Income Tax Rates

State	Tax Rate (%)	Income Brackets ($)	Num. of Brackets	Financial Institution Tax Rate (%)[a]	Federal Income Tax Ded.
Tennessee	6.5	Flat rate	1	6.5	No

Note: Tax rates as of January 1, 2023; (a) Rates listed are the corporate income tax rate applied to financial institutions or excise taxes based on income. Some states have other taxes based upon the value of deposits or shares.
Source: Federation of Tax Administrators, State Corporate Income Tax Rates, January 1, 2023

State Individual Income Tax Rates

State	Tax Rate (%)	Income Brackets ($)	Personal Exemptions ($) Single	Married	Depend.	Standard Ded. ($) Single	Married
Tennessee						– No state income tax –	

Note: Tax rates as of January 1, 2023; Local- and county-level taxes are not included
Source: Federation of Tax Administrators, State Individual Income Tax Rates, January 1, 2023

Various State Sales and Excise Tax Rates

State	State Sales Tax (%)	Gasoline[1] ($/gal.)	Cigarette[2] ($/pack)	Spirits[3] ($/gal.)	Wine[4] ($/gal.)	Beer[5] ($/gal.)	Recreational Marijuana (%)
Tennessee	7	0.274	0.62	4.46	1.27	1.29	Not legal

Note: All tax rates as of January 1, 2023; (1) The American Petroleum Institute has developed a methodology for determining the average tax rate on a gallon of fuel. Rates may include any of the following: excise taxes, environmental fees, storage tank fees, other fees or taxes, general sales tax, and local taxes; (2) The federal excise tax of $1.0066 per pack and local taxes are not included; (3) Rates are those applicable to off-premise sales of 40% alcohol by volume (a.b.v.) distilled spirits in 750ml containers. Local excise taxes are excluded; (4) Rates are those applicable to off-premise sales of 11% a.b.v. non-carbonated wine in 750ml containers; (5) Rates are those applicable to off-premise sales of 4.7% a.b.v. beer in 12 ounce containers.
Source: Tax Foundation, 2023 Facts & Figures: How Does Your State Compare?

State Business Tax Climate Index Rankings

State	Overall Rank	Corporate Tax Rank	Individual Income Tax Rank	Sales Tax Rank	Property Tax Rank	Unemployment Insurance Tax Rank
Tennessee	14	45	6	46	33	21

Note: The index is a measure of how each state's tax laws affect economic performance. The lower the rank, the more favorable a state's tax system is for business. States without a given tax are given a ranking of 1. The scores/rankings for the District of Columbia do not affect other states. The 2023 index represents the tax climate as of July 1, 2022.
Source: Tax Foundation, State Business Tax Climate Index 2023

TRANSPORTATION

Means of Transportation to Work

Area	Car/Truck/Van Drove Alone	Car-pooled	Public Transportation Bus	Subway	Railroad	Bicycle	Walked	Other Means	Worked at Home
City	84.5	7.7	0.7	0.0	0.0	0.0	1.2	1.4	4.5
MSA[1]	82.2	8.6	0.5	0.0	0.0	0.2	2.9	1.3	4.3
U.S.	73.2	8.6	2.0	1.6	0.5	0.5	2.5	1.5	9.7

Note: Figures are percentages and cover workers 16 years of age and older; (1) Figures cover the Clarksville, TN-KY Metropolitan Statistical Area
Source: U.S. Census Bureau, 2017-2021 American Community Survey 5-Year Estimates

Travel Time to Work

Area	Less Than 10 Minutes	10 to 19 Minutes	20 to 29 Minutes	30 to 44 Minutes	45 to 59 Minutes	60 to 89 Minutes	90 Minutes or More
City	10.3	33.0	25.3	14.1	6.8	8.5	2.2
MSA[1]	14.8	31.0	22.4	16.1	6.5	6.5	2.7
U.S.	12.4	28.5	21.0	20.9	8.2	6.2	2.9

Note: Note: Figures are percentages and include workers 16 years old and over; (1) Figures cover the Clarksville, TN-KY Metropolitan Statistical Area
Source: U.S. Census Bureau, 2017-2021 American Community Survey 5-Year Estimates

Key Congestion Measures

Measure	1990	2000	2010	2015	2020
Annual Hours of Delay, Total (000)	n/a	n/a	n/a	3,611	1,474
Annual Hours of Delay, Per Auto Commuter	n/a	n/a	n/a	21	8
Annual Congestion Cost, Per Auto Commuter ($)	n/a	n/a	n/a	453	191

Note: n/a not available
Source: Texas A&M Transportation Institute, 2021 Urban Mobility Report

Freeway Travel Time Index

Measure	1985	1990	1995	2000	2005	2010	2015	2020
Urban Area Index[1]	n/a	n/a	n/a	n/a	n/a	n/a	1.11	1.04
Urban Area Rank[1,2]	n/a	n/a	n/a	n/a	n/a	n/a	n/a	n/a

Note: Freeway Travel Time Index—the ratio of travel time in the peak period to the travel time at free-flow conditions. For example, a value of 1.30 indicates a 20-minute free-flow trip takes 26 minutes in the peak (20 minutes x 1.30 = 26 minutes); (1) Covers the Clarksville TN-KY urban area; (2) Rank is based on 101 larger urban areas (#1 = highest travel time index); n/a not available
Source: Texas A&M Transportation Institute, 2021 Urban Mobility Report

Public Transportation

Agency Name / Mode of Transportation	Vehicles Operated in Maximum Service[1]	Annual Unlinked Passenger Trips[2] (in thous.)	Annual Passenger Miles[3] (in thous.)
Clarksville Transit System (CTS)			
Bus (directly operated)	18	436.7	n/a
Demand Response (directly operated)	11	29.1	n/a

Note: (1) Number of revenue vehicles operated by the given mode and type of service to meet the annual maximum service requirement. This is the revenue vehicle count during the peak season of the year; on the week and day that maximum service is provided. Vehicles operated in maximum service (VOMS) exclude atypical days and one-time special events; (2) Number of passengers who boarded public transportation vehicles. Passengers are counted each time they board a vehicle no matter how many vehicles they use to travel from their origin to their destination. (3) Sum of the distances ridden by all passengers during the entire fiscal year.
Source: Federal Transit Administration, National Transit Database, 2021

Air Transportation

Airport Name and Code / Type of Service	Passenger Airlines[1]	Passenger Enplanements	Freight Carriers[2]	Freight (lbs)
Nashville International (53 miles) (BNA)				
Domestic service (U.S. carriers - 2022)	39	9,686,383	17	83,946,848
International service (U.S. carriers - 2021)	8	18,031	2	1,128

Note: (1) Includes all U.S.-based major, minor and commuter airlines that carried at least one passenger during the year; (2) Includes all U.S.-based airlines and freight carriers that transported at least one pound of freight during the year.
Source: Bureau of Transportation Statistics, The Intermodal Transportation Database, Air Carriers: T-100 Domestic Market (U.S. Carriers), 2022; Bureau of Transportation Statistics, The Intermodal Transportation Database, Air Carriers: T-100 International Market (U.S. Carriers), 2021

BUSINESSES

Major Business Headquarters

Company Name	Industry	Rankings Fortune[1]	Forbes[2]
No companies listed	-	-	-

Note: (1) Companies that produce a 10-K are ranked 1 to 500 based on 2021 revenue; (2) All private companies with at least $2 billion in annual revenue through the end of their most current fiscal year are ranked 1 to 246; companies listed are headquartered in the city; dashes indicate no ranking
Source: Fortune, "Fortune 500," 2022; Forbes, "America's Largest Private Companies," 2022

Living Environment

COST OF LIVING

Cost of Living Index

Composite Index	Groceries	Housing	Utilities	Transportation	Health Care	Misc. Goods/Services
n/a	n/a	n/a	n/a	n/a	n/a	n/a

Note: The Cost of Living Index measures regional differences in the cost of consumer goods and services, excluding taxes and non-consumer expenditures, for professional and managerial households in the top income quintile. It is based on more than 50,000 prices covering almost 60 different items for which prices are collected three times a year by chambers of commerce, economic development organizations or university applied economic centers in each participating urban area. The numbers shown should be read as a percentage above or below the national average of 100. For example, a value of 115.4 in the groceries column indicates that grocery prices are 15.4% higher than the national average. Small differences in the index numbers should not be interpreted as significant; n/a not available.
Source: The Council for Community and Economic Research, Cost of Living Index, 2022

Grocery Prices

Area[1]	T-Bone Steak ($/pound)	Frying Chicken ($/pound)	Whole Milk ($/half gal.)	Eggs ($/dozen)	Orange Juice ($/64 oz.)	Coffee ($/11.5 oz.)
City[2]	n/a	n/a	n/a	n/a	n/a	n/a
Avg.	13.81	1.59	2.43	2.25	3.85	4.95
Min.	10.17	0.90	1.51	1.30	2.90	3.46
Max.	19.35	3.30	4.32	4.32	5.31	8.59

*Note: (1) Values for the local area are compared with the average, minimum and maximum values for all 286 areas in the Cost of Living Index; (2) Figures cover the Clarksville TN urban area; n/a not available; **T-Bone Steak** (price per pound); **Frying Chicken** (price per pound, whole fryer); **Whole Milk** (half gallon carton); **Eggs** (price per dozen, Grade A, large); **Orange Juice** (64 oz. Tropicana or Florida Natural); **Coffee** (11.5 oz. can, vacuum-packed, Maxwell House, Hills Bros, or Folgers).*
Source: The Council for Community and Economic Research, Cost of Living Index, 2022

Housing and Utility Costs

Area[1]	New Home Price ($)	Apartment Rent ($/month)	All Electric ($/month)	Part Electric ($/month)	Other Energy ($/month)	Telephone ($/month)
City[2]	n/a	n/a	n/a	n/a	n/a	n/a
Avg.	450,913	1,371	176.41	99.93	76.96	190.22
Min.	229,283	546	100.84	31.56	27.15	174.27
Max.	2,434,977	4,569	356.86	249.59	272.24	208.31

*Note: (1) Values for the local area are compared with the average, minimum and maximum values for all 286 areas in the Cost of Living Index; (2) Figures cover the Clarksville TN urban area; n/a not available; **New Home Price** (2,400 sf living area, 8,000 sf lot, in urban area with full utilities); **Apartment Rent** (950 sf 2 bedroom/1.5 or 2 bath, unfurnished, excluding all utilities except water); **All Electric** (average monthly cost for an all-electric home); **Part Electric** (average monthly cost for a part-electric home); **Other Energy** (average monthly cost for natural gas, fuel oil, coal, wood, and any other forms of energy except electricity); **Telephone** (price includes the base monthly rate plus taxes and fees for three lines of mobile phone service).*
Source: The Council for Community and Economic Research, Cost of Living Index, 2022

Health Care, Transportation, and Other Costs

Area[1]	Doctor ($/visit)	Dentist ($/visit)	Optometrist ($/visit)	Gasoline ($/gallon)	Beauty Salon ($/visit)	Men's Shirt ($)
City[2]	n/a	n/a	n/a	n/a	n/a	n/a
Avg.	124.91	107.77	117.66	3.86	43.31	34.21
Min.	36.61	58.25	51.79	2.90	22.18	13.05
Max.	250.21	162.58	371.96	5.54	85.61	63.54

*Note: (1) Values for the local area are compared with the average, minimum and maximum values for all 286 areas in the Cost of Living Index; (2) Figures cover the Clarksville TN urban area; n/a not available; **Doctor** (general practitioners routine exam of an established patient); **Dentist** (adult teeth cleaning and periodic oral examination); **Optometrist** (full vision eye exam for established adult patient); **Gasoline** (one gallon regular unleaded, national brand, including all taxes, cash price at self-service pump if available); **Beauty Salon** (woman's shampoo, trim, and blow-dry); **Men's Shirt** (cotton/polyester dress shirt, pinpoint weave, long sleeves).*
Source: The Council for Community and Economic Research, Cost of Living Index, 2022

HOUSING

Homeownership Rate

Area	2015 (%)	2016 (%)	2017 (%)	2018 (%)	2019 (%)	2020 (%)	2021 (%)	2022 (%)
MSA[1]	n/a	n/a	n/a	n/a	n/a	n/a	n/a	n/a
U.S.	63.7	63.4	63.9	64.4	64.6	66.6	65.5	65.8

Note: (1) Figures cover the Clarksville, TN-KY Metropolitan Statistical Area; n/a not available
Source: U.S. Census Bureau, Housing Vacancies and Homeownership Annual Statistics: 2015-2022

House Price Index (HPI)

Area	National Ranking[2]	Quarterly Change (%)	One-Year Change (%)	Five-Year Change (%)	Since 1991Q1 (%)
MSA[1]	n/a	n/a	n/a	n/a	n/a
U.S.[3]	—	0.34	8.41	58.44	289.08

Note: The HPI is a weighted repeat sales index. It measures average price changes in repeat sales or refinancings on the same properties. This information is obtained by reviewing repeat mortgage transactions on single-family properties whose mortgages have been purchased or securitized by Fannie Mae or Freddie Mac since January 1975; (1) Figures cover the , Metropolitan Statistical Area; (2) Rankings are based on annual percentage change for all metro areas containing at least 15,000 transactions over the last 10 years and ranges from 1 to 257; (3) figures based on a weighted average of Census Division estimates using a seasonally adjusted, purchase-only index; all figures are for the period ending December 31, 2022; n/a not available
Source: Federal Housing Finance Agency, Change in FHFA Metropolitan Area House Price Indexes, 2022Q4

Median Single-Family Home Prices

Area	2020	2021	2022p	Percent Change 2021 to 2022
MSA[1]	n/a	n/a	n/a	n/a
U.S. Average	300.2	357.1	392.6	9.9

Note: Figures are median sales prices of existing single-family homes in thousands of dollars; (p) preliminary; n/a not available; (1) Figures cover the Clarksville, TN-KY Metropolitan Statistical Area
Source: National Association of Realtors, Median Sales Price of Existing Single-Family Homes for Metropolitan Areas, 4th Quarter 2022

Qualifying Income Based on Median Sales Price of Existing Single-Family Homes

Area	With 5% Down ($)	With 10% Down ($)	With 20% Down ($)
MSA[1]	n/a	n/a	n/a
U.S. Average	112,234	106,237	94,513

Note: Figures are preliminary; Qualifying income is based on a mortgage rate of 6.77%. Monthly principal and interest payment is limited to 25% of income; n/a not available; (1) Figures cover the Clarksville, TN-KY Metropolitan Statistical Area
Source: National Association of Realtors, Qualifying Income Based on Median Sales Price of Existing Single-Family Homes for Metropolitan Areas, 4th Quarter 2022

Home Value

Area	Under $100,000	$100,000 -$199,999	$200,000 -$299,999	$300,000 -$399,999	$400,000 -$499,999	$500,000 -$999,999	$1,000,000 or more	Median ($)
City	13.0	51.0	25.3	6.3	1.6	2.6	0.3	172,700
MSA[1]	19.0	41.2	23.4	9.2	2.9	3.7	0.7	174,300
U.S.	16.2	24.2	20.1	13.6	8.3	13.6	4.1	244,900

Note: Figures are percentages except for median and cover owner-occupied housing units; (1) Figures cover the Clarksville, TN-KY Metropolitan Statistical Area
Source: U.S. Census Bureau, 2017-2021 American Community Survey 5-Year Estimates

Year Housing Structure Built

Area	2020 or Later	2010 -2019	2000 -2009	1990 -1999	1980 -1989	1970 -1979	1960 -1969	1950 -1959	1940 -1949	Before 1940	Median Year
City	0.2	15.6	22.2	20.2	12.9	12.0	7.2	4.8	2.8	2.1	1994
MSA[1]	0.4	13.8	19.7	20.2	12.2	13.9	7.9	6.0	2.9	3.0	1992
U.S.	0.2	7.3	13.6	13.6	13.2	14.8	10.3	10.0	4.7	12.2	1979

Note: Figures are percentages except for Median Year; Note: (1) Figures cover the Clarksville, TN-KY Metropolitan Statistical Area
Source: U.S. Census Bureau, 2017-2021 American Community Survey 5-Year Estimates

Gross Monthly Rent

Area	Under $500	$500 -$999	$1,000 -$1,499	$1,500 -$1,999	$2,000 -$2,499	$2,500 -$2,999	$3,000 and up	Median ($)
City	4.2	44.4	38.0	10.4	2.6	0.3	0.1	1,016
MSA[1]	7.7	45.9	35.8	8.3	1.9	0.2	0.1	967
U.S.	8.1	30.5	30.8	16.8	7.3	3.1	3.5	1,163

Note: Figures are percentages except for median; Gross rent is the contract rent plus the estimated average monthly cost of utilities (electricity, gas, and water and sewer) and fuels (oil, coal, kerosene, wood, etc.) if these are paid by the renter (or paid for the renter by someone else); (1) Figures cover the Clarksville, TN-KY Metropolitan Statistical Area
Source: U.S. Census Bureau, 2017-2021 American Community Survey 5-Year Estimates

HEALTH

Health Risk Factors

Category	MSA[1] (%)	U.S. (%)
Adults aged 18–64 who have any kind of health care coverage	n/a	90.9
Adults who reported being in good or better health	n/a	85.2
Adults who have been told they have high blood cholesterol	n/a	35.7
Adults who have been told they have high blood pressure	n/a	32.4
Adults who are current smokers	n/a	14.4
Adults who currently use e-cigarettes	n/a	6.7
Adults who currently use chewing tobacco, snuff, or snus	n/a	3.5
Adults who are heavy drinkers[2]	n/a	6.3
Adults who are binge drinkers[3]	n/a	15.4
Adults who are overweight (BMI 25.0 - 29.9)	n/a	34.4
Adults who are obese (BMI 30.0 - 99.8)	n/a	33.9
Adults who participated in any physical activities in the past month	n/a	76.3

*Note: (1) Figures for the Clarksville, TN-KY Metropolitan Statistical Area were not available.
(2) Heavy drinkers are classified as adult men having more than 14 drinks per week and adult women having more than 7 drinks per week; (3) Binge drinkers are classified as males having five or more drinks on one occasion or females having four or more drinks on one occasion
Source: Centers for Disease Control and Prevention, Behaviorial Risk Factor Surveillance System, SMART: Selected Metropolitan Area Risk Trends, 2021*

Acute and Chronic Health Conditions

Category	MSA[1] (%)	U.S. (%)
Adults who have ever been told they had a heart attack	n/a	4.0
Adults who have ever been told they have angina or coronary heart disease	n/a	3.8
Adults who have ever been told they had a stroke	n/a	3.0
Adults who have ever been told they have asthma	n/a	14.9
Adults who have ever been told they have arthritis	n/a	25.8
Adults who have ever been told they have diabetes[2]	n/a	10.9
Adults who have ever been told they had skin cancer	n/a	6.6
Adults who have ever been told they had any other types of cancer	n/a	7.5
Adults who have ever been told they have COPD	n/a	6.1
Adults who have ever been told they have kidney disease	n/a	3.0
Adults who have ever been told they have a form of depression	n/a	20.5

*Note: (1) Figures for the Clarksville, TN-KY Metropolitan Statistical Area were not available.
(2) Figures do not include pregnancy-related, borderline, or pre-diabetes
Source: Centers for Disease Control and Prevention, Behaviorial Risk Factor Surveillance System, SMART: Selected Metropolitan Area Risk Trends, 2021*

Health Screening and Vaccination Rates

Category	MSA[1] (%)	U.S. (%)
Adults who have ever been tested for HIV	n/a	34.9
Adults who have had their blood cholesterol checked within the last five years	n/a	85.2
Adults aged 65+ who have had flu shot within the past year	n/a	68.6
Adults aged 65+ who have ever had a pneumonia vaccination	n/a	71.0

*Note: (1) Figures for the Clarksville, TN-KY Metropolitan Statistical Area were not available.
Source: Centers for Disease Control and Prevention, Behaviorial Risk Factor Surveillance System, SMART: Selected Metropolitan Area Risk Trends, 2021*

Disability Status

Category	MSA[1] (%)	U.S. (%)
Adults who reported being deaf	n/a	7.2
Are you blind or have serious difficulty seeing, even when wearing glasses?	n/a	4.8
Are you limited in any way in any of your usual activities due to arthritis?	n/a	11.1
Do you have difficulty doing errands alone?	n/a	7.0
Do you have difficulty dressing or bathing?	n/a	3.6
Do you have serious difficulty concentrating/remembering/making decisions?	n/a	12.1
Do you have serious difficulty walking or climbing stairs?	n/a	12.8

*Note: (1) Figures for the Clarksville, TN-KY Metropolitan Statistical Area were not available.
Source: Centers for Disease Control and Prevention, Behaviorial Risk Factor Surveillance System, SMART: Selected Metropolitan Area Risk Trends, 2021*

Mortality Rates for the Top 10 Causes of Death in the U.S.

ICD-10[a] Sub-Chapter	ICD-10[a] Code	Crude Mortality Rate[1] per 100,000 population County[2]	U.S.
Malignant neoplasms	C00-C97	136.8	182.6
Ischaemic heart diseases	I20-I25	86.5	113.1
Other forms of heart disease	I30-I51	28.7	64.4
Other degenerative diseases of the nervous system	G30-G31	36.2	51.0
Cerebrovascular diseases	I60-I69	39.5	47.8
Other external causes of accidental injury	W00-X59	55.0	46.4
Chronic lower respiratory diseases	J40-J47	49.3	45.7
Organic, including symptomatic, mental disorders	F01-F09	18.6	35.9
Hypertensive diseases	I10-I15	27.8	35.0
Diabetes mellitus	E10-E14	26.6	29.6

Note: (a) ICD-10 = International Classification of Diseases 10th Revision; (1) Crude mortality rates are a three-year average covering 2019-2021; (2) Figures cover Montgomery County.
Source: Centers for Disease Control and Prevention, National Center for Health Statistics. National Vital Statistics System, Mortality 2018-2021 on CDC WONDER Online Database

Mortality Rates for Selected Causes of Death

ICD-10[a] Sub-Chapter	ICD-10[a] Code	Crude Mortality Rate[1] per 100,000 population County[2]	U.S.
Assault	X85-Y09	9.7	7.0
Diseases of the liver	K70-K76	14.1	19.8
Human immunodeficiency virus (HIV) disease	B20-B24	Suppressed	1.5
Influenza and pneumonia	J09-J18	12.4	14.7
Intentional self-harm	X60-X84	19.8	14.3
Malnutrition	E40-E46	Unreliable	4.3
Obesity and other hyperalimentation	E65-E68	6.5	3.0
Renal failure	N17-N19	7.5	15.7
Transport accidents	V01-V99	16.6	13.6
Viral hepatitis	B15-B19	Unreliable	1.2

Note: (a) ICD-10 = International Classification of Diseases 10th Revision; (1) Crude mortality rates are a three-year average covering 2019-2021; (2) Figures cover Montgomery County; Data are suppressed when the data meet the criteria for confidentiality constraints; Crude mortality rates are flagged as unreliable when the rate would be calculated with a numerator of 20 or less.
Source: Centers for Disease Control and Prevention, National Center for Health Statistics. National Vital Statistics System, Mortality 2018-2021 on CDC WONDER Online Database

Health Insurance Coverage

Area	With Health Insurance	With Private Health Insurance	With Public Health Insurance	Without Health Insurance	Population Under Age 19 Without Health Insurance
City	91.5	71.6	34.9	8.5	3.5
MSA[1]	91.6	69.8	36.8	8.4	5.6
U.S.	91.2	67.8	35.4	8.8	5.3

Note: Figures are percentages that cover the civilian noninstitutionalized population; (1) Figures cover the Clarksville, TN-KY Metropolitan Statistical Area
Source: U.S. Census Bureau, 2017-2021 American Community Survey 5-Year Estimates

Number of Medical Professionals

Area	MDs[3]	DOs[3,4]	Dentists	Podiatrists	Chiropractors	Optometrists
County[1] (number)	216	36	98	5	28	27
County[1] (rate[2])	97.7	16.3	43.0	2.2	12.3	11.8
U.S. (rate[2])	289.3	23.5	72.5	6.2	28.7	17.4

Note: Data as of 2021 unless noted; (1) Data covers Montgomery County; (2) Rate per 100,000 population; (3) Data as of 2020 and includes all active, non-federal physicians; (4) Doctor of Osteopathic Medicine
Source: U.S. Department of Health and Human Services, Health Resources and Services Administration, Bureau of Health Professions, Area Resource File (ARF) 2021-2022

EDUCATION

Public School District Statistics

District Name	Schls	Pupils	Pupil/Teacher Ratio	Minority Pupils[1] (%)	LEP/ELL[2] (%)	IEP[3] (%)
Montgomery County	42	37,680	17.7	52.0	2.0	13.8

Note: Table includes school districts with 2,000 or more students; (1) Percentage of students that are not non-Hispanic white; (2) Percentage of students that are Limited English Proficient or English Language Learners (2018-19); (3) Percentage of students that have an Individualized Education Program (2019-20).
Source: U.S. Department of Education, National Center for Education Statistics, Common Core of Data, Local Education Agency (School District) Universe Survey: School Year 2021-2022

Highest Level of Education

Area	Less than H.S.	H.S. Diploma	Some College, No Deg.	Associate Degree	Bachelor's Degree	Master's Degree	Prof. School Degree	Doctorate Degree
City	6.4	26.9	26.3	11.6	18.7	8.2	0.8	1.1
MSA[1]	8.6	28.9	25.1	11.0	17.0	7.4	1.2	0.9
U.S.	11.1	26.5	20.0	8.7	20.6	9.3	2.2	1.5

Note: Figures cover persons age 25 and over; (1) Figures cover the Clarksville, TN-KY Metropolitan Statistical Area
Source: U.S. Census Bureau, 2017-2021 American Community Survey 5-Year Estimates

Educational Attainment by Race

Area	High School Graduate or Higher (%) Total	White	Black	Asian	Hisp.[2]	Bachelor's Degree or Higher (%) Total	White	Black	Asian	Hisp.[2]
City	93.6	94.2	94.0	87.4	87.1	28.7	30.6	25.3	37.3	17.2
MSA[1]	91.4	91.9	90.6	87.5	85.7	26.5	27.3	23.3	42.7	18.7
U.S.	88.9	91.4	87.2	87.6	71.2	33.7	35.5	23.3	55.6	18.4

Note: Figures shown cover persons 25 years old and over; (1) Figures cover the Clarksville, TN-KY Metropolitan Statistical Area; (2) People of Hispanic origin can be of any race
Source: U.S. Census Bureau, 2017-2021 American Community Survey 5-Year Estimates

School Enrollment by Grade and Control

Area	Preschool (%) Public	Private	Kindergarten (%) Public	Private	Grades 1 - 4 (%) Public	Private	Grades 5 - 8 (%) Public	Private	Grades 9 - 12 (%) Public	Private
City	61.1	38.9	85.7	14.3	93.4	6.6	92.1	7.9	87.1	12.9
MSA[1]	62.6	37.4	88.2	11.8	86.8	13.2	88.6	11.4	87.0	13.0
U.S.	58.8	41.2	86.3	13.7	88.3	11.7	88.6	11.4	89.4	10.6

Note: Figures shown cover persons 3 years old and over; (1) Figures cover the Clarksville, TN-KY Metropolitan Statistical Area
Source: U.S. Census Bureau, 2017-2021 American Community Survey 5-Year Estimates

Higher Education

Four-Year Colleges Public	Private Non-profit	Private For-profit	Two-Year Colleges Public	Private Non-profit	Private For-profit	Medical Schools[1]	Law Schools[2]	Voc/Tech[3]
1	0	1	1	0	2	0	0	2

Note: Figures cover institutions located within the Clarksville, TN-KY Metropolitan Statistical Area and include main campuses only; (1) includes schools accredited by the Liaison Committee on Medical Education and the American Osteopathic Association's Commission on Osteopathic College Accreditation; (2) includes ABA-accredited schools, schools with provisional ABA accreditation, and state accredited schools; (3) includes all schools with programs that are less than 2 years.
Source: National Center for Education Statistics, Integrated Postsecondary Education System (IPEDS), 2021-22; Wikipedia, List of Medical Schools in the United States, accessed April 10, 2023; Wikipedia, List of Law Schools in the United States, accessed April 10, 2023

EMPLOYERS

Major Employers

Company Name	Industry
Agero	Call center
Akebono	Hubs, rotors
AT&T	Engineering services
Austin Peay State University	University
Bridgestone Metalpha U.S.A.	Steel tire cords & tire cord fabrics
City of Clarksville	Municipal government
Clarksville-Montgomery School System	Education
Gateway Medical Center	General medical & surgical hospitals
Jennie Stuart Medical Center	General medical & surgical hospitals
Jostens	Yearbooks & commercial printing
Montgomery County Government	Government
Trane Company	Heating & air conditioners
Trigg County Board of Education	Elementary & secondary schools
U.S. Army	U.S. military
Wal-Mart Stores	Department stores, discount

Note: Companies shown are located within the Clarksville, TN-KY Metropolitan Statistical Area.
Source: Hoovers.com; Wikipedia

PUBLIC SAFETY

Crime Rate

Area	Total Crime	Violent Crime Rate				Property Crime Rate		
		Murder	Rape[3]	Robbery	Aggrav. Assault	Burglary	Larceny-Theft	Motor Vehicle Theft
City	2,852.9	9.3	52.1	48.4	500.1	273.6	1,715.6	253.8
Suburbs[1]	1,659.2	4.0	32.5	25.9	161.9	300.0	988.2	146.7
Metro[2]	2,276.1	6.7	42.6	37.5	336.7	286.4	1,364.1	202.0
U.S.	2,356.7	6.5	38.4	73.9	279.7	314.2	1,398.0	246.0

Note: Figures are crimes per 100,000 population; (1) All areas within the metro area that are located outside the city limits; (2) Figures cover the Clarksville, TN-KY Metropolitan Statistical Area; (3) All figures shown were reported using the revised Uniform Crime Reporting (UCR) definition of rape; Due to the transition to the National Incident-Based Reporting System (NIBRS), limited city and metro area data was released for 2021.
Source: FBI Uniform Crime Reports, 2020

Hate Crimes

Area	Number of Quarters Reported	Number of Incidents per Bias Motivation					
		Race/Ethnicity/Ancestry	Religion	Sexual Orientation	Disability	Gender	Gender Identity
City	4	0	0	0	0	0	0
U.S.	4	5,227	1,244	1,110	130	75	266

Note: Due to the transition to the National Incident-Based Reporting System (NIBRS), limited crime data was released for 2021.
Source: Federal Bureau of Investigation, Hate Crime Statistics 2020

Identity Theft Consumer Reports

Area	Reports	Reports per 100,000 Population	Rank[2]
MSA[1]	808	265	92
U.S.	1,108,609	339	-

Note: (1) Figures cover the Clarksville, TN-KY Metropolitan Statistical Area; (2) Rank ranges from 1 to 391 where 1 indicates greatest number of identity theft reports per 100,000 population
Source: Federal Trade Commission, Consumer Sentinel Network Data Book 2022

Fraud and Other Consumer Reports

Area	Reports	Reports per 100,000 Population	Rank[2]
MSA[1]	3,630	1,192	42
U.S.	4,064,520	1,245	-

Note: (1) Figures cover the Clarksville, TN-KY Metropolitan Statistical Area; (2) Rank ranges from 1 to 391 where 1 indicates greatest number of fraud and other consumer reports per 100,000 population
Source: Federal Trade Commission, Consumer Sentinel Network Data Book 2022

POLITICS

2020 Presidential Election Results

Area	Biden	Trump	Jorgensen	Hawkins	Other
Montgomery County	42.3	55.0	1.9	0.2	0.7
U.S.	51.3	46.8	1.2	0.3	0.5

Note: Results are percentages and may not add to 100% due to rounding
Source: Dave Leip's Atlas of U.S. Presidential Elections

SPORTS

Professional Sports Teams

Team Name	League	Year Established

No teams are located in the metro area
Source: Wikipedia, Major Professional Sports Teams of the United States and Canada, April 12, 2023

CLIMATE

Average and Extreme Temperatures

Temperature	Jan	Feb	Mar	Apr	May	Jun	Jul	Aug	Sep	Oct	Nov	Dec	Yr.
Extreme High (°F)	78	84	86	91	95	106	107	104	105	94	84	79	107
Average High (°F)	47	51	60	71	79	87	90	89	83	72	60	50	70
Average Temp. (°F)	38	41	50	60	68	76	80	79	72	61	49	41	60
Average Low (°F)	28	31	39	48	57	65	69	68	61	48	39	31	49
Extreme Low (°F)	-17	-13	2	23	34	42	54	49	36	26	-1	-10	-17

Note: Figures cover the years 1948-1990
Source: National Climatic Data Center, International Station Meteorological Climate Summary, 9/96

Average Precipitation/Snowfall/Humidity

Precip./Humidity	Jan	Feb	Mar	Apr	May	Jun	Jul	Aug	Sep	Oct	Nov	Dec	Yr.
Avg. Precip. (in.)	4.4	4.2	5.0	4.1	4.6	3.7	3.8	3.3	3.2	2.6	3.9	4.6	47.4
Avg. Snowfall (in.)	4	3	1	Tr	0	0	0	0	0	Tr	1	1	11
Avg. Rel. Hum. 6am (%)	81	81	80	81	86	86	88	90	90	87	83	82	85
Avg. Rel. Hum. 3pm (%)	61	57	51	48	52	52	54	53	52	49	55	59	54

Note: Figures cover the years 1948-1990; Tr = Trace amounts (<0.05 in. of rain; <0.5 in. of snow)
Source: National Climatic Data Center, International Station Meteorological Climate Summary, 9/96

Weather Conditions

Temperature			Daytime Sky			Precipitation		
10°F & below	32°F & below	90°F & above	Clear	Partly cloudy	Cloudy	0.01 inch or more precip.	0.1 inch or more snow/ice	Thunder-storms
5	76	51	98	135	132	119	8	54

Note: Figures are average number of days per year and cover the years 1948-1990
Source: National Climatic Data Center, International Station Meteorological Climate Summary, 9/96

HAZARDOUS WASTE

Superfund Sites

The Clarksville, TN-KY metro area has no sites on the EPA's Superfund Final National Priorities List. There are a total of 1,165 Superfund sites with a status of proposed or final on the list in the U.S.
U.S. Environmental Protection Agency, National Priorities List, April 12, 2023

AIR QUALITY

Air Quality Trends: Ozone

	1990	1995	2000	2005	2010	2015	2018	2019	2020	2021
MSA[1]	n/a	n/a	n/a	n/a	n/a	n/a	n/a	n/a	n/a	n/a
U.S.	0.087	0.089	0.081	0.080	0.072	0.067	0.069	0.065	0.065	0.067

Note: (1) Data covers the Clarksville, TN-KY Metropolitan Statistical Area; n/a not available. The values shown are the composite ozone concentration averages among trend sites based on the highest fourth daily maximum 8-hour concentration in parts per million. These trends are based on sites having an adequate record of monitoring data during the trend period. Data from exceptional events are included.
Source: U.S. Environmental Protection Agency, Air Quality Monitoring Information, "Air Quality Trends by City, 1990-2021"

Air Quality Index

Area	Percent of Days when Air Quality was...[2]					AQI Statistics[2]	
	Good	Moderate	Unhealthy for Sensitive Groups	Unhealthy	Very Unhealthy	Maximum	Median
MSA[1]	70.4	29.3	0.3	0.0	0.0	138	43

Note: (1) Data covers the Clarksville, TN-KY Metropolitan Statistical Area; (2) Based on 365 days with AQI data in 2021. Air Quality Index (AQI) is an index for reporting daily air quality. EPA calculates the AQI for five major air pollutants regulated by the Clean Air Act: ground-level ozone, particle pollution (aka particulate matter), carbon monoxide, sulfur dioxide, and nitrogen dioxide. The AQI runs from 0 to 500. The higher the AQI value, the greater the level of air pollution and the greater the health concern. There are six AQI categories: "Good" AQI is between 0 and 50. Air quality is considered satisfactory; "Moderate" AQI is between 51 and 100. Air quality is acceptable; "Unhealthy for Sensitive Groups" When AQI values are between 101 and 150, members of sensitive groups may experience health effects; "Unhealthy" When AQI values are between 151 and 200 everyone may begin to experience health effects; "Very Unhealthy" AQI values between 201 and 300 trigger a health alert; "Hazardous" AQI values over 300 trigger warnings of emergency conditions (not shown).
Source: U.S. Environmental Protection Agency, Air Quality Index Report, 2021

Air Quality Index Pollutants

Area	Percent of Days when AQI Pollutant was...[2]					
	Carbon Monoxide	Nitrogen Dioxide	Ozone	Sulfur Dioxide	Particulate Matter 2.5	Particulate Matter 10
MSA[1]	0.0	0.0	47.4	(3)	52.6	0.0

Note: (1) Data covers the Clarksville, TN-KY Metropolitan Statistical Area; (2) Based on 365 days with AQI data in 2021. The Air Quality Index (AQI) is an index for reporting daily air quality. EPA calculates the AQI for five major air pollutants regulated by the Clean Air Act: ground-level ozone, particle pollution (also known as particulate matter), carbon monoxide, sulfur dioxide, and nitrogen dioxide. The AQI runs from 0 to 500. The higher the AQI value, the greater the level of air pollution and the greater the health concern; (3) Sulfur dioxide is no longer included in this table (as of December 8, 2021) because SO_2 concentrations tend to be very localized and not necessarily representative of broad geographical areas like counties and CBSAs.
Source: U.S. Environmental Protection Agency, Air Quality Index Report, 2021

Maximum Air Pollutant Concentrations: Particulate Matter, Ozone, CO and Lead

	Particulate Matter 10 (ug/m³)	Particulate Matter 2.5 Wtd AM (ug/m³)	Particulate Matter 2.5 24-Hr (ug/m³)	Ozone (ppm)	Carbon Monoxide (ppm)	Lead (ug/m³)
MSA[1] Level	n/a	10.4	27	0.06	n/a	n/a
NAAQS[2]	150	15	35	0.075	9	0.15
Met NAAQS[2]	n/a	Yes	Yes	Yes	n/a	n/a

Note: (1) Data covers the Clarksville, TN-KY Metropolitan Statistical Area; Data from exceptional events are included; (2) National Ambient Air Quality Standards; ppm = parts per million; ug/m³ = micrograms per cubic meter; n/a not available.
Concentrations: Particulate Matter 10 (coarse particulate)—highest second maximum 24-hour concentration; Particulate Matter 2.5 Wtd AM (fine particulate)—highest weighted annual mean concentration; Particulate Matter 2.5 24-Hour (fine particulate)—highest 98th percentile 24-hour concentration; Ozone—highest fourth daily maximum 8-hour concentration; Carbon Monoxide—highest second maximum non-overlapping 8-hour concentration; Lead—maximum running 3-month average
Source: U.S. Environmental Protection Agency, Air Quality Monitoring Information, "Air Quality Statistics by City, 2021"

Maximum Air Pollutant Concentrations: Nitrogen Dioxide and Sulfur Dioxide

	Nitrogen Dioxide AM (ppb)	Nitrogen Dioxide 1-Hr (ppb)	Sulfur Dioxide AM (ppb)	Sulfur Dioxide 1-Hr (ppb)	Sulfur Dioxide 24-Hr (ppb)
MSA[1] Level	n/a	n/a	n/a	n/a	n/a
NAAQS[2]	53	100	30	75	140
Met NAAQS[2]	n/a	n/a	n/a	n/a	n/a

Note: (1) Data covers the Clarksville, TN-KY Metropolitan Statistical Area; Data from exceptional events are included; (2) National Ambient Air Quality Standards; ppm = parts per million; ug/m³ = micrograms per cubic meter; n/a not available.
Concentrations: Nitrogen Dioxide AM—highest arithmetic mean concentration; Nitrogen Dioxide 1-Hr—highest 98th percentile 1-hour daily maximum concentration; Sulfur Dioxide AM—highest annual mean concentration; Sulfur Dioxide 1-Hr—highest 99th percentile 1-hour daily maximum concentration; Sulfur Dioxide 24-Hr—highest second maximum 24-hour concentration
Source: U.S. Environmental Protection Agency, Air Quality Monitoring Information, "Air Quality Statistics by City, 2021"

College Station, Texas

Background

College Station is located 367 feet above sea level in the center of the Texas Triangle within Brazos County and shares a border with the city of Bryan to the northwest. Named the most educated city in Texas, College Station was built alongside the prestigious Texas A&M University during the nation's centennial in 1876. The city's origins date back to 1860, when Houston and Texas Central Railway began to build through the region during the height of railroad expansion in the mid-1800s. Though this railway no longer exists, College Station's location and the university make it important to the state.

Although College Station has always been upheld by Texas A&M, the city was not incorporated until 1938. In 1942, the so-called "Father of College Station," Mayor Ernest Langford, gave the community its own, unique identity over his 26-year run. During Langford's first term, the city also adopted a council-manager system of government.

College Station is comprised of three major districts. Northgate, Wolf Pen Creek, and Wellborn combine to create a bustling city populated by students, professors, and their families. The city's population is young, mostly comprised of college-age individuals.

The economy of the city largely relies on the university itself, with many of its employees doing double time both attending the school and working in the city's shops and restaurants. Unemployment was among the lowest in Texas in recent years, but underemployment continues to be an issue among the overqualified college students. Post Oak Mall provides much of the business within College Station, being the first to open in the area and the largest mall in Brazos Valley. Over 75 percent of retail sales in the Brazos Valley are comprised here.

The largest employer of the city is Texas A&M University. Previously known as the Agricultural and Mechanical College of Texas, TAMU is known for its triple designation as a Land-, Sea-, and Space-Grant institution, housing ongoing research projects funded by NASA, the National Institutes of Health, the National Science Foundation, and others.

The city's nightlife and entertainment attract its young crowd to events such as the four-day Northgate Music Festival and the live music at Church Street BBQ and Hurricane Harry's. The Texas country music scene thrives here, with many notable musicians getting their start at these smaller stages, among them Robert Earl Keen, Grammy-award winner Lyle Lovett, and Roger Creager.

Alongside these celebrities are important landmarks and areas within College Station, including Church Street, made famous by the Lyle Lovett/Robert Earl Keen duet "The Front Porch Song," and the George Bush Presidential Library, which was dedicated in 1997 in honor of President George H.W. Bush. The population and popularity of this relatively small city continues to grow every year, with predictions of the population doubling by the year 2030.

With the climate sitting comfortably in the subtropical and temperate zone, College Station enjoys mild winters with its low-temperature period lasting less than two months. While snow and ice during winter months are very rare, February 2021 saw unprecedented frigid temperatures and snowfall that led to days-long power outages. In turn, the summers are hot with occasional rain showers. The city's average temperature is 69 degrees with annual rainfall averaging 39 inches.

Rankings

Business/Finance Rankings

- The College Station metro area appeared on the Milken Institute "2022 Best Performing Cities" list. Rank: #27 out of 201 small metro areas (population over 60,000). Criteria: job growth; wage and salary growth; high-tech output growth; housing affordability; household broadband access. *Milken Institute, "Best-Performing Cities 2022," March 28, 2022*

- *Forbes* ranked 203 smaller metro areas (population under 268,000) to determine the nation's "Best Small Places for Business and Careers." The College Station metro area was ranked #2. Criteria: costs (business and living); job growth (past and projected); income growth; quality of life; educational attainment (college and high school); projected economic growth; cultural and leisure opportunities; workplace tolerance laws; net migration patterns. *Forbes, "The Best Small Places for Business and Careers 2019," October 30, 2019*

Real Estate Rankings

- College Station was ranked #132 out of 235 metro areas in terms of housing affordability in 2022 by the National Association of Home Builders (#1 = most affordable). Criteria: the share of homes sold in that area affordable to a family earning the local median income, based on standard mortgage underwriting criteria. *National Association of Home Builders®, NAHB-Wells Fargo Housing Opportunity Index, 4th Quarter 2022*

Safety Rankings

- The National Insurance Crime Bureau ranked 390 metro areas in the U.S. in terms of per capita rates of vehicle theft. The College Station metro area ranked #233 (#1 = highest rate). Criteria: number of vehicle theft offenses per 100,000 inhabitants in 2021. *National Insurance Crime Bureau, "Hot Spots 2021," September 1, 2022*

Seniors/Retirement Rankings

- From its Best Cities for Successful Aging indexes, the Milken Institute generated rankings for metropolitan areas, weighing data in nine categories—health care, wellness, living arrangements, transportation and convenience, financial characteristics, education, employment, community engagement, and overall livability. The College Station metro area was ranked #28 overall in the small metro area category. *Milken Institute, "Best Cities for Successful Aging, 2017" March 14, 2017*

- College Station made the 2022 *Forbes* list of "25 Best Places to Retire." Criteria, focused on overall affordability as well as quality of life indicators, include: housing/living costs compared to the national average and state taxes; air quality; crime rates; home price appreciation; risk associated with climate-change/natural hazards; availability of medical care; bikeability; walkability; healthy living. *Forbes.com, "The Best Places to Retire in 2022," May 13, 2022*

Business Environment

DEMOGRAPHICS

Population Growth

Area	1990 Census	2000 Census	2010 Census	2020 Census	Population Growth (%) 1990-2020	Population Growth (%) 2010-2020
City	53,318	67,890	93,857	120,511	126.0	28.4
MSA[1]	150,998	184,885	228,660	268,248	77.7	17.3
U.S.	248,709,873	281,421,906	308,745,538	331,449,281	33.3	7.4

Note: (1) Figures cover the College Station-Bryan, TX Metropolitan Statistical Area
Source: U.S. Census Bureau, 1990 Census, 2000 Census, 2010 Census, 2020 Census

Race

Area	White Alone[2] (%)	Black Alone[2] (%)	Asian Alone[2] (%)	AIAN[3] Alone[2] (%)	NHOPI[4] Alone[2] (%)	Other Race Alone[2] (%)	Two or More Races (%)
City	63.5	8.1	10.2	0.5	0.1	7.4	10.2
MSA[1]	60.7	11.0	5.6	0.7	0.1	9.8	12.1
U.S.	61.6	12.4	6.0	1.1	0.2	8.4	10.2

Note: (1) Figures cover the College Station-Bryan, TX Metropolitan Statistical Area; (2) Alone is defined as not being in combination with one or more other races; (3) American Indian and Alaska Native; (4) Native Hawaiian and Other Pacific Islander
Source: U.S. Census Bureau, 2020 Census

Hispanic or Latino Origin

Area	Total (%)	Mexican (%)	Puerto Rican (%)	Cuban (%)	Other (%)
City	17.7	12.8	0.7	0.2	4.1
MSA[1]	25.7	21.8	0.4	0.3	3.1
U.S.	18.4	11.2	1.8	0.7	4.7

Note: Persons of Hispanic or Latino origin can be of any race; (1) Figures cover the College Station-Bryan, TX Metropolitan Statistical Area
Source: U.S. Census Bureau, 2017-2021 American Community Survey 5-Year Estimates

Age

Area	Under Age 5	Age 5–19	Age 20–34	Age 35–44	Age 45–54	Age 55–64	Age 65–74	Age 75–84	Age 85+	Median Age
City	5.4	24.3	43.8	8.4	6.3	5.2	3.8	2.1	0.6	22.5
MSA[1]	5.9	22.0	32.3	10.5	8.8	9.1	6.8	3.3	1.3	27.5
U.S.	5.6	19.2	20.2	12.7	12.4	13.1	10.0	4.9	1.9	38.8

Note: (1) Figures cover the College Station-Bryan, TX Metropolitan Statistical Area
Source: U.S. Census Bureau, 2020 Census

Disability by Age

Area	All Ages	Under 18 Years Old	18 to 64 Years Old	65 Years and Over
City	6.8	5.1	5.3	27.8
MSA[1]	9.9	5.5	7.6	33.3
U.S.	12.6	4.4	10.3	33.4

Note: Figures show percent of the civilian noninstitutionalized population that reported having a disability. Disability status is determined from six types of difficulty: vision, hearing, cognitive, ambulatory, self-care, and independent living. For children under 5 years old, hearing and vision difficulty are used to determine disability status. For children between the ages of 5 and 14, disability status is determined from hearing, vision, cognitive, ambulatory, and self-care difficulties. For people aged 15 years and older, they are considered to have a disability if they have difficulty with any one of the six difficulty types; Note: (1) Figures cover the College Station-Bryan, TX Metropolitan Statistical Area
Source: U.S. Census Bureau, 2017-2021 American Community Survey 5-Year Estimates

Ancestry

Area	German	Irish	English	American	Italian	Polish	French[2]	Scottish	Dutch
City	15.9	8.4	8.8	3.3	3.5	1.8	2.9	1.7	0.8
MSA[1]	13.5	7.6	7.6	3.8	2.8	1.8	2.4	1.6	0.7
U.S.	12.8	9.6	8.1	5.7	5.0	2.7	2.2	1.6	1.1

Note: Figures are the percentage of the total population reporting a particular ancestry. The nine most commonly reported ancestries in the U.S. are shown. Figures include multiple ancestries (e.g. if a person reported being Irish and Italian, they were included in both columns); (1) Figures cover the College Station-Bryan, TX Metropolitan Statistical Area; (2) Excludes Basque
Source: U.S. Census Bureau, 2017-2021 American Community Survey 5-Year Estimates

148　College Station, Texas

Foreign-born Population

Area	Any Foreign Country	Asia	Mexico	Europe	Caribbean	Central America[2]	South America	Africa	Canada
City	12.3	7.3	1.5	0.9	0.2	0.3	1.1	0.8	0.2
MSA[1]	11.5	3.8	5.0	0.7	0.2	0.5	0.7	0.5	0.1
U.S.	13.6	4.2	3.3	1.5	1.4	1.1	1.1	0.8	0.2

Note: (1) Figures cover the College Station-Bryan, TX Metropolitan Statistical Area; (2) Excludes Mexico.
Source: U.S. Census Bureau, 2017-2021 American Community Survey 5-Year Estimates

Household Size

Area	One	Two	Three	Four	Five	Six	Seven or More	Average Household Size
City	32.5	31.2	14.9	15.0	3.6	2.5	0.5	2.50
MSA[1]	30.9	32.6	14.7	12.7	5.3	2.6	1.2	2.60
U.S.	28.1	33.8	15.5	12.9	6.0	2.3	1.4	2.60

Note: (1) Figures cover the College Station-Bryan, TX Metropolitan Statistical Area
Source: U.S. Census Bureau, 2017-2021 American Community Survey 5-Year Estimates

Household Relationships

Area	Householder	Opposite-sex Spouse	Same-sex Spouse	Opposite-sex Unmarried Partner	Same-sex Unmarried Partner	Child[2]	Grandchild	Other Relatives	Non-relatives
City	35.2	11.2	0.2	1.8	0.1	19.7	0.7	2.7	13.7
MSA[1]	36.9	14.6	0.1	2.0	0.1	24.7	1.9	3.5	8.3
U.S.	38.3	17.5	0.2	2.5	0.2	28.3	2.4	4.8	3.4

Note: Figures are percent of the total population; (1) Figures cover the College Station-Bryan, TX Metropolitan Statistical Area; (2) Includes biological, adopted, and stepchildren of the householder
Source: U.S. Census Bureau, 2020 Census

Gender

Area	Males	Females	Males per 100 Females
City	61,203	59,308	103.2
MSA[1]	134,329	133,919	100.3
U.S.	162,685,811	168,763,470	96.4

Note: (1) Figures cover the College Station-Bryan, TX Metropolitan Statistical Area
Source: U.S. Census Bureau, 2020 Census

Marital Status

Area	Never Married	Now Married[2]	Separated	Widowed	Divorced
City	59.4	31.9	0.8	2.4	5.5
MSA[1]	45.5	40.1	1.8	4.1	8.5
U.S.	33.8	48.0	1.8	5.6	10.8

Note: Figures are percentages and cover the population 15 years of age and older; (1) Figures cover the College Station-Bryan, TX Metropolitan Statistical Area; (2) Excludes separated
Source: U.S. Census Bureau, 2017-2021 American Community Survey 5-Year Estimates

Religious Groups by Family

Area	Catholic	Baptist	Methodist	LDS[2]	Pentecostal	Lutheran	Islam	Adventist	Other
MSA[1]	17.2	10.6	4.3	1.7	0.5	1.1	0.6	0.5	6.8
U.S.	18.7	7.3	3.0	2.0	1.8	1.7	1.3	1.3	11.6

Note: Figures are the number of adherents as a percentage of the total population and cover the eight largest religious groups in the U.S; (1) Figures cover the College Station-Bryan, TX Metropolitan Statistical Area; (2) Church of Jesus Christ of Latter-day Saints
Sources: 2020 U.S. Religion Census, Association of Statisticians of American Religious Bodies; The Association of Religion Data Archives (ARDA)

Religious Groups by Tradition

Area	Catholic	Evangelical Protestant	Mainline Protestant	Black Protestant	Islam	Judaism	Hinduism	Orthodox	Buddhism
MSA[1]	17.2	16.1	5.3	1.8	0.6	n/a	0.1	0.1	n/a
U.S.	18.7	16.5	5.2	2.3	1.3	0.6	0.4	0.4	0.3

Note: Figures are the number of adherents as a percentage of the total population; (1) Figures cover the College Station-Bryan, TX Metropolitan Statistical Area
Sources: 2020 U.S. Religion Census, Association of Statisticians of American Religious Bodies; The Association of Religion Data Archives (ARDA)

College Station, Texas   149

ECONOMY

Gross Metropolitan Product

Area	2020	2021	2022	2023	Rank[2]
MSA[1]	13.6	14.9	16.6	17.4	185

Note: Figures are in billions of dollars; (1) Figures cover the College Station-Bryan, TX Metropolitan Statistical Area; (2) Rank is based on 2021 data and ranges from 1 to 381
Source: U.S. Conference of Mayors, U.S. Metro Economies: U.S. Metros Compared to Global and State Economies, June 2022

Economic Growth

Area	2018-20 (%)	2021 (%)	2022 (%)	2023 (%)	Rank[2]
MSA[1]	1.1	5.1	4.2	2.8	61
U.S.	-0.6	5.7	3.1	2.9	—

Note: Figures are real gross metropolitan product (GMP) growth rates and represent average annual percent change; (1) Figures cover the College Station-Bryan, TX Metropolitan Statistical Area; (2) Rank is based on 2020 2-year average annual percent change and ranges from 1 to 381
Source: U.S. Conference of Mayors, U.S. Metro Economies: U.S. Metros Compared to Global and State Economies, June 2022

Metropolitan Area Exports

Area	2016	2017	2018	2019	2020	2021	Rank[2]
MSA[1]	113.2	145.4	153.0	160.5	114.9	110.3	346

Note: Figures are in millions of dollars; (1) Figures cover the College Station-Bryan, TX Metropolitan Statistical Area; (2) Rank is based on 2021 data and ranges from 1 to 388
Source: U.S. Department of Commerce, International Trade Administration, Office of Trade and Economic Analysis, Industry and Analysis, Exports by Metropolitan Area, data extracted March 16, 2023

Building Permits

Area	Single-Family 2021	Single-Family 2022	Pct. Chg.	Multi-Family 2021	Multi-Family 2022	Pct. Chg.	Total 2021	Total 2022	Pct. Chg.
City	674	592	-12.2	318	97	-69.5	992	689	-30.5
MSA[1]	1,765	1,545	-12.5	535	230	-57.0	2,300	1,775	-22.8
U.S.	1,115,400	975,600	-12.5	621,600	689,500	10.9	1,737,000	1,665,100	-4.1

Note: (1) Figures cover the College Station-Bryan, TX Metropolitan Statistical Area; Figures represent new, privately-owned housing units authorized (unadjusted data); All permit data are based on estimates with imputation
Source: U.S. Census Bureau, Manufacturing, Mining, and Construction Statistics, Building Permits, 2021, 2022

Bankruptcy Filings

Area	Business Filings 2021	Business Filings 2022	% Chg.	Nonbusiness Filings 2021	Nonbusiness Filings 2022	% Chg.
Brazos County	8	4	-50.0	66	47	-28.8
U.S.	14,347	13,481	-6.0	399,269	374,240	-6.3

Note: Business filings include Chapter 7, Chapter 9, Chapter 11, Chapter 12, Chapter 13, Chapter 15, and Section 304; Nonbusiness filings include Chapter 7, Chapter 11, and Chapter 13
Source: Administrative Office of the U.S. Courts, Business and Nonbusiness Bankruptcy, County Cases Commenced by Chapter of the Bankruptcy Code, During the 12-Month Period Ending December 31, 2021 and Business and Nonbusiness Bankruptcy, County Cases Commenced by Chapter of the Bankruptcy Code, During the 12-Month Period Ending December 31, 2022

Housing Vacancy Rates

Area	Gross Vacancy Rate[2] (%) 2020	2021	2022	Year-Round Vacancy Rate[3] (%) 2020	2021	2022	Rental Vacancy Rate[4] (%) 2020	2021	2022	Homeowner Vacancy Rate[5] (%) 2020	2021	2022
MSA[1]	n/a	n/a	n/a	n/a	n/a	n/a	n/a	n/a	n/a	n/a	n/a	n/a
U.S.	10.6	10.8	10.5	8.2	8.4	8.2	6.3	6.1	5.8	1.0	0.9	0.8

Note: (1) Figures cover the College Station-Bryan, TX Metropolitan Statistical Area; (2) The percentage of the total housing inventory that is vacant; (3) The percentage of the housing inventory (excluding seasonal units) that is year-round vacant; (4) The percentage of rental inventory that is vacant for rent; (5) The percentage of homeowner inventory that is vacant for sale; n/a not available
Source: U.S. Census Bureau, Housing Vacancies and Homeownership Annual Statistics: 2020, 2021, 2022

INCOME

Income

Area	Per Capita ($)	Median Household ($)	Average Household ($)
City	28,705	50,089	76,307
MSA[1]	30,182	53,541	78,104
U.S.	37,638	69,021	97,196

Note: (1) Figures cover the College Station-Bryan, TX Metropolitan Statistical Area
Source: U.S. Census Bureau, 2017-2021 American Community Survey 5-Year Estimates

Household Income Distribution

Area	Under $15,000	$15,000 -$24,999	$25,000 -$34,999	$35,000 -$49,999	$50,000 -$74,999	$75,000 -$99,999	$100,000 -$149,999	$150,000 and up
City	19.7	10.2	8.8	11.2	15.3	10.0	12.3	12.4
MSA[1]	16.0	9.6	8.9	12.5	17.0	11.2	13.1	11.7
U.S.	9.4	7.8	8.2	11.4	16.8	12.8	16.3	17.3

Note: (1) Figures cover the College Station-Bryan, TX Metropolitan Statistical Area
Source: U.S. Census Bureau, 2017-2021 American Community Survey 5-Year Estimates

Poverty Rate

Area	All Ages	Under 18 Years Old	18 to 64 Years Old	65 Years and Over
City	28.2	13.2	34.3	5.9
MSA[1]	22.3	20.5	25.3	8.6
U.S.	12.6	17.0	11.8	9.6

Note: Figures are percentage of people whose income during the past 12 months was below the poverty level; (1) Figures cover the College Station-Bryan, TX Metropolitan Statistical Area
Source: U.S. Census Bureau, 2017-2021 American Community Survey 5-Year Estimates

EMPLOYMENT

Labor Force and Employment

Area	Civilian Labor Force Dec. 2021	Civilian Labor Force Dec. 2022	% Chg.	Workers Employed Dec. 2021	Workers Employed Dec. 2022	% Chg.
City	63,443	64,403	1.5	61,598	62,625	1.7
MSA[1]	138,941	140,832	1.4	134,636	136,870	1.7
U.S.	161,696,000	164,224,000	1.6	155,732,000	158,872,000	2.0

Note: Data is not seasonally adjusted and covers workers 16 years of age and older; (1) Figures cover the College Station-Bryan, TX Metropolitan Statistical Area
Source: Bureau of Labor Statistics, Local Area Unemployment Statistics

Unemployment Rate

Area	Jan.	Feb.	Mar.	Apr.	May	Jun.	Jul.	Aug.	Sep.	Oct.	Nov.	Dec.
City	3.5	3.4	2.7	2.6	2.8	3.6	3.3	3.3	3.0	3.0	3.2	2.8
MSA[1]	3.7	3.5	2.9	2.7	2.9	3.6	3.5	3.5	3.1	3.1	3.1	2.8
U.S.	4.4	4.1	3.8	3.3	3.4	3.8	3.8	3.8	3.3	3.4	3.4	3.3

Note: Data is not seasonally adjusted and covers workers 16 years of age and older; (1) Figures cover the College Station-Bryan, TX Metropolitan Statistical Area
Source: Bureau of Labor Statistics, Local Area Unemployment Statistics

Average Wages

Occupation	$/Hr.	Occupation	$/Hr.
Accountants and Auditors	36.77	Maintenance and Repair Workers	18.38
Automotive Mechanics	21.75	Marketing Managers	57.23
Bookkeepers	19.34	Network and Computer Systems Admin.	37.16
Carpenters	20.12	Nurses, Licensed Practical	23.08
Cashiers	12.47	Nurses, Registered	37.59
Computer Programmers	36.69	Nursing Assistants	14.34
Computer Systems Analysts	39.40	Office Clerks, General	15.70
Computer User Support Specialists	22.57	Physical Therapists	46.21
Construction Laborers	17.19	Physicians	n/a
Cooks, Restaurant	13.51	Plumbers, Pipefitters and Steamfitters	24.11
Customer Service Representatives	16.40	Police and Sheriff's Patrol Officers	31.36
Dentists	n/a	Postal Service Mail Carriers	26.30
Electricians	25.15	Real Estate Sales Agents	31.28
Engineers, Electrical	44.21	Retail Salespersons	14.39
Fast Food and Counter Workers	10.89	Sales Representatives, Technical/Scientific	39.76
Financial Managers	65.41	Secretaries, Exc. Legal/Medical/Executive	18.70
First-Line Supervisors of Office Workers	26.24	Security Guards	14.38
General and Operations Managers	47.87	Surgeons	n/a
Hairdressers/Cosmetologists	13.68	Teacher Assistants, Exc. Postsecondary*	13.43
Home Health and Personal Care Aides	11.46	Teachers, Secondary School, Exc. Sp. Ed.*	25.97
Janitors and Cleaners	13.57	Telemarketers	n/a
Landscaping/Groundskeeping Workers	15.78	Truck Drivers, Heavy/Tractor-Trailer	22.43
Lawyers	75.98	Truck Drivers, Light/Delivery Services	22.97
Maids and Housekeeping Cleaners	12.68	Waiters and Waitresses	12.47

Note: Wage data covers the College Station-Bryan, TX Metropolitan Statistical Area; (*) Hourly wages were calculated from annual wage data based on a 40 hour work week; n/a not available.
Source: Bureau of Labor Statistics, Metro Area Occupational Employment & Wage Estimates, May 2022

Employment by Industry

Sector	MSA[1] Number of Employees	MSA[1] Percent of Total	U.S. Percent of Total
Construction, Mining, and Logging	8,000	5.7	5.4
Private Education and Health Services	15,700	11.3	16.1
Financial Activities	4,400	3.2	5.9
Government	47,800	34.3	14.5
Information	1,600	1.1	2.0
Leisure and Hospitality	19,400	13.9	10.3
Manufacturing	6,200	4.4	8.4
Other Services	3,600	2.6	3.7
Professional and Business Services	13,200	9.5	14.7
Retail Trade	14,000	10.0	10.2
Transportation, Warehousing, and Utilities	2,700	1.9	4.9
Wholesale Trade	2,900	2.1	3.9

Note: Figures are non-farm employment as of December 2022. Figures are not seasonally adjusted and include workers 16 years of age and older; (1) Figures cover the College Station-Bryan, TX Metropolitan Statistical Area
Source: Bureau of Labor Statistics, Current Employment Statistics, Employment, Hours, and Earnings

Employment by Occupation

Occupation Classification	City (%)	MSA[1] (%)	U.S. (%)
Management, Business, Science, and Arts	50.0	42.0	40.3
Natural Resources, Construction, and Maintenance	4.3	9.2	8.7
Production, Transportation, and Material Moving	8.1	10.8	13.1
Sales and Office	20.9	20.3	20.9
Service	16.8	17.6	17.0

Note: Figures cover employed civilians 16 years of age and older; (1) Figures cover the College Station-Bryan, TX Metropolitan Statistical Area
Source: U.S. Census Bureau, 2017-2021 American Community Survey 5-Year Estimates

Occupations with Greatest Projected Employment Growth: 2022 – 2024

Occupation[1]	2022 Employment	2024 Projected Employment	Numeric Employment Change	Percent Employment Change
Home Health and Personal Care Aides	338,130	364,760	26,630	7.9
General and Operations Managers	395,700	416,100	20,400	5.2
Heavy and Tractor-Trailer Truck Drivers	206,850	222,220	15,370	7.4
Software Developers	119,810	134,060	14,250	11.9
Laborers and Freight, Stock, and Material Movers, Hand	214,680	228,680	14,000	6.5
Farmers, Ranchers, and Other Agricultural Managers	274,740	287,430	12,690	4.6
Stockers and Order Fillers	212,180	224,670	12,490	5.9
Construction Laborers	153,220	164,330	11,110	7.3
Cooks, Restaurant	131,480	141,860	10,380	7.9
Industrial Truck and Tractor Operators	83,270	93,190	9,920	11.9

Note: Projections cover Texas; (1) Sorted by numeric employment change
Source: www.projectionscentral.com, State Occupational Projections, 2022–2024 Short-Term Projections

Fastest-Growing Occupations: 2022 – 2024

Occupation[1]	2022 Employment	2024 Projected Employment	Numeric Employment Change	Percent Employment Change
Wind Turbine Service Technicians	5,240	5,990	750	14.3
Information Security Analysts (SOC 2018)	14,170	16,110	1,940	13.7
Solar Photovoltaic Installers	2,240	2,540	300	13.4
Veterinary Technologists and Technicians	16,140	18,200	2,060	12.8
Actuaries	1,810	2,040	230	12.7
Data Scientists	7,340	8,270	930	12.7
Web Developers	6,920	7,790	870	12.6
Veterinarians	6,830	7,670	840	12.3
Veterinary Assistants and Laboratory Animal Caretakers	5,990	6,720	730	12.2
Ushers, Lobby Attendants, and Ticket Takers	9,100	10,190	1,090	12.0

Note: Projections cover Texas; (1) Sorted by percent employment change and excludes occupations with numeric employment change less than 50
Source: www.projectionscentral.com, State Occupational Projections, 2022–2024 Short-Term Projections

CITY FINANCES

City Government Finances

Component	2020 ($000)	2020 ($ per capita)
Total Revenues	267,043	2,265
Total Expenditures	174,055	1,476
Debt Outstanding	405,395	3,438
Cash and Securities[1]	529,978	4,495

Note: (1) Cash and security holdings of a government at the close of its fiscal year, including those of its dependent agencies, utilities, and liquor stores.
Source: U.S. Census Bureau, State & Local Government Finances 2020

City Government Revenue by Source

Source	2020 ($000)	2020 ($ per capita)	2020 (%)
General Revenue			
From Federal Government	2,074	18	0.8
From State Government	980	8	0.4
From Local Governments	403	3	0.2
Taxes			
Property	46,865	397	17.5
Sales and Gross Receipts	35,729	303	13.4
Personal Income	0	0	0.0
Corporate Income	0	0	0.0
Motor Vehicle License	0	0	0.0
Other Taxes	4,390	37	1.6
Current Charges	38,086	323	14.3
Liquor Store	0	0	0.0
Utility	122,913	1,042	46.0

Source: U.S. Census Bureau, State & Local Government Finances 2020

City Government Expenditures by Function

Function	2020 ($000)	2020 ($ per capita)	2020 (%)
General Direct Expenditures			
Air Transportation	0	0	0.0
Corrections	0	0	0.0
Education	0	0	0.0
Employment Security Administration	0	0	0.0
Financial Administration	2,937	24	1.7
Fire Protection	15,236	129	8.8
General Public Buildings	7,901	67	4.5
Governmental Administration, Other	9,506	80	5.5
Health	0	0	0.0
Highways	7,901	67	4.5
Hospitals	0	0	0.0
Housing and Community Development	2,059	17	1.2
Interest on General Debt	2,049	17	1.2
Judicial and Legal	2,229	18	1.3
Libraries	1,249	10	0.7
Parking	716	6	0.4
Parks and Recreation	12,713	107	7.3
Police Protection	29	< 1	< 0.1
Public Welfare	0	0	0.0
Sewerage	3,562	30	2.0
Solid Waste Management	7,604	64	4.4
Veterans' Services	0	0	0.0
Liquor Store	0	0	0.0
Utility	90,452	767	52.0

Source: U.S. Census Bureau, State & Local Government Finances 2020

TAXES

State Corporate Income Tax Rates

State	Tax Rate (%)	Income Brackets ($)	Num. of Brackets	Financial Institution Tax Rate (%)[a]	Federal Income Tax Ded.
Texas	(u)	–	–	(u)	No

Note: Tax rates as of January 1, 2023; (a) Rates listed are the corporate income tax rate applied to financial institutions or excise taxes based on income. Some states have other taxes based upon the value of deposits or shares; (u) Texas imposes a Franchise Tax, otherwise known as margin tax, imposed on entities with more than $1,230,000 total revenues at rate of 0.75%, or 0.375% for entities primarily engaged in retail or wholesale trade, on lesser of 70% of total revenues or 100% of gross receipts after deductions for either compensation or cost of goods sold.
Source: Federation of Tax Administrators, State Corporate Income Tax Rates, January 1, 2023

State Individual Income Tax Rates

State	Tax Rate (%)	Income Brackets ($)	Personal Exemptions ($) Single	Personal Exemptions ($) Married	Personal Exemptions ($) Depend.	Standard Ded. ($) Single	Standard Ded. ($) Married
Texas					– No state income tax –		

Note: Tax rates as of January 1, 2023; Local- and county-level taxes are not included
Source: Federation of Tax Administrators, State Individual Income Tax Rates, January 1, 2023

Various State Sales and Excise Tax Rates

State	State Sales Tax (%)	Gasoline[1] ($/gal.)	Cigarette[2] ($/pack)	Spirits[3] ($/gal.)	Wine[4] ($/gal.)	Beer[5] ($/gal.)	Recreational Marijuana (%)
Texas	6.25	0.20	1.41	2.40	0.20	0.19	Not legal

Note: All tax rates as of January 1, 2023; (1) The American Petroleum Institute has developed a methodology for determining the average tax rate on a gallon of fuel. Rates may include any of the following: excise taxes, environmental fees, storage tank fees, other fees or taxes, general sales tax, and local taxes; (2) The federal excise tax of $1.0066 per pack and local taxes are not included; (3) Rates are those applicable to off-premise sales of 40% alcohol by volume (a.b.v.) distilled spirits in 750ml containers. Local excise taxes are excluded; (4) Rates are those applicable to off-premise sales of 11% a.b.v. non-carbonated wine in 750ml containers; (5) Rates are those applicable to off-premise sales of 4.7% a.b.v. beer in 12 ounce containers.
Source: Tax Foundation, 2023 Facts & Figures: How Does Your State Compare?

State Business Tax Climate Index Rankings

State	Overall Rank	Corporate Tax Rank	Individual Income Tax Rank	Sales Tax Rank	Property Tax Rank	Unemployment Insurance Tax Rank
Texas	13	47	7	37	38	12

Note: The index is a measure of how each state's tax laws affect economic performance. The lower the rank, the more favorable a state's tax system is for business. States without a given tax are given a ranking of 1. The scores/rankings for the District of Columbia do not affect other states. The 2023 index represents the tax climate as of July 1, 2022.
Source: Tax Foundation, State Business Tax Climate Index 2023

TRANSPORTATION

Means of Transportation to Work

Area	Car/Truck/Van Drove Alone	Car/Truck/Van Carpooled	Public Transportation Bus	Public Transportation Subway	Public Transportation Railroad	Bicycle	Walked	Other Means	Worked at Home
City	74.7	8.8	2.1	0.0	0.0	1.8	2.6	0.9	9.0
MSA[1]	78.2	9.5	1.1	0.0	0.0	1.1	1.7	1.2	7.2
U.S.	73.2	8.6	2.0	1.6	0.5	0.5	2.5	1.5	9.7

Note: Figures are percentages and cover workers 16 years of age and older; (1) Figures cover the College Station-Bryan, TX Metropolitan Statistical Area
Source: U.S. Census Bureau, 2017-2021 American Community Survey 5-Year Estimates

Travel Time to Work

Area	Less Than 10 Minutes	10 to 19 Minutes	20 to 29 Minutes	30 to 44 Minutes	45 to 59 Minutes	60 to 89 Minutes	90 Minutes or More
City	17.6	55.5	17.1	6.2	0.5	2.0	1.1
MSA[1]	16.1	49.4	18.4	10.4	2.3	2.1	1.4
U.S.	12.4	28.5	21.0	20.9	8.2	6.2	2.9

Note: Note: Figures are percentages and include workers 16 years old and over; (1) Figures cover the College Station-Bryan, TX Metropolitan Statistical Area
Source: U.S. Census Bureau, 2017-2021 American Community Survey 5-Year Estimates

Key Congestion Measures

Measure	1990	2000	2010	2015	2020
Annual Hours of Delay, Total (000)	n/a	n/a	n/a	5,235	2,659
Annual Hours of Delay, Per Auto Commuter	n/a	n/a	n/a	31	15
Annual Congestion Cost, Per Auto Commuter ($)	n/a	n/a	n/a	661	334

Note: n/a not available
Source: Texas A&M Transportation Institute, 2021 Urban Mobility Report

Freeway Travel Time Index

Measure	1985	1990	1995	2000	2005	2010	2015	2020
Urban Area Index[1]	n/a	n/a	n/a	n/a	n/a	n/a	1.15	1.05
Urban Area Rank[1,2]	n/a	n/a	n/a	n/a	n/a	n/a	n/a	n/a

Note: Freeway Travel Time Index—the ratio of travel time in the peak period to the travel time at free-flow conditions. For example, a value of 1.30 indicates a 20-minute free-flow trip takes 26 minutes in the peak (20 minutes x 1.30 = 26 minutes); (1) Covers the College Station-Bryan TX urban area; (2) Rank is based on 101 larger urban areas (#1 = highest travel time index); n/a not available
Source: Texas A&M Transportation Institute, 2021 Urban Mobility Report

Public Transportation

Agency Name / Mode of Transportation	Vehicles Operated in Maximum Service[1]	Annual Unlinked Passenger Trips[2] (in thous.)	Annual Passenger Miles[3] (in thous.)
Brazos Transit District			
Bus (directly operated)	17	218.9	1,396.8
Demand Response (directly operated)	48	61.5	967.3

Note: (1) Number of revenue vehicles operated by the given mode and type of service to meet the annual maximum service requirement. This is the revenue vehicle count during the peak season of the year; on the week and day that maximum service is provided. Vehicles operated in maximum service (VOMS) exclude atypical days and one-time special events; (2) Number of passengers who boarded public transportation vehicles. Passengers are counted each time they board a vehicle no matter how many vehicles they use to travel from their origin to their destination. (3) Sum of the distances ridden by all passengers during the entire fiscal year.
Source: Federal Transit Administration, National Transit Database, 2021

Air Transportation

Airport Name and Code / Type of Service	Passenger Airlines[1]	Passenger Enplanements	Freight Carriers[2]	Freight (lbs)
Easterwood Airport (CLL)				
Domestic service (U.S. carriers - 2022)	17	54,689	3	52,287
International service (U.S. carriers - 2021)	0	0	0	0

Note: (1) Includes all U.S.-based major, minor and commuter airlines that carried at least one passenger during the year; (2) Includes all U.S.-based airlines and freight carriers that transported at least one pound of freight during the year.
Source: Bureau of Transportation Statistics, The Intermodal Transportation Database, Air Carriers: T-100 Domestic Market (U.S. Carriers), 2022; Bureau of Transportation Statistics, The Intermodal Transportation Database, Air Carriers: T-100 International Market (U.S. Carriers), 2021

BUSINESSES

Major Business Headquarters

Company Name	Industry	Rankings Fortune[1]	Forbes[2]
No companies listed	-	-	-

Note: (1) Companies that produce a 10-K are ranked 1 to 500 based on 2021 revenue; (2) All private companies with at least $2 billion in annual revenue through the end of their most current fiscal year are ranked 1 to 246; companies listed are headquartered in the city; dashes indicate no ranking
Source: Fortune, "Fortune 500," 2022; Forbes, "America's Largest Private Companies," 2022

Living Environment

COST OF LIVING

Cost of Living Index

Composite Index	Groceries	Housing	Utilities	Transportation	Health Care	Misc. Goods/Services
n/a	n/a	n/a	n/a	n/a	n/a	n/a

Note: The Cost of Living Index measures regional differences in the cost of consumer goods and services, excluding taxes and non-consumer expenditures, for professional and managerial households in the top income quintile. It is based on more than 50,000 prices covering almost 60 different items for which prices are collected three times a year by chambers of commerce, economic development organizations or university applied economic centers in each participating urban area. The numbers shown should be read as a percentage above or below the national average of 100. For example, a value of 115.4 in the groceries column indicates that grocery prices are 15.4% higher than the national average. Small differences in the index numbers should not be interpreted as significant; n/a not available.
Source: The Council for Community and Economic Research, Cost of Living Index, 2022

Grocery Prices

Area[1]	T-Bone Steak ($/pound)	Frying Chicken ($/pound)	Whole Milk ($/half gal.)	Eggs ($/dozen)	Orange Juice ($/64 oz.)	Coffee ($/11.5 oz.)
City[2]	n/a	n/a	n/a	n/a	n/a	n/a
Avg.	13.81	1.59	2.43	2.25	3.85	4.95
Min.	10.17	0.90	1.51	1.30	2.90	3.46
Max.	19.35	3.30	4.32	4.32	5.31	8.59

Note: (1) Values for the local area are compared with the average, minimum and maximum values for all 286 areas in the Cost of Living Index; (2) Figures cover the College Station TX urban area; n/a not available;
T-Bone Steak *(price per pound);* ***Frying Chicken*** *(price per pound, whole fryer);* ***Whole Milk*** *(half gallon carton);* ***Eggs*** *(price per dozen, Grade A, large);* ***Orange Juice*** *(64 oz. Tropicana or Florida Natural);* ***Coffee*** *(11.5 oz. can, vacuum-packed, Maxwell House, Hills Bros, or Folgers).*
Source: The Council for Community and Economic Research, Cost of Living Index, 2022

Housing and Utility Costs

Area[1]	New Home Price ($)	Apartment Rent ($/month)	All Electric ($/month)	Part Electric ($/month)	Other Energy ($/month)	Telephone ($/month)
City[2]	n/a	n/a	n/a	n/a	n/a	n/a
Avg.	450,913	1,371	176.41	99.93	76.96	190.22
Min.	229,283	546	100.84	31.56	27.15	174.27
Max.	2,434,977	4,569	356.86	249.59	272.24	208.31

Note: (1) Values for the local area are compared with the average, minimum and maximum values for all 286 areas in the Cost of Living Index; (2) Figures cover the College Station TX urban area; n/a not available; ***New Home Price*** *(2,400 sf living area, 8,000 sf lot, in urban area with full utilities);* ***Apartment Rent*** *(950 sf 2 bedroom/1.5 or 2 bath, unfurnished, excluding all utilities except water);* ***All Electric*** *(average monthly cost for an all-electric home);* ***Part Electric*** *(average monthly cost for a part-electric home);* ***Other Energy*** *(average monthly cost for natural gas, fuel oil, coal, wood, and any other forms of energy except electricity);* ***Telephone*** *(price includes the base monthly rate plus taxes and fees for three lines of mobile phone service).*
Source: The Council for Community and Economic Research, Cost of Living Index, 2022

Health Care, Transportation, and Other Costs

Area[1]	Doctor ($/visit)	Dentist ($/visit)	Optometrist ($/visit)	Gasoline ($/gallon)	Beauty Salon ($/visit)	Men's Shirt ($)
City[2]	n/a	n/a	n/a	n/a	n/a	n/a
Avg.	124.91	107.77	117.66	3.86	43.31	34.21
Min.	36.61	58.25	51.79	2.90	22.18	13.05
Max.	250.21	162.58	371.96	5.54	85.61	63.54

Note: (1) Values for the local area are compared with the average, minimum and maximum values for all 286 areas in the Cost of Living Index; (2) Figures cover the College Station TX urban area; n/a not available;
Doctor *(general practitioners routine exam of an established patient);* ***Dentist*** *(adult teeth cleaning and periodic oral examination);* ***Optometrist*** *(full vision eye exam for established adult patient);* ***Gasoline*** *(one gallon regular unleaded, national brand, including all taxes, cash price at self-service pump if available);* ***Beauty Salon*** *(woman's shampoo, trim, and blow-dry);* ***Men's Shirt*** *(cotton/polyester dress shirt, pinpoint weave, long sleeves).*
Source: The Council for Community and Economic Research, Cost of Living Index, 2022

HOUSING

Homeownership Rate

Area	2015 (%)	2016 (%)	2017 (%)	2018 (%)	2019 (%)	2020 (%)	2021 (%)	2022 (%)
MSA[1]	n/a	n/a	n/a	n/a	n/a	n/a	n/a	n/a
U.S.	63.7	63.4	63.9	64.4	64.6	66.6	65.5	65.8

Note: (1) Figures cover the College Station-Bryan, TX Metropolitan Statistical Area; n/a not available
Source: U.S. Census Bureau, Housing Vacancies and Homeownership Annual Statistics: 2015-2022

House Price Index (HPI)

Area	National Ranking[2]	Quarterly Change (%)	One-Year Change (%)	Five-Year Change (%)	Since 1991Q1 (%)
MSA[1]	n/a	n/a	n/a	n/a	n/a
U.S.[3]	—	0.34	8.41	58.44	289.08

Note: The HPI is a weighted repeat sales index. It measures average price changes in repeat sales or refinancings on the same properties. This information is obtained by reviewing repeat mortgage transactions on single-family properties whose mortgages have been purchased or securitized by Fannie Mae or Freddie Mac since January 1975; (1) Figures cover the , Metropolitan Statistical Area; (2) Rankings are based on annual percentage change for all metro areas containing at least 15,000 transactions over the last 10 years and ranges from 1 to 257; (3) figures based on a weighted average of Census Division estimates using a seasonally adjusted, purchase-only index; all figures are for the period ending December 31, 2022; n/a not available
Source: Federal Housing Finance Agency, Change in FHFA Metropolitan Area House Price Indexes, 2022Q4

Median Single-Family Home Prices

Area	2020	2021	2022p	Percent Change 2021 to 2022
MSA[1]	n/a	n/a	n/a	n/a
U.S. Average	300.2	357.1	392.6	9.9

Note: Figures are median sales prices of existing single-family homes in thousands of dollars; (p) preliminary; n/a not available; (1) Figures cover the College Station-Bryan, TX Metropolitan Statistical Area
Source: National Association of Realtors, Median Sales Price of Existing Single-Family Homes for Metropolitan Areas, 4th Quarter 2022

Qualifying Income Based on Median Sales Price of Existing Single-Family Homes

Area	With 5% Down ($)	With 10% Down ($)	With 20% Down ($)
MSA[1]	n/a	n/a	n/a
U.S. Average	112,234	106,237	94,513

Note: Figures are preliminary; Qualifying income is based on a mortgage rate of 6.77%. Monthly principal and interest payment is limited to 25% of income; n/a not available; (1) Figures cover the College Station-Bryan, TX Metropolitan Statistical Area
Source: National Association of Realtors, Qualifying Income Based on Median Sales Price of Existing Single-Family Homes for Metropolitan Areas, 4th Quarter 2022

Home Value

Area	Under $100,000	$100,000 -$199,999	$200,000 -$299,999	$300,000 -$399,999	$400,000 -$499,999	$500,000 -$999,999	$1,000,000 or more	Median ($)
City	2.2	18.2	39.2	25.7	7.6	6.3	0.7	269,100
MSA[1]	20.3	25.9	24.8	14.8	5.2	7.7	1.3	213,600
U.S.	16.2	24.2	20.1	13.6	8.3	13.6	4.1	244,900

Note: Figures are percentages except for median and cover owner-occupied housing units; (1) Figures cover the College Station-Bryan, TX Metropolitan Statistical Area
Source: U.S. Census Bureau, 2017-2021 American Community Survey 5-Year Estimates

Year Housing Structure Built

Area	2020 or Later	2010 -2019	2000 -2009	1990 -1999	1980 -1989	1970 -1979	1960 -1969	1950 -1959	1940 -1949	Before 1940	Median Year
City	0.6	20.8	20.7	20.0	16.6	14.8	3.5	2.0	0.4	0.6	1996
MSA[1]	0.6	17.0	18.8	18.0	16.6	14.4	6.0	4.3	2.1	2.3	1992
U.S.	0.2	7.3	13.6	13.6	13.2	14.8	10.3	10.0	4.7	12.2	1979

Note: Figures are percentages except for Median Year; Note: (1) Figures cover the College Station-Bryan, TX Metropolitan Statistical Area
Source: U.S. Census Bureau, 2017-2021 American Community Survey 5-Year Estimates

Gross Monthly Rent

Area	Under $500	$500 -$999	$1,000 -$1,499	$1,500 -$1,999	$2,000 -$2,499	$2,500 -$2,999	$3,000 and up	Median ($)
City	2.2	44.2	33.0	14.9	3.9	1.4	0.5	1,042
MSA[1]	5.0	44.7	32.9	12.3	3.1	1.2	0.7	1,003
U.S.	8.1	30.5	30.8	16.8	7.3	3.1	3.5	1,163

Note: Figures are percentages except for median; Gross rent is the contract rent plus the estimated average monthly cost of utilities (electricity, gas, and water and sewer) and fuels (oil, coal, kerosene, wood, etc.) if these are paid by the renter (or paid for the renter by someone else); (1) Figures cover the College Station-Bryan, TX Metropolitan Statistical Area
Source: U.S. Census Bureau, 2017-2021 American Community Survey 5-Year Estimates

College Station, Texas   157

HEALTH

Health Risk Factors

Category	MSA[1] (%)	U.S. (%)
Adults aged 18–64 who have any kind of health care coverage	n/a	90.9
Adults who reported being in good or better health	n/a	85.2
Adults who have been told they have high blood cholesterol	n/a	35.7
Adults who have been told they have high blood pressure	n/a	32.4
Adults who are current smokers	n/a	14.4
Adults who currently use e-cigarettes	n/a	6.7
Adults who currently use chewing tobacco, snuff, or snus	n/a	3.5
Adults who are heavy drinkers[2]	n/a	6.3
Adults who are binge drinkers[3]	n/a	15.4
Adults who are overweight (BMI 25.0 - 29.9)	n/a	34.4
Adults who are obese (BMI 30.0 - 99.8)	n/a	33.9
Adults who participated in any physical activities in the past month	n/a	76.3

*Note: (1) Figures for the College Station-Bryan, TX Metropolitan Statistical Area were not available.
(2) Heavy drinkers are classified as adult men having more than 14 drinks per week and adult women having more than 7 drinks per week; (3) Binge drinkers are classified as males having five or more drinks on one occasion or females having four or more drinks on one occasion*
Source: Centers for Disease Control and Prevention, Behaviorial Risk Factor Surveillance System, SMART: Selected Metropolitan Area Risk Trends, 2021

Acute and Chronic Health Conditions

Category	MSA[1] (%)	U.S. (%)
Adults who have ever been told they had a heart attack	n/a	4.0
Adults who have ever been told they have angina or coronary heart disease	n/a	3.8
Adults who have ever been told they had a stroke	n/a	3.0
Adults who have ever been told they have asthma	n/a	14.9
Adults who have ever been told they have arthritis	n/a	25.8
Adults who have ever been told they have diabetes[2]	n/a	10.9
Adults who have ever been told they had skin cancer	n/a	6.6
Adults who have ever been told they had any other types of cancer	n/a	7.5
Adults who have ever been told they have COPD	n/a	6.1
Adults who have ever been told they have kidney disease	n/a	3.0
Adults who have ever been told they have a form of depression	n/a	20.5

*Note: (1) Figures for the College Station-Bryan, TX Metropolitan Statistical Area were not available.
(2) Figures do not include pregnancy-related, borderline, or pre-diabetes*
Source: Centers for Disease Control and Prevention, Behaviorial Risk Factor Surveillance System, SMART: Selected Metropolitan Area Risk Trends, 2021

Health Screening and Vaccination Rates

Category	MSA[1] (%)	U.S. (%)
Adults who have ever been tested for HIV	n/a	34.9
Adults who have had their blood cholesterol checked within the last five years	n/a	85.2
Adults aged 65+ who have had flu shot within the past year	n/a	68.6
Adults aged 65+ who have ever had a pneumonia vaccination	n/a	71.0

Note: (1) Figures for the College Station-Bryan, TX Metropolitan Statistical Area were not available.
Source: Centers for Disease Control and Prevention, Behaviorial Risk Factor Surveillance System, SMART: Selected Metropolitan Area Risk Trends, 2021

Disability Status

Category	MSA[1] (%)	U.S. (%)
Adults who reported being deaf	n/a	7.2
Are you blind or have serious difficulty seeing, even when wearing glasses?	n/a	4.8
Are you limited in any way in any of your usual activities due to arthritis?	n/a	11.1
Do you have difficulty doing errands alone?	n/a	7.0
Do you have difficulty dressing or bathing?	n/a	3.6
Do you have serious difficulty concentrating/remembering/making decisions?	n/a	12.1
Do you have serious difficulty walking or climbing stairs?	n/a	12.8

Note: (1) Figures for the College Station-Bryan, TX Metropolitan Statistical Area were not available.
Source: Centers for Disease Control and Prevention, Behaviorial Risk Factor Surveillance System, SMART: Selected Metropolitan Area Risk Trends, 2021

Mortality Rates for the Top 10 Causes of Death in the U.S.

ICD-10[a] Sub-Chapter	ICD-10[a] Code	Crude Mortality Rate[1] per 100,000 population County[2]	U.S.
Malignant neoplasms	C00-C97	96.3	182.6
Ischaemic heart diseases	I20-I25	64.1	113.1
Other forms of heart disease	I30-I51	49.7	64.4
Other degenerative diseases of the nervous system	G30-G31	31.1	51.0
Cerebrovascular diseases	I60-I69	21.0	47.8
Other external causes of accidental injury	W00-X59	20.2	46.4
Chronic lower respiratory diseases	J40-J47	21.0	45.7
Organic, including symptomatic, mental disorders	F01-F09	20.0	35.9
Hypertensive diseases	I10-I15	20.2	35.0
Diabetes mellitus	E10-E14	16.7	29.6

Note: (a) ICD-10 = International Classification of Diseases 10th Revision; (1) Crude mortality rates are a three-year average covering 2019-2021; (2) Figures cover Brazos County.
Source: Centers for Disease Control and Prevention, National Center for Health Statistics. National Vital Statistics System, Mortality 2018-2021 on CDC WONDER Online Database

Mortality Rates for Selected Causes of Death

ICD-10[a] Sub-Chapter	ICD-10[a] Code	Crude Mortality Rate[1] per 100,000 population County[2]	U.S.
Assault	X85-Y09	5.0	7.0
Diseases of the liver	K70-K76	13.6	19.8
Human immunodeficiency virus (HIV) disease	B20-B24	Suppressed	1.5
Influenza and pneumonia	J09-J18	5.2	14.7
Intentional self-harm	X60-X84	9.4	14.3
Malnutrition	E40-E46	Unreliable	4.3
Obesity and other hyperalimentation	E65-E68	Unreliable	3.0
Renal failure	N17-N19	8.0	15.7
Transport accidents	V01-V99	8.6	13.6
Viral hepatitis	B15-B19	Suppressed	1.2

Note: (a) ICD-10 = International Classification of Diseases 10th Revision; (1) Crude mortality rates are a three-year average covering 2019-2021; (2) Figures cover Brazos County; Data are suppressed when the data meet the criteria for confidentiality constraints; Crude mortality rates are flagged as unreliable when the rate would be calculated with a numerator of 20 or less.
Source: Centers for Disease Control and Prevention, National Center for Health Statistics. National Vital Statistics System, Mortality 2018-2021 on CDC WONDER Online Database

Health Insurance Coverage

Area	With Health Insurance	With Private Health Insurance	With Public Health Insurance	Without Health Insurance	Population Under Age 19 Without Health Insurance
City	91.3	84.1	14.3	8.7	5.6
MSA[1]	87.5	73.3	23.8	12.5	8.4
U.S.	91.2	67.8	35.4	8.8	5.3

Note: Figures are percentages that cover the civilian noninstitutionalized population; (1) Figures cover the College Station-Bryan, TX Metropolitan Statistical Area
Source: U.S. Census Bureau, 2017-2021 American Community Survey 5-Year Estimates

Number of Medical Professionals

Area	MDs[3]	DOs[3,4]	Dentists	Podiatrists	Chiropractors	Optometrists
County[1] (number)	635	38	131	8	42	39
County[1] (rate[2])	270.8	16.2	55.3	3.4	17.7	16.5
U.S. (rate[2])	289.3	23.5	72.5	6.2	28.7	17.4

Note: Data as of 2021 unless noted; (1) Data covers Brazos County; (2) Rate per 100,000 population; (3) Data as of 2020 and includes all active, non-federal physicians; (4) Doctor of Osteopathic Medicine
Source: U.S. Department of Health and Human Services, Health Resources and Services Administration, Bureau of Health Professions, Area Resource File (ARF) 2021-2022

EDUCATION

Public School District Statistics

District Name	Schls	Pupils	Pupil/ Teacher Ratio	Minority Pupils[1] (%)	LEP/ELL[2] (%)	IEP[3] (%)
College Station ISD	20	14,187	14.1	48.8	7.5	12.5

Note: Table includes school districts with 2,000 or more students; (1) Percentage of students that are not non-Hispanic white; (2) Percentage of students that are Limited English Proficient or English Language Learners (2018-19); (3) Percentage of students that have an Individualized Education Program (2019-20).
Source: U.S. Department of Education, National Center for Education Statistics, Common Core of Data, Local Education Agency (School District) Universe Survey: School Year 2021-2022

Highest Level of Education

Area	Less than H.S.	H.S. Diploma	Some College, No Deg.	Associate Degree	Bachelor's Degree	Master's Degree	Prof. School Degree	Doctorate Degree
City	5.2	13.1	17.0	6.7	30.3	15.4	2.1	10.3
MSA[1]	12.1	23.4	19.3	6.7	21.6	9.8	2.0	5.1
U.S.	11.1	26.5	20.0	8.7	20.6	9.3	2.2	1.5

Note: Figures cover persons age 25 and over; (1) Figures cover the College Station-Bryan, TX Metropolitan Statistical Area
Source: U.S. Census Bureau, 2017-2021 American Community Survey 5-Year Estimates

Educational Attainment by Race

Area	High School Graduate or Higher (%) Total	White	Black	Asian	Hisp.[2]	Bachelor's Degree or Higher (%) Total	White	Black	Asian	Hisp.[2]
City	94.8	95.9	91.0	94.2	87.1	58.0	58.7	31.9	78.7	41.2
MSA[1]	87.9	89.3	87.7	94.5	67.8	38.6	40.7	18.3	76.8	17.3
U.S.	88.9	91.4	87.2	87.6	71.2	33.7	35.5	23.3	55.6	18.4

Note: Figures shown cover persons 25 years old and over; (1) Figures cover the College Station-Bryan, TX Metropolitan Statistical Area; (2) People of Hispanic origin can be of any race
Source: U.S. Census Bureau, 2017-2021 American Community Survey 5-Year Estimates

School Enrollment by Grade and Control

Area	Preschool (%) Public	Private	Kindergarten (%) Public	Private	Grades 1-4 (%) Public	Private	Grades 5-8 (%) Public	Private	Grades 9-12 (%) Public	Private
City	51.4	48.6	86.9	13.1	91.0	9.0	93.9	6.1	88.3	11.7
MSA[1]	59.9	40.1	86.3	13.7	91.4	8.6	92.1	7.9	92.3	7.7
U.S.	58.8	41.2	86.3	13.7	88.3	11.7	88.6	11.4	89.4	10.6

Note: Figures shown cover persons 3 years old and over; (1) Figures cover the College Station-Bryan, TX Metropolitan Statistical Area
Source: U.S. Census Bureau, 2017-2021 American Community Survey 5-Year Estimates

Higher Education

Four-Year Colleges Public	Private Non-profit	Private For-profit	Two-Year Colleges Public	Private Non-profit	Private For-profit	Medical Schools[1]	Law Schools[2]	Voc/Tech[3]
1	0	0	0	0	0	1	0	2

Note: Figures cover institutions located within the College Station-Bryan, TX Metropolitan Statistical Area and include main campuses only; (1) includes schools accredited by the Liaison Committee on Medical Education and the American Osteopathic Association's Commission on Osteopathic College Accreditation; (2) includes ABA-accredited schools, schools with provisional ABA accreditation, and state accredited schools; (3) includes all schools with programs that are less than 2 years.
Source: National Center for Education Statistics, Integrated Postsecondary Education System (IPEDS), 2021-22; Wikipedia, List of Medical Schools in the United States, accessed April 10, 2023; Wikipedia, List of Law Schools in the United States, accessed April 10, 2023

According to *U.S. News & World Report,* the College Station-Bryan, TX metro area is home to one of the top 200 national universities in the U.S.: **Texas A&M University** (#67 tie). The indicators used to capture academic quality fall into a number of categories: assessment by administrators at peer institutions; retention of students; faculty resources; student selectivity; financial resources; alumni giving; high school counselor ratings of colleges; and graduation rate. *U.S. News & World Report, "America's Best Colleges 2023"*

According to *U.S. News & World Report,* the College Station-Bryan, TX metro area is home to one of the top 75 business schools in the U.S.: **Texas A&M University—College Station (Mays)** (#41 tie). The rankings are based on a weighted average of the following nine measures: quality assessment; peer assessment; recruiter assessment; placement success; mean starting salary and bonus; student selectivity; mean GMAT and GRE scores; mean undergraduate GPA; and acceptance rate. *U.S. News & World Report, "America's Best Graduate Schools, Business, 2023"*

160 College Station, Texas

EMPLOYERS

Major Employers

Company Name	Industry
Bryan Independent School District	Education
City of Bryan	Municipal government
City of College Station	Municipal government
College Station ISD	Education
H-E-B Grocery	Grocery stores
New Alenco Windows	Fabricated metal products
Reynolds and Reynolds/Rentsys	Computer hardware/software
Sanderson Farms	Poultry processing
St. Joseph Regional Health Center	Health services
Texas A&M University System	Education
Wal-Mart Stores	Retail

Note: Companies shown are located within the College Station-Bryan, TX Metropolitan Statistical Area.
Source: Hoovers.com; Wikipedia

PUBLIC SAFETY

Crime Rate

Area	Total Crime	Violent Crime Rate				Property Crime Rate		
		Murder	Rape[3]	Robbery	Aggrav. Assault	Burglary	Larceny-Theft	Motor Vehicle Theft
City	2,082.2	1.7	45.5	22.3	110.1	265.7	1,463.2	173.8
Suburbs[1]	2,209.2	5.4	86.2	41.4	262.1	349.1	1,310.7	154.2
Metro[2]	2,152.0	3.7	67.9	32.8	193.6	311.5	1,379.4	163.0
U.S.	2,356.7	6.5	38.4	73.9	279.7	314.2	1,398.0	246.0

Note: Figures are crimes per 100,000 population; (1) All areas within the metro area that are located outside the city limits; (2) Figures cover the College Station-Bryan, TX Metropolitan Statistical Area; (3) All figures shown were reported using the revised Uniform Crime Reporting (UCR) definition of rape; Due to the transition to the National Incident-Based Reporting System (NIBRS), limited city and metro area data was released for 2021.
Source: FBI Uniform Crime Reports, 2020

Hate Crimes

Area	Number of Quarters Reported	Number of Incidents per Bias Motivation					
		Race/Ethnicity/Ancestry	Religion	Sexual Orientation	Disability	Gender	Gender Identity
City	4	1	1	0	0	0	0
U.S.	4	5,227	1,244	1,110	130	75	266

Note: Due to the transition to the National Incident-Based Reporting System (NIBRS), limited crime data was released for 2021.
Source: Federal Bureau of Investigation, Hate Crime Statistics 2020

Identity Theft Consumer Reports

Area	Reports	Reports per 100,000 Population	Rank[2]
MSA[1]	484	185	190
U.S.	1,108,609	339	-

Note: (1) Figures cover the College Station-Bryan, TX Metropolitan Statistical Area; (2) Rank ranges from 1 to 391 where 1 indicates greatest number of identity theft reports per 100,000 population
Source: Federal Trade Commission, Consumer Sentinel Network Data Book 2022

Fraud and Other Consumer Reports

Area	Reports	Reports per 100,000 Population	Rank[2]
MSA[1]	1,862	711	286
U.S.	4,064,520	1,245	-

Note: (1) Figures cover the College Station-Bryan, TX Metropolitan Statistical Area; (2) Rank ranges from 1 to 391 where 1 indicates greatest number of fraud and other consumer reports per 100,000 population
Source: Federal Trade Commission, Consumer Sentinel Network Data Book 2022

POLITICS

2020 Presidential Election Results

Area	Biden	Trump	Jorgensen	Hawkins	Other
Brazos County	41.4	55.7	2.1	0.3	0.4
U.S.	51.3	46.8	1.2	0.3	0.5

Note: Results are percentages and may not add to 100% due to rounding
Source: Dave Leip's Atlas of U.S. Presidential Elections

SPORTS

Professional Sports Teams

Team Name	League	Year Established

No teams are located in the metro area
Source: Wikipedia, Major Professional Sports Teams of the United States and Canada, April 12, 2023

CLIMATE

Average and Extreme Temperatures

Temperature	Jan	Feb	Mar	Apr	May	Jun	Jul	Aug	Sep	Oct	Nov	Dec	Yr.
Extreme High (°F)	90	97	98	98	100	105	109	106	104	98	91	90	109
Average High (°F)	60	64	72	79	85	91	95	96	90	81	70	63	79
Average Temp. (°F)	50	53	61	69	75	82	85	85	80	70	60	52	69
Average Low (°F)	39	43	50	58	65	72	74	74	69	59	49	41	58
Extreme Low (°F)	-2	7	18	35	43	53	64	61	47	32	20	4	-2

Note: Figures cover the years 1948-1990
Source: National Climatic Data Center, International Station Meteorological Climate Summary, 9/96

Average Precipitation/Snowfall/Humidity

Precip./Humidity	Jan	Feb	Mar	Apr	May	Jun	Jul	Aug	Sep	Oct	Nov	Dec	Yr.
Avg. Precip. (in.)	1.6	2.3	1.8	2.9	4.3	3.5	1.9	1.9	3.3	3.5	2.1	1.9	31.1
Avg. Snowfall (in.)	1	Tr	Tr	0	0	0	0	0	0	0	Tr	Tr	1
Avg. Rel. Hum. 6am (%)	79	80	79	83	88	89	88	87	86	84	81	79	84
Avg. Rel. Hum. 3pm (%)	53	51	47	50	53	49	43	42	47	47	49	51	48

Note: Figures cover the years 1948-1990; Tr = Trace amounts (<0.05 in. of rain; <0.5 in. of snow)
Source: National Climatic Data Center, International Station Meteorological Climate Summary, 9/96

Weather Conditions

Temperature			Daytime Sky			Precipitation		
10°F & below	32°F & below	90°F & above	Clear	Partly cloudy	Cloudy	0.01 inch or more precip.	0.1 inch or more snow/ice	Thunder-storms
< 1	20	111	105	148	112	83	1	41

Note: Figures are average number of days per year and cover the years 1948-1990
Source: National Climatic Data Center, International Station Meteorological Climate Summary, 9/96

HAZARDOUS WASTE

Superfund Sites

The College Station-Bryan, TX metro area has no sites on the EPA's Superfund Final National Priorities List. There are a total of 1,165 Superfund sites with a status of proposed or final on the list in the U.S. *U.S. Environmental Protection Agency, National Priorities List, April 12, 2023*

AIR QUALITY

Air Quality Trends: Ozone

	1990	1995	2000	2005	2010	2015	2018	2019	2020	2021
MSA[1]	n/a	n/a	n/a	n/a	n/a	n/a	n/a	n/a	n/a	n/a
U.S.	0.087	0.089	0.081	0.080	0.072	0.067	0.069	0.065	0.065	0.067

Note: (1) Data covers the College Station-Bryan, TX Metropolitan Statistical Area; n/a not available. The values shown are the composite ozone concentration averages among trend sites based on the highest fourth daily maximum 8-hour concentration in parts per million. These trends are based on sites having an adequate record of monitoring data during the trend period. Data from exceptional events are included.
Source: U.S. Environmental Protection Agency, Air Quality Monitoring Information, "Air Quality Trends by City, 1990-2021"

Air Quality Index

Area	Percent of Days when Air Quality was...[2]					AQI Statistics[2]	
	Good	Moderate	Unhealthy for Sensitive Groups	Unhealthy	Very Unhealthy	Maximum	Median
MSA[1]	87.6	12.4	0.0	0.0	0.0	84	30

Note: (1) Data covers the College Station-Bryan, TX Metropolitan Statistical Area; (2) Based on 356 days with AQI data in 2021. Air Quality Index (AQI) is an index for reporting daily air quality. EPA calculates the AQI for five major air pollutants regulated by the Clean Air Act: ground-level ozone, particle pollution (aka particulate matter), carbon monoxide, sulfur dioxide, and nitrogen dioxide. The AQI runs from 0 to 500. The higher the AQI value, the greater the level of air pollution and the greater the health concern. There are six AQI categories: "Good" AQI is between 0 and 50. Air quality is considered satisfactory; "Moderate" AQI is between 51 and 100. Air quality is acceptable; "Unhealthy for Sensitive Groups" When AQI values are between 101 and 150, members of sensitive groups may experience health effects; "Unhealthy" When AQI values are between 151 and 200 everyone may begin to experience health effects; "Very Unhealthy" AQI values between 201 and 300 trigger a health alert; "Hazardous" AQI values over 300 trigger warnings of emergency conditions (not shown).
Source: U.S. Environmental Protection Agency, Air Quality Index Report, 2021

Air Quality Index Pollutants

Area	Percent of Days when AQI Pollutant was...[2]					
	Carbon Monoxide	Nitrogen Dioxide	Ozone	Sulfur Dioxide	Particulate Matter 2.5	Particulate Matter 10
MSA[1]	0.0	0.0	0.0	(3)	100.0	0.0

Note: (1) Data covers the College Station-Bryan, TX Metropolitan Statistical Area; (2) Based on 356 days with AQI data in 2021. The Air Quality Index (AQI) is an index for reporting daily air quality. EPA calculates the AQI for five major air pollutants regulated by the Clean Air Act: ground-level ozone, particle pollution (also known as particulate matter), carbon monoxide, sulfur dioxide, and nitrogen dioxide. The AQI runs from 0 to 500. The higher the AQI value, the greater the level of air pollution and the greater the health concern; (3) Sulfur dioxide is no longer included in this table (as of December 8, 2021) because SO_2 concentrations tend to be very localized and not necessarily representative of broad geographical areas like counties and CBSAs.
Source: U.S. Environmental Protection Agency, Air Quality Index Report, 2021

Maximum Air Pollutant Concentrations: Particulate Matter, Ozone, CO and Lead

	Particulate Matter 10 (ug/m³)	Particulate Matter 2.5 Wtd AM (ug/m³)	Particulate Matter 2.5 24-Hr (ug/m³)	Ozone (ppm)	Carbon Monoxide (ppm)	Lead (ug/m³)
MSA[1] Level	n/a	8	21	n/a	n/a	n/a
NAAQS[2]	150	15	35	0.075	9	0.15
Met NAAQS[2]	n/a	Yes	Yes	n/a	n/a	n/a

Note: (1) Data covers the College Station-Bryan, TX Metropolitan Statistical Area; Data from exceptional events are included; (2) National Ambient Air Quality Standards; ppm = parts per million; ug/m³ = micrograms per cubic meter; n/a not available.
Concentrations: Particulate Matter 10 (coarse particulate)—highest second maximum 24-hour concentration; Particulate Matter 2.5 Wtd AM (fine particulate)—highest weighted annual mean concentration; Particulate Matter 2.5 24-Hour (fine particulate)—highest 98th percentile 24-hour concentration; Ozone—highest fourth daily maximum 8-hour concentration; Carbon Monoxide—highest second maximum non-overlapping 8-hour concentration; Lead—maximum running 3-month average
Source: U.S. Environmental Protection Agency, Air Quality Monitoring Information, "Air Quality Statistics by City, 2021"

Maximum Air Pollutant Concentrations: Nitrogen Dioxide and Sulfur Dioxide

	Nitrogen Dioxide AM (ppb)	Nitrogen Dioxide 1-Hr (ppb)	Sulfur Dioxide AM (ppb)	Sulfur Dioxide 1-Hr (ppb)	Sulfur Dioxide 24-Hr (ppb)
MSA[1] Level	n/a	n/a	n/a	11	n/a
NAAQS[2]	53	100	30	75	140
Met NAAQS[2]	n/a	n/a	n/a	Yes	n/a

Note: (1) Data covers the College Station-Bryan, TX Metropolitan Statistical Area; Data from exceptional events are included; (2) National Ambient Air Quality Standards; ppm = parts per million; ug/m³ = micrograms per cubic meter; n/a not available.
Concentrations: Nitrogen Dioxide AM—highest arithmetic mean concentration; Nitrogen Dioxide 1-Hr—highest 98th percentile 1-hour daily maximum concentration; Sulfur Dioxide AM—highest annual mean concentration; Sulfur Dioxide 1-Hr—highest 99th percentile 1-hour daily maximum concentration; Sulfur Dioxide 24-Hr—highest second maximum 24-hour concentration
Source: U.S. Environmental Protection Agency, Air Quality Monitoring Information, "Air Quality Statistics by City, 2021"

Columbia, South Carolina

Background

Located on the Congaree River, Columbia is South Carolina's capital and largest city, and the seat of Richland County. It is a center for local and state government, and an important financial, insurance, and medical center.

The region has depended on trade since a trading post opened south of the present-day city in 1718. In 1786, Columbia was chosen as the new state capital due to its location in the center of South Carolina, a compromise between residents on the coast and those living further inland.

The nation's second planned city, Columbia was originally 400 acres along the river. The main thoroughfares were designed 150 feet wide and other streets were also wider than most. Much of this spacious layout survives, lending an expansive feel to the city. Columbia was chartered as a town in 1805. Its first mayor—or "intendent"—John Taylor, later served in the state general assembly, the U.S. Congress, and as governor of the state. Columbia was staunchly Confederate during the Civil War, attacked in 1865 by General Sherman's troops and set ablaze by both Union attackers and Confederate evacuees. After the war and Reconstruction, Columbia was revitalized as the state's industrial and farm products hub.

Today, a brisk renewal continues in Columbia's downtown thanks to the state's first Business Improvement District. The City Center Partnership, Inc., manages the district and works to bring businesses and residents into the area, via, among other things, the free ZeRover shuttle. The area's Central Business District has seen record office space occupancy. A major CanalSide mixed use development on the Congaree River was completed in 2018, with 750 residential apartments.

Columbia is home to the University of South Carolina, a major employer alongside BlueCross BlueShield of SC. The USC/Columbia Technology Incubator's more than 40 companies have generated more than $45 million in total revenue by member companies, which employ more than 650. The university has also created the 500-acre Innovista Research District to provide office and lab space to tech and innovation businesses and startups. The health care industry is also significant. The Medical University of South Carolina and the area's largest employer, Palmetto Health, merged their medical practices in 2016 under the banner of Palmetto Health-USC Medical Group. The city's two venerable Providence Hospitals—operated by the Sisters of Charity since 1938—were recently acquired by LifePoint Health, a Tennessee-based for-profit company that operates health care facilities in 22 states.

Other large employers include Fort Jackson, the U.S. Army's largest initial entry training installation (and home to Fort Jackson National Cemetery), and the United Parcel Service, which operates a freight service center in West Columbia.

Columbia is the cultural center for the area, known as South Carolina's Midlands. The Columbia Museum of Art, with its collection of Renaissance and Baroque art, is a major regional museum. The performing arts are onstage year-round at the Koger Center for the Arts at USC. The city's Town Theatre, hosting its 103rd season in 2023, is the country's oldest community theatre in continuous use. The South Carolina State Museum "Windows to New Worlds" includes a planetarium, observatory, and 4-D theater. Major historic architecture in Columbia includes City Hall, designed by President Ulysses S. Grant's federal architect, Alfred B. Mullet, and the Lutheran Survey Print Building.

In addition to USC, Columbia's other institutions of higher learning are Lutheran Theological Seminary, Columbia College, Benedict College, Allen University, and Columbia International University.

In March 2015, the Confederate battle flag was removed from the state house flagpole by a protester motivated by the Charleston Massacre. Although the flag was raised again minutes after this action, it was permanently removed in July of that year.

Located about 150 miles southeast of the Appalachian Mountains, Columbia has a relatively temperate climate. Summers are long and often hot and humid with frequent thunderstorms, thanks to the Bermuda high-pressure force. Winters are mild with little snow, while spring is changeable withinfrequent tornadoes or hail. Fall is considered the most pleasant season.

Rankings

General Rankings

- For its "Best for Vets: Places to Live 2019" rankings, *Military Times* evaluated 599 cities (83 large, 234 medium, 282 small) and compared the locations across three broad categories: veteran and military culture/services; economic indicators; and livability factors such as health, crime, traffic, and school quality. Columbia ranked #39 out of the top 50, in the medium-sized city category (population of 100,000-249,999). Data points more specific to veterans and the military weighed more heavily than others. *rebootcamp.militarytimes.com, "Military Times Best Places to Live 2019," September 10, 2018*

Business/Finance Rankings

- The Brookings Institution ranked the nation's largest cities based on income inequality. Columbia was ranked #38 (#1 = greatest inequality). Criteria: the "95/20 ratio," a figure representing the income at which a household earns more than 95 percent of all other households, divided by the income at which a household earns more than only 20 percent of all other households. *Brookings Institution, "Household Income Inequality, Largest Cities of 97 Large U.S. Metro Areas, 2014-2016," February 5, 2018*

- The Brookings Institution ranked the 100 largest metro areas in the U.S. based on income inequality. Columbia was ranked #63 (#1 = greatest inequality). Criteria: the "95/20 ratio," a figure representing the income at which a household earns more than 95 percent of all other households, divided by the income at which a household earns more than only 20 percent of all other households. *Brookings Institution, "Household Income Inequality, 100 Largest U.S. Metro Areas, 2014-2016," February 5, 2018*

- The Columbia metro area appeared on the Milken Institute "2022 Best Performing Cities" list. Rank: #100 out of 200 large metro areas (population over 250,000). Criteria: job growth; wage and salary growth; high-tech output growth; housing affordability; household broadband access. *Milken Institute, "Best-Performing Cities 2022," March 28, 2022*

- *Forbes* ranked the 200 most populous metro areas to determine the nation's "Best Places for Business and Careers." The Columbia metro area was ranked #102. Criteria: costs (business and living); job growth (past and projected); income growth; quality of life; educational attainment (college and high school); projected economic growth; cultural and leisure opportunities; workplace tolerance laws; net migration patterns. *Forbes, "The Best Places for Business and Careers 2019: Seattle Still On Top," October 30, 2019*

Children/Family Rankings

- Columbia was selected as one of the most playful cities in the U.S. by KaBOOM! The organization's Playful City USA initiative honors cities and towns across the nation that have made their communities more playable. Criteria: pledging to integrate play as a solution to challenges in their communities; making it easy for children to get active and balanced play; creating more family-friendly and innovative communities as a result. *KaBOOM! National Campaign for Play, "2017 Playful City USA Communities"*

Dating/Romance Rankings

- Columbia was selected as one of the nation's most romantic cities with 100,000 or more residents by Amazon.com. The city ranked #11 of 20. Criteria: per capita sales of romance novels, relationship books, romantic comedy movies, romantic music, and sexual wellness products. *Amazon.com, "Top 20 Most Romantic Cities in the U.S.," February 1, 2017*

Education Rankings

- Personal finance website *WalletHub* analyzed the 150 largest U.S. metropolitan statistical areas to determine where the most educated Americans are putting their degrees to work. Criteria: education levels; percentage of workers with degrees; education quality and attainment gap; public school quality rankings; quality and enrollment of each metro area's universities. Columbia was ranked #66 (#1 = most educated city). *www.WalletHub.com, "Most & Least Educated Cities in America," July 18, 2022*

Health/Fitness Rankings

- Columbia was identified as a "2022 Spring Allergy Capital." The area ranked #12 out of 100. Three groups of factors were used to identify the most challenging cities for people with allergies during the spring season: annual spring pollen scores; over the counter allergy medicine use; number of board-certified allergy specialists. *Asthma and Allergy Foundation of America, "Spring Allergy Capitals 2022," March 2, 2022*

- Columbia was identified as a "2022 Fall Allergy Capital." The area ranked #16 out of 100. Three groups of factors were used to identify the most challenging cities for people with allergies during the fall season: annual fall pollen scores; over the counter allergy medicine use; number of board-certified allergy specialists. *Asthma and Allergy Foundation of America, "Fall Allergy Capitals 2022," March 2, 2022*

- Columbia was identified as a "2022 Asthma Capital." The area ranked #39 out of the nation's 100 largest metropolitan areas. Criteria: estimated asthma prevalence; asthma-related mortality; and ER visits due to asthma. Risk factors analyzed but not factored in the rankings: annual pollen score; annual air quality; public smoking laws; access to board-certified asthma specialists; rescue and controller medication use; uninsured rate; poverty rate. *Asthma and Allergy Foundation of America, "Asthma Capitals 2022: The Most Challenging Places to Live With Asthma," September 14, 2022*

Real Estate Rankings

- *WalletHub* compared the most populated U.S. cities to determine which had the best markets for real estate agents. Columbia ranked #80 where demand was high and pay was the best. Criteria: sales per agent; annual median wage for real-estate agents; monthly average starting salary for real estate agents; real estate job density and competition; unemployment rate; home turnover rate; housing-market health index; and other relevant metrics. *www.WalletHub.com, "2021 Best Places to Be a Real Estate Agent," May 12, 2021*

- The Columbia metro area appeared on Realtor.com's list of hot housing markets to watch in 2023. The area ranked #8. Criteria: forecasted home price and sales growth; overall economy; population trends. *Realtor.com®, "Top 10 Housing Markets Positioned for Growth in 2023," December 7, 2022*

- Columbia was ranked #11 in the top 20 out of the 100 largest metro areas in terms of house price appreciation in 2022 (#1 = highest rate). *Federal Housing Finance Agency, House Price Index, 4th Quarter 2022*

- Columbia was ranked #54 out of 235 metro areas in terms of housing affordability in 2022 by the National Association of Home Builders (#1 = most affordable). Criteria: the share of homes sold in that area affordable to a family earning the local median income, based on standard mortgage underwriting criteria. *National Association of Home Builders®, NAHB-Wells Fargo Housing Opportunity Index, 4th Quarter 2022*

- The nation's largest metro areas were analyzed in terms of the percentage of households entering some stage of foreclosure in 2022. The Columbia metro area ranked #4 out of 8 (#1 = highest foreclosure rate). *ATTOM Data Solutions, "2022 Year-End U.S. Foreclosure Market Report™," January 12, 2023*

Safety Rankings

- The National Insurance Crime Bureau ranked 390 metro areas in the U.S. in terms of per capita rates of vehicle theft. The Columbia metro area ranked #57 (#1 = highest rate). Criteria: number of vehicle theft offenses per 100,000 inhabitants in 2021. *National Insurance Crime Bureau, "Hot Spots 2021," September 1, 2022*

Seniors/Retirement Rankings

- From its Best Cities for Successful Aging indexes, the Milken Institute generated rankings for metropolitan areas, weighing data in nine categories—health care, wellness, living arrangements, transportation and convenience, financial characteristics, education, employment, community engagement, and overall livability. The Columbia metro area was ranked #54 overall in the large metro area category. *Milken Institute, "Best Cities for Successful Aging, 2017" March 14, 2017*

Women/Minorities Rankings

- Personal finance website *WalletHub* compared more than 180 U.S. cities across two key dimensions, "Hispanic Business-Friendliness" and "Hispanic Purchasing Power," to arrive at the most favorable conditions for Hispanic entrepreneurs. Columbia was ranked #149 out of 182. Criteria includes: share of Hispanic-Owned Businesses; Hispanic entrepreneurship rate to median annual income of Hispanics; Small Business-Friendliness score; cost of living; and number of Hispanics with at least a bachelor's degree. *WalletHub.com, "2019's Best Cities for Hispanic Entrepreneurs," May 1, 2019*

Miscellaneous Rankings

- *WalletHub* compared the 150 most populated U.S. cities to determine their operating efficiency. A "Quality of Services" score was constructed for each city and then divided by the total budget per capita to reveal which were managed the best. Columbia ranked #79. Criteria: financial stability; economy; education; safety; health; infrastructure and pollution. *www.WalletHub.com, "2022's Best- & Worst-Run Cities in America," June 21, 2022*

Business Environment

DEMOGRAPHICS

Population Growth

Area	1990 Census	2000 Census	2010 Census	2020 Census	Population Growth (%) 1990-2020	Population Growth (%) 2010-2020
City	115,475	116,278	129,272	136,632	18.3	5.7
MSA[1]	548,325	647,158	767,598	829,470	51.3	8.1
U.S.	248,709,873	281,421,906	308,745,538	331,449,281	33.3	7.4

Note: (1) Figures cover the Columbia, SC Metropolitan Statistical Area
Source: U.S. Census Bureau, 1990 Census, 2000 Census, 2010 Census, 2020 Census

Race

Area	White Alone[2] (%)	Black Alone[2] (%)	Asian Alone[2] (%)	AIAN[3] Alone[2] (%)	NHOPI[4] Alone[2] (%)	Other Race Alone[2] (%)	Two or More Races (%)
City	50.7	38.5	3.1	0.3	0.1	2.3	5.1
MSA[1]	55.7	32.4	2.3	0.4	0.1	3.1	6.0
U.S.	61.6	12.4	6.0	1.1	0.2	8.4	10.2

Note: (1) Figures cover the Columbia, SC Metropolitan Statistical Area; (2) Alone is defined as not being in combination with one or more other races; (3) American Indian and Alaska Native; (4) Native Hawaiian and Other Pacific Islander
Source: U.S. Census Bureau, 2020 Census

Hispanic or Latino Origin

Area	Total (%)	Mexican (%)	Puerto Rican (%)	Cuban (%)	Other (%)
City	5.6	2.4	1.1	0.3	1.8
MSA[1]	5.8	2.8	1.1	0.2	1.7
U.S.	18.4	11.2	1.8	0.7	4.7

Note: Persons of Hispanic or Latino origin can be of any race; (1) Figures cover the Columbia, SC Metropolitan Statistical Area
Source: U.S. Census Bureau, 2017-2021 American Community Survey 5-Year Estimates

Age

Area	Under Age 5	Age 5–19	Age 20–34	Age 35–44	Age 45–54	Age 55–64	Age 65–74	Age 75–84	Age 85+	Median Age
City	4.6	22.1	30.7	11.1	9.5	9.8	7.7	3.2	1.3	29.9
MSA[1]	5.4	20.2	20.1	12.4	12.4	13.2	10.2	4.6	1.6	38.4
U.S.	5.6	19.2	20.2	12.7	12.4	13.1	10.0	4.9	1.9	38.8

Note: (1) Figures cover the Columbia, SC Metropolitan Statistical Area
Source: U.S. Census Bureau, 2020 Census

Disability by Age

Area	All Ages	Under 18 Years Old	18 to 64 Years Old	65 Years and Over
City	12.8	5.1	10.7	38.5
MSA[1]	14.2	4.7	12.3	36.3
U.S.	12.6	4.4	10.3	33.4

Note: Figures show percent of the civilian noninstitutionalized population that reported having a disability. Disability status is determined from six types of difficulty: vision, hearing, cognitive, ambulatory, self-care, and independent living. For children under 5 years old, hearing and vision difficulty are used to determine disability status. For children between the ages of 5 and 14, disability status is determined from hearing, vision, cognitive, ambulatory, and self-care difficulties. For people aged 15 years and older, they are considered to have a disability if they have difficulty with any one of the six difficulty types; Note: (1) Figures cover the Columbia, SC Metropolitan Statistical Area
Source: U.S. Census Bureau, 2017-2021 American Community Survey 5-Year Estimates

Ancestry

Area	German	Irish	English	American	Italian	Polish	French[2]	Scottish	Dutch
City	9.6	6.9	7.7	5.5	3.3	1.1	1.9	1.9	0.6
MSA[1]	9.5	7.1	8.3	7.5	2.3	1.3	1.4	1.8	0.6
U.S.	12.8	9.6	8.1	5.7	5.0	2.7	2.2	1.6	1.1

Note: Figures are the percentage of the total population reporting a particular ancestry. The nine most commonly reported ancestries in the U.S. are shown. Figures include multiple ancestries (e.g. if a person reported being Irish and Italian, they were included in both columns); (1) Figures cover the Columbia, SC Metropolitan Statistical Area; (2) Excludes Basque
Source: U.S. Census Bureau, 2017-2021 American Community Survey 5-Year Estimates

Foreign-born Population

Area	Any Foreign Country	Asia	Mexico	Europe	Caribbean	Central America[2]	South America	Africa	Canada
City	4.8	2.1	0.3	0.6	0.6	0.2	0.4	0.5	0.1
MSA[1]	5.3	1.8	1.0	0.7	0.4	0.6	0.3	0.3	0.1
U.S.	13.6	4.2	3.3	1.5	1.4	1.1	1.1	0.8	0.2

Note: (1) Figures cover the Columbia, SC Metropolitan Statistical Area; (2) Excludes Mexico.
Source: U.S. Census Bureau, 2017-2021 American Community Survey 5-Year Estimates

Household Size

Area	One	Two	Three	Four	Five	Six	Seven or More	Average Household Size
City	39.1	32.7	13.4	9.0	4.1	1.4	0.3	2.20
MSA[1]	30.4	34.2	15.5	11.9	5.1	2.0	0.9	2.50
U.S.	28.1	33.8	15.5	12.9	6.0	2.3	1.4	2.60

Note: (1) Figures cover the Columbia, SC Metropolitan Statistical Area
Source: U.S. Census Bureau, 2017-2021 American Community Survey 5-Year Estimates

Household Relationships

Area	House-holder	Opposite-sex Spouse	Same-sex Spouse	Opposite-sex Unmarried Partner	Same-sex Unmarried Partner	Child[2]	Grand-child	Other Relatives	Non-relatives
City	39.2	10.5	0.2	2.1	0.2	19.5	1.6	2.8	5.8
MSA[1]	39.9	17.0	0.2	2.1	0.2	27.5	2.7	3.8	3.0
U.S.	38.3	17.5	0.2	2.5	0.2	28.3	2.4	4.8	3.4

Note: Figures are percent of the total population; (1) Figures cover the Columbia, SC Metropolitan Statistical Area; (2) Includes biological, adopted, and stepchildren of the householder
Source: U.S. Census Bureau, 2020 Census

Gender

Area	Males	Females	Males per 100 Females
City	67,155	69,477	96.7
MSA[1]	398,440	431,030	92.4
U.S.	162,685,811	168,763,470	96.4

Note: (1) Figures cover the Columbia, SC Metropolitan Statistical Area
Source: U.S. Census Bureau, 2020 Census

Marital Status

Area	Never Married	Now Married[2]	Separated	Widowed	Divorced
City	55.7	29.6	2.3	4.0	8.4
MSA[1]	36.3	45.0	2.6	5.6	10.6
U.S.	33.8	48.0	1.8	5.6	10.8

Note: Figures are percentages and cover the population 15 years of age and older; (1) Figures cover the Columbia, SC Metropolitan Statistical Area; (2) Excludes separated
Source: U.S. Census Bureau, 2017-2021 American Community Survey 5-Year Estimates

Religious Groups by Family

Area	Catholic	Baptist	Methodist	LDS[2]	Pentecostal	Lutheran	Islam	Adventist	Other
MSA[1]	6.6	15.1	8.5	1.2	3.8	2.3	0.3	1.3	15.4
U.S.	18.7	7.3	3.0	2.0	1.8	1.7	1.3	1.3	11.6

Note: Figures are the number of adherents as a percentage of the total population and cover the eight largest religious groups in the U.S; (1) Figures cover the Columbia, SC Metropolitan Statistical Area; (2) Church of Jesus Christ of Latter-day Saints
Sources: 2020 U.S. Religion Census, Association of Statisticians of American Religious Bodies; The Association of Religion Data Archives (ARDA)

Religious Groups by Tradition

Area	Catholic	Evangelical Protestant	Mainline Protestant	Black Protestant	Islam	Judaism	Hinduism	Orthodox	Buddhism
MSA[1]	6.6	27.9	10.7	5.6	0.3	0.2	0.4	0.1	0.3
U.S.	18.7	16.5	5.2	2.3	1.3	0.6	0.4	0.4	0.3

Note: Figures are the number of adherents as a percentage of the total population; (1) Figures cover the Columbia, SC Metropolitan Statistical Area
Sources: 2020 U.S. Religion Census, Association of Statisticians of American Religious Bodies; The Association of Religion Data Archives (ARDA)

ECONOMY

Gross Metropolitan Product

Area	2020	2021	2022	2023	Rank[2]
MSA[1]	44.4	48.2	51.8	55.2	74

Note: Figures are in billions of dollars; (1) Figures cover the Columbia, SC Metropolitan Statistical Area; (2) Rank is based on 2021 data and ranges from 1 to 381
Source: U.S. Conference of Mayors, U.S. Metro Economies: U.S. Metros Compared to Global and State Economies, June 2022

Economic Growth

Area	2018-20 (%)	2021 (%)	2022 (%)	2023 (%)	Rank[2]
MSA[1]	0.1	4.4	1.7	3.2	137
U.S.	-0.6	5.7	3.1	2.9	—

Note: Figures are real gross metropolitan product (GMP) growth rates and represent average annual percent change; (1) Figures cover the Columbia, SC Metropolitan Statistical Area; (2) Rank is based on 2020 2-year average annual percent change and ranges from 1 to 381
Source: U.S. Conference of Mayors, U.S. Metro Economies: U.S. Metros Compared to Global and State Economies, June 2022

Metropolitan Area Exports

Area	2016	2017	2018	2019	2020	2021	Rank[2]
MSA[1]	2,007.7	2,123.9	2,083.8	2,184.6	2,058.8	2,100.2	104

Note: Figures are in millions of dollars; (1) Figures cover the Columbia, SC Metropolitan Statistical Area; (2) Rank is based on 2021 data and ranges from 1 to 388
Source: U.S. Department of Commerce, International Trade Administration, Office of Trade and Economic Analysis, Industry and Analysis, Exports by Metropolitan Area, data extracted March 16, 2023

Building Permits

Area	Single-Family 2021	2022	Pct. Chg.	Multi-Family 2021	2022	Pct. Chg.	Total 2021	2022	Pct. Chg.
City	804	772	-4.0	896	1,359	51.7	1,700	2,131	25.4
MSA[1]	5,853	4,101	-29.9	1,028	1,703	65.7	6,881	5,804	-15.7
U.S.	1,115,400	975,600	-12.5	621,600	689,500	10.9	1,737,000	1,665,100	-4.1

Note: (1) Figures cover the Columbia, SC Metropolitan Statistical Area; Figures represent new, privately-owned housing units authorized (unadjusted data); All permit data are based on estimates with imputation
Source: U.S. Census Bureau, Manufacturing, Mining, and Construction Statistics, Building Permits, 2021, 2022

Bankruptcy Filings

Area	Business Filings 2021	2022	% Chg.	Nonbusiness Filings 2021	2022	% Chg.
Richland County	8	13	62.5	348	424	21.8
U.S.	14,347	13,481	-6.0	399,269	374,240	-6.3

Note: Business filings include Chapter 7, Chapter 9, Chapter 11, Chapter 12, Chapter 13, Chapter 15, and Section 304; Nonbusiness filings include Chapter 7, Chapter 11, and Chapter 13
Source: Administrative Office of the U.S. Courts, Business and Nonbusiness Bankruptcy, County Cases Commenced by Chapter of the Bankruptcy Code, During the 12-Month Period Ending December 31, 2021 and Business and Nonbusiness Bankruptcy, County Cases Commenced by Chapter of the Bankruptcy Code, During the 12-Month Period Ending December 31, 2022

Housing Vacancy Rates

Area	Gross Vacancy Rate[2] (%) 2020	2021	2022	Year-Round Vacancy Rate[3] (%) 2020	2021	2022	Rental Vacancy Rate[4] (%) 2020	2021	2022	Homeowner Vacancy Rate[5] (%) 2020	2021	2022
MSA[1]	7.2	7.6	12.0	7.1	7.6	12.0	4.5	4.7	6.1	0.7	1.1	0.6
U.S.	10.6	10.8	10.5	8.2	8.4	8.2	6.3	6.1	5.8	1.0	0.9	0.8

Note: (1) Figures cover the Columbia, SC Metropolitan Statistical Area; (2) The percentage of the total housing inventory that is vacant; (3) The percentage of the housing inventory (excluding seasonal units) that is year-round vacant; (4) The percentage of rental inventory that is vacant for rent; (5) The percentage of homeowner inventory that is vacant for sale
Source: U.S. Census Bureau, Housing Vacancies and Homeownership Annual Statistics: 2020, 2021, 2022

INCOME

Income

Area	Per Capita ($)	Median Household ($)	Average Household ($)
City	32,954	48,791	79,637
MSA[1]	32,508	58,992	79,903
U.S.	37,638	69,021	97,196

Note: (1) Figures cover the Columbia, SC Metropolitan Statistical Area
Source: U.S. Census Bureau, 2017-2021 American Community Survey 5-Year Estimates

Columbia, South Carolina

Household Income Distribution

Area	Under $15,000	$15,000 -$24,999	$25,000 -$34,999	$35,000 -$49,999	$50,000 -$74,999	$75,000 -$99,999	$100,000 -$149,999	$150,000 and up
City	18.9	10.2	9.7	12.6	14.8	10.5	11.2	12.1
MSA[1]	12.0	8.3	9.4	12.8	18.2	13.1	14.4	11.8
U.S.	9.4	7.8	8.2	11.4	16.8	12.8	16.3	17.3

Note: (1) Figures cover the Columbia, SC Metropolitan Statistical Area
Source: U.S. Census Bureau, 2017-2021 American Community Survey 5-Year Estimates

Poverty Rate

Area	All Ages	Under 18 Years Old	18 to 64 Years Old	65 Years and Over
City	24.3	31.3	23.5	16.7
MSA[1]	14.9	19.9	14.2	10.6
U.S.	12.6	17.0	11.8	9.6

Note: Figures are percentage of people whose income during the past 12 months was below the poverty level; (1) Figures cover the Columbia, SC Metropolitan Statistical Area
Source: U.S. Census Bureau, 2017-2021 American Community Survey 5-Year Estimates

EMPLOYMENT

Labor Force and Employment

Area	Civilian Labor Force Dec. 2021	Civilian Labor Force Dec. 2022	% Chg.	Workers Employed Dec. 2021	Workers Employed Dec. 2022	% Chg.
City	56,736	55,816	-1.6	54,797	54,043	-1.4
MSA[1]	399,511	392,721	-1.7	387,182	381,702	-1.4
U.S.	161,696,000	164,224,000	1.6	155,732,000	158,872,000	2.0

Note: Data is not seasonally adjusted and covers workers 16 years of age and older; (1) Figures cover the Columbia, SC Metropolitan Statistical Area
Source: Bureau of Labor Statistics, Local Area Unemployment Statistics

Unemployment Rate

Area	Jan.	Feb.	Mar.	Apr.	May	Jun.	Jul.	Aug.	Sep.	Oct.	Nov.	Dec.
City	3.7	4.3	3.5	2.9	3.9	4.0	3.9	3.7	3.4	4.2	3.3	3.2
MSA[1]	3.5	3.8	3.1	2.5	3.0	3.3	3.1	3.1	2.9	3.4	2.6	2.8
U.S.	4.4	4.1	3.8	3.3	3.4	3.8	3.8	3.8	3.3	3.4	3.4	3.3

Note: Data is not seasonally adjusted and covers workers 16 years of age and older; (1) Figures cover the Columbia, SC Metropolitan Statistical Area
Source: Bureau of Labor Statistics, Local Area Unemployment Statistics

Average Wages

Occupation	$/Hr.	Occupation	$/Hr.
Accountants and Auditors	31.51	Maintenance and Repair Workers	20.68
Automotive Mechanics	22.42	Marketing Managers	59.00
Bookkeepers	19.63	Network and Computer Systems Admin.	43.75
Carpenters	22.23	Nurses, Licensed Practical	25.20
Cashiers	11.56	Nurses, Registered	35.37
Computer Programmers	46.56	Nursing Assistants	15.81
Computer Systems Analysts	41.41	Office Clerks, General	16.30
Computer User Support Specialists	26.44	Physical Therapists	41.97
Construction Laborers	18.07	Physicians	142.61
Cooks, Restaurant	14.25	Plumbers, Pipefitters and Steamfitters	22.81
Customer Service Representatives	17.29	Police and Sheriff's Patrol Officers	24.96
Dentists	76.98	Postal Service Mail Carriers	25.68
Electricians	25.73	Real Estate Sales Agents	28.52
Engineers, Electrical	41.58	Retail Salespersons	14.63
Fast Food and Counter Workers	10.98	Sales Representatives, Technical/Scientific	40.39
Financial Managers	59.98	Secretaries, Exc. Legal/Medical/Executive	18.64
First-Line Supervisors of Office Workers	30.75	Security Guards	13.48
General and Operations Managers	48.46	Surgeons	n/a
Hairdressers/Cosmetologists	15.32	Teacher Assistants, Exc. Postsecondary*	12.00
Home Health and Personal Care Aides	12.35	Teachers, Secondary School, Exc. Sp. Ed.*	26.34
Janitors and Cleaners	13.42	Telemarketers	10.78
Landscaping/Groundskeeping Workers	15.84	Truck Drivers, Heavy/Tractor-Trailer	23.99
Lawyers	53.72	Truck Drivers, Light/Delivery Services	19.35
Maids and Housekeeping Cleaners	12.62	Waiters and Waitresses	10.82

Note: Wage data covers the Columbia, SC Metropolitan Statistical Area; (*) Hourly wages were calculated from annual wage data based on a 40 hour work week; n/a not available.
Source: Bureau of Labor Statistics, Metro Area Occupational Employment & Wage Estimates, May 2022

Employment by Industry

Sector	MSA[1] Number of Employees	MSA[1] Percent of Total	U.S. Percent of Total
Construction, Mining, and Logging	16,900	4.0	5.4
Private Education and Health Services	53,400	12.8	16.1
Financial Activities	36,000	8.6	5.9
Government	83,100	19.9	14.5
Information	5,200	1.2	2.0
Leisure and Hospitality	38,600	9.2	10.3
Manufacturing	31,600	7.6	8.4
Other Services	17,100	4.1	3.7
Professional and Business Services	57,500	13.7	14.7
Retail Trade	45,100	10.8	10.2
Transportation, Warehousing, and Utilities	17,700	4.2	4.9
Wholesale Trade	16,000	3.8	3.9

Note: Figures are non-farm employment as of December 2022. Figures are not seasonally adjusted and include workers 16 years of age and older; (1) Figures cover the Columbia, SC Metropolitan Statistical Area
Source: Bureau of Labor Statistics, Current Employment Statistics, Employment, Hours, and Earnings

Employment by Occupation

Occupation Classification	City (%)	MSA[1] (%)	U.S. (%)
Management, Business, Science, and Arts	44.7	39.9	40.3
Natural Resources, Construction, and Maintenance	4.3	8.1	8.7
Production, Transportation, and Material Moving	10.1	13.2	13.1
Sales and Office	22.6	22.3	20.9
Service	18.3	16.5	17.0

Note: Figures cover employed civilians 16 years of age and older; (1) Figures cover the Columbia, SC Metropolitan Statistical Area
Source: U.S. Census Bureau, 2017-2021 American Community Survey 5-Year Estimates

Occupations with Greatest Projected Employment Growth: 2022 – 2024

Occupation[1]	2022 Employment	2024 Projected Employment	Numeric Employment Change	Percent Employment Change
Laborers and Freight, Stock, and Material Movers, Hand	65,510	67,830	2,320	3.5
Cooks, Restaurant	24,980	26,740	1,760	7.0
Home Health and Personal Care Aides	32,690	34,380	1,690	5.2
Retail Salespersons	71,670	73,260	1,590	2.2
Stockers and Order Fillers	32,230	33,820	1,590	4.9
Fast Food and Counter Workers	68,620	69,700	1,080	1.6
Miscellaneous Assemblers and Fabricators	42,810	43,730	920	2.1
General and Operations Managers	32,800	33,630	830	2.5
Waiters and Waitresses	37,090	37,880	790	2.1
Customer Service Representatives	59,220	59,970	750	1.3

Note: Projections cover South Carolina; (1) Sorted by numeric employment change
Source: www.projectionscentral.com, State Occupational Projections, 2022–2024 Short-Term Projections

Fastest-Growing Occupations: 2022 – 2024

Occupation[1]	2022 Employment	2024 Projected Employment	Numeric Employment Change	Percent Employment Change
Nurse Practitioners	3,070	3,400	330	10.7
Logisticians	3,160	3,440	280	8.9
Chemical Engineers	600	650	50	8.3
Software Developers and Software Quality Assurance Analysts and Testers	8,510	9,190	680	8.0
Physician Assistants	1,660	1,790	130	7.8
Electrical, Electronic, and Electromechanical Assemblers, Except Coil Winders, Tapers, and Fini	4,730	5,100	370	7.8
Information Security Analysts (SOC 2018)	1,700	1,830	130	7.6
Financial Examiners	700	750	50	7.1
Personal Financial Advisors	2,700	2,890	190	7.0
Cooks, Restaurant	24,980	26,740	1,760	7.0

Note: Projections cover South Carolina; (1) Sorted by percent employment change and excludes occupations with numeric employment change less than 50
Source: www.projectionscentral.com, State Occupational Projections, 2022–2024 Short-Term Projections

CITY FINANCES

City Government Finances

Component	2020 ($000)	2020 ($ per capita)
Total Revenues	404,736	3,074
Total Expenditures	414,955	3,151
Debt Outstanding	824,201	6,259
Cash and Securities[1]	600,665	4,562

Note: (1) Cash and security holdings of a government at the close of its fiscal year, including those of its dependent agencies, utilities, and liquor stores.
Source: U.S. Census Bureau, State & Local Government Finances 2020

City Government Revenue by Source

Source	2020 ($000)	2020 ($ per capita)	2020 (%)
General Revenue			
From Federal Government	10,640	81	2.6
From State Government	29,395	223	7.3
From Local Governments	31,458	239	7.8
Taxes			
Property	47,949	364	11.8
Sales and Gross Receipts	16,707	127	4.1
Personal Income	0	0	0.0
Corporate Income	0	0	0.0
Motor Vehicle License	0	0	0.0
Other Taxes	40,667	309	10.0
Current Charges	94,857	720	23.4
Liquor Store	0	0	0.0
Utility	101,264	769	25.0

Source: U.S. Census Bureau, State & Local Government Finances 2020

City Government Expenditures by Function

Function	2020 ($000)	2020 ($ per capita)	2020 (%)
General Direct Expenditures			
Air Transportation	0	0	0.0
Corrections	0	0	0.0
Education	0	0	0.0
Employment Security Administration	0	0	0.0
Financial Administration	6,491	49	1.6
Fire Protection	50,120	380	12.1
General Public Buildings	8,299	63	2.0
Governmental Administration, Other	12,766	97	3.1
Health	1,859	14	0.4
Highways	6,471	49	1.6
Hospitals	0	0	0.0
Housing and Community Development	11,793	89	2.8
Interest on General Debt	4,398	33	1.1
Judicial and Legal	4,465	33	1.1
Libraries	0	0	0.0
Parking	4,685	35	1.1
Parks and Recreation	15,603	118	3.8
Police Protection	51,832	393	12.5
Public Welfare	1,111	8	0.3
Sewerage	87,734	666	21.1
Solid Waste Management	11,853	90	2.9
Veterans' Services	0	0	0.0
Liquor Store	0	0	0.0
Utility	101,065	767	24.4

Source: U.S. Census Bureau, State & Local Government Finances 2020

TAXES

State Corporate Income Tax Rates

State	Tax Rate (%)	Income Brackets ($)	Num. of Brackets	Financial Institution Tax Rate (%)[a]	Federal Income Tax Ded.
South Carolina	5.0	Flat rate	1	4.5 (t)	No

Note: Tax rates as of January 1, 2023; (a) Rates listed are the corporate income tax rate applied to financial institutions or excise taxes based on income. Some states have other taxes based upon the value of deposits or shares; (t) South Carolina taxes savings and loans at a 6% rate.
Source: Federation of Tax Administrators, State Corporate Income Tax Rates, January 1, 2023

State Individual Income Tax Rates

State	Tax Rate (%)	Income Brackets ($)	Personal Exemptions ($) Single	Personal Exemptions ($) Married	Personal Exemptions ($) Depend.	Standard Ded. ($) Single	Standard Ded. ($) Married
South Carolina (a)	0.0 - 6.4 (bb)	3,200 - 16,040	(d)	(d)	(d)	13,850	27,700 (d)

Note: Tax rates as of January 1, 2023; Local- and county-level taxes are not included; Federal income tax is not deductible on state income tax returns; (a) 16 states have statutory provision for automatically adjusting to the rate of inflation the dollar values of the income tax brackets, standard deductions, and/or personal exemptions. Oregon does not index the income brackets for $125,000 and over; (d) These states use the personal exemption/standard deduction amounts provided in the federal Internal Revenue Code; (bb) Louisiana tax rates may be adjusted down if revenue trigger is met on April 1st. Iowa is phasing-in a flat rate by 2027, while Nebraska and South Carolina is phasing-in a reduced top rate by 2027.
Source: Federation of Tax Administrators, State Individual Income Tax Rates, January 1, 2023

Various State Sales and Excise Tax Rates

State	State Sales Tax (%)	Gasoline[1] ($/gal.)	Cigarette[2] ($/pack)	Spirits[3] ($/gal.)	Wine[4] ($/gal.)	Beer[5] ($/gal.)	Recreational Marijuana (%)
South Carolina	6	0.2875	0.57	5.42	1.08	0.77	Not legal

Note: All tax rates as of January 1, 2023; (1) The American Petroleum Institute has developed a methodology for determining the average tax rate on a gallon of fuel. Rates may include any of the following: excise taxes, environmental fees, storage tank fees, other fees or taxes, general sales tax, and local taxes; (2) The federal excise tax of $1.0066 per pack and local taxes are not included; (3) Rates are those applicable to off-premise sales of 40% alcohol by volume (a.b.v.) distilled spirits in 750ml containers. Local excise taxes are excluded; (4) Rates are those applicable to off-premise sales of 11% a.b.v. non-carbonated wine in 750ml containers; (5) Rates are those applicable to off-premise sales of 4.7% a.b.v. beer in 12 ounce containers.
Source: Tax Foundation, 2023 Facts & Figures: How Does Your State Compare?

State Business Tax Climate Index Rankings

State	Overall Rank	Corporate Tax Rank	Individual Income Tax Rank	Sales Tax Rank	Property Tax Rank	Unemployment Insurance Tax Rank
South Carolina	31	6	28	32	35	29

Note: The index is a measure of how each state's tax laws affect economic performance. The lower the rank, the more favorable a state's tax system is for business. States without a given tax are given a ranking of 1. The scores/rankings for the District of Columbia do not affect other states. The 2023 index represents the tax climate as of July 1, 2022.
Source: Tax Foundation, State Business Tax Climate Index 2023

TRANSPORTATION

Means of Transportation to Work

Area	Car/Truck/Van Drove Alone	Car/Truck/Van Carpooled	Public Transportation Bus	Public Transportation Subway	Public Transportation Railroad	Bicycle	Walked	Other Means	Worked at Home
City	63.8	5.7	1.5	0.0	0.0	0.4	20.3	1.6	6.7
MSA[1]	78.7	8.1	0.6	0.0	0.0	0.1	4.2	1.6	6.7
U.S.	73.2	8.6	2.0	1.6	0.5	0.5	2.5	1.5	9.7

Note: Figures are percentages and cover workers 16 years of age and older; (1) Figures cover the Columbia, SC Metropolitan Statistical Area
Source: U.S. Census Bureau, 2017-2021 American Community Survey 5-Year Estimates

Travel Time to Work

Area	Less Than 10 Minutes	10 to 19 Minutes	20 to 29 Minutes	30 to 44 Minutes	45 to 59 Minutes	60 to 89 Minutes	90 Minutes or More
City	29.8	36.0	19.0	10.0	2.1	1.8	1.4
MSA[1]	12.6	28.8	24.1	22.2	6.9	3.3	2.2
U.S.	12.4	28.5	21.0	20.9	8.2	6.2	2.9

Note: Note: Figures are percentages and include workers 16 years old and over; (1) Figures cover the Columbia, SC Metropolitan Statistical Area
Source: U.S. Census Bureau, 2017-2021 American Community Survey 5-Year Estimates

Key Congestion Measures

Measure	1990	2000	2010	2015	2020
Annual Hours of Delay, Total (000)	3,176	7,111	13,675	15,687	7,362
Annual Hours of Delay, Per Auto Commuter	18	29	41	44	19
Annual Congestion Cost, Per Auto Commuter ($)	287	482	732	776	370

Note: Covers the Columbia SC urban area
Source: Texas A&M Transportation Institute, 2021 Urban Mobility Report

Freeway Travel Time Index

Measure	1985	1990	1995	2000	2005	2010	2015	2020
Urban Area Index[1]	1.05	1.07	1.08	1.12	1.14	1.15	1.15	1.05
Urban Area Rank[1,2]	64	74	84	77	73	65	67	85

Note: Freeway Travel Time Index—the ratio of travel time in the peak period to the travel time at free-flow conditions. For example, a value of 1.30 indicates a 20-minute free-flow trip takes 26 minutes in the peak (20 minutes x 1.30 = 26 minutes); (1) Covers the Columbia SC urban area; (2) Rank is based on 101 larger urban areas (#1 = highest travel time index)
Source: Texas A&M Transportation Institute, 2021 Urban Mobility Report

Public Transportation

Agency Name / Mode of Transportation	Vehicles Operated in Maximum Service[1]	Annual Unlinked Passenger Trips[2] (in thous.)	Annual Passenger Miles[3] (in thous.)
Central Midlands Regional Transit Authority			
Bus (purchased transportation)	58	2,028.1	6,558.1
Commuter Bus (purchased transportation)	2	1.2	62.1
Demand Response (purchased transportation)	24	49.6	677.2
Demand Response - Transportation Network Company	13	5.9	18.9
Vanpool (purchased transportation)	14	31.1	1,871.1

Note: (1) Number of revenue vehicles operated by the given mode and type of service to meet the annual maximum service requirement. This is the revenue vehicle count during the peak season of the year; on the week and day that maximum service is provided. Vehicles operated in maximum service (VOMS) exclude atypical days and one-time special events; (2) Number of passengers who boarded public transportation vehicles. Passengers are counted each time they board a vehicle no matter how many vehicles they use to travel from their origin to their destination. (3) Sum of the distances ridden by all passengers during the entire fiscal year.
Source: Federal Transit Administration, National Transit Database, 2021

Air Transportation

Airport Name and Code / Type of Service	Passenger Airlines[1]	Passenger Enplanements	Freight Carriers[2]	Freight (lbs)
Columbia Metropolitan (CAE)				
Domestic service (U.S. carriers - 2022)	23	504,046	9	57,409,926
International service (U.S. carriers - 2021)	0	0	1	4,250

Note: (1) Includes all U.S.-based major, minor and commuter airlines that carried at least one passenger during the year; (2) Includes all U.S.-based airlines and freight carriers that transported at least one pound of freight during the year.
Source: Bureau of Transportation Statistics, The Intermodal Transportation Database, Air Carriers: T-100 Domestic Market (U.S. Carriers), 2022; Bureau of Transportation Statistics, The Intermodal Transportation Database, Air Carriers: T-100 International Market (U.S. Carriers), 2021

BUSINESSES

Major Business Headquarters

Company Name	Industry	Rankings Fortune[1]	Forbes[2]
No companies listed	-	-	-

Note: (1) Companies that produce a 10-K are ranked 1 to 500 based on 2021 revenue; (2) All private companies with at least $2 billion in annual revenue through the end of their most current fiscal year are ranked 1 to 246; companies listed are headquartered in the city; dashes indicate no ranking
Source: Fortune, "Fortune 500," 2022; Forbes, "America's Largest Private Companies," 2022

Living Environment

COST OF LIVING

Cost of Living Index

Composite Index	Groceries	Housing	Utilities	Transportation	Health Care	Misc. Goods/Services
94.5	102.0	74.3	134.2	76.7	87.4	102.6

Note: The Cost of Living Index measures regional differences in the cost of consumer goods and services, excluding taxes and non-consumer expenditures, for professional and managerial households in the top income quintile. It is based on more than 50,000 prices covering almost 60 different items for which prices are collected three times a year by chambers of commerce, economic development organizations or university applied economic centers in each participating urban area. The numbers shown should be read as a percentage above or below the national average of 100. For example, a value of 115.4 in the groceries column indicates that grocery prices are 15.4% higher than the national average. Small differences in the index numbers should not be interpreted as significant; Figures cover the Columbia SC urban area.
Source: The Council for Community and Economic Research, Cost of Living Index, 2022

Grocery Prices

Area[1]	T-Bone Steak ($/pound)	Frying Chicken ($/pound)	Whole Milk ($/half gal.)	Eggs ($/dozen)	Orange Juice ($/64 oz.)	Coffee ($/11.5 oz.)
City[2]	12.03	1.56	2.36	2.02	3.66	4.95
Avg.	13.81	1.59	2.43	2.25	3.85	4.95
Min.	10.17	0.90	1.51	1.30	2.90	3.46
Max.	19.35	3.30	4.32	4.32	5.31	8.59

Note: (1) Values for the local area are compared with the average, minimum and maximum values for all 286 areas in the Cost of Living Index; (2) Figures cover the Columbia SC urban area; **T-Bone Steak** (price per pound); **Frying Chicken** (price per pound, whole fryer); **Whole Milk** (half gallon carton); **Eggs** (price per dozen, Grade A, large); **Orange Juice** (64 oz. Tropicana or Florida Natural); **Coffee** (11.5 oz. can, vacuum-packed, Maxwell House, Hills Bros, or Folgers).
Source: The Council for Community and Economic Research, Cost of Living Index, 2022

Housing and Utility Costs

Area[1]	New Home Price ($)	Apartment Rent ($/month)	All Electric ($/month)	Part Electric ($/month)	Other Energy ($/month)	Telephone ($/month)
City[2]	322,903	1,107	-	112.85	167.25	190.68
Avg.	450,913	1,371	176.41	99.93	76.96	190.22
Min.	229,283	546	100.84	31.56	27.15	174.27
Max.	2,434,977	4,569	356.86	249.59	272.24	208.31

Note: (1) Values for the local area are compared with the average, minimum and maximum values for all 286 areas in the Cost of Living Index; (2) Figures cover the Columbia SC urban area; **New Home Price** (2,400 sf living area, 8,000 sf lot, in urban area with full utilities); **Apartment Rent** (950 sf 2 bedroom/1.5 or 2 bath, unfurnished, excluding all utilities except water); **All Electric** (average monthly cost for an all-electric home); **Part Electric** (average monthly cost for a part-electric home); **Other Energy** (average monthly cost for natural gas, fuel oil, coal, wood, and any other forms of energy except electricity); **Telephone** (price includes the base monthly rate plus taxes and fees for three lines of mobile phone service).
Source: The Council for Community and Economic Research, Cost of Living Index, 2022

Health Care, Transportation, and Other Costs

Area[1]	Doctor ($/visit)	Dentist ($/visit)	Optometrist ($/visit)	Gasoline ($/gallon)	Beauty Salon ($/visit)	Men's Shirt ($)
City[2]	124.17	82.50	53.00	3.26	42.36	37.12
Avg.	124.91	107.77	117.66	3.86	43.31	34.21
Min.	36.61	58.25	51.79	2.90	22.18	13.05
Max.	250.21	162.58	371.96	5.54	85.61	63.54

Note: (1) Values for the local area are compared with the average, minimum and maximum values for all 286 areas in the Cost of Living Index; (2) Figures cover the Columbia SC urban area; **Doctor** (general practitioners routine exam of an established patient); **Dentist** (adult teeth cleaning and periodic oral examination); **Optometrist** (full vision eye exam for established adult patient); **Gasoline** (one gallon regular unleaded, national brand, including all taxes, cash price at self-service pump if available); **Beauty Salon** (woman's shampoo, trim, and blow-dry); **Men's Shirt** (cotton/polyester dress shirt, pinpoint weave, long sleeves).
Source: The Council for Community and Economic Research, Cost of Living Index, 2022

HOUSING

Homeownership Rate

Area	2015 (%)	2016 (%)	2017 (%)	2018 (%)	2019 (%)	2020 (%)	2021 (%)	2022 (%)
MSA[1]	66.1	63.9	70.7	69.3	65.9	69.7	69.4	70.9
U.S.	63.7	63.4	63.9	64.4	64.6	66.6	65.5	65.8

Note: (1) Figures cover the Columbia, SC Metropolitan Statistical Area
Source: U.S. Census Bureau, Housing Vacancies and Homeownership Annual Statistics: 2015-2022

House Price Index (HPI)

Area	National Ranking[2]	Quarterly Change (%)	One-Year Change (%)	Five-Year Change (%)	Since 1991Q1 (%)
MSA[1]	23	1.44	18.32	59.58	209.37
U.S.[3]	—	0.34	8.41	58.44	289.08

Note: The HPI is a weighted repeat sales index. It measures average price changes in repeat sales or refinancings on the same properties. This information is obtained by reviewing repeat mortgage transactions on single-family properties whose mortgages have been purchased or securitized by Fannie Mae or Freddie Mac since January 1975; (1) Figures cover the Columbia, SC Metropolitan Statistical Area; (2) Rankings are based on annual percentage change for all metro areas containing at least 15,000 transactions over the last 10 years and ranges from 1 to 257; (3) figures based on a weighted average of Census Division estimates using a seasonally adjusted, purchase-only index; all figures are for the period ending December 31, 2022
Source: Federal Housing Finance Agency, Change in FHFA Metropolitan Area House Price Indexes, 2022Q4

Median Single-Family Home Prices

Area	2020	2021	2022[p]	Percent Change 2021 to 2022
MSA[1]	202.9	233.2	269.9	15.7
U.S. Average	300.2	357.1	392.6	9.9

Note: Figures are median sales prices of existing single-family homes in thousands of dollars; (p) preliminary; (1) Figures cover the Columbia, SC Metropolitan Statistical Area
Source: National Association of Realtors, Median Sales Price of Existing Single-Family Homes for Metropolitan Areas, 4th Quarter 2022

Qualifying Income Based on Median Sales Price of Existing Single-Family Homes

Area	With 5% Down ($)	With 10% Down ($)	With 20% Down ($)
MSA[1]	78,985	74,827	66,513
U.S. Average	112,234	106,237	94,513

Note: Figures are preliminary; Qualifying income is based on a mortgage rate of 6.77%. Monthly principal and interest payment is limited to 25% of income; (1) Figures cover the Columbia, SC Metropolitan Statistical Area
Source: National Association of Realtors, Qualifying Income Based on Median Sales Price of Existing Single-Family Homes for Metropolitan Areas, 4th Quarter 2022

Home Value

Area	Under $100,000	$100,000 -$199,999	$200,000 -$299,999	$300,000 -$399,999	$400,000 -$499,999	$500,000 -$999,999	$1,000,000 or more	Median ($)
City	17.9	34.1	18.9	9.7	5.5	11.7	2.2	193,100
MSA[1]	22.5	38.6	19.7	9.2	4.2	4.9	1.0	167,800
U.S.	16.2	24.2	20.1	13.6	8.3	13.6	4.1	244,900

Note: Figures are percentages except for median and cover owner-occupied housing units; (1) Figures cover the Columbia, SC Metropolitan Statistical Area
Source: U.S. Census Bureau, 2017-2021 American Community Survey 5-Year Estimates

Year Housing Structure Built

Area	2020 or Later	2010 -2019	2000 -2009	1990 -1999	1980 -1989	1970 -1979	1960 -1969	1950 -1959	1940 -1949	Before 1940	Median Year
City	0.2	9.3	15.2	11.3	10.2	10.2	10.2	13.9	10.1	9.5	1976
MSA[1]	0.3	11.3	18.6	18.3	13.7	14.9	9.2	6.7	3.2	3.7	1989
U.S.	0.2	7.3	13.6	13.6	13.2	14.8	10.3	10.0	4.7	12.2	1979

Note: Figures are percentages except for Median Year; Note: (1) Figures cover the Columbia, SC Metropolitan Statistical Area
Source: U.S. Census Bureau, 2017-2021 American Community Survey 5-Year Estimates

Gross Monthly Rent

Area	Under $500	$500 -$999	$1,000 -$1,499	$1,500 -$1,999	$2,000 -$2,499	$2,500 -$2,999	$3,000 and up	Median ($)
City	10.3	38.9	37.0	11.2	2.0	0.3	0.3	1,007
MSA[1]	7.1	43.7	35.6	9.8	2.7	0.5	0.5	993
U.S.	8.1	30.5	30.8	16.8	7.3	3.1	3.5	1,163

Note: Figures are percentages except for median; Gross rent is the contract rent plus the estimated average monthly cost of utilities (electricity, gas, and water and sewer) and fuels (oil, coal, kerosene, wood, etc.) if these are paid by the renter (or paid for the renter by someone else); (1) Figures cover the Columbia, SC Metropolitan Statistical Area
Source: U.S. Census Bureau, 2017-2021 American Community Survey 5-Year Estimates

HEALTH

Health Risk Factors

Category	MSA[1] (%)	U.S. (%)
Adults aged 18–64 who have any kind of health care coverage	88.4	90.9
Adults who reported being in good or better health	82.2	85.2
Adults who have been told they have high blood cholesterol	37.6	35.7
Adults who have been told they have high blood pressure	33.7	32.4
Adults who are current smokers	17.2	14.4
Adults who currently use e-cigarettes	8.0	6.7
Adults who currently use chewing tobacco, snuff, or snus	2.3	3.5
Adults who are heavy drinkers[2]	7.1	6.3
Adults who are binge drinkers[3]	17.4	15.4
Adults who are overweight (BMI 25.0 - 29.9)	36.5	34.4
Adults who are obese (BMI 30.0 - 99.8)	35.1	33.9
Adults who participated in any physical activities in the past month	75.3	76.3

Note: (1) Figures cover the Columbia, SC Metropolitan Statistical Area; (2) Heavy drinkers are classified as adult men having more than 14 drinks per week and adult women having more than 7 drinks per week; (3) Binge drinkers are classified as males having five or more drinks on one occasion or females having four or more drinks on one occasion
Source: Centers for Disease Control and Prevention, Behaviorial Risk Factor Surveillance System, SMART: Selected Metropolitan Area Risk Trends, 2021

Acute and Chronic Health Conditions

Category	MSA[1] (%)	U.S. (%)
Adults who have ever been told they had a heart attack	4.2	4.0
Adults who have ever been told they have angina or coronary heart disease	4.3	3.8
Adults who have ever been told they had a stroke	2.7	3.0
Adults who have ever been told they have asthma	15.7	14.9
Adults who have ever been told they have arthritis	29.5	25.8
Adults who have ever been told they have diabetes[2]	13.2	10.9
Adults who have ever been told they had skin cancer	5.7	6.6
Adults who have ever been told they had any other types of cancer	7.4	7.5
Adults who have ever been told they have COPD	7.2	6.1
Adults who have ever been told they have kidney disease	2.9	3.0
Adults who have ever been told they have a form of depression	20.5	20.5

Note: (1) Figures cover the Columbia, SC Metropolitan Statistical Area; (2) Figures do not include pregnancy-related, borderline, or pre-diabetes
Source: Centers for Disease Control and Prevention, Behaviorial Risk Factor Surveillance System, SMART: Selected Metropolitan Area Risk Trends, 2021

Health Screening and Vaccination Rates

Category	MSA[1] (%)	U.S. (%)
Adults who have ever been tested for HIV	43.9	34.9
Adults who have had their blood cholesterol checked within the last five years	86.0	85.2
Adults aged 65+ who have had flu shot within the past year	59.7	68.6
Adults aged 65+ who have ever had a pneumonia vaccination	69.9	71.0

Note: (1) Figures cover the Columbia, SC Metropolitan Statistical Area.
Source: Centers for Disease Control and Prevention, Behaviorial Risk Factor Surveillance System, SMART: Selected Metropolitan Area Risk Trends, 2021

Disability Status

Category	MSA[1] (%)	U.S. (%)
Adults who reported being deaf	6.5	7.2
Are you blind or have serious difficulty seeing, even when wearing glasses?	6.2	4.8
Are you limited in any way in any of your usual activities due to arthritis?	12.6	11.1
Do you have difficulty doing errands alone?	9.2	7.0
Do you have difficulty dressing or bathing?	4.4	3.6
Do you have serious difficulty concentrating/remembering/making decisions?	13.8	12.1
Do you have serious difficulty walking or climbing stairs?	16.6	12.8

Note: (1) Figures cover the Columbia, SC Metropolitan Statistical Area.
Source: Centers for Disease Control and Prevention, Behaviorial Risk Factor Surveillance System, SMART: Selected Metropolitan Area Risk Trends, 2021

Mortality Rates for the Top 10 Causes of Death in the U.S.

ICD-10[a] Sub-Chapter	ICD-10[a] Code	Crude Mortality Rate[1] per 100,000 population County[2]	U.S.
Malignant neoplasms	C00-C97	166.6	182.6
Ischaemic heart diseases	I20-I25	92.1	113.1
Other forms of heart disease	I30-I51	42.4	64.4
Other degenerative diseases of the nervous system	G30-G31	47.1	51.0
Cerebrovascular diseases	I60-I69	35.6	47.8
Other external causes of accidental injury	W00-X59	39.2	46.4
Chronic lower respiratory diseases	J40-J47	28.7	45.7
Organic, including symptomatic, mental disorders	F01-F09	32.6	35.9
Hypertensive diseases	I10-I15	44.0	35.0
Diabetes mellitus	E10-E14	25.9	29.6

Note: (a) ICD-10 = International Classification of Diseases 10th Revision; (1) Crude mortality rates are a three-year average covering 2019-2021; (2) Figures cover Richland County.
Source: Centers for Disease Control and Prevention, National Center for Health Statistics. National Vital Statistics System, Mortality 2018-2021 on CDC WONDER Online Database

Mortality Rates for Selected Causes of Death

ICD-10[a] Sub-Chapter	ICD-10[a] Code	Crude Mortality Rate[1] per 100,000 population County[2]	U.S.
Assault	X85-Y09	14.2	7.0
Diseases of the liver	K70-K76	17.7	19.8
Human immunodeficiency virus (HIV) disease	B20-B24	3.8	1.5
Influenza and pneumonia	J09-J18	8.8	14.7
Intentional self-harm	X60-X84	12.0	14.3
Malnutrition	E40-E46	7.6	4.3
Obesity and other hyperalimentation	E65-E68	Unreliable	3.0
Renal failure	N17-N19	13.6	15.7
Transport accidents	V01-V99	17.3	13.6
Viral hepatitis	B15-B19	Unreliable	1.2

Note: (a) ICD-10 = International Classification of Diseases 10th Revision; (1) Crude mortality rates are a three-year average covering 2019-2021; (2) Figures cover Richland County; Data are suppressed when the data meet the criteria for confidentiality constraints; Crude mortality rates are flagged as unreliable when the rate would be calculated with a numerator of 20 or less.
Source: Centers for Disease Control and Prevention, National Center for Health Statistics. National Vital Statistics System, Mortality 2018-2021 on CDC WONDER Online Database

Health Insurance Coverage

Area	With Health Insurance	With Private Health Insurance	With Public Health Insurance	Without Health Insurance	Population Under Age 19 Without Health Insurance
City	91.4	70.7	30.7	8.6	3.4
MSA[1]	90.4	69.8	34.4	9.6	4.5
U.S.	91.2	67.8	35.4	8.8	5.3

Note: Figures are percentages that cover the civilian noninstitutionalized population; (1) Figures cover the Columbia, SC Metropolitan Statistical Area
Source: U.S. Census Bureau, 2017-2021 American Community Survey 5-Year Estimates

Number of Medical Professionals

Area	MDs[3]	DOs[3,4]	Dentists	Podiatrists	Chiropractors	Optometrists
County[1] (number)	1,488	64	392	30	94	83
County[1] (rate[2])	357.2	15.4	93.7	7.2	22.5	19.8
U.S. (rate[2])	289.3	23.5	72.5	6.2	28.7	17.4

Note: Data as of 2021 unless noted; (1) Data covers Richland County; (2) Rate per 100,000 population; (3) Data as of 2020 and includes all active, non-federal physicians; (4) Doctor of Osteopathic Medicine
Source: U.S. Department of Health and Human Services, Health Resources and Services Administration, Bureau of Health Professions, Area Resource File (ARF) 2021-2022

EDUCATION

Public School District Statistics

District Name	Schls	Pupils	Pupil/Teacher Ratio	Minority Pupils[1] (%)	LEP/ELL[2] (%)	IEP[3] (%)
Charter Institute at Erskine	26	24,409	22.9	42.1	3.6	11.6
Richland 01	48	22,151	11.6	82.2	3.3	13.9
Richland 02	32	28,303	14.4	82.1	4.7	13.4
SC Public Charter School District	38	17,097	13.5	47.7	3.5	11.3

Note: Table includes school districts with 2,000 or more students; (1) Percentage of students that are not non-Hispanic white; (2) Percentage of students that are Limited English Proficient or English Language Learners (2018-19); (3) Percentage of students that have an Individualized Education Program (2019-20).
Source: U.S. Department of Education, National Center for Education Statistics, Common Core of Data, Local Education Agency (School District) Universe Survey: School Year 2021-2022

Highest Level of Education

Area	Less than H.S.	H.S. Diploma	Some College, No Deg.	Associate Degree	Bachelor's Degree	Master's Degree	Prof. School Degree	Doctorate Degree
City	9.5	19.3	18.8	7.7	25.1	11.7	4.5	3.3
MSA[1]	9.4	26.0	21.5	9.5	20.5	9.2	2.1	1.8
U.S.	11.1	26.5	20.0	8.7	20.6	9.3	2.2	1.5

Note: Figures cover persons age 25 and over; (1) Figures cover the Columbia, SC Metropolitan Statistical Area
Source: U.S. Census Bureau, 2017-2021 American Community Survey 5-Year Estimates

Educational Attainment by Race

Area	High School Graduate or Higher (%)					Bachelor's Degree or Higher (%)				
	Total	White	Black	Asian	Hisp.[2]	Total	White	Black	Asian	Hisp.[2]
City	90.5	96.2	83.5	95.7	87.6	44.7	63.4	21.6	76.0	35.4
MSA[1]	90.6	92.8	88.1	92.3	70.0	33.6	37.9	24.7	62.2	23.1
U.S.	88.9	91.4	87.2	87.6	71.2	33.7	35.5	23.3	55.6	18.4

Note: Figures shown cover persons 25 years old and over; (1) Figures cover the Columbia, SC Metropolitan Statistical Area; (2) People of Hispanic origin can be of any race
Source: U.S. Census Bureau, 2017-2021 American Community Survey 5-Year Estimates

School Enrollment by Grade and Control

Area	Preschool (%)		Kindergarten (%)		Grades 1 - 4 (%)		Grades 5 - 8 (%)		Grades 9 - 12 (%)	
	Public	Private	Public	Private	Public	Private	Public	Private	Public	Private
City	50.6	49.4	75.0	25.0	88.4	11.6	86.6	13.4	91.7	8.3
MSA[1]	58.5	41.5	90.7	9.3	92.0	8.0	92.7	7.3	92.9	7.1
U.S.	58.8	41.2	86.3	13.7	88.3	11.7	88.6	11.4	89.4	10.6

Note: Figures shown cover persons 3 years old and over; (1) Figures cover the Columbia, SC Metropolitan Statistical Area
Source: U.S. Census Bureau, 2017-2021 American Community Survey 5-Year Estimates

Higher Education

Four-Year Colleges			Two-Year Colleges			Medical Schools[1]	Law Schools[2]	Voc/Tech[3]
Public	Private Non-profit	Private For-profit	Public	Private Non-profit	Private For-profit			
1	5	1	1	0	2	1	1	6

Note: Figures cover institutions located within the Columbia, SC Metropolitan Statistical Area and include main campuses only; (1) includes schools accredited by the Liaison Committee on Medical Education and the American Osteopathic Association's Commission on Osteopathic College Accreditation; (2) includes ABA-accredited schools, schools with provisional ABA accreditation, and state accredited schools; (3) includes all schools with programs that are less than 2 years.
Source: National Center for Education Statistics, Integrated Postsecondary Education System (IPEDS), 2021-22; Wikipedia, List of Medical Schools in the United States, accessed April 10, 2023; Wikipedia, List of Law Schools in the United States, accessed April 10, 2023

According to *U.S. News & World Report,* the Columbia, SC metro area is home to one of the top 200 national universities in the U.S.: **University of South Carolina** (#115 tie). The indicators used to capture academic quality fall into a number of categories: assessment by administrators at peer institutions; retention of students; faculty resources; student selectivity; financial resources; alumni giving; high school counselor ratings of colleges; and graduation rate. *U.S. News & World Report, "America's Best Colleges 2023"*

According to *U.S. News & World Report,* the Columbia, SC metro area is home to one of the top 100 law schools in the U.S.: **University of South Carolina** (#84 tie). The rankings are based on a weighted average of 12 measures of quality: peer assessment score; assessment score by lawyers/judges; median LSAT scores; median undergrad GPA; acceptance rate; employment rates for graduates; placement success; bar passage rate; faculty resources; expenditures per student; student/faculty ratio; and library resources. *U.S. News & World Report, "America's Best Graduate Schools, Law, 2023"*

According to *U.S. News & World Report,* the Columbia, SC metro area is home to one of the top 75 business schools in the U.S.: **University of South Carolina (Moore)** (#47 tie). The rankings are based on a weighted average of the following nine measures: quality assessment; peer assessment; recruiter assessment; placement success; mean starting salary and bonus; student selectivity; mean GMAT and GRE scores; mean undergraduate GPA; and acceptance rate. *U.S. News & World Report, "America's Best Graduate Schools, Business, 2023"*

EMPLOYERS

Major Employers

Company Name	Industry
AnMed Health	Healthcare
Baldor Electric Co	Utilities
Ben Arnold Beverage Co	Beverages
Berkeley County School Dist	Education
BlueCross BlueShield of SC	Finance, insurance and real estate
BMW Manufacturing Co	Manufacturing
Bon Secours St Francis Hosp	Healthcare
Charleston AIR Force Base	U.S. military
City of Columbia	Municipal government
Clemson University Research	Healthcare
Continental Tire North America	Wholesaling/manufacturing
Corrections Dept.	Government
Crescent Moon Diving	Professional, scientific, technical
Fluor Enterprises Inc	Engineering services
Greenville Memorial Hospital	Healthcare
Lexington Medical Ctr	Healthcare
McLeod Health	Healthcare
Medical University of SC	Healthcare/university
Palmetto Health	Health care & social assistance
Piggly Wiggly	Grocery stores
Pilgrim's Pride Corp	Poultry processing
Richland County	Government
Richland School District 1 & 2	Education
Robert Bosch	Manufacturing
Shaw Air Force Base	U.S. military
Sonoco Plastics Inc	Manufacturing
Spartanburg Regional Healthcre	Healthcare
University of South Carolina	Education
Women's Imaging Center	Healthcare

Note: Companies shown are located within the Columbia, SC Metropolitan Statistical Area.
Source: Hoovers.com; Wikipedia

PUBLIC SAFETY

Crime Rate

Area	Total Crime	Violent Crime Rate				Property Crime Rate		
		Murder	Rape[3]	Robbery	Aggrav. Assault	Burglary	Larceny-Theft	Motor Vehicle Theft
City	5,227.8	14.4	65.3	156.3	516.0	552.4	3,442.2	481.1
Suburbs[1]	3,572.6	8.2	37.6	61.2	415.2	504.0	2,183.1	363.3
Metro[2]	3,830.0	9.2	41.9	76.0	430.9	511.5	2,378.9	381.6
U.S.	2,356.7	6.5	38.4	73.9	279.7	314.2	1,398.0	246.0

Note: Figures are crimes per 100,000 population; (1) All areas within the metro area that are located outside the city limits; (2) Figures cover the Columbia, SC Metropolitan Statistical Area; (3) All figures shown were reported using the revised Uniform Crime Reporting (UCR) definition of rape; Due to the transition to the National Incident-Based Reporting System (NIBRS), limited city and metro area data was released for 2021.
Source: FBI Uniform Crime Reports, 2020

Hate Crimes

Area	Number of Quarters Reported	Number of Incidents per Bias Motivation					
		Race/Ethnicity/Ancestry	Religion	Sexual Orientation	Disability	Gender	Gender Identity
City	4	2	0	0	0	0	0
U.S.	4	5,227	1,244	1,110	130	75	266

Note: Due to the transition to the National Incident-Based Reporting System (NIBRS), limited crime data was released for 2021.
Source: Federal Bureau of Investigation, Hate Crime Statistics 2020

Identity Theft Consumer Reports

Area	Reports	Reports per 100,000 Population	Rank[2]
MSA[1]	4,455	535	14
U.S.	1,108,609	339	-

Note: (1) Figures cover the Columbia, SC Metropolitan Statistical Area; (2) Rank ranges from 1 to 391 where 1 indicates greatest number of identity theft reports per 100,000 population
Source: Federal Trade Commission, Consumer Sentinel Network Data Book 2022

Fraud and Other Consumer Reports

Area	Reports	Reports per 100,000 Population	Rank[2]
MSA[1]	11,022	1,323	24
U.S.	4,064,520	1,245	-

Note: (1) Figures cover the Columbia, SC Metropolitan Statistical Area; (2) Rank ranges from 1 to 391 where 1 indicates greatest number of fraud and other consumer reports per 100,000 population
Source: Federal Trade Commission, Consumer Sentinel Network Data Book 2022

POLITICS

2020 Presidential Election Results

Area	Biden	Trump	Jorgensen	Hawkins	Other
Richland County	68.4	30.1	1.0	0.4	0.1
U.S.	51.3	46.8	1.2	0.3	0.5

Note: Results are percentages and may not add to 100% due to rounding
Source: Dave Leip's Atlas of U.S. Presidential Elections

SPORTS

Professional Sports Teams

Team Name	League	Year Established

No teams are located in the metro area
Source: Wikipedia, Major Professional Sports Teams of the United States and Canada, April 12, 2023

CLIMATE

Average and Extreme Temperatures

Temperature	Jan	Feb	Mar	Apr	May	Jun	Jul	Aug	Sep	Oct	Nov	Dec	Yr.
Extreme High (°F)	84	84	91	94	101	107	107	107	101	101	90	83	107
Average High (°F)	56	60	67	77	84	90	92	91	85	77	67	59	75
Average Temp. (°F)	45	48	55	64	72	78	82	80	75	64	54	47	64
Average Low (°F)	33	35	42	50	59	66	70	69	64	51	41	35	51
Extreme Low (°F)	-1	5	4	26	34	44	54	53	40	23	12	4	-1

Note: Figures cover the years 1948-1990
Source: National Climatic Data Center, International Station Meteorological Climate Summary, 9/96

Average Precipitation/Snowfall/Humidity

Precip./Humidity	Jan	Feb	Mar	Apr	May	Jun	Jul	Aug	Sep	Oct	Nov	Dec	Yr.
Avg. Precip. (in.)	4.0	4.0	4.7	3.4	3.6	4.2	5.5	5.9	4.0	2.9	2.7	3.4	48.3
Avg. Snowfall (in.)	1	1	Tr	0	0	0	0	0	0	0	Tr	Tr	2
Avg. Rel. Hum. 7am (%)	83	83	84	82	84	85	88	91	91	90	88	84	86
Avg. Rel. Hum. 4pm (%)	51	47	44	41	46	50	54	56	54	49	48	51	49

Note: Figures cover the years 1948-1990; Tr = Trace amounts (<0.05 in. of rain; <0.5 in. of snow)
Source: National Climatic Data Center, International Station Meteorological Climate Summary, 9/96

Weather Conditions

Temperature			Daytime Sky			Precipitation		
10°F & below	32°F & below	90°F & above	Clear	Partly cloudy	Cloudy	0.01 inch or more precip.	0.1 inch or more snow/ice	Thunder-storms
<1	58	77	97	149	119	110	1	53

Note: Figures are average number of days per year and cover the years 1948-1990
Source: National Climatic Data Center, International Station Meteorological Climate Summary, 9/96

HAZARDOUS WASTE

Superfund Sites

The Columbia, SC metro area is home to four sites on the EPA's Superfund National Priorities List: **Lexington County Landfill Area** (final); **Palmetto Wood Preserving** (final); **SCRDI Bluff Road** (final); **SCRDI Dixiana** (final). There are a total of 1,165 Superfund sites with a status of proposed or final on the list in the U.S. *U.S. Environmental Protection Agency, National Priorities List, April 12, 2023*

AIR QUALITY

Air Quality Trends: Ozone

	1990	1995	2000	2005	2010	2015	2018	2019	2020	2021
MSA[1]	0.091	0.079	0.089	0.082	0.069	0.058	0.059	0.063	0.053	0.061
U.S.	0.087	0.089	0.081	0.080	0.072	0.067	0.069	0.065	0.065	0.067

Note: (1) Data covers the Columbia, SC Metropolitan Statistical Area. The values shown are the composite ozone concentration averages among trend sites based on the highest fourth daily maximum 8-hour concentration in parts per million. These trends are based on sites having an adequate record of monitoring data during the trend period. Data from exceptional events are included.
Source: U.S. Environmental Protection Agency, Air Quality Monitoring Information, "Air Quality Trends by City, 1990-2021"

Air Quality Index

Area	\multicolumn{5}{c}{Percent of Days when Air Quality was...[2]}	\multicolumn{2}{c}{AQI Statistics[2]}
	Good	Moderate	Unhealthy for Sensitive Groups	Unhealthy	Very Unhealthy	Maximum	Median
MSA[1]	74.0	25.5	0.5	0.0	0.0	102	41

Note: (1) Data covers the Columbia, SC Metropolitan Statistical Area; (2) Based on 365 days with AQI data in 2021. Air Quality Index (AQI) is an index for reporting daily air quality. EPA calculates the AQI for five major air pollutants regulated by the Clean Air Act: ground-level ozone, particle pollution (aka particulate matter), carbon monoxide, sulfur dioxide, and nitrogen dioxide. The AQI runs from 0 to 500. The higher the AQI value, the greater the level of air pollution and the greater the health concern. There are six AQI categories: "Good" AQI is between 0 and 50. Air quality is considered satisfactory; "Moderate" AQI is between 51 and 100. Air quality is acceptable; "Unhealthy for Sensitive Groups" When AQI values are between 101 and 150, members of sensitive groups may experience health effects; "Unhealthy" When AQI values are between 151 and 200 everyone may begin to experience health effects; "Very Unhealthy" AQI values between 201 and 300 trigger a health alert; "Hazardous" AQI values over 300 trigger warnings of emergency conditions (not shown).
Source: U.S. Environmental Protection Agency, Air Quality Index Report, 2021

Air Quality Index Pollutants

Area	\multicolumn{6}{c}{Percent of Days when AQI Pollutant was...[2]}
	Carbon Monoxide	Nitrogen Dioxide	Ozone	Sulfur Dioxide	Particulate Matter 2.5	Particulate Matter 10
MSA[1]	0.0	0.0	51.8	(3)	48.2	0.0

Note: (1) Data covers the Columbia, SC Metropolitan Statistical Area; (2) Based on 365 days with AQI data in 2021. The Air Quality Index (AQI) is an index for reporting daily air quality. EPA calculates the AQI for five major air pollutants regulated by the Clean Air Act: ground-level ozone, particle pollution (also known as particulate matter), carbon monoxide, sulfur dioxide, and nitrogen dioxide. The AQI runs from 0 to 500. The higher the AQI value, the greater the level of air pollution and the greater the health concern; (3) Sulfur dioxide is no longer included in this table (as of December 8, 2021) because SO_2 concentrations tend to be very localized and not necessarily representative of broad geographical areas like counties and CBSAs.
Source: U.S. Environmental Protection Agency, Air Quality Index Report, 2021

Maximum Air Pollutant Concentrations: Particulate Matter, Ozone, CO and Lead

	Particulate Matter 10 (ug/m³)	Particulate Matter 2.5 Wtd AM (ug/m³)	Particulate Matter 2.5 24-Hr (ug/m³)	Ozone (ppm)	Carbon Monoxide (ppm)	Lead (ug/m³)
MSA[1] Level	42	9	22	0.064	1	n/a
NAAQS[2]	150	15	35	0.075	9	0.15
Met NAAQS[2]	Yes	Yes	Yes	Yes	Yes	n/a

Note: (1) Data covers the Columbia, SC Metropolitan Statistical Area; Data from exceptional events are included; (2) National Ambient Air Quality Standards; ppm = parts per million; ug/m³ = micrograms per cubic meter; n/a not available.
Concentrations: Particulate Matter 10 (coarse particulate)—highest second maximum 24-hour concentration; Particulate Matter 2.5 Wtd AM (fine particulate)—highest weighted annual mean concentration; Particulate Matter 2.5 24-Hour (fine particulate)—highest 98th percentile 24-hour concentration; Ozone—highest fourth daily maximum 8-hour concentration; Carbon Monoxide—highest second maximum non-overlapping 8-hour concentration; Lead—maximum running 3-month average
Source: U.S. Environmental Protection Agency, Air Quality Monitoring Information, "Air Quality Statistics by City, 2021"

Maximum Air Pollutant Concentrations: Nitrogen Dioxide and Sulfur Dioxide

	Nitrogen Dioxide AM (ppb)	Nitrogen Dioxide 1-Hr (ppb)	Sulfur Dioxide AM (ppb)	Sulfur Dioxide 1-Hr (ppb)	Sulfur Dioxide 24-Hr (ppb)
MSA[1] Level	n/a	n/a	n/a	1	n/a
NAAQS[2]	53	100	30	75	140
Met NAAQS[2]	n/a	n/a	n/a	Yes	n/a

Note: (1) Data covers the Columbia, SC Metropolitan Statistical Area; Data from exceptional events are included; (2) National Ambient Air Quality Standards; ppm = parts per million; ug/m³ = micrograms per cubic meter; n/a not available.
Concentrations: Nitrogen Dioxide AM—highest arithmetic mean concentration; Nitrogen Dioxide 1-Hr—highest 98th percentile 1-hour daily maximum concentration; Sulfur Dioxide AM—highest annual mean concentration; Sulfur Dioxide 1-Hr—highest 99th percentile 1-hour daily maximum concentration; Sulfur Dioxide 24-Hr—highest second maximum 24-hour concentration
Source: U.S. Environmental Protection Agency, Air Quality Monitoring Information, "Air Quality Statistics by City, 2021"

Dallas, Texas

Background

Dallas is one of those cities that offer everything. Founded in 1841 by Tennessee lawyer and trader, John Neely Bryan, Dallas has come to symbolize all that is big, exciting, and affluent. The city itself is in the top ten worldwide among cities with the most billionaires. When combined with those billionaires who live in Dallas's neighboring city of Fort Worth, the area has one of the greatest concentrations of billionaires in the world.

Originally one of the largest markets for cotton in the U.S., Dallas moved on to become one of the largest markets for oil in the country. In the 1930s, oil was struck on the eastern fields of Texas. As a result, oil companies were founded and billions were made, creating the face we now associate with Dallas and the state of Texas.

Today, oil still plays a dominant role in the Dallas economy. Outside of Alaska, Texas holds most of the U.S. oil reserves. For that reason, many oil companies choose to headquarter in the silver skyscrapers of Dallas, which is also home to 12 Fortune 500 companies.

In addition to employment opportunities in the oil industry, the Dallas branch of the Federal Reserve Bank, and a host of other banks and investment firms clustering around the Federal Reserve hub employ thousands. Other opportunities are offered in aircraft, advertising, film, and publishing industries. The city is sometimes referred to as Texas's "Silicon Prairie" because of a high concentration of telecommunications companies.

The Kay Bailey Hutchison Convention Center Dallas, with more than two million square feet (over one million in exhibit space), is the largest convention center in Texas, and one of the largest in the country. Each year it welcomes over a million visitors. In 2022, the Dallas City Council approved plans for a new, 2.5 million-square-foot replacement; construction is expected to begin in 2024 and be complete in 2029. Dallas also has a significant cultural presence with independent theater groups sponsored by Southern Methodist University; Museum of Art with its collection of modern, especially American, art; and Winspear Opera House as part of the AT&T Performing Arts Center.

Dallas Opera has showcased Maria Callas, Joan Sutherland, and Monserrat Caballe. Dallas is the only city in the world with four buildings within one contiguous block designed by Pritzker Architecture Prize winners. The city also boasts historical districts such as the Swiss Avenue District, and elegant buildings such as the City Hall Building designed by I.M. Pei. A notable city event is the State Fair of Texas, which has been held annually at Fair Park since 1886 with exceptions during WWI and II and COVID-19. Recent numbers report the total annual attendance at about 2 million with an estimated $50 million to the city's economy.

The area's high concentration of wealth contributes to Dallas's wide array of shopping centers and high-end boutiques. Downtown Dallas is home to many cafes, restaurants, clubs, and its centrally located "Arts District," named for its many independent theaters and art galleries Northern districts of the city and the central downtown have seen much urban revival in the last 30 years.

Colleges and universities in the Dallas area include Southern Methodist University, University of Dallas, and University of Texas at Dallas. In 2006, University of North Texas opened a branch in the southern part of the city, in part, to help accelerate development south of downtown Dallas. The city maintains 21,000 acres of park land, with over 400 parks.

The climate of Dallas is generally temperate. Occasional periods of extreme cold are short-lived, and extremely high temperatures that sometimes occur in summer usually do not last for extended periods. In February 2021, a series of severe winter storms caused record low temperatures in Dallas, causing a massive power disruption in the state.

Rankings

General Rankings

- The Dallas metro area was identified as one of America's fastest-growing areas in terms of population and business growth by *MagnifyMoney*. The area ranked #7 out of 35. The 100 most populous metro areas in the U.S. were evaluated on their change from 2011 to 2016 in the following categories: people and housing; workforce and employment opportunities; growing industry. *www.businessinsider.com, "The 35 Cities in the US with the Biggest Influx of People, the Most Work Opportunities, and the Hottest Business Growth," August 12, 2018*

- The Dallas metro area was identified as one of America's fastest-growing areas in terms of population and economy by *Forbes*. The area ranked #3 out of 25. The 100 most populous metro areas in the U.S. were evaluated on the following criteria: estimated population growth; employment; economic output; wages; home values. *Forbes, "America's Fastest-Growing Cities 2018," February 28, 2018*

- The human resources consulting firm Mercer ranked 231 major cities worldwide in terms of overall quality of life. Dallas ranked #63. Criteria: political, social, economic, and socio-cultural factors; medical and health considerations; schools and education; public services and transportation; recreation; consumer goods; housing; and natural environment. *Mercer, "Mercer 2019 Quality of Living Survey," March 13, 2019*

Business/Finance Rankings

- Based on metro area social media reviews, the employment opinion group Glassdoor surveyed 50 of the most populous U.S. metro areas and equally weighed cost of living, hiring opportunity, and job satisfaction to compose a list of "25 Best Cities for Jobs." Median pay and home value, and number of active job openings were also factored in. The Dallas metro area was ranked #25 in overall job satisfaction. *www.glassdoor.com, "Best Cities for Jobs," February 25, 2020*

- The Brookings Institution ranked the nation's largest cities based on income inequality. Dallas was ranked #33 (#1 = greatest inequality). Criteria: the "95/20 ratio," a figure representing the income at which a household earns more than 95 percent of all other households, divided by the income at which a household earns more than only 20 percent of all other households. *Brookings Institution, "Household Income Inequality, Largest Cities of 97 Large U.S. Metro Areas, 2014-2016," February 5, 2018*

- The Brookings Institution ranked the 100 largest metro areas in the U.S. based on income inequality. Dallas was ranked #60 (#1 = greatest inequality). Criteria: the "95/20 ratio," a figure representing the income at which a household earns more than 95 percent of all other households, divided by the income at which a household earns more than only 20 percent of all other households. *Brookings Institution, "Household Income Inequality, 100 Largest U.S. Metro Areas, 2014-2016," February 5, 2018*

- The Dallas metro area was identified as one of the most debt-ridden places in America by the finance site Credit.com. The metro area was ranked #2. Criteria: residents' average credit card debt as well as median income. *Credit.com, "25 Cities With the Most Credit Card Debt," February 28, 2018*

- Dallas was identified as one of America's most frugal metro areas by *Coupons.com*. The city ranked #2 out of 25. Criteria: digital coupon usage. *Coupons.com, "America's Most Frugal Cities of 2017," March 22, 2018*

- *Forbes* ranked the 200 most populous metro areas to determine the nation's "Best Places for Business and Careers." The Dallas metro area was ranked #2. Criteria: costs (business and living); job growth (past and projected); income growth; quality of life; educational attainment (college and high school); projected economic growth; cultural and leisure opportunities; workplace tolerance laws; net migration patterns. *Forbes, "The Best Places for Business and Careers 2019: Seattle Still On Top," October 30, 2019*

- Mercer Human Resources Consulting ranked 227 cities worldwide in terms of cost-of-living. Dallas ranked #75 (the lower the ranking, the higher the cost-of-living). The survey measured the comparative cost of over 200 items (such as housing, food, clothing, domestic supplies, transportation, and recreation/entertainment) in each location. *Mercer, "2022 Cost of Living City Ranking," June 29, 2022*

Culture/Performing Arts Rankings

- Dallas was selected as one of the 25 best cities for moviemakers in North America. Great film cities are places where filmmaking dreams can come true, that offer more creative space, lower costs, and great outdoor locations. NYC & LA were intentionally excluded. Criteria: longstanding reputations as film-friendly communities; film community and culture; affordability; and quality of life. The city was ranked #20. *MovieMaker Magazine, "Best Places to Live and Work as a Moviemaker, 2023," January 18, 2023*

Dating/Romance Rankings

- *Apartment List* conducted its Annual Renter Satisfaction Survey and asked renters "how satisfied are you with opportunities for dating in your current city." The cities were ranked from highest to lowest based on their satisfaction scores. Dallas ranked #10 out of 85 cities. *Apartment List, "Best Cities for Dating 2022 with Local Dating Insights from Bumble," February 7, 2022*

Education Rankings

- Dallas was selected as one of the best cities for post grads by *Rent.com*. The city ranked among the top 10. Criteria: jobs per capita; unemployment rate; mean annual income; cost of living; rental inventory. *Rent.com, "Best Cities for College Grads," December 11, 2018*

- Dallas was selected as one of America's most literate cities. The city ranked #36 out of the 84 largest U.S. cities. Criteria: number of booksellers; library resources; Internet resources; educational attainment; periodical publishing resources; newspaper circulation. *Central Connecticut State University, "America's Most Literate Cities, 2018," February 2019*

Environmental Rankings

- Sperling's BestPlaces assessed the 50 largest metropolitan areas of the United States for the likelihood of dangerously extreme weather events or earthquakes. In general the Southeast and South-Central regions have the highest risk of weather extremes and earthquakes, while the Pacific Northwest enjoys the lowest risk. Of the most risky metropolitan areas, the Dallas metro area was ranked #4. *www.bestplaces.net, "Avoid Natural Disasters: BestPlaces Reveals The Top 10 Safest Places to Live," October 25, 2017*

- The U.S. Environmental Protection Agency (EPA) released its list of U.S. metropolitan areas with the most ENERGY STAR certified buildings in 2022. The Dallas metro area was ranked #8 out of 25. *U.S. Environmental Protection Agency, "2023 Energy Star Top Cities," April 26, 2023*

- Dallas was highlighted as one of the 25 most ozone-polluted metro areas in the U.S. during 2019 through 2021. The area ranked #18. *American Lung Association, "State of the Air 2023," April 19, 2023*

Food/Drink Rankings

- Globe Life Park was selected as one of PETA's "Top 10 Vegan-Friendly Ballparks" for 2019. The park ranked #1. *People for the Ethical Treatment of Animals, "Top 10 Vegan-Friendly Ballparks," May 23, 2019*

Health/Fitness Rankings

- For each of the 100 largest cities in the United States, the American Fitness Index®, compiled in partnership between the American College of Sports Medicine and the Elevance Health Foundation, evaluated community infrastructure and 34 health behaviors including preventive health, levels of chronic disease conditions, food insecurity, sleep quality, pedestrian safety, air quality, and community/environment resources that support physical activity. Dallas ranked #57 for "community fitness." *americanfitnessindex.org, "2022 ACSM American Fitness Index Summary Report," July 12, 2022*

- Dallas was identified as a "2022 Spring Allergy Capital." The area ranked #32 out of 100. Three groups of factors were used to identify the most challenging cities for people with allergies during the spring season: annual spring pollen scores; over the counter allergy medicine use; number of board-certified allergy specialists. *Asthma and Allergy Foundation of America, "Spring Allergy Capitals 2022," March 2, 2022*

- Dallas was identified as a "2022 Fall Allergy Capital." The area ranked #22 out of 100. Three groups of factors were used to identify the most challenging cities for people with allergies during the fall season: annual fall pollen scores; over the counter allergy medicine use; number of board-certified allergy specialists. *Asthma and Allergy Foundation of America, "Fall Allergy Capitals 2022," March 2, 2022*

- Dallas was identified as a "2022 Asthma Capital." The area ranked #45 out of the nation's 100 largest metropolitan areas. Criteria: estimated asthma prevalence; asthma-related mortality; and ER visits due to asthma. Risk factors analyzed but not factored in the rankings: annual pollen score; annual air quality; public smoking laws; access to board-certified asthma specialists; rescue and controller medication use; uninsured rate; poverty rate. *Asthma and Allergy Foundation of America, "Asthma Capitals 2022: The Most Challenging Places to Live With Asthma," September 14, 2022*

Real Estate Rankings

- *WalletHub* compared the most populated U.S. cities to determine which had the best markets for real estate agents. Dallas ranked #62 where demand was high and pay was the best. Criteria: sales per agent; annual median wage for real-estate agents; monthly average starting salary for real estate agents; real estate job density and competition; unemployment rate; home turnover rate; housing-market health index; and other relevant metrics. *www.WalletHub.com, "2021 Best Places to Be a Real Estate Agent," May 12, 2021*

Safety Rankings

- Allstate ranked the 200 largest cities in America in terms of driver safety. Dallas ranked #172. Criteria: internal property damage claims over a two-year period from January 2016 to December 2017. The report helps increase the importance of safety and awareness behind the wheel. *Allstate, "Allstate America's Best Drivers Report, 2019" June 24, 2019*

Transportation Rankings

- According to the INRIX "2022 Global Traffic Scorecard," Dallas was identified as one of the most congested metro areas in the U.S. The area ranked #14 out of 25. Criteria: average annual time spent in traffic and average cost of congestion per motorist. *Inrix.com, "Return to Work, Higher Gas Prices & Inflation Drove Americans to Spend Hundreds More in Time and Money Commuting," January 10, 2023*

Women/Minorities Rankings

- The *Houston Chronicle* listed the Dallas metro area as #7 in top places for young Latinos to live in the U.S. Research was largely based on housing and occupational data from the largest metropolitan areas performed by *Forbes* and NBC Universo. Criteria: percentage of 18-34 year-olds; Latino college grad rates; and diversity. *blog.chron.com, "The 15 Best Big Cities for Latino Millenials," January 26, 2016*

- Personal finance website *WalletHub* compared more than 180 U.S. cities across two key dimensions, "Hispanic Business-Friendliness" and "Hispanic Purchasing Power," to arrive at the most favorable conditions for Hispanic entrepreneurs. Dallas was ranked #28 out of 182. Criteria includes: share of Hispanic-Owned Businesses; Hispanic entrepreneurship rate to median annual income of Hispanics; Small Business-Friendliness score; cost of living; and number of Hispanics with at least a bachelor's degree. *WalletHub.com, "2019's Best Cities for Hispanic Entrepreneurs," May 1, 2019*

Miscellaneous Rankings

- Dallas was selected as a 2022 Digital Cities Survey winner. The city ranked #10 in the large city (500,000 or more population) category. The survey examined and assessed how city governments are utilizing technology to continue innovation, engage with residents, and persevere through the challenges of the pandemic. Survey questions focused on ten initiatives: cybersecurity; citizen experience; disaster recovery; business intelligence; IT personnel; data governance; business automation; IT governance; infrastructure modernization; and broadband connectivity. *Center for Digital Government, "2022 Digital Cities Survey," November 10, 2022*

- The watchdog site, Charity Navigator, conducted a study of charities in major markets both to analyze statistical differences in their financial, accountability, and transparency practices and to track year-to-year variations in individual philanthropic communities. The Dallas metro area was ranked #5 among the 30 metro markets in the rating category of Overall Score. *www.charitynavigator.org, "2017 Metro Market Study," May 1, 2017*

- *WalletHub* compared the 150 most populated U.S. cities to determine their operating efficiency. A "Quality of Services" score was constructed for each city and then divided by the total budget per capita to reveal which were managed the best. Dallas ranked #101. Criteria: financial stability; economy; education; safety; health; infrastructure and pollution. *www.WalletHub.com, "2022's Best- & Worst-Run Cities in America," June 21, 2022*

Business Environment

DEMOGRAPHICS

Population Growth

Area	1990 Census	2000 Census	2010 Census	2020 Census	Population Growth (%) 1990-2020	Population Growth (%) 2010-2020
City	1,006,971	1,188,580	1,197,816	1,304,379	29.5	8.9
MSA[1]	3,989,294	5,161,544	6,371,773	7,637,387	91.4	19.9
U.S.	248,709,873	281,421,906	308,745,538	331,449,281	33.3	7.4

Note: (1) Figures cover the Dallas-Fort Worth-Arlington, TX Metropolitan Statistical Area
Source: U.S. Census Bureau, 1990 Census, 2000 Census, 2010 Census, 2020 Census

Race

Area	White Alone[2] (%)	Black Alone[2] (%)	Asian Alone[2] (%)	AIAN[3] Alone[2] (%)	NHOPI[4] Alone[2] (%)	Other Race Alone[2] (%)	Two or More Races (%)
City	36.1	23.3	3.7	1.2	0.1	19.5	16.2
MSA[1]	48.9	16.0	7.9	1.0	0.1	12.2	13.9
U.S.	61.6	12.4	6.0	1.1	0.2	8.4	10.2

Note: (1) Figures cover the Dallas-Fort Worth-Arlington, TX Metropolitan Statistical Area; (2) Alone is defined as not being in combination with one or more other races; (3) American Indian and Alaska Native; (4) Native Hawaiian and Other Pacific Islander
Source: U.S. Census Bureau, 2020 Census

Hispanic or Latino Origin

Area	Total (%)	Mexican (%)	Puerto Rican (%)	Cuban (%)	Other (%)
City	42.0	34.7	0.6	0.3	6.4
MSA[1]	29.3	23.6	0.8	0.3	4.5
U.S.	18.4	11.2	1.8	0.7	4.7

Note: Persons of Hispanic or Latino origin can be of any race; (1) Figures cover the Dallas-Fort Worth-Arlington, TX Metropolitan Statistical Area
Source: U.S. Census Bureau, 2017-2021 American Community Survey 5-Year Estimates

Age

Area	Under Age 5	Age 5–19	Age 20–34	Age 35–44	Age 45–54	Age 55–64	Age 65–74	Age 75–84	Age 85+	Median Age
City	6.5	19.3	26.6	14.2	11.7	10.6	6.8	3.1	1.3	33.6
MSA[1]	6.2	21.8	21.4	14.1	13.0	11.4	7.4	3.4	1.1	35.3
U.S.	5.6	19.2	20.2	12.7	12.4	13.1	10.0	4.9	1.9	38.8

Note: (1) Figures cover the Dallas-Fort Worth-Arlington, TX Metropolitan Statistical Area
Source: U.S. Census Bureau, 2020 Census

Disability by Age

Area	All Ages	Under 18 Years Old	18 to 64 Years Old	65 Years and Over
City	10.5	4.5	9.0	34.3
MSA[1]	9.5	3.8	8.0	32.1
U.S.	12.6	4.4	10.3	33.4

Note: Figures show percent of the civilian noninstitutionalized population that reported having a disability. Disability status is determined from six types of difficulty: vision, hearing, cognitive, ambulatory, self-care, and independent living. For children under 5 years old, hearing and vision difficulty are used to determine disability status. For children between the ages of 5 and 14, disability status is determined from hearing, vision, cognitive, ambulatory, and self-care difficulties. For people aged 15 years and older, they are considered to have a disability if they have difficulty with any one of the six difficulty types; Note: (1) Figures cover the Dallas-Fort Worth-Arlington, TX Metropolitan Statistical Area
Source: U.S. Census Bureau, 2017-2021 American Community Survey 5-Year Estimates

Ancestry

Area	German	Irish	English	American	Italian	Polish	French[2]	Scottish	Dutch
City	5.1	4.2	5.1	4.2	1.7	0.8	1.2	1.1	0.4
MSA[1]	8.2	6.5	7.6	5.9	2.1	1.0	1.5	1.5	0.6
U.S.	12.8	9.6	8.1	5.7	5.0	2.7	2.2	1.6	1.1

Note: Figures are the percentage of the total population reporting a particular ancestry. The nine most commonly reported ancestries in the U.S. are shown. Figures include multiple ancestries (e.g. if a person reported being Irish and Italian, they were included in both columns); (1) Figures cover the Dallas-Fort Worth-Arlington, TX Metropolitan Statistical Area; (2) Excludes Basque
Source: U.S. Census Bureau, 2017-2021 American Community Survey 5-Year Estimates

Foreign-born Population

Area	Any Foreign Country	Asia	Mexico	Europe	Caribbean	Central America[2]	South America	Africa	Canada
City	23.8	2.8	13.9	0.8	0.4	2.9	0.7	2.1	0.2
MSA[1]	18.7	5.7	7.8	0.8	0.3	1.6	0.7	1.6	0.2
U.S.	13.6	4.2	3.3	1.5	1.4	1.1	1.1	0.8	0.2

Note: (1) Figures cover the Dallas-Fort Worth-Arlington, TX Metropolitan Statistical Area; (2) Excludes Mexico.
Source: U.S. Census Bureau, 2017-2021 American Community Survey 5-Year Estimates

Household Size

Area	One	Two	Three	Four	Five	Six	Seven or More	Average Household Size
City	36.4	29.5	13.1	10.4	6.5	2.5	1.7	2.50
MSA[1]	25.1	30.8	16.8	15.0	7.7	2.9	1.8	2.80
U.S.	28.1	33.8	15.5	12.9	6.0	2.3	1.4	2.60

Note: (1) Figures cover the Dallas-Fort Worth-Arlington, TX Metropolitan Statistical Area
Source: U.S. Census Bureau, 2017-2021 American Community Survey 5-Year Estimates

Household Relationships

Area	Householder	Opposite-sex Spouse	Same-sex Spouse	Opposite-sex Unmarried Partner	Same-sex Unmarried Partner	Child[2]	Grandchild	Other Relatives	Non-relatives
City	40.1	13.4	0.4	2.6	0.3	28.6	3.2	6.2	4.0
MSA[1]	36.2	17.6	0.2	2.0	0.2	31.7	2.7	5.5	2.9
U.S.	38.3	17.5	0.2	2.5	0.2	28.3	2.4	4.8	3.4

Note: Figures are percent of the total population; (1) Figures cover the Dallas-Fort Worth-Arlington, TX Metropolitan Statistical Area; (2) Includes biological, adopted, and stepchildren of the householder
Source: U.S. Census Bureau, 2020 Census

Gender

Area	Males	Females	Males per 100 Females
City	647,963	656,416	98.7
MSA[1]	3,753,384	3,884,003	96.6
U.S.	162,685,811	168,763,470	96.4

Note: (1) Figures cover the Dallas-Fort Worth-Arlington, TX Metropolitan Statistical Area
Source: U.S. Census Bureau, 2020 Census

Marital Status

Area	Never Married	Now Married[2]	Separated	Widowed	Divorced
City	42.3	40.2	2.9	4.3	10.3
MSA[1]	32.8	50.8	1.9	4.2	10.3
U.S.	33.8	48.0	1.8	5.6	10.8

Note: Figures are percentages and cover the population 15 years of age and older; (1) Figures cover the Dallas-Fort Worth-Arlington, TX Metropolitan Statistical Area; (2) Excludes separated
Source: U.S. Census Bureau, 2017-2021 American Community Survey 5-Year Estimates

Religious Groups by Family

Area	Catholic	Baptist	Methodist	LDS[2]	Pentecostal	Lutheran	Islam	Adventist	Other
MSA[1]	14.2	14.3	4.7	1.4	2.2	0.5	1.8	1.3	13.8
U.S.	18.7	7.3	3.0	2.0	1.8	1.7	1.3	1.3	11.6

Note: Figures are the number of adherents as a percentage of the total population and cover the eight largest religious groups in the U.S; (1) Figures cover the Dallas-Fort Worth-Arlington, TX Metropolitan Statistical Area; (2) Church of Jesus Christ of Latter-day Saints
Sources: 2020 U.S. Religion Census, Association of Statisticians of American Religious Bodies; The Association of Religion Data Archives (ARDA)

Religious Groups by Tradition

Area	Catholic	Evangelical Protestant	Mainline Protestant	Black Protestant	Islam	Judaism	Hinduism	Orthodox	Buddhism
MSA[1]	14.2	25.4	5.9	3.3	1.8	0.3	0.5	0.3	0.2
U.S.	18.7	16.5	5.2	2.3	1.3	0.6	0.4	0.4	0.3

Note: Figures are the number of adherents as a percentage of the total population; (1) Figures cover the Dallas-Fort Worth-Arlington, TX Metropolitan Statistical Area
Sources: 2020 U.S. Religion Census, Association of Statisticians of American Religious Bodies; The Association of Religion Data Archives (ARDA)

Dallas, Texas   189

ECONOMY

Gross Metropolitan Product

Area	2020	2021	2022	2023	Rank[2]
MSA[1]	538.4	608.8	686.1	722.1	5

Note: Figures are in billions of dollars; (1) Figures cover the Dallas-Fort Worth-Arlington, TX Metropolitan Statistical Area; (2) Rank is based on 2021 data and ranges from 1 to 381
Source: U.S. Conference of Mayors, U.S. Metro Economies: U.S. Metros Compared to Global and State Economies, June 2022

Economic Growth

Area	2018-20 (%)	2021 (%)	2022 (%)	2023 (%)	Rank[2]
MSA[1]	0.8	8.3	5.3	3.2	84
U.S.	-0.6	5.7	3.1	2.9	—

Note: Figures are real gross metropolitan product (GMP) growth rates and represent average annual percent change; (1) Figures cover the Dallas-Fort Worth-Arlington, TX Metropolitan Statistical Area; (2) Rank is based on 2020 2-year average annual percent change and ranges from 1 to 381
Source: U.S. Conference of Mayors, U.S. Metro Economies: U.S. Metros Compared to Global and State Economies, June 2022

Metropolitan Area Exports

Area	2016	2017	2018	2019	2020	2021	Rank[2]
MSA[1]	27,187.8	30,269.1	36,260.9	39,474.0	35,642.0	43,189.0	6

Note: Figures are in millions of dollars; (1) Figures cover the Dallas-Fort Worth-Arlington, TX Metropolitan Statistical Area; (2) Rank is based on 2021 data and ranges from 1 to 388
Source: U.S. Department of Commerce, International Trade Administration, Office of Trade and Economic Analysis, Industry and Analysis, Exports by Metropolitan Area, data extracted March 16, 2023

Building Permits

	Single-Family			Multi-Family			Total		
Area	2021	2022	Pct. Chg.	2021	2022	Pct. Chg.	2021	2022	Pct. Chg.
City	2,245	2,349	4.6	7,769	7,880	1.4	10,014	10,229	2.1
MSA[1]	51,996	43,645	-16.1	26,709	34,249	28.2	78,705	77,894	-1.0
U.S.	1,115,400	975,600	-12.5	621,600	689,500	10.9	1,737,000	1,665,100	-4.1

Note: (1) Figures cover the Dallas-Fort Worth-Arlington, TX Metropolitan Statistical Area; Figures represent new, privately-owned housing units authorized (unadjusted data); All permit data are based on estimates with imputation
Source: U.S. Census Bureau, Manufacturing, Mining, and Construction Statistics, Building Permits, 2021, 2022

Bankruptcy Filings

	Business Filings			Nonbusiness Filings		
Area	2021	2022	% Chg.	2021	2022	% Chg.
Dallas County	186	237	27.4	1,797	1,984	10.4
U.S.	14,347	13,481	-6.0	399,269	374,240	-6.3

Note: Business filings include Chapter 7, Chapter 9, Chapter 11, Chapter 12, Chapter 13, Chapter 15, and Section 304; Nonbusiness filings include Chapter 7, Chapter 11, and Chapter 13
Source: Administrative Office of the U.S. Courts, Business and Nonbusiness Bankruptcy, County Cases Commenced by Chapter of the Bankruptcy Code, During the 12-Month Period Ending December 31, 2021 and Business and Nonbusiness Bankruptcy, County Cases Commenced by Chapter of the Bankruptcy Code, During the 12-Month Period Ending December 31, 2022

Housing Vacancy Rates

	Gross Vacancy Rate[2] (%)			Year-Round Vacancy Rate[3] (%)			Rental Vacancy Rate[4] (%)			Homeowner Vacancy Rate[5] (%)		
Area	2020	2021	2022	2020	2021	2022	2020	2021	2022	2020	2021	2022
MSA[1]	6.4	6.6	6.6	6.4	6.5	6.3	7.2	7.0	6.8	0.7	0.7	0.7
U.S.	10.6	10.8	10.5	8.2	8.4	8.2	6.3	6.1	5.8	1.0	0.9	0.8

Note: (1) Figures cover the Dallas-Fort Worth-Arlington, TX Metropolitan Statistical Area; (2) The percentage of the total housing inventory that is vacant; (3) The percentage of the housing inventory (excluding seasonal units) that is year-round vacant; (4) The percentage of rental inventory that is vacant for rent; (5) The percentage of homeowner inventory that is vacant for sale
Source: U.S. Census Bureau, Housing Vacancies and Homeownership Annual Statistics: 2020, 2021, 2022

INCOME

Income

Area	Per Capita ($)	Median Household ($)	Average Household ($)
City	37,719	58,231	92,785
MSA[1]	38,609	76,916	105,647
U.S.	37,638	69,021	97,196

Note: (1) Figures cover the Dallas-Fort Worth-Arlington, TX Metropolitan Statistical Area
Source: U.S. Census Bureau, 2017-2021 American Community Survey 5-Year Estimates

Household Income Distribution

Area	Under $15,000	$15,000 -$24,999	$25,000 -$34,999	$35,000 -$49,999	$50,000 -$74,999	$75,000 -$99,999	$100,000 -$149,999	$150,000 and up
City	11.3	8.6	9.6	13.7	18.4	11.3	12.1	14.8
MSA[1]	7.1	6.0	7.4	11.1	17.3	13.3	17.9	20.0
U.S.	9.4	7.8	8.2	11.4	16.8	12.8	16.3	17.3

Note: (1) Figures cover the Dallas-Fort Worth-Arlington, TX Metropolitan Statistical Area
Source: U.S. Census Bureau, 2017-2021 American Community Survey 5-Year Estimates

Poverty Rate

Area	All Ages	Under 18 Years Old	18 to 64 Years Old	65 Years and Over
City	17.7	26.9	14.7	14.7
MSA[1]	10.9	15.4	9.4	8.9
U.S.	12.6	17.0	11.8	9.6

Note: Figures are percentage of people whose income during the past 12 months was below the poverty level;
(1) Figures cover the Dallas-Fort Worth-Arlington, TX Metropolitan Statistical Area
Source: U.S. Census Bureau, 2017-2021 American Community Survey 5-Year Estimates

EMPLOYMENT

Labor Force and Employment

Area	Civilian Labor Force Dec. 2021	Civilian Labor Force Dec. 2022	% Chg.	Workers Employed Dec. 2021	Workers Employed Dec. 2022	% Chg.
City	707,758	735,922	4.0	679,409	711,095	4.7
MD[1]	2,825,024	2,943,498	4.2	2,723,620	2,851,201	4.7
U.S.	161,696,000	164,224,000	1.6	155,732,000	158,872,000	2.0

Note: Data is not seasonally adjusted and covers workers 16 years of age and older; (1) Figures cover the Dallas-Plano-Irving, TX Metropolitan Division
Source: Bureau of Labor Statistics, Local Area Unemployment Statistics

Unemployment Rate

Area	Jan.	Feb.	Mar.	Apr.	May	Jun.	Jul.	Aug.	Sep.	Oct.	Nov.	Dec.
City	4.5	4.4	3.6	3.4	3.5	4.0	4.0	3.9	3.6	3.6	3.5	3.4
MD[1]	4.1	4.0	3.3	3.1	3.3	3.8	3.7	3.6	3.4	3.3	3.2	3.1
U.S.	4.4	4.1	3.8	3.3	3.4	3.8	3.8	3.8	3.3	3.4	3.4	3.3

Note: Data is not seasonally adjusted and covers workers 16 years of age and older; (1) Figures cover the Dallas-Plano-Irving, TX Metropolitan Division
Source: Bureau of Labor Statistics, Local Area Unemployment Statistics

Average Wages

Occupation	$/Hr.	Occupation	$/Hr.
Accountants and Auditors	43.06	Maintenance and Repair Workers	21.23
Automotive Mechanics	24.09	Marketing Managers	67.66
Bookkeepers	22.81	Network and Computer Systems Admin.	45.36
Carpenters	23.70	Nurses, Licensed Practical	26.59
Cashiers	13.14	Nurses, Registered	42.24
Computer Programmers	46.27	Nursing Assistants	16.34
Computer Systems Analysts	54.07	Office Clerks, General	18.59
Computer User Support Specialists	28.45	Physical Therapists	50.76
Construction Laborers	18.68	Physicians	118.86
Cooks, Restaurant	15.57	Plumbers, Pipefitters and Steamfitters	26.94
Customer Service Representatives	19.64	Police and Sheriff's Patrol Officers	35.82
Dentists	76.46	Postal Service Mail Carriers	27.30
Electricians	26.46	Real Estate Sales Agents	38.08
Engineers, Electrical	50.66	Retail Salespersons	16.19
Fast Food and Counter Workers	12.14	Sales Representatives, Technical/Scientific	43.31
Financial Managers	79.36	Secretaries, Exc. Legal/Medical/Executive	20.33
First-Line Supervisors of Office Workers	31.46	Security Guards	16.99
General and Operations Managers	56.66	Surgeons	142.82
Hairdressers/Cosmetologists	16.24	Teacher Assistants, Exc. Postsecondary*	14.09
Home Health and Personal Care Aides	11.66	Teachers, Secondary School, Exc. Sp. Ed.*	30.46
Janitors and Cleaners	14.42	Telemarketers	18.24
Landscaping/Groundskeeping Workers	16.86	Truck Drivers, Heavy/Tractor-Trailer	24.73
Lawyers	87.42	Truck Drivers, Light/Delivery Services	22.27
Maids and Housekeeping Cleaners	13.78	Waiters and Waitresses	13.17

Note: Wage data covers the Dallas-Fort Worth-Arlington, TX Metropolitan Statistical Area; (*) Hourly wages were calculated from annual wage data based on a 40 hour work week; n/a not available.
Source: Bureau of Labor Statistics, Metro Area Occupational Employment & Wage Estimates, May 2022

Employment by Industry

Sector	MD[1] Number of Employees	MD[1] Percent of Total	U.S. Percent of Total
Construction, Mining, and Logging	161,300	5.3	5.4
Private Education and Health Services	345,100	11.4	16.1
Financial Activities	293,500	9.7	5.9
Government	328,100	10.9	14.5
Information	83,300	2.8	2.0
Leisure and Hospitality	276,700	9.2	10.3
Manufacturing	196,000	6.5	8.4
Other Services	90,200	3.0	3.7
Professional and Business Services	623,300	20.6	14.7
Retail Trade	269,900	8.9	10.2
Transportation, Warehousing, and Utilities	178,600	5.9	4.9
Wholesale Trade	177,800	5.9	3.9

Note: Figures are non-farm employment as of December 2022. Figures are not seasonally adjusted and include workers 16 years of age and older; (1) Figures cover the Dallas-Plano-Irving, TX Metropolitan Division
Source: Bureau of Labor Statistics, Current Employment Statistics, Employment, Hours, and Earnings

Employment by Occupation

Occupation Classification	City (%)	MSA[1] (%)	U.S. (%)
Management, Business, Science, and Arts	38.1	41.4	40.3
Natural Resources, Construction, and Maintenance	11.5	9.1	8.7
Production, Transportation, and Material Moving	13.0	12.7	13.1
Sales and Office	20.9	22.0	20.9
Service	16.5	14.7	17.0

Note: Figures cover employed civilians 16 years of age and older; (1) Figures cover the Dallas-Fort Worth-Arlington, TX Metropolitan Statistical Area
Source: U.S. Census Bureau, 2017-2021 American Community Survey 5-Year Estimates

Occupations with Greatest Projected Employment Growth: 2022 – 2024

Occupation[1]	2022 Employment	2024 Projected Employment	Numeric Employment Change	Percent Employment Change
Home Health and Personal Care Aides	338,130	364,760	26,630	7.9
General and Operations Managers	395,700	416,100	20,400	5.2
Heavy and Tractor-Trailer Truck Drivers	206,850	222,220	15,370	7.4
Software Developers	119,810	134,060	14,250	11.9
Laborers and Freight, Stock, and Material Movers, Hand	214,680	228,680	14,000	6.5
Farmers, Ranchers, and Other Agricultural Managers	274,740	287,430	12,690	4.6
Stockers and Order Fillers	212,180	224,670	12,490	5.9
Construction Laborers	153,220	164,330	11,110	7.3
Cooks, Restaurant	131,480	141,860	10,380	7.9
Industrial Truck and Tractor Operators	83,270	93,190	9,920	11.9

Note: Projections cover Texas; (1) Sorted by numeric employment change
Source: www.projectionscentral.com, State Occupational Projections, 2022–2024 Short-Term Projections

Fastest-Growing Occupations: 2022 – 2024

Occupation[1]	2022 Employment	2024 Projected Employment	Numeric Employment Change	Percent Employment Change
Wind Turbine Service Technicians	5,240	5,990	750	14.3
Information Security Analysts (SOC 2018)	14,170	16,110	1,940	13.7
Solar Photovoltaic Installers	2,240	2,540	300	13.4
Veterinary Technologists and Technicians	16,140	18,200	2,060	12.8
Actuaries	1,810	2,040	230	12.7
Data Scientists	7,340	8,270	930	12.7
Web Developers	6,920	7,790	870	12.6
Veterinarians	6,830	7,670	840	12.3
Veterinary Assistants and Laboratory Animal Caretakers	5,990	6,720	730	12.2
Ushers, Lobby Attendants, and Ticket Takers	9,100	10,190	1,090	12.0

Note: Projections cover Texas; (1) Sorted by percent employment change and excludes occupations with numeric employment change less than 50
Source: www.projectionscentral.com, State Occupational Projections, 2022–2024 Short-Term Projections

CITY FINANCES

City Government Finances

Component	2020 ($000)	2020 ($ per capita)
Total Revenues	4,334,095	3,226
Total Expenditures	4,001,495	2,978
Debt Outstanding	11,366,409	8,460
Cash and Securities[1]	4,730,951	3,521

Note: (1) Cash and security holdings of a government at the close of its fiscal year, including those of its dependent agencies, utilities, and liquor stores.
Source: U.S. Census Bureau, State & Local Government Finances 2020

City Government Revenue by Source

Source	2020 ($000)	2020 ($ per capita)	2020 (%)
General Revenue			
From Federal Government	95,212	71	2.2
From State Government	59,013	44	1.4
From Local Governments	13,682	10	0.3
Taxes			
Property	1,074,313	800	24.8
Sales and Gross Receipts	490,973	365	11.3
Personal Income	0	0	0.0
Corporate Income	0	0	0.0
Motor Vehicle License	0	0	0.0
Other Taxes	50,937	38	1.2
Current Charges	1,944,886	1,448	44.9
Liquor Store	0	0	0.0
Utility	371,729	277	8.6

Source: U.S. Census Bureau, State & Local Government Finances 2020

City Government Expenditures by Function

Function	2020 ($000)	2020 ($ per capita)	2020 (%)
General Direct Expenditures			
Air Transportation	1,051,104	782	26.3
Corrections	2,408	1	0.1
Education	0	0	0.0
Employment Security Administration	0	0	0.0
Financial Administration	36,695	27	0.9
Fire Protection	261,889	194	6.5
General Public Buildings	30,570	22	0.8
Governmental Administration, Other	28,288	21	0.7
Health	32,663	24	0.8
Highways	238,612	177	6.0
Hospitals	0	0	0.0
Housing and Community Development	20,143	15	0.5
Interest on General Debt	373,346	277	9.3
Judicial and Legal	36,863	27	0.9
Libraries	31,817	23	0.8
Parking	323	< 1	< 0.1
Parks and Recreation	256,384	190	6.4
Police Protection	437,933	325	10.9
Public Welfare	12,903	9	0.3
Sewerage	264,776	197	6.6
Solid Waste Management	91,177	67	2.3
Veterans' Services	0	0	0.0
Liquor Store	0	0	0.0
Utility	436,683	325	10.9

Source: U.S. Census Bureau, State & Local Government Finances 2020

TAXES

State Corporate Income Tax Rates

State	Tax Rate (%)	Income Brackets ($)	Num. of Brackets	Financial Institution Tax Rate (%)[a]	Federal Income Tax Ded.
Texas	(u)	–	–	(u)	No

Note: Tax rates as of January 1, 2023; (a) Rates listed are the corporate income tax rate applied to financial institutions or excise taxes based on income. Some states have other taxes based upon the value of deposits or shares; (u) Texas imposes a Franchise Tax, otherwise known as margin tax, imposed on entities with more than $1,230,000 total revenues at rate of 0.75%, or 0.375% for entities primarily engaged in retail or wholesale trade, on lesser of 70% of total revenues or 100% of gross receipts after deductions for either compensation or cost of goods sold.
Source: Federation of Tax Administrators, State Corporate Income Tax Rates, January 1, 2023

State Individual Income Tax Rates

State	Tax Rate (%)	Income Brackets ($)	Personal Exemptions ($) Single	Personal Exemptions ($) Married	Personal Exemptions ($) Depend.	Standard Ded. ($) Single	Standard Ded. ($) Married
Texas				— No state income tax —			

Note: Tax rates as of January 1, 2023; Local- and county-level taxes are not included
Source: Federation of Tax Administrators, State Individual Income Tax Rates, January 1, 2023

Various State Sales and Excise Tax Rates

State	State Sales Tax (%)	Gasoline[1] ($/gal.)	Cigarette[2] ($/pack)	Spirits[3] ($/gal.)	Wine[4] ($/gal.)	Beer[5] ($/gal.)	Recreational Marijuana (%)
Texas	6.25	0.20	1.41	2.40	0.20	0.19	Not legal

Note: All tax rates as of January 1, 2023; (1) The American Petroleum Institute has developed a methodology for determining the average tax rate on a gallon of fuel. Rates may include any of the following: excise taxes, environmental fees, storage tank fees, other fees or taxes, general sales tax, and local taxes; (2) The federal excise tax of $1.0066 per pack and local taxes are not included; (3) Rates are those applicable to off-premise sales of 40% alcohol by volume (a.b.v.) distilled spirits in 750ml containers. Local excise taxes are excluded; (4) Rates are those applicable to off-premise sales of 11% a.b.v. non-carbonated wine in 750ml containers; (5) Rates are those applicable to off-premise sales of 4.7% a.b.v. beer in 12 ounce containers.
Source: Tax Foundation, 2023 Facts & Figures: How Does Your State Compare?

State Business Tax Climate Index Rankings

State	Overall Rank	Corporate Tax Rank	Individual Income Tax Rank	Sales Tax Rank	Property Tax Rank	Unemployment Insurance Tax Rank
Texas	13	47	7	37	38	12

Note: The index is a measure of how each state's tax laws affect economic performance. The lower the rank, the more favorable a state's tax system is for business. States without a given tax are given a ranking of 1. The scores/rankings for the District of Columbia do not affect other states. The 2023 index represents the tax climate as of July 1, 2022.
Source: Tax Foundation, State Business Tax Climate Index 2023

TRANSPORTATION

Means of Transportation to Work

Area	Car/Truck/Van Drove Alone	Car/Truck/Van Carpooled	Public Transportation Bus	Public Transportation Subway	Public Transportation Railroad	Bicycle	Walked	Other Means	Worked at Home
City	72.3	11.2	2.3	0.3	0.2	0.2	2.2	1.6	9.7
MSA[1]	75.8	9.5	0.6	0.1	0.2	0.1	1.2	1.3	11.1
U.S.	73.2	8.6	2.0	1.6	0.5	0.5	2.5	1.5	9.7

Note: Figures are percentages and cover workers 16 years of age and older; (1) Figures cover the Dallas-Fort Worth-Arlington, TX Metropolitan Statistical Area
Source: U.S. Census Bureau, 2017-2021 American Community Survey 5-Year Estimates

Travel Time to Work

Area	Less Than 10 Minutes	10 to 19 Minutes	20 to 29 Minutes	30 to 44 Minutes	45 to 59 Minutes	60 to 89 Minutes	90 Minutes or More
City	8.2	26.9	23.3	25.8	8.0	5.9	1.9
MSA[1]	8.6	25.2	21.7	25.6	10.3	6.7	2.0
U.S.	12.4	28.5	21.0	20.9	8.2	6.2	2.9

Note: Note: Figures are percentages and include workers 16 years old and over; (1) Figures cover the Dallas-Fort Worth-Arlington, TX Metropolitan Statistical Area
Source: U.S. Census Bureau, 2017-2021 American Community Survey 5-Year Estimates

Key Congestion Measures

Measure	1990	2000	2010	2015	2020
Annual Hours of Delay, Total (000)	77,977	129,786	175,068	214,718	136,953
Annual Hours of Delay, Per Auto Commuter	40	47	50	63	40
Annual Congestion Cost, Per Auto Commuter ($)	844	1,056	1,132	1,283	848

Note: Covers the Dallas-Fort Worth-Arlington TX urban area
Source: Texas A&M Transportation Institute, 2021 Urban Mobility Report

Freeway Travel Time Index

Measure	1985	1990	1995	2000	2005	2010	2015	2020
Urban Area Index[1]	1.19	1.20	1.23	1.24	1.26	1.25	1.26	1.12
Urban Area Rank[1,2]	6	9	8	18	22	21	23	10

Note: Freeway Travel Time Index—the ratio of travel time in the peak period to the travel time at free-flow conditions. For example, a value of 1.30 indicates a 20-minute free-flow trip takes 26 minutes in the peak (20 minutes x 1.30 = 26 minutes); (1) Covers the Dallas-Fort Worth-Arlington TX urban area; (2) Rank is based on 101 larger urban areas (#1 = highest travel time index)
Source: Texas A&M Transportation Institute, 2021 Urban Mobility Report

Public Transportation

Agency Name / Mode of Transportation	Vehicles Operated in Maximum Service[1]	Annual Unlinked Passenger Trips[2] (in thous.)	Annual Passenger Miles[3] (in thous.)
Dallas Area Rapid Transit Authority (DART)			
Bus (directly operated)	453	19,432.2	78,169.1
Commuter Rail (purchased transportation)	23	795.3	12,709.6
Demand Response (purchased transportation)	149	578.0	6,164.7
Demand Response - Taxi	1	2.2	18.8
Light Rail (directly operated)	89	14,487.2	121,236.0
Streetcar Rail (directly operated)	2	116.0	191.0
Vanpool (purchased transportation)	13	24.1	726.8

Note: (1) Number of revenue vehicles operated by the given mode and type of service to meet the annual maximum service requirement. This is the revenue vehicle count during the peak season of the year; on the week and day that maximum service is provided. Vehicles operated in maximum service (VOMS) exclude atypical days and one-time special events; (2) Number of passengers who boarded public transportation vehicles. Passengers are counted each time they board a vehicle no matter how many vehicles they use to travel from their origin to their destination. (3) Sum of the distances ridden by all passengers during the entire fiscal year.
Source: Federal Transit Administration, National Transit Database, 2021

Air Transportation

Airport Name and Code / Type of Service	Passenger Airlines[1]	Passenger Enplanements	Freight Carriers[2]	Freight (lbs)
Dallas-Fort Worth International (DFW)				
Domestic service (U.S. carriers - 2022)	29	30,640,857	22	539,257,244
International service (U.S. carriers - 2021)	8	2,517,818	5	81,848,301
Dallas Love Field (DAL)				
Domestic service (U.S. carriers - 2022)	23	7,816,836	6	14,872,355
International service (U.S. carriers - 2021)	5	248	0	0

Note: (1) Includes all U.S.-based major, minor and commuter airlines that carried at least one passenger during the year; (2) Includes all U.S.-based airlines and freight carriers that transported at least one pound of freight during the year.
Source: Bureau of Transportation Statistics, The Intermodal Transportation Database, Air Carriers: T-100 Domestic Market (U.S. Carriers), 2022; Bureau of Transportation Statistics, The Intermodal Transportation Database, Air Carriers: T-100 International Market (U.S. Carriers), 2021

BUSINESSES

Major Business Headquarters

Company Name	Industry	Fortune[1]	Forbes[2]
AT&T	Telecommunications	13	-
Austin Industries	Construction	-	192
Builders FirstSource	Building materials, glass	176	-
EnLink Midstream	Pipelines	485	-
Energy Transfer	Pipelines	54	-
HF Sinclair	Petroleum refining	197	-
Hunt Consolidated/Hunt Oil	Oil & gas operations	-	124
Jacobs Engineering Group	Engineering, architecture, construction	262	-
Mode Transportation	Transportation	-	159
Neiman Marcus Group	Retailing	-	107
Sammons Enterprises	Multicompany	-	44
Southwest Airlines	Airlines	234	-
Tenet Healthcare	Health care, medical facilities	181	-
Texas Instruments	Semiconductors and other electronic components	198	-

Note: (1) Companies that produce a 10-K are ranked 1 to 500 based on 2021 revenue; (2) All private companies with at least $2 billion in annual revenue through the end of their most current fiscal year are ranked 1 to 246; companies listed are headquartered in the city; dashes indicate no ranking
Source: Fortune, "Fortune 500," 2022; Forbes, "America's Largest Private Companies," 2022

Fastest-Growing Businesses

According to *Inc.*, Dallas is home to five of America's 500 fastest-growing private companies: **Blue Hammer Roofing** (#17); **Forester Haynie** (#172); **Avara** (#406); **Tradebloc** (#425); **Archer Review** (#466). Criteria: must be an independent, privately-held, for-profit, U.S. corporation, proprietorship or partnership as of December 31, 2021; revenues must be at least $100,000 in 2018 and $2 million in 2021; must have four-year operating/sales history. *Inc.*, "America's 500 Fastest-Growing Private Companies," 2022

According to *Initiative for a Competitive Inner City (ICIC)*, Dallas is home to two of America's 100 fastest-growing "inner city" companies: **Ordermygear** (#47); **Artifacture** (#92). Criteria for inclusion: company must be headquartered in or have 51 percent or more of its physical operations in an economically distressed urban area; must be an independent, for-profit corporation, partnership or proprietorship; must have 10 or more employees and have a five-year sales history that includes sales of at least $200,000 in the base year and at least $1 million in the current year with no decrease in sales over the two most recent years. Companies were ranked overall by revenue growth over the five-year period between 2017 and 2021. *Initiative for a Competitive Inner City (ICIC), "Inner City 100 Companies," 2022*

According to Deloitte, Dallas is home to five of North America's 500 fastest-growing high-technology companies: **ACCELQ** (#212); **o9 Solutions** (#396); **Qentelli** (#426); **Appspace** (#461); **Zimperium** (#481). Companies are ranked by percentage growth in revenue over a four-year period. Criteria for inclusion: company must be headquartered within North America; must own proprietary intellectual property or technology that is sold to customers in products that contributes to a significant portion of the company's operating revenue; must have been in business for a minumum of four years with 2018 operating revenues of at least $50,000 USD/CD and 2021 operating revenues of at least $5 million USD/CD. *Deloitte, 2022 Technology Fast 500*™

Dallas, Texas

Living Environment

COST OF LIVING

Cost of Living Index

Composite Index	Groceries	Housing	Utilities	Transportation	Health Care	Misc. Goods/Services
102.5	95.3	96.5	114.3	85.5	112.6	110.6

Note: The Cost of Living Index measures regional differences in the cost of consumer goods and services, excluding taxes and non-consumer expenditures, for professional and managerial households in the top income quintile. It is based on more than 50,000 prices covering almost 60 different items for which prices are collected three times a year by chambers of commerce, economic development organizations or university applied economic centers in each participating urban area. The numbers shown should be read as a percentage above or below the national average of 100. For example, a value of 115.4 in the groceries column indicates that grocery prices are 15.4% higher than the national average. Small differences in the index numbers should not be interpreted as significant; Figures cover the Dallas TX urban area.
Source: The Council for Community and Economic Research, Cost of Living Index, 2022

Grocery Prices

Area[1]	T-Bone Steak ($/pound)	Frying Chicken ($/pound)	Whole Milk ($/half gal.)	Eggs ($/dozen)	Orange Juice ($/64 oz.)	Coffee ($/11.5 oz.)
City[2]	12.76	1.26	2.34	2.12	3.60	4.62
Avg.	13.81	1.59	2.43	2.25	3.85	4.95
Min.	10.17	0.90	1.51	1.30	2.90	3.46
Max.	19.35	3.30	4.32	4.32	5.31	8.59

Note: (1) Values for the local area are compared with the average, minimum and maximum values for all 286 areas in the Cost of Living Index; (2) Figures cover the Dallas TX urban area; **T-Bone Steak** (price per pound); **Frying Chicken** (price per pound, whole fryer); **Whole Milk** (half gallon carton); **Eggs** (price per dozen, Grade A, large); **Orange Juice** (64 oz. Tropicana or Florida Natural); **Coffee** (11.5 oz. can, vacuum-packed, Maxwell House, Hills Bros, or Folgers).
Source: The Council for Community and Economic Research, Cost of Living Index, 2022

Housing and Utility Costs

Area[1]	New Home Price ($)	Apartment Rent ($/month)	All Electric ($/month)	Part Electric ($/month)	Other Energy ($/month)	Telephone ($/month)
City[2]	439,403	1,563	-	136.69	79.10	196.79
Avg.	450,913	1,371	176.41	99.93	76.96	190.22
Min.	229,283	546	100.84	31.56	27.15	174.27
Max.	2,434,977	4,569	356.86	249.59	272.24	208.31

Note: (1) Values for the local area are compared with the average, minimum and maximum values for all 286 areas in the Cost of Living Index; (2) Figures cover the Dallas TX urban area; **New Home Price** (2,400 sf living area, 8,000 sf lot, in urban area with full utilities); **Apartment Rent** (950 sf 2 bedroom/1.5 or 2 bath, unfurnished, excluding all utilities except water); **All Electric** (average monthly cost for an all-electric home); **Part Electric** (average monthly cost for a part-electric home); **Other Energy** (average monthly cost for natural gas, fuel oil, coal, wood, and any other forms of energy except electricity); **Telephone** (price includes the base monthly rate plus taxes and fees for three lines of mobile phone service).
Source: The Council for Community and Economic Research, Cost of Living Index, 2022

Health Care, Transportation, and Other Costs

Area[1]	Doctor ($/visit)	Dentist ($/visit)	Optometrist ($/visit)	Gasoline ($/gallon)	Beauty Salon ($/visit)	Men's Shirt ($)
City[2]	141.13	129.77	139.62	3.39	64.32	38.33
Avg.	124.91	107.77	117.66	3.86	43.31	34.21
Min.	36.61	58.25	51.79	2.90	22.18	13.05
Max.	250.21	162.58	371.96	5.54	85.61	63.54

Note: (1) Values for the local area are compared with the average, minimum and maximum values for all 286 areas in the Cost of Living Index; (2) Figures cover the Dallas TX urban area; **Doctor** (general practitioners routine exam of an established patient); **Dentist** (adult teeth cleaning and periodic oral examination); **Optometrist** (full vision eye exam for established adult patient); **Gasoline** (one gallon regular unleaded, national brand, including all taxes, cash price at self-service pump if available); **Beauty Salon** (woman's shampoo, trim, and blow-dry); **Men's Shirt** (cotton/polyester dress shirt, pinpoint weave, long sleeves).
Source: The Council for Community and Economic Research, Cost of Living Index, 2022

HOUSING

Homeownership Rate

Area	2015 (%)	2016 (%)	2017 (%)	2018 (%)	2019 (%)	2020 (%)	2021 (%)	2022 (%)
MSA[1]	57.8	59.7	61.8	62.0	60.6	64.7	61.8	60.4
U.S.	63.7	63.4	63.9	64.4	64.6	66.6	65.5	65.8

Note: (1) Figures cover the Dallas-Fort Worth-Arlington, TX Metropolitan Statistical Area
Source: U.S. Census Bureau, Housing Vacancies and Homeownership Annual Statistics: 2015-2022

House Price Index (HPI)

Area	National Ranking[2]	Quarterly Change (%)	One-Year Change (%)	Five-Year Change (%)	Since 1991Q1 (%)
MD[1]	43	-1.44	15.77	61.60	325.13
U.S.[3]	–	0.34	8.41	58.44	289.08

Note: The HPI is a weighted repeat sales index. It measures average price changes in repeat sales or refinancings on the same properties. This information is obtained by reviewing repeat mortgage transactions on single-family properties whose mortgages have been purchased or securitized by Fannie Mae or Freddie Mac since January 1975; (1) Figures cover the Dallas-Plano-Irving, TX Metropolitan Division; (2) Rankings are based on annual percentage change for all metro areas containing at least 15,000 transactions over the last 10 years and ranges from 1 to 257; (3) figures based on a weighted average of Census Division estimates using a seasonally adjusted, purchase-only index; all figures are for the period ending December 31, 2022
Source: Federal Housing Finance Agency, Change in FHFA Metropolitan Area House Price Indexes, 2022Q4

Median Single-Family Home Prices

Area	2020	2021	2022p	Percent Change 2021 to 2022
MSA[1]	287.2	336.7	385.5	14.5
U.S. Average	300.2	357.1	392.6	9.9

Note: Figures are median sales prices of existing single-family homes in thousands of dollars; (p) preliminary; (1) Figures cover the Dallas-Fort Worth-Arlington, TX Metropolitan Statistical Area
Source: National Association of Realtors, Median Sales Price of Existing Single-Family Homes for Metropolitan Areas, 4th Quarter 2022

Qualifying Income Based on Median Sales Price of Existing Single-Family Homes

Area	With 5% Down ($)	With 10% Down ($)	With 20% Down ($)
MSA[1]	112,194	106,289	94,479
U.S. Average	112,234	106,237	94,513

Note: Figures are preliminary; Qualifying income is based on a mortgage rate of 6.77%. Monthly principal and interest payment is limited to 25% of income; (1) Figures cover the Dallas-Fort Worth-Arlington, TX Metropolitan Statistical Area
Source: National Association of Realtors, Qualifying Income Based on Median Sales Price of Existing Single-Family Homes for Metropolitan Areas, 4th Quarter 2022

Home Value

Area	Under $100,000	$100,000 -$199,999	$200,000 -$299,999	$300,000 -$399,999	$400,000 -$499,999	$500,000 -$999,999	$1,000,000 or more	Median ($)
City	17.6	27.3	15.3	11.0	8.6	14.8	5.5	230,000
MSA[1]	10.9	24.1	26.2	17.0	9.3	10.2	2.4	255,600
U.S.	16.2	24.2	20.1	13.6	8.3	13.6	4.1	244,900

Note: Figures are percentages except for median and cover owner-occupied housing units; (1) Figures cover the Dallas-Fort Worth-Arlington, TX Metropolitan Statistical Area
Source: U.S. Census Bureau, 2017-2021 American Community Survey 5-Year Estimates

Year Housing Structure Built

Area	2020 or Later	2010 -2019	2000 -2009	1990 -1999	1980 -1989	1970 -1979	1960 -1969	1950 -1959	1940 -1949	Before 1940	Median Year
City	0.2	9.8	10.5	10.8	16.4	16.5	12.5	13.2	4.9	5.2	1979
MSA[1]	0.4	14.0	19.1	15.6	17.3	13.3	8.3	7.1	2.4	2.6	1989
U.S.	0.2	7.3	13.6	13.2	14.8	10.3	10.0	4.7	12.2		1979

Note: Figures are percentages except for Median Year; Note: (1) Figures cover the Dallas-Fort Worth-Arlington, TX Metropolitan Statistical Area
Source: U.S. Census Bureau, 2017-2021 American Community Survey 5-Year Estimates

Gross Monthly Rent

Area	Under $500	$500 -$999	$1,000 -$1,499	$1,500 -$1,999	$2,000 -$2,499	$2,500 -$2,999	$3,000 and up	Median ($)
City	3.5	28.7	42.6	16.5	5.2	1.7	1.8	1,178
MSA[1]	2.6	22.1	43.0	21.2	7.7	1.9	1.5	1,264
U.S.	8.1	30.5	30.8	16.8	7.3	3.1	3.5	1,163

Note: Figures are percentages except for median; Gross rent is the contract rent plus the estimated average monthly cost of utilities (electricity, gas, and water and sewer) and fuels (oil, coal, kerosene, wood, etc.) if these are paid by the renter (or paid for the renter by someone else); (1) Figures cover the Dallas-Fort Worth-Arlington, TX Metropolitan Statistical Area
Source: U.S. Census Bureau, 2017-2021 American Community Survey 5-Year Estimates

HEALTH

Health Risk Factors

Category	MD[1] (%)	U.S. (%)
Adults aged 18–64 who have any kind of health care coverage	77.2	90.9
Adults who reported being in good or better health	83.9	85.2
Adults who have been told they have high blood cholesterol	35.8	35.7
Adults who have been told they have high blood pressure	31.9	32.4
Adults who are current smokers	11.4	14.4
Adults who currently use e-cigarettes	6.1	6.7
Adults who currently use chewing tobacco, snuff, or snus	2.1	3.5
Adults who are heavy drinkers[2]	5.2	6.3
Adults who are binge drinkers[3]	15.6	15.4
Adults who are overweight (BMI 25.0 - 29.9)	35.7	34.4
Adults who are obese (BMI 30.0 - 99.8)	31.8	33.9
Adults who participated in any physical activities in the past month	75.8	76.3

Note: (1) Figures cover the Dallas-Plano-Irving, TX Metropolitan Division; (2) Heavy drinkers are classified as adult men having more than 14 drinks per week and adult women having more than 7 drinks per week; (3) Binge drinkers are classified as males having five or more drinks on one occasion or females having four or more drinks on one occasion
Source: Centers for Disease Control and Prevention, Behaviorial Risk Factor Surveillance System, SMART: Selected Metropolitan Area Risk Trends, 2021

Acute and Chronic Health Conditions

Category	MD[1] (%)	U.S. (%)
Adults who have ever been told they had a heart attack	3.3	4.0
Adults who have ever been told they have angina or coronary heart disease	2.5	3.8
Adults who have ever been told they had a stroke	2.9	3.0
Adults who have ever been told they have asthma	12.4	14.9
Adults who have ever been told they have arthritis	19.8	25.8
Adults who have ever been told they have diabetes[2]	10.0	10.9
Adults who have ever been told they had skin cancer	5.2	6.6
Adults who have ever been told they had any other types of cancer	5.2	7.5
Adults who have ever been told they have COPD	4.5	6.1
Adults who have ever been told they have kidney disease	3.3	3.0
Adults who have ever been told they have a form of depression	18.1	20.5

Note: (1) Figures cover the Dallas-Plano-Irving, TX Metropolitan Division; (2) Figures do not include pregnancy-related, borderline, or pre-diabetes
Source: Centers for Disease Control and Prevention, Behaviorial Risk Factor Surveillance System, SMART: Selected Metropolitan Area Risk Trends, 2021

Health Screening and Vaccination Rates

Category	MD[1] (%)	U.S. (%)
Adults who have ever been tested for HIV	41.0	34.9
Adults who have had their blood cholesterol checked within the last five years	88.8	85.2
Adults aged 65+ who have had flu shot within the past year	61.8	68.6
Adults aged 65+ who have ever had a pneumonia vaccination	71.0	71.0

Note: (1) Figures cover the Dallas-Plano-Irving, TX Metropolitan Division.
Source: Centers for Disease Control and Prevention, Behaviorial Risk Factor Surveillance System, SMART: Selected Metropolitan Area Risk Trends, 2021

Disability Status

Category	MD[1] (%)	U.S. (%)
Adults who reported being deaf	4.7	7.2
Are you blind or have serious difficulty seeing, even when wearing glasses?	5.9	4.8
Are you limited in any way in any of your usual activities due to arthritis?	8.2	11.1
Do you have difficulty doing errands alone?	6.2	7.0
Do you have difficulty dressing or bathing?	3.3	3.6
Do you have serious difficulty concentrating/remembering/making decisions?	10.9	12.1
Do you have serious difficulty walking or climbing stairs?	10.2	12.8

Note: (1) Figures cover the Dallas-Plano-Irving, TX Metropolitan Division.
Source: Centers for Disease Control and Prevention, Behaviorial Risk Factor Surveillance System, SMART: Selected Metropolitan Area Risk Trends, 2021

Mortality Rates for the Top 10 Causes of Death in the U.S.

ICD-10[a] Sub-Chapter	ICD-10[a] Code	Crude Mortality Rate[1] per 100,000 population County[2]	U.S.
Malignant neoplasms	C00-C97	129.2	182.6
Ischaemic heart diseases	I20-I25	79.4	113.1
Other forms of heart disease	I30-I51	36.4	64.4
Other degenerative diseases of the nervous system	G30-G31	49.2	51.0
Cerebrovascular diseases	I60-I69	37.7	47.8
Other external causes of accidental injury	W00-X59	31.4	46.4
Chronic lower respiratory diseases	J40-J47	25.9	45.7
Organic, including symptomatic, mental disorders	F01-F09	16.5	35.9
Hypertensive diseases	I10-I15	31.6	35.0
Diabetes mellitus	E10-E14	22.9	29.6

Note: (a) ICD-10 = International Classification of Diseases 10th Revision; (1) Crude mortality rates are a three-year average covering 2019-2021; (2) Figures cover Dallas County.
Source: Centers for Disease Control and Prevention, National Center for Health Statistics. National Vital Statistics System, Mortality 2018-2021 on CDC WONDER Online Database

Mortality Rates for Selected Causes of Death

ICD-10[a] Sub-Chapter	ICD-10[a] Code	Crude Mortality Rate[1] per 100,000 population County[2]	U.S.
Assault	X85-Y09	10.6	7.0
Diseases of the liver	K70-K76	16.4	19.8
Human immunodeficiency virus (HIV) disease	B20-B24	2.9	1.5
Influenza and pneumonia	J09-J18	9.4	14.7
Intentional self-harm	X60-X84	10.7	14.3
Malnutrition	E40-E46	3.6	4.3
Obesity and other hyperalimentation	E65-E68	2.8	3.0
Renal failure	N17-N19	13.9	15.7
Transport accidents	V01-V99	13.8	13.6
Viral hepatitis	B15-B19	1.5	1.2

Note: (a) ICD-10 = International Classification of Diseases 10th Revision; (1) Crude mortality rates are a three-year average covering 2019-2021; (2) Figures cover Dallas County; Data are suppressed when the data meet the criteria for confidentiality constraints; Crude mortality rates are flagged as unreliable when the rate would be calculated with a numerator of 20 or less.
Source: Centers for Disease Control and Prevention, National Center for Health Statistics. National Vital Statistics System, Mortality 2018-2021 on CDC WONDER Online Database

Health Insurance Coverage

Area	With Health Insurance	With Private Health Insurance	With Public Health Insurance	Without Health Insurance	Population Under Age 19 Without Health Insurance
City	76.5	53.3	29.3	23.5	16.0
MSA[1]	83.4	66.4	24.5	16.6	11.7
U.S.	91.2	67.8	35.4	8.8	5.3

Note: Figures are percentages that cover the civilian noninstitutionalized population; (1) Figures cover the Dallas-Fort Worth-Arlington, TX Metropolitan Statistical Area
Source: U.S. Census Bureau, 2017-2021 American Community Survey 5-Year Estimates

Number of Medical Professionals

Area	MDs[3]	DOs[3,4]	Dentists	Podiatrists	Chiropractors	Optometrists
County[1] (number)	9,324	556	2,416	110	973	379
County[1] (rate[2])	357.1	21.3	93.4	4.3	37.6	14.7
U.S. (rate[2])	289.3	23.5	72.5	6.2	28.7	17.4

Note: Data as of 2021 unless noted; (1) Data covers Dallas County; (2) Rate per 100,000 population; (3) Data as of 2020 and includes all active, non-federal physicians; (4) Doctor of Osteopathic Medicine
Source: U.S. Department of Health and Human Services, Health Resources and Services Administration, Bureau of Health Professions, Area Resource File (ARF) 2021-2022

Best Hospitals

According to *U.S. News*, the Dallas-Plano-Irving, TX metro area is home to four of the best hospitals in the U.S.: **Baylor Scott and White Institute for Rehabilitation-Dallas** (1 adult specialty); **Baylor Scott and White The Heart Hospital Plano** (1 adult specialty); **Baylor University Medical Center** (1 adult specialty); **UT Southwestern Medical Center** (9 adult specialties). The hospitals listed were nationally ranked in at least one of 15 adult or 10 pediatric specialties. The number of specialties shown cover the parent hospital. Only 164 U.S. hospitals performed well enough to be nationally ranked in one or more specialties. Twenty hospitals in the U.S. made the Honor Roll. The Best Hospitals Honor Roll takes both the national rankings and the procedure and condition ratings into account. Hospitals received points if they were nationally ranked in one of the 15 adult specialties—the higher

EDUCATION

Public School District Statistics

District Name	Schls	Pupils	Pupil/Teacher Ratio	Minority Pupils[1] (%)	LEP/ELL[2] (%)	IEP[3] (%)
Dallas ISD	237	143,558	14.5	94.0	40.7	9.4
Harmony Science Academy (Waco)	16	9,892	14.2	86.1	26.7	9.2
Highland Park ISD	8	6,724	14.8	18.3	1.3	9.4
Texans Can Academies	13	5,037	19.5	97.9	16.8	7.6
Trinity Basin Preparatory	3	4,211	14.5	98.5	51.3	8.9

Note: Table includes school districts with 2,000 or more students; (1) Percentage of students that are not non-Hispanic white; (2) Percentage of students that are Limited English Proficient or English Language Learners (2018-19); (3) Percentage of students that have an Individualized Education Program (2019-20).
Source: U.S. Department of Education, National Center for Education Statistics, Common Core of Data, Local Education Agency (School District) Universe Survey: School Year 2021-2022

Best High Schools

According to *U.S. News*, Dallas is home to 12 of the top 500 high schools in the U.S.: **The School for the Talented and Gifted (TAG)** (#8); **Irma Lerma Rangel Young Women's Leadership School** (#20); **Science and Engineering Magnet School (SEM)** (#22); **Judge Barefoot Sanders Law Magnet** (#48); **Trinidad Garza Early College at Mt View** (#118); **School of Health Professions** (#141); **School of Business and Management** (#173); **Booker T. Washington SPVA** (#219); **Barack Obama Male Leadership Academy** (#272); **Highland Park High School** (#281); **Dr. Wright L Lassiter Jr Early College High School** (#333); **Rosie Sorrells Education and Social Services High School** (#343). Nearly 18,000 public, magnet and charter schools were ranked based on their performance on state assessments and how well they prepare students for college. *U.S. News & World Report, "Best High Schools 2022"*

Highest Level of Education

Area	Less than H.S.	H.S. Diploma	Some College, No Deg.	Associate Degree	Bachelor's Degree	Master's Degree	Prof. School Degree	Doctorate Degree
City	20.4	21.8	17.4	4.8	22.1	9.0	3.2	1.3
MSA[1]	13.4	22.0	20.6	7.3	23.8	9.8	1.9	1.2
U.S.	11.1	26.5	20.0	8.7	20.6	9.3	2.2	1.5

Note: Figures cover persons age 25 and over; (1) Figures cover the Dallas-Fort Worth-Arlington, TX Metropolitan Statistical Area
Source: U.S. Census Bureau, 2017-2021 American Community Survey 5-Year Estimates

Educational Attainment by Race

Area	High School Graduate or Higher (%)					Bachelor's Degree or Higher (%)				
	Total	White	Black	Asian	Hisp.[2]	Total	White	Black	Asian	Hisp.[2]
City	79.6	80.5	88.4	87.4	55.4	35.6	44.3	22.3	66.0	13.5
MSA[1]	86.6	88.9	91.8	88.8	63.9	36.8	38.9	30.0	62.8	16.2
U.S.	88.9	91.4	87.2	87.6	71.2	33.7	35.5	23.3	55.6	18.4

Note: Figures shown cover persons 25 years old and over; (1) Figures cover the Dallas-Fort Worth-Arlington, TX Metropolitan Statistical Area; (2) People of Hispanic origin can be of any race
Source: U.S. Census Bureau, 2017-2021 American Community Survey 5-Year Estimates

School Enrollment by Grade and Control

Area	Preschool (%)		Kindergarten (%)		Grades 1 - 4 (%)		Grades 5 - 8 (%)		Grades 9 - 12 (%)	
	Public	Private	Public	Private	Public	Private	Public	Private	Public	Private
City	71.3	28.7	91.0	9.0	91.3	8.7	91.4	8.6	90.6	9.4
MSA[1]	59.0	41.0	88.8	11.2	91.3	8.7	91.6	8.4	91.9	8.1
U.S.	58.8	41.2	86.3	13.7	88.3	11.7	88.6	11.4	89.4	10.6

Note: Figures shown cover persons 3 years old and over; (1) Figures cover the Dallas-Fort Worth-Arlington, TX Metropolitan Statistical Area
Source: U.S. Census Bureau, 2017-2021 American Community Survey 5-Year Estimates

Dallas, Texas

Higher Education

| Four-Year Colleges ||| Two-Year Colleges ||| Medical Schools[1] | Law Schools[2] | Voc/Tech[3] |
Public	Private Non-profit	Private For-profit	Public	Private Non-profit	Private For-profit			
11	23	5	1	3	12	3	3	34

Note: Figures cover institutions located within the Dallas-Fort Worth-Arlington, TX Metropolitan Statistical Area and include main campuses only; (1) includes schools accredited by the Liaison Committee on Medical Education and the American Osteopathic Association's Commission on Osteopathic College Accreditation; (2) includes ABA-accredited schools, schools with provisional ABA accreditation, and state accredited schools; (3) includes all schools with programs that are less than 2 years.
Source: National Center for Education Statistics, Integrated Postsecondary Education System (IPEDS), 2021-22; Wikipedia, List of Medical Schools in the United States, accessed April 10, 2023; Wikipedia, List of Law Schools in the United States, accessed April 10, 2023

According to *U.S. News & World Report,* the Dallas-Plano-Irving, TX metro division is home to two of the top 200 national universities in the U.S.: **Southern Methodist University** (#72 tie); **The University of Texas at Dallas** (#151 tie). The indicators used to capture academic quality fall into a number of categories: assessment by administrators at peer institutions; retention of students; faculty resources; student selectivity; financial resources; alumni giving; high school counselor ratings of colleges; and graduation rate. *U.S. News & World Report, "America's Best Colleges 2023"*

According to *U.S. News & World Report,* the Dallas-Plano-Irving, TX metro division is home to one of the top 100 law schools in the U.S.: **SMU (Dedman)** (#58 tie). The rankings are based on a weighted average of 12 measures of quality: peer assessment score; assessment score by lawyers/judges; median LSAT scores; median undergrad GPA; acceptance rate; employment rates for graduates; placement success; bar passage rate; faculty resources; expenditures per student; student/faculty ratio; and library resources. *U.S. News & World Report, "America's Best Graduate Schools, Law, 2023"*

According to *U.S. News & World Report,* the Dallas-Plano-Irving, TX metro division is home to one of the top 75 medical schools for research in the U.S.: **University of Texas Southwestern Medical Center** (#25 tie). The rankings are based on a weighted average of 11 measures of quality: quality assessment; peer assessment score; assessment score by residency directors; research activity; total research activity; average research activity per faculty member; student selectivity; median MCAT total score; median undergraduate GPA; acceptance rate; and faculty resources. *U.S. News & World Report, "America's Best Graduate Schools, Medical, 2023"*

According to *U.S. News & World Report,* the Dallas-Plano-Irving, TX metro division is home to two of the top 75 business schools in the U.S.: **The University of Texas at Dallas (Jindal)** (#29 tie); **Southern Methodist University (Cox)** (#41 tie). The rankings are based on a weighted average of the following nine measures: quality assessment; peer assessment; recruiter assessment; placement success; mean starting salary and bonus; student selectivity; mean GMAT and GRE scores; mean undergraduate GPA; and acceptance rate. *U.S. News & World Report, "America's Best Graduate Schools, Business, 2023"*

EMPLOYERS

Major Employers

Company Name	Industry
AMR Corporation	Air transportation, scheduled
Associates First Capital Corporation	Mortgage bankers
Baylor University Medical Center	General medical & surgical hospitals
Children's Medical Center Dallas	Specialty hospitals, except psychiatric
Combat Support Associates	Engineering services
County of Dallas	County government
Dallas County Hospital District	General medical & surgical hospitals
Fort Worth Independent School District	Public elementary & secondary schools
Housewares Holding Company	Toasters, electric: household
HP Enterprise Services	Computer integrated systems design
J.C. Penney Company	Department stores
JCP Publications Corp.	Department stores
L-3 Communications Corporation	Business economic service
Odyssey HealthCare	Home health care services
Romano's Macaroni Grill	Italian restaurant
SFG Management	Milk processing (pasteurizing, homogenizing, bottling)
Texas Instruments Incorporated	Semiconductors & related devices
University of North Texas	Colleges & universities
University of Texas SW Medical Center	Accident & health insurance
Verizon Business Global	Telephone communication, except radio

Note: Companies shown are located within the Dallas-Fort Worth-Arlington, TX Metropolitan Statistical Area.
Source: Hoovers.com; Wikipedia

Best Companies to Work For

Ryan, headquartered in Dallas, is among "The 100 Best Companies to Work For." To pick the best companies, *Fortune* partnered with the Great Place to Work Institute. Two-thirds of a company's score is based on the results of the Institute's Trust Index survey, which is sent to a random sample of employees from each company. The questions related to attitudes about management's credibility, job satisfaction, and camaraderie. The other third of the scoring is based on the company's responses to the Institute's Culture Audit, which includes detailed questions about pay and benefit programs, and a series of open-ended questions about hiring practices, internal communication, training, recognition programs, and diversity efforts. Any company that is at least five years old with more than 1,000 U.S. employees is eligible. *Fortune, "The 100 Best Companies to Work For," 2023*

PMG; PrimeLending; Ryan, headquartered in Dallas, are among "Fortune's Best Workplaces for Women." To pick the best companies, *Fortune* partnered with the Great Place to Work Institute. To be considered for the list, companies must be Great Place To Work-Certified. Companies must also employ at least 50 women, at least 20% of their non-executive managers must be female, and at least one executive must be female. To determine the Best Workplaces for Women, Great Place To Work measured the differences in women's survey responses to those of their peers and assesses the impact of demographics and roles on the quality and consistency of women's experiences. Great Place To Work also analyzed the gender balance of each workplace, how it compared to each company's industry, and patterns in representation as women rise from front-line positions to the board of directors. *Fortune, "Best Workplaces for Women," 2022*

Astanza Laser; Enhabit Home Health & Hospice; ProPath, headquartered in Dallas, are among "Best Workplaces in Health Care." To determine the Best Workplaces in Health Care list, Great Place To Work analyzed the survey responses of over 161,000 employees from Great Place To Work-Certified companies in the health care industry. Survey data analysis and company-provided datapoints are then factored into a combined score to compare and rank the companies that create the most consistently positive experience for all employees in this industry. *Fortune, "Best Workplaces in Health Care," 2022*

Bestow; PMG; PrimeLending; Ryan, headquartered in Dallas, are among "Fortune's Best Workplaces for Parents." To pick the best companies, *Fortune* partnered with the Great Place to Work Institute. To be considered for the list, companies must be Great Place To Work-Certified and have at least 50 responses from parents in the US. The survey enables employees to share confidential quantitative and qualitative feedback about their organization's culture by responding to 60 statements on a 5-point scale and answering two open-ended questions. Collectively, these statements describe a great employee experience, defined by high levels of trust, respect, credibility, fairness, pride, and camaraderie. In addition, companies provide organizational data like size, location, industry, demographics, roles, and levels; and provide information about parental leave, adoption, flexible schedule, childcare and dependent health care benefits. *Fortune, "Best Workplaces for Parents," 2022*

Axxess, headquartered in Dallas, is among the "100 Best Places to Work in IT." To qualify, companies had to have a minimum of 100 total employees and five IT employees. The best places to work were selected based on DEI (diversity, equity, and inclusion) practices; IT turnover, promotions, and growth; IT retention and engagement programs; remote/hybrid working; benefits and perks (such as elder care and child care, flextime, and reimbursement for college tuition); and training and career development opportunities. *Computerworld, "Best Places to Work in IT," 2023*

PUBLIC SAFETY

Crime Rate

Area	Total Crime	Violent Crime Rate				Property Crime Rate		
		Murder	Rape[3]	Robbery	Aggrav. Assault	Burglary	Larceny-Theft	Motor Vehicle Theft
City	4,291.0	17.3	41.7	241.5	544.2	727.6	1,955.6	763.1
Suburbs[1]	n/a	n/a	n/a	n/a	n/a	n/a	n/a	n/a
Metro[2]	n/a	n/a	n/a	n/a	n/a	n/a	n/a	n/a
U.S.	2,356.7	6.5	38.4	73.9	279.7	314.2	1,398.0	246.0

Note: Figures are crimes per 100,000 population; (1) All areas within the metro area that are located outside the city limits; (2) Figures cover the Dallas-Plano-Irving, TX Metropolitan Division; n/a not available; (3) All figures shown were reported using the revised Uniform Crime Reporting (UCR) definition of rape; Due to the transition to the National Incident-Based Reporting System (NIBRS), limited city and metro area data was released for 2021.
Source: FBI Uniform Crime Reports, 2020

Hate Crimes

Area	Number of Quarters Reported	Race/Ethnicity/Ancestry	Religion	Sexual Orientation	Disability	Gender	Gender Identity
City	4	24	3	11	0	0	0
U.S.	4	5,227	1,244	1,110	130	75	266

Note: Due to the transition to the National Incident-Based Reporting System (NIBRS), limited crime data was released for 2021.
Source: Federal Bureau of Investigation, Hate Crime Statistics 2020

Identity Theft Consumer Reports

Area	Reports	Reports per 100,000 Population	Rank[2]
MSA[1]	34,005	456	23
U.S.	1,108,609	339	-

Note: (1) Figures cover the Dallas-Fort Worth-Arlington, TX Metropolitan Statistical Area; (2) Rank ranges from 1 to 391 where 1 indicates greatest number of identity theft reports per 100,000 population
Source: Federal Trade Commission, Consumer Sentinel Network Data Book 2022

Fraud and Other Consumer Reports

Area	Reports	Reports per 100,000 Population	Rank[2]
MSA[1]	93,393	1,253	37
U.S.	4,064,520	1,245	-

Note: (1) Figures cover the Dallas-Fort Worth-Arlington, TX Metropolitan Statistical Area; (2) Rank ranges from 1 to 391 where 1 indicates greatest number of fraud and other consumer reports per 100,000 population
Source: Federal Trade Commission, Consumer Sentinel Network Data Book 2022

POLITICS

2020 Presidential Election Results

Area	Biden	Trump	Jorgensen	Hawkins	Other
Dallas County	64.9	33.3	1.0	0.4	0.4
U.S.	51.3	46.8	1.2	0.3	0.5

Note: Results are percentages and may not add to 100% due to rounding
Source: Dave Leip's Atlas of U.S. Presidential Elections

SPORTS

Professional Sports Teams

Team Name	League	Year Established
Dallas Cowboys	National Football League (NFL)	1960
Dallas Mavericks	National Basketball Association (NBA)	1980
Dallas Stars	National Hockey League (NHL)	1993
FC Dallas	Major League Soccer (MLS)	1996
Texas Rangers	Major League Baseball (MLB)	1972

Note: Includes teams located in the Dallas-Fort Worth-Arlington, TX Metropolitan Statistical Area.
Source: Wikipedia, Major Professional Sports Teams of the United States and Canada, April 12, 2023

CLIMATE

Average and Extreme Temperatures

Temperature	Jan	Feb	Mar	Apr	May	Jun	Jul	Aug	Sep	Oct	Nov	Dec	Yr.
Extreme High (°F)	85	90	100	100	101	112	111	109	107	101	91	87	112
Average High (°F)	55	60	68	76	84	92	96	96	89	79	67	58	77
Average Temp. (°F)	45	50	57	66	74	82	86	86	79	68	56	48	67
Average Low (°F)	35	39	47	56	64	72	76	75	68	57	46	38	56
Extreme Low (°F)	-2	9	12	30	39	53	58	58	42	24	16	0	-2

Note: Figures cover the years 1945-1993
Source: National Climatic Data Center, International Station Meteorological Climate Summary, 9/96

Average Precipitation/Snowfall/Humidity

Precip./Humidity	Jan	Feb	Mar	Apr	May	Jun	Jul	Aug	Sep	Oct	Nov	Dec	Yr.
Avg. Precip. (in.)	1.9	2.3	2.6	3.8	4.9	3.4	2.1	2.3	2.9	3.3	2.3	2.1	33.9
Avg. Snowfall (in.)	1	1	Tr	Tr	0	0	0	0	0	Tr	Tr	Tr	3
Avg. Rel. Hum. 6am (%)	78	77	75	77	82	81	77	76	80	79	78	77	78
Avg. Rel. Hum. 3pm (%)	53	51	47	49	51	48	43	41	46	46	48	51	48

Note: Figures cover the years 1945-1993; Tr = Trace amounts (<0.05 in. of rain; <0.5 in. of snow)
Source: National Climatic Data Center, International Station Meteorological Climate Summary, 9/96

Weather Conditions

Temperature			Daytime Sky			Precipitation		
10°F & below	32°F & below	90°F & above	Clear	Partly cloudy	Cloudy	0.01 inch or more precip.	0.1 inch or more snow/ice	Thunder-storms
1	34	102	108	160	97	78	2	49

Note: Figures are average number of days per year and cover the years 1945-1993
Source: National Climatic Data Center, International Station Meteorological Climate Summary, 9/96

HAZARDOUS WASTE

Superfund Sites

The Dallas-Plano-Irving, TX metro division is home to three sites on the EPA's Superfund National Priorities List: **Delfasco Forge** (final); **Lane Plating Works, Inc** (final); **RSR Corporation** (final). There are a total of 1,165 Superfund sites with a status of proposed or final on the list in the U.S. *U.S. Environmental Protection Agency, National Priorities List, April 12, 2023*

AIR QUALITY

Air Quality Trends: Ozone

	1990	1995	2000	2005	2010	2015	2018	2019	2020	2021
MSA[1]	0.094	0.103	0.096	0.096	0.079	0.078	0.079	0.070	0.070	0.076
U.S.	0.087	0.089	0.081	0.080	0.072	0.067	0.069	0.065	0.065	0.067

Note: (1) Data covers the Dallas-Fort Worth-Arlington, TX Metropolitan Statistical Area. The values shown are the composite ozone concentration averages among trend sites based on the highest fourth daily maximum 8-hour concentration in parts per million. These trends are based on sites having an adequate record of monitoring data during the trend period. Data from exceptional events are included.
Source: U.S. Environmental Protection Agency, Air Quality Monitoring Information, "Air Quality Trends by City, 1990-2021"

Air Quality Index

Area	Percent of Days when Air Quality was...[2]					AQI Statistics[2]	
	Good	Moderate	Unhealthy for Sensitive Groups	Unhealthy	Very Unhealthy	Maximum	Median
MSA[1]	54.0	37.5	7.4	0.8	0.3	209	49

Note: (1) Data covers the Dallas-Fort Worth-Arlington, TX Metropolitan Statistical Area; (2) Based on 365 days with AQI data in 2021. Air Quality Index (AQI) is an index for reporting daily air quality. EPA calculates the AQI for five major air pollutants regulated by the Clean Air Act: ground-level ozone, particle pollution (aka particulate matter), carbon monoxide, sulfur dioxide, and nitrogen dioxide. The AQI runs from 0 to 500. The higher the AQI value, the greater the level of air pollution and the greater the health concern. There are six AQI categories: "Good" AQI is between 0 and 50. Air quality is considered satisfactory; "Moderate" AQI is between 51 and 100. Air quality is acceptable; "Unhealthy for Sensitive Groups" When AQI values are between 101 and 150, members of sensitive groups may experience health effects; "Unhealthy" When AQI values are between 151 and 200 everyone may begin to experience health effects; "Very Unhealthy" AQI values between 201 and 300 trigger a health alert; "Hazardous" AQI values over 300 trigger warnings of emergency conditions (not shown).
Source: U.S. Environmental Protection Agency, Air Quality Index Report, 2021

Air Quality Index Pollutants

Area	Percent of Days when AQI Pollutant was...[2]					
	Carbon Monoxide	Nitrogen Dioxide	Ozone	Sulfur Dioxide	Particulate Matter 2.5	Particulate Matter 10
MSA[1]	0.0	3.3	61.4	(3)	35.3	0.0

Note: (1) Data covers the Dallas-Fort Worth-Arlington, TX Metropolitan Statistical Area; (2) Based on 365 days with AQI data in 2021. The Air Quality Index (AQI) is an index for reporting daily air quality. EPA calculates the AQI for five major air pollutants regulated by the Clean Air Act: ground-level ozone, particle pollution (also known as particulate matter), carbon monoxide, sulfur dioxide, and nitrogen dioxide. The AQI runs from 0 to 500. The higher the AQI value, the greater the level of air pollution and the greater the health concern; (3) Sulfur dioxide is no longer included in this table (as of December 8, 2021) because SO_2 concentrations tend to be very localized and not necessarily representative of broad geographical areas like counties and CBSAs.
Source: U.S. Environmental Protection Agency, Air Quality Index Report, 2021

Maximum Air Pollutant Concentrations: Particulate Matter, Ozone, CO and Lead

	Particulate Matter 10 (ug/m³)	Particulate Matter 2.5 Wtd AM (ug/m³)	Particulate Matter 2.5 24-Hr (ug/m³)	Ozone (ppm)	Carbon Monoxide (ppm)	Lead (ug/m³)
MSA[1] Level	56	9.6	23	0.085	1	0.02
NAAQS[2]	150	15	35	0.075	9	0.15
Met NAAQS[2]	Yes	Yes	Yes	No	Yes	Yes

Note: (1) Data covers the Dallas-Fort Worth-Arlington, TX Metropolitan Statistical Area; Data from exceptional events are included; (2) National Ambient Air Quality Standards; ppm = parts per million; ug/m³ = micrograms per cubic meter; n/a not available.
Concentrations: Particulate Matter 10 (coarse particulate)—highest second maximum 24-hour concentration; Particulate Matter 2.5 Wtd AM (fine particulate)—highest weighted annual mean concentration; Particulate Matter 2.5 24-Hour (fine particulate)—highest 98th percentile 24-hour concentration; Ozone—highest fourth daily maximum 8-hour concentration; Carbon Monoxide—highest second maximum non-overlapping 8-hour concentration; Lead—maximum running 3-month average
Source: U.S. Environmental Protection Agency, Air Quality Monitoring Information, "Air Quality Statistics by City, 2021"

Maximum Air Pollutant Concentrations: Nitrogen Dioxide and Sulfur Dioxide

	Nitrogen Dioxide AM (ppb)	Nitrogen Dioxide 1-Hr (ppb)	Sulfur Dioxide AM (ppb)	Sulfur Dioxide 1-Hr (ppb)	Sulfur Dioxide 24-Hr (ppb)
MSA[1] Level	13	48	n/a	8	n/a
NAAQS[2]	53	100	30	75	140
Met NAAQS[2]	Yes	Yes	n/a	Yes	n/a

Note: (1) Data covers the Dallas-Fort Worth-Arlington, TX Metropolitan Statistical Area; Data from exceptional events are included; (2) National Ambient Air Quality Standards; ppm = parts per million; ug/m³ = micrograms per cubic meter; n/a not available.
Concentrations: Nitrogen Dioxide AM—highest arithmetic mean concentration; Nitrogen Dioxide 1-Hr—highest 98th percentile 1-hour daily maximum concentration; Sulfur Dioxide AM—highest annual mean concentration; Sulfur Dioxide 1-Hr—highest 99th percentile 1-hour daily maximum concentration; Sulfur Dioxide 24-Hr—highest second maximum 24-hour concentration
Source: U.S. Environmental Protection Agency, Air Quality Monitoring Information, "Air Quality Statistics by City, 2021"

El Paso, Texas

Background

El Paso, is named so because it sits in a spectacular pass through the Franklin Mountains. With an average elevation of 3,700 feet and direct view of peaks that rise to 7,200 feet, El Paso is the fourth-largest city in Texas. It lies just south of New Mexico on the Rio Grande and just north of Juarez, Mexico.

Although there is evidence that early Spanish explorer Alvar Nunez Cabeza de Vaca (circa 1530) passed through this area, the city was named in 1598 by Juan de Onante, El Paso del Rio del Norte—The Pass at the River of the North. It was also Onante who declared the area Spanish, on the authority of King Philip II, but a mission was not established until 1649. For some time, El Paso del Norte was the seat of government for northern Mexico, but settlement in and around the present-day city was sparse for many years.

This changed considerably by 1807, when Zebulon A. Pike, a United States Army officer, was interned in El Paso after being convicted of trespassing on Spanish territory. He found the area pleasant and well-tended, with many irrigated fields and vineyards and a thriving trade in brandy and wine. Despite Pike's attraction and interest in the area, El Paso remained for many years a Mexican region, escaping most of the military action connected to the Texas Revolution.

In the wake of the Mexican War (1846-1848) and in response to the California gold rush in 1849, El Paso emerged as a significant way station on the road west. Federal garrison Fort Bliss was established there in 1849 and was briefly occupied by Confederate sympathizers in 1862. Federal forces quickly reoccupied the fort, however, and the area was firmly controlled by Union armies. El Paso was incorporated in 1873, and several years later, growth accelerated considerably with the building of rail links through the city, giving rise to ironworks, mills, and breweries.

After the Mexican Revolution (1911), El Paso was an important and disputed city, with Pancho Villa a frequent visitor, and many of his followers' becoming residents of the town. Mexico's national history continued to affect El Paso until 1967 when, by way of settling a historic border dispute, 437 acres of the city was ceded to Mexico. Much of the disputed area on both sides of the border was made into parkland. The U.S. National Parks Service maintains the Chamizal Park on the U.S. side and plays host to a variety of community events during the year including the Chamizal Film Festival and the summer concert series, Music Under the Stars.

El Paso is one of the major points of entry to the United States from Mexico, often with hundreds reaching the El Paso's Processing Center daily. El Paso is a vitally important international city and a burgeoning center of rail, road, and air transportation. During the 1990s, the city's economy shifted more toward a service-oriented economy and away from a manufacturing base. In 2021, Amazon opened a 625,000 square-foot fulfillment center in the city and employs about 700.

Transportation services and tourism are growing segments of the economy. Government and military are also sources of employment, with Fort Bliss being the largest Air Defense Artillery Training Center in the world. The city hosts the University of Texas at El Paso, and a community college. Cultural amenities include the Tigua Indian Cultural Center, Wilderness Park Museum, El Paso Zoo, a symphony orchestra, a ballet company, and many theaters. The city's "Wild West" qualities have long made it a popular destination for musicians, many of whom have recorded albums at El Paso's Sonic Ranch recording studio.

In 2019, El Paso was awarded its own United Soccer League team.

El Paso's revitalized downtown has increased the city's aesthetic appeal. It includes an open-air mall and "lifestyle center" in the city's central area, Doubletree by Hilton Hotel, and renovations of several historic downtown buildings.

El Paso is home to the world's largest inland desalination plant, designed to produce 27.5 million gallons of fresh water daily making it a critical component of the region's water portfolio.

The weather in El Paso is of the mountain-desert type, with very little precipitation. Summers are hot, humidity is low, and winters are mild. However, temperatures in the flat Rio Grande Valley nearby are notably cooler at night year-round. There is plenty of sunshine and clear skies generally more than 200 days of the year.

Rankings

General Rankings

- For its "Best for Vets: Places to Live 2019" rankings, *Military Times* evaluated 599 cities (83 large, 234 medium, 282 small) and compared the locations across three broad categories: veteran and military culture/services; economic indicators; and livability factors such as health, crime, traffic, and school quality. El Paso ranked #20 out of the top 25, in the large city category (population of more than 250,000). Data points more specific to veterans and the military weighed more heavily than others. *rebootcamp.militarytimes.com*, "Military Times Best Places to Live 2019," September 10, 2018

- The El Paso metro area was identified as one of America's fastest-growing areas in terms of population and business growth by *MagnifyMoney*. The area ranked #24 out of 35. The 100 most populous metro areas in the U.S. were evaluated on their change from 2011 to 2016 in the following categories: people and housing; workforce and employment opportunities; growing industry. *www.businessinsider.com*, "The 35 Cities in the US with the Biggest Influx of People, the Most Work Opportunities, and the Hottest Business Growth," August 12, 2018

Business/Finance Rankings

- El Paso was the #1-ranked city for savers, according to a study by the finance site GOBankingRates, which considered the prospects for people trying to save money. Criteria: average monthly cost of grocery items; median home listing price; median rent; median income; transportation costs; gas prices; and the cost of eating out for an inexpensive and mid-range meal in 100 U.S. cities. *www.gobankingrates.com*, "The 20 Best (and Worst) Places to Live If You're Trying to Save Money," August 27, 2019

- El Paso was ranked #1 among 100 U.S. cities for most difficult conditions for savers, according to a study by the finance site GOBankingRates. Criteria: average monthly cost of grocery items; median home listing price; median rent; median income; transportation costs; gas prices; and the cost of eating out for an inexpensive and mid-range meal. *www.gobankingrates.com*, "The 20 Best (and Worst) Places to Live If You're Trying to Save Money," August 27, 2019

- The Brookings Institution ranked the nation's largest cities based on income inequality. El Paso was ranked #59 (#1 = greatest inequality). Criteria: the "95/20 ratio," a figure representing the income at which a household earns more than 95 percent of all other households, divided by the income at which a household earns more than only 20 percent of all other households. *Brookings Institution*, "Household Income Inequality, Largest Cities of 97 Large U.S. Metro Areas, 2014-2016," February 5, 2018

- The Brookings Institution ranked the 100 largest metro areas in the U.S. based on income inequality. El Paso was ranked #39 (#1 = greatest inequality). Criteria: the "95/20 ratio," a figure representing the income at which a household earns more than 95 percent of all other households, divided by the income at which a household earns more than only 20 percent of all other households. *Brookings Institution*, "Household Income Inequality, 100 Largest U.S. Metro Areas, 2014-2016," February 5, 2018

- The El Paso metro area appeared on the Milken Institute "2022 Best Performing Cities" list. Rank: #73 out of 200 large metro areas (population over 250,000). Criteria: job growth; wage and salary growth; high-tech output growth; housing affordability; household broadband access. *Milken Institute*, "Best-Performing Cities 2022," March 28, 2022

- *Forbes* ranked the 200 most populous metro areas to determine the nation's "Best Places for Business and Careers." The El Paso metro area was ranked #171. Criteria: costs (business and living); job growth (past and projected); income growth; quality of life; educational attainment (college and high school); projected economic growth; cultural and leisure opportunities; workplace tolerance laws; net migration patterns. *Forbes*, "The Best Places for Business and Careers 2019: Seattle Still On Top," October 30, 2019

Education Rankings

- Personal finance website *WalletHub* analyzed the 150 largest U.S. metropolitan statistical areas to determine where the most educated Americans are putting their degrees to work. Criteria: education levels; percentage of workers with degrees; education quality and attainment gap; public school quality rankings; quality and enrollment of each metro area's universities. El Paso was ranked #138 (#1 = most educated city). *www.WalletHub.com*, "Most & Least Educated Cities in America," July 18, 2022

El Paso, Texas

- El Paso was selected as one of America's most literate cities. The city ranked #80 out of the 84 largest U.S. cities. Criteria: number of booksellers; library resources; Internet resources; educational attainment; periodical publishing resources; newspaper circulation. *Central Connecticut State University, "America's Most Literate Cities, 2018," February 2019*

Environmental Rankings

- El Paso was highlighted as one of the 25 most ozone-polluted metro areas in the U.S. during 2019 through 2021. The area ranked #14. *American Lung Association, "State of the Air 2023," April 19, 2023*

Health/Fitness Rankings

- For each of the 100 largest cities in the United States, the American Fitness Index®, compiled in partnership between the American College of Sports Medicine and the Elevance Health Foundation, evaluated community infrastructure and 34 health behaviors including preventive health, levels of chronic disease conditions, food insecurity, sleep quality, pedestrian safety, air quality, and community/environment resources that support physical activity. El Paso ranked #77 for "community fitness." *americanfitnessindex.org, "2022 ACSM American Fitness Index Summary Report," July 12, 2022*

- El Paso was identified as a "2022 Spring Allergy Capital." The area ranked #30 out of 100. Three groups of factors were used to identify the most challenging cities for people with allergies during the spring season: annual spring pollen scores; over the counter allergy medicine use; number of board-certified allergy specialists. *Asthma and Allergy Foundation of America, "Spring Allergy Capitals 2022," March 2, 2022*

- El Paso was identified as a "2022 Fall Allergy Capital." The area ranked #6 out of 100. Three groups of factors were used to identify the most challenging cities for people with allergies during the fall season: annual fall pollen scores; over the counter allergy medicine use; number of board-certified allergy specialists. *Asthma and Allergy Foundation of America, "Fall Allergy Capitals 2022," March 2, 2022*

- El Paso was identified as a "2022 Asthma Capital." The area ranked #56 out of the nation's 100 largest metropolitan areas. Criteria: estimated asthma prevalence; asthma-related mortality; and ER visits due to asthma. Risk factors analyzed but not factored in the rankings: annual pollen score; annual air quality; public smoking laws; access to board-certified asthma specialists; rescue and controller medication use; uninsured rate; poverty rate. *Asthma and Allergy Foundation of America, "Asthma Capitals 2022: The Most Challenging Places to Live With Asthma," September 14, 2022*

Real Estate Rankings

- *WalletHub* compared the most populated U.S. cities to determine which had the best markets for real estate agents. El Paso ranked #156 where demand was high and pay was the best. Criteria: sales per agent; annual median wage for real-estate agents; monthly average starting salary for real estate agents; real estate job density and competition; unemployment rate; home turnover rate; housing-market health index; and other relevant metrics. *www.WalletHub.com, "2021 Best Places to Be a Real Estate Agent," May 12, 2021*

- The El Paso metro area appeared on Realtor.com's list of hot housing markets to watch in 2023. The area ranked #2. Criteria: forecasted home price and sales growth; overall economy; population trends. *Realtor.com®, "Top 10 Housing Markets Positioned for Growth in 2023," December 7, 2022*

- The El Paso metro area was identified as one of the 20 best housing markets in the U.S. in 2022. The area ranked #8 out of 187 markets. Criteria: year-over-year change of median sales price of existing single-family homes between the 4th quarter of 2021 and the 4th quarter of 2022. *National Association of Realtors®, Median Sales Price of Existing Single-Family Homes for Metropolitan Areas, 4th Quarter 2022*

- El Paso was ranked #178 out of 235 metro areas in terms of housing affordability in 2022 by the National Association of Home Builders (#1 = most affordable). Criteria: the share of homes sold in that area affordable to a family earning the local median income, based on standard mortgage underwriting criteria. *National Association of Home Builders®, NAHB-Wells Fargo Housing Opportunity Index, 4th Quarter 2022*

Safety Rankings

- Allstate ranked the 200 largest cities in America in terms of driver safety. El Paso ranked #48. Criteria: internal property damage claims over a two-year period from January 2016 to December 2017. The report helps increase the importance of safety and awareness behind the wheel. *Allstate, "Allstate America's Best Drivers Report, 2019" June 24, 2019*

- The National Insurance Crime Bureau ranked 390 metro areas in the U.S. in terms of per capita rates of vehicle theft. The El Paso metro area ranked #247 (#1 = highest rate). Criteria: number of vehicle theft offenses per 100,000 inhabitants in 2021. *National Insurance Crime Bureau, "Hot Spots 2021," September 1, 2022*

Seniors/Retirement Rankings

- From its Best Cities for Successful Aging indexes, the Milken Institute generated rankings for metropolitan areas, weighing data in nine categories—health care, wellness, living arrangements, transportation and convenience, financial characteristics, education, employment, community engagement, and overall livability. The El Paso metro area was ranked #80 overall in the large metro area category. *Milken Institute, "Best Cities for Successful Aging, 2017" March 14, 2017*

Women/Minorities Rankings

- The *Houston Chronicle* listed the El Paso metro area as #14 in top places for young Latinos to live in the U.S. Research was largely based on housing and occupational data from the largest metropolitan areas performed by *Forbes* and NBC Universo. Criteria: percentage of 18-34 year-olds; Latino college grad rates; and diversity. *blog.chron.com, "The 15 Best Big Cities for Latino Millenials," January 26, 2016*

- Personal finance website *WalletHub* compared more than 180 U.S. cities across two key dimensions, "Hispanic Business-Friendliness" and "Hispanic Purchasing Power," to arrive at the most favorable conditions for Hispanic entrepreneurs. El Paso was ranked #9 out of 182. Criteria includes: share of Hispanic-Owned Businesses; Hispanic entrepreneurship rate to median annual income of Hispanics; Small Business-Friendliness score; cost of living; and number of Hispanics with at least a bachelor's degree. *WalletHub.com, "2019's Best Cities for Hispanic Entrepreneurs," May 1, 2019*

Miscellaneous Rankings

- El Paso was selected as a 2022 Digital Cities Survey winner. The city ranked #9 in the large city (500,000 or more population) category. The survey examined and assessed how city governments are utilizing technology to continue innovation, engage with residents, and persevere through the challenges of the pandemic. Survey questions focused on ten initiatives: cybersecurity; citizen experience; disaster recovery; business intelligence; IT personnel; data governance; business automation; IT governance; infrastructure modernization; and broadband connectivity. *Center for Digital Government, "2022 Digital Cities Survey," November 10, 2022*

- *WalletHub* compared the 150 most populated U.S. cities to determine their operating efficiency. A "Quality of Services" score was constructed for each city and then divided by the total budget per capita to reveal which were managed the best. El Paso ranked #38. Criteria: financial stability; economy; education; safety; health; infrastructure and pollution. *www.WalletHub.com, "2022's Best- & Worst-Run Cities in America," June 21, 2022*

Business Environment

DEMOGRAPHICS

Population Growth

Area	1990 Census	2000 Census	2010 Census	2020 Census	Population Growth (%) 1990-2020	Population Growth (%) 2010-2020
City	515,541	563,662	649,121	678,815	31.7	4.6
MSA[1]	591,610	679,622	800,647	868,859	46.9	8.5
U.S.	248,709,873	281,421,906	308,745,538	331,449,281	33.3	7.4

Note: (1) Figures cover the El Paso, TX Metropolitan Statistical Area
Source: U.S. Census Bureau, 1990 Census, 2000 Census, 2010 Census, 2020 Census

Race

Area	White Alone[2] (%)	Black Alone[2] (%)	Asian Alone[2] (%)	AIAN[3] Alone[2] (%)	NHOPI[4] Alone[2] (%)	Other Race Alone[2] (%)	Two or More Races (%)
City	36.8	3.7	1.5	1.1	0.2	20.6	36.0
MSA[1]	36.3	3.3	1.4	1.2	0.2	21.7	35.8
U.S.	61.6	12.4	6.0	1.1	0.2	8.4	10.2

Note: (1) Figures cover the El Paso, TX Metropolitan Statistical Area; (2) Alone is defined as not being in combination with one or more other races; (3) American Indian and Alaska Native; (4) Native Hawaiian and Other Pacific Islander
Source: U.S. Census Bureau, 2020 Census

Hispanic or Latino Origin

Area	Total (%)	Mexican (%)	Puerto Rican (%)	Cuban (%)	Other (%)
City	81.6	76.9	1.0	0.2	3.5
MSA[1]	82.9	78.1	0.9	0.2	3.6
U.S.	18.4	11.2	1.8	0.7	4.7

Note: Persons of Hispanic or Latino origin can be of any race; (1) Figures cover the El Paso, TX Metropolitan Statistical Area
Source: U.S. Census Bureau, 2017-2021 American Community Survey 5-Year Estimates

Age

Area	Under Age 5	Age 5–19	Age 20–34	Age 35–44	Age 45–54	Age 55–64	Age 65–74	Age 75–84	Age 85+	Median Age
City	5.9	21.7	21.9	11.9	11.9	11.9	8.6	4.3	1.9	35.4
MSA[1]	6.1	22.6	22.4	12.1	11.8	11.5	8.0	3.9	1.7	34.2
U.S.	5.6	19.2	20.2	12.7	12.4	13.1	10.0	4.9	1.9	38.8

Note: (1) Figures cover the El Paso, TX Metropolitan Statistical Area
Source: U.S. Census Bureau, 2020 Census

Disability by Age

Area	All Ages	Under 18 Years Old	18 to 64 Years Old	65 Years and Over
City	13.6	5.2	11.1	42.1
MSA[1]	13.3	5.4	10.9	43.0
U.S.	12.6	4.4	10.3	33.4

Note: Figures show percent of the civilian noninstitutionalized population that reported having a disability. Disability status is determined from six types of difficulty: vision, hearing, cognitive, ambulatory, self-care, and independent living. For children under 5 years old, hearing and vision difficulty are used to determine disability status. For children between the ages of 5 and 14, disability status is determined from hearing, vision, cognitive, ambulatory, and self-care difficulties. For people aged 15 years and older, they are considered to have a disability if they have difficulty with any one of the six difficulty types; Note: (1) Figures cover the El Paso, TX Metropolitan Statistical Area
Source: U.S. Census Bureau, 2017-2021 American Community Survey 5-Year Estimates

Ancestry

Area	German	Irish	English	American	Italian	Polish	French[2]	Scottish	Dutch
City	3.8	2.5	1.9	2.2	1.3	0.5	0.7	0.4	0.2
MSA[1]	3.5	2.3	1.8	2.2	1.2	0.5	0.6	0.4	0.2
U.S.	12.8	9.6	8.1	5.7	5.0	2.7	2.2	1.6	1.1

Note: Figures are the percentage of the total population reporting a particular ancestry. The nine most commonly reported ancestries in the U.S. are shown. Figures include multiple ancestries (e.g. if a person reported being Irish and Italian, they were included in both columns); (1) Figures cover the El Paso, TX Metropolitan Statistical Area; (2) Excludes Basque
Source: U.S. Census Bureau, 2017-2021 American Community Survey 5-Year Estimates

Foreign-born Population

Area	Any Foreign Country	Asia	Mexico	Europe	Caribbean	Central America[2]	South America	Africa	Canada
City	22.8	1.0	20.2	0.5	0.2	0.3	0.2	0.3	0.0
MSA[1]	23.7	0.9	21.3	0.4	0.2	0.3	0.2	0.2	0.0
U.S.	13.6	4.2	3.3	1.5	1.4	1.1	1.1	0.8	0.2

Note: (1) Figures cover the El Paso, TX Metropolitan Statistical Area; (2) Excludes Mexico.
Source: U.S. Census Bureau, 2017-2021 American Community Survey 5-Year Estimates

Household Size

Area	One	Two	Three	Four	Five	Six	Seven or More	Average Household Size
City	25.4	28.6	17.6	15.6	8.2	3.1	1.5	2.80
MSA[1]	23.7	27.8	17.7	16.3	9.2	3.6	1.7	2.90
U.S.	28.1	33.8	15.5	12.9	6.0	2.3	1.4	2.60

Note: (1) Figures cover the El Paso, TX Metropolitan Statistical Area
Source: U.S. Census Bureau, 2017-2021 American Community Survey 5-Year Estimates

Household Relationships

Area	Householder	Opposite-sex Spouse	Same-sex Spouse	Opposite-sex Unmarried Partner	Same-sex Unmarried Partner	Child[2]	Grandchild	Other Relatives	Non-relatives
City	35.9	15.8	0.2	1.8	0.1	32.7	3.9	6.4	2.0
MSA[1]	34.2	15.8	0.2	1.7	0.1	33.5	4.2	6.5	1.8
U.S.	38.3	17.5	0.2	2.5	0.2	28.3	2.4	4.8	3.4

Note: Figures are percent of the total population; (1) Figures cover the El Paso, TX Metropolitan Statistical Area; (2) Includes biological, adopted, and stepchildren of the householder
Source: U.S. Census Bureau, 2020 Census

Gender

Area	Males	Females	Males per 100 Females
City	326,540	352,275	92.7
MSA[1]	422,688	446,171	94.7
U.S.	162,685,811	168,763,470	96.4

Note: (1) Figures cover the El Paso, TX Metropolitan Statistical Area
Source: U.S. Census Bureau, 2020 Census

Marital Status

Area	Never Married	Now Married[2]	Separated	Widowed	Divorced
City	34.9	44.8	3.6	5.7	11.1
MSA[1]	34.9	45.8	3.5	5.4	10.4
U.S.	33.8	48.0	1.8	5.6	10.8

Note: Figures are percentages and cover the population 15 years of age and older; (1) Figures cover the El Paso, TX Metropolitan Statistical Area; (2) Excludes separated
Source: U.S. Census Bureau, 2017-2021 American Community Survey 5-Year Estimates

Religious Groups by Family

Area	Catholic	Baptist	Methodist	LDS[2]	Pentecostal	Lutheran	Islam	Adventist	Other
MSA[1]	47.9	2.5	0.4	1.2	1.1	0.2	0.1	2.1	6.9
U.S.	18.7	7.3	3.0	2.0	1.8	1.7	1.3	1.3	11.6

Note: Figures are the number of adherents as a percentage of the total population and cover the eight largest religious groups in the U.S; (1) Figures cover the El Paso, TX Metropolitan Statistical Area; (2) Church of Jesus Christ of Latter-day Saints
Sources: 2020 U.S. Religion Census, Association of Statisticians of American Religious Bodies; The Association of Religion Data Archives (ARDA)

Religious Groups by Tradition

Area	Catholic	Evangelical Protestant	Mainline Protestant	Black Protestant	Islam	Judaism	Hinduism	Orthodox	Buddhism
MSA[1]	47.9	9.9	0.6	0.4	0.1	0.2	<0.1	<0.1	0.2
U.S.	18.7	16.5	5.2	2.3	1.3	0.6	0.4	0.4	0.3

Note: Figures are the number of adherents as a percentage of the total population; (1) Figures cover the El Paso, TX Metropolitan Statistical Area
Sources: 2020 U.S. Religion Census, Association of Statisticians of American Religious Bodies; The Association of Religion Data Archives (ARDA)

ECONOMY

Gross Metropolitan Product

Area	2020	2021	2022	2023	Rank[2]
MSA[1]	34.1	37.5	40.5	42.6	89

Note: Figures are in billions of dollars; (1) Figures cover the El Paso, TX Metropolitan Statistical Area; (2) Rank is based on 2021 data and ranges from 1 to 381
Source: U.S. Conference of Mayors, U.S. Metro Economies: U.S. Metros Compared to Global and State Economies, June 2022

Economic Growth

Area	2018-20 (%)	2021 (%)	2022 (%)	2023 (%)	Rank[2]
MSA[1]	2.0	5.5	2.3	1.9	36
U.S.	-0.6	5.7	3.1	2.9	—

Note: Figures are real gross metropolitan product (GMP) growth rates and represent average annual percent change; (1) Figures cover the El Paso, TX Metropolitan Statistical Area; (2) Rank is based on 2020 2-year average annual percent change and ranges from 1 to 381
Source: U.S. Conference of Mayors, U.S. Metro Economies: U.S. Metros Compared to Global and State Economies, June 2022

Metropolitan Area Exports

Area	2016	2017	2018	2019	2020	2021	Rank[2]
MSA[1]	26,452.8	25,814.1	30,052.0	32,749.6	27,154.4	32,397.9	11

Note: Figures are in millions of dollars; (1) Figures cover the El Paso, TX Metropolitan Statistical Area; (2) Rank is based on 2021 data and ranges from 1 to 388
Source: U.S. Department of Commerce, International Trade Administration, Office of Trade and Economic Analysis, Industry and Analysis, Exports by Metropolitan Area, data extracted March 16, 2023

Building Permits

Area	Single-Family 2021	Single-Family 2022	Pct. Chg.	Multi-Family 2021	Multi-Family 2022	Pct. Chg.	Total 2021	Total 2022	Pct. Chg.
City	1,961	1,649	-15.9	272	319	17.3	2,233	1,968	-11.9
MSA[1]	2,655	2,147	-19.1	334	319	-4.5	2,989	2,466	-17.5
U.S.	1,115,400	975,600	-12.5	621,600	689,500	10.9	1,737,000	1,665,100	-4.1

Note: (1) Figures cover the El Paso, TX Metropolitan Statistical Area; Figures represent new, privately-owned housing units authorized (unadjusted data); All permit data are based on estimates with imputation
Source: U.S. Census Bureau, Manufacturing, Mining, and Construction Statistics, Building Permits, 2021, 2022

Bankruptcy Filings

Area	Business Filings 2021	Business Filings 2022	% Chg.	Nonbusiness Filings 2021	Nonbusiness Filings 2022	% Chg.
El Paso County	46	41	-10.9	961	1,092	13.6
U.S.	14,347	13,481	-6.0	399,269	374,240	-6.3

Note: Business filings include Chapter 7, Chapter 9, Chapter 11, Chapter 12, Chapter 13, Chapter 15, and Section 304; Nonbusiness filings include Chapter 7, Chapter 11, and Chapter 13
Source: Administrative Office of the U.S. Courts, Business and Nonbusiness Bankruptcy, County Cases Commenced by Chapter of the Bankruptcy Code, During the 12-Month Period Ending December 31, 2021 and Business and Nonbusiness Bankruptcy, County Cases Commenced by Chapter of the Bankruptcy Code, During the 12-Month Period Ending December 31, 2022

Housing Vacancy Rates

Area	Gross Vacancy Rate[2] (%) 2020	2021	2022	Year-Round Vacancy Rate[3] (%) 2020	2021	2022	Rental Vacancy Rate[4] (%) 2020	2021	2022	Homeowner Vacancy Rate[5] (%) 2020	2021	2022
MSA[1]	n/a	n/a	n/a	n/a	n/a	n/a	n/a	n/a	n/a	n/a	n/a	n/a
U.S.	10.6	10.8	10.5	8.2	8.4	8.2	6.3	6.1	5.8	1.0	0.9	0.8

Note: (1) Figures cover the El Paso, TX Metropolitan Statistical Area; (2) The percentage of the total housing inventory that is vacant; (3) The percentage of the housing inventory (excluding seasonal units) that is year-round vacant; (4) The percentage of rental inventory that is vacant for rent; (5) The percentage of homeowner inventory that is vacant for sale; n/a not available
Source: U.S. Census Bureau, Housing Vacancies and Homeownership Annual Statistics: 2020, 2021, 2022

INCOME

Income

Area	Per Capita ($)	Median Household ($)	Average Household ($)
City	25,165	51,325	69,692
MSA[1]	23,934	50,849	68,522
U.S.	37,638	69,021	97,196

Note: (1) Figures cover the El Paso, TX Metropolitan Statistical Area
Source: U.S. Census Bureau, 2017-2021 American Community Survey 5-Year Estimates

Household Income Distribution

Area	Under $15,000	$15,000 -$24,999	$25,000 -$34,999	$35,000 -$49,999	$50,000 -$74,999	$75,000 -$99,999	$100,000 -$149,999	$150,000 and up
City	13.8	11.4	10.6	13.3	18.8	10.7	12.7	8.8
MSA[1]	13.8	11.2	10.7	13.5	19.0	10.9	12.5	8.3
U.S.	9.4	7.8	8.2	11.4	16.8	12.8	16.3	17.3

Note: (1) Figures cover the El Paso, TX Metropolitan Statistical Area
Source: U.S. Census Bureau, 2017-2021 American Community Survey 5-Year Estimates

Poverty Rate

Area	All Ages	Under 18 Years Old	18 to 64 Years Old	65 Years and Over
City	18.3	25.3	15.1	19.1
MSA[1]	19.3	26.5	15.9	20.0
U.S.	12.6	17.0	11.8	9.6

Note: Figures are percentage of people whose income during the past 12 months was below the poverty level; (1) Figures cover the El Paso, TX Metropolitan Statistical Area
Source: U.S. Census Bureau, 2017-2021 American Community Survey 5-Year Estimates

EMPLOYMENT

Labor Force and Employment

Area	Civilian Labor Force Dec. 2021	Civilian Labor Force Dec. 2022	% Chg.	Workers Employed Dec. 2021	Workers Employed Dec. 2022	% Chg.
City	302,469	303,815	0.4	288,907	292,314	1.2
MSA[1]	365,233	366,661	0.4	347,953	352,057	1.2
U.S.	161,696,000	164,224,000	1.6	155,732,000	158,872,000	2.0

Note: Data is not seasonally adjusted and covers workers 16 years of age and older; (1) Figures cover the El Paso, TX Metropolitan Statistical Area
Source: Bureau of Labor Statistics, Local Area Unemployment Statistics

Unemployment Rate

Area	Jan.	Feb.	Mar.	Apr.	May	Jun.	Jul.	Aug.	Sep.	Oct.	Nov.	Dec.
City	5.1	5.0	4.1	4.0	4.2	4.7	4.5	4.4	4.1	4.1	4.1	3.8
MSA[1]	5.4	5.3	4.3	4.2	4.3	4.9	4.8	4.6	4.4	4.3	4.2	4.0
U.S.	4.4	4.1	3.8	3.3	3.4	3.8	3.8	3.8	3.3	3.4	3.4	3.3

Note: Data is not seasonally adjusted and covers workers 16 years of age and older; (1) Figures cover the El Paso, TX Metropolitan Statistical Area
Source: Bureau of Labor Statistics, Local Area Unemployment Statistics

Average Wages

Occupation	$/Hr.	Occupation	$/Hr.
Accountants and Auditors	33.19	Maintenance and Repair Workers	16.87
Automotive Mechanics	19.58	Marketing Managers	49.29
Bookkeepers	18.00	Network and Computer Systems Admin.	37.25
Carpenters	18.84	Nurses, Licensed Practical	22.95
Cashiers	11.04	Nurses, Registered	36.36
Computer Programmers	32.89	Nursing Assistants	13.69
Computer Systems Analysts	38.82	Office Clerks, General	15.17
Computer User Support Specialists	20.96	Physical Therapists	45.54
Construction Laborers	15.44	Physicians	105.87
Cooks, Restaurant	12.46	Plumbers, Pipefitters and Steamfitters	22.73
Customer Service Representatives	15.69	Police and Sheriff's Patrol Officers	30.10
Dentists	78.62	Postal Service Mail Carriers	26.59
Electricians	21.95	Real Estate Sales Agents	27.97
Engineers, Electrical	40.61	Retail Salespersons	14.09
Fast Food and Counter Workers	10.10	Sales Representatives, Technical/Scientific	n/a
Financial Managers	62.87	Secretaries, Exc. Legal/Medical/Executive	16.30
First-Line Supervisors of Office Workers	24.90	Security Guards	15.14
General and Operations Managers	40.58	Surgeons	n/a
Hairdressers/Cosmetologists	13.11	Teacher Assistants, Exc. Postsecondary*	12.23
Home Health and Personal Care Aides	9.83	Teachers, Secondary School, Exc. Sp. Ed.*	27.72
Janitors and Cleaners	12.05	Telemarketers	14.74
Landscaping/Groundskeeping Workers	13.79	Truck Drivers, Heavy/Tractor-Trailer	20.95
Lawyers	65.20	Truck Drivers, Light/Delivery Services	18.70
Maids and Housekeeping Cleaners	11.07	Waiters and Waitresses	11.05

Note: Wage data covers the El Paso, TX Metropolitan Statistical Area; (*) Hourly wages were calculated from annual wage data based on a 40 hour work week; n/a not available.
Source: Bureau of Labor Statistics, Metro Area Occupational Employment & Wage Estimates, May 2022

Employment by Industry

Sector	MSA[1] Number of Employees	MSA[1] Percent of Total	U.S. Percent of Total
Construction, Mining, and Logging	17,400	5.1	5.4
Private Education and Health Services	49,600	14.5	16.1
Financial Activities	13,400	3.9	5.9
Government	70,900	20.7	14.5
Information	6,100	1.8	2.0
Leisure and Hospitality	40,100	11.7	10.3
Manufacturing	18,700	5.5	8.4
Other Services	9,400	2.7	3.7
Professional and Business Services	41,700	12.2	14.7
Retail Trade	41,400	12.1	10.2
Transportation, Warehousing, and Utilities	21,800	6.4	4.9
Wholesale Trade	12,200	3.6	3.9

Note: Figures are non-farm employment as of December 2022. Figures are not seasonally adjusted and include workers 16 years of age and older; (1) Figures cover the El Paso, TX Metropolitan Statistical Area
Source: Bureau of Labor Statistics, Current Employment Statistics, Employment, Hours, and Earnings

Employment by Occupation

Occupation Classification	City (%)	MSA[1] (%)	U.S. (%)
Management, Business, Science, and Arts	33.9	32.1	40.3
Natural Resources, Construction, and Maintenance	8.6	9.9	8.7
Production, Transportation, and Material Moving	12.3	13.3	13.1
Sales and Office	24.0	23.8	20.9
Service	21.2	20.9	17.0

Note: Figures cover employed civilians 16 years of age and older; (1) Figures cover the El Paso, TX Metropolitan Statistical Area
Source: U.S. Census Bureau, 2017-2021 American Community Survey 5-Year Estimates

Occupations with Greatest Projected Employment Growth: 2022 – 2024

Occupation[1]	2022 Employment	2024 Projected Employment	Numeric Employment Change	Percent Employment Change
Home Health and Personal Care Aides	338,130	364,760	26,630	7.9
General and Operations Managers	395,700	416,100	20,400	5.2
Heavy and Tractor-Trailer Truck Drivers	206,850	222,220	15,370	7.4
Software Developers	119,810	134,060	14,250	11.9
Laborers and Freight, Stock, and Material Movers, Hand	214,680	228,680	14,000	6.5
Farmers, Ranchers, and Other Agricultural Managers	274,740	287,430	12,690	4.6
Stockers and Order Fillers	212,180	224,670	12,490	5.9
Construction Laborers	153,220	164,330	11,110	7.3
Cooks, Restaurant	131,480	141,860	10,380	7.9
Industrial Truck and Tractor Operators	83,270	93,190	9,920	11.9

Note: Projections cover Texas; (1) Sorted by numeric employment change
Source: www.projectionscentral.com, State Occupational Projections, 2022–2024 Short-Term Projections

Fastest-Growing Occupations: 2022 – 2024

Occupation[1]	2022 Employment	2024 Projected Employment	Numeric Employment Change	Percent Employment Change
Wind Turbine Service Technicians	5,240	5,990	750	14.3
Information Security Analysts (SOC 2018)	14,170	16,110	1,940	13.7
Solar Photovoltaic Installers	2,240	2,540	300	13.4
Veterinary Technologists and Technicians	16,140	18,200	2,060	12.8
Actuaries	1,810	2,040	230	12.7
Data Scientists	7,340	8,270	930	12.7
Web Developers	6,920	7,790	870	12.6
Veterinarians	6,830	7,670	840	12.3
Veterinary Assistants and Laboratory Animal Caretakers	5,990	6,720	730	12.2
Ushers, Lobby Attendants, and Ticket Takers	9,100	10,190	1,090	12.0

Note: Projections cover Texas; (1) Sorted by percent employment change and excludes occupations with numeric employment change less than 50
Source: www.projectionscentral.com, State Occupational Projections, 2022–2024 Short-Term Projections

CITY FINANCES

City Government Finances

Component	2020 ($000)	2020 ($ per capita)
Total Revenues	1,264,213	1,854
Total Expenditures	1,181,885	1,734
Debt Outstanding	2,327,339	3,414
Cash and Securities[1]	808,793	1,186

Note: (1) Cash and security holdings of a government at the close of its fiscal year, including those of its dependent agencies, utilities, and liquor stores.
Source: U.S. Census Bureau, State & Local Government Finances 2020

City Government Revenue by Source

Source	2020 ($000)	2020 ($ per capita)	2020 (%)
General Revenue			
From Federal Government	131,544	193	10.4
From State Government	20,808	31	1.6
From Local Governments	3,855	6	0.3
Taxes			
Property	299,295	439	23.7
Sales and Gross Receipts	227,420	334	18.0
Personal Income	0	0	0.0
Corporate Income	0	0	0.0
Motor Vehicle License	0	0	0.0
Other Taxes	16,190	24	1.3
Current Charges	302,961	444	24.0
Liquor Store	0	0	0.0
Utility	170,741	250	13.5

Source: U.S. Census Bureau, State & Local Government Finances 2020

City Government Expenditures by Function

Function	2020 ($000)	2020 ($ per capita)	2020 (%)
General Direct Expenditures			
Air Transportation	60,423	88	5.1
Corrections	0	0	0.0
Education	0	0	0.0
Employment Security Administration	0	0	0.0
Financial Administration	9,941	14	0.8
Fire Protection	100,982	148	8.5
General Public Buildings	4	<1	<0.1
Governmental Administration, Other	9,586	14	0.8
Health	24,679	36	2.1
Highways	89,211	130	7.5
Hospitals	0	0	0.0
Housing and Community Development	11,556	17	1.0
Interest on General Debt	80,036	117	6.8
Judicial and Legal	10,655	15	0.9
Libraries	9,007	13	0.8
Parking	0	0	0.0
Parks and Recreation	59,157	86	5.0
Police Protection	131,938	193	11.2
Public Welfare	917	1	0.1
Sewerage	98,247	144	8.3
Solid Waste Management	38,589	56	3.3
Veterans' Services	0	0	0.0
Liquor Store	0	0	0.0
Utility	275,323	403	23.3

Source: U.S. Census Bureau, State & Local Government Finances 2020

TAXES

State Corporate Income Tax Rates

State	Tax Rate (%)	Income Brackets ($)	Num. of Brackets	Financial Institution Tax Rate (%)[a]	Federal Income Tax Ded.
Texas	(u)	–	–	(u)	No

Note: Tax rates as of January 1, 2023; (a) Rates listed are the corporate income tax rate applied to financial institutions or excise taxes based on income. Some states have other taxes based upon the value of deposits or shares; (u) Texas imposes a Franchise Tax, otherwise known as margin tax, imposed on entities with more than $1,230,000 total revenues at rate of 0.75%, or 0.375% for entities primarily engaged in retail or wholesale trade, on lesser of 70% of total revenues or 100% of gross receipts after deductions for either compensation or cost of goods sold.
Source: Federation of Tax Administrators, State Corporate Income Tax Rates, January 1, 2023

State Individual Income Tax Rates

State	Tax Rate (%)	Income Brackets ($)	Personal Exemptions ($) Single	Married	Depend.	Standard Ded. ($) Single	Married
Texas			– No state income tax –				

Note: Tax rates as of January 1, 2023; Local- and county-level taxes are not included
Source: Federation of Tax Administrators, State Individual Income Tax Rates, January 1, 2023

Various State Sales and Excise Tax Rates

State	State Sales Tax (%)	Gasoline[1] ($/gal.)	Cigarette[2] ($/pack)	Spirits[3] ($/gal.)	Wine[4] ($/gal.)	Beer[5] ($/gal.)	Recreational Marijuana (%)
Texas	6.25	0.20	1.41	2.40	0.20	0.19	Not legal

Note: All tax rates as of January 1, 2023; (1) The American Petroleum Institute has developed a methodology for determining the average tax rate on a gallon of fuel. Rates may include any of the following: excise taxes, environmental fees, storage tank fees, other fees or taxes, general sales tax, and local taxes; (2) The federal excise tax of $1.0066 per pack and local taxes are not included; (3) Rates are those applicable to off-premise sales of 40% alcohol by volume (a.b.v.) distilled spirits in 750ml containers. Local excise taxes are excluded; (4) Rates are those applicable to off-premise sales of 11% a.b.v. non-carbonated wine in 750ml containers; (5) Rates are those applicable to off-premise sales of 4.7% a.b.v. beer in 12 ounce containers.
Source: Tax Foundation, 2023 Facts & Figures: How Does Your State Compare?

State Business Tax Climate Index Rankings

State	Overall Rank	Corporate Tax Rank	Individual Income Tax Rank	Sales Tax Rank	Property Tax Rank	Unemployment Insurance Tax Rank
Texas	13	47	7	37	38	12

Note: The index is a measure of how each state's tax laws affect economic performance. The lower the rank, the more favorable a state's tax system is for business. States without a given tax are given a ranking of 1. The scores/rankings for the District of Columbia do not affect other states. The 2023 index represents the tax climate as of July 1, 2022.
Source: Tax Foundation, State Business Tax Climate Index 2023

TRANSPORTATION

Means of Transportation to Work

Area	Car/Truck/Van Drove Alone	Car-pooled	Public Transportation Bus	Subway	Railroad	Bicycle	Walked	Other Means	Worked at Home
City	79.1	10.2	1.4	0.0	0.0	0.1	1.1	2.4	5.7
MSA[1]	78.6	10.6	1.1	0.0	0.0	0.1	1.4	2.3	5.8
U.S.	73.2	8.6	2.0	1.6	0.5	0.5	2.5	1.5	9.7

Note: Figures are percentages and cover workers 16 years of age and older; (1) Figures cover the El Paso, TX Metropolitan Statistical Area
Source: U.S. Census Bureau, 2017-2021 American Community Survey 5-Year Estimates

Travel Time to Work

Area	Less Than 10 Minutes	10 to 19 Minutes	20 to 29 Minutes	30 to 44 Minutes	45 to 59 Minutes	60 to 89 Minutes	90 Minutes or More
City	9.5	33.5	28.5	19.7	4.7	2.2	1.8
MSA[1]	10.3	31.9	27.4	21.0	5.2	2.3	1.9
U.S.	12.4	28.5	21.0	20.9	8.2	6.2	2.9

Note: Note: Figures are percentages and include workers 16 years old and over; (1) Figures cover the El Paso, TX Metropolitan Statistical Area
Source: U.S. Census Bureau, 2017-2021 American Community Survey 5-Year Estimates

Key Congestion Measures

Measure	1990	2000	2010	2015	2020
Annual Hours of Delay, Total (000)	6,571	13,636	18,665	21,604	17,490
Annual Hours of Delay, Per Auto Commuter	20	32	36	39	32
Annual Congestion Cost, Per Auto Commuter ($)	438	684	746	796	688

Note: Covers the El Paso TX-NM urban area
Source: Texas A&M Transportation Institute, 2021 Urban Mobility Report

Freeway Travel Time Index

Measure	1985	1990	1995	2000	2005	2010	2015	2020
Urban Area Index[1]	1.05	1.09	1.13	1.16	1.18	1.17	1.16	1.13
Urban Area Rank[1,2]	64	56	47	43	41	41	57	6

Note: Freeway Travel Time Index—the ratio of travel time in the peak period to the travel time at free-flow conditions. For example, a value of 1.30 indicates a 20-minute free-flow trip takes 26 minutes in the peak (20 minutes x 1.30 = 26 minutes); (1) Covers the El Paso TX-NM urban area; (2) Rank is based on 101 larger urban areas (#1 = highest travel time index)
Source: Texas A&M Transportation Institute, 2021 Urban Mobility Report

Public Transportation

Agency Name / Mode of Transportation	Vehicles Operated in Maximum Service[1]	Annual Unlinked Passenger Trips[2] (in thous.)	Annual Passenger Miles[3] (in thous.)
Mass Transit Department-City of El Paso (Sun Metro)			
Bus (directly operated)	112	3,663.3	24,952.9
Demand Response (purchased transportation)	61	182.8	1,687.8
Streetcar Rail (directly operated)	4	4.1	9.6

Note: (1) Number of revenue vehicles operated by the given mode and type of service to meet the annual maximum service requirement. This is the revenue vehicle count during the peak season of the year; on the week and day that maximum service is provided. Vehicles operated in maximum service (VOMS) exclude atypical days and one-time special events; (2) Number of passengers who boarded public transportation vehicles. Passengers are counted each time they board a vehicle no matter how many vehicles they use to travel from their origin to their destination. (3) Sum of the distances ridden by all passengers during the entire fiscal year.
Source: Federal Transit Administration, National Transit Database, 2021

Air Transportation

Airport Name and Code / Type of Service	Passenger Airlines[1]	Passenger Enplanements	Freight Carriers[2]	Freight (lbs)
El Paso International (ELP)				
Domestic service (U.S. carriers - 2022)	25	1,929,158	20	99,385,532
International service (U.S. carriers - 2021)	2	2,571	7	719,648

Note: (1) Includes all U.S.-based major, minor and commuter airlines that carried at least one passenger during the year; (2) Includes all U.S.-based airlines and freight carriers that transported at least one pound of freight during the year.
Source: Bureau of Transportation Statistics, The Intermodal Transportation Database, Air Carriers: T-100 Domestic Market (U.S. Carriers), 2022; Bureau of Transportation Statistics, The Intermodal Transportation Database, Air Carriers: T-100 International Market (U.S. Carriers), 2021

BUSINESSES

Major Business Headquarters

Company Name	Industry	Rankings Fortune[1]	Forbes[2]
No companies listed	-	-	-

Note: (1) Companies that produce a 10-K are ranked 1 to 500 based on 2021 revenue; (2) All private companies with at least $2 billion in annual revenue through the end of their most current fiscal year are ranked 1 to 246; companies listed are headquartered in the city; dashes indicate no ranking
Source: Fortune, "Fortune 500," 2022; Forbes, "America's Largest Private Companies," 2022

Living Environment

COST OF LIVING

Cost of Living Index

Composite Index	Groceries	Housing	Utilities	Transportation	Health Care	Misc. Goods/Services
89.7	102.0	70.2	90.5	97.4	97.7	96.9

Note: The Cost of Living Index measures regional differences in the cost of consumer goods and services, excluding taxes and non-consumer expenditures, for professional and managerial households in the top income quintile. It is based on more than 50,000 prices covering almost 60 different items for which prices are collected three times a year by chambers of commerce, economic development organizations or university applied economic centers in each participating urban area. The numbers shown should be read as a percentage above or below the national average of 100. For example, a value of 115.4 in the groceries column indicates that grocery prices are 15.4% higher than the national average. Small differences in the index numbers should not be interpreted as significant; Figures cover the El Paso TX urban area.
Source: The Council for Community and Economic Research, Cost of Living Index, 2022

Grocery Prices

Area[1]	T-Bone Steak ($/pound)	Frying Chicken ($/pound)	Whole Milk ($/half gal.)	Eggs ($/dozen)	Orange Juice ($/64 oz.)	Coffee ($/11.5 oz.)
City[2]	14.35	2.08	2.19	2.14	3.96	5.58
Avg.	13.81	1.59	2.43	2.25	3.85	4.95
Min.	10.17	0.90	1.51	1.30	2.90	3.46
Max.	19.35	3.30	4.32	4.32	5.31	8.59

Note: (1) Values for the local area are compared with the average, minimum and maximum values for all 286 areas in the Cost of Living Index; (2) Figures cover the El Paso TX urban area; **T-Bone Steak** (price per pound); **Frying Chicken** (price per pound, whole fryer); **Whole Milk** (half gallon carton); **Eggs** (price per dozen, Grade A, large); **Orange Juice** (64 oz. Tropicana or Florida Natural); **Coffee** (11.5 oz. can, vacuum-packed, Maxwell House, Hills Bros, or Folgers).
Source: The Council for Community and Economic Research, Cost of Living Index, 2022

Housing and Utility Costs

Area[1]	New Home Price ($)	Apartment Rent ($/month)	All Electric ($/month)	Part Electric ($/month)	Other Energy ($/month)	Telephone ($/month)
City[2]	292,519	1,130	-	93.81	47.74	200.02
Avg.	450,913	1,371	176.41	99.93	76.96	190.22
Min.	229,283	546	100.84	31.56	27.15	174.27
Max.	2,434,977	4,569	356.86	249.59	272.24	208.31

Note: (1) Values for the local area are compared with the average, minimum and maximum values for all 286 areas in the Cost of Living Index; (2) Figures cover the El Paso TX urban area; **New Home Price** (2,400 sf living area, 8,000 sf lot, in urban area with full utilities); **Apartment Rent** (950 sf 2 bedroom/1.5 or 2 bath, unfurnished, excluding all utilities except water); **All Electric** (average monthly cost for an all-electric home); **Part Electric** (average monthly cost for a part-electric home); **Other Energy** (average monthly cost for natural gas, fuel oil, coal, wood, and any other forms of energy except electricity); **Telephone** (price includes the base monthly rate plus taxes and fees for three lines of mobile phone service).
Source: The Council for Community and Economic Research, Cost of Living Index, 2022

Health Care, Transportation, and Other Costs

Area[1]	Doctor ($/visit)	Dentist ($/visit)	Optometrist ($/visit)	Gasoline ($/gallon)	Beauty Salon ($/visit)	Men's Shirt ($)
City[2]	146.74	84.59	98.23	3.61	28.33	30.52
Avg.	124.91	107.77	117.66	3.86	43.31	34.21
Min.	36.61	58.25	51.79	2.90	22.18	13.05
Max.	250.21	162.58	371.96	5.54	85.61	63.54

Note: (1) Values for the local area are compared with the average, minimum and maximum values for all 286 areas in the Cost of Living Index; (2) Figures cover the El Paso TX urban area; **Doctor** (general practitioners routine exam of an established patient); **Dentist** (adult teeth cleaning and periodic oral examination); **Optometrist** (full vision eye exam for established adult patient); **Gasoline** (one gallon regular unleaded, national brand, including all taxes, cash price at self-service pump if available); **Beauty Salon** (woman's shampoo, trim, and blow-dry); **Men's Shirt** (cotton/polyester dress shirt, pinpoint weave, long sleeves).
Source: The Council for Community and Economic Research, Cost of Living Index, 2022

HOUSING

Homeownership Rate

Area	2015 (%)	2016 (%)	2017 (%)	2018 (%)	2019 (%)	2020 (%)	2021 (%)	2022 (%)
MSA[1]	n/a	n/a	n/a	n/a	n/a	n/a	n/a	n/a
U.S.	63.7	63.4	63.9	64.4	64.6	66.6	65.5	65.8

Note: (1) Figures cover the El Paso, TX Metropolitan Statistical Area; n/a not available
Source: U.S. Census Bureau, Housing Vacancies and Homeownership Annual Statistics: 2015-2022

House Price Index (HPI)

Area	National Ranking[2]	Quarterly Change (%)	One-Year Change (%)	Five-Year Change (%)	Since 1991Q1 (%)
MSA[1]	21	2.05	18.42	54.29	201.64
U.S.[3]	–	0.34	8.41	58.44	289.08

Note: The HPI is a weighted repeat sales index. It measures average price changes in repeat sales or refinancings on the same properties. This information is obtained by reviewing repeat mortgage transactions on single-family properties whose mortgages have been purchased or securitized by Fannie Mae or Freddie Mac since January 1975; (1) Figures cover the El Paso, TX Metropolitan Statistical Area; (2) Rankings are based on annual percentage change for all metro areas containing at least 15,000 transactions over the last 10 years and ranges from 1 to 257; (3) figures based on a weighted average of Census Division estimates using a seasonally adjusted, purchase-only index; all figures are for the period ending December 31, 2022
Source: Federal Housing Finance Agency, Change in FHFA Metropolitan Area House Price Indexes, 2022Q4

Median Single-Family Home Prices

Area	2020	2021	2022p	Percent Change 2021 to 2022
MSA[1]	177.8	200.8	237.1	18.1
U.S. Average	300.2	357.1	392.6	9.9

Note: Figures are median sales prices of existing single-family homes in thousands of dollars; (p) preliminary; (1) Figures cover the El Paso, TX Metropolitan Statistical Area
Source: National Association of Realtors, Median Sales Price of Existing Single-Family Homes for Metropolitan Areas, 4th Quarter 2022

Qualifying Income Based on Median Sales Price of Existing Single-Family Homes

Area	With 5% Down ($)	With 10% Down ($)	With 20% Down ($)
MSA[1]	73,150	69,300	61,600
U.S. Average	112,234	106,237	94,513

Note: Figures are preliminary; Qualifying income is based on a mortgage rate of 6.77%. Monthly principal and interest payment is limited to 25% of income; (1) Figures cover the El Paso, TX Metropolitan Statistical Area
Source: National Association of Realtors, Qualifying Income Based on Median Sales Price of Existing Single-Family Homes for Metropolitan Areas, 4th Quarter 2022

Home Value

Area	Under $100,000	$100,000 -$199,999	$200,000 -$299,999	$300,000 -$399,999	$400,000 -$499,999	$500,000 -$999,999	$1,000,000 or more	Median ($)
City	25.7	52.3	14.1	4.5	1.7	1.4	0.3	137,600
MSA[1]	29.8	49.6	13.5	4.1	1.4	1.2	0.3	131,200
U.S.	16.2	24.2	20.1	13.6	8.3	13.6	4.1	244,900

Note: Figures are percentages except for median and cover owner-occupied housing units; (1) Figures cover the El Paso, TX Metropolitan Statistical Area
Source: U.S. Census Bureau, 2017-2021 American Community Survey 5-Year Estimates

Year Housing Structure Built

Area	2020 or Later	2010 -2019	2000 -2009	1990 -1999	1980 -1989	1970 -1979	1960 -1969	1950 -1959	1940 -1949	Before 1940	Median Year
City	0.1	12.1	14.1	12.9	14.4	16.3	10.5	11.1	3.7	4.8	1982
MSA[1]	0.2	14.0	15.8	14.1	14.5	15.2	9.2	9.4	3.3	4.3	1986
U.S.	0.2	7.3	13.6	13.6	13.2	14.8	10.3	10.0	4.7	12.2	1979

Note: Figures are percentages except for Median Year; Note: (1) Figures cover the El Paso, TX Metropolitan Statistical Area
Source: U.S. Census Bureau, 2017-2021 American Community Survey 5-Year Estimates

Gross Monthly Rent

Area	Under $500	$500 -$999	$1,000 -$1,499	$1,500 -$1,999	$2,000 -$2,499	$2,500 -$2,999	$3,000 and up	Median ($)
City	12.3	48.4	31.0	6.7	1.2	0.3	0.2	910
MSA[1]	12.0	48.6	30.8	7.0	1.2	0.2	0.2	908
U.S.	8.1	30.5	30.8	16.8	7.3	3.1	3.5	1,163

Note: Figures are percentages except for median; Gross rent is the contract rent plus the estimated average monthly cost of utilities (electricity, gas, and water and sewer) and fuels (oil, coal, kerosene, wood, etc.) if these are paid by the renter (or paid for the renter by someone else); (1) Figures cover the El Paso, TX Metropolitan Statistical Area
Source: U.S. Census Bureau, 2017-2021 American Community Survey 5-Year Estimates

HEALTH

Health Risk Factors

Category	MSA[1] (%)	U.S. (%)
Adults aged 18–64 who have any kind of health care coverage	71.5	90.9
Adults who reported being in good or better health	81.9	85.2
Adults who have been told they have high blood cholesterol	30.3	35.7
Adults who have been told they have high blood pressure	29.4	32.4
Adults who are current smokers	13.5	14.4
Adults who currently use e-cigarettes	6.0	6.7
Adults who currently use chewing tobacco, snuff, or snus	3.5	3.5
Adults who are heavy drinkers[2]	4.7	6.3
Adults who are binge drinkers[3]	15.9	15.4
Adults who are overweight (BMI 25.0 - 29.9)	37.8	34.4
Adults who are obese (BMI 30.0 - 99.8)	38.1	33.9
Adults who participated in any physical activities in the past month	74.6	76.3

Note: (1) Figures cover the El Paso, TX Metropolitan Statistical Area; (2) Heavy drinkers are classified as adult men having more than 14 drinks per week and adult women having more than 7 drinks per week; (3) Binge drinkers are classified as males having five or more drinks on one occasion or females having four or more drinks on one occasion
Source: Centers for Disease Control and Prevention, Behavioral Risk Factor Surveillance System, SMART: Selected Metropolitan Area Risk Trends, 2021

Acute and Chronic Health Conditions

Category	MSA[1] (%)	U.S. (%)
Adults who have ever been told they had a heart attack	3.3	4.0
Adults who have ever been told they have angina or coronary heart disease	n/a	3.8
Adults who have ever been told they had a stroke	3.2	3.0
Adults who have ever been told they have asthma	10.2	14.9
Adults who have ever been told they have arthritis	16.1	25.8
Adults who have ever been told they have diabetes[2]	11.4	10.9
Adults who have ever been told they had skin cancer	2.0	6.6
Adults who have ever been told they had any other types of cancer	4.2	7.5
Adults who have ever been told they have COPD	4.9	6.1
Adults who have ever been told they have kidney disease	2.0	3.0
Adults who have ever been told they have a form of depression	22.6	20.5

Note: (1) Figures cover the El Paso, TX Metropolitan Statistical Area; (2) Figures do not include pregnancy-related, borderline, or pre-diabetes
Source: Centers for Disease Control and Prevention, Behavioral Risk Factor Surveillance System, SMART: Selected Metropolitan Area Risk Trends, 2021

Health Screening and Vaccination Rates

Category	MSA[1] (%)	U.S. (%)
Adults who have ever been tested for HIV	37.9	34.9
Adults who have had their blood cholesterol checked within the last five years	79.9	85.2
Adults aged 65+ who have had flu shot within the past year	65.8	68.6
Adults aged 65+ who have ever had a pneumonia vaccination	67.3	71.0

Note: (1) Figures cover the El Paso, TX Metropolitan Statistical Area.
Source: Centers for Disease Control and Prevention, Behavioral Risk Factor Surveillance System, SMART: Selected Metropolitan Area Risk Trends, 2021

Disability Status

Category	MSA[1] (%)	U.S. (%)
Adults who reported being deaf	5.1	7.2
Are you blind or have serious difficulty seeing, even when wearing glasses?	5.8	4.8
Are you limited in any way in any of your usual activities due to arthritis?	6.7	11.1
Do you have difficulty doing errands alone?	6.8	7.0
Do you have difficulty dressing or bathing?	3.6	3.6
Do you have serious difficulty concentrating/remembering/making decisions?	11.4	12.1
Do you have serious difficulty walking or climbing stairs?	11.9	12.8

Note: (1) Figures cover the El Paso, TX Metropolitan Statistical Area.
Source: Centers for Disease Control and Prevention, Behavioral Risk Factor Surveillance System, SMART: Selected Metropolitan Area Risk Trends, 2021

Mortality Rates for the Top 10 Causes of Death in the U.S.

ICD-10[a] Sub-Chapter	ICD-10[a] Code	Crude Mortality Rate[1] per 100,000 population County[2]	U.S.
Malignant neoplasms	C00-C97	130.4	182.6
Ischaemic heart diseases	I20-I25	87.5	113.1
Other forms of heart disease	I30-I51	31.0	64.4
Other degenerative diseases of the nervous system	G30-G31	51.6	51.0
Cerebrovascular diseases	I60-I69	27.9	47.8
Other external causes of accidental injury	W00-X59	27.8	46.4
Chronic lower respiratory diseases	J40-J47	25.7	45.7
Organic, including symptomatic, mental disorders	F01-F09	14.0	35.9
Hypertensive diseases	I10-I15	37.0	35.0
Diabetes mellitus	E10-E14	39.1	29.6

Note: (a) ICD-10 = International Classification of Diseases 10th Revision; (1) Crude mortality rates are a three-year average covering 2019-2021; (2) Figures cover El Paso County.
Source: Centers for Disease Control and Prevention, National Center for Health Statistics. National Vital Statistics System, Mortality 2018-2021 on CDC WONDER Online Database

Mortality Rates for Selected Causes of Death

ICD-10[a] Sub-Chapter	ICD-10[a] Code	Crude Mortality Rate[1] per 100,000 population County[2]	U.S.
Assault	X85-Y09	4.0	7.0
Diseases of the liver	K70-K76	32.4	19.8
Human immunodeficiency virus (HIV) disease	B20-B24	1.2	1.5
Influenza and pneumonia	J09-J18	9.2	14.7
Intentional self-harm	X60-X84	11.5	14.3
Malnutrition	E40-E46	2.4	4.3
Obesity and other hyperalimentation	E65-E68	2.6	3.0
Renal failure	N17-N19	18.6	15.7
Transport accidents	V01-V99	13.2	13.6
Viral hepatitis	B15-B19	1.4	1.2

Note: (a) ICD-10 = International Classification of Diseases 10th Revision; (1) Crude mortality rates are a three-year average covering 2019-2021; (2) Figures cover El Paso County; Data are suppressed when the data meet the criteria for confidentiality constraints; Crude mortality rates are flagged as unreliable when the rate would be calculated with a numerator of 20 or less.
Source: Centers for Disease Control and Prevention, National Center for Health Statistics. National Vital Statistics System, Mortality 2018-2021 on CDC WONDER Online Database

Health Insurance Coverage

Area	With Health Insurance	With Private Health Insurance	With Public Health Insurance	Without Health Insurance	Population Under Age 19 Without Health Insurance
City	80.0	54.6	33.9	20.0	10.2
MSA[1]	78.7	52.8	33.7	21.3	10.9
U.S.	91.2	67.8	35.4	8.8	5.3

Note: Figures are percentages that cover the civilian noninstitutionalized population; (1) Figures cover the El Paso, TX Metropolitan Statistical Area
Source: U.S. Census Bureau, 2017-2021 American Community Survey 5-Year Estimates

Number of Medical Professionals

Area	MDs[3]	DOs[3,4]	Dentists	Podiatrists	Chiropractors	Optometrists
County[1] (number)	1,768	115	411	34	79	90
County[1] (rate[2])	204.1	13.3	47.4	3.9	9.1	10.4
U.S. (rate[2])	289.3	23.5	72.5	6.2	28.7	17.4

Note: Data as of 2021 unless noted; (1) Data covers El Paso County; (2) Rate per 100,000 population; (3) Data as of 2020 and includes all active, non-federal physicians; (4) Doctor of Osteopathic Medicine
Source: U.S. Department of Health and Human Services, Health Resources and Services Administration, Bureau of Health Professions, Area Resource File (ARF) 2021-2022

EDUCATION

Public School District Statistics

District Name	Schls	Pupils	Pupil/Teacher Ratio	Minority Pupils[1] (%)	LEP/ELL[2] (%)	IEP[3] (%)
Canutillo ISD	10	6,091	14.7	95.4	28.9	10.2
Clint ISD	14	10,494	15.2	96.2	34.0	10.0
El Paso ISD	80	50,769	14.5	91.0	28.2	11.6
Harmony Science Acad. (El Paso)	6	4,573	14.4	90.9	22.7	10.1
Socorro ISD	52	47,278	16.2	95.8	21.8	11.4
Ysleta ISD	57	37,244	14.6	97.2	25.7	13.8

Note: Table includes school districts with 2,000 or more students; (1) Percentage of students that are not non-Hispanic white; (2) Percentage of students that are Limited English Proficient or English Language Learners (2018-19); (3) Percentage of students that have an Individualized Education Program (2019-20).
Source: U.S. Department of Education, National Center for Education Statistics, Common Core of Data, Local Education Agency (School District) Universe Survey: School Year 2021-2022

Best High Schools

According to *U.S. News*, El Paso is home to three of the top 500 high schools in the U.S.: **Valle Verde Early College High School** (#345); **Transmountain Early College High School** (#428); **Northwest Early College High School (NWECHS)** (#449). Nearly 18,000 public, magnet and charter schools were ranked based on their performance on state assessments and how well they prepare students for college. *U.S. News & World Report, "Best High Schools 2022"*

Highest Level of Education

Area	Less than H.S.	H.S. Diploma	Some College, No Deg.	Associate Degree	Bachelor's Degree	Master's Degree	Prof. School Degree	Doctorate Degree
City	18.6	23.1	22.7	8.8	17.7	6.6	1.4	1.0
MSA[1]	20.4	23.8	22.3	9.0	16.5	6.0	1.3	0.8
U.S.	11.1	26.5	20.0	8.7	20.6	9.3	2.2	1.5

Note: Figures cover persons age 25 and over; (1) Figures cover the El Paso, TX Metropolitan Statistical Area
Source: U.S. Census Bureau, 2017-2021 American Community Survey 5-Year Estimates

Educational Attainment by Race

Area	High School Graduate or Higher (%) Total	White	Black	Asian	Hisp.[2]	Bachelor's Degree or Higher (%) Total	White	Black	Asian	Hisp.[2]
City	81.4	84.1	96.1	88.5	77.8	26.7	28.7	32.3	56.8	22.7
MSA[1]	79.6	82.4	96.1	89.2	76.0	24.6	26.5	32.2	54.0	20.8
U.S.	88.9	91.4	87.2	87.6	71.2	33.7	35.5	23.3	55.6	18.4

Note: Figures shown cover persons 25 years old and over; (1) Figures cover the El Paso, TX Metropolitan Statistical Area; (2) People of Hispanic origin can be of any race
Source: U.S. Census Bureau, 2017-2021 American Community Survey 5-Year Estimates

School Enrollment by Grade and Control

Area	Preschool (%) Public	Private	Kindergarten (%) Public	Private	Grades 1 - 4 (%) Public	Private	Grades 5 - 8 (%) Public	Private	Grades 9 - 12 (%) Public	Private
City	88.6	11.4	92.5	7.5	94.3	5.7	94.0	6.0	95.8	4.2
MSA[1]	88.3	11.7	93.1	6.9	94.3	5.7	94.7	5.3	96.3	3.7
U.S.	58.8	41.2	86.3	13.7	88.3	11.7	88.6	11.4	89.4	10.6

Note: Figures shown cover persons 3 years old and over; (1) Figures cover the El Paso, TX Metropolitan Statistical Area
Source: U.S. Census Bureau, 2017-2021 American Community Survey 5-Year Estimates

Higher Education

Four-Year Colleges			Two-Year Colleges			Medical Schools[1]	Law Schools[2]	Voc/Tech[3]
Public	Private Non-profit	Private For-profit	Public	Private Non-profit	Private For-profit			
2	0	3	1	0	1	1	0	5

Note: Figures cover institutions located within the El Paso, TX Metropolitan Statistical Area and include main campuses only; (1) includes schools accredited by the Liaison Committee on Medical Education and the American Osteopathic Association's Commission on Osteopathic College Accreditation; (2) includes ABA-accredited schools, schools with provisional ABA accreditation, and state accredited schools; (3) includes all schools with programs that are less than 2 years.
Source: National Center for Education Statistics, Integrated Postsecondary Education System (IPEDS), 2021-22; Wikipedia, List of Medical Schools in the United States, accessed April 10, 2023; Wikipedia, List of Law Schools in the United States, accessed April 10, 2023

EMPLOYERS

Major Employers

Company Name	Industry
Alorica	Inbound customer service
Automatic Data Processing	Contact center - private
Coca-Cola Enterprises	Bottling & distributing
Datamark	Data processing & related service
Del Sol Medical Center	Health care - private
Dish Network	Technical support center
El Paso Electric Corporation	Electric utilities
GC Services	Inbound customer service
Las Palmas Medical Center	Health care - private
Redcats USA	Inbound customer service
RM Personnel	Employment services
T&T Staff Management	Employment services
Texas Tech University Health Sci Ctr	Higher education & health care
Union Pacific Railroad Co.	Transportation
University Medical Center	Health care - public
Visiting Nurse Association of El Paso	Health care & social assistance
West Customer Management Group	Inbound customer service
Western Refining	Corporate headquarters petro chemical refinery

Note: Companies shown are located within the El Paso, TX Metropolitan Statistical Area.
Source: Hoovers.com; Wikipedia

PUBLIC SAFETY

Crime Rate

Area	Total Crime	Violent Crime Rate — Murder	Rape[3]	Robbery	Aggrav. Assault	Property Crime Rate — Burglary	Larceny-Theft	Motor Vehicle Theft
City	1,557.6	4.1	38.1	42.2	231.9	123.6	1,057.2	60.6
Suburbs[1]	1,026.7	3.1	36.2	20.0	217.8	121.7	554.9	73.0
Metro[2]	1,457.0	3.9	37.7	38.0	229.2	123.2	962.0	62.9
U.S.	2,356.7	6.5	38.4	73.9	279.7	314.2	1,398.0	246.0

Note: Figures are crimes per 100,000 population; (1) All areas within the metro area that are located outside the city limits; (2) Figures cover the El Paso, TX Metropolitan Statistical Area; (3) All figures shown were reported using the revised Uniform Crime Reporting (UCR) definition of rape; Due to the transition to the National Incident-Based Reporting System (NIBRS), limited city and metro area data was released for 2021.
Source: FBI Uniform Crime Reports, 2020

Hate Crimes

Area	Number of Quarters Reported	Race/Ethnicity/Ancestry	Religion	Sexual Orientation	Disability	Gender	Gender Identity
City	4	2	0	0	0	5	0
U.S.	4	5,227	1,244	1,110	130	75	266

Note: Due to the transition to the National Incident-Based Reporting System (NIBRS), limited crime data was released for 2021.
Source: Federal Bureau of Investigation, Hate Crime Statistics 2020

Identity Theft Consumer Reports

Area	Reports	Reports per 100,000 Population	Rank[2]
MSA[1]	1,968	234	126
U.S.	1,108,609	339	-

Note: (1) Figures cover the El Paso, TX Metropolitan Statistical Area; (2) Rank ranges from 1 to 391 where 1 indicates greatest number of identity theft reports per 100,000 population
Source: Federal Trade Commission, Consumer Sentinel Network Data Book 2022

Fraud and Other Consumer Reports

Area	Reports	Reports per 100,000 Population	Rank[2]
MSA[1]	5,587	664	316
U.S.	4,064,520	1,245	-

Note: (1) Figures cover the El Paso, TX Metropolitan Statistical Area; (2) Rank ranges from 1 to 391 where 1 indicates greatest number of fraud and other consumer reports per 100,000 population
Source: Federal Trade Commission, Consumer Sentinel Network Data Book 2022

POLITICS

2020 Presidential Election Results

Area	Biden	Trump	Jorgensen	Hawkins	Other
El Paso County	66.7	31.6	1.0	0.5	0.2
U.S.	51.3	46.8	1.2	0.3	0.5

Note: Results are percentages and may not add to 100% due to rounding
Source: Dave Leip's Atlas of U.S. Presidential Elections

SPORTS

Professional Sports Teams

Team Name	League	Year Established

No teams are located in the metro area
Source: Wikipedia, Major Professional Sports Teams of the United States and Canada, April 12, 2023

CLIMATE

Average and Extreme Temperatures

Temperature	Jan	Feb	Mar	Apr	May	Jun	Jul	Aug	Sep	Oct	Nov	Dec	Yr.
Extreme High (°F)	80	83	89	98	104	114	112	108	104	96	87	80	114
Average High (°F)	57	63	70	79	87	96	95	93	88	79	66	58	78
Average Temp. (°F)	44	49	56	64	73	81	83	81	75	65	52	45	64
Average Low (°F)	31	35	41	49	58	66	70	68	62	50	38	32	50
Extreme Low (°F)	-8	8	14	23	31	46	57	56	42	25	1	5	-8

Note: Figures cover the years 1948-1995
Source: National Climatic Data Center, International Station Meteorological Climate Summary, 9/96

Average Precipitation/Snowfall/Humidity

Precip./Humidity	Jan	Feb	Mar	Apr	May	Jun	Jul	Aug	Sep	Oct	Nov	Dec	Yr.
Avg. Precip. (in.)	0.4	0.4	0.3	0.2	0.3	0.7	1.6	1.5	1.4	0.7	0.3	0.6	8.6
Avg. Snowfall (in.)	1	1	Tr	Tr	0	0	0	0	0	Tr	1	2	6
Avg. Rel. Hum. 6am (%)	68	60	50	43	44	46	63	69	72	66	63	68	59
Avg. Rel. Hum. 3pm (%)	34	27	21	17	17	17	28	30	32	29	30	36	26

Note: Figures cover the years 1948-1995; Tr = Trace amounts (<0.05 in. of rain; <0.5 in. of snow)
Source: National Climatic Data Center, International Station Meteorological Climate Summary, 9/96

Weather Conditions

Temperature			Daytime Sky			Precipitation		
10°F & below	32°F & below	90°F & above	Clear	Partly cloudy	Cloudy	0.01 inch or more precip.	0.1 inch or more snow/ice	Thunderstorms
1	59	106	147	164	54	49	3	35

Note: Figures are average number of days per year and cover the years 1948-1995
Source: National Climatic Data Center, International Station Meteorological Climate Summary, 9/96

HAZARDOUS WASTE

Superfund Sites

The El Paso, TX metro area has no sites on the EPA's Superfund Final National Priorities List. There are a total of 1,165 Superfund sites with a status of proposed or final on the list in the U.S. *U.S. Environmental Protection Agency, National Priorities List, April 12, 2023*

AIR QUALITY

Air Quality Trends: Ozone

	1990	1995	2000	2005	2010	2015	2018	2019	2020	2021
MSA[1]	0.080	0.078	0.082	0.074	0.072	0.071	0.077	0.074	0.076	0.071
U.S.	0.087	0.089	0.081	0.080	0.072	0.067	0.069	0.065	0.065	0.067

Note: (1) Data covers the El Paso, TX Metropolitan Statistical Area. The values shown are the composite ozone concentration averages among trend sites based on the highest fourth daily maximum 8-hour concentration in parts per million. These trends are based on sites having an adequate record of monitoring data during the trend period. Data from exceptional events are included.
Source: U.S. Environmental Protection Agency, Air Quality Monitoring Information, "Air Quality Trends by City, 1990-2021"

Air Quality Index

Area	Percent of Days when Air Quality was...[2]					AQI Statistics[2]	
	Good	Moderate	Unhealthy for Sensitive Groups	Unhealthy	Very Unhealthy	Maximum	Median
MSA[1]	38.6	56.2	5.2	0.0	0.0	150	54

Note: (1) Data covers the El Paso, TX Metropolitan Statistical Area; (2) Based on 365 days with AQI data in 2021. Air Quality Index (AQI) is an index for reporting daily air quality. EPA calculates the AQI for five major air pollutants regulated by the Clean Air Act: ground-level ozone, particle pollution (aka particulate matter), carbon monoxide, sulfur dioxide, and nitrogen dioxide. The AQI runs from 0 to 500. The higher the AQI value, the greater the level of air pollution and the greater the health concern. There are six AQI categories: "Good" AQI is between 0 and 50. Air quality is considered satisfactory; "Moderate" AQI is between 51 and 100. Air quality is acceptable; "Unhealthy for Sensitive Groups" When AQI values are between 101 and 150, members of sensitive groups may experience health effects; "Unhealthy" When AQI values are between 151 and 200 everyone may begin to experience health effects; "Very Unhealthy" AQI values between 201 and 300 trigger a health alert; "Hazardous" AQI values over 300 trigger warnings of emergency conditions (not shown).
Source: U.S. Environmental Protection Agency, Air Quality Index Report, 2021

Air Quality Index Pollutants

Area	Percent of Days when AQI Pollutant was...[2]						
	Carbon Monoxide	Nitrogen Dioxide	Ozone	Sulfur Dioxide	Particulate Matter 2.5	Particulate Matter 10
MSA[1]	0.0	5.8	53.2	(3)	35.9	5.2

Note: (1) Data covers the El Paso, TX Metropolitan Statistical Area; (2) Based on 365 days with AQI data in 2021. The Air Quality Index (AQI) is an index for reporting daily air quality. EPA calculates the AQI for five major air pollutants regulated by the Clean Air Act: ground-level ozone, particle pollution (also known as particulate matter), carbon monoxide, sulfur dioxide, and nitrogen dioxide. The AQI runs from 0 to 500. The higher the AQI value, the greater the level of air pollution and the greater the health concern; (3) Sulfur dioxide is no longer included in this table (as of December 8, 2021) because SO_2 concentrations tend to be very localized and not necessarily representative of broad geographical areas like counties and CBSAs.
Source: U.S. Environmental Protection Agency, Air Quality Index Report, 2021

Maximum Air Pollutant Concentrations: Particulate Matter, Ozone, CO and Lead

	Particulate Matter 10 (ug/m^3)	Particulate Matter 2.5 Wtd AM (ug/m^3)	Particulate Matter 2.5 24-Hr (ug/m^3)	Ozone (ppm)	Carbon Monoxide (ppm)	Lead (ug/m^3)
MSA[1] Level	153	9.2	37	0.073	3	n/a
NAAQS[2]	150	15	35	0.075	9	0.15
Met NAAQS[2]	No	Yes	No	Yes	Yes	n/a

Note: (1) Data covers the El Paso, TX Metropolitan Statistical Area; Data from exceptional events are included; (2) National Ambient Air Quality Standards; ppm = parts per million; ug/m^3 = micrograms per cubic meter; n/a not available.
Concentrations: Particulate Matter 10 (coarse particulate)—highest second maximum 24-hour concentration; Particulate Matter 2.5 Wtd AM (fine particulate)—highest weighted annual mean concentration; Particulate Matter 2.5 24-Hour (fine particulate)—highest 98th percentile 24-hour concentration; Ozone—highest fourth daily maximum 8-hour concentration; Carbon Monoxide—highest second maximum non-overlapping 8-hour concentration; Lead—maximum running 3-month average
Source: U.S. Environmental Protection Agency, Air Quality Monitoring Information, "Air Quality Statistics by City, 2021"

Maximum Air Pollutant Concentrations: Nitrogen Dioxide and Sulfur Dioxide

	Nitrogen Dioxide AM (ppb)	Nitrogen Dioxide 1-Hr (ppb)	Sulfur Dioxide AM (ppb)	Sulfur Dioxide 1-Hr (ppb)	Sulfur Dioxide 24-Hr (ppb)
MSA[1] Level	14	57	n/a	n/a	n/a
NAAQS[2]	53	100	30	75	140
Met NAAQS[2]	Yes	Yes	n/a	n/a	n/a

Note: (1) Data covers the El Paso, TX Metropolitan Statistical Area; Data from exceptional events are included; (2) National Ambient Air Quality Standards; ppm = parts per million; ug/m^3 = micrograms per cubic meter; n/a not available.
Concentrations: Nitrogen Dioxide AM—highest arithmetic mean concentration; Nitrogen Dioxide 1-Hr—highest 98th percentile 1-hour daily maximum concentration; Sulfur Dioxide AM—highest annual mean concentration; Sulfur Dioxide 1-Hr—highest 99th percentile 1-hour daily maximum concentration; Sulfur Dioxide 24-Hr—highest second maximum 24-hour concentration
Source: U.S. Environmental Protection Agency, Air Quality Monitoring Information, "Air Quality Statistics by City, 2021"

Fort Worth, Texas

Background

Fort Worth lies in north central Texas near the headwaters of the Trinity River. Despite its modern skyscrapers, multiple freeways, shopping malls, and extensive industry, the city is known for its easy-going atmosphere.

The area has seen many travelers. Nomadic Native Americans of the plains rode through on horses bred from those brought by Spanish explorers. The 1840s saw American-Anglos settle in the region. On June 6, 1849, Major Ripley A. Arnold and his U.S. Cavalry troop established an outpost on the Trinity River to protect settlers moving westward. The fort was named for General William J. Worth, Commander of the U.S. Army's Texas department. When the fort was abandoned in 1853, settlers moved in and converted the vacant barracks into trading establishments and homes, stealing the county seat from Birdville (an act made legal in the 1860 election).

In the 1860s, Fort Worth, which was close to the Chisholm Trail, became an oasis for cowboys traveling to and from Kansas. Although the town's growth virtually stopped during the Civil War, Fort Worth was incorporated as a city in 1873. In a race against time, the final 26 miles of the Texas & Pacific Line were completed, and Fort Worth survived to be a part of the West Texas oil boom in 1917.

Real prosperity followed at the end of World War II when the city became a center for several military installations. Aviation is the city's principal source of economic growth. Its leading industries include the manufacture of aircraft, automobiles, machinery, and containers, as well as food processing and brewing. Emerging economic sectors in the 21st century include semiconductor manufacturing, and communications equipment manufacturing and distribution.

Since it first began testing DNA samples in 2003, the DNA Identity Laboratory at the University of North Texas Health Science Center has made over 100 matches, helping to solve missing-persons cases and close criminal cases. The university is also home to the national Osteopathic Research Center, the only academic DNA Lab qualified to work with the FBI, the Texas Center for Health Disparities, and the Health Institutes of Texas. Other colleges in Fort Worth include Texas Christian University, Southwestern Baptist Seminary, and Texas Wesleyan University.

Fort Worth's most comprehensive mixed-use project at Walsh Ranch was completed in 2017 with space for residential, commercial, office and retail. The 7,275-acre planned community is named after the original owners of the property, F. Howard and Mary D. Walsh, who were well-known ranchers, philanthropists and civic leaders. Walsh Ranch has room for 50,000 Fort Worth residents.

The Omni Fort Worth Hotel was host to the 2011 AFC champion Pittsburgh Steelers during Super Bowl XLV, and the city's 3,600-acre Greer Island Nature Center and Refuge will celebrate its 60th anniversary in 2024.

Winter temperatures and rainfall are modified by the northeast-northwest mountain barrier, which prevents shallow cold air masses from crossing over from the west. Summer temperatures vary with cloud and shower activity but are generally mild. Summer precipitation is largely from local thunderstorms and varies from year to year. Damaging rains are infrequent. Hurricanes have produced heavy rainfall but are usually not accompanied by destructive winds. In February 2021, record-breaking low temperatures (-2) caused icy roads, a 133-car pile-up, and major disruption in electricity across the state.

Rankings

General Rankings

- For its "Best for Vets: Places to Live 2019" rankings, *Military Times* evaluated 599 cities (83 large, 234 medium, 282 small) and compared the locations across three broad categories: veteran and military culture/services; economic indicators; and livability factors such as health, crime, traffic, and school quality. Fort Worth ranked #22 out of the top 25, in the large city category (population of more than 250,000). Data points more specific to veterans and the military weighed more heavily than others. *rebootcamp.militarytimes.com, "Military Times Best Places to Live 2019," September 10, 2018*

- The Dallas metro area was identified as one of America's fastest-growing areas in terms of population and business growth by *MagnifyMoney*. The area ranked #7 out of 35. The 100 most populous metro areas in the U.S. were evaluated on their change from 2011 to 2016 in the following categories: people and housing; workforce and employment opportunities; growing industry. *www.businessinsider.com, "The 35 Cities in the US with the Biggest Influx of People, the Most Work Opportunities, and the Hottest Business Growth," August 12, 2018*

- The Fort Worth metro area was identified as one of America's fastest-growing areas in terms of population and economy by *Forbes*. The area ranked #5 out of 25. The 100 most populous metro areas in the U.S. were evaluated on the following criteria: estimated population growth; employment; economic output; wages; home values. *Forbes, "America's Fastest-Growing Cities 2018," February 28, 2018*

Business/Finance Rankings

- WalletHub's latest report ranked over 2,500 cities by the average credit score of its residents. Fort Worth was ranked #4 among the ten cities with the lowest average credit score, based on TransUnion data as of October 2022. *www.wallethub.com, "2023's Cities With the Highest & Lowest Credit Scores," March 29, 2023*

- Based on metro area social media reviews, the employment opinion group Glassdoor surveyed 50 of the most populous U.S. metro areas and equally weighed cost of living, hiring opportunity, and job satisfaction to compose a list of "25 Best Cities for Jobs." Median pay and home value, and number of active job openings were also factored in. The Dallas metro area was ranked #25 in overall job satisfaction. *www.glassdoor.com, "Best Cities for Jobs," February 25, 2020*

- The Brookings Institution ranked the 100 largest metro areas in the U.S. based on income inequality. Dallas was ranked #60 (#1 = greatest inequality). Criteria: the "95/20 ratio," a figure representing the income at which a household earns more than 95 percent of all other households, divided by the income at which a household earns more than only 20 percent of all other households. *Brookings Institution, "Household Income Inequality, 100 Largest U.S. Metro Areas, 2014-2016," February 5, 2018*

- The Dallas metro area was identified as one of the most debt-ridden places in America by the finance site Credit.com. The metro area was ranked #2. Criteria: residents' average credit card debt as well as median income. *Credit.com, "25 Cities With the Most Credit Card Debt," February 28, 2018*

- Dallas was identified as one of America's most frugal metro areas by *Coupons.com*. The city ranked #2 out of 25. Criteria: digital coupon usage. *Coupons.com, "America's Most Frugal Cities of 2017," March 22, 2018*

- Fort Worth was cited as one of America's top metros for total corporate facility investment in 2022. The area ranked #2 in the large metro area category (population over 1 million). *Site Selection, "Top Metros of 2022," March 2023*

- Fort Worth was identified as one of the unhappiest cities to work in by CareerBliss.com, an online community for career advancement. The city ranked #2 out of 5. Criteria: an employee's relationship with his or her boss and co-workers; general work environment; compensation; opportunities for advancement; company culture and job reputation; and resources. *Businesswire.com, "CareerBliss Unhappiest Cities to Work 2019," February 12, 2019*

- The Fort Worth metro area appeared on the Milken Institute "2022 Best Performing Cities" list. Rank: #40 out of 200 large metro areas (population over 250,000). Criteria: job growth; wage and salary growth; high-tech output growth; housing affordability; household broadband access. *Milken Institute, "Best-Performing Cities 2022," March 28, 2022*

- *Forbes* ranked the 200 most populous metro areas to determine the nation's "Best Places for Business and Careers." The Fort Worth metro area was ranked #20. Criteria: costs (business and living); job growth (past and projected); income growth; quality of life; educational attainment (college and high school); projected economic growth; cultural and leisure opportunities; workplace tolerance laws; net migration patterns. *Forbes, "The Best Places for Business and Careers 2019: Seattle Still On Top," October 30, 2019*

Culture/Performing Arts Rankings

- Fort Worth was selected as one of the 25 best cities for moviemakers in North America. Great film cities are places where filmmaking dreams can come true, that offer more creative space, lower costs, and great outdoor locations. NYC & LA were intentionally excluded. Criteria: longstanding reputations as film-friendly communities; film community and culture; affordability; and quality of life. The city was ranked #25. *MovieMaker Magazine, "Best Places to Live and Work as a Moviemaker, 2023," January 18, 2023*

- Fort Worth was selected as one of "America's Favorite Cities." The city ranked #15 in the "Architecture" category. Respondents to an online survey were asked to rate their favorite place (population over 100,000) in over 65 categories. *Travelandleisure.com, "America's Favorite Cities for Architecture 2016," March 2, 2017*

Education Rankings

- Personal finance website *WalletHub* analyzed the 150 largest U.S. metropolitan statistical areas to determine where the most educated Americans are putting their degrees to work. Criteria: education levels; percentage of workers with degrees; education quality and attainment gap; public school quality rankings; quality and enrollment of each metro area's universities. Fort Worth was ranked #73 (#1 = most educated city). *www.WalletHub.com, "Most & Least Educated Cities in America," July 18, 2022*

- Fort Worth was selected as one of America's most literate cities. The city ranked #65 out of the 84 largest U.S. cities. Criteria: number of booksellers; library resources; Internet resources; educational attainment; periodical publishing resources; newspaper circulation. *Central Connecticut State University, "America's Most Literate Cities, 2018," February 2019*

Environmental Rankings

- Sperling's BestPlaces assessed the 50 largest metropolitan areas of the United States for the likelihood of dangerously extreme weather events or earthquakes. In general the Southeast and South-Central regions have the highest risk of weather extremes and earthquakes, while the Pacific Northwest enjoys the lowest risk. Of the most risky metropolitan areas, the Fort Worth metro area was ranked #4. *www.bestplaces.net, "Avoid Natural Disasters: BestPlaces Reveals The Top 10 Safest Places to Live," October 25, 2017*

- The U.S. Environmental Protection Agency (EPA) released its list of U.S. metropolitan areas with the most ENERGY STAR certified buildings in 2022. The Dallas metro area was ranked #8 out of 25. *U.S. Environmental Protection Agency, "2023 Energy Star Top Cities," April 26, 2023*

- Fort Worth was highlighted as one of the 25 most ozone-polluted metro areas in the U.S. during 2019 through 2021. The area ranked #18. *American Lung Association, "State of the Air 2023," April 19, 2023*

Food/Drink Rankings

- Globe Life Park was selected as one of PETA's "Top 10 Vegan-Friendly Ballparks" for 2019. The park ranked #1. *People for the Ethical Treatment of Animals, "Top 10 Vegan-Friendly Ballparks," May 23, 2019*

Health/Fitness Rankings

- For each of the 100 largest cities in the United States, the American Fitness Index®, compiled in partnership between the American College of Sports Medicine and the Elevance Health Foundation, evaluated community infrastructure and 34 health behaviors including preventive health, levels of chronic disease conditions, food insecurity, sleep quality, pedestrian safety, air quality, and community/environment resources that support physical activity. Fort Worth ranked #82 for "community fitness." *americanfitnessindex.org, "2022 ACSM American Fitness Index Summary Report," July 12, 2022*

- Dallas was identified as a "2022 Spring Allergy Capital." The area ranked #32 out of 100. Three groups of factors were used to identify the most challenging cities for people with allergies during the spring season: annual spring pollen scores; over the counter allergy medicine use; number of board-certified allergy specialists. *Asthma and Allergy Foundation of America, "Spring Allergy Capitals 2022," March 2, 2022*

- Dallas was identified as a "2022 Fall Allergy Capital." The area ranked #22 out of 100. Three groups of factors were used to identify the most challenging cities for people with allergies during the fall season: annual fall pollen scores; over the counter allergy medicine use; number of board-certified allergy specialists. *Asthma and Allergy Foundation of America, "Fall Allergy Capitals 2022," March 2, 2022*

- Dallas was identified as a "2022 Asthma Capital." The area ranked #45 out of the nation's 100 largest metropolitan areas. Criteria: estimated asthma prevalence; asthma-related mortality; and ER visits due to asthma. Risk factors analyzed but not factored in the rankings: annual pollen score; annual air quality; public smoking laws; access to board-certified asthma specialists; rescue and controller medication use; uninsured rate; poverty rate. *Asthma and Allergy Foundation of America, "Asthma Capitals 2022: The Most Challenging Places to Live With Asthma," September 14, 2022*

Pet Rankings

- Fort Worth appeared on *The Dogington Post* site as one of the top cities for dog lovers, ranking #12 out of 15. The real estate marketplace, Zillow®, and Rover, the largest pet sitter and dog walker network, introduced a new list of "Top Emerging Dog-Friendly Cities" for 2021. Criteria: number of new dog accounts on the Rover platform; and rentals and listings that mention features that attract dog owners (fenced-in yards, dog houses, dog door or proximity to a dog park). *www.dogingtonpost.com, "15 Cities Emerging as Dog-Friendliest in 2021," May 11, 2021*

Real Estate Rankings

- *WalletHub* compared the most populated U.S. cities to determine which had the best markets for real estate agents. Fort Worth ranked #76 where demand was high and pay was the best. Criteria: sales per agent; annual median wage for real-estate agents; monthly average starting salary for real estate agents; real estate job density and competition; unemployment rate; home turnover rate; housing-market health index; and other relevant metrics. *www.WalletHub.com, "2021 Best Places to Be a Real Estate Agent," May 12, 2021*

- Fort Worth was ranked #157 out of 235 metro areas in terms of housing affordability in 2022 by the National Association of Home Builders (#1 = most affordable). Criteria: the share of homes sold in that area affordable to a family earning the local median income, based on standard mortgage underwriting criteria. *National Association of Home Builders®, NAHB-Wells Fargo Housing Opportunity Index, 4th Quarter 2022*

Safety Rankings

- Allstate ranked the 200 largest cities in America in terms of driver safety. Fort Worth ranked #139. Criteria: internal property damage claims over a two-year period from January 2016 to December 2017. The report helps increase the importance of safety and awareness behind the wheel. *Allstate, "Allstate America's Best Drivers Report, 2019" June 24, 2019*

- The National Insurance Crime Bureau ranked 390 metro areas in the U.S. in terms of per capita rates of vehicle theft. The Fort Worth metro area ranked #72 (#1 = highest rate). Criteria: number of vehicle theft offenses per 100,000 inhabitants in 2021. *National Insurance Crime Bureau, "Hot Spots 2021," September 1, 2022*

Seniors/Retirement Rankings

- *AARP the Magazine* selected Fort Worth as one of the great places in the United States for seniors, as well as younger generations, that represent "a place to call home." For the list, the magazine recognized the change in criteria due to the pandemic, and looked for cities with easy access to exercise/outdoors, quality healthcare, sense of community, relatively affordable housing costs, job markets that accommodate working from home, and reliable internet access. *www.aarp.org/magazine, "Best Places to Live and Retire Now," November 29, 2021*

Transportation Rankings

- According to the INRIX "2022 Global Traffic Scorecard," Dallas was identified as one of the most congested metro areas in the U.S. The area ranked #14 out of 25. Criteria: average annual time spent in traffic and average cost of congestion per motorist. *Inrix.com, "Return to Work, Higher Gas Prices & Inflation Drove Americans to Spend Hundreds More in Time and Money Commuting," January 10, 2023*

Women/Minorities Rankings

- The *Houston Chronicle* listed the Dallas metro area as #7 in top places for young Latinos to live in the U.S. Research was largely based on housing and occupational data from the largest metropolitan areas performed by *Forbes* and NBC Universo. Criteria: percentage of 18-34 year-olds; Latino college grad rates; and diversity. *blog.chron.com, "The 15 Best Big Cities for Latino Millenials," January 26, 2016*

- Personal finance website *WalletHub* compared more than 180 U.S. cities across two key dimensions, "Hispanic Business-Friendliness" and "Hispanic Purchasing Power," to arrive at the most favorable conditions for Hispanic entrepreneurs. Fort Worth was ranked #14 out of 182. Criteria includes: share of Hispanic-Owned Businesses; Hispanic entrepreneurship rate to median annual income of Hispanics; Small Business-Friendliness score; cost of living; and number of Hispanics with at least a bachelor's degree. *WalletHub.com, "2019's Best Cities for Hispanic Entrepreneurs," May 1, 2019*

Miscellaneous Rankings

- The watchdog site, Charity Navigator, conducted a study of charities in major markets both to analyze statistical differences in their financial, accountability, and transparency practices and to track year-to-year variations in individual philanthropic communities. The Dallas metro area was ranked #5 among the 30 metro markets in the rating category of Overall Score. *www.charitynavigator.org, "2017 Metro Market Study," May 1, 2017*

- *WalletHub* compared the 150 most populated U.S. cities to determine their operating efficiency. A "Quality of Services" score was constructed for each city and then divided by the total budget per capita to reveal which were managed the best. Fort Worth ranked #49. Criteria: financial stability; economy; education; safety; health; infrastructure and pollution. *www.WalletHub.com, "2022's Best- & Worst-Run Cities in America," June 21, 2022*

- Fort Worth was selected as one of "America's Friendliest Cities." The city ranked #9 in the "Friendliest" category. Respondents to an online survey were asked to rate 38 top urban destinations in the United States as to general friendliness, as well as manners, politeness and warm disposition. *Travel + Leisure, "America's Friendliest Cities," October 20, 2017*

Business Environment

DEMOGRAPHICS

Population Growth

Area	1990 Census	2000 Census	2010 Census	2020 Census	Population Growth (%) 1990-2020	Population Growth (%) 2010-2020
City	448,311	534,694	741,206	918,915	105.0	24.0
MSA[1]	3,989,294	5,161,544	6,371,773	7,637,387	91.4	19.9
U.S.	248,709,873	281,421,906	308,745,538	331,449,281	33.3	7.4

Note: (1) Figures cover the Dallas-Fort Worth-Arlington, TX Metropolitan Statistical Area
Source: U.S. Census Bureau, 1990 Census, 2000 Census, 2010 Census, 2020 Census

Race

Area	White Alone[2] (%)	Black Alone[2] (%)	Asian Alone[2] (%)	AIAN[3] Alone[2] (%)	NHOPI[4] Alone[2] (%)	Other Race Alone[2] (%)	Two or More Races (%)
City	44.9	19.6	5.2	0.9	0.1	14.2	15.1
MSA[1]	48.9	16.0	7.9	1.0	0.1	12.2	13.9
U.S.	61.6	12.4	6.0	1.1	0.2	8.4	10.2

Note: (1) Figures cover the Dallas-Fort Worth-Arlington, TX Metropolitan Statistical Area; (2) Alone is defined as not being in combination with one or more other races; (3) American Indian and Alaska Native; (4) Native Hawaiian and Other Pacific Islander
Source: U.S. Census Bureau, 2020 Census

Hispanic or Latino Origin

Area	Total (%)	Mexican (%)	Puerto Rican (%)	Cuban (%)	Other (%)
City	35.3	29.8	1.2	0.4	3.9
MSA[1]	29.3	23.6	0.8	0.3	4.5
U.S.	18.4	11.2	1.8	0.7	4.7

Note: Persons of Hispanic or Latino origin can be of any race; (1) Figures cover the Dallas-Fort Worth-Arlington, TX Metropolitan Statistical Area
Source: U.S. Census Bureau, 2017-2021 American Community Survey 5-Year Estimates

Age

Area	Under Age 5	Age 5–19	Age 20–34	Age 35–44	Age 45–54	Age 55–64	Age 65–74	Age 75–84	Age 85+	Median Age
City	7.0	22.7	23.1	14.3	12.1	10.3	6.6	2.9	1.1	33.2
MSA[1]	6.2	21.8	21.4	14.1	13.0	11.4	7.4	3.4	1.1	35.3
U.S.	5.6	19.2	20.2	12.7	12.4	13.1	10.0	4.9	1.9	38.8

Note: (1) Figures cover the Dallas-Fort Worth-Arlington, TX Metropolitan Statistical Area
Source: U.S. Census Bureau, 2020 Census

Disability by Age

Area	All Ages	Under 18 Years Old	18 to 64 Years Old	65 Years and Over
City	9.7	3.4	8.6	34.4
MSA[1]	9.5	3.8	8.0	32.1
U.S.	12.6	4.4	10.3	33.4

Note: Figures show percent of the civilian noninstitutionalized population that reported having a disability. Disability status is determined from six types of difficulty: vision, hearing, cognitive, ambulatory, self-care, and independent living. For children under 5 years old, hearing and vision difficulty are used to determine disability status. For children between the ages of 5 and 14, disability status is determined from hearing, vision, cognitive, ambulatory, and self-care difficulties. For people aged 15 years and older, they are considered to have a disability if they have difficulty with any one of the six difficulty types; Note: (1) Figures cover the Dallas-Fort Worth-Arlington, TX Metropolitan Statistical Area
Source: U.S. Census Bureau, 2017-2021 American Community Survey 5-Year Estimates

Ancestry

Area	German	Irish	English	American	Italian	Polish	French[2]	Scottish	Dutch
City	7.2	6.1	6.5	4.2	1.8	1.0	1.3	1.5	0.7
MSA[1]	8.2	6.5	7.6	5.9	2.1	1.0	1.5	1.5	0.6
U.S.	12.8	9.6	8.1	5.7	5.0	2.7	2.2	1.6	1.1

Note: Figures are the percentage of the total population reporting a particular ancestry. The nine most commonly reported ancestries in the U.S. are shown. Figures include multiple ancestries (e.g. if a person reported being Irish and Italian, they were included in both columns); (1) Figures cover the Dallas-Fort Worth-Arlington, TX Metropolitan Statistical Area; (2) Excludes Basque
Source: U.S. Census Bureau, 2017-2021 American Community Survey 5-Year Estimates

Foreign-born Population

Area	Any Foreign Country	Asia	Mexico	Europe	Caribbean	Central America[2]	South America	Africa	Canada
City	16.7	3.7	9.2	0.6	0.3	0.8	0.6	1.3	0.2
MSA[1]	18.7	5.7	7.8	0.8	0.3	1.6	0.7	1.6	0.2
U.S.	13.6	4.2	3.3	1.5	1.4	1.1	1.1	0.8	0.2

Percent of Population Born in

Note: (1) Figures cover the Dallas-Fort Worth-Arlington, TX Metropolitan Statistical Area; (2) Excludes Mexico.
Source: U.S. Census Bureau, 2017-2021 American Community Survey 5-Year Estimates

Household Size

Area	One	Two	Three	Four	Five	Six	Seven or More	Average Household Size
City	26.6	29.4	16.5	14.6	7.5	3.2	2.0	2.80
MSA[1]	25.1	30.8	16.8	15.0	7.7	2.9	1.8	2.80
U.S.	28.1	33.8	15.5	12.9	6.0	2.3	1.4	2.60

Note: (1) Figures cover the Dallas-Fort Worth-Arlington, TX Metropolitan Statistical Area
Source: U.S. Census Bureau, 2017-2021 American Community Survey 5-Year Estimates

Household Relationships

Area	House-holder	Opposite-sex Spouse	Same-sex Spouse	Opposite-sex Unmarried Partner	Same-sex Unmarried Partner	Child[2]	Grand-child	Other Relatives	Non-relatives
City	35.2	15.8	0.2	2.1	0.1	33.0	3.1	5.6	3.0
MSA[1]	36.2	17.6	0.2	2.0	0.2	31.7	2.7	5.5	2.9
U.S.	38.3	17.5	0.2	2.5	0.2	28.3	2.4	4.8	3.4

Note: Figures are percent of the total population; (1) Figures cover the Dallas-Fort Worth-Arlington, TX Metropolitan Statistical Area; (2) Includes biological, adopted, and stepchildren of the householder
Source: U.S. Census Bureau, 2020 Census

Gender

Area	Males	Females	Males per 100 Females
City	449,923	468,992	95.9
MSA[1]	3,753,384	3,884,003	96.6
U.S.	162,685,811	168,763,470	96.4

Note: (1) Figures cover the Dallas-Fort Worth-Arlington, TX Metropolitan Statistical Area
Source: U.S. Census Bureau, 2020 Census

Marital Status

Area	Never Married	Now Married[2]	Separated	Widowed	Divorced
City	35.5	46.7	2.2	4.4	11.1
MSA[1]	32.8	50.8	1.9	4.2	10.3
U.S.	33.8	48.0	1.8	5.6	10.8

Note: Figures are percentages and cover the population 15 years of age and older; (1) Figures cover the Dallas-Fort Worth-Arlington, TX Metropolitan Statistical Area; (2) Excludes separated
Source: U.S. Census Bureau, 2017-2021 American Community Survey 5-Year Estimates

Religious Groups by Family

Area	Catholic	Baptist	Methodist	LDS[2]	Pentecostal	Lutheran	Islam	Adventist	Other
MSA[1]	14.2	14.3	4.7	1.4	2.2	0.5	1.8	1.3	13.8
U.S.	18.7	7.3	3.0	2.0	1.8	1.7	1.3	1.3	11.6

Note: Figures are the number of adherents as a percentage of the total population and cover the eight largest religious groups in the U.S; (1) Figures cover the Dallas-Fort Worth-Arlington, TX Metropolitan Statistical Area; (2) Church of Jesus Christ of Latter-day Saints
Sources: 2020 U.S. Religion Census, Association of Statisticians of American Religious Bodies; The Association of Religion Data Archives (ARDA)

Religious Groups by Tradition

Area	Catholic	Evangelical Protestant	Mainline Protestant	Black Protestant	Islam	Judaism	Hinduism	Orthodox	Buddhism
MSA[1]	14.2	25.4	5.9	3.3	1.8	0.3	0.5	0.3	0.2
U.S.	18.7	16.5	5.2	2.3	1.3	0.6	0.4	0.4	0.3

Note: Figures are the number of adherents as a percentage of the total population; (1) Figures cover the Dallas-Fort Worth-Arlington, TX Metropolitan Statistical Area
Sources: 2020 U.S. Religion Census, Association of Statisticians of American Religious Bodies; The Association of Religion Data Archives (ARDA)

ECONOMY

Gross Metropolitan Product

Area	2020	2021	2022	2023	Rank[2]
MSA[1]	538.4	608.8	686.1	722.1	5

Note: Figures are in billions of dollars; (1) Figures cover the Dallas-Fort Worth-Arlington, TX Metropolitan Statistical Area; (2) Rank is based on 2021 data and ranges from 1 to 381
Source: U.S. Conference of Mayors, U.S. Metro Economies: U.S. Metros Compared to Global and State Economies, June 2022

Economic Growth

Area	2018-20 (%)	2021 (%)	2022 (%)	2023 (%)	Rank[2]
MSA[1]	0.8	8.3	5.3	3.2	84
U.S.	-0.6	5.7	3.1	2.9	—

Note: Figures are real gross metropolitan product (GMP) growth rates and represent average annual percent change; (1) Figures cover the Dallas-Fort Worth-Arlington, TX Metropolitan Statistical Area; (2) Rank is based on 2020 2-year average annual percent change and ranges from 1 to 381
Source: U.S. Conference of Mayors, U.S. Metro Economies: U.S. Metros Compared to Global and State Economies, June 2022

Metropolitan Area Exports

Area	2016	2017	2018	2019	2020	2021	Rank[2]
MSA[1]	27,187.8	30,269.1	36,260.9	39,474.0	35,642.0	43,189.0	6

Note: Figures are in millions of dollars; (1) Figures cover the Dallas-Fort Worth-Arlington, TX Metropolitan Statistical Area; (2) Rank is based on 2021 data and ranges from 1 to 388
Source: U.S. Department of Commerce, International Trade Administration, Office of Trade and Economic Analysis, Industry and Analysis, Exports by Metropolitan Area, data extracted March 16, 2023

Building Permits

Area	Single-Family 2021	Single-Family 2022	Pct. Chg.	Multi-Family 2021	Multi-Family 2022	Pct. Chg.	Total 2021	Total 2022	Pct. Chg.
City	7,236	7,421	2.6	4,338	4,557	5.0	11,574	11,978	3.5
MSA[1]	51,996	43,645	-16.1	26,709	34,249	28.2	78,705	77,894	-1.0
U.S.	1,115,400	975,600	-12.5	621,600	689,500	10.9	1,737,000	1,665,100	-4.1

Note: (1) Figures cover the Dallas-Fort Worth-Arlington, TX Metropolitan Statistical Area; Figures represent new, privately-owned housing units authorized (unadjusted data); All permit data are based on estimates with imputation
Source: U.S. Census Bureau, Manufacturing, Mining, and Construction Statistics, Building Permits, 2021, 2022

Bankruptcy Filings

Area	Business Filings 2021	Business Filings 2022	% Chg.	Nonbusiness Filings 2021	Nonbusiness Filings 2022	% Chg.
Tarrant County	151	200	32.5	2,277	2,447	7.5
U.S.	14,347	13,481	-6.0	399,269	374,240	-6.3

Note: Business filings include Chapter 7, Chapter 9, Chapter 11, Chapter 12, Chapter 13, Chapter 15, and Section 304; Nonbusiness filings include Chapter 7, Chapter 11, and Chapter 13
Source: Administrative Office of the U.S. Courts, Business and Nonbusiness Bankruptcy, County Cases Commenced by Chapter of the Bankruptcy Code, During the 12-Month Period Ending December 31, 2021 and Business and Nonbusiness Bankruptcy, County Cases Commenced by Chapter of the Bankruptcy Code, During the 12-Month Period Ending December 31, 2022

Housing Vacancy Rates

Area	Gross Vacancy Rate[2] (%) 2020	2021	2022	Year-Round Vacancy Rate[3] (%) 2020	2021	2022	Rental Vacancy Rate[4] (%) 2020	2021	2022	Homeowner Vacancy Rate[5] (%) 2020	2021	2022
MSA[1]	6.4	6.6	6.6	6.4	6.5	6.3	7.2	7.0	6.8	0.7	0.7	0.7
U.S.	10.6	10.8	10.5	8.2	8.4	8.2	6.3	6.1	5.8	1.0	0.9	0.8

Note: (1) Figures cover the Dallas-Fort Worth-Arlington, TX Metropolitan Statistical Area; (2) The percentage of the total housing inventory that is vacant; (3) The percentage of the housing inventory (excluding seasonal units) that is year-round vacant; (4) The percentage of rental inventory that is vacant for rent; (5) The percentage of homeowner inventory that is vacant for sale
Source: U.S. Census Bureau, Housing Vacancies and Homeownership Annual Statistics: 2020, 2021, 2022

INCOME

Income

Area	Per Capita ($)	Median Household ($)	Average Household ($)
City	32,569	67,927	90,141
MSA[1]	38,609	76,916	105,647
U.S.	37,638	69,021	97,196

Note: (1) Figures cover the Dallas-Fort Worth-Arlington, TX Metropolitan Statistical Area
Source: U.S. Census Bureau, 2017-2021 American Community Survey 5-Year Estimates

Household Income Distribution

Area	Percent of Households Earning							
	Under $15,000	$15,000 -$24,999	$25,000 -$34,999	$35,000 -$49,999	$50,000 -$74,999	$75,000 -$99,999	$100,000 -$149,999	$150,000 and up
City	8.7	7.0	8.7	11.6	18.6	13.5	17.2	14.6
MSA[1]	7.1	6.0	7.4	11.1	17.3	13.3	17.9	20.0
U.S.	9.4	7.8	8.2	11.4	16.8	12.8	16.3	17.3

Note: (1) Figures cover the Dallas-Fort Worth-Arlington, TX Metropolitan Statistical Area
Source: U.S. Census Bureau, 2017-2021 American Community Survey 5-Year Estimates

Poverty Rate

Area	All Ages	Under 18 Years Old	18 to 64 Years Old	65 Years and Over
City	13.4	19.1	11.3	10.7
MSA[1]	10.9	15.4	9.4	8.9
U.S.	12.6	17.0	11.8	9.6

Note: Figures are percentage of people whose income during the past 12 months was below the poverty level; (1) Figures cover the Dallas-Fort Worth-Arlington, TX Metropolitan Statistical Area
Source: U.S. Census Bureau, 2017-2021 American Community Survey 5-Year Estimates

EMPLOYMENT

Labor Force and Employment

Area	Civilian Labor Force			Workers Employed		
	Dec. 2021	Dec. 2022	% Chg.	Dec. 2021	Dec. 2022	% Chg.
City	462,444	475,802	2.9	444,256	459,728	3.5
MD[1]	1,345,295	1,384,350	2.9	1,295,323	1,340,078	3.5
U.S.	161,696,000	164,224,000	1.6	155,732,000	158,872,000	2.0

Note: Data is not seasonally adjusted and covers workers 16 years of age and older; (1) Figures cover the Fort Worth-Arlington-Grapevine, TX Metropolitan Division
Source: Bureau of Labor Statistics, Local Area Unemployment Statistics

Unemployment Rate

Area	2022											
	Jan.	Feb.	Mar.	Apr.	May	Jun.	Jul.	Aug.	Sep.	Oct.	Nov.	Dec.
City	4.5	4.4	3.6	3.4	3.6	4.2	4.2	4.0	3.7	3.6	3.5	3.4
MD[1]	4.2	4.2	3.4	3.2	3.4	3.9	3.9	3.8	3.5	3.4	3.4	3.2
U.S.	4.4	4.1	3.8	3.3	3.4	3.8	3.8	3.8	3.3	3.4	3.4	3.3

Note: Data is not seasonally adjusted and covers workers 16 years of age and older; (1) Figures cover the Fort Worth-Arlington-Grapevine, TX Metropolitan Division
Source: Bureau of Labor Statistics, Local Area Unemployment Statistics

Average Wages

Occupation	$/Hr.	Occupation	$/Hr.
Accountants and Auditors	43.06	Maintenance and Repair Workers	21.23
Automotive Mechanics	24.09	Marketing Managers	67.66
Bookkeepers	22.81	Network and Computer Systems Admin.	45.36
Carpenters	23.70	Nurses, Licensed Practical	26.59
Cashiers	13.14	Nurses, Registered	42.24
Computer Programmers	46.27	Nursing Assistants	16.34
Computer Systems Analysts	54.07	Office Clerks, General	18.59
Computer User Support Specialists	28.45	Physical Therapists	50.76
Construction Laborers	18.68	Physicians	118.86
Cooks, Restaurant	15.57	Plumbers, Pipefitters and Steamfitters	26.94
Customer Service Representatives	19.64	Police and Sheriff's Patrol Officers	35.82
Dentists	76.46	Postal Service Mail Carriers	27.30
Electricians	26.46	Real Estate Sales Agents	38.08
Engineers, Electrical	50.66	Retail Salespersons	16.19
Fast Food and Counter Workers	12.14	Sales Representatives, Technical/Scientific	43.31
Financial Managers	79.36	Secretaries, Exc. Legal/Medical/Executive	20.33
First-Line Supervisors of Office Workers	31.46	Security Guards	16.99
General and Operations Managers	56.66	Surgeons	142.82
Hairdressers/Cosmetologists	16.24	Teacher Assistants, Exc. Postsecondary*	14.09
Home Health and Personal Care Aides	11.66	Teachers, Secondary School, Exc. Sp. Ed.*	30.46
Janitors and Cleaners	14.42	Telemarketers	18.24
Landscaping/Groundskeeping Workers	16.86	Truck Drivers, Heavy/Tractor-Trailer	24.73
Lawyers	87.42	Truck Drivers, Light/Delivery Services	22.27
Maids and Housekeeping Cleaners	13.78	Waiters and Waitresses	13.17

Note: Wage data covers the Dallas-Fort Worth-Arlington, TX Metropolitan Statistical Area; (*) Hourly wages were calculated from annual wage data based on a 40 hour work week; n/a not available.
Source: Bureau of Labor Statistics, Metro Area Occupational Employment & Wage Estimates, May 2022

Employment by Industry

Sector	MD[1] Number of Employees	MD[1] Percent of Total	U.S. Percent of Total
Construction, Mining, and Logging	79,600	6.6	5.4
Private Education and Health Services	153,200	12.8	16.1
Financial Activities	77,200	6.4	5.9
Government	142,700	11.9	14.5
Information	11,300	0.9	2.0
Leisure and Hospitality	126,200	10.5	10.3
Manufacturing	111,400	9.3	8.4
Other Services	41,300	3.4	3.7
Professional and Business Services	161,200	13.4	14.7
Retail Trade	128,200	10.7	10.2
Transportation, Warehousing, and Utilities	108,300	9.0	4.9
Wholesale Trade	59,000	4.9	3.9

Note: Figures are non-farm employment as of December 2022. Figures are not seasonally adjusted and include workers 16 years of age and older; (1) Figures cover the Fort Worth-Arlington-Grapevine, TX Metropolitan Division
Source: Bureau of Labor Statistics, Current Employment Statistics, Employment, Hours, and Earnings

Employment by Occupation

Occupation Classification	City (%)	MSA[1] (%)	U.S. (%)
Management, Business, Science, and Arts	37.1	41.4	40.3
Natural Resources, Construction, and Maintenance	10.0	9.1	8.7
Production, Transportation, and Material Moving	15.6	12.7	13.1
Sales and Office	21.5	22.0	20.9
Service	15.8	14.7	17.0

Note: Figures cover employed civilians 16 years of age and older; (1) Figures cover the Dallas-Fort Worth-Arlington, TX Metropolitan Statistical Area
Source: U.S. Census Bureau, 2017-2021 American Community Survey 5-Year Estimates

Occupations with Greatest Projected Employment Growth: 2022 – 2024

Occupation[1]	2022 Employment	2024 Projected Employment	Numeric Employment Change	Percent Employment Change
Home Health and Personal Care Aides	338,130	364,760	26,630	7.9
General and Operations Managers	395,700	416,100	20,400	5.2
Heavy and Tractor-Trailer Truck Drivers	206,850	222,220	15,370	7.4
Software Developers	119,810	134,060	14,250	11.9
Laborers and Freight, Stock, and Material Movers, Hand	214,680	228,680	14,000	6.5
Farmers, Ranchers, and Other Agricultural Managers	274,740	287,430	12,690	4.6
Stockers and Order Fillers	212,180	224,670	12,490	5.9
Construction Laborers	153,220	164,330	11,110	7.3
Cooks, Restaurant	131,480	141,860	10,380	7.9
Industrial Truck and Tractor Operators	83,270	93,190	9,920	11.9

Note: Projections cover Texas; (1) Sorted by numeric employment change
Source: www.projectionscentral.com, State Occupational Projections, 2022–2024 Short-Term Projections

Fastest-Growing Occupations: 2022 – 2024

Occupation[1]	2022 Employment	2024 Projected Employment	Numeric Employment Change	Percent Employment Change
Wind Turbine Service Technicians	5,240	5,990	750	14.3
Information Security Analysts (SOC 2018)	14,170	16,110	1,940	13.7
Solar Photovoltaic Installers	2,240	2,540	300	13.4
Veterinary Technologists and Technicians	16,140	18,200	2,060	12.8
Actuaries	1,810	2,040	230	12.7
Data Scientists	7,340	8,270	930	12.7
Web Developers	6,920	7,790	870	12.6
Veterinarians	6,830	7,670	840	12.3
Veterinary Assistants and Laboratory Animal Caretakers	5,990	6,720	730	12.2
Ushers, Lobby Attendants, and Ticket Takers	9,100	10,190	1,090	12.0

Note: Projections cover Texas; (1) Sorted by percent employment change and excludes occupations with numeric employment change less than 50
Source: www.projectionscentral.com, State Occupational Projections, 2022–2024 Short-Term Projections

Fort Worth, Texas

CITY FINANCES

City Government Finances

Component	2020 ($000)	2020 ($ per capita)
Total Revenues	1,732,805	1,905
Total Expenditures	1,670,478	1,837
Debt Outstanding	2,236,267	2,459
Cash and Securities[1]	1,954,863	2,149

Note: (1) Cash and security holdings of a government at the close of its fiscal year, including those of its dependent agencies, utilities, and liquor stores.
Source: U.S. Census Bureau, State & Local Government Finances 2020

City Government Revenue by Source

Source	2020 ($000)	2020 ($ per capita)	2020 (%)
General Revenue			
From Federal Government	39,953	44	2.3
From State Government	60,771	67	3.5
From Local Governments	3,399	4	0.2
Taxes			
Property	517,382	569	29.9
Sales and Gross Receipts	331,503	364	19.1
Personal Income	0	0	0.0
Corporate Income	0	0	0.0
Motor Vehicle License	0	0	0.0
Other Taxes	41,035	45	2.4
Current Charges	346,967	381	20.0
Liquor Store	0	0	0.0
Utility	269,795	297	15.6

Source: U.S. Census Bureau, State & Local Government Finances 2020

City Government Expenditures by Function

Function	2020 ($000)	2020 ($ per capita)	2020 (%)
General Direct Expenditures			
Air Transportation	25,606	28	1.5
Corrections	0	0	0.0
Education	0	0	0.0
Employment Security Administration	0	0	0.0
Financial Administration	14,216	15	0.9
Fire Protection	156,836	172	9.4
General Public Buildings	20,475	22	1.2
Governmental Administration, Other	40,420	44	2.4
Health	11,017	12	0.7
Highways	194,954	214	11.7
Hospitals	0	0	0.0
Housing and Community Development	32,265	35	1.9
Interest on General Debt	47,111	51	2.8
Judicial and Legal	22,096	24	1.3
Libraries	20,296	22	1.2
Parking	4,027	4	0.2
Parks and Recreation	126,524	139	7.6
Police Protection	330,875	363	19.8
Public Welfare	0	0	0.0
Sewerage	196,091	215	11.7
Solid Waste Management	63,321	69	3.8
Veterans' Services	0	0	0.0
Liquor Store	0	0	0.0
Utility	224,136	246	13.4

Source: U.S. Census Bureau, State & Local Government Finances 2020

TAXES

State Corporate Income Tax Rates

State	Tax Rate (%)	Income Brackets ($)	Num. of Brackets	Financial Institution Tax Rate (%)[a]	Federal Income Tax Ded.
Texas	(u)	–	–	(u)	No

Note: Tax rates as of January 1, 2023; (a) Rates listed are the corporate income tax rate applied to financial institutions or excise taxes based on income. Some states have other taxes based upon the value of deposits or shares; (u) Texas imposes a Franchise Tax, otherwise known as margin tax, imposed on entities with more than $1,230,000 total revenues at rate of 0.75%, or 0.375% for entities primarily engaged in retail or wholesale trade, on lesser of 70% of total revenues or 100% of gross receipts after deductions for either compensation or cost of goods sold.
Source: Federation of Tax Administrators, State Corporate Income Tax Rates, January 1, 2023

State Individual Income Tax Rates

State	Tax Rate (%)	Income Brackets ($)	Personal Exemptions ($) Single	Personal Exemptions ($) Married	Personal Exemptions ($) Depend.	Standard Ded. ($) Single	Standard Ded. ($) Married
Texas				– No state income tax –			

Note: Tax rates as of January 1, 2023; Local- and county-level taxes are not included
Source: Federation of Tax Administrators, State Individual Income Tax Rates, January 1, 2023

Various State Sales and Excise Tax Rates

State	State Sales Tax (%)	Gasoline[1] ($/gal.)	Cigarette[2] ($/pack)	Spirits[3] ($/gal.)	Wine[4] ($/gal.)	Beer[5] ($/gal.)	Recreational Marijuana (%)
Texas	6.25	0.20	1.41	2.40	0.20	0.19	Not legal

Note: All tax rates as of January 1, 2023; (1) The American Petroleum Institute has developed a methodology for determining the average tax rate on a gallon of fuel. Rates may include any of the following: excise taxes, environmental fees, storage tank fees, other fees or taxes, general sales tax, and local taxes; (2) The federal excise tax of $1.0066 per pack and local taxes are not included; (3) Rates are those applicable to off-premise sales of 40% alcohol by volume (a.b.v.) distilled spirits in 750ml containers. Local excise taxes are excluded; (4) Rates are those applicable to off-premise sales of 11% a.b.v. non-carbonated wine in 750ml containers; (5) Rates are those applicable to off-premise sales of 4.7% a.b.v. beer in 12 ounce containers.
Source: Tax Foundation, 2023 Facts & Figures: How Does Your State Compare?

State Business Tax Climate Index Rankings

State	Overall Rank	Corporate Tax Rank	Individual Income Tax Rank	Sales Tax Rank	Property Tax Rank	Unemployment Insurance Tax Rank
Texas	13	47	7	37	38	12

Note: The index is a measure of how each state's tax laws affect economic performance. The lower the rank, the more favorable a state's tax system is for business. States without a given tax are given a ranking of 1. The scores/rankings for the District of Columbia do not affect other states. The 2023 index represents the tax climate as of July 1, 2022.
Source: Tax Foundation, State Business Tax Climate Index 2023

TRANSPORTATION

Means of Transportation to Work

Area	Car/Truck/Van Drove Alone	Car/Truck/Van Carpooled	Bus	Subway	Railroad	Bicycle	Walked	Other Means	Worked at Home
City	77.3	11.0	0.5	0.0	0.1	0.2	1.3	1.0	8.6
MSA[1]	75.8	9.5	0.6	0.1	0.2	0.1	1.2	1.3	11.1
U.S.	73.2	8.6	2.0	1.6	0.5	0.5	2.5	1.5	9.7

Note: Figures are percentages and cover workers 16 years of age and older; (1) Figures cover the Dallas-Fort Worth-Arlington, TX Metropolitan Statistical Area
Source: U.S. Census Bureau, 2017-2021 American Community Survey 5-Year Estimates

Travel Time to Work

Area	Less Than 10 Minutes	10 to 19 Minutes	20 to 29 Minutes	30 to 44 Minutes	45 to 59 Minutes	60 to 89 Minutes	90 Minutes or More
City	7.7	29.0	22.9	23.9	8.7	5.8	2.0
MSA[1]	8.6	25.2	21.7	25.6	10.3	6.7	2.0
U.S.	12.4	28.5	21.0	20.9	8.2	6.2	2.9

Note: Note: Figures are percentages and include workers 16 years old and over; (1) Figures cover the Dallas-Fort Worth-Arlington, TX Metropolitan Statistical Area
Source: U.S. Census Bureau, 2017-2021 American Community Survey 5-Year Estimates

Key Congestion Measures

Measure	1990	2000	2010	2015	2020
Annual Hours of Delay, Total (000)	77,977	129,786	175,068	214,718	136,953
Annual Hours of Delay, Per Auto Commuter	40	47	50	63	40
Annual Congestion Cost, Per Auto Commuter ($)	844	1,056	1,132	1,283	848

Note: Covers the Dallas-Fort Worth-Arlington TX urban area
Source: Texas A&M Transportation Institute, 2021 Urban Mobility Report

Freeway Travel Time Index

Measure	1985	1990	1995	2000	2005	2010	2015	2020
Urban Area Index[1]	1.19	1.20	1.23	1.24	1.26	1.25	1.26	1.12
Urban Area Rank[1,2]	6	9	8	18	22	21	23	10

Note: Freeway Travel Time Index—the ratio of travel time in the peak period to the travel time at free-flow conditions. For example, a value of 1.30 indicates a 20-minute free-flow trip takes 26 minutes in the peak (20 minutes x 1.30 = 26 minutes); (1) Covers the Dallas-Fort Worth-Arlington TX urban area; (2) Rank is based on 101 larger urban areas (#1 = highest travel time index)
Source: Texas A&M Transportation Institute, 2021 Urban Mobility Report

Public Transportation

Agency Name / Mode of Transportation	Vehicles Operated in Maximum Service[1]	Annual Unlinked Passenger Trips[2] (in thous.)	Annual Passenger Miles[3] (in thous.)
Fort Worth Transportation Authority (The T)			
Bus (directly operated)	122	2,952.1	15,208.3
Commuter Rail (purchased transportation)	20	304.5	4,652.0
Demand Response (directly operated)	34	80.5	786.0
Demand Response (purchased transportation)	49	133.5	1,222.8
Vanpool (purchased transportation)	70	129.9	5,032.1

Note: (1) Number of revenue vehicles operated by the given mode and type of service to meet the annual maximum service requirement. This is the revenue vehicle count during the peak season of the year; on the week and day that maximum service is provided. Vehicles operated in maximum service (VOMS) exclude atypical days and one-time special events; (2) Number of passengers who boarded public transportation vehicles. Passengers are counted each time they board a vehicle no matter how many vehicles they use to travel from their origin to their destination. (3) Sum of the distances ridden by all passengers during the entire fiscal year.
Source: Federal Transit Administration, National Transit Database, 2021

Air Transportation

Airport Name and Code / Type of Service	Passenger Airlines[1]	Passenger Enplanements	Freight Carriers[2]	Freight (lbs)
Dallas-Fort Worth International (DFW)				
Domestic service (U.S. carriers - 2022)	29	30,640,857	22	539,257,244
International service (U.S. carriers - 2021)	8	2,517,818	5	81,848,301
Dallas Love Field (DAL)				
Domestic service (U.S. carriers - 2022)	23	7,816,836	6	14,872,355
International service (U.S. carriers - 2021)	5	248	0	0

Note: (1) Includes all U.S.-based major, minor and commuter airlines that carried at least one passenger during the year; (2) Includes all U.S.-based airlines and freight carriers that transported at least one pound of freight during the year.
Source: Bureau of Transportation Statistics, The Intermodal Transportation Database, Air Carriers: T-100 Domestic Market (U.S. Carriers), 2022; Bureau of Transportation Statistics, The Intermodal Transportation Database, Air Carriers: T-100 International Market (U.S. Carriers), 2021

BUSINESSES

Major Business Headquarters

Company Name	Industry	Fortune[1]	Forbes[2]
American Airlines Group	Airlines	114	-
Ben E Keith	Food, drink & tobacco	-	102
D.R. Horton	Homebuilders	124	-

Note: (1) Companies that produce a 10-K are ranked 1 to 500 based on 2021 revenue; (2) All private companies with at least $2 billion in annual revenue through the end of their most current fiscal year are ranked 1 to 246; companies listed are headquartered in the city; dashes indicate no ranking
Source: Fortune, "Fortune 500," 2022; Forbes, "America's Largest Private Companies," 2022

Fastest-Growing Businesses

According to *Inc.*, Fort Worth is home to five of America's 500 fastest-growing private companies: **Blue Hammer Roofing** (#17); **Forester Haynie** (#172); **Avara** (#406); **Tradebloc** (#425); **Archer Review** (#466). Criteria: must be an independent, privately-held, for-profit, U.S. corporation, proprietorship or partnership as of December 31, 2021; revenues must be at least $100,000 in 2018 and $2 million in 2021; must have four-year operating/sales history. *Inc., "America's 500 Fastest-Growing Private Companies," 2022*

Living Environment

COST OF LIVING

Cost of Living Index

Composite Index	Groceries	Housing	Utilities	Transportation	Health Care	Misc. Goods/Services
95.1	93.1	86.4	114.0	90.5	86.8	100.5

Note: The Cost of Living Index measures regional differences in the cost of consumer goods and services, excluding taxes and non-consumer expenditures, for professional and managerial households in the top income quintile. It is based on more than 50,000 prices covering almost 60 different items for which prices are collected three times a year by chambers of commerce, economic development organizations or university applied economic centers in each participating urban area. The numbers shown should be read as a percentage above or below the national average of 100. For example, a value of 115.4 in the groceries column indicates that grocery prices are 15.4% higher than the national average. Small differences in the index numbers should not be interpreted as significant; Figures cover the Fort Worth TX urban area.
Source: The Council for Community and Economic Research, Cost of Living Index, 2022

Grocery Prices

Area[1]	T-Bone Steak ($/pound)	Frying Chicken ($/pound)	Whole Milk ($/half gal.)	Eggs ($/dozen)	Orange Juice ($/64 oz.)	Coffee ($/11.5 oz.)
City[2]	13.46	1.51	2.16	2.25	3.40	4.73
Avg.	13.81	1.59	2.43	2.25	3.85	4.95
Min.	10.17	0.90	1.51	1.30	2.90	3.46
Max.	19.35	3.30	4.32	4.32	5.31	8.59

*Note: (1) Values for the local area are compared with the average, minimum and maximum values for all 286 areas in the Cost of Living Index; (2) Figures cover the Fort Worth TX urban area; **T-Bone Steak** (price per pound); **Frying Chicken** (price per pound, whole fryer); **Whole Milk** (half gallon carton); **Eggs** (price per dozen, Grade A, large); **Orange Juice** (64 oz. Tropicana or Florida Natural); **Coffee** (11.5 oz. can, vacuum-packed, Maxwell House, Hills Bros, or Folgers).*
Source: The Council for Community and Economic Research, Cost of Living Index, 2022

Housing and Utility Costs

Area[1]	New Home Price ($)	Apartment Rent ($/month)	All Electric ($/month)	Part Electric ($/month)	Other Energy ($/month)	Telephone ($/month)
City[2]	372,205	1,327	-	137.89	75.49	199.27
Avg.	450,913	1,371	176.41	99.93	76.96	190.22
Min.	229,283	546	100.84	31.56	27.15	174.27
Max.	2,434,977	4,569	356.86	249.59	272.24	208.31

*Note: (1) Values for the local area are compared with the average, minimum and maximum values for all 286 areas in the Cost of Living Index; (2) Figures cover the Fort Worth TX urban area; **New Home Price** (2,400 sf living area, 8,000 sf lot, in urban area with full utilities); **Apartment Rent** (950 sf 2 bedroom/1.5 or 2 bath, unfurnished, excluding all utilities except water); **All Electric** (average monthly cost for an all-electric home); **Part Electric** (average monthly cost for a part-electric home); **Other Energy** (average monthly cost for natural gas, fuel oil, coal, wood, and any other forms of energy except electricity); **Telephone** (price includes the base monthly rate plus taxes and fees for three lines of mobile phone service).*
Source: The Council for Community and Economic Research, Cost of Living Index, 2022

Health Care, Transportation, and Other Costs

Area[1]	Doctor ($/visit)	Dentist ($/visit)	Optometrist ($/visit)	Gasoline ($/gallon)	Beauty Salon ($/visit)	Men's Shirt ($)
City[2]	92.61	96.41	111.17	3.58	55.08	32.87
Avg.	124.91	107.77	117.66	3.86	43.31	34.21
Min.	36.61	58.25	51.79	2.90	22.18	13.05
Max.	250.21	162.58	371.96	5.54	85.61	63.54

*Note: (1) Values for the local area are compared with the average, minimum and maximum values for all 286 areas in the Cost of Living Index; (2) Figures cover the Fort Worth TX urban area; **Doctor** (general practitioners routine exam of an established patient); **Dentist** (adult teeth cleaning and periodic oral examination); **Optometrist** (full vision eye exam for established adult patient); **Gasoline** (one gallon regular unleaded, national brand, including all taxes, cash price at self-service pump if available); **Beauty Salon** (woman's shampoo, trim, and blow-dry); **Men's Shirt** (cotton/polyester dress shirt, pinpoint weave, long sleeves).*
Source: The Council for Community and Economic Research, Cost of Living Index, 2022

HOUSING

Homeownership Rate

Area	2015 (%)	2016 (%)	2017 (%)	2018 (%)	2019 (%)	2020 (%)	2021 (%)	2022 (%)
MSA[1]	57.8	59.7	61.8	62.0	60.6	64.7	61.8	60.4
U.S.	63.7	63.4	63.9	64.4	64.6	66.6	65.5	65.8

Note: (1) Figures cover the Dallas-Fort Worth-Arlington, TX Metropolitan Statistical Area
Source: U.S. Census Bureau, Housing Vacancies and Homeownership Annual Statistics: 2015-2022

House Price Index (HPI)

Area	National Ranking[2]	Quarterly Change (%)	One-Year Change (%)	Five-Year Change (%)	Since 1991Q1 (%)
MD[1]	53	-1.47	15.09	66.00	306.95
U.S.[3]	—	0.34	8.41	58.44	289.08

Note: The HPI is a weighted repeat sales index. It measures average price changes in repeat sales or refinancings on the same properties. This information is obtained by reviewing repeat mortgage transactions on single-family properties whose mortgages have been purchased or securitized by Fannie Mae or Freddie Mac since January 1975; (1) Figures cover the Fort Worth-Arlington, TX Metropolitan Division; (2) Rankings are based on annual percentage change for all metro areas containing at least 15,000 transactions over the last 10 years and ranges from 1 to 257; (3) figures based on a weighted average of Census Division estimates using a seasonally adjusted, purchase-only index; all figures are for the period ending December 31, 2022
Source: Federal Housing Finance Agency, Change in FHFA Metropolitan Area House Price Indexes, 2022Q4

Median Single-Family Home Prices

Area	2020	2021	2022p	Percent Change 2021 to 2022
MSA[1]	287.2	336.7	385.5	14.5
U.S. Average	300.2	357.1	392.6	9.9

Note: Figures are median sales prices of existing single-family homes in thousands of dollars; (p) preliminary; (1) Figures cover the Dallas-Fort Worth-Arlington, TX Metropolitan Statistical Area
Source: National Association of Realtors, Median Sales Price of Existing Single-Family Homes for Metropolitan Areas, 4th Quarter 2022

Qualifying Income Based on Median Sales Price of Existing Single-Family Homes

Area	With 5% Down ($)	With 10% Down ($)	With 20% Down ($)
MSA[1]	112,194	106,289	94,479
U.S. Average	112,234	106,237	94,513

Note: Figures are preliminary; Qualifying income is based on a mortgage rate of 6.77%. Monthly principal and interest payment is limited to 25% of income; (1) Figures cover the Dallas-Fort Worth-Arlington, TX Metropolitan Statistical Area
Source: National Association of Realtors, Qualifying Income Based on Median Sales Price of Existing Single-Family Homes for Metropolitan Areas, 4th Quarter 2022

Home Value

Area	Under $100,000	$100,000 -$199,999	$200,000 -$299,999	$300,000 -$399,999	$400,000 -$499,999	$500,000 -$999,999	$1,000,000 or more	Median ($)
City	15.9	29.7	31.6	12.1	4.7	4.8	1.2	212,300
MSA[1]	10.9	24.1	26.2	17.0	9.3	10.2	2.4	255,600
U.S.	16.2	24.2	20.1	13.6	8.3	13.6	4.1	244,900

Note: Figures are percentages except for median and cover owner-occupied housing units; (1) Figures cover the Dallas-Fort Worth-Arlington, TX Metropolitan Statistical Area
Source: U.S. Census Bureau, 2017-2021 American Community Survey 5-Year Estimates

Year Housing Structure Built

Area	2020 or Later	2010 -2019	2000 -2009	1990 -1999	1980 -1989	1970 -1979	1960 -1969	1950 -1959	1940 -1949	Before 1940	Median Year
City	0.3	14.8	21.3	12.3	13.5	9.4	7.7	10.2	4.9	5.7	1989
MSA[1]	0.4	14.0	19.1	15.6	17.3	13.3	8.3	7.1	2.4	2.6	1989
U.S.	0.2	7.3	13.6	13.6	13.2	14.8	10.3	10.0	4.7	12.2	1979

Note: Figures are percentages except for Median Year; Note: (1) Figures cover the Dallas-Fort Worth-Arlington, TX Metropolitan Statistical Area
Source: U.S. Census Bureau, 2017-2021 American Community Survey 5-Year Estimates

Gross Monthly Rent

Area	Under $500	$500 -$999	$1,000 -$1,499	$1,500 -$1,999	$2,000 -$2,499	$2,500 -$2,999	$3,000 and up	Median ($)
City	3.7	28.4	40.5	19.2	5.9	1.4	0.9	1,187
MSA[1]	2.6	22.1	43.0	21.2	7.7	1.9	1.5	1,264
U.S.	8.1	30.5	30.8	16.8	7.3	3.1	3.5	1,163

Note: Figures are percentages except for median; Gross rent is the contract rent plus the estimated average monthly cost of utilities (electricity, gas, and water and sewer) and fuels (oil, coal, kerosene, wood, etc.) if these are paid by the renter (or paid for the renter by someone else); (1) Figures cover the Dallas-Fort Worth-Arlington, TX Metropolitan Statistical Area
Source: U.S. Census Bureau, 2017-2021 American Community Survey 5-Year Estimates

HEALTH

Health Risk Factors

Category	MD[1] (%)	U.S. (%)
Adults aged 18–64 who have any kind of health care coverage	80.8	90.9
Adults who reported being in good or better health	81.6	85.2
Adults who have been told they have high blood cholesterol	40.3	35.7
Adults who have been told they have high blood pressure	33.1	32.4
Adults who are current smokers	15.1	14.4
Adults who currently use e-cigarettes	5.9	6.7
Adults who currently use chewing tobacco, snuff, or snus	4.7	3.5
Adults who are heavy drinkers[2]	7.0	6.3
Adults who are binge drinkers[3]	16.9	15.4
Adults who are overweight (BMI 25.0 - 29.9)	36.2	34.4
Adults who are obese (BMI 30.0 - 99.8)	36.5	33.9
Adults who participated in any physical activities in the past month	76.4	76.3

Note: (1) Figures cover the Fort Worth-Arlington, TX Metropolitan Division; (2) Heavy drinkers are classified as adult men having more than 14 drinks per week and adult women having more than 7 drinks per week; (3) Binge drinkers are classified as males having five or more drinks on one occasion or females having four or more drinks on one occasion
Source: Centers for Disease Control and Prevention, Behaviorial Risk Factor Surveillance System, SMART: Selected Metropolitan Area Risk Trends, 2021

Acute and Chronic Health Conditions

Category	MD[1] (%)	U.S. (%)
Adults who have ever been told they had a heart attack	4.5	4.0
Adults who have ever been told they have angina or coronary heart disease	2.4	3.8
Adults who have ever been told they had a stroke	3.2	3.0
Adults who have ever been told they have asthma	13.3	14.9
Adults who have ever been told they have arthritis	21.8	25.8
Adults who have ever been told they have diabetes[2]	11.0	10.9
Adults who have ever been told they had skin cancer	7.1	6.6
Adults who have ever been told they had any other types of cancer	7.2	7.5
Adults who have ever been told they have COPD	8.2	6.1
Adults who have ever been told they have kidney disease	3.4	3.0
Adults who have ever been told they have a form of depression	19.5	20.5

Note: (1) Figures cover the Fort Worth-Arlington, TX Metropolitan Division; (2) Figures do not include pregnancy-related, borderline, or pre-diabetes
Source: Centers for Disease Control and Prevention, Behaviorial Risk Factor Surveillance System, SMART: Selected Metropolitan Area Risk Trends, 2021

Health Screening and Vaccination Rates

Category	MD[1] (%)	U.S. (%)
Adults who have ever been tested for HIV	40.5	34.9
Adults who have had their blood cholesterol checked within the last five years	87.6	85.2
Adults aged 65+ who have had flu shot within the past year	72.4	68.6
Adults aged 65+ who have ever had a pneumonia vaccination	70.5	71.0

Note: (1) Figures cover the Fort Worth-Arlington, TX Metropolitan Division.
Source: Centers for Disease Control and Prevention, Behaviorial Risk Factor Surveillance System, SMART: Selected Metropolitan Area Risk Trends, 2021

Disability Status

Category	MD[1] (%)	U.S. (%)
Adults who reported being deaf	7.9	7.2
Are you blind or have serious difficulty seeing, even when wearing glasses?	4.1	4.8
Are you limited in any way in any of your usual activities due to arthritis?	7.9	11.1
Do you have difficulty doing errands alone?	9.2	7.0
Do you have difficulty dressing or bathing?	4.8	3.6
Do you have serious difficulty concentrating/remembering/making decisions?	13.2	12.1
Do you have serious difficulty walking or climbing stairs?	14.8	12.8

Note: (1) Figures cover the Fort Worth-Arlington, TX Metropolitan Division.
Source: Centers for Disease Control and Prevention, Behaviorial Risk Factor Surveillance System, SMART: Selected Metropolitan Area Risk Trends, 2021

Mortality Rates for the Top 10 Causes of Death in the U.S.

ICD-10[a] Sub-Chapter	ICD-10[a] Code	Crude Mortality Rate[1] per 100,000 population County[2]	U.S.
Malignant neoplasms	C00-C97	135.7	182.6
Ischaemic heart diseases	I20-I25	65.2	113.1
Other forms of heart disease	I30-I51	38.9	64.4
Other degenerative diseases of the nervous system	G30-G31	57.6	51.0
Cerebrovascular diseases	I60-I69	41.4	47.8
Other external causes of accidental injury	W00-X59	26.4	46.4
Chronic lower respiratory diseases	J40-J47	32.4	45.7
Organic, including symptomatic, mental disorders	F01-F09	16.9	35.9
Hypertensive diseases	I10-I15	38.3	35.0
Diabetes mellitus	E10-E14	25.8	29.6

Note: (a) ICD-10 = International Classification of Diseases 10th Revision; (1) Crude mortality rates are a three-year average covering 2019-2021; (2) Figures cover Tarrant County.
Source: Centers for Disease Control and Prevention, National Center for Health Statistics. National Vital Statistics System, Mortality 2018-2021 on CDC WONDER Online Database

Mortality Rates for Selected Causes of Death

ICD-10[a] Sub-Chapter	ICD-10[a] Code	Crude Mortality Rate[1] per 100,000 population County[2]	U.S.
Assault	X85-Y09	7.6	7.0
Diseases of the liver	K70-K76	17.0	19.8
Human immunodeficiency virus (HIV) disease	B20-B24	1.3	1.5
Influenza and pneumonia	J09-J18	10.5	14.7
Intentional self-harm	X60-X84	12.9	14.3
Malnutrition	E40-E46	3.8	4.3
Obesity and other hyperalimentation	E65-E68	3.7	3.0
Renal failure	N17-N19	13.7	15.7
Transport accidents	V01-V99	12.5	13.6
Viral hepatitis	B15-B19	1.3	1.2

Note: (a) ICD-10 = International Classification of Diseases 10th Revision; (1) Crude mortality rates are a three-year average covering 2019-2021; (2) Figures cover Tarrant County; Data are suppressed when the data meet the criteria for confidentiality constraints; Crude mortality rates are flagged as unreliable when the rate would be calculated with a numerator of 20 or less.
Source: Centers for Disease Control and Prevention, National Center for Health Statistics. National Vital Statistics System, Mortality 2018-2021 on CDC WONDER Online Database

Health Insurance Coverage

Area	With Health Insurance	With Private Health Insurance	With Public Health Insurance	Without Health Insurance	Population Under Age 19 Without Health Insurance
City	81.2	61.1	26.9	18.8	12.5
MSA[1]	83.4	66.4	24.5	16.6	11.7
U.S.	91.2	67.8	35.4	8.8	5.3

Note: Figures are percentages that cover the civilian noninstitutionalized population; (1) Figures cover the Dallas-Fort Worth-Arlington, TX Metropolitan Statistical Area
Source: U.S. Census Bureau, 2017-2021 American Community Survey 5-Year Estimates

Number of Medical Professionals

Area	MDs[3]	DOs[3,4]	Dentists	Podiatrists	Chiropractors	Optometrists
County[1] (number)	4,021	717	1,337	96	620	353
County[1] (rate[2])	190.1	33.9	62.9	4.5	29.2	16.6
U.S. (rate[2])	289.3	23.5	72.5	6.2	28.7	17.4

Note: Data as of 2021 unless noted; (1) Data covers Tarrant County; (2) Rate per 100,000 population; (3) Data as of 2020 and includes all active, non-federal physicians; (4) Doctor of Osteopathic Medicine
Source: U.S. Department of Health and Human Services, Health Resources and Services Administration, Bureau of Health Professions, Area Resource File (ARF) 2021-2022

Best Hospitals

According to *U.S. News*, the Fort Worth-Arlington-Grapevine, TX metro area is home to one of the best children's hospitals in the U.S.: **Cook Children's Medical Center** (6 pediatric specialties). The hospital listed was highly ranked in at least one of 10 pediatric specialties. Eighty-six children's hospitals in the U.S. were nationally ranked in at least one specialty. Hospitals received points for being ranked in a specialty, and the 10 hospitals with the most points across the 10 specialties make up the Honor Roll. *U.S. News Online, "America's Best Children's Hospitals 2022-23"*

EDUCATION

Public School District Statistics

District Name	Schls	Pupils	Pupil/Teacher Ratio	Minority Pupils[1] (%)	LEP/ELL[2] (%)	IEP[3] (%)
Castleberry ISD	8	3,639	15.1	85.9	30.8	12.1
Eagle Mt-Saginaw ISD	29	22,464	15.7	65.5	10.0	10.6
Everman ISD	10	5,463	13.6	96.3	26.3	10.2
Fort Worth ISD	140	74,850	14.8	88.8	30.4	9.9
Uplift Education	43	22,183	15.9	96.9	31.0	7.8

Note: Table includes school districts with 2,000 or more students; (1) Percentage of students that are not non-Hispanic white; (2) Percentage of students that are Limited English Proficient or English Language Learners (2018-19); (3) Percentage of students that have an Individualized Education Program (2019-20).
Source: U.S. Department of Education, National Center for Education Statistics, Common Core of Data, Local Education Agency (School District) Universe Survey: School Year 2021-2022

Best High Schools

According to *U.S. News,* Fort Worth is home to two of the top 500 high schools in the U.S.: **Young Women's Leadership Academy** (#130); **Texas Academy of Biomedical** (#258). Nearly 18,000 public, magnet and charter schools were ranked based on their performance on state assessments and how well they prepare students for college. *U.S. News & World Report, "Best High Schools 2022"*

Highest Level of Education

Area	Less than H.S.	H.S. Diploma	Some College, No Deg.	Associate Degree	Bachelor's Degree	Master's Degree	Prof. School Degree	Doctorate Degree
City	16.5	24.5	20.8	7.2	20.6	7.8	1.6	1.1
MSA[1]	13.4	22.0	20.6	7.3	23.8	9.8	1.9	1.2
U.S.	11.1	26.5	20.0	8.7	20.6	9.3	2.2	1.5

Note: Figures cover persons age 25 and over; (1) Figures cover the Dallas-Fort Worth-Arlington, TX Metropolitan Statistical Area
Source: U.S. Census Bureau, 2017-2021 American Community Survey 5-Year Estimates

Educational Attainment by Race

Area	High School Graduate or Higher (%)					Bachelor's Degree or Higher (%)				
	Total	White	Black	Asian	Hisp.[2]	Total	White	Black	Asian	Hisp.[2]
City	83.5	88.1	89.1	80.9	63.5	31.0	37.5	22.7	44.5	14.4
MSA[1]	86.6	88.9	91.8	88.8	63.9	36.8	38.9	30.0	62.8	16.2
U.S.	88.9	91.4	87.2	87.6	71.2	33.7	35.5	23.3	55.6	18.4

Note: Figures shown cover persons 25 years old and over; (1) Figures cover the Dallas-Fort Worth-Arlington, TX Metropolitan Statistical Area; (2) People of Hispanic origin can be of any race
Source: U.S. Census Bureau, 2017-2021 American Community Survey 5-Year Estimates

School Enrollment by Grade and Control

Area	Preschool (%)		Kindergarten (%)		Grades 1 - 4 (%)		Grades 5 - 8 (%)		Grades 9 - 12 (%)	
	Public	Private	Public	Private	Public	Private	Public	Private	Public	Private
City	62.1	37.9	83.6	16.4	90.6	9.4	90.1	9.9	92.2	7.8
MSA[1]	59.0	41.0	88.8	11.2	91.3	8.7	91.6	8.4	91.9	8.1
U.S.	58.8	41.2	86.3	13.7	88.3	11.7	88.6	11.4	89.4	10.6

Note: Figures shown cover persons 3 years old and over; (1) Figures cover the Dallas-Fort Worth-Arlington, TX Metropolitan Statistical Area
Source: U.S. Census Bureau, 2017-2021 American Community Survey 5-Year Estimates

Higher Education

Four-Year Colleges			Two-Year Colleges			Medical Schools[1]	Law Schools[2]	Voc/Tech[3]
Public	Private Non-profit	Private For-profit	Public	Private Non-profit	Private For-profit			
11	23	5	1	3	12	3	3	34

Note: Figures cover institutions located within the Dallas-Fort Worth-Arlington, TX Metropolitan Statistical Area and include main campuses only; (1) includes schools accredited by the Liaison Committee on Medical Education and the American Osteopathic Association's Commission on Osteopathic College Accreditation; (2) includes ABA-accredited schools, schools with provisional ABA accreditation, and state accredited schools; (3) includes all schools with programs that are less than 2 years.
Source: National Center for Education Statistics, Integrated Postsecondary Education System (IPEDS), 2021-22; Wikipedia, List of Medical Schools in the United States, accessed April 10, 2023; Wikipedia, List of Law Schools in the United States, accessed April 10, 2023

According to *U.S. News & World Report,* the Fort Worth-Arlington-Grapevine, TX metro division is home to one of the top 200 national universities in the U.S.: **Texas Christian University** (#89 tie). The indicators used to capture academic quality fall into a number of categories: assessment by administrators at peer institutions; retention of students; faculty resources; student selectivity; financial resources; alumni giving; high school counselor ratings of colleges; and graduation rate. *U.S. News & World Report, "America's Best Colleges 2023"*

According to *U.S. News & World Report,* the Fort Worth-Arlington-Grapevine, TX metro division is home to one of the top 100 law schools in the U.S.: **Texas A&M University** (#46). The rankings are based on a weighted average of 12 measures of quality: peer assessment score; assessment score by lawyers/judges; median LSAT scores; median undergrad GPA; acceptance rate; employment rates for graduates; placement success; bar passage rate; faculty resources; expenditures per student; student/faculty ratio; and library resources. *U.S. News & World Report, "America's Best Graduate Schools, Law, 2023"*

According to *U.S. News & World Report,* the Fort Worth-Arlington-Grapevine, TX metro division is home to one of the top 75 business schools in the U.S.: **Texas Christian University (Neeley)** (#67 tie). The rankings are based on a weighted average of the following nine measures: quality assessment; peer assessment; recruiter assessment; placement success; mean starting salary and bonus; student selectivity; mean GMAT and GRE scores; mean undergraduate GPA; and acceptance rate. *U.S. News & World Report, "America's Best Graduate Schools, Business, 2023"*

EMPLOYERS

Major Employers

Company Name	Industry
AMR Corporation	Air transportation, scheduled
Associates First Capital Corporation	Mortgage bankers
Baylor University Medical Center	General medical & surgical hospitals
Children's Medical Center Dallas	Specialty hospitals, except psychiatric
Combat Support Associates	Engineering services
County of Dallas	County government
Dallas County Hospital District	General medical & surgical hospitals
Fort Worth Independent School District	Public elementary & secondary schools
Housewares Holding Company	Toasters, electric: household
HP Enterprise Services	Computer integrated systems design
J.C. Penney Company	Department stores
JCP Publications Corp.	Department stores
L-3 Communications Corporation	Business economic service
Odyssey HealthCare	Home health care services
Romano's Macaroni Grill	Italian restaurant
SFG Management	Milk processing (pasteurizing, homogenizing, bottling)
Texas Instruments Incorporated	Semiconductors & related devices
University of North Texas	Colleges & universities
University of Texas SW Medical Center	Accident & health insurance
Verizon Business Global	Telephone communication, except radio

Note: Companies shown are located within the Dallas-Fort Worth-Arlington, TX Metropolitan Statistical Area.
Source: Hoovers.com; Wikipedia

PUBLIC SAFETY

Crime Rate

Area	Total Crime	Violent Crime Rate				Property Crime Rate		
		Murder	Rape[3]	Robbery	Aggrav. Assault	Burglary	Larceny-Theft	Motor Vehicle Theft
City	3,274.2	11.8	48.0	93.3	387.9	366.9	1,988.9	377.4
Suburbs[1]	n/a	n/a	n/a	n/a	n/a	n/a	n/a	n/a
Metro[2]	n/a	n/a	n/a	n/a	n/a	n/a	n/a	n/a
U.S.	2,356.7	6.5	38.4	73.9	279.7	314.2	1,398.0	246.0

Note: Figures are crimes per 100,000 population; (1) All areas within the metro area that are located outside the city limits; (2) Figures cover the Fort Worth-Arlington, TX Metropolitan Division; n/a not available; (3) All figures shown were reported using the revised Uniform Crime Reporting (UCR) definition of rape; Due to the transition to the National Incident-Based Reporting System (NIBRS), limited city and metro area data was released for 2021.
Source: FBI Uniform Crime Reports, 2020

Hate Crimes

Area	Number of Quarters Reported	Number of Incidents per Bias Motivation					
		Race/Ethnicity/Ancestry	Religion	Sexual Orientation	Disability	Gender	Gender Identity
City	4	4	1	5	1	0	0
U.S.	4	5,227	1,244	1,110	130	75	266

Note: Due to the transition to the National Incident-Based Reporting System (NIBRS), limited crime data was released for 2021.
Source: Federal Bureau of Investigation, Hate Crime Statistics 2020

Identity Theft Consumer Reports

Area	Reports	Reports per 100,000 Population	Rank[2]
MSA[1]	34,005	456	23
U.S.	1,108,609	339	-

Note: (1) Figures cover the Dallas-Fort Worth-Arlington, TX Metropolitan Statistical Area; (2) Rank ranges from 1 to 391 where 1 indicates greatest number of identity theft reports per 100,000 population
Source: Federal Trade Commission, Consumer Sentinel Network Data Book 2022

Fraud and Other Consumer Reports

Area	Reports	Reports per 100,000 Population	Rank[2]
MSA[1]	93,393	1,253	37
U.S.	4,064,520	1,245	-

Note: (1) Figures cover the Dallas-Fort Worth-Arlington, TX Metropolitan Statistical Area; (2) Rank ranges from 1 to 391 where 1 indicates greatest number of fraud and other consumer reports per 100,000 population
Source: Federal Trade Commission, Consumer Sentinel Network Data Book 2022

POLITICS

2020 Presidential Election Results

Area	Biden	Trump	Jorgensen	Hawkins	Other
Tarrant County	49.3	49.1	1.2	0.3	0.0
U.S.	51.3	46.8	1.2	0.3	0.5

Note: Results are percentages and may not add to 100% due to rounding
Source: Dave Leip's Atlas of U.S. Presidential Elections

SPORTS

Professional Sports Teams

Team Name	League	Year Established
Dallas Cowboys	National Football League (NFL)	1960
Dallas Mavericks	National Basketball Association (NBA)	1980
Dallas Stars	National Hockey League (NHL)	1993
FC Dallas	Major League Soccer (MLS)	1996
Texas Rangers	Major League Baseball (MLB)	1972

Note: Includes teams located in the Dallas-Fort Worth-Arlington, TX Metropolitan Statistical Area.
Source: Wikipedia, Major Professional Sports Teams of the United States and Canada, April 12, 2023

CLIMATE

Average and Extreme Temperatures

Temperature	Jan	Feb	Mar	Apr	May	Jun	Jul	Aug	Sep	Oct	Nov	Dec	Yr.
Extreme High (°F)	88	88	96	98	103	113	110	108	107	106	89	90	113
Average High (°F)	54	59	67	76	83	92	96	96	88	79	67	58	76
Average Temp. (°F)	44	49	57	66	73	81	85	85	78	68	56	47	66
Average Low (°F)	33	38	45	54	63	71	75	74	67	56	45	37	55
Extreme Low (°F)	4	6	11	29	41	51	59	56	43	29	19	-1	-1

Note: Figures cover the years 1953-1990
Source: National Climatic Data Center, International Station Meteorological Climate Summary, 9/96

Average Precipitation/Snowfall/Humidity

Precip./Humidity	Jan	Feb	Mar	Apr	May	Jun	Jul	Aug	Sep	Oct	Nov	Dec	Yr.
Avg. Precip. (in.)	1.8	2.2	2.6	3.7	4.9	2.8	2.1	1.9	3.0	3.3	2.1	1.7	32.3
Avg. Snowfall (in.)	1	1	Tr	0	0	0	0	0	0	0	Tr	Tr	3
Avg. Rel. Hum. 6am (%)	79	79	79	81	86	85	80	79	83	82	80	79	81
Avg. Rel. Hum. 3pm (%)	52	51	48	50	53	47	42	41	46	47	49	51	48

Note: Figures cover the years 1953-1990; Tr = Trace amounts (<0.05 in. of rain; <0.5 in. of snow)
Source: National Climatic Data Center, International Station Meteorological Climate Summary, 9/96

Weather Conditions

Temperature			Daytime Sky			Precipitation		
10°F & below	32°F & below	90°F & above	Clear	Partly cloudy	Cloudy	0.01 inch or more precip.	0.1 inch or more snow/ice	Thunderstorms
1	40	100	123	136	106	79	3	47

Note: Figures are average number of days per year and cover the years 1953-1990
Source: National Climatic Data Center, International Station Meteorological Climate Summary, 9/96

HAZARDOUS WASTE

Superfund Sites

The Fort Worth-Arlington-Grapevine, TX metro division is home to three sites on the EPA's Superfund National Priorities List: **Air Force Plant #4 (General Dynamics)** (final); **Circle Court Ground Water Plume** (final); **Sandy Beach Road Ground Water Plume** (final). There are a total of 1,165 Superfund sites with a status of proposed or final on the list in the U.S. *U.S. Environmental Protection Agency, National Priorities List, April 12, 2023*

AIR QUALITY

Air Quality Trends: Ozone

	1990	1995	2000	2005	2010	2015	2018	2019	2020	2021
MSA[1]	0.094	0.103	0.096	0.096	0.079	0.078	0.079	0.070	0.070	0.076
U.S.	0.087	0.089	0.081	0.080	0.072	0.067	0.069	0.065	0.065	0.067

Note: (1) Data covers the Dallas-Fort Worth-Arlington, TX Metropolitan Statistical Area. The values shown are the composite ozone concentration averages among trend sites based on the highest fourth daily maximum 8-hour concentration in parts per million. These trends are based on sites having an adequate record of monitoring data during the trend period. Data from exceptional events are included.
Source: U.S. Environmental Protection Agency, Air Quality Monitoring Information, "Air Quality Trends by City, 1990-2021"

Air Quality Index

Area	\multicolumn{5}{c}{Percent of Days when Air Quality was...[2]}	\multicolumn{2}{c}{AQI Statistics[2]}
	Good	Moderate	Unhealthy for Sensitive Groups	Unhealthy	Very Unhealthy	Maximum	Median
MSA[1]	54.0	37.5	7.4	0.8	0.3	209	49

Note: (1) Data covers the Dallas-Fort Worth-Arlington, TX Metropolitan Statistical Area; (2) Based on 365 days with AQI data in 2021. Air Quality Index (AQI) is an index for reporting daily air quality. EPA calculates the AQI for five major air pollutants regulated by the Clean Air Act: ground-level ozone, particle pollution (aka particulate matter), carbon monoxide, sulfur dioxide, and nitrogen dioxide. The AQI runs from 0 to 500. The higher the AQI value, the greater the level of air pollution and the greater the health concern. There are six AQI categories: "Good" AQI is between 0 and 50. Air quality is considered satisfactory; "Moderate" AQI is between 51 and 100. Air quality is acceptable; "Unhealthy for Sensitive Groups" When AQI values are between 101 and 150, members of sensitive groups may experience health effects; "Unhealthy" When AQI values are between 151 and 200 everyone may begin to experience health effects; "Very Unhealthy" AQI values between 201 and 300 trigger a health alert; "Hazardous" AQI values over 300 trigger warnings of emergency conditions (not shown).
Source: U.S. Environmental Protection Agency, Air Quality Index Report, 2021

Air Quality Index Pollutants

Area	\multicolumn{6}{c}{Percent of Days when AQI Pollutant was...[2]}
	Carbon Monoxide	Nitrogen Dioxide	Ozone	Sulfur Dioxide	Particulate Matter 2.5	Particulate Matter 10
MSA[1]	0.0	3.3	61.4	(3)	35.3	0.0

Note: (1) Data covers the Dallas-Fort Worth-Arlington, TX Metropolitan Statistical Area; (2) Based on 365 days with AQI data in 2021. The Air Quality Index (AQI) is an index for reporting daily air quality. EPA calculates the AQI for five major air pollutants regulated by the Clean Air Act: ground-level ozone, particle pollution (also known as particulate matter), carbon monoxide, sulfur dioxide, and nitrogen dioxide. The AQI runs from 0 to 500. The higher the AQI value, the greater the level of air pollution and the greater the health concern; (3) Sulfur dioxide is no longer included in this table (as of December 8, 2021) because SO_2 concentrations tend to be very localized and not necessarily representative of broad geographical areas like counties and CBSAs.
Source: U.S. Environmental Protection Agency, Air Quality Index Report, 2021

Maximum Air Pollutant Concentrations: Particulate Matter, Ozone, CO and Lead

	Particulate Matter 10 (ug/m³)	Particulate Matter 2.5 Wtd AM (ug/m³)	Particulate Matter 2.5 24-Hr (ug/m³)	Ozone (ppm)	Carbon Monoxide (ppm)	Lead (ug/m³)
MSA[1] Level	56	9.6	23	0.085	1	0.02
NAAQS[2]	150	15	35	0.075	9	0.15
Met NAAQS[2]	Yes	Yes	Yes	No	Yes	Yes

Note: (1) Data covers the Dallas-Fort Worth-Arlington, TX Metropolitan Statistical Area; Data from exceptional events are included; (2) National Ambient Air Quality Standards; ppm = parts per million; ug/m³ = micrograms per cubic meter; n/a not available.
Concentrations: Particulate Matter 10 (coarse particulate)—highest second maximum 24-hour concentration; Particulate Matter 2.5 Wtd AM (fine particulate)—highest weighted annual mean concentration; Particulate Matter 2.5 24-Hour (fine particulate)—highest 98th percentile 24-hour concentration; Ozone—highest fourth daily maximum 8-hour concentration; Carbon Monoxide—highest second maximum non-overlapping 8-hour concentration; Lead—maximum running 3-month average
Source: U.S. Environmental Protection Agency, Air Quality Monitoring Information, "Air Quality Statistics by City, 2021"

Maximum Air Pollutant Concentrations: Nitrogen Dioxide and Sulfur Dioxide

	Nitrogen Dioxide AM (ppb)	Nitrogen Dioxide 1-Hr (ppb)	Sulfur Dioxide AM (ppb)	Sulfur Dioxide 1-Hr (ppb)	Sulfur Dioxide 24-Hr (ppb)
MSA[1] Level	13	48	n/a	8	n/a
NAAQS[2]	53	100	30	75	140
Met NAAQS[2]	Yes	Yes	n/a	Yes	n/a

Note: (1) Data covers the Dallas-Fort Worth-Arlington, TX Metropolitan Statistical Area; Data from exceptional events are included; (2) National Ambient Air Quality Standards; ppm = parts per million; ug/m³ = micrograms per cubic meter; n/a not available.
Concentrations: Nitrogen Dioxide AM—highest arithmetic mean concentration; Nitrogen Dioxide 1-Hr—highest 98th percentile 1-hour daily maximum concentration; Sulfur Dioxide AM—highest annual mean concentration; Sulfur Dioxide 1-Hr—highest 99th percentile 1-hour daily maximum concentration; Sulfur Dioxide 24-Hr—highest second maximum 24-hour concentration
Source: U.S. Environmental Protection Agency, Air Quality Monitoring Information, "Air Quality Statistics by City, 2021"

Houston, Texas

Background

In 1836, brothers John K. and Augustus C. Allen bought a 6,642-acre tract of marshy, mosquito-infested land 56 miles north of the Gulf of Mexico and named it Houston, after the hero of San Jacinto. From that moment on, Houston has experienced continued growth.

By the end of its first year in the Republic of Texas, Houston claimed 1,500 residents and one theater. The first churches came three years later. By the end of its second year, Houston saw its first steamship, establishing its position as one of the top-ranking ports in the country.

Certainly, Houston owes much to the Houston ship channel, the "golden strip" on which oil refineries, chemical plants, cement factories, and grain elevators conduct their bustling economic activity. The diversity of these industries is a testament to Houston's economy in general.

Tonnage through the Port of Houston has grown to number one in the nation for foreign tonnage. The port is important to the cruise industry as well, and the Norwegian Cruise Line sails out of Houston.

As Texas' biggest city, Houston has also enjoyed manufacturing expansion in its diversified economy. The city is home to 24 Fortune 500 companies, second only to New York City.

Houston is also one of the major scientific research areas in the world. The presence of the Johnson Space Center has spawned several related industries in medical and technological research. The Texas Medical Center oversees a network of 45 medical institutions, including St. Luke's Episcopal Hospital, the Texas Children's Hospital, and the Methodist Hospital. As a city whose reputation rests upon advanced research, Houston is also devoted to education and the arts. Rice University, for example, whose admission standards rank as one of the highest in the nation, is in Houston, as are Dominican College and the University of St. Thomas.

Today, this relatively young city is home to a diverse range of ethnicities, including Mexican American, Nigerian, American Indian, and Pakistani.

Houston also is patron to the Museum of Fine Arts, the Contemporary Arts Museum, and the Houston Ballet and Grand Opera. A host of smaller cultural institutions, such as the Gilbert and Sullivan Society, the Virtuoso Quartet, and the Houston Harpsichord Society enliven the scene. Two privately funded museums, the Holocaust Museum Houston, and the Houston Museum of Natural Science, are historical and educational attractions, and baseball's Minute Maid Park sits in the city's downtown.

Houstonians eagerly embrace continued revitalization. Recent years have seen an explosion of dining and entertainment options in the heart of the city. The opening of the Bayou Place, Houston's largest entertainment complex, has especially generated excitement, providing a variety of restaurants and entertainment options in one facility. An active urban park sits on 12 acres in front of the George R. Brown Convention Center. Reliant Stadium in downtown Houston and home to the NFL's Houston Texans, hosted Superbowl XXXVIII in 2004 and LI in 2017, and WrestleMania XXV in 2009. Major league baseball team Houston Astros won the 2017 and 2022 World Series. In fact, the city has sports teams for every major professional league except the National Hockey League.

Located in the flat coastal plains, Houston's climate is predominantly marine. The terrain includes many small streams and bayous which, together with the nearness to Galveston Bay, favor the development of fog. Temperatures are moderated by the influence of winds from the Gulf of Mexico, which is 50 miles away. Mild winters are the norm, as is abundant rainfall. Polar air penetrates the area frequently enough to provide variability in the weather.

In August 2017, Hurricane Harvey caused severe flooding in the Houston area, with some regions receiving over 50 inches of rain. Damage from the hurricane is estimated at $125 billion. It is considered one of the worst natural disasters in the history of the United States. In 2018, Houston City Council forgave the large water bills thousands of households faced in the aftermath of Hurricane Harvey. In February 2021, record-low temperatures and severe winter weather caused major power outages across the state.

Rankings

General Rankings

- The Houston metro area was identified as one of America's fastest-growing areas in terms of population and business growth by *MagnifyMoney*. The area ranked #11 out of 35. The 100 most populous metro areas in the U.S. were evaluated on their change from 2011 to 2016 in the following categories: people and housing; workforce and employment opportunities; growing industry. *www.businessinsider.com, "The 35 Cities in the US with the Biggest Influx of People, the Most Work Opportunities, and the Hottest Business Growth," August 12, 2018*

- The human resources consulting firm Mercer ranked 231 major cities worldwide in terms of overall quality of life. Houston ranked #66. Criteria: political, social, economic, and socio-cultural factors; medical and health considerations; schools and education; public services and transportation; recreation; consumer goods; housing; and natural environment. *Mercer, "Mercer 2019 Quality of Living Survey," March 13, 2019*

Business/Finance Rankings

- The Brookings Institution ranked the nation's largest cities based on income inequality. Houston was ranked #25 (#1 = greatest inequality). Criteria: the "95/20 ratio," a figure representing the income at which a household earns more than 95 percent of all other households, divided by the income at which a household earns more than only 20 percent of all other households. *Brookings Institution, "Household Income Inequality, Largest Cities of 97 Large U.S. Metro Areas, 2014-2016," February 5, 2018*

- The Brookings Institution ranked the 100 largest metro areas in the U.S. based on income inequality. Houston was ranked #8 (#1 = greatest inequality). Criteria: the "95/20 ratio," a figure representing the income at which a household earns more than 95 percent of all other households, divided by the income at which a household earns more than only 20 percent of all other households. *Brookings Institution, "Household Income Inequality, 100 Largest U.S. Metro Areas, 2014-2016," February 5, 2018*

- Payscale.com ranked the 32 largest metro areas in terms of wage growth. The Houston metro area ranked #22. Criteria: quarterly changes in private industry employee and education professional wage growth from the previous year. *PayScale, "Wage Trends by Metro Area-1st Quarter," April 20, 2023*

- The Houston metro area was identified as one of the most debt-ridden places in America by the finance site Credit.com. The metro area was ranked #4. Criteria: residents' average credit card debt as well as median income. *Credit.com, "25 Cities With the Most Credit Card Debt," February 28, 2018*

- Houston was identified as one of America's most frugal metro areas by *Coupons.com*. The city ranked #19 out of 25. Criteria: digital coupon usage. *Coupons.com, "America's Most Frugal Cities of 2017," March 22, 2018*

- Houston was cited as one of America's top metros for total corporate facility investment in 2022. The area ranked #3 in the large metro area category (population over 1 million). *Site Selection, "Top Metros of 2022," March 2023*

- The Houston metro area appeared on the Milken Institute "2022 Best Performing Cities" list. Rank: #145 out of 200 large metro areas (population over 250,000). Criteria: job growth; wage and salary growth; high-tech output growth; housing affordability; household broadband access. *Milken Institute, "Best-Performing Cities 2022," March 28, 2022*

- *Forbes* ranked the 200 most populous metro areas to determine the nation's "Best Places for Business and Careers." The Houston metro area was ranked #34. Criteria: costs (business and living); job growth (past and projected); income growth; quality of life; educational attainment (college and high school); projected economic growth; cultural and leisure opportunities; workplace tolerance laws; net migration patterns. *Forbes, "The Best Places for Business and Careers 2019: Seattle Still On Top," October 30, 2019*

- Mercer Human Resources Consulting ranked 227 cities worldwide in terms of cost-of-living. Houston ranked #85 (the lower the ranking, the higher the cost-of-living). The survey measured the comparative cost of over 200 items (such as housing, food, clothing, domestic supplies, transportation, and recreation/entertainment) in each location. *Mercer, "2022 Cost of Living City Ranking," June 29, 2022*

Culture/Performing Arts Rankings

- Houston was selected as one of the 25 best cities for moviemakers in North America. Great film cities are places where filmmaking dreams can come true, that offer more creative space, lower costs, and great outdoor locations. NYC & LA were intentionally excluded. Criteria: longstanding reputations as film-friendly communities; film community and culture; affordability; and quality of life. The city was ranked #21. *MovieMaker Magazine, "Best Places to Live and Work as a Moviemaker, 2023," January 18, 2023*

Dating/Romance Rankings

- *Apartment List* conducted its Annual Renter Satisfaction Survey and asked renters "how satisfied are you with opportunities for dating in your current city." The cities were ranked from highest to lowest based on their satisfaction scores. Houston ranked #3 out of 85 cities. *Apartment List, "Best Cities for Dating 2022 with Local Dating Insights from Bumble," February 7, 2022*

Education Rankings

- Personal finance website *WalletHub* analyzed the 150 largest U.S. metropolitan statistical areas to determine where the most educated Americans are putting their degrees to work. Criteria: education levels; percentage of workers with degrees; education quality and attainment gap; public school quality rankings; quality and enrollment of each metro area's universities. Houston was ranked #88 (#1 = most educated city). *www.WalletHub.com, "Most & Least Educated Cities in America," July 18, 2022*

- Houston was selected as one of the best cities for post grads by *Rent.com*. The city ranked among the top 10. Criteria: jobs per capita; unemployment rate; mean annual income; cost of living; rental inventory. *Rent.com, "Best Cities for College Grads," December 11, 2018*

- Houston was selected as one of America's most literate cities. The city ranked #68 out of the 84 largest U.S. cities. Criteria: number of booksellers; library resources; Internet resources; educational attainment; periodical publishing resources; newspaper circulation. *Central Connecticut State University, "America's Most Literate Cities, 2018," February 2019*

Environmental Rankings

- Sperling's BestPlaces assessed the 50 largest metropolitan areas of the United States for the likelihood of dangerously extreme weather events or earthquakes. In general the Southeast and South-Central regions have the highest risk of weather extremes and earthquakes, while the Pacific Northwest enjoys the lowest risk. Of the most risky metropolitan areas, the Houston metro area was ranked #5. *www.bestplaces.net, "Avoid Natural Disasters: BestPlaces Reveals The Top 10 Safest Places to Live," October 25, 2017*

- The U.S. Environmental Protection Agency (EPA) released its list of U.S. metropolitan areas with the most ENERGY STAR certified buildings in 2022. The Houston metro area was ranked #11 out of 25. *U.S. Environmental Protection Agency, "2023 Energy Star Top Cities," April 26, 2023*

- Houston was highlighted as one of the 25 most ozone-polluted metro areas in the U.S. during 2019 through 2021. The area ranked #9. *American Lung Association, "State of the Air 2023," April 19, 2023*

- Houston was highlighted as one of the 25 metro areas most polluted by year-round particle pollution (Annual PM 2.5) in the U.S. during 2019 through 2021. The area ranked #15. *American Lung Association, "State of the Air 2023," April 19, 2023*

Food/Drink Rankings

- The U.S. Chamber of Commerce Foundation conducted an in-depth study on local food truck regulations, surveyed 288 food truck owners, and ranked 20 major American cities based on how friendly they are for operating a food truck. The compiled index assessed the following: procedures for obtaining permits and licenses; complying with restrictions; and financial obligations associated with operating a food truck. Houston ranked #6 overall (1 being the best). *www.foodtrucknation.us, "Food Truck Nation," March 20, 2018*

Health/Fitness Rankings

- For each of the 100 largest cities in the United States, the American Fitness Index®, compiled in partnership between the American College of Sports Medicine and the Elevance Health Foundation, evaluated community infrastructure and 34 health behaviors including preventive health, levels of chronic disease conditions, food insecurity, sleep quality, pedestrian safety, air quality, and community/environment resources that support physical activity. Houston ranked #61 for "community fitness." *americanfitnessindex.org, "2022 ACSM American Fitness Index Summary Report," July 12, 2022*

- The Houston metro area was identified as one of the worst cities for bed bugs in America by pest control company Orkin. The area ranked #44 out of 50 based on the number of bed bug treatments Orkin performed from December 2021 to November 2022. *Orkin, "The Windy City Can't Blow Bed Bugs Away: Chicago Ranks #1 For Third Consecutive Year On Orkin's Bed Bug Cities List," January 9, 2023*

- Houston was identified as a "2022 Spring Allergy Capital." The area ranked #44 out of 100. Three groups of factors were used to identify the most challenging cities for people with allergies during the spring season: annual spring pollen scores; over the counter allergy medicine use; number of board-certified allergy specialists. *Asthma and Allergy Foundation of America, "Spring Allergy Capitals 2022," March 2, 2022*

- Houston was identified as a "2022 Fall Allergy Capital." The area ranked #27 out of 100. Three groups of factors were used to identify the most challenging cities for people with allergies during the fall season: annual fall pollen scores; over the counter allergy medicine use; number of board-certified allergy specialists. *Asthma and Allergy Foundation of America, "Fall Allergy Capitals 2022," March 2, 2022*

- Houston was identified as a "2022 Asthma Capital." The area ranked #64 out of the nation's 100 largest metropolitan areas. Criteria: estimated asthma prevalence; asthma-related mortality; and ER visits due to asthma. Risk factors analyzed but not factored in the rankings: annual pollen score; annual air quality; public smoking laws; access to board-certified asthma specialists; rescue and controller medication use; uninsured rate; poverty rate. *Asthma and Allergy Foundation of America, "Asthma Capitals 2022: The Most Challenging Places to Live With Asthma," September 14, 2022*

Real Estate Rankings

- *WalletHub* compared the most populated U.S. cities to determine which had the best markets for real estate agents. Houston ranked #149 where demand was high and pay was the best. Criteria: sales per agent; annual median wage for real-estate agents; monthly average starting salary for real estate agents; real estate job density and competition; unemployment rate; home turnover rate; housing-market health index; and other relevant metrics. *www.WalletHub.com, "2021 Best Places to Be a Real Estate Agent," May 12, 2021*

- According to Penske Truck Rental, the Houston metro area was named the #1 moving destination in 2022, based on one-way consumer truck rental reservations made through Penske's website, rental locations, and reservations call center. *gopenske.com/blog, "Penske Truck Rental's 2022 Top Moving Destinations," April 27, 2023*

- Houston was ranked #133 out of 235 metro areas in terms of housing affordability in 2022 by the National Association of Home Builders (#1 = most affordable). Criteria: the share of homes sold in that area affordable to a family earning the local median income, based on standard mortgage underwriting criteria. *National Association of Home Builders®, NAHB-Wells Fargo Housing Opportunity Index, 4th Quarter 2022*

Safety Rankings

- To identify the most dangerous cities in America, *24/7 Wall St.* focused on violent crime categories—murder, non-negligent manslaughter, rape, robbery, and aggravated assault—as reported for every 100,000 residents using data from the FBI's 2020 annual Uniform Crime Report. For cities with populations over 25,000, Houston was ranked #34. *247wallst.com, "America's Most Dangerous Cities" November 12, 2021*

- Statistics drawn from the FBI's Uniform Crime Report were used to rank the cities where violent crime rose the most year over year from 2019 to 2020. Only cities with 25,000 or more residents were included. *24/7 Wall St.* found that Houston placed #38 of those with a notable surge in incidents of violent crime. *247wallst.com, "American Cities Where Crime Is Soaring," March 4, 2022*

- Allstate ranked the 200 largest cities in America in terms of driver safety. Houston ranked #158. Criteria: internal property damage claims over a two-year period from January 2016 to December 2017. The report helps increase the importance of safety and awareness behind the wheel. *Allstate, "Allstate America's Best Drivers Report, 2019" June 24, 2019*

- Houston was identified as one of the most dangerous cities in America by NeighborhoodScout. The city ranked #43 out of 100 (#1 = most dangerous). Criteria: number of violent crimes per 1,000 residents. The editors evaluated cities with 25,000 or more residents. *NeighborhoodScout.com, "2023 Top 100 Most Dangerous Cities in the U.S.," January 12, 2023*

- The National Insurance Crime Bureau ranked 390 metro areas in the U.S. in terms of per capita rates of vehicle theft. The Houston metro area ranked #44 (#1 = highest rate). Criteria: number of vehicle theft offenses per 100,000 inhabitants in 2021. *National Insurance Crime Bureau, "Hot Spots 2021," September 1, 2022*

Seniors/Retirement Rankings

- From its Best Cities for Successful Aging indexes, the Milken Institute generated rankings for metropolitan areas, weighing data in nine categories—health care, wellness, living arrangements, transportation and convenience, financial characteristics, education, employment, community engagement, and overall livability. The Houston metro area was ranked #25 overall in the large metro area category. *Milken Institute, "Best Cities for Successful Aging, 2017" March 14, 2017*

Sports/Recreation Rankings

- Houston was chosen as a bicycle friendly community by the League of American Bicyclists. A "Bicycle Friendly Community" welcomes cyclists by providing safe and supportive accommodation for cycling and encouraging people to bike for transportation and recreation. There are five award levels: Diamond; Platinum; Gold; Silver; and Bronze. The community achieved an award level of Bronze. *League of American Bicyclists, "Fall 2022 Awards-New & Renewing Bicycle Friendly Communities List," December 14, 2022*

Transportation Rankings

- According to the INRIX "2022 Global Traffic Scorecard," Houston was identified as one of the most congested metro areas in the U.S. The area ranked #9 out of 25. Criteria: average annual time spent in traffic and average cost of congestion per motorist. *Inrix.com, "Return to Work, Higher Gas Prices & Inflation Drove Americans to Spend Hundreds More in Time and Money Commuting," January 10, 2023*

Women/Minorities Rankings

- The *Houston Chronicle* listed the Houston metro area as #11 in top places for young Latinos to live in the U.S. Research was largely based on housing and occupational data from the largest metropolitan areas performed by *Forbes* and NBC Universo. Criteria: percentage of 18-34 year-olds; Latino college grad rates; and diversity. *blog.chron.com, "The 15 Best Big Cities for Latino Millenials," January 26, 2016*

- Personal finance website *WalletHub* compared more than 180 U.S. cities across two key dimensions, "Hispanic Business-Friendliness" and "Hispanic Purchasing Power," to arrive at the most favorable conditions for Hispanic entrepreneurs. Houston was ranked #27 out of 182. Criteria includes: share of Hispanic-Owned Businesses; Hispanic entrepreneurship rate to median annual income of Hispanics; Small Business-Friendliness score; cost of living; and number of Hispanics with at least a bachelor's degree. *WalletHub.com, "2019's Best Cities for Hispanic Entrepreneurs," May 1, 2019*

Miscellaneous Rankings

- The watchdog site, Charity Navigator, conducted a study of charities in major markets both to analyze statistical differences in their financial, accountability, and transparency practices and to track year-to-year variations in individual philanthropic communities. The Houston metro area was ranked #2 among the 30 metro markets in the rating category of Overall Score. *www.charitynavigator.org, "2017 Metro Market Study," May 1, 2017*

- *WalletHub* compared the 150 most populated U.S. cities to determine their operating efficiency. A "Quality of Services" score was constructed for each city and then divided by the total budget per capita to reveal which were managed the best. Houston ranked #82. Criteria: financial stability; economy; education; safety; health; infrastructure and pollution. *www.WalletHub.com, "2022's Best- & Worst-Run Cities in America," June 21, 2022*

- The National Alliance to End Homelessness listed the 25 most populous metro areas with the highest rate of homelessness. The Houston metro area had a high rate of homelessness. Criteria: number of homeless people per 10,000 population in 2016. *National Alliance to End Homelessness, "Homelessness in the 25 Most Populous U.S. Metro Areas," September 1, 2017*

Business Environment

DEMOGRAPHICS

Population Growth

Area	1990 Census	2000 Census	2010 Census	2020 Census	Population Growth (%) 1990-2020	Population Growth (%) 2010-2020
City	1,697,610	1,953,631	2,099,451	2,304,580	35.8	9.8
MSA[1]	3,767,335	4,715,407	5,946,800	7,122,240	89.1	19.8
U.S.	248,709,873	281,421,906	308,745,538	331,449,281	33.3	7.4

Note: (1) Figures cover the Houston-The Woodlands-Sugar Land, TX Metropolitan Statistical Area
Source: U.S. Census Bureau, 1990 Census, 2000 Census, 2010 Census, 2020 Census

Race

Area	White Alone[2] (%)	Black Alone[2] (%)	Asian Alone[2] (%)	AIAN[3] Alone[2] (%)	NHOPI[4] Alone[2] (%)	Other Race Alone[2] (%)	Two or More Races (%)
City	32.1	22.6	7.3	1.2	0.1	20.7	16.1
MSA[1]	41.4	17.4	8.4	1.0	0.1	16.0	15.7
U.S.	61.6	12.4	6.0	1.1	0.2	8.4	10.2

Note: (1) Figures cover the Houston-The Woodlands-Sugar Land, TX Metropolitan Statistical Area; (2) Alone is defined as not being in combination with one or more other races; (3) American Indian and Alaska Native; (4) Native Hawaiian and Other Pacific Islander
Source: U.S. Census Bureau, 2020 Census

Hispanic or Latino Origin

Area	Total (%)	Mexican (%)	Puerto Rican (%)	Cuban (%)	Other (%)
City	44.5	30.3	0.7	0.8	12.8
MSA[1]	37.9	27.3	0.7	0.7	9.2
U.S.	18.4	11.2	1.8	0.7	4.7

Note: Persons of Hispanic or Latino origin can be of any race; (1) Figures cover the Houston-The Woodlands-Sugar Land, TX Metropolitan Statistical Area
Source: U.S. Census Bureau, 2017-2021 American Community Survey 5-Year Estimates

Age

Area	Under Age 5	Age 5–19	Age 20–34	Age 35–44	Age 45–54	Age 55–64	Age 65–74	Age 75–84	Age 85+	Median Age
City	6.6	19.7	25.1	14.3	11.6	10.7	7.3	3.4	1.3	34.2
MSA[1]	6.5	22.1	21.0	14.3	12.7	11.4	7.7	3.3	1.1	35.3
U.S.	5.6	19.2	20.2	12.7	12.4	13.1	10.0	4.9	1.9	38.8

Note: (1) Figures cover the Houston-The Woodlands-Sugar Land, TX Metropolitan Statistical Area
Source: U.S. Census Bureau, 2020 Census

Disability by Age

Area	All Ages	Under 18 Years Old	18 to 64 Years Old	65 Years and Over
City	9.9	3.9	8.0	34.7
MSA[1]	9.6	3.8	7.9	32.6
U.S.	12.6	4.4	10.3	33.4

Note: Figures show percent of the civilian noninstitutionalized population that reported having a disability. Disability status is determined from six types of difficulty: vision, hearing, cognitive, ambulatory, self-care, and independent living. For children under 5 years old, hearing and vision difficulty are used to determine disability status. For children between the ages of 5 and 14, disability status is determined from hearing, vision, cognitive, ambulatory, and self-care difficulties. For people aged 15 years and older, they are considered to have a disability if they have difficulty with any one of the six difficulty types; Note: (1) Figures cover the Houston-The Woodlands-Sugar Land, TX Metropolitan Statistical Area
Source: U.S. Census Bureau, 2017-2021 American Community Survey 5-Year Estimates

Ancestry

Area	German	Irish	English	American	Italian	Polish	French[2]	Scottish	Dutch
City	4.8	3.5	4.3	3.4	1.6	0.9	1.4	0.9	0.4
MSA[1]	7.3	5.0	5.8	3.8	2.0	1.1	1.9	1.1	0.6
U.S.	12.8	9.6	8.1	5.7	5.0	2.7	2.2	1.6	1.1

Note: Figures are the percentage of the total population reporting a particular ancestry. The nine most commonly reported ancestries in the U.S. are shown. Figures include multiple ancestries (e.g. if a person reported being Irish and Italian, they were included in both columns); (1) Figures cover the Houston-The Woodlands-Sugar Land, TX Metropolitan Statistical Area; (2) Excludes Basque
Source: U.S. Census Bureau, 2017-2021 American Community Survey 5-Year Estimates

Foreign-born Population

Area	Any Foreign Country	Asia	Mexico	Europe	Caribbean	Central America[2]	South America	Africa	Canada
City	28.9	5.9	10.6	1.1	1.0	6.5	1.6	2.0	0.2
MSA[1]	23.5	6.0	8.4	1.1	0.8	3.8	1.6	1.5	0.3
U.S.	13.6	4.2	3.3	1.5	1.4	1.1	1.1	0.8	0.2

Note: (1) Figures cover the Houston-The Woodlands-Sugar Land, TX Metropolitan Statistical Area; (2) Excludes Mexico.
Source: U.S. Census Bureau, 2017-2021 American Community Survey 5-Year Estimates

Household Size

Area	One	Two	Three	Four	Five	Six	Seven or More	Average Household Size
City	32.8	29.2	15.7	12.0	6.3	2.5	1.6	2.60
MSA[1]	24.2	29.7	17.3	15.8	8.1	3.1	1.9	2.80
U.S.	28.1	33.8	15.5	12.9	6.0	2.3	1.4	2.60

Note: (1) Figures cover the Houston-The Woodlands-Sugar Land, TX Metropolitan Statistical Area
Source: U.S. Census Bureau, 2017-2021 American Community Survey 5-Year Estimates

Household Relationships

Area	House-holder	Opposite-sex Spouse	Same-sex Spouse	Opposite-sex Unmarried Partner	Same-sex Unmarried Partner	Child[2]	Grand-child	Other Relatives	Non-relatives
City	38.9	14.0	0.3	2.4	0.2	29.5	2.9	6.5	3.6
MSA[1]	35.2	17.1	0.2	2.0	0.1	32.7	2.8	6.1	2.6
U.S.	38.3	17.5	0.2	2.5	0.2	28.3	2.4	4.8	3.4

Note: Figures are percent of the total population; (1) Figures cover the Houston-The Woodlands-Sugar Land, TX Metropolitan Statistical Area; (2) Includes biological, adopted, and stepchildren of the householder
Source: U.S. Census Bureau, 2020 Census

Gender

Area	Males	Females	Males per 100 Females
City	1,140,598	1,163,982	98.0
MSA[1]	3,505,374	3,616,866	96.9
U.S.	162,685,811	168,763,470	96.4

Note: (1) Figures cover the Houston-The Woodlands-Sugar Land, TX Metropolitan Statistical Area
Source: U.S. Census Bureau, 2020 Census

Marital Status

Area	Never Married	Now Married[2]	Separated	Widowed	Divorced
City	41.1	41.2	3.0	4.5	10.2
MSA[1]	33.8	50.2	2.3	4.3	9.4
U.S.	33.8	48.0	1.8	5.6	10.8

Note: Figures are percentages and cover the population 15 years of age and older; (1) Figures cover the Houston-The Woodlands-Sugar Land, TX Metropolitan Statistical Area; (2) Excludes separated
Source: U.S. Census Bureau, 2017-2021 American Community Survey 5-Year Estimates

Religious Groups by Family

Area	Catholic	Baptist	Methodist	LDS[2]	Pentecostal	Lutheran	Islam	Adventist	Other
MSA[1]	18.3	13.1	3.7	1.2	1.6	0.7	1.7	1.5	13.1
U.S.	18.7	7.3	3.0	2.0	1.8	1.7	1.3	1.3	11.6

Note: Figures are the number of adherents as a percentage of the total population and cover the eight largest religious groups in the U.S; (1) Figures cover the Houston-The Woodlands-Sugar Land, TX Metropolitan Statistical Area; (2) Church of Jesus Christ of Latter-day Saints
Sources: 2020 U.S. Religion Census, Association of Statisticians of American Religious Bodies; The Association of Religion Data Archives (ARDA)

Religious Groups by Tradition

Area	Catholic	Evangelical Protestant	Mainline Protestant	Black Protestant	Islam	Judaism	Hinduism	Orthodox	Buddhism
MSA[1]	18.3	23.8	4.7	2.3	1.7	0.3	0.7	0.3	0.3
U.S.	18.7	16.5	5.2	2.3	1.3	0.6	0.4	0.4	0.3

Note: Figures are the number of adherents as a percentage of the total population; (1) Figures cover the Houston-The Woodlands-Sugar Land, TX Metropolitan Statistical Area
Sources: 2020 U.S. Religion Census, Association of Statisticians of American Religious Bodies; The Association of Religion Data Archives (ARDA)

ECONOMY

Gross Metropolitan Product

Area	2020	2021	2022	2023	Rank[2]
MSA[1]	488.1	543.0	619.8	654.0	7

Note: Figures are in billions of dollars; (1) Figures cover the Houston-The Woodlands-Sugar Land, TX Metropolitan Statistical Area; (2) Rank is based on 2021 data and ranges from 1 to 381
Source: U.S. Conference of Mayors, U.S. Metro Economies: U.S. Metros Compared to Global and State Economies, June 2022

Economic Growth

Area	2018-20 (%)	2021 (%)	2022 (%)	2023 (%)	Rank[2]
MSA[1]	-1.6	4.9	4.4	4.7	254
U.S.	-0.6	5.7	3.1	2.9	—

Note: Figures are real gross metropolitan product (GMP) growth rates and represent average annual percent change; (1) Figures cover the Houston-The Woodlands-Sugar Land, TX Metropolitan Statistical Area; (2) Rank is based on 2020 2-year average annual percent change and ranges from 1 to 381
Source: U.S. Conference of Mayors, U.S. Metro Economies: U.S. Metros Compared to Global and State Economies, June 2022

Metropolitan Area Exports

Area	2016	2017	2018	2019	2020	2021	Rank[2]
MSA[1]	84,105.5	95,760.3	120,714.3	129,656.0	104,538.2	140,750.4	1

Note: Figures are in millions of dollars; (1) Figures cover the Houston-The Woodlands-Sugar Land, TX Metropolitan Statistical Area; (2) Rank is based on 2021 data and ranges from 1 to 388
Source: U.S. Department of Commerce, International Trade Administration, Office of Trade and Economic Analysis, Industry and Analysis, Exports by Metropolitan Area, data extracted March 16, 2023

Building Permits

Area	Single-Family 2021	Single-Family 2022	Pct. Chg.	Multi-Family 2021	Multi-Family 2022	Pct. Chg.	Total 2021	Total 2022	Pct. Chg.
City	7,146	6,800	-4.8	8,103	8,945	10.4	15,249	15,745	3.3
MSA[1]	52,719	47,701	-9.5	16,544	28,027	69.4	69,263	75,728	9.3
U.S.	1,115,400	975,600	-12.5	621,600	689,500	10.9	1,737,000	1,665,100	-4.1

Note: (1) Figures cover the Houston-The Woodlands-Sugar Land, TX Metropolitan Statistical Area; Figures represent new, privately-owned housing units authorized (unadjusted data); All permit data are based on estimates with imputation
Source: U.S. Census Bureau, Manufacturing, Mining, and Construction Statistics, Building Permits, 2021, 2022

Bankruptcy Filings

Area	Business Filings 2021	Business Filings 2022	% Chg.	Nonbusiness Filings 2021	Nonbusiness Filings 2022	% Chg.
Harris County	269	213	-20.8	2,310	2,541	10.0
U.S.	14,347	13,481	-6.0	399,269	374,240	-6.3

Note: Business filings include Chapter 7, Chapter 9, Chapter 11, Chapter 12, Chapter 13, Chapter 15, and Section 304; Nonbusiness filings include Chapter 7, Chapter 11, and Chapter 13
Source: Administrative Office of the U.S. Courts, Business and Nonbusiness Bankruptcy, County Cases Commenced by Chapter of the Bankruptcy Code, During the 12-Month Period Ending December 31, 2021 and Business and Nonbusiness Bankruptcy, County Cases Commenced by Chapter of the Bankruptcy Code, During the 12-Month Period Ending December 31, 2022

Housing Vacancy Rates

Area	Gross Vacancy Rate[2] (%) 2020	2021	2022	Year-Round Vacancy Rate[3] (%) 2020	2021	2022	Rental Vacancy Rate[4] (%) 2020	2021	2022	Homeowner Vacancy Rate[5] (%) 2020	2021	2022
MSA[1]	6.8	7.2	6.9	6.3	6.6	6.3	9.7	8.8	8.9	1.1	0.8	0.6
U.S.	10.6	10.8	10.5	8.2	8.4	8.2	6.3	6.1	5.8	1.0	0.9	0.8

Note: (1) Figures cover the Houston-The Woodlands-Sugar Land, TX Metropolitan Statistical Area; (2) The percentage of the total housing inventory that is vacant; (3) The percentage of the housing inventory (excluding seasonal units) that is year-round vacant; (4) The percentage of rental inventory that is vacant for rent; (5) The percentage of homeowner inventory that is vacant for sale
Source: U.S. Census Bureau, Housing Vacancies and Homeownership Annual Statistics: 2020, 2021, 2022

INCOME

Income

Area	Per Capita ($)	Median Household ($)	Average Household ($)
City	35,578	56,019	90,511
MSA[1]	36,821	72,551	103,497
U.S.	37,638	69,021	97,196

Note: (1) Figures cover the Houston-The Woodlands-Sugar Land, TX Metropolitan Statistical Area
Source: U.S. Census Bureau, 2017-2021 American Community Survey 5-Year Estimates

Household Income Distribution

Area	Percent of Households Earning							
	Under $15,000	$15,000 -$24,999	$25,000 -$34,999	$35,000 -$49,999	$50,000 -$74,999	$75,000 -$99,999	$100,000 -$149,999	$150,000 and up
City	11.9	9.5	10.6	13.1	17.1	10.7	12.1	14.9
MSA[1]	8.4	7.1	8.2	11.0	16.6	12.3	16.5	19.8
U.S.	9.4	7.8	8.2	11.4	16.8	12.8	16.3	17.3

Note: (1) Figures cover the Houston-The Woodlands-Sugar Land, TX Metropolitan Statistical Area
Source: U.S. Census Bureau, 2017-2021 American Community Survey 5-Year Estimates

Poverty Rate

Area	All Ages	Under 18 Years Old	18 to 64 Years Old	65 Years and Over
City	19.5	29.7	16.3	15.1
MSA[1]	13.3	18.9	11.5	10.5
U.S.	12.6	17.0	11.8	9.6

Note: Figures are percentage of people whose income during the past 12 months was below the poverty level;
(1) Figures cover the Houston-The Woodlands-Sugar Land, TX Metropolitan Statistical Area
Source: U.S. Census Bureau, 2017-2021 American Community Survey 5-Year Estimates

EMPLOYMENT

Labor Force and Employment

Area	Civilian Labor Force			Workers Employed		
	Dec. 2021	Dec. 2022	% Chg.	Dec. 2021	Dec. 2022	% Chg.
City	1,138,573	1,173,802	3.1	1,085,474	1,128,659	4.0
MSA[1]	3,460,832	3,565,905	3.0	3,294,015	3,425,418	4.0
U.S.	161,696,000	164,224,000	1.6	155,732,000	158,872,000	2.0

Note: Data is not seasonally adjusted and covers workers 16 years of age and older; (1) Figures cover the Houston-The Woodlands-Sugar Land, TX Metropolitan Statistical Area
Source: Bureau of Labor Statistics, Local Area Unemployment Statistics

Unemployment Rate

Area	2022											
	Jan.	Feb.	Mar.	Apr.	May	Jun.	Jul.	Aug.	Sep.	Oct.	Nov.	Dec.
City	5.3	5.2	4.3	4.1	4.2	4.7	4.8	4.6	4.2	4.1	4.0	3.8
MSA[1]	5.5	5.3	4.4	4.1	4.3	4.8	4.8	4.6	4.2	4.1	4.0	3.9
U.S.	4.4	4.1	3.8	3.3	3.4	3.8	3.8	3.8	3.3	3.4	3.4	3.3

Note: Data is not seasonally adjusted and covers workers 16 years of age and older; (1) Figures cover the Houston-The Woodlands-Sugar Land, TX Metropolitan Statistical Area
Source: Bureau of Labor Statistics, Local Area Unemployment Statistics

Average Wages

Occupation	$/Hr.	Occupation	$/Hr.
Accountants and Auditors	45.35	Maintenance and Repair Workers	20.87
Automotive Mechanics	24.26	Marketing Managers	71.45
Bookkeepers	22.16	Network and Computer Systems Admin.	47.28
Carpenters	23.53	Nurses, Licensed Practical	26.65
Cashiers	12.84	Nurses, Registered	42.73
Computer Programmers	44.09	Nursing Assistants	16.18
Computer Systems Analysts	53.59	Office Clerks, General	18.74
Computer User Support Specialists	27.70	Physical Therapists	52.20
Construction Laborers	18.56	Physicians	138.31
Cooks, Restaurant	14.67	Plumbers, Pipefitters and Steamfitters	28.24
Customer Service Representatives	18.59	Police and Sheriff's Patrol Officers	32.31
Dentists	74.27	Postal Service Mail Carriers	26.87
Electricians	27.69	Real Estate Sales Agents	38.86
Engineers, Electrical	55.91	Retail Salespersons	16.04
Fast Food and Counter Workers	11.74	Sales Representatives, Technical/Scientific	46.77
Financial Managers	84.66	Secretaries, Exc. Legal/Medical/Executive	20.43
First-Line Supervisors of Office Workers	31.01	Security Guards	15.78
General and Operations Managers	56.99	Surgeons	162.09
Hairdressers/Cosmetologists	13.81	Teacher Assistants, Exc. Postsecondary*	13.73
Home Health and Personal Care Aides	11.18	Teachers, Secondary School, Exc. Sp. Ed.*	30.64
Janitors and Cleaners	13.63	Telemarketers	17.46
Landscaping/Groundskeeping Workers	16.29	Truck Drivers, Heavy/Tractor-Trailer	24.72
Lawyers	84.79	Truck Drivers, Light/Delivery Services	22.19
Maids and Housekeeping Cleaners	14.27	Waiters and Waitresses	13.02

Note: Wage data covers the Houston-The Woodlands-Sugar Land, TX Metropolitan Statistical Area; (*) Hourly wages were calculated from annual wage data based on a 40 hour work week; n/a not available.
Source: Bureau of Labor Statistics, Metro Area Occupational Employment & Wage Estimates, May 2022

Employment by Industry

Sector	MSA[1] Number of Employees	MSA[1] Percent of Total	U.S. Percent of Total
Construction	224,600	6.7	5.0
Private Education and Health Services	438,900	13.2	16.1
Financial Activities	183,400	5.5	5.9
Government	446,400	13.4	14.5
Information	33,400	1.0	2.0
Leisure and Hospitality	343,900	10.3	10.3
Manufacturing	229,700	6.9	8.4
Mining and Logging	67,400	2.0	0.4
Other Services	116,700	3.5	3.7
Professional and Business Services	554,700	16.6	14.7
Retail Trade	326,400	9.8	10.2
Transportation, Warehousing, and Utilities	197,200	5.9	4.9
Wholesale Trade	173,100	5.2	3.9

Note: Figures are non-farm employment as of December 2022. Figures are not seasonally adjusted and include workers 16 years of age and older; (1) Figures cover the Houston-The Woodlands-Sugar Land, TX Metropolitan Statistical Area
Source: Bureau of Labor Statistics, Current Employment Statistics, Employment, Hours, and Earnings

Employment by Occupation

Occupation Classification	City (%)	MSA[1] (%)	U.S. (%)
Management, Business, Science, and Arts	37.9	40.0	40.3
Natural Resources, Construction, and Maintenance	12.0	10.7	8.7
Production, Transportation, and Material Moving	12.6	12.9	13.1
Sales and Office	19.6	20.6	20.9
Service	17.9	15.7	17.0

Note: Figures cover employed civilians 16 years of age and older; (1) Figures cover the Houston-The Woodlands-Sugar Land, TX Metropolitan Statistical Area
Source: U.S. Census Bureau, 2017-2021 American Community Survey 5-Year Estimates

Occupations with Greatest Projected Employment Growth: 2022 – 2024

Occupation[1]	2022 Employment	2024 Projected Employment	Numeric Employment Change	Percent Employment Change
Home Health and Personal Care Aides	338,130	364,760	26,630	7.9
General and Operations Managers	395,700	416,100	20,400	5.2
Heavy and Tractor-Trailer Truck Drivers	206,850	222,220	15,370	7.4
Software Developers	119,810	134,060	14,250	11.9
Laborers and Freight, Stock, and Material Movers, Hand	214,680	228,680	14,000	6.5
Farmers, Ranchers, and Other Agricultural Managers	274,740	287,430	12,690	4.6
Stockers and Order Fillers	212,180	224,670	12,490	5.9
Construction Laborers	153,220	164,330	11,110	7.3
Cooks, Restaurant	131,480	141,860	10,380	7.9
Industrial Truck and Tractor Operators	83,270	93,190	9,920	11.9

Note: Projections cover Texas; (1) Sorted by numeric employment change
Source: www.projectionscentral.com, State Occupational Projections, 2022–2024 Short-Term Projections

Fastest-Growing Occupations: 2022 – 2024

Occupation[1]	2022 Employment	2024 Projected Employment	Numeric Employment Change	Percent Employment Change
Wind Turbine Service Technicians	5,240	5,990	750	14.3
Information Security Analysts (SOC 2018)	14,170	16,110	1,940	13.7
Solar Photovoltaic Installers	2,240	2,540	300	13.4
Veterinary Technologists and Technicians	16,140	18,200	2,060	12.8
Actuaries	1,810	2,040	230	12.7
Data Scientists	7,340	8,270	930	12.7
Web Developers	6,920	7,790	870	12.6
Veterinarians	6,830	7,670	840	12.3
Veterinary Assistants and Laboratory Animal Caretakers	5,990	6,720	730	12.2
Ushers, Lobby Attendants, and Ticket Takers	9,100	10,190	1,090	12.0

Note: Projections cover Texas; (1) Sorted by percent employment change and excludes occupations with numeric employment change less than 50
Source: www.projectionscentral.com, State Occupational Projections, 2022–2024 Short-Term Projections

Houston, Texas 259

CITY FINANCES

City Government Finances

Component	2020 ($000)	2020 ($ per capita)
Total Revenues	5,564,702	2,398
Total Expenditures	5,246,003	2,261
Debt Outstanding	14,590,458	6,288
Cash and Securities[1]	7,247,645	3,124

Note: (1) Cash and security holdings of a government at the close of its fiscal year, including those of its dependent agencies, utilities, and liquor stores.
Source: U.S. Census Bureau, State & Local Government Finances 2020

City Government Revenue by Source

Source	2020 ($000)	2020 ($ per capita)	2020 (%)
General Revenue			
From Federal Government	293,947	127	5.3
From State Government	211,470	91	3.8
From Local Governments	107,001	46	1.9
Taxes			
Property	1,512,641	652	27.2
Sales and Gross Receipts	926,632	399	16.7
Personal Income	0	0	0.0
Corporate Income	0	0	0.0
Motor Vehicle License	0	0	0.0
Other Taxes	163,591	71	2.9
Current Charges	1,268,420	547	22.8
Liquor Store	0	0	0.0
Utility	581,779	251	10.5

Source: U.S. Census Bureau, State & Local Government Finances 2020

City Government Expenditures by Function

Function	2020 ($000)	2020 ($ per capita)	2020 (%)
General Direct Expenditures			
Air Transportation	417,153	179	8.0
Corrections	0	0	0.0
Education	0	0	0.0
Employment Security Administration	0	0	0.0
Financial Administration	63,031	27	1.2
Fire Protection	400,639	172	7.6
General Public Buildings	44,100	19	0.8
Governmental Administration, Other	337,400	145	6.4
Health	117,635	50	2.2
Highways	220,642	95	4.2
Hospitals	0	0	0.0
Housing and Community Development	113,048	48	2.2
Interest on General Debt	610,231	263	11.6
Judicial and Legal	49,449	21	0.9
Libraries	38,192	16	0.7
Parking	9,172	4	0.2
Parks and Recreation	89,814	38	1.7
Police Protection	788,706	339	15.0
Public Welfare	0	0	0.0
Sewerage	764,919	329	14.6
Solid Waste Management	114,900	49	2.2
Veterans' Services	0	0	0.0
Liquor Store	0	0	0.0
Utility	578,957	249	11.0

Source: U.S. Census Bureau, State & Local Government Finances 2020

TAXES

State Corporate Income Tax Rates

State	Tax Rate (%)	Income Brackets ($)	Num. of Brackets	Financial Institution Tax Rate (%)[a]	Federal Income Tax Ded.
Texas	(u)	–	–	(u)	No

Note: Tax rates as of January 1, 2023; (a) Rates listed are the corporate income tax rate applied to financial institutions or excise taxes based on income. Some states have other taxes based upon the value of deposits or shares; (u) Texas imposes a Franchise Tax, otherwise known as margin tax, imposed on entities with more than $1,230,000 total revenues at rate of 0.75%, or 0.375% for entities primarily engaged in retail or wholesale trade, on lesser of 70% of total revenues or 100% of gross receipts after deductions for either compensation or cost of goods sold.
Source: Federation of Tax Administrators, State Corporate Income Tax Rates, January 1, 2023

State Individual Income Tax Rates

State	Tax Rate (%)	Income Brackets ($)	Personal Exemptions ($) Single	Personal Exemptions ($) Married	Personal Exemptions ($) Depend.	Standard Ded. ($) Single	Standard Ded. ($) Married
Texas				– No state income tax –			

Note: Tax rates as of January 1, 2023; Local- and county-level taxes are not included
Source: Federation of Tax Administrators, State Individual Income Tax Rates, January 1, 2023

Various State Sales and Excise Tax Rates

State	State Sales Tax (%)	Gasoline[1] ($/gal.)	Cigarette[2] ($/pack)	Spirits[3] ($/gal.)	Wine[4] ($/gal.)	Beer[5] ($/gal.)	Recreational Marijuana (%)
Texas	6.25	0.20	1.41	2.40	0.20	0.19	Not legal

Note: All tax rates as of January 1, 2023; (1) The American Petroleum Institute has developed a methodology for determining the average tax rate on a gallon of fuel. Rates may include any of the following: excise taxes, environmental fees, storage tank fees, other fees or taxes, general sales tax, and local taxes; (2) The federal excise tax of $1.0066 per pack and local taxes are not included; (3) Rates are those applicable to off-premise sales of 40% alcohol by volume (a.b.v.) distilled spirits in 750ml containers. Local excise taxes are excluded; (4) Rates are those applicable to off-premise sales of 11% a.b.v. non-carbonated wine in 750ml containers; (5) Rates are those applicable to off-premise sales of 4.7% a.b.v. beer in 12 ounce containers.
Source: Tax Foundation, 2023 Facts & Figures: How Does Your State Compare?

State Business Tax Climate Index Rankings

State	Overall Rank	Corporate Tax Rank	Individual Income Tax Rank	Sales Tax Rank	Property Tax Rank	Unemployment Insurance Tax Rank
Texas	13	47	7	37	38	12

Note: The index is a measure of how each state's tax laws affect economic performance. The lower the rank, the more favorable a state's tax system is for business. States without a given tax are given a ranking of 1. The scores/rankings for the District of Columbia do not affect other states. The 2023 index represents the tax climate as of July 1, 2022.
Source: Tax Foundation, State Business Tax Climate Index 2023

TRANSPORTATION

Means of Transportation to Work

Area	Car/Truck/Van Drove Alone	Car/Truck/Van Carpooled	Public Transportation Bus	Public Transportation Subway	Public Transportation Railroad	Bicycle	Walked	Other Means	Worked at Home
City	73.7	9.8	3.4	0.1	0.0	0.4	1.9	2.4	8.3
MSA[1]	77.1	9.3	1.7	0.0	0.0	0.3	1.2	1.6	8.7
U.S.	73.2	8.6	2.0	1.6	0.5	0.5	2.5	1.5	9.7

Note: Figures are percentages and cover workers 16 years of age and older; (1) Figures cover the Houston-The Woodlands-Sugar Land, TX Metropolitan Statistical Area
Source: U.S. Census Bureau, 2017-2021 American Community Survey 5-Year Estimates

Travel Time to Work

Area	Less Than 10 Minutes	10 to 19 Minutes	20 to 29 Minutes	30 to 44 Minutes	45 to 59 Minutes	60 to 89 Minutes	90 Minutes or More
City	7.2	25.5	23.0	27.7	8.9	5.9	1.8
MSA[1]	7.6	23.2	20.4	26.7	11.6	8.2	2.3
U.S.	12.4	28.5	21.0	20.9	8.2	6.2	2.9

Note: Note: Figures are percentages and include workers 16 years old and over; (1) Figures cover the Houston-The Woodlands-Sugar Land, TX Metropolitan Statistical Area
Source: U.S. Census Bureau, 2017-2021 American Community Survey 5-Year Estimates

Key Congestion Measures

Measure	1990	2000	2010	2015	2020
Annual Hours of Delay, Total (000)	70,147	111,210	176,796	236,989	169,765
Annual Hours of Delay, Per Auto Commuter	40	43	55	72	49
Annual Congestion Cost, Per Auto Commuter ($)	819	974	1,231	1,525	1,097

Note: Covers the Houston TX urban area
Source: Texas A&M Transportation Institute, 2021 Urban Mobility Report

Freeway Travel Time Index

Measure	1985	1990	1995	2000	2005	2010	2015	2020
Urban Area Index[1]	1.25	1.22	1.22	1.23	1.28	1.28	1.33	1.15
Urban Area Rank[1,2]	3	5	13	22	14	16	11	4

Note: Freeway Travel Time Index—the ratio of travel time in the peak period to the travel time at free-flow conditions. For example, a value of 1.30 indicates a 20-minute free-flow trip takes 26 minutes in the peak (20 minutes x 1.30 = 26 minutes); (1) Covers the Houston TX urban area; (2) Rank is based on 101 larger urban areas (#1 = highest travel time index)
Source: Texas A&M Transportation Institute, 2021 Urban Mobility Report

Houston, Texas 261

Public Transportation

Agency Name / Mode of Transportation	Vehicles Operated in Maximum Service[1]	Annual Unlinked Passenger Trips[2] (in thous.)	Annual Passenger Miles[3] (in thous.)
Metropolitan Transit Authority of Harris County (METRO)			
Bus (directly operated)	447	26,759.6	149,711.0
Bus (purchased transportation)	122	6,624.8	32,700.3
Bus Rapid Transit (directly operated)	8	231.4	742.6
Commuter Bus (directly operated)	104	1,005.8	19,572.5
Commuter Bus (purchased transportation)	22	302.1	6,425.8
Demand Response (purchased transportation)	322	1,065.4	10,976.7
Demand Response - Taxi	124	172.9	691.0
Light Rail (directly operated)	50	8,476.2	24,921.0
Vanpool (directly operated)	168	276.0	8,735.6

Note: (1) Number of revenue vehicles operated by the given mode and type of service to meet the annual maximum service requirement. This is the revenue vehicle count during the peak season of the year; on the week and day that maximum service is provided. Vehicles operated in maximum service (VOMS) exclude atypical days and one-time special events; (2) Number of passengers who boarded public transportation vehicles. Passengers are counted each time they board a vehicle no matter how many vehicles they use to travel from their origin to their destination. (3) Sum of the distances ridden by all passengers during the entire fiscal year.
Source: Federal Transit Administration, National Transit Database, 2021

Air Transportation

Airport Name and Code / Type of Service	Passenger Airlines[1]	Passenger Enplanements	Freight Carriers[2]	Freight (lbs)
George Bush Intercontinental (IAH)				
Domestic service (U.S. carriers - 2022)	26	15,176,932	19	309,576,727
International service (U.S. carriers - 2021)	9	2,387,150	8	37,583,500
William P. Hobby (HOU)				
Domestic service (U.S. carriers - 2022)	25	6,006,673	2	11,983,847
International service (U.S. carriers - 2021)	3	333,982	1	50,639

Note: (1) Includes all U.S.-based major, minor and commuter airlines that carried at least one passenger during the year; (2) Includes all U.S.-based airlines and freight carriers that transported at least one pound of freight during the year.
Source: Bureau of Transportation Statistics, The Intermodal Transportation Database, Air Carriers: T-100 Domestic Market (U.S. Carriers), 2022; Bureau of Transportation Statistics, The Intermodal Transportation Database, Air Carriers: T-100 International Market (U.S. Carriers), 2021

BUSINESSES

Major Business Headquarters

Company Name	Industry	Fortune[1]	Forbes[2]
APA	Hydrocarbon exploration	431	-
BMC Software	It software & services	-	231
Baker Hughes	Oil and gas equipment, services	170	-
Calpine	Utilities	-	45
CenterPoint Energy	Utilities, gas and electric	414	-
Cheniere Energy	Energy	233	-
ConocoPhillips	Mining, crude-oil production	77	-
EOG Resources	Mining, crude-oil production	193	-
Enterprise Products	Oil and gas	89	-
Fertitta Entertainment	Hotels, restaurants & leisure	-	135
Group 1 Automotive	Automotive retailing, services	273	-
Halliburton	Oil and gas equipment, services	241	-
KBR	Engineering, construction	460	-
Kinder Morgan	Pipelines	223	-
Occidental Petroleum	Mining, crude-oil production	135	-
Phillips 66	Petroleum refining	29	-
Plains GP Holdings	Pipelines	88	-
Quanta Services	Engineering, construction	285	-
Sysco	Wholesalers, food and grocery	70	-
Targa Resources	Pipelines	216	-
Tauber Oil	Oil & gas operations	-	160
The Friedkin Group	Consumer durables	-	42
Waste Management	Waste management	203	-
Westlake	Chemicals	320	-

Note: (1) Companies that produce a 10-K are ranked 1 to 500 based on 2021 revenue; (2) All private companies with at least $2 billion in annual revenue through the end of their most current fiscal year are ranked 1 to 246; companies listed are headquartered in the city; dashes indicate no ranking
Source: Fortune, "Fortune 500," 2022; Forbes, "America's Largest Private Companies," 2022

Fastest-Growing Businesses

According to *Inc.*, Houston is home to four of America's 500 fastest-growing private companies: **Simple Solar** (#44); **Specialty1 Partners** (#72); **Disrupt Equity** (#174); **Construction Concepts** (#497). Criteria: must be an independent, privately-held, for-profit, U.S. corporation, proprietorship or partnership as of December 31, 2021; revenues must be at least $100,000 in 2018 and $2 million in 2021; must have four-year operating/sales history. *Inc., "America's 500 Fastest-Growing Private Companies," 2022*

According to *Initiative for a Competitive Inner City (ICIC)*, Houston is home to four of America's 100 fastest-growing "inner city" companies: **Premier Wireless Business Technology Solutions** (#25); **Classy Art** (#39); **Green Light Safety** (#70); **Corporate Move Consulting** (#81). Criteria for inclusion: company must be headquartered in or have 51 percent or more of its physical operations in an economically distressed urban area; must be an independent, for-profit corporation, partnership or proprietorship; must have 10 or more employees and have a five-year sales history that includes sales of at least $200,000 in the base year and at least $1 million in the current year with no decrease in sales over the two most recent years. Companies were ranked overall by revenue growth over the five-year period between 2017 and 2021. *Initiative for a Competitive Inner City (ICIC), "Inner City 100 Companies," 2022*

According to Deloitte, Houston is home to one of North America's 500 fastest-growing high-technology companies: **Onit** (#372). Companies are ranked by percentage growth in revenue over a four-year period. Criteria for inclusion: company must be headquartered within North America; must own proprietary intellectual property or technology that is sold to customers in products that contributes to a significant portion of the company's operating revenue; must have been in business for a minumum of four years with 2018 operating revenues of at least $50,000 USD/CD and 2021 operating revenues of at least $5 million USD/CD. *Deloitte, 2022 Technology Fast 500*™

Living Environment

COST OF LIVING

Cost of Living Index

Composite Index	Groceries	Housing	Utilities	Transportation	Health Care	Misc. Goods/Services
92.1	94.0	82.2	98.5	94.1	95.4	96.8

Note: The Cost of Living Index measures regional differences in the cost of consumer goods and services, excluding taxes and non-consumer expenditures, for professional and managerial households in the top income quintile. It is based on more than 50,000 prices covering almost 60 different items for which prices are collected three times a year by chambers of commerce, economic development organizations or university applied economic centers in each participating urban area. The numbers shown should be read as a percentage above or below the national average of 100. For example, a value of 115.4 in the groceries column indicates that grocery prices are 15.4% higher than the national average. Small differences in the index numbers should not be interpreted as significant; Figures cover the Houston TX urban area.
Source: The Council for Community and Economic Research, Cost of Living Index, 2022

Grocery Prices

Area[1]	T-Bone Steak ($/pound)	Frying Chicken ($/pound)	Whole Milk ($/half gal.)	Eggs ($/dozen)	Orange Juice ($/64 oz.)	Coffee ($/11.5 oz.)
City[2]	11.65	1.42	2.10	2.00	3.76	4.58
Avg.	13.81	1.59	2.43	2.25	3.85	4.95
Min.	10.17	0.90	1.51	1.30	2.90	3.46
Max.	19.35	3.30	4.32	4.32	5.31	8.59

Note: (1) Values for the local area are compared with the average, minimum and maximum values for all 286 areas in the Cost of Living Index; (2) Figures cover the Houston TX urban area; **T-Bone Steak** (price per pound); **Frying Chicken** (price per pound, whole fryer); **Whole Milk** (half gallon carton); **Eggs** (price per dozen, Grade A, large); **Orange Juice** (64 oz. Tropicana or Florida Natural); **Coffee** (11.5 oz. can, vacuum-packed, Maxwell House, Hills Bros, or Folgers).
Source: The Council for Community and Economic Research, Cost of Living Index, 2022

Housing and Utility Costs

Area[1]	New Home Price ($)	Apartment Rent ($/month)	All Electric ($/month)	Part Electric ($/month)	Other Energy ($/month)	Telephone ($/month)
City[2]	378,106	1,292	-	123.18	45.33	195.79
Avg.	450,913	1,371	176.41	99.93	76.96	190.22
Min.	229,283	546	100.84	31.56	27.15	174.27
Max.	2,434,977	4,569	356.86	249.59	272.24	208.31

Note: (1) Values for the local area are compared with the average, minimum and maximum values for all 286 areas in the Cost of Living Index; (2) Figures cover the Houston TX urban area; **New Home Price** (2,400 sf living area, 8,000 sf lot, in urban area with full utilities); **Apartment Rent** (950 sf 2 bedroom/1.5 or 2 bath, unfurnished, excluding all utilities except water); **All Electric** (average monthly cost for an all-electric home); **Part Electric** (average monthly cost for a part-electric home); **Other Energy** (average monthly cost for natural gas, fuel oil, coal, wood, and any other forms of energy except electricity); **Telephone** (price includes the base monthly rate plus taxes and fees for three lines of mobile phone service).
Source: The Council for Community and Economic Research, Cost of Living Index, 2022

Health Care, Transportation, and Other Costs

Area[1]	Doctor ($/visit)	Dentist ($/visit)	Optometrist ($/visit)	Gasoline ($/gallon)	Beauty Salon ($/visit)	Men's Shirt ($)
City[2]	99.00	115.42	103.21	3.53	64.48	26.78
Avg.	124.91	107.77	117.66	3.86	43.31	34.21
Min.	36.61	58.25	51.79	2.90	22.18	13.05
Max.	250.21	162.58	371.96	5.54	85.61	63.54

Note: (1) Values for the local area are compared with the average, minimum and maximum values for all 286 areas in the Cost of Living Index; (2) Figures cover the Houston TX urban area; **Doctor** (general practitioners routine exam of an established patient); **Dentist** (adult teeth cleaning and periodic oral examination); **Optometrist** (full vision eye exam for established adult patient); **Gasoline** (one gallon regular unleaded, national brand, including all taxes, cash price at self-service pump if available); **Beauty Salon** (woman's shampoo, trim, and blow-dry); **Men's Shirt** (cotton/polyester dress shirt, pinpoint weave, long sleeves).
Source: The Council for Community and Economic Research, Cost of Living Index, 2022

HOUSING

Homeownership Rate

Area	2015 (%)	2016 (%)	2017 (%)	2018 (%)	2019 (%)	2020 (%)	2021 (%)	2022 (%)
MSA[1]	60.3	59.0	58.9	60.1	61.3	65.3	64.1	63.7
U.S.	63.7	63.4	63.9	64.4	64.6	66.6	65.5	65.8

Note: (1) Figures cover the Houston-The Woodlands-Sugar Land, TX Metropolitan Statistical Area
Source: U.S. Census Bureau, Housing Vacancies and Homeownership Annual Statistics: 2015-2022

House Price Index (HPI)

Area	National Ranking[2]	Quarterly Change (%)	One-Year Change (%)	Five-Year Change (%)	Since 1991Q1 (%)
MSA[1]	81	0.53	13.01	46.44	300.24
U.S.[3]	—	0.34	8.41	58.44	289.08

Note: The HPI is a weighted repeat sales index. It measures average price changes in repeat sales or refinancings on the same properties. This information is obtained by reviewing repeat mortgage transactions on single-family properties whose mortgages have been purchased or securitized by Fannie Mae or Freddie Mac since January 1975; (1) Figures cover the Houston-The Woodlands-Sugar Land, TX Metropolitan Statistical Area; (2) Rankings are based on annual percentage change for all metro areas containing at least 15,000 transactions over the last 10 years and ranges from 1 to 257; (3) figures based on a weighted average of Census Division estimates using a seasonally adjusted, purchase-only index; all figures are for the period ending December 31, 2022
Source: Federal Housing Finance Agency, Change in FHFA Metropolitan Area House Price Indexes, 2022Q4

Median Single-Family Home Prices

Area	2020	2021	2022p	Percent Change 2021 to 2022
MSA[1]	263.8	304.1	345.0	13.4
U.S. Average	300.2	357.1	392.6	9.9

Note: Figures are median sales prices of existing single-family homes in thousands of dollars; (p) preliminary; (1) Figures cover the Houston-The Woodlands-Sugar Land, TX Metropolitan Statistical Area
Source: National Association of Realtors, Median Sales Price of Existing Single-Family Homes for Metropolitan Areas, 4th Quarter 2022

Qualifying Income Based on Median Sales Price of Existing Single-Family Homes

Area	With 5% Down ($)	With 10% Down ($)	With 20% Down ($)
MSA[1]	101,094	95,773	85,132
U.S. Average	112,234	106,237	94,513

Note: Figures are preliminary; Qualifying income is based on a mortgage rate of 6.77%. Monthly principal and interest payment is limited to 25% of income; (1) Figures cover the Houston-The Woodlands-Sugar Land, TX Metropolitan Statistical Area
Source: National Association of Realtors, Qualifying Income Based on Median Sales Price of Existing Single-Family Homes for Metropolitan Areas, 4th Quarter 2022

Home Value

Area	Under $100,000	$100,000 -$199,999	$200,000 -$299,999	$300,000 -$399,999	$400,000 -$499,999	$500,000 -$999,999	$1,000,000 or more	Median ($)
City	19.1	30.8	17.1	11.0	6.7	11.3	4.0	200,700
MSA[1]	13.5	30.4	25.4	13.7	6.5	8.0	2.5	221,400
U.S.	16.2	24.2	20.1	13.6	8.3	13.6	4.1	244,900

Note: Figures are percentages except for median and cover owner-occupied housing units; (1) Figures cover the Houston-The Woodlands-Sugar Land, TX Metropolitan Statistical Area
Source: U.S. Census Bureau, 2017-2021 American Community Survey 5-Year Estimates

Year Housing Structure Built

Area	2020 or Later	2010 -2019	2000 -2009	1990 -1999	1980 -1989	1970 -1979	1960 -1969	1950 -1959	1940 -1949	Before 1940	Median Year
City	0.2	11.8	12.7	9.8	14.6	19.6	13.0	10.0	4.2	4.2	1980
MSA[1]	0.4	15.6	20.3	13.9	15.3	15.8	8.1	5.9	2.4	2.4	1990
U.S.	0.2	7.3	13.6	13.6	13.2	14.8	10.3	10.0	4.7	12.2	1979

Note: Figures are percentages except for Median Year; Note: (1) Figures cover the Houston-The Woodlands-Sugar Land, TX Metropolitan Statistical Area
Source: U.S. Census Bureau, 2017-2021 American Community Survey 5-Year Estimates

Gross Monthly Rent

Area	Under $500	$500 -$999	$1,000 -$1,499	$1,500 -$1,999	$2,000 -$2,499	$2,500 -$2,999	$3,000 and up	Median ($)
City	3.4	34.1	38.9	15.8	4.4	1.5	1.8	1,136
MSA[1]	3.3	29.1	39.7	19.2	5.7	1.5	1.6	1,189
U.S.	8.1	30.5	30.8	16.8	7.3	3.1	3.5	1,163

Note: Figures are percentages except for median; Gross rent is the contract rent plus the estimated average monthly cost of utilities (electricity, gas, and water and sewer) and fuels (oil, coal, kerosene, wood, etc.) if these are paid by the renter (or paid for the renter by someone else); (1) Figures cover the Houston-The Woodlands-Sugar Land, TX Metropolitan Statistical Area
Source: U.S. Census Bureau, 2017-2021 American Community Survey 5-Year Estimates

HEALTH

Health Risk Factors

Category	MSA[1] (%)	U.S. (%)
Adults aged 18–64 who have any kind of health care coverage	74.1	90.9
Adults who reported being in good or better health	85.4	85.2
Adults who have been told they have high blood cholesterol	33.4	35.7
Adults who have been told they have high blood pressure	30.0	32.4
Adults who are current smokers	11.3	14.4
Adults who currently use e-cigarettes	6.1	6.7
Adults who currently use chewing tobacco, snuff, or snus	3.2	3.5
Adults who are heavy drinkers[2]	5.7	6.3
Adults who are binge drinkers[3]	16.8	15.4
Adults who are overweight (BMI 25.0 - 29.9)	30.9	34.4
Adults who are obese (BMI 30.0 - 99.8)	32.8	33.9
Adults who participated in any physical activities in the past month	77.6	76.3

Note: (1) Figures cover the Houston-The Woodlands-Sugar Land, TX Metropolitan Statistical Area; (2) Heavy drinkers are classified as adult men having more than 14 drinks per week and adult women having more than 7 drinks per week; (3) Binge drinkers are classified as males having five or more drinks on one occasion or females having four or more drinks on one occasion
Source: Centers for Disease Control and Prevention, Behavioral Risk Factor Surveillance System, SMART: Selected Metropolitan Area Risk Trends, 2021

Acute and Chronic Health Conditions

Category	MSA[1] (%)	U.S. (%)
Adults who have ever been told they had a heart attack	2.0	4.0
Adults who have ever been told they have angina or coronary heart disease	2.3	3.8
Adults who have ever been told they had a stroke	2.8	3.0
Adults who have ever been told they have asthma	10.4	14.9
Adults who have ever been told they have arthritis	17.7	25.8
Adults who have ever been told they have diabetes[2]	10.5	10.9
Adults who have ever been told they had skin cancer	4.6	6.6
Adults who have ever been told they had any other types of cancer	6.2	7.5
Adults who have ever been told they have COPD	4.3	6.1
Adults who have ever been told they have kidney disease	n/a	3.0
Adults who have ever been told they have a form of depression	15.1	20.5

Note: (1) Figures cover the Houston-The Woodlands-Sugar Land, TX Metropolitan Statistical Area; (2) Figures do not include pregnancy-related, borderline, or pre-diabetes
Source: Centers for Disease Control and Prevention, Behavioral Risk Factor Surveillance System, SMART: Selected Metropolitan Area Risk Trends, 2021

Health Screening and Vaccination Rates

Category	MSA[1] (%)	U.S. (%)
Adults who have ever been tested for HIV	45.8	34.9
Adults who have had their blood cholesterol checked within the last five years	84.6	85.2
Adults aged 65+ who have had flu shot within the past year	74.0	68.6
Adults aged 65+ who have ever had a pneumonia vaccination	66.1	71.0

Note: (1) Figures cover the Houston-The Woodlands-Sugar Land, TX Metropolitan Statistical Area.
Source: Centers for Disease Control and Prevention, Behavioral Risk Factor Surveillance System, SMART: Selected Metropolitan Area Risk Trends, 2021

Disability Status

Category	MSA[1] (%)	U.S. (%)
Adults who reported being deaf	4.1	7.2
Are you blind or have serious difficulty seeing, even when wearing glasses?	6.3	4.8
Are you limited in any way in any of your usual activities due to arthritis?	6.1	11.1
Do you have difficulty doing errands alone?	4.8	7.0
Do you have difficulty dressing or bathing?	3.8	3.6
Do you have serious difficulty concentrating/remembering/making decisions?	12.2	12.1
Do you have serious difficulty walking or climbing stairs?	9.8	12.8

Note: (1) Figures cover the Houston-The Woodlands-Sugar Land, TX Metropolitan Statistical Area.
Source: Centers for Disease Control and Prevention, Behavioral Risk Factor Surveillance System, SMART: Selected Metropolitan Area Risk Trends, 2021

Mortality Rates for the Top 10 Causes of Death in the U.S.

ICD-10[a] Sub-Chapter	ICD-10[a] Code	Crude Mortality Rate[1] per 100,000 population County[2]	U.S.
Malignant neoplasms	C00-C97	119.3	182.6
Ischaemic heart diseases	I20-I25	74.6	113.1
Other forms of heart disease	I30-I51	40.4	64.4
Other degenerative diseases of the nervous system	G30-G31	33.5	51.0
Cerebrovascular diseases	I60-I69	34.7	47.8
Other external causes of accidental injury	W00-X59	33.3	46.4
Chronic lower respiratory diseases	J40-J47	20.4	45.7
Organic, including symptomatic, mental disorders	F01-F09	12.2	35.9
Hypertensive diseases	I10-I15	22.9	35.0
Diabetes mellitus	E10-E14	21.1	29.6

Note: (a) ICD-10 = International Classification of Diseases 10th Revision; (1) Crude mortality rates are a three-year average covering 2019-2021; (2) Figures cover Harris County.
Source: Centers for Disease Control and Prevention, National Center for Health Statistics. National Vital Statistics System, Mortality 2018-2021 on CDC WONDER Online Database

Mortality Rates for Selected Causes of Death

ICD-10[a] Sub-Chapter	ICD-10[a] Code	Crude Mortality Rate[1] per 100,000 population County[2]	U.S.
Assault	X85-Y09	11.2	7.0
Diseases of the liver	K70-K76	14.9	19.8
Human immunodeficiency virus (HIV) disease	B20-B24	3.0	1.5
Influenza and pneumonia	J09-J18	9.1	14.7
Intentional self-harm	X60-X84	11.3	14.3
Malnutrition	E40-E46	4.0	4.3
Obesity and other hyperalimentation	E65-E68	2.6	3.0
Renal failure	N17-N19	13.5	15.7
Transport accidents	V01-V99	12.4	13.6
Viral hepatitis	B15-B19	1.0	1.2

Note: (a) ICD-10 = International Classification of Diseases 10th Revision; (1) Crude mortality rates are a three-year average covering 2019-2021; (2) Figures cover Harris County; Data are suppressed when the data meet the criteria for confidentiality constraints; Crude mortality rates are flagged as unreliable when the rate would be calculated with a numerator of 20 or less.
Source: Centers for Disease Control and Prevention, National Center for Health Statistics. National Vital Statistics System, Mortality 2018-2021 on CDC WONDER Online Database

Health Insurance Coverage

Area	With Health Insurance	With Private Health Insurance	With Public Health Insurance	Without Health Insurance	Population Under Age 19 Without Health Insurance
City	76.2	51.7	30.5	23.8	14.5
MSA[1]	81.3	61.6	26.6	18.7	12.3
U.S.	91.2	67.8	35.4	8.8	5.3

Note: Figures are percentages that cover the civilian noninstitutionalized population; (1) Figures cover the Houston-The Woodlands-Sugar Land, TX Metropolitan Statistical Area
Source: U.S. Census Bureau, 2017-2021 American Community Survey 5-Year Estimates

Number of Medical Professionals

Area	MDs[3]	DOs[3,4]	Dentists	Podiatrists	Chiropractors	Optometrists
County[1] (number)	16,506	583	3,486	230	1,093	1,002
County[1] (rate[2])	348.8	12.3	73.7	4.9	23.1	21.2
U.S. (rate[2])	289.3	23.5	72.5	6.2	28.7	17.4

Note: Data as of 2021 unless noted; (1) Data covers Harris County; (2) Rate per 100,000 population; (3) Data as of 2020 and includes all active, non-federal physicians; (4) Doctor of Osteopathic Medicine
Source: U.S. Department of Health and Human Services, Health Resources and Services Administration, Bureau of Health Professions, Area Resource File (ARF) 2021-2022

Best Hospitals

According to *U.S. News*, the Houston-The Woodlands-Sugar Land, TX metro area is home to seven of the best hospitals in the U.S.: **Baylor St. Luke's Medical Center** (6 adult specialties); **Dan L Duncan Comprehensive Cancer Center at Baylor St. Luke's Medical Center** (6 adult specialties); **Houston Methodist Hospital** (Honor Roll/10 adult specialties); **Menninger Clinic** (1 adult specialty); **TIRR Memorial Hermann** (1 adult specialty); **Texas Heart Institute at Baylor St. Luke's Medical Center** (6 adult specialties); **University of Texas MD Anderson Cancer Center** (7 adult specialties and 1 pediatric specialty). The hospitals listed were nationally ranked in at least one of 15 adult or 10 pediatric specialties. The number of specialties shown cover the parent hospital. Only 164 U.S. hospitals performed well enough to be nationally ranked in one or more specialties.

Twenty hospitals in the U.S. made the Honor Roll. The Best Hospitals Honor Roll takes both the national rankings and the procedure and condition ratings into account. Hospitals received points if they were nationally ranked in one of the 15 adult specialties—the higher they ranked, the more points they got—and how many ratings of "high performing" they earned in the 17 procedures and conditions. *U.S. News Online, "America's Best Hospitals 2022-23"*

According to *U.S. News,* the Houston-The Woodlands-Sugar Land, TX metro area is home to two of the best children's hospitals in the U.S.: **Texas Children's Hospital** (Honor Roll/10 pediatric specialties); **Children's Memorial Hermann Hospital** (4 pediatric specialties). The hospitals listed were highly ranked in at least one of 10 pediatric specialties. Eighty-six children's hospitals in the U.S. were nationally ranked in at least one specialty. Hospitals received points for being ranked in a specialty, and the 10 hospitals with the most points across the 10 specialties make up the Honor Roll. *U.S. News Online, "America's Best Children's Hospitals 2022-23"*

EDUCATION

Public School District Statistics

District Name	Schls	Pupils	Pupil/Teacher Ratio	Minority Pupils[1] (%)	LEP/ELL[2] (%)	IEP[3] (%)
Aldine ISD	80	61,633	15.4	98.0	31.5	8.8
Alief ISD	46	40,664	12.8	96.7	40.3	8.7
Cypress-Fairbanks ISD	90	117,217	15.3	78.4	12.8	9.5
Galena Park ISD	25	21,431	15.3	96.6	31.5	9.6
Harmony School of Excellence	9	5,896	14.2	90.0	26.0	6.9
Houston Gateway Academy Inc	3	2,082	19.3	99.4	36.7	3.2
Houston ISD	274	194,607	17.7	90.3	28.6	8.0
Kipp Texas Public Schools	58	32,321	20.4	98.4	33.2	8.3
Sheldon ISD	13	10,570	16.8	95.5	28.0	8.6
Spring Branch ISD	49	33,545	15.3	72.6	30.9	9.2
Spring ISD	42	33,425	15.4	94.5	23.4	9.6
Yes Prep Public Schools Inc	19	14,562	17.0	99.0	24.9	6.4

Note: Table includes school districts with 2,000 or more students; (1) Percentage of students that are not non-Hispanic white; (2) Percentage of students that are Limited English Proficient or English Language Learners (2018-19); (3) Percentage of students that have an Individualized Education Program (2019-20).
Source: U.S. Department of Education, National Center for Education Statistics, Common Core of Data, Local Education Agency (School District) Universe Survey: School Year 2021-2022

Best High Schools

According to *U.S. News,* Houston is home to 18 of the top 500 high schools in the U.S.: **Carnegie Vanguard High School** (#40); **DeBakey High School for Health Professions** (#50); **Eastwood Academy** (#134); **Challenge Early College High School** (#140); **Young Women's College Prep Academy** (#148); **Kerr High School** (#159); **The High School for the Performing and Visual Arts** (#169); **Victory Early College High School** (#183); **YES Prep - Southeast** (#304); **YES Prep - Southwest** (#309); **East Early College High School** (#313); **YES Prep - West** (#346); **YES Prep - North Central** (#357); **Clear Horizons Early College High School** (#403); **North Houston Early College High School** (#409); **Sharpstown International School** (#422); **YES Prep - East End** (#445); **Houston Academy for International Studies** (#483). Nearly 18,000 public, magnet and charter schools were ranked based on their performance on state assessments and how well they prepare students for college. *U.S. News & World Report, "Best High Schools 2022"*

Highest Level of Education

Area	Less than H.S.	H.S. Diploma	Some College, No Deg.	Associate Degree	Bachelor's Degree	Master's Degree	Prof. School Degree	Doctorate Degree
City	20.5	21.6	17.2	6.0	20.9	9.1	3.0	1.8
MSA[1]	15.6	22.7	20.2	7.4	21.6	8.8	2.2	1.5
U.S.	11.1	26.5	20.0	8.7	20.6	9.3	2.2	1.5

Note: Figures cover persons age 25 and over; (1) Figures cover the Houston-The Woodlands-Sugar Land, TX Metropolitan Statistical Area
Source: U.S. Census Bureau, 2017-2021 American Community Survey 5-Year Estimates

Educational Attainment by Race

Area	High School Graduate or Higher (%)					Bachelor's Degree or Higher (%)				
	Total	White	Black	Asian	Hisp.[2]	Total	White	Black	Asian	Hisp.[2]
City	79.5	82.2	89.1	87.1	59.6	34.7	42.7	25.0	62.3	15.5
MSA[1]	84.4	86.6	91.8	87.3	66.4	34.2	36.5	30.0	56.9	16.7
U.S.	88.9	91.4	87.2	87.6	71.2	33.7	35.5	23.3	55.6	18.4

Note: Figures shown cover persons 25 years old and over; (1) Figures cover the Houston-The Woodlands-Sugar Land, TX Metropolitan Statistical Area; (2) People of Hispanic origin can be of any race
Source: U.S. Census Bureau, 2017-2021 American Community Survey 5-Year Estimates

School Enrollment by Grade and Control

Area	Preschool (%) Public	Preschool (%) Private	Kindergarten (%) Public	Kindergarten (%) Private	Grades 1 - 4 (%) Public	Grades 1 - 4 (%) Private	Grades 5 - 8 (%) Public	Grades 5 - 8 (%) Private	Grades 9 - 12 (%) Public	Grades 9 - 12 (%) Private
City	64.5	35.5	89.1	10.9	93.1	6.9	92.0	8.0	92.5	7.5
MSA[1]	56.6	43.4	88.9	11.1	92.0	8.0	92.4	7.6	92.5	7.5
U.S.	58.8	41.2	86.3	13.7	88.3	11.7	88.6	11.4	89.4	10.6

Note: Figures shown cover persons 3 years old and over; (1) Figures cover the Houston-The Woodlands-Sugar Land, TX Metropolitan Statistical Area
Source: U.S. Census Bureau, 2017-2021 American Community Survey 5-Year Estimates

Higher Education

Four-Year Colleges Public	Four-Year Colleges Private Non-profit	Four-Year Colleges Private For-profit	Two-Year Colleges Public	Two-Year Colleges Private Non-profit	Two-Year Colleges Private For-profit	Medical Schools[1]	Law Schools[2]	Voc/Tech[3]
13	11	6	3	3	17	5	3	26

Note: Figures cover institutions located within the Houston-The Woodlands-Sugar Land, TX Metropolitan Statistical Area and include main campuses only; (1) includes schools accredited by the Liaison Committee on Medical Education and the American Osteopathic Association's Commission on Osteopathic College Accreditation; (2) includes ABA-accredited schools, schools with provisional ABA accreditation, and state accredited schools; (3) includes all schools with programs that are less than 2 years.
Source: National Center for Education Statistics, Integrated Postsecondary Education System (IPEDS), 2021-22; Wikipedia, List of Medical Schools in the United States, accessed April 10, 2023; Wikipedia, List of Law Schools in the United States, accessed April 10, 2023

According to *U.S. News & World Report*, the Houston-The Woodlands-Sugar Land, TX metro area is home to two of the top 200 national universities in the U.S.: **Rice University** (#15 tie); **University of Houston** (#182 tie). The indicators used to capture academic quality fall into a number of categories: assessment by administrators at peer institutions; retention of students; faculty resources; student selectivity; financial resources; alumni giving; high school counselor ratings of colleges; and graduation rate. *U.S. News & World Report, "America's Best Colleges 2023"*

According to *U.S. News & World Report*, the Houston-The Woodlands-Sugar Land, TX metro area is home to one of the top 100 law schools in the U.S.: **University of Houston Law Center** (#58 tie). The rankings are based on a weighted average of 12 measures of quality: peer assessment score; assessment score by lawyers/judges; median LSAT scores; median undergrad GPA; acceptance rate; employment rates for graduates; placement success; bar passage rate; faculty resources; expenditures per student; student/faculty ratio; and library resources. *U.S. News & World Report, "America's Best Graduate Schools, Law, 2023"*

According to *U.S. News & World Report*, the Houston-The Woodlands-Sugar Land, TX metro area is home to two of the top 75 medical schools for research in the U.S.: **Baylor College of Medicine** (#22 tie); **University of Texas Health Science Center—Houston (McGovern)** (#53 tie). The rankings are based on a weighted average of 11 measures of quality: quality assessment; peer assessment score; assessment score by residency directors; research activity; total research activity; average research activity per faculty member; student selectivity; median MCAT total score; median undergraduate GPA; acceptance rate; and faculty resources. *U.S. News & World Report, "America's Best Graduate Schools, Medical, 2023"*

According to *U.S. News & World Report*, the Houston-The Woodlands-Sugar Land, TX metro area is home to one of the top 75 business schools in the U.S.: **Rice University (Jones)** (#27). The rankings are based on a weighted average of the following nine measures: quality assessment; peer assessment; recruiter assessment; placement success; mean starting salary and bonus; student selectivity; mean GMAT and GRE scores; mean undergraduate GPA; and acceptance rate. *U.S. News & World Report, "America's Best Graduate Schools, Business, 2023"*

EMPLOYERS

Major Employers

Company Name	Industry
Christus Health Gulf Coast	Management consulting services
Conoco Phillips	Petroleum refining
Continental Airlines	Air transportation, scheduled
Dibellos Dynamic Orthotics & Prosthetics	Surgical appliances & supplies
El Paso E&P Company	Petroleum refining
F Charles Brunicardi MD	Accounting, auditing, & bookkeeping
Grey Wolf	Drilling oil & gas wells
Kellogg Brown &Root	Industrial plant construction
Mustang Engineers and Constructors	Construction management consultant
Philip Industrial Services	Environmental consultant
Philips Petroleum Company	Oil & gas exploration services
Quaker State Corp	Lubricating oils & greases
St. Lukes Episcopal Health System	General medical & surgical hospitals
Texas Childrens Hospital	Specialty hospitals, except psychiatric
The Methodist Hospital	General medical & surgical hospitals
Tracer Industries	Plumbing
U.S. Dept of Veteran Affairs	Administration of veterans' affairs
Univ of Texas Medical Branch at Galveston	Accident & health insurance
University of Houston System	University
University of Texas System	General medical & surgical hospitals
Veterans Health Administration	Administration of veterans' affairs

Note: Companies shown are located within the Houston-The Woodlands-Sugar Land, TX Metropolitan Statistical Area.
Source: Hoovers.com; Wikipedia

Best Companies to Work For

Camden Property Trust; David Weekley Homes; Hewlett Packard Enterprise Company; Hilcorp Energy Company, headquartered in Houston, are among "The 100 Best Companies to Work For." To pick the best companies, *Fortune* partnered with the Great Place to Work Institute. Two-thirds of a company's score is based on the results of the Institute's Trust Index survey, which is sent to a random sample of employees from each company. The questions related to attitudes about management's credibility, job satisfaction, and camaraderie. The other third of the scoring is based on the company's responses to the Institute's Culture Audit, which includes detailed questions about pay and benefit programs, and a series of open-ended questions about hiring practices, internal communication, training, recognition programs, and diversity efforts. Any company that is at least five years old with more than 1,000 U.S. employees is eligible. *Fortune, "The 100 Best Companies to Work For," 2023*

Cornerstone Home Lending; David Weekley Homes, headquartered in Houston, are among "Fortune's Best Workplaces for Women." To pick the best companies, *Fortune* partnered with the Great Place to Work Institute. To be considered for the list, companies must be Great Place To Work-Certified. Companies must also employ at least 50 women, at least 20% of their non-executive managers must be female, and at least one executive must be female. To determine the Best Workplaces for Women, Great Place To Work measured the differences in women's survey responses to those of their peers and assesses the impact of demographics and roles on the quality and consistency of women's experiences. Great Place To Work also analyzed the gender balance of each workplace, how it compared to each company's industry, and patterns in representation as women rise from front-line positions to the board of directors. *Fortune, "Best Workplaces for Women," 2022*

Hewlett Packard Enterprise Company, headquartered in Houston, is among "Fortune's Best Workplaces for Parents." To pick the best companies, *Fortune* partnered with the Great Place to Work Institute. To be considered for the list, companies must be Great Place To Work-Certified and have at least 50 responses from parents in the US. The survey enables employees to share confidential quantitative and qualitative feedback about their organization's culture by responding to 60 statements on a 5-point scale and answering two open-ended questions. Collectively, these statements describe a great employee experience, defined by high levels of trust, respect, credibility, fairness, pride, and camaraderie. In addition, companies provide organizational data like size, location, industry, demographics, roles, and levels; and provide information about parental leave, adoption, flexible schedule, childcare and dependent health care benefits. *Fortune, "Best Workplaces for Parents," 2022*

PUBLIC SAFETY

Crime Rate

Area	Total Crime	Violent Crime Rate				Property Crime Rate		
		Murder	Rape[3]	Robbery	Aggrav. Assault	Burglary	Larceny-Theft	Motor Vehicle Theft
City	5,435.1	17.0	48.5	373.2	817.5	672.9	2,875.9	630.0
Suburbs[1]	2,188.3	5.4	42.8	68.3	212.3	270.6	1,338.7	250.2
Metro[2]	3,249.2	9.2	44.7	167.9	410.0	402.1	1,841.0	374.3
U.S.	2,356.7	6.5	38.4	73.9	279.7	314.2	1,398.0	246.0

Note: Figures are crimes per 100,000 population; (1) All areas within the metro area that are located outside the city limits; (2) Figures cover the Houston-The Woodlands-Sugar Land, TX Metropolitan Statistical Area; (3) All figures shown were reported using the revised Uniform Crime Reporting (UCR) definition of rape; Due to the transition to the National Incident-Based Reporting System (NIBRS), limited city and metro area data was released for 2021.
Source: FBI Uniform Crime Reports, 2020

Hate Crimes

Area	Number of Quarters Reported	Number of Incidents per Bias Motivation					
		Race/Ethnicity/Ancestry	Religion	Sexual Orientation	Disability	Gender	Gender Identity
City	4	31	1	8	0	0	3
U.S.	4	5,227	1,244	1,110	130	75	266

Note: Due to the transition to the National Incident-Based Reporting System (NIBRS), limited crime data was released for 2021.
Source: Federal Bureau of Investigation, Hate Crime Statistics 2020

Identity Theft Consumer Reports

Area	Reports	Reports per 100,000 Population	Rank[2]
MSA[1]	45,408	651	6
U.S.	1,108,609	339	-

Note: (1) Figures cover the Houston-The Woodlands-Sugar Land, TX Metropolitan Statistical Area; (2) Rank ranges from 1 to 391 where 1 indicates greatest number of identity theft reports per 100,000 population
Source: Federal Trade Commission, Consumer Sentinel Network Data Book 2022

Fraud and Other Consumer Reports

Area	Reports	Reports per 100,000 Population	Rank[2]
MSA[1]	87,472	1,253	38
U.S.	4,064,520	1,245	-

Note: (1) Figures cover the Houston-The Woodlands-Sugar Land, TX Metropolitan Statistical Area; (2) Rank ranges from 1 to 391 where 1 indicates greatest number of fraud and other consumer reports per 100,000 population
Source: Federal Trade Commission, Consumer Sentinel Network Data Book 2022

POLITICS

2020 Presidential Election Results

Area	Biden	Trump	Jorgensen	Hawkins	Other
Harris County	55.9	42.7	1.0	0.3	0.0
U.S.	51.3	46.8	1.2	0.3	0.5

Note: Results are percentages and may not add to 100% due to rounding
Source: Dave Leip's Atlas of U.S. Presidential Elections

SPORTS

Professional Sports Teams

Team Name	League	Year Established
Houston Astros	Major League Baseball (MLB)	1962
Houston Dynamo	Major League Soccer (MLS)	2006
Houston Rockets	National Basketball Association (NBA)	1971
Houston Texans	National Football League (NFL)	2002

Note: Includes teams located in the Houston-The Woodlands-Sugar Land, TX Metropolitan Statistical Area.
Source: Wikipedia, Major Professional Sports Teams of the United States and Canada, April 12, 2023

CLIMATE

Average and Extreme Temperatures

Temperature	Jan	Feb	Mar	Apr	May	Jun	Jul	Aug	Sep	Oct	Nov	Dec	Yr.
Extreme High (°F)	84	91	91	95	97	103	104	107	102	94	89	83	107
Average High (°F)	61	65	73	79	85	91	93	93	89	81	72	65	79
Average Temp. (°F)	51	54	62	69	75	81	83	83	79	70	61	54	69
Average Low (°F)	41	43	51	58	65	71	73	73	68	58	50	43	58
Extreme Low (°F)	12	20	22	31	44	52	62	62	48	32	19	7	7

Note: Figures cover the years 1969-1990
Source: National Climatic Data Center, International Station Meteorological Climate Summary, 9/96

Average Precipitation/Snowfall/Humidity

Precip./Humidity	Jan	Feb	Mar	Apr	May	Jun	Jul	Aug	Sep	Oct	Nov	Dec	Yr.
Avg. Precip. (in.)	3.3	2.7	3.3	3.3	5.6	4.9	3.7	3.7	4.8	4.7	3.7	3.3	46.9
Avg. Snowfall (in.)	Tr	Tr	0	0	0	0	0	0	0	0	Tr	Tr	Tr
Avg. Rel. Hum. 6am (%)	85	86	87	89	91	92	93	93	93	91	89	86	90
Avg. Rel. Hum. 3pm (%)	58	55	54	54	57	56	55	55	57	53	55	57	55

Note: Figures cover the years 1969-1990; Tr = Trace amounts (<0.05 in. of rain; <0.5 in. of snow)
Source: National Climatic Data Center, International Station Meteorological Climate Summary, 9/96

Weather Conditions

Temperature			Daytime Sky			Precipitation		
32°F & below	45°F & below	90°F & above	Clear	Partly cloudy	Cloudy	0.01 inch or more precip.	0.1 inch or more snow/ice	Thunderstorms
21	87	96	83	167	115	101	1	62

Note: Figures are average number of days per year and cover the years 1969-1990
Source: National Climatic Data Center, International Station Meteorological Climate Summary, 9/96

HAZARDOUS WASTE

Superfund Sites

The Houston-The Woodlands-Sugar Land, TX metro area is home to 18 sites on the EPA's Superfund National Priorities List: **Conroe Creosoting Co.** (final); **Crystal Chemical Co.** (final); **French, Ltd.** (final); **Geneva Industries/Fuhrmann Energy** (final); **Gulfco Marine Maintenance** (final); **Highlands Acid Pit** (final); **Jones Road Ground Water Plume** (final); **Malone Service Co - Swan Lake Plant** (final); **Many Diversified Interests, Inc.** (final); **Motco, Inc.** (final); **North Cavalcade Street** (final); **Patrick Bayou** (final); **Petro-Chemical Systems, Inc. (Turtle Bayou)** (final); **San Jacinto River Waste Pits** (final); **Sheridan Disposal Services** (final); **Sikes Disposal Pits** (final); **Sol Lynn/Industrial Transformers** (final); **South Cavalcade Street** (final). There are a total of 1,165 Superfund sites with a status of proposed or final on the list in the U.S. *U.S. Environmental Protection Agency, National Priorities List, April 12, 2023*

AIR QUALITY

Air Quality Trends: Ozone

	1990	1995	2000	2005	2010	2015	2018	2019	2020	2021
MSA[1]	0.119	0.114	0.102	0.087	0.079	0.083	0.073	0.074	0.067	0.072
U.S.	0.087	0.089	0.081	0.080	0.072	0.067	0.069	0.065	0.065	0.067

Note: (1) Data covers the Houston-The Woodlands-Sugar Land, TX Metropolitan Statistical Area. The values shown are the composite ozone concentration averages among trend sites based on the highest fourth daily maximum 8-hour concentration in parts per million. These trends are based on sites having an adequate record of monitoring data during the trend period. Data from exceptional events are included.
Source: U.S. Environmental Protection Agency, Air Quality Monitoring Information, "Air Quality Trends by City, 1990-2021"

Air Quality Index

Area	Percent of Days when Air Quality was...[2]					AQI Statistics[2]	
	Good	Moderate	Unhealthy for Sensitive Groups	Unhealthy	Very Unhealthy	Maximum	Median
MSA[1]	38.6	53.2	5.8	2.5	0.0	179	54

Note: (1) Data covers the Houston-The Woodlands-Sugar Land, TX Metropolitan Statistical Area; (2) Based on 365 days with AQI data in 2021. Air Quality Index (AQI) is an index for reporting daily air quality. EPA calculates the AQI for five major air pollutants regulated by the Clean Air Act: ground-level ozone, particle pollution (aka particulate matter), carbon monoxide, sulfur dioxide, and nitrogen dioxide. The AQI runs from 0 to 500. The higher the AQI value, the greater the level of air pollution and the greater the health concern. There are six AQI categories: "Good" AQI is between 0 and 50. Air quality is considered satisfactory; "Moderate" AQI is between 51 and 100. Air quality is acceptable; "Unhealthy for Sensitive Groups" When AQI values are between 101 and 150, members of sensitive groups may experience health effects; "Unhealthy" When AQI values are between 151 and 200 everyone may begin to experience health effects; "Very Unhealthy" AQI values between 201 and 300 trigger a health alert; "Hazardous" AQI values over 300 trigger warnings of emergency conditions (not shown).
Source: U.S. Environmental Protection Agency, Air Quality Index Report, 2021

Air Quality Index Pollutants

Area	Carbon Monoxide	Nitrogen Dioxide	Ozone	Sulfur Dioxide	Particulate Matter 2.5	Particulate Matter 10
MSA[1]	0.0	0.8	38.9	(3)	55.3	4.9

Percent of Days when AQI Pollutant was...[2]

Note: (1) Data covers the Houston-The Woodlands-Sugar Land, TX Metropolitan Statistical Area; (2) Based on 365 days with AQI data in 2021. The Air Quality Index (AQI) is an index for reporting daily air quality. EPA calculates the AQI for five major air pollutants regulated by the Clean Air Act: ground-level ozone, particle pollution (also known as particulate matter), carbon monoxide, sulfur dioxide, and nitrogen dioxide. The AQI runs from 0 to 500. The higher the AQI value, the greater the level of air pollution and the greater the health concern; (3) Sulfur dioxide is no longer included in this table (as of December 8, 2021) because SO_2 concentrations tend to be very localized and not necessarily representative of broad geographical areas like counties and CBSAs.
Source: U.S. Environmental Protection Agency, Air Quality Index Report, 2021

Maximum Air Pollutant Concentrations: Particulate Matter, Ozone, CO and Lead

	Particulate Matter 10 (ug/m³)	Particulate Matter 2.5 Wtd AM (ug/m³)	Particulate Matter 2.5 24-Hr (ug/m³)	Ozone (ppm)	Carbon Monoxide (ppm)	Lead (ug/m³)
MSA[1] Level	103	11.4	24	0.083	2	n/a
NAAQS[2]	150	15	35	0.075	9	0.15
Met NAAQS[2]	Yes	Yes	Yes	No	Yes	n/a

Note: (1) Data covers the Houston-The Woodlands-Sugar Land, TX Metropolitan Statistical Area; Data from exceptional events are included; (2) National Ambient Air Quality Standards; ppm = parts per million; ug/m³ = micrograms per cubic meter; n/a not available.
Concentrations: Particulate Matter 10 (coarse particulate)—highest second maximum 24-hour concentration; Particulate Matter 2.5 Wtd AM (fine particulate)—highest weighted annual mean concentration; Particulate Matter 2.5 24-Hour (fine particulate)—highest 98th percentile 24-hour concentration; Ozone—highest fourth daily maximum 8-hour concentration; Carbon Monoxide—highest second maximum non-overlapping 8-hour concentration; Lead—maximum running 3-month average
Source: U.S. Environmental Protection Agency, Air Quality Monitoring Information, "Air Quality Statistics by City, 2021"

Maximum Air Pollutant Concentrations: Nitrogen Dioxide and Sulfur Dioxide

	Nitrogen Dioxide AM (ppb)	Nitrogen Dioxide 1-Hr (ppb)	Sulfur Dioxide AM (ppb)	Sulfur Dioxide 1-Hr (ppb)	Sulfur Dioxide 24-Hr (ppb)
MSA[1] Level	12	49	n/a	16	n/a
NAAQS[2]	53	100	30	75	140
Met NAAQS[2]	Yes	Yes	n/a	Yes	n/a

Note: (1) Data covers the Houston-The Woodlands-Sugar Land, TX Metropolitan Statistical Area; Data from exceptional events are included; (2) National Ambient Air Quality Standards; ppm = parts per million; ug/m³ = micrograms per cubic meter; n/a not available.
Concentrations: Nitrogen Dioxide AM—highest arithmetic mean concentration; Nitrogen Dioxide 1-Hr—highest 98th percentile 1-hour daily maximum concentration; Sulfur Dioxide AM—highest annual mean concentration; Sulfur Dioxide 1-Hr—highest 99th percentile 1-hour daily maximum concentration; Sulfur Dioxide 24-Hr—highest second maximum 24-hour concentration
Source: U.S. Environmental Protection Agency, Air Quality Monitoring Information, "Air Quality Statistics by City, 2021"

Huntsville, Alabama

Background

Huntsville is richly evocative of the antebellum Deep South. It is also a uniquely cosmopolitan town that remains one of the South's fastest growing, with the highest per capita income in the Southeast.

Huntsville is the seat of Madison County, named for President James Madison. Originally home to Cherokee and Chickasaw Indians, Huntsville was rich in forests and game animals. The town is named for John Hunt, a Virginia Revolutionary War veteran who built a cabin in 1805 on the corner of today's Bank Street and Oak Avenue.

The fertility of the valley attracted both smaller farmers and wealthy plantation investors. Leroy Pope, having donated land to the municipality, wanted to rename it Twickenham, after a London suburb home to his kin, poet Alexander Pope, but resentment against all things British, prevented it.

Huntsville was the largest town in the Alabama Territory by 1819, the year Alabama received statehood. It was the site of the state's first constitutional convention and, briefly, the capital. It quickly became a hub for processing corn, tobacco, and cotton, which became its economic mainstay. In 1852, the Memphis and Charleston Railway was completed, and planters, merchants, and shippers transformed Huntsville into a main commercial southern city.

Because many wealthy residents had remained loyal to the Union at the outset of the Civil War, the town was largely undamaged by occupying forces and, as a result, Huntsville boasts one of the largest collections of antebellum houses in the South. Walking tours of the Twickenham historic district offer the 1819 Weeden House Museum and the 1860 Huntsville Depot Museum. Restored nineteenth-century cabins and farm buildings are displayed at the mountaintop Burritt Museum and Park.

Huntsville's U.S. Space and Rocket Center, the state's largest tourist attraction, showcases space technology and houses Space Camp, opportunities for children and adults that promote science, engineering, aviation, and exploration. The Huntsville Botanical Garden features year-long floral and aquatic gardens, and the Huntsville Museum of Art features both contemporary and classical exhibits.

In 2021, the Singing River Trail project, proposed as a 70-mile, 3-county hiking and biking trail, joined forces with the Tennessee RiverLine project, resulting in a 150-mile, 8-county system of hiking, biking, and on-water experience along the Tennessee River. Also in 2021 Huntsville saw the opening of a new Mazda Toyota manufacturing facility, which employs close to 4,000.

The city's modern Von Braun Center hosts national and international trade shows, local sports teams, concerts, and theater, and the city has a well-regarded symphony orchestra.

More than 25 biotechnology firms are in the city due to the Huntsville Biotech Initiative. The HudsonAlpha Institute for Biotechnology is the centerpiece of the Cummings Research Park Biotech Campus, and contributes genomics and genetics work to the Encyclopedia of DNA Elements (ENCODE). The University of Alabama in Huntsville's (UAH) doctoral program in biotechnology supports HudsonAlpha and the emerging biotechnology economy in Huntsville

Huntsville's institutions of higher learning include a campus of the University of Alabama, Oakwood College, and Alabama A&M University in nearby Normal, Alabama.

Redstone Arsenal, home to U.S. Army Aviation and Missile Command, propelled Huntsville into a high-tech hub, and is a strategic research site for rocketry, aviation, and related programs. In 1950, German rocket scientists, most notably the famous Wernher von Braun developed rockets for the U.S. Army here. The Redstone complex developed the rocket that launched America's first satellite into space, and rockets that put astronauts into space and landed them on the moon.

Huntsville enjoys a mild, temperate climate. Only four to five weeks during the middle of winter see temperatures below freezing. Huntsville has now gone about 15 years without significant snowfall. Rainfall is abundant.

Rankings

General Rankings

- *US News & World Report* conducted a survey of more than 3,600 people and analyzed the 150 largest metropolitan areas to determine what matters most when selecting where to settle down. Huntsville ranked #1 out of the top 25 as having the best combination of desirable factors. Criteria: cost of living; quality of life and education; net migration; job market; desirability; and other factors. *money.usnews.com, "The 25 Best Places to Live in the U.S. in 2022-2023," May 17, 2022*

- In their ninth annual survey, Livability.com looked at data for more than 2,300 mid-sized U.S. cities to determine the rankings for Livability's "Top 100 Best Places to Live" in 2022. Huntsville ranked #84. Criteria: housing and economy; social and civic engagement; education; demographics; health care options; transportation & infrastructure; and community amenities. *Livability.com, "Top 100 Best Places to Live 2022" July 19, 2022*

Business/Finance Rankings

- *24/7 Wall St.* used metro data from the Bureau of Labor Statistics' Occupational Employment database to identify the cities with the highest percentage of those employed in jobs requiring knowledge in the science, technology, engineering, and math (STEM) fields as well as average wages for STEM jobs. The Huntsville metro area was #3. *247wallst.com, "15 Cities with the Most High-Tech Jobs," January 11, 2020*

- The Huntsville metro area appeared on the Milken Institute "2022 Best Performing Cities" list. Rank: #12 out of 200 large metro areas (population over 250,000). Criteria: job growth; wage and salary growth; high-tech output growth; housing affordability; household broadband access. *Milken Institute, "Best-Performing Cities 2022," March 28, 2022*

- *Forbes* ranked the 200 most populous metro areas to determine the nation's "Best Places for Business and Careers." The Huntsville metro area was ranked #93. Criteria: costs (business and living); job growth (past and projected); income growth; quality of life; educational attainment (college and high school); projected economic growth; cultural and leisure opportunities; workplace tolerance laws; net migration patterns. *Forbes, "The Best Places for Business and Careers 2019: Seattle Still On Top," October 30, 2019*

Education Rankings

- Personal finance website *WalletHub* analyzed the 150 largest U.S. metropolitan statistical areas to determine where the most educated Americans are putting their degrees to work. Criteria: education levels; percentage of workers with degrees; education quality and attainment gap; public school quality rankings; quality and enrollment of each metro area's universities. Huntsville was ranked #21 (#1 = most educated city). *www.WalletHub.com, "Most & Least Educated Cities in America," July 18, 2022*

Environmental Rankings

- Huntsville was highlighted as one of the top 59 cleanest metro areas for short-term particle pollution (24-hour PM 2.5) in the U.S. during 2019 through 2021. Monitors in these cities reported no days with unhealthful PM 2.5 levels. *American Lung Association, "State of the Air 2023," April 19, 2023*

Real Estate Rankings

- *WalletHub* compared the most populated U.S. cities to determine which had the best markets for real estate agents. Huntsville ranked #8 where demand was high and pay was the best. Criteria: sales per agent; annual median wage for real-estate agents; monthly average starting salary for real estate agents; real estate job density and competition; unemployment rate; home turnover rate; housing-market health index; and other relevant metrics. *www.WalletHub.com, "2021 Best Places to Be a Real Estate Agent," May 12, 2021*

Safety Rankings

- Allstate ranked the 200 largest cities in America in terms of driver safety. Huntsville ranked #3. Criteria: internal property damage claims over a two-year period from January 2016 to December 2017. The report helps increase the importance of safety and awareness behind the wheel. *Allstate, "Allstate America's Best Drivers Report, 2019" June 24, 2019*

- Huntsville was identified as one of the most dangerous cities in America by NeighborhoodScout. The city ranked #84 out of 100 (#1 = most dangerous). Criteria: number of violent crimes per 1,000 residents. The editors evaluated cities with 25,000 or more residents. *NeighborhoodScout.com, "2023 Top 100 Most Dangerous Cities in the U.S.," January 12, 2023*

- The National Insurance Crime Bureau ranked 390 metro areas in the U.S. in terms of per capita rates of vehicle theft. The Huntsville metro area ranked #191 (#1 = highest rate). Criteria: number of vehicle theft offenses per 100,000 inhabitants in 2021. *National Insurance Crime Bureau, "Hot Spots 2021," September 1, 2022*

Seniors/Retirement Rankings

- From its Best Cities for Successful Aging indexes, the Milken Institute generated rankings for metropolitan areas, weighing data in nine categories—health care, wellness, living arrangements, transportation and convenience, financial characteristics, education, employment, community engagement, and overall livability. The Huntsville metro area was ranked #207 overall in the small metro area category. *Milken Institute, "Best Cities for Successful Aging, 2017" March 14, 2017*

Women/Minorities Rankings

- Personal finance website *WalletHub* compared more than 180 U.S. cities across two key dimensions, "Hispanic Business-Friendliness" and "Hispanic Purchasing Power," to arrive at the most favorable conditions for Hispanic entrepreneurs. Huntsville was ranked #128 out of 182. Criteria includes: share of Hispanic-Owned Businesses; Hispanic entrepreneurship rate to median annual income of Hispanics; Small Business-Friendliness score; cost of living; and number of Hispanics with at least a bachelor's degree. *WalletHub.com, "2019's Best Cities for Hispanic Entrepreneurs," May 1, 2019*

Business Environment

DEMOGRAPHICS

Population Growth

Area	1990 Census	2000 Census	2010 Census	2020 Census	Population Growth (%) 1990-2020	Population Growth (%) 2010-2020
City	161,842	158,216	180,105	215,006	32.8	19.4
MSA[1]	293,047	342,376	417,593	491,723	67.8	17.8
U.S.	248,709,873	281,421,906	308,745,538	331,449,281	33.3	7.4

Note: (1) Figures cover the Huntsville, AL Metropolitan Statistical Area
Source: U.S. Census Bureau, 1990 Census, 2000 Census, 2010 Census, 2020 Census

Race

Area	White Alone[2] (%)	Black Alone[2] (%)	Asian Alone[2] (%)	AIAN[3] Alone[2] (%)	NHOPI[4] Alone[2] (%)	Other Race Alone[2] (%)	Two or More Races (%)
City	56.6	29.3	2.5	0.7	0.1	3.4	7.3
MSA[1]	65.0	21.4	2.5	0.7	0.1	2.9	7.3
U.S.	61.6	12.4	6.0	1.1	0.2	8.4	10.2

Note: (1) Figures cover the Huntsville, AL Metropolitan Statistical Area; (2) Alone is defined as not being in combination with one or more other races; (3) American Indian and Alaska Native; (4) Native Hawaiian and Other Pacific Islander
Source: U.S. Census Bureau, 2020 Census

Hispanic or Latino Origin

Area	Total (%)	Mexican (%)	Puerto Rican (%)	Cuban (%)	Other (%)
City	6.4	3.6	1.1	0.2	1.6
MSA[1]	5.4	3.2	0.8	0.1	1.3
U.S.	18.4	11.2	1.8	0.7	4.7

Note: Persons of Hispanic or Latino origin can be of any race; (1) Figures cover the Huntsville, AL Metropolitan Statistical Area
Source: U.S. Census Bureau, 2017-2021 American Community Survey 5-Year Estimates

Age

Area	Under Age 5	Age 5–19	Age 20–34	Age 35–44	Age 45–54	Age 55–64	Age 65–74	Age 75–84	Age 85+	Median Age
City	5.6	17.7	24.2	12.0	11.2	13.1	9.0	5.2	2.2	36.9
MSA[1]	5.6	19.2	20.4	12.6	12.8	13.9	9.1	4.7	1.7	38.7
U.S.	5.6	19.2	20.2	12.7	12.4	13.1	10.0	4.9	1.9	38.8

Note: (1) Figures cover the Huntsville, AL Metropolitan Statistical Area
Source: U.S. Census Bureau, 2020 Census

Disability by Age

Area	All Ages	Under 18 Years Old	18 to 64 Years Old	65 Years and Over
City	13.5	4.4	11.3	33.7
MSA[1]	13.1	4.0	11.1	35.4
U.S.	12.6	4.4	10.3	33.4

Note: Figures show percent of the civilian noninstitutionalized population that reported having a disability. Disability status is determined from six types of difficulty: vision, hearing, cognitive, ambulatory, self-care, and independent living. For children under 5 years old, hearing and vision difficulty are used to determine disability status. For children between the ages of 5 and 14, disability status is determined from hearing, vision, cognitive, ambulatory, and self-care difficulties. For people aged 15 years and older, they are considered to have a disability if they have difficulty with any one of the six difficulty types; Note: (1) Figures cover the Huntsville, AL Metropolitan Statistical Area
Source: U.S. Census Bureau, 2017-2021 American Community Survey 5-Year Estimates

Ancestry

Area	German	Irish	English	American	Italian	Polish	French[2]	Scottish	Dutch
City	9.4	8.9	10.6	10.2	2.3	1.2	1.8	1.9	0.9
MSA[1]	8.9	9.5	11.1	11.7	2.2	1.3	1.6	1.9	0.8
U.S.	12.8	9.6	8.1	5.7	5.0	2.7	2.2	1.6	1.1

Note: Figures are the percentage of the total population reporting a particular ancestry. The nine most commonly reported ancestries in the U.S. are shown. Figures include multiple ancestries (e.g. if a person reported being Irish and Italian, they were included in both columns); (1) Figures cover the Huntsville, AL Metropolitan Statistical Area; (2) Excludes Basque
Source: U.S. Census Bureau, 2017-2021 American Community Survey 5-Year Estimates

Foreign-born Population

Area	Any Foreign Country	Asia	Mexico	Europe	Caribbean	Central America[2]	South America	Africa	Canada
City	6.4	1.9	1.5	0.8	0.3	0.5	0.3	0.7	0.1
MSA[1]	5.2	1.9	1.0	0.7	0.2	0.4	0.3	0.4	0.1
U.S.	13.6	4.2	3.3	1.5	1.4	1.1	1.1	0.8	0.2

Note: (1) Figures cover the Huntsville, AL Metropolitan Statistical Area; (2) Excludes Mexico.
Source: U.S. Census Bureau, 2017-2021 American Community Survey 5-Year Estimates

Household Size

Area	One	Two	Three	Four	Five	Six	Seven or More	Average Household Size
City	36.7	34.9	14.5	8.6	4.0	0.9	0.5	2.20
MSA[1]	29.4	36.1	15.3	12.0	5.0	1.6	0.6	2.40
U.S.	28.1	33.8	15.5	12.9	6.0	2.3	1.4	2.60

Note: (1) Figures cover the Huntsville, AL Metropolitan Statistical Area
Source: U.S. Census Bureau, 2017-2021 American Community Survey 5-Year Estimates

Household Relationships

Area	Householder	Opposite-sex Spouse	Same-sex Spouse	Opposite-sex Unmarried Partner	Same-sex Unmarried Partner	Child[2]	Grandchild	Other Relatives	Non-relatives
City	42.8	16.5	0.2	2.2	0.2	25.1	2.1	3.5	3.1
MSA[1]	40.1	19.3	0.1	1.9	0.1	27.8	2.3	3.4	2.3
U.S.	38.3	17.5	0.2	2.5	0.2	28.3	2.4	4.8	3.4

Note: Figures are percent of the total population; (1) Figures cover the Huntsville, AL Metropolitan Statistical Area; (2) Includes biological, adopted, and stepchildren of the householder
Source: U.S. Census Bureau, 2020 Census

Gender

Area	Males	Females	Males per 100 Females
City	104,200	110,806	94.0
MSA[1]	241,092	250,631	96.2
U.S.	162,685,811	168,763,470	96.4

Note: (1) Figures cover the Huntsville, AL Metropolitan Statistical Area
Source: U.S. Census Bureau, 2020 Census

Marital Status

Area	Never Married	Now Married[2]	Separated	Widowed	Divorced
City	36.1	43.6	2.1	5.9	12.4
MSA[1]	29.9	51.5	1.6	5.5	11.4
U.S.	33.8	48.0	1.8	5.6	10.8

Note: Figures are percentages and cover the population 15 years of age and older; (1) Figures cover the Huntsville, AL Metropolitan Statistical Area; (2) Excludes separated
Source: U.S. Census Bureau, 2017-2021 American Community Survey 5-Year Estimates

Religious Groups by Family

Area	Catholic	Baptist	Methodist	LDS[2]	Pentecostal	Lutheran	Islam	Adventist	Other
MSA[1]	7.5	23.6	6.6	1.4	1.2	0.4	0.8	2.7	17.5
U.S.	18.7	7.3	3.0	2.0	1.8	1.7	1.3	1.3	11.6

Note: Figures are the number of adherents as a percentage of the total population and cover the eight largest religious groups in the U.S; (1) Figures cover the Huntsville, AL Metropolitan Statistical Area; (2) Church of Jesus Christ of Latter-day Saints
Sources: 2020 U.S. Religion Census, Association of Statisticians of American Religious Bodies; The Association of Religion Data Archives (ARDA)

Religious Groups by Tradition

Area	Catholic	Evangelical Protestant	Mainline Protestant	Black Protestant	Islam	Judaism	Hinduism	Orthodox	Buddhism
MSA[1]	7.5	34.8	8.2	7.2	0.8	0.1	0.9	0.1	0.1
U.S.	18.7	16.5	5.2	2.3	1.3	0.6	0.4	0.4	0.3

Note: Figures are the number of adherents as a percentage of the total population; (1) Figures cover the Huntsville, AL Metropolitan Statistical Area
Sources: 2020 U.S. Religion Census, Association of Statisticians of American Religious Bodies; The Association of Religion Data Archives (ARDA)

ECONOMY

Gross Metropolitan Product

Area	2020	2021	2022	2023	Rank[2]
MSA[1]	30.9	33.5	36.5	39.2	98

Note: Figures are in billions of dollars; (1) Figures cover the Huntsville, AL Metropolitan Statistical Area; (2) Rank is based on 2021 data and ranges from 1 to 381
Source: U.S. Conference of Mayors, U.S. Metro Economies: U.S. Metros Compared to Global and State Economies, June 2022

Economic Growth

Area	2018-20 (%)	2021 (%)	2022 (%)	2023 (%)	Rank[2]
MSA[1]	1.8	4.9	3.4	3.9	42
U.S.	-0.6	5.7	3.1	2.9	—

Note: Figures are real gross metropolitan product (GMP) growth rates and represent average annual percent change; (1) Figures cover the Huntsville, AL Metropolitan Statistical Area; (2) Rank is based on 2020 2-year average annual percent change and ranges from 1 to 381
Source: U.S. Conference of Mayors, U.S. Metro Economies: U.S. Metros Compared to Global and State Economies, June 2022

Metropolitan Area Exports

Area	2016	2017	2018	2019	2020	2021	Rank[2]
MSA[1]	1,827.3	1,889.2	1,608.7	1,534.2	1,263.0	1,579.5	124

Note: Figures are in millions of dollars; (1) Figures cover the Huntsville, AL Metropolitan Statistical Area; (2) Rank is based on 2021 data and ranges from 1 to 388
Source: U.S. Department of Commerce, International Trade Administration, Office of Trade and Economic Analysis, Industry and Analysis, Exports by Metropolitan Area, data extracted March 16, 2023

Building Permits

Area	Single-Family 2021	Single-Family 2022	Pct. Chg.	Multi-Family 2021	Multi-Family 2022	Pct. Chg.	Total 2021	Total 2022	Pct. Chg.
City	1,483	1,083	-27.0	1,328	47	-96.5	2,811	1,130	-59.8
MSA[1]	4,230	3,617	-14.5	1,942	418	-78.5	6,172	4,035	-34.6
U.S.	1,115,400	975,600	-12.5	621,600	689,500	10.9	1,737,000	1,665,100	-4.1

Note: (1) Figures cover the Huntsville, AL Metropolitan Statistical Area; Figures represent new, privately-owned housing units authorized (unadjusted data); All permit data are based on estimates with imputation
Source: U.S. Census Bureau, Manufacturing, Mining, and Construction Statistics, Building Permits, 2021, 2022

Bankruptcy Filings

Area	Business Filings 2021	Business Filings 2022	% Chg.	Nonbusiness Filings 2021	Nonbusiness Filings 2022	% Chg.
Madison County	18	12	-33.3	894	806	-9.8
U.S.	14,347	13,481	-6.0	399,269	374,240	-6.3

Note: Business filings include Chapter 7, Chapter 9, Chapter 11, Chapter 12, Chapter 13, Chapter 15, and Section 304; Nonbusiness filings include Chapter 7, Chapter 11, and Chapter 13
Source: Administrative Office of the U.S. Courts, Business and Nonbusiness Bankruptcy, County Cases Commenced by Chapter of the Bankruptcy Code, During the 12-Month Period Ending December 31, 2021 and Business and Nonbusiness Bankruptcy, County Cases Commenced by Chapter of the Bankruptcy Code, During the 12-Month Period Ending December 31, 2022

Housing Vacancy Rates

Area	Gross Vacancy Rate[2] (%) 2020	2021	2022	Year-Round Vacancy Rate[3] (%) 2020	2021	2022	Rental Vacancy Rate[4] (%) 2020	2021	2022	Homeowner Vacancy Rate[5] (%) 2020	2021	2022
MSA[1]	n/a	n/a	n/a	n/a	n/a	n/a	n/a	n/a	n/a	n/a	n/a	n/a
U.S.	10.6	10.8	10.5	8.2	8.4	8.2	6.3	6.1	5.8	1.0	0.9	0.8

Note: (1) Figures cover the Huntsville, AL Metropolitan Statistical Area; (2) The percentage of the total housing inventory that is vacant; (3) The percentage of the housing inventory (excluding seasonal units) that is year-round vacant; (4) The percentage of rental inventory that is vacant for rent; (5) The percentage of homeowner inventory that is vacant for sale; n/a not available
Source: U.S. Census Bureau, Housing Vacancies and Homeownership Annual Statistics: 2020, 2021, 2022

INCOME

Income

Area	Per Capita ($)	Median Household ($)	Average Household ($)
City	38,838	60,959	87,475
MSA[1]	38,800	71,057	94,763
U.S.	37,638	69,021	97,196

Note: (1) Figures cover the Huntsville, AL Metropolitan Statistical Area
Source: U.S. Census Bureau, 2017-2021 American Community Survey 5-Year Estimates

Household Income Distribution

Area	Under $15,000	$15,000 -$24,999	$25,000 -$34,999	$35,000 -$49,999	$50,000 -$74,999	$75,000 -$99,999	$100,000 -$149,999	$150,000 and up
City	11.5	9.2	10.1	12.3	15.2	11.4	14.4	15.9
MSA[1]	8.8	8.0	8.2	11.7	15.4	12.8	16.9	18.2
U.S.	9.4	7.8	8.2	11.4	16.8	12.8	16.3	17.3

Note: (1) Figures cover the Huntsville, AL Metropolitan Statistical Area
Source: U.S. Census Bureau, 2017-2021 American Community Survey 5-Year Estimates

Poverty Rate

Area	All Ages	Under 18 Years Old	18 to 64 Years Old	65 Years and Over
City	14.6	21.8	13.9	8.3
MSA[1]	11.0	15.0	10.1	8.9
U.S.	12.6	17.0	11.8	9.6

Note: Figures are percentage of people whose income during the past 12 months was below the poverty level;
(1) Figures cover the Huntsville, AL Metropolitan Statistical Area
Source: U.S. Census Bureau, 2017-2021 American Community Survey 5-Year Estimates

EMPLOYMENT

Labor Force and Employment

Area	Civilian Labor Force Dec. 2021	Civilian Labor Force Dec. 2022	% Chg.	Workers Employed Dec. 2021	Workers Employed Dec. 2022	% Chg.
City	102,295	104,297	2.0	100,086	102,254	2.2
MSA[1]	239,285	244,014	2.0	234,543	239,596	2.2
U.S.	161,696,000	164,224,000	1.6	155,732,000	158,872,000	2.0

Note: Data is not seasonally adjusted and covers workers 16 years of age and older; (1) Figures cover the Huntsville, AL Metropolitan Statistical Area
Source: Bureau of Labor Statistics, Local Area Unemployment Statistics

Unemployment Rate

Area	Jan.	Feb.	Mar.	Apr.	May	Jun.	Jul.	Aug.	Sep.	Oct.	Nov.	Dec.
City	2.8	2.6	2.1	1.7	2.1	3.0	2.8	2.6	2.3	2.3	2.1	2.0
MSA[1]	2.6	2.4	1.9	1.6	1.9	2.7	2.6	2.3	2.1	2.2	2.0	1.8
U.S.	4.4	4.1	3.8	3.3	3.4	3.8	3.8	3.8	3.3	3.4	3.4	3.3

Note: Data is not seasonally adjusted and covers workers 16 years of age and older; (1) Figures cover the Huntsville, AL Metropolitan Statistical Area
Source: Bureau of Labor Statistics, Local Area Unemployment Statistics

Average Wages

Occupation	$/Hr.	Occupation	$/Hr.
Accountants and Auditors	38.65	Maintenance and Repair Workers	20.71
Automotive Mechanics	23.32	Marketing Managers	68.35
Bookkeepers	19.18	Network and Computer Systems Admin.	45.60
Carpenters	21.60	Nurses, Licensed Practical	22.75
Cashiers	12.06	Nurses, Registered	31.99
Computer Programmers	48.90	Nursing Assistants	14.59
Computer Systems Analysts	59.97	Office Clerks, General	13.92
Computer User Support Specialists	24.38	Physical Therapists	46.53
Construction Laborers	16.49	Physicians	139.48
Cooks, Restaurant	14.48	Plumbers, Pipefitters and Steamfitters	24.93
Customer Service Representatives	17.51	Police and Sheriff's Patrol Officers	25.54
Dentists	87.97	Postal Service Mail Carriers	26.36
Electricians	25.26	Real Estate Sales Agents	41.38
Engineers, Electrical	53.71	Retail Salespersons	14.54
Fast Food and Counter Workers	11.05	Sales Representatives, Technical/Scientific	38.34
Financial Managers	69.15	Secretaries, Exc. Legal/Medical/Executive	20.21
First-Line Supervisors of Office Workers	28.19	Security Guards	15.35
General and Operations Managers	67.02	Surgeons	n/a
Hairdressers/Cosmetologists	18.45	Teacher Assistants, Exc. Postsecondary*	10.75
Home Health and Personal Care Aides	12.03	Teachers, Secondary School, Exc. Sp. Ed.*	28.00
Janitors and Cleaners	13.17	Telemarketers	n/a
Landscaping/Groundskeeping Workers	15.92	Truck Drivers, Heavy/Tractor-Trailer	23.90
Lawyers	69.72	Truck Drivers, Light/Delivery Services	20.20
Maids and Housekeeping Cleaners	11.97	Waiters and Waitresses	11.55

Note: Wage data covers the Huntsville, AL Metropolitan Statistical Area; (*) Hourly wages were calculated from annual wage data based on a 40 hour work week; n/a not available.
Source: Bureau of Labor Statistics, Metro Area Occupational Employment & Wage Estimates, May 2022

Employment by Industry

Sector	MSA[1] Number of Employees	MSA[1] Percent of Total	U.S. Percent of Total
Construction, Mining, and Logging	10,500	3.9	5.4
Private Education and Health Services	22,800	8.5	16.1
Financial Activities	8,400	3.1	5.9
Government	55,100	20.4	14.5
Information	2,600	1.0	2.0
Leisure and Hospitality	22,200	8.2	10.3
Manufacturing	32,300	12.0	8.4
Other Services	8,800	3.3	3.7
Professional and Business Services	68,700	25.5	14.7
Retail Trade	27,300	10.1	10.2
Transportation, Warehousing, and Utilities	4,700	1.7	4.9
Wholesale Trade	6,400	2.4	3.9

Note: Figures are non-farm employment as of December 2022. Figures are not seasonally adjusted and include workers 16 years of age and older; (1) Figures cover the Huntsville, AL Metropolitan Statistical Area
Source: Bureau of Labor Statistics, Current Employment Statistics, Employment, Hours, and Earnings

Employment by Occupation

Occupation Classification	City (%)	MSA[1] (%)	U.S. (%)
Management, Business, Science, and Arts	49.0	47.5	40.3
Natural Resources, Construction, and Maintenance	5.6	7.1	8.7
Production, Transportation, and Material Moving	10.5	12.6	13.1
Sales and Office	18.7	19.0	20.9
Service	16.2	13.9	17.0

Note: Figures cover employed civilians 16 years of age and older; (1) Figures cover the Huntsville, AL Metropolitan Statistical Area
Source: U.S. Census Bureau, 2017-2021 American Community Survey 5-Year Estimates

Occupations with Greatest Projected Employment Growth: 2022 – 2024

Occupation[1]	2022 Employment	2024 Projected Employment	Numeric Employment Change	Percent Employment Change
Cooks, Restaurant	16,700	17,360	660	4.0
Industrial Machinery Mechanics	14,850	15,510	660	4.4
Software Developers	14,820	15,270	450	3.0
Accountants and Auditors	24,470	24,890	420	1.7
Sales Representatives, Wholesale and Manufacturing, Except Technical and Scientific Products	21,530	21,910	380	1.8
Medical and Health Services Managers	8,430	8,790	360	4.3
Janitors and Cleaners, Except Maids and Housekeeping Cleaners	28,680	29,040	360	1.3
Nurse Practitioners	4,550	4,880	330	7.3
General and Operations Managers	37,490	37,810	320	0.9
Logisticians	5,400	5,690	290	5.4

Note: Projections cover Alabama; (1) Sorted by numeric employment change
Source: www.projectionscentral.com, State Occupational Projections, 2022–2024 Short-Term Projections

Fastest-Growing Occupations: 2022 – 2024

Occupation[1]	2022 Employment	2024 Projected Employment	Numeric Employment Change	Percent Employment Change
Dental Laboratory Technicians	1,030	1,120	90	8.7
Nurse Practitioners	4,550	4,880	330	7.3
Molders, Shapers, and Casters, Except Metal and Plastic	850	910	60	7.1
Information Security Analysts (SOC 2018)	2,600	2,780	180	6.9
Logisticians	5,400	5,690	290	5.4
Telecommunications Equipment Installers and Repairers, Except Line Installers	2,720	2,860	140	5.1
Paralegals and Legal Assistants	3,850	4,020	170	4.4
Nursing Instructors and Teachers, Postsecondary	1,360	1,420	60	4.4
Industrial Machinery Mechanics	14,850	15,510	660	4.4
Medical and Health Services Managers	8,430	8,790	360	4.3

Note: Projections cover Alabama; (1) Sorted by percent employment change and excludes occupations with numeric employment change less than 50
Source: www.projectionscentral.com, State Occupational Projections, 2022–2024 Short-Term Projections

CITY FINANCES

City Government Finances

Component	2020 ($000)	2020 ($ per capita)
Total Revenues	1,126,357	5,616
Total Expenditures	1,097,975	5,474
Debt Outstanding	1,131,248	5,640
Cash and Securities[1]	564,568	2,815

Note: (1) Cash and security holdings of a government at the close of its fiscal year, including those of its dependent agencies, utilities, and liquor stores.
Source: U.S. Census Bureau, State & Local Government Finances 2020

City Government Revenue by Source

Source	2020 ($000)	2020 ($ per capita)	2020 (%)
General Revenue			
From Federal Government	2,575	13	0.2
From State Government	20,619	103	1.8
From Local Governments	0	0	0.0
Taxes			
Property	65,167	325	5.8
Sales and Gross Receipts	273,612	1,364	24.3
Personal Income	0	0	0.0
Corporate Income	0	0	0.0
Motor Vehicle License	0	0	0.0
Other Taxes	29,449	147	2.6
Current Charges	77,623	387	6.9
Liquor Store	0	0	0.0
Utility	623,621	3,109	55.4

Source: U.S. Census Bureau, State & Local Government Finances 2020

City Government Expenditures by Function

Function	2020 ($000)	2020 ($ per capita)	2020 (%)
General Direct Expenditures			
Air Transportation	0	0	0.0
Corrections	0	0	0.0
Education	0	0	0.0
Employment Security Administration	0	0	0.0
Financial Administration	5,939	29	0.5
Fire Protection	37,063	184	3.4
General Public Buildings	0	0	0.0
Governmental Administration, Other	9,172	45	0.8
Health	2,339	11	0.2
Highways	48,666	242	4.4
Hospitals	0	0	0.0
Housing and Community Development	4,024	20	0.4
Interest on General Debt	38,451	191	3.5
Judicial and Legal	7,537	37	0.7
Libraries	6,069	30	0.6
Parking	1,871	9	0.2
Parks and Recreation	49,226	245	4.5
Police Protection	50,668	252	4.6
Public Welfare	0	0	0.0
Sewerage	19,112	95	1.7
Solid Waste Management	0	0	0.0
Veterans' Services	0	0	0.0
Liquor Store	0	0	0.0
Utility	633,409	3,158	57.7

Source: U.S. Census Bureau, State & Local Government Finances 2020

TAXES

State Corporate Income Tax Rates

State	Tax Rate (%)	Income Brackets ($)	Num. of Brackets	Financial Institution Tax Rate (%)[a]	Federal Income Tax Ded.
Alabama	6.5	Flat rate	1	6.5	Yes

Note: Tax rates as of January 1, 2023; (a) Rates listed are the corporate income tax rate applied to financial institutions or excise taxes based on income. Some states have other taxes based upon the value of deposits or shares.
Source: Federation of Tax Administrators, State Corporate Income Tax Rates, January 1, 2023

State Individual Income Tax Rates

State	Tax Rate (%)	Income Brackets ($)	Personal Exemptions ($) Single	Personal Exemptions ($) Married	Personal Exemptions ($) Depend.	Standard Ded. ($) Single	Standard Ded. ($) Married
Alabama	2.0 - 5.0	500 - 3,001 (b)	1,500	3,000	500 (e)	3,000	8,500 (z)

Note: Tax rates as of January 1, 2023; Local- and county-level taxes are not included; Federal income tax is deductible on state income tax returns; (b) For joint returns, taxes are twice the tax on half the couple's income; (e) In Alabama, the per-dependent exemption is $1,000 for taxpayers with state AGI of $20,000 or less, $500 with AGI from $20,001 to $100,000, and $300 with AGI over $100,000; (z) Alabama standard deduction is phased out for incomes over $25,000. Rhode Island exemptions & standard deductions phased out for incomes over $233,750; Wisconsin standard deduciton phases out for income over $16,989.
Source: Federation of Tax Administrators, State Individual Income Tax Rates, January 1, 2023

Various State Sales and Excise Tax Rates

State	State Sales Tax (%)	Gasoline[1] ($/gal.)	Cigarette[2] ($/pack)	Spirits[3] ($/gal.)	Wine[4] ($/gal.)	Beer[5] ($/gal.)	Recreational Marijuana (%)
Alabama	4	0.3131	0.675	21.69	1.70	0.53	Not legal

Note: All tax rates as of January 1, 2023; (1) The American Petroleum Institute has developed a methodology for determining the average tax rate on a gallon of fuel. Rates may include any of the following: excise taxes, environmental fees, storage tank fees, other fees or taxes, general sales tax, and local taxes; (2) The federal excise tax of $1.0066 per pack and local taxes are not included; (3) Rates are those applicable to off-premise sales of 40% alcohol by volume (a.b.v.) distilled spirits in 750ml containers. Local excise taxes are excluded; (4) Rates are those applicable to off-premise sales of 11% a.b.v. non-carbonated wine in 750ml containers; (5) Rates are those applicable to off-premise sales of 4.7% a.b.v. beer in 12 ounce containers.
Source: Tax Foundation, 2023 Facts & Figures: How Does Your State Compare?

State Business Tax Climate Index Rankings

State	Overall Rank	Corporate Tax Rank	Individual Income Tax Rank	Sales Tax Rank	Property Tax Rank	Unemployment Insurance Tax Rank
Alabama	41	18	30	50	18	19

Note: The index is a measure of how each state's tax laws affect economic performance. The lower the rank, the more favorable a state's tax system is for business. States without a given tax are given a ranking of 1. The scores/rankings for the District of Columbia do not affect other states. The 2023 index represents the tax climate as of July 1, 2022.
Source: Tax Foundation, State Business Tax Climate Index 2023

TRANSPORTATION

Means of Transportation to Work

Area	Drove Alone	Car-pooled	Bus	Subway	Railroad	Bicycle	Walked	Other Means	Worked at Home
City	81.8	6.2	0.4	0.0	0.0	0.2	1.2	0.8	9.4
MSA[1]	83.6	5.8	0.2	0.0	0.0	0.1	0.7	1.0	8.6
U.S.	73.2	8.6	2.0	1.6	0.5	0.5	2.5	1.5	9.7

Note: Figures are percentages and cover workers 16 years of age and older; (1) Figures cover the Huntsville, AL Metropolitan Statistical Area
Source: U.S. Census Bureau, 2017-2021 American Community Survey 5-Year Estimates

Travel Time to Work

Area	Less Than 10 Minutes	10 to 19 Minutes	20 to 29 Minutes	30 to 44 Minutes	45 to 59 Minutes	60 to 89 Minutes	90 Minutes or More
City	13.1	41.0	26.2	15.5	2.5	1.0	0.8
MSA[1]	10.1	31.7	27.7	22.1	5.2	1.9	1.2
U.S.	12.4	28.5	21.0	20.9	8.2	6.2	2.9

Note: Note: Figures are percentages and include workers 16 years old and over; (1) Figures cover the Huntsville, AL Metropolitan Statistical Area
Source: U.S. Census Bureau, 2017-2021 American Community Survey 5-Year Estimates

Key Congestion Measures

Measure	1990	2000	2010	2015	2020
Annual Hours of Delay, Total (000)	n/a	n/a	n/a	7,460	5,232
Annual Hours of Delay, Per Auto Commuter	n/a	n/a	n/a	23	14
Annual Congestion Cost, Per Auto Commuter ($)	n/a	n/a	n/a	472	298

Note: n/a not available
Source: Texas A&M Transportation Institute, 2021 Urban Mobility Report

Freeway Travel Time Index

Measure	1985	1990	1995	2000	2005	2010	2015	2020
Urban Area Index[1]	n/a	n/a	n/a	n/a	n/a	n/a	1.11	1.06
Urban Area Rank[1,2]	n/a	n/a	n/a	n/a	n/a	n/a	n/a	n/a

Note: Freeway Travel Time Index—the ratio of travel time in the peak period to the travel time at free-flow conditions. For example, a value of 1.30 indicates a 20-minute free-flow trip takes 26 minutes in the peak (20 minutes x 1.30 = 26 minutes); (1) Covers the Huntsville AL urban area; (2) Rank is based on 101 larger urban areas (#1 = highest travel time index); n/a not available
Source: Texas A&M Transportation Institute, 2021 Urban Mobility Report

Public Transportation

Agency Name / Mode of Transportation	Vehicles Operated in Maximum Service[1]	Annual Unlinked Passenger Trips[2] (in thous.)	Annual Passenger Miles[3] (in thous.)
City of Huntsville - Public Transportation Division			
Bus (directly operated)	13	478.1	1,965.7
Demand Response (directly operated)	19	71.7	403.6

Note: (1) Number of revenue vehicles operated by the given mode and type of service to meet the annual maximum service requirement. This is the revenue vehicle count during the peak season of the year; on the week and day that maximum service is provided. Vehicles operated in maximum service (VOMS) exclude atypical days and one-time special events; (2) Number of passengers who boarded public transportation vehicles. Passengers are counted each time they board a vehicle no matter how many vehicles they use to travel from their origin to their destination. (3) Sum of the distances ridden by all passengers during the entire fiscal year.
Source: Federal Transit Administration, National Transit Database, 2021

Air Transportation

Airport Name and Code / Type of Service	Passenger Airlines[1]	Passenger Enplanements	Freight Carriers[2]	Freight (lbs)
Huntsville International (HSV)				
Domestic service (U.S. carriers - 2022)	21	587,497	9	33,045,712
International service (U.S. carriers - 2021)	1	6	2	681,889

Note: (1) Includes all U.S.-based major, minor and commuter airlines that carried at least one passenger during the year; (2) Includes all U.S.-based airlines and freight carriers that transported at least one pound of freight during the year.
Source: Bureau of Transportation Statistics, The Intermodal Transportation Database, Air Carriers: T-100 Domestic Market (U.S. Carriers), 2022; Bureau of Transportation Statistics, The Intermodal Transportation Database, Air Carriers: T-100 International Market (U.S. Carriers), 2021

BUSINESSES

Major Business Headquarters

Company Name	Industry	Fortune[1]	Forbes[2]
No companies listed	-	-	-

Note: (1) Companies that produce a 10-K are ranked 1 to 500 based on 2021 revenue; (2) All private companies with at least $2 billion in annual revenue through the end of their most current fiscal year are ranked 1 to 246; companies listed are headquartered in the city; dashes indicate no ranking
Source: Fortune, "Fortune 500," 2022; Forbes, "America's Largest Private Companies," 2022

Fastest-Growing Businesses

According to *Inc.*, Huntsville is home to one of America's 500 fastest-growing private companies: **LaunchTech** (#42). Criteria: must be an independent, privately-held, for-profit, U.S. corporation, proprietorship or partnership as of December 31, 2021; revenues must be at least $100,000 in 2018 and $2 million in 2021; must have four-year operating/sales history. *Inc.*, "America's 500 Fastest-Growing Private Companies," 2022

According to *Initiative for a Competitive Inner City (ICIC)*, Huntsville is home to one of America's 100 fastest-growing "inner city" companies: **ProjectXYZ** (#21). Criteria for inclusion: company must be headquartered in or have 51 percent or more of its physical operations in an economically distressed urban area; must be an independent, for-profit corporation, partnership or proprietorship; must have 10 or more employees and have a five-year sales history that includes sales of at least $200,000 in the base year and at least $1 million in the current year with no decrease in sales over the two most recent years. Companies were ranked overall by revenue growth over the five-year period between 2017 and 2021. *Initiative for a Competitive Inner City (ICIC), "Inner City 100 Companies," 2022*

Living Environment

COST OF LIVING

Cost of Living Index

Composite Index	Groceries	Housing	Utilities	Transportation	Health Care	Misc. Goods/Services
91.5	98.1	74.9	98.1	91.2	94.1	100.1

Note: The Cost of Living Index measures regional differences in the cost of consumer goods and services, excluding taxes and non-consumer expenditures, for professional and managerial households in the top income quintile. It is based on more than 50,000 prices covering almost 60 different items for which prices are collected three times a year by chambers of commerce, economic development organizations or university applied economic centers in each participating urban area. The numbers shown should be read as a percentage above or below the national average of 100. For example, a value of 115.4 in the groceries column indicates that grocery prices are 15.4% higher than the national average. Small differences in the index numbers should not be interpreted as significant; Figures cover the Huntsville AL urban area.
Source: The Council for Community and Economic Research, Cost of Living Index, 2022

Grocery Prices

Area[1]	T-Bone Steak ($/pound)	Frying Chicken ($/pound)	Whole Milk ($/half gal.)	Eggs ($/dozen)	Orange Juice ($/64 oz.)	Coffee ($/11.5 oz.)
City[2]	14.42	1.54	2.22	2.04	3.86	5.03
Avg.	13.81	1.59	2.43	2.25	3.85	4.95
Min.	10.17	0.90	1.51	1.30	2.90	3.46
Max.	19.35	3.30	4.32	4.32	5.31	8.59

*Note: (1) Values for the local area are compared with the average, minimum and maximum values for all 286 areas in the Cost of Living Index; (2) Figures cover the Huntsville AL urban area; **T-Bone Steak** (price per pound); **Frying Chicken** (price per pound, whole fryer); **Whole Milk** (half gallon carton); **Eggs** (price per dozen, Grade A, large); **Orange Juice** (64 oz. Tropicana or Florida Natural); **Coffee** (11.5 oz. can, vacuum-packed, Maxwell House, Hills Bros, or Folgers).*
Source: The Council for Community and Economic Research, Cost of Living Index, 2022

Housing and Utility Costs

Area[1]	New Home Price ($)	Apartment Rent ($/month)	All Electric ($/month)	Part Electric ($/month)	Other Energy ($/month)	Telephone ($/month)
City[2]	350,811	1,023	173.74	-	-	186.08
Avg.	450,913	1,371	176.41	99.93	76.96	190.22
Min.	229,283	546	100.84	31.56	27.15	174.27
Max.	2,434,977	4,569	356.86	249.59	272.24	208.31

*Note: (1) Values for the local area are compared with the average, minimum and maximum values for all 286 areas in the Cost of Living Index; (2) Figures cover the Huntsville AL urban area; **New Home Price** (2,400 sf living area, 8,000 sf lot, in urban area with full utilities); **Apartment Rent** (950 sf 2 bedroom/1.5 or 2 bath, unfurnished, excluding all utilities except water); **All Electric** (average monthly cost for an all-electric home); **Part Electric** (average monthly cost for a part-electric home); **Other Energy** (average monthly cost for natural gas, fuel oil, coal, wood, and any other forms of energy except electricity); **Telephone** (price includes the base monthly rate plus taxes and fees for three lines of mobile phone service).*
Source: The Council for Community and Economic Research, Cost of Living Index, 2022

Health Care, Transportation, and Other Costs

Area[1]	Doctor ($/visit)	Dentist ($/visit)	Optometrist ($/visit)	Gasoline ($/gallon)	Beauty Salon ($/visit)	Men's Shirt ($)
City[2]	124.50	99.17	88.78	3.55	49.33	33.22
Avg.	124.91	107.77	117.66	3.86	43.31	34.21
Min.	36.61	58.25	51.79	2.90	22.18	13.05
Max.	250.21	162.58	371.96	5.54	85.61	63.54

*Note: (1) Values for the local area are compared with the average, minimum and maximum values for all 286 areas in the Cost of Living Index; (2) Figures cover the Huntsville AL urban area; **Doctor** (general practitioners routine exam of an established patient); **Dentist** (adult teeth cleaning and periodic oral examination); **Optometrist** (full vision eye exam for established adult patient); **Gasoline** (one gallon regular unleaded, national brand, including all taxes, cash price at self-service pump if available); **Beauty Salon** (woman's shampoo, trim, and blow-dry); **Men's Shirt** (cotton/polyester dress shirt, pinpoint weave, long sleeves).*
Source: The Council for Community and Economic Research, Cost of Living Index, 2022

HOUSING

Homeownership Rate

Area	2015 (%)	2016 (%)	2017 (%)	2018 (%)	2019 (%)	2020 (%)	2021 (%)	2022 (%)
MSA[1]	n/a	n/a	n/a	n/a	n/a	n/a	n/a	n/a
U.S.	63.7	63.4	63.9	64.4	64.6	66.6	65.5	65.8

Note: (1) Figures cover the Huntsville, AL Metropolitan Statistical Area; n/a not available
Source: U.S. Census Bureau, Housing Vacancies and Homeownership Annual Statistics: 2015-2022

House Price Index (HPI)

Area	National Ranking[2]	Quarterly Change (%)	One-Year Change (%)	Five-Year Change (%)	Since 1991Q1 (%)
MSA[1]	109	-1.12	11.99	73.58	211.74
U.S.[3]	—	0.34	8.41	58.44	289.08

Note: The HPI is a weighted repeat sales index. It measures average price changes in repeat sales or refinancings on the same properties. This information is obtained by reviewing repeat mortgage transactions on single-family properties whose mortgages have been purchased or securitized by Fannie Mae or Freddie Mac since January 1975; (1) Figures cover the Huntsville, AL Metropolitan Statistical Area; (2) Rankings are based on annual percentage change for all metro areas containing at least 15,000 transactions over the last 10 years and ranges from 1 to 257; (3) figures based on a weighted average of Census Division estimates using a seasonally adjusted, purchase-only index; all figures are for the period ending December 31, 2022
Source: Federal Housing Finance Agency, Change in FHFA Metropolitan Area House Price Indexes, 2022Q4

Median Single-Family Home Prices

Area	2020	2021	2022p	Percent Change 2021 to 2022
MSA[1]	248.0	280.4	324.9	15.9
U.S. Average	300.2	357.1	392.6	9.9

Note: Figures are median sales prices of existing single-family homes in thousands of dollars; (p) preliminary; (1) Figures cover the Huntsville, AL Metropolitan Statistical Area
Source: National Association of Realtors, Median Sales Price of Existing Single-Family Homes for Metropolitan Areas, 4th Quarter 2022

Qualifying Income Based on Median Sales Price of Existing Single-Family Homes

Area	With 5% Down ($)	With 10% Down ($)	With 20% Down ($)
MSA[1]	100,167	94,895	84,351
U.S. Average	112,234	106,237	94,513

Note: Figures are preliminary; Qualifying income is based on a mortgage rate of 6.77%. Monthly principal and interest payment is limited to 25% of income; (1) Figures cover the Huntsville, AL Metropolitan Statistical Area
Source: National Association of Realtors, Qualifying Income Based on Median Sales Price of Existing Single-Family Homes for Metropolitan Areas, 4th Quarter 2022

Home Value

Area	Under $100,000	$100,000 -$199,999	$200,000 -$299,999	$300,000 -$399,999	$400,000 -$499,999	$500,000 -$999,999	$1,000,000 or more	Median ($)
City	21.0	30.5	21.8	12.5	6.6	6.4	1.1	194,500
MSA[1]	17.1	33.2	24.5	12.5	6.2	5.8	0.7	199,000
U.S.	16.2	24.2	20.1	13.6	8.3	13.6	4.1	244,900

Note: Figures are percentages except for median and cover owner-occupied housing units; (1) Figures cover the Huntsville, AL Metropolitan Statistical Area
Source: U.S. Census Bureau, 2017-2021 American Community Survey 5-Year Estimates

Year Housing Structure Built

Area	2020 or Later	2010 -2019	2000 -2009	1990 -1999	1980 -1989	1970 -1979	1960 -1969	1950 -1959	1940 -1949	Before 1940	Median Year
City	0.2	13.6	12.4	11.0	15.8	12.8	20.6	8.6	2.4	2.6	1982
MSA[1]	0.2	14.6	18.9	16.7	16.1	10.6	13.0	5.9	1.9	2.1	1990
U.S.	0.2	7.3	13.6	13.6	13.2	14.8	10.3	10.0	4.7	12.2	1979

Note: Figures are percentages except for Median Year; Note: (1) Figures cover the Huntsville, AL Metropolitan Statistical Area
Source: U.S. Census Bureau, 2017-2021 American Community Survey 5-Year Estimates

Gross Monthly Rent

Area	Under $500	$500 -$999	$1,000 -$1,499	$1,500 -$1,999	$2,000 -$2,499	$2,500 -$2,999	$3,000 and up	Median ($)
City	7.5	52.1	31.9	6.8	0.7	0.5	0.5	912
MSA[1]	8.0	51.8	30.9	7.1	1.1	0.6	0.5	912
U.S.	8.1	30.5	30.8	16.8	7.3	3.1	3.5	1,163

Note: Figures are percentages except for median; Gross rent is the contract rent plus the estimated average monthly cost of utilities (electricity, gas, and water and sewer) and fuels (oil, coal, kerosene, wood, etc.) if these are paid by the renter (or paid for the renter by someone else); (1) Figures cover the Huntsville, AL Metropolitan Statistical Area
Source: U.S. Census Bureau, 2017-2021 American Community Survey 5-Year Estimates

HEALTH

Health Risk Factors

Category	MSA[1] (%)	U.S. (%)
Adults aged 18–64 who have any kind of health care coverage	n/a	90.9
Adults who reported being in good or better health	n/a	85.2
Adults who have been told they have high blood cholesterol	n/a	35.7
Adults who have been told they have high blood pressure	n/a	32.4
Adults who are current smokers	n/a	14.4
Adults who currently use e-cigarettes	n/a	6.7
Adults who currently use chewing tobacco, snuff, or snus	n/a	3.5
Adults who are heavy drinkers[2]	n/a	6.3
Adults who are binge drinkers[3]	n/a	15.4
Adults who are overweight (BMI 25.0 - 29.9)	n/a	34.4
Adults who are obese (BMI 30.0 - 99.8)	n/a	33.9
Adults who participated in any physical activities in the past month	n/a	76.3

Note: (1) Figures for the Huntsville, AL Metropolitan Statistical Area were not available.
(2) Heavy drinkers are classified as adult men having more than 14 drinks per week and adult women having more than 7 drinks per week; (3) Binge drinkers are classified as males having five or more drinks on one occasion or females having four or more drinks on one occasion
Source: Centers for Disease Control and Prevention, Behavioral Risk Factor Surveillance System, SMART: Selected Metropolitan Area Risk Trends, 2021

Acute and Chronic Health Conditions

Category	MSA[1] (%)	U.S. (%)
Adults who have ever been told they had a heart attack	n/a	4.0
Adults who have ever been told they have angina or coronary heart disease	n/a	3.8
Adults who have ever been told they had a stroke	n/a	3.0
Adults who have ever been told they have asthma	n/a	14.9
Adults who have ever been told they have arthritis	n/a	25.8
Adults who have ever been told they have diabetes[2]	n/a	10.9
Adults who have ever been told they had skin cancer	n/a	6.6
Adults who have ever been told they had any other types of cancer	n/a	7.5
Adults who have ever been told they have COPD	n/a	6.1
Adults who have ever been told they have kidney disease	n/a	3.0
Adults who have ever been told they have a form of depression	n/a	20.5

Note: (1) Figures for the Huntsville, AL Metropolitan Statistical Area were not available.
(2) Figures do not include pregnancy-related, borderline, or pre-diabetes
Source: Centers for Disease Control and Prevention, Behavioral Risk Factor Surveillance System, SMART: Selected Metropolitan Area Risk Trends, 2021

Health Screening and Vaccination Rates

Category	MSA[1] (%)	U.S. (%)
Adults who have ever been tested for HIV	n/a	34.9
Adults who have had their blood cholesterol checked within the last five years	n/a	85.2
Adults aged 65+ who have had flu shot within the past year	n/a	68.6
Adults aged 65+ who have ever had a pneumonia vaccination	n/a	71.0

Note: (1) Figures for the Huntsville, AL Metropolitan Statistical Area were not available.
Source: Centers for Disease Control and Prevention, Behavioral Risk Factor Surveillance System, SMART: Selected Metropolitan Area Risk Trends, 2021

Disability Status

Category	MSA[1] (%)	U.S. (%)
Adults who reported being deaf	n/a	7.2
Are you blind or have serious difficulty seeing, even when wearing glasses?	n/a	4.8
Are you limited in any way in any of your usual activities due to arthritis?	n/a	11.1
Do you have difficulty doing errands alone?	n/a	7.0
Do you have difficulty dressing or bathing?	n/a	3.6
Do you have serious difficulty concentrating/remembering/making decisions?	n/a	12.1
Do you have serious difficulty walking or climbing stairs?	n/a	12.8

Note: (1) Figures for the Huntsville, AL Metropolitan Statistical Area were not available.
Source: Centers for Disease Control and Prevention, Behavioral Risk Factor Surveillance System, SMART: Selected Metropolitan Area Risk Trends, 2021

Mortality Rates for the Top 10 Causes of Death in the U.S.

ICD-10[a] Sub-Chapter	ICD-10[a] Code	Crude Mortality Rate[1] per 100,000 population County[2]	U.S.
Malignant neoplasms	C00-C97	173.8	182.6
Ischaemic heart diseases	I20-I25	78.9	113.1
Other forms of heart disease	I30-I51	115.5	64.4
Other degenerative diseases of the nervous system	G30-G31	68.9	51.0
Cerebrovascular diseases	I60-I69	53.2	47.8
Other external causes of accidental injury	W00-X59	40.1	46.4
Chronic lower respiratory diseases	J40-J47	43.7	45.7
Organic, including symptomatic, mental disorders	F01-F09	24.3	35.9
Hypertensive diseases	I10-I15	43.2	35.0
Diabetes mellitus	E10-E14	17.7	29.6

Note: (a) ICD-10 = International Classification of Diseases 10th Revision; (1) Crude mortality rates are a three-year average covering 2019-2021; (2) Figures cover Madison County.
Source: Centers for Disease Control and Prevention, National Center for Health Statistics. National Vital Statistics System, Mortality 2018-2021 on CDC WONDER Online Database

Mortality Rates for Selected Causes of Death

ICD-10[a] Sub-Chapter	ICD-10[a] Code	Crude Mortality Rate[1] per 100,000 population County[2]	U.S.
Assault	X85-Y09	7.8	7.0
Diseases of the liver	K70-K76	25.3	19.8
Human immunodeficiency virus (HIV) disease	B20-B24	Suppressed	1.5
Influenza and pneumonia	J09-J18	13.4	14.7
Intentional self-harm	X60-X84	15.9	14.3
Malnutrition	E40-E46	8.3	4.3
Obesity and other hyperalimentation	E65-E68	Unreliable	3.0
Renal failure	N17-N19	16.5	15.7
Transport accidents	V01-V99	15.1	13.6
Viral hepatitis	B15-B19	Suppressed	1.2

Note: (a) ICD-10 = International Classification of Diseases 10th Revision; (1) Crude mortality rates are a three-year average covering 2019-2021; (2) Figures cover Madison County; Data are suppressed when the data meet the criteria for confidentiality constraints; Crude mortality rates are flagged as unreliable when the rate would be calculated with a numerator of 20 or less.
Source: Centers for Disease Control and Prevention, National Center for Health Statistics. National Vital Statistics System, Mortality 2018-2021 on CDC WONDER Online Database

Health Insurance Coverage

Area	With Health Insurance	With Private Health Insurance	With Public Health Insurance	Without Health Insurance	Population Under Age 19 Without Health Insurance
City	90.1	72.6	33.3	9.9	3.9
MSA[1]	91.9	77.2	29.5	8.1	3.1
U.S.	91.2	67.8	35.4	8.8	5.3

Note: Figures are percentages that cover the civilian noninstitutionalized population; (1) Figures cover the Huntsville, AL Metropolitan Statistical Area
Source: U.S. Census Bureau, 2017-2021 American Community Survey 5-Year Estimates

Number of Medical Professionals

Area	MDs[3]	DOs[3,4]	Dentists	Podiatrists	Chiropractors	Optometrists
County[1] (number)	1,070	52	204	13	93	75
County[1] (rate[2])	274.6	13.3	51.6	3.3	23.5	19.0
U.S. (rate[2])	289.3	23.5	72.5	6.2	28.7	17.4

Note: Data as of 2021 unless noted; (1) Data covers Madison County; (2) Rate per 100,000 population; (3) Data as of 2020 and includes all active, non-federal physicians; (4) Doctor of Osteopathic Medicine
Source: U.S. Department of Health and Human Services, Health Resources and Services Administration, Bureau of Health Professions, Area Resource File (ARF) 2021-2022

EDUCATION

Public School District Statistics

District Name	Schls	Pupils	Pupil/Teacher Ratio	Minority Pupils[1] (%)	LEP/ELL[2] (%)	IEP[3] (%)
Huntsville City	46	23,939	18.2	61.4	5.8	13.2
Madison County	30	19,873	19.1	41.1	1.3	12.3

Note: Table includes school districts with 2,000 or more students; (1) Percentage of students that are not non-Hispanic white; (2) Percentage of students that are Limited English Proficient or English Language Learners (2018-19); (3) Percentage of students that have an Individualized Education Program (2019-20).
Source: U.S. Department of Education, National Center for Education Statistics, Common Core of Data, Local Education Agency (School District) Universe Survey: School Year 2021-2022

Best High Schools

According to *U.S. News*, Huntsville is home to one of the top 500 high schools in the U.S.: **New Century Tech Demo High School** (#166). Nearly 18,000 public, magnet and charter schools were ranked based on their performance on state assessments and how well they prepare students for college. *U.S. News & World Report, "Best High Schools 2022"*

Highest Level of Education

Area	Less than H.S.	H.S. Diploma	Some College, No Deg.	Associate Degree	Bachelor's Degree	Master's Degree	Prof. School Degree	Doctorate Degree
City	8.9	17.6	20.9	7.9	26.7	13.7	1.9	2.5
MSA[1]	9.2	20.9	21.0	8.0	25.2	12.4	1.5	1.8
U.S.	11.1	26.5	20.0	8.7	20.6	9.3	2.2	1.5

Note: Figures cover persons age 25 and over; (1) Figures cover the Huntsville, AL Metropolitan Statistical Area
Source: U.S. Census Bureau, 2017-2021 American Community Survey 5-Year Estimates

Educational Attainment by Race

Area	High School Graduate or Higher (%) Total	White	Black	Asian	Hisp.[2]	Bachelor's Degree or Higher (%) Total	White	Black	Asian	Hisp.[2]
City	91.1	93.8	86.8	88.8	72.3	44.8	51.8	29.4	56.2	29.2
MSA[1]	90.8	92.5	87.5	89.5	74.7	40.9	43.4	32.1	60.6	27.7
U.S.	88.9	91.4	87.2	87.6	71.2	33.7	35.5	23.3	55.6	18.4

Note: Figures shown cover persons 25 years old and over; (1) Figures cover the Huntsville, AL Metropolitan Statistical Area; (2) People of Hispanic origin can be of any race
Source: U.S. Census Bureau, 2017-2021 American Community Survey 5-Year Estimates

School Enrollment by Grade and Control

Area	Preschool (%) Public	Private	Kindergarten (%) Public	Private	Grades 1-4 (%) Public	Private	Grades 5-8 (%) Public	Private	Grades 9-12 (%) Public	Private
City	58.2	41.8	85.2	14.8	81.8	18.2	78.4	21.6	82.1	17.9
MSA[1]	57.2	42.8	80.7	19.3	82.7	17.3	81.5	18.5	81.8	18.2
U.S.	58.8	41.2	86.3	13.7	88.3	11.7	88.6	11.4	89.4	10.6

Note: Figures shown cover persons 3 years old and over; (1) Figures cover the Huntsville, AL Metropolitan Statistical Area
Source: U.S. Census Bureau, 2017-2021 American Community Survey 5-Year Estimates

Higher Education

Four-Year Colleges Public	Private Non-profit	Private For-profit	Two-Year Colleges Public	Private Non-profit	Private For-profit	Medical Schools[1]	Law Schools[2]	Voc/Tech[3]
3	2	0	2	0	0	0	0	3

Note: Figures cover institutions located within the Huntsville, AL Metropolitan Statistical Area and include main campuses only; (1) includes schools accredited by the Liaison Committee on Medical Education and the American Osteopathic Association's Commission on Osteopathic College Accreditation; (2) includes ABA-accredited schools, schools with provisional ABA accreditation, and state accredited schools; (3) includes all schools with programs that are less than 2 years.
Source: National Center for Education Statistics, Integrated Postsecondary Education System (IPEDS), 2021-22; Wikipedia, List of Medical Schools in the United States, accessed April 10, 2023; Wikipedia, List of Law Schools in the United States, accessed April 10, 2023

EMPLOYERS

Major Employers

Company Name	Industry
Avocent Corporation	Computer peripheral equip
City of Huntsville	Municipal government
City of Huntsville	Municipal government
COLSA Corporation	Commercial research laboratory
County of Madison	County government
Dynetics	Engineering laboratory/except testing
General Dynamics C4 Systems	Defense systems equipment
Healthcare Auth - City of Huntsville	General government
Intergraph Process & Bldg Solutions	Systems software development
Qualitest Products	Drugs & drug proprietaries
Science Applications Int'l Corporation	Computer processing services/commercial research lab
Teledyne Brown Engineering	Energy research
The Boeing Company	Aircraft/guided missiles/space vehicles
U.S. Army	U.S. military
United States Department of the Army	Army

Note: Companies shown are located within the Huntsville, AL Metropolitan Statistical Area.
Source: Hoovers.com; Wikipedia

Huntsville, Alabama

PUBLIC SAFETY

Crime Rate

Area	Total Crime	Violent Crime Rate				Property Crime Rate		
		Murder	Rape[3]	Robbery	Aggrav. Assault	Burglary	Larceny-Theft	Motor Vehicle Theft
City	n/a	n/a	n/a	n/a	n/a	n/a	n/a	n/a
Suburbs[1]	n/a	n/a	n/a	n/a	n/a	n/a	n/a	n/a
Metro[2]	n/a	n/a	n/a	n/a	n/a	n/a	n/a	n/a
U.S.	2,356.7	6.5	38.4	73.9	279.7	314.2	1,398.0	246.0

Note: Figures are crimes per 100,000 population; (1) All areas within the metro area that are located outside the city limits; (2) Figures cover the Huntsville, AL Metropolitan Statistical Area; n/a not available; (3) All figures shown were reported using the revised Uniform Crime Reporting (UCR) definition of rape; Due to the transition to the National Incident-Based Reporting System (NIBRS), limited city and metro area data was released for 2021.
Source: FBI Uniform Crime Reports, 2020

Hate Crimes

Area	Number of Quarters Reported	Number of Incidents per Bias Motivation					
		Race/Ethnicity/Ancestry	Religion	Sexual Orientation	Disability	Gender	Gender Identity
City	4	0	0	0	0	0	0
U.S.	4	5,227	1,244	1,110	130	75	266

Note: Due to the transition to the National Incident-Based Reporting System (NIBRS), limited crime data was released for 2021.
Source: Federal Bureau of Investigation, Hate Crime Statistics 2020

Identity Theft Consumer Reports

Area	Reports	Reports per 100,000 Population	Rank[2]
MSA[1]	1,382	297	71
U.S.	1,108,609	339	-

Note: (1) Figures cover the Huntsville, AL Metropolitan Statistical Area; (2) Rank ranges from 1 to 391 where 1 indicates greatest number of identity theft reports per 100,000 population
Source: Federal Trade Commission, Consumer Sentinel Network Data Book 2022

Fraud and Other Consumer Reports

Area	Reports	Reports per 100,000 Population	Rank[2]
MSA[1]	5,881	1,266	36
U.S.	4,064,520	1,245	-

Note: (1) Figures cover the Huntsville, AL Metropolitan Statistical Area; (2) Rank ranges from 1 to 391 where 1 indicates greatest number of fraud and other consumer reports per 100,000 population
Source: Federal Trade Commission, Consumer Sentinel Network Data Book 2022

POLITICS

2020 Presidential Election Results

Area	Biden	Trump	Jorgensen	Hawkins	Other
Madison County	44.8	52.8	1.9	0.0	0.5
U.S.	51.3	46.8	1.2	0.3	0.5

Note: Results are percentages and may not add to 100% due to rounding
Source: Dave Leip's Atlas of U.S. Presidential Elections

SPORTS

Professional Sports Teams

Team Name	League	Year Established

No teams are located in the metro area
Source: Wikipedia, Major Professional Sports Teams of the United States and Canada, April 12, 2023

CLIMATE

Average and Extreme Temperatures

Temperature	Jan	Feb	Mar	Apr	May	Jun	Jul	Aug	Sep	Oct	Nov	Dec	Yr.
Extreme High (°F)	76	82	88	92	96	101	104	103	101	91	84	77	104
Average High (°F)	49	54	63	73	80	87	90	89	83	73	62	52	71
Average Temp. (°F)	39	44	52	61	69	76	80	79	73	62	51	43	61
Average Low (°F)	30	33	41	49	58	65	69	68	62	50	40	33	50
Extreme Low (°F)	-11	5	6	26	36	45	53	52	37	28	15	-3	-11

Note: Figures cover the years 1958-1995
Source: National Climatic Data Center, International Station Meteorological Climate Summary, 9/96

Average Precipitation/Snowfall/Humidity

Precip./Humidity	Jan	Feb	Mar	Apr	May	Jun	Jul	Aug	Sep	Oct	Nov	Dec	Yr.
Avg. Precip. (in.)	5.0	5.0	6.6	4.8	5.1	4.3	4.6	3.5	4.1	3.3	4.7	5.7	56.8
Avg. Snowfall (in.)	2	1	1	Tr	0	0	0	0	0	Tr	Tr	1	4
Avg. Rel. Hum. 7am (%)	82	81	79	78	79	81	84	86	85	86	84	81	82
Avg. Rel. Hum. 4pm (%)	60	56	51	46	51	53	56	55	54	51	55	60	54

Note: Figures cover the years 1958-1995; Tr = Trace amounts (<0.05 in. of rain; <0.5 in. of snow)
Source: National Climatic Data Center, International Station Meteorological Climate Summary, 9/96

Weather Conditions

Temperature			Daytime Sky			Precipitation		
10°F & below	32°F & below	90°F & above	Clear	Partly cloudy	Cloudy	0.01 inch or more precip.	0.1 inch or more snow/ice	Thunder-storms
2	66	49	70	118	177	116	2	54

Note: Figures are average number of days per year and cover the years 1958-1995
Source: National Climatic Data Center, International Station Meteorological Climate Summary, 9/96

HAZARDOUS WASTE

Superfund Sites

The Huntsville, AL metro area has no sites on the EPA's Superfund Final National Priorities List. There are a total of 1,165 Superfund sites with a status of proposed or final on the list in the U.S. *U.S. Environmental Protection Agency, National Priorities List, April 12, 2023*

AIR QUALITY

Air Quality Trends: Ozone

	1990	1995	2000	2005	2010	2015	2018	2019	2020	2021
MSA[1]	0.079	0.080	0.088	0.075	0.071	0.063	0.065	0.063	0.057	0.061
U.S.	0.087	0.089	0.081	0.080	0.072	0.067	0.069	0.065	0.065	0.067

Note: (1) Data covers the Huntsville, AL Metropolitan Statistical Area. The values shown are the composite ozone concentration averages among trend sites based on the highest fourth daily maximum 8-hour concentration in parts per million. These trends are based on sites having an adequate record of monitoring data during the trend period. Data from exceptional events are included.
Source: U.S. Environmental Protection Agency, Air Quality Monitoring Information, "Air Quality Trends by City, 1990-2021"

Air Quality Index

Area	Percent of Days when Air Quality was...[2]					AQI Statistics[2]	
	Good	Moderate	Unhealthy for Sensitive Groups	Unhealthy	Very Unhealthy	Maximum	Median
MSA[1]	75.4	24.1	0.6	0.0	0.0	105	41

Note: (1) Data covers the Huntsville, AL Metropolitan Statistical Area; (2) Based on 357 days with AQI data in 2021. Air Quality Index (AQI) is an index for reporting daily air quality. EPA calculates the AQI for five major air pollutants regulated by the Clean Air Act: ground-level ozone, particle pollution (aka particulate matter), carbon monoxide, sulfur dioxide, and nitrogen dioxide. The AQI runs from 0 to 500. The higher the AQI value, the greater the level of air pollution and the greater the health concern. There are six AQI categories: "Good" AQI is between 0 and 50. Air quality is considered satisfactory; "Moderate" AQI is between 51 and 100. Air quality is acceptable; "Unhealthy for Sensitive Groups" When AQI values are between 101 and 150, members of sensitive groups may experience health effects; "Unhealthy" When AQI values are between 151 and 200 everyone may begin to experience health effects; "Very Unhealthy" AQI values between 201 and 300 trigger a health alert; "Hazardous" AQI values over 300 trigger warnings of emergency conditions (not shown).
Source: U.S. Environmental Protection Agency, Air Quality Index Report, 2021

Air Quality Index Pollutants

Area	Percent of Days when AQI Pollutant was...[2]					
	Carbon Monoxide	Nitrogen Dioxide	Ozone	Sulfur Dioxide	Particulate Matter 2.5	Particulate Matter 10
MSA[1]	0.0	0.0	33.3	(3)	63.0	3.6

Note: (1) Data covers the Huntsville, AL Metropolitan Statistical Area; (2) Based on 357 days with AQI data in 2021. The Air Quality Index (AQI) is an index for reporting daily air quality. EPA calculates the AQI for five major air pollutants regulated by the Clean Air Act: ground-level ozone, particle pollution (also known as particulate matter), carbon monoxide, sulfur dioxide, and nitrogen dioxide. The AQI runs from 0 to 500. The higher the AQI value, the greater the level of air pollution and the greater the health concern; (3) Sulfur dioxide is no longer included in this table (as of December 8, 2021) because SO_2 concentrations tend to be very localized and not necessarily representative of broad geographical areas like counties and CBSAs.
Source: U.S. Environmental Protection Agency, Air Quality Index Report, 2021

Maximum Air Pollutant Concentrations: Particulate Matter, Ozone, CO and Lead

	Particulate Matter 10 (ug/m³)	Particulate Matter 2.5 Wtd AM (ug/m³)	Particulate Matter 2.5 24-Hr (ug/m³)	Ozone (ppm)	Carbon Monoxide (ppm)	Lead (ug/m³)
MSA[1] Level	36	7.5	17	0.061	n/a	n/a
NAAQS[2]	150	15	35	0.075	9	0.15
Met NAAQS[2]	Yes	Yes	Yes	Yes	n/a	n/a

Note: (1) Data covers the Huntsville, AL Metropolitan Statistical Area; Data from exceptional events are included; (2) National Ambient Air Quality Standards; ppm = parts per million; ug/m³ = micrograms per cubic meter; n/a not available.
Concentrations: Particulate Matter 10 (coarse particulate)—highest second maximum 24-hour concentration; Particulate Matter 2.5 Wtd AM (fine particulate)—highest weighted annual mean concentration; Particulate Matter 2.5 24-Hour (fine particulate)—highest 98th percentile 24-hour concentration; Ozone—highest fourth daily maximum 8-hour concentration; Carbon Monoxide—highest second maximum non-overlapping 8-hour concentration; Lead—maximum running 3-month average
Source: U.S. Environmental Protection Agency, Air Quality Monitoring Information, "Air Quality Statistics by City, 2021"

Maximum Air Pollutant Concentrations: Nitrogen Dioxide and Sulfur Dioxide

	Nitrogen Dioxide AM (ppb)	Nitrogen Dioxide 1-Hr (ppb)	Sulfur Dioxide AM (ppb)	Sulfur Dioxide 1-Hr (ppb)	Sulfur Dioxide 24-Hr (ppb)
MSA[1] Level	n/a	n/a	n/a	n/a	n/a
NAAQS[2]	53	100	30	75	140
Met NAAQS[2]	n/a	n/a	n/a	n/a	n/a

Note: (1) Data covers the Huntsville, AL Metropolitan Statistical Area; Data from exceptional events are included; (2) National Ambient Air Quality Standards; ppm = parts per million; ug/m³ = micrograms per cubic meter; n/a not available.
Concentrations: Nitrogen Dioxide AM—highest arithmetic mean concentration; Nitrogen Dioxide 1-Hr—highest 98th percentile 1-hour daily maximum concentration; Sulfur Dioxide AM—highest annual mean concentration; Sulfur Dioxide 1-Hr—highest 99th percentile 1-hour daily maximum concentration; Sulfur Dioxide 24-Hr—highest second maximum 24-hour concentration
Source: U.S. Environmental Protection Agency, Air Quality Monitoring Information, "Air Quality Statistics by City, 2021"

Jacksonville, Florida

Background

Modern day Jacksonville is largely a product of the reconstruction that occurred during the 1940s after a fire razed 147 city blocks a few decades earlier. Lying under the modern structures, however, is a history that dates back earlier than the settlement of Plymouth by the Pilgrims.

Located in the northeast part of Florida on the St. John's River, Jacksonville, the largest city in land area in the contiguous United States, was settled by English, Spanish, and French explorers from the sixteenth through the eighteenth centuries. Sites commemorating their presence include Fort Caroline National Monument, marking the French settlement led by René de Goulaine Laudonnière in 1564; Spanish Pond one-quarter of a mile east of Fort Caroline, where Spanish forces led by Pedro Menendez captured the Fort; and Fort George Island, from which General James Oglethorpe led English attacks against the Spanish during the eighteenth century.

Jacksonville was attractive to these early settlers because of its easy access to the Atlantic Ocean, which meant a favorable port. Today, Jacksonville remains a military and civilian deep-water port. The city is home to Naval Station Mayport, Naval Air Station Jacksonville, the U.S. Marine Corps Bount Island command, and the Port of Jacksonville, Florida's third largest seaport. Jacksonville's military bases and the nearby Naval Submarine Base Kings Bay form the third largest military presence in the United States.

Jacksonville is the financial hub of Florida, and many business and financial companies are headquartered in the city. As with much of Florida, tourism is important to Jacksonville, particularly tourism related to golf.

Jacksonville voters approved The Better Jacksonville Plan in 2000, which authorized a half-penny sales tax to generate revenue for major improvement city projects, environmental protection and economic development. Recent improvements to the city's highway system are designed to reduce congestion, through 2030.

On the cultural front, Jacksonville boasts a range of options, including the Children's Museum, the Jacksonville Symphony Orchestra, the Gator Bowl, and beach facilities. The Jacksonville Jazz Festival, held every April, is the second-largest jazz festival in the nation. The city is home to several theaters, including Little Theatre, which, operating since 1919, is one of the oldest operating community theaters in the nation.

In 2005, the city hosted Super Bowl XXXIX at the former Alltel Stadium (now Jacksonville Municipal Stadium), home of the NFL's Jacksonville Jaguars.

The city also boasts the largest urban park system in the United States, providing services at more than 337 locations on more than 80,000 acres located throughout the city. Most recently, The Jacksonville Arboretum and Gardens was opened in 2008.

Summers are long, warm, and relatively humid. Winters are generally mild, although periodic invasions of cold northern air bring the temperature down. Temperatures along the beaches rarely rise above 90 degrees. Summer coastal thunderstorms usually occur before noon and move inland in the afternoons. The greatest rainfall, as localized thundershowers, occurs during the summer months. Although in the hurricane belt, this section of the coast has escaped hurricane-force winds in recent history until 2016, when Hurricane Matthew caused major flooding and damage to the city, Jacksonville Beach, Atlantic Beach, and Neptune Beach. In September 2017, Hurricane Irma caused record breaking floods in Jacksonville not seen since 1846.

Rankings

General Rankings

- For its "Best for Vets: Places to Live 2019" rankings, *Military Times* evaluated 599 cities (83 large, 234 medium, 282 small) and compared the locations across three broad categories: veteran and military culture/services; economic indicators; and livability factors such as health, crime, traffic, and school quality. Jacksonville ranked #10 out of the top 25, in the large city category (population of more than 250,000). Data points more specific to veterans and the military weighed more heavily than others. *rebootcamp.militarytimes.com, "Military Times Best Places to Live 2019," September 10, 2018*

- *US News & World Report* conducted a survey of more than 3,600 people and analyzed the 150 largest metropolitan areas to determine what matters most when selecting where to settle down. Jacksonville ranked #24 out of the top 25 as having the best combination of desirable factors. Criteria: cost of living; quality of life and education; net migration; job market; desirability; and other factors. *money.usnews.com, "The 25 Best Places to Live in the U.S. in 2022-2023," May 17, 2022*

- The Jacksonville metro area was identified as one of America's fastest-growing areas in terms of population and economy by *Forbes*. The area ranked #16 out of 25. The 100 most populous metro areas in the U.S. were evaluated on the following criteria: estimated population growth; employment; economic output; wages; home values. *Forbes, "America's Fastest-Growing Cities 2018," February 28, 2018*

- Jacksonville was selected as one of the best places to live in America by *Outside Magazine*. Criteria centered on diversity; sustainability; outdoor equity; and affordability. Local experts shared highlights from hands-on experience in each location. *Outside Magazine, "The 20 Most Livable Towns and Cities in America," October 15, 2021*

Business/Finance Rankings

- The Brookings Institution ranked the nation's largest cities based on income inequality. Jacksonville was ranked #91 (#1 = greatest inequality). Criteria: the "95/20 ratio," a figure representing the income at which a household earns more than 95 percent of all other households, divided by the income at which a household earns more than only 20 percent of all other households. *Brookings Institution, "Household Income Inequality, Largest Cities of 97 Large U.S. Metro Areas, 2014-2016," February 5, 2018*

- The Brookings Institution ranked the 100 largest metro areas in the U.S. based on income inequality. Jacksonville was ranked #77 (#1 = greatest inequality). Criteria: the "95/20 ratio," a figure representing the income at which a household earns more than 95 percent of all other households, divided by the income at which a household earns more than only 20 percent of all other households. *Brookings Institution, "Household Income Inequality, 100 Largest U.S. Metro Areas, 2014-2016," February 5, 2018*

- The Jacksonville metro area appeared on the Milken Institute "2022 Best Performing Cities" list. Rank: #24 out of 200 large metro areas (population over 250,000). Criteria: job growth; wage and salary growth; high-tech output growth; housing affordability; household broadband access. *Milken Institute, "Best-Performing Cities 2022," March 28, 2022*

- *Forbes* ranked the 200 most populous metro areas to determine the nation's "Best Places for Business and Careers." The Jacksonville metro area was ranked #22. Criteria: costs (business and living); job growth (past and projected); income growth; quality of life; educational attainment (college and high school); projected economic growth; cultural and leisure opportunities; workplace tolerance laws; net migration patterns. *Forbes, "The Best Places for Business and Careers 2019: Seattle Still On Top," October 30, 2019*

Dating/Romance Rankings

- Jacksonville was ranked #10 out of 25 cities that stood out for inspiring romance and attracting diners on the website OpenTable.com. Criteria: percentage of people who dined out on Valentine's Day in 2018; percentage of romantic restaurants as rated by OpenTable diner reviews; and percentage of tables seated for two. *OpenTable, "25 Most Romantic Cities in America for 2019," February 7, 2019*

Education Rankings

- Personal finance website *WalletHub* analyzed the 150 largest U.S. metropolitan statistical areas to determine where the most educated Americans are putting their degrees to work. Criteria: education levels; percentage of workers with degrees; education quality and attainment gap; public school quality rankings; quality and enrollment of each metro area's universities. Jacksonville was ranked #75 (#1 = most educated city). *www.WalletHub.com, "Most & Least Educated Cities in America," July 18, 2022*

- Jacksonville was selected as one of America's most literate cities. The city ranked #64 out of the 84 largest U.S. cities. Criteria: number of booksellers; library resources; Internet resources; educational attainment; periodical publishing resources; newspaper circulation. *Central Connecticut State University, "America's Most Literate Cities, 2018," February 2019*

Environmental Rankings

- Jacksonville was highlighted as one of the cleanest metro areas for ozone air pollution in the U.S. during 2019 through 2021. The list represents cities with no monitored ozone air pollution in unhealthful ranges. *American Lung Association, "State of the Air 2023," April 19, 2023*

Health/Fitness Rankings

- For each of the 100 largest cities in the United States, the American Fitness Index®, compiled in partnership between the American College of Sports Medicine and the Elevance Health Foundation, evaluated community infrastructure and 34 health behaviors including preventive health, levels of chronic disease conditions, food insecurity, sleep quality, pedestrian safety, air quality, and community/environment resources that support physical activity. Jacksonville ranked #71 for "community fitness." *americanfitnessindex.org, "2022 ACSM American Fitness Index Summary Report," July 12, 2022*

- Jacksonville was identified as a "2022 Spring Allergy Capital." The area ranked #20 out of 100. Three groups of factors were used to identify the most challenging cities for people with allergies during the spring season: annual spring pollen scores; over the counter allergy medicine use; number of board-certified allergy specialists. *Asthma and Allergy Foundation of America, "Spring Allergy Capitals 2022," March 2, 2022*

- Jacksonville was identified as a "2022 Fall Allergy Capital." The area ranked #26 out of 100. Three groups of factors were used to identify the most challenging cities for people with allergies during the fall season: annual fall pollen scores; over the counter allergy medicine use; number of board-certified allergy specialists. *Asthma and Allergy Foundation of America, "Fall Allergy Capitals 2022," March 2, 2022*

- Jacksonville was identified as a "2022 Asthma Capital." The area ranked #31 out of the nation's 100 largest metropolitan areas. Criteria: estimated asthma prevalence; asthma-related mortality; and ER visits due to asthma. Risk factors analyzed but not factored in the rankings: annual pollen score; annual air quality; public smoking laws; access to board-certified asthma specialists; rescue and controller medication use; uninsured rate; poverty rate. *Asthma and Allergy Foundation of America, "Asthma Capitals 2022: The Most Challenging Places to Live With Asthma," September 14, 2022*

Real Estate Rankings

- *WalletHub* compared the most populated U.S. cities to determine which had the best markets for real estate agents. Jacksonville ranked #21 where demand was high and pay was the best. Criteria: sales per agent; annual median wage for real-estate agents; monthly average starting salary for real estate agents; real estate job density and competition; unemployment rate; home turnover rate; housing-market health index; and other relevant metrics. *www.WalletHub.com, "2021 Best Places to Be a Real Estate Agent," May 12, 2021*

- According to Penske Truck Rental, the Jacksonville metro area was named the #8 moving destination in 2022, based on one-way consumer truck rental reservations made through Penske's website, rental locations, and reservations call center. *gopenske.com/blog, "Penske Truck Rental's 2022 Top Moving Destinations," April 27, 2023*

- Jacksonville was ranked #125 out of 235 metro areas in terms of housing affordability in 2022 by the National Association of Home Builders (#1 = most affordable). Criteria: the share of homes sold in that area affordable to a family earning the local median income, based on standard mortgage underwriting criteria. *National Association of Home Builders®, NAHB-Wells Fargo Housing Opportunity Index, 4th Quarter 2022*

- The nation's largest metro areas were analyzed in terms of the percentage of households entering some stage of foreclosure in 2022. The Jacksonville metro area ranked #7 out of 8 (#1 = highest foreclosure rate). *ATTOM Data Solutions, "2022 Year-End U.S. Foreclosure Market Report™," January 12, 2023*

Safety Rankings

- Allstate ranked the 200 largest cities in America in terms of driver safety. Jacksonville ranked #69. Criteria: internal property damage claims over a two-year period from January 2016 to December 2017. The report helps increase the importance of safety and awareness behind the wheel. *Allstate, "Allstate America's Best Drivers Report, 2019" June 24, 2019*

- The National Insurance Crime Bureau ranked 390 metro areas in the U.S. in terms of per capita rates of vehicle theft. The Jacksonville metro area ranked #158 (#1 = highest rate). Criteria: number of vehicle theft offenses per 100,000 inhabitants in 2021. *National Insurance Crime Bureau, "Hot Spots 2021," September 1, 2022*

Seniors/Retirement Rankings

- Jacksonville made *Southern Living's* list of southern places—by the beach, in the mountains, river or college town—to retire. From the incredible views and close knit communities, to the opportunities to put down new roots, and great places to eat and hike, these superb places are perfect for settling down. *Southern Living, "The Best Places to Retire in the South," March 7, 2022*

- From its Best Cities for Successful Aging indexes, the Milken Institute generated rankings for metropolitan areas, weighing data in nine categories—health care, wellness, living arrangements, transportation and convenience, financial characteristics, education, employment, community engagement, and overall livability. The Jacksonville metro area was ranked #63 overall in the large metro area category. *Milken Institute, "Best Cities for Successful Aging, 2017" March 14, 2017*

- Jacksonville made the 2022 *Forbes* list of "25 Best Places to Retire." Criteria, focused on overall affordability as well as quality of life indicators, include: housing/living costs compared to the national average and state taxes; air quality; crime rates; home price appreciation; risk associated with climate-change/natural hazards; availability of medical care; bikeability; walkability; healthy living. *Forbes.com, "The Best Places to Retire in 2022," May 13, 2022*

Women/Minorities Rankings

- Personal finance website *WalletHub* compared more than 180 U.S. cities across two key dimensions, "Hispanic Business-Friendliness" and "Hispanic Purchasing Power," to arrive at the most favorable conditions for Hispanic entrepreneurs. Jacksonville was ranked #32 out of 182. Criteria includes: share of Hispanic-Owned Businesses; Hispanic entrepreneurship rate to median annual income of Hispanics; Small Business-Friendliness score; cost of living; and number of Hispanics with at least a bachelor's degree. *WalletHub.com, "2019's Best Cities for Hispanic Entrepreneurs," May 1, 2019*

Miscellaneous Rankings

- *WalletHub* compared the 150 most populated U.S. cities to determine their operating efficiency. A "Quality of Services" score was constructed for each city and then divided by the total budget per capita to reveal which were managed the best. Jacksonville ranked #78. Criteria: financial stability; economy; education; safety; health; infrastructure and pollution. *www.WalletHub.com, "2022's Best- & Worst-Run Cities in America," June 21, 2022*

Business Environment

DEMOGRAPHICS

Population Growth

Area	1990 Census	2000 Census	2010 Census	2020 Census	Population Growth (%) 1990-2020	Population Growth (%) 2010-2020
City	635,221	735,617	821,784	949,611	49.5	15.6
MSA[1]	925,213	1,122,750	1,345,596	1,605,848	73.6	19.3
U.S.	248,709,873	281,421,906	308,745,538	331,449,281	33.3	7.4

Note: (1) Figures cover the Jacksonville, FL Metropolitan Statistical Area
Source: U.S. Census Bureau, 1990 Census, 2000 Census, 2010 Census, 2020 Census

Race

Area	White Alone[2] (%)	Black Alone[2] (%)	Asian Alone[2] (%)	AIAN[3] Alone[2] (%)	NHOPI[4] Alone[2] (%)	Other Race Alone[2] (%)	Two or More Races (%)
City	50.1	30.6	5.1	0.4	0.1	4.6	9.1
MSA[1]	61.6	21.2	4.2	0.4	0.1	3.6	8.8
U.S.	61.6	12.4	6.0	1.1	0.2	8.4	10.2

Note: (1) Figures cover the Jacksonville, FL Metropolitan Statistical Area; (2) Alone is defined as not being in combination with one or more other races; (3) American Indian and Alaska Native; (4) Native Hawaiian and Other Pacific Islander
Source: U.S. Census Bureau, 2020 Census

Hispanic or Latino Origin

Area	Total (%)	Mexican (%)	Puerto Rican (%)	Cuban (%)	Other (%)
City	10.9	2.0	3.4	1.6	3.9
MSA[1]	9.6	1.9	3.0	1.3	3.5
U.S.	18.4	11.2	1.8	0.7	4.7

Note: Persons of Hispanic or Latino origin can be of any race; (1) Figures cover the Jacksonville, FL Metropolitan Statistical Area
Source: U.S. Census Bureau, 2017-2021 American Community Survey 5-Year Estimates

Age

Area	Under Age 5	Age 5–19	Age 20–34	Age 35–44	Age 45–54	Age 55–64	Age 65–74	Age 75–84	Age 85+	Median Age
City	6.0	18.2	22.3	12.9	12.2	13.1	9.3	4.2	1.6	37.4
MSA[1]	5.6	18.9	19.5	12.8	12.6	13.6	10.4	4.8	1.7	39.6
U.S.	5.6	19.2	20.2	12.7	12.4	13.1	10.0	4.9	1.9	38.8

Note: (1) Figures cover the Jacksonville, FL Metropolitan Statistical Area
Source: U.S. Census Bureau, 2020 Census

Disability by Age

Area	All Ages	Under 18 Years Old	18 to 64 Years Old	65 Years and Over
City	13.1	4.8	11.3	35.3
MSA[1]	13.0	4.6	10.9	33.2
U.S.	12.6	4.4	10.3	33.4

Note: Figures show percent of the civilian noninstitutionalized population that reported having a disability. Disability status is determined from six types of difficulty: vision, hearing, cognitive, ambulatory, self-care, and independent living. For children under 5 years old, hearing and vision difficulty are used to determine disability status. For children between the ages of 5 and 14, disability status is determined from hearing, vision, cognitive, ambulatory, and self-care difficulties. For people aged 15 years and older, they are considered to have a disability if they have difficulty with any one of the six difficulty types; Note: (1) Figures cover the Jacksonville, FL Metropolitan Statistical Area
Source: U.S. Census Bureau, 2017-2021 American Community Survey 5-Year Estimates

Ancestry

Area	German	Irish	English	American	Italian	Polish	French[2]	Scottish	Dutch
City	7.5	7.6	6.5	5.7	3.7	1.4	1.3	1.5	0.6
MSA[1]	9.3	9.4	8.9	7.9	4.3	1.8	1.7	2.0	0.7
U.S.	12.8	9.6	8.1	5.7	5.0	2.7	2.2	1.6	1.1

Note: Figures are the percentage of the total population reporting a particular ancestry. The nine most commonly reported ancestries in the U.S. are shown. Figures include multiple ancestries (e.g. if a person reported being Irish and Italian, they were included in both columns); (1) Figures cover the Jacksonville, FL Metropolitan Statistical Area; (2) Excludes Basque
Source: U.S. Census Bureau, 2017-2021 American Community Survey 5-Year Estimates

Foreign-born Population

Area	Any Foreign Country	Asia	Mexico	Europe	Caribbean	Central America[2]	South America	Africa	Canada
City	12.0	4.2	0.6	1.9	2.2	0.8	1.4	0.6	0.2
MSA[1]	9.8	3.3	0.5	1.8	1.6	0.7	1.2	0.4	0.2
U.S.	13.6	4.2	3.3	1.5	1.4	1.1	1.1	0.8	0.2

Note: (1) Figures cover the Jacksonville, FL Metropolitan Statistical Area; (2) Excludes Mexico.
Source: U.S. Census Bureau, 2017-2021 American Community Survey 5-Year Estimates

Household Size

Area	One	Two	Three	Four	Five	Six	Seven or More	Average Household Size
City	32.3	32.8	16.3	10.7	5.2	1.6	1.0	2.50
MSA[1]	28.0	34.8	16.5	12.1	5.7	1.9	1.0	2.60
U.S.	28.1	33.8	15.5	12.9	6.0	2.3	1.4	2.60

Note: (1) Figures cover the Jacksonville, FL Metropolitan Statistical Area
Source: U.S. Census Bureau, 2017-2021 American Community Survey 5-Year Estimates

Household Relationships

Area	Householder	Opposite-sex Spouse	Same-sex Spouse	Opposite-sex Unmarried Partner	Same-sex Unmarried Partner	Child[2]	Grandchild	Other Relatives	Non-relatives
City	39.9	15.6	0.2	2.8	0.2	27.7	2.8	4.9	3.6
MSA[1]	39.1	17.9	0.2	2.6	0.2	28.0	2.6	4.3	3.2
U.S.	38.3	17.5	0.2	2.5	0.2	28.3	2.4	4.8	3.4

Note: Figures are percent of the total population; (1) Figures cover the Jacksonville, FL Metropolitan Statistical Area; (2) Includes biological, adopted, and stepchildren of the householder
Source: U.S. Census Bureau, 2020 Census

Gender

Area	Males	Females	Males per 100 Females
City	459,204	490,407	93.6
MSA[1]	779,083	826,765	94.2
U.S.	162,685,811	168,763,470	96.4

Note: (1) Figures cover the Jacksonville, FL Metropolitan Statistical Area
Source: U.S. Census Bureau, 2020 Census

Marital Status

Area	Never Married	Now Married[2]	Separated	Widowed	Divorced
City	36.0	42.4	2.1	5.5	14.0
MSA[1]	31.7	47.7	1.8	5.6	13.2
U.S.	33.8	48.0	1.8	5.6	10.8

Note: Figures are percentages and cover the population 15 years of age and older; (1) Figures cover the Jacksonville, FL Metropolitan Statistical Area; (2) Excludes separated
Source: U.S. Census Bureau, 2017-2021 American Community Survey 5-Year Estimates

Religious Groups by Family

Area	Catholic	Baptist	Methodist	LDS[2]	Pentecostal	Lutheran	Islam	Adventist	Other
MSA[1]	13.0	14.5	3.0	1.0	1.4	0.4	0.6	1.3	20.5
U.S.	18.7	7.3	3.0	2.0	1.8	1.7	1.3	1.3	11.6

Note: Figures are the number of adherents as a percentage of the total population and cover the eight largest religious groups in the U.S; (1) Figures cover the Jacksonville, FL Metropolitan Statistical Area; (2) Church of Jesus Christ of Latter-day Saints
Sources: 2020 U.S. Religion Census, Association of Statisticians of American Religious Bodies; The Association of Religion Data Archives (ARDA)

Religious Groups by Tradition

Area	Catholic	Evangelical Protestant	Mainline Protestant	Black Protestant	Islam	Judaism	Hinduism	Orthodox	Buddhism
MSA[1]	13.0	29.8	3.5	5.6	0.6	0.3	0.3	0.3	0.2
U.S.	18.7	16.5	5.2	2.3	1.3	0.6	0.4	0.4	0.3

Note: Figures are the number of adherents as a percentage of the total population; (1) Figures cover the Jacksonville, FL Metropolitan Statistical Area
Sources: 2020 U.S. Religion Census, Association of Statisticians of American Religious Bodies; The Association of Religion Data Archives (ARDA)

Jacksonville, Florida 299

ECONOMY

Gross Metropolitan Product

Area	2020	2021	2022	2023	Rank[2]
MSA[1]	91.0	100.3	109.1	115.5	42

Note: Figures are in billions of dollars; (1) Figures cover the Jacksonville, FL Metropolitan Statistical Area; (2) Rank is based on 2021 data and ranges from 1 to 381
Source: U.S. Conference of Mayors, U.S. Metro Economies: U.S. Metros Compared to Global and State Economies, June 2022

Economic Growth

Area	2018-20 (%)	2021 (%)	2022 (%)	2023 (%)	Rank[2]
MSA[1]	2.1	6.1	3.1	2.6	30
U.S.	-0.6	5.7	3.1	2.9	—

Note: Figures are real gross metropolitan product (GMP) growth rates and represent average annual percent change; (1) Figures cover the Jacksonville, FL Metropolitan Statistical Area; (2) Rank is based on 2020 2-year average annual percent change and ranges from 1 to 381
Source: U.S. Conference of Mayors, U.S. Metro Economies: U.S. Metros Compared to Global and State Economies, June 2022

Metropolitan Area Exports

Area	2016	2017	2018	2019	2020	2021	Rank[2]
MSA[1]	2,159.0	2,141.7	2,406.7	2,975.5	2,473.3	2,683.7	90

Note: Figures are in millions of dollars; (1) Figures cover the Jacksonville, FL Metropolitan Statistical Area; (2) Rank is based on 2021 data and ranges from 1 to 388
Source: U.S. Department of Commerce, International Trade Administration, Office of Trade and Economic Analysis, Industry and Analysis, Exports by Metropolitan Area, data extracted March 16, 2023

Building Permits

Area	Single-Family 2021	Single-Family 2022	Pct. Chg.	Multi-Family 2021	Multi-Family 2022	Pct. Chg.	Total 2021	Total 2022	Pct. Chg.
City	6,191	5,484	-11.4	3,778	5,862	55.2	9,969	11,346	13.8
MSA[1]	16,536	14,410	-12.9	6,202	8,759	41.2	22,738	23,169	1.9
U.S.	1,115,400	975,600	-12.5	621,600	689,500	10.9	1,737,000	1,665,100	-4.1

Note: (1) Figures cover the Jacksonville, FL Metropolitan Statistical Area; Figures represent new, privately-owned housing units authorized (unadjusted data); All permit data are based on estimates with imputation
Source: U.S. Census Bureau, Manufacturing, Mining, and Construction Statistics, Building Permits, 2021, 2022

Bankruptcy Filings

Area	Business Filings 2021	Business Filings 2022	% Chg.	Nonbusiness Filings 2021	Nonbusiness Filings 2022	% Chg.
Duval County	58	38	-34.5	1,336	1,226	-8.2
U.S.	14,347	13,481	-6.0	399,269	374,240	-6.3

Note: Business filings include Chapter 7, Chapter 9, Chapter 11, Chapter 12, Chapter 13, Chapter 15, and Section 304; Nonbusiness filings include Chapter 7, Chapter 11, and Chapter 13
Source: Administrative Office of the U.S. Courts, Business and Nonbusiness Bankruptcy, County Cases Commenced by Chapter of the Bankruptcy Code, During the 12-Month Period Ending December 31, 2021 and Business and Nonbusiness Bankruptcy, County Cases Commenced by Chapter of the Bankruptcy Code, During the 12-Month Period Ending December 31, 2022

Housing Vacancy Rates

Area	Gross Vacancy Rate[2] (%) 2020	2021	2022	Year-Round Vacancy Rate[3] (%) 2020	2021	2022	Rental Vacancy Rate[4] (%) 2020	2021	2022	Homeowner Vacancy Rate[5] (%) 2020	2021	2022
MSA[1]	9.5	8.3	8.9	9.3	7.6	7.7	7.5	5.6	6.2	1.5	0.4	1.7
U.S.	10.6	10.8	10.5	8.2	8.4	8.2	6.3	6.1	5.8	1.0	0.9	0.8

Note: (1) Figures cover the Jacksonville, FL Metropolitan Statistical Area; (2) The percentage of the total housing inventory that is vacant; (3) The percentage of the housing inventory (excluding seasonal units) that is year-round vacant; (4) The percentage of rental inventory that is vacant for rent; (5) The percentage of homeowner inventory that is vacant for sale
Source: U.S. Census Bureau, Housing Vacancies and Homeownership Annual Statistics: 2020, 2021, 2022

INCOME

Income

Area	Per Capita ($)	Median Household ($)	Average Household ($)
City	32,654	58,263	79,817
MSA[1]	36,316	66,664	91,361
U.S.	37,638	69,021	97,196

Note: (1) Figures cover the Jacksonville, FL Metropolitan Statistical Area
Source: U.S. Census Bureau, 2017-2021 American Community Survey 5-Year Estimates

Household Income Distribution

Area	Percent of Households Earning							
	Under $15,000	$15,000 -$24,999	$25,000 -$34,999	$35,000 -$49,999	$50,000 -$74,999	$75,000 -$99,999	$100,000 -$149,999	$150,000 and up
City	10.9	8.4	9.6	13.8	18.9	13.2	14.3	10.9
MSA[1]	9.0	7.1	8.6	12.5	18.3	13.7	15.8	15.0
U.S.	9.4	7.8	8.2	11.4	16.8	12.8	16.3	17.3

Note: (1) Figures cover the Jacksonville, FL Metropolitan Statistical Area
Source: U.S. Census Bureau, 2017-2021 American Community Survey 5-Year Estimates

Poverty Rate

Area	All Ages	Under 18 Years Old	18 to 64 Years Old	65 Years and Over
City	14.9	21.1	13.0	12.7
MSA[1]	12.3	17.2	11.3	9.3
U.S.	12.6	17.0	11.8	9.6

Note: Figures are percentage of people whose income during the past 12 months was below the poverty level; (1) Figures cover the Jacksonville, FL Metropolitan Statistical Area
Source: U.S. Census Bureau, 2017-2021 American Community Survey 5-Year Estimates

EMPLOYMENT

Labor Force and Employment

Area	Civilian Labor Force			Workers Employed		
	Dec. 2021	Dec. 2022	% Chg.	Dec. 2021	Dec. 2022	% Chg.
City	470,543	493,413	4.9	456,509	481,988	5.6
MSA[1]	806,862	847,564	5.0	785,663	829,550	5.6
U.S.	161,696,000	164,224,000	1.6	155,732,000	158,872,000	2.0

Note: Data is not seasonally adjusted and covers workers 16 years of age and older; (1) Figures cover the Jacksonville, FL Metropolitan Statistical Area
Source: Bureau of Labor Statistics, Local Area Unemployment Statistics

Unemployment Rate

Area	2022											
	Jan.	Feb.	Mar.	Apr.	May	Jun.	Jul.	Aug.	Sep.	Oct.	Nov.	Dec.
City	3.6	3.2	2.7	2.5	2.6	3.3	3.2	3.1	2.7	2.8	2.7	2.3
MSA[1]	3.2	2.9	2.5	2.2	2.3	2.9	2.8	2.8	2.5	2.5	2.5	2.1
U.S.	4.4	4.1	3.8	3.3	3.4	3.8	3.8	3.8	3.3	3.4	3.4	3.3

Note: Data is not seasonally adjusted and covers workers 16 years of age and older; (1) Figures cover the Jacksonville, FL Metropolitan Statistical Area
Source: Bureau of Labor Statistics, Local Area Unemployment Statistics

Average Wages

Occupation	$/Hr.	Occupation	$/Hr.
Accountants and Auditors	37.78	Maintenance and Repair Workers	20.57
Automotive Mechanics	21.66	Marketing Managers	72.46
Bookkeepers	22.39	Network and Computer Systems Admin.	43.58
Carpenters	21.96	Nurses, Licensed Practical	24.97
Cashiers	12.81	Nurses, Registered	37.74
Computer Programmers	45.61	Nursing Assistants	15.99
Computer Systems Analysts	47.46	Office Clerks, General	19.42
Computer User Support Specialists	27.33	Physical Therapists	44.49
Construction Laborers	18.20	Physicians	132.91
Cooks, Restaurant	15.75	Plumbers, Pipefitters and Steamfitters	23.81
Customer Service Representatives	19.12	Police and Sheriff's Patrol Officers	27.88
Dentists	82.64	Postal Service Mail Carriers	27.22
Electricians	24.62	Real Estate Sales Agents	29.37
Engineers, Electrical	48.04	Retail Salespersons	15.49
Fast Food and Counter Workers	12.07	Sales Representatives, Technical/Scientific	46.55
Financial Managers	73.04	Secretaries, Exc. Legal/Medical/Executive	19.30
First-Line Supervisors of Office Workers	31.15	Security Guards	15.13
General and Operations Managers	55.91	Surgeons	n/a
Hairdressers/Cosmetologists	16.72	Teacher Assistants, Exc. Postsecondary*	14.72
Home Health and Personal Care Aides	13.54	Teachers, Secondary School, Exc. Sp. Ed.*	31.72
Janitors and Cleaners	14.39	Telemarketers	15.08
Landscaping/Groundskeeping Workers	16.00	Truck Drivers, Heavy/Tractor-Trailer	24.87
Lawyers	62.74	Truck Drivers, Light/Delivery Services	21.39
Maids and Housekeeping Cleaners	13.79	Waiters and Waitresses	15.33

Note: Wage data covers the Jacksonville, FL Metropolitan Statistical Area; (*) Hourly wages were calculated from annual wage data based on a 40 hour work week; n/a not available.
Source: Bureau of Labor Statistics, Metro Area Occupational Employment & Wage Estimates, May 2022

Employment by Industry

Sector	MSA[1] Number of Employees	MSA[1] Percent of Total	U.S. Percent of Total
Construction	50,700	6.3	5.0
Private Education and Health Services	121,200	15.2	16.1
Financial Activities	75,400	9.4	5.9
Government	79,800	10.0	14.5
Information	13,900	1.7	2.0
Leisure and Hospitality	89,200	11.2	10.3
Manufacturing	35,700	4.5	8.4
Mining and Logging	400	0.1	0.4
Other Services	26,800	3.4	3.7
Professional and Business Services	130,500	16.3	14.7
Retail Trade	87,400	10.9	10.2
Transportation, Warehousing, and Utilities	59,000	7.4	4.9
Wholesale Trade	29,400	3.7	3.9

Note: Figures are non-farm employment as of December 2022. Figures are not seasonally adjusted and include workers 16 years of age and older; (1) Figures cover the Jacksonville, FL Metropolitan Statistical Area
Source: Bureau of Labor Statistics, Current Employment Statistics, Employment, Hours, and Earnings

Employment by Occupation

Occupation Classification	City (%)	MSA[1] (%)	U.S. (%)
Management, Business, Science, and Arts	37.6	39.7	40.3
Natural Resources, Construction, and Maintenance	8.2	8.2	8.7
Production, Transportation, and Material Moving	12.8	11.6	13.1
Sales and Office	23.7	23.6	20.9
Service	17.6	16.9	17.0

Note: Figures cover employed civilians 16 years of age and older; (1) Figures cover the Jacksonville, FL Metropolitan Statistical Area
Source: U.S. Census Bureau, 2017-2021 American Community Survey 5-Year Estimates

Occupations with Greatest Projected Employment Growth: 2022 – 2024

Occupation[1]	2022 Employment	2024 Projected Employment	Numeric Employment Change	Percent Employment Change
General and Operations Managers	196,430	209,480	13,050	6.6
Cooks, Restaurant	117,090	129,670	12,580	10.7
Registered Nurses	208,620	221,040	12,420	6.0
Waiters and Waitresses	194,570	206,380	11,810	6.1
Retail Salespersons	327,010	338,390	11,380	3.5
Stockers and Order Fillers	192,890	203,920	11,030	5.7
Customer Service Representatives	283,220	293,670	10,450	3.7
Fast Food and Counter Workers	203,420	212,470	9,050	4.4
Laborers and Freight, Stock, and Material Movers, Hand	138,200	146,930	8,730	6.3
Maids and Housekeeping Cleaners	77,330	85,600	8,270	10.7

Note: Projections cover Florida; (1) Sorted by numeric employment change
Source: www.projectionscentral.com, State Occupational Projections, 2022–2024 Short-Term Projections

Fastest-Growing Occupations: 2022 – 2024

Occupation[1]	2022 Employment	2024 Projected Employment	Numeric Employment Change	Percent Employment Change
Hotel, Motel, and Resort Desk Clerks	23,000	26,650	3,650	15.9
First-Line Supervisors of Gambling Services Workers	990	1,140	150	15.2
Baggage Porters and Bellhops	3,310	3,810	500	15.1
Solar Photovoltaic Installers	860	990	130	15.1
Nurse Practitioners	17,490	20,080	2,590	14.8
Motion Picture Projectionists	490	560	70	14.3
Lodging Managers	5,160	5,870	710	13.8
Transportation Workers, All Other	980	1,110	130	13.3
Information Security Analysts (SOC 2018)	11,910	13,480	1,570	13.2
Statisticians	1,370	1,550	180	13.1

Note: Projections cover Florida; (1) Sorted by percent employment change and excludes occupations with numeric employment change less than 50
Source: www.projectionscentral.com, State Occupational Projections, 2022–2024 Short-Term Projections

CITY FINANCES

City Government Finances

Component	2020 ($000)	2020 ($ per capita)
Total Revenues	4,048,615	4,442
Total Expenditures	4,111,000	4,510
Debt Outstanding	7,108,482	7,799
Cash and Securities[1]	2,441,761	2,679

Note: (1) Cash and security holdings of a government at the close of its fiscal year, including those of its dependent agencies, utilities, and liquor stores.
Source: U.S. Census Bureau, State & Local Government Finances 2020

City Government Revenue by Source

Source	2020 ($000)	2020 ($ per capita)	2020 (%)
General Revenue			
From Federal Government	88,771	97	2.2
From State Government	249,120	273	6.2
From Local Governments	272,110	299	6.7
Taxes			
Property	675,152	741	16.7
Sales and Gross Receipts	375,516	412	9.3
Personal Income	0	0	0.0
Corporate Income	0	0	0.0
Motor Vehicle License	0	0	0.0
Other Taxes	116,771	128	2.9
Current Charges	665,050	730	16.4
Liquor Store	0	0	0.0
Utility	1,464,996	1,607	36.2

Source: U.S. Census Bureau, State & Local Government Finances 2020

City Government Expenditures by Function

Function	2020 ($000)	2020 ($ per capita)	2020 (%)
General Direct Expenditures			
Air Transportation	104,440	114	2.5
Corrections	236	<1	<0.1
Education	0	0	0.0
Employment Security Administration	0	0	0.0
Financial Administration	248,647	272	6.0
Fire Protection	183,126	200	4.5
General Public Buildings	0	0	0.0
Governmental Administration, Other	26,120	28	0.6
Health	96,585	106	2.3
Highways	92,829	101	2.3
Hospitals	0	0	0.0
Housing and Community Development	18,783	20	0.5
Interest on General Debt	97,157	106	2.4
Judicial and Legal	42,895	47	1.0
Libraries	36,204	39	0.9
Parking	5,319	5	0.1
Parks and Recreation	151,291	166	3.7
Police Protection	451,200	495	11.0
Public Welfare	12,050	13	0.3
Sewerage	116,628	128	2.8
Solid Waste Management	81,528	89	2.0
Veterans' Services	0	0	0.0
Liquor Store	0	0	0.0
Utility	1,903,357	2,088	46.3

Source: U.S. Census Bureau, State & Local Government Finances 2020

TAXES

State Corporate Income Tax Rates

State	Tax Rate (%)	Income Brackets ($)	Num. of Brackets	Financial Institution Tax Rate (%)[a]	Federal Income Tax Ded.
Florida	5.5	Flat rate	1	5.5	No

Note: Tax rates as of January 1, 2023; (a) Rates listed are the corporate income tax rate applied to financial institutions or excise taxes based on income. Some states have other taxes based upon the value of deposits or shares.
Source: Federation of Tax Administrators, State Corporate Income Tax Rates, January 1, 2023

State Individual Income Tax Rates

State	Tax Rate (%)	Income Brackets ($)	Personal Exemptions ($) Single	Married	Depend.	Standard Ded. ($) Single	Married
Florida					– No state income tax –		

Note: Tax rates as of January 1, 2023; Local- and county-level taxes are not included
Source: Federation of Tax Administrators, State Individual Income Tax Rates, January 1, 2023

Various State Sales and Excise Tax Rates

State	State Sales Tax (%)	Gasoline[1] ($/gal.)	Cigarette[2] ($/pack)	Spirits[3] ($/gal.)	Wine[4] ($/gal.)	Beer[5] ($/gal.)	Recreational Marijuana (%)
Florida	6	0.4123	1.339	6.50	2.25	0.48	Not legal

Note: All tax rates as of January 1, 2023; (1) The American Petroleum Institute has developed a methodology for determining the average tax rate on a gallon of fuel. Rates may include any of the following: excise taxes, environmental fees, storage tank fees, other fees or taxes, general sales tax, and local taxes; (2) The federal excise tax of $1.0066 per pack and local taxes are not included; (3) Rates are those applicable to off-premise sales of 40% alcohol by volume (a.b.v.) distilled spirits in 750ml containers. Local excise taxes are excluded; (4) Rates are those applicable to off-premise sales of 11% a.b.v. non-carbonated wine in 750ml containers; (5) Rates are those applicable to off-premise sales of 4.7% a.b.v. beer in 12 ounce containers.
Source: Tax Foundation, 2023 Facts & Figures: How Does Your State Compare?

State Business Tax Climate Index Rankings

State	Overall Rank	Corporate Tax Rank	Individual Income Tax Rank	Sales Tax Rank	Property Tax Rank	Unemployment Insurance Tax Rank
Florida	4	10	1	21	12	3

Note: The index is a measure of how each state's tax laws affect economic performance. The lower the rank, the more favorable a state's tax system is for business. States without a given tax are given a ranking of 1. The scores/rankings for the District of Columbia do not affect other states. The 2023 index represents the tax climate as of July 1, 2022.
Source: Tax Foundation, State Business Tax Climate Index 2023

TRANSPORTATION

Means of Transportation to Work

Area	Car/Truck/Van Drove Alone	Car-pooled	Public Transportation Bus	Subway	Railroad	Bicycle	Walked	Other Means	Worked at Home
City	77.3	8.7	1.4	0.0	0.0	0.3	1.4	2.0	8.8
MSA[1]	76.8	8.2	0.9	0.0	0.0	0.4	1.3	1.9	10.5
U.S.	73.2	8.6	2.0	1.6	0.5	0.5	2.5	1.5	9.7

Note: Figures are percentages and cover workers 16 years of age and older; (1) Figures cover the Jacksonville, FL Metropolitan Statistical Area
Source: U.S. Census Bureau, 2017-2021 American Community Survey 5-Year Estimates

Travel Time to Work

Area	Less Than 10 Minutes	10 to 19 Minutes	20 to 29 Minutes	30 to 44 Minutes	45 to 59 Minutes	60 to 89 Minutes	90 Minutes or More
City	8.7	28.5	27.2	25.4	6.0	2.8	1.4
MSA[1]	9.1	26.1	24.3	26.1	8.6	4.2	1.6
U.S.	12.4	28.5	21.0	20.9	8.2	6.2	2.9

Note: Note: Figures are percentages and include workers 16 years old and over; (1) Figures cover the Jacksonville, FL Metropolitan Statistical Area
Source: U.S. Census Bureau, 2017-2021 American Community Survey 5-Year Estimates

Key Congestion Measures

Measure	1990	2000	2010	2015	2020
Annual Hours of Delay, Total (000)	10,620	21,108	29,864	33,457	16,143
Annual Hours of Delay, Per Auto Commuter	25	37	41	44	21
Annual Congestion Cost, Per Auto Commuter ($)	521	780	877	906	448

Note: Covers the Jacksonville FL urban area
Source: Texas A&M Transportation Institute, 2021 Urban Mobility Report

Freeway Travel Time Index

Measure	1985	1990	1995	2000	2005	2010	2015	2020
Urban Area Index[1]	1.08	1.12	1.14	1.17	1.20	1.18	1.19	1.06
Urban Area Rank[1,2]	40	35	41	36	36	38	38	75

Note: Freeway Travel Time Index—the ratio of travel time in the peak period to the travel time at free-flow conditions. For example, a value of 1.30 indicates a 20-minute free-flow trip takes 26 minutes in the peak (20 minutes x 1.30 = 26 minutes); (1) Covers the Jacksonville FL urban area; (2) Rank is based on 101 larger urban areas (#1 = highest travel time index)
Source: Texas A&M Transportation Institute, 2021 Urban Mobility Report

Public Transportation

Agency Name / Mode of Transportation	Vehicles Operated in Maximum Service[1]	Annual Unlinked Passenger Trips[2] (in thous.)	Annual Passenger Miles[3] (in thous.)
Jacksonville Transportation Authority (JTA)			
Bus (directly operated)	125	5,037.0	29,706.4
Bus (purchased transportation)	7	20.1	223.1
Commuter Bus (purchased transportation)	5	1.7	57.9
Demand Response (purchased transportation)	86	251.2	2,770.1
Ferryboat (purchased transportation)	1	323.7	145.7
Monorail and Automated Guideway (directly operated)	3	287.8	204.3

Note: (1) Number of revenue vehicles operated by the given mode and type of service to meet the annual maximum service requirement. This is the revenue vehicle count during the peak season of the year; on the week and day that maximum service is provided. Vehicles operated in maximum service (VOMS) exclude atypical days and one-time special events; (2) Number of passengers who boarded public transportation vehicles. Passengers are counted each time they board a vehicle no matter how many vehicles they use to travel from their origin to their destination. (3) Sum of the distances ridden by all passengers during the entire fiscal year.
Source: Federal Transit Administration, National Transit Database, 2021

Air Transportation

Airport Name and Code / Type of Service	Passenger Airlines[1]	Passenger Enplanements	Freight Carriers[2]	Freight (lbs)
Jacksonville International (JAX)				
Domestic service (U.S. carriers - 2022)	28	3,176,493	11	81,607,970
International service (U.S. carriers - 2021)	1	42	0	0

Note: (1) Includes all U.S.-based major, minor and commuter airlines that carried at least one passenger during the year; (2) Includes all U.S.-based airlines and freight carriers that transported at least one pound of freight during the year.
Source: Bureau of Transportation Statistics, The Intermodal Transportation Database, Air Carriers: T-100 Domestic Market (U.S. Carriers), 2022; Bureau of Transportation Statistics, The Intermodal Transportation Database, Air Carriers: T-100 International Market (U.S. Carriers), 2021

BUSINESSES

Major Business Headquarters

Company Name	Industry	Fortune[1]	Forbes[2]
CSX	Railroads	298	-
Crowley Maritime	Transportation	-	191
Fanatics	Clothing, shoes, sports equipment	-	137
Fidelity National Financial	Insurance, property and casualty (stock)	238	-
Fidelity National Information Services	Financial data services	268	-
Landstar System	Transportation	491	-
Southeastern Grocer	Food markets	-	52

Note: (1) Companies that produce a 10-K are ranked 1 to 500 based on 2021 revenue; (2) All private companies with at least $2 billion in annual revenue through the end of their most current fiscal year are ranked 1 to 246; companies listed are headquartered in the city; dashes indicate no ranking
Source: Fortune, "Fortune 500," 2022; Forbes, "America's Largest Private Companies," 2022

Fastest-Growing Businesses

According to *Inc.*, Jacksonville is home to one of America's 500 fastest-growing private companies: **Pulse Clinical Alliance** (#453). Criteria: must be an independent, privately-held, for-profit, U.S. corporation, proprietorship or partnership as of December 31, 2021; revenues must be at least $100,000 in 2018 and $2 million in 2021; must have four-year operating/sales history. *Inc.*, "America's 500 Fastest-Growing Private Companies," 2022

Living Environment

COST OF LIVING

Cost of Living Index

Composite Index	Groceries	Housing	Utilities	Transportation	Health Care	Misc. Goods/Services
94.2	97.8	94.3	104.9	83.2	82.6	94.0

Note: The Cost of Living Index measures regional differences in the cost of consumer goods and services, excluding taxes and non-consumer expenditures, for professional and managerial households in the top income quintile. It is based on more than 50,000 prices covering almost 60 different items for which prices are collected three times a year by chambers of commerce, economic development organizations or university applied economic centers in each participating urban area. The numbers shown should be read as a percentage above or below the national average of 100. For example, a value of 115.4 in the groceries column indicates that grocery prices are 15.4% higher than the national average. Small differences in the index numbers should not be interpreted as significant; Figures cover the Jacksonville FL urban area.
Source: The Council for Community and Economic Research, Cost of Living Index, 2022

Grocery Prices

Area[1]	T-Bone Steak ($/pound)	Frying Chicken ($/pound)	Whole Milk ($/half gal.)	Eggs ($/dozen)	Orange Juice ($/64 oz.)	Coffee ($/11.5 oz.)
City[2]	13.82	1.79	2.26	2.53	3.59	4.86
Avg.	13.81	1.59	2.43	2.25	3.85	4.95
Min.	10.17	0.90	1.51	1.30	2.90	3.46
Max.	19.35	3.30	4.32	4.32	5.31	8.59

Note: (1) Values for the local area are compared with the average, minimum and maximum values for all 286 areas in the Cost of Living Index; (2) Figures cover the Jacksonville FL urban area; **T-Bone Steak** (price per pound); **Frying Chicken** (price per pound, whole fryer); **Whole Milk** (half gallon carton); **Eggs** (price per dozen, Grade A, large); **Orange Juice** (64 oz. Tropicana or Florida Natural); **Coffee** (11.5 oz. can, vacuum-packed, Maxwell House, Hills Bros, or Folgers).
Source: The Council for Community and Economic Research, Cost of Living Index, 2022

Housing and Utility Costs

Area[1]	New Home Price ($)	Apartment Rent ($/month)	All Electric ($/month)	Part Electric ($/month)	Other Energy ($/month)	Telephone ($/month)
City[2]	385,800	1,507	187.84	-	-	196.12
Avg.	450,913	1,371	176.41	99.93	76.96	190.22
Min.	229,283	546	100.84	31.56	27.15	174.27
Max.	2,434,977	4,569	356.86	249.59	272.24	208.31

Note: (1) Values for the local area are compared with the average, minimum and maximum values for all 286 areas in the Cost of Living Index; (2) Figures cover the Jacksonville FL urban area; **New Home Price** (2,400 sf living area, 8,000 sf lot, in urban area with full utilities); **Apartment Rent** (950 sf 2 bedroom/1.5 or 2 bath, unfurnished, excluding all utilities except water); **All Electric** (average monthly cost for an all-electric home); **Part Electric** (average monthly cost for a part-electric home); **Other Energy** (average monthly cost for natural gas, fuel oil, coal, wood, and any other forms of energy except electricity); **Telephone** (price includes the base monthly rate plus taxes and fees for three lines of mobile phone service).
Source: The Council for Community and Economic Research, Cost of Living Index, 2022

Health Care, Transportation, and Other Costs

Area[1]	Doctor ($/visit)	Dentist ($/visit)	Optometrist ($/visit)	Gasoline ($/gallon)	Beauty Salon ($/visit)	Men's Shirt ($)
City[2]	90.43	93.90	72.66	3.68	63.00	25.84
Avg.	124.91	107.77	117.66	3.86	43.31	34.21
Min.	36.61	58.25	51.79	2.90	22.18	13.05
Max.	250.21	162.58	371.96	5.54	85.61	63.54

Note: (1) Values for the local area are compared with the average, minimum and maximum values for all 286 areas in the Cost of Living Index; (2) Figures cover the Jacksonville FL urban area; **Doctor** (general practitioners routine exam of an established patient); **Dentist** (adult teeth cleaning and periodic oral examination); **Optometrist** (full vision eye exam for established adult patient); **Gasoline** (one gallon regular unleaded, national brand, including all taxes, cash price at self-service pump if available); **Beauty Salon** (woman's shampoo, trim, and blow-dry); **Men's Shirt** (cotton/polyester dress shirt, pinpoint weave, long sleeves).
Source: The Council for Community and Economic Research, Cost of Living Index, 2022

HOUSING

Homeownership Rate

Area	2015 (%)	2016 (%)	2017 (%)	2018 (%)	2019 (%)	2020 (%)	2021 (%)	2022 (%)
MSA[1]	62.5	61.8	65.2	61.4	63.1	64.8	68.1	70.6
U.S.	63.7	63.4	63.9	64.4	64.6	66.6	65.5	65.8

Note: (1) Figures cover the Jacksonville, FL Metropolitan Statistical Area
Source: U.S. Census Bureau, Housing Vacancies and Homeownership Annual Statistics: 2015-2022

House Price Index (HPI)

Area	National Ranking[2]	Quarterly Change (%)	One-Year Change (%)	Five-Year Change (%)	Since 1991Q1 (%)
MSA[1]	35	-1.80	16.79	76.35	371.41
U.S.[3]	–	0.34	8.41	58.44	289.08

Note: The HPI is a weighted repeat sales index. It measures average price changes in repeat sales or refinancings on the same properties. This information is obtained by reviewing repeat mortgage transactions on single-family properties whose mortgages have been purchased or securitized by Fannie Mae or Freddie Mac since January 1975; (1) Figures cover the Jacksonville, FL Metropolitan Statistical Area; (2) Rankings are based on annual percentage change for all metro areas containing at least 15,000 transactions over the last 10 years and ranges from 1 to 257; (3) figures based on a weighted average of Census Division estimates using a seasonally adjusted, purchase-only index; all figures are for the period ending December 31, 2022
Source: Federal Housing Finance Agency, Change in FHFA Metropolitan Area House Price Indexes, 2022Q4

Median Single-Family Home Prices

Area	2020	2021	2022p	Percent Change 2021 to 2022
MSA[1]	279.0	325.0	386.5	18.9
U.S. Average	300.2	357.1	392.6	9.9

Note: Figures are median sales prices of existing single-family homes in thousands of dollars; (p) preliminary; (1) Figures cover the Jacksonville, FL Metropolitan Statistical Area
Source: National Association of Realtors, Median Sales Price of Existing Single-Family Homes for Metropolitan Areas, 4th Quarter 2022

Qualifying Income Based on Median Sales Price of Existing Single-Family Homes

Area	With 5% Down ($)	With 10% Down ($)	With 20% Down ($)
MSA[1]	115,485	109,407	97,250
U.S. Average	112,234	106,237	94,513

Note: Figures are preliminary; Qualifying income is based on a mortgage rate of 6.77%. Monthly principal and interest payment is limited to 25% of income; (1) Figures cover the Jacksonville, FL Metropolitan Statistical Area
Source: National Association of Realtors, Qualifying Income Based on Median Sales Price of Existing Single-Family Homes for Metropolitan Areas, 4th Quarter 2022

Home Value

Area	Under $100,000	$100,000 -$199,999	$200,000 -$299,999	$300,000 -$399,999	$400,000 -$499,999	$500,000 -$999,999	$1,000,000 or more	Median ($)
City	17.0	32.0	28.0	12.0	4.8	4.9	1.4	203,400
MSA[1]	13.2	26.5	26.7	15.0	7.8	8.5	2.2	235,300
U.S.	16.2	24.2	20.1	13.6	8.3	13.6	4.1	244,900

Note: Figures are percentages except for median and cover owner-occupied housing units; (1) Figures cover the Jacksonville, FL Metropolitan Statistical Area
Source: U.S. Census Bureau, 2017-2021 American Community Survey 5-Year Estimates

Year Housing Structure Built

Area	2020 or Later	2010 -2019	2000 -2009	1990 -1999	1980 -1989	1970 -1979	1960 -1969	1950 -1959	1940 -1949	Before 1940	Median Year
City	0.6	8.4	18.1	14.7	15.6	12.4	9.9	10.8	4.5	5.0	1985
MSA[1]	0.7	11.2	21.2	15.9	16.4	12.0	7.7	7.7	3.2	4.0	1989
U.S.	0.2	7.3	13.6	13.6	13.2	14.8	10.3	10.0	4.7	12.2	1979

Note: Figures are percentages except for Median Year; Note: (1) Figures cover the Jacksonville, FL Metropolitan Statistical Area
Source: U.S. Census Bureau, 2017-2021 American Community Survey 5-Year Estimates

Gross Monthly Rent

Area	Under $500	$500 -$999	$1,000 -$1,499	$1,500 -$1,999	$2,000 -$2,499	$2,500 -$2,999	$3,000 and up	Median ($)
City	5.4	29.0	43.7	17.5	3.6	0.5	0.4	1,146
MSA[1]	4.9	27.9	41.7	18.9	4.6	1.0	1.0	1,175
U.S.	8.1	30.5	30.8	16.8	7.3	3.1	3.5	1,163

Note: Figures are percentages except for median; Gross rent is the contract rent plus the estimated average monthly cost of utilities (electricity, gas, and water and sewer) and fuels (oil, coal, kerosene, wood, etc.) if these are paid by the renter (or paid for the renter by someone else); (1) Figures cover the Jacksonville, FL Metropolitan Statistical Area
Source: U.S. Census Bureau, 2017-2021 American Community Survey 5-Year Estimates

HEALTH

Health Risk Factors

Category	MSA[1] (%)	U.S. (%)
Adults aged 18–64 who have any kind of health care coverage	n/a	90.9
Adults who reported being in good or better health	n/a	85.2
Adults who have been told they have high blood cholesterol	n/a	35.7
Adults who have been told they have high blood pressure	n/a	32.4
Adults who are current smokers	n/a	14.4
Adults who currently use e-cigarettes	n/a	6.7
Adults who currently use chewing tobacco, snuff, or snus	n/a	3.5
Adults who are heavy drinkers[2]	n/a	6.3
Adults who are binge drinkers[3]	n/a	15.4
Adults who are overweight (BMI 25.0 - 29.9)	n/a	34.4
Adults who are obese (BMI 30.0 - 99.8)	n/a	33.9
Adults who participated in any physical activities in the past month	n/a	76.3

*Note: (1) Figures for the Jacksonville, FL Metropolitan Statistical Area were not available.
(2) Heavy drinkers are classified as adult men having more than 14 drinks per week and adult women having more than 7 drinks per week; (3) Binge drinkers are classified as males having five or more drinks on one occasion or females having four or more drinks on one occasion
Source: Centers for Disease Control and Prevention, Behaviorial Risk Factor Surveillance System, SMART: Selected Metropolitan Area Risk Trends, 2021*

Acute and Chronic Health Conditions

Category	MSA[1] (%)	U.S. (%)
Adults who have ever been told they had a heart attack	n/a	4.0
Adults who have ever been told they have angina or coronary heart disease	n/a	3.8
Adults who have ever been told they had a stroke	n/a	3.0
Adults who have ever been told they have asthma	n/a	14.9
Adults who have ever been told they have arthritis	n/a	25.8
Adults who have ever been told they have diabetes[2]	n/a	10.9
Adults who have ever been told they had skin cancer	n/a	6.6
Adults who have ever been told they had any other types of cancer	n/a	7.5
Adults who have ever been told they have COPD	n/a	6.1
Adults who have ever been told they have kidney disease	n/a	3.0
Adults who have ever been told they have a form of depression	n/a	20.5

*Note: (1) Figures for the Jacksonville, FL Metropolitan Statistical Area were not available.
(2) Figures do not include pregnancy-related, borderline, or pre-diabetes
Source: Centers for Disease Control and Prevention, Behavioral Risk Factor Surveillance System, SMART: Selected Metropolitan Area Risk Trends, 2021*

Health Screening and Vaccination Rates

Category	MSA[1] (%)	U.S. (%)
Adults who have ever been tested for HIV	n/a	34.9
Adults who have had their blood cholesterol checked within the last five years	n/a	85.2
Adults aged 65+ who have had flu shot within the past year	n/a	68.6
Adults aged 65+ who have ever had a pneumonia vaccination	n/a	71.0

*Note: (1) Figures for the Jacksonville, FL Metropolitan Statistical Area were not available.
Source: Centers for Disease Control and Prevention, Behavioral Risk Factor Surveillance System, SMART: Selected Metropolitan Area Risk Trends, 2021*

Disability Status

Category	MSA[1] (%)	U.S. (%)
Adults who reported being deaf	n/a	7.2
Are you blind or have serious difficulty seeing, even when wearing glasses?	n/a	4.8
Are you limited in any way in any of your usual activities due to arthritis?	n/a	11.1
Do you have difficulty doing errands alone?	n/a	7.0
Do you have difficulty dressing or bathing?	n/a	3.6
Do you have serious difficulty concentrating/remembering/making decisions?	n/a	12.1
Do you have serious difficulty walking or climbing stairs?	n/a	12.8

*Note: (1) Figures for the Jacksonville, FL Metropolitan Statistical Area were not available.
Source: Centers for Disease Control and Prevention, Behavioral Risk Factor Surveillance System, SMART: Selected Metropolitan Area Risk Trends, 2021*

Mortality Rates for the Top 10 Causes of Death in the U.S.

ICD-10[a] Sub-Chapter	ICD-10[a] Code	Crude Mortality Rate[1] per 100,000 population County[2]	U.S.
Malignant neoplasms	C00-C97	187.3	182.6
Ischaemic heart diseases	I20-I25	108.0	113.1
Other forms of heart disease	I30-I51	55.3	64.4
Other degenerative diseases of the nervous system	G30-G31	54.6	51.0
Cerebrovascular diseases	I60-I69	58.3	47.8
Other external causes of accidental injury	W00-X59	67.4	46.4
Chronic lower respiratory diseases	J40-J47	47.0	45.7
Organic, including symptomatic, mental disorders	F01-F09	25.1	35.9
Hypertensive diseases	I10-I15	36.2	35.0
Diabetes mellitus	E10-E14	30.9	29.6

Note: (a) ICD-10 = International Classification of Diseases 10th Revision; (1) Crude mortality rates are a three-year average covering 2019-2021; (2) Figures cover Duval County.
Source: Centers for Disease Control and Prevention, National Center for Health Statistics. National Vital Statistics System, Mortality 2018-2021 on CDC WONDER Online Database

Mortality Rates for Selected Causes of Death

ICD-10[a] Sub-Chapter	ICD-10[a] Code	Crude Mortality Rate[1] per 100,000 population County[2]	U.S.
Assault	X85-Y09	15.0	7.0
Diseases of the liver	K70-K76	24.0	19.8
Human immunodeficiency virus (HIV) disease	B20-B24	4.7	1.5
Influenza and pneumonia	J09-J18	12.2	14.7
Intentional self-harm	X60-X84	16.2	14.3
Malnutrition	E40-E46	6.0	4.3
Obesity and other hyperalimentation	E65-E68	2.9	3.0
Renal failure	N17-N19	21.5	15.7
Transport accidents	V01-V99	19.8	13.6
Viral hepatitis	B15-B19	1.2	1.2

Note: (a) ICD-10 = International Classification of Diseases 10th Revision; (1) Crude mortality rates are a three-year average covering 2019-2021; (2) Figures cover Duval County; Data are suppressed when the data meet the criteria for confidentiality constraints; Crude mortality rates are flagged as unreliable when the rate would be calculated with a numerator of 20 or less.
Source: Centers for Disease Control and Prevention, National Center for Health Statistics. National Vital Statistics System, Mortality 2018-2021 on CDC WONDER Online Database

Health Insurance Coverage

Area	With Health Insurance	With Private Health Insurance	With Public Health Insurance	Without Health Insurance	Population Under Age 19 Without Health Insurance
City	87.9	64.4	34.2	12.1	6.9
MSA[1]	89.3	68.7	33.1	10.7	6.7
U.S.	91.2	67.8	35.4	8.8	5.3

Note: Figures are percentages that cover the civilian noninstitutionalized population; (1) Figures cover the Jacksonville, FL Metropolitan Statistical Area
Source: U.S. Census Bureau, 2017-2021 American Community Survey 5-Year Estimates

Number of Medical Professionals

Area	MDs[3]	DOs[3,4]	Dentists	Podiatrists	Chiropractors	Optometrists
County[1] (number)	3,399	227	795	71	259	159
County[1] (rate[2])	341.1	22.8	79.5	7.1	25.9	15.9
U.S. (rate[2])	289.3	23.5	72.5	6.2	28.7	17.4

Note: Data as of 2021 unless noted; (1) Data covers Duval County; (2) Rate per 100,000 population; (3) Data as of 2020 and includes all active, non-federal physicians; (4) Doctor of Osteopathic Medicine
Source: U.S. Department of Health and Human Services, Health Resources and Services Administration, Bureau of Health Professions, Area Resource File (ARF) 2021-2022

Best Hospitals

According to *U.S. News,* the Jacksonville, FL metro area is home to two of the best hospitals in the U.S.: **Brooks Rehabilitation Hospital** (1 adult specialty); **Mayo Clinic-Jacksonville** (7 adult specialties). The hospitals listed were nationally ranked in at least one of 15 adult or 10 pediatric specialties. The number of specialties shown cover the parent hospital. Only 164 U.S. hospitals performed well enough to be nationally ranked in one or more specialties. Twenty hospitals in the U.S. made the Honor Roll. The Best Hospitals Honor Roll takes both the national rankings and the procedure and condition ratings into account. Hospitals received points if they were nationally ranked in one of the 15 adult specialties—the higher they ranked, the more points they got—and how many ratings of "high performing" they earned in the 17 procedures and conditions. *U.S. News Online, "America's Best Hospitals 2022-23"*

According to *U.S. News,* the Jacksonville, FL metro area is home to one of the best children's hospitals in the U.S.: **Wolfson Children's Hospital** (1 pediatric specialty). The hospital listed was highly ranked in at least one of 10 pediatric specialties. Eighty-six children's hospitals in the U.S. were nationally ranked in at least one specialty. Hospitals received points for being ranked in a specialty, and the 10 hospitals with the most points across the 10 specialties make up the Honor Roll. *U.S. News Online, "America's Best Children's Hospitals 2022-23"*

EDUCATION

Public School District Statistics

District Name	Schls	Pupils	Pupil/Teacher Ratio	Minority Pupils[1] (%)	LEP/ELL[2] (%)	IEP[3] (%)
Duval	205	128,948	18.1	68.3	5.5	16.3

Note: Table includes school districts with 2,000 or more students; (1) Percentage of students that are not non-Hispanic white; (2) Percentage of students that are Limited English Proficient or English Language Learners (2018-19); (3) Percentage of students that have an Individualized Education Program (2019-20).
Source: U.S. Department of Education, National Center for Education Statistics, Common Core of Data, Local Education Agency (School District) Universe Survey: School Year 2021-2022

Best High Schools

According to *U.S. News,* Jacksonville is home to four of the top 500 high schools in the U.S.: **Stanton College Preparatory School** (#75); **Darnell Cookman Middle/High School** (#142); **Paxon School/Advanced Studies** (#178); **Douglas Anderson School of the Arts** (#376). Nearly 18,000 public, magnet and charter schools were ranked based on their performance on state assessments and how well they prepare students for college. *U.S. News & World Report, "Best High Schools 2022"*

Highest Level of Education

Area	Less than H.S.	H.S. Diploma	Some College, No Deg.	Associate Degree	Bachelor's Degree	Master's Degree	Prof. School Degree	Doctorate Degree
City	9.7	28.7	21.5	9.9	20.3	7.2	1.6	1.0
MSA[1]	8.6	27.5	21.0	9.9	21.6	8.4	2.0	1.1
U.S.	11.1	26.5	20.0	8.7	20.6	9.3	2.2	1.5

Note: Figures cover persons age 25 and over; (1) Figures cover the Jacksonville, FL Metropolitan Statistical Area
Source: U.S. Census Bureau, 2017-2021 American Community Survey 5-Year Estimates

Educational Attainment by Race

Area	High School Graduate or Higher (%) Total	White	Black	Asian	Hisp.[2]	Bachelor's Degree or Higher (%) Total	White	Black	Asian	Hisp.[2]
City	90.3	92.0	88.2	87.8	83.9	30.2	33.0	21.3	49.4	27.0
MSA[1]	91.4	92.8	88.4	89.4	85.5	33.1	35.6	22.0	49.9	27.9
U.S.	88.9	91.4	87.2	87.6	71.2	33.7	35.5	23.3	55.6	18.4

Note: Figures shown cover persons 25 years old and over; (1) Figures cover the Jacksonville, FL Metropolitan Statistical Area; (2) People of Hispanic origin can be of any race
Source: U.S. Census Bureau, 2017-2021 American Community Survey 5-Year Estimates

School Enrollment by Grade and Control

Area	Preschool (%) Public	Private	Kindergarten (%) Public	Private	Grades 1 - 4 (%) Public	Private	Grades 5 - 8 (%) Public	Private	Grades 9 - 12 (%) Public	Private
City	54.4	45.6	85.0	15.0	83.7	16.3	80.4	19.6	84.8	15.2
MSA[1]	54.8	45.2	86.3	13.7	84.9	15.1	83.2	16.8	87.2	12.8
U.S.	58.8	41.2	86.3	13.7	88.3	11.7	88.6	11.4	89.4	10.6

Note: Figures shown cover persons 3 years old and over; (1) Figures cover the Jacksonville, FL Metropolitan Statistical Area
Source: U.S. Census Bureau, 2017-2021 American Community Survey 5-Year Estimates

Higher Education

Four-Year Colleges			Two-Year Colleges			Medical Schools[1]	Law Schools[2]	Voc/Tech[3]
Public	Private Non-profit	Private For-profit	Public	Private Non-profit	Private For-profit			
2	4	2	0	1	3	0	0	12

Note: Figures cover institutions located within the Jacksonville, FL Metropolitan Statistical Area and include main campuses only; (1) includes schools accredited by the Liaison Committee on Medical Education and the American Osteopathic Association's Commission on Osteopathic College Accreditation; (2) includes ABA-accredited schools, schools with provisional ABA accreditation, and state accredited schools; (3) includes all schools with programs that are less than 2 years.
Source: National Center for Education Statistics, Integrated Postsecondary Education System (IPEDS), 2021-22; Wikipedia, List of Medical Schools in the United States, accessed April 10, 2023; Wikipedia, List of Law Schools in the United States, accessed April 10, 2023

EMPLOYERS

Major Employers

Company Name	Industry
Bank of America, Merrill Lynch	Financial services
Baptist Health	Healthcare
Citi	Financial services
Fleet Readiness Center SE	Aviation & aerospace
Florida Blue	Financial services
Mayo Clinic	Healthcare
St. Vincent's Medical Center - Riverside	Healthcare
UF Health	Healthcare

Note: Companies shown are located within the Jacksonville, FL Metropolitan Statistical Area.
Source: Hoovers.com; Wikipedia

Best Companies to Work For

Availity, headquartered in Jacksonville, is among "Fortune's Best Workplaces for Women." To pick the best companies, *Fortune* partnered with the Great Place to Work Institute. To be considered for the list, companies must be Great Place To Work-Certified. Companies must also employ at least 50 women, at least 20% of their non-executive managers must be female, and at least one executive must be female. To determine the Best Workplaces for Women, Great Place To Work measured the differences in women's survey responses to those of their peers and assesses the impact of demographics and roles on the quality and consistency of women's experiences. Great Place To Work also analyzed the gender balance of each workplace, how it compared to each company's industry, and patterns in representation as women rise from front-line positions to the board of directors. *Fortune, "Best Workplaces for Women," 2022*

VyStar Credit Union, headquartered in Jacksonville, is among the "100 Best Places to Work in IT." To qualify, companies had to have a minimum of 100 total employees and five IT employees. The best places to work were selected based on DEI (diversity, equity, and inclusion) practices; IT turnover, promotions, and growth; IT retention and engagement programs; remote/hybrid working; benefits and perks (such as elder care and child care, flextime, and reimbursement for college tuition); and training and career development opportunities. *Computerworld, "Best Places to Work in IT," 2023*

PUBLIC SAFETY

Crime Rate

Area	Total Crime	Violent Crime Rate				Property Crime Rate		
		Murder	Rape[3]	Robbery	Aggrav. Assault	Burglary	Larceny-Theft	Motor Vehicle Theft
City	3,569.3	15.2	49.5	100.8	532.3	419.3	2,129.5	322.6
Suburbs[1]	1,375.4	2.4	28.0	23.8	169.5	172.0	880.2	99.5
Metro[2]	2,653.0	9.9	40.5	68.6	380.8	316.0	1,607.7	229.4
U.S.	2,356.7	6.5	38.4	73.9	279.7	314.2	1,398.0	246.0

Note: Figures are crimes per 100,000 population; (1) All areas within the metro area that are located outside the city limits; (2) Figures cover the Jacksonville, FL Metropolitan Statistical Area; (3) All figures shown were reported using the revised Uniform Crime Reporting (UCR) definition of rape; Due to the transition to the National Incident-Based Reporting System (NIBRS), limited city and metro area data was released for 2021.
Source: FBI Uniform Crime Reports, 2020

Hate Crimes

Area	Number of Quarters Reported	Number of Incidents per Bias Motivation					
		Race/Ethnicity/Ancestry	Religion	Sexual Orientation	Disability	Gender	Gender Identity
City	4	9	0	1	0	0	1
U.S.	4	5,227	1,244	1,110	130	75	266

Note: Due to the transition to the National Incident-Based Reporting System (NIBRS), limited crime data was released for 2021.
Source: Federal Bureau of Investigation, Hate Crime Statistics 2020

Identity Theft Consumer Reports

Area	Reports	Reports per 100,000 Population	Rank[2]
MSA[1]	5,279	344	48
U.S.	1,108,609	339	-

Note: (1) Figures cover the Jacksonville, FL Metropolitan Statistical Area; (2) Rank ranges from 1 to 391 where 1 indicates greatest number of identity theft reports per 100,000 population
Source: Federal Trade Commission, Consumer Sentinel Network Data Book 2022

Fraud and Other Consumer Reports

Area	Reports	Reports per 100,000 Population	Rank[2]
MSA[1]	23,065	1,504	10
U.S.	4,064,520	1,245	-

Note: (1) Figures cover the Jacksonville, FL Metropolitan Statistical Area; (2) Rank ranges from 1 to 391 where 1 indicates greatest number of fraud and other consumer reports per 100,000 population
Source: Federal Trade Commission, Consumer Sentinel Network Data Book 2022

POLITICS

2020 Presidential Election Results

Area	Biden	Trump	Jorgensen	Hawkins	Other
Duval County	51.1	47.3	1.0	0.2	0.5
U.S.	51.3	46.8	1.2	0.3	0.5

Note: Results are percentages and may not add to 100% due to rounding
Source: Dave Leip's Atlas of U.S. Presidential Elections

SPORTS

Professional Sports Teams

Team Name	League	Year Established
Jacksonville Jaguars	National Football League (NFL)	1995

Note: Includes teams located in the Jacksonville, FL Metropolitan Statistical Area.
Source: Wikipedia, Major Professional Sports Teams of the United States and Canada, April 12, 2023

CLIMATE

Average and Extreme Temperatures

Temperature	Jan	Feb	Mar	Apr	May	Jun	Jul	Aug	Sep	Oct	Nov	Dec	Yr.
Extreme High (°F)	84	88	91	95	100	103	103	102	98	96	88	84	103
Average High (°F)	65	68	74	80	86	90	92	91	87	80	73	67	79
Average Temp. (°F)	54	57	62	69	75	80	83	82	79	71	62	56	69
Average Low (°F)	43	45	51	57	64	70	73	73	70	61	51	44	58
Extreme Low (°F)	7	22	23	34	45	47	61	63	48	36	21	11	7

Note: Figures cover the years 1948-1990
Source: National Climatic Data Center, International Station Meteorological Climate Summary, 9/96

Average Precipitation/Snowfall/Humidity

Precip./Humidity	Jan	Feb	Mar	Apr	May	Jun	Jul	Aug	Sep	Oct	Nov	Dec	Yr.
Avg. Precip. (in.)	3.0	3.7	3.8	3.0	3.6	5.3	6.2	7.4	7.8	3.7	2.0	2.6	52.0
Avg. Snowfall (in.)	Tr	Tr	Tr	0	0	0	0	0	0	0	0	Tr	0
Avg. Rel. Hum. 7am (%)	86	86	87	86	86	88	89	91	92	91	89	88	88
Avg. Rel. Hum. 4pm (%)	56	53	50	49	54	61	64	65	66	62	58	58	58

Note: Figures cover the years 1948-1990; Tr = Trace amounts (<0.05 in. of rain; <0.5 in. of snow)
Source: National Climatic Data Center, International Station Meteorological Climate Summary, 9/96

Weather Conditions

Temperature			Daytime Sky			Precipitation		
10°F & below	32°F & below	90°F & above	Clear	Partly cloudy	Cloudy	0.01 inch or more precip.	0.1 inch or more snow/ice	Thunderstorms
<1	16	83	86	181	98	114	1	65

Note: Figures are average number of days per year and cover the years 1948-1990
Source: National Climatic Data Center, International Station Meteorological Climate Summary, 9/96

HAZARDOUS WASTE

Superfund Sites

The Jacksonville, FL metro area is home to three sites on the EPA's Superfund National Priorities List: **Jacksonville Naval Air Station** (final); **Kerr-Mcgee Chemical Corp - Jacksonville** (final); **Pickettville Road Landfill** (final). There are a total of 1,165 Superfund sites with a status of proposed or final on the list in the U.S. *U.S. Environmental Protection Agency, National Priorities List, April 12, 2023*

AIR QUALITY

Air Quality Trends: Ozone

	1990	1995	2000	2005	2010	2015	2018	2019	2020	2021
MSA[1]	0.080	0.068	0.072	0.076	0.068	0.060	0.060	0.062	0.057	0.061
U.S.	0.087	0.089	0.081	0.080	0.072	0.067	0.069	0.065	0.065	0.067

Note: (1) Data covers the Jacksonville, FL Metropolitan Statistical Area. The values shown are the composite ozone concentration averages among trend sites based on the highest fourth daily maximum 8-hour concentration in parts per million. These trends are based on sites having an adequate record of monitoring data during the trend period. Data from exceptional events are included.
Source: U.S. Environmental Protection Agency, Air Quality Monitoring Information, "Air Quality Trends by City, 1990-2021"

Air Quality Index

Area	\multicolumn{5}{c}{Percent of Days when Air Quality was...[2]}	AQI Statistics[2]	
	Good	Moderate	Unhealthy for Sensitive Groups	Unhealthy	Very Unhealthy	Maximum	Median
MSA[1]	73.4	26.6	0.0	0.0	0.0	93	43

Note: (1) Data covers the Jacksonville, FL Metropolitan Statistical Area; (2) Based on 365 days with AQI data in 2021. Air Quality Index (AQI) is an index for reporting daily air quality. EPA calculates the AQI for five major air pollutants regulated by the Clean Air Act: ground-level ozone, particle pollution (aka particulate matter), carbon monoxide, sulfur dioxide, and nitrogen dioxide. The AQI runs from 0 to 500. The higher the AQI value, the greater the level of air pollution and the greater the health concern. There are six AQI categories: "Good" AQI is between 0 and 50. Air quality is considered satisfactory; "Moderate" AQI is between 51 and 100. Air quality is acceptable; "Unhealthy for Sensitive Groups" When AQI values are between 101 and 150, members of sensitive groups may experience health effects; "Unhealthy" When AQI values are between 151 and 200 everyone may begin to experience health effects; "Very Unhealthy" AQI values between 201 and 300 trigger a health alert; "Hazardous" AQI values over 300 trigger warnings of emergency conditions (not shown).
Source: U.S. Environmental Protection Agency, Air Quality Index Report, 2021

Air Quality Index Pollutants

Area	\multicolumn{6}{c}{Percent of Days when AQI Pollutant was...[2]}
	Carbon Monoxide	Nitrogen Dioxide	Ozone	Sulfur Dioxide	Particulate Matter 2.5	Particulate Matter 10
MSA[1]	0.0	0.0	36.4	(3)	63.6	0.0

Note: (1) Data covers the Jacksonville, FL Metropolitan Statistical Area; (2) Based on 365 days with AQI data in 2021. The Air Quality Index (AQI) is an index for reporting daily air quality. EPA calculates the AQI for five major air pollutants regulated by the Clean Air Act: ground-level ozone, particle pollution (also known as particulate matter), carbon monoxide, sulfur dioxide, and nitrogen dioxide. The AQI runs from 0 to 500. The higher the AQI value, the greater the level of air pollution and the greater the health concern; (3) Sulfur dioxide is no longer included in this table (as of December 8, 2021) because SO_2 concentrations tend to be very localized and not necessarily representative of broad geographical areas like counties and CBSAs.
Source: U.S. Environmental Protection Agency, Air Quality Index Report, 2021

Maximum Air Pollutant Concentrations: Particulate Matter, Ozone, CO and Lead

	Particulate Matter 10 (ug/m³)	Particulate Matter 2.5 Wtd AM (ug/m³)	Particulate Matter 2.5 24-Hr (ug/m³)	Ozone (ppm)	Carbon Monoxide (ppm)	Lead (ug/m³)
MSA[1] Level	54	8.8	18	0.061	1	n/a
NAAQS[2]	150	15	35	0.075	9	0.15
Met NAAQS[2]	Yes	Yes	Yes	Yes	Yes	n/a

Note: (1) Data covers the Jacksonville, FL Metropolitan Statistical Area; Data from exceptional events are included; (2) National Ambient Air Quality Standards; ppm = parts per million; ug/m³ = micrograms per cubic meter; n/a not available.
Concentrations: Particulate Matter 10 (coarse particulate)—highest second maximum 24-hour concentration; Particulate Matter 2.5 Wtd AM (fine particulate)—highest weighted annual mean concentration; Particulate Matter 2.5 24-Hour (fine particulate)—highest 98th percentile 24-hour concentration; Ozone—highest fourth daily maximum 8-hour concentration; Carbon Monoxide—highest second maximum non-overlapping 8-hour concentration; Lead—maximum running 3-month average
Source: U.S. Environmental Protection Agency, Air Quality Monitoring Information, "Air Quality Statistics by City, 2021"

Maximum Air Pollutant Concentrations: Nitrogen Dioxide and Sulfur Dioxide

	Nitrogen Dioxide AM (ppb)	Nitrogen Dioxide 1-Hr (ppb)	Sulfur Dioxide AM (ppb)	Sulfur Dioxide 1-Hr (ppb)	Sulfur Dioxide 24-Hr (ppb)
MSA[1] Level	11	41	n/a	39	n/a
NAAQS[2]	53	100	30	75	140
Met NAAQS[2]	Yes	Yes	n/a	Yes	n/a

Note: (1) Data covers the Jacksonville, FL Metropolitan Statistical Area; Data from exceptional events are included; (2) National Ambient Air Quality Standards; ppm = parts per million; ug/m³ = micrograms per cubic meter; n/a not available.
Concentrations: Nitrogen Dioxide AM—highest arithmetic mean concentration; Nitrogen Dioxide 1-Hr—highest 98th percentile 1-hour daily maximum concentration; Sulfur Dioxide AM—highest annual mean concentration; Sulfur Dioxide 1-Hr—highest 99th percentile 1-hour daily maximum concentration; Sulfur Dioxide 24-Hr—highest second maximum 24-hour concentration
Source: U.S. Environmental Protection Agency, Air Quality Monitoring Information, "Air Quality Statistics by City, 2021"

Lafayette, Louisiana

Background

Lafayette's cultural origins originated far north of the city, in Nova Scotia, Canada. In 1755, the British governor, Charles Lawrence, expelled the entire population of Canadians known as the Acadians, whose roots were French and Catholic, when they refused to pledge loyalty to the British crown. Many lost their lives in their quest for a new home, as they settled all along the eastern seaboard of the United States. A large majority of Acadians settled in southern Louisiana, in the area surrounding New Orleans.

Prior to the Acadian expulsion, southern Louisiana had remained unsettled. The first known inhabitants were the Attakapas, a much feared and brutal tribe of Native Americans. A sparse population of French trappers, traders, and ranchers occupied the region until the Spanish occupation of 1766. The 1789 French Revolution brought teams of French immigrants fleeing the brutal conditions at home. In 1803, the French sold the Louisiana territory to the United States—known as the Louisiana Purchase.

The most important early event for Lafayette was the donation of land by an Acadian named Jean Mouton to the Catholic Church. The population began to grow in the parish then known as St. John the Evangelist of Vermillion. Lafayette's original name was Vermillionville, but it was renamed in 1884 in honor of the French Marquis de Lafayette, a Frenchman who fought under General George Washington in the American Revolution. Lafayette has been credited with bringing some of the ideals of the American Revolution to the French, partly precipitating the French Revolution. By the time of his death, Lafayette had visited all 24 of the United States, and was an American citizen.

The word "cajun," is derived from the early Acadian settlers. In French, "Les Acadians" became "le Cadiens," which later became just "'Cadien." The French pronunciation was difficult for non-French Americans to say, so Cadien became Cajun. A primary characteristic of the Acadian/Cajun culture is what's known as "joie de vivre" (joy of living). The Cajun reputation is one of hard work and hard play, full of passion that can turn on a dime. Contributions of the Cajun culture to the fabric of America have been many, but their food and their music have made an indelible mark.

Lafayette is about 40 miles north of the Gulf of Mexico, and 100 miles west of New Orleans. The city is often referred to as the center of Cajun culture not because of its geography, but because of the strong Cajun influence in everyday life. Celebration is a major part of the Cajun culture, and this is reflected in Lafayette's many festivals, one of the most famous annual festivals being Mari Gras. Others include The Festival International de Louisiana, which celebrates the French-speaking heritage of much of the population and Festival Acadians, which celebrates everything that is uniquely Cajun.

The 2018 Christmas film *The Christmas Contract* was set in the city.

With over 600 oil-related businesses in Lafayette Parish alone, the city is known for its oil and natural gas industries. Other important industry sectors are healthcare and education. The University of Louisiana at Lafayette started out as a small agricultural college with about 100 students, and today, more than 18,000 students in more than 100 programs roam the 1,300-acre campus. It is the second largest public university in the state. The university's focus is hands-on research—dubbed "research for a reason"—and all students are given the opportunity to have a meaningful impact in their area of study. UL is considered among the top universities in computer science, engineering, and nursing.

Lafayette's climate is humid and subtropical. It is typical of areas along the Gulf of Mexico with hot, humid summers and mild winters.

Rankings

Business/Finance Rankings

- The Lafayette metro area appeared on the Milken Institute "2022 Best Performing Cities" list. Rank: #186 out of 200 large metro areas (population over 250,000). Criteria: job growth; wage and salary growth; high-tech output growth; housing affordability; household broadband access. *Milken Institute, "Best-Performing Cities 2022," March 28, 2022*

- *Forbes* ranked the 200 most populous metro areas to determine the nation's "Best Places for Business and Careers." The Lafayette metro area was ranked #194. Criteria: costs (business and living); job growth (past and projected); income growth; quality of life; educational attainment (college and high school); projected economic growth; cultural and leisure opportunities; workplace tolerance laws; net migration patterns. *Forbes, "The Best Places for Business and Careers 2019: Seattle Still On Top," October 30, 2019*

Education Rankings

- Personal finance website *WalletHub* analyzed the 150 largest U.S. metropolitan statistical areas to determine where the most educated Americans are putting their degrees to work. Criteria: education levels; percentage of workers with degrees; education quality and attainment gap; public school quality rankings; quality and enrollment of each metro area's universities. Lafayette was ranked #133 (#1 = most educated city). *www.WalletHub.com, "Most & Least Educated Cities in America," July 18, 2022*

Environmental Rankings

- Lafayette was highlighted as one of the cleanest metro areas for ozone air pollution in the U.S. during 2019 through 2021. The list represents cities with no monitored ozone air pollution in unhealthful ranges. *American Lung Association, "State of the Air 2023," April 19, 2023*

Safety Rankings

- The National Insurance Crime Bureau ranked 390 metro areas in the U.S. in terms of per capita rates of vehicle theft. The Lafayette metro area ranked #151 (#1 = highest rate). Criteria: number of vehicle theft offenses per 100,000 inhabitants in 2021. *National Insurance Crime Bureau, "Hot Spots 2021," September 1, 2022*

Seniors/Retirement Rankings

- From its Best Cities for Successful Aging indexes, the Milken Institute generated rankings for metropolitan areas, weighing data in nine categories—health care, wellness, living arrangements, transportation and convenience, financial characteristics, education, employment, community engagement, and overall livability. The Lafayette metro area was ranked #85 overall in the small metro area category. *Milken Institute, "Best Cities for Successful Aging, 2017" March 14, 2017*

Business Environment

DEMOGRAPHICS

Population Growth

Area	1990 Census	2000 Census	2010 Census	2020 Census	Population Growth (%) 1990-2020	Population Growth (%) 2010-2020
City	104,735	110,257	120,623	121,374	15.9	0.6
MSA[1]	208,740	239,086	273,738	478,384	129.2	74.8
U.S.	248,709,873	281,421,906	308,745,538	331,449,281	33.3	7.4

Note: (1) Figures cover the Lafayette, LA Metropolitan Statistical Area
Source: U.S. Census Bureau, 1990 Census, 2000 Census, 2010 Census, 2020 Census

Race

Area	White Alone[2] (%)	Black Alone[2] (%)	Asian Alone[2] (%)	AIAN[3] Alone[2] (%)	NHOPI[4] Alone[2] (%)	Other Race Alone[2] (%)	Two or More Races (%)
City	58.1	30.7	2.6	0.4	0.0	2.3	5.8
MSA[1]	65.8	24.5	1.9	0.4	0.0	2.3	5.1
U.S.	61.6	12.4	6.0	1.1	0.2	8.4	10.2

Note: (1) Figures cover the Lafayette, LA Metropolitan Statistical Area; (2) Alone is defined as not being in combination with one or more other races; (3) American Indian and Alaska Native; (4) Native Hawaiian and Other Pacific Islander
Source: U.S. Census Bureau, 2020 Census

Hispanic or Latino Origin

Area	Total (%)	Mexican (%)	Puerto Rican (%)	Cuban (%)	Other (%)
City	4.6	1.4	0.1	0.2	2.9
MSA[1]	4.1	1.8	0.2	0.1	2.0
U.S.	18.4	11.2	1.8	0.7	4.7

Note: Persons of Hispanic or Latino origin can be of any race; (1) Figures cover the Lafayette, LA Metropolitan Statistical Area
Source: U.S. Census Bureau, 2017-2021 American Community Survey 5-Year Estimates

Age

Area	Under Age 5	Age 5–19	Age 20–34	Age 35–44	Age 45–54	Age 55–64	Age 65–74	Age 75–84	Age 85+	Median Age
City	5.6	17.9	23.5	12.4	10.9	13.0	10.2	4.6	2.0	37.3
MSA[1]	6.3	20.5	19.3	12.9	11.7	13.5	9.6	4.5	1.6	37.8
U.S.	5.6	19.2	20.2	12.7	12.4	13.1	10.0	4.9	1.9	38.8

Note: (1) Figures cover the Lafayette, LA Metropolitan Statistical Area
Source: U.S. Census Bureau, 2020 Census

Disability by Age

Area	All Ages	Under 18 Years Old	18 to 64 Years Old	65 Years and Over
City	12.1	2.8	9.7	34.5
MSA[1]	14.1	4.9	12.4	37.8
U.S.	12.6	4.4	10.3	33.4

Note: Figures show percent of the civilian noninstitutionalized population that reported having a disability. Disability status is determined from six types of difficulty: vision, hearing, cognitive, ambulatory, self-care, and independent living. For children under 5 years old, hearing and vision difficulty are used to determine disability status. For children between the ages of 5 and 14, disability status is determined from hearing, vision, cognitive, ambulatory, and self-care difficulties. For people aged 15 years and older, they are considered to have a disability if they have difficulty with any one of the six difficulty types; Note: (1) Figures cover the Lafayette, LA Metropolitan Statistical Area
Source: U.S. Census Bureau, 2017-2021 American Community Survey 5-Year Estimates

Ancestry

Area	German	Irish	English	American	Italian	Polish	French[2]	Scottish	Dutch
City	8.0	5.4	5.9	5.9	3.6	0.3	16.2	1.0	0.4
MSA[1]	6.3	4.3	4.2	6.4	2.6	0.4	16.5	0.6	0.3
U.S.	12.8	9.6	8.1	5.7	5.0	2.7	2.2	1.6	1.1

Note: Figures are the percentage of the total population reporting a particular ancestry. The nine most commonly reported ancestries in the U.S. are shown. Figures include multiple ancestries (e.g. if a person reported being Irish and Italian, they were included in both columns); (1) Figures cover the Lafayette, LA Metropolitan Statistical Area; (2) Excludes Basque
Source: U.S. Census Bureau, 2017-2021 American Community Survey 5-Year Estimates

Foreign-born Population

Area	Any Foreign Country	Asia	Mexico	Europe	Caribbean	Central America[2]	South America	Africa	Canada
City	5.5	2.3	0.4	0.7	0.2	1.1	0.6	0.1	0.1
MSA[1]	3.3	1.3	0.5	0.3	0.2	0.7	0.2	0.1	0.1
U.S.	13.6	4.2	3.3	1.5	1.4	1.1	1.1	0.8	0.2

Note: (1) Figures cover the Lafayette, LA Metropolitan Statistical Area; (2) Excludes Mexico.
Source: U.S. Census Bureau, 2017-2021 American Community Survey 5-Year Estimates

Household Size

Area	One	Two	Three	Four	Five	Six	Seven or More	Average Household Size
City	33.7	36.1	14.2	8.6	4.7	1.6	1.2	2.30
MSA[1]	27.6	33.6	16.7	13.1	5.8	2.0	1.1	2.60
U.S.	28.1	33.8	15.5	12.9	6.0	2.3	1.4	2.60

Note: (1) Figures cover the Lafayette, LA Metropolitan Statistical Area
Source: U.S. Census Bureau, 2017-2021 American Community Survey 5-Year Estimates

Household Relationships

Area	Householder	Opposite-sex Spouse	Same-sex Spouse	Opposite-sex Unmarried Partner	Same-sex Unmarried Partner	Child[2]	Grandchild	Other Relatives	Non-relatives
City	43.0	15.3	0.2	2.8	0.2	27.0	2.3	3.5	3.8
MSA[1]	39.5	17.1	0.2	2.7	0.2	30.4	2.9	3.5	2.5
U.S.	38.3	17.5	0.2	2.5	0.2	28.3	2.4	4.8	3.4

Note: Figures are percent of the total population; (1) Figures cover the Lafayette, LA Metropolitan Statistical Area; (2) Includes biological, adopted, and stepchildren of the householder
Source: U.S. Census Bureau, 2020 Census

Gender

Area	Males	Females	Males per 100 Females
City	58,213	63,161	92.2
MSA[1]	231,864	246,520	94.1
U.S.	162,685,811	168,763,470	96.4

Note: (1) Figures cover the Lafayette, LA Metropolitan Statistical Area
Source: U.S. Census Bureau, 2020 Census

Marital Status

Area	Never Married	Now Married[2]	Separated	Widowed	Divorced
City	40.6	41.4	2.1	6.0	9.9
MSA[1]	33.8	47.9	2.1	5.6	10.6
U.S.	33.8	48.0	1.8	5.6	10.8

Note: Figures are percentages and cover the population 15 years of age and older; (1) Figures cover the Lafayette, LA Metropolitan Statistical Area; (2) Excludes separated
Source: U.S. Census Bureau, 2017-2021 American Community Survey 5-Year Estimates

Religious Groups by Family

Area	Catholic	Baptist	Methodist	LDS[2]	Pentecostal	Lutheran	Islam	Adventist	Other
MSA[1]	44.3	9.3	2.0	0.4	1.8	0.1	0.1	0.8	7.0
U.S.	18.7	7.3	3.0	2.0	1.8	1.7	1.3	1.3	11.6

Note: Figures are the number of adherents as a percentage of the total population and cover the eight largest religious groups in the U.S; (1) Figures cover the Lafayette, LA Metropolitan Statistical Area; (2) Church of Jesus Christ of Latter-day Saints
Sources: 2020 U.S. Religion Census, Association of Statisticians of American Religious Bodies; The Association of Religion Data Archives (ARDA)

Religious Groups by Tradition

Area	Catholic	Evangelical Protestant	Mainline Protestant	Black Protestant	Islam	Judaism	Hinduism	Orthodox	Buddhism
MSA[1]	44.3	12.6	2.4	5.0	0.1	n/a	<0.1	<0.1	0.1
U.S.	18.7	16.5	5.2	2.3	1.3	0.6	0.4	0.4	0.3

Note: Figures are the number of adherents as a percentage of the total population; (1) Figures cover the Lafayette, LA Metropolitan Statistical Area
Sources: 2020 U.S. Religion Census, Association of Statisticians of American Religious Bodies; The Association of Religion Data Archives (ARDA)

ECONOMY

Gross Metropolitan Product

Area	2020	2021	2022	2023	Rank[2]
MSA[1]	20.6	22.6	24.8	26.2	135

Note: Figures are in billions of dollars; (1) Figures cover the Lafayette, LA Metropolitan Statistical Area; (2) Rank is based on 2021 data and ranges from 1 to 381
Source: U.S. Conference of Mayors, U.S. Metro Economies: U.S. Metros Compared to Global and State Economies, June 2022

Economic Growth

Area	2018-20 (%)	2021 (%)	2022 (%)	2023 (%)	Rank[2]
MSA[1]	-3.7	4.2	2.6	3.3	356
U.S.	-0.6	5.7	3.1	2.9	—

Note: Figures are real gross metropolitan product (GMP) growth rates and represent average annual percent change; (1) Figures cover the Lafayette, LA Metropolitan Statistical Area; (2) Rank is based on 2020 2-year average annual percent change and ranges from 1 to 381
Source: U.S. Conference of Mayors, U.S. Metro Economies: U.S. Metros Compared to Global and State Economies, June 2022

Metropolitan Area Exports

Area	2016	2017	2018	2019	2020	2021	Rank[2]
MSA[1]	1,335.2	954.8	1,001.7	1,086.2	946.2	895.7	167

Note: Figures are in millions of dollars; (1) Figures cover the Lafayette, LA Metropolitan Statistical Area; (2) Rank is based on 2021 data and ranges from 1 to 388
Source: U.S. Department of Commerce, International Trade Administration, Office of Trade and Economic Analysis, Industry and Analysis, Exports by Metropolitan Area, data extracted March 16, 2023

Building Permits

Area	Single-Family 2021	Single-Family 2022	Pct. Chg.	Multi-Family 2021	Multi-Family 2022	Pct. Chg.	Total 2021	Total 2022	Pct. Chg.
City	n/a	n/a	n/a	n/a	n/a	n/a	n/a	n/a	n/a
MSA[1]	3,040	2,051	-32.5	4	20	400.0	3,044	2,071	-32.0
U.S.	1,115,400	975,600	-12.5	621,600	689,500	10.9	1,737,000	1,665,100	-4.1

Note: (1) Figures cover the Lafayette, LA Metropolitan Statistical Area; Figures represent new, privately-owned housing units authorized (unadjusted data); All permit data are based on estimates with imputation
Source: U.S. Census Bureau, Manufacturing, Mining, and Construction Statistics, Building Permits, 2021, 2022

Bankruptcy Filings

Area	Business Filings 2021	Business Filings 2022	% Chg.	Nonbusiness Filings 2021	Nonbusiness Filings 2022	% Chg.
Lafayette Parish	17	29	70.6	263	296	12.5
U.S.	14,347	13,481	-6.0	399,269	374,240	-6.3

Note: Business filings include Chapter 7, Chapter 9, Chapter 11, Chapter 12, Chapter 13, Chapter 15, and Section 304; Nonbusiness filings include Chapter 7, Chapter 11, and Chapter 13
Source: Administrative Office of the U.S. Courts, Business and Nonbusiness Bankruptcy, County Cases Commenced by Chapter of the Bankruptcy Code, During the 12-Month Period Ending December 31, 2021 and Business and Nonbusiness Bankruptcy, County Cases Commenced by Chapter of the Bankruptcy Code, During the 12-Month Period Ending December 31, 2022

Housing Vacancy Rates

Area	Gross Vacancy Rate[2] (%) 2020	2021	2022	Year-Round Vacancy Rate[3] (%) 2020	2021	2022	Rental Vacancy Rate[4] (%) 2020	2021	2022	Homeowner Vacancy Rate[5] (%) 2020	2021	2022
MSA[1]	n/a	n/a	n/a	n/a	n/a	n/a	n/a	n/a	n/a	n/a	n/a	n/a
U.S.	10.6	10.8	10.5	8.2	8.4	8.2	6.3	6.1	5.8	1.0	0.9	0.8

Note: (1) Figures cover the Lafayette, LA Metropolitan Statistical Area; (2) The percentage of the total housing inventory that is vacant; (3) The percentage of the housing inventory (excluding seasonal units) that is year-round vacant; (4) The percentage of rental inventory that is vacant for rent; (5) The percentage of homeowner inventory that is vacant for sale; n/a not available
Source: U.S. Census Bureau, Housing Vacancies and Homeownership Annual Statistics: 2020, 2021, 2022

INCOME

Income

Area	Per Capita ($)	Median Household ($)	Average Household ($)
City	35,348	55,329	82,752
MSA[1]	30,758	55,539	77,448
U.S.	37,638	69,021	97,196

Note: (1) Figures cover the Lafayette, LA Metropolitan Statistical Area
Source: U.S. Census Bureau, 2017-2021 American Community Survey 5-Year Estimates

Household Income Distribution

Area	Percent of Households Earning							
	Under $15,000	$15,000 -$24,999	$25,000 -$34,999	$35,000 -$49,999	$50,000 -$74,999	$75,000 -$99,999	$100,000 -$149,999	$150,000 and up
City	16.0	8.5	9.7	11.5	15.4	11.4	13.3	14.2
MSA[1]	13.7	10.4	10.0	11.9	15.8	12.9	14.4	11.1
U.S.	9.4	7.8	8.2	11.4	16.8	12.8	16.3	17.3

Note: (1) Figures cover the Lafayette, LA Metropolitan Statistical Area
Source: U.S. Census Bureau, 2017-2021 American Community Survey 5-Year Estimates

Poverty Rate

Area	All Ages	Under 18 Years Old	18 to 64 Years Old	65 Years and Over
City	19.5	29.0	17.8	12.9
MSA[1]	18.5	26.6	16.6	12.9
U.S.	12.6	17.0	11.8	9.6

Note: Figures are percentage of people whose income during the past 12 months was below the poverty level; (1) Figures cover the Lafayette, LA Metropolitan Statistical Area
Source: U.S. Census Bureau, 2017-2021 American Community Survey 5-Year Estimates

EMPLOYMENT

Labor Force and Employment

Area	Civilian Labor Force			Workers Employed		
	Dec. 2021	Dec. 2022	% Chg.	Dec. 2021	Dec. 2022	% Chg.
City	59,534	60,606	1.8	57,818	58,830	1.8
MSA[1]	211,602	215,089	1.6	204,894	208,467	1.7
U.S.	161,696,000	164,224,000	1.6	155,732,000	158,872,000	2.0

Note: Data is not seasonally adjusted and covers workers 16 years of age and older; (1) Figures cover the Lafayette, LA Metropolitan Statistical Area
Source: Bureau of Labor Statistics, Local Area Unemployment Statistics

Unemployment Rate

Area	2022											
	Jan.	Feb.	Mar.	Apr.	May	Jun.	Jul.	Aug.	Sep.	Oct.	Nov.	Dec.
City	3.6	3.1	3.1	2.9	3.1	3.9	3.8	3.2	3.0	2.7	2.6	2.9
MSA[1]	3.8	3.4	3.4	3.1	3.2	4.1	4.0	3.3	3.2	2.8	2.7	3.1
U.S.	4.4	4.1	3.8	3.3	3.4	3.8	3.8	3.8	3.3	3.4	3.4	3.3

Note: Data is not seasonally adjusted and covers workers 16 years of age and older; (1) Figures cover the Lafayette, LA Metropolitan Statistical Area
Source: Bureau of Labor Statistics, Local Area Unemployment Statistics

Average Wages

Occupation	$/Hr.	Occupation	$/Hr.
Accountants and Auditors	33.20	Maintenance and Repair Workers	18.12
Automotive Mechanics	21.50	Marketing Managers	47.53
Bookkeepers	19.60	Network and Computer Systems Admin.	41.24
Carpenters	21.95	Nurses, Licensed Practical	21.48
Cashiers	10.71	Nurses, Registered	35.91
Computer Programmers	46.32	Nursing Assistants	12.92
Computer Systems Analysts	40.06	Office Clerks, General	13.92
Computer User Support Specialists	26.07	Physical Therapists	44.44
Construction Laborers	17.53	Physicians	140.81
Cooks, Restaurant	12.87	Plumbers, Pipefitters and Steamfitters	25.47
Customer Service Representatives	16.84	Police and Sheriff's Patrol Officers	22.67
Dentists	63.45	Postal Service Mail Carriers	26.29
Electricians	25.23	Real Estate Sales Agents	17.52
Engineers, Electrical	43.20	Retail Salespersons	13.84
Fast Food and Counter Workers	10.23	Sales Representatives, Technical/Scientific	40.17
Financial Managers	58.26	Secretaries, Exc. Legal/Medical/Executive	17.91
First-Line Supervisors of Office Workers	26.05	Security Guards	13.48
General and Operations Managers	58.46	Surgeons	n/a
Hairdressers/Cosmetologists	12.89	Teacher Assistants, Exc. Postsecondary*	11.25
Home Health and Personal Care Aides	9.92	Teachers, Secondary School, Exc. Sp. Ed.*	24.62
Janitors and Cleaners	12.05	Telemarketers	n/a
Landscaping/Groundskeeping Workers	14.42	Truck Drivers, Heavy/Tractor-Trailer	21.71
Lawyers	53.24	Truck Drivers, Light/Delivery Services	17.50
Maids and Housekeeping Cleaners	10.93	Waiters and Waitresses	11.88

Note: Wage data covers the Lafayette, LA Metropolitan Statistical Area; (*) Hourly wages were calculated from annual wage data based on a 40 hour work week; n/a not available.
Source: Bureau of Labor Statistics, Metro Area Occupational Employment & Wage Estimates, May 2022

Employment by Industry

Sector	MSA[1] Number of Employees	MSA[1] Percent of Total	U.S. Percent of Total
Construction	10,900	5.4	5.0
Private Education and Health Services	34,900	17.2	16.1
Financial Activities	11,100	5.5	5.9
Government	26,000	12.8	14.5
Information	1,800	0.9	2.0
Leisure and Hospitality	21,500	10.6	10.3
Manufacturing	16,500	8.1	8.4
Mining and Logging	10,500	5.2	0.4
Other Services	7,200	3.5	3.7
Professional and Business Services	21,100	10.4	14.7
Retail Trade	26,100	12.9	10.2
Transportation, Warehousing, and Utilities	6,600	3.2	4.9
Wholesale Trade	8,900	4.4	3.9

Note: Figures are non-farm employment as of December 2022. Figures are not seasonally adjusted and include workers 16 years of age and older; (1) Figures cover the Lafayette, LA Metropolitan Statistical Area
Source: Bureau of Labor Statistics, Current Employment Statistics, Employment, Hours, and Earnings

Employment by Occupation

Occupation Classification	City (%)	MSA[1] (%)	U.S. (%)
Management, Business, Science, and Arts	42.9	35.2	40.3
Natural Resources, Construction, and Maintenance	6.6	11.6	8.7
Production, Transportation, and Material Moving	7.9	13.2	13.1
Sales and Office	24.4	23.3	20.9
Service	18.3	16.8	17.0

Note: Figures cover employed civilians 16 years of age and older; (1) Figures cover the Lafayette, LA Metropolitan Statistical Area
Source: U.S. Census Bureau, 2017-2021 American Community Survey 5-Year Estimates

Occupations with Greatest Projected Employment Growth: 2022 – 2024

Occupation[1]	2022 Employment	2024 Projected Employment	Numeric Employment Change	Percent Employment Change
Waiters and Waitresses	30,970	32,690	1,720	5.6
Cooks, Restaurant	14,710	16,310	1,600	10.9
Home Health and Personal Care Aides	36,460	37,760	1,300	3.6
Fast Food and Counter Workers	25,550	26,760	1,210	4.7
Food Preparation Workers	31,490	32,540	1,050	3.3
Light Truck or Delivery Services Drivers	19,040	20,010	970	5.1
First-Line Supervisors of Food Preparation and Serving Workers	15,240	16,130	890	5.8
Laborers and Freight, Stock, and Material Movers, Hand	54,030	54,910	880	1.6
Security Guards	22,660	23,450	790	3.5
Registered Nurses	43,400	44,070	670	1.5

Note: Projections cover Louisiana; (1) Sorted by numeric employment change
Source: www.projectionscentral.com, State Occupational Projections, 2022–2024 Short-Term Projections

Fastest-Growing Occupations: 2022 – 2024

Occupation[1]	2022 Employment	2024 Projected Employment	Numeric Employment Change	Percent Employment Change
Cooks, Restaurant	14,710	16,310	1,600	10.9
Gaming Dealers	2,270	2,510	240	10.6
First-Line Supervisors of Gambling Services Workers	690	760	70	10.1
Tour and Travel Guides	1,090	1,200	110	10.1
Nurse Practitioners	4,190	4,600	410	9.8
Hotel, Motel, and Resort Desk Clerks	3,670	4,030	360	9.8
Lodging Managers	690	750	60	8.7
Parking Lot Attendants	1,420	1,540	120	8.5
Fitness Trainers and Aerobics Instructors	2,350	2,540	190	8.1
Audio and Video Equipment Technicians	880	950	70	8.0

Note: Projections cover Louisiana; (1) Sorted by percent employment change and excludes occupations with numeric employment change less than 50
Source: www.projectionscentral.com, State Occupational Projections, 2022–2024 Short-Term Projections

CITY FINANCES

City Government Finances

Component	2020 ($000)	2020 ($ per capita)
Total Revenues	686,085	5,437
Total Expenditures	656,559	5,203
Debt Outstanding	482,202	3,821
Cash and Securities[1]	726,443	5,757

Note: (1) Cash and security holdings of a government at the close of its fiscal year, including those of its dependent agencies, utilities, and liquor stores.
Source: U.S. Census Bureau, State & Local Government Finances 2020

City Government Revenue by Source

Source	2020 ($000)	2020 ($ per capita)	2020 (%)
General Revenue			
From Federal Government	21,825	173	3.2
From State Government	7,062	56	1.0
From Local Governments	5,617	45	0.8
Taxes			
Property	131,004	1,038	19.1
Sales and Gross Receipts	100,634	798	14.7
Personal Income	0	0	0.0
Corporate Income	0	0	0.0
Motor Vehicle License	0	0	0.0
Other Taxes	5,800	46	0.8
Current Charges	138,182	1,095	20.1
Liquor Store	0	0	0.0
Utility	249,928	1,981	36.4

Source: U.S. Census Bureau, State & Local Government Finances 2020

City Government Expenditures by Function

Function	2020 ($000)	2020 ($ per capita)	2020 (%)
General Direct Expenditures			
Air Transportation	7,358	58	1.1
Corrections	8,046	63	1.2
Education	0	0	0.0
Employment Security Administration	0	0	0.0
Financial Administration	28,230	223	4.3
Fire Protection	25,971	205	4.0
General Public Buildings	5,711	45	0.9
Governmental Administration, Other	7,880	62	1.2
Health	9,573	75	1.5
Highways	46,953	372	7.2
Hospitals	0	0	0.0
Housing and Community Development	19,549	154	3.0
Interest on General Debt	11,885	94	1.8
Judicial and Legal	21,284	168	3.2
Libraries	14,664	116	2.2
Parking	894	7	0.1
Parks and Recreation	27,040	214	4.1
Police Protection	101,948	807	15.5
Public Welfare	0	0	0.0
Sewerage	26,580	210	4.0
Solid Waste Management	15,356	121	2.3
Veterans' Services	0	0	0.0
Liquor Store	0	0	0.0
Utility	240,139	1,903	36.6

Source: U.S. Census Bureau, State & Local Government Finances 2020

TAXES

State Corporate Income Tax Rates

State	Tax Rate (%)	Income Brackets ($)	Num. of Brackets	Financial Institution Tax Rate (%)[a]	Federal Income Tax Ded.
Louisiana	3.5 - 7.5	50,000 - 150,000	3	3.5 - 7.5	Yes

Note: Tax rates as of January 1, 2023; (a) Rates listed are the corporate income tax rate applied to financial institutions or excise taxes based on income. Some states have other taxes based upon the value of deposits or shares.
Source: Federation of Tax Administrators, State Corporate Income Tax Rates, January 1, 2023

Lafayette, Louisiana

State Individual Income Tax Rates

State	Tax Rate (%)	Income Brackets ($)	Personal Exemptions ($) Single	Married	Depend.	Standard Ded. ($) Single	Married
Louisiana (aa)	1.85 - 4.25 (bb)	12,500 - 50,001 (b)	4,500	9,000	1,000 (k)	(k)	(k)

Note: Tax rates as of January 1, 2023; Local- and county-level taxes are not included; Federal income tax is deductible on state income tax returns; (b) For joint returns, taxes are twice the tax on half the couple's income; (k) The amounts reported for Louisiana are a combined personal exemption-standard deduction; (aa) Standard deduction amounts reported are maximums, Maryland standard deduction is 15% of AGI; (bb) Louisiana tax rates may be adjusted down if revenue trigger is met on April 1st. Iowa is phasing-in a flat rate by 2027, while Nebraska and South Carolina is phasing-in a reduced top rate by 2027.
Source: Federation of Tax Administrators, State Individual Income Tax Rates, January 1, 2023

Various State Sales and Excise Tax Rates

State	State Sales Tax (%)	Gasoline[1] ($/gal.)	Cigarette[2] ($/pack)	Spirits[3] ($/gal.)	Wine[4] ($/gal.)	Beer[5] ($/gal.)	Recreational Marijuana (%)
Louisiana	4.45	0.2013	1.08	3.03	0.76	0.40	Not legal

Note: All tax rates as of January 1, 2023; (1) The American Petroleum Institute has developed a methodology for determining the average tax rate on a gallon of fuel. Rates may include any of the following: excise taxes, environmental fees, storage tank fees, other fees or taxes, general sales tax, and local taxes; (2) The federal excise tax of $1.0066 per pack and local taxes are not included; (3) Rates are those applicable to off-premise sales of 40% alcohol by volume (a.b.v.) distilled spirits in 750ml containers. Local excise taxes are excluded; (4) Rates are those applicable to off-premise sales of 11% a.b.v. non-carbonated wine in 750ml containers; (5) Rates are those applicable to off-premise sales of 4.7% a.b.v. beer in 12 ounce containers.
Source: Tax Foundation, 2023 Facts & Figures: How Does Your State Compare?

State Business Tax Climate Index Rankings

State	Overall Rank	Corporate Tax Rank	Individual Income Tax Rank	Sales Tax Rank	Property Tax Rank	Unemployment Insurance Tax Rank
Louisiana	39	32	25	48	23	6

Note: The index is a measure of how each state's tax laws affect economic performance. The lower the rank, the more favorable a state's tax system is for business. States without a given tax are given a ranking of 1. The scores/rankings for the District of Columbia do not affect other states. The 2023 index represents the tax climate as of July 1, 2022.
Source: Tax Foundation, State Business Tax Climate Index 2023

TRANSPORTATION

Means of Transportation to Work

Area	Drove Alone	Car-pooled	Bus	Subway	Railroad	Bicycle	Walked	Other Means	Worked at Home
City	83.4	4.8	0.8	0.0	0.0	0.5	2.4	1.0	7.0
MSA[1]	83.9	6.7	0.3	0.0	0.0	0.2	1.9	1.2	5.8
U.S.	73.2	8.6	2.0	1.6	0.5	0.5	2.5	1.5	9.7

Note: Figures are percentages and cover workers 16 years of age and older; (1) Figures cover the Lafayette, LA Metropolitan Statistical Area
Source: U.S. Census Bureau, 2017-2021 American Community Survey 5-Year Estimates

Travel Time to Work

Area	Less Than 10 Minutes	10 to 19 Minutes	20 to 29 Minutes	30 to 44 Minutes	45 to 59 Minutes	60 to 89 Minutes	90 Minutes or More
City	15.8	44.0	19.3	11.9	2.8	3.6	2.6
MSA[1]	13.3	33.5	20.9	18.5	5.9	3.8	4.0
U.S.	12.4	28.5	21.0	20.9	8.2	6.2	2.9

Note: Note: Figures are percentages and include workers 16 years old and over; (1) Figures cover the Lafayette, LA Metropolitan Statistical Area
Source: U.S. Census Bureau, 2017-2021 American Community Survey 5-Year Estimates

Key Congestion Measures

Measure	1990	2000	2010	2015	2020
Annual Hours of Delay, Total (000)	n/a	n/a	n/a	8,208	3,331
Annual Hours of Delay, Per Auto Commuter	n/a	n/a	n/a	30	13
Annual Congestion Cost, Per Auto Commuter ($)	n/a	n/a	n/a	674	308

Note: n/a not available
Source: Texas A&M Transportation Institute, 2021 Urban Mobility Report

Freeway Travel Time Index

Measure	1985	1990	1995	2000	2005	2010	2015	2020
Urban Area Index[1]	n/a	n/a	n/a	n/a	n/a	n/a	1.13	1.06
Urban Area Rank[1,2]	n/a	n/a	n/a	n/a	n/a	n/a	n/a	n/a

Note: Freeway Travel Time Index—the ratio of travel time in the peak period to the travel time at free-flow conditions. For example, a value of 1.30 indicates a 20-minute free-flow trip takes 26 minutes in the peak (20 minutes x 1.30 = 26 minutes); (1) Covers the Lafayette LA urban area; (2) Rank is based on 101 larger urban areas (#1 = highest travel time index); n/a not available
Source: Texas A&M Transportation Institute, 2021 Urban Mobility Report

Public Transportation

Agency Name / Mode of Transportation	Vehicles Operated in Maximum Service[1]	Annual Unlinked Passenger Trips[2] (in thous.)	Annual Passenger Miles[3] (in thous.)
Lafayette Transit System			
Bus (directly operated)	11	751.2	5,379.0
Demand Response (purchased transportation)	7	28.2	335.1

Note: (1) Number of revenue vehicles operated by the given mode and type of service to meet the annual maximum service requirement. This is the revenue vehicle count during the peak season of the year; on the week and day that maximum service is provided. Vehicles operated in maximum service (VOMS) exclude atypical days and one-time special events; (2) Number of passengers who boarded public transportation vehicles. Passengers are counted each time they board a vehicle no matter how many vehicles they use to travel from their origin to their destination. (3) Sum of the distances ridden by all passengers during the entire fiscal year.
Source: Federal Transit Administration, National Transit Database, 2021

Air Transportation

Airport Name and Code / Type of Service	Passenger Airlines[1]	Passenger Enplanements	Freight Carriers[2]	Freight (lbs)
Lafayette Regional Airport (LFT)				
Domestic service (U.S. carriers - 2022)	11	225,747	5	13,777,988
International service (U.S. carriers - 2021)	0	0	0	0

Note: (1) Includes all U.S.-based major, minor and commuter airlines that carried at least one passenger during the year; (2) Includes all U.S.-based airlines and freight carriers that transported at least one pound of freight during the year.
Source: Bureau of Transportation Statistics, The Intermodal Transportation Database, Air Carriers: T-100 Domestic Market (U.S. Carriers), 2022; Bureau of Transportation Statistics, The Intermodal Transportation Database, Air Carriers: T-100 International Market (U.S. Carriers), 2021

BUSINESSES

Major Business Headquarters

Company Name	Industry	Rankings Fortune[1]	Forbes[2]
No companies listed	-	-	-

Note: (1) Companies that produce a 10-K are ranked 1 to 500 based on 2021 revenue; (2) All private companies with at least $2 billion in annual revenue through the end of their most current fiscal year are ranked 1 to 246; companies listed are headquartered in the city; dashes indicate no ranking
Source: Fortune, "Fortune 500," 2022; Forbes, "America's Largest Private Companies," 2022

Fastest-Growing Businesses

According to *Initiative for a Competitive Inner City (ICIC)*, Lafayette is home to one of America's 100 fastest-growing "inner city" companies: **Techneaux** (#56). Criteria for inclusion: company must be headquartered in or have 51 percent or more of its physical operations in an economically distressed urban area; must be an independent, for-profit corporation, partnership or proprietorship; must have 10 or more employees and have a five-year sales history that includes sales of at least $200,000 in the base year and at least $1 million in the current year with no decrease in sales over the two most recent years. Companies were ranked overall by revenue growth over the five-year period between 2017 and 2021. *Initiative for a Competitive Inner City (ICIC), "Inner City 100 Companies," 2022*

Lafayette, Louisiana

Living Environment

COST OF LIVING

Cost of Living Index

Composite Index	Groceries	Housing	Utilities	Transportation	Health Care	Misc. Goods/Services
88.1	99.3	68.8	89.5	97.9	94.3	95.1

Note: The Cost of Living Index measures regional differences in the cost of consumer goods and services, excluding taxes and non-consumer expenditures, for professional and managerial households in the top income quintile. It is based on more than 50,000 prices covering almost 60 different items for which prices are collected three times a year by chambers of commerce, economic development organizations or university applied economic centers in each participating urban area. The numbers shown should be read as a percentage above or below the national average of 100. For example, a value of 115.4 in the groceries column indicates that grocery prices are 15.4% higher than the national average. Small differences in the index numbers should not be interpreted as significant; Figures cover the Lafayette LA urban area.
Source: The Council for Community and Economic Research, Cost of Living Index, 2022

Grocery Prices

Area[1]	T-Bone Steak ($/pound)	Frying Chicken ($/pound)	Whole Milk ($/half gal.)	Eggs ($/dozen)	Orange Juice ($/64 oz.)	Coffee ($/11.5 oz.)
City[2]	12.53	1.49	2.57	3.19	3.66	5.04
Avg.	13.81	1.59	2.43	2.25	3.85	4.95
Min.	10.17	0.90	1.51	1.30	2.90	3.46
Max.	19.35	3.30	4.32	4.32	5.31	8.59

*Note: (1) Values for the local area are compared with the average, minimum and maximum values for all 286 areas in the Cost of Living Index; (2) Figures cover the Lafayette LA urban area; **T-Bone Steak** (price per pound); **Frying Chicken** (price per pound, whole fryer); **Whole Milk** (half gallon carton); **Eggs** (price per dozen, Grade A, large); **Orange Juice** (64 oz. Tropicana or Florida Natural); **Coffee** (11.5 oz. can, vacuum-packed, Maxwell House, Hills Bros, or Folgers).*
Source: The Council for Community and Economic Research, Cost of Living Index, 2022

Housing and Utility Costs

Area[1]	New Home Price ($)	Apartment Rent ($/month)	All Electric ($/month)	Part Electric ($/month)	Other Energy ($/month)	Telephone ($/month)
City[2]	284,856	1,063	-	89.62	58.12	186.23
Avg.	450,913	1,371	176.41	99.93	76.96	190.22
Min.	229,283	546	100.84	31.56	27.15	174.27
Max.	2,434,977	4,569	356.86	249.59	272.24	208.31

*Note: (1) Values for the local area are compared with the average, minimum and maximum values for all 286 areas in the Cost of Living Index; (2) Figures cover the Lafayette LA urban area; **New Home Price** (2,400 sf living area, 8,000 sf lot, in urban area with full utilities); **Apartment Rent** (950 sf 2 bedroom/1.5 or 2 bath, unfurnished, excluding all utilities except water); **All Electric** (average monthly cost for an all-electric home); **Part Electric** (average monthly cost for a part-electric home); **Other Energy** (average monthly cost for natural gas, fuel oil, coal, wood, and any other forms of energy except electricity); **Telephone** (price includes the base monthly rate plus taxes and fees for three lines of mobile phone service).*
Source: The Council for Community and Economic Research, Cost of Living Index, 2022

Health Care, Transportation, and Other Costs

Area[1]	Doctor ($/visit)	Dentist ($/visit)	Optometrist ($/visit)	Gasoline ($/gallon)	Beauty Salon ($/visit)	Men's Shirt ($)
City[2]	109.56	100.77	100.99	3.43	43.28	30.76
Avg.	124.91	107.77	117.66	3.86	43.31	34.21
Min.	36.61	58.25	51.79	2.90	22.18	13.05
Max.	250.21	162.58	371.96	5.54	85.61	63.54

*Note: (1) Values for the local area are compared with the average, minimum and maximum values for all 286 areas in the Cost of Living Index; (2) Figures cover the Lafayette LA urban area; **Doctor** (general practitioners routine exam of an established patient); **Dentist** (adult teeth cleaning and periodic oral examination); **Optometrist** (full vision eye exam for established adult patient); **Gasoline** (one gallon regular unleaded, national brand, including all taxes, cash price at self-service pump if available); **Beauty Salon** (woman's shampoo, trim, and blow-dry); **Men's Shirt** (cotton/polyester dress shirt, pinpoint weave, long sleeves).*
Source: The Council for Community and Economic Research, Cost of Living Index, 2022

HOUSING

Homeownership Rate

Area	2015 (%)	2016 (%)	2017 (%)	2018 (%)	2019 (%)	2020 (%)	2021 (%)	2022 (%)
MSA[1]	n/a	n/a	n/a	n/a	n/a	n/a	n/a	n/a
U.S.	63.7	63.4	63.9	64.4	64.6	66.6	65.5	65.8

Note: (1) Figures cover the Lafayette, LA Metropolitan Statistical Area; n/a not available
Source: U.S. Census Bureau, Housing Vacancies and Homeownership Annual Statistics: 2015-2022

House Price Index (HPI)

Area	National Ranking[2]	Quarterly Change (%)	One-Year Change (%)	Five-Year Change (%)	Since 1991Q1 (%)
MSA[1]	179	-0.60	9.73	25.29	232.27
U.S.[3]	—	0.34	8.41	58.44	289.08

Note: The HPI is a weighted repeat sales index. It measures average price changes in repeat sales or refinancings on the same properties. This information is obtained by reviewing repeat mortgage transactions on single-family properties whose mortgages have been purchased or securitized by Fannie Mae or Freddie Mac since January 1975; (1) Figures cover the Lafayette, LA Metropolitan Statistical Area; (2) Rankings are based on annual percentage change for all metro areas containing at least 15,000 transactions over the last 10 years and ranges from 1 to 257; (3) figures based on a weighted average of Census Division estimates using a seasonally adjusted, purchase-only index; all figures are for the period ending December 31, 2022
Source: Federal Housing Finance Agency, Change in FHFA Metropolitan Area House Price Indexes, 2022Q4

Median Single-Family Home Prices

Area	2020	2021	2022p	Percent Change 2021 to 2022
MSA[1]	n/a	n/a	n/a	n/a
U.S. Average	300.2	357.1	392.6	9.9

Note: Figures are median sales prices of existing single-family homes in thousands of dollars; (p) preliminary; n/a not available; (1) Figures cover the Lafayette, LA Metropolitan Statistical Area
Source: National Association of Realtors, Median Sales Price of Existing Single-Family Homes for Metropolitan Areas, 4th Quarter 2022

Qualifying Income Based on Median Sales Price of Existing Single-Family Homes

Area	With 5% Down ($)	With 10% Down ($)	With 20% Down ($)
MSA[1]	n/a	n/a	n/a
U.S. Average	112,234	106,237	94,513

Note: Figures are preliminary; Qualifying income is based on a mortgage rate of 6.77%. Monthly principal and interest payment is limited to 25% of income; n/a not available; (1) Figures cover the Lafayette, LA Metropolitan Statistical Area
Source: National Association of Realtors, Qualifying Income Based on Median Sales Price of Existing Single-Family Homes for Metropolitan Areas, 4th Quarter 2022

Home Value

Area	Under $100,000	$100,000 -$199,999	$200,000 -$299,999	$300,000 -$399,999	$400,000 -$499,999	$500,000 -$999,999	$1,000,000 or more	Median ($)
City	13.7	33.6	25.7	11.7	7.0	6.7	1.6	209,100
MSA[1]	28.0	34.1	21.1	9.0	3.7	3.3	0.7	167,400
U.S.	16.2	24.2	20.1	13.6	8.3	13.6	4.1	244,900

Note: Figures are percentages except for median and cover owner-occupied housing units; (1) Figures cover the Lafayette, LA Metropolitan Statistical Area
Source: U.S. Census Bureau, 2017-2021 American Community Survey 5-Year Estimates

Year Housing Structure Built

Area	2020 or Later	2010 -2019	2000 -2009	1990 -1999	1980 -1989	1970 -1979	1960 -1969	1950 -1959	1940 -1949	Before 1940	Median Year
City	<0.1	10.1	10.7	10.1	19.5	22.0	12.8	9.0	3.2	2.5	1980
MSA[1]	0.2	12.8	14.8	12.9	15.8	15.9	10.3	9.0	3.7	4.5	1984
U.S.	0.2	7.3	13.6	13.6	13.2	14.8	10.3	10.0	4.7	12.2	1979

Note: Figures are percentages except for Median Year; Note: (1) Figures cover the Lafayette, LA Metropolitan Statistical Area
Source: U.S. Census Bureau, 2017-2021 American Community Survey 5-Year Estimates

Gross Monthly Rent

Area	Under $500	$500 -$999	$1,000 -$1,499	$1,500 -$1,999	$2,000 -$2,499	$2,500 -$2,999	$3,000 and up	Median ($)
City	6.9	50.5	32.1	8.7	1.0	0.2	0.6	948
MSA[1]	13.8	54.5	25.3	4.8	1.1	0.1	0.4	853
U.S.	8.1	30.5	30.8	16.8	7.3	3.5	3.5	1,163

Note: Figures are percentages except for median; Gross rent is the contract rent plus the estimated average monthly cost of utilities (electricity, gas, and water and sewer) and fuels (oil, coal, kerosene, wood, etc.) if these are paid by the renter (or paid for the renter by someone else); (1) Figures cover the Lafayette, LA Metropolitan Statistical Area
Source: U.S. Census Bureau, 2017-2021 American Community Survey 5-Year Estimates

HEALTH

Health Risk Factors

Category	MSA[1] (%)	U.S. (%)
Adults aged 18–64 who have any kind of health care coverage	95.5	90.9
Adults who reported being in good or better health	82.0	85.2
Adults who have been told they have high blood cholesterol	35.2	35.7
Adults who have been told they have high blood pressure	41.0	32.4
Adults who are current smokers	19.9	14.4
Adults who currently use e-cigarettes	9.7	6.7
Adults who currently use chewing tobacco, snuff, or snus	5.4	3.5
Adults who are heavy drinkers[2]	9.0	6.3
Adults who are binge drinkers[3]	19.5	15.4
Adults who are overweight (BMI 25.0 - 29.9)	32.6	34.4
Adults who are obese (BMI 30.0 - 99.8)	39.6	33.9
Adults who participated in any physical activities in the past month	70.9	76.3

Note: (1) Figures cover the Lafayette, LA Metropolitan Statistical Area; (2) Heavy drinkers are classified as adult men having more than 14 drinks per week and adult women having more than 7 drinks per week; (3) Binge drinkers are classified as males having five or more drinks on one occasion or females having four or more drinks on one occasion
Source: Centers for Disease Control and Prevention, Behaviorial Risk Factor Surveillance System, SMART: Selected Metropolitan Area Risk Trends, 2021

Acute and Chronic Health Conditions

Category	MSA[1] (%)	U.S. (%)
Adults who have ever been told they had a heart attack	3.7	4.0
Adults who have ever been told they have angina or coronary heart disease	3.6	3.8
Adults who have ever been told they had a stroke	2.5	3.0
Adults who have ever been told they have asthma	13.0	14.9
Adults who have ever been told they have arthritis	28.2	25.8
Adults who have ever been told they have diabetes[2]	12.6	10.9
Adults who have ever been told they had skin cancer	5.1	6.6
Adults who have ever been told they had any other types of cancer	8.4	7.5
Adults who have ever been told they have COPD	8.7	6.1
Adults who have ever been told they have kidney disease	2.5	3.0
Adults who have ever been told they have a form of depression	27.2	20.5

Note: (1) Figures cover the Lafayette, LA Metropolitan Statistical Area; (2) Figures do not include pregnancy-related, borderline, or pre-diabetes
Source: Centers for Disease Control and Prevention, Behaviorial Risk Factor Surveillance System, SMART: Selected Metropolitan Area Risk Trends, 2021

Health Screening and Vaccination Rates

Category	MSA[1] (%)	U.S. (%)
Adults who have ever been tested for HIV	39.7	34.9
Adults who have had their blood cholesterol checked within the last five years	86.8	85.2
Adults aged 65+ who have had flu shot within the past year	64.4	68.6
Adults aged 65+ who have ever had a pneumonia vaccination	66.1	71.0

Note: (1) Figures cover the Lafayette, LA Metropolitan Statistical Area.
Source: Centers for Disease Control and Prevention, Behaviorial Risk Factor Surveillance System, SMART: Selected Metropolitan Area Risk Trends, 2021

Disability Status

Category	MSA[1] (%)	U.S. (%)
Adults who reported being deaf	9.1	7.2
Are you blind or have serious difficulty seeing, even when wearing glasses?	7.2	4.8
Are you limited in any way in any of your usual activities due to arthritis?	10.4	11.1
Do you have difficulty doing errands alone?	9.0	7.0
Do you have difficulty dressing or bathing?	5.0	3.6
Do you have serious difficulty concentrating/remembering/making decisions?	18.5	12.1
Do you have serious difficulty walking or climbing stairs?	15.5	12.8

Note: (1) Figures cover the Lafayette, LA Metropolitan Statistical Area.
Source: Centers for Disease Control and Prevention, Behaviorial Risk Factor Surveillance System, SMART: Selected Metropolitan Area Risk Trends, 2021

Mortality Rates for the Top 10 Causes of Death in the U.S.

ICD-10[a] Sub-Chapter	ICD-10[a] Code	Crude Mortality Rate[1] per 100,000 population County[2]	U.S.
Malignant neoplasms	C00-C97	169.8	182.6
Ischaemic heart diseases	I20-I25	65.7	113.1
Other forms of heart disease	I30-I51	58.4	64.4
Other degenerative diseases of the nervous system	G30-G31	63.8	51.0
Cerebrovascular diseases	I60-I69	45.2	47.8
Other external causes of accidental injury	W00-X59	50.7	46.4
Chronic lower respiratory diseases	J40-J47	29.8	45.7
Organic, including symptomatic, mental disorders	F01-F09	9.0	35.9
Hypertensive diseases	I10-I15	92.6	35.0
Diabetes mellitus	E10-E14	34.0	29.6

Note: (a) ICD-10 = International Classification of Diseases 10th Revision; (1) Crude mortality rates are a three-year average covering 2019-2021; (2) Figures cover Lafayette Parish.
Source: Centers for Disease Control and Prevention, National Center for Health Statistics. National Vital Statistics System, Mortality 2018-2021 on CDC WONDER Online Database

Mortality Rates for Selected Causes of Death

ICD-10[a] Sub-Chapter	ICD-10[a] Code	Crude Mortality Rate[1] per 100,000 population County[2]	U.S.
Assault	X85-Y09	10.7	7.0
Diseases of the liver	K70-K76	13.5	19.8
Human immunodeficiency virus (HIV) disease	B20-B24	Suppressed	1.5
Influenza and pneumonia	J09-J18	11.2	14.7
Intentional self-harm	X60-X84	15.0	14.3
Malnutrition	E40-E46	5.2	4.3
Obesity and other hyperalimentation	E65-E68	8.7	3.0
Renal failure	N17-N19	14.4	15.7
Transport accidents	V01-V99	14.1	13.6
Viral hepatitis	B15-B19	Suppressed	1.2

Note: (a) ICD-10 = International Classification of Diseases 10th Revision; (1) Crude mortality rates are a three-year average covering 2019-2021; (2) Figures cover Lafayette Parish; Data are suppressed when the data meet the criteria for confidentiality constraints; Crude mortality rates are flagged as unreliable when the rate would be calculated with a numerator of 20 or less.
Source: Centers for Disease Control and Prevention, National Center for Health Statistics. National Vital Statistics System, Mortality 2018-2021 on CDC WONDER Online Database

Health Insurance Coverage

Area	With Health Insurance	With Private Health Insurance	With Public Health Insurance	Without Health Insurance	Population Under Age 19 Without Health Insurance
City	91.5	64.4	38.6	8.5	4.0
MSA[1]	91.9	61.3	41.3	8.1	3.5
U.S.	91.2	67.8	35.4	8.8	5.3

Note: Figures are percentages that cover the civilian noninstitutionalized population; (1) Figures cover the Lafayette, LA Metropolitan Statistical Area
Source: U.S. Census Bureau, 2017-2021 American Community Survey 5-Year Estimates

Number of Medical Professionals

Area	MDs[3]	DOs[3,4]	Dentists	Podiatrists	Chiropractors	Optometrists
Parish[1] (number)	914	28	175	9	80	35
Parish[1] (rate[2])	377.7	11.6	71.7	3.7	32.8	14.3
U.S. (rate[2])	289.3	23.5	72.5	6.2	28.7	17.4

Note: Data as of 2021 unless noted; (1) Data covers Lafayette Parish; (2) Rate per 100,000 population; (3) Data as of 2020 and includes all active, non-federal physicians; (4) Doctor of Osteopathic Medicine
Source: U.S. Department of Health and Human Services, Health Resources and Services Administration, Bureau of Health Professions, Area Resource File (ARF) 2021-2022

EDUCATION

Public School District Statistics

District Name	Schls	Pupils	Pupil/ Teacher Ratio	Minority Pupils[1] (%)	LEP/ELL[2] (%)	IEP[3] (%)
Lafayette Parish	46	31,271	18.4	55.5	5.0	8.7

Note: Table includes school districts with 2,000 or more students; (1) Percentage of students that are not non-Hispanic white; (2) Percentage of students that are Limited English Proficient or English Language Learners (2018-19); (3) Percentage of students that have an Individualized Education Program (2019-20).
Source: U.S. Department of Education, National Center for Education Statistics, Common Core of Data, Local Education Agency (School District) Universe Survey: School Year 2021-2022

Highest Level of Education

Area	Less than H.S.	H.S. Diploma	Some College, No Deg.	Associate Degree	Bachelor's Degree	Master's Degree	Prof. School Degree	Doctorate Degree
City	9.7	26.2	19.5	5.2	24.9	8.7	3.9	1.9
MSA[1]	14.0	36.5	18.4	6.5	17.0	5.1	1.7	0.8
U.S.	11.1	26.5	20.0	8.7	20.6	9.3	2.2	1.5

Note: Figures cover persons age 25 and over; (1) Figures cover the Lafayette, LA Metropolitan Statistical Area
Source: U.S. Census Bureau, 2017-2021 American Community Survey 5-Year Estimates

Educational Attainment by Race

Area	High School Graduate or Higher (%) Total	White	Black	Asian	Hisp.[2]	Bachelor's Degree or Higher (%) Total	White	Black	Asian	Hisp.[2]
City	90.3	95.1	80.3	92.2	72.5	39.4	49.1	15.2	63.9	33.0
MSA[1]	86.0	88.8	79.2	76.0	70.7	24.6	27.7	13.2	38.0	19.1
U.S.	88.9	91.4	87.2	87.6	71.2	33.7	35.5	23.3	55.6	18.4

Note: Figures shown cover persons 25 years old and over; (1) Figures cover the Lafayette, LA Metropolitan Statistical Area; (2) People of Hispanic origin can be of any race
Source: U.S. Census Bureau, 2017-2021 American Community Survey 5-Year Estimates

School Enrollment by Grade and Control

Area	Preschool (%) Public	Private	Kindergarten (%) Public	Private	Grades 1 - 4 (%) Public	Private	Grades 5 - 8 (%) Public	Private	Grades 9 - 12 (%) Public	Private
City	63.6	36.4	67.4	32.6	70.2	29.8	72.4	27.6	79.5	20.5
MSA[1]	66.3	33.7	78.7	21.3	80.8	19.2	78.8	21.2	78.7	21.3
U.S.	58.8	41.2	86.3	13.7	88.3	11.7	88.6	11.4	89.4	10.6

Note: Figures shown cover persons 3 years old and over; (1) Figures cover the Lafayette, LA Metropolitan Statistical Area
Source: U.S. Census Bureau, 2017-2021 American Community Survey 5-Year Estimates

Higher Education

Four-Year Colleges Public	Private Non-profit	Private For-profit	Two-Year Colleges Public	Private Non-profit	Private For-profit	Medical Schools[1]	Law Schools[2]	Voc/Tech[3]
1	0	0	2	2	2	0	0	5

Note: Figures cover institutions located within the Lafayette, LA Metropolitan Statistical Area and include main campuses only; (1) includes schools accredited by the Liaison Committee on Medical Education and the American Osteopathic Association's Commission on Osteopathic College Accreditation; (2) includes ABA-accredited schools, schools with provisional ABA accreditation, and state accredited schools; (3) includes all schools with programs that are less than 2 years.
Source: National Center for Education Statistics, Integrated Postsecondary Education System (IPEDS), 2021-22; Wikipedia, List of Medical Schools in the United States, accessed April 10, 2023; Wikipedia, List of Law Schools in the United States, accessed April 10, 2023

EMPLOYERS

Major Employers

Company Name	Industry
Acadian Companies	Health care
American Legion Hospital	Health care
AT&T Wireless	Telecommunications
Baker Hughes	Oil field service
Cal Dive Intl Inc	Diving instruction
Cameron Valves & Measurement	Valves, manufacturers
Cheveron USA Production Co.	Oil & gas
Fieldwood Energy	Oil & gas
Frank's Casing Crew & Rental	Oil field service
Halliburton Energy SVC	Oil field service
Lafayette General Medical Ctr	Health care
LHC Group Inc	Health care
McDonald's of Acadiana	Services
Offshore Energy Inc	Oil field service
Opelousas Health Systems	Health care
Our Lady of Lourdes Regional Medical Ctr	Health care
Petroleum Helicopters	Transportation
Quality Construction & Production	General contractors
Regional Medical Center-Acadiana	Health care
Schlumberger	Oil field service
Stuller Inc	Jewelry-manufacturers
Superior Energy Svc	Oil field service
Wal-Mart Stores	Retail
Walmart Distribution Center	Distribution centers
Weatherford	Oil field service

Note: Companies shown are located within the Lafayette, LA Metropolitan Statistical Area.
Source: Hoovers.com; Wikipedia

PUBLIC SAFETY

Crime Rate

Area	Total Crime	Violent Crime Rate — Murder	Rape[3]	Robbery	Aggrav. Assault	Property Crime Rate — Burglary	Larceny-Theft	Motor Vehicle Theft
City	5,081.3	11.1	13.4	116.0	421.5	843.9	3,352.6	322.9
Suburbs[1]	2,189.8	7.4	23.9	35.5	344.1	400.2	1,210.2	168.4
Metro[2]	2,937.4	8.4	21.2	56.3	364.1	514.9	1,764.1	208.4
U.S.	2,356.7	6.5	38.4	73.9	279.7	314.2	1,398.0	246.0

Note: Figures are crimes per 100,000 population; (1) All areas within the metro area that are located outside the city limits; (2) Figures cover the Lafayette, LA Metropolitan Statistical Area; (3) All figures shown were reported using the revised Uniform Crime Reporting (UCR) definition of rape; Due to the transition to the National Incident-Based Reporting System (NIBRS), limited city and metro area data was released for 2021.
Source: FBI Uniform Crime Reports, 2020

Hate Crimes

Area	Number of Quarters Reported	Race/Ethnicity/Ancestry	Religion	Sexual Orientation	Disability	Gender	Gender Identity
City	4	0	0	0	0	0	0
U.S.	4	5,227	1,244	1,110	130	75	266

Note: Due to the transition to the National Incident-Based Reporting System (NIBRS), limited crime data was released for 2021.
Source: Federal Bureau of Investigation, Hate Crime Statistics 2020

Identity Theft Consumer Reports

Area	Reports	Reports per 100,000 Population	Rank[2]
MSA[1]	3,819	779	4
U.S.	1,108,609	339	-

Note: (1) Figures cover the Lafayette, LA Metropolitan Statistical Area; (2) Rank ranges from 1 to 391 where 1 indicates greatest number of identity theft reports per 100,000 population
Source: Federal Trade Commission, Consumer Sentinel Network Data Book 2022

Fraud and Other Consumer Reports

Area	Reports	Reports per 100,000 Population	Rank[2]
MSA[1]	4,927	1,005	97
U.S.	4,064,520	1,245	-

Note: (1) Figures cover the Lafayette, LA Metropolitan Statistical Area; (2) Rank ranges from 1 to 391 where 1 indicates greatest number of fraud and other consumer reports per 100,000 population
Source: Federal Trade Commission, Consumer Sentinel Network Data Book 2022

POLITICS

2020 Presidential Election Results

Area	Biden	Trump	Jorgensen	Hawkins	Other
Lafayette Parish	34.7	63.3	1.3	0.0	0.7
U.S.	51.3	46.8	1.2	0.3	0.5

Note: Results are percentages and may not add to 100% due to rounding
Source: Dave Leip's Atlas of U.S. Presidential Elections

SPORTS

Professional Sports Teams

Team Name	League	Year Established

No teams are located in the metro area
Source: Wikipedia, Major Professional Sports Teams of the United States and Canada, April 12, 2023

CLIMATE

Average and Extreme Temperatures

Temperature	Jan	Feb	Mar	Apr	May	Jun	Jul	Aug	Sep	Oct	Nov	Dec	Yr.
Extreme High (°F)	82	85	91	92	98	103	101	102	99	94	87	85	103
Average High (°F)	61	65	71	79	85	90	91	91	87	80	70	64	78
Average Temp. (°F)	51	54	61	68	75	81	82	82	78	69	59	53	68
Average Low (°F)	41	44	50	57	64	70	73	72	68	57	48	43	57
Extreme Low (°F)	9	13	20	32	44	53	58	59	43	30	21	8	8

Note: Figures cover the years 1948-1995
Source: National Climatic Data Center, International Station Meteorological Climate Summary, 9/96

Average Precipitation/Snowfall/Humidity

Precip./Humidity	Jan	Feb	Mar	Apr	May	Jun	Jul	Aug	Sep	Oct	Nov	Dec	Yr.
Avg. Precip. (in.)	4.9	5.1	4.8	5.5	5.0	4.4	6.6	5.4	4.1	3.1	4.2	5.3	58.5
Avg. Snowfall (in.)	Tr	Tr	Tr	0	0	0	0	0	0	0	Tr	Tr	Tr
Avg. Rel. Hum. 6am (%)	85	85	86	89	91	91	92	93	91	89	88	86	89
Avg. Rel. Hum. 3pm (%)	59	55	52	52	54	57	62	61	59	51	53	57	56

Note: Figures cover the years 1948-1995; Tr = Trace amounts (<0.05 in. of rain; <0.5 in. of snow)
Source: National Climatic Data Center, International Station Meteorological Climate Summary, 9/96

Weather Conditions

Temperature			Daytime Sky			Precipitation		
10°F & below	32°F & below	90°F & above	Clear	Partly cloudy	Cloudy	0.01 inch or more precip.	0.1 inch or more snow/ice	Thunder-storms
<1	21	86	99	150	116	113	<1	73

Note: Figures are average number of days per year and cover the years 1948-1995
Source: National Climatic Data Center, International Station Meteorological Climate Summary, 9/96

HAZARDOUS WASTE

Superfund Sites

The Lafayette, LA metro area is home to one site on the EPA's Superfund National Priorities List: **Evr-Wood Treating/Evangeline Refining Company** (final). There are a total of 1,165 Superfund sites with a status of proposed or final on the list in the U.S. *U.S. Environmental Protection Agency, National Priorities List, April 12, 2023*

AIR QUALITY

Air Quality Trends: Ozone

	1990	1995	2000	2005	2010	2015	2018	2019	2020	2021
MSA[1]	n/a	n/a	n/a	n/a	n/a	n/a	n/a	n/a	n/a	n/a
U.S.	0.087	0.089	0.081	0.080	0.072	0.067	0.069	0.065	0.065	0.067

Note: (1) Data covers the Lafayette, LA Metropolitan Statistical Area; n/a not available. The values shown are the composite ozone concentration averages among trend sites based on the highest fourth daily maximum 8-hour concentration in parts per million. These trends are based on sites having an adequate record of monitoring data during the trend period. Data from exceptional events are included.
Source: U.S. Environmental Protection Agency, Air Quality Monitoring Information, "Air Quality Trends by City, 1990-2021"

Air Quality Index

Area	Percent of Days when Air Quality was...[2]					AQI Statistics[2]	
	Good	Moderate	Unhealthy for Sensitive Groups	Unhealthy	Very Unhealthy	Maximum	Median
MSA[1]	81.6	18.4	0.0	0.0	0.0	87	38

Note: (1) Data covers the Lafayette, LA Metropolitan Statistical Area; (2) Based on 365 days with AQI data in 2021. Air Quality Index (AQI) is an index for reporting daily air quality. EPA calculates the AQI for five major air pollutants regulated by the Clean Air Act: ground-level ozone, particle pollution (aka particulate matter), carbon monoxide, sulfur dioxide, and nitrogen dioxide. The AQI runs from 0 to 500. The higher the AQI value, the greater the level of air pollution and the greater the health concern. There are six AQI categories: "Good" AQI is between 0 and 50. Air quality is considered satisfactory; "Moderate" AQI is between 51 and 100. Air quality is acceptable; "Unhealthy for Sensitive Groups" When AQI values are between 101 and 150, members of sensitive groups may experience health effects; "Unhealthy" When AQI values are between 151 and 200 everyone may begin to experience health effects; "Very Unhealthy" AQI values between 201 and 300 trigger a health alert; "Hazardous" AQI values over 300 trigger warnings of emergency conditions (not shown).
Source: U.S. Environmental Protection Agency, Air Quality Index Report, 2021

Air Quality Index Pollutants

Area	Percent of Days when AQI Pollutant was...[2]					
	Carbon Monoxide	Nitrogen Dioxide	Ozone	Sulfur Dioxide	Particulate Matter 2.5	Particulate Matter 10
MSA[1]	0.0	0.0	61.9	(3)	38.1	0.0

Note: (1) Data covers the Lafayette, LA Metropolitan Statistical Area; (2) Based on 365 days with AQI data in 2021. The Air Quality Index (AQI) is an index for reporting daily air quality. EPA calculates the AQI for five major air pollutants regulated by the Clean Air Act: ground-level ozone, particle pollution (also known as particulate matter), carbon monoxide, sulfur dioxide, and nitrogen dioxide. The AQI runs from 0 to 500. The higher the AQI value, the greater the level of air pollution and the greater the health concern; (3) Sulfur dioxide is no longer included in this table (as of December 8, 2021) because SO_2 concentrations tend to be very localized and not necessarily representative of broad geographical areas like counties and CBSAs.
Source: U.S. Environmental Protection Agency, Air Quality Index Report, 2021

Maximum Air Pollutant Concentrations: Particulate Matter, Ozone, CO and Lead

	Particulate Matter 10 (ug/m^3)	Particulate Matter 2.5 Wtd AM (ug/m^3)	Particulate Matter 2.5 24-Hr (ug/m^3)	Ozone (ppm)	Carbon Monoxide (ppm)	Lead (ug/m^3)
MSA[1] Level	56	7.6	16	0.063	n/a	n/a
NAAQS[2]	150	15	35	0.075	9	0.15
Met NAAQS[2]	Yes	Yes	Yes	Yes	n/a	n/a

Note: (1) Data covers the Lafayette, LA Metropolitan Statistical Area; Data from exceptional events are included; (2) National Ambient Air Quality Standards; ppm = parts per million; ug/m^3 = micrograms per cubic meter; n/a not available.
Concentrations: Particulate Matter 10 (coarse particulate)—highest second maximum 24-hour concentration; Particulate Matter 2.5 Wtd AM (fine particulate)—highest weighted annual mean concentration; Particulate Matter 2.5 24-Hour (fine particulate)—highest 98th percentile 24-hour concentration; Ozone—highest fourth daily maximum 8-hour concentration; Carbon Monoxide—highest second maximum non-overlapping 8-hour concentration; Lead—maximum running 3-month average
Source: U.S. Environmental Protection Agency, Air Quality Monitoring Information, "Air Quality Statistics by City, 2021"

Maximum Air Pollutant Concentrations: Nitrogen Dioxide and Sulfur Dioxide

	Nitrogen Dioxide AM (ppb)	Nitrogen Dioxide 1-Hr (ppb)	Sulfur Dioxide AM (ppb)	Sulfur Dioxide 1-Hr (ppb)	Sulfur Dioxide 24-Hr (ppb)
MSA[1] Level	n/a	n/a	n/a	n/a	n/a
NAAQS[2]	53	100	30	75	140
Met NAAQS[2]	n/a	n/a	n/a	n/a	n/a

Note: (1) Data covers the Lafayette, LA Metropolitan Statistical Area; Data from exceptional events are included; (2) National Ambient Air Quality Standards; ppm = parts per million; ug/m^3 = micrograms per cubic meter; n/a not available.
Concentrations: Nitrogen Dioxide AM—highest arithmetic mean concentration; Nitrogen Dioxide 1-Hr—highest 98th percentile 1-hour daily maximum concentration; Sulfur Dioxide AM—highest annual mean concentration; Sulfur Dioxide 1-Hr—highest 99th percentile 1-hour daily maximum concentration; Sulfur Dioxide 24-Hr—highest second maximum 24-hour concentration
Source: U.S. Environmental Protection Agency, Air Quality Monitoring Information, "Air Quality Statistics by City, 2021"

Miami, Florida

Background

Miami is a growing city comprised mostly of Latinos. Its large numbers of Cubans, Puerto Ricans, and Haitians give the city a flavorful mix with a Latin American and Caribbean accent. The City of Miami has three official languages: English, Spanish, and Haitian Creole.

In 1896 railroad magnate Henry Flagler extended the East Coast Railroad to Miami and within 15 years the city became known as the "Gold Coast." The land boom of the 1920s brought wealthy socialites, as well as African Americans in search of work. Pink- and aquamarine-hued art deco hotels were squeezed onto a tiny tract of land called Miami Beach, and the population of the Miami metro area swelled.

Miami's tourist economy is one of the largest in the country. The city offers many leisurely activities, including swimming, scuba diving, golf, tennis, and boating. For those who enjoy professional sports, the city is host to the Miami Dolphins, football; Florida Marlins, baseball; Miami Heat, basketball; and Florida Panthers, hockey. Cultural activities range from the Miami City Ballet and the Coconut Grove Playhouse to numerous art galleries and museums, including the Bass Museum of Art. The Villa Vizcaya, a gorgeous palazzo built by industrialist James Deering in the Italian Renaissance style, and the Miami MetroZoo are popular destinations.

Miami's prime location on Biscayne Bay in the southeastern United States makes it a perfect nexus for travel and trade. The Port of Miami is a bustling center for many cruise and cargo ships. The Port is also a base for the National Oceanic and Atmospheric Administration. The Miami International Airport is a busy one with over 1,000 flights daily to 167 destinations. It is expected to process 77 million passengers and 4 million tons of freight annually by 2040, and a $5 billion improvement plan is in the works, with a completion date of 2035.

Miami is at the trading crossroads of the Western Hemisphere as the chief shipment point for exports and imports with Latin America and the Caribbean. One out of every three North American cruise passengers sails from Miami. It is also the major U.S. coastal city most affected by climate change. Sea level in Miami has risen one foot over the last century, with the rate of sea rise doubling over the last 30 years.

The sultry, subtropical climate against a backdrop of Spanish, art deco, and modern architecture makes Miami a uniquely cosmopolitan city. The Art Deco Historic District, known as South Beach and located on the tip of Miami Beach, has an international reputation in the fashion, film, and music industries. Greater Miami is a national center for film, television, and print production.

In recent years Miami has witnessed its largest real estate boom since the 1920s, especially in the city's midtown, north of downtown and south of the Design District. More than 25,000 residential units have been added to the downtown skyline since 2005.

Long, warm summers and mild, dry winters are typical. The marine influence is evidenced by the city's narrow temperature range and the rapid warming of cold air. During the summer months, rainfall occurs in early morning near the ocean and in early afternoon further inland. Hurricanes occasionally affect the Miami area, usually in September and October, while destructive tornadoes are quite rare. Funnel clouds are occasionally sighted and a few touch the ground briefly, but significant destruction is unusual. Waterspouts are visible from the beaches during the summer months but seldom cause any damage. During June, July, and August, there are numerous beautiful, but dangerous, lightning events.

Rankings

General Rankings

- The Miami metro area was identified as one of America's fastest-growing areas in terms of population and business growth by *MagnifyMoney*. The area ranked #29 out of 35. The 100 most populous metro areas in the U.S. were evaluated on their change from 2011 to 2016 in the following categories: people and housing; workforce and employment opportunities; growing industry. *www.businessinsider.com, "The 35 Cities in the US with the Biggest Influx of People, the Most Work Opportunities, and the Hottest Business Growth," August 12, 2018*

- The human resources consulting firm Mercer ranked 231 major cities worldwide in terms of overall quality of life. Miami ranked #66. Criteria: political, social, economic, and socio-cultural factors; medical and health considerations; schools and education; public services and transportation; recreation; consumer goods; housing; and natural environment. *Mercer, "Mercer 2019 Quality of Living Survey," March 13, 2019*

Business/Finance Rankings

- The Brookings Institution ranked the nation's largest cities based on income inequality. Miami was ranked #5 (#1 = greatest inequality). Criteria: the "95/20 ratio," a figure representing the income at which a household earns more than 95 percent of all other households, divided by the income at which a household earns more than only 20 percent of all other households. *Brookings Institution, "Household Income Inequality, Largest Cities of 97 Large U.S. Metro Areas, 2014-2016," February 5, 2018*

- The Brookings Institution ranked the 100 largest metro areas in the U.S. based on income inequality. Miami was ranked #7 (#1 = greatest inequality). Criteria: the "95/20 ratio," a figure representing the income at which a household earns more than 95 percent of all other households, divided by the income at which a household earns more than only 20 percent of all other households. *Brookings Institution, "Household Income Inequality, 100 Largest U.S. Metro Areas, 2014-2016," February 5, 2018*

- The Miami metro area was identified as one of the most debt-ridden places in America by the finance site Credit.com. The metro area was ranked #14. Criteria: residents' average credit card debt as well as median income. *Credit.com, "25 Cities With the Most Credit Card Debt," February 28, 2018*

- Miami was identified as one of America's most frugal metro areas by *Coupons.com*. The city ranked #12 out of 25. Criteria: digital coupon usage. *Coupons.com, "America's Most Frugal Cities of 2017," March 22, 2018*

- *Forbes* ranked the 200 most populous metro areas to determine the nation's "Best Places for Business and Careers." The Miami metro area was ranked #85. Criteria: costs (business and living); job growth (past and projected); income growth; quality of life; educational attainment (college and high school); projected economic growth; cultural and leisure opportunities; workplace tolerance laws; net migration patterns. *Forbes, "The Best Places for Business and Careers 2019: Seattle Still On Top," October 30, 2019*

- Mercer Human Resources Consulting ranked 227 cities worldwide in terms of cost-of-living. Miami ranked #32 (the lower the ranking, the higher the cost-of-living). The survey measured the comparative cost of over 200 items (such as housing, food, clothing, domestic supplies, transportation, and recreation/entertainment) in each location. *Mercer, "2022 Cost of Living City Ranking," June 29, 2022*

Children/Family Rankings

- Miami was selected as one of the most playful cities in the U.S. by KaBOOM! The organization's Playful City USA initiative honors cities and towns across the nation that have made their communities more playable. Criteria: pledging to integrate play as a solution to challenges in their communities; making it easy for children to get active and balanced play; creating more family-friendly and innovative communities as a result. *KaBOOM! National Campaign for Play, "2017 Playful City USA Communities"*

Dating/Romance Rankings

- *Apartment List* conducted its Annual Renter Satisfaction Survey and asked renters "how satisfied are you with opportunities for dating in your current city." The cities were ranked from highest to lowest based on their satisfaction scores. Miami ranked #9 out of 85 cities. *Apartment List, "Best Cities for Dating 2022 with Local Dating Insights from Bumble," February 7, 2022*

- Miami was selected as one of the nation's most romantic cities with 100,000 or more residents by Amazon.com. The city ranked #2 of 20. Criteria: per capita sales of romance novels, relationship books, romantic comedy movies, romantic music, and sexual wellness products. *Amazon.com, "Top 20 Most Romantic Cities in the U.S.," February 1, 2017*

Education Rankings

- Miami was selected as one of America's most literate cities. The city ranked #47 out of the 84 largest U.S. cities. Criteria: number of booksellers; library resources; Internet resources; educational attainment; periodical publishing resources; newspaper circulation. *Central Connecticut State University, "America's Most Literate Cities, 2018," February 2019*

Environmental Rankings

- Sperling's BestPlaces assessed the 50 largest metropolitan areas of the United States for the likelihood of dangerously extreme weather events or earthquakes. In general the Southeast and South-Central regions have the highest risk of weather extremes and earthquakes, while the Pacific Northwest enjoys the lowest risk. Of the most risky metropolitan areas, the Miami metro area was ranked #1. *www.bestplaces.net, "Avoid Natural Disasters: BestPlaces Reveals The Top 10 Safest Places to Live," October 25, 2017*

- The U.S. Environmental Protection Agency (EPA) released its list of U.S. metropolitan areas with the most ENERGY STAR certified buildings in 2022. The Miami metro area was ranked #20 out of 25. *U.S. Environmental Protection Agency, "2023 Energy Star Top Cities," April 26, 2023*

Food/Drink Rankings

- Miami was identified as one of the cities in America ordering the most vegan food options by GrubHub.com. The city ranked #4 out of 5. Criteria: percentage of vegan, vegetarian and plant-based food orders compared to the overall number of orders. *GrubHub.com, "State of the Plate Report 2021: Top Cities for Vegans," June 20, 2021*

Health/Fitness Rankings

- For each of the 100 largest cities in the United States, the American Fitness Index®, compiled in partnership between the American College of Sports Medicine and the Elevance Health Foundation, evaluated community infrastructure and 34 health behaviors including preventive health, levels of chronic disease conditions, food insecurity, sleep quality, pedestrian safety, air quality, and community/environment resources that support physical activity. Miami ranked #40 for "community fitness." *americanfitnessindex.org, "2022 ACSM American Fitness Index Summary Report," July 12, 2022*

- Miami was identified as one of the 10 most walkable cities in the U.S. by Walk Score. The city ranked #5. Walk Score measures walkability by analyzing hundreds of walking routes to nearby amenities, and also measures pedestrian friendliness by analyzing population density and road metrics such as block length and intersection density. *WalkScore.com, April 13, 2021*

- Miami was identified as a "2022 Spring Allergy Capital." The area ranked #19 out of 100. Three groups of factors were used to identify the most challenging cities for people with allergies during the spring season: annual spring pollen scores; over the counter allergy medicine use; number of board-certified allergy specialists. *Asthma and Allergy Foundation of America, "Spring Allergy Capitals 2022," March 2, 2022*

- Miami was identified as a "2022 Fall Allergy Capital." The area ranked #18 out of 100. Three groups of factors were used to identify the most challenging cities for people with allergies during the fall season: annual fall pollen scores; over the counter allergy medicine use; number of board-certified allergy specialists. *Asthma and Allergy Foundation of America, "Fall Allergy Capitals 2022," March 2, 2022*

- Miami was identified as a "2022 Asthma Capital." The area ranked #22 out of the nation's 100 largest metropolitan areas. Criteria: estimated asthma prevalence; asthma-related mortality; and ER visits due to asthma. Risk factors analyzed but not factored in the rankings: annual pollen score; annual air quality; public smoking laws; access to board-certified asthma specialists; rescue and controller medication use; uninsured rate; poverty rate. *Asthma and Allergy Foundation of America, "Asthma Capitals 2022: The Most Challenging Places to Live With Asthma," September 14, 2022*

Pet Rankings

- Miami appeared on *The Dogington Post* site as one of the top cities for dog lovers, ranking #13 out of 15. The real estate marketplace, Zillow®, and Rover, the largest pet sitter and dog walker network, introduced a new list of "Top Emerging Dog-Friendly Cities" for 2021. Criteria: number of new dog accounts on the Rover platform; and rentals and listings that mention features that attract dog owners (fenced-in yards, dog houses, dog door or proximity to a dog park). *www.dogingtonpost.com, "15 Cities Emerging as Dog-Friendliest in 2021," May 11, 2021*

Real Estate Rankings

- *WalletHub* compared the most populated U.S. cities to determine which had the best markets for real estate agents. Miami ranked #155 where demand was high and pay was the best. Criteria: sales per agent; annual median wage for real-estate agents; monthly average starting salary for real estate agents; real estate job density and competition; unemployment rate; home turnover rate; housing-market health index; and other relevant metrics. *www.WalletHub.com, "2021 Best Places to Be a Real Estate Agent," May 12, 2021*

- Miami was ranked #14 in the top 20 out of the 100 largest metro areas in terms of house price appreciation in 2022 (#1 = highest rate). *Federal Housing Finance Agency, House Price Index, 4th Quarter 2022*

Safety Rankings

- Allstate ranked the 200 largest cities in America in terms of driver safety. Miami ranked #57. Criteria: internal property damage claims over a two-year period from January 2016 to December 2017. The report helps increase the importance of safety and awareness behind the wheel. *Allstate, "Allstate America's Best Drivers Report, 2019" June 24, 2019*

Sports/Recreation Rankings

- Miami was chosen as one of America's best cities for bicycling. The city ranked #50 out of 50. Criteria: cycling infrastructure that is safe and friendly for all ages; energy and bike culture. The editors evaluated cities with populations of 100,000 or more. *Bicycling, "The 50 Best Bike Cities in America," October 10, 2018*

Transportation Rankings

- Business Insider presented an AllTransit Performance Score ranking of public transportation in major U.S. cities and towns, with populations over 250,000, in which Miami earned the #11-ranked "Transit Score," awarded for frequency of service, access to jobs, quality and number of stops, and affordability. *www.businessinsider.com, "The 17 Major U.S. Cities with the Best Public Transportation," April 17, 2018*

- According to the INRIX "2022 Global Traffic Scorecard," Miami was identified as one of the most congested metro areas in the U.S. The area ranked #5 out of 25. Criteria: average annual time spent in traffic and average cost of congestion per motorist. *Inrix.com, "Return to Work, Higher Gas Prices & Inflation Drove Americans to Spend Hundreds More in Time and Money Commuting," January 10, 2023*

Women/Minorities Rankings

- Miami was selected as one of the queerest cities in America by *The Advocate*. The city ranked #16 out of 25. Criteria, among many: Trans Pride parades/festivals; gay rugby teams; lesbian bars; LGBTQ centers; theater screenings of "Moonlight"; LGBTQ-inclusive nondiscrimination ordinances; and gay bowling teams. *The Advocate, "Queerest Cities in America 2017" January 12, 2017*

- Personal finance website *WalletHub* compared more than 180 U.S. cities across two key dimensions, "Hispanic Business-Friendliness" and "Hispanic Purchasing Power," to arrive at the most favorable conditions for Hispanic entrepreneurs. Miami was ranked #4 out of 182. Criteria includes: share of Hispanic-Owned Businesses; Hispanic entrepreneurship rate to median annual income of Hispanics; Small Business-Friendliness score; cost of living; and number of Hispanics with at least a bachelor's degree. *WalletHub.com, "2019's Best Cities for Hispanic Entrepreneurs," May 1, 2019*

Miscellaneous Rankings

- *MoveHub* ranked 446 hipster cities across 20 countries, using its new and improved *alternative* Hipster Index and Miami came out as #7 among the top 50. Criteria: population over 150,000; number of vintage boutiques; density of tattoo parlors; vegan places to eat; coffee shops; and density of vinyl record stores. *www.movehub.com, "The Hipster Index: Brighton Pips Portland to Global Top Spot," July 28, 2021*

- The watchdog site, Charity Navigator, conducted a study of charities in major markets both to analyze statistical differences in their financial, accountability, and transparency practices and to track year-to-year variations in individual philanthropic communities. The Miami metro area was ranked #7 among the 30 metro markets in the rating category of Overall Score. *www.charitynavigator.org, "2017 Metro Market Study," May 1, 2017*

- *WalletHub* compared the 150 most populated U.S. cities to determine their operating efficiency. A "Quality of Services" score was constructed for each city and then divided by the total budget per capita to reveal which were managed the best. Miami ranked #75. Criteria: financial stability; economy; education; safety; health; infrastructure and pollution. *www.WalletHub.com, "2022's Best- & Worst-Run Cities in America," June 21, 2022*

Business Environment

DEMOGRAPHICS

Population Growth

Area	1990 Census	2000 Census	2010 Census	2020 Census	Population Growth (%) 1990-2020	Population Growth (%) 2010-2020
City	358,843	362,470	399,457	442,241	23.2	10.7
MSA[1]	4,056,100	5,007,564	5,564,635	6,138,333	51.3	10.3
U.S.	248,709,873	281,421,906	308,745,538	331,449,281	33.3	7.4

Note: (1) Figures cover the Miami-Fort Lauderdale-Pompano Beach, FL Metropolitan Statistical Area
Source: U.S. Census Bureau, 1990 Census, 2000 Census, 2010 Census, 2020 Census

Race

Area	White Alone[2] (%)	Black Alone[2] (%)	Asian Alone[2] (%)	AIAN[3] Alone[2] (%)	NHOPI[4] Alone[2] (%)	Other Race Alone[2] (%)	Two or More Races (%)
City	30.2	12.9	1.4	0.4	0.0	14.3	40.7
MSA[1]	39.6	19.5	2.7	0.4	0.0	9.7	28.1
U.S.	61.6	12.4	6.0	1.1	0.2	8.4	10.2

Note: (1) Figures cover the Miami-Fort Lauderdale-Pompano Beach, FL Metropolitan Statistical Area;
(2) Alone is defined as not being in combination with one or more other races; (3) American Indian and Alaska Native; (4) Native Hawaiian and Other Pacific Islander
Source: U.S. Census Bureau, 2020 Census

Hispanic or Latino Origin

Area	Total (%)	Mexican (%)	Puerto Rican (%)	Cuban (%)	Other (%)
City	72.3	1.9	3.5	33.4	33.5
MSA[1]	45.6	2.5	3.8	18.6	20.6
U.S.	18.4	11.2	1.8	0.7	4.7

Note: Persons of Hispanic or Latino origin can be of any race; (1) Figures cover the Miami-Fort Lauderdale-Pompano Beach, FL Metropolitan Statistical Area
Source: U.S. Census Bureau, 2017-2021 American Community Survey 5-Year Estimates

Age

Area	Under Age 5	Age 5–19	Age 20–34	Age 35–44	Age 45–54	Age 55–64	Age 65–74	Age 75–84	Age 85+	Median Age
City	4.8	13.6	24.0	15.0	13.5	12.4	8.8	5.5	2.5	39.7
MSA[1]	4.8	17.1	18.7	13.0	13.8	13.7	10.2	6.0	2.6	42.1
U.S.	5.6	19.2	20.2	12.7	12.4	13.1	10.0	4.9	1.9	38.8

Note: (1) Figures cover the Miami-Fort Lauderdale-Pompano Beach, FL Metropolitan Statistical Area
Source: U.S. Census Bureau, 2020 Census

Disability by Age

Area	All Ages	Under 18 Years Old	18 to 64 Years Old	65 Years and Over
City	11.9	4.5	7.6	37.2
MSA[1]	10.8	3.7	7.2	31.1
U.S.	12.6	4.4	10.3	33.4

Note: Figures show percent of the civilian noninstitutionalized population that reported having a disability. Disability status is determined from six types of difficulty: vision, hearing, cognitive, ambulatory, self-care, and independent living. For children under 5 years old, hearing and vision difficulty are used to determine disability status. For children between the ages of 5 and 14, disability status is determined from hearing, vision, cognitive, ambulatory, and self-care difficulties. For people aged 15 years and older, they are considered to have a disability if they have difficulty with any one of the six difficulty types; Note: (1) Figures cover the Miami-Fort Lauderdale-Pompano Beach, FL Metropolitan Statistical Area
Source: U.S. Census Bureau, 2017-2021 American Community Survey 5-Year Estimates

Ancestry

Area	German	Irish	English	American	Italian	Polish	French[2]	Scottish	Dutch
City	1.8	1.3	1.0	2.7	2.5	0.7	0.9	0.2	0.2
MSA[1]	4.3	4.2	2.9	5.9	4.9	1.8	1.2	0.6	0.4
U.S.	12.8	9.6	8.1	5.7	5.0	2.7	2.2	1.6	1.1

Note: Figures are the percentage of the total population reporting a particular ancestry. The nine most commonly reported ancestries in the U.S. are shown. Figures include multiple ancestries (e.g. if a person reported being Irish and Italian, they were included in both columns); (1) Figures cover the Miami-Fort Lauderdale-Pompano Beach, FL Metropolitan Statistical Area; (2) Excludes Basque
Source: U.S. Census Bureau, 2017-2021 American Community Survey 5-Year Estimates

Miami, Florida

Foreign-born Population

Area	Any Foreign Country	Asia	Mexico	Europe	Caribbean	Central America[2]	South America	Africa	Canada
City	58.1	1.4	1.1	1.9	31.0	11.9	10.3	0.3	0.2
MSA[1]	41.2	2.2	1.2	2.3	20.9	4.2	9.5	0.4	0.6
U.S.	13.6	4.2	3.3	1.5	1.4	1.1	1.1	0.8	0.2

Note: (1) Figures cover the Miami-Fort Lauderdale-Pompano Beach, FL Metropolitan Statistical Area; (2) Excludes Mexico.
Source: U.S. Census Bureau, 2017-2021 American Community Survey 5-Year Estimates

Household Size

Area	One	Two	Three	Four	Five	Six	Seven or More	Average Household Size
City	36.0	32.2	16.2	9.3	3.8	1.4	1.1	2.40
MSA[1]	28.0	32.4	17.0	13.3	6.0	2.1	1.2	2.70
U.S.	28.1	33.8	15.5	12.9	6.0	2.3	1.4	2.60

Note: (1) Figures cover the Miami-Fort Lauderdale-Pompano Beach, FL Metropolitan Statistical Area
Source: U.S. Census Bureau, 2017-2021 American Community Survey 5-Year Estimates

Household Relationships

Area	Householder	Opposite-sex Spouse	Same-sex Spouse	Opposite-sex Unmarried Partner	Same-sex Unmarried Partner	Child[2]	Grandchild	Other Relatives	Non-relatives
City	42.4	12.6	0.5	3.3	0.3	22.5	2.4	8.7	5.8
MSA[1]	38.0	16.0	0.3	2.6	0.2	27.6	2.5	7.8	3.7
U.S.	38.3	17.5	0.2	2.5	0.2	28.3	2.4	4.8	3.4

Note: Figures are percent of the total population; (1) Figures cover the Miami-Fort Lauderdale-Pompano Beach, FL Metropolitan Statistical Area; (2) Includes biological, adopted, and stepchildren of the householder
Source: U.S. Census Bureau, 2020 Census

Gender

Area	Males	Females	Males per 100 Females
City	218,706	223,535	97.8
MSA[1]	2,954,448	3,183,885	92.8
U.S.	162,685,811	168,763,470	96.4

Note: (1) Figures cover the Miami-Fort Lauderdale-Pompano Beach, FL Metropolitan Statistical Area
Source: U.S. Census Bureau, 2020 Census

Marital Status

Area	Never Married	Now Married[2]	Separated	Widowed	Divorced
City	39.7	37.3	3.5	6.0	13.6
MSA[1]	34.1	44.4	2.5	6.2	12.9
U.S.	33.8	48.0	1.8	5.6	10.8

Note: Figures are percentages and cover the population 15 years of age and older; (1) Figures cover the Miami-Fort Lauderdale-Pompano Beach, FL Metropolitan Statistical Area; (2) Excludes separated
Source: U.S. Census Bureau, 2017-2021 American Community Survey 5-Year Estimates

Religious Groups by Family

Area	Catholic	Baptist	Methodist	LDS[2]	Pentecostal	Lutheran	Islam	Adventist	Other
MSA[1]	23.8	5.1	0.9	0.5	1.3	0.3	0.8	2.4	11.1
U.S.	18.7	7.3	3.0	2.0	1.8	1.7	1.3	1.3	11.6

Note: Figures are the number of adherents as a percentage of the total population and cover the eight largest religious groups in the U.S; (1) Figures cover the Miami-Fort Lauderdale-Pompano Beach, FL Metropolitan Statistical Area; (2) Church of Jesus Christ of Latter-day Saints
Sources: 2020 U.S. Religion Census, Association of Statisticians of American Religious Bodies; The Association of Religion Data Archives (ARDA)

Religious Groups by Tradition

Area	Catholic	Evangelical Protestant	Mainline Protestant	Black Protestant	Islam	Judaism	Hinduism	Orthodox	Buddhism
MSA[1]	23.8	13.7	1.6	2.2	0.8	1.2	0.3	0.2	0.3
U.S.	18.7	16.5	5.2	2.3	1.3	0.6	0.4	0.4	0.3

Note: Figures are the number of adherents as a percentage of the total population; (1) Figures cover the Miami-Fort Lauderdale-Pompano Beach, FL Metropolitan Statistical Area
Sources: 2020 U.S. Religion Census, Association of Statisticians of American Religious Bodies; The Association of Religion Data Archives (ARDA)

ECONOMY

Gross Metropolitan Product

Area	2020	2021	2022	2023	Rank[2]
MSA[1]	365.0	402.9	442.8	471.0	12

Note: Figures are in billions of dollars; (1) Figures cover the Miami-Fort Lauderdale-Pompano Beach, FL Metropolitan Statistical Area; (2) Rank is based on 2021 data and ranges from 1 to 381
Source: U.S. Conference of Mayors, U.S. Metro Economies: U.S. Metros Compared to Global and State Economies, June 2022

Economic Growth

Area	2018-20 (%)	2021 (%)	2022 (%)	2023 (%)	Rank[2]
MSA[1]	-1.4	6.4	4.2	3.1	245
U.S.	-0.6	5.7	3.1	2.9	—

Note: Figures are real gross metropolitan product (GMP) growth rates and represent average annual percent change; (1) Figures cover the Miami-Fort Lauderdale-Pompano Beach, FL Metropolitan Statistical Area; (2) Rank is based on 2020 2-year average annual percent change and ranges from 1 to 381
Source: U.S. Conference of Mayors, U.S. Metro Economies: U.S. Metros Compared to Global and State Economies, June 2022

Metropolitan Area Exports

Area	2016	2017	2018	2019	2020	2021	Rank[2]
MSA[1]	32,734.5	34,780.5	35,650.2	35,498.9	29,112.1	36,011.3	7

Note: Figures are in millions of dollars; (1) Figures cover the Miami-Fort Lauderdale-Pompano Beach, FL Metropolitan Statistical Area; (2) Rank is based on 2021 data and ranges from 1 to 388
Source: U.S. Department of Commerce, International Trade Administration, Office of Trade and Economic Analysis, Industry and Analysis, Exports by Metropolitan Area, data extracted March 16, 2023

Building Permits

Area	Single-Family 2021	Single-Family 2022	Pct. Chg.	Multi-Family 2021	Multi-Family 2022	Pct. Chg.	Total 2021	Total 2022	Pct. Chg.
City	102	127	24.5	6,153	4,231	-31.2	6,255	4,358	-30.3
MSA[1]	8,316	6,970	-16.2	16,997	13,051	-23.2	25,313	20,021	-20.9
U.S.	1,115,400	975,600	-12.5	621,600	689,500	10.9	1,737,000	1,665,100	-4.1

Note: (1) Figures cover the Miami-Fort Lauderdale-Pompano Beach, FL Metropolitan Statistical Area; Figures represent new, privately-owned housing units authorized (unadjusted data); All permit data are based on estimates with imputation
Source: U.S. Census Bureau, Manufacturing, Mining, and Construction Statistics, Building Permits, 2021, 2022

Bankruptcy Filings

Area	Business Filings 2021	Business Filings 2022	% Chg.	Nonbusiness Filings 2021	Nonbusiness Filings 2022	% Chg.
Miami-Dade County	201	224	11.4	6,432	5,081	-21.0
U.S.	14,347	13,481	-6.0	399,269	374,240	-6.3

Note: Business filings include Chapter 7, Chapter 9, Chapter 11, Chapter 12, Chapter 13, Chapter 15, and Section 304; Nonbusiness filings include Chapter 7, Chapter 11, and Chapter 13
Source: Administrative Office of the U.S. Courts, Business and Nonbusiness Bankruptcy, County Cases Commenced by Chapter of the Bankruptcy Code, During the 12-Month Period Ending December 31, 2021 and Business and Nonbusiness Bankruptcy, County Cases Commenced by Chapter of the Bankruptcy Code, During the 12-Month Period Ending December 31, 2022

Housing Vacancy Rates

Area	Gross Vacancy Rate[2] (%) 2020	2021	2022	Year-Round Vacancy Rate[3] (%) 2020	2021	2022	Rental Vacancy Rate[4] (%) 2020	2021	2022	Homeowner Vacancy Rate[5] (%) 2020	2021	2022
MSA[1]	12.6	12.2	12.6	6.8	6.8	7.5	5.4	5.5	6.3	1.4	1.0	1.1
U.S.	10.6	10.8	10.5	8.2	8.4	8.2	6.3	6.1	5.8	1.0	0.9	0.8

Note: (1) Figures cover the Miami-Fort Lauderdale-Pompano Beach, FL Metropolitan Statistical Area; (2) The percentage of the total housing inventory that is vacant; (3) The percentage of the housing inventory (excluding seasonal units) that is year-round vacant; (4) The percentage of rental inventory that is vacant for rent; (5) The percentage of homeowner inventory that is vacant for sale
Source: U.S. Census Bureau, Housing Vacancies and Homeownership Annual Statistics: 2020, 2021, 2022

INCOME

Income

Area	Per Capita ($)	Median Household ($)	Average Household ($)
City	34,295	47,860	79,886
MSA[1]	36,174	62,870	94,059
U.S.	37,638	69,021	97,196

Note: (1) Figures cover the Miami-Fort Lauderdale-Pompano Beach, FL Metropolitan Statistical Area
Source: U.S. Census Bureau, 2017-2021 American Community Survey 5-Year Estimates

Miami, Florida

Household Income Distribution

Area	Under $15,000	$15,000 -$24,999	$25,000 -$34,999	$35,000 -$49,999	$50,000 -$74,999	$75,000 -$99,999	$100,000 -$149,999	$150,000 and up
				Percent of Households Earning				
City	17.7	11.8	10.1	11.8	16.1	9.4	11.1	12.0
MSA[1]	10.8	8.5	9.0	12.2	17.2	12.2	14.6	15.5
U.S.	9.4	7.8	8.2	11.4	16.8	12.8	16.3	17.3

Note: (1) Figures cover the Miami-Fort Lauderdale-Pompano Beach, FL Metropolitan Statistical Area
Source: U.S. Census Bureau, 2017-2021 American Community Survey 5-Year Estimates

Poverty Rate

Area	All Ages	Under 18 Years Old	18 to 64 Years Old	65 Years and Over
City	20.9	27.8	16.6	30.9
MSA[1]	13.6	18.0	11.6	15.6
U.S.	12.6	17.0	11.8	9.6

Note: Figures are percentage of people whose income during the past 12 months was below the poverty level;
(1) Figures cover the Miami-Fort Lauderdale-Pompano Beach, FL Metropolitan Statistical Area
Source: U.S. Census Bureau, 2017-2021 American Community Survey 5-Year Estimates

EMPLOYMENT

Labor Force and Employment

Area	Civilian Labor Force Dec. 2021	Civilian Labor Force Dec. 2022	% Chg.	Workers Employed Dec. 2021	Workers Employed Dec. 2022	% Chg.
City	227,422	231,754	1.9	220,939	228,420	3.4
MD[1]	1,345,385	1,397,307	3.9	1,304,718	1,369,536	5.0
U.S.	161,696,000	164,224,000	1.6	155,732,000	158,872,000	2.0

Note: Data is not seasonally adjusted and covers workers 16 years of age and older; (1) Figures cover the Miami-Miami Beach-Kendall, FL Metropolitan Division
Source: Bureau of Labor Statistics, Local Area Unemployment Statistics

Unemployment Rate

Area	Jan.	Feb.	Mar.	Apr.	May	Jun.	Jul.	Aug.	Sep.	Oct.	Nov.	Dec.
City	3.0	2.6	2.8	2.4	2.2	2.0	2.2	2.2	1.9	1.7	1.5	1.4
MD[1]	3.2	2.9	3.0	2.6	2.5	2.6	2.8	2.9	2.6	2.4	2.1	2.0
U.S.	4.4	4.1	3.8	3.3	3.4	3.8	3.8	3.8	3.3	3.4	3.4	3.3

Note: Data is not seasonally adjusted and covers workers 16 years of age and older; (1) Figures cover the Miami-Miami Beach-Kendall, FL Metropolitan Division
Source: Bureau of Labor Statistics, Local Area Unemployment Statistics

Average Wages

Occupation	$/Hr.	Occupation	$/Hr.
Accountants and Auditors	40.21	Maintenance and Repair Workers	20.30
Automotive Mechanics	23.98	Marketing Managers	73.31
Bookkeepers	22.09	Network and Computer Systems Admin.	45.42
Carpenters	23.23	Nurses, Licensed Practical	26.47
Cashiers	13.04	Nurses, Registered	39.33
Computer Programmers	57.52	Nursing Assistants	16.17
Computer Systems Analysts	49.49	Office Clerks, General	19.87
Computer User Support Specialists	27.62	Physical Therapists	42.11
Construction Laborers	18.58	Physicians	102.65
Cooks, Restaurant	16.91	Plumbers, Pipefitters and Steamfitters	24.64
Customer Service Representatives	19.16	Police and Sheriff's Patrol Officers	43.87
Dentists	80.27	Postal Service Mail Carriers	27.09
Electricians	25.35	Real Estate Sales Agents	26.19
Engineers, Electrical	47.59	Retail Salespersons	16.30
Fast Food and Counter Workers	12.93	Sales Representatives, Technical/Scientific	50.86
Financial Managers	81.34	Secretaries, Exc. Legal/Medical/Executive	20.66
First-Line Supervisors of Office Workers	31.90	Security Guards	16.16
General and Operations Managers	56.01	Surgeons	92.08
Hairdressers/Cosmetologists	15.37	Teacher Assistants, Exc. Postsecondary*	14.59
Home Health and Personal Care Aides	13.24	Teachers, Secondary School, Exc. Sp. Ed.*	31.87
Janitors and Cleaners	14.03	Telemarketers	16.79
Landscaping/Groundskeeping Workers	16.61	Truck Drivers, Heavy/Tractor-Trailer	24.62
Lawyers	69.69	Truck Drivers, Light/Delivery Services	21.37
Maids and Housekeeping Cleaners	14.17	Waiters and Waitresses	16.13

Note: Wage data covers the Miami-Fort Lauderdale-Pompano Beach, FL Metropolitan Statistical Area;
(*) Hourly wages were calculated from annual wage data based on a 40 hour work week; n/a not available.
Source: Bureau of Labor Statistics, Metro Area Occupational Employment & Wage Estimates, May 2022

Employment by Industry

Sector	MD[1] Number of Employees	MD[1] Percent of Total	U.S. Percent of Total
Construction	51,500	4.0	5.0
Private Education and Health Services	211,200	16.4	16.1
Financial Activities	91,300	7.1	5.9
Government	140,400	10.9	14.5
Information	24,200	1.9	2.0
Leisure and Hospitality	143,400	11.1	10.3
Manufacturing	44,200	3.4	8.4
Mining and Logging	500	<0.1	0.4
Other Services	48,200	3.7	3.7
Professional and Business Services	212,400	16.4	14.7
Retail Trade	149,800	11.6	10.2
Transportation, Warehousing, and Utilities	96,500	7.5	4.9
Wholesale Trade	77,900	6.0	3.9

Note: Figures are non-farm employment as of December 2022. Figures are not seasonally adjusted and include workers 16 years of age and older; (1) Figures cover the Miami-Miami Beach-Kendall, FL Metropolitan Division
Source: Bureau of Labor Statistics, Current Employment Statistics, Employment, Hours, and Earnings

Employment by Occupation

Occupation Classification	City (%)	MSA[1] (%)	U.S. (%)
Management, Business, Science, and Arts	34.5	37.0	40.3
Natural Resources, Construction, and Maintenance	11.4	9.2	8.7
Production, Transportation, and Material Moving	10.0	10.4	13.1
Sales and Office	21.7	23.7	20.9
Service	22.3	19.7	17.0

Note: Figures cover employed civilians 16 years of age and older; (1) Figures cover the Miami-Fort Lauderdale-Pompano Beach, FL Metropolitan Statistical Area
Source: U.S. Census Bureau, 2017-2021 American Community Survey 5-Year Estimates

Occupations with Greatest Projected Employment Growth: 2022 – 2024

Occupation[1]	2022 Employment	2024 Projected Employment	Numeric Employment Change	Percent Employment Change
General and Operations Managers	196,430	209,480	13,050	6.6
Cooks, Restaurant	117,090	129,670	12,580	10.7
Registered Nurses	208,620	221,040	12,420	6.0
Waiters and Waitresses	194,570	206,380	11,810	6.1
Retail Salespersons	327,010	338,390	11,380	3.5
Stockers and Order Fillers	192,890	203,920	11,030	5.7
Customer Service Representatives	283,220	293,670	10,450	3.7
Fast Food and Counter Workers	203,420	212,470	9,050	4.4
Laborers and Freight, Stock, and Material Movers, Hand	138,200	146,930	8,730	6.3
Maids and Housekeeping Cleaners	77,330	85,600	8,270	10.7

Note: Projections cover Florida; (1) Sorted by numeric employment change
Source: www.projectionscentral.com, State Occupational Projections, 2022–2024 Short-Term Projections

Fastest-Growing Occupations: 2022 – 2024

Occupation[1]	2022 Employment	2024 Projected Employment	Numeric Employment Change	Percent Employment Change
Hotel, Motel, and Resort Desk Clerks	23,000	26,650	3,650	15.9
First-Line Supervisors of Gambling Services Workers	990	1,140	150	15.2
Baggage Porters and Bellhops	3,310	3,810	500	15.1
Solar Photovoltaic Installers	860	990	130	15.1
Nurse Practitioners	17,490	20,080	2,590	14.8
Motion Picture Projectionists	490	560	70	14.3
Lodging Managers	5,160	5,870	710	13.8
Transportation Workers, All Other	980	1,110	130	13.3
Information Security Analysts (SOC 2018)	11,910	13,480	1,570	13.2
Statisticians	1,370	1,550	180	13.1

Note: Projections cover Florida; (1) Sorted by percent employment change and excludes occupations with numeric employment change less than 50
Source: www.projectionscentral.com, State Occupational Projections, 2022–2024 Short-Term Projections

Miami, Florida

CITY FINANCES

City Government Finances

Component	2020 ($000)	2020 ($ per capita)
Total Revenues	1,087,983	2,325
Total Expenditures	973,570	2,080
Debt Outstanding	601,914	1,286
Cash and Securities[1]	710,497	1,518

Note: (1) Cash and security holdings of a government at the close of its fiscal year, including those of its dependent agencies, utilities, and liquor stores.
Source: U.S. Census Bureau, State & Local Government Finances 2020

City Government Revenue by Source

Source	2020 ($000)	2020 ($ per capita)	2020 (%)
General Revenue			
From Federal Government	66,662	142	6.1
From State Government	68,893	147	6.3
From Local Governments	52,003	111	4.8
Taxes			
Property	444,756	950	40.9
Sales and Gross Receipts	113,630	243	10.4
Personal Income	0	0	0.0
Corporate Income	0	0	0.0
Motor Vehicle License	0	0	0.0
Other Taxes	114,674	245	10.5
Current Charges	141,025	301	13.0
Liquor Store	0	0	0.0
Utility	10	0	0.0

Source: U.S. Census Bureau, State & Local Government Finances 2020

City Government Expenditures by Function

Function	2020 ($000)	2020 ($ per capita)	2020 (%)
General Direct Expenditures			
Air Transportation	0	0	0.0
Corrections	0	0	0.0
Education	0	0	0.0
Employment Security Administration	0	0	0.0
Financial Administration	71,476	152	7.3
Fire Protection	169,397	362	17.4
General Public Buildings	0	0	0.0
Governmental Administration, Other	62,586	133	6.4
Health	0	0	0.0
Highways	23,794	50	2.4
Hospitals	0	0	0.0
Housing and Community Development	32,425	69	3.3
Interest on General Debt	24,567	52	2.5
Judicial and Legal	9,157	19	0.9
Libraries	0	0	0.0
Parking	40,581	86	4.2
Parks and Recreation	97,551	208	10.0
Police Protection	261,725	559	26.9
Public Welfare	7,146	15	0.7
Sewerage	0	0	0.0
Solid Waste Management	40,526	86	4.2
Veterans' Services	0	0	0.0
Liquor Store	0	0	0.0
Utility	0	0	0.0

Source: U.S. Census Bureau, State & Local Government Finances 2020

TAXES

State Corporate Income Tax Rates

State	Tax Rate (%)	Income Brackets ($)	Num. of Brackets	Financial Institution Tax Rate (%)[a]	Federal Income Tax Ded.
Florida	5.5	Flat rate	1	5.5	No

Note: Tax rates as of January 1, 2023; (a) Rates listed are the corporate income tax rate applied to financial institutions or excise taxes based on income. Some states have other taxes based upon the value of deposits or shares.
Source: Federation of Tax Administrators, State Corporate Income Tax Rates, January 1, 2023

State Individual Income Tax Rates

State	Tax Rate (%)	Income Brackets ($)	Personal Exemptions ($) Single	Married	Depend.	Standard Ded. ($) Single	Married
Florida			– No state income tax –				

Note: Tax rates as of January 1, 2023; Local- and county-level taxes are not included
Source: Federation of Tax Administrators, State Individual Income Tax Rates, January 1, 2023

Various State Sales and Excise Tax Rates

State	State Sales Tax (%)	Gasoline[1] ($/gal.)	Cigarette[2] ($/pack)	Spirits[3] ($/gal.)	Wine[4] ($/gal.)	Beer[5] ($/gal.)	Recreational Marijuana (%)
Florida	6	0.4123	1.339	6.50	2.25	0.48	Not legal

Note: All tax rates as of January 1, 2023; (1) The American Petroleum Institute has developed a methodology for determining the average tax rate on a gallon of fuel. Rates may include any of the following: excise taxes, environmental fees, storage tank fees, other fees or taxes, general sales tax, and local taxes; (2) The federal excise tax of $1.0066 per pack and local taxes are not included; (3) Rates are those applicable to off-premise sales of 40% alcohol by volume (a.b.v.) distilled spirits in 750ml containers. Local excise taxes are excluded; (4) Rates are those applicable to off-premise sales of 11% a.b.v. non-carbonated wine in 750ml containers; (5) Rates are those applicable to off-premise sales of 4.7% a.b.v. beer in 12 ounce containers.
Source: Tax Foundation, 2023 Facts & Figures: How Does Your State Compare?

State Business Tax Climate Index Rankings

State	Overall Rank	Corporate Tax Rank	Individual Income Tax Rank	Sales Tax Rank	Property Tax Rank	Unemployment Insurance Tax Rank
Florida	4	10	1	21	12	3

Note: The index is a measure of how each state's tax laws affect economic performance. The lower the rank, the more favorable a state's tax system is for business. States without a given tax are given a ranking of 1. The scores/rankings for the District of Columbia do not affect other states. The 2023 index represents the tax climate as of July 1, 2022.
Source: Tax Foundation, State Business Tax Climate Index 2023

TRANSPORTATION

Means of Transportation to Work

Area	Car/Truck/Van Drove Alone	Car-pooled	Public Transportation Bus	Subway	Railroad	Bicycle	Walked	Other Means	Worked at Home
City	65.9	7.7	6.1	1.1	0.1	0.8	4.8	3.5	10.1
MSA[1]	75.1	9.1	2.1	0.3	0.1	0.5	1.5	2.1	9.2
U.S.	73.2	8.6	2.0	1.6	0.5	0.5	2.5	1.5	9.7

Note: Figures are percentages and cover workers 16 years of age and older; (1) Figures cover the Miami-Fort Lauderdale-Pompano Beach, FL Metropolitan Statistical Area
Source: U.S. Census Bureau, 2017-2021 American Community Survey 5-Year Estimates

Travel Time to Work

Area	Less Than 10 Minutes	10 to 19 Minutes	20 to 29 Minutes	30 to 44 Minutes	45 to 59 Minutes	60 to 89 Minutes	90 Minutes or More
City	6.0	21.8	24.7	30.5	9.1	6.6	1.4
MSA[1]	6.6	22.6	22.7	27.7	10.2	7.6	2.6
U.S.	12.4	28.5	21.0	20.9	8.2	6.2	2.9

Note: Note: Figures are percentages and include workers 16 years old and over; (1) Figures cover the Miami-Fort Lauderdale-Pompano Beach, FL Metropolitan Statistical Area
Source: U.S. Census Bureau, 2017-2021 American Community Survey 5-Year Estimates

Key Congestion Measures

Measure	1990	2000	2010	2015	2020
Annual Hours of Delay, Total (000)	84,515	184,437	226,862	270,637	112,879
Annual Hours of Delay, Per Auto Commuter	32	49	55	65	27
Annual Congestion Cost, Per Auto Commuter ($)	796	1,307	1,277	1,408	608

Note: Covers the Miami FL urban area
Source: Texas A&M Transportation Institute, 2021 Urban Mobility Report

Freeway Travel Time Index

Measure	1985	1990	1995	2000	2005	2010	2015	2020
Urban Area Index[1]	1.16	1.18	1.21	1.27	1.29	1.28	1.31	1.11
Urban Area Rank[1,2]	10	15	16	13	16	14	15	20

Note: Freeway Travel Time Index—the ratio of travel time in the peak period to the travel time at free-flow conditions. For example, a value of 1.30 indicates a 20-minute free-flow trip takes 26 minutes in the peak (20 minutes x 1.30 = 26 minutes); (1) Covers the Miami FL urban area; (2) Rank is based on 101 larger urban areas (#1 = highest travel time index)
Source: Texas A&M Transportation Institute, 2021 Urban Mobility Report

Public Transportation

Agency Name / Mode of Transportation	Vehicles Operated in Maximum Service[1]	Annual Unlinked Passenger Trips[2] (in thous.)	Annual Passenger Miles[3] (in thous.)
Miami-Dade Transit (MDT)			
Bus (directly operated)	592	32,423.4	164,516.3
Bus (purchased transportation)	172	3,918.2	14,955.9
Commuter Bus (purchased transportation)	9	354.6	13,775.5
Demand Response (purchased transportation)	374	1,279.7	14,744.2
Heavy Rail (directly operated)	52	9,390.7	69,332.1
Monorail and Automated Guideway (directly operated)	21	3,487.2	3,275.6
Vanpool (purchased transportation)	166	306.0	9,280.5
South Florida Regional Transportation Authority (TRI-Rail)			
Bus (purchased transportation)	16	281.0	740.7
Commuter Rail (purchased transportation)	40	2,029.6	55,520.8

Note: (1) Number of revenue vehicles operated by the given mode and type of service to meet the annual maximum service requirement. This is the revenue vehicle count during the peak season of the year; on the week and day that maximum service is provided. Vehicles operated in maximum service (VOMS) exclude atypical days and one-time special events; (2) Number of passengers who boarded public transportation vehicles. Passengers are counted each time they board a vehicle no matter how many vehicles they use to travel from their origin to their destination. (3) Sum of the distances ridden by all passengers during the entire fiscal year.
Source: Federal Transit Administration, National Transit Database, 2021

Air Transportation

Airport Name and Code / Type of Service	Passenger Airlines[1]	Passenger Enplanements	Freight Carriers[2]	Freight (lbs)
Miami International (MIA)				
Domestic service (U.S. carriers - 2022)	29	14,144,426	20	420,160,240
International service (U.S. carriers - 2021)	18	4,253,088	19	829,297,038

Note: (1) Includes all U.S.-based major, minor and commuter airlines that carried at least one passenger during the year; (2) Includes all U.S.-based airlines and freight carriers that transported at least one pound of freight during the year.
Source: Bureau of Transportation Statistics, The Intermodal Transportation Database, Air Carriers: T-100 Domestic Market (U.S. Carriers), 2022; Bureau of Transportation Statistics, The Intermodal Transportation Database, Air Carriers: T-100 International Market (U.S. Carriers), 2021

BUSINESSES

Major Business Headquarters

Company Name	Industry	Fortune[1]	Forbes[2]
Greenberg Traurig	Business services & supplies	-	243
Lennar	Homebuilders	131	-
Ryder System	Trucking, truck leasing	365	-
Southern Glazer's Wine & Spirits	Food,, drink & tobacco	-	11
World Fuel Services	Wholesalers, diversified	111	-

Note: (1) Companies that produce a 10-K are ranked 1 to 500 based on 2021 revenue; (2) All private companies with at least $2 billion in annual revenue through the end of their most current fiscal year are ranked 1 to 246; companies listed are headquartered in the city; dashes indicate no ranking
Source: Fortune, "Fortune 500," 2022; Forbes, "America's Largest Private Companies," 2022

Fastest-Growing Businesses

According to *Inc.*, Miami is home to five of America's 500 fastest-growing private companies: **The Snow Agency** (#47); **Poseidon Management of Florida Get Staffed Up** (#67); **HCM Unlocked** (#99); **RapTV** (#431); **Sextant Stays** (#442). Criteria: must be an independent, privately-held, for-profit, U.S. corporation, proprietorship or partnership as of December 31, 2021; revenues must be at least $100,000 in 2018 and $2 million in 2021; must have four-year operating/sales history. *Inc., "America's 500 Fastest-Growing Private Companies," 2022*

According to *Initiative for a Competitive Inner City (ICIC)*, Miami is home to three of America's 100 fastest-growing "inner city" companies: **Rentingcarz Holdings** (#3); **Tissini** (#5); **Jassi & Co. Creative** (#33). Criteria for inclusion: company must be headquartered in or have 51 percent or more of its physical operations in an economically distressed urban area; must be an independent, for-profit corporation, partnership or proprietorship; must have 10 or more employees and have a five-year sales history that includes sales of at least $200,000 in the base year and at least $1 million in the current year with no decrease in sales over the two most recent years. Companies were ranked overall by revenue growth over the five-year period between 2017 and 2021. *Initiative for a Competitive Inner City (ICIC), "Inner City 100 Companies," 2022*

According to Deloitte, Miami is home to two of North America's 500 fastest-growing high-technology companies: **Taxfyle** (#381); **Veru** (#438). Companies are ranked by percentage growth in revenue over a four-year period. Criteria for inclusion: company must be headquartered within North America; must own proprietary intellectual property or technology that is sold to customers in products that contributes to a significant portion of the company's operating revenue; must have been in business for a minumum of four years with 2018 operating revenues of at least $50,000 USD/CD and 2021 operating revenues of at least $5 million USD/CD. *Deloitte, 2022 Technology Fast 500*™

Living Environment

COST OF LIVING

Cost of Living Index

Composite Index	Groceries	Housing	Utilities	Transportation	Health Care	Misc. Goods/Services
120.6	120.0	147.3	106.4	107.8	94.5	109.4

Note: The Cost of Living Index measures regional differences in the cost of consumer goods and services, excluding taxes and non-consumer expenditures, for professional and managerial households in the top income quintile. It is based on more than 50,000 prices covering almost 60 different items for which prices are collected three times a year by chambers of commerce, economic development organizations or university applied economic centers in each participating urban area. The numbers shown should be read as a percentage above or below the national average of 100. For example, a value of 115.4 in the groceries column indicates that grocery prices are 15.4% higher than the national average. Small differences in the index numbers should not be interpreted as significant; Figures cover the Miami-Dade County FL urban area.
Source: The Council for Community and Economic Research, Cost of Living Index, 2022

Grocery Prices

Area[1]	T-Bone Steak ($/pound)	Frying Chicken ($/pound)	Whole Milk ($/half gal.)	Eggs ($/dozen)	Orange Juice ($/64 oz.)	Coffee ($/11.5 oz.)
City[2]	11.37	1.69	3.62	2.72	4.62	5.14
Avg.	13.81	1.59	2.43	2.25	3.85	4.95
Min.	10.17	0.90	1.51	1.30	2.90	3.46
Max.	19.35	3.30	4.32	4.32	5.31	8.59

Note: (1) Values for the local area are compared with the average, minimum and maximum values for all 286 areas in the Cost of Living Index; (2) Figures cover the Miami-Dade County FL urban area; **T-Bone Steak** (price per pound); **Frying Chicken** (price per pound, whole fryer); **Whole Milk** (half gallon carton); **Eggs** (price per dozen, Grade A, large); **Orange Juice** (64 oz. Tropicana or Florida Natural); **Coffee** (11.5 oz. can, vacuum-packed, Maxwell House, Hills Bros, or Folgers).
Source: The Council for Community and Economic Research, Cost of Living Index, 2022

Housing and Utility Costs

Area[1]	New Home Price ($)	Apartment Rent ($/month)	All Electric ($/month)	Part Electric ($/month)	Other Energy ($/month)	Telephone ($/month)
City[2]	584,754	2,690	192.68	-	-	195.67
Avg.	450,913	1,371	176.41	99.93	76.96	190.22
Min.	229,283	546	100.84	31.56	27.15	174.27
Max.	2,434,977	4,569	356.86	249.59	272.24	208.31

Note: (1) Values for the local area are compared with the average, minimum and maximum values for all 286 areas in the Cost of Living Index; (2) Figures cover the Miami-Dade County FL urban area; **New Home Price** (2,400 sf living area, 8,000 sf lot, in urban area with full utilities); **Apartment Rent** (950 sf 2 bedroom/1.5 or 2 bath, unfurnished, excluding all utilities except water); **All Electric** (average monthly cost for an all-electric home); **Part Electric** (average monthly cost for a part-electric home); **Other Energy** (average monthly cost for natural gas, fuel oil, coal, wood, and any other forms of energy except electricity); **Telephone** (price includes the base monthly rate plus taxes and fees for three lines of mobile phone service).
Source: The Council for Community and Economic Research, Cost of Living Index, 2022

Health Care, Transportation, and Other Costs

Area[1]	Doctor ($/visit)	Dentist ($/visit)	Optometrist ($/visit)	Gasoline ($/gallon)	Beauty Salon ($/visit)	Men's Shirt ($)
City[2]	109.83	94.65	100.82	3.81	80.15	24.94
Avg.	124.91	107.77	117.66	3.86	43.31	34.21
Min.	36.61	58.25	51.79	2.90	22.18	13.05
Max.	250.21	162.58	371.96	5.54	85.61	63.54

Note: (1) Values for the local area are compared with the average, minimum and maximum values for all 286 areas in the Cost of Living Index; (2) Figures cover the Miami-Dade County FL urban area; **Doctor** (general practitioners routine exam of an established patient); **Dentist** (adult teeth cleaning and periodic oral examination); **Optometrist** (full vision eye exam for established adult patient); **Gasoline** (one gallon regular unleaded, national brand, including all taxes, cash price at self-service pump if available); **Beauty Salon** (woman's shampoo, trim, and blow-dry); **Men's Shirt** (cotton/polyester dress shirt, pinpoint weave, long sleeves).
Source: The Council for Community and Economic Research, Cost of Living Index, 2022

HOUSING

Homeownership Rate

Area	2015 (%)	2016 (%)	2017 (%)	2018 (%)	2019 (%)	2020 (%)	2021 (%)	2022 (%)
MSA[1]	58.6	58.4	57.9	59.9	60.4	60.6	59.4	58.3
U.S.	63.7	63.4	63.9	64.4	64.6	66.6	65.5	65.8

Note: (1) Figures cover the Miami-Fort Lauderdale-Pompano Beach, FL Metropolitan Statistical Area
Source: U.S. Census Bureau, Housing Vacancies and Homeownership Annual Statistics: 2015-2022

House Price Index (HPI)

Area	National Ranking[2]	Quarterly Change (%)	One-Year Change (%)	Five-Year Change (%)	Since 1991Q1 (%)
MD[1]	4	2.23	21.62	75.85	539.14
U.S.[3]	–	0.34	8.41	58.44	289.08

Note: The HPI is a weighted repeat sales index. It measures average price changes in repeat sales or refinancings on the same properties. This information is obtained by reviewing repeat mortgage transactions on single-family properties whose mortgages have been purchased or securitized by Fannie Mae or Freddie Mac since January 1975; (1) Figures cover the Miami-Miami Beach-Kendall, FL Metropolitan Division; (2) Rankings are based on annual percentage change for all metro areas containing at least 15,000 transactions over the last 10 years and ranges from 1 to 257; (3) figures based on a weighted average of Census Division estimates using a seasonally adjusted, purchase-only index; all figures are for the period ending December 31, 2022
Source: Federal Housing Finance Agency, Change in FHFA Metropolitan Area House Price Indexes, 2022Q4

Median Single-Family Home Prices

Area	2020	2021	2022p	Percent Change 2021 to 2022
MSA[1]	398.0	480.0	557.5	16.1
U.S. Average	300.2	357.1	392.6	9.9

Note: Figures are median sales prices of existing single-family homes in thousands of dollars; (p) preliminary; (1) Figures cover the Miami-Fort Lauderdale-Pompano Beach, FL Metropolitan Statistical Area
Source: National Association of Realtors, Median Sales Price of Existing Single-Family Homes for Metropolitan Areas, 4th Quarter 2022

Qualifying Income Based on Median Sales Price of Existing Single-Family Homes

Area	With 5% Down ($)	With 10% Down ($)	With 20% Down ($)
MSA[1]	164,551	155,891	138,569
U.S. Average	112,234	106,237	94,513

Note: Figures are preliminary; Qualifying income is based on a mortgage rate of 6.77%. Monthly principal and interest payment is limited to 25% of income; (1) Figures cover the Miami-Fort Lauderdale-Pompano Beach, FL Metropolitan Statistical Area
Source: National Association of Realtors, Qualifying Income Based on Median Sales Price of Existing Single-Family Homes for Metropolitan Areas, 4th Quarter 2022

Home Value

Area	Under $100,000	$100,000 -$199,999	$200,000 -$299,999	$300,000 -$399,999	$400,000 -$499,999	$500,000 -$999,999	$1,000,000 or more	Median ($)
City	4.5	9.8	20.4	22.1	14.7	20.0	8.4	369,100
MSA[1]	8.7	15.9	21.8	20.7	12.8	15.2	4.9	317,800
U.S.	16.2	24.2	20.1	13.6	8.3	13.6	4.1	244,900

Note: Figures are percentages except for median and cover owner-occupied housing units; (1) Figures cover the Miami-Fort Lauderdale-Pompano Beach, FL Metropolitan Statistical Area
Source: U.S. Census Bureau, 2017-2021 American Community Survey 5-Year Estimates

Year Housing Structure Built

Area	2020 or Later	2010 -2019	2000 -2009	1990 -1999	1980 -1989	1970 -1979	1960 -1969	1950 -1959	1940 -1949	Before 1940	Median Year
City	0.2	11.5	18.0	6.6	7.5	12.8	10.0	14.4	9.9	9.1	1975
MSA[1]	0.2	6.0	12.7	14.6	19.2	21.0	11.9	9.8	2.7	2.1	1981
U.S.	0.2	7.3	13.6	13.6	13.2	14.8	10.3	10.0	4.7	12.2	1979

Note: Figures are percentages except for Median Year; Note: (1) Figures cover the Miami-Fort Lauderdale-Pompano Beach, FL Metropolitan Statistical Area
Source: U.S. Census Bureau, 2017-2021 American Community Survey 5-Year Estimates

Gross Monthly Rent

Area	Under $500	$500 -$999	$1,000 -$1,499	$1,500 -$1,999	$2,000 -$2,499	$2,500 -$2,999	$3,000 and up	Median ($)
City	9.1	17.6	31.5	20.1	11.7	5.0	4.9	1,361
MSA[1]	4.5	11.5	34.6	28.5	12.9	4.5	3.6	1,492
U.S.	8.1	30.5	30.8	16.8	7.3	3.1	3.5	1,163

Note: Figures are percentages except for median; Gross rent is the contract rent plus the estimated average monthly cost of utilities (electricity, gas, and water and sewer) and fuels (oil, coal, kerosene, wood, etc.) if these are paid by the renter (or paid for the renter by someone else); (1) Figures cover the Miami-Fort Lauderdale-Pompano Beach, FL Metropolitan Statistical Area
Source: U.S. Census Bureau, 2017-2021 American Community Survey 5-Year Estimates

HEALTH

Health Risk Factors

Category	MSA[1] (%)	U.S. (%)
Adults aged 18–64 who have any kind of health care coverage	n/a	90.9
Adults who reported being in good or better health	n/a	85.2
Adults who have been told they have high blood cholesterol	n/a	35.7
Adults who have been told they have high blood pressure	n/a	32.4
Adults who are current smokers	n/a	14.4
Adults who currently use e-cigarettes	n/a	6.7
Adults who currently use chewing tobacco, snuff, or snus	n/a	3.5
Adults who are heavy drinkers[2]	n/a	6.3
Adults who are binge drinkers[3]	n/a	15.4
Adults who are overweight (BMI 25.0 - 29.9)	n/a	34.4
Adults who are obese (BMI 30.0 - 99.8)	n/a	33.9
Adults who participated in any physical activities in the past month	n/a	76.3

Note: (1) Figures for the Miami-Fort Lauderdale-Pompano Beach, FL Metropolitan Statistical Area were not available.
(2) Heavy drinkers are classified as adult men having more than 14 drinks per week and adult women having more than 7 drinks per week; (3) Binge drinkers are classified as males having five or more drinks on one occasion or females having four or more drinks on one occasion
Source: Centers for Disease Control and Prevention, Behavioral Risk Factor Surveillance System, SMART: Selected Metropolitan Area Risk Trends, 2021

Acute and Chronic Health Conditions

Category	MSA[1] (%)	U.S. (%)
Adults who have ever been told they had a heart attack	n/a	4.0
Adults who have ever been told they have angina or coronary heart disease	n/a	3.8
Adults who have ever been told they had a stroke	n/a	3.0
Adults who have ever been told they have asthma	n/a	14.9
Adults who have ever been told they have arthritis	n/a	25.8
Adults who have ever been told they have diabetes[2]	n/a	10.9
Adults who have ever been told they had skin cancer	n/a	6.6
Adults who have ever been told they had any other types of cancer	n/a	7.5
Adults who have ever been told they have COPD	n/a	6.1
Adults who have ever been told they have kidney disease	n/a	3.0
Adults who have ever been told they have a form of depression	n/a	20.5

Note: (1) Figures for the Miami-Fort Lauderdale-Pompano Beach, FL Metropolitan Statistical Area were not available.
(2) Figures do not include pregnancy-related, borderline, or pre-diabetes
Source: Centers for Disease Control and Prevention, Behavioral Risk Factor Surveillance System, SMART: Selected Metropolitan Area Risk Trends, 2021

Health Screening and Vaccination Rates

Category	MSA[1] (%)	U.S. (%)
Adults who have ever been tested for HIV	n/a	34.9
Adults who have had their blood cholesterol checked within the last five years	n/a	85.2
Adults aged 65+ who have had flu shot within the past year	n/a	68.6
Adults aged 65+ who have ever had a pneumonia vaccination	n/a	71.0

Note: (1) Figures for the Miami-Fort Lauderdale-Pompano Beach, FL Metropolitan Statistical Area were not available.
Source: Centers for Disease Control and Prevention, Behavioral Risk Factor Surveillance System, SMART: Selected Metropolitan Area Risk Trends, 2021

Disability Status

Category	MSA[1] (%)	U.S. (%)
Adults who reported being deaf	n/a	7.2
Are you blind or have serious difficulty seeing, even when wearing glasses?	n/a	4.8
Are you limited in any way in any of your usual activities due to arthritis?	n/a	11.1
Do you have difficulty doing errands alone?	n/a	7.0
Do you have difficulty dressing or bathing?	n/a	3.6
Do you have serious difficulty concentrating/remembering/making decisions?	n/a	12.1
Do you have serious difficulty walking or climbing stairs?	n/a	12.8

Note: (1) Figures for the Miami-Fort Lauderdale-Pompano Beach, FL Metropolitan Statistical Area were not available.
Source: Centers for Disease Control and Prevention, Behavioral Risk Factor Surveillance System, SMART: Selected Metropolitan Area Risk Trends, 2021

Mortality Rates for the Top 10 Causes of Death in the U.S.

ICD-10[a] Sub-Chapter	ICD-10[a] Code	Crude Mortality Rate[1] per 100,000 population County[2]	U.S.
Malignant neoplasms	C00-C97	160.3	182.6
Ischaemic heart diseases	I20-I25	127.0	113.1
Other forms of heart disease	I30-I51	39.1	64.4
Other degenerative diseases of the nervous system	G30-G31	44.3	51.0
Cerebrovascular diseases	I60-I69	72.1	47.8
Other external causes of accidental injury	W00-X59	24.5	46.4
Chronic lower respiratory diseases	J40-J47	32.8	45.7
Organic, including symptomatic, mental disorders	F01-F09	27.2	35.9
Hypertensive diseases	I10-I15	41.1	35.0
Diabetes mellitus	E10-E14	34.9	29.6

Note: (a) ICD-10 = International Classification of Diseases 10th Revision; (1) Crude mortality rates are a three-year average covering 2019-2021; (2) Figures cover Miami-Dade County.
Source: Centers for Disease Control and Prevention, National Center for Health Statistics. National Vital Statistics System, Mortality 2018-2021 on CDC WONDER Online Database

Mortality Rates for Selected Causes of Death

ICD-10[a] Sub-Chapter	ICD-10[a] Code	Crude Mortality Rate[1] per 100,000 population County[2]	U.S.
Assault	X85-Y09	8.4	7.0
Diseases of the liver	K70-K76	13.2	19.8
Human immunodeficiency virus (HIV) disease	B20-B24	4.8	1.5
Influenza and pneumonia	J09-J18	11.3	14.7
Intentional self-harm	X60-X84	9.1	14.3
Malnutrition	E40-E46	1.0	4.3
Obesity and other hyperalimentation	E65-E68	3.2	3.0
Renal failure	N17-N19	10.3	15.7
Transport accidents	V01-V99	13.5	13.6
Viral hepatitis	B15-B19	0.9	1.2

Note: (a) ICD-10 = International Classification of Diseases 10th Revision; (1) Crude mortality rates are a three-year average covering 2019-2021; (2) Figures cover Miami-Dade County; Data are suppressed when the data meet the criteria for confidentiality constraints; Crude mortality rates are flagged as unreliable when the rate would be calculated with a numerator of 20 or less.
Source: Centers for Disease Control and Prevention, National Center for Health Statistics. National Vital Statistics System, Mortality 2018-2021 on CDC WONDER Online Database

Health Insurance Coverage

Area	With Health Insurance	With Private Health Insurance	With Public Health Insurance	Without Health Insurance	Population Under Age 19 Without Health Insurance
City	81.0	49.9	34.5	19.0	8.1
MSA[1]	85.3	59.9	33.0	14.7	8.3
U.S.	91.2	67.8	35.4	8.8	5.3

Note: Figures are percentages that cover the civilian noninstitutionalized population; (1) Figures cover the Miami-Fort Lauderdale-Pompano Beach, FL Metropolitan Statistical Area
Source: U.S. Census Bureau, 2017-2021 American Community Survey 5-Year Estimates

Number of Medical Professionals

Area	MDs[3]	DOs[3,4]	Dentists	Podiatrists	Chiropractors	Optometrists
County[1] (number)	10,097	502	2,002	271	516	416
County[1] (rate[2])	375.0	18.6	75.2	10.2	19.4	15.6
U.S. (rate[2])	289.3	23.5	72.5	6.2	28.7	17.4

Note: Data as of 2021 unless noted; (1) Data covers Miami-Dade County; (2) Rate per 100,000 population; (3) Data as of 2020 and includes all active, non-federal physicians; (4) Doctor of Osteopathic Medicine
Source: U.S. Department of Health and Human Services, Health Resources and Services Administration, Bureau of Health Professions, Area Resource File (ARF) 2021-2022

Best Hospitals

According to *U.S. News*, the Miami-Miami Beach-Kendall, FL metro area is home to three of the best hospitals in the U.S.: **Bascom Palmer Eye Institute–University of Miami Hospital and Clinics** (3 adult specialties); **Sylvester Comprehensive Cancer Center-University of Miami Hospital and Clinics** (3 adult specialties); **University of Miami Hospital and Clinics-UHealth Tower** (3 adult specialties). The hospitals listed were nationally ranked in at least one of 15 adult or 10 pediatric specialties. The number of specialties shown cover the parent hospital. Only 164 U.S. hospitals performed well enough to be nationally ranked in one or more specialties. Twenty hospitals in the U.S. made the Honor Roll. The Best Hospitals Honor Roll takes both the national rankings and the procedure and condition ratings into account. Hospitals received points if they were nationally ranked in one of the 15 adult specialties—the higher they ranked, the more points they got—and how many ratings of "high performing" they earned in the 17 procedures and conditions. *U.S. News Online, "America's Best Hospitals 2022-23"*

According to *U.S. News,* the Miami-Miami Beach-Kendall, FL metro area is home to two of the best children's hospitals in the U.S.: **Nicklaus Children's Hospital** (5 pediatric specialties); **Holtz Children's Hospital at UM-Jackson Memorial Medical Center** (1 pediatric specialty). The hospitals listed were highly ranked in at least one of 10 pediatric specialties. Eighty-six children's hospitals in the U.S. were nationally ranked in at least one specialty. Hospitals received points for being ranked in a specialty, and the 10 hospitals with the most points across the 10 specialties make up the Honor Roll. *U.S. News Online, "America's Best Children's Hospitals 2022-23"*

EDUCATION

Public School District Statistics

District Name	Schls	Pupils	Pupil/Teacher Ratio	Minority Pupils[1] (%)	LEP/ELL[2] (%)	IEP[3] (%)
Miami-Dade	522	328,589	18.9	93.7	18.2	11.2

Note: Table includes school districts with 2,000 or more students; (1) Percentage of students that are not non-Hispanic white; (2) Percentage of students that are Limited English Proficient or English Language Learners (2018-19); (3) Percentage of students that have an Individualized Education Program (2019-20).
Source: U.S. Department of Education, National Center for Education Statistics, Common Core of Data, Local Education Agency (School District) Universe Survey: School Year 2021-2022

Best High Schools

According to *U.S. News,* Miami is home to nine of the top 500 high schools in the U.S.: **School for Advanced Studies (SAS)** (#4); **Archimedean Upper Conservatory Charter School** (#57); **Young Women's Preparatory Academy** (#60); **Design and Architecture Senior High School** (#74); **International Studies Charter High School** (#90); **iPrep Academy** (#99); **Terra Environmental Research Institute** (#144); **New World School of the Arts** (#299); **Coral Reef Senior High School** (#323). Nearly 18,000 public, magnet and charter schools were ranked based on their performance on state assessments and how well they prepare students for college. *U.S. News & World Report, "Best High Schools 2022"*

Highest Level of Education

Area	Less than H.S.	H.S. Diploma	Some College, No Deg.	Associate Degree	Bachelor's Degree	Master's Degree	Prof. School Degree	Doctorate Degree
City	20.8	25.8	12.6	7.8	19.8	8.2	3.9	1.1
MSA[1]	13.5	25.8	16.9	9.6	21.1	8.6	3.2	1.3
U.S.	11.1	26.5	20.0	8.7	20.6	9.3	2.2	1.5

Note: Figures cover persons age 25 and over; (1) Figures cover the Miami-Fort Lauderdale-Pompano Beach, FL Metropolitan Statistical Area
Source: U.S. Census Bureau, 2017-2021 American Community Survey 5-Year Estimates

Educational Attainment by Race

Area	High School Graduate or Higher (%)					Bachelor's Degree or Higher (%)				
	Total	White	Black	Asian	Hisp.[2]	Total	White	Black	Asian	Hisp.[2]
City	79.2	80.7	75.7	96.5	76.5	33.1	37.3	15.6	68.9	29.6
MSA[1]	86.5	88.7	83.6	87.9	81.2	34.1	38.5	21.2	54.3	29.8
U.S.	88.9	91.4	87.6	71.2	33.7	35.5	23.3	55.6	18.4

Note: Figures shown cover persons 25 years old and over; (1) Figures cover the Miami-Fort Lauderdale-Pompano Beach, FL Metropolitan Statistical Area; (2) People of Hispanic origin can be of any race
Source: U.S. Census Bureau, 2017-2021 American Community Survey 5-Year Estimates

School Enrollment by Grade and Control

Area	Preschool (%)		Kindergarten (%)		Grades 1 - 4 (%)		Grades 5 - 8 (%)		Grades 9 - 12 (%)	
	Public	Private	Public	Private	Public	Private	Public	Private	Public	Private
City	58.9	41.1	85.5	14.5	85.8	14.2	84.2	15.8	90.8	9.2
MSA[1]	51.1	48.9	82.4	17.6	85.2	14.8	85.6	14.4	86.1	13.9
U.S.	58.8	41.2	86.3	13.7	88.3	11.7	88.6	11.4	89.4	10.6

Note: Figures shown cover persons 3 years old and over; (1) Figures cover the Miami-Fort Lauderdale-Pompano Beach, FL Metropolitan Statistical Area
Source: U.S. Census Bureau, 2017-2021 American Community Survey 5-Year Estimates

Higher Education

Four-Year Colleges			Two-Year Colleges			Medical Schools[1]	Law Schools[2]	Voc/Tech[3]
Public	Private Non-profit	Private For-profit	Public	Private Non-profit	Private For-profit			
5	20	18	6	4	28	5	5	50

Note: Figures cover institutions located within the Miami-Fort Lauderdale-Pompano Beach, FL Metropolitan Statistical Area and include main campuses only; (1) includes schools accredited by the Liaison Committee on Medical Education and the American Osteopathic Association's Commission on Osteopathic College Accreditation; (2) includes ABA-accredited schools, schools with provisional ABA accreditation, and state accredited schools; (3) includes all schools with programs that are less than 2 years.
Source: National Center for Education Statistics, Integrated Postsecondary Education System (IPEDS), 2021-22; Wikipedia, List of Medical Schools in the United States, accessed April 10, 2023; Wikipedia, List of Law Schools in the United States, accessed April 10, 2023

According to *U.S. News & World Report,* the Miami-Miami Beach-Kendall, FL metro division is home to two of the top 200 national universities in the U.S.: **University of Miami** (#55 tie); **Florida International University** (#151 tie). The indicators used to capture academic quality fall into a number of categories: assessment by administrators at peer institutions; retention of students; faculty resources; student selectivity; financial resources; alumni giving; high school counselor ratings of colleges; and graduation rate. *U.S. News & World Report, "America's Best Colleges 2023"*

According to *U.S. News & World Report,* the Miami-Miami Beach-Kendall, FL metro division is home to two of the top 100 law schools in the U.S.: **University of Miami** (#73 tie); **Florida International University** (#98 tie). The rankings are based on a weighted average of 12 measures of quality: peer assessment score; assessment score by lawyers/judges; median LSAT scores; median undergrad GPA; acceptance rate; employment rates for graduates; placement success; bar passage rate; faculty resources; expenditures per student; student/faculty ratio; and library resources. *U.S. News & World Report, "America's Best Graduate Schools, Law, 2023"*

According to *U.S. News & World Report,* the Miami-Miami Beach-Kendall, FL metro division is home to one of the top 75 medical schools for research in the U.S.: **University of Miami (Miller)** (#43 tie). The rankings are based on a weighted average of 11 measures of quality: quality assessment; peer assessment score; assessment score by residency directors; research activity; total research activity; average research activity per faculty member; student selectivity; median MCAT total score; median undergraduate GPA; acceptance rate; and faculty resources. *U.S. News & World Report, "America's Best Graduate Schools, Medical, 2023"*

According to *U.S. News & World Report,* the Miami-Miami Beach-Kendall, FL metro division is home to one of the top 75 business schools in the U.S.: **University of Miami (Herbert)** (#67 tie). The rankings are based on a weighted average of the following nine measures: quality assessment; peer assessment; recruiter assessment; placement success; mean starting salary and bonus; student selectivity; mean GMAT and GRE scores; mean undergraduate GPA; and acceptance rate. *U.S. News & World Report, "America's Best Graduate Schools, Business, 2023"*

EMPLOYERS

Major Employers

Company Name	Industry
Baptist Health South Florida	General medical & surgical hospitals
Baptist Hospital of Miami	General medical & surgical hospitals
County of Miami-Dade	County government
Florida International University	Colleges & universities
Intercoastal Health Systems	Management services
Miami Dade College	Community college
Mount Sinai Medical Center of Florida	General medical & surgical hospitals
North Broward Hospital District	General medical & surgical hospitals
Palm Beach County	County government
Royal Caribbean Cruises Ltd	Deep sea passenger transportation, except ferry
School Board of Palm Beach County	Public elementary & secondary schools
Style View Products	Storm doors of windows, metal
The Answer Group	Custom computer programming services
University of Miami	Colleges & universities
Veterans Health Administration	General medical & surgical hospitals

Note: Companies shown are located within the Miami-Fort Lauderdale-Pompano Beach, FL Metropolitan Statistical Area.
Source: Hoovers.com; Wikipedia

Best Companies to Work For

ChenMed, headquartered in Miami, is among "Best Workplaces in Health Care." To determine the Best Workplaces in Health Care list, Great Place To Work analyzed the survey responses of over 161,000 employees from Great Place To Work-Certified companies in the health care industry. Survey data analysis and company-provided datapoints are then factored into a combined score to compare and rank the companies that create the most consistently positive experience for all employees in this industry. *Fortune, "Best Workplaces in Health Care," 2022*

Curity, a ChenMed company, headquartered in Miami, is among the "100 Best Places to Work in IT." To qualify, companies had to have a minimum of 100 total employees and five IT employees. The best places to work were selected based on DEI (diversity, equity, and inclusion) practices; IT turnover, promotions, and growth; IT retention and engagement programs; remote/hybrid working; benefits and perks (such as elder care and child care, flextime, and reimbursement for college tuition); and training and career development opportunities. *Computerworld, "Best Places to Work in IT," 2023*

PUBLIC SAFETY

Crime Rate

Area	Total Crime	Murder	Rape[3]	Robbery	Aggrav. Assault	Burglary	Larceny-Theft	Motor Vehicle Theft
City	3,305.4	12.8	19.7	128.1	394.9	305.2	2,104.0	340.7
Suburbs[1]	2,551.6	7.0	31.8	85.7	280.9	220.2	1,689.2	236.7
Metro[2]	2,609.4	7.5	30.9	88.9	289.6	226.7	1,721.0	244.7
U.S.	2,356.7	6.5	38.4	73.9	279.7	314.2	1,398.0	246.0

Note: Figures are crimes per 100,000 population; (1) All areas within the metro area that are located outside the city limits; (2) Figures cover the Miami-Miami Beach-Kendall, FL Metropolitan Division; (3) All figures shown were reported using the revised Uniform Crime Reporting (UCR) definition of rape; Due to the transition to the National Incident-Based Reporting System (NIBRS), limited city and metro area data was released for 2021.
Source: FBI Uniform Crime Reports, 2020

Hate Crimes

Area	Number of Quarters Reported	Race/Ethnicity/Ancestry	Religion	Sexual Orientation	Disability	Gender	Gender Identity
City	2	0	0	0	0	0	0
U.S.	4	5,227	1,244	1,110	130	75	266

Note: Due to the transition to the National Incident-Based Reporting System (NIBRS), limited crime data was released for 2021.
Source: Federal Bureau of Investigation, Hate Crime Statistics 2020

Identity Theft Consumer Reports

Area	Reports	Reports per 100,000 Population	Rank[2]
MSA[1]	53,201	868	3
U.S.	1,108,609	339	-

Note: (1) Figures cover the Miami-Fort Lauderdale-Pompano Beach, FL Metropolitan Statistical Area; (2) Rank ranges from 1 to 391 where 1 indicates greatest number of identity theft reports per 100,000 population
Source: Federal Trade Commission, Consumer Sentinel Network Data Book 2022

Fraud and Other Consumer Reports

Area	Reports	Reports per 100,000 Population	Rank[2]
MSA[1]	97,632	1,593	6
U.S.	4,064,520	1,245	-

Note: (1) Figures cover the Miami-Fort Lauderdale-Pompano Beach, FL Metropolitan Statistical Area; (2) Rank ranges from 1 to 391 where 1 indicates greatest number of fraud and other consumer reports per 100,000 population
Source: Federal Trade Commission, Consumer Sentinel Network Data Book 2022

POLITICS

2020 Presidential Election Results

Area	Biden	Trump	Jorgensen	Hawkins	Other
Miami-Dade County	53.3	46.0	0.3	0.1	0.3
U.S.	51.3	46.8	1.2	0.3	0.5

Note: Results are percentages and may not add to 100% due to rounding
Source: Dave Leip's Atlas of U.S. Presidential Elections

SPORTS

Professional Sports Teams

Team Name	League	Year Established
Florida Panthers	National Hockey League (NHL)	1993
Inter Miami CF	Major League Soccer (MLS)	2020
Miami Dolphins	National Football League (NFL)	1966
Miami Heat	National Basketball Association (NBA)	1988
Miami Marlins	Major League Baseball (MLB)	1993

Note: Includes teams located in the Miami-Fort Lauderdale-Pompano Beach, FL Metropolitan Statistical Area.
Source: Wikipedia, Major Professional Sports Teams of the United States and Canada, April 12, 2023

Miami, Florida

CLIMATE

Average and Extreme Temperatures

Temperature	Jan	Feb	Mar	Apr	May	Jun	Jul	Aug	Sep	Oct	Nov	Dec	Yr.
Extreme High (°F)	88	89	92	96	95	98	98	98	97	95	89	87	98
Average High (°F)	75	77	79	82	85	88	89	90	88	85	80	77	83
Average Temp. (°F)	68	69	72	75	79	82	83	83	82	78	73	69	76
Average Low (°F)	59	60	64	68	72	75	76	76	76	72	66	61	69
Extreme Low (°F)	30	35	32	42	55	60	69	68	68	53	39	30	30

Note: Figures cover the years 1948-1990
Source: National Climatic Data Center, International Station Meteorological Climate Summary, 9/96

Average Precipitation/Snowfall/Humidity

Precip./Humidity	Jan	Feb	Mar	Apr	May	Jun	Jul	Aug	Sep	Oct	Nov	Dec	Yr.
Avg. Precip. (in.)	1.9	2.0	2.3	3.0	6.2	8.7	6.1	7.5	8.2	6.6	2.7	1.8	57.1
Avg. Snowfall (in.)	0	0	0	0	0	0	0	0	0	0	0	0	0
Avg. Rel. Hum. 7am (%)	84	84	82	80	81	84	84	86	88	87	85	84	84
Avg. Rel. Hum. 4pm (%)	59	57	57	57	62	68	66	67	69	65	63	60	63

Note: Figures cover the years 1948-1990; Tr = Trace amounts (<0.05 in. of rain; <0.5 in. of snow)
Source: National Climatic Data Center, International Station Meteorological Climate Summary, 9/96

Weather Conditions

Temperature			Daytime Sky			Precipitation		
32°F & below	45°F & below	90°F & above	Clear	Partly cloudy	Cloudy	0.01 inch or more precip.	0.1 inch or more snow/ice	Thunder-storms
< 1	7	55	48	263	54	128	0	74

Note: Figures are average number of days per year and cover the years 1948-1990
Source: National Climatic Data Center, International Station Meteorological Climate Summary, 9/96

HAZARDOUS WASTE

Superfund Sites

The Miami-Miami Beach-Kendall, FL metro division is home to six sites on the EPA's Superfund National Priorities List: **Airco Plating Co.** (final); **Anodyne, Inc.** (final); **Continental Cleaners** (final); **Homestead Air Force Base** (final); **Miami Drum Services** (final); **Pepper Steel & Alloys, Inc.** (final). There are a total of 1,165 Superfund sites with a status of proposed or final on the list in the U.S. *U.S. Environmental Protection Agency, National Priorities List, April 12, 2023*

AIR QUALITY

Air Quality Trends: Ozone

	1990	1995	2000	2005	2010	2015	2018	2019	2020	2021
MSA[1]	0.068	0.072	0.075	0.065	0.064	0.061	0.064	0.058	0.058	0.057
U.S.	0.087	0.089	0.081	0.080	0.072	0.067	0.069	0.065	0.065	0.067

Note: (1) Data covers the Miami-Fort Lauderdale-Pompano Beach, FL Metropolitan Statistical Area. The values shown are the composite ozone concentration averages among trend sites based on the highest fourth daily maximum 8-hour concentration in parts per million. These trends are based on sites having an adequate record of monitoring data during the trend period. Data from exceptional events are included.
Source: U.S. Environmental Protection Agency, Air Quality Monitoring Information, "Air Quality Trends by City, 1990-2021"

Air Quality Index

Area	Percent of Days when Air Quality was...[2]					AQI Statistics[2]	
	Good	Moderate	Unhealthy for Sensitive Groups	Unhealthy	Very Unhealthy	Maximum	Median
MSA[1]	70.4	28.8	0.8	0.0	0.0	135	44

Note: (1) Data covers the Miami-Fort Lauderdale-Pompano Beach, FL Metropolitan Statistical Area; (2) Based on 365 days with AQI data in 2021. Air Quality Index (AQI) is an index for reporting daily air quality. EPA calculates the AQI for five major air pollutants regulated by the Clean Air Act: ground-level ozone, particle pollution (aka particulate matter), carbon monoxide, sulfur dioxide, and nitrogen dioxide. The AQI runs from 0 to 500. The higher the AQI value, the greater the level of air pollution and the greater the health concern. There are six AQI categories: "Good" AQI is between 0 and 50. Air quality is considered satisfactory; "Moderate" AQI is between 51 and 100. Air quality is acceptable; "Unhealthy for Sensitive Groups" When AQI values are between 101 and 150, members of sensitive groups may experience health effects; "Unhealthy" When AQI values are between 151 and 200 everyone may begin to experience health effects; "Very Unhealthy" AQI values between 201 and 300 trigger a health alert; "Hazardous" AQI values over 300 trigger warnings of emergency conditions (not shown).
Source: U.S. Environmental Protection Agency, Air Quality Index Report, 2021

Air Quality Index Pollutants

Area	Percent of Days when AQI Pollutant was...[2]					
	Carbon Monoxide	Nitrogen Dioxide	Ozone	Sulfur Dioxide	Particulate Matter 2.5	Particulate Matter 10
MSA[1]	0.0	6.8	33.7	(3)	59.5	0.0

Note: (1) Data covers the Miami-Fort Lauderdale-Pompano Beach, FL Metropolitan Statistical Area; (2) Based on 365 days with AQI data in 2021. The Air Quality Index (AQI) is an index for reporting daily air quality. EPA calculates the AQI for five major air pollutants regulated by the Clean Air Act: ground-level ozone, particle pollution (also known as particulate matter), carbon monoxide, sulfur dioxide, and nitrogen dioxide. The AQI runs from 0 to 500. The higher the AQI value, the greater the level of air pollution and the greater the health concern; (3) Sulfur dioxide is no longer included in this table (as of December 8, 2021) because SO_2 concentrations tend to be very localized and not necessarily representative of broad geographical areas like counties and CBSAs.
Source: U.S. Environmental Protection Agency, Air Quality Index Report, 2021

Maximum Air Pollutant Concentrations: Particulate Matter, Ozone, CO and Lead

	Particulate Matter 10 (ug/m^3)	Particulate Matter 2.5 Wtd AM (ug/m^3)	Particulate Matter 2.5 24-Hr (ug/m^3)	Ozone (ppm)	Carbon Monoxide (ppm)	Lead (ug/m^3)
MSA[1] Level	73	9.5	26	0.058	1	n/a
NAAQS[2]	150	15	35	0.075	9	0.15
Met NAAQS[2]	Yes	Yes	Yes	Yes	Yes	n/a

Note: (1) Data covers the Miami-Fort Lauderdale-Pompano Beach, FL Metropolitan Statistical Area; Data from exceptional events are included; (2) National Ambient Air Quality Standards; ppm = parts per million; ug/m^3 = micrograms per cubic meter; n/a not available.
Concentrations: Particulate Matter 10 (coarse particulate)—highest second maximum 24-hour concentration; Particulate Matter 2.5 Wtd AM (fine particulate)—highest weighted annual mean concentration; Particulate Matter 2.5 24-Hour (fine particulate)—highest 98th percentile 24-hour concentration; Ozone—highest fourth daily maximum 8-hour concentration; Carbon Monoxide—highest second maximum non-overlapping 8-hour concentration; Lead—maximum running 3-month average
Source: U.S. Environmental Protection Agency, Air Quality Monitoring Information, "Air Quality Statistics by City, 2021"

Maximum Air Pollutant Concentrations: Nitrogen Dioxide and Sulfur Dioxide

	Nitrogen Dioxide AM (ppb)	Nitrogen Dioxide 1-Hr (ppb)	Sulfur Dioxide AM (ppb)	Sulfur Dioxide 1-Hr (ppb)	Sulfur Dioxide 24-Hr (ppb)
MSA[1] Level	13	49	n/a	2	n/a
NAAQS[2]	53	100	30	75	140
Met NAAQS[2]	Yes	Yes	n/a	Yes	n/a

Note: (1) Data covers the Miami-Fort Lauderdale-Pompano Beach, FL Metropolitan Statistical Area; Data from exceptional events are included; (2) National Ambient Air Quality Standards; ppm = parts per million; ug/m^3 = micrograms per cubic meter; n/a not available.
Concentrations: Nitrogen Dioxide AM—highest arithmetic mean concentration; Nitrogen Dioxide 1-Hr—highest 98th percentile 1-hour daily maximum concentration; Sulfur Dioxide AM—highest annual mean concentration; Sulfur Dioxide 1-Hr—highest 99th percentile 1-hour daily maximum concentration; Sulfur Dioxide 24-Hr—highest second maximum 24-hour concentration
Source: U.S. Environmental Protection Agency, Air Quality Monitoring Information, "Air Quality Statistics by City, 2021"

Midland, Texas

Background

In 1881, Midland, Texas might have been called the middle of nowhere. It was almost exactly at the midpoint between Fort Worth and El Paso. Then barely a whistle-stop, Midland provided a small shelter where Texas and Pacific Railroad crews could rest and store maintenance equipment. Ten years later, it was a vital shipping center for the cattle trade. Today the locals like to say that Midland is in the middle of somewhere.

Little is known about the first inhabitants in the region, though they left plenty of evidence of their existence. The Pecos Trail region is rich with petroglyphs and pictographs. Anthropologists refer to these communities as the Karankawas (hunter-gatherers), and surmise these early scribes are the ancestors of the Comanche, Apache, Kiowa, and Kickapoo nations.

The first westerner to make Midland his permanent home in 1882 was Herman Garrett, a sheep rancher from California. Within three years, 100 families lived there, and by 1900, the population was 1,000. Midland became known as the "Windmill Town," as individual homes built windmills to pump water. After devastating fires in 1905 and 1909, the town put in a municipal water system and created a fire department.

Midland would remain a center of ranching and shipping until 1923, when a new industry—oil—overtook the town. Just southeast of Midland, the Santa Rita No. 1 oil rig "blew." From then on, Midland's economy and culture was defined by the price of oil, and its roller coaster ride of market highs and lows.

By 1929, there were thirty-six oil companies in Midland. Roads were paved and streetlights were raised as Midland's skyline began to rise from the wide-open landscape. The Hogal Building was twelve stories high. By 1930, the population blossomed to 5,484. When the Great Depression hit, the demand for petroleum decreased and prices plummeted. By 1932, one third of Midland's workers were unemployed.

World War II brought an increase in oil prices, along with the Midland Army Air Force Base, a training ground for bomber pilots, giving Midland's economy a much-needed boost. By 1950, 250 oil companies had set up shop in Midland.

Today, in addition to the oil industry, Midland's top employers include the school district, medical center, Dawson Geophysical who provides onshore seismic data acquisition services, and Walmart.

In 1972, Midland Community College was founded, and later, a satellite campus in Fort Stockton opened about 100 miles away. Twice a year, Midland College hosts free lectures by world-renowned speakers, including Ken Burns, Bill Moyers, Sandra Day O'Connor, Richard Rodriguez, John Updike and Neil deGrasse Tyson.

In recent years, interest in Midland has increased due to its association with the presidential Bush family. Laura Bush was born and raised in Midland. Both former presidents George W. Bush, and George H.W. Bush, as well as Barbara and Jeb Bush, lived in Midland. The George Bush Childhood Home Museum in Midland receives thousands of visitors a year.

Midland is a cultural mecca with six museums, as well as a community theater that offers fifteen shows each year. The Midland-Odessa Symphony & Chorale holds eighteen performances each year, with four masterworks, four Pops Concerts, six Chamber Concerts, two Chorale concerts, and a youth concert. The Marian Blakemore planetarium offers educational shows and lectures about the history of astronomy.

Midland features a semi-arid climate with long, hot summers and short, moderate winters. The city is occasionally subject to cold waves during the winter, but it rarely sees extended periods of below-freezing cold. Midland receives approximately 14.6 inches of precipitation per year, much of which falls in the summer. Highs exceed 90 degrees on 101 days per year, and 100 degrees on 16 days.

Rankings

Business/Finance Rankings

- The Midland metro area appeared on the Milken Institute "2022 Best Performing Cities" list. Rank: #104 out of 201 small metro areas (population over 60,000). Criteria: job growth; wage and salary growth; high-tech output growth; housing affordability; household broadband access. *Milken Institute, "Best-Performing Cities 2022," March 28, 2022*

- *Forbes* ranked 203 smaller metro areas (population under 268,000) to determine the nation's "Best Small Places for Business and Careers." The Midland metro area was ranked #81. Criteria: costs (business and living); job growth (past and projected); income growth; quality of life; educational attainment (college and high school); projected economic growth; cultural and leisure opportunities; workplace tolerance laws; net migration patterns. *Forbes, "The Best Small Places for Business and Careers 2019," October 30, 2019*

Environmental Rankings

- Midland was highlighted as one of the top 59 cleanest metro areas for short-term particle pollution (24-hour PM 2.5) in the U.S. during 2019 through 2021. Monitors in these cities reported no days with unhealthful PM 2.5 levels. *American Lung Association, "State of the Air 2023," April 19, 2023*

Real Estate Rankings

- Midland was ranked #59 out of 235 metro areas in terms of housing affordability in 2022 by the National Association of Home Builders (#1 = most affordable). Criteria: the share of homes sold in that area affordable to a family earning the local median income, based on standard mortgage underwriting criteria. *National Association of Home Builders®, NAHB-Wells Fargo Housing Opportunity Index, 4th Quarter 2022*

Safety Rankings

- The National Insurance Crime Bureau ranked 390 metro areas in the U.S. in terms of per capita rates of vehicle theft. The Midland metro area ranked #91 (#1 = highest rate). Criteria: number of vehicle theft offenses per 100,000 inhabitants in 2021. *National Insurance Crime Bureau, "Hot Spots 2021," September 1, 2022*

Seniors/Retirement Rankings

- From its Best Cities for Successful Aging indexes, the Milken Institute generated rankings for metropolitan areas, weighing data in nine categories—health care, wellness, living arrangements, transportation and convenience, financial characteristics, education, employment, community engagement, and overall livability. The Midland metro area was ranked #15 overall in the small metro area category. *Milken Institute, "Best Cities for Successful Aging, 2017" March 14, 2017*

Business Environment

DEMOGRAPHICS

Population Growth

Area	1990 Census	2000 Census	2010 Census	2020 Census	Population Growth (%) 1990-2020	Population Growth (%) 2010-2020
City	89,358	94,996	111,147	132,524	48.3	19.2
MSA[1]	106,611	116,009	136,872	175,220	64.4	28.0
U.S.	248,709,873	281,421,906	308,745,538	331,449,281	33.3	7.4

Note: (1) Figures cover the Midland, TX Metropolitan Statistical Area
Source: U.S. Census Bureau, 1990 Census, 2000 Census, 2010 Census, 2020 Census

Race

Area	White Alone[2] (%)	Black Alone[2] (%)	Asian Alone[2] (%)	AIAN[3] Alone[2] (%)	NHOPI[4] Alone[2] (%)	Other Race Alone[2] (%)	Two or More Races (%)
City	57.6	7.9	2.6	0.9	0.1	12.5	18.4
MSA[1]	58.2	6.4	2.3	0.9	0.1	13.2	18.9
U.S.	61.6	12.4	6.0	1.1	0.2	8.4	10.2

Note: (1) Figures cover the Midland, TX Metropolitan Statistical Area; (2) Alone is defined as not being in combination with one or more other races; (3) American Indian and Alaska Native; (4) Native Hawaiian and Other Pacific Islander
Source: U.S. Census Bureau, 2020 Census

Hispanic or Latino Origin

Area	Total (%)	Mexican (%)	Puerto Rican (%)	Cuban (%)	Other (%)
City	46.5	42.5	0.5	1.0	2.5
MSA[1]	46.3	42.7	0.4	0.9	2.3
U.S.	18.4	11.2	1.8	0.7	4.7

Note: Persons of Hispanic or Latino origin can be of any race; (1) Figures cover the Midland, TX Metropolitan Statistical Area
Source: U.S. Census Bureau, 2017-2021 American Community Survey 5-Year Estimates

Age

Area	Under Age 5	Age 5–19	Age 20–34	Age 35–44	Age 45–54	Age 55–64	Age 65–74	Age 75–84	Age 85+	Median Age
City	7.9	21.7	23.5	14.4	10.3	11.0	6.7	3.0	1.5	33.3
MSA[1]	7.8	22.3	22.9	14.3	10.7	11.2	6.7	2.9	1.3	33.3
U.S.	5.6	19.2	20.2	12.7	12.4	13.1	10.0	4.9	1.9	38.8

Note: (1) Figures cover the Midland, TX Metropolitan Statistical Area
Source: U.S. Census Bureau, 2020 Census

Disability by Age

Area	All Ages	Under 18 Years Old	18 to 64 Years Old	65 Years and Over
City	9.8	2.7	8.1	41.1
MSA[1]	9.9	2.6	8.2	41.3
U.S.	12.6	4.4	10.3	33.4

Note: Figures show percent of the civilian noninstitutionalized population that reported having a disability. Disability status is determined from six types of difficulty: vision, hearing, cognitive, ambulatory, self-care, and independent living. For children under 5 years old, hearing and vision difficulty are used to determine disability status. For children between the ages of 5 and 14, disability status is determined from hearing, vision, cognitive, ambulatory, and self-care difficulties. For people aged 15 years and older, they are considered to have a disability if they have difficulty with any one of the six difficulty types; Note: (1) Figures cover the Midland, TX Metropolitan Statistical Area
Source: U.S. Census Bureau, 2017-2021 American Community Survey 5-Year Estimates

Ancestry

Area	German	Irish	English	American	Italian	Polish	French[2]	Scottish	Dutch
City	5.8	5.2	6.0	4.7	1.0	0.5	1.5	1.4	0.3
MSA[1]	6.0	5.0	5.7	5.0	1.2	0.5	1.4	1.2	0.2
U.S.	12.8	9.6	8.1	5.7	5.0	2.7	2.2	1.6	1.1

Note: Figures are the percentage of the total population reporting a particular ancestry. The nine most commonly reported ancestries in the U.S. are shown. Figures include multiple ancestries (e.g. if a person reported being Irish and Italian, they were included in both columns); (1) Figures cover the Midland, TX Metropolitan Statistical Area; (2) Excludes Basque
Source: U.S. Census Bureau, 2017-2021 American Community Survey 5-Year Estimates

Foreign-born Population

Area	Any Foreign Country	Asia	Mexico	Europe	Caribbean	Central America[2]	South America	Africa	Canada
City	15.1	2.1	9.0	0.2	1.0	0.5	0.5	1.3	0.5
MSA[1]	13.7	1.9	8.5	0.3	0.8	0.4	0.4	1.0	0.4
U.S.	13.6	4.2	3.3	1.5	1.4	1.1	1.1	0.8	0.2

Note: (1) Figures cover the Midland, TX Metropolitan Statistical Area; (2) Excludes Mexico.
Source: U.S. Census Bureau, 2017-2021 American Community Survey 5-Year Estimates

Household Size

Area	One	Two	Three	Four	Five	Six	Seven or More	Average Household Size
City	26.8	28.3	17.2	15.3	8.2	2.8	1.4	2.60
MSA[1]	25.8	28.1	17.1	15.7	8.6	2.6	2.1	2.60
U.S.	28.1	33.8	15.5	12.9	6.0	2.3	1.4	2.60

Note: (1) Figures cover the Midland, TX Metropolitan Statistical Area
Source: U.S. Census Bureau, 2017-2021 American Community Survey 5-Year Estimates

Household Relationships

Area	Householder	Opposite-sex Spouse	Same-sex Spouse	Opposite-sex Unmarried Partner	Same-sex Unmarried Partner	Child[2]	Grandchild	Other Relatives	Non-relatives
City	36.4	18.5	0.1	2.1	0.1	31.9	3.0	4.2	2.5
MSA[1]	35.8	18.6	0.1	2.0	0.1	32.3	3.2	4.4	2.6
U.S.	38.3	17.5	0.2	2.5	0.2	28.3	2.4	4.8	3.4

Note: Figures are percent of the total population; (1) Figures cover the Midland, TX Metropolitan Statistical Area; (2) Includes biological, adopted, and stepchildren of the householder
Source: U.S. Census Bureau, 2020 Census

Gender

Area	Males	Females	Males per 100 Females
City	66,552	65,972	100.9
MSA[1]	88,457	86,763	102.0
U.S.	162,685,811	168,763,470	96.4

Note: (1) Figures cover the Midland, TX Metropolitan Statistical Area
Source: U.S. Census Bureau, 2020 Census

Marital Status

Area	Never Married	Now Married[2]	Separated	Widowed	Divorced
City	28.6	55.1	1.9	4.5	9.9
MSA[1]	27.9	55.4	1.7	4.5	10.5
U.S.	33.8	48.0	1.8	5.6	10.8

Note: Figures are percentages and cover the population 15 years of age and older; (1) Figures cover the Midland, TX Metropolitan Statistical Area; (2) Excludes separated
Source: U.S. Census Bureau, 2017-2021 American Community Survey 5-Year Estimates

Religious Groups by Family

Area	Catholic	Baptist	Methodist	LDS[2]	Pentecostal	Lutheran	Islam	Adventist	Other
MSA[1]	15.4	25.5	2.5	2.0	1.2	0.3	0.4	1.3	16.5
U.S.	18.7	7.3	3.0	2.0	1.8	1.7	1.3	1.3	11.6

Note: Figures are the number of adherents as a percentage of the total population and cover the eight largest religious groups in the U.S; (1) Figures cover the Midland, TX Metropolitan Statistical Area; (2) Church of Jesus Christ of Latter-day Saints
Sources: 2020 U.S. Religion Census, Association of Statisticians of American Religious Bodies; The Association of Religion Data Archives (ARDA)

Religious Groups by Tradition

Area	Catholic	Evangelical Protestant	Mainline Protestant	Black Protestant	Islam	Judaism	Hinduism	Orthodox	Buddhism
MSA[1]	15.4	35.5	3.0	7.6	0.4	n/a	0.2	n/a	n/a
U.S.	18.7	16.5	5.2	2.3	1.3	0.6	0.4	0.4	0.3

Note: Figures are the number of adherents as a percentage of the total population; (1) Figures cover the Midland, TX Metropolitan Statistical Area
Sources: 2020 U.S. Religion Census, Association of Statisticians of American Religious Bodies; The Association of Religion Data Archives (ARDA)

ECONOMY

Gross Metropolitan Product

Area	2020	2021	2022	2023	Rank[2]
MSA[1]	21.8	25.3	30.1	33.9	121

Note: Figures are in billions of dollars; (1) Figures cover the Midland, TX Metropolitan Statistical Area; (2) Rank is based on 2021 data and ranges from 1 to 381
Source: U.S. Conference of Mayors, U.S. Metro Economies: U.S. Metros Compared to Global and State Economies, June 2022

Economic Growth

Area	2018-20 (%)	2021 (%)	2022 (%)	2023 (%)	Rank[2]
MSA[1]	3.5	15.8	10.1	12.3	12
U.S.	-0.6	5.7	3.1	2.9	—

Note: Figures are real gross metropolitan product (GMP) growth rates and represent average annual percent change; (1) Figures cover the Midland, TX Metropolitan Statistical Area; (2) Rank is based on 2020 2-year average annual percent change and ranges from 1 to 381
Source: U.S. Conference of Mayors, U.S. Metro Economies: U.S. Metros Compared to Global and State Economies, June 2022

Metropolitan Area Exports

Area	2016	2017	2018	2019	2020	2021	Rank[2]
MSA[1]	69.6	69.4	63.6	63.7	57.7	49.9	372

Note: Figures are in millions of dollars; (1) Figures cover the Midland, TX Metropolitan Statistical Area; (2) Rank is based on 2021 data and ranges from 1 to 388
Source: U.S. Department of Commerce, International Trade Administration, Office of Trade and Economic Analysis, Industry and Analysis, Exports by Metropolitan Area, data extracted March 16, 2023

Building Permits

Area	Single-Family 2021	Single-Family 2022	Pct. Chg.	Multi-Family 2021	Multi-Family 2022	Pct. Chg.	Total 2021	Total 2022	Pct. Chg.
City	858	593	-30.9	0	0	0.0	858	593	-30.9
MSA[1]	872	594	-31.9	0	0	0.0	872	594	-31.9
U.S.	1,115,400	975,600	-12.5	621,600	689,500	10.9	1,737,000	1,665,100	-4.1

Note: (1) Figures cover the Midland, TX Metropolitan Statistical Area; Figures represent new, privately-owned housing units authorized (unadjusted data); All permit data are based on estimates with imputation
Source: U.S. Census Bureau, Manufacturing, Mining, and Construction Statistics, Building Permits, 2021, 2022

Bankruptcy Filings

Area	Business Filings 2021	Business Filings 2022	% Chg.	Nonbusiness Filings 2021	Nonbusiness Filings 2022	% Chg.
Midland County	18	7	-61.1	64	73	14.1
U.S.	14,347	13,481	-6.0	399,269	374,240	-6.3

Note: Business filings include Chapter 7, Chapter 9, Chapter 11, Chapter 12, Chapter 13, Chapter 15, and Section 304; Nonbusiness filings include Chapter 7, Chapter 11, and Chapter 13
Source: Administrative Office of the U.S. Courts, Business and Nonbusiness Bankruptcy, County Cases Commenced by Chapter of the Bankruptcy Code, During the 12-Month Period Ending December 31, 2021 and Business and Nonbusiness Bankruptcy, County Cases Commenced by Chapter of the Bankruptcy Code, During the 12-Month Period Ending December 31, 2022

Housing Vacancy Rates

Area	Gross Vacancy Rate[2] (%) 2020	2021	2022	Year-Round Vacancy Rate[3] (%) 2020	2021	2022	Rental Vacancy Rate[4] (%) 2020	2021	2022	Homeowner Vacancy Rate[5] (%) 2020	2021	2022
MSA[1]	n/a	n/a	n/a	n/a	n/a	n/a	n/a	n/a	n/a	n/a	n/a	n/a
U.S.	10.6	10.8	10.5	8.2	8.4	8.2	6.3	6.1	5.8	1.0	0.9	0.8

Note: (1) Figures cover the Midland, TX Metropolitan Statistical Area; (2) The percentage of the total housing inventory that is vacant; (3) The percentage of the housing inventory (excluding seasonal units) that is year-round vacant; (4) The percentage of rental inventory that is vacant for rent; (5) The percentage of homeowner inventory that is vacant for sale; n/a not available
Source: U.S. Census Bureau, Housing Vacancies and Homeownership Annual Statistics: 2020, 2021, 2022

INCOME

Income

Area	Per Capita ($)	Median Household ($)	Average Household ($)
City	44,218	87,900	115,425
MSA[1]	43,287	87,812	114,916
U.S.	37,638	69,021	97,196

Note: (1) Figures cover the Midland, TX Metropolitan Statistical Area
Source: U.S. Census Bureau, 2017-2021 American Community Survey 5-Year Estimates

Household Income Distribution

Area	Under $15,000	$15,000 -$24,999	$25,000 -$34,999	$35,000 -$49,999	$50,000 -$74,999	$75,000 -$99,999	$100,000 -$149,999	$150,000 and up
City	8.0	5.8	6.5	8.5	14.7	12.5	19.6	24.4
MSA[1]	7.6	5.8	7.1	8.8	14.1	12.8	19.2	24.6
U.S.	9.4	7.8	8.2	11.4	16.8	12.8	16.3	17.3

Note: (1) Figures cover the Midland, TX Metropolitan Statistical Area
Source: U.S. Census Bureau, 2017-2021 American Community Survey 5-Year Estimates

Poverty Rate

Area	All Ages	Under 18 Years Old	18 to 64 Years Old	65 Years and Over
City	10.6	13.5	9.1	11.8
MSA[1]	11.2	15.9	8.9	11.2
U.S.	12.6	17.0	11.8	9.6

Note: Figures are percentage of people whose income during the past 12 months was below the poverty level; (1) Figures cover the Midland, TX Metropolitan Statistical Area
Source: U.S. Census Bureau, 2017-2021 American Community Survey 5-Year Estimates

EMPLOYMENT

Labor Force and Employment

Area	Civilian Labor Force Dec. 2021	Civilian Labor Force Dec. 2022	% Chg.	Workers Employed Dec. 2021	Workers Employed Dec. 2022	% Chg.
City	83,370	84,916	1.9	80,102	82,715	3.3
MSA[1]	103,649	105,497	1.8	99,519	102,761	3.3
U.S.	161,696,000	164,224,000	1.6	155,732,000	158,872,000	2.0

Note: Data is not seasonally adjusted and covers workers 16 years of age and older; (1) Figures cover the Midland, TX Metropolitan Statistical Area
Source: Bureau of Labor Statistics, Local Area Unemployment Statistics

Unemployment Rate

Area	Jan.	Feb.	Mar.	Apr.	May	Jun.	Jul.	Aug.	Sep.	Oct.	Nov.	Dec.
City	4.3	4.3	3.4	3.2	3.2	3.6	3.5	3.3	3.0	3.0	2.8	2.6
MSA[1]	4.4	4.3	3.5	3.2	3.3	3.6	3.5	3.3	3.0	2.9	2.8	2.6
U.S.	4.4	4.1	3.8	3.3	3.4	3.8	3.8	3.8	3.3	3.4	3.4	3.3

Note: Data is not seasonally adjusted and covers workers 16 years of age and older; (1) Figures cover the Midland, TX Metropolitan Statistical Area
Source: Bureau of Labor Statistics, Local Area Unemployment Statistics

Average Wages

Occupation	$/Hr.	Occupation	$/Hr.
Accountants and Auditors	45.27	Maintenance and Repair Workers	20.19
Automotive Mechanics	22.73	Marketing Managers	76.35
Bookkeepers	23.16	Network and Computer Systems Admin.	46.75
Carpenters	24.74	Nurses, Licensed Practical	26.25
Cashiers	13.53	Nurses, Registered	39.34
Computer Programmers	46.24	Nursing Assistants	16.60
Computer Systems Analysts	60.82	Office Clerks, General	20.43
Computer User Support Specialists	29.09	Physical Therapists	50.09
Construction Laborers	19.01	Physicians	124.58
Cooks, Restaurant	15.29	Plumbers, Pipefitters and Steamfitters	26.81
Customer Service Representatives	19.91	Police and Sheriff's Patrol Officers	34.27
Dentists	n/a	Postal Service Mail Carriers	25.08
Electricians	29.47	Real Estate Sales Agents	48.44
Engineers, Electrical	42.56	Retail Salespersons	16.59
Fast Food and Counter Workers	12.27	Sales Representatives, Technical/Scientific	48.08
Financial Managers	94.45	Secretaries, Exc. Legal/Medical/Executive	20.58
First-Line Supervisors of Office Workers	32.60	Security Guards	17.08
General and Operations Managers	59.45	Surgeons	n/a
Hairdressers/Cosmetologists	14.46	Teacher Assistants, Exc. Postsecondary*	13.37
Home Health and Personal Care Aides	12.12	Teachers, Secondary School, Exc. Sp. Ed.*	30.50
Janitors and Cleaners	14.35	Telemarketers	n/a
Landscaping/Groundskeeping Workers	16.75	Truck Drivers, Heavy/Tractor-Trailer	25.69
Lawyers	87.92	Truck Drivers, Light/Delivery Services	20.91
Maids and Housekeeping Cleaners	13.55	Waiters and Waitresses	12.89

Note: Wage data covers the Midland, TX Metropolitan Statistical Area; (*) Hourly wages were calculated from annual wage data based on a 40 hour work week; n/a not available.
Source: Bureau of Labor Statistics, Metro Area Occupational Employment & Wage Estimates, May 2022

Employment by Industry

Sector	MSA[1] Number of Employees	MSA[1] Percent of Total	U.S. Percent of Total
Construction, Mining, and Logging	39,400	33.3	5.4
Private Education and Health Services	7,800	6.6	16.1
Financial Activities	5,300	4.5	5.9
Government	9,900	8.4	14.5
Information	1,200	1.0	2.0
Leisure and Hospitality	11,600	9.8	10.3
Manufacturing	5,000	4.2	8.4
Other Services	4,100	3.5	3.7
Professional and Business Services	11,600	9.8	14.7
Retail Trade	9,800	8.3	10.2
Transportation, Warehousing, and Utilities	5,800	4.9	4.9
Wholesale Trade	6,800	5.7	3.9

Note: Figures are non-farm employment as of December 2022. Figures are not seasonally adjusted and include workers 16 years of age and older; (1) Figures cover the Midland, TX Metropolitan Statistical Area
Source: Bureau of Labor Statistics, Current Employment Statistics, Employment, Hours, and Earnings

Employment by Occupation

Occupation Classification	City (%)	MSA[1] (%)	U.S. (%)
Management, Business, Science, and Arts	38.1	37.4	40.3
Natural Resources, Construction, and Maintenance	13.5	14.4	8.7
Production, Transportation, and Material Moving	12.0	12.4	13.1
Sales and Office	22.2	22.5	20.9
Service	14.2	13.3	17.0

Note: Figures cover employed civilians 16 years of age and older; (1) Figures cover the Midland, TX Metropolitan Statistical Area
Source: U.S. Census Bureau, 2017-2021 American Community Survey 5-Year Estimates

Occupations with Greatest Projected Employment Growth: 2022 – 2024

Occupation[1]	2022 Employment	2024 Projected Employment	Numeric Employment Change	Percent Employment Change
Home Health and Personal Care Aides	338,130	364,760	26,630	7.9
General and Operations Managers	395,700	416,100	20,400	5.2
Heavy and Tractor-Trailer Truck Drivers	206,850	222,220	15,370	7.4
Software Developers	119,810	134,060	14,250	11.9
Laborers and Freight, Stock, and Material Movers, Hand	214,680	228,680	14,000	6.5
Farmers, Ranchers, and Other Agricultural Managers	274,740	287,430	12,690	4.6
Stockers and Order Fillers	212,180	224,670	12,490	5.9
Construction Laborers	153,220	164,330	11,110	7.3
Cooks, Restaurant	131,480	141,860	10,380	7.9
Industrial Truck and Tractor Operators	83,270	93,190	9,920	11.9

Note: Projections cover Texas; (1) Sorted by numeric employment change
Source: www.projectionscentral.com, State Occupational Projections, 2022–2024 Short-Term Projections

Fastest-Growing Occupations: 2022 – 2024

Occupation[1]	2022 Employment	2024 Projected Employment	Numeric Employment Change	Percent Employment Change
Wind Turbine Service Technicians	5,240	5,990	750	14.3
Information Security Analysts (SOC 2018)	14,170	16,110	1,940	13.7
Solar Photovoltaic Installers	2,240	2,540	300	13.4
Veterinary Technologists and Technicians	16,140	18,200	2,060	12.8
Actuaries	1,810	2,040	230	12.7
Data Scientists	7,340	8,270	930	12.7
Web Developers	6,920	7,790	870	12.6
Veterinarians	6,830	7,670	840	12.3
Veterinary Assistants and Laboratory Animal Caretakers	5,990	6,720	730	12.2
Ushers, Lobby Attendants, and Ticket Takers	9,100	10,190	1,090	12.0

Note: Projections cover Texas; (1) Sorted by percent employment change and excludes occupations with numeric employment change less than 50
Source: www.projectionscentral.com, State Occupational Projections, 2022–2024 Short-Term Projections

CITY FINANCES

City Government Finances

Component	2020 ($000)	2020 ($ per capita)
Total Revenues	311,620	2,134
Total Expenditures	277,124	1,898
Debt Outstanding	181,095	1,240
Cash and Securities[1]	302,405	2,071

Note: (1) Cash and security holdings of a government at the close of its fiscal year, including those of its dependent agencies, utilities, and liquor stores.
Source: U.S. Census Bureau, State & Local Government Finances 2020

City Government Revenue by Source

Source	2020 ($000)	2020 ($ per capita)	2020 (%)
General Revenue			
From Federal Government	10,052	69	3.2
From State Government	1,649	11	0.5
From Local Governments	0	0	0.0
Taxes			
Property	52,513	360	16.9
Sales and Gross Receipts	94,217	645	30.2
Personal Income	0	0	0.0
Corporate Income	0	0	0.0
Motor Vehicle License	0	0	0.0
Other Taxes	4,386	30	1.4
Current Charges	61,411	421	19.7
Liquor Store	0	0	0.0
Utility	61,390	420	19.7

Source: U.S. Census Bureau, State & Local Government Finances 2020

City Government Expenditures by Function

Function	2020 ($000)	2020 ($ per capita)	2020 (%)
General Direct Expenditures			
Air Transportation	14,505	99	5.2
Corrections	0	0	0.0
Education	0	0	0.0
Employment Security Administration	0	0	0.0
Financial Administration	2,643	18	1.0
Fire Protection	29,481	201	10.6
General Public Buildings	3,418	23	1.2
Governmental Administration, Other	16,942	116	6.1
Health	2,233	15	0.8
Highways	32,992	225	11.9
Hospitals	0	0	0.0
Housing and Community Development	3,731	25	1.3
Interest on General Debt	1,090	7	0.4
Judicial and Legal	3,286	22	1.2
Libraries	0	0	0.0
Parking	0	0	0.0
Parks and Recreation	43,615	298	15.7
Police Protection	26,224	179	9.5
Public Welfare	0	0	0.0
Sewerage	252	1	0.1
Solid Waste Management	15,188	104	5.5
Veterans' Services	0	0	0.0
Liquor Store	0	0	0.0
Utility	80,720	552	29.1

Source: U.S. Census Bureau, State & Local Government Finances 2020

TAXES

State Corporate Income Tax Rates

State	Tax Rate (%)	Income Brackets ($)	Num. of Brackets	Financial Institution Tax Rate (%)[a]	Federal Income Tax Ded.
Texas	(u)	–	–	(u)	No

Note: Tax rates as of January 1, 2023; (a) Rates listed are the corporate income tax rate applied to financial institutions or excise taxes based on income. Some states have other taxes based upon the value of deposits or shares; (u) Texas imposes a Franchise Tax, otherwise known as margin tax, imposed on entities with more than $1,230,000 total revenues at rate of 0.75%, or 0.375% for entities primarily engaged in retail or wholesale trade, on lesser of 70% of total revenues or 100% of gross receipts after deductions for either compensation or cost of goods sold.
Source: Federation of Tax Administrators, State Corporate Income Tax Rates, January 1, 2023

State Individual Income Tax Rates

State	Tax Rate (%)	Income Brackets ($)	Personal Exemptions ($) Single	Married	Depend.	Standard Ded. ($) Single	Married
Texas				– No state income tax –			

Note: Tax rates as of January 1, 2023; Local- and county-level taxes are not included
Source: Federation of Tax Administrators, State Individual Income Tax Rates, January 1, 2023

Various State Sales and Excise Tax Rates

State	State Sales Tax (%)	Gasoline[1] ($/gal.)	Cigarette[2] ($/pack)	Spirits[3] ($/gal.)	Wine[4] ($/gal.)	Beer[5] ($/gal.)	Recreational Marijuana (%)
Texas	6.25	0.20	1.41	2.40	0.20	0.19	Not legal

Note: All tax rates as of January 1, 2023; (1) The American Petroleum Institute has developed a methodology for determining the average tax rate on a gallon of fuel. Rates may include any of the following: excise taxes, environmental fees, storage tank fees, other fees or taxes, general sales tax, and local taxes; (2) The federal excise tax of $1.0066 per pack and local taxes are not included; (3) Rates are those applicable to off-premise sales of 40% alcohol by volume (a.b.v.) distilled spirits in 750ml containers. Local excise taxes are excluded; (4) Rates are those applicable to off-premise sales of 11% a.b.v. non-carbonated wine in 750ml containers; (5) Rates are those applicable to off-premise sales of 4.7% a.b.v. beer in 12 ounce containers.
Source: Tax Foundation, 2023 Facts & Figures: How Does Your State Compare?

State Business Tax Climate Index Rankings

State	Overall Rank	Corporate Tax Rank	Individual Income Tax Rank	Sales Tax Rank	Property Tax Rank	Unemployment Insurance Tax Rank
Texas	13	47	7	37	38	12

Note: The index is a measure of how each state's tax laws affect economic performance. The lower the rank, the more favorable a state's tax system is for business. States without a given tax are given a ranking of 1. The scores/rankings for the District of Columbia do not affect other states. The 2023 index represents the tax climate as of July 1, 2022.
Source: Tax Foundation, State Business Tax Climate Index 2023

TRANSPORTATION

Means of Transportation to Work

Area	Car/Truck/Van Drove Alone	Car-pooled	Public Transportation Bus	Subway	Railroad	Bicycle	Walked	Other Means	Worked at Home
City	82.4	10.4	0.2	0.0	0.0	0.3	0.6	0.7	5.5
MSA[1]	82.7	9.9	0.1	0.0	0.0	0.2	1.2	0.7	5.1
U.S.	73.2	8.6	2.0	1.6	0.5	0.5	2.5	1.5	9.7

Note: Figures are percentages and cover workers 16 years of age and older; (1) Figures cover the Midland, TX Metropolitan Statistical Area
Source: U.S. Census Bureau, 2017-2021 American Community Survey 5-Year Estimates

Travel Time to Work

Area	Less Than 10 Minutes	10 to 19 Minutes	20 to 29 Minutes	30 to 44 Minutes	45 to 59 Minutes	60 to 89 Minutes	90 Minutes or More
City	14.2	47.3	18.9	12.0	2.9	2.4	2.4
MSA[1]	14.7	42.7	21.0	13.5	3.3	2.5	2.2
U.S.	12.4	28.5	21.0	20.9	8.2	6.2	2.9

Note: Note: Figures are percentages and include workers 16 years old and over; (1) Figures cover the Midland, TX Metropolitan Statistical Area
Source: U.S. Census Bureau, 2017-2021 American Community Survey 5-Year Estimates

Key Congestion Measures

Measure	1990	2000	2010	2015	2020
Annual Hours of Delay, Total (000)	n/a	n/a	n/a	2,945	3,167
Annual Hours of Delay, Per Auto Commuter	n/a	n/a	n/a	21	18
Annual Congestion Cost, Per Auto Commuter ($)	n/a	n/a	n/a	453	416

Note: n/a not available
Source: Texas A&M Transportation Institute, 2021 Urban Mobility Report

Freeway Travel Time Index

Measure	1985	1990	1995	2000	2005	2010	2015	2020
Urban Area Index[1]	n/a	n/a	n/a	n/a	n/a	n/a	1.08	1.09
Urban Area Rank[1,2]	n/a	n/a	n/a	n/a	n/a	n/a	n/a	n/a

Note: Freeway Travel Time Index—the ratio of travel time in the peak period to the travel time at free-flow conditions. For example, a value of 1.30 indicates a 20-minute free-flow trip takes 26 minutes in the peak (20 minutes x 1.30 = 26 minutes); (1) Covers the Midland TX urban area; (2) Rank is based on 101 larger urban areas (#1 = highest travel time index); n/a not available
Source: Texas A&M Transportation Institute, 2021 Urban Mobility Report

Public Transportation

Agency Name / Mode of Transportation	Vehicles Operated in Maximum Service[1]	Annual Unlinked Passenger Trips[2] (in thous.)	Annual Passenger Miles[3] (in thous.)
Midland-Odessa Urban Transit District			
Bus (directly operated)	12	155.3	n/a
Commuter Bus (directly operated)	2	9.6	n/a
Demand Response (directly operated)	7	19.1	n/a

Note: (1) Number of revenue vehicles operated by the given mode and type of service to meet the annual maximum service requirement. This is the revenue vehicle count during the peak season of the year; on the week and day that maximum service is provided. Vehicles operated in maximum service (VOMS) exclude atypical days and one-time special events; (2) Number of passengers who boarded public transportation vehicles. Passengers are counted each time they board a vehicle no matter how many vehicles they use to travel from their origin to their destination. (3) Sum of the distances ridden by all passengers during the entire fiscal year.
Source: Federal Transit Administration, National Transit Database, 2021

Air Transportation

Airport Name and Code / Type of Service	Passenger Airlines[1]	Passenger Enplanements	Freight Carriers[2]	Freight (lbs)
Midland International Airport (MAF)				
Domestic service (U.S. carriers - 2022)	13	633,792	5	2,844,269
International service (U.S. carriers - 2021)	0	0	0	0

Note: (1) Includes all U.S.-based major, minor and commuter airlines that carried at least one passenger during the year; (2) Includes all U.S.-based airlines and freight carriers that transported at least one pound of freight during the year.
Source: Bureau of Transportation Statistics, The Intermodal Transportation Database, Air Carriers: T-100 Domestic Market (U.S. Carriers), 2022; Bureau of Transportation Statistics, The Intermodal Transportation Database, Air Carriers: T-100 International Market (U.S. Carriers), 2021

BUSINESSES

Major Business Headquarters

Company Name	Industry	Rankings Fortune[1]	Forbes[2]
Diamondback Energy	Oil and natural gas	479	-

Note: (1) Companies that produce a 10-K are ranked 1 to 500 based on 2021 revenue; (2) All private companies with at least $2 billion in annual revenue through the end of their most current fiscal year are ranked 1 to 246; companies listed are headquartered in the city; dashes indicate no ranking
Source: Fortune, "Fortune 500," 2022; Forbes, "America's Largest Private Companies," 2022

Living Environment

COST OF LIVING

Cost of Living Index

Composite Index	Groceries	Housing	Utilities	Transportation	Health Care	Misc. Goods/Services
90.6	87.4	77.1	96.1	92.4	92.5	101.1

Note: The Cost of Living Index measures regional differences in the cost of consumer goods and services, excluding taxes and non-consumer expenditures, for professional and managerial households in the top income quintile. It is based on more than 50,000 prices covering almost 60 different items for which prices are collected three times a year by chambers of commerce, economic development organizations or university applied economic centers in each participating urban area. The numbers shown should be read as a percentage above or below the national average of 100. For example, a value of 115.4 in the groceries column indicates that grocery prices are 15.4% higher than the national average. Small differences in the index numbers should not be interpreted as significant; Figures cover the Midland TX urban area.
Source: The Council for Community and Economic Research, Cost of Living Index, 2022

Grocery Prices

Area[1]	T-Bone Steak ($/pound)	Frying Chicken ($/pound)	Whole Milk ($/half gal.)	Eggs ($/dozen)	Orange Juice ($/64 oz.)	Coffee ($/11.5 oz.)
City[2]	12.66	1.09	2.11	2.23	3.77	4.78
Avg.	13.81	1.59	2.43	2.25	3.85	4.95
Min.	10.17	0.90	1.51	1.30	2.90	3.46
Max.	19.35	3.30	4.32	4.32	5.31	8.59

Note: (1) Values for the local area are compared with the average, minimum and maximum values for all 286 areas in the Cost of Living Index; (2) Figures cover the Midland TX urban area; *T-Bone Steak* (price per pound); *Frying Chicken* (price per pound, whole fryer); *Whole Milk* (half gallon carton); *Eggs* (price per dozen, Grade A, large); *Orange Juice* (64 oz. Tropicana or Florida Natural); *Coffee* (11.5 oz. can, vacuum-packed, Maxwell House, Hills Bros, or Folgers).
Source: The Council for Community and Economic Research, Cost of Living Index, 2022

Housing and Utility Costs

Area[1]	New Home Price ($)	Apartment Rent ($/month)	All Electric ($/month)	Part Electric ($/month)	Other Energy ($/month)	Telephone ($/month)
City[2]	366,614	927	-	121.06	40.30	195.66
Avg.	450,913	1,371	176.41	99.93	76.96	190.22
Min.	229,283	546	100.84	31.56	27.15	174.27
Max.	2,434,977	4,569	356.86	249.59	272.24	208.31

Note: (1) Values for the local area are compared with the average, minimum and maximum values for all 286 areas in the Cost of Living Index; (2) Figures cover the Midland TX urban area; *New Home Price* (2,400 sf living area, 8,000 sf lot, in urban area with full utilities); *Apartment Rent* (950 sf 2 bedroom/1.5 or 2 bath, unfurnished, excluding all utilities except water); *All Electric* (average monthly cost for an all-electric home); *Part Electric* (average monthly cost for a part-electric home); *Other Energy* (average monthly cost for natural gas, fuel oil, coal, wood, and any other forms of energy except electricity); *Telephone* (price includes the base monthly rate plus taxes and fees for three lines of mobile phone service).
Source: The Council for Community and Economic Research, Cost of Living Index, 2022

Health Care, Transportation, and Other Costs

Area[1]	Doctor ($/visit)	Dentist ($/visit)	Optometrist ($/visit)	Gasoline ($/gallon)	Beauty Salon ($/visit)	Men's Shirt ($)
City[2]	118.20	107.50	108.50	3.51	45.00	25.17
Avg.	124.91	107.77	117.66	3.86	43.31	34.21
Min.	36.61	58.25	51.79	2.90	22.18	13.05
Max.	250.21	162.58	371.96	5.54	85.61	63.54

Note: (1) Values for the local area are compared with the average, minimum and maximum values for all 286 areas in the Cost of Living Index; (2) Figures cover the Midland TX urban area; *Doctor* (general practitioners routine exam of an established patient); *Dentist* (adult teeth cleaning and periodic oral examination); *Optometrist* (full vision eye exam for established adult patient); *Gasoline* (one gallon regular unleaded, national brand, including all taxes, cash price at self-service pump if available); *Beauty Salon* (woman's shampoo, trim, and blow-dry); *Men's Shirt* (cotton/polyester dress shirt, pinpoint weave, long sleeves).
Source: The Council for Community and Economic Research, Cost of Living Index, 2022

HOUSING

Homeownership Rate

Area	2015 (%)	2016 (%)	2017 (%)	2018 (%)	2019 (%)	2020 (%)	2021 (%)	2022 (%)
MSA[1]	n/a	n/a	n/a	n/a	n/a	n/a	n/a	n/a
U.S.	63.7	63.4	63.9	64.4	64.6	66.6	65.5	65.8

Note: (1) Figures cover the Midland, TX Metropolitan Statistical Area; n/a not available
Source: U.S. Census Bureau, Housing Vacancies and Homeownership Annual Statistics: 2015-2022

House Price Index (HPI)

Area	National Ranking[2]	Quarterly Change (%)	One-Year Change (%)	Five-Year Change (%)	Since 1991Q1 (%)
MSA[1]	n/a	n/a	n/a	n/a	n/a
U.S.[3]	—	0.34	8.41	58.44	289.08

Note: The HPI is a weighted repeat sales index. It measures average price changes in repeat sales or refinancings on the same properties. This information is obtained by reviewing repeat mortgage transactions on single-family properties whose mortgages have been purchased or securitized by Fannie Mae or Freddie Mac since January 1975; (1) Figures cover the , Metropolitan Statistical Area; (2) Rankings are based on annual percentage change for all metro areas containing at least 15,000 transactions over the last 10 years and ranges from 1 to 257; (3) figures based on a weighted average of Census Division estimates using a seasonally adjusted, purchase-only index; all figures are for the period ending December 31, 2022; n/a not available
Source: Federal Housing Finance Agency, Change in FHFA Metropolitan Area House Price Indexes, 2022Q4

Median Single-Family Home Prices

Area	2020	2021	2022p	Percent Change 2021 to 2022
MSA[1]	n/a	n/a	n/a	n/a
U.S. Average	300.2	357.1	392.6	9.9

Note: Figures are median sales prices of existing single-family homes in thousands of dollars; (p) preliminary; n/a not available; (1) Figures cover the Midland, TX Metropolitan Statistical Area
Source: National Association of Realtors, Median Sales Price of Existing Single-Family Homes for Metropolitan Areas, 4th Quarter 2022

Qualifying Income Based on Median Sales Price of Existing Single-Family Homes

Area	With 5% Down ($)	With 10% Down ($)	With 20% Down ($)
MSA[1]	n/a	n/a	n/a
U.S. Average	112,234	106,237	94,513

Note: Figures are preliminary; Qualifying income is based on a mortgage rate of 6.77%. Monthly principal and interest payment is limited to 25% of income; n/a not available; (1) Figures cover the Midland, TX Metropolitan Statistical Area
Source: National Association of Realtors, Qualifying Income Based on Median Sales Price of Existing Single-Family Homes for Metropolitan Areas, 4th Quarter 2022

Home Value

Area	Under $100,000	$100,000-$199,999	$200,000-$299,999	$300,000-$399,999	$400,000-$499,999	$500,000-$999,999	$1,000,000 or more	Median ($)
City	11.2	22.4	32.5	17.2	6.3	8.8	1.5	250,300
MSA[1]	16.5	20.8	29.5	16.1	6.9	8.7	1.4	243,400
U.S.	16.2	24.2	20.1	13.6	8.3	13.6	4.1	244,900

Note: Figures are percentages except for median and cover owner-occupied housing units; (1) Figures cover the Midland, TX Metropolitan Statistical Area
Source: U.S. Census Bureau, 2017-2021 American Community Survey 5-Year Estimates

Year Housing Structure Built

Area	2020 or Later	2010-2019	2000-2009	1990-1999	1980-1989	1970-1979	1960-1969	1950-1959	1940-1949	Before 1940	Median Year
City	0.2	18.2	8.1	13.4	18.0	11.7	8.9	17.8	2.6	1.2	1984
MSA[1]	0.2	19.5	11.0	14.2	17.8	10.9	7.8	14.6	2.6	1.4	1987
U.S.	0.2	7.3	13.6	13.6	13.2	14.8	10.3	10.0	4.7	12.2	1979

Note: Figures are percentages except for Median Year; Note: (1) Figures cover the Midland, TX Metropolitan Statistical Area
Source: U.S. Census Bureau, 2017-2021 American Community Survey 5-Year Estimates

Gross Monthly Rent

Area	Under $500	$500-$999	$1,000-$1,499	$1,500-$1,999	$2,000-$2,499	$2,500-$2,999	$3,000 and up	Median ($)
City	2.8	19.5	44.3	19.5	9.2	3.6	1.1	1,273
MSA[1]	4.2	19.9	43.6	19.0	9.0	3.3	1.0	1,271
U.S.	8.1	30.5	30.8	16.8	7.3	3.1	3.5	1,163

Note: Figures are percentages except for median; Gross rent is the contract rent plus the estimated average monthly cost of utilities (electricity, gas, and water and sewer) and fuels (oil, coal, kerosene, wood, etc.) if these are paid by the renter (or paid for the renter by someone else); (1) Figures cover the Midland, TX Metropolitan Statistical Area
Source: U.S. Census Bureau, 2017-2021 American Community Survey 5-Year Estimates

HEALTH

Health Risk Factors

Category	MSA[1] (%)	U.S. (%)
Adults aged 18–64 who have any kind of health care coverage	n/a	90.9
Adults who reported being in good or better health	n/a	85.2
Adults who have been told they have high blood cholesterol	n/a	35.7
Adults who have been told they have high blood pressure	n/a	32.4
Adults who are current smokers	n/a	14.4
Adults who currently use e-cigarettes	n/a	6.7
Adults who currently use chewing tobacco, snuff, or snus	n/a	3.5
Adults who are heavy drinkers[2]	n/a	6.3
Adults who are binge drinkers[3]	n/a	15.4
Adults who are overweight (BMI 25.0 - 29.9)	n/a	34.4
Adults who are obese (BMI 30.0 - 99.8)	n/a	33.9
Adults who participated in any physical activities in the past month	n/a	76.3

Note: (1) Figures for the Midland, TX Metropolitan Statistical Area were not available.
(2) Heavy drinkers are classified as adult men having more than 14 drinks per week and adult women having more than 7 drinks per week; (3) Binge drinkers are classified as males having five or more drinks on one occasion or females having four or more drinks on one occasion
Source: Centers for Disease Control and Prevention, Behaviorial Risk Factor Surveillance System, SMART: Selected Metropolitan Area Risk Trends, 2021

Acute and Chronic Health Conditions

Category	MSA[1] (%)	U.S. (%)
Adults who have ever been told they had a heart attack	n/a	4.0
Adults who have ever been told they have angina or coronary heart disease	n/a	3.8
Adults who have ever been told they had a stroke	n/a	3.0
Adults who have ever been told they have asthma	n/a	14.9
Adults who have ever been told they have arthritis	n/a	25.8
Adults who have ever been told they have diabetes[2]	n/a	10.9
Adults who have ever been told they had skin cancer	n/a	6.6
Adults who have ever been told they had any other types of cancer	n/a	7.5
Adults who have ever been told they have COPD	n/a	6.1
Adults who have ever been told they have kidney disease	n/a	3.0
Adults who have ever been told they have a form of depression	n/a	20.5

Note: (1) Figures for the Midland, TX Metropolitan Statistical Area were not available.
(2) Figures do not include pregnancy-related, borderline, or pre-diabetes
Source: Centers for Disease Control and Prevention, Behaviorial Risk Factor Surveillance System, SMART: Selected Metropolitan Area Risk Trends, 2021

Health Screening and Vaccination Rates

Category	MSA[1] (%)	U.S. (%)
Adults who have ever been tested for HIV	n/a	34.9
Adults who have had their blood cholesterol checked within the last five years	n/a	85.2
Adults aged 65+ who have had flu shot within the past year	n/a	68.6
Adults aged 65+ who have ever had a pneumonia vaccination	n/a	71.0

Note: (1) Figures for the Midland, TX Metropolitan Statistical Area were not available.
Source: Centers for Disease Control and Prevention, Behaviorial Risk Factor Surveillance System, SMART: Selected Metropolitan Area Risk Trends, 2021

Disability Status

Category	MSA[1] (%)	U.S. (%)
Adults who reported being deaf	n/a	7.2
Are you blind or have serious difficulty seeing, even when wearing glasses?	n/a	4.8
Are you limited in any way in any of your usual activities due to arthritis?	n/a	11.1
Do you have difficulty doing errands alone?	n/a	7.0
Do you have difficulty dressing or bathing?	n/a	3.6
Do you have serious difficulty concentrating/remembering/making decisions?	n/a	12.1
Do you have serious difficulty walking or climbing stairs?	n/a	12.8

Note: (1) Figures for the Midland, TX Metropolitan Statistical Area were not available.
Source: Centers for Disease Control and Prevention, Behaviorial Risk Factor Surveillance System, SMART: Selected Metropolitan Area Risk Trends, 2021

Mortality Rates for the Top 10 Causes of Death in the U.S.

ICD-10[a] Sub-Chapter	ICD-10[a] Code	Crude Mortality Rate[1] per 100,000 population County[2]	U.S.
Malignant neoplasms	C00-C97	117.3	182.6
Ischaemic heart diseases	I20-I25	90.1	113.1
Other forms of heart disease	I30-I51	36.4	64.4
Other degenerative diseases of the nervous system	G30-G31	66.8	51.0
Cerebrovascular diseases	I60-I69	36.7	47.8
Other external causes of accidental injury	W00-X59	23.9	46.4
Chronic lower respiratory diseases	J40-J47	34.1	45.7
Organic, including symptomatic, mental disorders	F01-F09	6.7	35.9
Hypertensive diseases	I10-I15	19.1	35.0
Diabetes mellitus	E10-E14	23.3	29.6

Note: (a) ICD-10 = International Classification of Diseases 10th Revision; (1) Crude mortality rates are a three-year average covering 2019-2021; (2) Figures cover Midland County.
Source: Centers for Disease Control and Prevention, National Center for Health Statistics. National Vital Statistics System, Mortality 2018-2021 on CDC WONDER Online Database

Mortality Rates for Selected Causes of Death

ICD-10[a] Sub-Chapter	ICD-10[a] Code	Crude Mortality Rate[1] per 100,000 population County[2]	U.S.
Assault	X85-Y09	7.3	7.0
Diseases of the liver	K70-K76	21.4	19.8
Human immunodeficiency virus (HIV) disease	B20-B24	Unreliable	1.5
Influenza and pneumonia	J09-J18	15.7	14.7
Intentional self-harm	X60-X84	17.6	14.3
Malnutrition	E40-E46	5.7	4.3
Obesity and other hyperalimentation	E65-E68	4.8	3.0
Renal failure	N17-N19	9.8	15.7
Transport accidents	V01-V99	18.8	13.6
Viral hepatitis	B15-B19	Suppressed	1.2

Note: (a) ICD-10 = International Classification of Diseases 10th Revision; (1) Crude mortality rates are a three-year average covering 2019-2021; (2) Figures cover Midland County; Data are suppressed when the data meet the criteria for confidentiality constraints; Crude mortality rates are flagged as unreliable when the rate would be calculated with a numerator of 20 or less.
Source: Centers for Disease Control and Prevention, National Center for Health Statistics. National Vital Statistics System, Mortality 2018-2021 on CDC WONDER Online Database

Health Insurance Coverage

Area	With Health Insurance	With Private Health Insurance	With Public Health Insurance	Without Health Insurance	Population Under Age 19 Without Health Insurance
City	83.5	69.9	20.7	16.5	14.2
MSA[1]	84.0	69.8	21.3	16.0	13.0
U.S.	91.2	67.8	35.4	8.8	5.3

Note: Figures are percentages that cover the civilian noninstitutionalized population; (1) Figures cover the Midland, TX Metropolitan Statistical Area
Source: U.S. Census Bureau, 2017-2021 American Community Survey 5-Year Estimates

Number of Medical Professionals

Area	MDs[3]	DOs[3,4]	Dentists	Podiatrists	Chiropractors	Optometrists
County[1] (number)	268	13	107	4	22	21
County[1] (rate[2])	157.4	7.6	63.7	2.4	13.1	12.5
U.S. (rate[2])	289.3	23.5	72.5	6.2	28.7	17.4

Note: Data as of 2021 unless noted; (1) Data covers Midland County; (2) Rate per 100,000 population; (3) Data as of 2020 and includes all active, non-federal physicians; (4) Doctor of Osteopathic Medicine
Source: U.S. Department of Health and Human Services, Health Resources and Services Administration, Bureau of Health Professions, Area Resource File (ARF) 2021-2022

EDUCATION

Public School District Statistics

District Name	Schls	Pupils	Pupil/ Teacher Ratio	Minority Pupils[1] (%)	LEP/ELL[2] (%)	IEP[3] (%)
Greenwood ISD	4	3,089	14.7	52.8	7.8	8.8
Midland ISD	41	26,398	15.8	77.3	11.8	7.8

Note: Table includes school districts with 2,000 or more students; (1) Percentage of students that are not non-Hispanic white; (2) Percentage of students that are Limited English Proficient or English Language Learners (2018-19); (3) Percentage of students that have an Individualized Education Program (2019-20).
Source: U.S. Department of Education, National Center for Education Statistics, Common Core of Data, Local Education Agency (School District) Universe Survey: School Year 2021-2022

Highest Level of Education

Area	Less than H.S.	H.S. Diploma	Some College, No Deg.	Associate Degree	Bachelor's Degree	Master's Degree	Prof. School Degree	Doctorate Degree
City	15.5	23.4	22.1	8.1	22.5	6.4	1.4	0.6
MSA[1]	15.6	24.5	23.1	8.2	20.0	6.8	1.2	0.5
U.S.	11.1	26.5	20.0	8.7	20.6	9.3	2.2	1.5

Note: Figures cover persons age 25 and over; (1) Figures cover the Midland, TX Metropolitan Statistical Area
Source: U.S. Census Bureau, 2017-2021 American Community Survey 5-Year Estimates

Educational Attainment by Race

Area	High School Graduate or Higher (%)					Bachelor's Degree or Higher (%)				
	Total	White	Black	Asian	Hisp.[2]	Total	White	Black	Asian	Hisp.[2]
City	84.5	88.0	88.2	72.1	71.2	30.9	35.0	16.2	45.8	15.5
MSA[1]	84.4	87.4	89.1	75.0	71.5	28.5	31.3	16.7	51.6	14.1
U.S.	88.9	91.4	87.2	87.6	71.2	33.7	35.5	23.3	55.6	18.4

Note: Figures shown cover persons 25 years old and over; (1) Figures cover the Midland, TX Metropolitan Statistical Area; (2) People of Hispanic origin can be of any race
Source: U.S. Census Bureau, 2017-2021 American Community Survey 5-Year Estimates

School Enrollment by Grade and Control

Area	Preschool (%)		Kindergarten (%)		Grades 1 - 4 (%)		Grades 5 - 8 (%)		Grades 9 - 12 (%)	
	Public	Private	Public	Private	Public	Private	Public	Private	Public	Private
City	70.6	29.4	83.7	16.3	83.1	16.9	77.6	22.4	83.9	16.1
MSA[1]	75.7	24.3	79.8	20.2	83.8	16.2	82.0	18.0	85.2	14.8
U.S.	58.8	41.2	86.3	13.7	88.3	11.7	88.6	11.4	89.4	10.6

Note: Figures shown cover persons 3 years old and over; (1) Figures cover the Midland, TX Metropolitan Statistical Area
Source: U.S. Census Bureau, 2017-2021 American Community Survey 5-Year Estimates

Higher Education

Four-Year Colleges			Two-Year Colleges			Medical Schools[1]	Law Schools[2]	Voc/Tech[3]
Public	Private Non-profit	Private For-profit	Public	Private Non-profit	Private For-profit			
1	0	0	0	0	0	0	0	0

Note: Figures cover institutions located within the Midland, TX Metropolitan Statistical Area and include main campuses only; (1) includes schools accredited by the Liaison Committee on Medical Education and the American Osteopathic Association's Commission on Osteopathic College Accreditation; (2) includes ABA-accredited schools, schools with provisional ABA accreditation, and state accredited schools; (3) includes all schools with programs that are less than 2 years.
Source: National Center for Education Statistics, Integrated Postsecondary Education System (IPEDS), 2021-22; Wikipedia, List of Medical Schools in the United States, accessed April 10, 2023; Wikipedia, List of Law Schools in the United States, accessed April 10, 2023

Midland, Texas

EMPLOYERS

Major Employers

Company Name	Industry
Albertsons Companies	Grocery stores
Bobby Cox Companies	Retail, restaurants
City of Odessa	Municipal government
Cudd Energy	Oil & gas
Dixie Electric	Electric
Ector County	Government
Ector County ISD	Public education
Family Dollar	Distribution
Halliburton Services	Oil & gas
HEB	Grocery stores
Holloman Construction	Oil field construction
Investment Corp. of America	Financial services
Lithia Motors	Automotive
Medical Center Hospital	County hospital
Nurses Unlimited	Medical
Odessa College	Education
Odessa Regional Medical Center	Medical
REXtac	Manufacturer
Saulsbury Companies	Electric & construction
Sewell Family of Dealerships	Automotive
Southwest Convenience Stores	Retail, service
Texas Tech University Health Sci Ctr	Education/medical
The University of Texas Permian Basin	Education
Wal-Mart Stores	Retail
Weatherford	Oil & gas

Note: Companies shown are located within the Midland, TX Metropolitan Statistical Area.
Source: Hoovers.com; Wikipedia

PUBLIC SAFETY

Crime Rate

Area	Total Crime	Violent Crime Rate - Murder	Rape[3]	Robbery	Aggrav. Assault	Property Crime Rate - Burglary	Larceny-Theft	Motor Vehicle Theft
City	2,436.7	6.6	53.8	33.2	271.0	268.4	1,494.1	309.6
Suburbs[1]	2,973.5	8.2	30.0	13.6	360.1	349.2	1,606.8	605.6
Metro[2]	2,541.9	6.9	49.1	29.4	288.5	284.2	1,516.1	367.5
U.S.	2,356.7	6.5	38.4	73.9	279.7	314.2	1,398.0	246.0

Note: Figures are crimes per 100,000 population; (1) All areas within the metro area that are located outside the city limits; (2) Figures cover the Midland, TX Metropolitan Statistical Area; (3) All figures shown were reported using the revised Uniform Crime Reporting (UCR) definition of rape; Due to the transition to the National Incident-Based Reporting System (NIBRS), limited city and metro area data was released for 2021.
Source: FBI Uniform Crime Reports, 2020

Hate Crimes

Area	Number of Quarters Reported	Race/Ethnicity/Ancestry	Religion	Sexual Orientation	Disability	Gender	Gender Identity
City	4	1	0	0	0	0	0
U.S.	4	5,227	1,244	1,110	130	75	266

Note: Due to the transition to the National Incident-Based Reporting System (NIBRS), limited crime data was released for 2021.
Source: Federal Bureau of Investigation, Hate Crime Statistics 2020

Identity Theft Consumer Reports

Area	Reports	Reports per 100,000 Population	Rank[2]
MSA[1]	342	193	179
U.S.	1,108,609	339	-

Note: (1) Figures cover the Midland, TX Metropolitan Statistical Area; (2) Rank ranges from 1 to 391 where 1 indicates greatest number of identity theft reports per 100,000 population
Source: Federal Trade Commission, Consumer Sentinel Network Data Book 2022

Fraud and Other Consumer Reports

Area	Reports	Reports per 100,000 Population	Rank[2]
MSA[1]	1,297	733	270
U.S.	4,064,520	1,245	-

Note: (1) Figures cover the Midland, TX Metropolitan Statistical Area; (2) Rank ranges from 1 to 391 where 1 indicates greatest number of fraud and other consumer reports per 100,000 population
Source: Federal Trade Commission, Consumer Sentinel Network Data Book 2022

Midland, Texas

POLITICS

2020 Presidential Election Results

Area	Biden	Trump	Jorgensen	Hawkins	Other
Midland County	20.9	77.3	1.3	0.2	0.2
U.S.	51.3	46.8	1.2	0.3	0.5

Note: Results are percentages and may not add to 100% due to rounding
Source: Dave Leip's Atlas of U.S. Presidential Elections

SPORTS

Professional Sports Teams

Team Name	League	Year Established

No teams are located in the metro area
Source: Wikipedia, Major Professional Sports Teams of the United States and Canada, April 12, 2023

CLIMATE

Average and Extreme Temperatures

Temperature	Jan	Feb	Mar	Apr	May	Jun	Jul	Aug	Sep	Oct	Nov	Dec	Yr.
Extreme High (°F)	84	90	95	101	108	116	112	107	107	100	89	85	116
Average High (°F)	57	62	70	79	86	93	94	93	86	78	66	59	77
Average Temp. (°F)	43	48	55	64	73	80	82	81	74	65	53	46	64
Average Low (°F)	30	34	40	49	59	67	69	68	62	51	39	32	50
Extreme Low (°F)	-8	-11	9	20	34	47	53	54	36	24	13	-1	-11

Note: Figures cover the years 1948-1995
Source: National Climatic Data Center, International Station Meteorological Climate Summary, 9/96

Average Precipitation/Snowfall/Humidity

Precip./Humidity	Jan	Feb	Mar	Apr	May	Jun	Jul	Aug	Sep	Oct	Nov	Dec	Yr.
Avg. Precip. (in.)	0.6	0.6	0.5	0.8	2.1	1.6	1.9	1.7	2.1	1.6	0.6	0.5	14.6
Avg. Snowfall (in.)	2	1	Tr	Tr	0	0	0	0	0	Tr	Tr	1	4
Avg. Rel. Hum. 6am (%)	72	72	65	67	75	76	73	74	79	78	74	71	73
Avg. Rel. Hum. 3pm (%)	38	35	27	27	31	32	34	34	40	37	35	37	34

Note: Figures cover the years 1948-1995; Tr = Trace amounts (<0.05 in. of rain; <0.5 in. of snow)
Source: National Climatic Data Center, International Station Meteorological Climate Summary, 9/96

Weather Conditions

Temperature			Daytime Sky			Precipitation		
10°F & below	32°F & below	90°F & above	Clear	Partly cloudy	Cloudy	0.01 inch or more precip.	0.1 inch or more snow/ice	Thunder-storms
1	62	102	144	138	83	52	3	38

Note: Figures are average number of days per year and cover the years 1948-1995
Source: National Climatic Data Center, International Station Meteorological Climate Summary, 9/96

HAZARDOUS WASTE

Superfund Sites

The Midland, TX metro area is home to one site on the EPA's Superfund National Priorities List: **Midessa Ground Water Plume** (final). There are a total of 1,165 Superfund sites with a status of proposed or final on the list in the U.S. *U.S. Environmental Protection Agency, National Priorities List, April 12, 2023*

AIR QUALITY

Air Quality Trends: Ozone

	1990	1995	2000	2005	2010	2015	2018	2019	2020	2021
MSA[1]	n/a	n/a	n/a	n/a	n/a	n/a	n/a	n/a	n/a	n/a
U.S.	0.087	0.089	0.081	0.080	0.072	0.067	0.069	0.065	0.065	0.067

Note: (1) Data covers the Midland, TX Metropolitan Statistical Area; n/a not available. The values shown are the composite ozone concentration averages among trend sites based on the highest fourth daily maximum 8-hour concentration in parts per million. These trends are based on sites having an adequate record of monitoring data during the trend period. Data from exceptional events are included.
Source: U.S. Environmental Protection Agency, Air Quality Monitoring Information, "Air Quality Trends by City, 1990-2021"

Air Quality Index

Area	Percent of Days when Air Quality was...[2]					AQI Statistics[2]	
	Good	Moderate	Unhealthy for Sensitive Groups	Unhealthy	Very Unhealthy	Maximum	Median
MSA[1]	n/a	n/a	n/a	n/a	n/a	n/a	n/a

Note: (1) Data covers the Midland, TX Metropolitan Statistical Area; (2) Based on days with AQI data in 2021. Air Quality Index (AQI) is an index for reporting daily air quality. EPA calculates the AQI for five major air pollutants regulated by the Clean Air Act: ground-level ozone, particle pollution (aka particulate matter), carbon monoxide, sulfur dioxide, and nitrogen dioxide. The AQI runs from 0 to 500. The higher the AQI value, the greater the level of air pollution and the greater the health concern. There are six AQI categories: "Good" AQI is between 0 and 50. Air quality is considered satisfactory; "Moderate" AQI is between 51 and 100. Air quality is acceptable; "Unhealthy for Sensitive Groups" When AQI values are between 101 and 150, members of sensitive groups may experience health effects; "Unhealthy" When AQI values are between 151 and 200 everyone may begin to experience health effects; "Very Unhealthy" AQI values between 201 and 300 trigger a health alert; "Hazardous" AQI values over 300 trigger warnings of emergency conditions (not shown).
Source: U.S. Environmental Protection Agency, Air Quality Index Report, 2021

Air Quality Index Pollutants

Area	Percent of Days when AQI Pollutant was...[2]					
	Carbon Monoxide	Nitrogen Dioxide	Ozone	Sulfur Dioxide	Particulate Matter 2.5	Particulate Matter 10
MSA[1]	n/a	n/a	n/a	(3)	n/a	n/a

Note: (1) Data covers the Midland, TX Metropolitan Statistical Area; (2) Based on days with AQI data in 2021. The Air Quality Index (AQI) is an index for reporting daily air quality. EPA calculates the AQI for five major air pollutants regulated by the Clean Air Act: ground-level ozone, particle pollution (also known as particulate matter), carbon monoxide, sulfur dioxide, and nitrogen dioxide. The AQI runs from 0 to 500. The higher the AQI value, the greater the level of air pollution and the greater the health concern; (3) Sulfur dioxide is no longer included in this table (as of December 8, 2021) because SO_2 concentrations tend to be very localized and not necessarily representative of broad geographical areas like counties and CBSAs.
Source: U.S. Environmental Protection Agency, Air Quality Index Report, 2021

Maximum Air Pollutant Concentrations: Particulate Matter, Ozone, CO and Lead

	Particulate Matter 10 (ug/m³)	Particulate Matter 2.5 Wtd AM (ug/m³)	Particulate Matter 2.5 24-Hr (ug/m³)	Ozone (ppm)	Carbon Monoxide (ppm)	Lead (ug/m³)
MSA[1] Level	n/a	n/a	n/a	n/a	n/a	n/a
NAAQS[2]	150	15	35	0.075	9	0.15
Met NAAQS[2]	Yes	Yes	Yes	Yes	Yes	Yes

Note: (1) Data covers the Midland, TX Metropolitan Statistical Area; Data from exceptional events are included; (2) National Ambient Air Quality Standards; ppm = parts per million; ug/m³ = micrograms per cubic meter; n/a not available.
Concentrations: Particulate Matter 10 (coarse particulate)—highest second maximum 24-hour concentration; Particulate Matter 2.5 Wtd AM (fine particulate)—highest weighted annual mean concentration; Particulate Matter 2.5 24-Hour (fine particulate)—highest 98th percentile 24-hour concentration; Ozone—highest fourth daily maximum 8-hour concentration; Carbon Monoxide—highest second maximum non-overlapping 8-hour concentration; Lead—maximum running 3-month average
Source: U.S. Environmental Protection Agency, Air Quality Monitoring Information, "Air Quality Statistics by City, 2021"

Maximum Air Pollutant Concentrations: Nitrogen Dioxide and Sulfur Dioxide

	Nitrogen Dioxide AM (ppb)	Nitrogen Dioxide 1-Hr (ppb)	Sulfur Dioxide AM (ppb)	Sulfur Dioxide 1-Hr (ppb)	Sulfur Dioxide 24-Hr (ppb)
MSA[1] Level	n/a	n/a	n/a	n/a	n/a
NAAQS[2]	53	100	30	75	140
Met NAAQS[2]	Yes	Yes	Yes	Yes	Yes

Note: (1) Data covers the Midland, TX Metropolitan Statistical Area; Data from exceptional events are included; (2) National Ambient Air Quality Standards; ppm = parts per million; ug/m³ = micrograms per cubic meter; n/a not available.
Concentrations: Nitrogen Dioxide AM—highest arithmetic mean concentration; Nitrogen Dioxide 1-Hr—highest 98th percentile 1-hour daily maximum concentration; Sulfur Dioxide AM—highest annual mean concentration; Sulfur Dioxide 1-Hr—highest 99th percentile 1-hour daily maximum concentration; Sulfur Dioxide 24-Hr—highest second maximum 24-hour concentration
Source: U.S. Environmental Protection Agency, Air Quality Monitoring Information, "Air Quality Statistics by City, 2021"

Nashville, Tennessee

Background

Nashville, the capital of Tennessee, was founded on Christmas Day in 1779 by James Robertson and John Donelson and is considered the country music capital of the world. It is home to the Grand Ole Opry—the longest-running radio show in the country—with millions of devoted listeners. It is no wonder, given how profoundly this industry has touched people, names like Dolly, Chet, Loretta, Hank, and Johnny are more familiar than the city's true native sons—Andrew Jackson, James Polk, and Sam Houston.

Nashville is home to Music Row, an area just to the southwest of downtown with hundreds of businesses related to the country music, gospel music, and contemporary Christian music industries. The USA Network's *Nashville Star*, a country music singing competition, is held in the Acuff Theatre. The magnitude of Nashville's recording industry is impressive, but other industries important to the city include health care management, automobile production, and printing and publishing.

The city is consistently ranked a high job-growth region and has been called "Nowville" and "It City." Nashville's first female mayor, Megan Barry, performed the city's first same-sex wedding in Nashville. The city recently received accolades for its economy and robust housing market.

Amazon's two new towers in downtown are nearly done, bringing with them more than 5,000 jobs. Global financial firm Alliance Bernstein moved its headquarters from New York to Nashville in 2021 and hired 1,250.

Nashville is a devoted patron of education. The Davidson Academy, forerunner of the George Peabody College for Teachers, was founded in Nashville, as were Vanderbilt and Fisk universities, the latter being the first private black university in the United States. Vanderbilt University and Medical Center is the region's largest non-governmental employer.

Nashville citizens take pride in their museums, including the Adventure Science Center, with its Sudekum Planetarium; the Aaron Douglas Gallery at Fisk University, which features a remarkable collection of African American art; and the Carl Van Vechten Gallery, also at Fisk University, home to works by Alfred Stieglitz, Picasso, Cezanne, and Georgia O'Keefe. The Cheekwood Botanical Garden and Museum of Art includes 55 acres of gardens and contemporary art galleries.

The city's majestic mansions and plantations testify to the nineteenth-century splendor for which the South is famous. The Belle Meade Plantation is an 1853 Greek Revival mansion crowning a 5,400-acre thoroughbred stud farm and nursery. The Belmont Mansion, built in 1850 by Adelicia Acklen, one of the wealthiest women in America, is constructed in the style of an Italian villa and was originally intended to be the summer home of the Acklens. Travelers' Rest Plantation, built in 1799, is Nashville's oldest plantation home open to the public. Carnton Plantation was the site of the Civil War's Battle of Franklin, and The Hermitage was the home of Andrew Jackson, the seventh president of the United States. Tennessee's historic State Capitol Building, completed in 1859, has had much of its interior restored to its nineteenth-century splendor.

The Nashville area comprises many urban, suburban, rural, and historic districts, which differ immensely from each other. Many restaurants, clubs, and shops are on the west side of the Cumberland River, while the east side encompasses fine neighborhoods, interesting homes, and upscale shopping. The club, CabaRay, opened in 2018, as a performance venue for American singer/songwriter Ray Stevens.

Plans for Amtrak service out of Nashville are being studied, with the goal of connecting Nashville to Atlanta through Murfreesboro, Tullahoma, and Chattanooga. Nashville is the third-largest city in the country without Amtrak service.

Outdoor activities include camping, fishing, hiking, and biking at the many scenic and accessible lakes in the region. Sports action in the city include the Tennessee Titans winning their fourth division championship in 2020, and the Nashville Super Speedway hosting their first NASCAR Cup Series in 2021.

Located on the Cumberland River in central Tennessee, Nashville's average relative humidity is moderate, as is its weather, with great temperature extremes a rarity. The city is not in the common path of storms that cross the country, but a tornado killed 25 in 2020.

Rankings

General Rankings

- *US News & World Report* conducted a survey of more than 3,600 people and analyzed the 150 largest metropolitan areas to determine what matters most when selecting where to settle down. Nashville ranked #25 out of the top 25 as having the best combination of desirable factors. Criteria: cost of living; quality of life and education; net migration; job market; desirability; and other factors. *money.usnews.com, "The 25 Best Places to Live in the U.S. in 2022-2023," May 17, 2022*

- *Insider* listed 23 places in the U.S. that travel industry trends reveal would be popular destinations in 2023. This year the list trends towards cultural and historical happenings, sports events, wellness experiences and invigorating outdoor escapes. According to the website insider.com Nashville is a place to visit in 2023. *Insider, "23 of the Best Places You Should Travel to in the U.S. in 2023," December 17, 2022*

- The Nashville metro area was identified as one of America's fastest-growing areas in terms of population and business growth by *MagnifyMoney*. The area ranked #5 out of 35. The 100 most populous metro areas in the U.S. were evaluated on their change from 2011 to 2016 in the following categories: people and housing; workforce and employment opportunities; growing industry. *www.businessinsider.com, "The 35 Cities in the US with the Biggest Influx of People, the Most Work Opportunities, and the Hottest Business Growth," August 12, 2018*

- The Nashville metro area was identified as one of America's fastest-growing areas in terms of population and economy by *Forbes*. The area ranked #7 out of 25. The 100 most populous metro areas in the U.S. were evaluated on the following criteria: estimated population growth; employment; economic output; wages; home values. *Forbes, "America's Fastest-Growing Cities 2018," February 28, 2018*

- Nashville appeared on *Travel + Leisure's* list of "The 15 Best Cities in the United States." The city was ranked #15. Criteria: sights/landmarks; culture; food; friendliness; shopping; and overall value. *Travel + Leisure, "The World's Best Awards 2022" July 12, 2022*

- For its 35th annual "Readers' Choice Awards" survey, *Condé Nast Traveler* ranked its readers' favorite cities in the U.S. Whether it be a longed-for visit or a first on the list, these are the places that inspired a return to travel. The list was broken into large cities and cities under 250,000. Nashville ranked #4 in the big city category. *Condé Nast Traveler, Readers' Choice Awards 2022, "Best Big Cities in the U.S." October 4, 2022*

Business/Finance Rankings

- The Brookings Institution ranked the nation's largest cities based on income inequality. Nashville was ranked #83 (#1 = greatest inequality). Criteria: the "95/20 ratio," a figure representing the income at which a household earns more than 95 percent of all other households, divided by the income at which a household earns more than only 20 percent of all other households. *Brookings Institution, "Household Income Inequality, Largest Cities of 97 Large U.S. Metro Areas, 2014-2016," February 5, 2018*

- The Brookings Institution ranked the 100 largest metro areas in the U.S. based on income inequality. Nashville was ranked #78 (#1 = greatest inequality). Criteria: the "95/20 ratio," a figure representing the income at which a household earns more than 95 percent of all other households, divided by the income at which a household earns more than only 20 percent of all other households. *Brookings Institution, "Household Income Inequality, 100 Largest U.S. Metro Areas, 2014-2016," February 5, 2018*

- Payscale.com ranked the 32 largest metro areas in terms of wage growth. The Nashville metro area ranked #7. Criteria: quarterly changes in private industry employee and education professional wage growth from the previous year. *PayScale, "Wage Trends by Metro Area-1st Quarter," April 20, 2023*

- Nashville was identified as one of America's most frugal metro areas by *Coupons.com*. The city ranked #9 out of 25. Criteria: digital coupon usage. *Coupons.com, "America's Most Frugal Cities of 2017," March 22, 2018*

- The Nashville metro area appeared on the Milken Institute "2022 Best Performing Cities" list. Rank: #25 out of 200 large metro areas (population over 250,000). Criteria: job growth; wage and salary growth; high-tech output growth; housing affordability; household broadband access. *Milken Institute, "Best-Performing Cities 2022," March 28, 2022*

- *Forbes* ranked the 200 most populous metro areas to determine the nation's "Best Places for Business and Careers." The Nashville metro area was ranked #15. Criteria: costs (business and living); job growth (past and projected); income growth; quality of life; educational attainment (college and high school); projected economic growth; cultural and leisure opportunities; workplace tolerance laws; net migration patterns. *Forbes, "The Best Places for Business and Careers 2019: Seattle Still On Top," October 30, 2019*

Children/Family Rankings

- Nashville was selected as one of the most playful cities in the U.S. by KaBOOM! The organization's Playful City USA initiative honors cities and towns across the nation that have made their communities more playable. Criteria: pledging to integrate play as a solution to challenges in their communities; making it easy for children to get active and balanced play; creating more family-friendly and innovative communities as a result. *KaBOOM! National Campaign for Play, "2017 Playful City USA Communities"*

Dating/Romance Rankings

- Nashville was selected as one of America's best cities for singles by the readers of *Travel + Leisure* in their annual "America's Favorite Cities" survey. Criteria included good-looking locals, cool shopping, an active bar scene and hipster-magnet coffee bars. *Travel + Leisure, "Best Cities in America for Singles," July 21, 2017*

Education Rankings

- Personal finance website *WalletHub* analyzed the 150 largest U.S. metropolitan statistical areas to determine where the most educated Americans are putting their degrees to work. Criteria: education levels; percentage of workers with degrees; education quality and attainment gap; public school quality rankings; quality and enrollment of each metro area's universities. Nashville was ranked #48 (#1 = most educated city). *www.WalletHub.com, "Most & Least Educated Cities in America," July 18, 2022*

- Nashville was selected as one of America's most literate cities. The city ranked #28 out of the 84 largest U.S. cities. Criteria: number of booksellers; library resources; Internet resources; educational attainment; periodical publishing resources; newspaper circulation. *Central Connecticut State University, "America's Most Literate Cities, 2018," February 2019*

Food/Drink Rankings

- The U.S. Chamber of Commerce Foundation conducted an in-depth study on local food truck regulations, surveyed 288 food truck owners, and ranked 20 major American cities based on how friendly they are for operating a food truck. The compiled index assessed the following: procedures for obtaining permits and licenses; complying with restrictions; and financial obligations associated with operating a food truck. Nashville ranked #10 overall (1 being the best). *www.foodtrucknation.us, "Food Truck Nation," March 20, 2018*

Health/Fitness Rankings

- For each of the 100 largest cities in the United States, the American Fitness Index®, compiled in partnership between the American College of Sports Medicine and the Elevance Health Foundation, evaluated community infrastructure and 34 health behaviors including preventive health, levels of chronic disease conditions, food insecurity, sleep quality, pedestrian safety, air quality, and community/environment resources that support physical activity. Nashville ranked #63 for "community fitness." *americanfitnessindex.org, "2022 ACSM American Fitness Index Summary Report," July 12, 2022*

- The Nashville metro area was identified as one of the worst cities for bed bugs in America by pest control company Orkin. The area ranked #33 out of 50 based on the number of bed bug treatments Orkin performed from December 2021 to November 2022. *Orkin, "The Windy City Can't Blow Bed Bugs Away: Chicago Ranks #1 For Third Consecutive Year On Orkin's Bed Bug Cities List," January 9, 2023*

- Nashville was identified as a "2022 Spring Allergy Capital." The area ranked #61 out of 100. Three groups of factors were used to identify the most challenging cities for people with allergies during the spring season: annual spring pollen scores; over the counter allergy medicine use; number of board-certified allergy specialists. *Asthma and Allergy Foundation of America, "Spring Allergy Capitals 2022," March 2, 2022*

- Nashville was identified as a "2022 Fall Allergy Capital." The area ranked #59 out of 100. Three groups of factors were used to identify the most challenging cities for people with allergies during the fall season: annual fall pollen scores; over the counter allergy medicine use; number of board-certified allergy specialists. *Asthma and Allergy Foundation of America, "Fall Allergy Capitals 2022," March 2, 2022*

- Nashville was identified as a "2022 Asthma Capital." The area ranked #44 out of the nation's 100 largest metropolitan areas. Criteria: estimated asthma prevalence; asthma-related mortality; and ER visits due to asthma. Risk factors analyzed but not factored in the rankings: annual pollen score; annual air quality; public smoking laws; access to board-certified asthma specialists; rescue and controller medication use; uninsured rate; poverty rate. *Asthma and Allergy Foundation of America, "Asthma Capitals 2022: The Most Challenging Places to Live With Asthma," September 14, 2022*

Pet Rankings

- Nashville appeared on *The Dogington Post* site as one of the top cities for dog lovers, ranking #14 out of 15. The real estate marketplace, Zillow®, and Rover, the largest pet sitter and dog walker network, introduced a new list of "Top Emerging Dog-Friendly Cities" for 2021. Criteria: number of new dog accounts on the Rover platform; and rentals and listings that mention features that attract dog owners (fenced-in yards, dog houses, dog door or proximity to a dog park). *www.dogingtonpost.com, "15 Cities Emerging as Dog-Friendliest in 2021," May 11, 2021*

Real Estate Rankings

- *WalletHub* compared the most populated U.S. cities to determine which had the best markets for real estate agents. Nashville ranked #6 where demand was high and pay was the best. Criteria: sales per agent; annual median wage for real-estate agents; monthly average starting salary for real estate agents; real estate job density and competition; unemployment rate; home turnover rate; housing-market health index; and other relevant metrics. *www.WalletHub.com, "2021 Best Places to Be a Real Estate Agent," May 12, 2021*

Safety Rankings

- To identify the most dangerous cities in America, *24/7 Wall St.* focused on violent crime categories—murder, non-negligent manslaughter, rape, robbery, and aggravated assault—as reported for every 100,000 residents using data from the FBI's 2020 annual Uniform Crime Report. For cities with populations over 25,000, Nashville was ranked #47. *247wallst.com, "America's Most Dangerous Cities" November 12, 2021*

- Allstate ranked the 200 largest cities in America in terms of driver safety. Nashville ranked #108. Criteria: internal property damage claims over a two-year period from January 2016 to December 2017. The report helps increase the importance of safety and awareness behind the wheel. *Allstate, "Allstate America's Best Drivers Report, 2019" June 24, 2019*

- Nashville was identified as one of the most dangerous cities in America by NeighborhoodScout. The city ranked #52 out of 100 (#1 = most dangerous). Criteria: number of violent crimes per 1,000 residents. The editors evaluated cities with 25,000 or more residents. *NeighborhoodScout.com, "2023 Top 100 Most Dangerous Cities in the U.S.," January 12, 2023*

- The National Insurance Crime Bureau ranked 390 metro areas in the U.S. in terms of per capita rates of vehicle theft. The Nashville metro area ranked #139 (#1 = highest rate). Criteria: number of vehicle theft offenses per 100,000 inhabitants in 2021. *National Insurance Crime Bureau, "Hot Spots 2021," September 1, 2022*

Seniors/Retirement Rankings

- From its Best Cities for Successful Aging indexes, the Milken Institute generated rankings for metropolitan areas, weighing data in nine categories—health care, wellness, living arrangements, transportation and convenience, financial characteristics, education, employment, community engagement, and overall livability. The Nashville metro area was ranked #30 overall in the large metro area category. *Milken Institute, "Best Cities for Successful Aging, 2017" March 14, 2017*

Transportation Rankings

- According to the INRIX "2022 Global Traffic Scorecard," Nashville was identified as one of the most congested metro areas in the U.S. The area ranked #24 out of 25. Criteria: average annual time spent in traffic and average cost of congestion per motorist. *Inrix.com, "Return to Work, Higher Gas Prices & Inflation Drove Americans to Spend Hundreds More in Time and Money Commuting," January 10, 2023*

Women/Minorities Rankings

- *Travel + Leisure* listed the best cities in and around the U.S. for a memorable and fun girls' trip, even on a budget. Whether it is for a special occasion, to make new memories or just to get away, Nashville is sure to have something for all the ladies in your tribe. *Travel + Leisure, "25 Affordable Girls Weekend Getaways That Won't Break the Bank," November 25, 2022*

- Personal finance website *WalletHub* compared more than 180 U.S. cities across two key dimensions, "Hispanic Business-Friendliness" and "Hispanic Purchasing Power," to arrive at the most favorable conditions for Hispanic entrepreneurs. Nashville was ranked #48 out of 182. Criteria includes: share of Hispanic-Owned Businesses; Hispanic entrepreneurship rate to median annual income of Hispanics; Small Business-Friendliness score; cost of living; and number of Hispanics with at least a bachelor's degree. *WalletHub.com, "2019's Best Cities for Hispanic Entrepreneurs," May 1, 2019*

Miscellaneous Rankings

- The watchdog site, Charity Navigator, conducted a study of charities in major markets both to analyze statistical differences in their financial, accountability, and transparency practices and to track year-to-year variations in individual philanthropic communities. The Nashville metro area was ranked #26 among the 30 metro markets in the rating category of Overall Score. *www.charitynavigator.org, "2017 Metro Market Study," May 1, 2017*

- In *Condé Nast Traveler* magazine's 2022 Readers' Choice Survey, Nashville made the top ten list of friendliest American cities. Nashville ranked #8. *www.cntraveler.com, "The 10 Friendliest Cities in the U.S.," December 20, 2022*

- *WalletHub* compared the 150 most populated U.S. cities to determine their operating efficiency. A "Quality of Services" score was constructed for each city and then divided by the total budget per capita to reveal which were managed the best. Nashville ranked #114. Criteria: financial stability; economy; education; safety; health; infrastructure and pollution. *www.WalletHub.com, "2022's Best- & Worst-Run Cities in America," June 21, 2022*

- Nashville was selected as one of "America's Friendliest Cities." The city ranked #7 in the "Friendliest" category. Respondents to an online survey were asked to rate 38 top urban destinations in the United States as to general friendliness, as well as manners, politeness and warm disposition. *Travel + Leisure, "America's Friendliest Cities," October 20, 2017*

Business Environment

DEMOGRAPHICS

Population Growth

Area	1990 Census	2000 Census	2010 Census	2020 Census	Population Growth (%) 1990-2020	Population Growth (%) 2010-2020
City	488,364	545,524	601,222	689,447	41.2	14.7
MSA[1]	1,048,218	1,311,789	1,589,934	1,989,519	89.8	25.1
U.S.	248,709,873	281,421,906	308,745,538	331,449,281	33.3	7.4

Note: (1) Figures cover the Nashville-Davidson—Murfreesboro—Franklin, TN Metropolitan Statistical Area
Source: U.S. Census Bureau, 1990 Census, 2000 Census, 2010 Census, 2020 Census

Race

Area	White Alone[2] (%)	Black Alone[2] (%)	Asian Alone[2] (%)	AIAN[3] Alone[2] (%)	NHOPI[4] Alone[2] (%)	Other Race Alone[2] (%)	Two or More Races (%)
City	55.2	24.6	4.0	0.6	0.0	8.1	7.6
MSA[1]	70.0	14.3	3.1	0.5	0.1	5.1	7.0
U.S.	61.6	12.4	6.0	1.1	0.2	8.4	10.2

Note: (1) Figures cover the Nashville-Davidson—Murfreesboro—Franklin, TN Metropolitan Statistical Area; (2) Alone is defined as not being in combination with one or more other races; (3) American Indian and Alaska Native; (4) Native Hawaiian and Other Pacific Islander
Source: U.S. Census Bureau, 2020 Census

Hispanic or Latino Origin

Area	Total (%)	Mexican (%)	Puerto Rican (%)	Cuban (%)	Other (%)
City	10.6	5.9	0.6	0.4	3.8
MSA[1]	7.7	4.3	0.6	0.3	2.5
U.S.	18.4	11.2	1.8	0.7	4.7

Note: Persons of Hispanic or Latino origin can be of any race; (1) Figures cover the Nashville-Davidson—Murfreesboro—Franklin, TN Metropolitan Statistical Area
Source: U.S. Census Bureau, 2017-2021 American Community Survey 5-Year Estimates

Age

Area	Under Age 5	Age 5–19	Age 20–34	Age 35–44	Age 45–54	Age 55–64	Age 65–74	Age 75–84	Age 85+	Median Age
City	6.1	16.6	29.5	14.1	10.7	10.8	7.5	3.3	1.3	33.8
MSA[1]	6.0	19.6	22.1	13.9	12.5	12.1	8.6	3.9	1.3	36.4
U.S.	5.6	19.2	20.2	12.7	12.4	13.1	10.0	4.9	1.9	38.8

Note: (1) Figures cover the Nashville-Davidson—Murfreesboro—Franklin, TN Metropolitan Statistical Area
Source: U.S. Census Bureau, 2020 Census

Disability by Age

Area	All Ages	Under 18 Years Old	18 to 64 Years Old	65 Years and Over
City	11.2	4.6	9.1	34.5
MSA[1]	11.6	4.0	9.7	33.6
U.S.	12.6	4.4	10.3	33.4

Note: Figures show percent of the civilian noninstitutionalized population that reported having a disability. Disability status is determined from six types of difficulty: vision, hearing, cognitive, ambulatory, self-care, and independent living. For children under 5 years old, hearing and vision difficulty are used to determine disability status. For children between the ages of 5 and 14, disability status is determined from hearing, vision, cognitive, ambulatory, and self-care difficulties. For people aged 15 years and older, they are considered to have a disability if they have difficulty with any one of the six difficulty types; Note: (1) Figures cover the Nashville-Davidson—Murfreesboro—Franklin, TN Metropolitan Statistical Area
Source: U.S. Census Bureau, 2017-2021 American Community Survey 5-Year Estimates

Ancestry

Area	German	Irish	English	American	Italian	Polish	French[2]	Scottish	Dutch
City	8.4	7.8	8.7	6.8	2.6	1.4	1.6	1.9	0.7
MSA[1]	9.9	9.3	11.1	10.2	2.7	1.3	1.7	2.1	0.8
U.S.	12.8	9.6	8.1	5.7	5.0	2.7	2.2	1.6	1.1

Note: Figures are the percentage of the total population reporting a particular ancestry. The nine most commonly reported ancestries in the U.S. are shown. Figures include multiple ancestries (e.g. if a person reported being Irish and Italian, they were included in both columns); (1) Figures cover the Nashville-Davidson—Murfreesboro—Franklin, TN Metropolitan Statistical Area; (2) Excludes Basque
Source: U.S. Census Bureau, 2017-2021 American Community Survey 5-Year Estimates

Foreign-born Population

Area	Any Foreign Country	Asia	Mexico	Europe	Caribbean	Central America[2]	South America	Africa	Canada
City	13.7	4.0	2.8	0.9	0.3	2.0	0.3	3.0	0.3
MSA[1]	8.5	2.6	1.9	0.7	0.3	1.1	0.4	1.3	0.2
U.S.	13.6	4.2	3.3	1.5	1.4	1.1	1.1	0.8	0.2

Percent of Population Born in

Note: (1) Figures cover the Nashville-Davidson—Murfreesboro—Franklin, TN Metropolitan Statistical Area; (2) Excludes Mexico.
Source: U.S. Census Bureau, 2017-2021 American Community Survey 5-Year Estimates

Household Size

Area	One	Two	Three	Four	Five	Six	Seven or More	Average Household Size
City	35.3	33.4	14.5	9.6	4.6	1.5	1.1	2.30
MSA[1]	26.9	34.8	16.3	13.2	5.8	1.9	1.1	2.60
U.S.	28.1	33.8	15.5	12.9	6.0	2.3	1.4	2.60

Note: (1) Figures cover the Nashville-Davidson—Murfreesboro—Franklin, TN Metropolitan Statistical Area
Source: U.S. Census Bureau, 2017-2021 American Community Survey 5-Year Estimates

Household Relationships

Area	Householder	Opposite-sex Spouse	Same-sex Spouse	Opposite-sex Unmarried Partner	Same-sex Unmarried Partner	Child[2]	Grandchild	Other Relatives	Non-relatives
City	42.1	14.3	0.3	3.0	0.3	24.0	1.9	4.7	5.7
MSA[1]	38.8	18.2	0.2	2.4	0.2	28.1	2.2	4.1	3.8
U.S.	38.3	17.5	0.2	2.5	0.2	28.3	2.4	4.8	3.4

Note: Figures are percent of the total population; (1) Figures cover the Nashville-Davidson—Murfreesboro—Franklin, TN Metropolitan Statistical Area; (2) Includes biological, adopted, and stepchildren of the householder
Source: U.S. Census Bureau, 2020 Census

Gender

Area	Males	Females	Males per 100 Females
City	332,568	356,879	93.2
MSA[1]	968,381	1,021,138	94.8
U.S.	162,685,811	168,763,470	96.4

Note: (1) Figures cover the Nashville-Davidson—Murfreesboro—Franklin, TN Metropolitan Statistical Area
Source: U.S. Census Bureau, 2020 Census

Marital Status

Area	Never Married	Now Married[2]	Separated	Widowed	Divorced
City	41.5	40.4	1.9	4.6	11.6
MSA[1]	32.6	50.0	1.5	4.9	11.0
U.S.	33.8	48.0	1.8	5.6	10.8

Note: Figures are percentages and cover the population 15 years of age and older; (1) Figures cover the Nashville-Davidson—Murfreesboro—Franklin, TN Metropolitan Statistical Area; (2) Excludes separated
Source: U.S. Census Bureau, 2017-2021 American Community Survey 5-Year Estimates

Religious Groups by Family

Area	Catholic	Baptist	Methodist	LDS[2]	Pentecostal	Lutheran	Islam	Adventist	Other
MSA[1]	6.2	16.4	4.8	0.9	1.6	0.4	0.8	1.3	19.4
U.S.	18.7	7.3	3.0	2.0	1.8	1.7	1.3	1.3	11.6

Note: Figures are the number of adherents as a percentage of the total population and cover the eight largest religious groups in the U.S; (1) Figures cover the Nashville-Davidson—Murfreesboro—Franklin, TN Metropolitan Statistical Area; (2) Church of Jesus Christ of Latter-day Saints
Sources: 2020 U.S. Religion Census, Association of Statisticians of American Religious Bodies; The Association of Religion Data Archives (ARDA)

Religious Groups by Tradition

Area	Catholic	Evangelical Protestant	Mainline Protestant	Black Protestant	Islam	Judaism	Hinduism	Orthodox	Buddhism
MSA[1]	6.2	30.1	6.0	5.2	0.8	0.2	0.4	1.1	0.2
U.S.	18.7	16.5	5.2	2.3	1.3	0.6	0.4	0.4	0.3

Note: Figures are the number of adherents as a percentage of the total population; (1) Figures cover the Nashville-Davidson—Murfreesboro—Franklin, TN Metropolitan Statistical Area
Sources: 2020 U.S. Religion Census, Association of Statisticians of American Religious Bodies; The Association of Religion Data Archives (ARDA)

ECONOMY

Gross Metropolitan Product

Area	2020	2021	2022	2023	Rank[2]
MSA[1]	136.6	157.4	173.7	184.5	31

Note: Figures are in billions of dollars; (1) Figures cover the Nashville-Davidson—Murfreesboro—Franklin, TN Metropolitan Statistical Area; (2) Rank is based on 2021 data and ranges from 1 to 381
Source: U.S. Conference of Mayors, U.S. Metro Economies: U.S. Metros Compared to Global and State Economies, June 2022

Economic Growth

Area	2018-20 (%)	2021 (%)	2022 (%)	2023 (%)	Rank[2]
MSA[1]	-1.2	10.6	4.4	3.0	228
U.S.	-0.6	5.7	3.1	2.9	—

Note: Figures are real gross metropolitan product (GMP) growth rates and represent average annual percent change; (1) Figures cover the Nashville-Davidson—Murfreesboro—Franklin, TN Metropolitan Statistical Area; (2) Rank is based on 2020 2-year average annual percent change and ranges from 1 to 381
Source: U.S. Conference of Mayors, U.S. Metro Economies: U.S. Metros Compared to Global and State Economies, June 2022

Metropolitan Area Exports

Area	2016	2017	2018	2019	2020	2021	Rank[2]
MSA[1]	9,460.1	10,164.3	8,723.7	7,940.7	6,569.9	8,256.1	42

Note: Figures are in millions of dollars; (1) Figures cover the Nashville-Davidson—Murfreesboro—Franklin, TN Metropolitan Statistical Area; (2) Rank is based on 2021 data and ranges from 1 to 388
Source: U.S. Department of Commerce, International Trade Administration, Office of Trade and Economic Analysis, Industry and Analysis, Exports by Metropolitan Area, data extracted March 16, 2023

Building Permits

Area	Single-Family 2021	Single-Family 2022	Pct. Chg.	Multi-Family 2021	Multi-Family 2022	Pct. Chg.	Total 2021	Total 2022	Pct. Chg.
City	3,932	3,977	1.1	12,205	10,818	-11.4	16,137	14,795	-8.3
MSA[1]	17,422	15,388	-11.7	14,769	12,804	-13.3	32,191	28,192	-12.4
U.S.	1,115,400	975,600	-12.5	621,600	689,500	10.9	1,737,000	1,665,100	-4.1

Note: (1) Figures cover the Nashville-Davidson—Murfreesboro—Franklin, TN Metropolitan Statistical Area; Figures represent new, privately-owned housing units authorized (unadjusted data); All permit data are based on estimates with imputation
Source: U.S. Census Bureau, Manufacturing, Mining, and Construction Statistics, Building Permits, 2021, 2022

Bankruptcy Filings

Area	Business Filings 2021	Business Filings 2022	% Chg.	Nonbusiness Filings 2021	Nonbusiness Filings 2022	% Chg.
Davidson County	37	32	-13.5	959	989	3.1
U.S.	14,347	13,481	-6.0	399,269	374,240	-6.3

Note: Business filings include Chapter 7, Chapter 9, Chapter 11, Chapter 12, Chapter 13, Chapter 15, and Section 304; Nonbusiness filings include Chapter 7, Chapter 11, and Chapter 13
Source: Administrative Office of the U.S. Courts, Business and Nonbusiness Bankruptcy, County Cases Commenced by Chapter of the Bankruptcy Code, During the 12-Month Period Ending December 31, 2021 and Business and Nonbusiness Bankruptcy, County Cases Commenced by Chapter of the Bankruptcy Code, During the 12-Month Period Ending December 31, 2022

Housing Vacancy Rates

Area	Gross Vacancy Rate[2] (%) 2020	2021	2022	Year-Round Vacancy Rate[3] (%) 2020	2021	2022	Rental Vacancy Rate[4] (%) 2020	2021	2022	Homeowner Vacancy Rate[5] (%) 2020	2021	2022
MSA[1]	6.5	7.1	7.6	6.1	6.8	7.1	7.3	7.9	6.4	0.7	1.0	0.9
U.S.	10.6	10.8	10.5	8.2	8.4	8.2	6.3	6.1	5.8	1.0	0.9	0.8

Note: (1) Figures cover the Nashville-Davidson—Murfreesboro—Franklin, TN Metropolitan Statistical Area; (2) The percentage of the total housing inventory that is vacant; (3) The percentage of the housing inventory (excluding seasonal units) that is year-round vacant; (4) The percentage of rental inventory that is vacant for rent; (5) The percentage of homeowner inventory that is vacant for sale
Source: U.S. Census Bureau, Housing Vacancies and Homeownership Annual Statistics: 2020, 2021, 2022

INCOME

Income

Area	Per Capita ($)	Median Household ($)	Average Household ($)
City	39,509	65,565	92,866
MSA[1]	39,269	72,537	99,987
U.S.	37,638	69,021	97,196

Note: (1) Figures cover the Nashville-Davidson—Murfreesboro—Franklin, TN Metropolitan Statistical Area
Source: U.S. Census Bureau, 2017-2021 American Community Survey 5-Year Estimates

Household Income Distribution

Area	Percent of Households Earning							
	Under $15,000	$15,000 -$24,999	$25,000 -$34,999	$35,000 -$49,999	$50,000 -$74,999	$75,000 -$99,999	$100,000 -$149,999	$150,000 and up
City	9.1	7.1	8.2	12.9	19.1	13.2	15.6	14.8
MSA[1]	7.4	6.5	7.4	12.1	18.2	13.9	17.5	16.9
U.S.	9.4	7.8	8.2	11.4	16.8	12.8	16.3	17.3

Note: (1) Figures cover the Nashville-Davidson—Murfreesboro—Franklin, TN Metropolitan Statistical Area
Source: U.S. Census Bureau, 2017-2021 American Community Survey 5-Year Estimates

Poverty Rate

Area	All Ages	Under 18 Years Old	18 to 64 Years Old	65 Years and Over
City	14.5	22.7	12.7	10.4
MSA[1]	10.9	14.6	10.2	8.3
U.S.	12.6	17.0	11.8	9.6

Note: Figures are percentage of people whose income during the past 12 months was below the poverty level; (1) Figures cover the Nashville-Davidson—Murfreesboro—Franklin, TN Metropolitan Statistical Area
Source: U.S. Census Bureau, 2017-2021 American Community Survey 5-Year Estimates

EMPLOYMENT

Labor Force and Employment

Area	Civilian Labor Force			Workers Employed		
	Dec. 2021	Dec. 2022	% Chg.	Dec. 2021	Dec. 2022	% Chg.
City	413,734	407,521	-1.5	402,245	397,879	-1.1
MSA[1]	1,124,910	1,111,047	-1.2	1,096,732	1,085,200	-1.1
U.S.	161,696,000	164,224,000	1.6	155,732,000	158,872,000	2.0

Note: Data is not seasonally adjusted and covers workers 16 years of age and older; (1) Figures cover the Nashville-Davidson—Murfreesboro—Franklin, TN Metropolitan Statistical Area
Source: Bureau of Labor Statistics, Local Area Unemployment Statistics

Unemployment Rate

Area	2022											
	Jan.	Feb.	Mar.	Apr.	May	Jun.	Jul.	Aug.	Sep.	Oct.	Nov.	Dec.
City	3.3	2.9	2.7	2.7	2.9	3.5	3.2	2.9	2.5	2.8	2.7	2.4
MSA[1]	2.9	2.7	2.4	2.5	2.8	3.4	3.1	2.7	2.4	2.7	2.6	2.3
U.S.	4.4	4.1	3.8	3.3	3.4	3.8	3.8	3.8	3.3	3.4	3.4	3.3

Note: Data is not seasonally adjusted and covers workers 16 years of age and older; (1) Figures cover the Nashville-Davidson—Murfreesboro—Franklin, TN Metropolitan Statistical Area
Source: Bureau of Labor Statistics, Local Area Unemployment Statistics

Average Wages

Occupation	$/Hr.	Occupation	$/Hr.
Accountants and Auditors	37.26	Maintenance and Repair Workers	21.40
Automotive Mechanics	23.62	Marketing Managers	76.32
Bookkeepers	22.19	Network and Computer Systems Admin.	44.89
Carpenters	23.17	Nurses, Licensed Practical	23.71
Cashiers	13.16	Nurses, Registered	37.13
Computer Programmers	55.27	Nursing Assistants	16.08
Computer Systems Analysts	45.76	Office Clerks, General	17.70
Computer User Support Specialists	25.45	Physical Therapists	44.33
Construction Laborers	19.33	Physicians	131.73
Cooks, Restaurant	15.20	Plumbers, Pipefitters and Steamfitters	26.77
Customer Service Representatives	18.93	Police and Sheriff's Patrol Officers	26.07
Dentists	89.30	Postal Service Mail Carriers	27.31
Electricians	28.19	Real Estate Sales Agents	19.02
Engineers, Electrical	47.79	Retail Salespersons	16.18
Fast Food and Counter Workers	12.17	Sales Representatives, Technical/Scientific	40.84
Financial Managers	72.46	Secretaries, Exc. Legal/Medical/Executive	20.51
First-Line Supervisors of Office Workers	32.48	Security Guards	15.94
General and Operations Managers	67.20	Surgeons	135.32
Hairdressers/Cosmetologists	19.75	Teacher Assistants, Exc. Postsecondary*	13.61
Home Health and Personal Care Aides	13.96	Teachers, Secondary School, Exc. Sp. Ed.*	26.44
Janitors and Cleaners	15.14	Telemarketers	n/a
Landscaping/Groundskeeping Workers	17.05	Truck Drivers, Heavy/Tractor-Trailer	26.23
Lawyers	73.05	Truck Drivers, Light/Delivery Services	21.56
Maids and Housekeeping Cleaners	13.44	Waiters and Waitresses	11.99

Note: Wage data covers the Nashville-Davidson—Murfreesboro—Franklin, TN Metropolitan Statistical Area; (*) Hourly wages were calculated from annual wage data based on a 40 hour work week; n/a not available.
Source: Bureau of Labor Statistics, Metro Area Occupational Employment & Wage Estimates, May 2022

Employment by Industry

Sector	MSA[1] Number of Employees	MSA[1] Percent of Total	U.S. Percent of Total
Construction, Mining, and Logging	59,900	5.2	5.4
Private Education and Health Services	168,500	14.6	16.1
Financial Activities	76,900	6.7	5.9
Government	126,200	10.9	14.5
Information	32,700	2.8	2.0
Leisure and Hospitality	126,700	11.0	10.3
Manufacturing	86,500	7.5	8.4
Other Services	47,000	4.1	3.7
Professional and Business Services	199,500	17.3	14.7
Retail Trade	106,500	9.2	10.2
Transportation, Warehousing, and Utilities	76,600	6.6	4.9
Wholesale Trade	48,500	4.2	3.9

Note: Figures are non-farm employment as of December 2022. Figures are not seasonally adjusted and include workers 16 years of age and older; (1) Figures cover the Nashville-Davidson—Murfreesboro—Franklin, TN Metropolitan Statistical Area
Source: Bureau of Labor Statistics, Current Employment Statistics, Employment, Hours, and Earnings

Employment by Occupation

Occupation Classification	City (%)	MSA[1] (%)	U.S. (%)
Management, Business, Science, and Arts	45.2	42.4	40.3
Natural Resources, Construction, and Maintenance	6.6	7.6	8.7
Production, Transportation, and Material Moving	11.9	13.6	13.1
Sales and Office	20.8	21.9	20.9
Service	15.5	14.6	17.0

Note: Figures cover employed civilians 16 years of age and older; (1) Figures cover the Nashville-Davidson—Murfreesboro—Franklin, TN Metropolitan Statistical Area
Source: U.S. Census Bureau, 2017-2021 American Community Survey 5-Year Estimates

Occupations with Greatest Projected Employment Growth: 2022 – 2024

Occupation[1]	2022 Employment	2024 Projected Employment	Numeric Employment Change	Percent Employment Change
Fast Food and Counter Workers	53,640	58,010	4,370	8.1
Waiters and Waitresses	49,450	53,640	4,190	8.5
General and Operations Managers	59,210	62,720	3,510	5.9
Cooks, Restaurant	22,120	25,260	3,140	14.2
Customer Service Representatives	71,500	74,270	2,770	3.9
First-Line Supervisors of Food Preparation and Serving Workers	26,470	29,030	2,560	9.7
Insurance Sales Agents	8,560	11,020	2,460	28.7
Managers, All Other	35,110	37,560	2,450	7.0
Construction Laborers	31,580	33,910	2,330	7.4
First-Line Supervisors of Office and Administrative Support Workers	54,390	56,690	2,300	4.2

Note: Projections cover Tennessee; (1) Sorted by numeric employment change
Source: www.projectionscentral.com, State Occupational Projections, 2022–2024 Short-Term Projections

Fastest-Growing Occupations: 2022 – 2024

Occupation[1]	2022 Employment	2024 Projected Employment	Numeric Employment Change	Percent Employment Change
Library Technicians	770	1,000	230	29.9
Insurance Sales Agents	8,560	11,020	2,460	28.7
Insurance Appraisers, Auto Damage	280	360	80	28.6
Athletes and Sports Competitors	1,280	1,630	350	27.3
Insurance Underwriters	2,060	2,560	500	24.3
Nursing Instructors and Teachers, Postsecondary	1,570	1,930	360	22.9
Biological Science Teachers, Postsecondary	1,240	1,510	270	21.8
Law Teachers, Postsecondary	230	280	50	21.7
English Language and Literature Teachers, Postsecondary	1,450	1,760	310	21.4
Mathematical Science Teachers, Postsecondary	900	1,090	190	21.1

Note: Projections cover Tennessee; (1) Sorted by percent employment change and excludes occupations with numeric employment change less than 50
Source: www.projectionscentral.com, State Occupational Projections, 2022–2024 Short-Term Projections

CITY FINANCES

City Government Finances

Component	2020 ($000)	2020 ($ per capita)
Total Revenues	5,053,837	7,444
Total Expenditures	5,235,445	7,712
Debt Outstanding	19,005,674	27,995
Cash and Securities[1]	11,988,432	17,659

Note: (1) Cash and security holdings of a government at the close of its fiscal year, including those of its dependent agencies, utilities, and liquor stores.
Source: U.S. Census Bureau, State & Local Government Finances 2020

City Government Revenue by Source

Source	2020 ($000)	2020 ($ per capita)	2020 (%)
General Revenue			
From Federal Government	62,614	92	1.2
From State Government	685,146	1,009	13.6
From Local Governments	885	1	0.0
Taxes			
Property	1,084,068	1,597	21.5
Sales and Gross Receipts	642,211	946	12.7
Personal Income	0	0	0.0
Corporate Income	0	0	0.0
Motor Vehicle License	33,132	49	0.7
Other Taxes	32,002	47	0.6
Current Charges	319,151	470	6.3
Liquor Store	0	0	0.0
Utility	1,397,243	2,058	27.6

Source: U.S. Census Bureau, State & Local Government Finances 2020

City Government Expenditures by Function

Function	2020 ($000)	2020 ($ per capita)	2020 (%)
General Direct Expenditures			
Air Transportation	0	0	0.0
Corrections	80,323	118	1.5
Education	1,118,964	1,648	21.4
Employment Security Administration	0	0	0.0
Financial Administration	35,737	52	0.7
Fire Protection	152,019	223	2.9
General Public Buildings	1,007	1	0.0
Governmental Administration, Other	91,472	134	1.7
Health	73,160	107	1.4
Highways	104,648	154	2.0
Hospitals	103,324	152	2.0
Housing and Community Development	0	0	0.0
Interest on General Debt	779,205	1,147	14.9
Judicial and Legal	109,451	161	2.1
Libraries	37,186	54	0.7
Parking	4,938	7	0.1
Parks and Recreation	134,896	198	2.6
Police Protection	283,212	417	5.4
Public Welfare	63,935	94	1.2
Sewerage	216,391	318	4.1
Solid Waste Management	30,080	44	0.6
Veterans' Services	0	0	0.0
Liquor Store	0	0	0.0
Utility	1,578,571	2,325	30.2

Source: U.S. Census Bureau, State & Local Government Finances 2020

TAXES

State Corporate Income Tax Rates

State	Tax Rate (%)	Income Brackets ($)	Num. of Brackets	Financial Institution Tax Rate (%)[a]	Federal Income Tax Ded.
Tennessee	6.5	Flat rate	1	6.5	No

Note: Tax rates as of January 1, 2023; (a) Rates listed are the corporate income tax rate applied to financial institutions or excise taxes based on income. Some states have other taxes based upon the value of deposits or shares.
Source: Federation of Tax Administrators, State Corporate Income Tax Rates, January 1, 2023

State Individual Income Tax Rates

State	Tax Rate (%)	Income Brackets ($)	Personal Exemptions ($) Single	Married	Depend.	Standard Ded. ($) Single	Married
Tennessee				– No state income tax –			

Note: Tax rates as of January 1, 2023; Local- and county-level taxes are not included
Source: Federation of Tax Administrators, State Individual Income Tax Rates, January 1, 2023

Various State Sales and Excise Tax Rates

State	State Sales Tax (%)	Gasoline[1] ($/gal.)	Cigarette[2] ($/pack)	Spirits[3] ($/gal.)	Wine[4] ($/gal.)	Beer[5] ($/gal.)	Recreational Marijuana (%)
Tennessee	7	0.274	0.62	4.46	1.27	1.29	Not legal

Note: All tax rates as of January 1, 2023; (1) The American Petroleum Institute has developed a methodology for determining the average tax rate on a gallon of fuel. Rates may include any of the following: excise taxes, environmental fees, storage tank fees, other fees or taxes, general sales tax, and local taxes; (2) The federal excise tax of $1.0066 per pack and local taxes are not included; (3) Rates are those applicable to off-premise sales of 40% alcohol by volume (a.b.v.) distilled spirits in 750ml containers. Local excise taxes are excluded; (4) Rates are those applicable to off-premise sales of 11% a.b.v. non-carbonated wine in 750ml containers; (5) Rates are those applicable to off-premise sales of 4.7% a.b.v. beer in 12 ounce containers.
Source: Tax Foundation, 2023 Facts & Figures: How Does Your State Compare?

State Business Tax Climate Index Rankings

State	Overall Rank	Corporate Tax Rank	Individual Income Tax Rank	Sales Tax Rank	Property Tax Rank	Unemployment Insurance Tax Rank
Tennessee	14	45	6	46	33	21

Note: The index is a measure of how each state's tax laws affect economic performance. The lower the rank, the more favorable a state's tax system is for business. States without a given tax are given a ranking of 1. The scores/rankings for the District of Columbia do not affect other states. The 2023 index represents the tax climate as of July 1, 2022.
Source: Tax Foundation, State Business Tax Climate Index 2023

TRANSPORTATION

Means of Transportation to Work

Area	Car/Truck/Van Drove Alone	Car-pooled	Public Transportation Bus	Subway	Railroad	Bicycle	Walked	Other Means	Worked at Home
City	72.8	9.1	1.6	0.0	0.1	0.2	2.2	1.3	12.7
MSA[1]	76.7	8.6	0.7	0.0	0.1	0.1	1.2	1.1	11.6
U.S.	73.2	8.6	2.0	1.6	0.5	0.5	2.5	1.5	9.7

Note: Figures are percentages and cover workers 16 years of age and older; (1) Figures cover the Nashville-Davidson—Murfreesboro—Franklin, TN Metropolitan Statistical Area
Source: U.S. Census Bureau, 2017-2021 American Community Survey 5-Year Estimates

Travel Time to Work

Area	Less Than 10 Minutes	10 to 19 Minutes	20 to 29 Minutes	30 to 44 Minutes	45 to 59 Minutes	60 to 89 Minutes	90 Minutes or More
City	9.1	29.0	26.6	23.2	7.0	3.6	1.5
MSA[1]	9.4	26.2	21.5	23.5	10.9	6.5	2.0
U.S.	12.4	28.5	21.0	20.9	8.2	6.2	2.9

Note: Note: Figures are percentages and include workers 16 years old and over; (1) Figures cover the Nashville-Davidson—Murfreesboro—Franklin, TN Metropolitan Statistical Area
Source: U.S. Census Bureau, 2017-2021 American Community Survey 5-Year Estimates

Key Congestion Measures

Measure	1990	2000	2010	2015	2020
Annual Hours of Delay, Total (000)	9,768	25,497	39,786	49,865	25,770
Annual Hours of Delay, Per Auto Commuter	26	43	46	57	28
Annual Congestion Cost, Per Auto Commuter ($)	437	853	1,058	1,226	659

Note: Covers the Nashville-Davidson TN urban area
Source: Texas A&M Transportation Institute, 2021 Urban Mobility Report

Freeway Travel Time Index

Measure	1985	1990	1995	2000	2005	2010	2015	2020
Urban Area Index[1]	1.10	1.12	1.15	1.19	1.22	1.20	1.22	1.06
Urban Area Rank[1,2]	27	35	36	34	32	36	34	75

Note: Freeway Travel Time Index—the ratio of travel time in the peak period to the travel time at free-flow conditions. For example, a value of 1.30 indicates a 20-minute free-flow trip takes 26 minutes in the peak (20 minutes x 1.30 = 26 minutes); (1) Covers the Nashville-Davidson TN urban area; (2) Rank is based on 101 larger urban areas (#1 = highest travel time index)
Source: Texas A&M Transportation Institute, 2021 Urban Mobility Report

Public Transportation

Agency Name / Mode of Transportation	Vehicles Operated in Maximum Service[1]	Annual Unlinked Passenger Trips[2] (in thous.)	Annual Passenger Miles[3] (in thous.)
Metropolitan Transit Authority (MTA)			
Bus (directly operated)	117	4,150.3	17,316.5
Demand Response (directly operated)	48	173.3	1,418.6
Demand Response - Taxi	28	43.4	487.2

*Note: (1) Number of revenue vehicles operated by the given mode and type of service to meet the annual maximum service requirement. This is the revenue vehicle count during the peak season of the year; on the week and day that maximum service is provided. Vehicles operated in maximum service (VOMS) exclude atypical days and one-time special events; (2) Number of passengers who boarded public transportation vehicles. Passengers are counted each time they board a vehicle no matter how many vehicles they use to travel from their origin to their destination. (3) Sum of the distances ridden by all passengers during the entire fiscal year.
Source: Federal Transit Administration, National Transit Database, 2021*

Air Transportation

Airport Name and Code / Type of Service	Passenger Airlines[1]	Passenger Enplanements	Freight Carriers[2]	Freight (lbs)
Nashville International (BNA)				
Domestic service (U.S. carriers - 2022)	39	9,686,383	17	83,946,848
International service (U.S. carriers - 2021)	8	18,031	2	1,128

*Note: (1) Includes all U.S.-based major, minor and commuter airlines that carried at least one passenger during the year; (2) Includes all U.S.-based airlines and freight carriers that transported at least one pound of freight during the year.
Source: Bureau of Transportation Statistics, The Intermodal Transportation Database, Air Carriers: T-100 Domestic Market (U.S. Carriers), 2022; Bureau of Transportation Statistics, The Intermodal Transportation Database, Air Carriers: T-100 International Market (U.S. Carriers), 2021*

BUSINESSES

Major Business Headquarters

Company Name	Industry	Fortune[1]	Forbes[2]
HCA Healthcare	Hospitals	62	-
Ingram Industries	Multicompany	-	227

*Note: (1) Companies that produce a 10-K are ranked 1 to 500 based on 2021 revenue; (2) All private companies with at least $2 billion in annual revenue through the end of their most current fiscal year are ranked 1 to 246; companies listed are headquartered in the city; dashes indicate no ranking
Source: Fortune, "Fortune 500," 2022; Forbes, "America's Largest Private Companies," 2022*

Fastest-Growing Businesses

According to *Inc.*, Nashville is home to one of America's 500 fastest-growing private companies: **Complete Health Partners** (#31). Criteria: must be an independent, privately-held, for-profit, U.S. corporation, proprietorship or partnership as of December 31, 2021; revenues must be at least $100,000 in 2018 and $2 million in 2021; must have four-year operating/sales history. *Inc., "America's 500 Fastest-Growing Private Companies," 2022*

According to Deloitte, Nashville is home to four of North America's 500 fastest-growing high-technology companies: **Revance Therapeutics** (#85); **LASSO** (#271); **XSOLIS** (#367); **TechnologyAdvice** (#394). Companies are ranked by percentage growth in revenue over a four-year period. Criteria for inclusion: company must be headquartered within North America; must own proprietary intellectual property or technology that is sold to customers in products that contributes to a significant portion of the company's operating revenue; must have been in business for a minumum of four years with 2018 operating revenues of at least $50,000 USD/CD and 2021 operating revenues of at least $5 million USD/CD. *Deloitte, 2022 Technology Fast 500™*

Living Environment

COST OF LIVING

Cost of Living Index

Composite Index	Groceries	Housing	Utilities	Transportation	Health Care	Misc. Goods/Services
97.7	97.5	106.1	88.7	91.3	90.9	95.9

Note: The Cost of Living Index measures regional differences in the cost of consumer goods and services, excluding taxes and non-consumer expenditures, for professional and managerial households in the top income quintile. It is based on more than 50,000 prices covering almost 60 different items for which prices are collected three times a year by chambers of commerce, economic development organizations or university applied economic centers in each participating urban area. The numbers shown should be read as a percentage above or below the national average of 100. For example, a value of 115.4 in the groceries column indicates that grocery prices are 15.4% higher than the national average. Small differences in the index numbers should not be interpreted as significant; Figures cover the Nashville-Murfreesboro TN urban area.
Source: The Council for Community and Economic Research, Cost of Living Index, 2022

Grocery Prices

Area[1]	T-Bone Steak ($/pound)	Frying Chicken ($/pound)	Whole Milk ($/half gal.)	Eggs ($/dozen)	Orange Juice ($/64 oz.)	Coffee ($/11.5 oz.)
City[2]	14.63	1.68	2.33	1.83	3.95	4.92
Avg.	13.81	1.59	2.43	2.25	3.85	4.95
Min.	10.17	0.90	1.51	1.30	2.90	3.46
Max.	19.35	3.30	4.32	4.32	5.31	8.59

Note: (1) Values for the local area are compared with the average, minimum and maximum values for all 286 areas in the Cost of Living Index; (2) Figures cover the Nashville-Murfreesboro TN urban area; **T-Bone Steak** (price per pound); **Frying Chicken** (price per pound, whole fryer); **Whole Milk** (half gallon carton); **Eggs** (price per dozen, Grade A, large); **Orange Juice** (64 oz. Tropicana or Florida Natural); **Coffee** (11.5 oz. can, vacuum-packed, Maxwell House, Hills Bros, or Folgers).
Source: The Council for Community and Economic Research, Cost of Living Index, 2022

Housing and Utility Costs

Area[1]	New Home Price ($)	Apartment Rent ($/month)	All Electric ($/month)	Part Electric ($/month)	Other Energy ($/month)	Telephone ($/month)
City[2]	483,320	1,465	-	90.92	51.95	190.02
Avg.	450,913	1,371	176.41	99.93	76.96	190.22
Min.	229,283	546	100.84	31.56	27.15	174.27
Max.	2,434,977	4,569	356.86	249.59	272.24	208.31

Note: (1) Values for the local area are compared with the average, minimum and maximum values for all 286 areas in the Cost of Living Index; (2) Figures cover the Nashville-Murfreesboro TN urban area; **New Home Price** (2,400 sf living area, 8,000 sf lot, in urban area with full utilities); **Apartment Rent** (950 sf 2 bedroom/1.5 or 2 bath, unfurnished, excluding all utilities except water); **All Electric** (average monthly cost for an all-electric home); **Part Electric** (average monthly cost for a part-electric home); **Other Energy** (average monthly cost for natural gas, fuel oil, coal, wood, and any other forms of energy except electricity); **Telephone** (price includes the base monthly rate plus taxes and fees for three lines of mobile phone service).
Source: The Council for Community and Economic Research, Cost of Living Index, 2022

Health Care, Transportation, and Other Costs

Area[1]	Doctor ($/visit)	Dentist ($/visit)	Optometrist ($/visit)	Gasoline ($/gallon)	Beauty Salon ($/visit)	Men's Shirt ($)
City[2]	106.23	100.08	86.77	3.57	41.35	27.39
Avg.	124.91	107.77	117.66	3.86	43.31	34.21
Min.	36.61	58.25	51.79	2.90	22.18	13.05
Max.	250.21	162.58	371.96	5.54	85.61	63.54

Note: (1) Values for the local area are compared with the average, minimum and maximum values for all 286 areas in the Cost of Living Index; (2) Figures cover the Nashville-Murfreesboro TN urban area; **Doctor** (general practitioners routine exam of an established patient); **Dentist** (adult teeth cleaning and periodic oral examination); **Optometrist** (full vision eye exam for established adult patient); **Gasoline** (one gallon regular unleaded, national brand, including all taxes, cash price at self-service pump if available); **Beauty Salon** (woman's shampoo, trim, and blow-dry); **Men's Shirt** (cotton/polyester dress shirt, pinpoint weave, long sleeves).
Source: The Council for Community and Economic Research, Cost of Living Index, 2022

HOUSING

Homeownership Rate

Area	2015 (%)	2016 (%)	2017 (%)	2018 (%)	2019 (%)	2020 (%)	2021 (%)	2022 (%)
MSA[1]	67.4	65.0	69.4	68.3	69.8	69.8	65.7	70.4
U.S.	63.7	63.4	63.9	64.4	64.6	66.6	65.5	65.8

Note: (1) Figures cover the Nashville-Davidson—Murfreesboro—Franklin, TN Metropolitan Statistical Area
Source: U.S. Census Bureau, Housing Vacancies and Homeownership Annual Statistics: 2015-2022

House Price Index (HPI)

Area	National Ranking[2]	Quarterly Change (%)	One-Year Change (%)	Five-Year Change (%)	Since 1991Q1 (%)
MSA[1]	34	-1.19	16.94	75.36	429.41
U.S.[3]	—	0.34	8.41	58.44	289.08

Note: The HPI is a weighted repeat sales index. It measures average price changes in repeat sales or refinancings on the same properties. This information is obtained by reviewing repeat mortgage transactions on single-family properties whose mortgages have been purchased or securitized by Fannie Mae or Freddie Mac since January 1975; (1) Figures cover the Nashville-Davidson—Murfreesboro—Franklin, TN Metropolitan Statistical Area; (2) Rankings are based on annual percentage change for all metro areas containing at least 15,000 transactions over the last 10 years and ranges from 1 to 257; (3) figures based on a weighted average of Census Division estimates using a seasonally adjusted, purchase-only index; all figures are for the period ending December 31, 2022
Source: Federal Housing Finance Agency, Change in FHFA Metropolitan Area House Price Indexes, 2022Q4

Median Single-Family Home Prices

Area	2020	2021	2022p	Percent Change 2021 to 2022
MSA[1]	298.9	349.5	403.7	15.5
U.S. Average	300.2	357.1	392.6	9.9

Note: Figures are median sales prices of existing single-family homes in thousands of dollars; (p) preliminary; (1) Figures cover the Nashville-Davidson—Murfreesboro—Franklin, TN Metropolitan Statistical Area
Source: National Association of Realtors, Median Sales Price of Existing Single-Family Homes for Metropolitan Areas, 4th Quarter 2022

Qualifying Income Based on Median Sales Price of Existing Single-Family Homes

Area	With 5% Down ($)	With 10% Down ($)	With 20% Down ($)
MSA[1]	119,703	113,403	100,803
U.S. Average	112,234	106,237	94,513

Note: Figures are preliminary; Qualifying income is based on a mortgage rate of 6.77%. Monthly principal and interest payment is limited to 25% of income; (1) Figures cover the Nashville-Davidson—Murfreesboro—Franklin, TN Metropolitan Statistical Area
Source: National Association of Realtors, Qualifying Income Based on Median Sales Price of Existing Single-Family Homes for Metropolitan Areas, 4th Quarter 2022

Home Value

Area	Under $100,000	$100,000 -$199,999	$200,000 -$299,999	$300,000 -$399,999	$400,000 -$499,999	$500,000 -$999,999	$1,000,000 or more	Median ($)
City	4.4	18.9	29.1	21.3	9.6	13.3	3.3	291,400
MSA[1]	6.6	19.5	27.4	19.2	9.9	14.1	3.2	286,800
U.S.	16.2	24.2	20.1	13.6	8.3	13.6	4.1	244,900

Note: Figures are percentages except for median and cover owner-occupied housing units; (1) Figures cover the Nashville-Davidson—Murfreesboro—Franklin, TN Metropolitan Statistical Area
Source: U.S. Census Bureau, 2017-2021 American Community Survey 5-Year Estimates

Year Housing Structure Built

Area	2020 or Later	2010 -2019	2000 -2009	1990 -1999	1980 -1989	1970 -1979	1960 -1969	1950 -1959	1940 -1949	Before 1940	Median Year
City	0.8	13.4	13.8	12.3	14.5	13.5	11.6	9.7	4.0	6.4	1983
MSA[1]	0.6	15.4	18.5	16.8	13.5	12.5	8.8	6.4	2.8	4.5	1991
U.S.	0.2	7.3	13.6	13.6	13.2	14.8	10.3	10.0	4.7	12.2	1979

Note: Figures are percentages except for Median Year; Note: (1) Figures cover the Nashville-Davidson—Murfreesboro—Franklin, TN Metropolitan Statistical Area
Source: U.S. Census Bureau, 2017-2021 American Community Survey 5-Year Estimates

Gross Monthly Rent

Area	Under $500	$500 -$999	$1,000 -$1,499	$1,500 -$1,999	$2,000 -$2,499	$2,500 -$2,999	$3,000 and up	Median ($)
City	7.4	20.6	41.1	20.6	6.9	1.9	1.5	1,250
MSA[1]	6.7	25.1	39.7	20.0	5.7	1.6	1.2	1,211
U.S.	8.1	30.5	30.8	16.8	7.3	3.1	3.5	1,163

Note: Figures are percentages except for median; Gross rent is the contract rent plus the estimated average monthly cost of utilities (electricity, gas, and water and sewer) and fuels (oil, coal, kerosene, wood, etc.) if these are paid by the renter (or paid for the renter by someone else); (1) Figures cover the Nashville-Davidson—Murfreesboro—Franklin, TN Metropolitan Statistical Area
Source: U.S. Census Bureau, 2017-2021 American Community Survey 5-Year Estimates

HEALTH

Health Risk Factors

Category	MSA[1] (%)	U.S. (%)
Adults aged 18–64 who have any kind of health care coverage	90.2	90.9
Adults who reported being in good or better health	87.2	85.2
Adults who have been told they have high blood cholesterol	32.3	35.7
Adults who have been told they have high blood pressure	30.0	32.4
Adults who are current smokers	18.4	14.4
Adults who currently use e-cigarettes	8.2	6.7
Adults who currently use chewing tobacco, snuff, or snus	4.1	3.5
Adults who are heavy drinkers[2]	5.9	6.3
Adults who are binge drinkers[3]	16.5	15.4
Adults who are overweight (BMI 25.0 - 29.9)	39.3	34.4
Adults who are obese (BMI 30.0 - 99.8)	30.4	33.9
Adults who participated in any physical activities in the past month	75.2	76.3

Note: (1) Figures cover the Nashville-Davidson—Murfreesboro—Franklin, TN Metropolitan Statistical Area; (2) Heavy drinkers are classified as adult men having more than 14 drinks per week and adult women having more than 7 drinks per week; (3) Binge drinkers are classified as males having five or more drinks on one occasion or females having four or more drinks on one occasion
Source: Centers for Disease Control and Prevention, Behavioral Risk Factor Surveillance System, SMART: Selected Metropolitan Area Risk Trends, 2021

Acute and Chronic Health Conditions

Category	MSA[1] (%)	U.S. (%)
Adults who have ever been told they had a heart attack	3.5	4.0
Adults who have ever been told they have angina or coronary heart disease	3.3	3.8
Adults who have ever been told they had a stroke	4.4	3.0
Adults who have ever been told they have asthma	16.1	14.9
Adults who have ever been told they have arthritis	25.2	25.8
Adults who have ever been told they have diabetes[2]	9.5	10.9
Adults who have ever been told they had skin cancer	6.3	6.6
Adults who have ever been told they had any other types of cancer	6.3	7.5
Adults who have ever been told they have COPD	7.5	6.1
Adults who have ever been told they have kidney disease	3.5	3.0
Adults who have ever been told they have a form of depression	23.8	20.5

Note: (1) Figures cover the Nashville-Davidson—Murfreesboro—Franklin, TN Metropolitan Statistical Area; (2) Figures do not include pregnancy-related, borderline, or pre-diabetes
Source: Centers for Disease Control and Prevention, Behavioral Risk Factor Surveillance System, SMART: Selected Metropolitan Area Risk Trends, 2021

Health Screening and Vaccination Rates

Category	MSA[1] (%)	U.S. (%)
Adults who have ever been tested for HIV	39.3	34.9
Adults who have had their blood cholesterol checked within the last five years	88.0	85.2
Adults aged 65+ who have had flu shot within the past year	65.7	68.6
Adults aged 65+ who have ever had a pneumonia vaccination	72.8	71.0

Note: (1) Figures cover the Nashville-Davidson—Murfreesboro—Franklin, TN Metropolitan Statistical Area.
Source: Centers for Disease Control and Prevention, Behavioral Risk Factor Surveillance System, SMART: Selected Metropolitan Area Risk Trends, 2021

Disability Status

Category	MSA[1] (%)	U.S. (%)
Adults who reported being deaf	6.7	7.2
Are you blind or have serious difficulty seeing, even when wearing glasses?	3.9	4.8
Are you limited in any way in any of your usual activities due to arthritis?	11.1	11.1
Do you have difficulty doing errands alone?	8.4	7.0
Do you have difficulty dressing or bathing?	3.6	3.6
Do you have serious difficulty concentrating/remembering/making decisions?	10.9	12.1
Do you have serious difficulty walking or climbing stairs?	11.7	12.8

Note: (1) Figures cover the Nashville-Davidson—Murfreesboro—Franklin, TN Metropolitan Statistical Area.
Source: Centers for Disease Control and Prevention, Behavioral Risk Factor Surveillance System, SMART: Selected Metropolitan Area Risk Trends, 2021

Mortality Rates for the Top 10 Causes of Death in the U.S.

ICD-10[a] Sub-Chapter	ICD-10[a] Code	Crude Mortality Rate[1] per 100,000 population County[2]	U.S.
Malignant neoplasms	C00-C97	151.0	182.6
Ischaemic heart diseases	I20-I25	91.5	113.1
Other forms of heart disease	I30-I51	42.6	64.4
Other degenerative diseases of the nervous system	G30-G31	50.2	51.0
Cerebrovascular diseases	I60-I69	40.1	47.8
Other external causes of accidental injury	W00-X59	84.1	46.4
Chronic lower respiratory diseases	J40-J47	39.0	45.7
Organic, including symptomatic, mental disorders	F01-F09	28.3	35.9
Hypertensive diseases	I10-I15	47.7	35.0
Diabetes mellitus	E10-E14	27.5	29.6

Note: (a) ICD-10 = International Classification of Diseases 10th Revision; (1) Crude mortality rates are a three-year average covering 2019-2021; (2) Figures cover Davidson County.
Source: Centers for Disease Control and Prevention, National Center for Health Statistics. National Vital Statistics System, Mortality 2018-2021 on CDC WONDER Online Database

Mortality Rates for Selected Causes of Death

ICD-10[a] Sub-Chapter	ICD-10[a] Code	Crude Mortality Rate[1] per 100,000 population County[2]	U.S.
Assault	X85-Y09	13.4	7.0
Diseases of the liver	K70-K76	16.3	19.8
Human immunodeficiency virus (HIV) disease	B20-B24	2.2	1.5
Influenza and pneumonia	J09-J18	11.6	14.7
Intentional self-harm	X60-X84	13.4	14.3
Malnutrition	E40-E46	1.2	4.3
Obesity and other hyperalimentation	E65-E68	3.4	3.0
Renal failure	N17-N19	10.3	15.7
Transport accidents	V01-V99	16.8	13.6
Viral hepatitis	B15-B19	1.4	1.2

Note: (a) ICD-10 = International Classification of Diseases 10th Revision; (1) Crude mortality rates are a three-year average covering 2019-2021; (2) Figures cover Davidson County; Data are suppressed when the data meet the criteria for confidentiality constraints; Crude mortality rates are flagged as unreliable when the rate would be calculated with a numerator of 20 or less.
Source: Centers for Disease Control and Prevention, National Center for Health Statistics. National Vital Statistics System, Mortality 2018-2021 on CDC WONDER Online Database

Health Insurance Coverage

Area	With Health Insurance	With Private Health Insurance	With Public Health Insurance	Without Health Insurance	Population Under Age 19 Without Health Insurance
City	87.6	68.7	29.3	12.4	8.2
MSA[1]	90.5	72.7	28.4	9.5	5.7
U.S.	91.2	67.8	35.4	8.8	5.3

Note: Figures are percentages that cover the civilian noninstitutionalized population; (1) Figures cover the Nashville-Davidson—Murfreesboro—Franklin, TN Metropolitan Statistical Area
Source: U.S. Census Bureau, 2017-2021 American Community Survey 5-Year Estimates

Number of Medical Professionals

Area	MDs[3]	DOs[3,4]	Dentists	Podiatrists	Chiropractors	Optometrists
County[1] (number)	4,630	101	570	37	189	123
County[1] (rate[2])	647.1	14.1	81.0	5.3	26.8	17.5
U.S. (rate[2])	289.3	23.5	72.5	6.2	28.7	17.4

Note: Data as of 2021 unless noted; (1) Data covers Davidson County; (2) Rate per 100,000 population; (3) Data as of 2020 and includes all active, non-federal physicians; (4) Doctor of Osteopathic Medicine
Source: U.S. Department of Health and Human Services, Health Resources and Services Administration, Bureau of Health Professions, Area Resource File (ARF) 2021-2022

Best Hospitals

According to *U.S. News*, the Nashville-Davidson—Murfreesboro—Franklin, TN metro area is home to one of the best hospitals in the U.S.: **Vanderbilt University Medical Center** (Honor Roll/9 adult specialties and 10 pediatric specialties). The hospital listed was nationally ranked in at least one of 15 adult or 10 pediatric specialties. The number of specialties shown cover the parent hospital. Only 164 U.S. hospitals performed well enough to be nationally ranked in one or more specialties. Twenty hospitals in the U.S. made the Honor Roll. The Best Hospitals Honor Roll takes both the national rankings and the procedure and condition ratings into account. Hospitals received points if they were nationally ranked in one of the 15 adult specialties—the higher they ranked, the more points they got—and how many ratings of "high performing" they earned in the 17 procedures and conditions. *U.S. News Online, "America's Best Hospitals 2022-23"*

According to *U.S. News,* the Nashville-Davidson—Murfreesboro—Franklin, TN metro area is home to one of the best children's hospitals in the U.S.: **Monroe Carell Jr. Children's Hospital at Vanderbilt** (10 pediatric specialties). The hospital listed was highly ranked in at least one of 10 pediatric specialties. Eighty-six children's hospitals in the U.S. were nationally ranked in at least one specialty. Hospitals received points for being ranked in a specialty, and the 10 hospitals with the most points across the 10 specialties make up the Honor Roll. *U.S. News Online, "America's Best Children's Hospitals 2022-23"*

EDUCATION

Public School District Statistics

District Name	Schls	Pupils	Pupil/Teacher Ratio	Minority Pupils[1] (%)	LEP/ELL[2] (%)	IEP[3] (%)
Achievement School District	26	8,616	20.6	97.6	3.4	11.4
Davidson County	162	80,381	16.6	74.9	16.2	12.1

Note: Table includes school districts with 2,000 or more students; (1) Percentage of students that are not non-Hispanic white; (2) Percentage of students that are Limited English Proficient or English Language Learners (2018-19); (3) Percentage of students that have an Individualized Education Program (2019-20).
Source: U.S. Department of Education, National Center for Education Statistics, Common Core of Data, Local Education Agency (School District) Universe Survey: School Year 2021-2022

Best High Schools

According to *U.S. News,* Nashville is home to two of the top 500 high schools in the U.S.: **Hume Fogg Magnet High School** (#70); **Martin Luther King Jr. Magnet School** (#170). Nearly 18,000 public, magnet and charter schools were ranked based on their performance on state assessments and how well they prepare students for college. *U.S. News & World Report, "Best High Schools 2022"*

Highest Level of Education

Area	Less than H.S.	H.S. Diploma	Some College, No Deg.	Associate Degree	Bachelor's Degree	Master's Degree	Prof. School Degree	Doctorate Degree
City	10.0	21.5	18.4	6.2	27.5	10.7	3.2	2.6
MSA[1]	9.0	25.7	19.6	7.3	24.9	9.4	2.3	1.8
U.S.	11.1	26.5	20.0	8.7	20.6	9.3	2.2	1.5

Note: Figures cover persons age 25 and over; (1) Figures cover the Nashville-Davidson—Murfreesboro—Franklin, TN Metropolitan Statistical Area
Source: U.S. Census Bureau, 2017-2021 American Community Survey 5-Year Estimates

Educational Attainment by Race

Area	High School Graduate or Higher (%)					Bachelor's Degree or Higher (%)				
	Total	White	Black	Asian	Hisp.[2]	Total	White	Black	Asian	Hisp.[2]
City	90.0	92.2	89.3	80.3	59.3	43.9	50.7	28.8	52.3	17.2
MSA[1]	91.0	92.2	90.0	86.0	64.9	38.4	39.9	30.0	55.3	19.4
U.S.	88.9	91.4	87.2	87.6	71.2	33.7	35.5	23.3	55.6	18.4

Note: Figures shown cover persons 25 years old and over; (1) Figures cover the Nashville-Davidson—Murfreesboro—Franklin, TN Metropolitan Statistical Area; (2) People of Hispanic origin can be of any race
Source: U.S. Census Bureau, 2017-2021 American Community Survey 5-Year Estimates

School Enrollment by Grade and Control

Area	Preschool (%)		Kindergarten (%)		Grades 1 - 4 (%)		Grades 5 - 8 (%)		Grades 9 - 12 (%)	
	Public	Private	Public	Private	Public	Private	Public	Private	Public	Private
City	48.4	51.6	84.0	16.0	84.6	15.4	80.0	20.0	81.9	18.1
MSA[1]	50.2	49.8	85.0	15.0	85.7	14.3	84.7	15.3	83.3	16.7
U.S.	58.8	41.2	86.3	13.7	88.3	11.7	88.6	11.4	89.4	10.6

Note: Figures shown cover persons 3 years old and over; (1) Figures cover the Nashville-Davidson—Murfreesboro—Franklin, TN Metropolitan Statistical Area
Source: U.S. Census Bureau, 2017-2021 American Community Survey 5-Year Estimates

Higher Education

| Four-Year Colleges ||| Two-Year Colleges ||| Medical Schools[1] | Law Schools[2] | Voc/Tech[3] |
Public	Private Non-profit	Private For-profit	Public	Private Non-profit	Private For-profit			
2	11	6	7	2	3	2	3	13

Note: Figures cover institutions located within the Nashville-Davidson—Murfreesboro—Franklin, TN Metropolitan Statistical Area and include main campuses only; (1) includes schools accredited by the Liaison Committee on Medical Education and the American Osteopathic Association's Commission on Osteopathic College Accreditation; (2) includes ABA-accredited schools, schools with provisional ABA accreditation, and state accredited schools; (3) includes all schools with programs that are less than 2 years.
Source: National Center for Education Statistics, Integrated Postsecondary Education System (IPEDS), 2021-22; Wikipedia, List of Medical Schools in the United States, accessed April 10, 2023; Wikipedia, List of Law Schools in the United States, accessed April 10, 2023

According to *U.S. News & World Report,* the Nashville-Davidson—Murfreesboro—Franklin, TN metro area is home to two of the top 200 national universities in the U.S.: **Vanderbilt University** (#13 tie); **Belmont University** (#182 tie). The indicators used to capture academic quality fall into a number of categories: assessment by administrators at peer institutions; retention of students; faculty resources; student selectivity; financial resources; alumni giving; high school counselor ratings of colleges; and graduation rate. *U.S. News & World Report, "America's Best Colleges 2023"*

According to *U.S. News & World Report,* the Nashville-Davidson—Murfreesboro—Franklin, TN metro area is home to one of the top 100 law schools in the U.S.: **Vanderbilt University** (#17 tie). The rankings are based on a weighted average of 12 measures of quality: peer assessment score; assessment score by lawyers/judges; median LSAT scores; median undergrad GPA; acceptance rate; employment rates for graduates; placement success; bar passage rate; faculty resources; expenditures per student; student/faculty ratio; and library resources. *U.S. News & World Report, "America's Best Graduate Schools, Law, 2023"*

According to *U.S. News & World Report,* the Nashville-Davidson—Murfreesboro—Franklin, TN metro area is home to one of the top 75 medical schools for research in the U.S.: **Vanderbilt University** (#13). The rankings are based on a weighted average of 11 measures of quality: quality assessment; peer assessment score; assessment score by residency directors; research activity; total research activity; average research activity per faculty member; student selectivity; median MCAT total score; median undergraduate GPA; acceptance rate; and faculty resources. *U.S. News & World Report, "America's Best Graduate Schools, Medical, 2023"*

According to *U.S. News & World Report,* the Nashville-Davidson—Murfreesboro—Franklin, TN metro area is home to one of the top 75 business schools in the U.S.: **Vanderbilt University (Owen)** (#25 tie). The rankings are based on a weighted average of the following nine measures: quality assessment; peer assessment; recruiter assessment; placement success; mean starting salary and bonus; student selectivity; mean GMAT and GRE scores; mean undergraduate GPA; and acceptance rate. *U.S. News & World Report, "America's Best Graduate Schools, Business, 2023"*

EMPLOYERS

Major Employers

Company Name	Industry
AHOM Holdings	Home health care services
Asurion Corporation	Business services nec
Baptist Hospital	General medical & surgical hospitals
Cannon County Knitting Mills	Apparel & outerwear broadwoven fabrics
County of Rutherford	County government
County of Sumner	County government
Gaylord Entertainment Company	Hotels & motels
Gaylord Opryland USA	Hotels & motels
Ingram Book Company	Books, periodicals, & newspapers
International Automotive	Automotive storage garage
LifeWay Christian Resources of the SBC	Religious organizations
Middle Tennessee State University	Colleges & universities
Newspaper Printing Corporation	Newspapers, publishing & printing
Nissan North America	Motor vehicles & car bodies
Primus Automotive Financial Services	Automobile loans including insurance
Psychiatric Solutions	Psychiatric clinic
State Industries	Hot water heaters, household
State of Tennessee	State government
Tennessee Department of Transportation	Regulation, administration of transportation
Vanderbilt Childrens Hospital	General medical & surgical hospitals
Vanderbilt University	Colleges & universities

Note: Companies shown are located within the Nashville-Davidson—Murfreesboro—Franklin, TN Metropolitan Statistical Area.
Source: Hoovers.com; Wikipedia

Best Companies to Work For

Pinnacle Financial Partners, headquartered in Nashville, is among "The 100 Best Companies to Work For." To pick the best companies, *Fortune* partnered with the Great Place to Work Institute. Two-thirds of a company's score is based on the results of the Institute's Trust Index survey, which is sent to a random sample of employees from each company. The questions related to attitudes about management's credibility, job satisfaction, and camaraderie. The other third of the scoring is based on the company's responses to the Institute's Culture Audit, which includes detailed questions about pay and benefit programs, and a series of open-ended questions about hiring practices, internal communication, training, recognition programs, and diversity efforts. Any company that is at least five years old with more than 1,000 U.S. employees is eligible. *Fortune, "The 100 Best Companies to Work For," 2023*

Pinnacle Financial Partners; The General, headquartered in Nashville, are among "Fortune's Best Workplaces for Women." To pick the best companies, *Fortune* partnered with the Great Place to Work Institute. To be considered for the list, companies must be Great Place To Work-Certified. Companies must also employ at least 50 women, at least 20% of their non-executive managers must be female, and at least one executive must be female. To determine the Best Workplaces for Women, Great Place To Work measured the differences in women's survey responses to those of their peers and assesses the impact of demographics and roles on the quality and consistency of women's experiences. Great Place To Work also analyzed the gender balance of each workplace, how it compared to each company's industry, and patterns in representation as women rise from front-line positions to the board of directors. *Fortune, "Best Workplaces for Women," 2022*

PUBLIC SAFETY

Crime Rate

Area	Total Crime	Murder	Rape[3]	Robbery	Aggrav. Assault	Burglary	Larceny-Theft	Motor Vehicle Theft
City	5,228.7	16.4	56.0	253.2	830.1	544.3	3,086.9	441.9
Suburbs[1]	1,755.3	3.0	29.0	27.7	266.9	199.9	1,090.1	138.6
Metro[2]	2,968.8	7.7	38.4	106.5	463.7	320.3	1,787.7	244.5
U.S.	2,356.7	6.5	38.4	73.9	279.7	314.2	1,398.0	246.0

Note: Figures are crimes per 100,000 population; (1) All areas within the metro area that are located outside the city limits; (2) Figures cover the Nashville-Davidson—Murfreesboro—Franklin, TN Metropolitan Statistical Area; (3) All figures shown were reported using the revised Uniform Crime Reporting (UCR) definition of rape; Due to the transition to the National Incident-Based Reporting System (NIBRS), limited city and metro area data was released for 2021.
Source: FBI Uniform Crime Reports, 2020

Hate Crimes

Area	Number of Quarters Reported	Race/Ethnicity/Ancestry	Religion	Sexual Orientation	Disability	Gender	Gender Identity
City	4	3	1	2	0	0	0
U.S.	4	5,227	1,244	1,110	130	75	266

Note: Due to the transition to the National Incident-Based Reporting System (NIBRS), limited crime data was released for 2021.
Source: Federal Bureau of Investigation, Hate Crime Statistics 2020

Identity Theft Consumer Reports

Area	Reports	Reports per 100,000 Population	Rank[2]
MSA[1]	5,176	272	87
U.S.	1,108,609	339	-

Note: (1) Figures cover the Nashville-Davidson—Murfreesboro—Franklin, TN Metropolitan Statistical Area; (2) Rank ranges from 1 to 391 where 1 indicates greatest number of identity theft reports per 100,000 population
Source: Federal Trade Commission, Consumer Sentinel Network Data Book 2022

Fraud and Other Consumer Reports

Area	Reports	Reports per 100,000 Population	Rank[2]
MSA[1]	22,581	1,186	44
U.S.	4,064,520	1,245	-

Note: (1) Figures cover the Nashville-Davidson—Murfreesboro—Franklin, TN Metropolitan Statistical Area; (2) Rank ranges from 1 to 391 where 1 indicates greatest number of fraud and other consumer reports per 100,000 population
Source: Federal Trade Commission, Consumer Sentinel Network Data Book 2022

POLITICS

2020 Presidential Election Results

Area	Biden	Trump	Jorgensen	Hawkins	Other
Davidson County	64.5	32.4	1.1	0.2	1.8
U.S.	51.3	46.8	1.2	0.3	0.5

Note: Results are percentages and may not add to 100% due to rounding
Source: Dave Leip's Atlas of U.S. Presidential Elections

SPORTS

Professional Sports Teams

Team Name	League	Year Established
Nashville Predators	National Hockey League (NHL)	1998
Nashville SC	Major League Soccer (MLS)	1997
Tennessee Titans	National Football League (NFL)	1997

Note: Includes teams located in the Nashville-Davidson—Murfreesboro—Franklin, TN Metropolitan Statistical Area.
Source: Wikipedia, Major Professional Sports Teams of the United States and Canada, April 12, 2023

CLIMATE

Average and Extreme Temperatures

Temperature	Jan	Feb	Mar	Apr	May	Jun	Jul	Aug	Sep	Oct	Nov	Dec	Yr.
Extreme High (°F)	78	84	86	91	95	106	107	104	105	94	84	79	107
Average High (°F)	47	51	60	71	79	87	90	89	83	72	60	50	70
Average Temp. (°F)	38	41	50	60	68	76	80	79	72	61	49	41	60
Average Low (°F)	28	31	39	48	57	65	69	68	61	48	39	31	49
Extreme Low (°F)	-17	-13	2	23	34	42	54	49	36	26	-1	-10	-17

Note: Figures cover the years 1948-1990
Source: National Climatic Data Center, International Station Meteorological Climate Summary, 9/96

Average Precipitation/Snowfall/Humidity

Precip./Humidity	Jan	Feb	Mar	Apr	May	Jun	Jul	Aug	Sep	Oct	Nov	Dec	Yr.
Avg. Precip. (in.)	4.4	4.2	5.0	4.1	4.6	3.7	3.8	3.3	3.2	2.6	3.9	4.6	47.4
Avg. Snowfall (in.)	4	3	1	Tr	0	0	0	0	0	Tr	1	1	11
Avg. Rel. Hum. 6am (%)	81	81	80	81	86	86	88	90	90	87	83	82	85
Avg. Rel. Hum. 3pm (%)	61	57	51	48	52	52	54	53	52	49	55	59	54

Note: Figures cover the years 1948-1990; Tr = Trace amounts (<0.05 in. of rain; <0.5 in. of snow)
Source: National Climatic Data Center, International Station Meteorological Climate Summary, 9/96

Weather Conditions

Temperature			Daytime Sky			Precipitation		
10°F & below	32°F & below	90°F & above	Clear	Partly cloudy	Cloudy	0.01 inch or more precip.	0.1 inch or more snow/ice	Thunderstorms
5	76	51	98	135	132	119	8	54

Note: Figures are average number of days per year and cover the years 1948-1990
Source: National Climatic Data Center, International Station Meteorological Climate Summary, 9/96

HAZARDOUS WASTE

Superfund Sites

The Nashville-Davidson—Murfreesboro—Franklin, TN metro area has no sites on the EPA's Superfund Final National Priorities List. There are a total of 1,165 Superfund sites with a status of proposed or final on the list in the U.S. *U.S. Environmental Protection Agency, National Priorities List, April 12, 2023*

AIR QUALITY

Air Quality Trends: Ozone

	1990	1995	2000	2005	2010	2015	2018	2019	2020	2021
MSA[1]	0.089	0.092	0.084	0.078	0.073	0.065	0.068	0.064	0.061	0.064
U.S.	0.087	0.089	0.081	0.080	0.072	0.067	0.069	0.065	0.065	0.067

Note: (1) Data covers the Nashville-Davidson—Murfreesboro—Franklin, TN Metropolitan Statistical Area. The values shown are the composite ozone concentration averages among trend sites based on the highest fourth daily maximum 8-hour concentration in parts per million. These trends are based on sites having an adequate record of monitoring data during the trend period. Data from exceptional events are included.
Source: U.S. Environmental Protection Agency, Air Quality Monitoring Information, "Air Quality Trends by City, 1990-2021"

Air Quality Index

Area	Percent of Days when Air Quality was...[2]					AQI Statistics[2]	
	Good	Moderate	Unhealthy for Sensitive Groups	Unhealthy	Very Unhealthy	Maximum	Median
MSA[1]	60.5	38.1	1.4	0.0	0.0	133	46

Note: (1) Data covers the Nashville-Davidson—Murfreesboro—Franklin, TN Metropolitan Statistical Area; (2) Based on 365 days with AQI data in 2021. Air Quality Index (AQI) is an index for reporting daily air quality. EPA calculates the AQI for five major air pollutants regulated by the Clean Air Act: ground-level ozone, particle pollution (aka particulate matter), carbon monoxide, sulfur dioxide, and nitrogen dioxide. The AQI runs from 0 to 500. The higher the AQI value, the greater the level of air pollution and the greater the health concern. There are six AQI categories: "Good" AQI is between 0 and 50. Air quality is considered satisfactory; "Moderate" AQI is between 51 and 100. Air quality is acceptable; "Unhealthy for Sensitive Groups" When AQI values are between 101 and 150, members of sensitive groups may experience health effects; "Unhealthy" When AQI values are between 151 and 200 everyone may begin to experience health effects; "Very Unhealthy" AQI values between 201 and 300 trigger a health alert; "Hazardous" AQI values over 300 trigger warnings of emergency conditions (not shown).
Source: U.S. Environmental Protection Agency, Air Quality Index Report, 2021

Air Quality Index Pollutants

Area	Percent of Days when AQI Pollutant was...[2]					
	Carbon Monoxide	Nitrogen Dioxide	Ozone	Sulfur Dioxide	Particulate Matter 2.5	Particulate Matter 10
MSA[1]	0.0	5.2	33.4	(3)	61.4	0.0

Note: (1) Data covers the Nashville-Davidson—Murfreesboro—Franklin, TN Metropolitan Statistical Area; (2) Based on 365 days with AQI data in 2021. The Air Quality Index (AQI) is an index for reporting daily air quality. EPA calculates the AQI for five major air pollutants regulated by the Clean Air Act: ground-level ozone, particle pollution (also known as particulate matter), carbon monoxide, sulfur dioxide, and nitrogen dioxide. The AQI runs from 0 to 500. The higher the AQI value, the greater the level of air pollution and the greater the health concern; (3) Sulfur dioxide is no longer included in this table (as of December 8, 2021) because SO_2 concentrations tend to be very localized and not necessarily representative of broad geographical areas like counties and CBSAs.
Source: U.S. Environmental Protection Agency, Air Quality Index Report, 2021

Maximum Air Pollutant Concentrations: Particulate Matter, Ozone, CO and Lead

	Particulate Matter 10 (ug/m^3)	Particulate Matter 2.5 Wtd AM (ug/m^3)	Particulate Matter 2.5 24-Hr (ug/m^3)	Ozone (ppm)	Carbon Monoxide (ppm)	Lead (ug/m^3)
MSA[1] Level	50	9.4	24	0.066	2	n/a
NAAQS[2]	150	15	35	0.075	9	0.15
Met NAAQS[2]	Yes	Yes	Yes	Yes	Yes	n/a

Note: (1) Data covers the Nashville-Davidson—Murfreesboro—Franklin, TN Metropolitan Statistical Area; Data from exceptional events are included; (2) National Ambient Air Quality Standards; ppm = parts per million; ug/m^3 = micrograms per cubic meter; n/a not available.
Concentrations: Particulate Matter 10 (coarse particulate)—highest second maximum 24-hour concentration; Particulate Matter 2.5 Wtd AM (fine particulate)—highest weighted annual mean concentration; Particulate Matter 2.5 24-Hour (fine particulate)—highest 98th percentile 24-hour concentration; Ozone—highest fourth daily maximum 8-hour concentration; Carbon Monoxide—highest second maximum non-overlapping 8-hour concentration; Lead—maximum running 3-month average
Source: U.S. Environmental Protection Agency, Air Quality Monitoring Information, "Air Quality Statistics by City, 2021"

Maximum Air Pollutant Concentrations: Nitrogen Dioxide and Sulfur Dioxide

	Nitrogen Dioxide AM (ppb)	Nitrogen Dioxide 1-Hr (ppb)	Sulfur Dioxide AM (ppb)	Sulfur Dioxide 1-Hr (ppb)	Sulfur Dioxide 24-Hr (ppb)
MSA[1] Level	13	52	n/a	4	n/a
NAAQS[2]	53	100	30	75	140
Met NAAQS[2]	Yes	Yes	n/a	Yes	n/a

Note: (1) Data covers the Nashville-Davidson—Murfreesboro—Franklin, TN Metropolitan Statistical Area; Data from exceptional events are included; (2) National Ambient Air Quality Standards; ppm = parts per million; ug/m^3 = micrograms per cubic meter; n/a not available.
Concentrations: Nitrogen Dioxide AM—highest arithmetic mean concentration; Nitrogen Dioxide 1-Hr—highest 98th percentile 1-hour daily maximum concentration; Sulfur Dioxide AM—highest annual mean concentration; Sulfur Dioxide 1-Hr—highest 99th percentile 1-hour daily maximum concentration; Sulfur Dioxide 24-Hr—highest second maximum 24-hour concentration
Source: U.S. Environmental Protection Agency, Air Quality Monitoring Information, "Air Quality Statistics by City, 2021"

New Orleans, Louisiana

Background

New Orleans, a port city upriver from the mouth of the Mississippi River, is one of the country's most interesting cities. This birthplace of jazz is rich in unique local history, distinctive neighborhoods, and an unmistakably individual character.

New Orleans was founded on behalf of France by the brothers Le Moyne, Sieurs d'Iberville, and de Bienville, in 1718. Despite disease, starvation, and an unwilling working class, New Orleans emerged as a genteel antebellum slave society, fashioning itself after the rigid social hierarchy of Versailles. After New Orleans was ceded to Spain after the French & Indian War, this unequal lifestyle persisted.

The port city briefly returned to French control, then became a crown jewel in the 1803 Louisiana Purchase to the U.S. The transfer of control changed New Orleans's Old-World isolation. American settlers introduced aggressive business acumen to the area, as well as the idea of respect for the self-made man. As trade opened with countries around the world, this made for a happy union. New Orleans became "Queen City of the South," growing prosperous from adventurous riverboat traders and speculators, as well as the cotton trade.

Today, much of the city's Old-World charm remains, resulting from Southern, Creole, African American, and European cultures. New Orleans' cuisine, indigenous music, unique festivals, and sultry, pleasing atmosphere, drew nearly 41 million visitors in 2021. The Ernest N. Morial Convention Center's numerous convention goers continuously fill more than 35,000 rooms. Another economic pillar is the Port of New Orleans, one of the nation's leading general cargo ports. In recent years, it has seen $400 million invested in new facilities.

New Orleans has a diverse economy with a focus on energy, advanced manufacturing, international trade, healthcare, and tourism.

In 2005, failure of federal levees following Hurricane Katrina put 80 percent of the city under floodwaters for weeks. The Crescent City's revival since then is a testament to her unique spirit, an influx of federal dollars, and an outpouring from volunteers ranging from church groups to spring breakers who returned year after year to help rebuild.

The influx of young people who arrived after Hurricane Katrina gave rise to a new start-up spirit. State tax breaks have helped to turn New Orleans into "Hollywood South," where more than 50 films and TV shows were produced in the last five years. New Orleans has given birth to a mother lode of cultural phenomena: Dixieland jazz, musicians Louis Armstrong, Mahalia Jackson, Dr. John, and chefs Emeril Lagasse and John Besh. The city is aware of its "cultural economy," which employs 12.5 percent of the local workforce. Popular tourist draws include the annual Mardi Gras celebration—which spans two long spring weekends leading up to Fat Tuesday—and the annual New Orleans Jazz & Heritage Festival.

The Louisiana Superdome - a home for the homeless after Katrina - was renovated and renamed in 2011 the Mercedes Benz Superdome. It is home to the 2010 Super Bowl champion New Orleans Saints and hosted the 2013 Super Bowl. In 2021 it was renamed Caesars Superdome

Louis Armstrong New Orleans International Airport was made more efficient for travelers by the expansion of the Consolidated Rental Car Facility project that has also brought scattered facilities under one roof. In addition, an effort to boost a medical economy that suffered after Hurricane Katrina, brought the city a new Louisiana State University teaching hospital.

Billions of dollars have been spent in recent years for bridge, airport, road, hospital, and school updates. Post Katrina, most New Orleans public schools became charter schools under the Recovery School District (RSD). In 2018, the RSD returned all its schools to the Orleans Parish School Board. Higher education campuses include Tulane University (including a medical school and law school), Loyola University, and the University of New Orleans. Louisiana State University has a medical school campus downtown.

Cultural amenities include the New Orleans Museum of Art located in the live oak filled City Park, the Ogden Museum of Southern Art, and Audubon Park, designed by John Charles Olmsted with its golf course and the Audubon Zoo.

The New Orleans metro area is virtually surrounded by water, which influences its climate. Between mid-June and September, temperatures are kept down by near-daily sporadic thunderstorms. Cold spells sometimes reach the area in winter but seldom last. Frequent and sometimes heavy rains are typical. Hurricane season officially runs from June 1 to November 30 but typically reaches its height in late summer.

Rankings

General Rankings

- *Insider* listed 23 places in the U.S. that travel industry trends reveal would be popular destinations in 2023. This year the list trends towards cultural and historical happenings, sports events, wellness experiences and invigorating outdoor escapes. According to the website insider.com New Orleans is a place to visit in 2023. *Insider, "23 of the Best Places You Should Travel to in the U.S. in 2023," December 17, 2022*

- The New Orleans metro area was identified as one of America's fastest-growing areas in terms of population and business growth by *MagnifyMoney*. The area ranked #30 out of 35. The 100 most populous metro areas in the U.S. were evaluated on their change from 2011 to 2016 in the following categories: people and housing; workforce and employment opportunities; growing industry. *www.businessinsider.com, "The 35 Cities in the US with the Biggest Influx of People, the Most Work Opportunities, and the Hottest Business Growth," August 12, 2018*

- New Orleans appeared on *Travel + Leisure's* list of "The 15 Best Cities in the United States." The city was ranked #2. Criteria: sights/landmarks; culture; food; friendliness; shopping; and overall value. *Travel + Leisure, "The World's Best Awards 2022" July 12, 2022*

- For its 35th annual "Readers' Choice Awards" survey, *Condé Nast Traveler* ranked its readers' favorite cities in the U.S. Whether it be a longed-for visit or a first on the list, these are the places that inspired a return to travel. The list was broken into large cities and cities under 250,000. New Orleans ranked #8 in the big city category. *Condé Nast Traveler, Readers' Choice Awards 2022, "Best Big Cities in the U.S." October 4, 2022*

Business/Finance Rankings

- WalletHub's latest report ranked over 2,500 cities by the average credit score of its residents. New Orleans was ranked #5 among the ten cities with the lowest average credit score, based on TransUnion data as of October 2022. *www.wallethub.com, "2023's Cities With the Highest & Lowest Credit Scores," March 29, 2023*

- The Brookings Institution ranked the nation's largest cities based on income inequality. New Orleans was ranked #4 (#1 = greatest inequality). Criteria: the "95/20 ratio," a figure representing the income at which a household earns more than 95 percent of all other households, divided by the income at which a household earns more than only 20 percent of all other households. *Brookings Institution, "Household Income Inequality, Largest Cities of 97 Large U.S. Metro Areas, 2014-2016," February 5, 2018*

- The Brookings Institution ranked the 100 largest metro areas in the U.S. based on income inequality. New Orleans was ranked #5 (#1 = greatest inequality). Criteria: the "95/20 ratio," a figure representing the income at which a household earns more than 95 percent of all other households, divided by the income at which a household earns more than only 20 percent of all other households. *Brookings Institution, "Household Income Inequality, 100 Largest U.S. Metro Areas, 2014-2016," February 5, 2018*

- The New Orleans metro area appeared on the Milken Institute "2022 Best Performing Cities" list. Rank: #198 out of 200 large metro areas (population over 250,000). Criteria: job growth; wage and salary growth; high-tech output growth; housing affordability; household broadband access. *Milken Institute, "Best-Performing Cities 2022," March 28, 2022*

- *Forbes* ranked the 200 most populous metro areas to determine the nation's "Best Places for Business and Careers." The New Orleans metro area was ranked #146. Criteria: costs (business and living); job growth (past and projected); income growth; quality of life; educational attainment (college and high school); projected economic growth; cultural and leisure opportunities; workplace tolerance laws; net migration patterns. *Forbes, "The Best Places for Business and Careers 2019: Seattle Still On Top," October 30, 2019*

Children/Family Rankings

- New Orleans was selected as one of the most playful cities in the U.S. by KaBOOM! The organization's Playful City USA initiative honors cities and towns across the nation that have made their communities more playable. Criteria: pledging to integrate play as a solution to challenges in their communities; making it easy for children to get active and balanced play; creating more family-friendly and innovative communities as a result. *KaBOOM! National Campaign for Play, "2017 Playful City USA Communities"*

Culture/Performing Arts Rankings

- New Orleans was selected as one of the 25 best cities for moviemakers in North America. Great film cities are places where filmmaking dreams can come true, that offer more creative space, lower costs, and great outdoor locations. NYC & LA were intentionally excluded. Criteria: longstanding reputations as film-friendly communities; film community and culture; affordability; and quality of life. The city was ranked #3. *MovieMaker Magazine, "Best Places to Live and Work as a Moviemaker, 2023," January 18, 2023*

- New Orleans was selected as one of "America's Favorite Cities." The city ranked #7 in the "Architecture" category. Respondents to an online survey were asked to rate their favorite place (population over 100,000) in over 65 categories. *Travelandleisure.com, "America's Favorite Cities for Architecture 2016," March 2, 2017*

Dating/Romance Rankings

- New Orleans was selected as one of America's best cities for singles by the readers of *Travel + Leisure* in their annual "America's Favorite Cities" survey. Criteria included good-looking locals, cool shopping, an active bar scene and hipster-magnet coffee bars. *Travel + Leisure, "Best Cities in America for Singles," July 21, 2017*

Education Rankings

- Personal finance website *WalletHub* analyzed the 150 largest U.S. metropolitan statistical areas to determine where the most educated Americans are putting their degrees to work. Criteria: education levels; percentage of workers with degrees; education quality and attainment gap; public school quality rankings; quality and enrollment of each metro area's universities. New Orleans was ranked #98 (#1 = most educated city). *www.WalletHub.com, "Most & Least Educated Cities in America," July 18, 2022*

- New Orleans was selected as one of America's most literate cities. The city ranked #28 out of the 84 largest U.S. cities. Criteria: number of booksellers; library resources; Internet resources; educational attainment; periodical publishing resources; newspaper circulation. *Central Connecticut State University, "America's Most Literate Cities, 2018," February 2019*

Environmental Rankings

- Sperling's BestPlaces assessed the 50 largest metropolitan areas of the United States for the likelihood of dangerously extreme weather events or earthquakes. In general the Southeast and South-Central regions have the highest risk of weather extremes and earthquakes, while the Pacific Northwest enjoys the lowest risk. Of the most risky metropolitan areas, the New Orleans metro area was ranked #10. *www.bestplaces.net, "Avoid Natural Disasters: BestPlaces Reveals The Top 10 Safest Places to Live," October 25, 2017*

- New Orleans was highlighted as one of the top 59 cleanest metro areas for short-term particle pollution (24-hour PM 2.5) in the U.S. during 2019 through 2021. Monitors in these cities reported no days with unhealthful PM 2.5 levels. *American Lung Association, "State of the Air 2023," April 19, 2023*

Health/Fitness Rankings

- For each of the 100 largest cities in the United States, the American Fitness Index®, compiled in partnership between the American College of Sports Medicine and the Elevance Health Foundation, evaluated community infrastructure and 34 health behaviors including preventive health, levels of chronic disease conditions, food insecurity, sleep quality, pedestrian safety, air quality, and community/environment resources that support physical activity. New Orleans ranked #46 for "community fitness." *americanfitnessindex.org, "2022 ACSM American Fitness Index Summary Report," July 12, 2022*

- New Orleans was identified as a "2022 Spring Allergy Capital." The area ranked #52 out of 100. Three groups of factors were used to identify the most challenging cities for people with allergies during the spring season: annual spring pollen scores; over the counter allergy medicine use; number of board-certified allergy specialists. *Asthma and Allergy Foundation of America, "Spring Allergy Capitals 2022," March 2, 2022*

- New Orleans was identified as a "2022 Fall Allergy Capital." The area ranked #47 out of 100. Three groups of factors were used to identify the most challenging cities for people with allergies during the fall season: annual fall pollen scores; over the counter allergy medicine use; number of board-certified allergy specialists. *Asthma and Allergy Foundation of America, "Fall Allergy Capitals 2022," March 2, 2022*

- New Orleans was identified as a "2022 Asthma Capital." The area ranked #35 out of the nation's 100 largest metropolitan areas. Criteria: estimated asthma prevalence; asthma-related mortality; and ER visits due to asthma. Risk factors analyzed but not factored in the rankings: annual pollen score; annual air quality; public smoking laws; access to board-certified asthma specialists; rescue and controller medication use; uninsured rate; poverty rate. *Asthma and Allergy Foundation of America, "Asthma Capitals 2022: The Most Challenging Places to Live With Asthma," September 14, 2022*

Pet Rankings

- New Orleans appeared on *The Dogington Post* site as one of the top cities for dog lovers, ranking #9 out of 15. The real estate marketplace, Zillow®, and Rover, the largest pet sitter and dog walker network, introduced a new list of "Top Emerging Dog-Friendly Cities" for 2021. Criteria: number of new dog accounts on the Rover platform; and rentals and listings that mention features that attract dog owners (fenced-in yards, dog houses, dog door or proximity to a dog park). *www.dogingtonpost.com, "15 Cities Emerging as Dog-Friendliest in 2021," May 11, 2021*

Real Estate Rankings

- *WalletHub* compared the most populated U.S. cities to determine which had the best markets for real estate agents. New Orleans ranked #148 where demand was high and pay was the best. Criteria: sales per agent; annual median wage for real-estate agents; monthly average starting salary for real estate agents; real estate job density and competition; unemployment rate; home turnover rate; housing-market health index; and other relevant metrics. *www.WalletHub.com, "2021 Best Places to Be a Real Estate Agent," May 12, 2021*

- The New Orleans metro area was identified as one of the 10 worst condo markets in the U.S. in 2022. The area ranked #62 out of 63 markets. Criteria: year-over-year change of median sales price of existing apartment condo-coop homes between the 4th quarter of 2021 and the 4th quarter of 2022. *National Association of Realtors®, Median Sales Price of Existing Apartment Condo-Coops Homes for Metropolitan Areas, 4th Quarter 2022*

Safety Rankings

- To identify the most dangerous cities in America, *24/7 Wall St.* focused on violent crime categories—murder, non-negligent manslaughter, rape, robbery, and aggravated assault—as reported for every 100,000 residents using data from the FBI's 2020 annual Uniform Crime Report. For cities with populations over 25,000, New Orleans was ranked #29. *247wallst.com, "America's Most Dangerous Cities" November 12, 2021*

- Statistics drawn from the FBI's Uniform Crime Report were used to rank the cities where violent crime rose the most year over year from 2019 to 2020. Only cities with 25,000 or more residents were included. *24/7 Wall St.* found that New Orleans placed #41 of those with a notable surge in incidents of violent crime. *247wallst.com, "American Cities Where Crime Is Soaring," March 4, 2022*

- Allstate ranked the 200 largest cities in America in terms of driver safety. New Orleans ranked #177. Criteria: internal property damage claims over a two-year period from January 2016 to December 2017. The report helps increase the importance of safety and awareness behind the wheel. *Allstate, "Allstate America's Best Drivers Report, 2019" June 24, 2019*

- New Orleans was identified as one of the most dangerous cities in America by NeighborhoodScout. The city ranked #33 out of 100 (#1 = most dangerous). Criteria: number of violent crimes per 1,000 residents. The editors evaluated cities with 25,000 or more residents. *NeighborhoodScout.com, "2023 Top 100 Most Dangerous Cities in the U.S.," January 12, 2023*

- The National Insurance Crime Bureau ranked 390 metro areas in the U.S. in terms of per capita rates of vehicle theft. The New Orleans metro area ranked #48 (#1 = highest rate). Criteria: number of vehicle theft offenses per 100,000 inhabitants in 2021. *National Insurance Crime Bureau, "Hot Spots 2021," September 1, 2022*

Seniors/Retirement Rankings

- From its Best Cities for Successful Aging indexes, the Milken Institute generated rankings for metropolitan areas, weighing data in nine categories—health care, wellness, living arrangements, transportation and convenience, financial characteristics, education, employment, community engagement, and overall livability. The New Orleans metro area was ranked #55 overall in the large metro area category. *Milken Institute, "Best Cities for Successful Aging, 2017" March 14, 2017*

Sports/Recreation Rankings

- New Orleans was chosen as one of America's best cities for bicycling. The city ranked #22 out of 50. Criteria: cycling infrastructure that is safe and friendly for all ages; energy and bike culture. The editors evaluated cities with populations of 100,000 or more. *Bicycling, "The 50 Best Bike Cities in America," October 10, 2018*

Transportation Rankings

- According to the INRIX "2022 Global Traffic Scorecard," New Orleans was identified as one of the most congested metro areas in the U.S. The area ranked #11 out of 25. Criteria: average annual time spent in traffic and average cost of congestion per motorist. *Inrix.com, "Return to Work, Higher Gas Prices & Inflation Drove Americans to Spend Hundreds More in Time and Money Commuting," January 10, 2023*

Women/Minorities Rankings

- *Travel + Leisure* listed the best cities in and around the U.S. for a memorable and fun girls' trip, even on a budget. Whether it is for a special occasion, to make new memories or just to get away, New Orleans is sure to have something for all the ladies in your tribe. *Travel + Leisure, "25 Affordable Girls Weekend Getaways That Won't Break the Bank," November 25, 2022*

- New Orleans was selected as one of the queerest cities in America by *The Advocate*. The city ranked #5 out of 25. Criteria, among many: Trans Pride parades/festivals; gay rugby teams; lesbian bars; LGBTQ centers; theater screenings of "Moonlight"; LGBTQ-inclusive nondiscrimination ordinances; and gay bowling teams. *The Advocate, "Queerest Cities in America 2017" January 12, 2017*

- Personal finance website *WalletHub* compared more than 180 U.S. cities across two key dimensions, "Hispanic Business-Friendliness" and "Hispanic Purchasing Power," to arrive at the most favorable conditions for Hispanic entrepreneurs. New Orleans was ranked #70 out of 182. Criteria includes: share of Hispanic-Owned Businesses; Hispanic entrepreneurship rate to median annual income of Hispanics; Small Business-Friendliness score; cost of living; and number of Hispanics with at least a bachelor's degree. *WalletHub.com, "2019's Best Cities for Hispanic Entrepreneurs," May 1, 2019*

Miscellaneous Rankings

- *MoveHub* ranked 446 hipster cities across 20 countries, using its new and improved *alternative* Hipster Index and New Orleans came out as #22 among the top 50. Criteria: population over 150,000; number of vintage boutiques; density of tattoo parlors; vegan places to eat; coffee shops; and density of vinyl record stores. *www.movehub.com, "The Hipster Index: Brighton Pips Portland to Global Top Spot," July 28, 2021*

- In its roundup of St. Patrick's Day parades "Gayot" listed the best festivals and parades of all things Irish. The festivities in New Orleans as among the best in North America. *www.gayot.com, "Best St. Patrick's Day Parades," March 2023*

- *WalletHub* compared the 150 most populated U.S. cities to determine their operating efficiency. A "Quality of Services" score was constructed for each city and then divided by the total budget per capita to reveal which were managed the best. New Orleans ranked #88. Criteria: financial stability; economy; education; safety; health; infrastructure and pollution. *www.WalletHub.com, "2022's Best- & Worst-Run Cities in America," June 21, 2022*

- New Orleans was selected as one of "America's Friendliest Cities." The city ranked #4 in the "Friendliest" category. Respondents to an online survey were asked to rate 38 top urban destinations in the United States as to general friendliness, as well as manners, politeness and warm disposition. *Travel + Leisure, "America's Friendliest Cities," October 20, 2017*

Business Environment

DEMOGRAPHICS

Population Growth

Area	1990 Census	2000 Census	2010 Census	2020 Census	Population Growth (%) 1990-2020	Population Growth (%) 2010-2020
City	496,938	484,674	343,829	383,997	-22.7	11.7
MSA[1]	1,264,391	1,316,510	1,167,764	1,271,845	0.6	8.9
U.S.	248,709,873	281,421,906	308,745,538	331,449,281	33.3	7.4

Note: (1) Figures cover the New Orleans-Metairie, LA Metropolitan Statistical Area
Source: U.S. Census Bureau, 1990 Census, 2000 Census, 2010 Census, 2020 Census

Race

Area	White Alone[2] (%)	Black Alone[2] (%)	Asian Alone[2] (%)	AIAN[3] Alone[2] (%)	NHOPI[4] Alone[2] (%)	Other Race Alone[2] (%)	Two or More Races (%)
City	32.9	54.2	2.8	0.3	0.0	3.2	6.4
MSA[1]	50.3	33.3	2.9	0.5	0.0	4.8	8.1
U.S.	61.6	12.4	6.0	1.1	0.2	8.4	10.2

Note: (1) Figures cover the New Orleans-Metairie, LA Metropolitan Statistical Area; (2) Alone is defined as not being in combination with one or more other races; (3) American Indian and Alaska Native; (4) Native Hawaiian and Other Pacific Islander
Source: U.S. Census Bureau, 2020 Census

Hispanic or Latino Origin

Area	Total (%)	Mexican (%)	Puerto Rican (%)	Cuban (%)	Other (%)
City	5.6	1.2	0.2	0.6	3.5
MSA[1]	9.1	1.7	0.5	0.6	6.3
U.S.	18.4	11.2	1.8	0.7	4.7

Note: Persons of Hispanic or Latino origin can be of any race; (1) Figures cover the New Orleans-Metairie, LA Metropolitan Statistical Area
Source: U.S. Census Bureau, 2017-2021 American Community Survey 5-Year Estimates

Age

Area	Under Age 5	Age 5–19	Age 20–34	Age 35–44	Age 45–54	Age 55–64	Age 65–74	Age 75–84	Age 85+	Median Age
City	5.5	17.5	24.9	14.0	11.1	12.3	9.4	3.9	1.5	36.2
MSA[1]	5.7	18.9	20.3	13.3	11.9	13.4	10.3	4.6	1.7	38.6
U.S.	5.6	19.2	20.2	12.7	12.4	13.1	10.0	4.9	1.9	38.8

Note: (1) Figures cover the New Orleans-Metairie, LA Metropolitan Statistical Area
Source: U.S. Census Bureau, 2020 Census

Disability by Age

Area	All Ages	Under 18 Years Old	18 to 64 Years Old	65 Years and Over
City	13.7	4.7	11.8	34.0
MSA[1]	14.9	5.4	12.7	36.4
U.S.	12.6	4.4	10.3	33.4

Note: Figures show percent of the civilian noninstitutionalized population that reported having a disability. Disability status is determined from six types of difficulty: vision, hearing, cognitive, ambulatory, self-care, and independent living. For children under 5 years old, hearing and vision difficulty are used to determine disability status. For children between the ages of 5 and 14, disability status is determined from hearing, vision, cognitive, ambulatory, and self-care difficulties. For people aged 15 years and older, they are considered to have a disability if they have difficulty with any one of the six difficulty types; Note: (1) Figures cover the New Orleans-Metairie, LA Metropolitan Statistical Area
Source: U.S. Census Bureau, 2017-2021 American Community Survey 5-Year Estimates

Ancestry

Area	German	Irish	English	American	Italian	Polish	French[2]	Scottish	Dutch
City	6.1	5.7	4.9	2.2	3.7	0.9	5.2	1.0	0.4
MSA[1]	9.6	7.9	5.5	4.8	7.3	0.7	11.0	1.0	0.4
U.S.	12.8	9.6	8.1	5.7	5.0	2.7	2.2	1.6	1.1

Note: Figures are the percentage of the total population reporting a particular ancestry. The nine most commonly reported ancestries in the U.S. are shown. Figures include multiple ancestries (e.g. if a person reported being Irish and Italian, they were included in both columns); (1) Figures cover the New Orleans-Metairie, LA Metropolitan Statistical Area; (2) Excludes Basque
Source: U.S. Census Bureau, 2017-2021 American Community Survey 5-Year Estimates

Foreign-born Population

Area	Any Foreign Country	Asia	Mexico	Europe	Caribbean	Central America[2]	South America	Africa	Canada
City	5.4	1.9	0.3	0.7	0.4	1.3	0.4	0.2	0.2
MSA[1]	7.6	2.1	0.5	0.5	0.9	2.7	0.4	0.3	0.1
U.S.	13.6	4.2	3.3	1.5	1.4	1.1	1.1	0.8	0.2

Percent of Population Born in

Note: (1) Figures cover the New Orleans-Metairie, LA Metropolitan Statistical Area; (2) Excludes Mexico.
Source: U.S. Census Bureau, 2017-2021 American Community Survey 5-Year Estimates

Household Size

Area	One	Two	Three	Four	Five	Six	Seven or More	Average Household Size
City	46.5	28.7	12.5	8.0	2.8	1.1	0.5	2.40
MSA[1]	34.1	32.0	15.3	11.3	4.7	1.7	1.0	2.50
U.S.	28.1	33.8	15.5	12.9	6.0	2.3	1.4	2.60

Note: (1) Figures cover the New Orleans-Metairie, LA Metropolitan Statistical Area
Source: U.S. Census Bureau, 2017-2021 American Community Survey 5-Year Estimates

Household Relationships

Area	Householder	Opposite-sex Spouse	Same-sex Spouse	Opposite-sex Unmarried Partner	Same-sex Unmarried Partner	Child[2]	Grandchild	Other Relatives	Non-relatives
City	43.0	11.0	0.3	3.1	0.4	26.1	3.2	4.6	4.3
MSA[1]	40.3	15.3	0.2	2.7	0.2	28.8	3.1	4.6	2.9
U.S.	38.3	17.5	0.2	2.5	0.2	28.3	2.4	4.8	3.4

Note: Figures are percent of the total population; (1) Figures cover the New Orleans-Metairie, LA Metropolitan Statistical Area; (2) Includes biological, adopted, and stepchildren of the householder
Source: U.S. Census Bureau, 2020 Census

Gender

Area	Males	Females	Males per 100 Females
City	181,171	202,826	89.3
MSA[1]	610,653	661,192	92.4
U.S.	162,685,811	168,763,470	96.4

Note: (1) Figures cover the New Orleans-Metairie, LA Metropolitan Statistical Area
Source: U.S. Census Bureau, 2020 Census

Marital Status

Area	Never Married	Now Married[2]	Separated	Widowed	Divorced
City	49.7	29.4	2.6	5.5	12.8
MSA[1]	37.8	41.7	2.3	6.0	12.1
U.S.	33.8	48.0	1.8	5.6	10.8

Note: Figures are percentages and cover the population 15 years of age and older; (1) Figures cover the New Orleans-Metairie, LA Metropolitan Statistical Area; (2) Excludes separated
Source: U.S. Census Bureau, 2017-2021 American Community Survey 5-Year Estimates

Religious Groups by Family

Area	Catholic	Baptist	Methodist	LDS[2]	Pentecostal	Lutheran	Islam	Adventist	Other
MSA[1]	42.1	9.3	2.5	0.5	2.1	0.5	1.4	1.0	8.0
U.S.	18.7	7.3	3.0	2.0	1.8	1.7	1.3	1.3	11.6

Note: Figures are the number of adherents as a percentage of the total population and cover the eight largest religious groups in the U.S; (1) Figures cover the New Orleans-Metairie, LA Metropolitan Statistical Area; (2) Church of Jesus Christ of Latter-day Saints
Sources: 2020 U.S. Religion Census, Association of Statisticians of American Religious Bodies; The Association of Religion Data Archives (ARDA)

Religious Groups by Tradition

Area	Catholic	Evangelical Protestant	Mainline Protestant	Black Protestant	Islam	Judaism	Hinduism	Orthodox	Buddhism
MSA[1]	42.1	13.5	3.0	4.9	1.4	0.4	0.3	0.1	0.3
U.S.	18.7	16.5	5.2	2.3	1.3	0.6	0.4	0.4	0.3

Note: Figures are the number of adherents as a percentage of the total population; (1) Figures cover the New Orleans-Metairie, LA Metropolitan Statistical Area
Sources: 2020 U.S. Religion Census, Association of Statisticians of American Religious Bodies; The Association of Religion Data Archives (ARDA)

ECONOMY

Gross Metropolitan Product

Area	2020	2021	2022	2023	Rank[2]
MSA[1]	76.4	82.6	91.2	96.5	48

Note: Figures are in billions of dollars; (1) Figures cover the New Orleans-Metairie, LA Metropolitan Statistical Area; (2) Rank is based on 2021 data and ranges from 1 to 381
Source: U.S. Conference of Mayors, U.S. Metro Economies: U.S. Metros Compared to Global and State Economies, June 2022

Economic Growth

Area	2018-20 (%)	2021 (%)	2022 (%)	2023 (%)	Rank[2]
MSA[1]	-2.2	2.6	1.8	3.3	304
U.S.	-0.6	5.7	3.1	2.9	—

Note: Figures are real gross metropolitan product (GMP) growth rates and represent average annual percent change; (1) Figures cover the New Orleans-Metairie, LA Metropolitan Statistical Area; (2) Rank is based on 2020 2-year average annual percent change and ranges from 1 to 381
Source: U.S. Conference of Mayors, U.S. Metro Economies: U.S. Metros Compared to Global and State Economies, June 2022

Metropolitan Area Exports

Area	2016	2017	2018	2019	2020	2021	Rank[2]
MSA[1]	29,518.8	31,648.5	36,570.4	34,109.6	31,088.4	35,773.5	8

Note: Figures are in millions of dollars; (1) Figures cover the New Orleans-Metairie, LA Metropolitan Statistical Area; (2) Rank is based on 2021 data and ranges from 1 to 388
Source: U.S. Department of Commerce, International Trade Administration, Office of Trade and Economic Analysis, Industry and Analysis, Exports by Metropolitan Area, data extracted March 16, 2023

Building Permits

Area	Single-Family 2021	Single-Family 2022	Pct. Chg.	Multi-Family 2021	Multi-Family 2022	Pct. Chg.	Total 2021	Total 2022	Pct. Chg.
City	716	615	-14.1	860	1,007	17.1	1,576	1,622	2.9
MSA[1]	4,018	3,101	-22.8	1,264	1,065	-15.7	5,282	4,166	-21.1
U.S.	1,115,400	975,600	-12.5	621,600	689,500	10.9	1,737,000	1,665,100	-4.1

Note: (1) Figures cover the New Orleans-Metairie, LA Metropolitan Statistical Area; Figures represent new, privately-owned housing units authorized (unadjusted data); All permit data are based on estimates with imputation
Source: U.S. Census Bureau, Manufacturing, Mining, and Construction Statistics, Building Permits, 2021, 2022

Bankruptcy Filings

Area	Business Filings 2021	Business Filings 2022	% Chg.	Nonbusiness Filings 2021	Nonbusiness Filings 2022	% Chg.
Orleans Parish	31	11	-64.5	263	287	9.1
U.S.	14,347	13,481	-6.0	399,269	374,240	-6.3

Note: Business filings include Chapter 7, Chapter 9, Chapter 11, Chapter 12, Chapter 13, Chapter 15, and Section 304; Nonbusiness filings include Chapter 7, Chapter 11, and Chapter 13
Source: Administrative Office of the U.S. Courts, Business and Nonbusiness Bankruptcy, County Cases Commenced by Chapter of the Bankruptcy Code, During the 12-Month Period Ending December 31, 2021 and Business and Nonbusiness Bankruptcy, County Cases Commenced by Chapter of the Bankruptcy Code, During the 12-Month Period Ending December 31, 2022

Housing Vacancy Rates

Area	Gross Vacancy Rate[2] (%) 2020	2021	2022	Year-Round Vacancy Rate[3] (%) 2020	2021	2022	Rental Vacancy Rate[4] (%) 2020	2021	2022	Homeowner Vacancy Rate[5] (%) 2020	2021	2022
MSA[1]	10.7	12.6	13.4	9.8	11.1	11.5	6.1	7.2	6.6	1.3	1.0	1.6
U.S.	10.6	10.8	10.5	8.2	8.4	8.2	6.3	6.1	5.8	1.0	0.9	0.8

Note: (1) Figures cover the New Orleans-Metairie, LA Metropolitan Statistical Area; (2) The percentage of the total housing inventory that is vacant; (3) The percentage of the housing inventory (excluding seasonal units) that is year-round vacant; (4) The percentage of rental inventory that is vacant for rent; (5) The percentage of homeowner inventory that is vacant for sale
Source: U.S. Census Bureau, Housing Vacancies and Homeownership Annual Statistics: 2020, 2021, 2022

INCOME

Income

Area	Per Capita ($)	Median Household ($)	Average Household ($)
City	34,036	45,594	76,715
MSA[1]	33,792	57,656	83,052
U.S.	37,638	69,021	97,196

Note: (1) Figures cover the New Orleans-Metairie, LA Metropolitan Statistical Area
Source: U.S. Census Bureau, 2017-2021 American Community Survey 5-Year Estimates

Household Income Distribution

Area	Under $15,000	$15,000 -$24,999	$25,000 -$34,999	$35,000 -$49,999	$50,000 -$74,999	$75,000 -$99,999	$100,000 -$149,999	$150,000 and up
City	21.3	11.3	9.5	10.4	15.0	9.4	10.8	12.3
MSA[1]	14.1	9.6	9.1	11.5	16.5	11.7	14.0	13.5
U.S.	9.4	7.8	8.2	11.4	16.8	12.8	16.3	17.3

Note: (1) Figures cover the New Orleans-Metairie, LA Metropolitan Statistical Area
Source: U.S. Census Bureau, 2017-2021 American Community Survey 5-Year Estimates

Poverty Rate

Area	All Ages	Under 18 Years Old	18 to 64 Years Old	65 Years and Over
City	23.8	33.8	21.5	20.6
MSA[1]	17.3	24.6	15.7	13.3
U.S.	12.6	17.0	11.8	9.6

Note: Figures are percentage of people whose income during the past 12 months was below the poverty level; (1) Figures cover the New Orleans-Metairie, LA Metropolitan Statistical Area
Source: U.S. Census Bureau, 2017-2021 American Community Survey 5-Year Estimates

EMPLOYMENT

Labor Force and Employment

Area	Civilian Labor Force Dec. 2021	Civilian Labor Force Dec. 2022	% Chg.	Workers Employed Dec. 2021	Workers Employed Dec. 2022	% Chg.
City	175,708	180,265	2.6	166,032	172,381	3.8
MSA[1]	582,640	600,820	3.1	558,375	579,744	3.8
U.S.	161,696,000	164,224,000	1.6	155,732,000	158,872,000	2.0

Note: Data is not seasonally adjusted and covers workers 16 years of age and older; (1) Figures cover the New Orleans-Metairie, LA Metropolitan Statistical Area
Source: Bureau of Labor Statistics, Local Area Unemployment Statistics

Unemployment Rate

Area	Jan.	Feb.	Mar.	Apr.	May	Jun.	Jul.	Aug.	Sep.	Oct.	Nov.	Dec.
City	6.5	6.0	5.9	5.5	5.5	6.5	6.6	5.5	4.8	4.1	4.0	4.4
MSA[1]	4.9	4.5	4.4	4.1	4.1	5.1	5.0	4.1	3.8	3.3	3.1	3.5
U.S.	4.4	4.1	3.8	3.3	3.4	3.8	3.8	3.8	3.3	3.4	3.4	3.3

Note: Data is not seasonally adjusted and covers workers 16 years of age and older; (1) Figures cover the New Orleans-Metairie, LA Metropolitan Statistical Area
Source: Bureau of Labor Statistics, Local Area Unemployment Statistics

Average Wages

Occupation	$/Hr.	Occupation	$/Hr.
Accountants and Auditors	35.71	Maintenance and Repair Workers	20.69
Automotive Mechanics	22.89	Marketing Managers	61.89
Bookkeepers	21.05	Network and Computer Systems Admin.	39.84
Carpenters	23.83	Nurses, Licensed Practical	24.25
Cashiers	11.45	Nurses, Registered	38.18
Computer Programmers	n/a	Nursing Assistants	14.49
Computer Systems Analysts	42.24	Office Clerks, General	14.52
Computer User Support Specialists	25.14	Physical Therapists	46.62
Construction Laborers	18.62	Physicians	151.73
Cooks, Restaurant	13.82	Plumbers, Pipefitters and Steamfitters	27.73
Customer Service Representatives	17.57	Police and Sheriff's Patrol Officers	23.68
Dentists	88.12	Postal Service Mail Carriers	26.86
Electricians	27.99	Real Estate Sales Agents	24.99
Engineers, Electrical	51.29	Retail Salespersons	14.66
Fast Food and Counter Workers	12.70	Sales Representatives, Technical/Scientific	40.90
Financial Managers	67.00	Secretaries, Exc. Legal/Medical/Executive	18.95
First-Line Supervisors of Office Workers	26.71	Security Guards	15.17
General and Operations Managers	61.48	Surgeons	n/a
Hairdressers/Cosmetologists	14.26	Teacher Assistants, Exc. Postsecondary*	14.50
Home Health and Personal Care Aides	11.09	Teachers, Secondary School, Exc. Sp. Ed.*	27.00
Janitors and Cleaners	12.91	Telemarketers	n/a
Landscaping/Groundskeeping Workers	14.72	Truck Drivers, Heavy/Tractor-Trailer	24.66
Lawyers	68.27	Truck Drivers, Light/Delivery Services	19.53
Maids and Housekeeping Cleaners	12.41	Waiters and Waitresses	12.15

Note: Wage data covers the New Orleans-Metairie, LA Metropolitan Statistical Area; (*) Hourly wages were calculated from annual wage data based on a 40 hour work week; n/a not available.
Source: Bureau of Labor Statistics, Metro Area Occupational Employment & Wage Estimates, May 2022

Employment by Industry

Sector	MSA[1] Number of Employees	MSA[1] Percent of Total	U.S. Percent of Total
Construction	28,700	5.1	5.0
Private Education and Health Services	108,000	19.0	16.1
Financial Activities	28,800	5.1	5.9
Government	68,600	12.1	14.5
Information	9,200	1.6	2.0
Leisure and Hospitality	79,700	14.0	10.3
Manufacturing	30,000	5.3	8.4
Mining and Logging	3,200	0.6	0.4
Other Services	22,900	4.0	3.7
Professional and Business Services	76,400	13.5	14.7
Retail Trade	60,100	10.6	10.2
Transportation, Warehousing, and Utilities	30,000	5.3	4.9
Wholesale Trade	22,100	3.9	3.9

Note: Figures are non-farm employment as of December 2022. Figures are not seasonally adjusted and include workers 16 years of age and older; (1) Figures cover the New Orleans-Metairie, LA Metropolitan Statistical Area
Source: Bureau of Labor Statistics, Current Employment Statistics, Employment, Hours, and Earnings

Employment by Occupation

Occupation Classification	City (%)	MSA[1] (%)	U.S. (%)
Management, Business, Science, and Arts	45.7	40.2	40.3
Natural Resources, Construction, and Maintenance	5.9	9.6	8.7
Production, Transportation, and Material Moving	8.2	10.6	13.1
Sales and Office	19.0	20.7	20.9
Service	21.1	18.9	17.0

Note: Figures cover employed civilians 16 years of age and older; (1) Figures cover the New Orleans-Metairie, LA Metropolitan Statistical Area
Source: U.S. Census Bureau, 2017-2021 American Community Survey 5-Year Estimates

Occupations with Greatest Projected Employment Growth: 2022 – 2024

Occupation[1]	2022 Employment	2024 Projected Employment	Numeric Employment Change	Percent Employment Change
Waiters and Waitresses	30,970	32,690	1,720	5.6
Cooks, Restaurant	14,710	16,310	1,600	10.9
Home Health and Personal Care Aides	36,460	37,760	1,300	3.6
Fast Food and Counter Workers	25,550	26,760	1,210	4.7
Food Preparation Workers	31,490	32,540	1,050	3.3
Light Truck or Delivery Services Drivers	19,040	20,010	970	5.1
First-Line Supervisors of Food Preparation and Serving Workers	15,240	16,130	890	5.8
Laborers and Freight, Stock, and Material Movers, Hand	54,030	54,910	880	1.6
Security Guards	22,660	23,450	790	3.5
Registered Nurses	43,400	44,070	670	1.5

Note: Projections cover Louisiana; (1) Sorted by numeric employment change
Source: www.projectionscentral.com, State Occupational Projections, 2022–2024 Short-Term Projections

Fastest-Growing Occupations: 2022 – 2024

Occupation[1]	2022 Employment	2024 Projected Employment	Numeric Employment Change	Percent Employment Change
Cooks, Restaurant	14,710	16,310	1,600	10.9
Gaming Dealers	2,270	2,510	240	10.6
First-Line Supervisors of Gambling Services Workers	690	760	70	10.1
Tour and Travel Guides	1,090	1,200	110	10.1
Nurse Practitioners	4,190	4,600	410	9.8
Hotel, Motel, and Resort Desk Clerks	3,670	4,030	360	9.8
Lodging Managers	690	750	60	8.7
Parking Lot Attendants	1,420	1,540	120	8.5
Fitness Trainers and Aerobics Instructors	2,350	2,540	190	8.1
Audio and Video Equipment Technicians	880	950	70	8.0

Note: Projections cover Louisiana; (1) Sorted by percent employment change and excludes occupations with numeric employment change less than 50
Source: www.projectionscentral.com, State Occupational Projections, 2022–2024 Short-Term Projections

CITY FINANCES

City Government Finances

Component	2020 ($000)	2020 ($ per capita)
Total Revenues	1,952,018	5,003
Total Expenditures	2,009,937	5,152
Debt Outstanding	825,142	2,115
Cash and Securities[1]	1,194,751	3,062

Note: (1) Cash and security holdings of a government at the close of its fiscal year, including those of its dependent agencies, utilities, and liquor stores.
Source: U.S. Census Bureau, State & Local Government Finances 2020

City Government Revenue by Source

Source	2020 ($000)	2020 ($ per capita)	2020 (%)
General Revenue			
From Federal Government	258,350	662	13.2
From State Government	203,669	522	10.4
From Local Governments	16,963	43	0.9
Taxes			
Property	299,666	768	15.4
Sales and Gross Receipts	295,447	757	15.1
Personal Income	0	0	0.0
Corporate Income	0	0	0.0
Motor Vehicle License	2,183	6	0.1
Other Taxes	40,736	104	2.1
Current Charges	583,243	1,495	29.9
Liquor Store	0	0	0.0
Utility	118,690	304	6.1

Source: U.S. Census Bureau, State & Local Government Finances 2020

City Government Expenditures by Function

Function	2020 ($000)	2020 ($ per capita)	2020 (%)
General Direct Expenditures			
Air Transportation	212,586	544	10.6
Corrections	85,773	219	4.3
Education	0	0	0.0
Employment Security Administration	0	0	0.0
Financial Administration	50,894	130	2.5
Fire Protection	117,125	300	5.8
General Public Buildings	10,025	25	0.5
Governmental Administration, Other	108,289	277	5.4
Health	42,782	109	2.1
Highways	83,219	213	4.1
Hospitals	58,382	149	2.9
Housing and Community Development	258,208	661	12.8
Interest on General Debt	40,140	102	2.0
Judicial and Legal	98,720	253	4.9
Libraries	43	<1	<0.1
Parking	12,466	32	0.6
Parks and Recreation	123,598	316	6.1
Police Protection	90,602	232	4.5
Public Welfare	595	1	0.0
Sewerage	206,036	528	10.3
Solid Waste Management	39,164	100	1.9
Veterans' Services	0	0	0.0
Liquor Store	0	0	0.0
Utility	168,575	432	8.4

Source: U.S. Census Bureau, State & Local Government Finances 2020

TAXES

State Corporate Income Tax Rates

State	Tax Rate (%)	Income Brackets ($)	Num. of Brackets	Financial Institution Tax Rate (%)[a]	Federal Income Tax Ded.
Louisiana	3.5 - 7.5	50,000 - 150,000	3	3.5 - 7.5	Yes

Note: Tax rates as of January 1, 2023; (a) Rates listed are the corporate income tax rate applied to financial institutions or excise taxes based on income. Some states have other taxes based upon the value of deposits or shares.
Source: Federation of Tax Administrators, State Corporate Income Tax Rates, January 1, 2023

State Individual Income Tax Rates

State	Tax Rate (%)	Income Brackets ($)	Personal Exemptions ($) Single	Married	Depend.	Standard Ded. ($) Single	Married
Louisiana (aa)	1.85 - 4.25 (bb)	12,500 - 50,001 (b)	4,500	9,000	1,000 (k)	(k)	(k)

Note: Tax rates as of January 1, 2023; Local- and county-level taxes are not included; Federal income tax is deductible on state income tax returns; (b) For joint returns, taxes are twice the tax on half the couple's income; (k) The amounts reported for Louisiana are a combined personal exemption-standard deduction; (aa) Standard deduction amounts reported are maximums, Maryland standard deduction is 15% of AGI; (bb) Louisiana tax rates may be adjusted down if revenue trigger is met on April 1st. Iowa is phasing-in a flat rate by 2027, while Nebraska and South Carolina is phasing-in a reduced top rate by 2027.
Source: Federation of Tax Administrators, State Individual Income Tax Rates, January 1, 2023

Various State Sales and Excise Tax Rates

State	State Sales Tax (%)	Gasoline[1] ($/gal.)	Cigarette[2] ($/pack)	Spirits[3] ($/gal.)	Wine[4] ($/gal.)	Beer[5] ($/gal.)	Recreational Marijuana (%)
Louisiana	4.45	0.2013	1.08	3.03	0.76	0.40	Not legal

Note: All tax rates as of January 1, 2023; (1) The American Petroleum Institute has developed a methodology for determining the average tax rate on a gallon of fuel. Rates may include any of the following: excise taxes, environmental fees, storage tank fees, other fees or taxes, general sales tax, and local taxes; (2) The federal excise tax of $1.0066 per pack and local taxes are not included; (3) Rates are those applicable to off-premise sales of 40% alcohol by volume (a.b.v.) distilled spirits in 750ml containers. Local excise taxes are excluded; (4) Rates are those applicable to off-premise sales of 11% a.b.v. non-carbonated wine in 750ml containers; (5) Rates are those applicable to off-premise sales of 4.7% a.b.v. beer in 12 ounce containers.
Source: Tax Foundation, 2023 Facts & Figures: How Does Your State Compare?

State Business Tax Climate Index Rankings

State	Overall Rank	Corporate Tax Rank	Individual Income Tax Rank	Sales Tax Rank	Property Tax Rank	Unemployment Insurance Tax Rank
Louisiana	39	32	25	48	23	6

Note: The index is a measure of how each state's tax laws affect economic performance. The lower the rank, the more favorable a state's tax system is for business. States without a given tax are given a ranking of 1. The scores/rankings for the District of Columbia do not affect other states. The 2023 index represents the tax climate as of July 1, 2022.
Source: Tax Foundation, State Business Tax Climate Index 2023

TRANSPORTATION

Means of Transportation to Work

Area	Car/Truck/Van Drove Alone	Car-pooled	Bus	Subway	Railroad	Bicycle	Walked	Other Means	Worked at Home
City	65.6	8.9	4.6	0.1	0.0	2.6	5.4	2.9	9.9
MSA[1]	76.2	9.6	1.7	0.0	0.0	0.9	2.4	1.7	7.4
U.S.	73.2	8.6	2.0	1.6	0.5	0.5	2.5	1.5	9.7

Note: Figures are percentages and cover workers 16 years of age and older; (1) Figures cover the New Orleans-Metairie, LA Metropolitan Statistical Area
Source: U.S. Census Bureau, 2017-2021 American Community Survey 5-Year Estimates

Travel Time to Work

Area	Less Than 10 Minutes	10 to 19 Minutes	20 to 29 Minutes	30 to 44 Minutes	45 to 59 Minutes	60 to 89 Minutes	90 Minutes or More
City	11.0	34.8	24.2	19.5	5.0	3.5	2.0
MSA[1]	10.9	30.8	21.8	20.7	8.0	5.5	2.4
U.S.	12.4	28.5	21.0	20.9	8.2	6.2	2.9

Note: Note: Figures are percentages and include workers 16 years old and over; (1) Figures cover the New Orleans-Metairie, LA Metropolitan Statistical Area
Source: U.S. Census Bureau, 2017-2021 American Community Survey 5-Year Estimates

Key Congestion Measures

Measure	1990	2000	2010	2015	2020
Annual Hours of Delay, Total (000)	23,513	35,168	47,211	53,514	24,668
Annual Hours of Delay, Per Auto Commuter	22	30	45	56	26
Annual Congestion Cost, Per Auto Commuter ($)	973	1,094	1,166	1,223	597

Note: Covers the New Orleans LA urban area
Source: Texas A&M Transportation Institute, 2021 Urban Mobility Report

Freeway Travel Time Index

Measure	1985	1990	1995	2000	2005	2010	2015	2020
Urban Area Index[1]	1.14	1.16	1.20	1.22	1.23	1.32	1.34	1.11
Urban Area Rank[1,2]	18	19	21	24	28	8	9	20

Note: Freeway Travel Time Index—the ratio of travel time in the peak period to the travel time at free-flow conditions. For example, a value of 1.30 indicates a 20-minute free-flow trip takes 26 minutes in the peak (20 minutes x 1.30 = 26 minutes); (1) Covers the New Orleans LA urban area; (2) Rank is based on 101 larger urban areas (#1 = highest travel time index)
Source: Texas A&M Transportation Institute, 2021 Urban Mobility Report

Public Transportation

Agency Name / Mode of Transportation	Vehicles Operated in Maximum Service[1]	Annual Unlinked Passenger Trips[2] (in thous.)	Annual Passenger Miles[3] (in thous.)
New Orleans Regional Transit Authority (NORTA)			
Bus (directly operated)	94	4,615.8	17,217.0
Demand Response (directly operated)	40	142.8	1,061.2
Ferryboat (purchased transportation)	3	626.8	313.4
Streetcar Rail (directly operated)	27	2,317.3	5,399.2

Note: (1) Number of revenue vehicles operated by the given mode and type of service to meet the annual maximum service requirement. This is the revenue vehicle count during the peak season of the year; on the week and day that maximum service is provided. Vehicles operated in maximum service (VOMS) exclude atypical days and one-time special events; (2) Number of passengers who boarded public transportation vehicles. Passengers are counted each time they board a vehicle no matter how many vehicles they use to travel from their origin to their destination. (3) Sum of the distances ridden by all passengers during the entire fiscal year.
Source: Federal Transit Administration, National Transit Database, 2021

Air Transportation

Airport Name and Code / Type of Service	Passenger Airlines[1]	Passenger Enplanements	Freight Carriers[2]	Freight (lbs)
New Orleans International (MSY)				
Domestic service (U.S. carriers - 2022)	31	5,848,525	15	58,756,297
International service (U.S. carriers - 2021)	4	15,472	1	13,567

Note: (1) Includes all U.S.-based major, minor and commuter airlines that carried at least one passenger during the year; (2) Includes all U.S.-based airlines and freight carriers that transported at least one pound of freight during the year.
Source: Bureau of Transportation Statistics, The Intermodal Transportation Database, Air Carriers: T-100 Domestic Market (U.S. Carriers), 2022; Bureau of Transportation Statistics, The Intermodal Transportation Database, Air Carriers: T-100 International Market (U.S. Carriers), 2021

BUSINESSES

Major Business Headquarters

Company Name	Industry	Fortune[1]	Forbes[2]
Entergy	Utilities, gas and electric	321	-

Note: (1) Companies that produce a 10-K are ranked 1 to 500 based on 2021 revenue; (2) All private companies with at least $2 billion in annual revenue through the end of their most current fiscal year are ranked 1 to 246; companies listed are headquartered in the city; dashes indicate no ranking
Source: Fortune, "Fortune 500," 2022; Forbes, "America's Largest Private Companies," 2022

Fastest-Growing Businesses

According to *Initiative for a Competitive Inner City (ICIC)*, New Orleans is home to one of America's 100 fastest-growing "inner city" companies: **High Level Speech & Hearing Center** (#68). Criteria for inclusion: company must be headquartered in or have 51 percent or more of its physical operations in an economically distressed urban area; must be an independent, for-profit corporation, partnership or proprietorship; must have 10 or more employees and have a five-year sales history that includes sales of at least $200,000 in the base year and at least $1 million in the current year with no decrease in sales over the two most recent years. Companies were ranked overall by revenue growth over the five-year period between 2017 and 2021. *Initiative for a Competitive Inner City (ICIC), "Inner City 100 Companies," 2022*

Living Environment

COST OF LIVING

Cost of Living Index

Composite Index	Groceries	Housing	Utilities	Transportation	Health Care	Misc. Goods/Services
111.5	96.6	143.5	80.0	99.0	119.6	102.2

Note: The Cost of Living Index measures regional differences in the cost of consumer goods and services, excluding taxes and non-consumer expenditures, for professional and managerial households in the top income quintile. It is based on more than 50,000 prices covering almost 60 different items for which prices are collected three times a year by chambers of commerce, economic development organizations or university applied economic centers in each participating urban area. The numbers shown should be read as a percentage above or below the national average of 100. For example, a value of 115.4 in the groceries column indicates that grocery prices are 15.4% higher than the national average. Small differences in the index numbers should not be interpreted as significant; Figures cover the New Orleans LA urban area.
Source: The Council for Community and Economic Research, Cost of Living Index, 2022

Grocery Prices

Area[1]	T-Bone Steak ($/pound)	Frying Chicken ($/pound)	Whole Milk ($/half gal.)	Eggs ($/dozen)	Orange Juice ($/64 oz.)	Coffee ($/11.5 oz.)
City[2]	15.23	1.37	2.57	2.32	3.68	4.26
Avg.	13.81	1.59	2.43	2.25	3.85	4.95
Min.	10.17	0.90	1.51	1.30	2.90	3.46
Max.	19.35	3.30	4.32	4.32	5.31	8.59

Note: (1) Values for the local area are compared with the average, minimum and maximum values for all 286 areas in the Cost of Living Index; (2) Figures cover the New Orleans LA urban area; **T-Bone Steak** (price per pound); **Frying Chicken** (price per pound, whole fryer); **Whole Milk** (half gallon carton); **Eggs** (price per dozen, Grade A, large); **Orange Juice** (64 oz. Tropicana or Florida Natural); **Coffee** (11.5 oz. can, vacuum-packed, Maxwell House, Hills Bros, or Folgers).
Source: The Council for Community and Economic Research, Cost of Living Index, 2022

Housing and Utility Costs

Area[1]	New Home Price ($)	Apartment Rent ($/month)	All Electric ($/month)	Part Electric ($/month)	Other Energy ($/month)	Telephone ($/month)
City[2]	654,349	1,851	-	71.40	46.62	187.68
Avg.	450,913	1,371	176.41	99.93	76.96	190.22
Min.	229,283	546	100.84	31.56	27.15	174.27
Max.	2,434,977	4,569	356.86	249.59	272.24	208.31

Note: (1) Values for the local area are compared with the average, minimum and maximum values for all 286 areas in the Cost of Living Index; (2) Figures cover the New Orleans LA urban area; **New Home Price** (2,400 sf living area, 8,000 sf lot, in urban area with full utilities); **Apartment Rent** (950 sf 2 bedroom/1.5 or 2 bath, unfurnished, excluding all utilities except water); **All Electric** (average monthly cost for an all-electric home); **Part Electric** (average monthly cost for a part-electric home); **Other Energy** (average monthly cost for natural gas, fuel oil, coal, wood, and any other forms of energy except electricity); **Telephone** (price includes the base monthly rate plus taxes and fees for three lines of mobile phone service).
Source: The Council for Community and Economic Research, Cost of Living Index, 2022

Health Care, Transportation, and Other Costs

Area[1]	Doctor ($/visit)	Dentist ($/visit)	Optometrist ($/visit)	Gasoline ($/gallon)	Beauty Salon ($/visit)	Men's Shirt ($)
City[2]	168.89	125.56	105.55	3.92	42.78	39.00
Avg.	124.91	107.77	117.66	3.86	43.31	34.21
Min.	36.61	58.25	51.79	2.90	22.18	13.05
Max.	250.21	162.58	371.96	5.54	85.61	63.54

Note: (1) Values for the local area are compared with the average, minimum and maximum values for all 286 areas in the Cost of Living Index; (2) Figures cover the New Orleans LA urban area; **Doctor** (general practitioners routine exam of an established patient); **Dentist** (adult teeth cleaning and periodic oral examination); **Optometrist** (full vision eye exam for established adult patient); **Gasoline** (one gallon regular unleaded, national brand, including all taxes, cash price at self-service pump if available); **Beauty Salon** (woman's shampoo, trim, and blow-dry); **Men's Shirt** (cotton/polyester dress shirt, pinpoint weave, long sleeves).
Source: The Council for Community and Economic Research, Cost of Living Index, 2022

HOUSING

Homeownership Rate

Area	2015 (%)	2016 (%)	2017 (%)	2018 (%)	2019 (%)	2020 (%)	2021 (%)	2022 (%)
MSA[1]	62.8	59.3	61.7	62.6	61.1	66.3	66.2	66.3
U.S.	63.7	63.4	63.9	64.4	64.6	66.6	65.5	65.8

Note: (1) Figures cover the New Orleans-Metairie, LA Metropolitan Statistical Area
Source: U.S. Census Bureau, Housing Vacancies and Homeownership Annual Statistics: 2015-2022

House Price Index (HPI)

Area	National Ranking[2]	Quarterly Change (%)	One-Year Change (%)	Five-Year Change (%)	Since 1991Q1 (%)
MSA[1]	202	0.06	8.58	36.52	291.68
U.S.[3]	—	0.34	8.41	58.44	289.08

Note: The HPI is a weighted repeat sales index. It measures average price changes in repeat sales or refinancings on the same properties. This information is obtained by reviewing repeat mortgage transactions on single-family properties whose mortgages have been purchased or securitized by Fannie Mae or Freddie Mac since January 1975; (1) Figures cover the New Orleans-Metairie, LA Metropolitan Statistical Area; (2) Rankings are based on annual percentage change for all metro areas containing at least 15,000 transactions over the last 10 years and ranges from 1 to 257; (3) figures based on a weighted average of Census Division estimates using a seasonally adjusted, purchase-only index; all figures are for the period ending December 31, 2022
Source: Federal Housing Finance Agency, Change in FHFA Metropolitan Area House Price Indexes, 2022Q4

Median Single-Family Home Prices

Area	2020	2021	2022p	Percent Change 2021 to 2022
MSA[1]	240.5	268.1	285.6	6.5
U.S. Average	300.2	357.1	392.6	9.9

Note: Figures are median sales prices of existing single-family homes in thousands of dollars; (p) preliminary; (1) Figures cover the New Orleans-Metairie, LA Metropolitan Statistical Area
Source: National Association of Realtors, Median Sales Price of Existing Single-Family Homes for Metropolitan Areas, 4th Quarter 2022

Qualifying Income Based on Median Sales Price of Existing Single-Family Homes

Area	With 5% Down ($)	With 10% Down ($)	With 20% Down ($)
MSA[1]	82,545	78,200	69,511
U.S. Average	112,234	106,237	94,513

Note: Figures are preliminary; Qualifying income is based on a mortgage rate of 6.77%. Monthly principal and interest payment is limited to 25% of income; (1) Figures cover the New Orleans-Metairie, LA Metropolitan Statistical Area
Source: National Association of Realtors, Qualifying Income Based on Median Sales Price of Existing Single-Family Homes for Metropolitan Areas, 4th Quarter 2022

Home Value

Area	Under $100,000	$100,000 -$199,999	$200,000 -$299,999	$300,000 -$399,999	$400,000 -$499,999	$500,000 -$999,999	$1,000,000 or more	Median ($)
City	9.7	28.7	20.4	13.4	8.3	15.2	4.2	255,500
MSA[1]	11.5	34.6	25.7	13.3	5.8	7.5	1.7	214,300
U.S.	16.2	24.2	20.1	13.6	8.3	13.6	4.1	244,900

Note: Figures are percentages except for median and cover owner-occupied housing units; (1) Figures cover the New Orleans-Metairie, LA Metropolitan Statistical Area
Source: U.S. Census Bureau, 2017-2021 American Community Survey 5-Year Estimates

Year Housing Structure Built

Area	2020 or Later	2010 -2019	2000 -2009	1990 -1999	1980 -1989	1970 -1979	1960 -1969	1950 -1959	1940 -1949	Before 1940	Median Year
City	0.1	4.4	6.9	3.3	7.6	13.9	10.9	12.1	7.3	33.4	1958
MSA[1]	0.2	5.1	12.1	10.0	13.3	19.0	12.9	9.7	4.6	13.0	1975
U.S.	0.2	7.3	13.6	13.6	13.2	14.8	10.3	10.0	4.7	12.2	1979

Note: Figures are percentages except for Median Year; Note: (1) Figures cover the New Orleans-Metairie, LA Metropolitan Statistical Area
Source: U.S. Census Bureau, 2017-2021 American Community Survey 5-Year Estimates

Gross Monthly Rent

Area	Under $500	$500 -$999	$1,000 -$1,499	$1,500 -$1,999	$2,000 -$2,499	$2,500 -$2,999	$3,000 and up	Median ($)
City	10.9	31.7	36.8	13.8	4.6	1.2	0.8	1,079
MSA[1]	8.0	35.7	39.3	12.2	3.5	0.7	0.6	1,064
U.S.	8.1	30.5	30.8	16.8	7.3	3.1	3.5	1,163

Note: Figures are percentages except for median; Gross rent is the contract rent plus the estimated average monthly cost of utilities (electricity, gas, and water and sewer) and fuels (oil, coal, kerosene, wood, etc.) if these are paid by the renter (or paid for the renter by someone else); (1) Figures cover the New Orleans-Metairie, LA Metropolitan Statistical Area
Source: U.S. Census Bureau, 2017-2021 American Community Survey 5-Year Estimates

HEALTH

Health Risk Factors

Category	MSA[1] (%)	U.S. (%)
Adults aged 18–64 who have any kind of health care coverage	92.6	90.9
Adults who reported being in good or better health	82.3	85.2
Adults who have been told they have high blood cholesterol	36.7	35.7
Adults who have been told they have high blood pressure	37.5	32.4
Adults who are current smokers	16.6	14.4
Adults who currently use e-cigarettes	8.0	6.7
Adults who currently use chewing tobacco, snuff, or snus	3.3	3.5
Adults who are heavy drinkers[2]	7.7	6.3
Adults who are binge drinkers[3]	18.9	15.4
Adults who are overweight (BMI 25.0 - 29.9)	33.8	34.4
Adults who are obese (BMI 30.0 - 99.8)	34.2	33.9
Adults who participated in any physical activities in the past month	75.9	76.3

Note: (1) Figures cover the New Orleans-Metairie, LA Metropolitan Statistical Area; (2) Heavy drinkers are classified as adult men having more than 14 drinks per week and adult women having more than 7 drinks per week; (3) Binge drinkers are classified as males having five or more drinks on one occasion or females having four or more drinks on one occasion
Source: Centers for Disease Control and Prevention, Behavioral Risk Factor Surveillance System, SMART: Selected Metropolitan Area Risk Trends, 2021

Acute and Chronic Health Conditions

Category	MSA[1] (%)	U.S. (%)
Adults who have ever been told they had a heart attack	4.4	4.0
Adults who have ever been told they have angina or coronary heart disease	4.0	3.8
Adults who have ever been told they had a stroke	4.0	3.0
Adults who have ever been told they have asthma	14.1	14.9
Adults who have ever been told they have arthritis	27.8	25.8
Adults who have ever been told they have diabetes[2]	13.0	10.9
Adults who have ever been told they had skin cancer	5.1	6.6
Adults who have ever been told they had any other types of cancer	7.8	7.5
Adults who have ever been told they have COPD	8.2	6.1
Adults who have ever been told they have kidney disease	3.4	3.0
Adults who have ever been told they have a form of depression	23.4	20.5

Note: (1) Figures cover the New Orleans-Metairie, LA Metropolitan Statistical Area; (2) Figures do not include pregnancy-related, borderline, or pre-diabetes
Source: Centers for Disease Control and Prevention, Behavioral Risk Factor Surveillance System, SMART: Selected Metropolitan Area Risk Trends, 2021

Health Screening and Vaccination Rates

Category	MSA[1] (%)	U.S. (%)
Adults who have ever been tested for HIV	50.6	34.9
Adults who have had their blood cholesterol checked within the last five years	88.2	85.2
Adults aged 65+ who have had flu shot within the past year	67.1	68.6
Adults aged 65+ who have ever had a pneumonia vaccination	69.6	71.0

Note: (1) Figures cover the New Orleans-Metairie, LA Metropolitan Statistical Area.
Source: Centers for Disease Control and Prevention, Behavioral Risk Factor Surveillance System, SMART: Selected Metropolitan Area Risk Trends, 2021

Disability Status

Category	MSA[1] (%)	U.S. (%)
Adults who reported being deaf	6.9	7.2
Are you blind or have serious difficulty seeing, even when wearing glasses?	6.0	4.8
Are you limited in any way in any of your usual activities due to arthritis?	13.1	11.1
Do you have difficulty doing errands alone?	7.3	7.0
Do you have difficulty dressing or bathing?	4.9	3.6
Do you have serious difficulty concentrating/remembering/making decisions?	14.4	12.1
Do you have serious difficulty walking or climbing stairs?	15.4	12.8

Note: (1) Figures cover the New Orleans-Metairie, LA Metropolitan Statistical Area.
Source: Centers for Disease Control and Prevention, Behavioral Risk Factor Surveillance System, SMART: Selected Metropolitan Area Risk Trends, 2021

Mortality Rates for the Top 10 Causes of Death in the U.S.

ICD-10[a] Sub-Chapter	ICD-10[a] Code	Crude Mortality Rate[1] per 100,000 population County[2]	U.S.
Malignant neoplasms	C00-C97	183.2	182.6
Ischaemic heart diseases	I20-I25	86.7	113.1
Other forms of heart disease	I30-I51	71.9	64.4
Other degenerative diseases of the nervous system	G30-G31	48.2	51.0
Cerebrovascular diseases	I60-I69	46.2	47.8
Other external causes of accidental injury	W00-X59	90.4	46.4
Chronic lower respiratory diseases	J40-J47	24.6	45.7
Organic, including symptomatic, mental disorders	F01-F09	16.4	35.9
Hypertensive diseases	I10-I15	41.0	35.0
Diabetes mellitus	E10-E14	53.3	29.6

Note: (a) ICD-10 = International Classification of Diseases 10th Revision; (1) Crude mortality rates are a three-year average covering 2019-2021; (2) Figures cover Orleans Parish.
Source: Centers for Disease Control and Prevention, National Center for Health Statistics. National Vital Statistics System, Mortality 2018-2021 on CDC WONDER Online Database

Mortality Rates for Selected Causes of Death

ICD-10[a] Sub-Chapter	ICD-10[a] Code	Crude Mortality Rate[1] per 100,000 population County[2]	U.S.
Assault	X85-Y09	42.2	7.0
Diseases of the liver	K70-K76	15.6	19.8
Human immunodeficiency virus (HIV) disease	B20-B24	5.5	1.5
Influenza and pneumonia	J09-J18	6.7	14.7
Intentional self-harm	X60-X84	10.3	14.3
Malnutrition	E40-E46	10.4	4.3
Obesity and other hyperalimentation	E65-E68	4.3	3.0
Renal failure	N17-N19	26.3	15.7
Transport accidents	V01-V99	15.0	13.6
Viral hepatitis	B15-B19	Unreliable	1.2

Note: (a) ICD-10 = International Classification of Diseases 10th Revision; (1) Crude mortality rates are a three-year average covering 2019-2021; (2) Figures cover Orleans Parish; Data are suppressed when the data meet the criteria for confidentiality constraints; Crude mortality rates are flagged as unreliable when the rate would be calculated with a numerator of 20 or less.
Source: Centers for Disease Control and Prevention, National Center for Health Statistics. National Vital Statistics System, Mortality 2018-2021 on CDC WONDER Online Database

Health Insurance Coverage

Area	With Health Insurance	With Private Health Insurance	With Public Health Insurance	Without Health Insurance	Population Under Age 19 Without Health Insurance
City	91.2	54.1	45.3	8.8	5.0
MSA[1]	91.2	58.8	42.8	8.8	4.5
U.S.	91.2	67.8	35.4	8.8	5.3

Note: Figures are percentages that cover the civilian noninstitutionalized population; (1) Figures cover the New Orleans-Metairie, LA Metropolitan Statistical Area
Source: U.S. Census Bureau, 2017-2021 American Community Survey 5-Year Estimates

Number of Medical Professionals

Area	MDs[3]	DOs[3,4]	Dentists	Podiatrists	Chiropractors	Optometrists
Parish[1] (number)	3,401	92	306	16	38	31
Parish[1] (rate[2])	887.3	24.0	81.2	4.2	10.1	8.2
U.S. (rate[2])	289.3	23.5	72.5	6.2	28.7	17.4

Note: Data as of 2021 unless noted; (1) Data covers Orleans Parish; (2) Rate per 100,000 population; (3) Data as of 2020 and includes all active, non-federal physicians; (4) Doctor of Osteopathic Medicine
Source: U.S. Department of Health and Human Services, Health Resources and Services Administration, Bureau of Health Professions, Area Resource File (ARF) 2021-2022

Best Hospitals

According to *U.S. News,* the New Orleans-Metairie, LA metro area is home to one of the best hospitals in the U.S.: **Ochsner Medical Center** (1 adult specialty and 3 pediatric specialties). The hospital listed was nationally ranked in at least one of 15 adult or 10 pediatric specialties. The number of specialties shown cover the parent hospital. Only 164 U.S. hospitals performed well enough to be nationally ranked in one or more specialties. Twenty hospitals in the U.S. made the Honor Roll. The Best Hospitals Honor Roll takes both the national rankings and the procedure and condition ratings into account. Hospitals received points if they were nationally ranked in one of the 15 adult specialties—the higher they ranked, the more points they got—and how many ratings of "high performing" they earned in the 17 procedures and conditions. *U.S. News Online, "America's Best Hospitals 2022-23"*

According to *U.S. News,* the New Orleans-Metairie, LA metro area is home to two of the best children's hospitals in the U.S.: **Children's Hospital New Orleans** (2 pediatric specialties); **Ochsner Hospital for Children** (3 pediatric specialties). The hospitals listed were highly ranked in at least one of 10 pediatric specialties. Eighty-six children's hospitals in the U.S. were nationally ranked in at least one specialty. Hospitals received points for being ranked in a specialty, and the 10 hospitals with the most points across the 10 specialties make up the Honor Roll. *U.S. News Online, "America's Best Children's Hospitals 2022-23"*

EDUCATION

Public School District Statistics

District Name	Schls	Pupils	Pupil/Teacher Ratio	Minority Pupils[1] (%)	LEP/ELL[2] (%)	IEP[3] (%)

Note: Table includes school districts with 2,000 or more students; (1) Percentage of students that are not non-Hispanic white; (2) Percentage of students that are Limited English Proficient or English Language Learners (2018-19); (3) Percentage of students that have an Individualized Education Program (2019-20).
Source: U.S. Department of Education, National Center for Education Statistics, Common Core of Data, Local Education Agency (School District) Universe Survey: School Year 2021-2022

Best High Schools

According to *U.S. News,* New Orleans is home to two of the top 500 high schools in the U.S.: **Benjamin Franklin High School** (#72); **Lusher Charter School** (#196). Nearly 18,000 public, magnet and charter schools were ranked based on their performance on state assessments and how well they prepare students for college. *U.S. News & World Report, "Best High Schools 2022"*

Highest Level of Education

Area	Less than H.S.	H.S. Diploma	Some College, No Deg.	Associate Degree	Bachelor's Degree	Master's Degree	Prof. School Degree	Doctorate Degree
City	11.8	22.4	21.6	5.0	21.9	10.4	4.5	2.2
MSA[1]	11.9	26.9	22.4	6.5	20.0	8.0	2.9	1.3
U.S.	11.1	26.5	20.0	8.7	20.6	9.3	2.2	1.5

Note: Figures cover persons age 25 and over; (1) Figures cover the New Orleans-Metairie, LA Metropolitan Statistical Area
Source: U.S. Census Bureau, 2017-2021 American Community Survey 5-Year Estimates

Educational Attainment by Race

Area	High School Graduate or Higher (%)					Bachelor's Degree or Higher (%)				
	Total	White	Black	Asian	Hisp.[2]	Total	White	Black	Asian	Hisp.[2]
City	88.2	96.4	83.7	76.7	80.9	39.1	65.3	21.0	47.9	40.4
MSA[1]	88.1	91.7	84.1	80.3	74.7	32.2	39.2	19.9	43.4	22.4
U.S.	88.9	91.4	87.2	87.6	71.2	33.7	35.5	23.3	55.6	18.4

Note: Figures shown cover persons 25 years old and over; (1) Figures cover the New Orleans-Metairie, LA Metropolitan Statistical Area; (2) People of Hispanic origin can be of any race
Source: U.S. Census Bureau, 2017-2021 American Community Survey 5-Year Estimates

School Enrollment by Grade and Control

Area	Preschool (%)		Kindergarten (%)		Grades 1 - 4 (%)		Grades 5 - 8 (%)		Grades 9 - 12 (%)	
	Public	Private	Public	Private	Public	Private	Public	Private	Public	Private
City	49.2	50.8	78.4	21.6	81.5	18.5	81.9	18.1	80.2	19.8
MSA[1]	54.1	45.9	76.7	23.3	77.8	22.2	77.5	22.5	74.9	25.1
U.S.	58.8	41.2	86.3	13.7	88.3	11.7	88.6	11.4	89.4	10.6

Note: Figures shown cover persons 3 years old and over; (1) Figures cover the New Orleans-Metairie, LA Metropolitan Statistical Area
Source: U.S. Census Bureau, 2017-2021 American Community Survey 5-Year Estimates

Higher Education

Four-Year Colleges			Two-Year Colleges			Medical Schools[1]	Law Schools[2]	Voc/ Tech[3]
Public	Private Non-profit	Private For-profit	Public	Private Non-profit	Private For-profit			
3	9	1	3	0	2	2	2	11

Note: Figures cover institutions located within the New Orleans-Metairie, LA Metropolitan Statistical Area and include main campuses only; (1) includes schools accredited by the Liaison Committee on Medical Education and the American Osteopathic Association's Commission on Osteopathic College Accreditation; (2) includes ABA-accredited schools, schools with provisional ABA accreditation, and state accredited schools; (3) includes all schools with programs that are less than 2 years.
Source: National Center for Education Statistics, Integrated Postsecondary Education System (IPEDS), 2021-22; Wikipedia, List of Medical Schools in the United States, accessed April 10, 2023; Wikipedia, List of Law Schools in the United States, accessed April 10, 2023

According to *U.S. News & World Report,* the New Orleans-Metairie, LA metro area is home to one of the top 200 national universities in the U.S.: **Tulane University** (#44 tie). The indicators used to capture academic quality fall into a number of categories: assessment by administrators at peer institutions; retention of students; faculty resources; student selectivity; financial resources; alumni giving; high school counselor ratings of colleges; and graduation rate. *U.S. News & World Report, "America's Best Colleges 2023"*

According to *U.S. News & World Report,* the New Orleans-Metairie, LA metro area is home to one of the top 100 law schools in the U.S.: **Tulane University** (#55). The rankings are based on a weighted average of 12 measures of quality: peer assessment score; assessment score by lawyers/judges; median LSAT scores; median undergrad GPA; acceptance rate; employment rates for graduates; placement success; bar passage rate; faculty resources; expenditures per student; student/faculty ratio; and library resources. *U.S. News & World Report, "America's Best Graduate Schools, Law, 2023"*

EMPLOYERS

Major Employers

Company Name	Industry
Al Copeland Investments	Restaurants & food manufacturing
Boh Bros. Construction Co.	General contractor
Capital One	Commercial banking
City of New Orleans	Municipal government
Dow Chemical Company	Chemical manufacturing
East Jefferson Hospital	Health care
Harrah's New Orleans Casino	Casinos
Jefferson Parish Government	Government
Jefferson Parish School Board	Elementary & secondary schools
Jefferson Parish Sheriff's Office	Government
Lockheed Martin Corp/Nasa Michoud	Space research & technology
LSU Health Sciences Center New Orleans	Colleges & universities
Naval Support Activity	Government
North Oaks Medical Center	Health care
Northrop Grumman	Ship building & repairing
Ochsner Health System	Health care
Saint Tammany Parish Hospital	General medical & surgical hospitals
Southeastern Louisiana University	Colleges & universities
St. Tammany Parish Public School Board	Elementary & secondary schools
Touro Infirmary	Health care
Tulane University	Colleges & universities
United States Postal Service	U.S. postal service
West Jefferson Medical Center	Health care

Note: Companies shown are located within the New Orleans-Metairie, LA Metropolitan Statistical Area.
Source: Hoovers.com; Wikipedia

PUBLIC SAFETY

Crime Rate

Area	Total Crime	Violent Crime Rate				Property Crime Rate		
		Murder	Rape[3]	Robbery	Aggrav. Assault	Burglary	Larceny -Theft	Motor Vehicle Theft
City	5,863.9	51.0	180.8	280.9	811.6	506.4	3,138.3	894.9
Suburbs[1]	2,268.4	8.6	24.1	45.2	233.6	244.1	1,581.0	131.9
Metro[2]	3,378.9	21.7	72.5	118.0	412.2	325.1	2,061.9	367.5
U.S.	2,356.7	6.5	38.4	73.9	279.7	314.2	1,398.0	246.0

Note: Figures are crimes per 100,000 population; (1) All areas within the metro area that are located outside the city limits; (2) Figures cover the New Orleans-Metairie, LA Metropolitan Statistical Area; (3) All figures shown were reported using the revised Uniform Crime Reporting (UCR) definition of rape; Due to the transition to the National Incident-Based Reporting System (NIBRS), limited city and metro area data was released for 2021.
Source: FBI Uniform Crime Reports, 2020

Hate Crimes

Area	Number of Quarters Reported	Race/Ethnicity/Ancestry	Religion	Sexual Orientation	Disability	Gender	Gender Identity
City	4	3	0	2	0	0	0
U.S.	4	5,227	1,244	1,110	130	75	266

Number of Incidents per Bias Motivation

Note: Due to the transition to the National Incident-Based Reporting System (NIBRS), limited crime data was released for 2021.
Source: Federal Bureau of Investigation, Hate Crime Statistics 2020

Identity Theft Consumer Reports

Area	Reports	Reports per 100,000 Population	Rank[2]
MSA[1]	6,109	480	21
U.S.	1,108,609	339	-

Note: (1) Figures cover the New Orleans-Metairie, LA Metropolitan Statistical Area; (2) Rank ranges from 1 to 391 where 1 indicates greatest number of identity theft reports per 100,000 population
Source: Federal Trade Commission, Consumer Sentinel Network Data Book 2022

Fraud and Other Consumer Reports

Area	Reports	Reports per 100,000 Population	Rank[2]
MSA[1]	14,428	1,135	54
U.S.	4,064,520	1,245	-

Note: (1) Figures cover the New Orleans-Metairie, LA Metropolitan Statistical Area; (2) Rank ranges from 1 to 391 where 1 indicates greatest number of fraud and other consumer reports per 100,000 population
Source: Federal Trade Commission, Consumer Sentinel Network Data Book 2022

POLITICS

2020 Presidential Election Results

Area	Biden	Trump	Jorgensen	Hawkins	Other
Orleans Parish	83.1	15.0	0.9	0.0	1.0
U.S.	51.3	46.8	1.2	0.3	0.5

Note: Results are percentages and may not add to 100% due to rounding
Source: Dave Leip's Atlas of U.S. Presidential Elections

SPORTS

Professional Sports Teams

Team Name	League	Year Established
New Orleans Pelicans	National Basketball Association (NBA)	2002
New Orleans Saints	National Football League (NFL)	1967

Note: Includes teams located in the New Orleans-Metairie, LA Metropolitan Statistical Area.
Source: Wikipedia, Major Professional Sports Teams of the United States and Canada, April 12, 2023

CLIMATE

Average and Extreme Temperatures

Temperature	Jan	Feb	Mar	Apr	May	Jun	Jul	Aug	Sep	Oct	Nov	Dec	Yr.
Extreme High (°F)	83	85	89	92	96	100	101	102	101	92	87	84	102
Average High (°F)	62	65	71	78	85	89	91	90	87	80	71	64	78
Average Temp. (°F)	53	56	62	69	75	81	82	82	79	70	61	55	69
Average Low (°F)	43	46	52	59	66	71	73	73	70	59	51	45	59
Extreme Low (°F)	14	19	25	32	41	50	60	60	42	35	24	11	11

Note: Figures cover the years 1948-1990
Source: National Climatic Data Center, International Station Meteorological Climate Summary, 9/96

Average Precipitation/Snowfall/Humidity

Precip./Humidity	Jan	Feb	Mar	Apr	May	Jun	Jul	Aug	Sep	Oct	Nov	Dec	Yr.
Avg. Precip. (in.)	4.7	5.6	5.2	4.7	4.4	5.4	6.4	5.9	5.5	2.8	4.4	5.5	60.6
Avg. Snowfall (in.)	Tr	Tr	Tr	0	0	0	0	0	0	0	0	Tr	Tr
Avg. Rel. Hum. 6am (%)	85	84	84	88	89	89	91	91	89	87	86	85	88
Avg. Rel. Hum. 3pm (%)	62	59	57	57	58	61	66	65	63	56	59	62	60

Note: Figures cover the years 1948-1990; Tr = Trace amounts (<0.05 in. of rain; <0.5 in. of snow)
Source: National Climatic Data Center, International Station Meteorological Climate Summary, 9/96

Weather Conditions

Temperature			Daytime Sky			Precipitation		
10°F & below	32°F & below	90°F & above	Clear	Partly cloudy	Cloudy	0.01 inch or more precip.	0.1 inch or more snow/ice	Thunder-storms
0	13	70	90	169	106	114	1	69

Note: Figures are average number of days per year and cover the years 1948-1990
Source: National Climatic Data Center, International Station Meteorological Climate Summary, 9/96

HAZARDOUS WASTE

Superfund Sites

The New Orleans-Metairie, LA metro area is home to three sites on the EPA's Superfund National Priorities List: **Agriculture Street Landfill** (final); **Bayou Bonfouca** (final); **Madisonville Creosote Works** (final). There are a total of 1,165 Superfund sites with a status of proposed or final on the list in the U.S. *U.S. Environmental Protection Agency, National Priorities List, April 12, 2023*

AIR QUALITY

Air Quality Trends: Ozone

	1990	1995	2000	2005	2010	2015	2018	2019	2020	2021
MSA[1]	0.082	0.088	0.091	0.079	0.074	0.067	0.065	0.062	0.061	0.060
U.S.	0.087	0.089	0.081	0.080	0.072	0.067	0.069	0.065	0.065	0.067

Note: (1) Data covers the New Orleans-Metairie, LA Metropolitan Statistical Area. The values shown are the composite ozone concentration averages among trend sites based on the highest fourth daily maximum 8-hour concentration in parts per million. These trends are based on sites having an adequate record of monitoring data during the trend period. Data from exceptional events are included.
Source: U.S. Environmental Protection Agency, Air Quality Monitoring Information, "Air Quality Trends by City, 1990-2021"

Air Quality Index

Area	Percent of Days when Air Quality was...[2]					AQI Statistics[2]	
	Good	Moderate	Unhealthy for Sensitive Groups	Unhealthy	Very Unhealthy	Maximum	Median
MSA[1]	76.4	22.7	0.8	0.0	0.0	108	42

Note: (1) Data covers the New Orleans-Metairie, LA Metropolitan Statistical Area; (2) Based on 365 days with AQI data in 2021. Air Quality Index (AQI) is an index for reporting daily air quality. EPA calculates the AQI for five major air pollutants regulated by the Clean Air Act: ground-level ozone, particle pollution (aka particulate matter), carbon monoxide, sulfur dioxide, and nitrogen dioxide. The AQI runs from 0 to 500. The higher the AQI value, the greater the level of air pollution and the greater the health concern. There are six AQI categories: "Good" AQI is between 0 and 50. Air quality is considered satisfactory; "Moderate" AQI is between 51 and 100. Air quality is acceptable; "Unhealthy for Sensitive Groups" When AQI values are between 101 and 150, members of sensitive groups may experience health effects; "Unhealthy" When AQI values are between 151 and 200 everyone may begin to experience health effects; "Very Unhealthy" AQI values between 201 and 300 trigger a health alert; "Hazardous" AQI values over 300 trigger warnings of emergency conditions (not shown).
Source: U.S. Environmental Protection Agency, Air Quality Index Report, 2021

Air Quality Index Pollutants

Area	Percent of Days when AQI Pollutant was...[2]						
	Carbon Monoxide	Nitrogen Dioxide	Ozone	Sulfur Dioxide	Particulate Matter 2.5	Particulate Matter 10
MSA[1]	0.0	0.0	48.2	(3)	51.5	0.3

Note: (1) Data covers the New Orleans-Metairie, LA Metropolitan Statistical Area; (2) Based on 365 days with AQI data in 2021. The Air Quality Index (AQI) is an index for reporting daily air quality. EPA calculates the AQI for five major air pollutants regulated by the Clean Air Act: ground-level ozone, particle pollution (also known as particulate matter), carbon monoxide, sulfur dioxide, and nitrogen dioxide. The AQI runs from 0 to 500. The higher the AQI value, the greater the level of air pollution and the greater the health concern; (3) Sulfur dioxide is no longer included in this table (as of December 8, 2021) because SO_2 concentrations tend to be very localized and not necessarily representative of broad geographical areas like counties and CBSAs.
Source: U.S. Environmental Protection Agency, Air Quality Index Report, 2021

Maximum Air Pollutant Concentrations: Particulate Matter, Ozone, CO and Lead

	Particulate Matter 10 (ug/m³)	Particulate Matter 2.5 Wtd AM (ug/m³)	Particulate Matter 2.5 24-Hr (ug/m³)	Ozone (ppm)	Carbon Monoxide (ppm)	Lead (ug/m³)
MSA[1] Level	45	7.6	17	0.063	1	0.05
NAAQS[2]	150	15	35	0.075	9	0.15
Met NAAQS[2]	Yes	Yes	Yes	Yes	Yes	Yes

Note: (1) Data covers the New Orleans-Metairie, LA Metropolitan Statistical Area; Data from exceptional events are included; (2) National Ambient Air Quality Standards; ppm = parts per million; ug/m³ = micrograms per cubic meter; n/a not available.
Concentrations: Particulate Matter 10 (coarse particulate)—highest second maximum 24-hour concentration; Particulate Matter 2.5 Wtd AM (fine particulate)—highest weighted annual mean concentration; Particulate Matter 2.5 24-Hour (fine particulate)—highest 98th percentile 24-hour concentration; Ozone—highest fourth daily maximum 8-hour concentration; Carbon Monoxide—highest second maximum non-overlapping 8-hour concentration; Lead—maximum running 3-month average
Source: U.S. Environmental Protection Agency, Air Quality Monitoring Information, "Air Quality Statistics by City, 2021"

Maximum Air Pollutant Concentrations: Nitrogen Dioxide and Sulfur Dioxide

	Nitrogen Dioxide AM (ppb)	Nitrogen Dioxide 1-Hr (ppb)	Sulfur Dioxide AM (ppb)	Sulfur Dioxide 1-Hr (ppb)	Sulfur Dioxide 24-Hr (ppb)
MSA[1] Level	9	37	n/a	56	n/a
NAAQS[2]	53	100	30	75	140
Met NAAQS[2]	Yes	Yes	n/a	Yes	n/a

Note: (1) Data covers the New Orleans-Metairie, LA Metropolitan Statistical Area; Data from exceptional events are included; (2) National Ambient Air Quality Standards; ppm = parts per million; ug/m³ = micrograms per cubic meter; n/a not available.
Concentrations: Nitrogen Dioxide AM—highest arithmetic mean concentration; Nitrogen Dioxide 1-Hr—highest 98th percentile 1-hour daily maximum concentration; Sulfur Dioxide AM—highest annual mean concentration; Sulfur Dioxide 1-Hr—highest 99th percentile 1-hour daily maximum concentration; Sulfur Dioxide 24-Hr—highest second maximum 24-hour concentration
Source: U.S. Environmental Protection Agency, Air Quality Monitoring Information, "Air Quality Statistics by City, 2021"

Orlando, Florida

Background

The city of Orlando is rampant with tourism. Not only is it home to the worldwide tourist attractions of Disney World, Epcot Center, and Sea World, but Orlando and its surrounding area also host Medieval Times Dinner & Tournament, Ripley's Believe It or Not Museum, and Sleuths Mystery Dinner Shows. No wonder the city is nicknamed "The Theme Park Capital of the World."

Orlando has its own high-tech corridor due to the University of Central Florida's College of Optics and Photonics. Manufacturing, government, business service, health care, high-tech research, and tourism supply significant numbers of jobs. The city is also one of the busiest American cities for conferences and conventions; Orange County Convention Center's annual numbers include approximately $3 billion to Central Florida's economy, 200 events, and more than 1.5 million attendees.

Aside from the glitz that pumps most of the money into its economy "The City Beautiful," with its warm climate and abundant rains, produce a variety of lush flora and fauna—an attractive setting for the many young people who settle in the area. There are numerous jazz clubs, restaurants, and pubs along Orange Avenue and Church Street. Known as the land of orange juice and sunshine, Orlando is also the city for young job seekers and professionals. It is one of Florida's fastest growing cities, and number two behind Miami in most new construction.

This genteel setting is a far cry from Orlando's rough-and-tumble origins. The city started out as a makeshift campsite in the middle of a cotton plantation. The Civil War and devastating rains brought an end to the cotton trade, and its settlers turned to raising livestock, a transition that resulted in daily chaotic brawls and senseless shootings. Martial law had to be imposed by a few large ranch families.

The greatest impetus toward modernity came when Cape Canaveral was founded in 1963, 50 miles away. Called Cape Kennedy until 1973, it brought missile assembly and electronic component production to the area. In 1971 the opening of Walt Disney World, created out of 27,000 acres of unexplored swampland, set the tone for Orlando as a tourist-oriented economy.

Orlando's University of Central Florida is the largest university campus in terms of enrollment in the United States and was listed as a "gamma" level global city in the World Cities Study Group's inventory.

Also a leading destination for film, television, commercial and web production, the city is home to Universal Studios, and a variety of arts and entertainment facilities. Amway Center opened in 2009 in Orlando, which is also home to the NBA's Orlando Magic, the Orlando Solar Bears of the ECHL (AA Hockey League) and the Orlando Predators of the National Arena League.

The city is also remembered for one of the deadliest mass shootings by a lone gunman when, in October 2016, more than 100 people were shot at Pulse, a gay nightclub in Orlando.

Orlando is surrounded by many lakes and its relative humidity remains high year-round, although winters are generally less humid. June through September is the rainy season, when scattered afternoon thunderstorms are an almost daily occurrence. During the winter months rainfall is light and the afternoons are most pleasant. Hurricanes are not usually considered a threat to the area.

Rankings

General Rankings

- *Insider* listed 23 places in the U.S. that travel industry trends reveal would be popular destinations in 2023. This year the list trends towards cultural and historical happenings, sports events, wellness experiences and invigorating outdoor escapes. According to the website insider.com Orlando is a place to visit in 2023. *Insider, "23 of the Best Places You Should Travel to in the U.S. in 2023," December 17, 2022*

- The Orlando metro area was identified as one of America's fastest-growing areas in terms of population and business growth by *MagnifyMoney*. The area ranked #14 out of 35. The 100 most populous metro areas in the U.S. were evaluated on their change from 2011 to 2016 in the following categories: people and housing; workforce and employment opportunities; growing industry. *www.businessinsider.com, "The 35 Cities in the US with the Biggest Influx of People, the Most Work Opportunities, and the Hottest Business Growth," August 12, 2018*

- The Orlando metro area was identified as one of America's fastest-growing areas in terms of population and economy by *Forbes*. The area ranked #4 out of 25. The 100 most populous metro areas in the U.S. were evaluated on the following criteria: estimated population growth; employment; economic output; wages; home values. *Forbes, "America's Fastest-Growing Cities 2018," February 28, 2018*

Business/Finance Rankings

- The Brookings Institution ranked the nation's largest cities based on income inequality. Orlando was ranked #69 (#1 = greatest inequality). Criteria: the "95/20 ratio," a figure representing the income at which a household earns more than 95 percent of all other households, divided by the income at which a household earns more than only 20 percent of all other households. *Brookings Institution, "Household Income Inequality, Largest Cities of 97 Large U.S. Metro Areas, 2014-2016," February 5, 2018*

- The Brookings Institution ranked the 100 largest metro areas in the U.S. based on income inequality. Orlando was ranked #69 (#1 = greatest inequality). Criteria: the "95/20 ratio," a figure representing the income at which a household earns more than 95 percent of all other households, divided by the income at which a household earns more than only 20 percent of all other households. *Brookings Institution, "Household Income Inequality, 100 Largest U.S. Metro Areas, 2014-2016," February 5, 2018*

- Payscale.com ranked the 32 largest metro areas in terms of wage growth. The Orlando metro area ranked #2. Criteria: quarterly changes in private industry employee and education professional wage growth from the previous year. *PayScale, "Wage Trends by Metro Area-1st Quarter," April 20, 2023*

- The Orlando metro area was identified as one of the most debt-ridden places in America by the finance site Credit.com. The metro area was ranked #23. Criteria: residents' average credit card debt as well as median income. *Credit.com, "25 Cities With the Most Credit Card Debt," February 28, 2018*

- Orlando was identified as one of America's most frugal metro areas by *Coupons.com*. The city ranked #5 out of 25. Criteria: digital coupon usage. *Coupons.com, "America's Most Frugal Cities of 2017," March 22, 2018*

- Orlando was identified as one of the unhappiest cities to work in by CareerBliss.com, an online community for career advancement. The city ranked #5 out of 5. Criteria: an employee's relationship with his or her boss and co-workers; general work environment; compensation; opportunities for advancement; company culture and job reputation; and resources. *Businesswire.com, "CareerBliss Unhappiest Cities to Work 2019," February 12, 2019*

- The Orlando metro area appeared on the Milken Institute "2022 Best Performing Cities" list. Rank: #57 out of 200 large metro areas (population over 250,000). Criteria: job growth; wage and salary growth; high-tech output growth; housing affordability; household broadband access. *Milken Institute, "Best-Performing Cities 2022," March 28, 2022*

- *Forbes* ranked the 200 most populous metro areas to determine the nation's "Best Places for Business and Careers." The Orlando metro area was ranked #23. Criteria: costs (business and living); job growth (past and projected); income growth; quality of life; educational attainment (college and high school); projected economic growth; cultural and leisure opportunities; workplace tolerance laws; net migration patterns. *Forbes, "The Best Places for Business and Careers 2019: Seattle Still On Top," October 30, 2019*

Children/Family Rankings

- Orlando was selected as one of the most playful cities in the U.S. by KaBOOM! The organization's Playful City USA initiative honors cities and towns across the nation that have made their communities more playable. Criteria: pledging to integrate play as a solution to challenges in their communities; making it easy for children to get active and balanced play; creating more family-friendly and innovative communities as a result. *KaBOOM! National Campaign for Play, "2017 Playful City USA Communities"*

Culture/Performing Arts Rankings

- Orlando was selected as one of the 25 best cities for moviemakers in North America. Great film cities are places where filmmaking dreams can come true, that offer more creative space, lower costs, and great outdoor locations. NYC & LA were intentionally excluded. Criteria: longstanding reputations as film-friendly communities; film community and culture; affordability; and quality of life. The city was ranked #25. *MovieMaker Magazine, "Best Places to Live and Work as a Moviemaker, 2023," January 18, 2023*

Dating/Romance Rankings

- Orlando was selected as one of America's best cities for singles by the readers of *Travel + Leisure* in their annual "America's Favorite Cities" survey. Criteria included good-looking locals, cool shopping, an active bar scene and hipster-magnet coffee bars. *Travel + Leisure, "Best Cities in America for Singles," July 21, 2017*

- Orlando was selected as one of the nation's most romantic cities with 100,000 or more residents by Amazon.com. The city ranked #4 of 20. Criteria: per capita sales of romance novels, relationship books, romantic comedy movies, romantic music, and sexual wellness products. *Amazon.com, "Top 20 Most Romantic Cities in the U.S.," February 1, 2017*

Education Rankings

- Personal finance website *WalletHub* analyzed the 150 largest U.S. metropolitan statistical areas to determine where the most educated Americans are putting their degrees to work. Criteria: education levels; percentage of workers with degrees; education quality and attainment gap; public school quality rankings; quality and enrollment of each metro area's universities. Orlando was ranked #60 (#1 = most educated city). *www.WalletHub.com, "Most & Least Educated Cities in America," July 18, 2022*

- Orlando was selected as one of America's most literate cities. The city ranked #41 out of the 84 largest U.S. cities. Criteria: number of booksellers; library resources; Internet resources; educational attainment; periodical publishing resources; newspaper circulation. *Central Connecticut State University, "America's Most Literate Cities, 2018," February 2019*

Environmental Rankings

- The U.S. Environmental Protection Agency (EPA) released its list of U.S. metropolitan areas with the most ENERGY STAR certified buildings in 2022. The Orlando metro area was ranked #23 out of 25. *U.S. Environmental Protection Agency, "2023 Energy Star Top Cities," April 26, 2023*

- Orlando was highlighted as one of the top 59 cleanest metro areas for short-term particle pollution (24-hour PM 2.5) in the U.S. during 2019 through 2021. Monitors in these cities reported no days with unhealthful PM 2.5 levels. *American Lung Association, "State of the Air 2023," April 19, 2023*

Food/Drink Rankings

- The U.S. Chamber of Commerce Foundation conducted an in-depth study on local food truck regulations, surveyed 288 food truck owners, and ranked 20 major American cities based on how friendly they are for operating a food truck. The compiled index assessed the following: procedures for obtaining permits and licenses; complying with restrictions; and financial obligations associated with operating a food truck. Orlando ranked #3 overall (1 being the best). *www.foodtrucknation.us, "Food Truck Nation," March 20, 2018*

Health/Fitness Rankings

- For each of the 100 largest cities in the United States, the American Fitness Index®, compiled in partnership between the American College of Sports Medicine and the Elevance Health Foundation, evaluated community infrastructure and 34 health behaviors including preventive health, levels of chronic disease conditions, food insecurity, sleep quality, pedestrian safety, air quality, and community/environment resources that support physical activity. Orlando ranked #51 for "community fitness." *americanfitnessindex.org, "2022 ACSM American Fitness Index Summary Report," July 12, 2022*

- The Orlando metro area was identified as one of the worst cities for bed bugs in America by pest control company Orkin. The area ranked #47 out of 50 based on the number of bed bug treatments Orkin performed from December 2021 to November 2022. *Orkin, "The Windy City Can't Blow Bed Bugs Away: Chicago Ranks #1 For Third Consecutive Year On Orkin's Bed Bug Cities List," January 9, 2023*

- Orlando was identified as a "2022 Spring Allergy Capital." The area ranked #47 out of 100. Three groups of factors were used to identify the most challenging cities for people with allergies during the spring season: annual spring pollen scores; over the counter allergy medicine use; number of board-certified allergy specialists. *Asthma and Allergy Foundation of America, "Spring Allergy Capitals 2022," March 2, 2022*

- Orlando was identified as a "2022 Fall Allergy Capital." The area ranked #38 out of 100. Three groups of factors were used to identify the most challenging cities for people with allergies during the fall season: annual fall pollen scores; over the counter allergy medicine use; number of board-certified allergy specialists. *Asthma and Allergy Foundation of America, "Fall Allergy Capitals 2022," March 2, 2022*

- Orlando was identified as a "2022 Asthma Capital." The area ranked #15 out of the nation's 100 largest metropolitan areas. Criteria: estimated asthma prevalence; asthma-related mortality; and ER visits due to asthma. Risk factors analyzed but not factored in the rankings: annual pollen score; annual air quality; public smoking laws; access to board-certified asthma specialists; rescue and controller medication use; uninsured rate; poverty rate. *Asthma and Allergy Foundation of America, "Asthma Capitals 2022: The Most Challenging Places to Live With Asthma," September 14, 2022*

Pet Rankings

- Orlando appeared on *The Dogington Post* site as one of the top cities for dog lovers, ranking #2 out of 15. The real estate marketplace, Zillow®, and Rover, the largest pet sitter and dog walker network, introduced a new list of "Top Emerging Dog-Friendly Cities" for 2021. Criteria: number of new dog accounts on the Rover platform; and rentals and listings that mention features that attract dog owners (fenced-in yards, dog houses, dog door or proximity to a dog park). *www.dogingtonpost.com, "15 Cities Emerging as Dog-Friendliest in 2021," May 11, 2021*

Real Estate Rankings

- *WalletHub* compared the most populated U.S. cities to determine which had the best markets for real estate agents. Orlando ranked #115 where demand was high and pay was the best. Criteria: sales per agent; annual median wage for real-estate agents; monthly average starting salary for real estate agents; real estate job density and competition; unemployment rate; home turnover rate; housing-market health index; and other relevant metrics. *www.WalletHub.com, "2021 Best Places to Be a Real Estate Agent," May 12, 2021*

- According to Penske Truck Rental, the Orlando metro area was named the #3 moving destination in 2022, based on one-way consumer truck rental reservations made through Penske's website, rental locations, and reservations call center. *gopenske.com/blog, "Penske Truck Rental's 2022 Top Moving Destinations," April 27, 2023*

- Orlando was ranked #4 in the top 20 out of the 100 largest metro areas in terms of house price appreciation in 2022 (#1 = highest rate). *Federal Housing Finance Agency, House Price Index, 4th Quarter 2022*

- Orlando was ranked #168 out of 235 metro areas in terms of housing affordability in 2022 by the National Association of Home Builders (#1 = most affordable). Criteria: the share of homes sold in that area affordable to a family earning the local median income, based on standard mortgage underwriting criteria. *National Association of Home Builders®, NAHB-Wells Fargo Housing Opportunity Index, 4th Quarter 2022*

Safety Rankings

- Allstate ranked the 200 largest cities in America in terms of driver safety. Orlando ranked #93. Criteria: internal property damage claims over a two-year period from January 2016 to December 2017. The report helps increase the importance of safety and awareness behind the wheel. *Allstate, "Allstate America's Best Drivers Report, 2019" June 24, 2019*

- The National Insurance Crime Bureau ranked 390 metro areas in the U.S. in terms of per capita rates of vehicle theft. The Orlando metro area ranked #209 (#1 = highest rate). Criteria: number of vehicle theft offenses per 100,000 inhabitants in 2021. *National Insurance Crime Bureau, "Hot Spots 2021," September 1, 2022*

Seniors/Retirement Rankings

- From its Best Cities for Successful Aging indexes, the Milken Institute generated rankings for metropolitan areas, weighing data in nine categories—health care, wellness, living arrangements, transportation and convenience, financial characteristics, education, employment, community engagement, and overall livability. The Orlando metro area was ranked #69 overall in the large metro area category. *Milken Institute, "Best Cities for Successful Aging, 2017" March 14, 2017*

Women/Minorities Rankings

- Orlando was selected as one of the queerest cities in America by *The Advocate*. The city ranked #2 out of 25. Criteria, among many: Trans Pride parades/festivals; gay rugby teams; lesbian bars; LGBTQ centers; theater screenings of "Moonlight"; LGBTQ-inclusive nondiscrimination ordinances; and gay bowling teams. *The Advocate, "Queerest Cities in America 2017" January 12, 2017*

- Personal finance website *WalletHub* compared more than 180 U.S. cities across two key dimensions, "Hispanic Business-Friendliness" and "Hispanic Purchasing Power," to arrive at the most favorable conditions for Hispanic entrepreneurs. Orlando was ranked #18 out of 182. Criteria includes: share of Hispanic-Owned Businesses; Hispanic entrepreneurship rate to median annual income of Hispanics; Small Business-Friendliness score; cost of living; and number of Hispanics with at least a bachelor's degree. *WalletHub.com, "2019's Best Cities for Hispanic Entrepreneurs," May 1, 2019*

Miscellaneous Rankings

- *MoveHub* ranked 446 hipster cities across 20 countries, using its new and improved *alternative* Hipster Index and Orlando came out as #8 among the top 50. Criteria: population over 150,000; number of vintage boutiques; density of tattoo parlors; vegan places to eat; coffee shops; and density of vinyl record stores. *www.movehub.com, "The Hipster Index: Brighton Pips Portland to Global Top Spot," July 28, 2021*

- The watchdog site, Charity Navigator, conducted a study of charities in major markets both to analyze statistical differences in their financial, accountability, and transparency practices and to track year-to-year variations in individual philanthropic communities. The Orlando metro area was ranked #15 among the 30 metro markets in the rating category of Overall Score. *www.charitynavigator.org, "2017 Metro Market Study," May 1, 2017*

- *WalletHub* compared the 150 most populated U.S. cities to determine their operating efficiency. A "Quality of Services" score was constructed for each city and then divided by the total budget per capita to reveal which were managed the best. Orlando ranked #104. Criteria: financial stability; economy; education; safety; health; infrastructure and pollution. *www.WalletHub.com, "2022's Best- & Worst-Run Cities in America," June 21, 2022*

- The National Alliance to End Homelessness listed the 25 most populous metro areas with the highest rate of homelessness. The Orlando metro area had a high rate of homelessness. Criteria: number of homeless people per 10,000 population in 2016. *National Alliance to End Homelessness, "Homelessness in the 25 Most Populous U.S. Metro Areas," September 1, 2017*

Business Environment

DEMOGRAPHICS

Population Growth

Area	1990 Census	2000 Census	2010 Census	2020 Census	Population Growth (%) 1990-2020	Population Growth (%) 2010-2020
City	161,172	185,951	238,300	307,573	90.8	29.1
MSA[1]	1,224,852	1,644,561	2,134,411	2,673,376	118.3	25.3
U.S.	248,709,873	281,421,906	308,745,538	331,449,281	33.3	7.4

Note: (1) Figures cover the Orlando-Kissimmee-Sanford, FL Metropolitan Statistical Area
Source: U.S. Census Bureau, 1990 Census, 2000 Census, 2010 Census, 2020 Census

Race

Area	White Alone[2] (%)	Black Alone[2] (%)	Asian Alone[2] (%)	AIAN[3] Alone[2] (%)	NHOPI[4] Alone[2] (%)	Other Race Alone[2] (%)	Two or More Races (%)
City	40.0	23.8	4.3	0.4	0.1	12.3	19.0
MSA[1]	50.4	15.4	4.7	0.4	0.1	11.4	17.7
U.S.	61.6	12.4	6.0	1.1	0.2	8.4	10.2

Note: (1) Figures cover the Orlando-Kissimmee-Sanford, FL Metropolitan Statistical Area; (2) Alone is defined as not being in combination with one or more other races; (3) American Indian and Alaska Native; (4) Native Hawaiian and Other Pacific Islander
Source: U.S. Census Bureau, 2020 Census

Hispanic or Latino Origin

Area	Total (%)	Mexican (%)	Puerto Rican (%)	Cuban (%)	Other (%)
City	34.2	1.8	15.8	3.0	13.6
MSA[1]	31.8	2.8	15.0	2.5	11.5
U.S.	18.4	11.2	1.8	0.7	4.7

Note: Persons of Hispanic or Latino origin can be of any race; (1) Figures cover the Orlando-Kissimmee-Sanford, FL Metropolitan Statistical Area
Source: U.S. Census Bureau, 2017-2021 American Community Survey 5-Year Estimates

Age

Area	Under Age 5	Age 5–19	Age 20–34	Age 35–44	Age 45–54	Age 55–64	Age 65–74	Age 75–84	Age 85+	Median Age
City	5.7	17.6	27.2	15.6	12.4	10.1	6.8	3.2	1.3	34.7
MSA[1]	5.2	19.5	21.2	13.5	12.9	12.2	9.2	4.6	1.7	37.9
U.S.	5.6	19.2	20.2	12.7	12.4	13.1	10.0	4.9	1.9	38.8

Note: (1) Figures cover the Orlando-Kissimmee-Sanford, FL Metropolitan Statistical Area
Source: U.S. Census Bureau, 2020 Census

Disability by Age

Area	All Ages	Under 18 Years Old	18 to 64 Years Old	65 Years and Over
City	9.6	4.9	7.7	32.0
MSA[1]	12.3	5.7	9.6	33.8
U.S.	12.6	4.4	10.3	33.4

Note: Figures show percent of the civilian noninstitutionalized population that reported having a disability. Disability status is determined from six types of difficulty: vision, hearing, cognitive, ambulatory, self-care, and independent living. For children under 5 years old, hearing and vision difficulty are used to determine disability status. For children between the ages of 5 and 14, disability status is determined from hearing, vision, cognitive, ambulatory, and self-care difficulties. For people aged 15 years and older, they are considered to have a disability if they have difficulty with any one of the six difficulty types; Note: (1) Figures cover the Orlando-Kissimmee-Sanford, FL Metropolitan Statistical Area
Source: U.S. Census Bureau, 2017-2021 American Community Survey 5-Year Estimates

Ancestry

Area	German	Irish	English	American	Italian	Polish	French[2]	Scottish	Dutch
City	6.2	5.7	5.7	5.6	4.7	1.6	1.5	1.0	0.6
MSA[1]	8.1	7.2	6.5	8.2	5.1	1.8	1.7	1.2	0.7
U.S.	12.8	9.6	8.1	5.7	5.0	2.7	2.2	1.6	1.1

Note: Figures are the percentage of the total population reporting a particular ancestry. The nine most commonly reported ancestries in the U.S. are shown. Figures include multiple ancestries (e.g. if a person reported being Irish and Italian, they were included in both columns); (1) Figures cover the Orlando-Kissimmee-Sanford, FL Metropolitan Statistical Area; (2) Excludes Basque
Source: U.S. Census Bureau, 2017-2021 American Community Survey 5-Year Estimates

Foreign-born Population

Area	Any Foreign Country	Asia	Mexico	Europe	Caribbean	Central America[2]	South America	Africa	Canada
City	22.8	2.8	0.6	2.0	6.7	1.1	8.8	0.5	0.3
MSA[1]	19.3	3.0	1.0	1.7	5.6	1.1	6.0	0.6	0.3
U.S.	13.6	4.2	3.3	1.5	1.4	1.1	1.1	0.8	0.2

Percent of Population Born in

Note: (1) Figures cover the Orlando-Kissimmee-Sanford, FL Metropolitan Statistical Area; (2) Excludes Mexico.
Source: U.S. Census Bureau, 2017-2021 American Community Survey 5-Year Estimates

Household Size

Area	One	Two	Three	Four	Five	Six	Seven or More	Average Household Size
City	32.8	33.5	16.0	10.8	4.3	1.4	1.0	2.50
MSA[1]	24.2	34.7	17.1	13.9	6.7	2.2	1.3	2.80
U.S.	28.1	33.8	15.5	12.9	6.0	2.3	1.4	2.60

Note: (1) Figures cover the Orlando-Kissimmee-Sanford, FL Metropolitan Statistical Area
Source: U.S. Census Bureau, 2017-2021 American Community Survey 5-Year Estimates

Household Relationships

Area	Householder	Opposite-sex Spouse	Same-sex Spouse	Opposite-sex Unmarried Partner	Same-sex Unmarried Partner	Child[2]	Grandchild	Other Relatives	Non-relatives
City	41.7	13.7	0.5	3.5	0.4	26.1	2.0	5.9	5.0
MSA[1]	37.0	17.0	0.3	2.7	0.2	28.4	2.4	6.0	4.2
U.S.	38.3	17.5	0.2	2.5	0.2	28.3	2.4	4.8	3.4

Note: Figures are percent of the total population; (1) Figures cover the Orlando-Kissimmee-Sanford, FL Metropolitan Statistical Area; (2) Includes biological, adopted, and stepchildren of the householder
Source: U.S. Census Bureau, 2020 Census

Gender

Area	Males	Females	Males per 100 Females
City	148,481	159,092	93.3
MSA[1]	1,296,256	1,377,120	94.1
U.S.	162,685,811	168,763,470	96.4

Note: (1) Figures cover the Orlando-Kissimmee-Sanford, FL Metropolitan Statistical Area
Source: U.S. Census Bureau, 2020 Census

Marital Status

Area	Never Married	Now Married[2]	Separated	Widowed	Divorced
City	43.2	37.8	2.4	3.9	12.7
MSA[1]	35.2	46.2	2.0	5.0	11.6
U.S.	33.8	48.0	1.8	5.6	10.8

Note: Figures are percentages and cover the population 15 years of age and older; (1) Figures cover the Orlando-Kissimmee-Sanford, FL Metropolitan Statistical Area; (2) Excludes separated
Source: U.S. Census Bureau, 2017-2021 American Community Survey 5-Year Estimates

Religious Groups by Family

Area	Catholic	Baptist	Methodist	LDS[2]	Pentecostal	Lutheran	Islam	Adventist	Other
MSA[1]	17.6	5.7	2.1	0.9	2.7	0.6	1.3	2.8	14.6
U.S.	18.7	7.3	3.0	2.0	1.8	1.7	1.3	1.3	11.6

Note: Figures are the number of adherents as a percentage of the total population and cover the eight largest religious groups in the U.S; (1) Figures cover the Orlando-Kissimmee-Sanford, FL Metropolitan Statistical Area; (2) Church of Jesus Christ of Latter-day Saints
Sources: 2020 U.S. Religion Census, Association of Statisticians of American Religious Bodies; The Association of Religion Data Archives (ARDA)

Religious Groups by Tradition

Area	Catholic	Evangelical Protestant	Mainline Protestant	Black Protestant	Islam	Judaism	Hinduism	Orthodox	Buddhism
MSA[1]	17.6	20.6	2.5	2.7	1.3	0.2	0.5	0.3	0.3
U.S.	18.7	16.5	5.2	2.3	1.3	0.6	0.4	0.4	0.3

Note: Figures are the number of adherents as a percentage of the total population; (1) Figures cover the Orlando-Kissimmee-Sanford, FL Metropolitan Statistical Area
Sources: 2020 U.S. Religion Census, Association of Statisticians of American Religious Bodies; The Association of Religion Data Archives (ARDA)

ECONOMY

Gross Metropolitan Product

Area	2020	2021	2022	2023	Rank[2]
MSA[1]	144.1	160.5	180.2	194.2	30

Note: Figures are in billions of dollars; (1) Figures cover the Orlando-Kissimmee-Sanford, FL Metropolitan Statistical Area; (2) Rank is based on 2021 data and ranges from 1 to 381
Source: U.S. Conference of Mayors, U.S. Metro Economies: U.S. Metros Compared to Global and State Economies, June 2022

Economic Growth

Area	2018-20 (%)	2021 (%)	2022 (%)	2023 (%)	Rank[2]
MSA[1]	-1.2	7.5	6.4	4.4	229
U.S.	-0.6	5.7	3.1	2.9	—

Note: Figures are real gross metropolitan product (GMP) growth rates and represent average annual percent change; (1) Figures cover the Orlando-Kissimmee-Sanford, FL Metropolitan Statistical Area; (2) Rank is based on 2020 2-year average annual percent change and ranges from 1 to 381
Source: U.S. Conference of Mayors, U.S. Metro Economies: U.S. Metros Compared to Global and State Economies, June 2022

Metropolitan Area Exports

Area	2016	2017	2018	2019	2020	2021	Rank[2]
MSA[1]	3,363.9	3,196.7	3,131.7	3,363.9	2,849.8	3,313.6	79

Note: Figures are in millions of dollars; (1) Figures cover the Orlando-Kissimmee-Sanford, FL Metropolitan Statistical Area; (2) Rank is based on 2021 data and ranges from 1 to 388
Source: U.S. Department of Commerce, International Trade Administration, Office of Trade and Economic Analysis, Industry and Analysis, Exports by Metropolitan Area, data extracted March 16, 2023

Building Permits

Area	Single-Family 2021	Single-Family 2022	Pct. Chg.	Multi-Family 2021	Multi-Family 2022	Pct. Chg.	Total 2021	Total 2022	Pct. Chg.
City	990	1,286	29.9	2,734	2,229	-18.5	3,724	3,515	-5.6
MSA[1]	17,795	16,213	-8.9	12,823	12,470	-2.8	30,618	28,683	-6.3
U.S.	1,115,400	975,600	-12.5	621,600	689,500	10.9	1,737,000	1,665,100	-4.1

Note: (1) Figures cover the Orlando-Kissimmee-Sanford, FL Metropolitan Statistical Area; Figures represent new, privately-owned housing units authorized (unadjusted data); All permit data are based on estimates with imputation
Source: U.S. Census Bureau, Manufacturing, Mining, and Construction Statistics, Building Permits, 2021, 2022

Bankruptcy Filings

Area	Business Filings 2021	Business Filings 2022	% Chg.	Nonbusiness Filings 2021	Nonbusiness Filings 2022	% Chg.
Orange County	100	127	27.0	1,909	1,588	-16.8
U.S.	14,347	13,481	-6.0	399,269	374,240	-6.3

Note: Business filings include Chapter 7, Chapter 9, Chapter 11, Chapter 12, Chapter 13, Chapter 15, and Section 304; Nonbusiness filings include Chapter 7, Chapter 11, and Chapter 13
Source: Administrative Office of the U.S. Courts, Business and Nonbusiness Bankruptcy, County Cases Commenced by Chapter of the Bankruptcy Code, During the 12-Month Period Ending December 31, 2021 and Business and Nonbusiness Bankruptcy, County Cases Commenced by Chapter of the Bankruptcy Code, During the 12-Month Period Ending December 31, 2022

Housing Vacancy Rates

Area	Gross Vacancy Rate[2] (%) 2020	2021	2022	Year-Round Vacancy Rate[3] (%) 2020	2021	2022	Rental Vacancy Rate[4] (%) 2020	2021	2022	Homeowner Vacancy Rate[5] (%) 2020	2021	2022
MSA[1]	12.9	9.5	9.6	9.8	7.5	7.4	8.6	7.5	6.5	1.2	0.5	1.4
U.S.	10.6	10.8	10.5	8.2	8.4	8.2	6.3	6.1	5.8	1.0	0.9	0.8

Note: (1) Figures cover the Orlando-Kissimmee-Sanford, FL Metropolitan Statistical Area; (2) The percentage of the total housing inventory that is vacant; (3) The percentage of the housing inventory (excluding seasonal units) that is year-round vacant; (4) The percentage of rental inventory that is vacant for rent; (5) The percentage of homeowner inventory that is vacant for sale
Source: U.S. Census Bureau, Housing Vacancies and Homeownership Annual Statistics: 2020, 2021, 2022

INCOME

Income

Area	Per Capita ($)	Median Household ($)	Average Household ($)
City	36,596	58,968	88,128
MSA[1]	32,999	65,086	89,689
U.S.	37,638	69,021	97,196

Note: (1) Figures cover the Orlando-Kissimmee-Sanford, FL Metropolitan Statistical Area
Source: U.S. Census Bureau, 2017-2021 American Community Survey 5-Year Estimates

Orlando, Florida

Household Income Distribution

Area	Under $15,000	$15,000 -$24,999	$25,000 -$34,999	$35,000 -$49,999	$50,000 -$74,999	$75,000 -$99,999	$100,000 -$149,999	$150,000 and up
City	11.2	9.3	8.7	13.6	17.9	11.7	13.0	14.5
MSA[1]	8.3	7.9	9.0	12.9	18.5	13.6	15.8	14.0
U.S.	9.4	7.8	8.2	11.4	16.8	12.8	16.3	17.3

Note: (1) Figures cover the Orlando-Kissimmee-Sanford, FL Metropolitan Statistical Area
Source: U.S. Census Bureau, 2017-2021 American Community Survey 5-Year Estimates

Poverty Rate

Area	All Ages	Under 18 Years Old	18 to 64 Years Old	65 Years and Over
City	15.5	21.5	13.7	14.5
MSA[1]	12.6	17.1	11.7	9.9
U.S.	12.6	17.0	11.8	9.6

Note: Figures are percentage of people whose income during the past 12 months was below the poverty level; (1) Figures cover the Orlando-Kissimmee-Sanford, FL Metropolitan Statistical Area
Source: U.S. Census Bureau, 2017-2021 American Community Survey 5-Year Estimates

EMPLOYMENT

Labor Force and Employment

Area	Civilian Labor Force Dec. 2021	Civilian Labor Force Dec. 2022	% Chg.	Workers Employed Dec. 2021	Workers Employed Dec. 2022	% Chg.
City	168,524	173,274	2.8	162,788	169,122	3.9
MSA[1]	1,366,646	1,407,116	3.0	1,323,163	1,374,399	3.9
U.S.	161,696,000	164,224,000	1.6	155,732,000	158,872,000	2.0

Note: Data is not seasonally adjusted and covers workers 16 years of age and older; (1) Figures cover the Orlando-Kissimmee-Sanford, FL Metropolitan Statistical Area
Source: Bureau of Labor Statistics, Local Area Unemployment Statistics

Unemployment Rate

Area	Jan.	Feb.	Mar.	Apr.	May	Jun.	Jul.	Aug.	Sep.	Oct.	Nov.	Dec.
City	3.9	3.6	3.1	2.9	2.9	3.3	3.1	3.1	2.7	2.8	2.7	2.4
MSA[1]	3.8	3.4	2.9	2.6	2.7	3.2	3.0	2.9	2.7	2.8	2.7	2.3
U.S.	4.4	4.1	3.8	3.3	3.4	3.8	3.8	3.8	3.3	3.4	3.4	3.3

Note: Data is not seasonally adjusted and covers workers 16 years of age and older; (1) Figures cover the Orlando-Kissimmee-Sanford, FL Metropolitan Statistical Area
Source: Bureau of Labor Statistics, Local Area Unemployment Statistics

Average Wages

Occupation	$/Hr.	Occupation	$/Hr.
Accountants and Auditors	39.04	Maintenance and Repair Workers	20.33
Automotive Mechanics	22.82	Marketing Managers	76.95
Bookkeepers	21.76	Network and Computer Systems Admin.	43.75
Carpenters	22.25	Nurses, Licensed Practical	26.40
Cashiers	13.41	Nurses, Registered	38.04
Computer Programmers	44.68	Nursing Assistants	16.41
Computer Systems Analysts	49.23	Office Clerks, General	18.94
Computer User Support Specialists	26.77	Physical Therapists	45.58
Construction Laborers	17.79	Physicians	133.16
Cooks, Restaurant	17.07	Plumbers, Pipefitters and Steamfitters	23.14
Customer Service Representatives	18.69	Police and Sheriff's Patrol Officers	29.83
Dentists	91.27	Postal Service Mail Carriers	26.72
Electricians	24.05	Real Estate Sales Agents	26.11
Engineers, Electrical	50.65	Retail Salespersons	15.51
Fast Food and Counter Workers	12.49	Sales Representatives, Technical/Scientific	46.62
Financial Managers	77.76	Secretaries, Exc. Legal/Medical/Executive	18.93
First-Line Supervisors of Office Workers	30.12	Security Guards	15.30
General and Operations Managers	55.62	Surgeons	n/a
Hairdressers/Cosmetologists	17.02	Teacher Assistants, Exc. Postsecondary*	13.42
Home Health and Personal Care Aides	13.54	Teachers, Secondary School, Exc. Sp. Ed.*	26.07
Janitors and Cleaners	13.87	Telemarketers	14.29
Landscaping/Groundskeeping Workers	16.23	Truck Drivers, Heavy/Tractor-Trailer	24.63
Lawyers	70.07	Truck Drivers, Light/Delivery Services	21.37
Maids and Housekeeping Cleaners	14.29	Waiters and Waitresses	16.41

Note: Wage data covers the Orlando-Kissimmee-Sanford, FL Metropolitan Statistical Area; (*) Hourly wages were calculated from annual wage data based on a 40 hour work week; n/a not available.
Source: Bureau of Labor Statistics, Metro Area Occupational Employment & Wage Estimates, May 2022

Employment by Industry

Sector	MSA[1] Number of Employees	MSA[1] Percent of Total	U.S. Percent of Total
Construction	86,600	6.0	5.0
Private Education and Health Services	180,400	12.6	16.1
Financial Activities	90,100	6.3	5.9
Government	127,900	8.9	14.5
Information	27,500	1.9	2.0
Leisure and Hospitality	278,100	19.4	10.3
Manufacturing	52,900	3.7	8.4
Mining and Logging	200	<0.1	0.4
Other Services	44,000	3.1	3.7
Professional and Business Services	277,000	19.3	14.7
Retail Trade	155,400	10.8	10.2
Transportation, Warehousing, and Utilities	64,900	4.5	4.9
Wholesale Trade	51,600	3.6	3.9

Note: Figures are non-farm employment as of December 2022. Figures are not seasonally adjusted and include workers 16 years of age and older; (1) Figures cover the Orlando-Kissimmee-Sanford, FL Metropolitan Statistical Area
Source: Bureau of Labor Statistics, Current Employment Statistics, Employment, Hours, and Earnings

Employment by Occupation

Occupation Classification	City (%)	MSA[1] (%)	U.S. (%)
Management, Business, Science, and Arts	40.0	37.9	40.3
Natural Resources, Construction, and Maintenance	6.1	8.1	8.7
Production, Transportation, and Material Moving	11.5	10.8	13.1
Sales and Office	24.2	24.4	20.9
Service	18.1	18.9	17.0

Note: Figures cover employed civilians 16 years of age and older; (1) Figures cover the Orlando-Kissimmee-Sanford, FL Metropolitan Statistical Area
Source: U.S. Census Bureau, 2017-2021 American Community Survey 5-Year Estimates

Occupations with Greatest Projected Employment Growth: 2022 – 2024

Occupation[1]	2022 Employment	2024 Projected Employment	Numeric Employment Change	Percent Employment Change
General and Operations Managers	196,430	209,480	13,050	6.6
Cooks, Restaurant	117,090	129,670	12,580	10.7
Registered Nurses	208,620	221,040	12,420	6.0
Waiters and Waitresses	194,570	206,380	11,810	6.1
Retail Salespersons	327,010	338,390	11,380	3.5
Stockers and Order Fillers	192,890	203,920	11,030	5.7
Customer Service Representatives	283,220	293,670	10,450	3.7
Fast Food and Counter Workers	203,420	212,470	9,050	4.4
Laborers and Freight, Stock, and Material Movers, Hand	138,200	146,930	8,730	6.3
Maids and Housekeeping Cleaners	77,330	85,600	8,270	10.7

Note: Projections cover Florida; (1) Sorted by numeric employment change
Source: www.projectionscentral.com, State Occupational Projections, 2022–2024 Short-Term Projections

Fastest-Growing Occupations: 2022 – 2024

Occupation[1]	2022 Employment	2024 Projected Employment	Numeric Employment Change	Percent Employment Change
Hotel, Motel, and Resort Desk Clerks	23,000	26,650	3,650	15.9
First-Line Supervisors of Gambling Services Workers	990	1,140	150	15.2
Baggage Porters and Bellhops	3,310	3,810	500	15.1
Solar Photovoltaic Installers	860	990	130	15.1
Nurse Practitioners	17,490	20,080	2,590	14.8
Motion Picture Projectionists	490	560	70	14.3
Lodging Managers	5,160	5,870	710	13.8
Transportation Workers, All Other	980	1,110	130	13.3
Information Security Analysts (SOC 2018)	11,910	13,480	1,570	13.2
Statisticians	1,370	1,550	180	13.1

Note: Projections cover Florida; (1) Sorted by percent employment change and excludes occupations with numeric employment change less than 50
Source: www.projectionscentral.com, State Occupational Projections, 2022–2024 Short-Term Projections

Orlando, Florida   429

CITY FINANCES

City Government Finances

Component	2020 ($000)	2020 ($ per capita)
Total Revenues	1,070,139	3,723
Total Expenditures	927,906	3,228
Debt Outstanding	972,887	3,385
Cash and Securities[1]	1,224,756	4,261

Note: (1) Cash and security holdings of a government at the close of its fiscal year, including those of its dependent agencies, utilities, and liquor stores.
Source: U.S. Census Bureau, State & Local Government Finances 2020

City Government Revenue by Source

Source	2020 ($000)	2020 ($ per capita)	2020 (%)
General Revenue			
From Federal Government	22,470	78	2.1
From State Government	70,488	245	6.6
From Local Governments	172,471	600	16.1
Taxes			
Property	200,652	698	18.8
Sales and Gross Receipts	63,109	220	5.9
Personal Income	0	0	0.0
Corporate Income	0	0	0.0
Motor Vehicle License	0	0	0.0
Other Taxes	73,094	254	6.8
Current Charges	291,349	1,014	27.2
Liquor Store	0	0	0.0
Utility	7	0	0.0

Source: U.S. Census Bureau, State & Local Government Finances 2020

City Government Expenditures by Function

Function	2020 ($000)	2020 ($ per capita)	2020 (%)
General Direct Expenditures			
Air Transportation	0	0	0.0
Corrections	0	0	0.0
Education	0	0	0.0
Employment Security Administration	0	0	0.0
Financial Administration	29,600	103	3.2
Fire Protection	116,242	404	12.5
General Public Buildings	0	0	0.0
Governmental Administration, Other	89,937	312	9.7
Health	0	0	0.0
Highways	25,203	87	2.7
Hospitals	0	0	0.0
Housing and Community Development	9,408	32	1.0
Interest on General Debt	40,446	140	4.4
Judicial and Legal	5,000	17	0.5
Libraries	0	0	0.0
Parking	17,726	61	1.9
Parks and Recreation	109,593	381	11.8
Police Protection	183,820	639	19.8
Public Welfare	0	0	0.0
Sewerage	102,419	356	11.0
Solid Waste Management	32,665	113	3.5
Veterans' Services	0	0	0.0
Liquor Store	0	0	0.0
Utility	0	0	0.0

Source: U.S. Census Bureau, State & Local Government Finances 2020

TAXES

State Corporate Income Tax Rates

State	Tax Rate (%)	Income Brackets ($)	Num. of Brackets	Financial Institution Tax Rate (%)[a]	Federal Income Tax Ded.
Florida	5.5	Flat rate	1	5.5	No

Note: Tax rates as of January 1, 2023; (a) Rates listed are the corporate income tax rate applied to financial institutions or excise taxes based on income. Some states have other taxes based upon the value of deposits or shares.
Source: Federation of Tax Administrators, State Corporate Income Tax Rates, January 1, 2023

State Individual Income Tax Rates

State	Tax Rate (%)	Income Brackets ($)	Personal Exemptions ($) Single	Personal Exemptions ($) Married	Personal Exemptions ($) Depend.	Standard Ded. ($) Single	Standard Ded. ($) Married
Florida			– No state income tax –				

Note: Tax rates as of January 1, 2023; Local- and county-level taxes are not included
Source: Federation of Tax Administrators, State Individual Income Tax Rates, January 1, 2023

Various State Sales and Excise Tax Rates

State	State Sales Tax (%)	Gasoline[1] ($/gal.)	Cigarette[2] ($/pack)	Spirits[3] ($/gal.)	Wine[4] ($/gal.)	Beer[5] ($/gal.)	Recreational Marijuana (%)
Florida	6	0.4123	1.339	6.50	2.25	0.48	Not legal

Note: All tax rates as of January 1, 2023; (1) The American Petroleum Institute has developed a methodology for determining the average tax rate on a gallon of fuel. Rates may include any of the following: excise taxes, environmental fees, storage tank fees, other fees or taxes, general sales tax, and local taxes; (2) The federal excise tax of $1.0066 per pack and local taxes are not included; (3) Rates are those applicable to off-premise sales of 40% alcohol by volume (a.b.v.) distilled spirits in 750ml containers. Local excise taxes are excluded; (4) Rates are those applicable to off-premise sales of 11% a.b.v. non-carbonated wine in 750ml containers; (5) Rates are those applicable to off-premise sales of 4.7% a.b.v. beer in 12 ounce containers.
Source: Tax Foundation, 2023 Facts & Figures: How Does Your State Compare?

State Business Tax Climate Index Rankings

State	Overall Rank	Corporate Tax Rank	Individual Income Tax Rank	Sales Tax Rank	Property Tax Rank	Unemployment Insurance Tax Rank
Florida	4	10	1	21	12	3

Note: The index is a measure of how each state's tax laws affect economic performance. The lower the rank, the more favorable a state's tax system is for business. States without a given tax are given a ranking of 1. The scores/rankings for the District of Columbia do not affect other states. The 2023 index represents the tax climate as of July 1, 2022.
Source: Tax Foundation, State Business Tax Climate Index 2023

TRANSPORTATION

Means of Transportation to Work

Area	Car/Truck/Van Drove Alone	Car/Truck/Van Carpooled	Public Transportation Bus	Public Transportation Subway	Public Transportation Railroad	Bicycle	Walked	Other Means	Worked at Home
City	75.2	8.1	2.3	0.0	0.0	0.6	1.4	2.7	9.7
MSA[1]	75.8	9.4	1.1	0.0	0.1	0.4	1.1	1.9	10.2
U.S.	73.2	8.6	2.0	1.6	0.5	0.5	2.5	1.5	9.7

Note: Figures are percentages and cover workers 16 years of age and older; (1) Figures cover the Orlando-Kissimmee-Sanford, FL Metropolitan Statistical Area
Source: U.S. Census Bureau, 2017-2021 American Community Survey 5-Year Estimates

Travel Time to Work

Area	Less Than 10 Minutes	10 to 19 Minutes	20 to 29 Minutes	30 to 44 Minutes	45 to 59 Minutes	60 to 89 Minutes	90 Minutes or More
City	7.2	25.4	27.6	26.6	7.2	3.9	2.2
MSA[1]	7.2	22.9	22.3	28.1	11.2	6.0	2.4
U.S.	12.4	28.5	21.0	20.9	8.2	6.2	2.9

Note: Note: Figures are percentages and include workers 16 years old and over; (1) Figures cover the Orlando-Kissimmee-Sanford, FL Metropolitan Statistical Area
Source: U.S. Census Bureau, 2017-2021 American Community Survey 5-Year Estimates

Key Congestion Measures

Measure	1990	2000	2010	2015	2020
Annual Hours of Delay, Total (000)	15,573	34,970	51,679	58,893	25,458
Annual Hours of Delay, Per Auto Commuter	30	43	48	53	22
Annual Congestion Cost, Per Auto Commuter ($)	520	877	1,030	1,084	471

Note: Covers the Orlando FL urban area
Source: Texas A&M Transportation Institute, 2021 Urban Mobility Report

Freeway Travel Time Index

Measure	1985	1990	1995	2000	2005	2010	2015	2020
Urban Area Index[1]	1.09	1.14	1.16	1.20	1.23	1.22	1.23	1.07
Urban Area Rank[1,2]	36	26	32	29	28	32	29	57

Note: Freeway Travel Time Index—the ratio of travel time in the peak period to the travel time at free-flow conditions. For example, a value of 1.30 indicates a 20-minute free-flow trip takes 26 minutes in the peak (20 minutes x 1.30 = 26 minutes); (1) Covers the Orlando FL urban area; (2) Rank is based on 101 larger urban areas (#1 = highest travel time index)
Source: Texas A&M Transportation Institute, 2021 Urban Mobility Report

Public Transportation

Agency Name / Mode of Transportation	Vehicles Operated in Maximum Service[1]	Annual Unlinked Passenger Trips[2] (in thous.)	Annual Passenger Miles[3] (in thous.)
Central Florida Regional Transportation Authority (Lynx)			
Bus (directly operated)	246	12,805.0	67,889.7
Bus (purchased transportation)	13	75.3	392.0
Bus Rapid Transit (directly operated)	11	456.5	455.2
Demand Response (purchased transportation)	142	530.2	5,679.0
Vanpool (purchased transportation)	146	263.4	5,404.3

Note: (1) Number of revenue vehicles operated by the given mode and type of service to meet the annual maximum service requirement. This is the revenue vehicle count during the peak season of the year; on the week and day that maximum service is provided. Vehicles operated in maximum service (VOMS) exclude atypical days and one-time special events; (2) Number of passengers who boarded public transportation vehicles. Passengers are counted each time they board a vehicle no matter how many vehicles they use to travel from their origin to their destination. (3) Sum of the distances ridden by all passengers during the entire fiscal year.
Source: Federal Transit Administration, National Transit Database, 2021

Air Transportation

Airport Name and Code / Type of Service	Passenger Airlines[1]	Passenger Enplanements	Freight Carriers[2]	Freight (lbs)
Orlando International (MCO)				
Domestic service (U.S. carriers - 2022)	28	21,838,068	19	162,445,831
International service (U.S. carriers - 2021)	10	467,342	2	283,118

Note: (1) Includes all U.S.-based major, minor and commuter airlines that carried at least one passenger during the year; (2) Includes all U.S.-based airlines and freight carriers that transported at least one pound of freight during the year.
Source: Bureau of Transportation Statistics, The Intermodal Transportation Database, Air Carriers: T-100 Domestic Market (U.S. Carriers), 2022; Bureau of Transportation Statistics, The Intermodal Transportation Database, Air Carriers: T-100 International Market (U.S. Carriers), 2021

BUSINESSES

Major Business Headquarters

Company Name	Industry	Fortune[1]	Forbes[2]
Darden Restaurants	Food services	465	-

Note: (1) Companies that produce a 10-K are ranked 1 to 500 based on 2021 revenue; (2) All private companies with at least $2 billion in annual revenue through the end of their most current fiscal year are ranked 1 to 246; companies listed are headquartered in the city; dashes indicate no ranking
Source: Fortune, "Fortune 500," 2022; Forbes, "America's Largest Private Companies," 2022

Fastest-Growing Businesses

According to *Inc.*, Orlando is home to three of America's 500 fastest-growing private companies: **HighKey** (#5); **OneRail** (#48); **The Desoto Group** (#219). Criteria: must be an independent, privately-held, for-profit, U.S. corporation, proprietorship or partnership as of December 31, 2021; revenues must be at least $100,000 in 2018 and $2 million in 2021; must have four-year operating/sales history. *Inc., "America's 500 Fastest-Growing Private Companies," 2022*

According to Deloitte, Orlando is home to one of North America's 500 fastest-growing high-technology companies: **Stax** (#148). Companies are ranked by percentage growth in revenue over a four-year period. Criteria for inclusion: company must be headquartered within North America; must own proprietary intellectual property or technology that is sold to customers in products that contributes to a significant portion of the company's operating revenue; must have been in business for a minumum of four years with 2018 operating revenues of at least $50,000 USD/CD and 2021 operating revenues of at least $5 million USD/CD. *Deloitte, 2022 Technology Fast 500™*

Living Environment

COST OF LIVING

Cost of Living Index

Composite Index	Groceries	Housing	Utilities	Transportation	Health Care	Misc. Goods/Services
104.8	103.0	110.9	93.0	100.7	91.7	106.6

Note: The Cost of Living Index measures regional differences in the cost of consumer goods and services, excluding taxes and non-consumer expenditures, for professional and managerial households in the top income quintile. It is based on more than 50,000 prices covering almost 60 different items for which prices are collected three times a year by chambers of commerce, economic development organizations or university applied economic centers in each participating urban area. The numbers shown should be read as a percentage above or below the national average of 100. For example, a value of 115.4 in the groceries column indicates that grocery prices are 15.4% higher than the national average. Small differences in the index numbers should not be interpreted as significant; Figures cover the Orlando FL urban area.
Source: The Council for Community and Economic Research, Cost of Living Index, 2022

Grocery Prices

Area[1]	T-Bone Steak ($/pound)	Frying Chicken ($/pound)	Whole Milk ($/half gal.)	Eggs ($/dozen)	Orange Juice ($/64 oz.)	Coffee ($/11.5 oz.)
City[2]	13.49	1.37	2.67	2.44	3.89	3.89
Avg.	13.81	1.59	2.43	2.25	3.85	4.95
Min.	10.17	0.90	1.51	1.30	2.90	3.46
Max.	19.35	3.30	4.32	4.32	5.31	8.59

Note: (1) Values for the local area are compared with the average, minimum and maximum values for all 286 areas in the Cost of Living Index; (2) Figures cover the Orlando FL urban area; **T-Bone Steak** (price per pound); **Frying Chicken** (price per pound, whole fryer); **Whole Milk** (half gallon carton); **Eggs** (price per dozen, Grade A, large); **Orange Juice** (64 oz. Tropicana or Florida Natural); **Coffee** (11.5 oz. can, vacuum-packed, Maxwell House, Hills Bros, or Folgers).
Source: The Council for Community and Economic Research, Cost of Living Index, 2022

Housing and Utility Costs

Area[1]	New Home Price ($)	Apartment Rent ($/month)	All Electric ($/month)	Part Electric ($/month)	Other Energy ($/month)	Telephone ($/month)
City[2]	448,493	1,766	154.33	-	-	192.14
Avg.	450,913	1,371	176.41	99.93	76.96	190.22
Min.	229,283	546	100.84	31.56	27.15	174.27
Max.	2,434,977	4,569	356.86	249.59	272.24	208.31

Note: (1) Values for the local area are compared with the average, minimum and maximum values for all 286 areas in the Cost of Living Index; (2) Figures cover the Orlando FL urban area; **New Home Price** (2,400 sf living area, 8,000 sf lot, in urban area with full utilities); **Apartment Rent** (950 sf 2 bedroom/1.5 or 2 bath, unfurnished, excluding all utilities except water); **All Electric** (average monthly cost for an all-electric home); **Part Electric** (average monthly cost for a part-electric home); **Other Energy** (average monthly cost for natural gas, fuel oil, coal, wood, and any other forms of energy except electricity); **Telephone** (price includes the base monthly rate plus taxes and fees for three lines of mobile phone service).
Source: The Council for Community and Economic Research, Cost of Living Index, 2022

Health Care, Transportation, and Other Costs

Area[1]	Doctor ($/visit)	Dentist ($/visit)	Optometrist ($/visit)	Gasoline ($/gallon)	Beauty Salon ($/visit)	Men's Shirt ($)
City[2]	98.00	108.72	79.50	3.83	60.44	45.42
Avg.	124.91	107.77	117.66	3.86	43.31	34.21
Min.	36.61	58.25	51.79	2.90	22.18	13.05
Max.	250.21	162.58	371.96	5.54	85.61	63.54

Note: (1) Values for the local area are compared with the average, minimum and maximum values for all 286 areas in the Cost of Living Index; (2) Figures cover the Orlando FL urban area; **Doctor** (general practitioners routine exam of an established patient); **Dentist** (adult teeth cleaning and periodic oral examination); **Optometrist** (full vision eye exam for established adult patient); **Gasoline** (one gallon regular unleaded, national brand, including all taxes, cash price at self-service pump if available); **Beauty Salon** (woman's shampoo, trim, and blow-dry); **Men's Shirt** (cotton/polyester dress shirt, pinpoint weave, long sleeves).
Source: The Council for Community and Economic Research, Cost of Living Index, 2022

HOUSING

Homeownership Rate

Area	2015 (%)	2016 (%)	2017 (%)	2018 (%)	2019 (%)	2020 (%)	2021 (%)	2022 (%)
MSA[1]	58.4	58.5	59.5	58.5	56.1	64.2	63.0	62.1
U.S.	63.7	63.4	63.9	64.4	64.6	66.6	65.5	65.8

Note: (1) Figures cover the Orlando-Kissimmee-Sanford, FL Metropolitan Statistical Area
Source: U.S. Census Bureau, Housing Vacancies and Homeownership Annual Statistics: 2015-2022

House Price Index (HPI)

Area	National Ranking[2]	Quarterly Change (%)	One-Year Change (%)	Five-Year Change (%)	Since 1991Q1 (%)
MSA[1]	13	0.53	19.76	74.99	330.12
U.S.[3]	–	0.34	8.41	58.44	289.08

Note: The HPI is a weighted repeat sales index. It measures average price changes in repeat sales or refinancings on the same properties. This information is obtained by reviewing repeat mortgage transactions on single-family properties whose mortgages have been purchased or securitized by Fannie Mae or Freddie Mac since January 1975; (1) Figures cover the Orlando-Kissimmee-Sanford, FL Metropolitan Statistical Area; (2) Rankings are based on annual percentage change for all metro areas containing at least 15,000 transactions over the last 10 years and ranges from 1 to 257; (3) figures based on a weighted average of Census Division estimates using a seasonally adjusted, purchase-only index; all figures are for the period ending December 31, 2022
Source: Federal Housing Finance Agency, Change in FHFA Metropolitan Area House Price Indexes, 2022Q4

Median Single-Family Home Prices

Area	2020	2021	2022p	Percent Change 2021 to 2022
MSA[1]	301.6	356.9	420.0	17.7
U.S. Average	300.2	357.1	392.6	9.9

Note: Figures are median sales prices of existing single-family homes in thousands of dollars; (p) preliminary; (1) Figures cover the Orlando-Kissimmee-Sanford, FL Metropolitan Statistical Area
Source: National Association of Realtors, Median Sales Price of Existing Single-Family Homes for Metropolitan Areas, 4th Quarter 2022

Qualifying Income Based on Median Sales Price of Existing Single-Family Homes

Area	With 5% Down ($)	With 10% Down ($)	With 20% Down ($)
MSA[1]	126,465	119,809	106,497
U.S. Average	112,234	106,237	94,513

Note: Figures are preliminary; Qualifying income is based on a mortgage rate of 6.77%. Monthly principal and interest payment is limited to 25% of income; (1) Figures cover the Orlando-Kissimmee-Sanford, FL Metropolitan Statistical Area
Source: National Association of Realtors, Qualifying Income Based on Median Sales Price of Existing Single-Family Homes for Metropolitan Areas, 4th Quarter 2022

Home Value

Area	Under $100,000	$100,000 -$199,999	$200,000 -$299,999	$300,000 -$399,999	$400,000 -$499,999	$500,000 -$999,999	$1,000,000 or more	Median ($)
City	7.5	23.3	22.9	20.6	10.8	12.3	2.6	283,700
MSA[1]	10.4	20.5	30.9	19.9	8.1	8.3	1.9	260,800
U.S.	16.2	24.2	20.1	13.6	8.3	13.6	4.1	244,900

Note: Figures are percentages except for median and cover owner-occupied housing units; (1) Figures cover the Orlando-Kissimmee-Sanford, FL Metropolitan Statistical Area
Source: U.S. Census Bureau, 2017-2021 American Community Survey 5-Year Estimates

Year Housing Structure Built

Area	2020 or Later	2010 -2019	2000 -2009	1990 -1999	1980 -1989	1970 -1979	1960 -1969	1950 -1959	1940 -1949	Before 1940	Median Year
City	0.2	13.7	20.3	14.7	15.6	14.5	7.2	8.3	2.8	2.8	1989
MSA[1]	0.3	12.7	22.2	19.4	19.4	12.6	5.8	5.1	1.2	1.5	1992
U.S.	0.2	7.3	13.6	13.6	13.2	14.8	10.3	10.0	4.7	12.2	1979

Note: Figures are percentages except for Median Year; Note: (1) Figures cover the Orlando-Kissimmee-Sanford, FL Metropolitan Statistical Area
Source: U.S. Census Bureau, 2017-2021 American Community Survey 5-Year Estimates

Gross Monthly Rent

Area	Under $500	$500 -$999	$1,000 -$1,499	$1,500 -$1,999	$2,000 -$2,499	$2,500 -$2,999	$3,000 and up	Median ($)
City	3.4	15.1	45.7	26.9	6.3	1.6	1.1	1,346
MSA[1]	2.7	16.2	43.2	27.2	7.5	1.9	1.2	1,363
U.S.	8.1	30.5	30.8	16.8	7.3	3.1	3.5	1,163

Note: Figures are percentages except for median; Gross rent is the contract rent plus the estimated average monthly cost of utilities (electricity, gas, and water and sewer) and fuels (oil, coal, kerosene, wood, etc.) if these are paid by the renter (or paid for the renter by someone else); (1) Figures cover the Orlando-Kissimmee-Sanford, FL Metropolitan Statistical Area
Source: U.S. Census Bureau, 2017-2021 American Community Survey 5-Year Estimates

HEALTH

Health Risk Factors

Category	MSA[1] (%)	U.S. (%)
Adults aged 18–64 who have any kind of health care coverage	n/a	90.9
Adults who reported being in good or better health	n/a	85.2
Adults who have been told they have high blood cholesterol	n/a	35.7
Adults who have been told they have high blood pressure	n/a	32.4
Adults who are current smokers	n/a	14.4
Adults who currently use e-cigarettes	n/a	6.7
Adults who currently use chewing tobacco, snuff, or snus	n/a	3.5
Adults who are heavy drinkers[2]	n/a	6.3
Adults who are binge drinkers[3]	n/a	15.4
Adults who are overweight (BMI 25.0 - 29.9)	n/a	34.4
Adults who are obese (BMI 30.0 - 99.8)	n/a	33.9
Adults who participated in any physical activities in the past month	n/a	76.3

Note: (1) Figures for the Orlando-Kissimmee-Sanford, FL Metropolitan Statistical Area were not available. (2) Heavy drinkers are classified as adult men having more than 14 drinks per week and adult women having more than 7 drinks per week; (3) Binge drinkers are classified as males having five or more drinks on one occasion or females having four or more drinks on one occasion
Source: Centers for Disease Control and Prevention, Behavioral Risk Factor Surveillance System, SMART: Selected Metropolitan Area Risk Trends, 2021

Acute and Chronic Health Conditions

Category	MSA[1] (%)	U.S. (%)
Adults who have ever been told they had a heart attack	n/a	4.0
Adults who have ever been told they have angina or coronary heart disease	n/a	3.8
Adults who have ever been told they had a stroke	n/a	3.0
Adults who have ever been told they have asthma	n/a	14.9
Adults who have ever been told they have arthritis	n/a	25.8
Adults who have ever been told they have diabetes[2]	n/a	10.9
Adults who have ever been told they had skin cancer	n/a	6.6
Adults who have ever been told they had any other types of cancer	n/a	7.5
Adults who have ever been told they have COPD	n/a	6.1
Adults who have ever been told they have kidney disease	n/a	3.0
Adults who have ever been told they have a form of depression	n/a	20.5

Note: (1) Figures for the Orlando-Kissimmee-Sanford, FL Metropolitan Statistical Area were not available. (2) Figures do not include pregnancy-related, borderline, or pre-diabetes
Source: Centers for Disease Control and Prevention, Behavioral Risk Factor Surveillance System, SMART: Selected Metropolitan Area Risk Trends, 2021

Health Screening and Vaccination Rates

Category	MSA[1] (%)	U.S. (%)
Adults who have ever been tested for HIV	n/a	34.9
Adults who have had their blood cholesterol checked within the last five years	n/a	85.2
Adults aged 65+ who have had flu shot within the past year	n/a	68.6
Adults aged 65+ who have ever had a pneumonia vaccination	n/a	71.0

Note: (1) Figures for the Orlando-Kissimmee-Sanford, FL Metropolitan Statistical Area were not available.
Source: Centers for Disease Control and Prevention, Behavioral Risk Factor Surveillance System, SMART: Selected Metropolitan Area Risk Trends, 2021

Disability Status

Category	MSA[1] (%)	U.S. (%)
Adults who reported being deaf	n/a	7.2
Are you blind or have serious difficulty seeing, even when wearing glasses?	n/a	4.8
Are you limited in any way in any of your usual activities due to arthritis?	n/a	11.1
Do you have difficulty doing errands alone?	n/a	7.0
Do you have difficulty dressing or bathing?	n/a	3.6
Do you have serious difficulty concentrating/remembering/making decisions?	n/a	12.1
Do you have serious difficulty walking or climbing stairs?	n/a	12.8

Note: (1) Figures for the Orlando-Kissimmee-Sanford, FL Metropolitan Statistical Area were not available.
Source: Centers for Disease Control and Prevention, Behavioral Risk Factor Surveillance System, SMART: Selected Metropolitan Area Risk Trends, 2021

Mortality Rates for the Top 10 Causes of Death in the U.S.

ICD-10[a] Sub-Chapter	ICD-10[a] Code	Crude Mortality Rate[1] per 100,000 population County[2]	U.S.
Malignant neoplasms	C00-C97	135.4	182.6
Ischaemic heart diseases	I20-I25	84.0	113.1
Other forms of heart disease	I30-I51	33.4	64.4
Other degenerative diseases of the nervous system	G30-G31	24.3	51.0
Cerebrovascular diseases	I60-I69	49.2	47.8
Other external causes of accidental injury	W00-X59	40.5	46.4
Chronic lower respiratory diseases	J40-J47	26.1	45.7
Organic, including symptomatic, mental disorders	F01-F09	23.5	35.9
Hypertensive diseases	I10-I15	24.5	35.0
Diabetes mellitus	E10-E14	21.6	29.6

Note: (a) ICD-10 = International Classification of Diseases 10th Revision; (1) Crude mortality rates are a three-year average covering 2019-2021; (2) Figures cover Orange County.
Source: Centers for Disease Control and Prevention, National Center for Health Statistics. National Vital Statistics System, Mortality 2018-2021 on CDC WONDER Online Database

Mortality Rates for Selected Causes of Death

ICD-10[a] Sub-Chapter	ICD-10[a] Code	Crude Mortality Rate[1] per 100,000 population County[2]	U.S.
Assault	X85-Y09	7.4	7.0
Diseases of the liver	K70-K76	12.8	19.8
Human immunodeficiency virus (HIV) disease	B20-B24	3.3	1.5
Influenza and pneumonia	J09-J18	7.9	14.7
Intentional self-harm	X60-X84	9.8	14.3
Malnutrition	E40-E46	3.4	4.3
Obesity and other hyperalimentation	E65-E68	1.7	3.0
Renal failure	N17-N19	10.5	15.7
Transport accidents	V01-V99	13.4	13.6
Viral hepatitis	B15-B19	1.2	1.2

Note: (a) ICD-10 = International Classification of Diseases 10th Revision; (1) Crude mortality rates are a three-year average covering 2019-2021; (2) Figures cover Orange County; Data are suppressed when the data meet the criteria for confidentiality constraints; Crude mortality rates are flagged as unreliable when the rate would be calculated with a numerator of 20 or less.
Source: Centers for Disease Control and Prevention, National Center for Health Statistics. National Vital Statistics System, Mortality 2018-2021 on CDC WONDER Online Database

Health Insurance Coverage

Area	With Health Insurance	With Private Health Insurance	With Public Health Insurance	Without Health Insurance	Population Under Age 19 Without Health Insurance
City	84.9	64.3	27.5	15.1	8.9
MSA[1]	87.8	65.8	31.3	12.2	6.8
U.S.	91.2	67.8	35.4	8.8	5.3

Note: Figures are percentages that cover the civilian noninstitutionalized population; (1) Figures cover the Orlando-Kissimmee-Sanford, FL Metropolitan Statistical Area
Source: U.S. Census Bureau, 2017-2021 American Community Survey 5-Year Estimates

Number of Medical Professionals

Area	MDs[3]	DOs[3,4]	Dentists	Podiatrists	Chiropractors	Optometrists
County[1] (number)	4,631	338	735	54	409	188
County[1] (rate[2])	323.9	23.6	51.7	3.8	28.7	13.2
U.S. (rate[2])	289.3	23.5	72.5	6.2	28.7	17.4

Note: Data as of 2021 unless noted; (1) Data covers Orange County; (2) Rate per 100,000 population; (3) Data as of 2020 and includes all active, non-federal physicians; (4) Doctor of Osteopathic Medicine
Source: U.S. Department of Health and Human Services, Health Resources and Services Administration, Bureau of Health Professions, Area Resource File (ARF) 2021-2022

Best Hospitals

According to *U.S. News,* the Orlando-Kissimmee-Sanford, FL metro area is home to one of the best hospitals in the U.S.: **AdventHealth Orlando** (6 adult specialties and 1 pediatric specialty). The hospital listed was nationally ranked in at least one of 15 adult or 10 pediatric specialties. The number of specialties shown cover the parent hospital. Only 164 U.S. hospitals performed well enough to be nationally ranked in one or more specialties. Twenty hospitals in the U.S. made the Honor Roll. The Best Hospitals Honor Roll takes both the national rankings and the procedure and condition ratings into account. Hospitals received points if they were nationally ranked in one of the 15 adult specialties—the higher they ranked, the more points they got—and how many ratings of "high performing" they earned in the 17 procedures and conditions. *U.S. News Online, "America's Best Hospitals 2022-23"*

According to *U.S. News,* the Orlando-Kissimmee-Sanford, FL metro area is home to three of the best children's hospitals in the U.S.: **Arnold Palmer Hospital for Children** (5 pediatric specialties); **AdventHealth for Children** (1 pediatric specialty); **Nemours Children's Hospital-Florida** (2 pediatric specialties). The hospitals listed were highly ranked in at least one of 10 pediatric specialties. Eighty-six children's hospitals in the U.S. were nationally ranked in at least one specialty. Hospitals received points for being ranked in a specialty, and the 10 hospitals with the most points across the 10 specialties make up the Honor Roll. *U.S. News Online, "America's Best Children's Hospitals 2022-23"*

EDUCATION

Public School District Statistics

District Name	Schls	Pupils	Pupil/Teacher Ratio	Minority Pupils[1] (%)	LEP/ELL[2] (%)	IEP[3] (%)
Orange	274	203,224	17.9	75.2	15.9	10.9

Note: Table includes school districts with 2,000 or more students; (1) Percentage of students that are not non-Hispanic white; (2) Percentage of students that are Limited English Proficient or English Language Learners (2018-19); (3) Percentage of students that have an Individualized Education Program (2019-20).
Source: U.S. Department of Education, National Center for Education Statistics, Common Core of Data, Local Education Agency (School District) Universe Survey: School Year 2021-2022

Best High Schools

According to *U.S. News,* Orlando is home to one of the top 500 high schools in the U.S.: **Orlando Science Middle High Charter** (#354). Nearly 18,000 public, magnet and charter schools were ranked based on their performance on state assessments and how well they prepare students for college. *U.S. News & World Report, "Best High Schools 2022"*

Highest Level of Education

Area	Less than H.S.	H.S. Diploma	Some College, No Deg.	Associate Degree	Bachelor's Degree	Master's Degree	Prof. School Degree	Doctorate Degree
City	8.4	23.2	16.8	11.5	25.0	10.3	3.1	1.7
MSA[1]	9.9	25.4	19.4	11.6	21.9	8.6	2.0	1.1
U.S.	11.1	26.5	20.0	8.7	20.6	9.3	2.2	1.5

Note: Figures cover persons age 25 and over; (1) Figures cover the Orlando-Kissimmee-Sanford, FL Metropolitan Statistical Area
Source: U.S. Census Bureau, 2017-2021 American Community Survey 5-Year Estimates

Educational Attainment by Race

Area	High School Graduate or Higher (%)					Bachelor's Degree or Higher (%)				
	Total	White	Black	Asian	Hisp.[2]	Total	White	Black	Asian	Hisp.[2]
City	91.6	94.7	84.5	92.5	90.2	40.1	48.5	20.6	54.5	32.2
MSA[1]	90.1	92.1	85.6	89.2	85.5	33.7	36.3	23.3	52.0	25.7
U.S.	88.9	91.4	87.2	87.6	71.2	33.7	35.5	23.3	55.6	18.4

Note: Figures shown cover persons 25 years old and over; (1) Figures cover the Orlando-Kissimmee-Sanford, FL Metropolitan Statistical Area; (2) People of Hispanic origin can be of any race
Source: U.S. Census Bureau, 2017-2021 American Community Survey 5-Year Estimates

School Enrollment by Grade and Control

Area	Preschool (%)		Kindergarten (%)		Grades 1 - 4 (%)		Grades 5 - 8 (%)		Grades 9 - 12 (%)	
	Public	Private	Public	Private	Public	Private	Public	Private	Public	Private
City	62.9	37.1	84.3	15.7	88.0	12.0	87.0	13.0	86.7	13.3
MSA[1]	50.4	49.6	81.5	18.5	84.1	15.9	85.5	14.5	87.5	12.5
U.S.	58.8	41.2	86.3	13.7	88.3	11.7	88.6	11.4	89.4	10.6

Note: Figures shown cover persons 3 years old and over; (1) Figures cover the Orlando-Kissimmee-Sanford, FL Metropolitan Statistical Area
Source: U.S. Census Bureau, 2017-2021 American Community Survey 5-Year Estimates

Higher Education

Four-Year Colleges			Two-Year Colleges			Medical Schools[1]	Law Schools[2]	Voc/ Tech[3]
Public	Private Non-profit	Private For-profit	Public	Private Non-profit	Private For-profit			
4	8	2	3	1	7	1	2	10

Note: Figures cover institutions located within the Orlando-Kissimmee-Sanford, FL Metropolitan Statistical Area and include main campuses only; (1) includes schools accredited by the Liaison Committee on Medical Education and the American Osteopathic Association's Commission on Osteopathic College Accreditation; (2) includes ABA-accredited schools, schools with provisional ABA accreditation, and state accredited schools; (3) includes all schools with programs that are less than 2 years.
Source: National Center for Education Statistics, Integrated Postsecondary Education System (IPEDS), 2021-22; Wikipedia, List of Medical Schools in the United States, accessed April 10, 2023; Wikipedia, List of Law Schools in the United States, accessed April 10, 2023

According to *U.S. News & World Report,* the Orlando-Kissimmee-Sanford, FL metro area is home to one of the top 200 national universities in the U.S.: **University of Central Florida** (#137 tie). The indicators used to capture academic quality fall into a number of categories: assessment by administrators at peer institutions; retention of students; faculty resources; student selectivity; financial resources; alumni giving; high school counselor ratings of colleges; and graduation rate. *U.S. News & World Report, "America's Best Colleges 2023"*

EMPLOYERS

Major Employers

Company Name	Industry
Adventist Health System/Sunbelt	General medical & surgical hospitals
Airtran Airways	Air passenger carrier, scheduled
Central Florida Health Alliance	Hospital management
CNL Lifestyle Properties	Real estate agents & managers
Connextions	Communication services, nec
Florida Department of Children & Families	Individual & family services
Florida Hospital Medical Center	General medical & surgical hospitals
Gaylord Palms Resort & Conv Ctr	Hotel franchised
Leesburg Regional Medical Center	General medical & surgical hospitals
Lockheed Martin Corporation	Aircraft
Marriott International	Hotels & motels
Orlando Health	General medical & surgical hospitals
Rosen 9939	Hotels & motels
Sea World of Florida	Theme park, amusement
Sears Termite & Pest Control	Pest control in structures
Siemens Energy	Power plant construction
Universal City Florida Partners	Amusement & theme parks
University of Central Florida	Colleges & universities
Winter Park Healthcare Group	Hospital affiliated with AMA residency

Note: Companies shown are located within the Orlando-Kissimmee-Sanford, FL Metropolitan Statistical Area.
Source: Hoovers.com; Wikipedia

PUBLIC SAFETY

Crime Rate

Area	Total Crime	Violent Crime Rate				Property Crime Rate		
		Murder	Rape[3]	Robbery	Aggrav. Assault	Burglary	Larceny -Theft	Motor Vehicle Theft
City	4,663.8	10.6	57.6	172.8	619.4	408.4	3,003.8	391.3
Suburbs[1]	1,994.4	5.4	40.1	59.7	267.8	251.1	1,217.2	153.1
Metro[2]	2,288.9	5.9	42.0	72.2	306.6	268.4	1,414.3	179.4
U.S.	2,356.7	6.5	38.4	73.9	279.7	314.2	1,398.0	246.0

Note: Figures are crimes per 100,000 population; (1) All areas within the metro area that are located outside the city limits; (2) Figures cover the Orlando-Kissimmee-Sanford, FL Metropolitan Statistical Area; (3) All figures shown were reported using the revised Uniform Crime Reporting (UCR) definition of rape; Due to the transition to the National Incident-Based Reporting System (NIBRS), limited city and metro area data was released for 2021.
Source: FBI Uniform Crime Reports, 2020

Hate Crimes

Area	Number of Quarters Reported	Number of Incidents per Bias Motivation					
		Race/Ethnicity/ Ancestry	Religion	Sexual Orientation	Disability	Gender	Gender Identity
City	3	1	0	1	0	0	0
U.S.	4	5,227	1,244	1,110	130	75	266

Note: Due to the transition to the National Incident-Based Reporting System (NIBRS), limited crime data was released for 2021.
Source: Federal Bureau of Investigation, Hate Crime Statistics 2020

Identity Theft Consumer Reports

Area	Reports	Reports per 100,000 Population	Rank[2]
MSA[1]	15,349	600	9
U.S.	1,108,609	339	-

Note: (1) Figures cover the Orlando-Kissimmee-Sanford, FL Metropolitan Statistical Area; (2) Rank ranges from 1 to 391 where 1 indicates greatest number of identity theft reports per 100,000 population
Source: Federal Trade Commission, Consumer Sentinel Network Data Book 2022

Fraud and Other Consumer Reports

Area	Reports	Reports per 100,000 Population	Rank[2]
MSA[1]	39,619	1,547	7
U.S.	4,064,520	1,245	-

Note: (1) Figures cover the Orlando-Kissimmee-Sanford, FL Metropolitan Statistical Area; (2) Rank ranges from 1 to 391 where 1 indicates greatest number of fraud and other consumer reports per 100,000 population
Source: Federal Trade Commission, Consumer Sentinel Network Data Book 2022

POLITICS

2020 Presidential Election Results

Area	Biden	Trump	Jorgensen	Hawkins	Other
Orange County	60.9	37.8	0.7	0.2	0.4
U.S.	51.3	46.8	1.2	0.3	0.5

Note: Results are percentages and may not add to 100% due to rounding
Source: Dave Leip's Atlas of U.S. Presidential Elections

SPORTS

Professional Sports Teams

Team Name	League	Year Established
Orlando City SC	Major League Soccer (MLS)	2015
Orlando Magic	National Basketball Association (NBA)	1989

Note: Includes teams located in the Orlando-Kissimmee-Sanford, FL Metropolitan Statistical Area.
Source: Wikipedia, Major Professional Sports Teams of the United States and Canada, April 12, 2023

CLIMATE

Average and Extreme Temperatures

Temperature	Jan	Feb	Mar	Apr	May	Jun	Jul	Aug	Sep	Oct	Nov	Dec	Yr.
Extreme High (°F)	86	89	90	95	100	100	99	100	98	95	89	90	100
Average High (°F)	70	72	77	82	87	90	91	91	89	83	78	72	82
Average Temp. (°F)	59	62	67	72	77	81	82	82	81	75	68	62	72
Average Low (°F)	48	51	56	60	66	71	73	74	72	66	58	51	62
Extreme Low (°F)	19	29	25	38	51	53	64	65	57	44	32	20	19

Note: Figures cover the years 1952-1990
Source: National Climatic Data Center, International Station Meteorological Climate Summary, 9/96

Average Precipitation/Snowfall/Humidity

Precip./Humidity	Jan	Feb	Mar	Apr	May	Jun	Jul	Aug	Sep	Oct	Nov	Dec	Yr.
Avg. Precip. (in.)	2.3	2.8	3.4	2.0	3.2	7.0	7.2	5.8	5.8	2.7	3.5	2.0	47.7
Avg. Snowfall (in.)	Tr	0	0	0	0	0	0	0	0	0	0	0	Tr
Avg. Rel. Hum. 7am (%)	87	87	88	87	88	89	90	92	92	89	89	87	89
Avg. Rel. Hum. 4pm (%)	53	51	49	47	51	61	65	66	66	59	56	55	57

Note: Figures cover the years 1952-1990; Tr = Trace amounts (<0.05 in. of rain; <0.5 in. of snow)
Source: National Climatic Data Center, International Station Meteorological Climate Summary, 9/96

Weather Conditions

Temperature			Daytime Sky			Precipitation		
32°F & below	45°F & below	90°F & above	Clear	Partly cloudy	Cloudy	0.01 inch or more precip.	0.1 inch or more snow/ice	Thunder-storms
3	35	90	76	208	81	115	0	80

Note: Figures are average number of days per year and cover the years 1952-1990
Source: National Climatic Data Center, International Station Meteorological Climate Summary, 9/96

HAZARDOUS WASTE

Superfund Sites

The Orlando-Kissimmee-Sanford, FL metro area is home to four sites on the EPA's Superfund National Priorities List: **Chevron Chemical Co. (Ortho Division)** (final); **City Industries, Inc.** (final); **General Dynamics Longwood** (final); **Sanford Dry Cleaners** (final). There are a total of 1,165 Superfund sites with a status of proposed or final on the list in the U.S. *U.S. Environmental Protection Agency, National Priorities List, April 12, 2023*

AIR QUALITY

Air Quality Trends: Ozone

	1990	1995	2000	2005	2010	2015	2018	2019	2020	2021
MSA[1]	0.081	0.075	0.080	0.083	0.069	0.060	0.062	0.062	0.059	0.061
U.S.	0.087	0.089	0.081	0.080	0.072	0.067	0.069	0.065	0.065	0.067

Note: (1) Data covers the Orlando-Kissimmee-Sanford, FL Metropolitan Statistical Area. The values shown are the composite ozone concentration averages among trend sites based on the highest fourth daily maximum 8-hour concentration in parts per million. These trends are based on sites having an adequate record of monitoring data during the trend period. Data from exceptional events are included.
Source: U.S. Environmental Protection Agency, Air Quality Monitoring Information, "Air Quality Trends by City, 1990-2021"

Air Quality Index

| Area | Percent of Days when Air Quality was...[2] ||||| AQI Statistics[2] ||
	Good	Moderate	Unhealthy for Sensitive Groups	Unhealthy	Very Unhealthy	Maximum	Median
MSA[1]	82.7	17.3	0.0	0.0	0.0	97	39

Note: (1) Data covers the Orlando-Kissimmee-Sanford, FL Metropolitan Statistical Area; (2) Based on 365 days with AQI data in 2021. Air Quality Index (AQI) is an index for reporting daily air quality. EPA calculates the AQI for five major air pollutants regulated by the Clean Air Act: ground-level ozone, particle pollution (aka particulate matter), carbon monoxide, sulfur dioxide, and nitrogen dioxide. The AQI runs from 0 to 500. The higher the AQI value, the greater the level of air pollution and the greater the health concern. There are six AQI categories: "Good" AQI is between 0 and 50. Air quality is considered satisfactory; "Moderate" AQI is between 51 and 100. Air quality is acceptable; "Unhealthy for Sensitive Groups" When AQI values are between 101 and 150, members of sensitive groups may experience health effects; "Unhealthy" When AQI values are between 151 and 200 everyone may begin to experience health effects; "Very Unhealthy" AQI values between 201 and 300 trigger a health alert; "Hazardous" AQI values over 300 trigger warnings of emergency conditions (not shown).
Source: U.S. Environmental Protection Agency, Air Quality Index Report, 2021

Air Quality Index Pollutants

| Area | Percent of Days when AQI Pollutant was...[2] ||||||
	Carbon Monoxide	Nitrogen Dioxide	Ozone	Sulfur Dioxide	Particulate Matter 2.5	Particulate Matter 10
MSA[1]	0.0	0.0	66.0	(3)	33.2	0.8

Note: (1) Data covers the Orlando-Kissimmee-Sanford, FL Metropolitan Statistical Area; (2) Based on 365 days with AQI data in 2021. The Air Quality Index (AQI) is an index for reporting daily air quality. EPA calculates the AQI for five major air pollutants regulated by the Clean Air Act: ground-level ozone, particle pollution (also known as particulate matter), carbon monoxide, sulfur dioxide, and nitrogen dioxide. The AQI runs from 0 to 500. The higher the AQI value, the greater the level of air pollution and the greater the health concern; (3) Sulfur dioxide is no longer included in this table (as of December 8, 2021) because SO_2 concentrations tend to be very localized and not necessarily representative of broad geographical areas like counties and CBSAs.
Source: U.S. Environmental Protection Agency, Air Quality Index Report, 2021

Maximum Air Pollutant Concentrations: Particulate Matter, Ozone, CO and Lead

	Particulate Matter 10 (ug/m^3)	Particulate Matter 2.5 Wtd AM (ug/m^3)	Particulate Matter 2.5 24-Hr (ug/m^3)	Ozone (ppm)	Carbon Monoxide (ppm)	Lead (ug/m^3)
MSA[1] Level	51	7.6	15	0.062	1	n/a
NAAQS[2]	150	15	35	0.075	9	0.15
Met NAAQS[2]	Yes	Yes	Yes	Yes	Yes	n/a

Note: (1) Data covers the Orlando-Kissimmee-Sanford, FL Metropolitan Statistical Area; Data from exceptional events are included; (2) National Ambient Air Quality Standards; ppm = parts per million; ug/m^3 = micrograms per cubic meter; n/a not available.
Concentrations: Particulate Matter 10 (coarse particulate)—highest second maximum 24-hour concentration; Particulate Matter 2.5 Wtd AM (fine particulate)—highest weighted annual mean concentration; Particulate Matter 2.5 24-Hour (fine particulate)—highest 98th percentile 24-hour concentration; Ozone—highest fourth daily maximum 8-hour concentration; Carbon Monoxide—highest second maximum non-overlapping 8-hour concentration; Lead—maximum running 3-month average
Source: U.S. Environmental Protection Agency, Air Quality Monitoring Information, "Air Quality Statistics by City, 2021"

Maximum Air Pollutant Concentrations: Nitrogen Dioxide and Sulfur Dioxide

	Nitrogen Dioxide AM (ppb)	Nitrogen Dioxide 1-Hr (ppb)	Sulfur Dioxide AM (ppb)	Sulfur Dioxide 1-Hr (ppb)	Sulfur Dioxide 24-Hr (ppb)
MSA[1] Level	n/a	n/a	n/a	n/a	n/a
NAAQS[2]	53	100	30	75	140
Met NAAQS[2]	n/a	n/a	n/a	n/a	n/a

Note: (1) Data covers the Orlando-Kissimmee-Sanford, FL Metropolitan Statistical Area; Data from exceptional events are included; (2) National Ambient Air Quality Standards; ppm = parts per million; ug/m³ = micrograms per cubic meter; n/a not available.
Concentrations: Nitrogen Dioxide AM—highest arithmetic mean concentration; Nitrogen Dioxide 1-Hr—highest 98th percentile 1-hour daily maximum concentration; Sulfur Dioxide AM—highest annual mean concentration; Sulfur Dioxide 1-Hr—highest 99th percentile 1-hour daily maximum concentration; Sulfur Dioxide 24-Hr—highest second maximum 24-hour concentration
Source: U.S. Environmental Protection Agency, Air Quality Monitoring Information, "Air Quality Statistics by City, 2021"

San Antonio, Texas

Background

San Antonio is a charming preservation of its Mexican-Spanish heritage. Walking along its famous Paseo Del Rio at night, with cream-colored stucco structures, seashell ornamented facades, and gently illuminating tiny lights is romantic and picturesque.

San Antonio began in the early eighteenth century as a cohesion of different Spanish missions, whose aim was to convert the Coahuiltecan natives to Christianity and European ways of farming. A debilitating epidemic, however, killed most of the natives, as well as the missions' goal, causing the city to be abandoned.

In 1836, San Antonio became of interest again, when a small band of American soldiers were unable to successfully defend themselves against an army of 4,000 Mexican soldiers, led by General Antonio de Lopez Santa Anna. Fighting desperately from within the walls of the Mission San Antonio de Valero, or The Alamo, all 183 men were killed. This inspired the cry "Remember the Alamo" from every American soldier led by General Sam Houston, who fought with determination to wrest Texas territory and independence from Mexico.

Despite the Anglo victory over the Mexicans more than 150 years ago, the Mexican culture and its influence remain strong. We see evidence of this in the architecture, the Franciscan educational system, the variety of Spanish-language media, and the fact that 64 percent of its population is Latino.

This blend of old and new makes San Antonio unique among American cities. It is home to the first museum of modern art in Texas, McNay Art Museum. Other art institutions and museums include ArtPace, Blue Star Contemporary Art Center, Briscoe Western Art Museum, Buckhorn Saloon & Museum (heavy on the cowboy culture), San Antonio Museum of Art, formerly Lonestar Brewery, Say Si (mentoring San Antonio artistic youth), Southwest School of Art, Texas Rangers Museum, Texas Transportation Museum, Witte Museum and the DoSeum. An outdoor display at North Star Mall features 40-foot-tall cowboy boots.

The five missions in the city, four in the San Antonio Missions National Historical Park and the Alamo, were named a UNESCO World Heritage Site on July 5, 2015. The San Antonio Missions became the 23rd U.S. site on the World Heritage List, which includes the Grand Canyon and the Statue of Liberty. It is the first such site in the state of Texas.

The city continues to draw tourists who come to visit the Alamo, theme parks like Six Flags Fiesta Texas and SeaWorld, and the famed River Walk. Kelly Air Force Base, decommissioned in 2001, is now a nearly 5,000-acre business park, Kelly USA. Port San Antonio, a warehouse on the site was used to house refugees from Hurricane Katrina. Sego Lily Dam was constructed in 2017 to prevent further flooding in the city.

Businesses at the port receive favorable property tax and pay no state, city, or corporate income taxes. With a continuing increase in professional jobs, San Antonio has become a destination for a college-education workforce. The city's economy focuses on military, healthcare, government, financial services, oil and gas, and tourism.

The city airport's current major renovation is ongoing. New gates opened in 2022, and a new, third terminal with more new gates is planned by 2030.

San Antonio's location on the edge of the Gulf Coastal Plains exposes it to a modified subtropical climate. Summers are hot, although extremely high temperatures are rare. Winters are mild. Located 140 miles from the Gulf of Mexico, tropical storms occasionally occur, bringing strong winds and heavy rains. In 2020, the city experienced a 5.7 magnitude earthquake. Relative humidity is high in the morning but tends to drop by late afternoon.

Rankings

General Rankings

- For its "Best for Vets: Places to Live 2019" rankings, *Military Times* evaluated 599 cities (83 large, 234 medium, 282 small) and compared the locations across three broad categories: veteran and military culture/services; economic indicators; and livability factors such as health, crime, traffic, and school quality. San Antonio ranked #3 out of the top 25, in the large city category (population of more than 250,000). Data points more specific to veterans and the military weighed more heavily than others. *rebootcamp.militarytimes.com, "Military Times Best Places to Live 2019," September 10, 2018*

- *Insider* listed 23 places in the U.S. that travel industry trends reveal would be popular destinations in 2023. This year the list trends towards cultural and historical happenings, sports events, wellness experiences and invigorating outdoor escapes. According to the website insider.com San Antonio is a place to visit in 2023. *Insider, "23 of the Best Places You Should Travel to in the U.S. in 2023," December 17, 2022*

- The San Antonio metro area was identified as one of America's fastest-growing areas in terms of population and business growth by *MagnifyMoney*. The area ranked #9 out of 35. The 100 most populous metro areas in the U.S. were evaluated on their change from 2011 to 2016 in the following categories: people and housing; workforce and employment opportunities; growing industry. *www.businessinsider.com, "The 35 Cities in the US with the Biggest Influx of People, the Most Work Opportunities, and the Hottest Business Growth," August 12, 2018*

- The San Antonio metro area was identified as one of America's fastest-growing areas in terms of population and economy by *Forbes*. The area ranked #21 out of 25. The 100 most populous metro areas in the U.S. were evaluated on the following criteria: estimated population growth; employment; economic output; wages; home values. *Forbes, "America's Fastest-Growing Cities 2018," February 28, 2018*

- San Antonio was selected as an "All-America City" by the National Civic League. The All-America City Award recognizes civic excellence and in 2022 honored 10 communities that best exemplify the spirit of grassroots citizen involvement and cross-sector collaborative problem solving to collectively tackle pressing and complex issues. This year's theme was: "Housing as a Platform to Promote Early School Success and Equitable Learning Recovery." *National Civic League, "2022 All-America City Awards," July 21, 2022*

- San Antonio appeared on *Travel + Leisure's* list of "The 15 Best Cities in the United States." The city was ranked #9. Criteria: sights/landmarks; culture; food; friendliness; shopping; and overall value. *Travel + Leisure, "The World's Best Awards 2022" July 12, 2022*

Business/Finance Rankings

- San Antonio was the #17-ranked city for savers, according to a study by the finance site GOBankingRates, which considered the prospects for people trying to save money. Criteria: average monthly cost of grocery items; median home listing price; median rent; median income; transportation costs; gas prices; and the cost of eating out for an inexpensive and mid-range meal in 100 U.S. cities. *www.gobankingrates.com, "The 20 Best (and Worst) Places to Live If You're Trying to Save Money," August 27, 2019*

- San Antonio was ranked #17 among 100 U.S. cities for most difficult conditions for savers, according to a study by the finance site GOBankingRates. Criteria: average monthly cost of grocery items; median home listing price; median rent; median income; transportation costs; gas prices; and the cost of eating out for an inexpensive and mid-range meal. *www.gobankingrates.com, "The 20 Best (and Worst) Places to Live If You're Trying to Save Money," August 27, 2019*

- The Brookings Institution ranked the nation's largest cities based on income inequality. San Antonio was ranked #79 (#1 = greatest inequality). Criteria: the "95/20 ratio," a figure representing the income at which a household earns more than 95 percent of all other households, divided by the income at which a household earns more than only 20 percent of all other households. *Brookings Institution, "Household Income Inequality, Largest Cities of 97 Large U.S. Metro Areas, 2014-2016," February 5, 2018*

- The Brookings Institution ranked the 100 largest metro areas in the U.S. based on income inequality. San Antonio was ranked #56 (#1 = greatest inequality). Criteria: the "95/20 ratio," a figure representing the income at which a household earns more than 95 percent of all other households, divided by the income at which a household earns more than only 20 percent of all other households. *Brookings Institution, "Household Income Inequality, 100 Largest U.S. Metro Areas, 2014-2016," February 5, 2018*

- The San Antonio metro area was identified as one of the most debt-ridden places in America by the finance site Credit.com. The metro area was ranked #5. Criteria: residents' average credit card debt as well as median income. *Credit.com, "25 Cities With the Most Credit Card Debt," February 28, 2018*
- San Antonio was identified as one of the unhappiest cities to work in by CareerBliss.com, an online community for career advancement. The city ranked #4 out of 5. Criteria: an employee's relationship with his or her boss and co-workers; general work environment; compensation; opportunities for advancement; company culture and job reputation; and resources. *Businesswire.com, "CareerBliss Unhappiest Cities to Work 2019," February 12, 2019*
- The San Antonio metro area appeared on the Milken Institute "2022 Best Performing Cities" list. Rank: #37 out of 200 large metro areas (population over 250,000). Criteria: job growth; wage and salary growth; high-tech output growth; housing affordability; household broadband access. *Milken Institute, "Best-Performing Cities 2022," March 28, 2022*
- *Forbes* ranked the 200 most populous metro areas to determine the nation's "Best Places for Business and Careers." The San Antonio metro area was ranked #48. Criteria: costs (business and living); job growth (past and projected); income growth; quality of life; educational attainment (college and high school); projected economic growth; cultural and leisure opportunities; workplace tolerance laws; net migration patterns. *Forbes, "The Best Places for Business and Careers 2019: Seattle Still On Top," October 30, 2019*

Children/Family Rankings

- San Antonio was selected as one of the most playful cities in the U.S. by KaBOOM! The organization's Playful City USA initiative honors cities and towns across the nation that have made their communities more playable. Criteria: pledging to integrate play as a solution to challenges in their communities; making it easy for children to get active and balanced play; creating more family-friendly and innovative communities as a result. *KaBOOM! National Campaign for Play, "2017 Playful City USA Communities"*

Culture/Performing Arts Rankings

- San Antonio was selected as one of the 25 best cities for moviemakers in North America. Great film cities are places where filmmaking dreams can come true, that offer more creative space, lower costs, and great outdoor locations. NYC & LA were intentionally excluded. Criteria: longstanding reputations as film-friendly communities; film community and culture; affordability; and quality of life. The city was ranked #22. *MovieMaker Magazine, "Best Places to Live and Work as a Moviemaker, 2023," January 18, 2023*

Dating/Romance Rankings

- *Apartment List* conducted its Annual Renter Satisfaction Survey and asked renters "how satisfied are you with opportunities for dating in your current city." The cities were ranked from highest to lowest based on their satisfaction scores. San Antonio ranked #8 out of 85 cities. *Apartment List, "Best Cities for Dating 2022 with Local Dating Insights from Bumble," February 7, 2022*
- San Antonio was selected as one of America's best cities for singles by the readers of *Travel + Leisure* in their annual "America's Favorite Cities" survey. Criteria included good-looking locals, cool shopping, an active bar scene and hipster-magnet coffee bars. *Travel + Leisure, "Best Cities in America for Singles," July 21, 2017*
- San Antonio was selected as one of the nation's most romantic cities with 100,000 or more residents by Amazon.com. The city ranked #1 of 20. Criteria: per capita sales of romance novels, relationship books, romantic comedy movies, romantic music, and sexual wellness products. *Amazon.com, "Top 20 Most Romantic Cities in the U.S.," February 1, 2017*

Education Rankings

- Personal finance website *WalletHub* analyzed the 150 largest U.S. metropolitan statistical areas to determine where the most educated Americans are putting their degrees to work. Criteria: education levels; percentage of workers with degrees; education quality and attainment gap; public school quality rankings; quality and enrollment of each metro area's universities. San Antonio was ranked #105 (#1 = most educated city). *www.WalletHub.com, "Most & Least Educated Cities in America," July 18, 2022*
- San Antonio was selected as one of America's most literate cities. The city ranked #76 out of the 84 largest U.S. cities. Criteria: number of booksellers; library resources; Internet resources; educational attainment; periodical publishing resources; newspaper circulation. *Central Connecticut State University, "America's Most Literate Cities, 2018," February 2019*

Environmental Rankings

- San Antonio was highlighted as one of the 25 most ozone-polluted metro areas in the U.S. during 2019 through 2021. The area ranked #23. *American Lung Association, "State of the Air 2023," April 19, 2023*

Health/Fitness Rankings

- For each of the 100 largest cities in the United States, the American Fitness Index®, compiled in partnership between the American College of Sports Medicine and the Elevance Health Foundation, evaluated community infrastructure and 34 health behaviors including preventive health, levels of chronic disease conditions, food insecurity, sleep quality, pedestrian safety, air quality, and community/environment resources that support physical activity. San Antonio ranked #69 for "community fitness." *americanfitnessindex.org, "2022 ACSM American Fitness Index Summary Report," July 12, 2022*

- San Antonio was identified as a "2022 Spring Allergy Capital." The area ranked #13 out of 100. Three groups of factors were used to identify the most challenging cities for people with allergies during the spring season: annual spring pollen scores; over the counter allergy medicine use; number of board-certified allergy specialists. *Asthma and Allergy Foundation of America, "Spring Allergy Capitals 2022," March 2, 2022*

- San Antonio was identified as a "2022 Fall Allergy Capital." The area ranked #4 out of 100. Three groups of factors were used to identify the most challenging cities for people with allergies during the fall season: annual fall pollen scores; over the counter allergy medicine use; number of board-certified allergy specialists. *Asthma and Allergy Foundation of America, "Fall Allergy Capitals 2022," March 2, 2022*

- San Antonio was identified as a "2022 Asthma Capital." The area ranked #40 out of the nation's 100 largest metropolitan areas. Criteria: estimated asthma prevalence; asthma-related mortality; and ER visits due to asthma. Risk factors analyzed but not factored in the rankings: annual pollen score; annual air quality; public smoking laws; access to board-certified asthma specialists; rescue and controller medication use; uninsured rate; poverty rate. *Asthma and Allergy Foundation of America, "Asthma Capitals 2022: The Most Challenging Places to Live With Asthma," September 14, 2022*

Real Estate Rankings

- *WalletHub* compared the most populated U.S. cities to determine which had the best markets for real estate agents. San Antonio ranked #133 where demand was high and pay was the best. Criteria: sales per agent; annual median wage for real-estate agents; monthly average starting salary for real estate agents; real estate job density and competition; unemployment rate; home turnover rate; housing-market health index; and other relevant metrics. *www.WalletHub.com, "2021 Best Places to Be a Real Estate Agent," May 12, 2021*

- According to Penske Truck Rental, the San Antonio metro area was named the #9 moving destination in 2022, based on one-way consumer truck rental reservations made through Penske's website, rental locations, and reservations call center. *gopenske.com/blog, "Penske Truck Rental's 2022 Top Moving Destinations," April 27, 2023*

- San Antonio was ranked #154 out of 235 metro areas in terms of housing affordability in 2022 by the National Association of Home Builders (#1 = most affordable). Criteria: the share of homes sold in that area affordable to a family earning the local median income, based on standard mortgage underwriting criteria. *National Association of Home Builders®, NAHB-Wells Fargo Housing Opportunity Index, 4th Quarter 2022*

Safety Rankings

- Allstate ranked the 200 largest cities in America in terms of driver safety. San Antonio ranked #138. Criteria: internal property damage claims over a two-year period from January 2016 to December 2017. The report helps increase the importance of safety and awareness behind the wheel. *Allstate, "Allstate America's Best Drivers Report, 2019" June 24, 2019*

- The National Insurance Crime Bureau ranked 390 metro areas in the U.S. in terms of per capita rates of vehicle theft. The San Antonio metro area ranked #35 (#1 = highest rate). Criteria: number of vehicle theft offenses per 100,000 inhabitants in 2021. *National Insurance Crime Bureau, "Hot Spots 2021," September 1, 2022*

Seniors/Retirement Rankings

- San Antonio made *Southern Living's* list of southern places—by the beach, in the mountains, river or college town—to retire. From the incredible views and close knit communities, to the opportunities to put down new roots, and great places to eat and hike, these superb places are perfect for settling down. *Southern Living, "The Best Places to Retire in the South," March 7, 2022*

- From its Best Cities for Successful Aging indexes, the Milken Institute generated rankings for metropolitan areas, weighing data in nine categories—health care, wellness, living arrangements, transportation and convenience, financial characteristics, education, employment, community engagement, and overall livability. The San Antonio metro area was ranked #64 overall in the large metro area category. *Milken Institute, "Best Cities for Successful Aging, 2017" March 14, 2017*

- San Antonio made the 2022 *Forbes* list of "25 Best Places to Retire." Criteria, focused on overall affordability as well as quality of life indicators, include: housing/living costs compared to the national average and state taxes; air quality; crime rates; home price appreciation; risk associated with climate-change/natural hazards; availability of medical care; bikeability; walkability; healthy living. *Forbes.com, "The Best Places to Retire in 2022," May 13, 2022*

- San Antonio was identified as #8 of 20 most popular places to retire in the Southwest region by *Topretirements.com*. The site separated its annual "Best Places to Retire" list by major U.S. regions for 2019. The list reflects the 20 cities that visitors to the website are most interested in for retirement, based on the number of times a city's review was viewed on the website. *Topretirements.com, "20 Most Popular Places to Retire in the Southwest for 2019," October 2, 2019*

Women/Minorities Rankings

- The *Houston Chronicle* listed the San Antonio metro area as #13 in top places for young Latinos to live in the U.S. Research was largely based on housing and occupational data from the largest metropolitan areas performed by *Forbes* and NBC Universo. Criteria: percentage of 18-34 year-olds; Latino college grad rates; and diversity. *blog.chron.com, "The 15 Best Big Cities for Latino Millenials," January 26, 2016*

- Personal finance website *WalletHub* compared more than 180 U.S. cities across two key dimensions, "Hispanic Business-Friendliness" and "Hispanic Purchasing Power," to arrive at the most favorable conditions for Hispanic entrepreneurs. San Antonio was ranked #5 out of 182. Criteria includes: share of Hispanic-Owned Businesses; Hispanic entrepreneurship rate to median annual income of Hispanics; Small Business-Friendliness score; cost of living; and number of Hispanics with at least a bachelor's degree. *WalletHub.com, "2019's Best Cities for Hispanic Entrepreneurs," May 1, 2019*

Miscellaneous Rankings

- *WalletHub* compared the 150 most populated U.S. cities to determine their operating efficiency. A "Quality of Services" score was constructed for each city and then divided by the total budget per capita to reveal which were managed the best. San Antonio ranked #86. Criteria: financial stability; economy; education; safety; health; infrastructure and pollution. *www.WalletHub.com, "2022's Best- & Worst-Run Cities in America," June 21, 2022*

- San Antonio was selected as one of "America's Friendliest Cities." The city ranked #5 in the "Friendliest" category. Respondents to an online survey were asked to rate 38 top urban destinations in the United States as to general friendliness, as well as manners, politeness and warm disposition. *Travel + Leisure, "America's Friendliest Cities," October 20, 2017*

- The National Alliance to End Homelessness listed the 25 most populous metro areas with the highest rate of homelessness. The San Antonio metro area had a high rate of homelessness. Criteria: number of homeless people per 10,000 population in 2016. *National Alliance to End Homelessness, "Homelessness in the 25 Most Populous U.S. Metro Areas," September 1, 2017*

Business Environment

DEMOGRAPHICS

Population Growth

Area	1990 Census	2000 Census	2010 Census	2020 Census	Population Growth (%) 1990-2020	Population Growth (%) 2010-2020
City	997,258	1,144,646	1,327,407	1,434,625	43.9	8.1
MSA[1]	1,407,745	1,711,703	2,142,508	2,558,143	81.7	19.4
U.S.	248,709,873	281,421,906	308,745,538	331,449,281	33.3	7.4

Note: (1) Figures cover the San Antonio-New Braunfels, TX Metropolitan Statistical Area
Source: U.S. Census Bureau, 1990 Census, 2000 Census, 2010 Census, 2020 Census

Race

Area	White Alone[2] (%)	Black Alone[2] (%)	Asian Alone[2] (%)	AIAN[3] Alone[2] (%)	NHOPI[4] Alone[2] (%)	Other Race Alone[2] (%)	Two or More Races (%)
City	44.3	7.2	3.3	1.2	0.1	16.7	27.1
MSA[1]	50.3	7.1	2.9	1.1	0.2	14.0	24.4
U.S.	61.6	12.4	6.0	1.1	0.2	8.4	10.2

Note: (1) Figures cover the San Antonio-New Braunfels, TX Metropolitan Statistical Area; (2) Alone is defined as not being in combination with one or more other races; (3) American Indian and Alaska Native; (4) Native Hawaiian and Other Pacific Islander
Source: U.S. Census Bureau, 2020 Census

Hispanic or Latino Origin

Area	Total (%)	Mexican (%)	Puerto Rican (%)	Cuban (%)	Other (%)
City	65.7	56.7	1.4	0.3	7.3
MSA[1]	56.0	48.2	1.4	0.3	6.0
U.S.	18.4	11.2	1.8	0.7	4.7

Note: Persons of Hispanic or Latino origin can be of any race; (1) Figures cover the San Antonio-New Braunfels, TX Metropolitan Statistical Area
Source: U.S. Census Bureau, 2017-2021 American Community Survey 5-Year Estimates

Age

Area	Under Age 5	Age 5–19	Age 20–34	Age 35–44	Age 45–54	Age 55–64	Age 65–74	Age 75–84	Age 85+	Median Age
City	6.1	20.6	23.4	13.0	11.8	11.4	8.2	3.9	1.6	34.9
MSA[1]	6.1	21.4	21.0	13.2	12.2	11.8	8.7	4.1	1.5	36.0
U.S.	5.6	19.2	20.2	12.7	12.4	13.1	10.0	4.9	1.9	38.8

Note: (1) Figures cover the San Antonio-New Braunfels, TX Metropolitan Statistical Area
Source: U.S. Census Bureau, 2020 Census

Disability by Age

Area	All Ages	Under 18 Years Old	18 to 64 Years Old	65 Years and Over
City	15.0	6.3	13.2	41.6
MSA[1]	14.1	5.9	12.3	38.7
U.S.	12.6	4.4	10.3	33.4

Note: Figures show percent of the civilian noninstitutionalized population that reported having a disability. Disability status is determined from six types of difficulty: vision, hearing, cognitive, ambulatory, self-care, and independent living. For children under 5 years old, hearing and vision difficulty are used to determine disability status. For children between the ages of 5 and 14, disability status is determined from hearing, vision, cognitive, ambulatory, and self-care difficulties. For people aged 15 years and older, they are considered to have a disability if they have difficulty with any one of the six difficulty types; Note: (1) Figures cover the San Antonio-New Braunfels, TX Metropolitan Statistical Area
Source: U.S. Census Bureau, 2017-2021 American Community Survey 5-Year Estimates

Ancestry

Area	German	Irish	English	American	Italian	Polish	French[2]	Scottish	Dutch
City	7.0	4.3	4.0	3.2	1.8	1.0	1.4	0.8	0.3
MSA[1]	10.0	5.7	5.8	3.6	2.1	1.4	1.7	1.2	0.4
U.S.	12.8	9.6	8.1	5.7	5.0	2.7	2.2	1.6	1.1

Note: Figures are the percentage of the total population reporting a particular ancestry. The nine most commonly reported ancestries in the U.S. are shown. Figures include multiple ancestries (e.g. if a person reported being Irish and Italian, they were included in both columns); (1) Figures cover the San Antonio-New Braunfels, TX Metropolitan Statistical Area; (2) Excludes Basque
Source: U.S. Census Bureau, 2017-2021 American Community Survey 5-Year Estimates

Foreign-born Population

Area	Any Foreign Country	Asia	Mexico	Europe	Caribbean	Central America[2]	South America	Africa	Canada
City	14.2	2.5	8.9	0.5	0.3	0.9	0.5	0.4	0.1
MSA[1]	11.7	2.1	7.1	0.6	0.3	0.7	0.4	0.3	0.1
U.S.	13.6	4.2	3.3	1.5	1.4	1.1	1.1	0.8	0.2

Note: (1) Figures cover the San Antonio-New Braunfels, TX Metropolitan Statistical Area; (2) Excludes Mexico.
Source: U.S. Census Bureau, 2017-2021 American Community Survey 5-Year Estimates

Household Size

Area	One	Two	Three	Four	Five	Six	Seven or More	Average Household Size
City	30.6	29.5	15.4	12.8	7.0	2.9	1.7	2.60
MSA[1]	26.3	31.0	16.2	14.0	7.6	3.0	1.9	2.70
U.S.	28.1	33.8	15.5	12.9	6.0	2.3	1.4	2.60

Note: (1) Figures cover the San Antonio-New Braunfels, TX Metropolitan Statistical Area
Source: U.S. Census Bureau, 2017-2021 American Community Survey 5-Year Estimates

Household Relationships

Area	House-holder	Opposite-sex Spouse	Same-sex Spouse	Opposite-sex Unmarried Partner	Same-sex Unmarried Partner	Child[2]	Grand-child	Other Relatives	Non-relatives
City	37.5	14.7	0.3	2.7	0.2	30.3	3.8	5.5	3.2
MSA[1]	36.2	16.9	0.2	2.3	0.2	31.0	3.5	5.1	2.8
U.S.	38.3	17.5	0.2	2.5	0.2	28.3	2.4	4.8	3.4

Note: Figures are percent of the total population; (1) Figures cover the San Antonio-New Braunfels, TX Metropolitan Statistical Area; (2) Includes biological, adopted, and stepchildren of the householder
Source: U.S. Census Bureau, 2020 Census

Gender

Area	Males	Females	Males per 100 Females
City	699,905	734,720	95.3
MSA[1]	1,254,014	1,304,129	96.2
U.S.	162,685,811	168,763,470	96.4

Note: (1) Figures cover the San Antonio-New Braunfels, TX Metropolitan Statistical Area
Source: U.S. Census Bureau, 2020 Census

Marital Status

Area	Never Married	Now Married[2]	Separated	Widowed	Divorced
City	38.3	41.7	2.8	5.1	12.0
MSA[1]	34.0	47.6	2.4	4.9	11.1
U.S.	33.8	48.0	1.8	5.6	10.8

Note: Figures are percentages and cover the population 15 years of age and older; (1) Figures cover the San Antonio-New Braunfels, TX Metropolitan Statistical Area; (2) Excludes separated
Source: U.S. Census Bureau, 2017-2021 American Community Survey 5-Year Estimates

Religious Groups by Family

Area	Catholic	Baptist	Methodist	LDS[2]	Pentecostal	Lutheran	Islam	Adventist	Other
MSA[1]	27.3	6.4	2.1	1.4	1.6	1.1	0.5	1.5	11.0
U.S.	18.7	7.3	3.0	2.0	1.8	1.7	1.3	1.3	11.6

Note: Figures are the number of adherents as a percentage of the total population and cover the eight largest religious groups in the U.S; (1) Figures cover the San Antonio-New Braunfels, TX Metropolitan Statistical Area; (2) Church of Jesus Christ of Latter-day Saints
Sources: 2020 U.S. Religion Census, Association of Statisticians of American Religious Bodies; The Association of Religion Data Archives (ARDA)

Religious Groups by Tradition

Area	Catholic	Evangelical Protestant	Mainline Protestant	Black Protestant	Islam	Judaism	Hinduism	Orthodox	Buddhism
MSA[1]	27.3	17.7	3.1	0.8	0.5	0.2	0.1	0.1	0.3
U.S.	18.7	16.5	5.2	2.3	1.3	0.6	0.4	0.4	0.3

Note: Figures are the number of adherents as a percentage of the total population; (1) Figures cover the San Antonio-New Braunfels, TX Metropolitan Statistical Area
Sources: 2020 U.S. Religion Census, Association of Statisticians of American Religious Bodies; The Association of Religion Data Archives (ARDA)

ECONOMY

Gross Metropolitan Product

Area	2020	2021	2022	2023	Rank[2]
MSA[1]	132.1	146.4	161.1	169.2	34

Note: Figures are in billions of dollars; (1) Figures cover the San Antonio-New Braunfels, TX Metropolitan Statistical Area; (2) Rank is based on 2021 data and ranges from 1 to 381
Source: U.S. Conference of Mayors, U.S. Metro Economies: U.S. Metros Compared to Global and State Economies, June 2022

Economic Growth

Area	2018-20 (%)	2021 (%)	2022 (%)	2023 (%)	Rank[2]
MSA[1]	0.8	6.2	3.7	2.4	88
U.S.	-0.6	5.7	3.1	2.9	—

Note: Figures are real gross metropolitan product (GMP) growth rates and represent average annual percent change; (1) Figures cover the San Antonio-New Braunfels, TX Metropolitan Statistical Area; (2) Rank is based on 2020 2-year average annual percent change and ranges from 1 to 381
Source: U.S. Conference of Mayors, U.S. Metro Economies: U.S. Metros Compared to Global and State Economies, June 2022

Metropolitan Area Exports

Area	2016	2017	2018	2019	2020	2021	Rank[2]
MSA[1]	5,621.2	9,184.1	11,678.1	11,668.0	10,987.9	13,086.4	29

Note: Figures are in millions of dollars; (1) Figures cover the San Antonio-New Braunfels, TX Metropolitan Statistical Area; (2) Rank is based on 2021 data and ranges from 1 to 388
Source: U.S. Department of Commerce, International Trade Administration, Office of Trade and Economic Analysis, Industry and Analysis, Exports by Metropolitan Area, data extracted March 16, 2023

Building Permits

Area	Single-Family 2021	Single-Family 2022	Pct. Chg.	Multi-Family 2021	Multi-Family 2022	Pct. Chg.	Total 2021	Total 2022	Pct. Chg.
City	6,567	4,686	-28.6	4,591	9,496	106.8	11,158	14,182	27.1
MSA[1]	13,945	10,226	-26.7	8,319	14,113	69.6	22,264	24,339	9.3
U.S.	1,115,400	975,600	-12.5	621,600	689,500	10.9	1,737,000	1,665,100	-4.1

Note: (1) Figures cover the San Antonio-New Braunfels, TX Metropolitan Statistical Area; Figures represent new, privately-owned housing units authorized (unadjusted data); All permit data are based on estimates with imputation
Source: U.S. Census Bureau, Manufacturing, Mining, and Construction Statistics, Building Permits, 2021, 2022

Bankruptcy Filings

Area	Business Filings 2021	Business Filings 2022	% Chg.	Nonbusiness Filings 2021	Nonbusiness Filings 2022	% Chg.
Bexar County	143	84	-41.3	1,102	1,028	-6.7
U.S.	14,347	13,481	-6.0	399,269	374,240	-6.3

Note: Business filings include Chapter 7, Chapter 9, Chapter 11, Chapter 12, Chapter 13, Chapter 15, and Section 304; Nonbusiness filings include Chapter 7, Chapter 11, and Chapter 13
Source: Administrative Office of the U.S. Courts, Business and Nonbusiness Bankruptcy, County Cases Commenced by Chapter of the Bankruptcy Code, During the 12-Month Period Ending December 31, 2021 and Business and Nonbusiness Bankruptcy, County Cases Commenced by Chapter of the Bankruptcy Code, During the 12-Month Period Ending December 31, 2022

Housing Vacancy Rates

Area	Gross Vacancy Rate[2] (%) 2020	2021	2022	Year-Round Vacancy Rate[3] (%) 2020	2021	2022	Rental Vacancy Rate[4] (%) 2020	2021	2022	Homeowner Vacancy Rate[5] (%) 2020	2021	2022
MSA[1]	7.4	7.6	7.5	6.7	6.9	7.1	7.2	8.4	8.1	1.0	1.1	0.9
U.S.	10.6	10.8	10.5	8.2	8.4	8.2	6.3	6.1	5.8	1.0	0.9	0.8

Note: (1) Figures cover the San Antonio-New Braunfels, TX Metropolitan Statistical Area; (2) The percentage of the total housing inventory that is vacant; (3) The percentage of the housing inventory (excluding seasonal units) that is year-round vacant; (4) The percentage of rental inventory that is vacant for rent; (5) The percentage of homeowner inventory that is vacant for sale
Source: U.S. Census Bureau, Housing Vacancies and Homeownership Annual Statistics: 2020, 2021, 2022

INCOME

Income

Area	Per Capita ($)	Median Household ($)	Average Household ($)
City	28,579	55,084	74,154
MSA[1]	32,580	65,355	88,127
U.S.	37,638	69,021	97,196

Note: (1) Figures cover the San Antonio-New Braunfels, TX Metropolitan Statistical Area
Source: U.S. Census Bureau, 2017-2021 American Community Survey 5-Year Estimates

San Antonio, Texas

Household Income Distribution

Area	Percent of Households Earning							
	Under $15,000	$15,000 -$24,999	$25,000 -$34,999	$35,000 -$49,999	$50,000 -$74,999	$75,000 -$99,999	$100,000 -$149,999	$150,000 and up
City	12.2	9.5	10.3	13.6	19.1	12.0	13.3	10.0
MSA[1]	9.6	7.9	8.9	12.0	18.2	13.0	16.1	14.4
U.S.	9.4	7.8	8.2	11.4	16.8	12.8	16.3	17.3

Note: (1) Figures cover the San Antonio-New Braunfels, TX Metropolitan Statistical Area
Source: U.S. Census Bureau, 2017-2021 American Community Survey 5-Year Estimates

Poverty Rate

Area	All Ages	Under 18 Years Old	18 to 64 Years Old	65 Years and Over
City	17.6	25.8	15.3	13.6
MSA[1]	13.8	19.4	12.1	10.7
U.S.	12.6	17.0	11.8	9.6

Note: Figures are percentage of people whose income during the past 12 months was below the poverty level; (1) Figures cover the San Antonio-New Braunfels, TX Metropolitan Statistical Area
Source: U.S. Census Bureau, 2017-2021 American Community Survey 5-Year Estimates

EMPLOYMENT

Labor Force and Employment

Area	Civilian Labor Force			Workers Employed		
	Dec. 2021	Dec. 2022	% Chg.	Dec. 2021	Dec. 2022	% Chg.
City	735,449	751,540	2.2	707,860	727,368	2.8
MSA[1]	1,217,217	1,244,094	2.2	1,171,224	1,203,295	2.7
U.S.	161,696,000	164,224,000	1.6	155,732,000	158,872,000	2.0

Note: Data is not seasonally adjusted and covers workers 16 years of age and older; (1) Figures cover the San Antonio-New Braunfels, TX Metropolitan Statistical Area
Source: Bureau of Labor Statistics, Local Area Unemployment Statistics

Unemployment Rate

Area	2022											
	Jan.	Feb.	Mar.	Apr.	May	Jun.	Jul.	Aug.	Sep.	Oct.	Nov.	Dec.
City	4.3	4.2	3.5	3.3	3.5	4.0	3.9	3.8	3.5	3.5	3.4	3.2
MSA[1]	4.3	4.2	3.5	3.3	3.5	4.0	4.0	3.8	3.5	3.5	3.4	3.3
U.S.	4.4	4.1	3.8	3.3	3.4	3.8	3.8	3.8	3.3	3.4	3.4	3.3

Note: Data is not seasonally adjusted and covers workers 16 years of age and older; (1) Figures cover the San Antonio-New Braunfels, TX Metropolitan Statistical Area
Source: Bureau of Labor Statistics, Local Area Unemployment Statistics

Average Wages

Occupation	$/Hr.	Occupation	$/Hr.
Accountants and Auditors	40.79	Maintenance and Repair Workers	19.50
Automotive Mechanics	22.70	Marketing Managers	60.00
Bookkeepers	21.14	Network and Computer Systems Admin.	41.81
Carpenters	21.56	Nurses, Licensed Practical	25.93
Cashiers	13.19	Nurses, Registered	39.92
Computer Programmers	42.04	Nursing Assistants	15.47
Computer Systems Analysts	48.72	Office Clerks, General	18.02
Computer User Support Specialists	26.07	Physical Therapists	45.42
Construction Laborers	18.15	Physicians	145.35
Cooks, Restaurant	14.44	Plumbers, Pipefitters and Steamfitters	24.88
Customer Service Representatives	18.47	Police and Sheriff's Patrol Officers	31.55
Dentists	90.08	Postal Service Mail Carriers	26.74
Electricians	25.79	Real Estate Sales Agents	32.87
Engineers, Electrical	50.10	Retail Salespersons	15.92
Fast Food and Counter Workers	11.50	Sales Representatives, Technical/Scientific	41.27
Financial Managers	73.39	Secretaries, Exc. Legal/Medical/Executive	19.44
First-Line Supervisors of Office Workers	30.02	Security Guards	15.80
General and Operations Managers	50.98	Surgeons	n/a
Hairdressers/Cosmetologists	14.16	Teacher Assistants, Exc. Postsecondary*	14.17
Home Health and Personal Care Aides	10.89	Teachers, Secondary School, Exc. Sp. Ed.*	29.61
Janitors and Cleaners	14.02	Telemarketers	17.04
Landscaping/Groundskeeping Workers	15.69	Truck Drivers, Heavy/Tractor-Trailer	22.61
Lawyers	68.81	Truck Drivers, Light/Delivery Services	20.69
Maids and Housekeeping Cleaners	13.15	Waiters and Waitresses	13.14

Note: Wage data covers the San Antonio-New Braunfels, TX Metropolitan Statistical Area; (*) Hourly wages were calculated from annual wage data based on a 40 hour work week; n/a not available.
Source: Bureau of Labor Statistics, Metro Area Occupational Employment & Wage Estimates, May 2022

Employment by Industry

Sector	MSA[1] Number of Employees	MSA[1] Percent of Total	U.S. Percent of Total
Construction	61,100	5.3	5.0
Private Education and Health Services	171,300	14.9	16.1
Financial Activities	102,600	8.9	5.9
Government	179,300	15.6	14.5
Information	19,200	1.7	2.0
Leisure and Hospitality	140,700	12.2	10.3
Manufacturing	58,500	5.1	8.4
Mining and Logging	7,000	0.6	0.4
Other Services	40,100	3.5	3.7
Professional and Business Services	161,100	14.0	14.7
Retail Trade	125,600	10.9	10.2
Transportation, Warehousing, and Utilities	47,300	4.1	4.9
Wholesale Trade	38,500	3.3	3.9

Note: Figures are non-farm employment as of December 2022. Figures are not seasonally adjusted and include workers 16 years of age and older; (1) Figures cover the San Antonio-New Braunfels, TX Metropolitan Statistical Area
Source: Bureau of Labor Statistics, Current Employment Statistics, Employment, Hours, and Earnings

Employment by Occupation

Occupation Classification	City (%)	MSA[1] (%)	U.S. (%)
Management, Business, Science, and Arts	34.8	37.6	40.3
Natural Resources, Construction, and Maintenance	10.1	9.9	8.7
Production, Transportation, and Material Moving	11.4	11.5	13.1
Sales and Office	23.6	23.1	20.9
Service	20.1	17.9	17.0

Note: Figures cover employed civilians 16 years of age and older; (1) Figures cover the San Antonio-New Braunfels, TX Metropolitan Statistical Area
Source: U.S. Census Bureau, 2017-2021 American Community Survey 5-Year Estimates

Occupations with Greatest Projected Employment Growth: 2022 – 2024

Occupation[1]	2022 Employment	2024 Projected Employment	Numeric Employment Change	Percent Employment Change
Home Health and Personal Care Aides	338,130	364,760	26,630	7.9
General and Operations Managers	395,700	416,100	20,400	5.2
Heavy and Tractor-Trailer Truck Drivers	206,850	222,220	15,370	7.4
Software Developers	119,810	134,060	14,250	11.9
Laborers and Freight, Stock, and Material Movers, Hand	214,680	228,680	14,000	6.5
Farmers, Ranchers, and Other Agricultural Managers	274,740	287,430	12,690	4.6
Stockers and Order Fillers	212,180	224,670	12,490	5.9
Construction Laborers	153,220	164,330	11,110	7.3
Cooks, Restaurant	131,480	141,860	10,380	7.9
Industrial Truck and Tractor Operators	83,270	93,190	9,920	11.9

Note: Projections cover Texas; (1) Sorted by numeric employment change
Source: www.projectionscentral.com, State Occupational Projections, 2022–2024 Short-Term Projections

Fastest-Growing Occupations: 2022 – 2024

Occupation[1]	2022 Employment	2024 Projected Employment	Numeric Employment Change	Percent Employment Change
Wind Turbine Service Technicians	5,240	5,990	750	14.3
Information Security Analysts (SOC 2018)	14,170	16,110	1,940	13.7
Solar Photovoltaic Installers	2,240	2,540	300	13.4
Veterinary Technologists and Technicians	16,140	18,200	2,060	12.8
Actuaries	1,810	2,040	230	12.7
Data Scientists	7,340	8,270	930	12.7
Web Developers	6,920	7,790	870	12.6
Veterinarians	6,830	7,670	840	12.3
Veterinary Assistants and Laboratory Animal Caretakers	5,990	6,720	730	12.2
Ushers, Lobby Attendants, and Ticket Takers	9,100	10,190	1,090	12.0

Note: Projections cover Texas; (1) Sorted by percent employment change and excludes occupations with numeric employment change less than 50
Source: www.projectionscentral.com, State Occupational Projections, 2022–2024 Short-Term Projections

San Antonio, Texas

CITY FINANCES

City Government Finances

Component	2020 ($000)	2020 ($ per capita)
Total Revenues	5,742,941	3,712
Total Expenditures	5,597,102	3,617
Debt Outstanding	12,091,172	7,815
Cash and Securities[1]	5,155,509	3,332

Note: (1) Cash and security holdings of a government at the close of its fiscal year, including those of its dependent agencies, utilities, and liquor stores.
Source: U.S. Census Bureau, State & Local Government Finances 2020

City Government Revenue by Source

Source	2020 ($000)	2020 ($ per capita)	2020 (%)
General Revenue			
From Federal Government	105,440	68	1.8
From State Government	158,212	102	2.8
From Local Governments	92,086	60	1.6
Taxes			
Property	588,815	381	10.3
Sales and Gross Receipts	502,079	324	8.7
Personal Income	0	0	0.0
Corporate Income	0	0	0.0
Motor Vehicle License	0	0	0.0
Other Taxes	64,286	42	1.1
Current Charges	742,374	480	12.9
Liquor Store	0	0	0.0
Utility	3,027,838	1,957	52.7

Source: U.S. Census Bureau, State & Local Government Finances 2020

City Government Expenditures by Function

Function	2020 ($000)	2020 ($ per capita)	2020 (%)
General Direct Expenditures			
Air Transportation	113,481	73	2.0
Corrections	0	0	0.0
Education	103,419	66	1.8
Employment Security Administration	0	0	0.0
Financial Administration	61,382	39	1.1
Fire Protection	288,722	186	5.2
General Public Buildings	17,782	11	0.3
Governmental Administration, Other	31,504	20	0.6
Health	34,025	22	0.6
Highways	189,347	122	3.4
Hospitals	0	0	0.0
Housing and Community Development	68,699	44	1.2
Interest on General Debt	179,276	115	3.2
Judicial and Legal	28,845	18	0.5
Libraries	42,544	27	0.8
Parking	8,225	5	0.1
Parks and Recreation	164,238	106	2.9
Police Protection	425,314	274	7.6
Public Welfare	112,693	72	2.0
Sewerage	295,674	191	5.3
Solid Waste Management	135,242	87	2.4
Veterans' Services	0	0	0.0
Liquor Store	0	0	0.0
Utility	3,048,209	1,970	54.5

Source: U.S. Census Bureau, State & Local Government Finances 2020

TAXES

State Corporate Income Tax Rates

State	Tax Rate (%)	Income Brackets ($)	Num. of Brackets	Financial Institution Tax Rate (%)[a]	Federal Income Tax Ded.
Texas	(u)	—	—	(u)	No

Note: Tax rates as of January 1, 2023; (a) Rates listed are the corporate income tax rate applied to financial institutions or excise taxes based on income. Some states have other taxes based upon the value of deposits or shares; (u) Texas imposes a Franchise Tax, otherwise known as margin tax, imposed on entities with more than $1,230,000 total revenues at rate of 0.75%, or 0.375% for entities primarily engaged in retail or wholesale trade, on lesser of 70% of total revenues or 100% of gross receipts after deductions for either compensation or cost of goods sold.
Source: Federation of Tax Administrators, State Corporate Income Tax Rates, January 1, 2023

State Individual Income Tax Rates

State	Tax Rate (%)	Income Brackets ($)	Personal Exemptions ($) Single	Personal Exemptions ($) Married	Personal Exemptions ($) Depend.	Standard Ded. ($) Single	Standard Ded. ($) Married
Texas							

– No state income tax –

Note: Tax rates as of January 1, 2023; Local- and county-level taxes are not included
Source: Federation of Tax Administrators, State Individual Income Tax Rates, January 1, 2023

Various State Sales and Excise Tax Rates

State	State Sales Tax (%)	Gasoline[1] ($/gal.)	Cigarette[2] ($/pack)	Spirits[3] ($/gal.)	Wine[4] ($/gal.)	Beer[5] ($/gal.)	Recreational Marijuana (%)
Texas	6.25	0.20	1.41	2.40	0.20	0.19	Not legal

Note: All tax rates as of January 1, 2023; (1) The American Petroleum Institute has developed a methodology for determining the average tax rate on a gallon of fuel. Rates may include any of the following: excise taxes, environmental fees, storage tank fees, other fees or taxes, general sales tax, and local taxes; (2) The federal excise tax of $1.0066 per pack and local taxes are not included; (3) Rates are those applicable to off-premise sales of 40% alcohol by volume (a.b.v.) distilled spirits in 750ml containers. Local excise taxes are excluded; (4) Rates are those applicable to off-premise sales of 11% a.b.v. non-carbonated wine in 750ml containers; (5) Rates are those applicable to off-premise sales of 4.7% a.b.v. beer in 12 ounce containers.
Source: Tax Foundation, 2023 Facts & Figures: How Does Your State Compare?

State Business Tax Climate Index Rankings

State	Overall Rank	Corporate Tax Rank	Individual Income Tax Rank	Sales Tax Rank	Property Tax Rank	Unemployment Insurance Tax Rank
Texas	13	47	7	37	38	12

Note: The index is a measure of how each state's tax laws affect economic performance. The lower the rank, the more favorable a state's tax system is for business. States without a given tax are given a ranking of 1. The scores/rankings for the District of Columbia do not affect other states. The 2023 index represents the tax climate as of July 1, 2022.
Source: Tax Foundation, State Business Tax Climate Index 2023

TRANSPORTATION

Means of Transportation to Work

Area	Car/Truck/Van Drove Alone	Car/Truck/Van Carpooled	Public Transportation Bus	Public Transportation Subway	Public Transportation Railroad	Bicycle	Walked	Other Means	Worked at Home
City	74.6	11.8	2.1	0.0	0.0	0.2	1.8	1.6	8.0
MSA[1]	75.6	10.7	1.3	0.0	0.0	0.2	1.6	1.4	9.1
U.S.	73.2	8.6	2.0	1.6	0.5	0.5	2.5	1.5	9.7

Note: Figures are percentages and cover workers 16 years of age and older; (1) Figures cover the San Antonio-New Braunfels, TX Metropolitan Statistical Area
Source: U.S. Census Bureau, 2017-2021 American Community Survey 5-Year Estimates

Travel Time to Work

Area	Less Than 10 Minutes	10 to 19 Minutes	20 to 29 Minutes	30 to 44 Minutes	45 to 59 Minutes	60 to 89 Minutes	90 Minutes or More
City	9.4	31.4	26.3	21.8	6.0	3.4	1.7
MSA[1]	9.2	27.8	24.1	23.2	8.7	4.8	2.2
U.S.	12.4	28.5	21.0	20.9	8.2	6.2	2.9

Note: Note: Figures are percentages and include workers 16 years old and over; (1) Figures cover the San Antonio-New Braunfels, TX Metropolitan Statistical Area
Source: U.S. Census Bureau, 2017-2021 American Community Survey 5-Year Estimates

Key Congestion Measures

Measure	1990	2000	2010	2015	2020
Annual Hours of Delay, Total (000)	15,248	38,579	54,651	66,862	44,999
Annual Hours of Delay, Per Auto Commuter	22	40	42	48	32
Annual Congestion Cost, Per Auto Commuter ($)	401	765	861	974	682

Note: Covers the San Antonio TX urban area
Source: Texas A&M Transportation Institute, 2021 Urban Mobility Report

Freeway Travel Time Index

Measure	1985	1990	1995	2000	2005	2010	2015	2020
Urban Area Index[1]	1.11	1.12	1.19	1.22	1.24	1.23	1.23	1.12
Urban Area Rank[1,2]	25	35	23	24	27	28	29	10

Note: Freeway Travel Time Index—the ratio of travel time in the peak period to the travel time at free-flow conditions. For example, a value of 1.30 indicates a 20-minute free-flow trip takes 26 minutes in the peak (20 minutes x 1.30 = 26 minutes); (1) Covers the San Antonio TX urban area; (2) Rank is based on 101 larger urban areas (#1 = highest travel time index)
Source: Texas A&M Transportation Institute, 2021 Urban Mobility Report

Public Transportation

Agency Name / Mode of Transportation	Vehicles Operated in Maximum Service[1]	Annual Unlinked Passenger Trips[2] (in thous.)	Annual Passenger Miles[3] (in thous.)
VIA Metropolitan Transit (VIA)			
Bus (directly operated)	503	23,032.6	94,848.7
Demand Response (directly operated)	84	236.3	2,731.0
Demand Response (purchased transportation)	86	414.9	3,645.1
Demand Response - Taxi	33	32.2	387.8
Vanpool (purchased transportation)	117	270.3	16,191.0

Note: (1) Number of revenue vehicles operated by the given mode and type of service to meet the annual maximum service requirement. This is the revenue vehicle count during the peak season of the year; on the week and day that maximum service is provided. Vehicles operated in maximum service (VOMS) exclude atypical days and one-time special events; (2) Number of passengers who boarded public transportation vehicles. Passengers are counted each time they board a vehicle no matter how many vehicles they use to travel from their origin to their destination. (3) Sum of the distances ridden by all passengers during the entire fiscal year.
Source: Federal Transit Administration, National Transit Database, 2021

Air Transportation

Airport Name and Code / Type of Service	Passenger Airlines[1]	Passenger Enplanements	Freight Carriers[2]	Freight (lbs)
San Antonio International (SAT)				
Domestic service (U.S. carriers - 2022)	27	4,473,117	15	111,944,248
International service (U.S. carriers - 2021)	7	15,814	1	10,660,534

Note: (1) Includes all U.S.-based major, minor and commuter airlines that carried at least one passenger during the year; (2) Includes all U.S.-based airlines and freight carriers that transported at least one pound of freight during the year.
Source: Bureau of Transportation Statistics, The Intermodal Transportation Database, Air Carriers: T-100 Domestic Market (U.S. Carriers), 2022; Bureau of Transportation Statistics, The Intermodal Transportation Database, Air Carriers: T-100 International Market (U.S. Carriers), 2021

BUSINESSES

Major Business Headquarters

Company Name	Industry	Fortune[1]	Forbes[2]
H-E-B	Food markets	-	6
USAA	Insurance, property and casualty (stock)	96	-
Valero Energy	Petroleum refining	30	-
Zachry Group	Construction	-	223

Note: (1) Companies that produce a 10-K are ranked 1 to 500 based on 2021 revenue; (2) All private companies with at least $2 billion in annual revenue through the end of their most current fiscal year are ranked 1 to 246; companies listed are headquartered in the city; dashes indicate no ranking
Source: Fortune, "Fortune 500," 2022; Forbes, "America's Largest Private Companies," 2022

Fastest-Growing Businesses

According to *Inc.*, San Antonio is home to one of America's 500 fastest-growing private companies: **Texas Solar Integrated** (#209). Criteria: must be an independent, privately-held, for-profit, U.S. corporation, proprietorship or partnership as of December 31, 2021; revenues must be at least $100,000 in 2018 and $2 million in 2021; must have four-year operating/sales history. *Inc., "America's 500 Fastest-Growing Private Companies," 2022*

According to Deloitte, San Antonio is home to one of North America's 500 fastest-growing high-technology companies: **Stirista** (#402). Companies are ranked by percentage growth in revenue over a four-year period. Criteria for inclusion: company must be headquartered within North America; must own proprietary intellectual property or technology that is sold to customers in products that contributes to a significant portion of the company's operating revenue; must have been in business for a minumum of four years with 2018 operating revenues of at least $50,000 USD/CD and 2021 operating revenues of at least $5 million USD/CD. *Deloitte, 2022 Technology Fast 500™*

Living Environment

COST OF LIVING

Cost of Living Index

Composite Index	Groceries	Housing	Utilities	Transportation	Health Care	Misc. Goods/Services
92.0	88.6	79.9	88.7	96.0	101.6	102.3

Note: The Cost of Living Index measures regional differences in the cost of consumer goods and services, excluding taxes and non-consumer expenditures, for professional and managerial households in the top income quintile. It is based on more than 50,000 prices covering almost 60 different items for which prices are collected three times a year by chambers of commerce, economic development organizations or university applied economic centers in each participating urban area. The numbers shown should be read as a percentage above or below the national average of 100. For example, a value of 115.4 in the groceries column indicates that grocery prices are 15.4% higher than the national average. Small differences in the index numbers should not be interpreted as significant; Figures cover the San Antonio TX urban area.
Source: The Council for Community and Economic Research, Cost of Living Index, 2022

Grocery Prices

Area[1]	T-Bone Steak ($/pound)	Frying Chicken ($/pound)	Whole Milk ($/half gal.)	Eggs ($/dozen)	Orange Juice ($/64 oz.)	Coffee ($/11.5 oz.)
City[2]	11.06	1.05	2.20	1.86	3.41	4.07
Avg.	13.81	1.59	2.43	2.25	3.85	4.95
Min.	10.17	0.90	1.51	1.30	2.90	3.46
Max.	19.35	3.30	4.32	4.32	5.31	8.59

Note: (1) Values for the local area are compared with the average, minimum and maximum values for all 286 areas in the Cost of Living Index; (2) Figures cover the San Antonio TX urban area; **T-Bone Steak** (price per pound); **Frying Chicken** (price per pound, whole fryer); **Whole Milk** (half gallon carton); **Eggs** (price per dozen, Grade A, large); **Orange Juice** (64 oz. Tropicana or Florida Natural); **Coffee** (11.5 oz. can, vacuum-packed, Maxwell House, Hills Bros, or Folgers).
Source: The Council for Community and Economic Research, Cost of Living Index, 2022

Housing and Utility Costs

Area[1]	New Home Price ($)	Apartment Rent ($/month)	All Electric ($/month)	Part Electric ($/month)	Other Energy ($/month)	Telephone ($/month)
City[2]	327,632	1,388	-	99.94	37.03	198.89
Avg.	450,913	1,371	176.41	99.93	76.96	190.22
Min.	229,283	546	100.84	31.56	27.15	174.27
Max.	2,434,977	4,569	356.86	249.59	272.24	208.31

Note: (1) Values for the local area are compared with the average, minimum and maximum values for all 286 areas in the Cost of Living Index; (2) Figures cover the San Antonio TX urban area; **New Home Price** (2,400 sf living area, 8,000 sf lot, in urban area with full utilities); **Apartment Rent** (950 sf 2 bedroom/1.5 or 2 bath, unfurnished, excluding all utilities except water); **All Electric** (average monthly cost for an all-electric home); **Part Electric** (average monthly cost for a part-electric home); **Other Energy** (average monthly cost for natural gas, fuel oil, coal, wood, and any other forms of energy except electricity); **Telephone** (price includes the base monthly rate plus taxes and fees for three lines of mobile phone service).
Source: The Council for Community and Economic Research, Cost of Living Index, 2022

Health Care, Transportation, and Other Costs

Area[1]	Doctor ($/visit)	Dentist ($/visit)	Optometrist ($/visit)	Gasoline ($/gallon)	Beauty Salon ($/visit)	Men's Shirt ($)
City[2]	123.35	111.47	125.52	3.43	58.84	35.83
Avg.	124.91	107.77	117.66	3.86	43.31	34.21
Min.	36.61	58.25	51.79	2.90	22.18	13.05
Max.	250.21	162.58	371.96	5.54	85.61	63.54

Note: (1) Values for the local area are compared with the average, minimum and maximum values for all 286 areas in the Cost of Living Index; (2) Figures cover the San Antonio TX urban area; **Doctor** (general practitioners routine exam of an established patient); **Dentist** (adult teeth cleaning and periodic oral examination); **Optometrist** (full vision eye exam for established adult patient); **Gasoline** (one gallon regular unleaded, national brand, including all taxes, cash price at self-service pump if available); **Beauty Salon** (woman's shampoo, trim, and blow-dry); **Men's Shirt** (cotton/polyester dress shirt, pinpoint weave, long sleeves).
Source: The Council for Community and Economic Research, Cost of Living Index, 2022

HOUSING

Homeownership Rate

Area	2015 (%)	2016 (%)	2017 (%)	2018 (%)	2019 (%)	2020 (%)	2021 (%)	2022 (%)
MSA[1]	66.0	61.6	62.5	64.4	62.6	64.2	62.7	62.9
U.S.	63.7	63.4	63.9	64.4	64.6	66.6	65.5	65.8

Note: (1) Figures cover the San Antonio-New Braunfels, TX Metropolitan Statistical Area
Source: U.S. Census Bureau, Housing Vacancies and Homeownership Annual Statistics: 2015-2022

House Price Index (HPI)

Area	National Ranking[2]	Quarterly Change (%)	One-Year Change (%)	Five-Year Change (%)	Since 1991Q1 (%)
MSA[1]	50	0.79	15.27	62.24	345.76
U.S.[3]	–	0.34	8.41	58.44	289.08

Note: The HPI is a weighted repeat sales index. It measures average price changes in repeat sales or refinancings on the same properties. This information is obtained by reviewing repeat mortgage transactions on single-family properties whose mortgages have been purchased or securitized by Fannie Mae or Freddie Mac since January 1975; (1) Figures cover the San Antonio-New Braunfels, TX Metropolitan Statistical Area; (2) Rankings are based on annual percentage change for all metro areas containing at least 15,000 transactions over the last 10 years and ranges from 1 to 257; (3) figures based on a weighted average of Census Division estimates using a seasonally adjusted, purchase-only index; all figures are for the period ending December 31, 2022
Source: Federal Housing Finance Agency, Change in FHFA Metropolitan Area House Price Indexes, 2022Q4

Median Single-Family Home Prices

Area	2020	2021	2022p	Percent Change 2021 to 2022
MSA[1]	254.3	291.2	337.7	16.0
U.S. Average	300.2	357.1	392.6	9.9

Note: Figures are median sales prices of existing single-family homes in thousands of dollars; (p) preliminary; (1) Figures cover the San Antonio-New Braunfels, TX Metropolitan Statistical Area
Source: National Association of Realtors, Median Sales Price of Existing Single-Family Homes for Metropolitan Areas, 4th Quarter 2022

Qualifying Income Based on Median Sales Price of Existing Single-Family Homes

Area	With 5% Down ($)	With 10% Down ($)	With 20% Down ($)
MSA[1]	98,671	93,478	83,091
U.S. Average	112,234	106,237	94,513

Note: Figures are preliminary; Qualifying income is based on a mortgage rate of 6.77%. Monthly principal and interest payment is limited to 25% of income; (1) Figures cover the San Antonio-New Braunfels, TX Metropolitan Statistical Area
Source: National Association of Realtors, Qualifying Income Based on Median Sales Price of Existing Single-Family Homes for Metropolitan Areas, 4th Quarter 2022

Home Value

Area	Under $100,000	$100,000 -$199,999	$200,000 -$299,999	$300,000 -$399,999	$400,000 -$499,999	$500,000 -$999,999	$1,000,000 or more	Median ($)
City	24.0	38.4	21.9	8.7	3.3	3.1	0.6	167,700
MSA[1]	18.7	31.5	24.5	12.0	5.8	6.2	1.3	199,200
U.S.	16.2	24.2	20.1	13.6	8.3	13.6	4.1	244,900

Note: Figures are percentages except for median and cover owner-occupied housing units; (1) Figures cover the San Antonio-New Braunfels, TX Metropolitan Statistical Area
Source: U.S. Census Bureau, 2017-2021 American Community Survey 5-Year Estimates

Year Housing Structure Built

Area	2020 or Later	2010 -2019	2000 -2009	1990 -1999	1980 -1989	1970 -1979	1960 -1969	1950 -1959	1940 -1949	Before 1940	Median Year
City	0.2	10.2	14.9	12.9	16.2	14.4	10.3	9.9	5.5	5.4	1983
MSA[1]	0.5	16.2	19.2	13.9	14.5	12.4	8.0	7.2	3.8	4.3	1990
U.S.	0.2	7.3	13.6	13.6	13.2	14.8	10.3	10.0	4.7	12.2	1979

Note: Figures are percentages except for Median Year; Note: (1) Figures cover the San Antonio-New Braunfels, TX Metropolitan Statistical Area
Source: U.S. Census Bureau, 2017-2021 American Community Survey 5-Year Estimates

Gross Monthly Rent

Area	Under $500	$500 -$999	$1,000 -$1,499	$1,500 -$1,999	$2,000 -$2,499	$2,500 -$2,999	$3,000 and up	Median ($)
City	6.2	34.8	41.6	13.5	2.6	0.7	0.6	1,090
MSA[1]	5.6	32.5	41.5	15.3	3.5	0.9	0.7	1,122
U.S.	8.1	30.5	30.8	16.8	7.3	3.1	3.5	1,163

Note: Figures are percentages except for median; Gross rent is the contract rent plus the estimated average monthly cost of utilities (electricity, gas, and water and sewer) and fuels (oil, coal, kerosene, wood, etc.) if these are paid by the renter (or paid for the renter by someone else); (1) Figures cover the San Antonio-New Braunfels, TX Metropolitan Statistical Area
Source: U.S. Census Bureau, 2017-2021 American Community Survey 5-Year Estimates

HEALTH

Health Risk Factors

Category	MSA[1] (%)	U.S. (%)
Adults aged 18–64 who have any kind of health care coverage	79.1	90.9
Adults who reported being in good or better health	78.5	85.2
Adults who have been told they have high blood cholesterol	34.8	35.7
Adults who have been told they have high blood pressure	31.6	32.4
Adults who are current smokers	10.4	14.4
Adults who currently use e-cigarettes	5.8	6.7
Adults who currently use chewing tobacco, snuff, or snus	2.9	3.5
Adults who are heavy drinkers[2]	5.5	6.3
Adults who are binge drinkers[3]	16.3	15.4
Adults who are overweight (BMI 25.0 - 29.9)	37.2	34.4
Adults who are obese (BMI 30.0 - 99.8)	40.2	33.9
Adults who participated in any physical activities in the past month	75.6	76.3

Note: (1) Figures cover the San Antonio-New Braunfels, TX Metropolitan Statistical Area; (2) Heavy drinkers are classified as adult men having more than 14 drinks per week and adult women having more than 7 drinks per week; (3) Binge drinkers are classified as males having five or more drinks on one occasion or females having four or more drinks on one occasion
Source: Centers for Disease Control and Prevention, Behaviorial Risk Factor Surveillance System, SMART: Selected Metropolitan Area Risk Trends, 2021

Acute and Chronic Health Conditions

Category	MSA[1] (%)	U.S. (%)
Adults who have ever been told they had a heart attack	3.8	4.0
Adults who have ever been told they have angina or coronary heart disease	3.4	3.8
Adults who have ever been told they had a stroke	3.8	3.0
Adults who have ever been told they have asthma	14.8	14.9
Adults who have ever been told they have arthritis	24.2	25.8
Adults who have ever been told they have diabetes[2]	11.2	10.9
Adults who have ever been told they had skin cancer	5.0	6.6
Adults who have ever been told they had any other types of cancer	6.4	7.5
Adults who have ever been told they have COPD	6.5	6.1
Adults who have ever been told they have kidney disease	4.1	3.0
Adults who have ever been told they have a form of depression	23.4	20.5

Note: (1) Figures cover the San Antonio-New Braunfels, TX Metropolitan Statistical Area; (2) Figures do not include pregnancy-related, borderline, or pre-diabetes
Source: Centers for Disease Control and Prevention, Behaviorial Risk Factor Surveillance System, SMART: Selected Metropolitan Area Risk Trends, 2021

Health Screening and Vaccination Rates

Category	MSA[1] (%)	U.S. (%)
Adults who have ever been tested for HIV	43.3	34.9
Adults who have had their blood cholesterol checked within the last five years	84.6	85.2
Adults aged 65+ who have had flu shot within the past year	71.1	68.6
Adults aged 65+ who have ever had a pneumonia vaccination	74.7	71.0

Note: (1) Figures cover the San Antonio-New Braunfels, TX Metropolitan Statistical Area.
Source: Centers for Disease Control and Prevention, Behaviorial Risk Factor Surveillance System, SMART: Selected Metropolitan Area Risk Trends, 2021

Disability Status

Category	MSA[1] (%)	U.S. (%)
Adults who reported being deaf	6.0	7.2
Are you blind or have serious difficulty seeing, even when wearing glasses?	4.8	4.8
Are you limited in any way in any of your usual activities due to arthritis?	12.0	11.1
Do you have difficulty doing errands alone?	8.7	7.0
Do you have difficulty dressing or bathing?	5.4	3.6
Do you have serious difficulty concentrating/remembering/making decisions?	12.9	12.1
Do you have serious difficulty walking or climbing stairs?	16.4	12.8

Note: (1) Figures cover the San Antonio-New Braunfels, TX Metropolitan Statistical Area.
Source: Centers for Disease Control and Prevention, Behaviorial Risk Factor Surveillance System, SMART: Selected Metropolitan Area Risk Trends, 2021

Mortality Rates for the Top 10 Causes of Death in the U.S.

ICD-10[a] Sub-Chapter	ICD-10[a] Code	Crude Mortality Rate[1] per 100,000 population County[2]	U.S.
Malignant neoplasms	C00-C97	132.1	182.6
Ischaemic heart diseases	I20-I25	86.4	113.1
Other forms of heart disease	I30-I51	57.1	64.4
Other degenerative diseases of the nervous system	G30-G31	62.8	51.0
Cerebrovascular diseases	I60-I69	43.3	47.8
Other external causes of accidental injury	W00-X59	31.4	46.4
Chronic lower respiratory diseases	J40-J47	27.8	45.7
Organic, including symptomatic, mental disorders	F01-F09	12.6	35.9
Hypertensive diseases	I10-I15	29.4	35.0
Diabetes mellitus	E10-E14	31.3	29.6

Note: (a) ICD-10 = International Classification of Diseases 10th Revision; (1) Crude mortality rates are a three-year average covering 2019-2021; (2) Figures cover Bexar County.
Source: Centers for Disease Control and Prevention, National Center for Health Statistics. National Vital Statistics System, Mortality 2018-2021 on CDC WONDER Online Database

Mortality Rates for Selected Causes of Death

ICD-10[a] Sub-Chapter	ICD-10[a] Code	Crude Mortality Rate[1] per 100,000 population County[2]	U.S.
Assault	X85-Y09	8.9	7.0
Diseases of the liver	K70-K76	25.4	19.8
Human immunodeficiency virus (HIV) disease	B20-B24	2.3	1.5
Influenza and pneumonia	J09-J18	8.3	14.7
Intentional self-harm	X60-X84	13.1	14.3
Malnutrition	E40-E46	5.5	4.3
Obesity and other hyperalimentation	E65-E68	3.1	3.0
Renal failure	N17-N19	14.7	15.7
Transport accidents	V01-V99	12.9	13.6
Viral hepatitis	B15-B19	1.2	1.2

Note: (a) ICD-10 = International Classification of Diseases 10th Revision; (1) Crude mortality rates are a three-year average covering 2019-2021; (2) Figures cover Bexar County; Data are suppressed when the data meet the criteria for confidentiality constraints; Crude mortality rates are flagged as unreliable when the rate would be calculated with a numerator of 20 or less.
Source: Centers for Disease Control and Prevention, National Center for Health Statistics. National Vital Statistics System, Mortality 2018-2021 on CDC WONDER Online Database

Health Insurance Coverage

Area	With Health Insurance	With Private Health Insurance	With Public Health Insurance	Without Health Insurance	Population Under Age 19 Without Health Insurance
City	82.8	58.9	33.4	17.2	9.2
MSA[1]	85.0	64.7	31.2	15.0	8.9
U.S.	91.2	67.8	35.4	8.8	5.3

Note: Figures are percentages that cover the civilian noninstitutionalized population; (1) Figures cover the San Antonio-New Braunfels, TX Metropolitan Statistical Area
Source: U.S. Census Bureau, 2017-2021 American Community Survey 5-Year Estimates

Number of Medical Professionals

Area	MDs[3]	DOs[3,4]	Dentists	Podiatrists	Chiropractors	Optometrists
County[1] (number)	6,626	381	1,910	110	348	383
County[1] (rate[2])	329.0	18.9	94.2	5.4	17.2	18.9
U.S. (rate[2])	289.3	23.5	72.5	6.2	28.7	17.4

Note: Data as of 2021 unless noted; (1) Data covers Bexar County; (2) Rate per 100,000 population; (3) Data as of 2020 and includes all active, non-federal physicians; (4) Doctor of Osteopathic Medicine
Source: U.S. Department of Health and Human Services, Health Resources and Services Administration, Bureau of Health Professions, Area Resource File (ARF) 2021-2022

EDUCATION

Public School District Statistics

District Name	Schls	Pupils	Pupil/ Teacher Ratio	Minority Pupils[1] (%)	LEP/ELL[2] (%)	IEP[3] (%)
Alamo Heights ISD	5	4,824	13.6	47.7	5.9	9.2
Basis Texas	7	3,421	15.7	81.7	14.2	2.1
Brooks Academies Of Texas	4	3,141	16.3	91.2	6.7	12.8
East Central ISD	15	10,006	17.0	85.9	10.9	11.7
Edgewood ISD	24	8,393	15.9	99.3	17.9	11.4
Great Hearts Texas	11	8,136	17.6	63.2	5.0	6.6
Harlandale ISD	28	12,080	13.2	98.4	15.5	11.1
Harmony Science Academy	8	4,466	12.5	96.7	31.4	9.5
Jubilee Academies	13	5,764	17.2	93.8	20.1	7.7
North East ISD	75	59,830	15.0	76.5	12.4	11.4
Northside ISD	124	102,377	15.1	82.6	8.5	13.1
San Antonio ISD	100	44,710	14.3	96.9	17.4	12.3
School of Science and Technology	6	5,288	14.5	86.1	10.3	8.5
South San Antonio ISD	20	7,922	14.6	97.6	16.3	11.4
Southside ISD	9	5,520	14.2	92.6	15.8	13.3
Southwest ISD	18	13,277	13.6	95.3	15.8	14.6

Note: Table includes school districts with 2,000 or more students; (1) Percentage of students that are not non-Hispanic white; (2) Percentage of students that are Limited English Proficient or English Language Learners (2018-19); (3) Percentage of students that have an Individualized Education Program (2019-20).
Source: U.S. Department of Education, National Center for Education Statistics, Common Core of Data, Local Education Agency (School District) Universe Survey: School Year 2021-2022

Best High Schools

According to *U.S. News,* San Antonio is home to five of the top 500 high schools in the U.S.: **BASIS San Antonio- Shavano Campus** (#77); **Young Women's Leadership Academy** (#78); **Health Careers High School** (#102); **IDEA Carver College Preparatory** (#207); **Travis Early College High School** (#326). Nearly 18,000 public, magnet and charter schools were ranked based on their performance on state assessments and how well they prepare students for college. *U.S. News & World Report, "Best High Schools 2022"*

Highest Level of Education

Area	Less than H.S.	H.S. Diploma	Some College, No Deg.	Associate Degree	Bachelor's Degree	Master's Degree	Prof. School Degree	Doctorate Degree
City	16.7	25.5	22.5	8.0	16.9	7.2	2.0	1.2
MSA[1]	13.6	25.2	22.7	8.2	19.0	8.2	1.9	1.2
U.S.	11.1	26.5	20.0	8.7	20.6	9.3	2.2	1.5

Note: Figures cover persons age 25 and over; (1) Figures cover the San Antonio-New Braunfels, TX Metropolitan Statistical Area
Source: U.S. Census Bureau, 2017-2021 American Community Survey 5-Year Estimates

Educational Attainment by Race

Area	High School Graduate or Higher (%)					Bachelor's Degree or Higher (%)				
	Total	White	Black	Asian	Hisp.[2]	Total	White	Black	Asian	Hisp.[2]
City	83.3	84.8	91.5	86.1	76.7	27.3	28.9	25.7	55.7	18.0
MSA[1]	86.4	88.1	92.7	87.8	78.4	30.3	32.0	31.4	53.9	19.4
U.S.	88.9	91.4	87.2	87.6	71.2	33.7	35.5	23.3	55.6	18.4

Note: Figures shown cover persons 25 years old and over; (1) Figures cover the San Antonio-New Braunfels, TX Metropolitan Statistical Area; (2) People of Hispanic origin can be of any race
Source: U.S. Census Bureau, 2017-2021 American Community Survey 5-Year Estimates

School Enrollment by Grade and Control

Area	Preschool (%)		Kindergarten (%)		Grades 1 - 4 (%)		Grades 5 - 8 (%)		Grades 9 - 12 (%)	
	Public	Private	Public	Private	Public	Private	Public	Private	Public	Private
City	74.0	26.0	89.7	10.3	92.1	7.9	92.3	7.7	91.5	8.5
MSA[1]	67.2	32.8	89.3	10.7	91.6	8.4	91.2	8.8	91.1	8.9
U.S.	58.8	41.2	86.3	13.7	88.3	11.7	88.6	11.4	89.4	10.6

Note: Figures shown cover persons 3 years old and over; (1) Figures cover the San Antonio-New Braunfels, TX Metropolitan Statistical Area
Source: U.S. Census Bureau, 2017-2021 American Community Survey 5-Year Estimates

Higher Education

Four-Year Colleges			Two-Year Colleges			Medical Schools[1]	Law Schools[2]	Voc/Tech[3]
Public	Private Non-profit	Private For-profit	Public	Private Non-profit	Private For-profit			
3	9	3	5	0	6	2	1	21

Note: Figures cover institutions located within the San Antonio-New Braunfels, TX Metropolitan Statistical Area and include main campuses only; (1) includes schools accredited by the Liaison Committee on Medical Education and the American Osteopathic Association's Commission on Osteopathic College Accreditation; (2) includes ABA-accredited schools, schools with provisional ABA accreditation, and state accredited schools; (3) includes all schools with programs that are less than 2 years.
Source: National Center for Education Statistics, Integrated Postsecondary Education System (IPEDS), 2021-22; Wikipedia, List of Medical Schools in the United States, accessed April 10, 2023; Wikipedia, List of Law Schools in the United States, accessed April 10, 2023

According to *U.S. News & World Report,* the San Antonio-New Braunfels, TX metro area is home to one of the top 100 liberal arts colleges in the U.S.: **Trinity University** (#55 tie). The indicators used to capture academic quality fall into a number of categories: assessment by administrators at peer institutions; retention of students; faculty resources; student selectivity; financial resources; alumni giving; high school counselor ratings of colleges; and graduation rate. *U.S. News & World Report, "America's Best Colleges 2023"*

According to *U.S. News & World Report,* the San Antonio-New Braunfels, TX metro area is home to one of the top 75 medical schools for research in the U.S.: **University of Texas Health Science Center—San Antonio** (#47 tie). The rankings are based on a weighted average of 11 measures of quality: quality assessment; peer assessment score; assessment score by residency directors; research activity; total research activity; average research activity per faculty member; student selectivity; median MCAT total score; median undergraduate GPA; acceptance rate; and faculty resources. *U.S. News & World Report, "America's Best Graduate Schools, Medical, 2023"*

EMPLOYERS

Major Employers

Company Name	Industry
AT&T	Phone, wireless & internet services
Baptist Health System	Health care services
Bill Miller BBQ	Restaurant chain
Christus Santa Rosa Health Care	Health care services
City of San Antonio	Municipal government
Clear Channel Communications	TV & radio stations, outdoor ads
CPS Energy	Utilities
Fort Sam Houston-U.S. Army	U.S. military
H-E-B	Super market chain
JPMorgan Chase	Financial services
Lackland Air Force Base	U.S. military
Methodist Healthcare System	Health care services
North East ISD	School districts
Northside ISD	School districts
Rackspace	IT managed hosting solutions
Randolph Air Force Base	U.S. military
San Antonio ISD	School districts
Toyota Motor Manufacturing	Manufacturing
USAA	Financial services & insurance
Wells Fargo	Financial services

Note: Companies shown are located within the San Antonio-New Braunfels, TX Metropolitan Statistical Area.
Source: Hoovers.com; Wikipedia

Best Companies to Work For

NuStar Energy, headquartered in San Antonio, is among "The 100 Best Companies to Work For." To pick the best companies, *Fortune* partnered with the Great Place to Work Institute. Two-thirds of a company's score is based on the results of the Institute's Trust Index survey, which is sent to a random sample of employees from each company. The questions related to attitudes about management's credibility, job satisfaction, and camaraderie. The other third of the scoring is based on the company's responses to the Institute's Culture Audit, which includes detailed questions about pay and benefit programs, and a series of open-ended questions about hiring practices, internal communication, training, recognition programs, and diversity efforts. Any company that is at least five years old with more than 1,000 U.S. employees is eligible. *Fortune, "The 100 Best Companies to Work For," 2023*

PUBLIC SAFETY

Crime Rate

Area	Total Crime	Violent Crime Rate				Property Crime Rate		
		Murder	Rape[3]	Robbery	Aggrav. Assault	Burglary	Larceny-Theft	Motor Vehicle Theft
City	4,362.2	8.3	75.5	137.5	514.2	503.4	2,679.8	443.7
Suburbs[1]	1,759.0	3.9	36.2	22.5	151.5	297.8	1,074.4	172.6
Metro[2]	3,339.5	6.6	60.1	92.3	371.7	422.6	2,049.1	337.2
U.S.	2,356.7	6.5	38.4	73.9	279.7	314.2	1,398.0	246.0

Note: Figures are crimes per 100,000 population; (1) All areas within the metro area that are located outside the city limits; (2) Figures cover the San Antonio-New Braunfels, TX Metropolitan Statistical Area; (3) All figures shown were reported using the revised Uniform Crime Reporting (UCR) definition of rape; Due to the transition to the National Incident-Based Reporting System (NIBRS), limited city and metro area data was released for 2021.
Source: FBI Uniform Crime Reports, 2020

Hate Crimes

Area	Number of Quarters Reported	Number of Incidents per Bias Motivation					
		Race/Ethnicity/Ancestry	Religion	Sexual Orientation	Disability	Gender	Gender Identity
City	4	10	2	3	0	0	1
U.S.	4	5,227	1,244	1,110	130	75	266

Note: Due to the transition to the National Incident-Based Reporting System (NIBRS), limited crime data was released for 2021.
Source: Federal Bureau of Investigation, Hate Crime Statistics 2020

Identity Theft Consumer Reports

Area	Reports	Reports per 100,000 Population	Rank[2]
MSA[1]	6,858	273	86
U.S.	1,108,609	339	-

Note: (1) Figures cover the San Antonio-New Braunfels, TX Metropolitan Statistical Area; (2) Rank ranges from 1 to 391 where 1 indicates greatest number of identity theft reports per 100,000 population
Source: Federal Trade Commission, Consumer Sentinel Network Data Book 2022

Fraud and Other Consumer Reports

Area	Reports	Reports per 100,000 Population	Rank[2]
MSA[1]	25,048	998	100
U.S.	4,064,520	1,245	-

Note: (1) Figures cover the San Antonio-New Braunfels, TX Metropolitan Statistical Area; (2) Rank ranges from 1 to 391 where 1 indicates greatest number of fraud and other consumer reports per 100,000 population
Source: Federal Trade Commission, Consumer Sentinel Network Data Book 2022

POLITICS

2020 Presidential Election Results

Area	Biden	Trump	Jorgensen	Hawkins	Other
Bexar County	58.2	40.1	1.1	0.4	0.2
U.S.	51.3	46.8	1.2	0.3	0.5

Note: Results are percentages and may not add to 100% due to rounding
Source: Dave Leip's Atlas of U.S. Presidential Elections

SPORTS

Professional Sports Teams

Team Name	League	Year Established
San Antonio Spurs	National Basketball Association (NBA)	1973

Note: Includes teams located in the San Antonio-New Braunfels, TX Metropolitan Statistical Area.
Source: Wikipedia, Major Professional Sports Teams of the United States and Canada, April 12, 2023

CLIMATE

Average and Extreme Temperatures

Temperature	Jan	Feb	Mar	Apr	May	Jun	Jul	Aug	Sep	Oct	Nov	Dec	Yr.
Extreme High (°F)	89	97	100	100	103	105	106	108	103	98	94	90	108
Average High (°F)	62	66	74	80	86	92	95	95	90	82	71	64	80
Average Temp. (°F)	51	55	62	70	76	82	85	85	80	71	60	53	69
Average Low (°F)	39	43	50	58	66	72	74	74	69	59	49	41	58
Extreme Low (°F)	0	6	19	31	43	53	62	61	46	33	21	6	0

Note: Figures cover the years 1948-1990
Source: National Climatic Data Center, International Station Meteorological Climate Summary, 9/96

Average Precipitation/Snowfall/Humidity

Precip./Humidity	Jan	Feb	Mar	Apr	May	Jun	Jul	Aug	Sep	Oct	Nov	Dec	Yr.
Avg. Precip. (in.)	1.5	1.8	1.5	2.6	3.8	3.6	2.0	2.5	3.3	3.2	2.3	1.4	29.6
Avg. Snowfall (in.)	1	Tr	Tr	0	0	0	0	0	0	0	Tr	Tr	1
Avg. Rel. Hum. 6am (%)	79	80	79	82	87	87	87	86	85	83	81	79	83
Avg. Rel. Hum. 3pm (%)	51	48	45	48	51	48	43	42	47	46	48	49	47

Note: Figures cover the years 1948-1990; Tr = Trace amounts (<0.05 in. of rain; <0.5 in. of snow)
Source: National Climatic Data Center, International Station Meteorological Climate Summary, 9/96

Weather Conditions

Temperature			Daytime Sky			Precipitation		
32°F & below	45°F & below	90°F & above	Clear	Partly cloudy	Cloudy	0.01 inch or more precip.	0.1 inch or more snow/ice	Thunder-storms
23	91	112	97	153	115	81	1	36

Note: Figures are average number of days per year and cover the years 1948-1990
Source: National Climatic Data Center, International Station Meteorological Climate Summary, 9/96

HAZARDOUS WASTE

Superfund Sites

The San Antonio-New Braunfels, TX metro area is home to three sites on the EPA's Superfund National Priorities List: **Bandera Road Ground Water Plume** (final); **Eldorado Chemical Co., Inc.** (final); **R & H Oil/Tropicana** (proposed). There are a total of 1,165 Superfund sites with a status of proposed or final on the list in the U.S. *U.S. Environmental Protection Agency, National Priorities List, April 12, 2023*

AIR QUALITY

Air Quality Trends: Ozone

	1990	1995	2000	2005	2010	2015	2018	2019	2020	2021
MSA[1]	0.090	0.095	0.078	0.084	0.072	0.079	0.072	0.075	0.069	0.070
U.S.	0.087	0.089	0.081	0.080	0.072	0.067	0.069	0.065	0.065	0.067

Note: (1) Data covers the San Antonio-New Braunfels, TX Metropolitan Statistical Area. The values shown are the composite ozone concentration averages among trend sites based on the highest fourth daily maximum 8-hour concentration in parts per million. These trends are based on sites having an adequate record of monitoring data during the trend period. Data from exceptional events are included.
Source: U.S. Environmental Protection Agency, Air Quality Monitoring Information, "Air Quality Trends by City, 1990-2021"

Air Quality Index

Area	Percent of Days when Air Quality was...[2]					AQI Statistics[2]	
	Good	Moderate	Unhealthy for Sensitive Groups	Unhealthy	Very Unhealthy	Maximum	Median
MSA[1]	54.5	42.2	3.3	0.0	0.0	147	48

Note: (1) Data covers the San Antonio-New Braunfels, TX Metropolitan Statistical Area; (2) Based on 365 days with AQI data in 2021. Air Quality Index (AQI) is an index for reporting daily air quality. EPA calculates the AQI for five major air pollutants regulated by the Clean Air Act: ground-level ozone, particle pollution (aka particulate matter), carbon monoxide, sulfur dioxide, and nitrogen dioxide. The AQI runs from 0 to 500. The higher the AQI value, the greater the level of air pollution and the greater the health concern. There are six AQI categories: "Good" AQI is between 0 and 50. Air quality is considered satisfactory; "Moderate" AQI is between 51 and 100. Air quality is acceptable; "Unhealthy for Sensitive Groups" When AQI values are between 101 and 150, members of sensitive groups may experience health effects; "Unhealthy" When AQI values are between 151 and 200 everyone may begin to experience health effects; "Very Unhealthy" AQI values between 201 and 300 trigger a health alert; "Hazardous" AQI values over 300 trigger warnings of emergency conditions (not shown).
Source: U.S. Environmental Protection Agency, Air Quality Index Report, 2021

Air Quality Index Pollutants

Area	Percent of Days when AQI Pollutant was...[2]						
	Carbon Monoxide	Nitrogen Dioxide	Ozone	Sulfur Dioxide	Particulate Matter 2.5	Particulate Matter 10
MSA[1]	0.0	0.3	44.9	(3)	54.2	0.5

Note: (1) Data covers the San Antonio-New Braunfels, TX Metropolitan Statistical Area; (2) Based on 365 days with AQI data in 2021. The Air Quality Index (AQI) is an index for reporting daily air quality. EPA calculates the AQI for five major air pollutants regulated by the Clean Air Act: ground-level ozone, particle pollution (also known as particulate matter), carbon monoxide, sulfur dioxide, and nitrogen dioxide. The AQI runs from 0 to 500. The higher the AQI value, the greater the level of air pollution and the greater the health concern; (3) Sulfur dioxide is no longer included in this table (as of December 8, 2021) because SO_2 concentrations tend to be very localized and not necessarily representative of broad geographical areas like counties and CBSAs.
Source: U.S. Environmental Protection Agency, Air Quality Index Report, 2021

Maximum Air Pollutant Concentrations: Particulate Matter, Ozone, CO and Lead

	Particulate Matter 10 (ug/m^3)	Particulate Matter 2.5 Wtd AM (ug/m^3)	Particulate Matter 2.5 24-Hr (ug/m^3)	Ozone (ppm)	Carbon Monoxide (ppm)	Lead (ug/m^3)
MSA[1] Level	87	8.9	22	0.078	1	n/a
NAAQS[2]	150	15	35	0.075	9	0.15
Met NAAQS[2]	Yes	Yes	Yes	No	Yes	n/a

Note: (1) Data covers the San Antonio-New Braunfels, TX Metropolitan Statistical Area; Data from exceptional events are included; (2) National Ambient Air Quality Standards; ppm = parts per million; ug/m^3 = micrograms per cubic meter; n/a not available.
Concentrations: Particulate Matter 10 (coarse particulate)—highest second maximum 24-hour concentration; Particulate Matter 2.5 Wtd AM (fine particulate)—highest weighted annual mean concentration; Particulate Matter 2.5 24-Hour (fine particulate)—highest 98th percentile 24-hour concentration; Ozone—highest fourth daily maximum 8-hour concentration; Carbon Monoxide—highest second maximum non-overlapping 8-hour concentration; Lead—maximum running 3-month average
Source: U.S. Environmental Protection Agency, Air Quality Monitoring Information, "Air Quality Statistics by City, 2021"

Maximum Air Pollutant Concentrations: Nitrogen Dioxide and Sulfur Dioxide

	Nitrogen Dioxide AM (ppb)	Nitrogen Dioxide 1-Hr (ppb)	Sulfur Dioxide AM (ppb)	Sulfur Dioxide 1-Hr (ppb)	Sulfur Dioxide 24-Hr (ppb)
MSA[1] Level	7	32	n/a	3	n/a
NAAQS[2]	53	100	30	75	140
Met NAAQS[2]	Yes	Yes	n/a	Yes	n/a

Note: (1) Data covers the San Antonio-New Braunfels, TX Metropolitan Statistical Area; Data from exceptional events are included; (2) National Ambient Air Quality Standards; ppm = parts per million; ug/m^3 = micrograms per cubic meter; n/a not available.
Concentrations: Nitrogen Dioxide AM—highest arithmetic mean concentration; Nitrogen Dioxide 1-Hr—highest 98th percentile 1-hour daily maximum concentration; Sulfur Dioxide AM—highest annual mean concentration; Sulfur Dioxide 1-Hr—highest 99th percentile 1-hour daily maximum concentration; Sulfur Dioxide 24-Hr—highest second maximum 24-hour concentration
Source: U.S. Environmental Protection Agency, Air Quality Monitoring Information, "Air Quality Statistics by City, 2021"

Savannah, Georgia

Background

Savannah sits at the mouth of the Savannah River on the border between Georgia and South Carolina. It was established in 1733 when General James Oglethorpe landed with a group of settlers in the sailing vessel *Anne*, after a voyage of more than three months. City Hall now stands at the spot where Oglethorpe and his followers first camped on a small bluff overlooking the river.

Savannah is unique among American cities in that it was extensively planned while Oglethorpe was still in England. Each new settler was given a package of property, including a town lot, a garden space, and an outlying farm area. The town was planned in quadrants, the north and south for residences, and the east and west for public buildings.

The quadrant design was inspired in part by considerations of public defense, given the unsettled character of relations with Native Americans. In fact, an early treaty between the settlers and the Creek Indian Chief Tomochichi allowed Savannah to develop quite peacefully, with little of the hostility between Europeans and Indians that marred much of the development elsewhere in the colonies.

Savannah was taken by the British during the American Revolution and, in the patriotic siege that followed, many lives were lost. Savannah was eventually retaken in 1782 by the American Generals Nathaniel Greene and Anthony Wayne. In the post-Revolutionary period, Savannah grew dramatically, its economic strength being driven in large part by Eli Whitney's cotton gin. As the world's leader in the cotton trade, Savannah also hosted a great development in export activity, and the first American steamboat built in the United States to cross the Atlantic was launched in its busy port.

Savannah's physical structure had been saved from the worst ravages of war, but the destruction of the area's infrastructure slowed its further development for an extended period. In the long period of slow recovery that followed, the Girl Scouts was established in the city in 1912 by Juliette Gordeon Low—a true Savannah success story.

In 1954, an extensive fire destroyed a large portion of the historic City Market, and the area was bulldozed to make room for a parking garage. The Historic Savannah Foundation has worked continuously since to maintain and improve Savannah's considerable architectural charms. As a result, Savannah's Historic District was designated a Registered National Historic Landmark, and the city has been a favored site for movie makers for decades. More than forty major movies have been filmed in Savannah including *Roots* (1976), *East of Eden* (1980), *Forrest Gump* (1994), *Midnight in the Garden of Good and Evil* (1997) and *The Legend of Bagger Vance* (2000), and a segment of the Colbert Report (2005).

The Port of Savannah, manufacturing, the military, and tourism are the city's major economic drivers in the twenty-first century. Its port facilities, operated by the Georgia Ports Authority, have seen notable growth in container tonnage in recent years. Garden City Terminal is the fourth largest container port in the United States, and the largest single-terminal operation in North America. In 2019, a second passenger airport, Paine Field, opened for business. Military installations in the area include Hunter Army Airfield and Fort Stewart military bases, employing nearly 50,000.

Museums include Juliette Gordon Low Museum, Flannery O'Connor Childhood Home/Museum, Telfair Museum of Art, and the Mighty 8th Air Force Museum. Savannah hosted the sailing competitions during the 1996 Summer Olympics held in Atlanta, and the Savannah Book Festival is a popular annual fair held on President's Day weekend. Football's XFL league resumed play in the city in 2022.

The city's beauty draws not just tourists, but conventioneers. The Savannah International Trade & Convention Center is a state-of-the-art facility with more than 100,000 square feet of exhibition space, accommodating nearly 10,000 people.

Colleges and universities in the city include the Savannah College of Art and Design, Savannah State University, and South University.

Savannah's climate is subtropical and is at risk for hurricanes. With hot summers and mild winters, however, the city is ideal for all-year outside activities.

Rankings

General Rankings

- Savannah appeared on *Travel + Leisure's* list of "The 15 Best Cities in the United States." The city was ranked #4. Criteria: sights/landmarks; culture; food; friendliness; shopping; and overall value. *Travel + Leisure, "The World's Best Awards 2022" July 12, 2022*

- For its 35th annual "Readers' Choice Awards" survey, *Condé Nast Traveler* ranked its readers' favorite cities in the U.S. Whether it be a longed-for visit or a first on the list, these are the places that inspired a return to travel. The list was broken into large cities and cities under 250,000. Savannah ranked #5 in the small city category. *Condé Nast Traveler, Readers' Choice Awards 2022, "Best Small Cities in the U.S." October 4, 2022*

Business/Finance Rankings

- Savannah was cited as one of America's top metros for total major capital investment facility projects in 2022. The area ranked #9 in the mid-sized metro area category (population 200,000 to 1 million). *Site Selection, "Top Metros of 2022," March 2023*

- The Savannah metro area appeared on the Milken Institute "2022 Best Performing Cities" list. Rank: #78 out of 200 large metro areas (population over 250,000). Criteria: job growth; wage and salary growth; high-tech output growth; housing affordability; household broadband access. *Milken Institute, "Best-Performing Cities 2022," March 28, 2022*

- *Forbes* ranked the 200 most populous metro areas to determine the nation's "Best Places for Business and Careers." The Savannah metro area was ranked #74. Criteria: costs (business and living); job growth (past and projected); income growth; quality of life; educational attainment (college and high school); projected economic growth; cultural and leisure opportunities; workplace tolerance laws; net migration patterns. *Forbes, "The Best Places for Business and Careers 2019: Seattle Still On Top," October 30, 2019*

Children/Family Rankings

- Savannah was selected as one of the most playful cities in the U.S. by KaBOOM! The organization's Playful City USA initiative honors cities and towns across the nation that have made their communities more playable. Criteria: pledging to integrate play as a solution to challenges in their communities; making it easy for children to get active and balanced play; creating more family-friendly and innovative communities as a result. *KaBOOM! National Campaign for Play, "2017 Playful City USA Communities"*

Culture/Performing Arts Rankings

- Savannah was selected as one of the ten best small North American cities and towns for moviemakers. Of cities with smaller populations, the area ranked #3. As with the 2023 list for bigger cities, the philosophy of freedom to pursue filmmaking dreams were highly factored in. Other criteria: film community and culture; access to equipment and facilities; affordability; tax incentives; and quality of life. *MovieMaker Magazine, "Best Places to Live and Work as a Moviemaker, 2023," January 18, 2023*

- Savannah was selected as one of "America's Favorite Cities." The city ranked #2 in the "Architecture" category. Respondents to an online survey were asked to rate their favorite place (population over 100,000) in over 65 categories. *Travelandleisure.com, "America's Favorite Cities for Architecture 2016," March 2, 2017*

Education Rankings

- Personal finance website *WalletHub* analyzed the 150 largest U.S. metropolitan statistical areas to determine where the most educated Americans are putting their degrees to work. Criteria: education levels; percentage of workers with degrees; education quality and attainment gap; public school quality rankings; quality and enrollment of each metro area's universities. Savannah was ranked #83 (#1 = most educated city). *www.WalletHub.com, "Most & Least Educated Cities in America," July 18, 2022*

Environmental Rankings

- Savannah was highlighted as one of the cleanest metro areas for ozone air pollution in the U.S. during 2019 through 2021. The list represents cities with no monitored ozone air pollution in unhealthful ranges. *American Lung Association, "State of the Air 2023," April 19, 2023*

Safety Rankings

- Allstate ranked the 200 largest cities in America in terms of driver safety. Savannah ranked #157. Criteria: internal property damage claims over a two-year period from January 2016 to December 2017. The report helps increase the importance of safety and awareness behind the wheel. *Allstate, "Allstate America's Best Drivers Report, 2019" June 24, 2019*

- The National Insurance Crime Bureau ranked 390 metro areas in the U.S. in terms of per capita rates of vehicle theft. The Savannah metro area ranked #103 (#1 = highest rate). Criteria: number of vehicle theft offenses per 100,000 inhabitants in 2021. *National Insurance Crime Bureau, "Hot Spots 2021," September 1, 2022*

Seniors/Retirement Rankings

- From its Best Cities for Successful Aging indexes, the Milken Institute generated rankings for metropolitan areas, weighing data in nine categories—health care, wellness, living arrangements, transportation and convenience, financial characteristics, education, employment, community engagement, and overall livability. The Savannah metro area was ranked #99 overall in the small metro area category. *Milken Institute, "Best Cities for Successful Aging, 2017" March 14, 2017*

- Savannah made the 2022 *Forbes* list of "25 Best Places to Retire." Criteria, focused on overall affordability as well as quality of life indicators, include: housing/living costs compared to the national average and state taxes; air quality; crime rates; home price appreciation; risk associated with climate-change/natural hazards; availability of medical care; bikeability; walkability; healthy living. *Forbes.com, "The Best Places to Retire in 2022," May 13, 2022*

Miscellaneous Rankings

- Despite the freedom to now travel internationally, plugged-in travel influencers and experts continue to rediscover their local regions. Savannah appeared on a *Forbes* list of places in the U.S. that provide solace as well as local inspiration. Whether it be quirky things to see and do, delicious take out, outdoor exploring and daytrips, these places are must-see destinations. *Forbes, "The Best Places To Travel In The U.S. In 2023, According To The Experts," April 13, 2023*

- In its roundup of St. Patrick's Day parades "Gayot" listed the best festivals and parades of all things Irish. The festivities in Savannah as among the best in North America. *www.gayot.com, "Best St. Patrick's Day Parades," March 2023*

- In *Condé Nast Traveler* magazine's 2022 Readers' Choice Survey, Savannah made the top ten list of friendliest American cities. Savannah ranked #1. *www.cntraveler.com, "The 10 Friendliest Cities in the U.S.," December 20, 2022*

Business Environment

DEMOGRAPHICS

Population Growth

Area	1990 Census	2000 Census	2010 Census	2020 Census	Population Growth (%) 1990-2020	Population Growth (%) 2010-2020
City	138,038	131,510	136,286	147,780	7.1	8.4
MSA[1]	258,060	293,000	347,611	404,798	56.9	16.5
U.S.	248,709,873	281,421,906	308,745,538	331,449,281	33.3	7.4

Note: (1) Figures cover the Savannah, GA Metropolitan Statistical Area
Source: U.S. Census Bureau, 1990 Census, 2000 Census, 2010 Census, 2020 Census

Race

Area	White Alone[2] (%)	Black Alone[2] (%)	Asian Alone[2] (%)	AIAN[3] Alone[2] (%)	NHOPI[4] Alone[2] (%)	Other Race Alone[2] (%)	Two or More Races (%)
City	37.9	49.1	3.8	0.3	0.2	3.1	5.5
MSA[1]	55.6	30.8	3.1	0.4	0.1	3.4	6.6
U.S.	61.6	12.4	6.0	1.1	0.2	8.4	10.2

Note: (1) Figures cover the Savannah, GA Metropolitan Statistical Area; (2) Alone is defined as not being in combination with one or more other races; (3) American Indian and Alaska Native; (4) Native Hawaiian and Other Pacific Islander
Source: U.S. Census Bureau, 2020 Census

Hispanic or Latino Origin

Area	Total (%)	Mexican (%)	Puerto Rican (%)	Cuban (%)	Other (%)
City	6.5	2.1	2.0	0.4	2.0
MSA[1]	6.5	2.9	1.6	0.5	1.6
U.S.	18.4	11.2	1.8	0.7	4.7

Note: Persons of Hispanic or Latino origin can be of any race; (1) Figures cover the Savannah, GA Metropolitan Statistical Area
Source: U.S. Census Bureau, 2017-2021 American Community Survey 5-Year Estimates

Age

Area	Under Age 5	Age 5–19	Age 20–34	Age 35–44	Age 45–54	Age 55–64	Age 65–74	Age 75–84	Age 85+	Median Age
City	5.8	18.4	28.0	12.2	10.2	11.2	8.6	4.0	1.6	33.5
MSA[1]	5.9	19.7	22.5	13.0	11.7	12.2	9.3	4.3	1.5	36.3
U.S.	5.6	19.2	20.2	12.7	12.4	13.1	10.0	4.9	1.9	38.8

Note: (1) Figures cover the Savannah, GA Metropolitan Statistical Area
Source: U.S. Census Bureau, 2020 Census

Disability by Age

Area	All Ages	Under 18 Years Old	18 to 64 Years Old	65 Years and Over
City	15.7	6.4	13.1	42.3
MSA[1]	14.2	4.9	12.5	36.6
U.S.	12.6	4.4	10.3	33.4

Note: Figures show percent of the civilian noninstitutionalized population that reported having a disability. Disability status is determined from six types of difficulty: vision, hearing, cognitive, ambulatory, self-care, and independent living. For children under 5 years old, hearing and vision difficulty are used to determine disability status. For children between the ages of 5 and 14, disability status is determined from hearing, vision, cognitive, ambulatory, and self-care difficulties. For people aged 15 years and older, they are considered to have a disability if they have difficulty with any one of the six difficulty types; Note: (1) Figures cover the Savannah, GA Metropolitan Statistical Area
Source: U.S. Census Bureau, 2017-2021 American Community Survey 5-Year Estimates

Ancestry

Area	German	Irish	English	American	Italian	Polish	French[2]	Scottish	Dutch
City	6.5	7.6	5.4	4.0	3.1	1.5	1.6	1.3	0.6
MSA[1]	9.1	9.9	8.7	7.4	3.5	1.4	1.7	1.7	0.6
U.S.	12.8	9.6	8.1	5.7	5.0	2.7	2.2	1.6	1.1

Note: Figures are the percentage of the total population reporting a particular ancestry. The nine most commonly reported ancestries in the U.S. are shown. Figures include multiple ancestries (e.g. if a person reported being Irish and Italian, they were included in both columns); (1) Figures cover the Savannah, GA Metropolitan Statistical Area; (2) Excludes Basque
Source: U.S. Census Bureau, 2017-2021 American Community Survey 5-Year Estimates

Foreign-born Population

Area	Any Foreign Country	Asia	Mexico	Europe	Caribbean	Central America[2]	South America	Africa	Canada
City	6.1	2.5	0.8	0.8	0.5	0.5	0.5	0.3	0.2
MSA[1]	6.0	1.9	1.2	1.0	0.6	0.3	0.4	0.3	0.2
U.S.	13.6	4.2	3.3	1.5	1.4	1.1	1.1	0.8	0.2

Note: (1) Figures cover the Savannah, GA Metropolitan Statistical Area; (2) Excludes Mexico.
Source: U.S. Census Bureau, 2017-2021 American Community Survey 5-Year Estimates

Household Size

Area	One	Two	Three	Four	Five	Six	Seven or More	Average Household Size
City	32.8	35.5	15.2	9.6	4.6	1.4	0.9	2.50
MSA[1]	28.0	36.7	15.9	12.2	4.8	1.5	0.9	2.60
U.S.	28.1	33.8	15.5	12.9	6.0	2.3	1.4	2.60

Note: (1) Figures cover the Savannah, GA Metropolitan Statistical Area
Source: U.S. Census Bureau, 2017-2021 American Community Survey 5-Year Estimates

Household Relationships

Area	House-holder	Opposite-sex Spouse	Same-sex Spouse	Opposite-sex Unmarried Partner	Same-sex Unmarried Partner	Child[2]	Grand-child	Other Relatives	Non-relatives
City	39.9	11.2	0.3	2.7	0.3	24.9	3.2	4.4	5.0
MSA[1]	38.7	16.6	0.2	2.4	0.2	28.0	2.8	4.1	3.4
U.S.	38.3	17.5	0.2	2.5	0.2	28.3	2.4	4.8	3.4

Note: Figures are percent of the total population; (1) Figures cover the Savannah, GA Metropolitan Statistical Area; (2) Includes biological, adopted, and stepchildren of the householder
Source: U.S. Census Bureau, 2020 Census

Gender

Area	Males	Females	Males per 100 Females
City	69,878	77,902	89.7
MSA[1]	194,814	209,984	92.8
U.S.	162,685,811	168,763,470	96.4

Note: (1) Figures cover the Savannah, GA Metropolitan Statistical Area
Source: U.S. Census Bureau, 2020 Census

Marital Status

Area	Never Married	Now Married[2]	Separated	Widowed	Divorced
City	47.5	32.1	2.6	5.6	12.2
MSA[1]	35.7	45.2	2.3	5.3	11.7
U.S.	33.8	48.0	1.8	5.6	10.8

Note: Figures are percentages and cover the population 15 years of age and older; (1) Figures cover the Savannah, GA Metropolitan Statistical Area; (2) Excludes separated
Source: U.S. Census Bureau, 2017-2021 American Community Survey 5-Year Estimates

Religious Groups by Family

Area	Catholic	Baptist	Methodist	LDS[2]	Pentecostal	Lutheran	Islam	Adventist	Other
MSA[1]	5.5	11.9	4.8	0.8	1.5	1.1	0.2	1.4	12.3
U.S.	18.7	7.3	3.0	2.0	1.8	1.7	1.3	1.3	11.6

Note: Figures are the number of adherents as a percentage of the total population and cover the eight largest religious groups in the U.S; (1) Figures cover the Savannah, GA Metropolitan Statistical Area; (2) Church of Jesus Christ of Latter-day Saints
Sources: 2020 U.S. Religion Census, Association of Statisticians of American Religious Bodies; The Association of Religion Data Archives (ARDA)

Religious Groups by Tradition

Area	Catholic	Evangelical Protestant	Mainline Protestant	Black Protestant	Islam	Judaism	Hinduism	Orthodox	Buddhism
MSA[1]	5.5	19.0	5.7	5.9	0.2	0.7	0.5	0.1	n/a
U.S.	18.7	16.5	5.2	2.3	1.3	0.6	0.4	0.4	0.3

Note: Figures are the number of adherents as a percentage of the total population; (1) Figures cover the Savannah, GA Metropolitan Statistical Area
Sources: 2020 U.S. Religion Census, Association of Statisticians of American Religious Bodies; The Association of Religion Data Archives (ARDA)

ECONOMY

Gross Metropolitan Product

Area	2020	2021	2022	2023	Rank[2]
MSA[1]	22.0	25.3	27.7	28.7	122

Note: Figures are in billions of dollars; (1) Figures cover the Savannah, GA Metropolitan Statistical Area; (2) Rank is based on 2021 data and ranges from 1 to 381
Source: U.S. Conference of Mayors, U.S. Metro Economies: U.S. Metros Compared to Global and State Economies, June 2022

Economic Growth

Area	2018-20 (%)	2021 (%)	2022 (%)	2023 (%)	Rank[2]
MSA[1]	-1.6	10.3	4.8	0.1	262
U.S.	-0.6	5.7	3.1	2.9	—

Note: Figures are real gross metropolitan product (GMP) growth rates and represent average annual percent change; (1) Figures cover the Savannah, GA Metropolitan Statistical Area; (2) Rank is based on 2020 2-year average annual percent change and ranges from 1 to 381
Source: U.S. Conference of Mayors, U.S. Metro Economies: U.S. Metros Compared to Global and State Economies, June 2022

Metropolitan Area Exports

Area	2016	2017	2018	2019	2020	2021	Rank[2]
MSA[1]	4,263.4	4,472.0	5,407.8	4,925.5	4,557.0	5,520.5	55

Note: Figures are in millions of dollars; (1) Figures cover the Savannah, GA Metropolitan Statistical Area; (2) Rank is based on 2021 data and ranges from 1 to 388
Source: U.S. Department of Commerce, International Trade Administration, Office of Trade and Economic Analysis, Industry and Analysis, Exports by Metropolitan Area, data extracted March 16, 2023

Building Permits

Area	Single-Family 2021	Single-Family 2022	Pct. Chg.	Multi-Family 2021	Multi-Family 2022	Pct. Chg.	Total 2021	Total 2022	Pct. Chg.
City	487	408	-16.2	5	24	380.0	492	432	-12.2
MSA[1]	2,752	2,228	-19.0	475	966	103.4	3,227	3,194	-1.0
U.S.	1,115,400	975,600	-12.5	621,600	689,500	10.9	1,737,000	1,665,100	-4.1

Note: (1) Figures cover the Savannah, GA Metropolitan Statistical Area; Figures represent new, privately-owned housing units authorized (unadjusted data); All permit data are based on estimates with imputation
Source: U.S. Census Bureau, Manufacturing, Mining, and Construction Statistics, Building Permits, 2021, 2022

Bankruptcy Filings

Area	Business Filings 2021	Business Filings 2022	% Chg.	Nonbusiness Filings 2021	Nonbusiness Filings 2022	% Chg.
Chatham County	9	7	-22.2	546	591	8.2
U.S.	14,347	13,481	-6.0	399,269	374,240	-6.3

Note: Business filings include Chapter 7, Chapter 9, Chapter 11, Chapter 12, Chapter 13, Chapter 15, and Section 304; Nonbusiness filings include Chapter 7, Chapter 11, and Chapter 13
Source: Administrative Office of the U.S. Courts, Business and Nonbusiness Bankruptcy, County Cases Commenced by Chapter of the Bankruptcy Code, During the 12-Month Period Ending December 31, 2021 and Business and Nonbusiness Bankruptcy, County Cases Commenced by Chapter of the Bankruptcy Code, During the 12-Month Period Ending December 31, 2022

Housing Vacancy Rates

Area	Gross Vacancy Rate[2] (%) 2020	2021	2022	Year-Round Vacancy Rate[3] (%) 2020	2021	2022	Rental Vacancy Rate[4] (%) 2020	2021	2022	Homeowner Vacancy Rate[5] (%) 2020	2021	2022
MSA[1]	n/a	n/a	n/a	n/a	n/a	n/a	n/a	n/a	n/a	n/a	n/a	n/a
U.S.	10.6	10.8	10.5	8.2	8.4	8.2	6.3	6.1	5.8	1.0	0.9	0.8

Note: (1) Figures cover the Savannah, GA Metropolitan Statistical Area; (2) The percentage of the total housing inventory that is vacant; (3) The percentage of the housing inventory (excluding seasonal units) that is year-round vacant; (4) The percentage of rental inventory that is vacant for rent; (5) The percentage of homeowner inventory that is vacant for sale; n/a not available
Source: U.S. Census Bureau, Housing Vacancies and Homeownership Annual Statistics: 2020, 2021, 2022

INCOME

Income

Area	Per Capita ($)	Median Household ($)	Average Household ($)
City	27,952	49,832	69,653
MSA[1]	34,908	64,703	89,172
U.S.	37,638	69,021	97,196

Note: (1) Figures cover the Savannah, GA Metropolitan Statistical Area
Source: U.S. Census Bureau, 2017-2021 American Community Survey 5-Year Estimates

Savannah, Georgia

Household Income Distribution

Area	Under $15,000	$15,000 -$24,999	$25,000 -$34,999	$35,000 -$49,999	$50,000 -$74,999	$75,000 -$99,999	$100,000 -$149,999	$150,000 and up
City	14.7	11.5	10.4	13.6	18.3	11.2	11.7	8.6
MSA[1]	9.4	7.9	8.6	12.0	18.6	14.1	15.9	13.5
U.S.	9.4	7.8	8.2	11.4	16.8	12.8	16.3	17.3

Note: (1) Figures cover the Savannah, GA Metropolitan Statistical Area
Source: U.S. Census Bureau, 2017-2021 American Community Survey 5-Year Estimates

Poverty Rate

Area	All Ages	Under 18 Years Old	18 to 64 Years Old	65 Years and Over
City	19.8	29.7	18.1	12.1
MSA[1]	12.5	17.5	11.5	8.6
U.S.	12.6	17.0	11.8	9.6

Note: Figures are percentage of people whose income during the past 12 months was below the poverty level; (1) Figures cover the Savannah, GA Metropolitan Statistical Area
Source: U.S. Census Bureau, 2017-2021 American Community Survey 5-Year Estimates

EMPLOYMENT

Labor Force and Employment

Area	Civilian Labor Force Dec. 2021	Civilian Labor Force Dec. 2022	% Chg.	Workers Employed Dec. 2021	Workers Employed Dec. 2022	% Chg.
City	69,179	68,684	-0.7	66,698	66,661	-0.1
MSA[1]	199,752	198,853	-0.5	194,065	193,933	-0.1
U.S.	161,696,000	164,224,000	1.6	155,732,000	158,872,000	2.0

Note: Data is not seasonally adjusted and covers workers 16 years of age and older; (1) Figures cover the Savannah, GA Metropolitan Statistical Area
Source: Bureau of Labor Statistics, Local Area Unemployment Statistics

Unemployment Rate

Area	Jan.	Feb.	Mar.	Apr.	May	Jun.	Jul.	Aug.	Sep.	Oct.	Nov.	Dec.
City	4.2	4.0	4.1	3.1	3.2	3.8	3.3	3.5	3.0	3.4	3.1	2.9
MSA[1]	3.3	3.2	3.2	2.4	2.6	3.1	2.7	2.9	2.5	2.9	2.6	2.5
U.S.	4.4	4.1	3.8	3.3	3.4	3.8	3.8	3.8	3.3	3.4	3.4	3.3

Note: Data is not seasonally adjusted and covers workers 16 years of age and older; (1) Figures cover the Savannah, GA Metropolitan Statistical Area
Source: Bureau of Labor Statistics, Local Area Unemployment Statistics

Average Wages

Occupation	$/Hr.	Occupation	$/Hr.
Accountants and Auditors	37.20	Maintenance and Repair Workers	20.32
Automotive Mechanics	21.80	Marketing Managers	68.95
Bookkeepers	21.94	Network and Computer Systems Admin.	44.17
Carpenters	22.17	Nurses, Licensed Practical	24.10
Cashiers	12.01	Nurses, Registered	40.41
Computer Programmers	40.03	Nursing Assistants	14.89
Computer Systems Analysts	51.98	Office Clerks, General	18.02
Computer User Support Specialists	26.01	Physical Therapists	45.44
Construction Laborers	17.96	Physicians	100.61
Cooks, Restaurant	15.06	Plumbers, Pipefitters and Steamfitters	28.19
Customer Service Representatives	16.30	Police and Sheriff's Patrol Officers	25.28
Dentists	n/a	Postal Service Mail Carriers	26.97
Electricians	25.68	Real Estate Sales Agents	23.15
Engineers, Electrical	56.50	Retail Salespersons	14.40
Fast Food and Counter Workers	11.64	Sales Representatives, Technical/Scientific	40.36
Financial Managers	71.42	Secretaries, Exc. Legal/Medical/Executive	18.89
First-Line Supervisors of Office Workers	27.26	Security Guards	15.54
General and Operations Managers	51.37	Surgeons	n/a
Hairdressers/Cosmetologists	16.53	Teacher Assistants, Exc. Postsecondary*	15.18
Home Health and Personal Care Aides	12.70	Teachers, Secondary School, Exc. Sp. Ed.*	29.79
Janitors and Cleaners	14.18	Telemarketers	n/a
Landscaping/Groundskeeping Workers	15.94	Truck Drivers, Heavy/Tractor-Trailer	24.85
Lawyers	n/a	Truck Drivers, Light/Delivery Services	20.20
Maids and Housekeeping Cleaners	11.85	Waiters and Waitresses	13.87

Note: Wage data covers the Savannah, GA Metropolitan Statistical Area; (*) Hourly wages were calculated from annual wage data based on a 40 hour work week; n/a not available.
Source: Bureau of Labor Statistics, Metro Area Occupational Employment & Wage Estimates, May 2022

Employment by Industry

Sector	MSA[1] Number of Employees	MSA[1] Percent of Total	U.S. Percent of Total
Construction, Mining, and Logging	9,400	4.7	5.4
Private Education and Health Services	28,500	14.1	16.1
Financial Activities	7,000	3.5	5.9
Government	23,800	11.8	14.5
Information	1,700	0.8	2.0
Leisure and Hospitality	27,700	13.7	10.3
Manufacturing	19,700	9.8	8.4
Other Services	8,100	4.0	3.7
Professional and Business Services	25,400	12.6	14.7
Retail Trade	24,200	12.0	10.2
Transportation, Warehousing, and Utilities	19,100	9.5	4.9
Wholesale Trade	7,100	3.5	3.9

Note: Figures are non-farm employment as of December 2022. Figures are not seasonally adjusted and include workers 16 years of age and older; (1) Figures cover the Savannah, GA Metropolitan Statistical Area
Source: Bureau of Labor Statistics, Current Employment Statistics, Employment, Hours, and Earnings

Employment by Occupation

Occupation Classification	City (%)	MSA[1] (%)	U.S. (%)
Management, Business, Science, and Arts	34.2	38.1	40.3
Natural Resources, Construction, and Maintenance	5.7	7.9	8.7
Production, Transportation, and Material Moving	14.2	14.3	13.1
Sales and Office	21.5	21.1	20.9
Service	24.4	18.5	17.0

Note: Figures cover employed civilians 16 years of age and older; (1) Figures cover the Savannah, GA Metropolitan Statistical Area
Source: U.S. Census Bureau, 2017-2021 American Community Survey 5-Year Estimates

Occupations with Greatest Projected Employment Growth: 2022 – 2024

Occupation[1]	2022 Employment	2024 Projected Employment	Numeric Employment Change	Percent Employment Change
Laborers and Freight, Stock, and Material Movers, Hand	124,130	131,700	7,570	6.1
Retail Salespersons	139,030	146,370	7,340	5.3
Industrial Truck and Tractor Operators	48,230	54,230	6,000	12.4
General and Operations Managers	95,580	101,230	5,650	5.9
Fast Food and Counter Workers	116,760	122,340	5,580	4.8
Stockers and Order Fillers	73,270	78,260	4,990	6.8
Software Developers and Software Quality Assurance Analysts and Testers	58,710	63,610	4,900	8.3
Cooks, Restaurant	42,420	47,160	4,740	11.2
Heavy and Tractor-Trailer Truck Drivers	68,660	73,100	4,440	6.5
Project Management Specialists and Business Operations Specialists, All Other	93,000	97,320	4,320	4.6

Note: Projections cover Georgia; (1) Sorted by numeric employment change
Source: www.projectionscentral.com, State Occupational Projections, 2022–2024 Short-Term Projections

Fastest-Growing Occupations: 2022 – 2024

Occupation[1]	2022 Employment	2024 Projected Employment	Numeric Employment Change	Percent Employment Change
Musicians and Singers	710	850	140	19.7
Amusement and Recreation Attendants	6,720	8,030	1,310	19.5
Reservation and Transportation Ticket Agents and Travel Clerks	4,000	4,710	710	17.8
Fitness Trainers and Aerobics Instructors	4,620	5,420	800	17.3
Manicurists and Pedicurists	1,810	2,120	310	17.1
Hotel, Motel, and Resort Desk Clerks	7,700	9,000	1,300	16.9
Machine Feeders and Offbearers	3,020	3,490	470	15.6
Massage Therapists	2,980	3,430	450	15.1
Skincare Specialists	1,730	1,990	260	15.0
Parking Lot Attendants	2,820	3,240	420	14.9

Note: Projections cover Georgia; (1) Sorted by percent employment change and excludes occupations with numeric employment change less than 50
Source: www.projectionscentral.com, State Occupational Projections, 2022–2024 Short-Term Projections

Savannah, Georgia

CITY FINANCES

City Government Finances

Component	2020 ($000)	2020 ($ per capita)
Total Revenues	553,786	3,833
Total Expenditures	440,458	3,049
Debt Outstanding	261,914	1,813
Cash and Securities[1]	736,657	5,099

Note: (1) Cash and security holdings of a government at the close of its fiscal year, including those of its dependent agencies, utilities, and liquor stores.
Source: U.S. Census Bureau, State & Local Government Finances 2020

City Government Revenue by Source

Source	2020 ($000)	2020 ($ per capita)	2020 (%)
General Revenue			
From Federal Government	22,376	155	4.0
From State Government	3,227	22	0.6
From Local Governments	87,791	608	15.9
Taxes			
Property	78,126	541	14.1
Sales and Gross Receipts	51,632	357	9.3
Personal Income	0	0	0.0
Corporate Income	0	0	0.0
Motor Vehicle License	0	0	0.0
Other Taxes	13,488	93	2.4
Current Charges	166,204	1,150	30.0
Liquor Store	0	0	0.0
Utility	19,725	137	3.6

Source: U.S. Census Bureau, State & Local Government Finances 2020

City Government Expenditures by Function

Function	2020 ($000)	2020 ($ per capita)	2020 (%)
General Direct Expenditures			
Air Transportation	49,990	346	11.3
Corrections	0	0	0.0
Education	0	0	0.0
Employment Security Administration	0	0	0.0
Financial Administration	5,206	36	1.2
Fire Protection	33,087	229	7.5
General Public Buildings	22,289	154	5.1
Governmental Administration, Other	18,696	129	4.2
Health	0	0	0.0
Highways	59,341	410	13.5
Hospitals	0	0	0.0
Housing and Community Development	0	0	0.0
Interest on General Debt	10,952	75	2.5
Judicial and Legal	5,755	39	1.3
Libraries	0	0	0.0
Parking	8,876	61	2.0
Parks and Recreation	24,590	170	5.6
Police Protection	61,046	422	13.9
Public Welfare	14,225	98	3.2
Sewerage	38,893	269	8.8
Solid Waste Management	25,853	179	5.9
Veterans' Services	0	0	0.0
Liquor Store	0	0	0.0
Utility	26,254	181	6.0

Source: U.S. Census Bureau, State & Local Government Finances 2020

TAXES

State Corporate Income Tax Rates

State	Tax Rate (%)	Income Brackets ($)	Num. of Brackets	Financial Institution Tax Rate (%)[a]	Federal Income Tax Ded.
Georgia	5.75	Flat rate	1	5.75	No

Note: Tax rates as of January 1, 2023; (a) Rates listed are the corporate income tax rate applied to financial institutions or excise taxes based on income. Some states have other taxes based upon the value of deposits or shares.
Source: Federation of Tax Administrators, State Corporate Income Tax Rates, January 1, 2023

State Individual Income Tax Rates

State	Tax Rate (%)	Income Brackets ($)	Personal Exemptions ($) Single	Personal Exemptions ($) Married	Personal Exemptions ($) Depend.	Standard Ded. ($) Single	Standard Ded. ($) Married
Georgia	1.0 - 5.75	750 - 7,001 (i)	2,700	7,400	3,000	5,400	7,100

Note: Tax rates as of January 1, 2023; Local- and county-level taxes are not included; Federal income tax is not deductible on state income tax returns; (i) The Georgia income brackets reported are for single individuals. For married couples filing jointly, the same tax rates apply to income brackets ranging from $1,000, to $10,000.
Source: Federation of Tax Administrators, State Individual Income Tax Rates, January 1, 2023

Various State Sales and Excise Tax Rates

State	State Sales Tax (%)	Gasoline[1] ($/gal.)	Cigarette[2] ($/pack)	Spirits[3] ($/gal.)	Wine[4] ($/gal.)	Beer[5] ($/gal.)	Recreational Marijuana (%)
Georgia	4	0.4005	0.37	3.79	1.51	0.48	Not legal

Note: All tax rates as of January 1, 2023; (1) The American Petroleum Institute has developed a methodology for determining the average tax rate on a gallon of fuel. Rates may include any of the following: excise taxes, environmental fees, storage tank fees, other fees or taxes, general sales tax, and local taxes; (2) The federal excise tax of $1.0066 per pack and local taxes are not included; (3) Rates are those applicable to off-premise sales of 40% alcohol by volume (a.b.v.) distilled spirits in 750ml containers. Local excise taxes are excluded; (4) Rates are those applicable to off-premise sales of 11% a.b.v. non-carbonated wine in 750ml containers; (5) Rates are those applicable to off-premise sales of 4.7% a.b.v. beer in 12 ounce containers.
Source: Tax Foundation, 2023 Facts & Figures: How Does Your State Compare?

State Business Tax Climate Index Rankings

State	Overall Rank	Corporate Tax Rank	Individual Income Tax Rank	Sales Tax Rank	Property Tax Rank	Unemployment Insurance Tax Rank
Georgia	32	8	35	31	28	35

Note: The index is a measure of how each state's tax laws affect economic performance. The lower the rank, the more favorable a state's tax system is for business. States without a given tax are given a ranking of 1. The scores/rankings for the District of Columbia do not affect other states. The 2023 index represents the tax climate as of July 1, 2022.
Source: Tax Foundation, State Business Tax Climate Index 2023

TRANSPORTATION

Means of Transportation to Work

Area	Car/Truck/Van Drove Alone	Car/Truck/Van Car-pooled	Public Transportation Bus	Public Transportation Subway	Public Transportation Railroad	Bicycle	Walked	Other Means	Worked at Home
City	71.7	10.7	3.1	0.0	0.0	1.2	4.2	1.8	7.3
MSA[1]	79.8	8.6	1.3	0.0	0.0	0.6	1.9	1.7	6.2
U.S.	73.2	8.6	2.0	1.6	0.5	0.5	2.5	1.5	9.7

Note: Figures are percentages and cover workers 16 years of age and older; (1) Figures cover the Savannah, GA Metropolitan Statistical Area
Source: U.S. Census Bureau, 2017-2021 American Community Survey 5-Year Estimates

Travel Time to Work

Area	Less Than 10 Minutes	10 to 19 Minutes	20 to 29 Minutes	30 to 44 Minutes	45 to 59 Minutes	60 to 89 Minutes	90 Minutes or More
City	15.7	39.1	22.8	13.3	4.8	2.8	1.5
MSA[1]	11.0	29.3	24.8	21.8	8.2	3.6	1.5
U.S.	12.4	28.5	21.0	20.9	8.2	6.2	2.9

Note: Note: Figures are percentages and include workers 16 years old and over; (1) Figures cover the Savannah, GA Metropolitan Statistical Area
Source: U.S. Census Bureau, 2017-2021 American Community Survey 5-Year Estimates

Key Congestion Measures

Measure	1990	2000	2010	2015	2020
Annual Hours of Delay, Total (000)	n/a	n/a	n/a	9,791	4,060
Annual Hours of Delay, Per Auto Commuter	n/a	n/a	n/a	34	14
Annual Congestion Cost, Per Auto Commuter ($)	n/a	n/a	n/a	704	320

Note: n/a not available
Source: Texas A&M Transportation Institute, 2021 Urban Mobility Report

Freeway Travel Time Index

Measure	1985	1990	1995	2000	2005	2010	2015	2020
Urban Area Index[1]	n/a	n/a	n/a	n/a	n/a	n/a	1.11	1.06
Urban Area Rank[1,2]	n/a	n/a	n/a	n/a	n/a	n/a	n/a	n/a

Note: Freeway Travel Time Index—the ratio of travel time in the peak period to the travel time at free-flow conditions. For example, a value of 1.30 indicates a 20-minute free-flow trip takes 26 minutes in the peak (20 minutes x 1.30 = 26 minutes); (1) Covers the Savannah GA urban area; (2) Rank is based on 101 larger urban areas (#1 = highest travel time index); n/a not available
Source: Texas A&M Transportation Institute, 2021 Urban Mobility Report

Public Transportation

Agency Name / Mode of Transportation	Vehicles Operated in Maximum Service[1]	Annual Unlinked Passenger Trips[2] (in thous.)	Annual Passenger Miles[3] (in thous.)
Chatham Area Transit Authority (CAT)			
Bus (directly operated)	36	1,314.8	4,444.0
Demand Response (directly operated)	28	90.9	709.4
Ferryboat (directly operated)	2	370.0	140.6

Note: (1) Number of revenue vehicles operated by the given mode and type of service to meet the annual maximum service requirement. This is the revenue vehicle count during the peak season of the year; on the week and day that maximum service is provided. Vehicles operated in maximum service (VOMS) exclude atypical days and one-time special events; (2) Number of passengers who boarded public transportation vehicles. Passengers are counted each time they board a vehicle no matter how many vehicles they use to travel from their origin to their destination. (3) Sum of the distances ridden by all passengers during the entire fiscal year.
Source: Federal Transit Administration, National Transit Database, 2021

Air Transportation

Airport Name and Code / Type of Service	Passenger Airlines[1]	Passenger Enplanements	Freight Carriers[2]	Freight (lbs)
Savannah International (SAV)				
Domestic service (U.S. carriers - 2022)	30	1,726,156	7	5,616,644
International service (U.S. carriers - 2021)	0	0	0	0

Note: (1) Includes all U.S.-based major, minor and commuter airlines that carried at least one passenger during the year; (2) Includes all U.S.-based airlines and freight carriers that transported at least one pound of freight during the year.
Source: Bureau of Transportation Statistics, The Intermodal Transportation Database, Air Carriers: T-100 Domestic Market (U.S. Carriers), 2022; Bureau of Transportation Statistics, The Intermodal Transportation Database, Air Carriers: T-100 International Market (U.S. Carriers), 2021

BUSINESSES

Major Business Headquarters

Company Name	Industry	Rankings Fortune[1]	Rankings Forbes[2]
Colonial Group	Oil & gas operations	-	199

Note: (1) Companies that produce a 10-K are ranked 1 to 500 based on 2021 revenue; (2) All private companies with at least $2 billion in annual revenue through the end of their most current fiscal year are ranked 1 to 246; companies listed are headquartered in the city; dashes indicate no ranking
Source: Fortune, "Fortune 500," 2022; Forbes, "America's Largest Private Companies," 2022

Living Environment

COST OF LIVING

Cost of Living Index

Composite Index	Groceries	Housing	Utilities	Transportation	Health Care	Misc. Goods/Services
90.1	95.2	71.9	93.1	92.1	107.5	99.0

Note: The Cost of Living Index measures regional differences in the cost of consumer goods and services, excluding taxes and non-consumer expenditures, for professional and managerial households in the top income quintile. It is based on more than 50,000 prices covering almost 60 different items for which prices are collected three times a year by chambers of commerce, economic development organizations or university applied economic centers in each participating urban area. The numbers shown should be read as a percentage above or below the national average of 100. For example, a value of 115.4 in the groceries column indicates that grocery prices are 15.4% higher than the national average. Small differences in the index numbers should not be interpreted as significant; Figures cover the Savannah GA urban area.
Source: The Council for Community and Economic Research, Cost of Living Index, 2022

Grocery Prices

Area[1]	T-Bone Steak ($/pound)	Frying Chicken ($/pound)	Whole Milk ($/half gal.)	Eggs ($/dozen)	Orange Juice ($/64 oz.)	Coffee ($/11.5 oz.)
City[2]	13.73	1.29	2.24	1.99	3.42	4.55
Avg.	13.81	1.59	2.43	2.25	3.85	4.95
Min.	10.17	0.90	1.51	1.30	2.90	3.46
Max.	19.35	3.30	4.32	4.32	5.31	8.59

*Note: (1) Values for the local area are compared with the average, minimum and maximum values for all 286 areas in the Cost of Living Index; (2) Figures cover the Savannah GA urban area; **T-Bone Steak** (price per pound); **Frying Chicken** (price per pound, whole fryer); **Whole Milk** (half gallon carton); **Eggs** (price per dozen, Grade A, large); **Orange Juice** (64 oz. Tropicana or Florida Natural); **Coffee** (11.5 oz. can, vacuum-packed, Maxwell House, Hills Bros, or Folgers).*
Source: The Council for Community and Economic Research, Cost of Living Index, 2022

Housing and Utility Costs

Area[1]	New Home Price ($)	Apartment Rent ($/month)	All Electric ($/month)	Part Electric ($/month)	Other Energy ($/month)	Telephone ($/month)
City[2]	297,041	1,176	158.44	-	-	186.50
Avg.	450,913	1,371	176.41	99.93	76.96	190.22
Min.	229,283	546	100.84	31.56	27.15	174.27
Max.	2,434,977	4,569	356.86	249.59	272.24	208.31

*Note: (1) Values for the local area are compared with the average, minimum and maximum values for all 286 areas in the Cost of Living Index; (2) Figures cover the Savannah GA urban area; **New Home Price** (2,400 sf living area, 8,000 sf lot, in urban area with full utilities); **Apartment Rent** (950 sf 2 bedroom/1.5 or 2 bath, unfurnished, excluding all utilities except water); **All Electric** (average monthly cost for an all-electric home); **Part Electric** (average monthly cost for a part-electric home); **Other Energy** (average monthly cost for natural gas, fuel oil, coal, wood, and any other forms of energy except electricity); **Telephone** (price includes the base monthly rate plus taxes and fees for three lines of mobile phone service).*
Source: The Council for Community and Economic Research, Cost of Living Index, 2022

Health Care, Transportation, and Other Costs

Area[1]	Doctor ($/visit)	Dentist ($/visit)	Optometrist ($/visit)	Gasoline ($/gallon)	Beauty Salon ($/visit)	Men's Shirt ($)
City[2]	119.64	141.34	89.22	3.40	37.92	35.96
Avg.	124.91	107.77	117.66	3.86	43.31	34.21
Min.	36.61	58.25	51.79	2.90	22.18	13.05
Max.	250.21	162.58	371.96	5.54	85.61	63.54

*Note: (1) Values for the local area are compared with the average, minimum and maximum values for all 286 areas in the Cost of Living Index; (2) Figures cover the Savannah GA urban area; **Doctor** (general practitioners routine exam of an established patient); **Dentist** (adult teeth cleaning and periodic oral examination); **Optometrist** (full vision eye exam for established adult patient); **Gasoline** (one gallon regular unleaded, national brand, including all taxes, cash price at self-service pump if available); **Beauty Salon** (woman's shampoo, trim, and blow-dry); **Men's Shirt** (cotton/polyester dress shirt, pinpoint weave, long sleeves).*
Source: The Council for Community and Economic Research, Cost of Living Index, 2022

HOUSING

Homeownership Rate

Area	2015 (%)	2016 (%)	2017 (%)	2018 (%)	2019 (%)	2020 (%)	2021 (%)	2022 (%)
MSA[1]	n/a	n/a	n/a	n/a	n/a	n/a	n/a	n/a
U.S.	63.7	63.4	63.9	64.4	64.6	66.6	65.5	65.8

Note: (1) Figures cover the Savannah, GA Metropolitan Statistical Area; n/a not available
Source: U.S. Census Bureau, Housing Vacancies and Homeownership Annual Statistics: 2015-2022

House Price Index (HPI)

Area	National Ranking[2]	Quarterly Change (%)	One-Year Change (%)	Five-Year Change (%)	Since 1991Q1 (%)
MSA[1]	12	1.20	19.86	70.81	361.13
U.S.[3]	–	0.34	8.41	58.44	289.08

Note: The HPI is a weighted repeat sales index. It measures average price changes in repeat sales or refinancings on the same properties. This information is obtained by reviewing repeat mortgage transactions on single-family properties whose mortgages have been purchased or securitized by Fannie Mae or Freddie Mac since January 1975; (1) Figures cover the Savannah, GA Metropolitan Statistical Area; (2) Rankings are based on annual percentage change for all metro areas containing at least 15,000 transactions over the last 10 years and ranges from 1 to 257; (3) figures based on a weighted average of Census Division estimates using a seasonally adjusted, purchase-only index; all figures are for the period ending December 31, 2022
Source: Federal Housing Finance Agency, Change in FHFA Metropolitan Area House Price Indexes, 2022Q4

Median Single-Family Home Prices

Area	2020	2021	2022p	Percent Change 2021 to 2022
MSA[1]	n/a	n/a	n/a	n/a
U.S. Average	300.2	357.1	392.6	9.9

Note: Figures are median sales prices of existing single-family homes in thousands of dollars; (p) preliminary; n/a not available; (1) Figures cover the Savannah, GA Metropolitan Statistical Area
Source: National Association of Realtors, Median Sales Price of Existing Single-Family Homes for Metropolitan Areas, 4th Quarter 2022

Qualifying Income Based on Median Sales Price of Existing Single-Family Homes

Area	With 5% Down ($)	With 10% Down ($)	With 20% Down ($)
MSA[1]	n/a	n/a	n/a
U.S. Average	112,234	106,237	94,513

Note: Figures are preliminary; Qualifying income is based on a mortgage rate of 6.77%. Monthly principal and interest payment is limited to 25% of income; n/a not available; (1) Figures cover the Savannah, GA Metropolitan Statistical Area
Source: National Association of Realtors, Qualifying Income Based on Median Sales Price of Existing Single-Family Homes for Metropolitan Areas, 4th Quarter 2022

Home Value

Area	Under $100,000	$100,000 -$199,999	$200,000 -$299,999	$300,000 -$399,999	$400,000 -$499,999	$500,000 -$999,999	$1,000,000 or more	Median ($)
City	19.1	41.2	21.4	6.7	4.4	5.9	1.3	170,500
MSA[1]	14.2	32.9	25.4	11.2	5.1	9.1	2.1	210,400
U.S.	16.2	24.2	20.1	13.6	8.3	13.6	4.1	244,900

Note: Figures are percentages except for median and cover owner-occupied housing units; (1) Figures cover the Savannah, GA Metropolitan Statistical Area
Source: U.S. Census Bureau, 2017-2021 American Community Survey 5-Year Estimates

Year Housing Structure Built

Area	2020 or Later	2010 -2019	2000 -2009	1990 -1999	1980 -1989	1970 -1979	1960 -1969	1950 -1959	1940 -1949	Before 1940	Median Year
City	0.1	9.6	9.7	6.5	10.9	11.5	12.2	14.5	8.0	17.0	1969
MSA[1]	0.3	13.3	19.8	14.7	13.2	11.2	7.6	7.8	4.2	8.0	1989
U.S.	0.2	7.3	13.6	13.6	13.2	14.8	10.3	10.0	4.7	12.2	1979

Note: Figures are percentages except for Median Year; Note: (1) Figures cover the Savannah, GA Metropolitan Statistical Area
Source: U.S. Census Bureau, 2017-2021 American Community Survey 5-Year Estimates

Gross Monthly Rent

Area	Under $500	$500 -$999	$1,000 -$1,499	$1,500 -$1,999	$2,000 -$2,499	$2,500 -$2,999	$3,000 and up	Median ($)
City	8.6	29.0	45.1	13.3	2.8	0.5	0.7	1,116
MSA[1]	5.5	26.3	47.1	16.1	3.7	0.6	0.6	1,161
U.S.	8.1	30.5	30.8	16.8	7.3	3.1	3.5	1,163

Note: Figures are percentages except for median; Gross rent is the contract rent plus the estimated average monthly cost of utilities (electricity, gas, and water and sewer) and fuels (oil, coal, kerosene, wood, etc.) if these are paid by the renter (or paid for the renter by someone else); (1) Figures cover the Savannah, GA Metropolitan Statistical Area
Source: U.S. Census Bureau, 2017-2021 American Community Survey 5-Year Estimates

HEALTH

Health Risk Factors

Category	MSA[1] (%)	U.S. (%)
Adults aged 18–64 who have any kind of health care coverage	n/a	90.9
Adults who reported being in good or better health	n/a	85.2
Adults who have been told they have high blood cholesterol	n/a	35.7
Adults who have been told they have high blood pressure	n/a	32.4
Adults who are current smokers	n/a	14.4
Adults who currently use e-cigarettes	n/a	6.7
Adults who currently use chewing tobacco, snuff, or snus	n/a	3.5
Adults who are heavy drinkers[2]	n/a	6.3
Adults who are binge drinkers[3]	n/a	15.4
Adults who are overweight (BMI 25.0 - 29.9)	n/a	34.4
Adults who are obese (BMI 30.0 - 99.8)	n/a	33.9
Adults who participated in any physical activities in the past month	n/a	76.3

Note: (1) Figures for the Savannah, GA Metropolitan Statistical Area were not available.
(2) Heavy drinkers are classified as adult men having more than 14 drinks per week and adult women having more than 7 drinks per week; (3) Binge drinkers are classified as males having five or more drinks on one occasion or females having four or more drinks on one occasion
Source: Centers for Disease Control and Prevention, Behavioral Risk Factor Surveillance System, SMART: Selected Metropolitan Area Risk Trends, 2021

Acute and Chronic Health Conditions

Category	MSA[1] (%)	U.S. (%)
Adults who have ever been told they had a heart attack	n/a	4.0
Adults who have ever been told they have angina or coronary heart disease	n/a	3.8
Adults who have ever been told they had a stroke	n/a	3.0
Adults who have ever been told they have asthma	n/a	14.9
Adults who have ever been told they have arthritis	n/a	25.8
Adults who have ever been told they have diabetes[2]	n/a	10.9
Adults who have ever been told they had skin cancer	n/a	6.6
Adults who have ever been told they had any other types of cancer	n/a	7.5
Adults who have ever been told they have COPD	n/a	6.1
Adults who have ever been told they have kidney disease	n/a	3.0
Adults who have ever been told they have a form of depression	n/a	20.5

Note: (1) Figures for the Savannah, GA Metropolitan Statistical Area were not available.
(2) Figures do not include pregnancy-related, borderline, or pre-diabetes
Source: Centers for Disease Control and Prevention, Behavioral Risk Factor Surveillance System, SMART: Selected Metropolitan Area Risk Trends, 2021

Health Screening and Vaccination Rates

Category	MSA[1] (%)	U.S. (%)
Adults who have ever been tested for HIV	n/a	34.9
Adults who have had their blood cholesterol checked within the last five years	n/a	85.2
Adults aged 65+ who have had flu shot within the past year	n/a	68.6
Adults aged 65+ who have ever had a pneumonia vaccination	n/a	71.0

Note: (1) Figures for the Savannah, GA Metropolitan Statistical Area were not available.
Source: Centers for Disease Control and Prevention, Behavioral Risk Factor Surveillance System, SMART: Selected Metropolitan Area Risk Trends, 2021

Disability Status

Category	MSA[1] (%)	U.S. (%)
Adults who reported being deaf	n/a	7.2
Are you blind or have serious difficulty seeing, even when wearing glasses?	n/a	4.8
Are you limited in any way in any of your usual activities due to arthritis?	n/a	11.1
Do you have difficulty doing errands alone?	n/a	7.0
Do you have difficulty dressing or bathing?	n/a	3.6
Do you have serious difficulty concentrating/remembering/making decisions?	n/a	12.1
Do you have serious difficulty walking or climbing stairs?	n/a	12.8

Note: (1) Figures for the Savannah, GA Metropolitan Statistical Area were not available.
Source: Centers for Disease Control and Prevention, Behavioral Risk Factor Surveillance System, SMART: Selected Metropolitan Area Risk Trends, 2021

Mortality Rates for the Top 10 Causes of Death in the U.S.

ICD-10[a] Sub-Chapter	ICD-10[a] Code	Crude Mortality Rate[1] per 100,000 population County[2]	U.S.
Malignant neoplasms	C00-C97	167.5	182.6
Ischaemic heart diseases	I20-I25	79.1	113.1
Other forms of heart disease	I30-I51	67.3	64.4
Other degenerative diseases of the nervous system	G30-G31	59.3	51.0
Cerebrovascular diseases	I60-I69	48.8	47.8
Other external causes of accidental injury	W00-X59	39.5	46.4
Chronic lower respiratory diseases	J40-J47	52.1	45.7
Organic, including symptomatic, mental disorders	F01-F09	25.3	35.9
Hypertensive diseases	I10-I15	83.3	35.0
Diabetes mellitus	E10-E14	21.1	29.6

Note: (a) ICD-10 = International Classification of Diseases 10th Revision; (1) Crude mortality rates are a three-year average covering 2019-2021; (2) Figures cover Chatham County.
Source: Centers for Disease Control and Prevention, National Center for Health Statistics. National Vital Statistics System, Mortality 2018-2021 on CDC WONDER Online Database

Mortality Rates for Selected Causes of Death

ICD-10[a] Sub-Chapter	ICD-10[a] Code	Crude Mortality Rate[1] per 100,000 population County[2]	U.S.
Assault	X85-Y09	12.1	7.0
Diseases of the liver	K70-K76	21.5	19.8
Human immunodeficiency virus (HIV) disease	B20-B24	3.4	1.5
Influenza and pneumonia	J09-J18	18.7	14.7
Intentional self-harm	X60-X84	15.1	14.3
Malnutrition	E40-E46	5.4	4.3
Obesity and other hyperalimentation	E65-E68	Unreliable	3.0
Renal failure	N17-N19	18.3	15.7
Transport accidents	V01-V99	12.7	13.6
Viral hepatitis	B15-B19	Unreliable	1.2

Note: (a) ICD-10 = International Classification of Diseases 10th Revision; (1) Crude mortality rates are a three-year average covering 2019-2021; (2) Figures cover Chatham County; Data are suppressed when the data meet the criteria for confidentiality constraints; Crude mortality rates are flagged as unreliable when the rate would be calculated with a numerator of 20 or less.
Source: Centers for Disease Control and Prevention, National Center for Health Statistics. National Vital Statistics System, Mortality 2018-2021 on CDC WONDER Online Database

Health Insurance Coverage

Area	With Health Insurance	With Private Health Insurance	With Public Health Insurance	Without Health Insurance	Population Under Age 19 Without Health Insurance
City	84.3	58.4	35.4	15.7	7.7
MSA[1]	87.2	68.1	30.9	12.8	6.3
U.S.	91.2	67.8	35.4	8.8	5.3

Note: Figures are percentages that cover the civilian noninstitutionalized population; (1) Figures cover the Savannah, GA Metropolitan Statistical Area
Source: U.S. Census Bureau, 2017-2021 American Community Survey 5-Year Estimates

Number of Medical Professionals

Area	MDs[3]	DOs[3,4]	Dentists	Podiatrists	Chiropractors	Optometrists
County[1] (number)	1,039	56	203	20	60	41
County[1] (rate[2])	352.3	19.0	68.5	6.7	20.2	13.8
U.S. (rate[2])	289.3	23.5	72.5	6.2	28.7	17.4

Note: Data as of 2021 unless noted; (1) Data covers Chatham County; (2) Rate per 100,000 population; (3) Data as of 2020 and includes all active, non-federal physicians; (4) Doctor of Osteopathic Medicine
Source: U.S. Department of Health and Human Services, Health Resources and Services Administration, Bureau of Health Professions, Area Resource File (ARF) 2021-2022

EDUCATION

Public School District Statistics

District Name	Schls	Pupils	Pupil/Teacher Ratio	Minority Pupils[1] (%)	LEP/ELL[2] (%)	IEP[3] (%)
Savannah-Chatham County	60	35,925	13.2	79.1	3.8	12.9

Note: Table includes school districts with 2,000 or more students; (1) Percentage of students that are not non-Hispanic white; (2) Percentage of students that are Limited English Proficient or English Language Learners (2018-19); (3) Percentage of students that have an Individualized Education Program (2019-20).
Source: U.S. Department of Education, National Center for Education Statistics, Common Core of Data, Local Education Agency (School District) Universe Survey: School Year 2021-2022

Best High Schools

According to *U.S. News*, Savannah is home to one of the top 500 high schools in the U.S.: **Savannah Arts Academy** (#276). Nearly 18,000 public, magnet and charter schools were ranked based on their performance on state assessments and how well they prepare students for college. *U.S. News & World Report, "Best High Schools 2022"*

Highest Level of Education

Area	Less than H.S.	H.S. Diploma	Some College, No Deg.	Associate Degree	Bachelor's Degree	Master's Degree	Prof. School Degree	Doctorate Degree
City	11.2	26.9	24.6	6.8	19.3	7.9	2.1	1.2
MSA[1]	9.3	26.5	22.9	7.8	20.7	9.0	2.4	1.5
U.S.	11.1	26.5	20.0	8.7	20.6	9.3	2.2	1.5

Note: Figures cover persons age 25 and over; (1) Figures cover the Savannah, GA Metropolitan Statistical Area
Source: U.S. Census Bureau, 2017-2021 American Community Survey 5-Year Estimates

Educational Attainment by Race

Area	\multicolumn{5}{c	}{High School Graduate or Higher (%)}	\multicolumn{5}{c	}{Bachelor's Degree or Higher (%)}
	Total	White	Black	Asian	Hisp.[2]	Total	White	Black	Asian	Hisp.[2]
City	88.8	94.8	84.1	78.6	84.0	30.5	45.4	16.3	50.7	31.9
MSA[1]	90.7	93.4	87.0	83.3	84.4	33.6	39.7	21.0	51.4	25.1
U.S.	88.9	91.4	87.2	87.6	71.2	33.7	35.5	23.3	55.6	18.4

Note: Figures shown cover persons 25 years old and over; (1) Figures cover the Savannah, GA Metropolitan Statistical Area; (2) People of Hispanic origin can be of any race
Source: U.S. Census Bureau, 2017-2021 American Community Survey 5-Year Estimates

School Enrollment by Grade and Control

Area	Preschool (%) Public	Preschool (%) Private	Kindergarten (%) Public	Kindergarten (%) Private	Grades 1 - 4 (%) Public	Grades 1 - 4 (%) Private	Grades 5 - 8 (%) Public	Grades 5 - 8 (%) Private	Grades 9 - 12 (%) Public	Grades 9 - 12 (%) Private
City	77.0	23.0	89.0	11.0	91.9	8.1	91.5	8.5	88.5	11.5
MSA[1]	53.9	46.1	81.7	18.3	85.0	15.0	88.0	12.0	85.4	14.6
U.S.	58.8	41.2	86.3	13.7	88.3	11.7	88.6	11.4	89.4	10.6

Note: Figures shown cover persons 3 years old and over; (1) Figures cover the Savannah, GA Metropolitan Statistical Area
Source: U.S. Census Bureau, 2017-2021 American Community Survey 5-Year Estimates

Higher Education

\multicolumn{3}{c	}{Four-Year Colleges}	\multicolumn{3}{c	}{Two-Year Colleges}	Medical Schools[1]	Law Schools[2]	Voc/Tech[3]
Public	Private Non-profit	Private For-profit	Public	Private Non-profit	Private For-profit			
1	1	2	1	0	0	0	0	1

Note: Figures cover institutions located within the Savannah, GA Metropolitan Statistical Area and include main campuses only; (1) includes schools accredited by the Liaison Committee on Medical Education and the American Osteopathic Association's Commission on Osteopathic College Accreditation; (2) includes ABA-accredited schools, schools with provisional ABA accreditation, and state accredited schools; (3) includes all schools with programs that are less than 2 years.
Source: National Center for Education Statistics, Integrated Postsecondary Education System (IPEDS), 2021-22; Wikipedia, List of Medical Schools in the United States, accessed April 10, 2023; Wikipedia, List of Law Schools in the United States, accessed April 10, 2023

EMPLOYERS

Major Employers

Company Name	Industry
Ceres Marine Terminals	Marine cargo handling
Coastal Home Care	Medical care
Colonial Group	Petroleum products
CSX	Railroad
Dollar Tree	Retail
Effingham County Hospital Authority	Hospital
Georgia Power Company	Electric utility
Georgia Regional Hospital	Hospital
Goodwill Industries of the Coastal Empire	Adult vocational rehabilitation
Kroger Company	Retail food
Marine Terminals Corp.	Marine cargo handling
McDonalds	Restaurants
Memorial University Medical Center	Hospital
Publix Supermarkets	Retail grocery
SouthCoast Health	Healthcare services
SSA Cooper	Marine cargo handling
St. Joseph's/Candler	Hospital
The Landings Club	Private membership club
TMX Finance	Financial services
Trace Staffing Solutions	Employment services
UTC Overseas	Logistics solutions
Wal-Mart Stores	Retail

Note: Companies shown are located within the Savannah, GA Metropolitan Statistical Area.
Source: Hoovers.com; Wikipedia

PUBLIC SAFETY

Crime Rate

Area	Total Crime	Violent Crime Rate				Property Crime Rate		
		Murder	Rape[3]	Robbery	Aggrav. Assault	Burglary	Larceny-Theft	Motor Vehicle Theft
City	2,865.5	11.6	35.1	110.2	248.5	364.9	1,824.4	270.8
Suburbs[1]	3,497.3	5.3	37.2	67.1	245.2	497.1	2,366.1	279.1
Metro[2]	3,107.5	9.2	35.9	93.7	247.2	415.6	2,032.0	274.0
U.S.	2,593.1	5.0	44.0	86.1	248.2	378.0	1,601.6	230.2

Note: Figures are crimes per 100,000 population; (1) All areas within the metro area that are located outside the city limits; (2) Figures cover the Savannah, GA Metropolitan Statistical Area; (3) All figures shown were reported using the revised Uniform Crime Reporting (UCR) definition of rape; Due to the transition to the National Incident-Based Reporting System (NIBRS), limited city and metro area data was released for 2021.
Source: FBI Uniform Crime Reports, 2018 (data for 2020 was not available)

Hate Crimes

Area	Number of Quarters Reported	Number of Incidents per Bias Motivation					
		Race/Ethnicity/Ancestry	Religion	Sexual Orientation	Disability	Gender	Gender Identity
City	n/a	n/a	n/a	n/a	n/a	n/a	n/a
U.S.	4	5,227	1,244	1,110	130	75	266

Note: n/a not available; Due to the transition to the National Incident-Based Reporting System (NIBRS), limited crime data was released for 2021.
Source: Federal Bureau of Investigation, Hate Crime Statistics 2020

Identity Theft Consumer Reports

Area	Reports	Reports per 100,000 Population	Rank[2]
MSA[1]	2,407	617	8
U.S.	1,108,609	339	-

Note: (1) Figures cover the Savannah, GA Metropolitan Statistical Area; (2) Rank ranges from 1 to 391 where 1 indicates greatest number of identity theft reports per 100,000 population
Source: Federal Trade Commission, Consumer Sentinel Network Data Book 2022

Fraud and Other Consumer Reports

Area	Reports	Reports per 100,000 Population	Rank[2]
MSA[1]	5,236	1,342	22
U.S.	4,064,520	1,245	-

Note: (1) Figures cover the Savannah, GA Metropolitan Statistical Area; (2) Rank ranges from 1 to 391 where 1 indicates greatest number of fraud and other consumer reports per 100,000 population
Source: Federal Trade Commission, Consumer Sentinel Network Data Book 2022

POLITICS

2020 Presidential Election Results

Area	Biden	Trump	Jorgensen	Hawkins	Other
Chatham County	58.6	39.9	1.4	0.0	0.0
U.S.	51.3	46.8	1.2	0.3	0.5

Note: Results are percentages and may not add to 100% due to rounding
Source: Dave Leip's Atlas of U.S. Presidential Elections

SPORTS

Professional Sports Teams

Team Name	League	Year Established

No teams are located in the metro area
Source: Wikipedia, Major Professional Sports Teams of the United States and Canada, April 12, 2023

CLIMATE

Average and Extreme Temperatures

Temperature	Jan	Feb	Mar	Apr	May	Jun	Jul	Aug	Sep	Oct	Nov	Dec	Yr.
Extreme High (°F)	84	86	91	95	100	104	105	104	98	97	89	83	105
Average High (°F)	60	64	70	78	84	89	92	90	86	78	70	62	77
Average Temp. (°F)	49	53	59	66	74	79	82	81	77	68	59	52	67
Average Low (°F)	38	41	48	54	62	69	72	72	68	57	47	40	56
Extreme Low (°F)	3	14	20	32	39	51	61	57	43	28	15	9	3

Note: Figures cover the years 1950-1995
Source: National Climatic Data Center, International Station Meteorological Climate Summary, 9/96

Average Precipitation/Snowfall/Humidity

Precip./Humidity	Jan	Feb	Mar	Apr	May	Jun	Jul	Aug	Sep	Oct	Nov	Dec	Yr.
Avg. Precip. (in.)	3.5	3.1	3.9	3.2	4.2	5.6	6.8	7.2	5.0	2.9	2.2	2.7	50.3
Avg. Snowfall (in.)	Tr	Tr	Tr	0	0	0	0	0	0	0	Tr	Tr	Tr
Avg. Rel. Hum. 7am (%)	83	82	83	84	85	87	88	91	91	88	86	83	86
Avg. Rel. Hum. 4pm (%)	53	50	49	48	52	58	61	63	62	55	53	54	55

Note: Figures cover the years 1950-1995; Tr = Trace amounts (<0.05 in. of rain; <0.5 in. of snow)
Source: National Climatic Data Center, International Station Meteorological Climate Summary, 9/96

Weather Conditions

Temperature			Daytime Sky			Precipitation		
10°F & below	32°F & below	90°F & above	Clear	Partly cloudy	Cloudy	0.01 inch or more precip.	0.1 inch or more snow/ice	Thunder-storms
< 1	29	70	97	155	113	111	< 1	63

Note: Figures are average number of days per year and cover the years 1950-1995
Source: National Climatic Data Center, International Station Meteorological Climate Summary, 9/96

HAZARDOUS WASTE

Superfund Sites

The Savannah, GA metro area has no sites on the EPA's Superfund Final National Priorities List. There are a total of 1,165 Superfund sites with a status of proposed or final on the list in the U.S. *U.S. Environmental Protection Agency, National Priorities List, April 12, 2023*

AIR QUALITY

Air Quality Trends: Ozone

	1990	1995	2000	2005	2010	2015	2018	2019	2020	2021
MSA[1]	n/a	n/a	n/a	n/a	n/a	n/a	n/a	n/a	n/a	n/a
U.S.	0.087	0.089	0.081	0.080	0.072	0.067	0.069	0.065	0.065	0.067

Note: (1) Data covers the Savannah, GA Metropolitan Statistical Area; n/a not available. The values shown are the composite ozone concentration averages among trend sites based on the highest fourth daily maximum 8-hour concentration in parts per million. These trends are based on sites having an adequate record of monitoring data during the trend period. Data from exceptional events are included.
Source: U.S. Environmental Protection Agency, Air Quality Monitoring Information, "Air Quality Trends by City, 1990-2021"

Savannah, Georgia

Air Quality Index

Area	Percent of Days when Air Quality was...[2]					AQI Statistics[2]	
	Good	Moderate	Unhealthy for Sensitive Groups	Unhealthy	Very Unhealthy	Maximum	Median
MSA[1]	75.8	24.0	0.3	0.0	0.0	103	41

Note: (1) Data covers the Savannah, GA Metropolitan Statistical Area; (2) Based on 363 days with AQI data in 2021. Air Quality Index (AQI) is an index for reporting daily air quality. EPA calculates the AQI for five major air pollutants regulated by the Clean Air Act: ground-level ozone, particle pollution (aka particulate matter), carbon monoxide, sulfur dioxide, and nitrogen dioxide. The AQI runs from 0 to 500. The higher the AQI value, the greater the level of air pollution and the greater the health concern. There are six AQI categories: "Good" AQI is between 0 and 50. Air quality is considered satisfactory; "Moderate" AQI is between 51 and 100. Air quality is acceptable; "Unhealthy for Sensitive Groups" When AQI values are between 101 and 150, members of sensitive groups may experience health effects; "Unhealthy" When AQI values are between 151 and 200 everyone may begin to experience health effects; "Very Unhealthy" AQI values between 201 and 300 trigger a health alert; "Hazardous" AQI values over 300 trigger warnings of emergency conditions (not shown).
Source: U.S. Environmental Protection Agency, Air Quality Index Report, 2021

Air Quality Index Pollutants

Area	Percent of Days when AQI Pollutant was...[2]					
	Carbon Monoxide	Nitrogen Dioxide	Ozone	Sulfur Dioxide	Particulate Matter 2.5	Particulate Matter 10
MSA[1]	0.0	0.0	24.5	(3)	75.5	0.0

Note: (1) Data covers the Savannah, GA Metropolitan Statistical Area; (2) Based on 363 days with AQI data in 2021. The Air Quality Index (AQI) is an index for reporting daily air quality. EPA calculates the AQI for five major air pollutants regulated by the Clean Air Act: ground-level ozone, particle pollution (also known as particulate matter), carbon monoxide, sulfur dioxide, and nitrogen dioxide. The AQI runs from 0 to 500. The higher the AQI value, the greater the level of air pollution and the greater the health concern; (3) Sulfur dioxide is no longer included in this table (as of December 8, 2021) because SO_2 concentrations tend to be very localized and not necessarily representative of broad geographical areas like counties and CBSAs.
Source: U.S. Environmental Protection Agency, Air Quality Index Report, 2021

Maximum Air Pollutant Concentrations: Particulate Matter, Ozone, CO and Lead

	Particulate Matter 10 (ug/m³)	Particulate Matter 2.5 Wtd AM (ug/m³)	Particulate Matter 2.5 24-Hr (ug/m³)	Ozone (ppm)	Carbon Monoxide (ppm)	Lead (ug/m³)
MSA[1] Level	n/a	10.1	22	0.058	n/a	n/a
NAAQS[2]	150	15	35	0.075	9	0.15
Met NAAQS[2]	n/a	Yes	Yes	Yes	n/a	n/a

Note: (1) Data covers the Savannah, GA Metropolitan Statistical Area; Data from exceptional events are included; (2) National Ambient Air Quality Standards; ppm = parts per million; ug/m³ = micrograms per cubic meter; n/a not available.
Concentrations: Particulate Matter 10 (coarse particulate)—highest second maximum 24-hour concentration; Particulate Matter 2.5 Wtd AM (fine particulate)—highest weighted annual mean concentration; Particulate Matter 2.5 24-Hour (fine particulate)—highest 98th percentile 24-hour concentration; Ozone—highest fourth daily maximum 8-hour concentration; Carbon Monoxide—highest second maximum non-overlapping 8-hour concentration; Lead—maximum running 3-month average
Source: U.S. Environmental Protection Agency, Air Quality Monitoring Information, "Air Quality Statistics by City, 2021"

Maximum Air Pollutant Concentrations: Nitrogen Dioxide and Sulfur Dioxide

	Nitrogen Dioxide AM (ppb)	Nitrogen Dioxide 1-Hr (ppb)	Sulfur Dioxide AM (ppb)	Sulfur Dioxide 1-Hr (ppb)	Sulfur Dioxide 24-Hr (ppb)
MSA[1] Level	n/a	n/a	n/a	50	n/a
NAAQS[2]	53	100	30	75	140
Met NAAQS[2]	n/a	n/a	n/a	Yes	n/a

Note: (1) Data covers the Savannah, GA Metropolitan Statistical Area; Data from exceptional events are included; (2) National Ambient Air Quality Standards; ppm = parts per million; ug/m³ = micrograms per cubic meter; n/a not available.
Concentrations: Nitrogen Dioxide AM—highest arithmetic mean concentration; Nitrogen Dioxide 1-Hr—highest 98th percentile 1-hour daily maximum concentration; Sulfur Dioxide AM—highest annual mean concentration; Sulfur Dioxide 1-Hr—highest 99th percentile 1-hour daily maximum concentration; Sulfur Dioxide 24-Hr—highest second maximum 24-hour concentration
Source: U.S. Environmental Protection Agency, Air Quality Monitoring Information, "Air Quality Statistics by City, 2021"

Tampa, Florida

Background

Although Tampa was visited by Spanish explorers, including Ponce de Leon and Hernando de Soto as early as 1521, this city on the mouth of the Hillsborough River on Tampa Bay, did not see significant growth until the mid-nineteenth century.

Like many cities in northern Florida, Tampa was a fort during the Seminole War and was captured by the Union Army during the Civil War. Later in the 19th century, Tampa prospered when the railroad transported tourists from up north to enjoy the warmth and sunshine of Florida.

Tampa distinguished itself from other Florida cities due to its significant role as a main port for American troops travelling to Cuba during the Spanish-American War in 1898 and Colonel Theodore Roosevelt occupied a Tampa hotel as his military headquarters. A cigar factory in nearby Ybor City also played a part in the city's importance at this time when Jose Marti (the George Washington of Cuba) exhorted factory workers to take up arms against the tyranny of Spanish rule.

By 1900, Tampa was known as the Cigar Capital of the World. In the peak year of 1929, factories in Tampa and Ybor City hand rolled 500 million cigars. When machines pushed handmade production offshore, Tampa remained a major spot for machine-made cigars until 2009, when the last Hav A-Tampa Jewel came off the machines. Today, the cigar legacy of Tampa lives on, and the city hosts The Tampa Cigar Week every year.

The city saw its share of organized crime, with crime family alliances in New York and Cuba, from the late nineteenth century to the 1950s. Rampant and open corruption ended with crime and the sensational misconduct of local officials.

Today, Tampa is the largest port in the state and host to many cruise ships. Major industries in and around Tampa include finance, retail, healthcare, insurance, shipping by air and sea, national defense, professional sports, and real estate. Like most of Florida, the city's economy is heavily based on tourism. Attractions include Tampa Riverwalk, Glazer Children's Museum, and Tampa Museum of Art.

Redeveloping Tampa's downtown continues; phase one of Water Street Tampa opened in 2022 comprising three new residential towers, an office tower, a new Publix GreenWise Market, and two hotels. Phase two with more horizontal infrastructure, like pedestrian walkways, is expected to be complete by 2027.

Public transportation in the city includes Amtrak's Silver Star Line at Tampa Union Station and the TECO Line Streetcar System. Several sites have been designated historical landmarks. Tampa is also home to Big Cat Rescue, one of the largest accredited sanctuaries in the world dedicated entirely to abused and abandoned big cats, including lions, tigers, bobcats, and cougars.

Significant employers in the city include BayCare Health, Publix, WellCare Health, University of South Florida, Tampa General Hospital, Verizon, and JP Morgan Chase. It is also home to 300 computer servers that run Wikipedia, the online encyclopedia. Companies with headquarters in the city include TD Synnex, Mosaic, Raymond James Financial, Bloomin' Brands, and Masonite

The city boasts National Football's Tampa Bay Buccaneers, which won the Superbowl in 2022. The city also hosts Major League Baseball's Devil Rays baseball team, and National Hockey League's Lightning, which won the Stanley Cup in 2020. Other attractions include Florida's Latin Quarter known as Ybor City, Busch Gardens, and a Museum of Science and Industry. Two popular annual events are the MacDill Air Force Base air show, and the Gasparilla Pirate Festival, referred to as Tampa's "mardi gras."

Winters are mild, while summers are long, warm, and humid. Freezing temperatures occur on one or two mornings per year during November through March. Dramatic thunderstorms occur during the summer season, most during late afternoon, sometimes causing dramatic temperature drops. With an elevation of less than 15 feet above sea level, the city is vulnerable to tidal surges. Three major hurricanes have seriously threatened Tampa—Donna in 1960, Charley in 2004, and Irma in 2017, the last of which caused significant damage to the city's electrical grid.

Rankings

General Rankings

- For its "Best for Vets: Places to Live 2019" rankings, *Military Times* evaluated 599 cities (83 large, 234 medium, 282 small) and compared the locations across three broad categories: veteran and military culture/services; economic indicators; and livability factors such as health, crime, traffic, and school quality. Tampa ranked #13 out of the top 25, in the large city category (population of more than 250,000). Data points more specific to veterans and the military weighed more heavily than others. *rebootcamp.militarytimes.com, "Military Times Best Places to Live 2019," September 10, 2018*

- The Tampa metro area was identified as one of America's fastest-growing areas in terms of population and economy by *Forbes*. The area ranked #23 out of 25. The 100 most populous metro areas in the U.S. were evaluated on the following criteria: estimated population growth; employment; economic output; wages; home values. *Forbes, "America's Fastest-Growing Cities 2018," February 28, 2018*

- Tampa was selected as one of the best places to live in the United States by *Money* magazine. The city ranked #9 out of 50. This year's list focused on cities that would be welcoming to a broader group of people and with populations of at least 20,000. Beginning with a pool of 1,370 candidates, editors looked at 350 data points, organized into the these nine categories: income and personal finance, cost of living, economic opportunity, housing market, fun and amenities, health and safety, education, diversity, and quality of life. *Money, "The 50 Best Places to Live in the U.S. in 2022-2023" September 29, 2022*

Business/Finance Rankings

- The Brookings Institution ranked the nation's largest cities based on income inequality. Tampa was ranked #13 (#1 = greatest inequality). Criteria: the "95/20 ratio," a figure representing the income at which a household earns more than 95 percent of all other households, divided by the income at which a household earns more than only 20 percent of all other households. *Brookings Institution, "Household Income Inequality, Largest Cities of 97 Large U.S. Metro Areas, 2014-2016," February 5, 2018*

- The Brookings Institution ranked the 100 largest metro areas in the U.S. based on income inequality. Tampa was ranked #38 (#1 = greatest inequality). Criteria: the "95/20 ratio," a figure representing the income at which a household earns more than 95 percent of all other households, divided by the income at which a household earns more than only 20 percent of all other households. *Brookings Institution, "Household Income Inequality, 100 Largest U.S. Metro Areas, 2014-2016," February 5, 2018*

- Payscale.com ranked the 32 largest metro areas in terms of wage growth. The Tampa metro area ranked #1. Criteria: quarterly changes in private industry employee and education professional wage growth from the previous year. *PayScale, "Wage Trends by Metro Area-1st Quarter," April 20, 2023*

- The Tampa metro area was identified as one of the most debt-ridden places in America by the finance site Credit.com. The metro area was ranked #19. Criteria: residents' average credit card debt as well as median income. *Credit.com, "25 Cities With the Most Credit Card Debt," February 28, 2018*

- Tampa was identified as one of America's most frugal metro areas by *Coupons.com*. The city ranked #7 out of 25. Criteria: digital coupon usage. *Coupons.com, "America's Most Frugal Cities of 2017," March 22, 2018*

- The Tampa metro area appeared on the Milken Institute "2022 Best Performing Cities" list. Rank: #17 out of 200 large metro areas (population over 250,000). Criteria: job growth; wage and salary growth; high-tech output growth; housing affordability; household broadband access. *Milken Institute, "Best-Performing Cities 2022," March 28, 2022*

- *Forbes* ranked the 200 most populous metro areas to determine the nation's "Best Places for Business and Careers." The Tampa metro area was ranked #35. Criteria: costs (business and living); job growth (past and projected); income growth; quality of life; educational attainment (college and high school); projected economic growth; cultural and leisure opportunities; workplace tolerance laws; net migration patterns. *Forbes, "The Best Places for Business and Careers 2019: Seattle Still On Top," October 30, 2019*

Children/Family Rankings

- Tampa was selected as one of the most playful cities in the U.S. by KaBOOM! The organization's Playful City USA initiative honors cities and towns across the nation that have made their communities more playable. Criteria: pledging to integrate play as a solution to challenges in their communities; making it easy for children to get active and balanced play; creating more family-friendly and innovative communities as a result. *KaBOOM! National Campaign for Play, "2017 Playful City USA Communities"*

Dating/Romance Rankings

- Tampa was selected as one of the nation's most romantic cities with 100,000 or more residents by Amazon.com. The city ranked #16 of 20. Criteria: per capita sales of romance novels, relationship books, romantic comedy movies, romantic music, and sexual wellness products. *Amazon.com, "Top 20 Most Romantic Cities in the U.S.," February 1, 2017*

Education Rankings

- Personal finance website *WalletHub* analyzed the 150 largest U.S. metropolitan statistical areas to determine where the most educated Americans are putting their degrees to work. Criteria: education levels; percentage of workers with degrees; education quality and attainment gap; public school quality rankings; quality and enrollment of each metro area's universities. Tampa was ranked #85 (#1 = most educated city). *www.WalletHub.com, "Most & Least Educated Cities in America," July 18, 2022*

- Tampa was selected as one of America's most literate cities. The city ranked #49 out of the 84 largest U.S. cities. Criteria: number of booksellers; library resources; Internet resources; educational attainment; periodical publishing resources; newspaper circulation. *Central Connecticut State University, "America's Most Literate Cities, 2018," February 2019*

Environmental Rankings

- Sperling's BestPlaces assessed the 50 largest metropolitan areas of the United States for the likelihood of dangerously extreme weather events or earthquakes. In general the Southeast and South-Central regions have the highest risk of weather extremes and earthquakes, while the Pacific Northwest enjoys the lowest risk. Of the most risky metropolitan areas, the Tampa metro area was ranked #8. *www.bestplaces.net, "Avoid Natural Disasters: BestPlaces Reveals The Top 10 Safest Places to Live," October 25, 2017*

- The U.S. Environmental Protection Agency (EPA) released its list of U.S. metropolitan areas with the most ENERGY STAR certified buildings in 2022. The Tampa metro area was ranked #12 out of 25. *U.S. Environmental Protection Agency, "2023 Energy Star Top Cities," April 26, 2023*

Health/Fitness Rankings

- For each of the 100 largest cities in the United States, the American Fitness Index®, compiled in partnership between the American College of Sports Medicine and the Elevance Health Foundation, evaluated community infrastructure and 34 health behaviors including preventive health, levels of chronic disease conditions, food insecurity, sleep quality, pedestrian safety, air quality, and community/environment resources that support physical activity. Tampa ranked #25 for "community fitness." *americanfitnessindex.org, "2022 ACSM American Fitness Index Summary Report," July 12, 2022*

- The Tampa metro area was identified as one of the worst cities for bed bugs in America by pest control company Orkin. The area ranked #41 out of 50 based on the number of bed bug treatments Orkin performed from December 2021 to November 2022. *Orkin, "The Windy City Can't Blow Bed Bugs Away: Chicago Ranks #1 For Third Consecutive Year On Orkin's Bed Bug Cities List," January 9, 2023*

- Tampa was identified as a "2022 Spring Allergy Capital." The area ranked #53 out of 100. Three groups of factors were used to identify the most challenging cities for people with allergies during the spring season: annual spring pollen scores; over the counter allergy medicine use; number of board-certified allergy specialists. *Asthma and Allergy Foundation of America, "Spring Allergy Capitals 2022," March 2, 2022*

- Tampa was identified as a "2022 Fall Allergy Capital." The area ranked #52 out of 100. Three groups of factors were used to identify the most challenging cities for people with allergies during the fall season: annual fall pollen scores; over the counter allergy medicine use; number of board-certified allergy specialists. *Asthma and Allergy Foundation of America, "Fall Allergy Capitals 2022," March 2, 2022*

- Tampa was identified as a "2022 Asthma Capital." The area ranked #33 out of the nation's 100 largest metropolitan areas. Criteria: estimated asthma prevalence; asthma-related mortality; and ER visits due to asthma. Risk factors analyzed but not factored in the rankings: annual pollen score; annual air quality; public smoking laws; access to board-certified asthma specialists; rescue and controller medication use; uninsured rate; poverty rate. *Asthma and Allergy Foundation of America, "Asthma Capitals 2022: The Most Challenging Places to Live With Asthma," September 14, 2022*

Pet Rankings

- Tampa appeared on *The Dogington Post* site as one of the top cities for dog lovers, ranking #10 out of 15. The real estate marketplace, Zillow®, and Rover, the largest pet sitter and dog walker network, introduced a new list of "Top Emerging Dog-Friendly Cities" for 2021. Criteria: number of new dog accounts on the Rover platform; and rentals and listings that mention features that attract dog owners (fenced-in yards, dog houses, dog door or proximity to a dog park). *www.dogingtonpost.com, "15 Cities Emerging as Dog-Friendliest in 2021," May 11, 2021*

Real Estate Rankings

- *WalletHub* compared the most populated U.S. cities to determine which had the best markets for real estate agents. Tampa ranked #39 where demand was high and pay was the best. Criteria: sales per agent; annual median wage for real-estate agents; monthly average starting salary for real estate agents; real estate job density and competition; unemployment rate; home turnover rate; housing-market health index; and other relevant metrics. *www.WalletHub.com, "2021 Best Places to Be a Real Estate Agent," May 12, 2021*

- Tampa was ranked #7 in the top 20 out of the 100 largest metro areas in terms of house price appreciation in 2022 (#1 = highest rate). *Federal Housing Finance Agency, House Price Index, 4th Quarter 2022*

- The Tampa metro area was identified as one of the 20 best housing markets in the U.S. in 2022. The area ranked #17 out of 187 markets. Criteria: year-over-year change of median sales price of existing single-family homes between the 4th quarter of 2021 and the 4th quarter of 2022. *National Association of Realtors®, Median Sales Price of Existing Single-Family Homes for Metropolitan Areas, 4th Quarter 2022*

- The Tampa metro area was identified as one of the 10 best condo markets in the U.S. in 2022. The area ranked #3 out of 63 markets. Criteria: year-over-year change of median sales price of existing apartment condo-coop homes between the 4th quarter of 2021 and the 4th quarter of 2022. *National Association of Realtors®, Median Sales Price of Existing Apartment Condo-Coops Homes for Metropolitan Areas, 4th Quarter 2022*

- Tampa was ranked #153 out of 235 metro areas in terms of housing affordability in 2022 by the National Association of Home Builders (#1 = most affordable). Criteria: the share of homes sold in that area affordable to a family earning the local median income, based on standard mortgage underwriting criteria. *National Association of Home Builders®, NAHB-Wells Fargo Housing Opportunity Index, 4th Quarter 2022*

Safety Rankings

- Allstate ranked the 200 largest cities in America in terms of driver safety. Tampa ranked #101. Criteria: internal property damage claims over a two-year period from January 2016 to December 2017. The report helps increase the importance of safety and awareness behind the wheel. *Allstate, "Allstate America's Best Drivers Report, 2019" June 24, 2019*

- The National Insurance Crime Bureau ranked 390 metro areas in the U.S. in terms of per capita rates of vehicle theft. The Tampa metro area ranked #238 (#1 = highest rate). Criteria: number of vehicle theft offenses per 100,000 inhabitants in 2021. *National Insurance Crime Bureau, "Hot Spots 2021," September 1, 2022*

Seniors/Retirement Rankings

- From its Best Cities for Successful Aging indexes, the Milken Institute generated rankings for metropolitan areas, weighing data in nine categories—health care, wellness, living arrangements, transportation and convenience, financial characteristics, education, employment, community engagement, and overall livability. The Tampa metro area was ranked #84 overall in the large metro area category. *Milken Institute, "Best Cities for Successful Aging, 2017" March 14, 2017*

Sports/Recreation Rankings

- Tampa was chosen as one of America's best cities for bicycling. The city ranked #48 out of 50. Criteria: cycling infrastructure that is safe and friendly for all ages; energy and bike culture. The editors evaluated cities with populations of 100,000 or more. *Bicycling, "The 50 Best Bike Cities in America," October 10, 2018*

Women/Minorities Rankings

- Tampa was selected as one of the queerest cities in America by *The Advocate*. The city ranked #19 out of 25. Criteria, among many: Trans Pride parades/festivals; gay rugby teams; lesbian bars; LGBTQ centers; theater screenings of "Moonlight"; LGBTQ-inclusive nondiscrimination ordinances; and gay bowling teams. *The Advocate, "Queerest Cities in America 2017" January 12, 2017*

- Personal finance website *WalletHub* compared more than 180 U.S. cities across two key dimensions, "Hispanic Business-Friendliness" and "Hispanic Purchasing Power," to arrive at the most favorable conditions for Hispanic entrepreneurs. Tampa was ranked #7 out of 182. Criteria includes: share of Hispanic-Owned Businesses; Hispanic entrepreneurship rate to median annual income of Hispanics; Small Business-Friendliness score; cost of living; and number of Hispanics with at least a bachelor's degree. *WalletHub.com, "2019's Best Cities for Hispanic Entrepreneurs," May 1, 2019*

Miscellaneous Rankings

- *MoveHub* ranked 446 hipster cities across 20 countries, using its new and improved *alternative* Hipster Index and Tampa came out as #11 among the top 50. Criteria: population over 150,000; number of vintage boutiques; density of tattoo parlors; vegan places to eat; coffee shops; and density of vinyl record stores. *www.movehub.com, "The Hipster Index: Brighton Pips Portland to Global Top Spot," July 28, 2021*

- The watchdog site, Charity Navigator, conducted a study of charities in major markets both to analyze statistical differences in their financial, accountability, and transparency practices and to track year-to-year variations in individual philanthropic communities. The Tampa metro area was ranked #4 among the 30 metro markets in the rating category of Overall Score. *www.charitynavigator.org, "2017 Metro Market Study," May 1, 2017*

- *WalletHub* compared the 150 most populated U.S. cities to determine their operating efficiency. A "Quality of Services" score was constructed for each city and then divided by the total budget per capita to reveal which were managed the best. Tampa ranked #84. Criteria: financial stability; economy; education; safety; health; infrastructure and pollution. *www.WalletHub.com, "2022's Best- & Worst-Run Cities in America," June 21, 2022*

- The National Alliance to End Homelessness listed the 25 most populous metro areas with the highest rate of homelessness. The Tampa metro area had a high rate of homelessness. Criteria: number of homeless people per 10,000 population in 2016. *National Alliance to End Homelessness, "Homelessness in the 25 Most Populous U.S. Metro Areas," September 1, 2017*

Business Environment

DEMOGRAPHICS

Population Growth

Area	1990 Census	2000 Census	2010 Census	2020 Census	Population Growth (%) 1990-2020	Population Growth (%) 2010-2020
City	279,960	303,447	335,709	384,959	37.5	14.7
MSA[1]	2,067,959	2,395,997	2,783,243	3,175,275	53.5	14.1
U.S.	248,709,873	281,421,906	308,745,538	331,449,281	33.3	7.4

Note: (1) Figures cover the Tampa-St. Petersburg-Clearwater, FL Metropolitan Statistical Area
Source: U.S. Census Bureau, 1990 Census, 2000 Census, 2010 Census, 2020 Census

Race

Area	White Alone[2] (%)	Black Alone[2] (%)	Asian Alone[2] (%)	AIAN[3] Alone[2] (%)	NHOPI[4] Alone[2] (%)	Other Race Alone[2] (%)	Two or More Races (%)
City	49.7	21.9	5.4	0.4	0.1	7.6	14.8
MSA[1]	64.4	11.8	3.9	0.4	0.1	6.2	13.1
U.S.	61.6	12.4	6.0	1.1	0.2	8.4	10.2

Note: (1) Figures cover the Tampa-St. Petersburg-Clearwater, FL Metropolitan Statistical Area; (2) Alone is defined as not being in combination with one or more other races; (3) American Indian and Alaska Native; (4) Native Hawaiian and Other Pacific Islander
Source: U.S. Census Bureau, 2020 Census

Hispanic or Latino Origin

Area	Total (%)	Mexican (%)	Puerto Rican (%)	Cuban (%)	Other (%)
City	26.2	3.1	6.9	8.0	8.3
MSA[1]	20.5	3.7	6.3	4.3	6.3
U.S.	18.4	11.2	1.8	0.7	4.7

Note: Persons of Hispanic or Latino origin can be of any race; (1) Figures cover the Tampa-St. Petersburg-Clearwater, FL Metropolitan Statistical Area
Source: U.S. Census Bureau, 2017-2021 American Community Survey 5-Year Estimates

Age

Area	Under Age 5	Age 5–19	Age 20–34	Age 35–44	Age 45–54	Age 55–64	Age 65–74	Age 75–84	Age 85+	Median Age
City	5.4	18.7	24.6	13.6	12.4	11.9	8.0	3.8	1.5	35.8
MSA[1]	4.8	17.1	18.3	12.3	12.8	14.2	11.8	6.2	2.3	42.7
U.S.	5.6	19.2	20.2	12.7	12.4	13.1	10.0	4.9	1.9	38.8

Note: (1) Figures cover the Tampa-St. Petersburg-Clearwater, FL Metropolitan Statistical Area
Source: U.S. Census Bureau, 2020 Census

Disability by Age

Area	All Ages	Under 18 Years Old	18 to 64 Years Old	65 Years and Over
City	12.1	3.7	9.6	38.9
MSA[1]	14.1	5.0	10.8	33.6
U.S.	12.6	4.4	10.3	33.4

Note: Figures show percent of the civilian noninstitutionalized population that reported having a disability. Disability status is determined from six types of difficulty: vision, hearing, cognitive, ambulatory, self-care, and independent living. For children under 5 years old, hearing and vision difficulty are used to determine disability status. For children between the ages of 5 and 14, disability status is determined from hearing, vision, cognitive, ambulatory, and self-care difficulties. For people aged 15 years and older, they are considered to have a disability if they have difficulty with any one of the six difficulty types; Note: (1) Figures cover the Tampa-St. Petersburg-Clearwater, FL Metropolitan Statistical Area
Source: U.S. Census Bureau, 2017-2021 American Community Survey 5-Year Estimates

Ancestry

Area	German	Irish	English	American	Italian	Polish	French[2]	Scottish	Dutch
City	8.7	7.5	6.7	6.5	6.2	2.0	1.8	1.4	0.7
MSA[1]	11.6	10.3	8.5	8.6	7.3	2.9	2.4	1.7	0.9
U.S.	12.8	9.6	8.1	5.7	5.0	2.7	2.2	1.6	1.1

Note: Figures are the percentage of the total population reporting a particular ancestry. The nine most commonly reported ancestries in the U.S. are shown. Figures include multiple ancestries (e.g. if a person reported being Irish and Italian, they were included in both columns); (1) Figures cover the Tampa-St. Petersburg-Clearwater, FL Metropolitan Statistical Area; (2) Excludes Basque
Source: U.S. Census Bureau, 2017-2021 American Community Survey 5-Year Estimates

Foreign-born Population

Area	Any Foreign Country	Asia	Mexico	Europe	Caribbean	Central America[2]	South America	Africa	Canada
City	18.1	3.8	1.1	1.8	7.1	1.2	2.3	0.5	0.3
MSA[1]	14.4	2.8	1.3	2.2	4.0	0.8	2.2	0.5	0.6
U.S.	13.6	4.2	3.3	1.5	1.4	1.1	1.1	0.8	0.2

Note: (1) Figures cover the Tampa-St. Petersburg-Clearwater, FL Metropolitan Statistical Area; (2) Excludes Mexico.
Source: U.S. Census Bureau, 2017-2021 American Community Survey 5-Year Estimates

Household Size

Area	One	Two	Three	Four	Five	Six	Seven or More	Average Household Size
City	36.0	31.2	15.7	10.7	4.3	1.5	0.7	2.40
MSA[1]	30.7	36.4	15.0	10.9	4.6	1.6	0.9	2.50
U.S.	28.1	33.8	15.5	12.9	6.0	2.3	1.4	2.60

Note: (1) Figures cover the Tampa-St. Petersburg-Clearwater, FL Metropolitan Statistical Area
Source: U.S. Census Bureau, 2017-2021 American Community Survey 5-Year Estimates

Household Relationships

Area	Householder	Opposite-sex Spouse	Same-sex Spouse	Opposite-sex Unmarried Partner	Same-sex Unmarried Partner	Child[2]	Grandchild	Other Relatives	Non-relatives
City	40.9	13.8	0.3	3.2	0.3	25.8	2.3	4.9	4.5
MSA[1]	41.2	17.6	0.3	3.1	0.2	25.5	2.2	4.6	3.4
U.S.	38.3	17.5	0.2	2.5	0.2	28.3	2.4	4.8	3.4

Note: Figures are percent of the total population; (1) Figures cover the Tampa-St. Petersburg-Clearwater, FL Metropolitan Statistical Area; (2) Includes biological, adopted, and stepchildren of the householder
Source: U.S. Census Bureau, 2020 Census

Gender

Area	Males	Females	Males per 100 Females
City	187,761	197,198	95.2
MSA[1]	1,535,385	1,639,890	93.6
U.S.	162,685,811	168,763,470	96.4

Note: (1) Figures cover the Tampa-St. Petersburg-Clearwater, FL Metropolitan Statistical Area
Source: U.S. Census Bureau, 2020 Census

Marital Status

Area	Never Married	Now Married[2]	Separated	Widowed	Divorced
City	40.3	39.1	2.5	5.0	13.1
MSA[1]	31.3	46.5	1.9	6.8	13.5
U.S.	33.8	48.0	1.8	5.6	10.8

Note: Figures are percentages and cover the population 15 years of age and older; (1) Figures cover the Tampa-St. Petersburg-Clearwater, FL Metropolitan Statistical Area; (2) Excludes separated
Source: U.S. Census Bureau, 2017-2021 American Community Survey 5-Year Estimates

Religious Groups by Family

Area	Catholic	Baptist	Methodist	LDS[2]	Pentecostal	Lutheran	Islam	Adventist	Other
MSA[1]	23.1	6.3	2.9	0.5	1.9	0.6	0.7	1.8	12.1
U.S.	18.7	7.3	3.0	2.0	1.8	1.7	1.3	1.3	11.6

Note: Figures are the number of adherents as a percentage of the total population and cover the eight largest religious groups in the U.S; (1) Figures cover the Tampa-St. Petersburg-Clearwater, FL Metropolitan Statistical Area; (2) Church of Jesus Christ of Latter-day Saints
Sources: 2020 U.S. Religion Census, Association of Statisticians of American Religious Bodies; The Association of Religion Data Archives (ARDA)

Religious Groups by Tradition

Area	Catholic	Evangelical Protestant	Mainline Protestant	Black Protestant	Islam	Judaism	Hinduism	Orthodox	Buddhism
MSA[1]	23.1	16.9	3.8	1.7	0.7	0.4	0.3	0.8	0.4
U.S.	18.7	16.5	5.2	2.3	1.3	0.6	0.4	0.4	0.3

Note: Figures are the number of adherents as a percentage of the total population; (1) Figures cover the Tampa-St. Petersburg-Clearwater, FL Metropolitan Statistical Area
Sources: 2020 U.S. Religion Census, Association of Statisticians of American Religious Bodies; The Association of Religion Data Archives (ARDA)

Tampa, Florida

ECONOMY

Gross Metropolitan Product

Area	2020	2021	2022	2023	Rank[2]
MSA[1]	169.3	187.4	205.4	217.8	24

Note: Figures are in billions of dollars; (1) Figures cover the Tampa-St. Petersburg-Clearwater, FL Metropolitan Statistical Area; (2) Rank is based on 2021 data and ranges from 1 to 381
Source: U.S. Conference of Mayors, U.S. Metro Economies: U.S. Metros Compared to Global and State Economies, June 2022

Economic Growth

Area	2018-20 (%)	2021 (%)	2022 (%)	2023 (%)	Rank[2]
MSA[1]	1.0	7.2	4.1	2.8	72
U.S.	-0.6	5.7	3.1	2.9	—

Note: Figures are real gross metropolitan product (GMP) growth rates and represent average annual percent change; (1) Figures cover the Tampa-St. Petersburg-Clearwater, FL Metropolitan Statistical Area; (2) Rank is based on 2020 2-year average annual percent change and ranges from 1 to 381
Source: U.S. Conference of Mayors, U.S. Metro Economies: U.S. Metros Compared to Global and State Economies, June 2022

Metropolitan Area Exports

Area	2016	2017	2018	2019	2020	2021	Rank[2]
MSA[1]	5,702.9	6,256.0	4,966.7	6,219.7	5,082.2	5,754.7	53

Note: Figures are in millions of dollars; (1) Figures cover the Tampa-St. Petersburg-Clearwater, FL Metropolitan Statistical Area; (2) Rank is based on 2021 data and ranges from 1 to 388
Source: U.S. Department of Commerce, International Trade Administration, Office of Trade and Economic Analysis, Industry and Analysis, Exports by Metropolitan Area, data extracted March 16, 2023

Building Permits

Area	Single-Family 2021	Single-Family 2022	Pct. Chg.	Multi-Family 2021	Multi-Family 2022	Pct. Chg.	Total 2021	Total 2022	Pct. Chg.
City	1,312	1,058	-19.4	1,093	3,753	243.4	2,405	4,811	100.0
MSA[1]	19,305	15,678	-18.8	5,526	14,291	158.6	24,831	29,969	20.7
U.S.	1,115,400	975,600	-12.5	621,600	689,500	10.9	1,737,000	1,665,100	-4.1

Note: (1) Figures cover the Tampa-St. Petersburg-Clearwater, FL Metropolitan Statistical Area; Figures represent new, privately-owned housing units authorized (unadjusted data); All permit data are based on estimates with imputation
Source: U.S. Census Bureau, Manufacturing, Mining, and Construction Statistics, Building Permits, 2021, 2022

Bankruptcy Filings

Area	Business Filings 2021	Business Filings 2022	% Chg.	Nonbusiness Filings 2021	Nonbusiness Filings 2022	% Chg.
Hillsborough County	87	94	8.0	2,061	1,686	-18.2
U.S.	14,347	13,481	-6.0	399,269	374,240	-6.3

Note: Business filings include Chapter 7, Chapter 9, Chapter 11, Chapter 12, Chapter 13, Chapter 15, and Section 304; Nonbusiness filings include Chapter 7, Chapter 11, and Chapter 13
Source: Administrative Office of the U.S. Courts, Business and Nonbusiness Bankruptcy, County Cases Commenced by Chapter of the Bankruptcy Code, During the 12-Month Period Ending December 31, 2021 and Business and Nonbusiness Bankruptcy, County Cases Commenced by Chapter of the Bankruptcy Code, During the 12-Month Period Ending December 31, 2022

Housing Vacancy Rates

Area	Gross Vacancy Rate[2] (%) 2020	2021	2022	Year-Round Vacancy Rate[3] (%) 2020	2021	2022	Rental Vacancy Rate[4] (%) 2020	2021	2022	Homeowner Vacancy Rate[5] (%) 2020	2021	2022
MSA[1]	13.0	14.2	13.3	10.1	10.5	9.9	8.9	7.3	8.1	1.5	1.0	1.2
U.S.	10.6	10.8	10.5	8.2	8.4	8.2	6.3	6.1	5.8	1.0	0.9	0.8

Note: (1) Figures cover the Tampa-St. Petersburg-Clearwater, FL Metropolitan Statistical Area; (2) The percentage of the total housing inventory that is vacant; (3) The percentage of the housing inventory (excluding seasonal units) that is year-round vacant; (4) The percentage of rental inventory that is vacant for rent; (5) The percentage of homeowner inventory that is vacant for sale
Source: U.S. Census Bureau, Housing Vacancies and Homeownership Annual Statistics: 2020, 2021, 2022

INCOME

Income

Area	Per Capita ($)	Median Household ($)	Average Household ($)
City	40,962	59,893	97,942
MSA[1]	35,879	61,121	86,382
U.S.	37,638	69,021	97,196

Note: (1) Figures cover the Tampa-St. Petersburg-Clearwater, FL Metropolitan Statistical Area
Source: U.S. Census Bureau, 2017-2021 American Community Survey 5-Year Estimates

Household Income Distribution

Area	Percent of Households Earning							
	Under $15,000	$15,000 -$24,999	$25,000 -$34,999	$35,000 -$49,999	$50,000 -$74,999	$75,000 -$99,999	$100,000 -$149,999	$150,000 and up
City	12.9	8.5	9.4	12.0	15.8	10.8	13.3	17.3
MSA[1]	9.9	8.6	9.5	13.2	18.0	12.7	14.6	13.7
U.S.	9.4	7.8	8.2	11.4	16.8	12.8	16.3	17.3

Note: (1) Figures cover the Tampa-St. Petersburg-Clearwater, FL Metropolitan Statistical Area
Source: U.S. Census Bureau, 2017-2021 American Community Survey 5-Year Estimates

Poverty Rate

Area	All Ages	Under 18 Years Old	18 to 64 Years Old	65 Years and Over
City	17.2	23.7	14.6	19.3
MSA[1]	12.9	17.4	12.1	10.9
U.S.	12.6	17.0	11.8	9.6

Note: Figures are percentage of people whose income during the past 12 months was below the poverty level;
(1) Figures cover the Tampa-St. Petersburg-Clearwater, FL Metropolitan Statistical Area
Source: U.S. Census Bureau, 2017-2021 American Community Survey 5-Year Estimates

EMPLOYMENT

Labor Force and Employment

Area	Civilian Labor Force			Workers Employed		
	Dec. 2021	Dec. 2022	% Chg.	Dec. 2021	Dec. 2022	% Chg.
City	211,042	219,467	4.0	205,058	214,586	4.6
MSA[1]	1,596,468	1,661,495	4.1	1,552,983	1,625,105	4.6
U.S.	161,696,000	164,224,000	1.6	155,732,000	158,872,000	2.0

Note: Data is not seasonally adjusted and covers workers 16 years of age and older; (1) Figures cover the Tampa-St. Petersburg-Clearwater, FL Metropolitan Statistical Area
Source: Bureau of Labor Statistics, Local Area Unemployment Statistics

Unemployment Rate

Area	2022											
	Jan.	Feb.	Mar.	Apr.	May	Jun.	Jul.	Aug.	Sep.	Oct.	Nov.	Dec.
City	3.5	3.0	2.6	2.3	2.4	2.9	2.8	2.8	2.6	2.7	2.6	2.2
MSA[1]	3.3	2.9	2.5	2.3	2.4	2.9	2.7	2.7	2.5	2.6	2.6	2.2
U.S.	4.4	4.1	3.8	3.3	3.4	3.8	3.8	3.8	3.3	3.4	3.4	3.3

Note: Data is not seasonally adjusted and covers workers 16 years of age and older; (1) Figures cover the Tampa-St. Petersburg-Clearwater, FL Metropolitan Statistical Area
Source: Bureau of Labor Statistics, Local Area Unemployment Statistics

Average Wages

Occupation	$/Hr.	Occupation	$/Hr.
Accountants and Auditors	39.60	Maintenance and Repair Workers	19.72
Automotive Mechanics	22.77	Marketing Managers	72.41
Bookkeepers	21.91	Network and Computer Systems Admin.	44.44
Carpenters	22.26	Nurses, Licensed Practical	25.31
Cashiers	12.70	Nurses, Registered	38.42
Computer Programmers	42.78	Nursing Assistants	16.72
Computer Systems Analysts	47.41	Office Clerks, General	19.64
Computer User Support Specialists	29.20	Physical Therapists	46.29
Construction Laborers	18.14	Physicians	132.49
Cooks, Restaurant	15.73	Plumbers, Pipefitters and Steamfitters	23.00
Customer Service Representatives	18.73	Police and Sheriff's Patrol Officers	33.26
Dentists	77.98	Postal Service Mail Carriers	26.91
Electricians	24.40	Real Estate Sales Agents	27.94
Engineers, Electrical	49.32	Retail Salespersons	16.01
Fast Food and Counter Workers	12.44	Sales Representatives, Technical/Scientific	45.68
Financial Managers	76.40	Secretaries, Exc. Legal/Medical/Executive	18.84
First-Line Supervisors of Office Workers	30.65	Security Guards	15.00
General and Operations Managers	53.47	Surgeons	191.11
Hairdressers/Cosmetologists	17.46	Teacher Assistants, Exc. Postsecondary*	14.33
Home Health and Personal Care Aides	13.80	Teachers, Secondary School, Exc. Sp. Ed.*	32.73
Janitors and Cleaners	13.88	Telemarketers	14.35
Landscaping/Groundskeeping Workers	15.63	Truck Drivers, Heavy/Tractor-Trailer	23.41
Lawyers	66.40	Truck Drivers, Light/Delivery Services	20.06
Maids and Housekeeping Cleaners	13.55	Waiters and Waitresses	15.84

Note: Wage data covers the Tampa-St. Petersburg-Clearwater, FL Metropolitan Statistical Area; (*) Hourly wages were calculated from annual wage data based on a 40 hour work week; n/a not available.
Source: Bureau of Labor Statistics, Metro Area Occupational Employment & Wage Estimates, May 2022

Employment by Industry

Sector	MSA[1] Number of Employees	MSA[1] Percent of Total	U.S. Percent of Total
Construction	94,600	6.2	5.0
Private Education and Health Services	230,900	15.2	16.1
Financial Activities	139,200	9.1	5.9
Government	155,500	10.2	14.5
Information	29,000	1.9	2.0
Leisure and Hospitality	165,100	10.8	10.3
Manufacturing	74,900	4.9	8.4
Mining and Logging	300	<0.1	0.4
Other Services	50,900	3.3	3.7
Professional and Business Services	293,300	19.3	14.7
Retail Trade	171,700	11.3	10.2
Transportation, Warehousing, and Utilities	55,200	3.6	4.9
Wholesale Trade	62,400	4.1	3.9

Note: Figures are non-farm employment as of December 2022. Figures are not seasonally adjusted and include workers 16 years of age and older; (1) Figures cover the Tampa-St. Petersburg-Clearwater, FL Metropolitan Statistical Area
Source: Bureau of Labor Statistics, Current Employment Statistics, Employment, Hours, and Earnings

Employment by Occupation

Occupation Classification	City (%)	MSA[1] (%)	U.S. (%)
Management, Business, Science, and Arts	45.0	40.5	40.3
Natural Resources, Construction, and Maintenance	6.5	8.3	8.7
Production, Transportation, and Material Moving	9.6	9.9	13.1
Sales and Office	22.0	24.3	20.9
Service	16.9	17.1	17.0

Note: Figures cover employed civilians 16 years of age and older; (1) Figures cover the Tampa-St. Petersburg-Clearwater, FL Metropolitan Statistical Area
Source: U.S. Census Bureau, 2017-2021 American Community Survey 5-Year Estimates

Occupations with Greatest Projected Employment Growth: 2022 – 2024

Occupation[1]	2022 Employment	2024 Projected Employment	Numeric Employment Change	Percent Employment Change
General and Operations Managers	196,430	209,480	13,050	6.6
Cooks, Restaurant	117,090	129,670	12,580	10.7
Registered Nurses	208,620	221,040	12,420	6.0
Waiters and Waitresses	194,570	206,380	11,810	6.1
Retail Salespersons	327,010	338,390	11,380	3.5
Stockers and Order Fillers	192,890	203,920	11,030	5.7
Customer Service Representatives	283,220	293,670	10,450	3.7
Fast Food and Counter Workers	203,420	212,470	9,050	4.4
Laborers and Freight, Stock, and Material Movers, Hand	138,200	146,930	8,730	6.3
Maids and Housekeeping Cleaners	77,330	85,600	8,270	10.7

Note: Projections cover Florida; (1) Sorted by numeric employment change
Source: www.projectionscentral.com, State Occupational Projections, 2022–2024 Short-Term Projections

Fastest-Growing Occupations: 2022 – 2024

Occupation[1]	2022 Employment	2024 Projected Employment	Numeric Employment Change	Percent Employment Change
Hotel, Motel, and Resort Desk Clerks	23,000	26,650	3,650	15.9
First-Line Supervisors of Gambling Services Workers	990	1,140	150	15.2
Baggage Porters and Bellhops	3,310	3,810	500	15.1
Solar Photovoltaic Installers	860	990	130	15.1
Nurse Practitioners	17,490	20,080	2,590	14.8
Motion Picture Projectionists	490	560	70	14.3
Lodging Managers	5,160	5,870	710	13.8
Transportation Workers, All Other	980	1,110	130	13.3
Information Security Analysts (SOC 2018)	11,910	13,480	1,570	13.2
Statisticians	1,370	1,550	180	13.1

Note: Projections cover Florida; (1) Sorted by percent employment change and excludes occupations with numeric employment change less than 50
Source: www.projectionscentral.com, State Occupational Projections, 2022–2024 Short-Term Projections

CITY FINANCES

City Government Finances

Component	2020 ($000)	2020 ($ per capita)
Total Revenues	990,724	2,479
Total Expenditures	1,172,762	2,934
Debt Outstanding	1,672,158	4,184
Cash and Securities[1]	1,846,374	4,619

Note: (1) Cash and security holdings of a government at the close of its fiscal year, including those of its dependent agencies, utilities, and liquor stores.
Source: U.S. Census Bureau, State & Local Government Finances 2020

City Government Revenue by Source

Source	2020 ($000)	2020 ($ per capita)	2020 (%)
General Revenue			
From Federal Government	16,345	41	1.6
From State Government	62,850	157	6.3
From Local Governments	28,825	72	2.9
Taxes			
Property	202,879	508	20.5
Sales and Gross Receipts	149,593	374	15.1
Personal Income	0	0	0.0
Corporate Income	0	0	0.0
Motor Vehicle License	0	0	0.0
Other Taxes	60,547	151	6.1
Current Charges	280,468	702	28.3
Liquor Store	0	0	0.0
Utility	111,554	279	11.3

Source: U.S. Census Bureau, State & Local Government Finances 2020

City Government Expenditures by Function

Function	2020 ($000)	2020 ($ per capita)	2020 (%)
General Direct Expenditures			
Air Transportation	0	0	0.0
Corrections	0	0	0.0
Education	0	0	0.0
Employment Security Administration	0	0	0.0
Financial Administration	253,102	633	21.6
Fire Protection	95,161	238	8.1
General Public Buildings	14,204	35	1.2
Governmental Administration, Other	3,800	9	0.3
Health	0	0	0.0
Highways	50,551	126	4.3
Hospitals	0	0	0.0
Housing and Community Development	37,206	93	3.2
Interest on General Debt	15,124	37	1.3
Judicial and Legal	6,206	15	0.5
Libraries	0	0	0.0
Parking	16,421	41	1.4
Parks and Recreation	71,252	178	6.1
Police Protection	166,013	415	14.2
Public Welfare	0	0	0.0
Sewerage	123,387	308	10.5
Solid Waste Management	80,968	202	6.9
Veterans' Services	0	0	0.0
Liquor Store	0	0	0.0
Utility	127,990	320	10.9

Source: U.S. Census Bureau, State & Local Government Finances 2020

TAXES

State Corporate Income Tax Rates

State	Tax Rate (%)	Income Brackets ($)	Num. of Brackets	Financial Institution Tax Rate (%)[a]	Federal Income Tax Ded.
Florida	5.5	Flat rate	1	5.5	No

Note: Tax rates as of January 1, 2023; (a) Rates listed are the corporate income tax rate applied to financial institutions or excise taxes based on income. Some states have other taxes based upon the value of deposits or shares.
Source: Federation of Tax Administrators, State Corporate Income Tax Rates, January 1, 2023

State Individual Income Tax Rates

State	Tax Rate (%)	Income Brackets ($)	Personal Exemptions ($) Single	Personal Exemptions ($) Married	Personal Exemptions ($) Depend.	Standard Ded. ($) Single	Standard Ded. ($) Married
Florida				– No state income tax –			

Note: Tax rates as of January 1, 2023; Local- and county-level taxes are not included
Source: Federation of Tax Administrators, State Individual Income Tax Rates, January 1, 2023

Various State Sales and Excise Tax Rates

State	State Sales Tax (%)	Gasoline[1] ($/gal.)	Cigarette[2] ($/pack)	Spirits[3] ($/gal.)	Wine[4] ($/gal.)	Beer[5] ($/gal.)	Recreational Marijuana (%)
Florida	6	0.4123	1.339	6.50	2.25	0.48	Not legal

Note: All tax rates as of January 1, 2023; (1) The American Petroleum Institute has developed a methodology for determining the average tax rate on a gallon of fuel. Rates may include any of the following: excise taxes, environmental fees, storage tank fees, other fees or taxes, general sales tax, and local taxes; (2) The federal excise tax of $1.0066 per pack and local taxes are not included; (3) Rates are those applicable to off-premise sales of 40% alcohol by volume (a.b.v.) distilled spirits in 750ml containers. Local excise taxes are excluded; (4) Rates are those applicable to off-premise sales of 11% a.b.v. non-carbonated wine in 750ml containers; (5) Rates are those applicable to off-premise sales of 4.7% a.b.v. beer in 12 ounce containers.
Source: Tax Foundation, 2023 Facts & Figures: How Does Your State Compare?

State Business Tax Climate Index Rankings

State	Overall Rank	Corporate Tax Rank	Individual Income Tax Rank	Sales Tax Rank	Property Tax Rank	Unemployment Insurance Tax Rank
Florida	4	10	1	21	12	3

Note: The index is a measure of how each state's tax laws affect economic performance. The lower the rank, the more favorable a state's tax system is for business. States without a given tax are given a ranking of 1. The scores/rankings for the District of Columbia do not affect other states. The 2023 index represents the tax climate as of July 1, 2022.
Source: Tax Foundation, State Business Tax Climate Index 2023

TRANSPORTATION

Means of Transportation to Work

Area	Car/Truck/Van Drove Alone	Car/Truck/Van Car-pooled	Public Transportation Bus	Public Transportation Subway	Public Transportation Railroad	Bicycle	Walked	Other Means	Worked at Home
City	71.9	8.2	1.9	0.0	0.0	0.8	2.1	1.9	13.2
MSA[1]	74.8	8.2	1.0	0.0	0.0	0.5	1.3	1.6	12.4
U.S.	73.2	8.6	2.0	1.6	0.5	0.5	2.5	1.5	9.7

Note: Figures are percentages and cover workers 16 years of age and older; (1) Figures cover the Tampa-St. Petersburg-Clearwater, FL Metropolitan Statistical Area
Source: U.S. Census Bureau, 2017-2021 American Community Survey 5-Year Estimates

Travel Time to Work

Area	Less Than 10 Minutes	10 to 19 Minutes	20 to 29 Minutes	30 to 44 Minutes	45 to 59 Minutes	60 to 89 Minutes	90 Minutes or More
City	11.1	30.2	22.5	23.4	6.8	4.3	1.8
MSA[1]	9.6	26.9	21.0	23.7	10.2	6.3	2.3
U.S.	12.4	28.5	21.0	20.9	8.2	6.2	2.9

Note: Note: Figures are percentages and include workers 16 years old and over; (1) Figures cover the Tampa-St. Petersburg-Clearwater, FL Metropolitan Statistical Area
Source: U.S. Census Bureau, 2017-2021 American Community Survey 5-Year Estimates

Key Congestion Measures

Measure	1990	2000	2010	2015	2020
Annual Hours of Delay, Total (000)	28,408	45,586	70,452	83,008	34,479
Annual Hours of Delay, Per Auto Commuter	28	36	42	47	18
Annual Congestion Cost, Per Auto Commuter ($)	624	754	926	997	401

Note: Covers the Tampa-St. Petersburg FL urban area
Source: Texas A&M Transportation Institute, 2021 Urban Mobility Report

Freeway Travel Time Index

Measure	1985	1990	1995	2000	2005	2010	2015	2020
Urban Area Index[1]	1.12	1.15	1.18	1.19	1.22	1.21	1.22	1.08
Urban Area Rank[1,2]	21	22	26	34	32	33	34	44

Note: Freeway Travel Time Index—the ratio of travel time in the peak period to the travel time at free-flow conditions. For example, a value of 1.30 indicates a 20-minute free-flow trip takes 26 minutes in the peak (20 minutes x 1.30 = 26 minutes); (1) Covers the Tampa-St. Petersburg FL urban area; (2) Rank is based on 101 larger urban areas (#1 = highest travel time index)
Source: Texas A&M Transportation Institute, 2021 Urban Mobility Report

Public Transportation

Agency Name / Mode of Transportation	Vehicles Operated in Maximum Service[1]	Annual Unlinked Passenger Trips[2] (in thous.)	Annual Passenger Miles[3] (in thous.)
Hillsborough Area Regional Transit Authority (HART)			
Bus (directly operated)	125	9,570.8	40,146.8
Demand Response (directly operated)	45	134.3	1,128.0
Demand Response - Taxi	25	8.0	33.5
Streetcar Rail (directly operated)	4	735.1	1,062.3

Note: (1) Number of revenue vehicles operated by the given mode and type of service to meet the annual maximum service requirement. This is the revenue vehicle count during the peak season of the year; on the week and day that maximum service is provided. Vehicles operated in maximum service (VOMS) exclude atypical days and one-time special events; (2) Number of passengers who boarded public transportation vehicles. Passengers are counted each time they board a vehicle no matter how many vehicles they use to travel from their origin to their destination. (3) Sum of the distances ridden by all passengers during the entire fiscal year.
Source: Federal Transit Administration, National Transit Database, 2021

Air Transportation

Airport Name and Code / Type of Service	Passenger Airlines[1]	Passenger Enplanements	Freight Carriers[2]	Freight (lbs)
Tampa International (TPA)				
Domestic service (U.S. carriers - 2022)	28	10,126,595	15	218,693,493
International service (U.S. carriers - 2021)	6	33,875	0	0

Note: (1) Includes all U.S.-based major, minor and commuter airlines that carried at least one passenger during the year; (2) Includes all U.S.-based airlines and freight carriers that transported at least one pound of freight during the year.
Source: Bureau of Transportation Statistics, The Intermodal Transportation Database, Air Carriers: T-100 Domestic Market (U.S. Carriers), 2022; Bureau of Transportation Statistics, The Intermodal Transportation Database, Air Carriers: T-100 International Market (U.S. Carriers), 2021

BUSINESSES

Major Business Headquarters

Company Name	Industry	Fortune[1]	Forbes[2]
No companies listed	-	-	-

Note: (1) Companies that produce a 10-K are ranked 1 to 500 based on 2021 revenue; (2) All private companies with at least $2 billion in annual revenue through the end of their most current fiscal year are ranked 1 to 246; companies listed are headquartered in the city; dashes indicate no ranking
Source: Fortune, "Fortune 500," 2022; Forbes, "America's Largest Private Companies," 2022

Fastest-Growing Businesses

According to *Inc.*, Tampa is home to six of America's 500 fastest-growing private companies: **Ideal Agent** (#73); **Soma Global** (#141); **PainTEQ** (#149); **Snapcell** (#366); **Iron EagleX** (#370); **Onicx Group** (#441). Criteria: must be an independent, privately-held, for-profit, U.S. corporation, proprietorship or partnership as of December 31, 2021; revenues must be at least $100,000 in 2018 and $2 million in 2021; must have four-year operating/sales history. *Inc., "America's 500 Fastest-Growing Private Companies," 2022*

According to Deloitte, Tampa is home to one of North America's 500 fastest-growing high-technology companies: **Ideal Agent** (#34). Companies are ranked by percentage growth in revenue over a four-year period. Criteria for inclusion: company must be headquartered within North America; must own proprietary intellectual property or technology that is sold to customers in products that contributes to a significant portion of the company's operating revenue; must have been in business for a minumum of four years with 2018 operating revenues of at least $50,000 USD/CD and 2021 operating revenues of at least $5 million USD/CD. *Deloitte, 2022 Technology Fast 500™*

Living Environment

COST OF LIVING

Cost of Living Index

Composite Index	Groceries	Housing	Utilities	Transportation	Health Care	Misc. Goods/Services
99.8	108.0	96.7	97.4	100.2	92.2	100.2

Note: The Cost of Living Index measures regional differences in the cost of consumer goods and services, excluding taxes and non-consumer expenditures, for professional and managerial households in the top income quintile. It is based on more than 50,000 prices covering almost 60 different items for which prices are collected three times a year by chambers of commerce, economic development organizations or university applied economic centers in each participating urban area. The numbers shown should be read as a percentage above or below the national average of 100. For example, a value of 115.4 in the groceries column indicates that grocery prices are 15.4% higher than the national average. Small differences in the index numbers should not be interpreted as significant; Figures cover the Tampa FL urban area.
Source: The Council for Community and Economic Research, Cost of Living Index, 2022

Grocery Prices

Area[1]	T-Bone Steak ($/pound)	Frying Chicken ($/pound)	Whole Milk ($/half gal.)	Eggs ($/dozen)	Orange Juice ($/64 oz.)	Coffee ($/11.5 oz.)
City[2]	12.92	1.93	2.78	2.83	4.18	4.31
Avg.	13.81	1.59	2.43	2.25	3.85	4.95
Min.	10.17	0.90	1.51	1.30	2.90	3.46
Max.	19.35	3.30	4.32	4.32	5.31	8.59

Note: (1) Values for the local area are compared with the average, minimum and maximum values for all 286 areas in the Cost of Living Index; (2) Figures cover the Tampa FL urban area; **T-Bone Steak** (price per pound); **Frying Chicken** (price per pound, whole fryer); **Whole Milk** (half gallon carton); **Eggs** (price per dozen, Grade A, large); **Orange Juice** (64 oz. Tropicana or Florida Natural); **Coffee** (11.5 oz. can, vacuum-packed, Maxwell House, Hills Bros, or Folgers).
Source: The Council for Community and Economic Research, Cost of Living Index, 2022

Housing and Utility Costs

Area[1]	New Home Price ($)	Apartment Rent ($/month)	All Electric ($/month)	Part Electric ($/month)	Other Energy ($/month)	Telephone ($/month)
City[2]	414,223	1,528	167.09	-	-	192.89
Avg.	450,913	1,371	176.41	99.93	76.96	190.22
Min.	229,283	546	100.84	31.56	27.15	174.27
Max.	2,434,977	4,569	356.86	249.59	272.24	208.31

Note: (1) Values for the local area are compared with the average, minimum and maximum values for all 286 areas in the Cost of Living Index; (2) Figures cover the Tampa FL urban area; **New Home Price** (2,400 sf living area, 8,000 sf lot, in urban area with full utilities); **Apartment Rent** (950 sf 2 bedroom/1.5 or 2 bath, unfurnished, excluding all utilities except water); **All Electric** (average monthly cost for an all-electric home); **Part Electric** (average monthly cost for a part-electric home); **Other Energy** (average monthly cost for natural gas, fuel oil, coal, wood, and any other forms of energy except electricity); **Telephone** (price includes the base monthly rate plus taxes and fees for three lines of mobile phone service).
Source: The Council for Community and Economic Research, Cost of Living Index, 2022

Health Care, Transportation, and Other Costs

Area[1]	Doctor ($/visit)	Dentist ($/visit)	Optometrist ($/visit)	Gasoline ($/gallon)	Beauty Salon ($/visit)	Men's Shirt ($)
City[2]	100.17	104.90	106.73	3.80	31.35	28.97
Avg.	124.91	107.77	117.66	3.86	43.31	34.21
Min.	36.61	58.25	51.79	2.90	22.18	13.05
Max.	250.21	162.58	371.96	5.54	85.61	63.54

Note: (1) Values for the local area are compared with the average, minimum and maximum values for all 286 areas in the Cost of Living Index; (2) Figures cover the Tampa FL urban area; **Doctor** (general practitioners routine exam of an established patient); **Dentist** (adult teeth cleaning and periodic oral examination); **Optometrist** (full vision eye exam for established adult patient); **Gasoline** (one gallon regular unleaded, national brand, including all taxes, cash price at self-service pump if available); **Beauty Salon** (woman's shampoo, trim, and blow-dry); **Men's Shirt** (cotton/polyester dress shirt, pinpoint weave, long sleeves).
Source: The Council for Community and Economic Research, Cost of Living Index, 2022

HOUSING

Homeownership Rate

Area	2015 (%)	2016 (%)	2017 (%)	2018 (%)	2019 (%)	2020 (%)	2021 (%)	2022 (%)
MSA[1]	64.9	62.9	60.4	64.9	68.0	72.2	68.3	68.4
U.S.	63.7	63.4	63.9	64.4	64.6	66.6	65.5	65.8

Note: (1) Figures cover the Tampa-St. Petersburg-Clearwater, FL Metropolitan Statistical Area
Source: U.S. Census Bureau, Housing Vacancies and Homeownership Annual Statistics: 2015-2022

House Price Index (HPI)

Area	National Ranking[2]	Quarterly Change (%)	One-Year Change (%)	Five-Year Change (%)	Since 1991Q1 (%)
MSA[1]	10	-0.71	19.98	91.22	438.13
U.S.[3]	—	0.34	8.41	58.44	289.08

Note: The HPI is a weighted repeat sales index. It measures average price changes in repeat sales or refinancings on the same properties. This information is obtained by reviewing repeat mortgage transactions on single-family properties whose mortgages have been purchased or securitized by Fannie Mae or Freddie Mac since January 1975; (1) Figures cover the Tampa-St. Petersburg-Clearwater, FL Metropolitan Statistical Area; (2) Rankings are based on annual percentage change for all metro areas containing at least 15,000 transactions over the last 10 years and ranges from 1 to 257; (3) figures based on a weighted average of Census Division estimates using a seasonally adjusted, purchase-only index; all figures are for the period ending December 31, 2022
Source: Federal Housing Finance Agency, Change in FHFA Metropolitan Area House Price Indexes, 2022Q4

Median Single-Family Home Prices

Area	2020	2021	2022p	Percent Change 2021 to 2022
MSA[1]	272.0	330.0	400.0	21.2
U.S. Average	300.2	357.1	392.6	9.9

Note: Figures are median sales prices of existing single-family homes in thousands of dollars; (p) preliminary; (1) Figures cover the Tampa-St. Petersburg-Clearwater, FL Metropolitan Statistical Area
Source: National Association of Realtors, Median Sales Price of Existing Single-Family Homes for Metropolitan Areas, 4th Quarter 2022

Qualifying Income Based on Median Sales Price of Existing Single-Family Homes

Area	With 5% Down ($)	With 10% Down ($)	With 20% Down ($)
MSA[1]	119,374	113,091	100,526
U.S. Average	112,234	106,237	94,513

Note: Figures are preliminary; Qualifying income is based on a mortgage rate of 6.77%. Monthly principal and interest payment is limited to 25% of income; (1) Figures cover the Tampa-St. Petersburg-Clearwater, FL Metropolitan Statistical Area
Source: National Association of Realtors, Qualifying Income Based on Median Sales Price of Existing Single-Family Homes for Metropolitan Areas, 4th Quarter 2022

Home Value

Area	Under $100,000	$100,000 -$199,999	$200,000 -$299,999	$300,000 -$399,999	$400,000 -$499,999	$500,000 -$999,999	$1,000,000 or more	Median ($)
City	9.0	22.7	22.8	14.6	9.9	14.9	6.1	277,700
MSA[1]	16.4	25.3	26.4	14.8	6.9	8.1	2.0	229,400
U.S.	16.2	24.2	20.1	13.6	8.3	13.6	4.1	244,900

Note: Figures are percentages except for median and cover owner-occupied housing units; (1) Figures cover the Tampa-St. Petersburg-Clearwater, FL Metropolitan Statistical Area
Source: U.S. Census Bureau, 2017-2021 American Community Survey 5-Year Estimates

Year Housing Structure Built

Area	2020 or Later	2010 -2019	2000 -2009	1990 -1999	1980 -1989	1970 -1979	1960 -1969	1950 -1959	1940 -1949	Before 1940	Median Year
City	0.3	10.8	17.3	12.5	11.9	11.3	9.3	13.0	5.1	8.6	1982
MSA[1]	0.3	8.2	15.8	14.0	19.9	19.9	9.1	8.3	2.0	2.6	1984
U.S.	0.2	7.3	13.6	13.6	13.2	14.8	10.3	10.0	4.7	12.2	1979

Note: Figures are percentages except for Median Year; Note: (1) Figures cover the Tampa-St. Petersburg-Clearwater, FL Metropolitan Statistical Area
Source: U.S. Census Bureau, 2017-2021 American Community Survey 5-Year Estimates

Gross Monthly Rent

Area	Under $500	$500 -$999	$1,000 -$1,499	$1,500 -$1,999	$2,000 -$2,499	$2,500 -$2,999	$3,000 and up	Median ($)
City	7.4	21.2	39.2	19.4	8.2	2.4	2.1	1,249
MSA[1]	4.1	24.2	42.4	19.8	6.2	1.8	1.5	1,230
U.S.	8.1	30.5	30.8	16.8	7.3	3.1	3.5	1,163

Note: Figures are percentages except for median; Gross rent is the contract rent plus the estimated average monthly cost of utilities (electricity, gas, and water and sewer) and fuels (oil, coal, kerosene, wood, etc.) if these are paid by the renter (or paid for the renter by someone else); (1) Figures cover the Tampa-St. Petersburg-Clearwater, FL Metropolitan Statistical Area
Source: U.S. Census Bureau, 2017-2021 American Community Survey 5-Year Estimates

HEALTH

Health Risk Factors

Category	MSA[1] (%)	U.S. (%)
Adults aged 18–64 who have any kind of health care coverage	n/a	90.9
Adults who reported being in good or better health	n/a	85.2
Adults who have been told they have high blood cholesterol	n/a	35.7
Adults who have been told they have high blood pressure	n/a	32.4
Adults who are current smokers	n/a	14.4
Adults who currently use e-cigarettes	n/a	6.7
Adults who currently use chewing tobacco, snuff, or snus	n/a	3.5
Adults who are heavy drinkers[2]	n/a	6.3
Adults who are binge drinkers[3]	n/a	15.4
Adults who are overweight (BMI 25.0 - 29.9)	n/a	34.4
Adults who are obese (BMI 30.0 - 99.8)	n/a	33.9
Adults who participated in any physical activities in the past month	n/a	76.3

Note: (1) Figures for the Tampa-St. Petersburg-Clearwater, FL Metropolitan Statistical Area were not available.
(2) Heavy drinkers are classified as adult men having more than 14 drinks per week and adult women having more than 7 drinks per week; (3) Binge drinkers are classified as males having five or more drinks on one occasion or females having four or more drinks on one occasion
Source: Centers for Disease Control and Prevention, Behavioral Risk Factor Surveillance System, SMART: Selected Metropolitan Area Risk Trends, 2021

Acute and Chronic Health Conditions

Category	MSA[1] (%)	U.S. (%)
Adults who have ever been told they had a heart attack	n/a	4.0
Adults who have ever been told they have angina or coronary heart disease	n/a	3.8
Adults who have ever been told they had a stroke	n/a	3.0
Adults who have ever been told they have asthma	n/a	14.9
Adults who have ever been told they have arthritis	n/a	25.8
Adults who have ever been told they have diabetes[2]	n/a	10.9
Adults who have ever been told they had skin cancer	n/a	6.6
Adults who have ever been told they had any other types of cancer	n/a	7.5
Adults who have ever been told they have COPD	n/a	6.1
Adults who have ever been told they have kidney disease	n/a	3.0
Adults who have ever been told they have a form of depression	n/a	20.5

Note: (1) Figures for the Tampa-St. Petersburg-Clearwater, FL Metropolitan Statistical Area were not available.
(2) Figures do not include pregnancy-related, borderline, or pre-diabetes
Source: Centers for Disease Control and Prevention, Behavioral Risk Factor Surveillance System, SMART: Selected Metropolitan Area Risk Trends, 2021

Health Screening and Vaccination Rates

Category	MSA[1] (%)	U.S. (%)
Adults who have ever been tested for HIV	n/a	34.9
Adults who have had their blood cholesterol checked within the last five years	n/a	85.2
Adults aged 65+ who have had flu shot within the past year	n/a	68.6
Adults aged 65+ who have ever had a pneumonia vaccination	n/a	71.0

Note: (1) Figures for the Tampa-St. Petersburg-Clearwater, FL Metropolitan Statistical Area were not available.
Source: Centers for Disease Control and Prevention, Behavioral Risk Factor Surveillance System, SMART: Selected Metropolitan Area Risk Trends, 2021

Disability Status

Category	MSA[1] (%)	U.S. (%)
Adults who reported being deaf	n/a	7.2
Are you blind or have serious difficulty seeing, even when wearing glasses?	n/a	4.8
Are you limited in any way in any of your usual activities due to arthritis?	n/a	11.1
Do you have difficulty doing errands alone?	n/a	7.0
Do you have difficulty dressing or bathing?	n/a	3.6
Do you have serious difficulty concentrating/remembering/making decisions?	n/a	12.1
Do you have serious difficulty walking or climbing stairs?	n/a	12.8

Note: (1) Figures for the Tampa-St. Petersburg-Clearwater, FL Metropolitan Statistical Area were not available.
Source: Centers for Disease Control and Prevention, Behavioral Risk Factor Surveillance System, SMART: Selected Metropolitan Area Risk Trends, 2021

Mortality Rates for the Top 10 Causes of Death in the U.S.

ICD-10[a] Sub-Chapter	ICD-10[a] Code	Crude Mortality Rate[1] per 100,000 population County[2]	U.S.
Malignant neoplasms	C00-C97	160.6	182.6
Ischaemic heart diseases	I20-I25	99.7	113.1
Other forms of heart disease	I30-I51	40.0	64.4
Other degenerative diseases of the nervous system	G30-G31	47.5	51.0
Cerebrovascular diseases	I60-I69	36.2	47.8
Other external causes of accidental injury	W00-X59	47.3	46.4
Chronic lower respiratory diseases	J40-J47	37.1	45.7
Organic, including symptomatic, mental disorders	F01-F09	32.9	35.9
Hypertensive diseases	I10-I15	44.4	35.0
Diabetes mellitus	E10-E14	24.9	29.6

Note: (a) ICD-10 = International Classification of Diseases 10th Revision; (1) Crude mortality rates are a three-year average covering 2019-2021; (2) Figures cover Hillsborough County.
Source: Centers for Disease Control and Prevention, National Center for Health Statistics. National Vital Statistics System, Mortality 2018-2021 on CDC WONDER Online Database

Mortality Rates for Selected Causes of Death

ICD-10[a] Sub-Chapter	ICD-10[a] Code	Crude Mortality Rate[1] per 100,000 population County[2]	U.S.
Assault	X85-Y09	6.1	7.0
Diseases of the liver	K70-K76	15.2	19.8
Human immunodeficiency virus (HIV) disease	B20-B24	2.6	1.5
Influenza and pneumonia	J09-J18	13.0	14.7
Intentional self-harm	X60-X84	13.8	14.3
Malnutrition	E40-E46	2.1	4.3
Obesity and other hyperalimentation	E65-E68	2.3	3.0
Renal failure	N17-N19	11.8	15.7
Transport accidents	V01-V99	15.7	13.6
Viral hepatitis	B15-B19	1.0	1.2

Note: (a) ICD-10 = International Classification of Diseases 10th Revision; (1) Crude mortality rates are a three-year average covering 2019-2021; (2) Figures cover Hillsborough County; Data are suppressed when the data meet the criteria for confidentiality constraints; Crude mortality rates are flagged as unreliable when the rate would be calculated with a numerator of 20 or less.
Source: Centers for Disease Control and Prevention, National Center for Health Statistics. National Vital Statistics System, Mortality 2018-2021 on CDC WONDER Online Database

Health Insurance Coverage

Area	With Health Insurance	With Private Health Insurance	With Public Health Insurance	Without Health Insurance	Population Under Age 19 Without Health Insurance
City	88.9	63.5	33.0	11.1	5.1
MSA[1]	88.3	63.7	36.4	11.7	6.2
U.S.	91.2	67.8	35.4	8.8	5.3

Note: Figures are percentages that cover the civilian noninstitutionalized population; (1) Figures cover the Tampa-St. Petersburg-Clearwater, FL Metropolitan Statistical Area
Source: U.S. Census Bureau, 2017-2021 American Community Survey 5-Year Estimates

Number of Medical Professionals

Area	MDs[3]	DOs[3,4]	Dentists	Podiatrists	Chiropractors	Optometrists
County[1] (number)	5,360	465	911	89	410	222
County[1] (rate[2])	366.3	31.8	61.6	6.0	27.7	15.0
U.S. (rate[2])	289.3	23.5	72.5	6.2	28.7	17.4

Note: Data as of 2021 unless noted; (1) Data covers Hillsborough County; (2) Rate per 100,000 population; (3) Data as of 2020 and includes all active, non-federal physicians; (4) Doctor of Osteopathic Medicine
Source: U.S. Department of Health and Human Services, Health Resources and Services Administration, Bureau of Health Professions, Area Resource File (ARF) 2021-2022

Best Hospitals

According to *U.S. News*, the Tampa-St. Petersburg-Clearwater, FL metro area is home to three of the best hospitals in the U.S.: **Florida Orthopaedic Institute at Tampa General Hospital** (7 adult specialties); **H. Lee Moffitt Cancer Center and Research Institute** (1 adult specialty); **Tampa General Hospital** (7 adult specialties). The hospitals listed were nationally ranked in at least one of 15 adult or 10 pediatric specialties. The number of specialties shown cover the parent hospital. Only 164 U.S. hospitals performed well enough to be nationally ranked in one or more specialties. Twenty hospitals in the U.S. made the Honor Roll. The Best Hospitals Honor Roll takes both the national rankings and the procedure and condition ratings into account. Hospitals received points if they were nationally ranked in one of the 15 adult specialties—the higher they ranked, the more points they got—and how many ratings of "high performing" they earned in the 17 procedures and conditions. *U.S. News Online, "America's Best Hospitals 2022-23"*

According to *U.S. News*, the Tampa-St. Petersburg-Clearwater, FL metro area is home to one of the best children's hospitals in the U.S.: **Johns Hopkins All Children's Hospital** (4 pediatric specialties). The hospital listed was highly ranked in at least one of 10 pediatric specialties. Eighty-six children's hospitals in the U.S. were nationally ranked in at least one specialty. Hospitals received points for being ranked in a specialty, and the 10 hospitals with the most points across the 10 specialties make up the Honor Roll. *U.S. News Online, "America's Best Children's Hospitals 2022-23"*

EDUCATION

Public School District Statistics

District Name	Schls	Pupils	Pupil/Teacher Ratio	Minority Pupils[1] (%)	LEP/ELL[2] (%)	IEP[3] (%)
Hillsborough	304	224,149	17.2	68.8	10.7	15.0

Note: Table includes school districts with 2,000 or more students; (1) Percentage of students that are not non-Hispanic white; (2) Percentage of students that are Limited English Proficient or English Language Learners (2018-19); (3) Percentage of students that have an Individualized Education Program (2019-20).
Source: U.S. Department of Education, National Center for Education Statistics, Common Core of Data, Local Education Agency (School District) Universe Survey: School Year 2021-2022

Highest Level of Education

Area	Less than H.S.	H.S. Diploma	Some College, No Deg.	Associate Degree	Bachelor's Degree	Master's Degree	Prof. School Degree	Doctorate Degree
City	11.6	23.4	15.3	7.9	24.8	10.6	4.4	2.0
MSA[1]	9.6	28.1	20.0	9.8	20.8	8.2	2.2	1.2
U.S.	11.1	26.5	20.0	8.7	20.6	9.3	2.2	1.5

Note: Figures cover persons age 25 and over; (1) Figures cover the Tampa-St. Petersburg-Clearwater, FL Metropolitan Statistical Area
Source: U.S. Census Bureau, 2017-2021 American Community Survey 5-Year Estimates

Educational Attainment by Race

Area	High School Graduate or Higher (%)					Bachelor's Degree or Higher (%)				
	Total	White	Black	Asian	Hisp.[2]	Total	White	Black	Asian	Hisp.[2]
City	88.4	91.9	84.1	87.7	78.2	41.8	49.8	18.7	65.4	26.7
MSA[1]	90.4	91.9	88.7	85.1	81.4	32.4	33.1	25.0	51.8	24.6
U.S.	88.9	91.4	87.2	87.6	71.2	33.7	35.5	23.3	55.6	18.4

Note: Figures shown cover persons 25 years old and over; (1) Figures cover the Tampa-St. Petersburg-Clearwater, FL Metropolitan Statistical Area; (2) People of Hispanic origin can be of any race
Source: U.S. Census Bureau, 2017-2021 American Community Survey 5-Year Estimates

School Enrollment by Grade and Control

Area	Preschool (%)		Kindergarten (%)		Grades 1 - 4 (%)		Grades 5 - 8 (%)		Grades 9 - 12 (%)	
	Public	Private	Public	Private	Public	Private	Public	Private	Public	Private
City	51.4	48.6	81.9	18.1	87.9	12.1	83.5	16.5	82.2	17.8
MSA[1]	54.7	45.3	82.3	17.7	84.8	15.2	85.9	14.1	87.4	12.6
U.S.	58.8	41.2	86.3	13.7	88.3	11.7	88.6	11.4	89.4	10.6

Note: Figures shown cover persons 3 years old and over; (1) Figures cover the Tampa-St. Petersburg-Clearwater, FL Metropolitan Statistical Area
Source: U.S. Census Bureau, 2017-2021 American Community Survey 5-Year Estimates

Higher Education

Four-Year Colleges			Two-Year Colleges			Medical Schools[1]	Law Schools[2]	Voc/Tech[3]
Public	Private Non-profit	Private For-profit	Public	Private Non-profit	Private For-profit			
3	7	5	5	2	4	1	2	15

Note: Figures cover institutions located within the Tampa-St. Petersburg-Clearwater, FL Metropolitan Statistical Area and include main campuses only; (1) includes schools accredited by the Liaison Committee on Medical Education and the American Osteopathic Association's Commission on Osteopathic College Accreditation; (2) includes ABA-accredited schools, schools with provisional ABA accreditation, and state accredited schools; (3) includes all schools with programs that are less than 2 years.
Source: National Center for Education Statistics, Integrated Postsecondary Education Data System (IPEDS), 2021-22; Wikipedia, List of Medical Schools in the United States, accessed April 10, 2023; Wikipedia, List of Law Schools in the United States, accessed April 10, 2023

According to *U.S. News & World Report*, the Tampa-St. Petersburg-Clearwater, FL metro area is home to one of the top 200 national universities in the U.S.: **University of South Florida** (#97 tie). The indicators used to capture academic quality fall into a number of categories: assessment by administrators at peer institutions; retention of students; faculty resources; student selectivity; financial resources; alumni giving; high school counselor ratings of colleges; and graduation rate. *U.S. News & World Report, "America's Best Colleges 2023"*

According to *U.S. News & World Report,* the Tampa-St. Petersburg-Clearwater, FL metro area is home to one of the top 75 medical schools for research in the U.S.: **University of South Florida (Morsani)** (#46). The rankings are based on a weighted average of 11 measures of quality: quality assessment; peer assessment score; assessment score by residency directors; research activity; total research activity; average research activity per faculty member; student selectivity; median MCAT total score; median undergraduate GPA; acceptance rate; and faculty resources. *U.S. News & World Report, "America's Best Graduate Schools, Medical, 2023"*

EMPLOYERS

Major Employers

Company Name	Industry
Baycare Health System	General medical & surgical hospitals
Beall's	Manufacturing
Busch Gardens	Arts, entertainment & recreation
Caspers Company	Accommodation & food services
Citi	Finance & insurance
Florida Hospital	Health care & social assistance
Gerdau Ameristeel US	Manufacturing
HCA Healthcare	Health care & social assistance
Home Shopping Network	Information
JPMorgan Chase	Finance & insurance
MacDill Air Force Base	Public administration
Moffitt Cancer Center & Research Institute	Health care & social assistance
Progressive	Finance & insurance
Publix Supermarkets	Retail grocery
Raymond James Financial	Finance & insurance
Tampa General Hospital	Health care & social assistance
Tech Data Corp	Wholesale trade
University of South Florida	Educational services
Verizon	Information
WellCare	Finance & insurance

Note: Companies shown are located within the Tampa-St. Petersburg-Clearwater, FL Metropolitan Statistical Area.
Source: Hoovers.com; Wikipedia

Best Companies to Work For

WilsonHCG, headquartered in Tampa, is among "Fortune's Best Workplaces for Women." To pick the best companies, *Fortune* partnered with the Great Place to Work Institute. To be considered for the list, companies must be Great Place To Work-Certified. Companies must also employ at least 50 women, at least 20% of their non-executive managers must be female, and at least one executive must be female. To determine the Best Workplaces for Women, Great Place To Work measured the differences in women's survey responses to those of their peers and assesses the impact of demographics and roles on the quality and consistency of women's experiences. Great Place To Work also analyzed the gender balance of each workplace, how it compared to each company's industry, and patterns in representation as women rise from front-line positions to the board of directors. *Fortune, "Best Workplaces for Women," 2022*

Healthcare Solutions Direct, headquartered in Tampa, is among "Best Workplaces in Health Care." To determine the Best Workplaces in Health Care list, Great Place To Work analyzed the survey responses of over 161,000 employees from Great Place To Work-Certified companies in the health care industry. Survey data analysis and company-provided datapoints are then factored into a combined score to compare and rank the companies that create the most consistently positive experience for all employees in this industry. *Fortune, "Best Workplaces in Health Care," 2022*

PUBLIC SAFETY

Crime Rate

Area	Total Crime	Violent Crime Rate				Property Crime Rate		
		Murder	Rape[3]	Robbery	Aggrav. Assault	Burglary	Larceny-Theft	Motor Vehicle Theft
City	1,885.4	10.1	24.8	79.8	405.5	227.1	980.2	157.8
Suburbs[1]	1,648.1	3.1	34.5	42.4	204.3	176.5	1,068.6	118.6
Metro[2]	1,678.0	4.0	33.3	47.1	229.7	182.8	1,057.5	123.6
U.S.	2,356.7	6.5	38.4	73.9	279.7	314.2	1,398.0	246.0

Note: Figures are crimes per 100,000 population; (1) All areas within the metro area that are located outside the city limits; (2) Figures cover the Tampa-St. Petersburg-Clearwater, FL Metropolitan Statistical Area; (3) All figures shown were reported using the revised Uniform Crime Reporting (UCR) definition of rape; Due to the transition to the National Incident-Based Reporting System (NIBRS), limited city and metro area data was released for 2021.
Source: FBI Uniform Crime Reports, 2020

Hate Crimes

Area	Number of Quarters Reported	Race/Ethnicity/ Ancestry	Religion	Sexual Orientation	Disability	Gender	Gender Identity
City	4	0	0	1	0	0	0
U.S.	4	5,227	1,244	1,110	130	75	266

Note: Due to the transition to the National Incident-Based Reporting System (NIBRS), limited crime data was released for 2021.
Source: Federal Bureau of Investigation, Hate Crime Statistics 2020

Identity Theft Consumer Reports

Area	Reports	Reports per 100,000 Population	Rank[2]
MSA[1]	12,078	383	36
U.S.	1,108,609	339	-

Note: (1) Figures cover the Tampa-St. Petersburg-Clearwater, FL Metropolitan Statistical Area; (2) Rank ranges from 1 to 391 where 1 indicates greatest number of identity theft reports per 100,000 population
Source: Federal Trade Commission, Consumer Sentinel Network Data Book 2022

Fraud and Other Consumer Reports

Area	Reports	Reports per 100,000 Population	Rank[2]
MSA[1]	47,325	1,501	11
U.S.	4,064,520	1,245	-

Note: (1) Figures cover the Tampa-St. Petersburg-Clearwater, FL Metropolitan Statistical Area; (2) Rank ranges from 1 to 391 where 1 indicates greatest number of fraud and other consumer reports per 100,000 population
Source: Federal Trade Commission, Consumer Sentinel Network Data Book 2022

POLITICS

2020 Presidential Election Results

Area	Biden	Trump	Jorgensen	Hawkins	Other
Hillsborough County	52.7	45.8	0.8	0.2	0.5
U.S.	51.3	46.8	1.2	0.3	0.5

Note: Results are percentages and may not add to 100% due to rounding
Source: Dave Leip's Atlas of U.S. Presidential Elections

SPORTS

Professional Sports Teams

Team Name	League	Year Established
Tampa Bay Buccaneers	National Football League (NFL)	1976
Tampa Bay Lightning	National Hockey League (NHL)	1993
Tampa Bay Rays	Major League Baseball (MLB)	1998

Note: Includes teams located in the Tampa-St. Petersburg-Clearwater, FL Metropolitan Statistical Area.
Source: Wikipedia, Major Professional Sports Teams of the United States and Canada, April 12, 2023

CLIMATE

Average and Extreme Temperatures

Temperature	Jan	Feb	Mar	Apr	May	Jun	Jul	Aug	Sep	Oct	Nov	Dec	Yr.
Extreme High (°F)	85	88	91	93	98	99	97	98	96	94	90	86	99
Average High (°F)	70	72	76	82	87	90	90	90	89	84	77	72	82
Average Temp. (°F)	60	62	67	72	78	81	82	83	81	75	68	62	73
Average Low (°F)	50	52	56	61	67	73	74	74	73	66	57	52	63
Extreme Low (°F)	21	24	29	40	49	53	63	67	57	40	23	18	18

Note: Figures cover the years 1948-1990
Source: National Climatic Data Center, International Station Meteorological Climate Summary, 9/96

Average Precipitation/Snowfall/Humidity

Precip./Humidity	Jan	Feb	Mar	Apr	May	Jun	Jul	Aug	Sep	Oct	Nov	Dec	Yr.
Avg. Precip. (in.)	2.1	2.8	3.5	1.8	3.0	5.6	7.3	7.9	6.5	2.3	1.8	2.1	46.7
Avg. Snowfall (in.)	Tr	Tr	Tr	0	0	0	0	0	0	0	0	Tr	Tr
Avg. Rel. Hum. 7am (%)	87	87	86	86	85	86	88	90	91	89	88	87	88
Avg. Rel. Hum. 4pm (%)	56	55	54	51	52	60	65	66	64	57	56	57	58

Note: Figures cover the years 1948-1990; Tr = Trace amounts (<0.05 in. of rain; <0.5 in. of snow)
Source: National Climatic Data Center, International Station Meteorological Climate Summary, 9/96

Tampa, Florida 503

Weather Conditions

Temperature			Daytime Sky			Precipitation		
32°F & below	45°F & below	90°F & above	Clear	Partly cloudy	Cloudy	0.01 inch or more precip.	0.1 inch or more snow/ice	Thunder-storms
3	35	85	81	204	80	107	< 1	87

Note: Figures are average number of days per year and cover the years 1948-1990
Source: National Climatic Data Center, International Station Meteorological Climate Summary, 9/96

HAZARDOUS WASTE

Superfund Sites

The Tampa-St. Petersburg-Clearwater, FL metro area is home to nine sites on the EPA's Superfund National Priorities List: **Alaric Area Gw Plume** (final); **Arkla Terra Property** (final); **Helena Chemical Co. (Tampa Plant)** (final); **JJ Seifert Machine** (final); **MRI Corp (Tampa)** (final); **Normandy Park Apartments** (proposed); **Peak Oil Co./Bay Drum Co.** (final); **Raleigh Street Dump** (final); **Reeves Southeastern Galvanizing Corp.** (final). There are a total of 1,165 Superfund sites with a status of proposed or final on the list in the U.S. *U.S. Environmental Protection Agency, National Priorities List, April 12, 2023*

AIR QUALITY

Air Quality Trends: Ozone

	1990	1995	2000	2005	2010	2015	2018	2019	2020	2021
MSA[1]	0.080	0.075	0.081	0.075	0.067	0.062	0.065	0.065	0.063	0.060
U.S.	0.087	0.089	0.081	0.080	0.072	0.067	0.069	0.065	0.065	0.067

Note: (1) Data covers the Tampa-St. Petersburg-Clearwater, FL Metropolitan Statistical Area. The values shown are the composite ozone concentration averages among trend sites based on the highest fourth daily maximum 8-hour concentration in parts per million. These trends are based on sites having an adequate record of monitoring data during the trend period. Data from exceptional events are included.
Source: U.S. Environmental Protection Agency, Air Quality Monitoring Information, "Air Quality Trends by City, 1990-2021"

Air Quality Index

Area	Percent of Days when Air Quality was...[2]					AQI Statistics[2]	
	Good	Moderate	Unhealthy for Sensitive Groups	Unhealthy	Very Unhealthy	Maximum	Median
MSA[1]	72.9	26.8	0.3	0.0	0.0	129	44

Note: (1) Data covers the Tampa-St. Petersburg-Clearwater, FL Metropolitan Statistical Area; (2) Based on 365 days with AQI data in 2021. Air Quality Index (AQI) is an index for reporting daily air quality. EPA calculates the AQI for five major air pollutants regulated by the Clean Air Act: ground-level ozone, particle pollution (aka particulate matter), carbon monoxide, sulfur dioxide, and nitrogen dioxide. The AQI runs from 0 to 500. The higher the AQI value, the greater the level of air pollution and the greater the health concern. There are six AQI categories: "Good" AQI is between 0 and 50. Air quality is considered satisfactory; "Moderate" AQI is between 51 and 100. Air quality is acceptable; "Unhealthy for Sensitive Groups" When AQI values are between 101 and 150, members of sensitive groups may experience health effects; "Unhealthy" When AQI values are between 151 and 200 everyone may begin to experience health effects; "Very Unhealthy" AQI values between 201 and 300 trigger a health alert; "Hazardous" AQI values over 300 trigger warnings of emergency conditions (not shown).
Source: U.S. Environmental Protection Agency, Air Quality Index Report, 2021

Air Quality Index Pollutants

Area	Percent of Days when AQI Pollutant was...[2]					
	Carbon Monoxide	Nitrogen Dioxide	Ozone	Sulfur Dioxide	Particulate Matter 2.5	Particulate Matter 10
MSA[1]	0.0	0.0	51.2	(3)	48.2	0.5

Note: (1) Data covers the Tampa-St. Petersburg-Clearwater, FL Metropolitan Statistical Area; (2) Based on 365 days with AQI data in 2021. The Air Quality Index (AQI) is an index for reporting daily air quality. EPA calculates the AQI for five major air pollutants regulated by the Clean Air Act: ground-level ozone, particle pollution (also known as particulate matter), carbon monoxide, sulfur dioxide, and nitrogen dioxide. The AQI runs from 0 to 500. The higher the AQI value, the greater the level of air pollution and the greater the health concern; (3) Sulfur dioxide is no longer included in this table (as of December 8, 2021) because SO_2 concentrations tend to be very localized and not necessarily representative of broad geographical areas like counties and CBSAs.
Source: U.S. Environmental Protection Agency, Air Quality Index Report, 2021

Maximum Air Pollutant Concentrations: Particulate Matter, Ozone, CO and Lead

	Particulate Matter 10 (ug/m^3)	Particulate Matter 2.5 Wtd AM (ug/m^3)	Particulate Matter 2.5 24-Hr (ug/m^3)	Ozone (ppm)	Carbon Monoxide (ppm)	Lead (ug/m^3)
MSA[1] Level	61	8.5	18	0.063	1	0.08
NAAQS[2]	150	15	35	0.075	9	0.15
Met NAAQS[2]	Yes	Yes	Yes	Yes	Yes	Yes

Note: (1) Data covers the Tampa-St. Petersburg-Clearwater, FL Metropolitan Statistical Area; Data from exceptional events are included; (2) National Ambient Air Quality Standards; ppm = parts per million; ug/m^3 = micrograms per cubic meter; n/a not available.
Concentrations: Particulate Matter 10 (coarse particulate)—highest second maximum 24-hour concentration; Particulate Matter 2.5 Wtd AM (fine particulate)—highest weighted annual mean concentration; Particulate Matter 2.5 24-Hour (fine particulate)—highest 98th percentile 24-hour concentration; Ozone—highest fourth daily maximum 8-hour concentration; Carbon Monoxide—highest second maximum non-overlapping 8-hour concentration; Lead—maximum running 3-month average
Source: U.S. Environmental Protection Agency, Air Quality Monitoring Information, "Air Quality Statistics by City, 2021"

Maximum Air Pollutant Concentrations: Nitrogen Dioxide and Sulfur Dioxide

	Nitrogen Dioxide AM (ppb)	Nitrogen Dioxide 1-Hr (ppb)	Sulfur Dioxide AM (ppb)	Sulfur Dioxide 1-Hr (ppb)	Sulfur Dioxide 24-Hr (ppb)
MSA[1] Level	9	37	n/a	29	n/a
NAAQS[2]	53	100	30	75	140
Met NAAQS[2]	Yes	Yes	n/a	Yes	n/a

Note: (1) Data covers the Tampa-St. Petersburg-Clearwater, FL Metropolitan Statistical Area; Data from exceptional events are included; (2) National Ambient Air Quality Standards; ppm = parts per million; ug/m^3 = micrograms per cubic meter; n/a not available.
Concentrations: Nitrogen Dioxide AM—highest arithmetic mean concentration; Nitrogen Dioxide 1-Hr—highest 98th percentile 1-hour daily maximum concentration; Sulfur Dioxide AM—highest annual mean concentration; Sulfur Dioxide 1-Hr—highest 99th percentile 1-hour daily maximum concentration; Sulfur Dioxide 24-Hr—highest second maximum 24-hour concentration
Source: U.S. Environmental Protection Agency, Air Quality Monitoring Information, "Air Quality Statistics by City, 2021"

Tuscaloosa, Alabama

Background

Tuscaloosa is located on the Black Warrior River in west central Alabama. This seat of Tuscaloosa County is situated between the Appalachian Highland and the Gulf Coastal Plain, giving the city a diverse geography. The city celebrated its 200th birthday in 2019.

Originally inhabited by the Creek or Muskogee people, these native inhabitants were relocated following the passage of the Indian Removal Act in 1830 and were sent to Indian Territory. The capital of Alabama, from 1826 to 1846, Tuscaloosa grew rapidly once the University of Alabama was founded there in 1831, although moving the capital to Montgomery in 1846 reversed a good deal of this growth. The Civil War caused widespread damage including the burning of the University, and the Reconstruction period caused additional economic damage. In 1890s the U.S. Army Corps of Engineers constructed a series of locks and dams on the Black Warrior River, linking Tuscaloosa to the city of Mobile and the Gulf Coast. As a result, Tuscaloosa became active in trade and its economy began to flourish, helped by mining and metallurgical industries that took root in the city at this time.

Tuscaloosa continued to experience steady growth, with its population increasing by 75 percent between 1880 and 1890. The city's economy diversified throughout the 20th century and into the 21st century, although mining and construction and higher education continued to be integral to the economy. Retail trade and transportation, hospitality, government, and finance have also become key fields of employment, and manufacturing retains a healthy presence, with BF Goodrich Tire, GAF Materials Corporation, and JVC America all in Tuscaloosa. Nearby, Mercedes-Benz's U.S. International Assembly employs many city residents.

Tuscaloosa played a key role in the Civil Rights Movement of the 1960s, much of it revolving around university admissions. In 1956, Autherine Lucy became the first African American admitted to a white public university in the state—University of Alabama. On her first day, she was met with a mob of more than a thousand white male students who threw objects at her car and who were expelled by the University. In 1963, Alabama governor George Wallace stood at the entrance of the University, attempting to prevent two African American students from entering.

Tuscaloosa was also home to many brave protestors who fought valiantly for civil rights. Today, the University is integrated with a diverse student population.

Although much of the cultural life of Tuscaloosa is centered on the University, the city is home to the world-class, 1,094-seat Bama Theater in downtown, and the massive Tuscaloosa Amphitheater hosts many of the world's biggest musical acts. The city's museums include the Murphy African American Museum, Alabama Museum of Natural History, and Westervelt Warner Museum of American Art.

In the world of sports, Tuscaloosa is best known for the University of Alabama's football team, the Crimson Tide. Among the most successful programs in the country, Alabama has won five national championships since 2009 and regularly turns out star N.F.L. players under Coach Nick Saban. The Tide play in the 101,821-seat Bryant-Denny stadium. The University features competitive baseball, softball, golf, and women's gymnastics programs. Nearby Stillman College features additional sports programs.

Tuscaloosa is marked by a humid subtropical climate. Although the city experiences four distinct seasons, winter, from mid-December to late-February, is notably mild, with temperatures in January reaching 44 degrees. On average, the city records 71 days of temperatures 90 degrees or above. Tuscaloosa also experiences severe thunderstorms and the occasional tornado. In 2011, two tornadoes struck the city in a span of 12 days, killing over 50 people and causing much structural damage.

Rankings

Business/Finance Rankings

- The Tuscaloosa metro area appeared on the Milken Institute "2022 Best Performing Cities" list. Rank: #155 out of 201 small metro areas (population over 60,000). Criteria: job growth; wage and salary growth; high-tech output growth; housing affordability; household broadband access. *Milken Institute, "Best-Performing Cities 2022," March 28, 2022*

- *Forbes* ranked 203 smaller metro areas (population under 268,000) to determine the nation's "Best Small Places for Business and Careers." The Tuscaloosa metro area was ranked #49. Criteria: costs (business and living); job growth (past and projected); income growth; quality of life; educational attainment (college and high school); projected economic growth; cultural and leisure opportunities; workplace tolerance laws; net migration patterns. *Forbes, "The Best Small Places for Business and Careers 2019," October 30, 2019*

Environmental Rankings

- Tuscaloosa was highlighted as one of the cleanest metro areas for ozone air pollution in the U.S. during 2019 through 2021. The list represents cities with no monitored ozone air pollution in unhealthful ranges. *American Lung Association, "State of the Air 2023," April 19, 2023*

- Tuscaloosa was highlighted as one of the top 59 cleanest metro areas for short-term particle pollution (24-hour PM 2.5) in the U.S. during 2019 through 2021. Monitors in these cities reported no days with unhealthful PM 2.5 levels. *American Lung Association, "State of the Air 2023," April 19, 2023*

Safety Rankings

- The National Insurance Crime Bureau ranked 390 metro areas in the U.S. in terms of per capita rates of vehicle theft. The Tuscaloosa metro area ranked #185 (#1 = highest rate). Criteria: number of vehicle theft offenses per 100,000 inhabitants in 2021. *National Insurance Crime Bureau, "Hot Spots 2021," September 1, 2022*

Seniors/Retirement Rankings

- From its Best Cities for Successful Aging indexes, the Milken Institute generated rankings for metropolitan areas, weighing data in nine categories—health care, wellness, living arrangements, transportation and convenience, financial characteristics, education, employment, community engagement, and overall livability. The Tuscaloosa metro area was ranked #129 overall in the small metro area category. *Milken Institute, "Best Cities for Successful Aging, 2017" March 14, 2017*

Business Environment

DEMOGRAPHICS

Population Growth

Area	1990 Census	2000 Census	2010 Census	2020 Census	Population Growth (%) 1990-2020	Population Growth (%) 2010-2020
City	81,075	77,906	90,468	99,600	22.8	10.1
MSA[1]	176,123	192,034	219,461	268,674	52.5	22.4
U.S.	248,709,873	281,421,906	308,745,538	331,449,281	33.3	7.4

Note: (1) Figures cover the Tuscaloosa, AL Metropolitan Statistical Area
Source: U.S. Census Bureau, 1990 Census, 2000 Census, 2010 Census, 2020 Census

Race

Area	White Alone[2] (%)	Black Alone[2] (%)	Asian Alone[2] (%)	AIAN[3] Alone[2] (%)	NHOPI[4] Alone[2] (%)	Other Race Alone[2] (%)	Two or More Races (%)
City	48.7	41.2	2.4	0.3	0.1	2.1	5.3
MSA[1]	57.5	33.9	1.3	0.4	0.0	2.5	4.3
U.S.	61.6	12.4	6.0	1.1	0.2	8.4	10.2

Note: (1) Figures cover the Tuscaloosa, AL Metropolitan Statistical Area; (2) Alone is defined as not being in combination with one or more other races; (3) American Indian and Alaska Native; (4) Native Hawaiian and Other Pacific Islander
Source: U.S. Census Bureau, 2020 Census

Hispanic or Latino Origin

Area	Total (%)	Mexican (%)	Puerto Rican (%)	Cuban (%)	Other (%)
City	4.4	2.5	0.6	0.3	0.9
MSA[1]	3.8	2.4	0.3	0.2	0.9
U.S.	18.4	11.2	1.8	0.7	4.7

Note: Persons of Hispanic or Latino origin can be of any race; (1) Figures cover the Tuscaloosa, AL Metropolitan Statistical Area
Source: U.S. Census Bureau, 2017-2021 American Community Survey 5-Year Estimates

Age

Area	Under Age 5	Age 5–19	Age 20–34	Age 35–44	Age 45–54	Age 55–64	Age 65–74	Age 75–84	Age 85+	Median Age
City	5.1	20.8	34.3	10.0	8.8	9.0	7.2	3.3	1.5	27.1
MSA[1]	5.8	20.1	24.7	11.9	11.1	11.8	9.0	4.1	1.5	34.5
U.S.	5.6	19.2	20.2	12.7	12.4	13.1	10.0	4.9	1.9	38.8

Note: (1) Figures cover the Tuscaloosa, AL Metropolitan Statistical Area
Source: U.S. Census Bureau, 2020 Census

Disability by Age

Area	All Ages	Under 18 Years Old	18 to 64 Years Old	65 Years and Over
City	9.9	2.9	8.3	28.0
MSA[1]	14.3	4.5	12.5	37.4
U.S.	12.6	4.4	10.3	33.4

Note: Figures show percent of the civilian noninstitutionalized population that reported having a disability. Disability status is determined from six types of difficulty: vision, hearing, cognitive, ambulatory, self-care, and independent living. For children under 5 years old, hearing and vision difficulty are used to determine disability status. For children between the ages of 5 and 14, disability status is determined from hearing, vision, cognitive, ambulatory, and self-care difficulties. For people aged 15 years and older, they are considered to have a disability if they have difficulty with any one of the six difficulty types; Note: (1) Figures cover the Tuscaloosa, AL Metropolitan Statistical Area
Source: U.S. Census Bureau, 2017-2021 American Community Survey 5-Year Estimates

Ancestry

Area	German	Irish	English	American	Italian	Polish	French[2]	Scottish	Dutch
City	5.2	6.1	6.4	5.7	1.9	0.7	1.3	2.1	0.5
MSA[1]	5.0	6.5	6.9	10.9	1.5	0.4	0.9	1.9	0.5
U.S.	12.8	9.6	8.1	5.7	5.0	2.7	2.2	1.6	1.1

Note: Figures are the percentage of the total population reporting a particular ancestry. The nine most commonly reported ancestries in the U.S. are shown. Figures include multiple ancestries (e.g. if a person reported being Irish and Italian, they were included in both columns); (1) Figures cover the Tuscaloosa, AL Metropolitan Statistical Area; (2) Excludes Basque
Source: U.S. Census Bureau, 2017-2021 American Community Survey 5-Year Estimates

Foreign-born Population

Area	Any Foreign Country	Asia	Mexico	Europe	Caribbean	Central America[2]	South America	Africa	Canada
City	4.5	2.3	1.0	0.4	0.1	0.3	0.1	0.2	0.1
MSA[1]	3.3	1.2	1.1	0.3	0.1	0.4	0.1	0.1	0.1
U.S.	13.6	4.2	3.3	1.5	1.4	1.1	1.1	0.8	0.2

Note: (1) Figures cover the Tuscaloosa, AL Metropolitan Statistical Area; (2) Excludes Mexico.
Source: U.S. Census Bureau, 2017-2021 American Community Survey 5-Year Estimates

Household Size

Area	One	Two	Three	Four	Five	Six	Seven or More	Average Household Size
City	37.2	32.9	14.0	9.9	3.9	1.3	0.7	2.50
MSA[1]	30.2	34.6	15.6	11.8	5.5	1.5	0.9	2.60
U.S.	28.1	33.8	15.5	12.9	6.0	2.3	1.4	2.60

Note: (1) Figures cover the Tuscaloosa, AL Metropolitan Statistical Area
Source: U.S. Census Bureau, 2017-2021 American Community Survey 5-Year Estimates

Household Relationships

Area	Householder	Opposite-sex Spouse	Same-sex Spouse	Opposite-sex Unmarried Partner	Same-sex Unmarried Partner	Child[2]	Grandchild	Other Relatives	Non-relatives
City	41.0	10.6	0.1	2.1	0.1	21.3	2.4	3.5	8.7
MSA[1]	39.8	15.2	0.1	1.9	0.1	26.5	3.2	3.9	4.5
U.S.	38.3	17.5	0.2	2.5	0.2	28.3	2.4	4.8	3.4

Note: Figures are percent of the total population; (1) Figures cover the Tuscaloosa, AL Metropolitan Statistical Area; (2) Includes biological, adopted, and stepchildren of the householder
Source: U.S. Census Bureau, 2020 Census

Gender

Area	Males	Females	Males per 100 Females
City	47,020	52,580	89.4
MSA[1]	127,913	140,761	90.9
U.S.	162,685,811	168,763,470	96.4

Note: (1) Figures cover the Tuscaloosa, AL Metropolitan Statistical Area
Source: U.S. Census Bureau, 2020 Census

Marital Status

Area	Never Married	Now Married[2]	Separated	Widowed	Divorced
City	52.3	32.6	1.8	4.0	9.4
MSA[1]	39.5	43.1	1.7	5.4	10.3
U.S.	33.8	48.0	1.8	5.6	10.8

Note: Figures are percentages and cover the population 15 years of age and older; (1) Figures cover the Tuscaloosa, AL Metropolitan Statistical Area; (2) Excludes separated
Source: U.S. Census Bureau, 2017-2021 American Community Survey 5-Year Estimates

Religious Groups by Family

Area	Catholic	Baptist	Methodist	LDS[2]	Pentecostal	Lutheran	Islam	Adventist	Other
MSA[1]	2.6	25.1	6.2	0.6	1.5	0.1	0.3	0.7	13.3
U.S.	18.7	7.3	3.0	2.0	1.8	1.7	1.3	1.3	11.6

Note: Figures are the number of adherents as a percentage of the total population and cover the eight largest religious groups in the U.S; (1) Figures cover the Tuscaloosa, AL Metropolitan Statistical Area; (2) Church of Jesus Christ of Latter-day Saints
Sources: 2020 U.S. Religion Census, Association of Statisticians of American Religious Bodies; The Association of Religion Data Archives (ARDA)

Religious Groups by Tradition

Area	Catholic	Evangelical Protestant	Mainline Protestant	Black Protestant	Islam	Judaism	Hinduism	Orthodox	Buddhism
MSA[1]	2.6	34.3	4.6	7.3	0.3	0.1	n/a	n/a	n/a
U.S.	18.7	16.5	5.2	2.3	1.3	0.6	0.4	0.4	0.3

Note: Figures are the number of adherents as a percentage of the total population; (1) Figures cover the Tuscaloosa, AL Metropolitan Statistical Area
Sources: 2020 U.S. Religion Census, Association of Statisticians of American Religious Bodies; The Association of Religion Data Archives (ARDA)

ECONOMY

Gross Metropolitan Product

Area	2020	2021	2022	2023	Rank[2]
MSA[1]	11.4	12.2	13.2	13.9	205

Note: Figures are in billions of dollars; (1) Figures cover the Tuscaloosa, AL Metropolitan Statistical Area; (2) Rank is based on 2021 data and ranges from 1 to 381
Source: U.S. Conference of Mayors, U.S. Metro Economies: U.S. Metros Compared to Global and State Economies, June 2022

Economic Growth

Area	2018-20 (%)	2021 (%)	2022 (%)	2023 (%)	Rank[2]
MSA[1]	0.9	3.1	3.9	2.4	80
U.S.	-0.6	5.7	3.1	2.9	–

Note: Figures are real gross metropolitan product (GMP) growth rates and represent average annual percent change; (1) Figures cover the Tuscaloosa, AL Metropolitan Statistical Area; (2) Rank is based on 2020 2-year average annual percent change and ranges from 1 to 381
Source: U.S. Conference of Mayors, U.S. Metro Economies: U.S. Metros Compared to Global and State Economies, June 2022

Metropolitan Area Exports

Area	2016	2017	2018	2019	2020	2021	Rank[2]
MSA[1]	n/a	n/a	n/a	n/a	5,175.0	6,675.5	50

Note: Figures are in millions of dollars; (1) Figures cover the Tuscaloosa, AL Metropolitan Statistical Area; (2) Rank is based on 2021 data and ranges from 1 to 388
Source: U.S. Department of Commerce, International Trade Administration, Office of Trade and Economic Analysis, Industry and Analysis, Exports by Metropolitan Area, data extracted March 16, 2023

Building Permits

Area	Single-Family 2021	Single-Family 2022	Pct. Chg.	Multi-Family 2021	Multi-Family 2022	Pct. Chg.	Total 2021	Total 2022	Pct. Chg.
City	401	299	-25.4	725	329	-54.6	1,126	628	-44.2
MSA[1]	771	714	-7.4	725	329	-54.6	1,496	1,043	-30.3
U.S.	1,115,400	975,600	-12.5	621,600	689,500	10.9	1,737,000	1,665,100	-4.1

Note: (1) Figures cover the Tuscaloosa, AL Metropolitan Statistical Area; Figures represent new, privately-owned housing units authorized (unadjusted data); All permit data are based on estimates with imputation
Source: U.S. Census Bureau, Manufacturing, Mining, and Construction Statistics, Building Permits, 2021, 2022

Bankruptcy Filings

Area	Business Filings 2021	Business Filings 2022	% Chg.	Nonbusiness Filings 2021	Nonbusiness Filings 2022	% Chg.
Tuscaloosa County	4	9	125.0	679	821	20.9
U.S.	14,347	13,481	-6.0	399,269	374,240	-6.3

Note: Business filings include Chapter 7, Chapter 9, Chapter 11, Chapter 12, Chapter 13, Chapter 15, and Section 304; Nonbusiness filings include Chapter 7, Chapter 11, and Chapter 13
Source: Administrative Office of the U.S. Courts, Business and Nonbusiness Bankruptcy, County Cases Commenced by Chapter of the Bankruptcy Code, During the 12-Month Period Ending December 31, 2021 and Business and Nonbusiness Bankruptcy, County Cases Commenced by Chapter of the Bankruptcy Code, During the 12-Month Period Ending December 31, 2022

Housing Vacancy Rates

Area	Gross Vacancy Rate[2] (%) 2020	2021	2022	Year-Round Vacancy Rate[3] (%) 2020	2021	2022	Rental Vacancy Rate[4] (%) 2020	2021	2022	Homeowner Vacancy Rate[5] (%) 2020	2021	2022
MSA[1]	n/a	n/a	n/a	n/a	n/a	n/a	n/a	n/a	n/a	n/a	n/a	n/a
U.S.	10.6	10.8	10.5	8.2	8.4	8.2	6.3	6.1	5.8	1.0	0.9	0.8

Note: (1) Figures cover the Tuscaloosa, AL Metropolitan Statistical Area; (2) The percentage of the total housing inventory that is vacant; (3) The percentage of the housing inventory (excluding seasonal units) that is year-round vacant; (4) The percentage of rental inventory that is vacant for rent; (5) The percentage of homeowner inventory that is vacant for sale; n/a not available
Source: U.S. Census Bureau, Housing Vacancies and Homeownership Annual Statistics: 2020, 2021, 2022

INCOME

Income

Area	Per Capita ($)	Median Household ($)	Average Household ($)
City	27,789	44,880	69,736
MSA[1]	28,204	54,449	72,452
U.S.	37,638	69,021	97,196

Note: (1) Figures cover the Tuscaloosa, AL Metropolitan Statistical Area
Source: U.S. Census Bureau, 2017-2021 American Community Survey 5-Year Estimates

Household Income Distribution

Area	Under $15,000	$15,000-$24,999	$25,000-$34,999	$35,000-$49,999	$50,000-$74,999	$75,000-$99,999	$100,000-$149,999	$150,000 and up
City	19.5	10.8	10.9	11.9	15.4	8.7	12.8	10.0
MSA[1]	14.3	9.9	10.2	12.1	17.3	12.0	14.5	9.6
U.S.	9.4	7.8	8.2	11.4	16.8	12.8	16.3	17.3

Note: (1) Figures cover the Tuscaloosa, AL Metropolitan Statistical Area
Source: U.S. Census Bureau, 2017-2021 American Community Survey 5-Year Estimates

Poverty Rate

Area	All Ages	Under 18 Years Old	18 to 64 Years Old	65 Years and Over
City	22.6	21.7	24.5	14.8
MSA[1]	17.5	22.8	17.0	11.8
U.S.	12.6	17.0	11.8	9.6

Note: Figures are percentage of people whose income during the past 12 months was below the poverty level; (1) Figures cover the Tuscaloosa, AL Metropolitan Statistical Area
Source: U.S. Census Bureau, 2017-2021 American Community Survey 5-Year Estimates

EMPLOYMENT

Labor Force and Employment

Area	Civilian Labor Force Dec. 2021	Civilian Labor Force Dec. 2022	% Chg.	Workers Employed Dec. 2021	Workers Employed Dec. 2022	% Chg.
City	46,912	47,393	1.0	45,459	46,256	1.8
MSA[1]	114,876	116,118	1.1	111,656	113,579	1.7
U.S.	161,696,000	164,224,000	1.6	155,732,000	158,872,000	2.0

Note: Data is not seasonally adjusted and covers workers 16 years of age and older; (1) Figures cover the Tuscaloosa, AL Metropolitan Statistical Area
Source: Bureau of Labor Statistics, Local Area Unemployment Statistics

Unemployment Rate

Area	Jan.	Feb.	Mar.	Apr.	May	Jun.	Jul.	Aug.	Sep.	Oct.	Nov.	Dec.
City	3.6	3.4	2.6	2.4	2.9	4.1	4.0	3.4	2.9	3.1	2.7	2.4
MSA[1]	3.5	3.2	2.5	2.1	2.5	3.6	3.4	3.0	2.6	2.7	2.4	2.2
U.S.	4.4	4.1	3.8	3.3	3.4	3.8	3.8	3.8	3.3	3.4	3.4	3.3

Note: Data is not seasonally adjusted and covers workers 16 years of age and older; (1) Figures cover the Tuscaloosa, AL Metropolitan Statistical Area
Source: Bureau of Labor Statistics, Local Area Unemployment Statistics

Average Wages

Occupation	$/Hr.	Occupation	$/Hr.
Accountants and Auditors	35.59	Maintenance and Repair Workers	18.71
Automotive Mechanics	21.58	Marketing Managers	54.09
Bookkeepers	19.16	Network and Computer Systems Admin.	37.32
Carpenters	21.27	Nurses, Licensed Practical	21.53
Cashiers	11.34	Nurses, Registered	30.81
Computer Programmers	40.66	Nursing Assistants	14.13
Computer Systems Analysts	45.86	Office Clerks, General	13.87
Computer User Support Specialists	29.58	Physical Therapists	48.68
Construction Laborers	15.23	Physicians	105.13
Cooks, Restaurant	14.27	Plumbers, Pipefitters and Steamfitters	23.92
Customer Service Representatives	17.16	Police and Sheriff's Patrol Officers	27.48
Dentists	93.58	Postal Service Mail Carriers	27.01
Electricians	25.75	Real Estate Sales Agents	29.05
Engineers, Electrical	55.16	Retail Salespersons	14.09
Fast Food and Counter Workers	11.34	Sales Representatives, Technical/Scientific	n/a
Financial Managers	62.63	Secretaries, Exc. Legal/Medical/Executive	19.12
First-Line Supervisors of Office Workers	28.60	Security Guards	15.31
General and Operations Managers	55.95	Surgeons	n/a
Hairdressers/Cosmetologists	17.32	Teacher Assistants, Exc. Postsecondary*	10.07
Home Health and Personal Care Aides	11.32	Teachers, Secondary School, Exc. Sp. Ed.*	26.64
Janitors and Cleaners	14.40	Telemarketers	n/a
Landscaping/Groundskeeping Workers	15.89	Truck Drivers, Heavy/Tractor-Trailer	24.19
Lawyers	55.63	Truck Drivers, Light/Delivery Services	20.50
Maids and Housekeeping Cleaners	11.48	Waiters and Waitresses	10.78

Note: Wage data covers the Tuscaloosa, AL Metropolitan Statistical Area; (*) Hourly wages were calculated from annual wage data based on a 40 hour work week; n/a not available.
Source: Bureau of Labor Statistics, Metro Area Occupational Employment & Wage Estimates, May 2022

Employment by Industry

Sector	MSA[1] Number of Employees	MSA[1] Percent of Total	U.S. Percent of Total
Construction, Mining, and Logging	6,400	5.7	5.4
Private Education and Health Services	9,600	8.5	16.1
Financial Activities	4,000	3.5	5.9
Government	29,100	25.7	14.5
Information	800	0.7	2.0
Leisure and Hospitality	11,600	10.3	10.3
Manufacturing	19,000	16.8	8.4
Other Services	4,600	4.1	3.7
Professional and Business Services	10,500	9.3	14.7
Retail Trade	11,800	10.4	10.2
Transportation, Warehousing, and Utilities	3,500	3.1	4.9
Wholesale Trade	2,200	1.9	3.9

Note: Figures are non-farm employment as of December 2022. Figures are not seasonally adjusted and include workers 16 years of age and older; (1) Figures cover the Tuscaloosa, AL Metropolitan Statistical Area
Source: Bureau of Labor Statistics, Current Employment Statistics, Employment, Hours, and Earnings

Employment by Occupation

Occupation Classification	City (%)	MSA[1] (%)	U.S. (%)
Management, Business, Science, and Arts	37.6	35.5	40.3
Natural Resources, Construction, and Maintenance	5.5	9.6	8.7
Production, Transportation, and Material Moving	16.8	18.0	13.1
Sales and Office	22.0	20.4	20.9
Service	18.2	16.5	17.0

Note: Figures cover employed civilians 16 years of age and older; (1) Figures cover the Tuscaloosa, AL Metropolitan Statistical Area
Source: U.S. Census Bureau, 2017-2021 American Community Survey 5-Year Estimates

Occupations with Greatest Projected Employment Growth: 2022 – 2024

Occupation[1]	2022 Employment	2024 Projected Employment	Numeric Employment Change	Percent Employment Change
Cooks, Restaurant	16,700	17,360	660	4.0
Industrial Machinery Mechanics	14,850	15,510	660	4.4
Software Developers	14,820	15,270	450	3.0
Accountants and Auditors	24,470	24,890	420	1.7
Sales Representatives, Wholesale and Manufacturing, Except Technical and Scientific Products	21,530	21,910	380	1.8
Medical and Health Services Managers	8,430	8,790	360	4.3
Janitors and Cleaners, Except Maids and Housekeeping Cleaners	28,680	29,040	360	1.3
Nurse Practitioners	4,550	4,880	330	7.3
General and Operations Managers	37,490	37,810	320	0.9
Logisticians	5,400	5,690	290	5.4

Note: Projections cover Alabama; (1) Sorted by numeric employment change
Source: www.projectionscentral.com, State Occupational Projections, 2022–2024 Short-Term Projections

Fastest-Growing Occupations: 2022 – 2024

Occupation[1]	2022 Employment	2024 Projected Employment	Numeric Employment Change	Percent Employment Change
Dental Laboratory Technicians	1,030	1,120	90	8.7
Nurse Practitioners	4,550	4,880	330	7.3
Molders, Shapers, and Casters, Except Metal and Plastic	850	910	60	7.1
Information Security Analysts (SOC 2018)	2,600	2,780	180	6.9
Logisticians	5,400	5,690	290	5.4
Telecommunications Equipment Installers and Repairers, Except Line Installers	2,720	2,860	140	5.1
Paralegals and Legal Assistants	3,850	4,020	170	4.4
Nursing Instructors and Teachers, Postsecondary	1,360	1,420	60	4.4
Industrial Machinery Mechanics	14,850	15,510	660	4.4
Medical and Health Services Managers	8,430	8,790	360	4.3

Note: Projections cover Alabama; (1) Sorted by percent employment change and excludes occupations with numeric employment change less than 50
Source: www.projectionscentral.com, State Occupational Projections, 2022–2024 Short-Term Projections

CITY FINANCES

City Government Finances

Component	2020 ($000)	2020 ($ per capita)
Total Revenues	237,928	2,353
Total Expenditures	214,925	2,125
Debt Outstanding	181,567	1,795
Cash and Securities[1]	85,727	848

Note: (1) Cash and security holdings of a government at the close of its fiscal year, including those of its dependent agencies, utilities, and liquor stores.
Source: U.S. Census Bureau, State & Local Government Finances 2020

City Government Revenue by Source

Source	2020 ($000)	2020 ($ per capita)	2020 (%)
General Revenue			
From Federal Government	6,364	63	2.7
From State Government	19,211	190	8.1
From Local Governments	38,341	379	16.1
Taxes			
Property	18,496	183	7.8
Sales and Gross Receipts	62,001	613	26.1
Personal Income	0	0	0.0
Corporate Income	0	0	0.0
Motor Vehicle License	0	0	0.0
Other Taxes	24,299	240	10.2
Current Charges	41,943	415	17.6
Liquor Store	0	0	0.0
Utility	15,298	151	6.4

Source: U.S. Census Bureau, State & Local Government Finances 2020

City Government Expenditures by Function

Function	2020 ($000)	2020 ($ per capita)	2020 (%)
General Direct Expenditures			
Air Transportation	1,109	11	0.5
Corrections	557	5	0.3
Education	0	0	0.0
Employment Security Administration	0	0	0.0
Financial Administration	8,451	83	3.9
Fire Protection	24,432	241	11.4
General Public Buildings	4,421	43	2.1
Governmental Administration, Other	5,004	49	2.3
Health	71	<1	<0.1
Highways	31,388	310	14.6
Hospitals	0	0	0.0
Housing and Community Development	1,662	16	0.8
Interest on General Debt	4,189	41	1.9
Judicial and Legal	3,074	30	1.4
Libraries	1,842	18	0.9
Parking	0	0	0.0
Parks and Recreation	8,968	88	4.2
Police Protection	43,329	428	20.2
Public Welfare	0	0	0.0
Sewerage	8,408	83	3.9
Solid Waste Management	7,920	78	3.7
Veterans' Services	0	0	0.0
Liquor Store	0	0	0.0
Utility	33,036	326	15.4

Source: U.S. Census Bureau, State & Local Government Finances 2020

TAXES

State Corporate Income Tax Rates

State	Tax Rate (%)	Income Brackets ($)	Num. of Brackets	Financial Institution Tax Rate (%)[a]	Federal Income Tax Ded.
Alabama	6.5	Flat rate	1	6.5	Yes

Note: Tax rates as of January 1, 2023; (a) Rates listed are the corporate income tax rate applied to financial institutions or excise taxes based on income. Some states have other taxes based upon the value of deposits or shares.
Source: Federation of Tax Administrators, State Corporate Income Tax Rates, January 1, 2023

State Individual Income Tax Rates

State	Tax Rate (%)	Income Brackets ($)	Personal Exemptions ($) Single	Personal Exemptions ($) Married	Personal Exemptions ($) Depend.	Standard Ded. ($) Single	Standard Ded. ($) Married
Alabama	2.0 - 5.0	500 - 3,001 (b)	1,500	3,000	500 (e)	3,000	8,500 (z)

Note: Tax rates as of January 1, 2023; Local- and county-level taxes are not included; Federal income tax is deductible on state income tax returns; (b) For joint returns, taxes are twice the tax on half the couple's income; (e) In Alabama, the per-dependent exemption is $1,000 for taxpayers with state AGI of $20,000 or less, $500 with AGI from $20,001 to $100,000, and $300 with AGI over $100,000; (z) Alabama standard deduction is phased out for incomes over $25,000. Rhode Island exemptions & standard deductions phased out for incomes over $233,750; Wisconsin standard deduciton phases out for income over $16,989.
Source: Federation of Tax Administrators, State Individual Income Tax Rates, January 1, 2023

Various State Sales and Excise Tax Rates

State	State Sales Tax (%)	Gasoline[1] ($/gal.)	Cigarette[2] ($/pack)	Spirits[3] ($/gal.)	Wine[4] ($/gal.)	Beer[5] ($/gal.)	Recreational Marijuana (%)
Alabama	4	0.3131	0.675	21.69	1.70	0.53	Not legal

Note: All tax rates as of January 1, 2023; (1) The American Petroleum Institute has developed a methodology for determining the average tax rate on a gallon of fuel. Rates may include any of the following: excise taxes, environmental fees, storage tank fees, other fees or taxes, general sales tax, and local taxes; (2) The federal excise tax of $1.0066 per pack and local taxes are not included; (3) Rates are those applicable to off-premise sales of 40% alcohol by volume (a.b.v.) distilled spirits in 750ml containers. Local excise taxes are excluded; (4) Rates are those applicable to off-premise sales of 11% a.b.v. non-carbonated wine in 750ml containers; (5) Rates are those applicable to off-premise sales of 4.7% a.b.v. beer in 12 ounce containers.
Source: Tax Foundation, 2023 Facts & Figures: How Does Your State Compare?

State Business Tax Climate Index Rankings

State	Overall Rank	Corporate Tax Rank	Individual Income Tax Rank	Sales Tax Rank	Property Tax Rank	Unemployment Insurance Tax Rank
Alabama	41	18	30	50	18	19

Note: The index is a measure of how each state's tax laws affect economic performance. The lower the rank, the more favorable a state's tax system is for business. States without a given tax are given a ranking of 1. The scores/rankings for the District of Columbia do not affect other states. The 2023 index represents the tax climate as of July 1, 2022.
Source: Tax Foundation, State Business Tax Climate Index 2023

TRANSPORTATION

Means of Transportation to Work

Area	Car/Truck/Van Drove Alone	Car/Truck/Van Car-pooled	Public Transportation Bus	Public Transportation Subway	Public Transportation Railroad	Bicycle	Walked	Other Means	Worked at Home
City	80.0	9.7	1.4	0.0	0.0	0.5	1.8	1.0	5.6
MSA[1]	82.3	10.3	0.8	0.0	0.0	0.2	0.9	0.6	5.0
U.S.	73.2	8.6	2.0	1.6	0.5	0.5	2.5	1.5	9.7

Note: Figures are percentages and cover workers 16 years of age and older; (1) Figures cover the Tuscaloosa, AL Metropolitan Statistical Area
Source: U.S. Census Bureau, 2017-2021 American Community Survey 5-Year Estimates

Travel Time to Work

Area	Less Than 10 Minutes	10 to 19 Minutes	20 to 29 Minutes	30 to 44 Minutes	45 to 59 Minutes	60 to 89 Minutes	90 Minutes or More
City	16.8	46.6	21.7	7.6	3.1	3.1	1.1
MSA[1]	11.1	33.8	23.3	17.4	6.7	5.7	2.0
U.S.	12.4	28.5	21.0	20.9	8.2	6.2	2.9

Note: Note: Figures are percentages and include workers 16 years old and over; (1) Figures cover the Tuscaloosa, AL Metropolitan Statistical Area
Source: U.S. Census Bureau, 2017-2021 American Community Survey 5-Year Estimates

Key Congestion Measures

Measure	1990	2000	2010	2015	2020
Annual Hours of Delay, Total (000)	n/a	n/a	n/a	4,816	1,883
Annual Hours of Delay, Per Auto Commuter	n/a	n/a	n/a	30	11
Annual Congestion Cost, Per Auto Commuter ($)	n/a	n/a	n/a	613	255

Note: n/a not available
Source: Texas A&M Transportation Institute, 2021 Urban Mobility Report

Freeway Travel Time Index

Measure	1985	1990	1995	2000	2005	2010	2015	2020
Urban Area Index[1]	n/a	n/a	n/a	n/a	n/a	n/a	1.11	1.04
Urban Area Rank[1,2]	n/a	n/a	n/a	n/a	n/a	n/a	n/a	n/a

Note: Freeway Travel Time Index—the ratio of travel time in the peak period to the travel time at free-flow conditions. For example, a value of 1.30 indicates a 20-minute free-flow trip takes 26 minutes in the peak (20 minutes x 1.30 = 26 minutes); (1) Covers the Tuscaloosa AL urban area; (2) Rank is based on 101 larger urban areas (#1 = highest travel time index); n/a not available
Source: Texas A&M Transportation Institute, 2021 Urban Mobility Report

Public Transportation

Agency Name / Mode of Transportation	Vehicles Operated in Maximum Service[1]	Annual Unlinked Passenger Trips[2] (in thous.)	Annual Passenger Miles[3] (in thous.)
Tuscaloosa County Parking and Transit Authority			
Bus (directly operated)	7	167.9	n/a
Demand Response (directly operated)	5	11.3	n/a

Note: (1) Number of revenue vehicles operated by the given mode and type of service to meet the annual maximum service requirement. This is the revenue vehicle count during the peak season of the year; on the week and day that maximum service is provided. Vehicles operated in maximum service (VOMS) exclude atypical days and one-time special events; (2) Number of passengers who boarded public transportation vehicles. Passengers are counted each time they board a vehicle no matter how many vehicles they use to travel from their origin to their destination. (3) Sum of the distances ridden by all passengers during the entire fiscal year.
Source: Federal Transit Administration, National Transit Database, 2021

Air Transportation

Airport Name and Code / Type of Service	Passenger Airlines[1]	Passenger Enplanements	Freight Carriers[2]	Freight (lbs)
Birmingham-Shuttlesworth International Airport (BHM)				
Domestic service (U.S. carriers - 2022)	28	1,330,588	11	17,030,068
International service (U.S. carriers - 2021)	0	0	0	0

Note: (1) Includes all U.S.-based major, minor and commuter airlines that carried at least one passenger during the year; (2) Includes all U.S.-based airlines and freight carriers that transported at least one pound of freight during the year.
Source: Bureau of Transportation Statistics, The Intermodal Transportation Database, Air Carriers: T-100 Domestic Market (U.S. Carriers), 2022; Bureau of Transportation Statistics, The Intermodal Transportation Database, Air Carriers: T-100 International Market (U.S. Carriers), 2021

BUSINESSES

Major Business Headquarters

Company Name	Industry	Rankings Fortune[1]	Forbes[2]
No companies listed	-	-	-

Note: (1) Companies that produce a 10-K are ranked 1 to 500 based on 2021 revenue; (2) All private companies with at least $2 billion in annual revenue through the end of their most current fiscal year are ranked 1 to 246; companies listed are headquartered in the city; dashes indicate no ranking
Source: Fortune, "Fortune 500," 2022; Forbes, "America's Largest Private Companies," 2022

Fastest-Growing Businesses

According to *Inc.*, Tuscaloosa is home to one of America's 500 fastest-growing private companies: **GRO** (#157). Criteria: must be an independent, privately-held, for-profit, U.S. corporation, proprietorship or partnership as of December 31, 2021; revenues must be at least $100,000 in 2018 and $2 million in 2021; must have four-year operating/sales history. *Inc.*, "America's 500 Fastest-Growing Private Companies," 2022

Living Environment

COST OF LIVING

Cost of Living Index

Composite Index	Groceries	Housing	Utilities	Transportation	Health Care	Misc. Goods/Services
n/a	n/a	n/a	n/a	n/a	n/a	n/a

Note: The Cost of Living Index measures regional differences in the cost of consumer goods and services, excluding taxes and non-consumer expenditures, for professional and managerial households in the top income quintile. It is based on more than 50,000 prices covering almost 60 different items for which prices are collected three times a year by chambers of commerce, economic development organizations or university applied economic centers in each participating urban area. The numbers shown should be read as a percentage above or below the national average of 100. For example, a value of 115.4 in the groceries column indicates that grocery prices are 15.4% higher than the national average. Small differences in the index numbers should not be interpreted as significant; n/a not available.
Source: The Council for Community and Economic Research, Cost of Living Index, 2022

Grocery Prices

Area[1]	T-Bone Steak ($/pound)	Frying Chicken ($/pound)	Whole Milk ($/half gal.)	Eggs ($/dozen)	Orange Juice ($/64 oz.)	Coffee ($/11.5 oz.)
City[2]	n/a	n/a	n/a	n/a	n/a	n/a
Avg.	13.81	1.59	2.43	2.25	3.85	4.95
Min.	10.17	0.90	1.51	1.30	2.90	3.46
Max.	19.35	3.30	4.32	4.32	5.31	8.59

*Note: (1) Values for the local area are compared with the average, minimum and maximum values for all 286 areas in the Cost of Living Index; (2) Figures cover the Tuscaloosa AL urban area; n/a not available; **T-Bone Steak** (price per pound); **Frying Chicken** (price per pound, whole fryer); **Whole Milk** (half gallon carton); **Eggs** (price per dozen, Grade A, large); **Orange Juice** (64 oz. Tropicana or Florida Natural); **Coffee** (11.5 oz. can, vacuum-packed, Maxwell House, Hills Bros, or Folgers).*
Source: The Council for Community and Economic Research, Cost of Living Index, 2022

Housing and Utility Costs

Area[1]	New Home Price ($)	Apartment Rent ($/month)	All Electric ($/month)	Part Electric ($/month)	Other Energy ($/month)	Telephone ($/month)
City[2]	n/a	n/a	n/a	n/a	n/a	n/a
Avg.	450,913	1,371	176.41	99.93	76.96	190.22
Min.	229,283	546	100.84	31.56	27.15	174.27
Max.	2,434,977	4,569	356.86	249.59	272.24	208.31

*Note: (1) Values for the local area are compared with the average, minimum and maximum values for all 286 areas in the Cost of Living Index; (2) Figures cover the Tuscaloosa AL urban area; n/a not available; **New Home Price** (2,400 sf living area, 8,000 sf lot, in urban area with full utilities); **Apartment Rent** (950 sf 2 bedroom/1.5 or 2 bath, unfurnished, excluding all utilities except water); **All Electric** (average monthly cost for an all-electric home); **Part Electric** (average monthly cost for a part-electric home); **Other Energy** (average monthly cost for natural gas, fuel oil, coal, wood, and any other forms of energy except electricity); **Telephone** (price includes the base monthly rate plus taxes and fees for three lines of mobile phone service).*
Source: The Council for Community and Economic Research, Cost of Living Index, 2022

Health Care, Transportation, and Other Costs

Area[1]	Doctor ($/visit)	Dentist ($/visit)	Optometrist ($/visit)	Gasoline ($/gallon)	Beauty Salon ($/visit)	Men's Shirt ($)
City[2]	n/a	n/a	n/a	n/a	n/a	n/a
Avg.	124.91	107.77	117.66	3.86	43.31	34.21
Min.	36.61	58.25	51.79	2.90	22.18	13.05
Max.	250.21	162.58	371.96	5.54	85.61	63.54

*Note: (1) Values for the local area are compared with the average, minimum and maximum values for all 286 areas in the Cost of Living Index; (2) Figures cover the Tuscaloosa AL urban area; n/a not available; **Doctor** (general practitioners routine exam of an established patient); **Dentist** (adult teeth cleaning and periodic oral examination); **Optometrist** (full vision eye exam for established adult patient); **Gasoline** (one gallon regular unleaded, national brand, including all taxes, cash price at self-service pump if available); **Beauty Salon** (woman's shampoo, trim, and blow-dry); **Men's Shirt** (cotton/polyester dress shirt, pinpoint weave, long sleeves).*
Source: The Council for Community and Economic Research, Cost of Living Index, 2022

HOUSING

Homeownership Rate

Area	2015 (%)	2016 (%)	2017 (%)	2018 (%)	2019 (%)	2020 (%)	2021 (%)	2022 (%)
MSA[1]	n/a	n/a	n/a	n/a	n/a	n/a	n/a	n/a
U.S.	63.7	63.4	63.9	64.4	64.6	66.6	65.5	65.8

Note: (1) Figures cover the Tuscaloosa, AL Metropolitan Statistical Area; n/a not available
Source: U.S. Census Bureau, Housing Vacancies and Homeownership Annual Statistics: 2015-2022

House Price Index (HPI)

Area	National Ranking[2]	Quarterly Change (%)	One-Year Change (%)	Five-Year Change (%)	Since 1991Q1 (%)
MSA[1]	n/a	n/a	n/a	n/a	n/a
U.S.[3]	—	0.34	8.41	58.44	289.08

Note: The HPI is a weighted repeat sales index. It measures average price changes in repeat sales or refinancings on the same properties. This information is obtained by reviewing repeat mortgage transactions on single-family properties whose mortgages have been purchased or securitized by Fannie Mae or Freddie Mac since January 1975; (1) Figures cover the , Metropolitan Statistical Area; (2) Rankings are based on annual percentage change for all metro areas containing at least 15,000 transactions over the last 10 years and ranges from 1 to 257; (3) figures based on a weighted average of Census Division estimates using a seasonally adjusted, purchase-only index; all figures are for the period ending December 31, 2022; n/a not available
Source: Federal Housing Finance Agency, Change in FHFA Metropolitan Area House Price Indexes, 2022Q4

Median Single-Family Home Prices

Area	2020	2021	2022p	Percent Change 2021 to 2022
MSA[1]	n/a	n/a	n/a	n/a
U.S. Average	300.2	357.1	392.6	9.9

Note: Figures are median sales prices of existing single-family homes in thousands of dollars; (p) preliminary; n/a not available; (1) Figures cover the Tuscaloosa, AL Metropolitan Statistical Area
Source: National Association of Realtors, Median Sales Price of Existing Single-Family Homes for Metropolitan Areas, 4th Quarter 2022

Qualifying Income Based on Median Sales Price of Existing Single-Family Homes

Area	With 5% Down ($)	With 10% Down ($)	With 20% Down ($)
MSA[1]	n/a	n/a	n/a
U.S. Average	112,234	106,237	94,513

Note: Figures are preliminary; Qualifying income is based on a mortgage rate of 6.77%. Monthly principal and interest payment is limited to 25% of income; n/a not available; (1) Figures cover the Tuscaloosa, AL Metropolitan Statistical Area
Source: National Association of Realtors, Qualifying Income Based on Median Sales Price of Existing Single-Family Homes for Metropolitan Areas, 4th Quarter 2022

Home Value

Area	Under $100,000	$100,000 -$199,999	$200,000 -$299,999	$300,000 -$399,999	$400,000 -$499,999	$500,000 -$999,999	$1,000,000 or more	Median ($)
City	14.2	37.7	19.5	11.1	6.0	10.0	1.6	194,500
MSA[1]	24.9	35.9	20.8	9.4	3.6	4.6	0.8	171,100
U.S.	16.2	24.2	20.1	13.6	8.3	13.6	4.1	244,900

Note: Figures are percentages except for median and cover owner-occupied housing units; (1) Figures cover the Tuscaloosa, AL Metropolitan Statistical Area
Source: U.S. Census Bureau, 2017-2021 American Community Survey 5-Year Estimates

Year Housing Structure Built

Area	2020 or Later	2010 -2019	2000 -2009	1990 -1999	1980 -1989	1970 -1979	1960 -1969	1950 -1959	1940 -1949	Before 1940	Median Year
City	0.1	16.7	16.7	14.4	11.6	14.9	9.8	8.3	3.9	3.6	1988
MSA[1]	0.1	12.4	18.5	18.3	13.5	14.7	9.0	6.6	3.2	3.6	1989
U.S.	0.2	7.3	13.6	13.6	13.2	14.8	10.3	10.0	4.7	12.2	1979

Note: Figures are percentages except for Median Year; Note: (1) Figures cover the Tuscaloosa, AL Metropolitan Statistical Area
Source: U.S. Census Bureau, 2017-2021 American Community Survey 5-Year Estimates

Gross Monthly Rent

Area	Under $500	$500 -$999	$1,000 -$1,499	$1,500 -$1,999	$2,000 -$2,499	$2,500 -$2,999	$3,000 and up	Median ($)
City	11.0	51.3	28.3	5.9	2.0	0.6	0.9	907
MSA[1]	14.9	50.5	27.1	4.8	1.5	0.6	0.5	879
U.S.	8.1	30.5	30.8	16.8	7.3	3.1	3.5	1,163

Note: Figures are percentages except for median; Gross rent is the contract rent plus the estimated average monthly cost of utilities (electricity, gas, and water and sewer) and fuels (oil, coal, kerosene, wood, etc.) if these are paid by the renter (or paid for the renter by someone else); (1) Figures cover the Tuscaloosa, AL Metropolitan Statistical Area
Source: U.S. Census Bureau, 2017-2021 American Community Survey 5-Year Estimates

HEALTH

Health Risk Factors

Category	MSA[1] (%)	U.S. (%)
Adults aged 18–64 who have any kind of health care coverage	n/a	90.9
Adults who reported being in good or better health	n/a	85.2
Adults who have been told they have high blood cholesterol	n/a	35.7
Adults who have been told they have high blood pressure	n/a	32.4
Adults who are current smokers	n/a	14.4
Adults who currently use e-cigarettes	n/a	6.7
Adults who currently use chewing tobacco, snuff, or snus	n/a	3.5
Adults who are heavy drinkers[2]	n/a	6.3
Adults who are binge drinkers[3]	n/a	15.4
Adults who are overweight (BMI 25.0 - 29.9)	n/a	34.4
Adults who are obese (BMI 30.0 - 99.8)	n/a	33.9
Adults who participated in any physical activities in the past month	n/a	76.3

Note: (1) Figures for the Tuscaloosa, AL Metropolitan Statistical Area were not available.
(2) Heavy drinkers are classified as adult men having more than 14 drinks per week and adult women having more than 7 drinks per week; (3) Binge drinkers are classified as males having five or more drinks on one occasion or females having four or more drinks on one occasion
Source: Centers for Disease Control and Prevention, Behavioral Risk Factor Surveillance System, SMART: Selected Metropolitan Area Risk Trends, 2021

Acute and Chronic Health Conditions

Category	MSA[1] (%)	U.S. (%)
Adults who have ever been told they had a heart attack	n/a	4.0
Adults who have ever been told they have angina or coronary heart disease	n/a	3.8
Adults who have ever been told they had a stroke	n/a	3.0
Adults who have ever been told they have asthma	n/a	14.9
Adults who have ever been told they have arthritis	n/a	25.8
Adults who have ever been told they have diabetes[2]	n/a	10.9
Adults who have ever been told they had skin cancer	n/a	6.6
Adults who have ever been told they had any other types of cancer	n/a	7.5
Adults who have ever been told they have COPD	n/a	6.1
Adults who have ever been told they have kidney disease	n/a	3.0
Adults who have ever been told they have a form of depression	n/a	20.5

Note: (1) Figures for the Tuscaloosa, AL Metropolitan Statistical Area were not available.
(2) Figures do not include pregnancy-related, borderline, or pre-diabetes
Source: Centers for Disease Control and Prevention, Behavioral Risk Factor Surveillance System, SMART: Selected Metropolitan Area Risk Trends, 2021

Health Screening and Vaccination Rates

Category	MSA[1] (%)	U.S. (%)
Adults who have ever been tested for HIV	n/a	34.9
Adults who have had their blood cholesterol checked within the last five years	n/a	85.2
Adults aged 65+ who have had flu shot within the past year	n/a	68.6
Adults aged 65+ who have ever had a pneumonia vaccination	n/a	71.0

Note: (1) Figures for the Tuscaloosa, AL Metropolitan Statistical Area were not available.
Source: Centers for Disease Control and Prevention, Behavioral Risk Factor Surveillance System, SMART: Selected Metropolitan Area Risk Trends, 2021

Disability Status

Category	MSA[1] (%)	U.S. (%)
Adults who reported being deaf	n/a	7.2
Are you blind or have serious difficulty seeing, even when wearing glasses?	n/a	4.8
Are you limited in any way in any of your usual activities due to arthritis?	n/a	11.1
Do you have difficulty doing errands alone?	n/a	7.0
Do you have difficulty dressing or bathing?	n/a	3.6
Do you have serious difficulty concentrating/remembering/making decisions?	n/a	12.1
Do you have serious difficulty walking or climbing stairs?	n/a	12.8

Note: (1) Figures for the Tuscaloosa, AL Metropolitan Statistical Area were not available.
Source: Centers for Disease Control and Prevention, Behavioral Risk Factor Surveillance System, SMART: Selected Metropolitan Area Risk Trends, 2021

Mortality Rates for the Top 10 Causes of Death in the U.S.

ICD-10[a] Sub-Chapter	ICD-10[a] Code	Crude Mortality Rate[1] per 100,000 population County[2]	U.S.
Malignant neoplasms	C00-C97	149.1	182.6
Ischaemic heart diseases	I20-I25	74.6	113.1
Other forms of heart disease	I30-I51	107.6	64.4
Other degenerative diseases of the nervous system	G30-G31	70.5	51.0
Cerebrovascular diseases	I60-I69	55.5	47.8
Other external causes of accidental injury	W00-X59	36.8	46.4
Chronic lower respiratory diseases	J40-J47	42.7	45.7
Organic, including symptomatic, mental disorders	F01-F09	34.0	35.9
Hypertensive diseases	I10-I15	47.8	35.0
Diabetes mellitus	E10-E14	13.1	29.6

Note: (a) ICD-10 = International Classification of Diseases 10th Revision; (1) Crude mortality rates are a three-year average covering 2019-2021; (2) Figures cover Tuscaloosa County.
Source: Centers for Disease Control and Prevention, National Center for Health Statistics. National Vital Statistics System, Mortality 2018-2021 on CDC WONDER Online Database

Mortality Rates for Selected Causes of Death

ICD-10[a] Sub-Chapter	ICD-10[a] Code	Crude Mortality Rate[1] per 100,000 population County[2]	U.S.
Assault	X85-Y09	9.7	7.0
Diseases of the liver	K70-K76	16.4	19.8
Human immunodeficiency virus (HIV) disease	B20-B24	Suppressed	1.5
Influenza and pneumonia	J09-J18	20.6	14.7
Intentional self-harm	X60-X84	12.8	14.3
Malnutrition	E40-E46	3.4	4.3
Obesity and other hyperalimentation	E65-E68	Suppressed	3.0
Renal failure	N17-N19	15.9	15.7
Transport accidents	V01-V99	13.4	13.6
Viral hepatitis	B15-B19	Suppressed	1.2

Note: (a) ICD-10 = International Classification of Diseases 10th Revision; (1) Crude mortality rates are a three-year average covering 2019-2021; (2) Figures cover Tuscaloosa County; Data are suppressed when the data meet the criteria for confidentiality constraints; Crude mortality rates are flagged as unreliable when the rate would be calculated with a numerator of 20 or less.
Source: Centers for Disease Control and Prevention, National Center for Health Statistics. National Vital Statistics System, Mortality 2018-2021 on CDC WONDER Online Database

Health Insurance Coverage

Area	With Health Insurance	With Private Health Insurance	With Public Health Insurance	Without Health Insurance	Population Under Age 19 Without Health Insurance
City	92.1	70.9	32.9	7.9	2.3
MSA[1]	92.6	70.5	34.5	7.4	2.6
U.S.	91.2	67.8	35.4	8.8	5.3

Note: Figures are percentages that cover the civilian noninstitutionalized population; (1) Figures cover the Tuscaloosa, AL Metropolitan Statistical Area
Source: U.S. Census Bureau, 2017-2021 American Community Survey 5-Year Estimates

Number of Medical Professionals

Area	MDs[3]	DOs[3,4]	Dentists	Podiatrists	Chiropractors	Optometrists
County[1] (number)	507	21	102	9	43	36
County[1] (rate[2])	223.2	9.2	44.9	4.0	18.9	15.9
U.S. (rate[2])	289.3	23.5	72.5	6.2	28.7	17.4

Note: Data as of 2021 unless noted; (1) Data covers Tuscaloosa County; (2) Rate per 100,000 population; (3) Data as of 2020 and includes all active, non-federal physicians; (4) Doctor of Osteopathic Medicine
Source: U.S. Department of Health and Human Services, Health Resources and Services Administration, Bureau of Health Professions, Area Resource File (ARF) 2021-2022

EDUCATION

Public School District Statistics

District Name	Schls	Pupils	Pupil/Teacher Ratio	Minority Pupils[1] (%)	LEP/ELL[2] (%)	IEP[3] (%)
Tuscaloosa City	20	10,964	17.5	77.6	3.3	12.7
Tuscaloosa County	36	19,111	20.3	43.6	5.1	15.4

Note: Table includes school districts with 2,000 or more students; (1) Percentage of students that are not non-Hispanic white; (2) Percentage of students that are Limited English Proficient or English Language Learners (2018-19); (3) Percentage of students that have an Individualized Education Program (2019-20).
Source: U.S. Department of Education, National Center for Education Statistics, Common Core of Data, Local Education Agency (School District) Universe Survey: School Year 2021-2022

Highest Level of Education

Area	Less than H.S.	H.S. Diploma	Some College, No Deg.	Associate Degree	Bachelor's Degree	Master's Degree	Prof. School Degree	Doctorate Degree
City	9.9	27.1	18.6	6.8	20.5	11.0	2.1	4.0
MSA[1]	11.5	31.7	20.2	8.8	16.6	7.6	1.2	2.4
U.S.	11.1	26.5	20.0	8.7	20.6	9.3	2.2	1.5

Note: Figures cover persons age 25 and over; (1) Figures cover the Tuscaloosa, AL Metropolitan Statistical Area
Source: U.S. Census Bureau, 2017-2021 American Community Survey 5-Year Estimates

Educational Attainment by Race

Area	High School Graduate or Higher (%) Total	White	Black	Asian	Hisp.[2]	Bachelor's Degree or Higher (%) Total	White	Black	Asian	Hisp.[2]
City	90.1	95.5	85.9	91.4	66.5	37.6	57.4	15.7	67.5	20.2
MSA[1]	88.5	91.2	84.9	86.9	64.6	27.8	34.2	15.3	61.0	17.4
U.S.	88.9	91.4	87.2	87.6	71.2	33.7	35.5	23.3	55.6	18.4

Note: Figures shown cover persons 25 years old and over; (1) Figures cover the Tuscaloosa, AL Metropolitan Statistical Area; (2) People of Hispanic origin can be of any race
Source: U.S. Census Bureau, 2017-2021 American Community Survey 5-Year Estimates

School Enrollment by Grade and Control

Area	Preschool (%) Public	Private	Kindergarten (%) Public	Private	Grades 1 - 4 (%) Public	Private	Grades 5 - 8 (%) Public	Private	Grades 9 - 12 (%) Public	Private
City	78.7	21.3	94.7	5.3	84.3	15.7	96.4	3.6	94.9	5.1
MSA[1]	71.4	28.6	87.3	12.7	86.8	13.2	89.9	10.1	88.1	11.9
U.S.	58.8	41.2	86.3	13.7	88.3	11.7	88.6	11.4	89.4	10.6

Note: Figures shown cover persons 3 years old and over; (1) Figures cover the Tuscaloosa, AL Metropolitan Statistical Area
Source: U.S. Census Bureau, 2017-2021 American Community Survey 5-Year Estimates

Higher Education

Four-Year Colleges Public	Private Non-profit	Private For-profit	Two-Year Colleges Public	Private Non-profit	Private For-profit	Medical Schools[1]	Law Schools[2]	Voc/Tech[3]
1	1	0	1	0	0	0	1	1

Note: Figures cover institutions located within the Tuscaloosa, AL Metropolitan Statistical Area and include main campuses only; (1) includes schools accredited by the Liaison Committee on Medical Education and the American Osteopathic Association's Commission on Osteopathic College Accreditation; (2) includes ABA-accredited schools, schools with provisional ABA accreditation, and state accredited schools; (3) includes all schools with programs that are less than 2 years.
Source: National Center for Education Statistics, Integrated Postsecondary Education System (IPEDS), 2021-22; Wikipedia, List of Medical Schools in the United States, accessed April 10, 2023; Wikipedia, List of Law Schools in the United States, accessed April 10, 2023

According to *U.S. News & World Report,* the Tuscaloosa, AL metro area is home to one of the top 200 national universities in the U.S.: **University of Alabama** (#137 tie). The indicators used to capture academic quality fall into a number of categories: assessment by administrators at peer institutions; retention of students; faculty resources; student selectivity; financial resources; alumni giving; high school counselor ratings of colleges; and graduation rate. *U.S. News & World Report, "America's Best Colleges 2023"*

According to *U.S. News & World Report,* the Tuscaloosa, AL metro area is home to one of the top 100 law schools in the U.S.: **University of Alabama** (#25 tie). The rankings are based on a weighted average of 12 measures of quality: peer assessment score; assessment score by lawyers/judges; median LSAT scores; median undergrad GPA; acceptance rate; employment rates for graduates; placement success; bar passage rate; faculty resources; expenditures per student; student/faculty ratio; and library resources. *U.S. News & World Report, "America's Best Graduate Schools, Law, 2023"*

According to *U.S. News & World Report,* the Tuscaloosa, AL metro area is home to one of the top 75 business schools in the U.S.: **University of Alabama (Manderson)** (#57 tie). The rankings are based on a weighted average of the following nine measures: quality assessment; peer assessment; recruiter assessment; placement success; mean starting salary and bonus; student selectivity; mean GMAT and GRE scores; mean undergraduate GPA; and acceptance rate. *U.S. News & World Report, "America's Best Graduate Schools, Business, 2023"*

EMPLOYERS

Major Employers

Company Name	Industry
City Board of Education	Public education
City of Tuscaloosa	Municipal government
County Board of Education	Public education
DCH Regional Medical Center	Medical services
Mercedes-Benz U.S. International	Automobile manufacturing
Michelin/BFGoodrich Tire Manufacturing	Aftermarket tire manufacturing
Phifer Incorporated	Aluminum/fiberglass screening, mfg
The University of Alabama	Higher education
Veterans Administration Hospital	Specialized health care
Warrior Met Coal	Metallurgical coal mining

Note: Companies shown are located within the Tuscaloosa, AL Metropolitan Statistical Area.
Source: Hoovers.com; Wikipedia

PUBLIC SAFETY

Crime Rate

Area	Total Crime	Violent Crime Rate				Property Crime Rate		
		Murder	Rape[3]	Robbery	Aggrav. Assault	Burglary	Larceny-Theft	Motor Vehicle Theft
City	4,843.6	4.9	46.2	137.6	316.4	739.9	3,289.0	309.5
Suburbs[1]	2,503.0	3.3	28.5	41.7	249.6	518.3	1,449.1	212.5
Metro[2]	3,445.1	4.0	35.6	80.3	276.5	607.5	2,189.7	251.6
U.S.	2,593.1	5.0	44.0	86.1	248.2	378.0	1,601.6	230.2

Note: Figures are crimes per 100,000 population; (1) All areas within the metro area that are located outside the city limits; (2) Figures cover the Tuscaloosa, AL Metropolitan Statistical Area; (3) All figures shown were reported using the revised Uniform Crime Reporting (UCR) definition of rape; Due to the transition to the National Incident-Based Reporting System (NIBRS), limited city and metro area data was released for 2021.
Source: FBI Uniform Crime Reports, 2018 (data for 2020 was not available)

Hate Crimes

Area	Number of Quarters Reported	Number of Incidents per Bias Motivation					
		Race/Ethnicity/Ancestry	Religion	Sexual Orientation	Disability	Gender	Gender Identity
City	4	0	0	0	0	0	0
U.S.	4	5,227	1,244	1,110	130	75	266

Note: Due to the transition to the National Incident-Based Reporting System (NIBRS), limited crime data was released for 2021.
Source: Federal Bureau of Investigation, Hate Crime Statistics 2020

Identity Theft Consumer Reports

Area	Reports	Reports per 100,000 Population	Rank[2]
MSA[1]	2,829	1,123	1
U.S.	1,108,609	339	-

Note: (1) Figures cover the Tuscaloosa, AL Metropolitan Statistical Area; (2) Rank ranges from 1 to 391 where 1 indicates greatest number of identity theft reports per 100,000 population
Source: Federal Trade Commission, Consumer Sentinel Network Data Book 2022

Fraud and Other Consumer Reports

Area	Reports	Reports per 100,000 Population	Rank[2]
MSA[1]	5,702	2,264	1
U.S.	4,064,520	1,245	-

Note: (1) Figures cover the Tuscaloosa, AL Metropolitan Statistical Area; (2) Rank ranges from 1 to 391 where 1 indicates greatest number of fraud and other consumer reports per 100,000 population
Source: Federal Trade Commission, Consumer Sentinel Network Data Book 2022

POLITICS

2020 Presidential Election Results

Area	Biden	Trump	Jorgensen	Hawkins	Other
Tuscaloosa County	41.9	56.7	1.0	0.0	0.4
U.S.	51.3	46.8	1.2	0.3	0.5

Note: Results are percentages and may not add to 100% due to rounding
Source: Dave Leip's Atlas of U.S. Presidential Elections

SPORTS

Professional Sports Teams

Team Name	League	Year Established

No teams are located in the metro area
Source: Wikipedia, Major Professional Sports Teams of the United States and Canada, April 12, 2023

CLIMATE

Average and Extreme Temperatures

Temperature	Jan	Feb	Mar	Apr	May	Jun	Jul	Aug	Sep	Oct	Nov	Dec	Yr.
Extreme High (°F)	81	83	89	92	99	102	106	103	100	94	84	80	106
Average High (°F)	53	58	66	75	82	88	90	90	84	75	64	56	74
Average Temp. (°F)	43	47	54	63	70	77	80	80	74	63	53	46	63
Average Low (°F)	33	36	42	50	58	66	70	69	63	51	41	35	51
Extreme Low (°F)	-6	3	2	26	36	42	51	52	37	27	5	1	-6

Note: Figures cover the years 1948-1995
Source: National Climatic Data Center, International Station Meteorological Climate Summary, 9/96

Average Precipitation/Snowfall/Humidity

Precip./Humidity	Jan	Feb	Mar	Apr	May	Jun	Jul	Aug	Sep	Oct	Nov	Dec	Yr.
Avg. Precip. (in.)	5.0	4.8	5.9	4.6	4.4	3.8	5.1	3.8	4.1	2.9	4.3	4.8	53.5
Avg. Snowfall (in.)	1	Tr	Tr	Tr	0	0	0	0	0	Tr	Tr	Tr	2
Avg. Rel. Hum. 7am (%)	82	81	78	76	76	78	81	82	81	82	82	82	80
Avg. Rel. Hum. 4pm (%)	57	53	48	46	51	54	58	55	54	50	52	58	53

Note: Figures cover the years 1948-1995; Tr = Trace amounts (<0.05 in. of rain; <0.5 in. of snow)
Source: National Climatic Data Center, International Station Meteorological Climate Summary, 9/96

Weather Conditions

Temperature			Daytime Sky			Precipitation		
10°F & below	32°F & below	90°F & above	Clear	Partly cloudy	Cloudy	0.01 inch or more precip.	0.1 inch or more snow/ice	Thunderstorms
1	57	59	91	161	113	119	1	57

Note: Figures are average number of days per year and cover the years 1948-1995
Source: National Climatic Data Center, International Station Meteorological Climate Summary, 9/96

HAZARDOUS WASTE

Superfund Sites

The Tuscaloosa, AL metro area has no sites on the EPA's Superfund Final National Priorities List. There are a total of 1,165 Superfund sites with a status of proposed or final on the list in the U.S. *U.S. Environmental Protection Agency, National Priorities List, April 12, 2023*

AIR QUALITY

Air Quality Trends: Ozone

	1990	1995	2000	2005	2010	2015	2018	2019	2020	2021
MSA[1]	n/a	n/a	n/a	n/a	n/a	n/a	n/a	n/a	n/a	n/a
U.S.	0.087	0.089	0.081	0.080	0.072	0.067	0.069	0.065	0.065	0.067

Note: (1) Data covers the Tuscaloosa, AL Metropolitan Statistical Area; n/a not available. The values shown are the composite ozone concentration averages among trend sites based on the highest fourth daily maximum 8-hour concentration in parts per million. These trends are based on sites having an adequate record of monitoring data during the trend period. Data from exceptional events are included.
Source: U.S. Environmental Protection Agency, Air Quality Monitoring Information, "Air Quality Trends by City, 1990-2021"

Air Quality Index

Area	Percent of Days when Air Quality was...[2]					AQI Statistics[2]	
	Good	Moderate	Unhealthy for Sensitive Groups	Unhealthy	Very Unhealthy	Maximum	Median
MSA[1]	94.3	5.7	0.0	0.0	0.0	90	31

Note: (1) Data covers the Tuscaloosa, AL Metropolitan Statistical Area; (2) Based on 281 days with AQI data in 2021. Air Quality Index (AQI) is an index for reporting daily air quality. EPA calculates the AQI for five major air pollutants regulated by the Clean Air Act: ground-level ozone, particle pollution (aka particulate matter), carbon monoxide, sulfur dioxide, and nitrogen dioxide. The AQI runs from 0 to 500. The higher the AQI value, the greater the level of air pollution and the greater the health concern. There are six AQI categories: "Good" AQI is between 0 and 50. Air quality is considered satisfactory; "Moderate" AQI is between 51 and 100. Air quality is acceptable; "Unhealthy for Sensitive Groups" When AQI values are between 101 and 150, members of sensitive groups may experience health effects; "Unhealthy" When AQI values are between 151 and 200 everyone may begin to experience health effects; "Very Unhealthy" AQI values between 201 and 300 trigger a health alert; "Hazardous" AQI values over 300 trigger warnings of emergency conditions (not shown).
Source: U.S. Environmental Protection Agency, Air Quality Index Report, 2021

Air Quality Index Pollutants

Area	Percent of Days when AQI Pollutant was...[2]					
	Carbon Monoxide	Nitrogen Dioxide	Ozone	Sulfur Dioxide	Particulate Matter 2.5	Particulate Matter 10
MSA[1]	0.0	0.0	72.6	(3)	27.4	0.0

Note: (1) Data covers the Tuscaloosa, AL Metropolitan Statistical Area; (2) Based on 281 days with AQI data in 2021. The Air Quality Index (AQI) is an index for reporting daily air quality. EPA calculates the AQI for five major air pollutants regulated by the Clean Air Act: ground-level ozone, particle pollution (also known as particulate matter), carbon monoxide, sulfur dioxide, and nitrogen dioxide. The AQI runs from 0 to 500. The higher the AQI value, the greater the level of air pollution and the greater the health concern; (3) Sulfur dioxide is no longer included in this table (as of December 8, 2021) because SO_2 concentrations tend to be very localized and not necessarily representative of broad geographical areas like counties and CBSAs.
Source: U.S. Environmental Protection Agency, Air Quality Index Report, 2021

Maximum Air Pollutant Concentrations: Particulate Matter, Ozone, CO and Lead

	Particulate Matter 10 (ug/m³)	Particulate Matter 2.5 Wtd AM (ug/m³)	Particulate Matter 2.5 24-Hr (ug/m³)	Ozone (ppm)	Carbon Monoxide (ppm)	Lead (ug/m³)
MSA[1] Level	n/a	7.8	20	0.053	n/a	n/a
NAAQS[2]	150	15	35	0.075	9	0.15
Met NAAQS[2]	n/a	Yes	Yes	Yes	n/a	n/a

Note: (1) Data covers the Tuscaloosa, AL Metropolitan Statistical Area; Data from exceptional events are included; (2) National Ambient Air Quality Standards; ppm = parts per million; ug/m³ = micrograms per cubic meter; n/a not available.
Concentrations: Particulate Matter 10 (coarse particulate)—highest second maximum 24-hour concentration; Particulate Matter 2.5 Wtd AM (fine particulate)—highest weighted annual mean concentration; Particulate Matter 2.5 24-Hour (fine particulate)—highest 98th percentile 24-hour concentration; Ozone—highest fourth daily maximum 8-hour concentration; Carbon Monoxide—highest second maximum non-overlapping 8-hour concentration; Lead—maximum running 3-month average
Source: U.S. Environmental Protection Agency, Air Quality Monitoring Information, "Air Quality Statistics by City, 2021"

Maximum Air Pollutant Concentrations: Nitrogen Dioxide and Sulfur Dioxide

	Nitrogen Dioxide AM (ppb)	Nitrogen Dioxide 1-Hr (ppb)	Sulfur Dioxide AM (ppb)	Sulfur Dioxide 1-Hr (ppb)	Sulfur Dioxide 24-Hr (ppb)
MSA[1] Level	n/a	n/a	n/a	n/a	n/a
NAAQS[2]	53	100	30	75	140
Met NAAQS[2]	n/a	n/a	n/a	n/a	n/a

Note: (1) Data covers the Tuscaloosa, AL Metropolitan Statistical Area; Data from exceptional events are included; (2) National Ambient Air Quality Standards; ppm = parts per million; ug/m³ = micrograms per cubic meter; n/a not available.
Concentrations: Nitrogen Dioxide AM—highest arithmetic mean concentration; Nitrogen Dioxide 1-Hr—highest 98th percentile 1-hour daily maximum concentration; Sulfur Dioxide AM—highest annual mean concentration; Sulfur Dioxide 1-Hr—highest 99th percentile 1-hour daily maximum concentration; Sulfur Dioxide 24-Hr—highest second maximum 24-hour concentration
Source: U.S. Environmental Protection Agency, Air Quality Monitoring Information, "Air Quality Statistics by City, 2021"

Appendixes

Appendix A: Comparative Statistics

Table of Contents

Demographics
Population Growth: City............................... A-4
Population Growth: Metro Area....................... A-6
Male/Female Ratio: City............................. A-8
Male/Female Ratio: Metro Area..................... A-10
Race: City... A-12
Race: Metro Area................................... A-14
Hispanic Origin: City.............................. A-16
Hispanic Origin: Metro Area........................ A-18
Household Size: City............................... A-20
Household Size: Metro Area......................... A-22
Household Relationships: City...................... A-24
Household Relationships: Metro Area................ A-26
Age: City.. A-28
Age: Metro Area.................................... A-30
Ancestry: City..................................... A-32
Ancestry: Metro Area............................... A-34
Foreign-born Population: City...................... A-36
Foreign-born Population: Metro Area................ A-38
Marital Status: City............................... A-40
Marital Status: Metro Area......................... A-42
Disability by Age: City............................ A-44
Disability by Age: Metro Area...................... A-46
Religious Groups by Family......................... A-48
Religious Groups by Tradition...................... A-50

Economy
Gross Metropolitan Product......................... A-52
Economic Growth.................................... A-54
Metropolitan Area Exports.......................... A-56
Building Permits: City............................. A-58
Building Permits: Metro Area....................... A-60
Housing Vacancy Rates.............................. A-62
Bankruptcy Filings................................. A-64

Income and Poverty
Income: City....................................... A-66
Income: Metro Area................................. A-68
Household Income Distribution: City................ A-70
Household Income Distribution: Metro Area.......... A-72
Poverty Rate: City................................. A-74
Poverty Rate: Metro Area........................... A-76

Employment and Earnings
Employment by Industry............................. A-78
Labor Force, Employment and Job Growth: City....... A-80
Labor Force, Employment and Job Growth: Metro Area.... A-82
Unemployment Rate: City............................ A-84
Unemployment Rate: Metro Area...................... A-86
Average Hourly Wages: Occupations A - C............ A-88
Average Hourly Wages: Occupations C - E............ A-90
Average Hourly Wages: Occupations F - J............ A-92
Average Hourly Wages: Occupations L - N............ A-94
Average Hourly Wages: Occupations N - P............ A-96
Average Hourly Wages: Occupations P - S............ A-98

Average Hourly Wages: Occupations T - W............ A-100
Means of Transportation to Work: City.............. A-102
Means of Transportation to Work: Metro Area........ A-104
Travel Time to Work: City.......................... A-106
Travel Time to Work: Metro Area.................... A-108

Election Results
2020 Presidential Election Results................. A-110

Housing
House Price Index (HPI)............................ A-112
Home Value: City................................... A-114
Home Value: Metro Area............................. A-116
Homeownership Rate................................. A-118
Year Housing Structure Built: City................. A-120
Year Housing Structure Built: Metro Area........... A-122
Gross Monthly Rent: City........................... A-124
Gross Monthly Rent: Metro Area..................... A-126

Education
Highest Level of Education: City................... A-128
Highest Level of Education: Metro Area............. A-130
School Enrollment by Grade and Control: City....... A-132
School Enrollment by Grade and Control: Metro Area.... A-134
Educational Attainment by Race: City............... A-136
Educational Attainment by Race: Metro Area......... A-138

Cost of Living
Cost of Living Index............................... A-140
Grocery Prices..................................... A-142
Housing and Utility Costs.......................... A-144
Health Care, Transportation, and Other Costs....... A-146

Health Care
Number of Medical Professionals.................... A-148
Health Insurance Coverage: City.................... A-150
Health Insurance Coverage: Metro Area.............. A-152

Public Safety
Crime Rate: City................................... A-154
Crime Rate: Suburbs................................ A-156
Crime Rate: Metro Area............................. A-158

Climate
Temperature & Precipitation: Yearly Averages
    and Extremes................................... A-160
Weather Conditions................................. A-162

Air Quality
Air Quality Index.................................. A-164
Air Quality Index Pollutants....................... A-166
Air Quality Trends: Ozone.......................... A-168
Maximum Air Pollutant Concentrations:
    Particulate Matter, Ozone, CO and Lead......... A-170
Maximum Air Pollutant Concentrations:
    Nitrogen Dioxide and Sulfur Dioxide............ A-172

Population Growth: City

Area	1990 Census	2000 Census	2010 Census	2020 Census	Population Growth (%) 1990-2020	Population Growth (%) 2010-2020
Albuquerque, NM	388,375	448,607	545,852	564,559	45.4	3.4
Allentown, PA	105,066	106,632	118,032	125,845	19.8	6.6
Anchorage, AK	226,338	260,283	291,826	291,247	28.7	-0.2
Ann Arbor, MI	111,018	114,024	113,934	123,851	11.6	8.7
Athens, GA	86,561	100,266	115,452	127,315	47.1	10.3
Atlanta, GA	394,092	416,474	420,003	498,715	26.5	18.7
Austin, TX	499,053	656,562	790,390	961,855	92.7	21.7
Baltimore, MD	736,014	651,154	620,961	585,708	-20.4	-5.7
Boise City, ID	144,317	185,787	205,671	235,684	63.3	14.6
Boston, MA	574,283	589,141	617,594	675,647	17.7	9.4
Boulder, CO	87,737	94,673	97,385	108,250	23.4	11.2
Brownsville, TX	114,025	139,722	175,023	186,738	63.8	6.7
Cape Coral, FL	75,507	102,286	154,305	194,016	157.0	25.7
Cedar Rapids, IA	110,829	120,758	126,326	137,710	24.3	9.0
Charleston, SC	96,102	96,650	120,083	150,227	56.3	25.1
Charlotte, NC	428,283	540,828	731,424	874,579	104.2	19.6
Chicago, IL	2,783,726	2,896,016	2,695,598	2,746,388	-1.3	1.9
Cincinnati, OH	363,974	331,285	296,943	309,317	-15.0	4.2
Clarksville, TN	78,569	103,455	132,929	166,722	112.2	25.4
Cleveland, OH	505,333	478,403	396,815	372,624	-26.3	-6.1
College Station, TX	53,318	67,890	93,857	120,511	126.0	28.4
Colorado Springs, CO	283,798	360,890	416,427	478,961	68.8	15.0
Columbia, MO	71,069	84,531	108,500	126,254	77.6	16.4
Columbia, SC	115,475	116,278	129,272	136,632	18.3	5.7
Columbus, OH	648,656	711,470	787,033	905,748	39.6	15.1
Dallas, TX	1,006,971	1,188,580	1,197,816	1,304,379	29.5	8.9
Davenport, IA	95,705	98,359	99,685	101,724	6.3	2.0
Denver, CO	467,153	554,636	600,158	715,522	53.2	19.2
Des Moines, IA	193,569	198,682	203,433	214,133	10.6	5.3
Durham, NC	151,737	187,035	228,330	283,506	86.8	24.2
Edison, NJ	88,680	97,687	99,967	107,588	21.3	7.6
El Paso, TX	515,541	563,662	649,121	678,815	31.7	4.6
Fargo, ND	74,372	90,599	105,549	125,990	69.4	19.4
Fort Collins, CO	89,555	118,652	143,986	169,810	89.6	17.9
Fort Wayne, IN	205,671	205,727	253,691	263,886	28.3	4.0
Fort Worth, TX	448,311	534,694	741,206	918,915	105.0	24.0
Grand Rapids, MI	189,145	197,800	188,040	198,917	5.2	5.8
Greeley, CO	60,887	76,930	92,889	108,795	78.7	17.1
Green Bay, WI	96,466	102,313	104,057	107,395	11.3	3.2
Greensboro, NC	193,389	223,891	269,666	299,035	54.6	10.9
Honolulu, HI	376,465	371,657	337,256	350,964	-6.8	4.1
Houston, TX	1,697,610	1,953,631	2,099,451	2,304,580	35.8	9.8
Huntsville, AL	161,842	158,216	180,105	215,006	32.8	19.4
Indianapolis, IN	730,993	781,870	820,445	887,642	21.4	8.2
Jacksonville, FL	635,221	735,617	821,784	949,611	49.5	15.6
Kansas City, MO	434,967	441,545	459,787	508,090	16.8	10.5
Lafayette, LA	104,735	110,257	120,623	121,374	15.9	0.6
Las Cruces, NM	63,267	74,267	97,618	111,385	76.1	14.1
Las Vegas, NV	261,374	478,434	583,756	641,903	145.6	10.0
Lexington, KY	225,366	260,512	295,803	322,570	43.1	9.0
Lincoln, NE	193,629	225,581	258,379	291,082	50.3	12.7
Little Rock, AR	177,519	183,133	193,524	202,591	14.1	4.7
Los Angeles, CA	3,487,671	3,694,820	3,792,621	3,898,747	11.8	2.8
Louisville, KY	269,160	256,231	597,337	386,884	43.7	-35.2
Madison, WI	193,451	208,054	233,209	269,840	39.5	15.7

Table continued on following page.

Area	1990 Census	2000 Census	2010 Census	2020 Census	Population Growth (%) 1990-2020	Population Growth (%) 2010-2020
Manchester, NH	99,567	107,006	109,565	115,644	16.1	5.5
Miami, FL	358,843	362,470	399,457	442,241	23.2	10.7
Midland, TX	89,358	94,996	111,147	132,524	48.3	19.2
Milwaukee, WI	628,095	596,974	594,833	577,222	-8.1	-3.0
Minneapolis, MN	368,383	382,618	382,578	429,954	16.7	12.4
Nashville, TN	488,364	545,524	601,222	689,447	41.2	14.7
New Haven, CT	130,474	123,626	129,779	134,023	2.7	3.3
New Orleans, LA	496,938	484,674	343,829	383,997	-22.7	11.7
New York, NY	7,322,552	8,008,278	8,175,133	8,804,190	20.2	7.7
Oklahoma City, OK	445,065	506,132	579,999	681,054	53.0	17.4
Omaha, NE	371,972	390,007	408,958	486,051	30.7	18.9
Orlando, FL	161,172	185,951	238,300	307,573	90.8	29.1
Philadelphia, PA	1,585,577	1,517,550	1,526,006	1,603,797	1.1	5.1
Phoenix, AZ	989,873	1,321,045	1,445,632	1,608,139	62.5	11.2
Pittsburgh, PA	369,785	334,563	305,704	302,971	-18.1	-0.9
Portland, OR	485,833	529,121	583,776	652,503	34.3	11.8
Providence, RI	160,734	173,618	178,042	190,934	18.8	7.2
Provo, UT	87,148	105,166	112,488	115,162	32.1	2.4
Raleigh, NC	226,841	276,093	403,892	467,665	106.2	15.8
Reno, NV	139,950	180,480	225,221	264,165	88.8	17.3
Richmond, VA	202,783	197,790	204,214	226,610	11.7	11.0
Rochester, MN	74,151	85,806	106,769	121,395	63.7	13.7
Sacramento, CA	368,923	407,018	466,488	524,943	42.3	12.5
St. Louis, MO	396,685	348,189	319,294	301,578	-24.0	-5.5
Salem, OR	112,046	136,924	154,637	175,535	56.7	13.5
Salt Lake City, UT	159,796	181,743	186,440	199,723	25.0	7.1
San Antonio, TX	997,258	1,144,646	1,327,407	1,434,625	43.9	8.1
San Diego, CA	1,111,048	1,223,400	1,307,402	1,386,932	24.8	6.1
San Francisco, CA	723,959	776,733	805,235	873,965	20.7	8.5
San Jose, CA	784,324	894,943	945,942	1,013,240	29.2	7.1
Santa Rosa, CA	123,297	147,595	167,815	178,127	44.5	6.1
Savannah, GA	138,038	131,510	136,286	147,780	7.1	8.4
Seattle, WA	516,262	563,374	608,660	737,015	42.8	21.1
Sioux Falls, SD	102,262	123,975	153,888	192,517	88.3	25.1
Springfield, IL	108,997	111,454	116,250	114,394	5.0	-1.6
Tampa, FL	279,960	303,447	335,709	384,959	37.5	14.7
Tucson, AZ	417,942	486,699	520,116	542,629	29.8	4.3
Tulsa, OK	367,241	393,049	391,906	413,066	12.5	5.4
Tuscaloosa, AL	81,075	77,906	90,468	99,600	22.8	10.1
Virginia Beach, VA	393,069	425,257	437,994	459,470	16.9	4.9
Washington, DC	606,900	572,059	601,723	689,545	13.6	14.6
Wichita, KS	313,693	344,284	382,368	397,532	26.7	4.0
Wilmington, NC	64,609	75,838	106,476	115,451	78.7	8.4
Winston-Salem, NC	168,139	185,776	229,617	249,545	48.4	8.7
Worcester, MA	169,759	172,648	181,045	206,518	21.7	14.1
U.S.	248,709,873	281,421,906	308,745,538	331,449,281	33.3	7.4

Source: U.S. Census Bureau, 1990 Census,, 2000 Census,, 2010 Census,, 2020 Census

Appendix A: Comparative Statistics

Population Growth: Metro Area

Area	1990 Census	2000 Census	2010 Census	2020 Census	Population Growth (%) 1990-2020	Population Growth (%) 2010-2020
Albuquerque, NM	599,416	729,649	887,077	916,528	52.9	3.3
Allentown, PA	686,666	740,395	821,173	861,889	25.5	5.0
Anchorage, AK	266,021	319,605	380,821	398,328	49.7	4.6
Ann Arbor, MI	282,937	322,895	344,791	372,258	31.6	8.0
Athens, GA	136,025	166,079	192,541	215,415	58.4	11.9
Atlanta, GA	3,069,411	4,247,981	5,268,860	6,089,815	98.4	15.6
Austin, TX	846,217	1,249,763	1,716,289	2,283,371	169.8	33.0
Baltimore, MD	2,382,172	2,552,994	2,710,489	2,844,510	19.4	4.9
Boise City, ID	319,596	464,840	616,561	764,718	139.3	24.0
Boston, MA	4,133,895	4,391,344	4,552,402	4,941,632	19.5	8.5
Boulder, CO	208,898	269,758	294,567	330,758	58.3	12.3
Brownsville, TX	260,120	335,227	406,220	421,017	61.9	3.6
Cape Coral, FL	335,113	440,888	618,754	760,822	127.0	23.0
Cedar Rapids, IA	210,640	237,230	257,940	276,520	31.3	7.2
Charleston, SC	506,875	549,033	664,607	799,636	57.8	20.3
Charlotte, NC	1,024,331	1,330,448	1,758,038	2,660,329	159.7	51.3
Chicago, IL	8,182,076	9,098,316	9,461,105	9,618,502	17.6	1.7
Cincinnati, OH	1,844,917	2,009,632	2,130,151	2,256,884	22.3	5.9
Clarksville, TN	189,277	232,000	273,949	320,535	69.3	17.0
Cleveland, OH	2,102,219	2,148,143	2,077,240	2,088,251	-0.7	0.5
College Station, TX	150,998	184,885	228,660	268,248	77.7	17.3
Colorado Springs, CO	409,482	537,484	645,613	755,105	84.4	17.0
Columbia, MO	122,010	145,666	172,786	210,864	72.8	22.0
Columbia, SC	548,325	647,158	767,598	829,470	51.3	8.1
Columbus, OH	1,405,176	1,612,694	1,836,536	2,138,926	52.2	16.5
Dallas, TX	3,989,294	5,161,544	6,371,773	7,637,387	91.4	19.9
Davenport, IA	368,151	376,019	379,690	384,324	4.4	1.2
Denver, CO	1,666,935	2,179,296	2,543,482	2,963,821	77.8	16.5
Des Moines, IA	416,346	481,394	569,633	709,466	70.4	24.5
Durham, NC	344,646	426,493	504,357	649,903	88.6	28.9
Edison, NJ	16,845,992	18,323,002	18,897,109	20,140,470	19.6	6.6
El Paso, TX	591,610	679,622	800,647	868,859	46.9	8.5
Fargo, ND	153,296	174,367	208,777	249,843	63.0	19.7
Fort Collins, CO	186,136	251,494	299,630	359,066	92.9	19.8
Fort Wayne, IN	354,435	390,156	416,257	419,601	18.4	0.8
Fort Worth, TX	3,989,294	5,161,544	6,371,773	7,637,387	91.4	19.9
Grand Rapids, MI	645,914	740,482	774,160	1,087,592	68.4	40.5
Greeley, CO	131,816	180,926	252,825	328,981	149.6	30.1
Green Bay, WI	243,698	282,599	306,241	328,268	34.7	7.2
Greensboro, NC	540,257	643,430	723,801	776,566	43.7	7.3
Honolulu, HI	836,231	876,156	953,207	1,016,508	21.6	6.6
Houston, TX	3,767,335	4,715,407	5,946,800	7,122,240	89.1	19.8
Huntsville, AL	293,047	342,376	417,593	491,723	67.8	17.8
Indianapolis, IN	1,294,217	1,525,104	1,756,241	2,111,040	63.1	20.2
Jacksonville, FL	925,213	1,122,750	1,345,596	1,605,848	73.6	19.3
Kansas City, MO	1,636,528	1,836,038	2,035,334	2,192,035	33.9	7.7
Lafayette, LA	208,740	239,086	273,738	478,384	129.2	74.8
Las Cruces, NM	135,510	174,682	209,233	219,561	62.0	4.9
Las Vegas, NV	741,459	1,375,765	1,951,269	2,265,461	205.5	16.1
Lexington, KY	348,428	408,326	472,099	516,811	48.3	9.5
Lincoln, NE	229,091	266,787	302,157	340,217	48.5	12.6
Little Rock, AR	535,034	610,518	699,757	748,031	39.8	6.9
Los Angeles, CA	11,273,720	12,365,627	12,828,837	13,200,998	17.1	2.9
Louisville, KY	1,055,973	1,161,975	1,283,566	1,285,439	21.7	0.1
Madison, WI	432,323	501,774	568,593	680,796	57.5	19.7

Table continued on following page.

Area	1990 Census	2000 Census	2010 Census	2020 Census	Population Growth (%) 1990-2020	Population Growth (%) 2010-2020
Manchester, NH	336,073	380,841	400,721	422,937	25.8	5.5
Miami, FL	4,056,100	5,007,564	5,564,635	6,138,333	51.3	10.3
Midland, TX	106,611	116,009	136,872	175,220	64.4	28.0
Milwaukee, WI	1,432,149	1,500,741	1,555,908	1,574,731	10.0	1.2
Minneapolis, MN	2,538,834	2,968,806	3,279,833	3,690,261	45.4	12.5
Nashville, TN	1,048,218	1,311,789	1,589,934	1,989,519	89.8	25.1
New Haven, CT	804,219	824,008	862,477	864,835	7.5	0.3
New Orleans, LA	1,264,391	1,316,510	1,167,764	1,271,845	0.6	8.9
New York, NY	16,845,992	18,323,002	18,897,109	20,140,470	19.6	6.6
Oklahoma City, OK	971,042	1,095,421	1,252,987	1,425,695	46.8	13.8
Omaha, NE	685,797	767,041	865,350	967,604	41.1	11.8
Orlando, FL	1,224,852	1,644,561	2,134,411	2,673,376	118.3	25.3
Philadelphia, PA	5,435,470	5,687,147	5,965,343	6,245,051	14.9	4.7
Phoenix, AZ	2,238,480	3,251,876	4,192,887	4,845,832	116.5	15.6
Pittsburgh, PA	2,468,289	2,431,087	2,356,285	2,370,930	-3.9	0.6
Portland, OR	1,523,741	1,927,881	2,226,009	2,512,859	64.9	12.9
Providence, RI	1,509,789	1,582,997	1,600,852	1,676,579	11.0	4.7
Provo, UT	269,407	376,774	526,810	671,185	149.1	27.4
Raleigh, NC	541,081	797,071	1,130,490	1,413,982	161.3	25.1
Reno, NV	257,193	342,885	425,417	490,596	90.8	15.3
Richmond, VA	949,244	1,096,957	1,258,251	1,314,434	38.5	4.5
Rochester, MN	141,945	163,618	186,011	226,329	59.4	21.7
Sacramento, CA	1,481,126	1,796,857	2,149,127	2,397,382	61.9	11.6
St. Louis, MO	2,580,897	2,698,687	2,812,896	2,820,253	9.3	0.3
Salem, OR	278,024	347,214	390,738	433,353	55.9	10.9
Salt Lake City, UT	768,075	968,858	1,124,197	1,257,936	63.8	11.9
San Antonio, TX	1,407,745	1,711,703	2,142,508	2,558,143	81.7	19.4
San Diego, CA	2,498,016	2,813,833	3,095,313	3,298,634	32.1	6.6
San Francisco, CA	3,686,592	4,123,740	4,335,391	4,749,008	28.8	9.5
San Jose, CA	1,534,280	1,735,819	1,836,911	2,000,468	30.4	8.9
Santa Rosa, CA	388,222	458,614	483,878	488,863	25.9	1.0
Savannah, GA	258,060	293,000	347,611	404,798	56.9	16.5
Seattle, WA	2,559,164	3,043,878	3,439,809	4,018,762	57.0	16.8
Sioux Falls, SD	153,500	187,093	228,261	276,730	80.3	21.2
Springfield, IL	189,550	201,437	210,170	208,640	10.1	-0.7
Tampa, FL	2,067,959	2,395,997	2,783,243	3,175,275	53.5	14.1
Tucson, AZ	666,880	843,746	980,263	1,043,433	56.5	6.4
Tulsa, OK	761,019	859,532	937,478	1,015,331	33.4	8.3
Tuscaloosa, AL	176,123	192,034	219,461	268,674	52.5	22.4
Virginia Beach, VA	1,449,389	1,576,370	1,671,683	1,799,674	24.2	7.7
Washington, DC	4,122,914	4,796,183	5,582,170	6,385,162	54.9	14.4
Wichita, KS	511,111	571,166	623,061	647,610	26.7	3.9
Wilmington, NC	200,124	274,532	362,315	285,905	42.9	-21.1
Winston-Salem, NC	361,091	421,961	477,717	675,966	87.2	41.5
Worcester, MA	709,728	750,963	798,552	978,529	37.9	22.5
U.S.	248,709,873	281,421,906	308,745,538	331,449,281	33.3	7.4

Note: Figures cover the Metropolitan Statistical Area (MSA)
Source: U.S. Census Bureau, 1990 Census,, 2000 Census,, 2010 Census,, 2020 Census

Male/Female Ratio: City

City	Males	Females	Males per 100 Females
Albuquerque, NM	274,173	290,386	94.4
Allentown, PA	60,577	65,268	92.8
Anchorage, AK	147,894	143,353	103.2
Ann Arbor, MI	61,263	62,588	97.9
Athens, GA	59,963	67,352	89.0
Atlanta, GA	245,444	253,271	96.9
Austin, TX	485,739	476,116	102.0
Baltimore, MD	274,635	311,073	88.3
Boise City, ID	116,758	118,926	98.2
Boston, MA	319,326	356,321	89.6
Boulder, CO	55,982	52,268	107.1
Brownsville, TX	89,293	97,445	91.6
Cape Coral, FL	95,028	98,988	96.0
Cedar Rapids, IA	67,218	70,492	95.4
Charleston, SC	71,681	78,546	91.3
Charlotte, NC	421,316	453,263	93.0
Chicago, IL	1,332,725	1,413,663	94.3
Cincinnati, OH	149,736	159,581	93.8
Clarksville, TN	81,849	84,873	96.4
Cleveland, OH	180,991	191,633	94.4
College Station, TX	61,203	59,308	103.2
Colorado Springs, CO	236,731	242,230	97.7
Columbia, MO	60,766	65,488	92.8
Columbia, SC	67,155	69,477	96.7
Columbus, OH	441,869	463,879	95.3
Dallas, TX	647,963	656,416	98.7
Davenport, IA	49,751	51,973	95.7
Denver, CO	358,405	357,117	100.4
Des Moines, IA	105,618	108,515	97.3
Durham, NC	133,353	150,153	88.8
Edison, NJ	53,123	54,465	97.5
El Paso, TX	326,540	352,275	92.7
Fargo, ND	63,707	62,283	102.3
Fort Collins, CO	84,217	85,593	98.4
Fort Wayne, IN	128,678	135,208	95.2
Fort Worth, TX	449,923	468,992	95.9
Grand Rapids, MI	97,037	101,880	95.2
Greeley, CO	53,848	54,947	98.0
Green Bay, WI	53,407	53,988	98.9
Greensboro, NC	138,465	160,570	86.2
Honolulu, HI	172,783	178,181	97.0
Houston, TX	1,140,598	1,163,982	98.0
Huntsville, AL	104,200	110,806	94.0
Indianapolis, IN	430,358	457,284	94.1
Jacksonville, FL	459,204	490,407	93.6
Kansas City, MO	247,776	260,314	95.2
Lafayette, LA	58,213	63,161	92.2
Las Cruces, NM	53,571	57,814	92.7
Las Vegas, NV	317,700	324,203	98.0
Lexington, KY	155,876	166,694	93.5
Lincoln, NE	145,790	145,292	100.3
Little Rock, AR	96,018	106,573	90.1
Los Angeles, CA	1,925,675	1,973,072	97.6
Louisville, KY	186,813	200,071	93.4
Madison, WI	133,922	135,918	98.5

Table continued on following page.

City	Males	Females	Males per 100 Females
Manchester, NH	57,668	57,976	99.5
Miami, FL	218,706	223,535	97.8
Midland, TX	66,552	65,972	100.9
Milwaukee, WI	278,386	298,836	93.2
Minneapolis, MN	216,381	213,573	101.3
Nashville, TN	332,568	356,879	93.2
New Haven, CT	64,141	69,882	91.8
New Orleans, LA	181,171	202,826	89.3
New York, NY	4,184,548	4,619,642	90.6
Oklahoma City, OK	335,613	345,441	97.2
Omaha, NE	239,675	246,376	97.3
Orlando, FL	148,481	159,092	93.3
Philadelphia, PA	760,383	843,414	90.2
Phoenix, AZ	799,456	808,683	98.9
Pittsburgh, PA	148,157	154,814	95.7
Portland, OR	322,690	329,813	97.8
Providence, RI	92,861	98,073	94.7
Provo, UT	56,944	58,218	97.8
Raleigh, NC	224,994	242,671	92.7
Reno, NV	134,002	130,163	102.9
Richmond, VA	107,678	118,932	90.5
Rochester, MN	58,643	62,752	93.5
Sacramento, CA	255,987	268,956	95.2
St. Louis, MO	147,340	154,238	95.5
Salem, OR	87,574	87,961	99.6
Salt Lake City, UT	102,530	97,193	105.5
San Antonio, TX	699,905	734,720	95.3
San Diego, CA	694,107	692,825	100.2
San Francisco, CA	446,144	427,821	104.3
San Jose, CA	509,260	503,980	101.0
Santa Rosa, CA	86,767	91,360	95.0
Savannah, GA	69,878	77,902	89.7
Seattle, WA	371,247	365,768	101.5
Sioux Falls, SD	95,676	96,841	98.8
Springfield, IL	54,215	60,179	90.1
Tampa, FL	187,761	197,198	95.2
Tucson, AZ	269,110	273,519	98.4
Tulsa, OK	201,814	211,252	95.5
Tuscaloosa, AL	47,020	52,580	89.4
Virginia Beach, VA	224,059	235,411	95.2
Washington, DC	322,777	366,768	88.0
Wichita, KS	196,575	200,957	97.8
Wilmington, NC	54,189	61,262	88.5
Winston-Salem, NC	116,698	132,847	87.8
Worcester, MA	100,540	105,978	94.9
U.S.	162,685,811	168,763,470	96.4

Source: U.S. Census Bureau, 2020 Census

Male/Female Ratio: Metro Area

Metro Area	Males	Females	Males per 100 Females
Albuquerque, NM	449,092	467,436	96.1
Allentown, PA	419,780	442,109	94.9
Anchorage, AK	203,277	195,051	104.2
Ann Arbor, MI	182,825	189,433	96.5
Athens, GA	103,235	112,180	92.0
Atlanta, GA	2,933,974	3,155,841	93.0
Austin, TX	1,138,942	1,144,429	99.5
Baltimore, MD	1,365,439	1,479,071	92.3
Boise City, ID	380,892	383,826	99.2
Boston, MA	2,390,705	2,550,927	93.7
Boulder, CO	166,794	163,964	101.7
Brownsville, TX	203,223	217,794	93.3
Cape Coral, FL	371,444	389,378	95.4
Cedar Rapids, IA	136,845	139,675	98.0
Charleston, SC	389,850	409,786	95.1
Charlotte, NC	1,289,221	1,371,108	94.0
Chicago, IL	4,694,560	4,923,942	95.3
Cincinnati, OH	1,107,410	1,149,474	96.3
Clarksville, TN	159,552	160,983	99.1
Cleveland, OH	1,008,568	1,079,683	93.4
College Station, TX	134,329	133,919	100.3
Colorado Springs, CO	379,052	376,053	100.8
Columbia, MO	102,929	107,935	95.4
Columbia, SC	398,440	431,030	92.4
Columbus, OH	1,050,767	1,088,159	96.6
Dallas, TX	3,753,384	3,884,003	96.6
Davenport, IA	189,247	195,077	97.0
Denver, CO	1,481,349	1,482,472	99.9
Des Moines, IA	349,805	359,661	97.3
Durham, NC	312,256	337,647	92.5
Edison, NJ	9,693,702	10,446,768	92.8
El Paso, TX	422,688	446,171	94.7
Fargo, ND	125,674	124,169	101.2
Fort Collins, CO	177,804	181,262	98.1
Fort Wayne, IN	205,785	213,816	96.2
Fort Worth, TX	3,753,384	3,884,003	96.6
Grand Rapids, MI	540,561	547,031	98.8
Greeley, CO	164,843	164,138	100.4
Green Bay, WI	163,689	164,579	99.5
Greensboro, NC	370,483	406,083	91.2
Honolulu, HI	509,569	506,939	100.5
Houston, TX	3,505,374	3,616,866	96.9
Huntsville, AL	241,092	250,631	96.2
Indianapolis, IN	1,033,439	1,077,601	95.9
Jacksonville, FL	779,083	826,765	94.2
Kansas City, MO	1,076,104	1,115,931	96.4
Lafayette, LA	231,864	246,520	94.1
Las Cruces, NM	107,150	112,411	95.3
Las Vegas, NV	1,126,444	1,139,017	98.9
Lexington, KY	250,691	266,120	94.2
Lincoln, NE	170,718	169,499	100.7
Little Rock, AR	361,694	386,337	93.6
Los Angeles, CA	6,469,965	6,731,033	96.1
Louisville, KY	628,220	657,219	95.6
Madison, WI	338,757	342,039	99.0

Table continued on following page.

Metro Area	Males	Females	Males per 100 Females
Manchester, NH	209,879	213,058	98.5
Miami, FL	2,954,448	3,183,885	92.8
Midland, TX	88,457	86,763	102.0
Milwaukee, WI	766,278	808,453	94.8
Minneapolis, MN	1,824,100	1,866,161	97.7
Nashville, TN	968,381	1,021,138	94.8
New Haven, CT	415,391	449,444	92.4
New Orleans, LA	610,653	661,192	92.4
New York, NY	9,693,702	10,446,768	92.8
Oklahoma City, OK	702,324	723,371	97.1
Omaha, NE	478,627	488,977	97.9
Orlando, FL	1,296,256	1,377,120	94.1
Philadelphia, PA	3,015,319	3,229,732	93.4
Phoenix, AZ	2,395,320	2,450,512	97.7
Pittsburgh, PA	1,157,964	1,212,966	95.5
Portland, OR	1,240,947	1,271,912	97.6
Providence, RI	812,496	864,083	94.0
Provo, UT	336,952	334,233	100.8
Raleigh, NC	687,440	726,542	94.6
Reno, NV	247,924	242,672	102.2
Richmond, VA	632,849	681,585	92.8
Rochester, MN	111,433	114,896	97.0
Sacramento, CA	1,170,850	1,226,532	95.5
St. Louis, MO	1,369,631	1,450,622	94.4
Salem, OR	214,703	218,650	98.2
Salt Lake City, UT	632,295	625,641	101.1
San Antonio, TX	1,254,014	1,304,129	96.2
San Diego, CA	1,642,796	1,655,838	99.2
San Francisco, CA	2,344,775	2,404,233	97.5
San Jose, CA	1,007,254	993,214	101.4
Santa Rosa, CA	238,535	250,328	95.3
Savannah, GA	194,814	209,984	92.8
Seattle, WA	2,007,150	2,011,612	99.8
Sioux Falls, SD	138,437	138,293	100.1
Springfield, IL	100,412	108,228	92.8
Tampa, FL	1,535,385	1,639,890	93.6
Tucson, AZ	512,753	530,680	96.6
Tulsa, OK	499,555	515,776	96.9
Tuscaloosa, AL	127,913	140,761	90.9
Virginia Beach, VA	879,439	920,235	95.6
Washington, DC	3,091,711	3,293,451	93.9
Wichita, KS	321,349	326,261	98.5
Wilmington, NC	137,791	148,114	93.0
Winston-Salem, NC	324,467	351,499	92.3
Worcester, MA	482,355	496,174	97.2
U.S.	162,685,811	168,763,470	96.4

Note: Figures cover the Metropolitan Statistical Area (MSA)
Source: U.S. Census Bureau, 2020 Census

Appendix A: Comparative Statistics

Race: City

City	White Alone[1] (%)	Black Alone[1] (%)	Asian Alone[1] (%)	AIAN[2] Alone[1] (%)	NHOPI[3] Alone[1] (%)	Other Race Alone[1] (%)	Two or More Races (%)
Albuquerque, NM	52.2	3.5	3.4	5.6	0.1	14.2	21.0
Allentown, PA	38.3	13.2	2.1	0.8	0.1	30.1	15.5
Anchorage, AK	56.5	5.0	9.5	8.1	3.4	3.5	14.0
Ann Arbor, MI	67.6	6.8	15.7	0.2	0.1	1.8	7.9
Athens, GA	58.1	24.7	3.9	0.5	0.1	6.1	6.7
Atlanta, GA	39.8	47.2	4.5	0.3	0.0	2.4	5.8
Austin, TX	54.7	7.3	9.0	1.0	0.1	11.9	16.1
Baltimore, MD	27.8	57.8	3.6	0.4	0.0	4.8	5.5
Boise City, ID	81.2	2.3	3.6	0.7	0.3	3.5	8.5
Boston, MA	47.1	20.6	11.3	0.4	0.1	10.1	10.5
Boulder, CO	78.8	1.3	6.4	0.6	0.1	4.7	8.1
Brownsville, TX	34.9	0.3	0.6	0.7	0.0	20.5	42.9
Cape Coral, FL	72.3	4.3	1.7	0.3	0.1	5.8	15.6
Cedar Rapids, IA	77.8	10.4	2.7	0.3	0.4	1.7	6.8
Charleston, SC	73.5	17.0	2.2	0.3	0.1	1.6	5.3
Charlotte, NC	41.7	33.1	7.1	0.6	0.1	9.6	7.9
Chicago, IL	35.9	29.2	7.0	1.3	0.0	15.8	10.8
Cincinnati, OH	47.7	40.6	2.5	0.3	0.1	3.0	5.8
Clarksville, TN	57.0	24.4	2.5	0.5	0.5	4.2	10.9
Cleveland, OH	34.5	48.4	2.8	0.4	0.0	6.3	7.6
College Station, TX	63.5	8.1	10.2	0.5	0.1	7.4	10.2
Colorado Springs, CO	70.3	5.9	3.4	1.1	0.3	6.2	12.8
Columbia, MO	72.5	11.9	5.6	0.3	0.1	2.2	7.4
Columbia, SC	50.7	38.5	3.1	0.3	0.1	2.3	5.1
Columbus, OH	53.2	28.6	6.2	0.4	0.0	4.3	7.2
Dallas, TX	36.1	23.3	3.7	1.2	0.1	19.5	16.2
Davenport, IA	74.1	12.0	2.2	0.4	0.0	2.6	8.7
Denver, CO	60.6	8.9	3.9	1.5	0.2	11.3	13.5
Des Moines, IA	64.5	11.7	6.8	0.7	0.1	6.6	9.6
Durham, NC	40.2	36.2	5.6	0.7	0.0	9.8	7.4
Edison, NJ	28.1	7.6	53.7	0.4	0.0	4.7	5.5
El Paso, TX	36.8	3.7	1.5	1.1	0.2	20.6	36.0
Fargo, ND	78.9	8.8	4.1	1.6	0.1	1.2	5.3
Fort Collins, CO	80.8	1.5	3.6	0.8	0.1	3.6	9.6
Fort Wayne, IN	65.0	15.3	5.8	0.5	0.0	5.6	7.8
Fort Worth, TX	44.9	19.6	5.2	0.9	0.1	14.2	15.1
Grand Rapids, MI	60.3	18.9	2.3	0.9	0.0	9.0	8.7
Greeley, CO	62.0	2.7	2.0	1.8	0.1	14.8	16.6
Green Bay, WI	66.6	5.5	4.4	4.4	0.1	8.4	10.6
Greensboro, NC	40.0	42.0	5.1	0.6	0.0	5.6	6.6
Honolulu, HI	16.4	1.7	52.9	0.2	9.2	1.3	18.2
Houston, TX	32.1	22.6	7.3	1.2	0.1	20.7	16.1
Huntsville, AL	56.6	29.3	2.5	0.7	0.1	3.4	7.3
Indianapolis, IN	52.0	27.9	4.3	0.5	0.0	7.7	7.5
Jacksonville, FL	50.1	30.6	5.1	0.4	0.1	4.6	9.1
Kansas City, MO	55.3	26.1	3.1	0.6	0.3	5.5	9.0
Lafayette, LA	58.1	30.7	2.6	0.4	0.0	2.3	5.8
Las Cruces, NM	51.9	2.7	1.9	2.3	0.1	16.6	24.5
Las Vegas, NV	46.0	12.9	7.2	1.1	0.7	17.0	15.0
Lexington, KY	68.3	14.9	4.2	0.3	0.0	5.2	7.1
Lincoln, NE	78.7	4.7	4.8	0.9	0.1	3.5	7.5
Little Rock, AR	43.5	40.6	3.5	0.6	0.0	6.0	5.7
Los Angeles, CA	34.9	8.6	11.9	1.7	0.2	29.5	13.3
Louisville, KY	66.3	17.5	3.5	0.3	0.1	4.2	8.0

Table continued on following page.

Appendix A: Comparative Statistics A-13

City	White Alone[1] (%)	Black Alone[1] (%)	Asian Alone[1] (%)	AIAN[2] Alone[1] (%)	NHOPI[3] Alone[1] (%)	Other Race Alone[1] (%)	Two or More Races (%)
Madison, WI	71.0	7.4	9.5	0.5	0.1	3.8	7.8
Manchester, NH	76.7	5.5	4.2	0.3	0.0	5.2	7.9
Miami, FL	30.2	12.9	1.4	0.4	0.0	14.3	40.7
Midland, TX	57.6	7.9	2.6	0.9	0.1	12.5	18.4
Milwaukee, WI	36.1	38.6	5.2	0.9	0.0	9.0	10.1
Minneapolis, MN	59.5	19.1	5.8	1.7	0.0	5.9	8.0
Nashville, TN	55.2	24.6	4.0	0.6	0.0	8.1	7.6
New Haven, CT	32.7	32.2	6.8	1.0	0.1	15.3	12.0
New Orleans, LA	32.9	54.2	2.8	0.3	0.0	3.2	6.4
New York, NY	34.1	22.1	15.7	1.0	0.1	17.0	10.1
Oklahoma City, OK	53.6	14.0	4.6	3.4	0.2	11.1	13.1
Omaha, NE	65.5	12.4	4.6	1.1	0.1	7.2	9.1
Orlando, FL	40.0	23.8	4.3	0.4	0.1	12.3	19.0
Philadelphia, PA	36.3	39.3	8.3	0.4	0.1	8.7	6.9
Phoenix, AZ	49.7	7.8	4.1	2.6	0.2	20.1	15.5
Pittsburgh, PA	62.7	22.8	6.5	0.2	0.0	1.8	5.9
Portland, OR	68.8	5.9	8.1	1.1	0.6	4.8	10.7
Providence, RI	37.7	13.5	6.1	1.5	0.1	26.9	14.2
Provo, UT	74.6	0.9	2.5	1.0	1.5	8.2	11.3
Raleigh, NC	53.3	26.3	5.0	0.6	0.1	7.5	7.4
Reno, NV	62.7	3.1	7.1	1.4	0.8	12.0	13.0
Richmond, VA	43.3	40.4	2.8	0.4	0.1	6.8	6.2
Rochester, MN	73.2	8.9	7.9	0.4	0.1	2.9	6.6
Sacramento, CA	34.8	13.2	19.9	1.4	1.6	15.3	13.8
St. Louis, MO	43.9	43.0	4.1	0.3	0.0	2.6	6.1
Salem, OR	69.1	1.7	3.2	1.7	1.4	10.9	12.1
Salt Lake City, UT	68.4	2.9	5.5	1.4	2.1	9.7	9.9
San Antonio, TX	44.3	7.2	3.3	1.2	0.1	16.7	27.1
San Diego, CA	46.4	5.9	17.9	0.9	0.4	14.1	14.4
San Francisco, CA	41.3	5.3	33.9	0.7	0.4	8.4	9.9
San Jose, CA	27.3	2.9	38.5	1.4	0.4	18.2	11.2
Santa Rosa, CA	55.7	2.3	6.1	2.3	0.6	19.1	13.9
Savannah, GA	37.9	49.1	3.8	0.3	0.2	3.1	5.5
Seattle, WA	61.3	7.0	17.1	0.7	0.3	3.2	10.5
Sioux Falls, SD	79.0	6.3	2.8	2.7	0.0	2.9	6.1
Springfield, IL	68.9	20.4	2.9	0.3	0.0	1.1	6.4
Tampa, FL	49.7	21.9	5.4	0.4	0.1	7.6	14.8
Tucson, AZ	54.5	5.6	3.2	2.9	0.3	15.2	18.3
Tulsa, OK	51.8	14.9	3.5	5.2	0.2	9.8	14.6
Tuscaloosa, AL	48.7	41.2	2.4	0.3	0.1	2.1	5.3
Virginia Beach, VA	60.7	18.6	7.5	0.4	0.2	3.0	9.6
Washington, DC	39.6	41.4	4.9	0.5	0.1	5.4	8.1
Wichita, KS	63.4	11.0	5.1	1.3	0.1	7.4	11.7
Wilmington, NC	70.9	16.5	1.6	0.4	0.1	3.9	6.6
Winston-Salem, NC	45.8	32.5	2.5	0.7	0.1	10.7	7.6
Worcester, MA	53.3	14.8	7.1	0.5	0.0	12.9	11.3
U.S.	61.6	12.4	6.0	1.1	0.2	8.4	10.2

Note: (1) Alone is defined as not being in combination with one or more other races; (2) American Indian and Alaska Native; (3) Native Hawaiian and Other Pacific Islander
Source: U.S. Census Bureau, 2020 Census

Appendix A: Comparative Statistics

Race: Metro Area

Metro Area	White Alone[1] (%)	Black Alone[1] (%)	Asian Alone[1] (%)	AIAN[2] Alone[1] (%)	NHOPI[3] Alone[1] (%)	Other Race Alone[1] (%)	Two or More Races (%)
Albuquerque, NM	52.8	2.8	2.5	6.6	0.1	14.5	20.6
Allentown, PA	72.9	6.3	3.2	0.3	0.0	8.5	8.8
Anchorage, AK	62.1	3.9	7.3	7.7	2.6	3.0	13.3
Ann Arbor, MI	69.2	11.5	9.0	0.3	0.1	2.0	7.9
Athens, GA	67.0	17.9	3.6	0.4	0.0	4.7	6.3
Atlanta, GA	45.5	33.6	6.6	0.5	0.0	6.0	7.7
Austin, TX	57.3	7.0	7.1	0.9	0.1	11.1	16.5
Baltimore, MD	53.9	28.5	6.3	0.4	0.0	4.0	6.8
Boise City, ID	80.0	1.3	2.1	0.9	0.3	5.9	9.6
Boston, MA	68.4	7.4	8.7	0.3	0.0	6.9	8.4
Boulder, CO	77.4	1.0	5.0	0.8	0.1	5.8	10.0
Brownsville, TX	38.6	0.5	0.7	0.7	0.0	19.0	40.4
Cape Coral, FL	69.7	7.7	1.7	0.5	0.0	7.5	12.8
Cedar Rapids, IA	84.7	6.1	2.0	0.2	0.2	1.2	5.6
Charleston, SC	64.0	23.0	2.0	0.5	0.1	3.9	6.5
Charlotte, NC	59.5	21.9	4.3	0.6	0.1	6.4	7.2
Chicago, IL	54.0	16.4	7.1	0.9	0.0	11.3	10.2
Cincinnati, OH	76.7	12.1	3.0	0.3	0.1	2.1	5.7
Clarksville, TN	65.8	19.1	2.0	0.5	0.4	3.2	9.0
Cleveland, OH	68.9	19.6	2.6	0.2	0.0	2.6	6.0
College Station, TX	60.7	11.0	5.6	0.7	0.1	9.8	12.1
Colorado Springs, CO	71.3	5.8	3.0	1.0	0.4	5.8	12.7
Columbia, MO	77.7	9.3	3.8	0.3	0.1	1.8	7.1
Columbia, SC	55.7	32.4	2.3	0.4	0.1	3.1	6.0
Columbus, OH	70.1	15.7	4.9	0.3	0.0	2.7	6.3
Dallas, TX	48.9	16.0	7.9	1.0	0.1	12.2	13.9
Davenport, IA	78.2	8.3	2.4	0.4	0.0	3.2	7.5
Denver, CO	66.7	5.6	4.6	1.2	0.2	8.8	12.8
Des Moines, IA	79.8	5.6	4.3	0.4	0.1	3.2	6.7
Durham, NC	54.3	25.0	4.9	0.7	0.0	7.9	7.2
Edison, NJ	46.5	16.1	12.5	0.8	0.1	14.1	10.0
El Paso, TX	36.3	3.3	1.4	1.2	0.2	21.7	35.8
Fargo, ND	82.8	6.5	2.7	1.5	0.0	1.1	5.3
Fort Collins, CO	82.4	1.1	2.4	0.8	0.1	3.8	9.4
Fort Wayne, IN	73.7	10.6	4.4	0.4	0.0	4.0	6.8
Fort Worth, TX	48.9	16.0	7.9	1.0	0.1	12.2	13.9
Grand Rapids, MI	78.0	6.9	2.8	0.6	0.0	4.7	7.0
Greeley, CO	70.5	1.4	1.8	1.3	0.1	11.2	13.8
Green Bay, WI	81.8	2.6	2.7	2.5	0.0	3.8	6.6
Greensboro, NC	56.7	26.7	4.1	0.6	0.0	5.5	6.4
Honolulu, HI	18.5	2.0	43.0	0.2	10.0	1.7	24.5
Houston, TX	41.4	17.4	8.4	1.0	0.1	16.0	15.7
Huntsville, AL	65.0	21.4	2.5	0.7	0.1	2.9	7.3
Indianapolis, IN	69.6	15.0	3.9	0.4	0.0	4.5	6.6
Jacksonville, FL	61.6	21.2	4.2	0.4	0.1	3.6	8.8
Kansas City, MO	70.9	12.0	3.1	0.6	0.2	4.2	9.0
Lafayette, LA	65.8	24.5	1.9	0.4	0.0	2.3	5.1
Las Cruces, NM	47.5	1.9	1.2	1.9	0.1	20.1	27.4
Las Vegas, NV	44.9	12.7	10.5	1.0	0.9	15.4	14.7
Lexington, KY	74.9	11.1	2.9	0.3	0.0	4.2	6.6
Lincoln, NE	80.8	4.1	4.2	0.8	0.1	3.1	6.9
Little Rock, AR	64.0	23.2	1.8	0.6	0.1	3.7	6.6
Los Angeles, CA	35.2	6.4	16.7	1.5	0.3	25.2	14.7
Louisville, KY	72.7	14.8	2.5	0.3	0.1	2.9	6.8

Table continued on following page.

Metro Area	White Alone[1] (%)	Black Alone[1] (%)	Asian Alone[1] (%)	AIAN[2] Alone[1] (%)	NHOPI[3] Alone[1] (%)	Other Race Alone[1] (%)	Two or More Races (%)
Madison, WI	80.2	4.7	5.4	0.4	0.0	2.9	6.4
Manchester, NH	82.8	2.6	3.9	0.2	0.0	3.5	6.9
Miami, FL	39.6	19.5	2.7	0.4	0.0	9.7	28.1
Midland, TX	58.2	6.4	2.3	0.9	0.1	13.2	18.9
Milwaukee, WI	66.7	16.3	4.2	0.6	0.0	4.6	7.6
Minneapolis, MN	73.0	9.1	7.2	0.8	0.0	3.3	6.6
Nashville, TN	70.0	14.3	3.1	0.5	0.1	5.1	7.0
New Haven, CT	62.9	13.8	4.3	0.5	0.1	9.0	9.5
New Orleans, LA	50.3	33.3	2.9	0.5	0.0	4.8	8.1
New York, NY	46.5	16.1	12.5	0.8	0.1	14.1	10.0
Oklahoma City, OK	62.5	10.3	3.3	4.0	0.1	7.2	12.6
Omaha, NE	74.9	7.7	3.5	0.8	0.1	5.0	8.0
Orlando, FL	50.4	15.4	4.7	0.4	0.1	11.4	17.7
Philadelphia, PA	60.7	20.4	6.6	0.3	0.0	5.1	6.8
Phoenix, AZ	60.2	5.8	4.3	2.5	0.3	13.4	13.5
Pittsburgh, PA	82.7	8.4	2.9	0.1	0.0	0.9	4.9
Portland, OR	71.5	3.0	7.1	1.1	0.6	6.0	10.7
Providence, RI	73.9	5.2	3.1	0.6	0.0	8.0	9.1
Provo, UT	81.8	0.7	1.6	0.7	1.0	5.4	8.9
Raleigh, NC	60.1	18.3	7.0	0.6	0.0	6.4	7.6
Reno, NV	64.2	2.5	5.9	1.8	0.7	11.8	13.0
Richmond, VA	56.5	27.7	4.3	0.5	0.1	4.4	6.4
Rochester, MN	82.3	5.1	4.7	0.3	0.0	2.2	5.4
Sacramento, CA	52.5	7.0	14.9	1.1	0.9	10.4	13.2
St. Louis, MO	71.2	18.0	2.9	0.3	0.0	1.6	6.0
Salem, OR	69.6	1.1	2.1	2.0	1.0	12.2	12.0
Salt Lake City, UT	72.3	1.9	4.1	1.1	1.8	9.1	9.8
San Antonio, TX	50.3	7.1	2.9	1.1	0.2	14.0	24.4
San Diego, CA	49.5	4.7	12.5	1.2	0.5	15.8	15.8
San Francisco, CA	39.3	7.1	27.5	1.0	0.7	12.7	11.7
San Jose, CA	32.5	2.3	38.1	1.2	0.4	14.6	11.0
Santa Rosa, CA	62.7	1.6	4.7	1.8	0.4	15.3	13.5
Savannah, GA	55.6	30.8	3.1	0.4	0.1	3.4	6.6
Seattle, WA	60.1	6.1	15.4	1.1	1.1	5.3	11.0
Sioux Falls, SD	83.4	4.6	2.0	2.2	0.0	2.3	5.5
Springfield, IL	78.4	12.5	2.1	0.2	0.0	0.9	5.8
Tampa, FL	64.4	11.8	3.9	0.4	0.1	6.2	13.1
Tucson, AZ	60.7	3.8	3.0	3.3	0.2	12.2	16.7
Tulsa, OK	61.3	7.9	2.8	8.1	0.1	5.4	14.2
Tuscaloosa, AL	57.5	33.9	1.3	0.4	0.0	2.5	4.3
Virginia Beach, VA	54.0	30.3	4.1	0.4	0.2	2.9	8.1
Washington, DC	44.5	24.5	11.0	0.6	0.1	9.3	10.1
Wichita, KS	71.7	7.5	3.7	1.2	0.1	5.4	10.4
Wilmington, NC	75.6	12.2	1.3	0.5	0.1	3.8	6.4
Winston-Salem, NC	67.0	17.2	1.8	0.6	0.1	6.7	6.5
Worcester, MA	74.5	5.2	4.9	0.4	0.0	6.3	8.6
U.S.	61.6	12.4	6.0	1.1	0.2	8.4	10.2

Note: Figures cover the Metropolitan Statistical Area (MSA); (1) Alone is defined as not being in combination with one or more other races; (2) American Indian and Alaska Native; (3) Native Hawaiian & Other Pacific Islander
Source: U.S. Census Bureau, 2020 Census

Hispanic Origin: City

City	Hispanic or Latino (%)	Mexican (%)	Puerto Rican (%)	Cuban (%)	Other Hispanic or Latino (%)
Albuquerque, NM	49.8	29.7	0.7	0.4	19.0
Allentown, PA	54.5	2.6	27.6	0.8	23.5
Anchorage, AK	9.5	4.6	1.5	0.4	3.0
Ann Arbor, MI	4.6	2.4	0.3	0.3	1.7
Athens, GA	11.0	5.9	0.4	0.6	4.0
Atlanta, GA	5.0	1.9	0.8	0.3	2.0
Austin, TX	33.1	25.6	1.0	0.7	5.8
Baltimore, MD	5.6	1.1	0.8	0.3	3.3
Boise City, ID	8.8	6.4	0.5	0.1	1.9
Boston, MA	19.8	1.1	5.2	0.4	13.1
Boulder, CO	10.6	6.3	0.4	0.4	3.6
Brownsville, TX	94.7	90.5	0.2	0.1	3.8
Cape Coral, FL	23.2	1.7	4.9	9.7	7.0
Cedar Rapids, IA	4.4	3.2	0.2	0.1	1.0
Charleston, SC	4.2	1.9	0.6	0.1	1.6
Charlotte, NC	14.9	5.3	1.1	0.6	7.9
Chicago, IL	28.7	21.2	3.5	0.3	3.8
Cincinnati, OH	4.4	1.4	0.6	0.2	2.2
Clarksville, TN	11.7	5.6	3.0	0.4	2.8
Cleveland, OH	12.2	1.6	8.6	0.2	1.8
College Station, TX	17.7	12.8	0.7	0.2	4.1
Colorado Springs, CO	18.4	12.1	1.2	0.3	4.9
Columbia, MO	3.7	2.1	0.3	0.0	1.2
Columbia, SC	5.6	2.4	1.1	0.3	1.8
Columbus, OH	6.5	3.1	1.0	0.1	2.3
Dallas, TX	42.0	34.7	0.6	0.3	6.4
Davenport, IA	8.9	8.2	0.3	0.1	0.3
Denver, CO	29.4	22.6	0.7	0.3	5.9
Des Moines, IA	14.6	11.6	0.3	0.2	2.4
Durham, NC	13.2	6.4	0.9	0.3	5.7
Edison, NJ	10.8	1.4	2.8	0.7	6.0
El Paso, TX	81.6	76.9	1.0	0.2	3.5
Fargo, ND	3.2	2.0	0.3	0.0	0.9
Fort Collins, CO	12.6	9.0	0.5	0.1	3.0
Fort Wayne, IN	9.5	7.2	0.6	0.1	1.6
Fort Worth, TX	35.3	29.8	1.2	0.4	3.9
Grand Rapids, MI	15.7	9.6	1.6	0.3	4.1
Greeley, CO	40.3	33.0	0.9	0.1	6.3
Green Bay, WI	16.6	13.0	1.9	0.0	1.8
Greensboro, NC	8.4	4.5	1.1	0.2	2.6
Honolulu, HI	7.2	2.2	2.0	0.1	2.8
Houston, TX	44.5	30.3	0.7	0.8	12.8
Huntsville, AL	6.4	3.6	1.1	0.2	1.6
Indianapolis, IN	10.8	7.3	0.7	0.2	2.6
Jacksonville, FL	10.9	2.0	3.4	1.6	3.9
Kansas City, MO	10.7	7.7	0.4	0.4	2.2
Lafayette, LA	4.6	1.4	0.1	0.2	2.9
Las Cruces, NM	61.8	51.1	0.6	0.2	9.9
Las Vegas, NV	34.1	24.9	1.2	1.4	6.5
Lexington, KY	7.4	4.7	0.6	0.2	1.9
Lincoln, NE	8.1	5.5	0.4	0.2	2.0
Little Rock, AR	7.8	4.7	0.2	0.3	2.5
Los Angeles, CA	48.4	31.5	0.5	0.4	16.1
Louisville, KY	6.5	2.3	0.4	2.3	1.4
Madison, WI	7.8	4.5	0.7	0.2	2.4

Table continued on following page.

City	Hispanic or Latino (%)	Mexican (%)	Puerto Rican (%)	Cuban (%)	Other Hispanic or Latino (%)
Manchester, NH	11.0	1.6	3.9	0.1	5.4
Miami, FL	72.3	1.9	3.5	33.4	33.5
Midland, TX	46.5	42.5	0.5	1.0	2.5
Milwaukee, WI	19.9	13.4	4.9	0.2	1.4
Minneapolis, MN	9.8	5.3	0.5	0.2	3.8
Nashville, TN	10.6	5.9	0.6	0.4	3.8
New Haven, CT	30.3	5.3	16.5	0.4	8.1
New Orleans, LA	5.6	1.2	0.2	0.6	3.5
New York, NY	28.9	3.8	7.7	0.5	16.9
Oklahoma City, OK	19.9	16.1	0.4	0.1	3.3
Omaha, NE	14.5	10.9	0.5	0.2	2.9
Orlando, FL	34.2	1.8	15.8	3.0	13.6
Philadelphia, PA	15.4	1.3	8.7	0.3	5.1
Phoenix, AZ	42.7	37.9	0.7	0.4	3.8
Pittsburgh, PA	3.5	1.2	0.7	0.1	1.6
Portland, OR	10.3	7.0	0.5	0.4	2.3
Providence, RI	42.9	1.3	7.9	0.3	33.4
Provo, UT	17.8	11.3	0.7	0.2	5.6
Raleigh, NC	11.3	5.0	1.4	0.4	4.5
Reno, NV	23.3	17.8	0.7	0.3	4.6
Richmond, VA	7.3	1.3	0.8	0.3	4.9
Rochester, MN	5.8	3.7	0.6	0.1	1.4
Sacramento, CA	28.9	24.1	0.9	0.2	3.7
St. Louis, MO	4.2	2.5	0.2	0.2	1.3
Salem, OR	22.4	19.5	0.6	0.1	2.2
Salt Lake City, UT	19.9	14.2	0.4	0.3	5.0
San Antonio, TX	65.7	56.7	1.4	0.3	7.3
San Diego, CA	30.1	25.6	0.8	0.3	3.4
San Francisco, CA	15.4	7.8	0.7	0.3	6.7
San Jose, CA	31.0	26.0	0.5	0.2	4.3
Santa Rosa, CA	34.0	29.3	0.5	0.1	4.1
Savannah, GA	6.5	2.1	2.0	0.4	2.0
Seattle, WA	7.2	4.2	0.4	0.2	2.4
Sioux Falls, SD	5.5	2.6	0.3	0.1	2.6
Springfield, IL	2.9	1.5	0.6	0.1	0.7
Tampa, FL	26.2	3.1	6.9	8.0	8.3
Tucson, AZ	44.6	39.8	0.9	0.2	3.7
Tulsa, OK	17.1	13.4	0.6	0.1	3.0
Tuscaloosa, AL	4.4	2.5	0.6	0.3	0.9
Virginia Beach, VA	8.6	2.7	2.2	0.3	3.4
Washington, DC	11.3	1.9	0.9	0.5	8.0
Wichita, KS	17.6	15.1	0.5	0.1	1.9
Wilmington, NC	7.1	2.7	1.3	0.4	2.7
Winston-Salem, NC	16.2	9.7	1.5	0.2	4.8
Worcester, MA	23.9	0.8	14.7	0.3	8.1
U.S.	18.4	11.2	1.8	0.7	4.7

Note: Persons of Hispanic or Latino origin can be of any race
Source: U.S. Census Bureau, 2017-2021 American Community Survey 5-Year Estimates

Hispanic Origin: Metro Area

Metro Area	Hispanic or Latino (%)	Mexican (%)	Puerto Rican (%)	Cuban (%)	Other Hispanic or Latino (%)
Albuquerque, NM	49.7	29.0	0.7	0.4	19.7
Allentown, PA	18.4	1.3	9.3	0.4	7.3
Anchorage, AK	8.4	4.1	1.3	0.4	2.6
Ann Arbor, MI	5.0	2.8	0.5	0.2	1.5
Athens, GA	8.9	4.7	0.8	0.4	2.9
Atlanta, GA	11.0	5.5	1.1	0.4	3.9
Austin, TX	32.7	26.3	1.0	0.5	5.0
Baltimore, MD	6.2	1.4	1.0	0.2	3.6
Boise City, ID	14.1	11.5	0.5	0.1	2.0
Boston, MA	11.6	0.7	2.8	0.3	7.8
Boulder, CO	14.0	9.9	0.5	0.3	3.3
Brownsville, TX	90.0	86.0	0.3	0.1	3.6
Cape Coral, FL	22.6	5.4	4.6	5.7	6.8
Cedar Rapids, IA	3.2	2.4	0.1	0.0	0.7
Charleston, SC	5.9	2.7	0.8	0.1	2.3
Charlotte, NC	10.6	4.6	1.1	0.4	4.6
Chicago, IL	22.5	17.5	2.2	0.3	2.6
Cincinnati, OH	3.5	1.6	0.4	0.1	1.4
Clarksville, TN	9.3	4.7	2.4	0.2	2.0
Cleveland, OH	6.2	1.4	3.5	0.1	1.1
College Station, TX	25.7	21.8	0.4	0.3	3.1
Colorado Springs, CO	17.5	10.9	1.4	0.4	4.9
Columbia, MO	3.4	2.1	0.2	0.1	1.0
Columbia, SC	5.8	2.8	1.1	0.2	1.7
Columbus, OH	4.5	2.1	0.8	0.1	1.6
Dallas, TX	29.3	23.6	0.8	0.3	4.5
Davenport, IA	9.1	8.0	0.3	0.1	0.7
Denver, CO	23.4	17.5	0.6	0.2	5.0
Des Moines, IA	7.4	5.5	0.3	0.1	1.5
Durham, NC	11.3	5.9	0.8	0.3	4.3
Edison, NJ	24.8	2.9	5.9	0.8	15.3
El Paso, TX	82.9	78.1	0.9	0.2	3.6
Fargo, ND	3.4	2.4	0.3	0.0	0.7
Fort Collins, CO	12.0	8.8	0.4	0.2	2.6
Fort Wayne, IN	7.4	5.6	0.4	0.1	1.3
Fort Worth, TX	29.3	23.6	0.8	0.3	4.5
Grand Rapids, MI	9.9	6.8	0.9	0.3	1.9
Greeley, CO	30.0	24.5	0.5	0.2	4.8
Green Bay, WI	8.1	6.1	0.9	0.1	1.0
Greensboro, NC	8.8	5.7	1.0	0.2	1.9
Honolulu, HI	10.2	3.2	3.5	0.1	3.5
Houston, TX	37.9	27.3	0.7	0.7	9.2
Huntsville, AL	5.4	3.2	0.8	0.1	1.3
Indianapolis, IN	7.1	4.6	0.6	0.1	1.8
Jacksonville, FL	9.6	1.9	3.0	1.3	3.5
Kansas City, MO	9.4	7.0	0.4	0.2	1.8
Lafayette, LA	4.1	1.8	0.2	0.1	2.0
Las Cruces, NM	68.9	60.8	0.4	0.1	7.6
Las Vegas, NV	31.8	23.3	1.1	1.5	5.9
Lexington, KY	6.3	4.2	0.5	0.1	1.5
Lincoln, NE	7.2	4.9	0.3	0.2	1.7
Little Rock, AR	5.5	3.7	0.2	0.1	1.5
Los Angeles, CA	45.2	34.5	0.5	0.4	9.8
Louisville, KY	5.3	2.4	0.4	1.3	1.1
Madison, WI	6.1	3.7	0.5	0.1	1.7

Table continued on following page.

Metro Area	Hispanic or Latino (%)	Mexican (%)	Puerto Rican (%)	Cuban (%)	Other Hispanic or Latino (%)
Manchester, NH	7.4	1.1	2.5	0.2	3.5
Miami, FL	45.6	2.5	3.8	18.6	20.6
Midland, TX	46.3	42.7	0.4	0.9	2.3
Milwaukee, WI	11.3	7.5	2.6	0.2	1.1
Minneapolis, MN	6.1	3.8	0.4	0.1	1.8
Nashville, TN	7.7	4.3	0.6	0.3	2.5
New Haven, CT	19.2	2.2	10.6	0.4	6.0
New Orleans, LA	9.1	1.7	0.5	0.6	6.3
New York, NY	24.8	2.9	5.9	0.8	15.3
Oklahoma City, OK	13.9	10.9	0.4	0.1	2.5
Omaha, NE	11.0	8.2	0.5	0.1	2.1
Orlando, FL	31.8	2.8	15.0	2.5	11.5
Philadelphia, PA	9.9	1.9	4.6	0.3	3.2
Phoenix, AZ	31.5	27.1	0.7	0.3	3.4
Pittsburgh, PA	1.9	0.6	0.5	0.1	0.7
Portland, OR	12.5	9.4	0.4	0.3	2.4
Providence, RI	13.7	0.9	4.4	0.2	8.3
Provo, UT	12.1	7.5	0.3	0.1	4.1
Raleigh, NC	10.8	5.6	1.4	0.4	3.5
Reno, NV	25.1	19.3	0.7	0.4	4.6
Richmond, VA	6.7	1.6	1.0	0.2	3.8
Rochester, MN	4.7	2.9	0.4	0.1	1.3
Sacramento, CA	22.2	17.8	0.7	0.2	3.5
St. Louis, MO	3.2	2.0	0.3	0.1	0.9
Salem, OR	24.9	22.1	0.4	0.1	2.3
Salt Lake City, UT	18.5	13.1	0.5	0.2	4.7
San Antonio, TX	56.0	48.2	1.4	0.3	6.0
San Diego, CA	34.3	29.9	0.8	0.2	3.4
San Francisco, CA	22.0	14.1	0.7	0.2	7.0
San Jose, CA	26.2	21.5	0.5	0.2	4.1
Santa Rosa, CA	27.5	22.7	0.4	0.2	4.2
Savannah, GA	6.5	2.9	1.6	0.5	1.6
Seattle, WA	10.5	7.3	0.6	0.2	2.5
Sioux Falls, SD	4.6	2.3	0.2	0.1	2.1
Springfield, IL	2.4	1.4	0.4	0.1	0.5
Tampa, FL	20.5	3.7	6.3	4.3	6.3
Tucson, AZ	38.0	33.7	0.9	0.2	3.2
Tulsa, OK	10.5	8.1	0.4	0.1	1.9
Tuscaloosa, AL	3.8	2.4	0.3	0.2	0.9
Virginia Beach, VA	7.2	2.4	1.9	0.3	2.5
Washington, DC	16.2	2.3	1.2	0.3	12.4
Wichita, KS	13.6	11.5	0.4	0.1	1.6
Wilmington, NC	6.2	2.5	1.0	0.3	2.4
Winston-Salem, NC	10.8	6.7	1.1	0.2	2.8
Worcester, MA	12.3	0.9	7.2	0.2	4.0
U.S.	18.4	11.2	1.8	0.7	4.7

Note: Persons of Hispanic or Latino origin can be of any race; Figures cover the Metropolitan Statistical Area (MSA)
Source: U.S. Census Bureau, 2017-2021 American Community Survey 5-Year Estimates

Household Size: City

City	One	Two	Three	Four	Five	Six	Seven or More	Average Household Size
Albuquerque, NM	36.4	32.9	13.6	10.1	4.7	1.2	0.7	2.36
Allentown, PA	29.4	29.5	14.0	14.3	7.3	3.0	2.1	2.65
Anchorage, AK	26.8	32.9	15.5	13.5	6.2	2.6	2.1	2.68
Ann Arbor, MI	33.6	37.5	13.0	10.6	2.8	1.6	0.5	2.21
Athens, GA	34.2	34.4	14.9	11.1	3.4	1.1	0.6	2.22
Atlanta, GA	45.8	31.9	10.9	6.7	2.5	1.1	0.7	2.06
Austin, TX	34.7	33.7	14.3	10.4	4.2	1.5	0.8	2.28
Baltimore, MD	41.4	29.8	13.8	8.1	3.7	1.6	1.1	2.32
Boise City, ID	31.6	36.5	14.9	9.9	4.9	1.3	0.5	2.37
Boston, MA	36.2	32.7	15.1	9.4	3.9	1.6	0.9	2.30
Boulder, CO	35.7	35.9	13.9	10.5	2.7	0.4	0.5	2.21
Brownsville, TX	19.2	23.6	17.0	19.2	12.4	4.6	3.5	3.31
Cape Coral, FL	26.0	42.6	13.7	10.6	5.0	1.1	0.7	2.59
Cedar Rapids, IA	33.7	34.3	14.6	10.3	4.4	1.4	0.9	2.31
Charleston, SC	35.0	38.5	13.2	9.6	2.7	0.6	0.1	2.23
Charlotte, NC	34.1	31.7	15.0	11.9	4.6	1.5	0.9	2.47
Chicago, IL	38.2	29.5	13.5	10.0	4.9	2.1	1.4	2.41
Cincinnati, OH	44.5	30.2	11.4	8.4	3.0	1.3	0.8	2.11
Clarksville, TN	24.5	32.7	17.0	15.9	6.0	2.3	1.4	2.69
Cleveland, OH	46.0	27.9	12.0	7.3	3.7	1.7	1.0	2.15
College Station, TX	32.4	31.1	14.8	14.9	3.5	2.4	0.5	2.51
Colorado Springs, CO	27.5	36.0	15.0	12.4	5.5	2.2	1.1	2.48
Columbia, MO	35.6	31.7	13.7	11.1	5.7	1.2	0.7	2.33
Columbia, SC	39.1	32.6	13.4	8.9	4.0	1.4	0.2	2.19
Columbus, OH	35.8	32.6	13.3	10.1	4.8	1.7	1.3	2.32
Dallas, TX	36.3	29.5	13.1	10.3	6.4	2.4	1.6	2.49
Davenport, IA	34.3	35.7	13.1	9.1	5.0	1.7	0.8	2.36
Denver, CO	38.5	33.5	11.7	9.4	3.8	1.5	1.2	2.21
Des Moines, IA	34.8	30.5	14.3	10.8	5.1	2.5	1.6	2.40
Durham, NC	35.5	33.9	14.1	9.6	4.3	1.6	0.7	2.27
Edison, NJ	17.7	28.6	20.6	22.7	6.3	2.2	1.7	2.90
El Paso, TX	25.4	28.5	17.5	15.6	8.2	3.0	1.4	2.83
Fargo, ND	38.0	33.9	13.2	9.0	4.1	1.1	0.4	2.15
Fort Collins, CO	25.2	37.4	17.6	14.0	4.0	1.1	0.4	2.36
Fort Wayne, IN	32.8	32.7	14.1	10.8	5.6	2.6	1.1	2.42
Fort Worth, TX	26.6	29.4	16.5	14.6	7.5	3.1	2.0	2.81
Grand Rapids, MI	33.2	30.9	15.1	10.2	6.0	2.2	2.1	2.47
Greeley, CO	25.4	32.8	16.1	13.5	7.3	3.0	1.6	2.73
Green Bay, WI	34.9	32.2	13.5	10.6	5.5	1.5	1.3	2.36
Greensboro, NC	35.1	31.9	15.5	10.3	4.5	1.4	0.9	2.36
Honolulu, HI	34.9	30.4	14.1	10.5	4.9	2.1	2.8	2.54
Houston, TX	32.7	29.1	15.6	11.9	6.2	2.5	1.5	2.57
Huntsville, AL	36.6	34.9	14.4	8.5	3.9	0.8	0.5	2.21
Indianapolis, IN	36.8	32.2	12.9	9.7	5.1	1.8	1.1	2.46
Jacksonville, FL	32.2	32.8	16.3	10.7	5.1	1.6	0.9	2.50
Kansas City, MO	36.7	32.0	12.7	10.8	4.4	1.9	1.1	2.31
Lafayette, LA	33.6	36.0	14.1	8.6	4.7	1.5	1.1	2.30
Las Cruces, NM	31.9	31.4	15.8	12.6	5.5	1.6	0.7	2.46
Las Vegas, NV	30.2	31.3	15.5	12.1	6.1	2.7	1.7	2.65
Lexington, KY	33.0	34.2	14.3	11.4	4.2	1.7	0.8	2.30
Lincoln, NE	31.6	33.7	13.7	11.8	5.4	2.4	0.9	2.37
Little Rock, AR	37.6	31.8	13.8	9.9	4.4	1.4	0.7	2.33
Los Angeles, CA	30.5	28.5	15.4	13.1	6.7	2.9	2.5	2.75
Louisville, KY	33.8	32.9	15.1	10.7	4.9	1.4	0.9	2.39

Table continued on following page.

City	\multicolumn{7}{c	}{Persons in Household (%)}	Average Household Size
	One	Two	Three	Four	Five	Six	Seven or More	
Madison, WI	37.7	35.2	12.4	9.4	3.4	1.0	0.5	2.16
Manchester, NH	33.9	33.2	15.8	10.3	3.5	1.9	1.0	2.32
Miami, FL	35.9	32.2	16.2	9.2	3.8	1.3	1.0	2.38
Midland, TX	26.8	28.2	17.2	15.2	8.2	2.8	1.3	2.57
Milwaukee, WI	37.7	28.8	13.7	10.0	5.7	2.3	1.5	2.45
Minneapolis, MN	40.4	31.6	11.5	9.5	3.4	1.7	1.5	2.24
Nashville, TN	35.2	33.3	14.5	9.6	4.6	1.4	1.1	2.34
New Haven, CT	36.7	29.1	16.1	9.0	5.3	2.0	1.4	2.48
New Orleans, LA	46.4	28.7	12.5	7.9	2.7	1.1	0.4	2.37
New York, NY	32.4	28.6	16.3	12.1	5.7	2.5	2.0	2.63
Oklahoma City, OK	31.3	31.8	15.1	11.6	6.4	2.5	1.0	2.49
Omaha, NE	33.6	31.6	13.6	10.7	6.1	2.5	1.6	2.44
Orlando, FL	32.8	33.5	16.0	10.8	4.3	1.3	1.0	2.53
Philadelphia, PA	37.1	29.4	14.9	10.2	4.8	1.8	1.3	2.40
Phoenix, AZ	27.9	30.0	15.2	13.0	7.4	3.6	2.7	2.71
Pittsburgh, PA	44.2	32.4	12.4	6.7	2.5	1.0	0.5	2.04
Portland, OR	34.9	35.2	13.7	10.3	3.5	1.2	0.8	2.26
Providence, RI	33.6	29.0	15.5	11.1	7.0	1.9	1.6	2.56
Provo, UT	15.1	34.8	17.3	14.9	7.2	6.9	3.4	3.10
Raleigh, NC	34.6	32.8	14.4	12.0	4.2	1.2	0.5	2.37
Reno, NV	31.9	34.0	14.6	11.2	5.3	1.4	1.2	2.37
Richmond, VA	42.4	33.0	12.0	7.6	2.8	1.3	0.5	2.19
Rochester, MN	31.0	34.7	13.0	12.2	5.5	1.9	1.4	2.40
Sacramento, CA	30.5	30.3	14.6	13.0	6.1	2.8	2.4	2.63
St. Louis, MO	46.2	30.2	10.8	7.3	3.2	0.9	1.0	2.08
Salem, OR	29.6	33.2	14.8	11.0	6.4	2.7	2.0	2.58
Salt Lake City, UT	38.2	32.7	11.9	9.3	4.1	1.9	1.7	2.32
San Antonio, TX	30.6	29.5	15.4	12.7	6.9	2.9	1.7	2.64
San Diego, CA	27.8	34.0	15.7	12.9	5.6	2.1	1.5	2.64
San Francisco, CA	36.5	32.9	13.9	10.1	3.6	1.4	1.3	2.34
San Jose, CA	19.7	28.9	18.8	17.9	8.0	3.2	3.2	3.08
Santa Rosa, CA	28.4	32.4	15.0	13.8	6.6	2.0	1.3	2.60
Savannah, GA	32.8	35.4	15.2	9.6	4.5	1.3	0.9	2.46
Seattle, WA	39.9	35.0	12.1	8.9	2.5	0.8	0.5	2.08
Sioux Falls, SD	32.2	33.4	14.0	11.2	6.1	1.8	1.0	2.37
Springfield, IL	39.3	32.5	12.3	9.5	3.8	1.2	1.0	2.18
Tampa, FL	35.9	31.1	15.6	10.7	4.2	1.5	0.6	2.41
Tucson, AZ	34.9	31.0	14.2	11.2	5.2	2.0	1.2	2.35
Tulsa, OK	35.5	32.2	13.2	10.4	5.0	2.2	1.1	2.41
Tuscaloosa, AL	37.2	32.9	14.0	9.9	3.8	1.3	0.6	2.45
Virginia Beach, VA	24.5	35.5	17.6	13.7	6.0	1.7	0.6	2.53
Washington, DC	45.4	30.6	11.6	7.3	3.1	1.0	0.6	2.08
Wichita, KS	32.8	32.4	13.0	11.2	6.2	2.5	1.7	2.51
Wilmington, NC	39.9	36.9	11.5	7.4	3.0	0.6	0.3	2.10
Winston-Salem, NC	36.0	31.7	14.7	9.3	4.6	2.4	1.0	2.43
Worcester, MA	34.9	28.3	17.0	11.9	4.4	2.1	1.0	2.40
U.S.	28.0	33.8	15.5	12.8	5.9	2.2	1.4	2.60

U.S. Census Bureau, 2017-2021 American Community Survey 5-Year Estimates

Appendix A: Comparative Statistics

Household Size: Metro Area

Metro Area	One	Two	Three	Four	Five	Six	Seven or More	Average Household Size
Albuquerque, NM	32.3	34.7	14.2	10.7	5.1	1.7	1.0	2.49
Allentown, PA	26.5	35.6	15.2	13.6	5.8	1.9	1.1	2.52
Anchorage, AK	25.7	33.3	15.5	13.4	6.7	2.8	2.3	2.70
Ann Arbor, MI	29.9	36.6	14.7	11.7	4.2	1.8	0.8	2.39
Athens, GA	28.7	34.5	16.6	13.2	4.5	1.3	0.9	2.46
Atlanta, GA	26.7	31.7	17.0	14.2	6.2	2.4	1.4	2.69
Austin, TX	27.2	33.7	15.9	13.5	5.9	2.2	1.2	2.54
Baltimore, MD	29.1	32.7	16.1	12.9	5.6	2.0	1.1	2.55
Boise City, ID	24.7	36.0	15.3	12.5	6.5	3.1	1.6	2.67
Boston, MA	27.5	33.0	16.6	14.4	5.5	1.7	0.9	2.50
Boulder, CO	29.4	36.3	14.8	13.1	4.2	1.5	0.4	2.41
Brownsville, TX	20.4	26.8	16.4	17.5	10.4	4.9	3.3	3.21
Cape Coral, FL	28.6	44.2	11.5	8.8	4.6	1.3	0.7	2.49
Cedar Rapids, IA	29.5	36.6	14.1	11.9	5.1	1.6	0.9	2.41
Charleston, SC	28.7	36.1	16.2	11.8	4.9	1.4	0.7	2.50
Charlotte, NC	27.4	34.0	16.1	13.8	5.6	1.8	0.9	2.59
Chicago, IL	29.2	31.1	15.6	13.6	6.5	2.3	1.4	2.61
Cincinnati, OH	29.2	33.9	15.0	12.8	5.5	2.1	1.1	2.49
Clarksville, TN	25.1	33.1	17.6	13.9	6.1	2.5	1.3	2.68
Cleveland, OH	34.8	33.5	13.9	10.5	4.5	1.5	0.8	2.32
College Station, TX	30.8	32.6	14.6	12.7	5.3	2.6	1.1	2.56
Colorado Springs, CO	24.5	35.7	15.9	13.2	6.6	2.3	1.5	2.60
Columbia, MO	31.5	35.1	13.7	11.9	5.3	1.4	0.8	2.41
Columbia, SC	30.4	34.2	15.4	11.8	5.1	1.9	0.9	2.46
Columbus, OH	28.8	33.9	15.2	12.8	5.8	2.0	1.2	2.49
Dallas, TX	25.1	30.7	16.7	14.9	7.7	2.9	1.7	2.77
Davenport, IA	31.2	36.3	13.2	11.4	5.0	1.8	0.8	2.39
Denver, CO	28.4	34.4	15.0	13.1	5.3	2.2	1.3	2.51
Des Moines, IA	28.5	34.1	14.2	13.7	6.2	2.0	1.0	2.48
Durham, NC	30.7	36.0	15.0	11.2	4.8	1.4	0.7	2.40
Edison, NJ	28.0	29.5	17.0	14.4	6.4	2.5	1.9	2.71
El Paso, TX	23.6	27.7	17.7	16.2	9.1	3.6	1.7	2.94
Fargo, ND	33.2	33.8	13.9	11.2	5.4	1.4	0.8	2.33
Fort Collins, CO	24.8	39.8	15.7	12.2	4.9	1.4	0.8	2.38
Fort Wayne, IN	29.0	34.3	14.1	12.1	6.1	2.6	1.4	2.51
Fort Worth, TX	25.1	30.7	16.7	14.9	7.7	2.9	1.7	2.77
Grand Rapids, MI	25.0	34.3	15.2	14.3	7.2	2.4	1.4	2.61
Greeley, CO	20.1	34.4	16.3	15.8	8.1	3.2	1.6	2.84
Green Bay, WI	28.3	37.5	14.0	11.7	5.5	1.7	0.9	2.41
Greensboro, NC	30.0	34.5	16.1	11.5	4.9	1.8	0.9	2.47
Honolulu, HI	24.5	30.4	16.5	13.4	7.1	3.7	4.0	2.96
Houston, TX	24.2	29.6	17.2	15.7	8.0	3.0	1.8	2.83
Huntsville, AL	29.3	36.0	15.3	11.9	5.0	1.5	0.6	2.42
Indianapolis, IN	29.2	34.1	14.7	12.9	5.8	1.8	1.1	2.54
Jacksonville, FL	28.0	34.8	16.4	12.1	5.7	1.8	1.0	2.57
Kansas City, MO	29.1	34.4	14.3	13.0	5.7	2.0	1.2	2.50
Lafayette, LA	27.5	33.6	16.7	13.1	5.7	2.0	1.1	2.56
Las Cruces, NM	27.3	33.2	15.7	13.5	6.4	2.0	1.5	2.66
Las Vegas, NV	28.0	32.7	15.5	12.2	6.7	2.7	1.8	2.71
Lexington, KY	29.8	35.1	15.5	12.1	4.5	1.8	0.8	2.39
Lincoln, NE	29.9	35.2	13.6	12.0	5.6	2.4	1.0	2.41
Little Rock, AR	30.3	34.4	15.8	11.7	5.1	1.7	0.7	2.47
Los Angeles, CA	24.6	28.6	17.0	15.4	7.9	3.3	2.8	2.95
Louisville, KY	30.3	34.4	15.5	11.7	5.2	1.7	0.9	2.47

Table continued on following page.

Appendix A: Comparative Statistics

Metro Area	One	Two	Three	Four	Five	Six	Seven or More	Average Household Size
Madison, WI	31.5	36.8	13.6	11.4	4.3	1.4	0.7	2.31
Manchester, NH	27.1	35.7	16.3	13.0	4.8	2.1	0.7	2.50
Miami, FL	28.0	32.4	17.0	13.3	5.9	2.0	1.1	2.68
Midland, TX	25.7	28.1	17.0	15.7	8.6	2.6	2.0	2.61
Milwaukee, WI	32.2	34.3	13.7	11.5	5.2	1.7	0.9	2.40
Minneapolis, MN	28.1	34.1	14.7	13.5	5.8	2.1	1.4	2.53
Nashville, TN	26.9	34.8	16.2	13.1	5.7	1.8	1.1	2.57
New Haven, CT	30.6	33.1	16.4	12.2	4.7	1.6	0.9	2.49
New Orleans, LA	34.1	32.0	15.3	11.2	4.6	1.6	0.9	2.52
New York, NY	28.0	29.5	17.0	14.4	6.4	2.5	1.9	2.71
Oklahoma City, OK	28.5	33.4	15.7	12.2	6.3	2.5	1.1	2.53
Omaha, NE	28.9	33.5	14.5	12.2	6.6	2.4	1.4	2.53
Orlando, FL	24.1	34.6	17.0	13.9	6.6	2.2	1.2	2.83
Philadelphia, PA	29.2	32.1	16.1	13.4	5.7	1.9	1.1	2.53
Phoenix, AZ	25.9	34.5	14.6	12.7	6.8	3.0	2.2	2.65
Pittsburgh, PA	33.7	35.3	14.1	10.7	4.1	1.2	0.5	2.27
Portland, OR	26.9	35.5	15.4	13.3	5.3	2.0	1.3	2.53
Providence, RI	29.6	33.1	16.7	12.7	5.1	1.6	0.8	2.46
Provo, UT	12.4	28.6	15.5	15.9	12.5	8.9	5.9	3.52
Raleigh, NC	25.4	34.1	16.6	14.8	5.9	1.9	0.9	2.61
Reno, NV	27.4	34.9	15.5	12.5	5.8	2.0	1.5	2.51
Richmond, VA	29.4	34.5	15.7	12.3	5.3	1.7	0.8	2.51
Rochester, MN	27.4	36.9	13.3	13.0	6.1	1.9	1.1	2.46
Sacramento, CA	24.6	32.9	15.9	14.7	6.9	2.7	1.9	2.73
St. Louis, MO	30.5	34.5	15.0	12.2	5.1	1.5	0.8	2.43
Salem, OR	25.3	34.1	15.2	12.4	7.4	3.3	2.0	2.74
Salt Lake City, UT	23.1	30.9	15.7	13.8	8.5	4.6	3.1	2.92
San Antonio, TX	26.2	30.9	16.2	14.0	7.5	3.0	1.8	2.74
San Diego, CA	24.0	32.8	16.8	14.6	6.8	2.7	1.9	2.81
San Francisco, CA	26.4	31.8	16.8	14.8	6.1	2.2	1.6	2.71
San Jose, CA	20.4	30.4	19.1	17.7	7.2	2.7	2.2	2.94
Santa Rosa, CA	26.9	35.1	14.8	13.7	6.1	1.9	1.1	2.56
Savannah, GA	27.9	36.7	15.8	12.1	4.8	1.5	0.9	2.56
Seattle, WA	27.2	33.9	16.0	13.9	5.4	1.9	1.3	2.53
Sioux Falls, SD	28.7	34.4	14.5	12.2	6.8	2.0	1.1	2.45
Springfield, IL	33.7	35.4	13.4	10.4	4.6	1.3	0.9	2.28
Tampa, FL	30.7	36.3	14.9	10.8	4.6	1.5	0.8	2.46
Tucson, AZ	30.7	35.4	13.4	11.3	5.2	2.3	1.3	2.41
Tulsa, OK	28.8	33.7	15.2	12.2	6.0	2.5	1.3	2.57
Tuscaloosa, AL	30.1	34.6	15.5	11.7	5.4	1.5	0.8	2.62
Virginia Beach, VA	27.8	34.4	16.9	12.5	5.5	1.8	0.8	2.49
Washington, DC	27.8	30.7	16.1	14.5	6.5	2.6	1.6	2.67
Wichita, KS	29.7	33.4	13.9	11.8	6.6	2.5	1.8	2.56
Wilmington, NC	33.6	36.4	14.4	10.1	3.6	1.2	0.4	2.30
Winston-Salem, NC	30.1	35.7	15.6	10.7	4.7	2.0	0.9	2.47
Worcester, MA	27.0	33.0	17.4	14.5	5.3	1.6	0.8	2.52
U.S.	28.0	33.8	15.5	12.8	5.9	2.2	1.4	2.60

Note: Figures cover the Metropolitan Statistical Area (MSA)
Source: U.S. Census Bureau, 2017-2021 American Community Survey 5-Year Estimates

Household Relationships: City

City	House-holder	Opposite-sex Spouse	Same-sex Spouse	Opposite-sex Unmarried Partner	Same-sex Unmarried Partner	Child[1]	Grand-child	Other Relatives	Non-relatives
Albuquerque, NM	42.1	15.1	0.3	3.4	0.3	27.0	2.5	4.6	3.2
Allentown, PA	36.3	11.6	0.2	3.7	0.2	30.6	3.2	6.8	4.1
Anchorage, AK	37.5	17.0	0.2	3.0	0.2	28.3	1.9	4.6	4.2
Ann Arbor, MI	40.3	13.3	0.3	2.4	0.2	17.1	0.5	1.6	11.5
Athens, GA	40.1	11.6	0.2	2.7	0.2	20.8	2.0	3.7	10.7
Atlanta, GA	45.7	10.4	0.5	3.1	0.6	20.7	2.1	3.9	5.9
Austin, TX	42.7	14.5	0.4	3.6	0.4	23.2	1.5	4.1	6.4
Baltimore, MD	42.9	9.6	0.3	3.3	0.3	24.9	3.7	5.8	6.1
Boise City, ID	41.4	17.8	0.2	3.2	0.2	24.7	1.3	2.9	5.4
Boston, MA	41.4	10.4	0.5	3.1	0.4	20.6	1.7	5.3	9.7
Boulder, CO	40.2	13.0	0.3	3.1	0.2	16.4	0.3	1.6	12.3
Brownsville, TX	30.8	15.0	0.1	1.4	0.1	36.7	4.7	8.3	1.6
Cape Coral, FL	39.5	21.2	0.3	3.2	0.1	25.5	2.1	4.8	2.8
Cedar Rapids, IA	42.2	16.7	0.2	3.5	0.2	26.8	1.3	2.9	3.4
Charleston, SC	45.0	17.0	0.3	3.1	0.2	21.8	1.4	2.7	5.3
Charlotte, NC	40.6	15.2	0.2	2.8	0.2	28.0	2.1	4.9	4.2
Chicago, IL	41.6	12.2	0.3	3.0	0.3	26.6	3.0	6.4	4.8
Cincinnati, OH	45.1	10.2	0.3	3.4	0.3	24.6	2.2	3.4	5.3
Clarksville, TN	36.6	16.9	0.2	2.5	0.1	31.2	2.4	3.9	3.5
Cleveland, OH	45.0	8.5	0.2	3.5	0.3	27.0	3.3	5.0	3.8
College Station, TX	35.2	11.2	0.2	1.8	0.1	19.7	0.7	2.7	13.7
Colorado Springs, CO	39.7	18.3	0.3	2.6	0.2	27.5	1.9	3.6	4.3
Columbia, MO	40.5	14.1	0.2	2.8	0.2	22.4	1.0	2.5	7.8
Columbia, SC	39.2	10.5	0.2	2.1	0.2	19.5	1.6	2.8	5.8
Columbus, OH	42.2	12.9	0.3	3.6	0.3	26.2	2.1	4.4	5.2
Dallas, TX	40.1	13.4	0.4	2.6	0.3	28.6	3.2	6.2	4.0
Davenport, IA	41.9	15.9	0.2	3.7	0.2	27.0	2.0	3.0	3.2
Denver, CO	44.4	14.0	0.5	4.1	0.4	22.3	1.9	4.4	5.9
Des Moines, IA	41.1	14.2	0.3	3.5	0.2	27.9	2.0	4.4	3.9
Durham, NC	42.0	14.8	0.4	2.9	0.3	24.6	1.8	4.4	4.6
Edison, NJ	34.3	21.2	0.1	1.1	0.1	32.2	1.4	6.8	1.9
El Paso, TX	35.9	15.8	0.2	1.8	0.1	32.7	3.9	6.4	2.0
Fargo, ND	44.5	15.5	0.1	3.6	0.2	23.5	0.7	2.5	5.0
Fort Collins, CO	39.9	16.0	0.2	3.3	0.2	22.1	0.9	2.4	9.0
Fort Wayne, IN	40.7	15.6	0.2	3.1	0.2	29.7	2.0	3.4	3.0
Fort Worth, TX	35.2	15.8	0.2	2.1	0.1	33.0	3.1	5.6	3.0
Grand Rapids, MI	40.2	13.1	0.3	3.6	0.3	26.1	2.1	4.0	6.6
Greeley, CO	34.9	15.8	0.2	2.5	0.1	29.4	2.6	5.0	5.1
Green Bay, WI	40.7	15.2	0.2	4.0	0.2	28.6	1.6	3.4	3.0
Greensboro, NC	40.9	13.6	0.2	2.6	0.2	26.4	2.0	4.1	3.6
Honolulu, HI	39.1	15.0	0.3	2.4	0.2	22.2	3.1	9.1	5.6
Houston, TX	38.9	14.0	0.3	2.4	0.2	29.5	2.9	6.5	3.6
Huntsville, AL	42.8	16.5	0.2	2.2	0.2	25.1	2.1	3.5	3.1
Indianapolis, IN	40.7	14.0	0.3	3.4	0.3	28.6	2.5	4.5	3.9
Jacksonville, FL	39.9	15.6	0.2	2.8	0.2	27.7	2.8	4.9	3.6
Kansas City, MO	42.6	14.5	0.3	3.3	0.3	27.2	2.3	4.0	3.8
Lafayette, LA	43.0	15.3	0.2	2.8	0.2	27.0	2.3	3.5	3.8
Las Cruces, NM	41.1	14.9	0.2	3.4	0.3	28.5	2.5	4.5	3.6
Las Vegas, NV	37.5	15.2	0.3	2.9	0.2	29.3	2.7	6.7	4.3
Lexington, KY	41.7	16.0	0.3	2.9	0.3	25.3	1.6	3.4	4.4
Lincoln, NE	40.1	16.9	0.2	2.8	0.1	26.6	1.1	2.7	4.6
Little Rock, AR	43.5	14.5	0.3	2.4	0.3	27.1	2.3	3.9	3.1
Los Angeles, CA	36.2	13.1	0.3	2.8	0.3	26.5	2.8	9.0	6.3
Louisville, KY	40.0	18.0	0.2	2.9	0.2	28.8	2.6	4.2	2.7
Madison, WI	44.8	14.5	0.4	3.8	0.3	19.7	0.7	2.4	8.2

Table continued on following page.

Appendix A: Comparative Statistics

City	House-holder	Opposite-sex Spouse	Same-sex Spouse	Opposite-sex Unmarried Partner	Same-sex Unmarried Partner	Child[1]	Grand-child	Other Relatives	Non-relatives
Manchester, NH	42.5	14.9	0.3	4.3	0.2	24.3	1.6	4.3	4.7
Miami, FL	42.4	12.6	0.5	3.3	0.3	22.5	2.4	8.7	5.8
Midland, TX	36.4	18.5	0.1	2.1	0.1	31.9	3.0	4.2	2.5
Milwaukee, WI	40.8	10.2	0.2	3.6	0.2	30.2	2.7	4.9	4.4
Minneapolis, MN	43.7	12.0	0.6	3.9	0.5	22.1	1.1	3.5	8.0
Nashville, TN	42.1	14.3	0.3	3.0	0.3	24.0	1.9	4.7	5.7
New Haven, CT	39.0	9.4	0.3	2.9	0.2	27.0	2.5	5.0	5.7
New Orleans, LA	43.0	11.0	0.3	3.1	0.4	26.1	3.2	4.6	4.3
New York, NY	38.3	12.7	0.3	2.2	0.2	27.6	2.5	8.3	5.3
Oklahoma City, OK	39.4	16.6	0.2	2.6	0.2	29.4	2.3	4.3	3.1
Omaha, NE	39.8	16.0	0.2	2.8	0.2	29.6	1.8	3.7	3.6
Orlando, FL	41.7	13.7	0.5	3.5	0.4	26.1	2.0	5.9	5.0
Philadelphia, PA	41.0	10.9	0.3	3.1	0.3	26.8	3.6	5.9	5.2
Phoenix, AZ	36.3	14.4	0.3	3.1	0.3	30.2	2.9	6.6	4.2
Pittsburgh, PA	46.1	11.5	0.3	3.6	0.4	19.3	1.7	3.1	6.7
Portland, OR	43.2	14.9	0.7	4.4	0.6	21.2	1.1	3.7	7.2
Providence, RI	36.5	10.5	0.3	2.9	0.3	27.3	1.9	5.7	6.1
Provo, UT	29.6	15.9	0.1	0.6	0.0	25.7	1.6	4.0	12.7
Raleigh, NC	41.8	15.1	0.2	2.9	0.2	25.5	1.4	3.9	5.0
Reno, NV	41.1	15.2	0.3	3.8	0.2	24.8	1.7	4.7	5.7
Richmond, VA	45.2	10.4	0.4	4.0	0.4	20.8	2.1	4.3	7.4
Rochester, MN	41.1	18.5	0.2	2.8	0.1	27.8	0.9	2.8	3.3
Sacramento, CA	36.7	13.5	0.4	3.0	0.3	28.0	2.6	7.5	4.7
St. Louis, MO	48.0	10.3	0.4	3.7	0.4	22.5	2.6	4.0	4.3
Salem, OR	36.6	16.0	0.2	3.1	0.2	28.1	1.9	4.6	4.2
Salt Lake City, UT	42.3	13.9	0.5	3.4	0.4	22.1	1.7	4.2	7.6
San Antonio, TX	37.5	14.7	0.3	2.7	0.2	30.3	3.8	5.5	3.2
San Diego, CA	37.2	15.7	0.4	2.6	0.3	25.0	2.0	6.2	6.1
San Francisco, CA	42.6	13.6	0.8	3.3	0.6	17.6	1.3	6.8	10.3
San Jose, CA	32.4	17.1	0.2	1.9	0.1	28.6	2.3	9.8	6.1
Santa Rosa, CA	37.6	16.2	0.4	3.0	0.2	27.3	1.8	6.2	5.5
Savannah, GA	39.9	11.2	0.3	2.7	0.3	24.9	3.2	4.4	5.0
Seattle, WA	46.9	15.2	0.8	4.3	0.6	17.5	0.7	2.8	7.3
Sioux Falls, SD	40.7	18.0	0.1	3.2	0.1	28.4	1.1	2.7	3.1
Springfield, IL	44.8	15.5	0.2	3.2	0.2	25.7	1.9	2.8	2.8
Tampa, FL	40.9	13.8	0.3	3.2	0.3	25.8	2.3	4.9	4.5
Tucson, AZ	41.1	13.3	0.3	3.3	0.3	25.4	2.8	4.8	4.5
Tulsa, OK	41.6	14.8	0.2	2.9	0.2	27.8	2.3	4.3	3.4
Tuscaloosa, AL	41.0	10.6	0.1	2.1	0.1	21.3	2.4	3.5	8.7
Virginia Beach, VA	38.8	18.6	0.2	2.4	0.1	28.7	2.2	4.0	3.5
Washington, DC	45.3	10.3	0.6	3.1	0.5	20.4	2.4	4.2	7.1
Wichita, KS	40.0	16.4	0.2	2.7	0.2	29.1	2.2	3.7	3.1
Wilmington, NC	45.7	14.9	0.3	3.4	0.3	21.2	1.5	3.0	5.9
Winston-Salem, NC	40.9	14.6	0.2	2.5	0.2	28.1	2.4	4.3	2.7
Worcester, MA	38.3	12.2	0.3	2.8	0.2	26.3	1.7	5.7	5.3
U.S.	38.3	17.5	0.2	2.5	0.2	28.3	2.4	4.8	3.4

Note: Figures are percent of the total population; (1) Includes biological, adopted, and stepchildren of the householder
Source: U.S. Census Bureau, 2020 Census

Appendix A: Comparative Statistics

Household Relationships: Metro Area

Metro Area	House-holder	Opposite-sex Spouse	Same-sex Spouse	Opposite-sex Unmarried Partner	Same-sex Unmarried Partner	Child[1]	Grand-child	Other Relatives	Non-relatives
Albuquerque, NM	40.1	16.3	0.3	3.1	0.3	27.7	3.1	4.6	2.9
Allentown, PA	38.8	18.7	0.2	2.9	0.1	28.2	2.0	4.1	2.5
Anchorage, AK	37.1	17.6	0.2	2.9	0.1	29.1	1.9	4.2	4.0
Ann Arbor, MI	39.7	17.0	0.3	2.4	0.2	24.3	1.3	2.5	5.8
Athens, GA	38.6	15.6	0.2	2.3	0.2	25.1	2.3	3.7	7.3
Atlanta, GA	37.1	16.7	0.2	2.1	0.2	30.4	2.7	5.7	3.5
Austin, TX	38.6	17.3	0.3	2.7	0.3	27.8	1.9	4.4	4.6
Baltimore, MD	38.7	16.8	0.2	2.4	0.2	28.7	2.5	4.8	3.5
Boise City, ID	36.6	19.5	0.2	2.5	0.1	29.7	1.9	3.5	3.8
Boston, MA	38.7	17.4	0.3	2.5	0.2	27.1	1.6	4.5	4.4
Boulder, CO	40.1	18.0	0.3	2.8	0.2	23.8	1.0	2.6	6.8
Brownsville, TX	31.5	15.3	0.1	1.7	0.1	36.1	5.2	7.4	1.7
Cape Coral, FL	41.8	20.9	0.3	3.0	0.2	22.4	1.8	4.4	3.3
Cedar Rapids, IA	40.9	19.3	0.1	3.0	0.1	27.9	1.2	2.3	2.5
Charleston, SC	39.9	18.1	0.2	2.4	0.1	27.3	2.6	3.8	3.5
Charlotte, NC	38.9	18.3	0.2	2.4	0.2	29.2	2.4	4.2	2.8
Chicago, IL	38.2	17.1	0.2	2.3	0.1	30.3	2.4	5.1	2.8
Cincinnati, OH	39.5	18.1	0.2	2.7	0.1	28.9	2.3	3.2	2.9
Clarksville, TN	36.7	18.2	0.2	2.2	0.1	30.5	2.5	3.6	3.0
Cleveland, OH	42.5	17.1	0.1	2.7	0.1	27.7	2.1	3.3	2.3
College Station, TX	36.9	14.6	0.1	2.0	0.1	24.7	1.9	3.5	8.3
Colorado Springs, CO	37.5	19.3	0.2	2.2	0.1	28.5	2.0	3.6	3.8
Columbia, MO	39.8	16.5	0.2	2.8	0.2	24.9	1.4	2.5	5.7
Columbia, SC	39.9	17.0	0.2	2.1	0.2	27.5	2.7	3.8	3.0
Columbus, OH	39.4	17.4	0.2	2.9	0.2	28.5	2.0	3.5	3.3
Dallas, TX	36.2	17.6	0.2	2.0	0.2	31.7	2.7	5.5	2.9
Davenport, IA	41.4	18.8	0.2	2.9	0.1	27.9	1.8	2.5	2.2
Denver, CO	39.4	17.9	0.3	2.9	0.2	27.4	1.9	4.4	4.3
Des Moines, IA	39.6	19.2	0.2	2.7	0.1	29.6	1.3	2.8	2.6
Durham, NC	40.3	17.2	0.3	2.5	0.2	25.1	1.9	3.8	3.9
Edison, NJ	36.8	15.8	0.2	2.0	0.2	29.7	2.1	7.1	4.1
El Paso, TX	34.2	15.8	0.2	1.7	0.1	33.5	4.2	6.5	1.8
Fargo, ND	41.5	17.7	0.1	3.2	0.1	27.0	0.7	2.2	3.9
Fort Collins, CO	40.2	19.4	0.2	2.8	0.2	24.0	1.2	2.7	6.0
Fort Wayne, IN	39.5	18.0	0.2	2.7	0.1	30.5	1.9	2.9	2.5
Fort Worth, TX	36.2	17.6	0.2	2.0	0.2	31.7	2.7	5.5	2.9
Grand Rapids, MI	37.3	19.0	0.1	2.5	0.1	29.6	1.7	2.9	3.5
Greeley, CO	34.6	19.3	0.1	2.2	0.1	31.5	2.4	4.6	3.6
Green Bay, WI	40.5	19.8	0.1	3.3	0.1	28.1	1.2	2.2	2.2
Greensboro, NC	40.2	17.1	0.2	2.4	0.2	27.4	2.3	3.9	2.6
Honolulu, HI	33.1	16.3	0.2	1.9	0.1	26.2	4.5	9.2	4.9
Houston, TX	35.2	17.1	0.2	2.0	0.1	32.7	2.8	6.1	2.6
Huntsville, AL	40.1	19.3	0.1	1.9	0.1	27.8	2.3	3.4	2.3
Indianapolis, IN	39.2	17.9	0.2	2.8	0.2	29.6	2.1	3.5	2.8
Jacksonville, FL	39.1	17.9	0.2	2.6	0.2	28.0	2.6	4.3	3.2
Kansas City, MO	39.6	18.4	0.2	2.6	0.2	29.4	2.0	3.3	2.7
Lafayette, LA	39.5	17.1	0.2	2.7	0.2	30.4	2.9	3.5	2.5
Las Cruces, NM	37.5	15.9	0.2	2.7	0.2	30.0	3.6	5.1	2.7
Las Vegas, NV	37.3	15.5	0.3	3.0	0.2	28.7	2.6	7.0	4.4
Lexington, KY	40.5	17.4	0.2	2.8	0.2	26.5	2.0	3.4	3.7
Lincoln, NE	39.5	17.9	0.2	2.6	0.1	27.2	1.1	2.6	4.1
Little Rock, AR	40.8	17.7	0.2	2.3	0.2	27.9	2.6	3.6	2.7
Los Angeles, CA	34.0	15.2	0.2	2.3	0.2	29.0	3.0	9.1	5.1
Louisville, KY	40.5	17.7	0.2	2.8	0.2	27.6	2.5	3.6	2.9
Madison, WI	42.2	18.6	0.3	3.3	0.2	25.0	0.8	2.1	4.5

Table continued on following page.

Appendix A: Comparative Statistics

Metro Area	House-holder	Opposite-sex Spouse	Same-sex Spouse	Opposite-sex Unmarried Partner	Same-sex Unmarried Partner	Child[1]	Grand-child	Other Relatives	Non-relatives
Manchester, NH	39.7	19.2	0.3	3.2	0.1	27.2	1.6	3.5	3.2
Miami, FL	38.0	16.0	0.3	2.6	0.2	27.6	2.5	7.8	3.7
Midland, TX	35.8	18.6	0.1	2.0	0.1	32.3	3.2	4.4	2.6
Milwaukee, WI	41.3	17.5	0.2	2.9	0.2	28.7	1.6	3.1	2.7
Minneapolis, MN	38.9	18.7	0.2	2.8	0.2	29.4	1.2	3.3	3.3
Nashville, TN	38.8	18.2	0.2	2.4	0.2	28.1	2.2	4.1	3.8
New Haven, CT	39.7	16.5	0.2	2.6	0.2	28.1	2.0	4.4	2.9
New Orleans, LA	40.3	15.3	0.2	2.7	0.2	28.8	3.1	4.6	2.9
New York, NY	36.8	15.8	0.2	2.0	0.2	29.7	2.1	7.1	4.1
Oklahoma City, OK	38.8	17.7	0.2	2.4	0.2	29.0	2.3	3.8	3.1
Omaha, NE	38.8	18.4	0.2	2.6	0.1	30.6	1.6	3.1	2.8
Orlando, FL	37.0	17.0	0.3	2.7	0.2	28.4	2.4	6.0	4.2
Philadelphia, PA	38.7	16.9	0.2	2.5	0.2	29.2	2.5	4.4	3.0
Phoenix, AZ	36.9	17.2	0.2	2.8	0.2	29.0	2.5	5.4	3.7
Pittsburgh, PA	43.2	19.0	0.2	2.8	0.2	25.6	1.6	2.6	2.4
Portland, OR	39.0	18.1	0.4	3.2	0.3	26.7	1.6	4.2	4.9
Providence, RI	40.0	16.9	0.2	3.0	0.2	27.2	1.9	4.1	3.0
Provo, UT	28.0	18.8	0.1	0.7	0.0	39.0	2.1	4.0	4.8
Raleigh, NC	38.4	19.2	0.2	2.2	0.2	30.0	1.5	3.7	3.0
Reno, NV	39.5	17.2	0.2	3.4	0.2	26.1	2.1	5.0	4.9
Richmond, VA	39.5	17.3	0.2	2.5	0.2	27.7	2.4	4.0	3.3
Rochester, MN	40.1	20.5	0.1	2.7	0.1	28.9	1.0	2.2	2.5
Sacramento, CA	36.2	17.1	0.3	2.4	0.2	29.4	2.2	6.0	4.2
St. Louis, MO	40.8	18.2	0.2	2.6	0.2	28.5	2.2	3.0	2.4
Salem, OR	35.7	17.6	0.2	2.7	0.1	29.3	2.3	5.0	4.1
Salt Lake City, UT	34.0	17.4	0.3	2.1	0.2	32.4	2.5	5.3	4.4
San Antonio, TX	36.2	16.9	0.2	2.3	0.2	31.0	3.5	5.1	2.8
San Diego, CA	35.1	16.9	0.3	2.3	0.2	27.8	2.3	6.6	5.1
San Francisco, CA	36.7	17.0	0.4	2.3	0.3	26.3	1.8	6.9	5.9
San Jose, CA	33.8	18.4	0.2	1.8	0.1	28.3	1.9	7.9	5.6
Santa Rosa, CA	38.4	17.6	0.4	2.9	0.2	26.1	1.9	5.2	5.5
Savannah, GA	38.7	16.6	0.2	2.4	0.2	28.0	2.8	4.1	3.4
Seattle, WA	38.9	18.3	0.3	2.9	0.2	26.7	1.5	4.6	4.7
Sioux Falls, SD	39.5	19.4	0.1	2.9	0.1	29.8	1.1	2.3	2.6
Springfield, IL	42.9	18.2	0.2	3.0	0.2	27.2	1.8	2.4	2.4
Tampa, FL	41.2	17.6	0.3	3.1	0.2	25.5	2.2	4.6	3.4
Tucson, AZ	40.9	17.2	0.3	2.9	0.2	25.5	2.6	4.4	3.4
Tulsa, OK	39.1	18.2	0.2	2.4	0.1	29.0	2.6	3.9	2.7
Tuscaloosa, AL	39.8	15.2	0.1	1.9	0.1	26.5	3.2	3.9	4.5
Virginia Beach, VA	39.0	17.4	0.2	2.3	0.1	27.7	2.5	4.0	3.3
Washington, DC	37.0	17.3	0.3	2.0	0.2	29.3	2.0	5.9	4.4
Wichita, KS	39.0	18.2	0.1	2.4	0.1	29.8	2.1	3.2	2.6
Wilmington, NC	42.3	18.7	0.2	2.9	0.2	24.4	1.9	3.1	3.9
Winston-Salem, NC	40.9	18.6	0.2	2.3	0.1	27.5	2.4	3.7	2.2
Worcester, MA	38.6	17.9	0.2	2.9	0.1	28.1	1.7	4.0	3.1
U.S.	38.3	17.5	0.2	2.5	0.2	28.3	2.4	4.8	3.4

Note: Figures are percent of the total population; Figures cover the Metropolitan Statistical Area; (1) Includes biological, adopted, and stepchildren of the householder
Source: U.S. Census Bureau, 2020 Census

Age: City

City	Under Age 5	Age 5–19	Age 20–34	Age 35–44	Age 45–54	Age 55–64	Age 65–74	Age 75–84	Age 85+	Median Age
Albuquerque, NM	5.1	18.6	21.8	13.2	11.7	12.7	10.2	4.9	1.9	38.2
Allentown, PA	6.8	21.0	23.3	12.4	11.4	11.6	7.8	3.9	1.7	34.2
Anchorage, AK	6.4	19.6	23.4	13.7	11.7	12.6	8.3	3.1	0.9	35.2
Ann Arbor, MI	3.9	15.5	42.4	9.6	7.8	8.1	7.3	3.6	1.7	27.9
Athens, GA	5.1	16.6	38.4	10.7	8.8	8.5	7.3	3.5	1.2	28.2
Atlanta, GA	4.9	15.5	33.3	14.3	11.2	9.5	6.8	3.3	1.3	33.1
Austin, TX	5.5	16.7	31.8	16.1	11.4	9.0	6.1	2.5	1.0	33.0
Baltimore, MD	5.5	16.6	27.0	13.1	10.7	12.6	8.9	4.0	1.6	35.5
Boise City, ID	5.1	18.4	23.4	13.6	11.7	12.0	9.5	4.5	1.8	37.1
Boston, MA	4.5	14.1	37.6	12.0	9.6	9.8	7.2	3.7	1.5	31.7
Boulder, CO	3.0	19.4	34.9	10.4	10.3	9.1	7.7	3.6	1.6	30.0
Brownsville, TX	6.6	25.8	20.0	12.3	12.0	10.1	7.9	3.8	1.5	32.9
Cape Coral, FL	4.5	16.6	14.9	11.3	13.4	16.0	14.5	6.8	2.1	47.2
Cedar Rapids, IA	6.3	19.1	22.5	13.0	11.2	12.0	8.9	4.6	2.4	36.4
Charleston, SC	5.6	14.6	28.5	13.9	10.3	11.2	9.7	4.4	1.8	35.7
Charlotte, NC	6.1	19.3	25.8	14.6	12.6	10.5	6.9	3.0	1.1	34.2
Chicago, IL	5.5	16.9	27.5	14.4	11.9	11.1	7.7	3.7	1.4	35.1
Cincinnati, OH	6.1	18.3	29.2	11.9	10.0	11.5	8.0	3.3	1.7	32.7
Clarksville, TN	8.3	21.9	28.4	13.0	9.9	9.2	5.8	2.5	0.8	29.9
Cleveland, OH	6.0	18.2	24.2	11.8	11.5	13.9	9.0	3.9	1.7	36.1
College Station, TX	5.4	24.3	43.8	8.4	6.3	5.2	3.8	2.1	0.6	22.5
Colorado Springs, CO	5.9	19.0	23.7	13.2	11.3	12.2	8.9	4.1	1.6	35.9
Columbia, MO	5.5	20.5	32.8	11.4	9.1	8.9	7.0	3.3	1.5	29.2
Columbia, SC	4.6	22.1	30.7	11.1	9.5	9.8	7.7	3.2	1.3	29.9
Columbus, OH	6.6	18.1	30.0	13.4	10.7	10.3	6.9	2.9	1.2	32.3
Dallas, TX	6.5	19.3	26.6	14.2	11.7	10.6	6.8	3.1	1.3	33.6
Davenport, IA	6.1	18.8	21.8	12.5	11.5	12.8	9.7	4.6	2.1	37.5
Denver, CO	5.4	15.5	31.0	15.8	11.1	9.4	7.4	3.2	1.3	34.1
Des Moines, IA	6.6	19.7	24.0	13.1	11.3	11.8	8.2	3.6	1.7	34.8
Durham, NC	6.0	17.6	28.2	13.9	11.1	10.4	8.1	3.4	1.3	33.9
Edison, NJ	5.3	19.7	18.1	16.5	13.3	12.2	8.9	4.2	1.9	39.0
El Paso, TX	5.9	21.7	21.9	11.9	11.9	11.9	8.6	4.3	1.9	35.4
Fargo, ND	6.2	17.8	30.1	13.0	9.7	10.3	7.7	3.5	1.8	32.5
Fort Collins, CO	4.4	19.4	31.1	12.7	10.2	9.5	7.7	3.4	1.6	31.7
Fort Wayne, IN	6.9	20.8	21.9	12.4	11.2	11.9	9.1	4.1	1.9	35.3
Fort Worth, TX	7.0	22.7	23.1	14.3	12.1	10.3	6.6	2.9	1.1	33.2
Grand Rapids, MI	6.4	18.1	31.1	12.2	9.3	10.1	7.3	3.4	2.1	31.7
Greeley, CO	6.9	22.5	25.0	12.3	10.2	9.8	7.9	3.9	1.6	31.9
Green Bay, WI	6.5	20.6	22.5	12.9	11.1	12.4	8.6	3.7	1.5	35.2
Greensboro, NC	5.5	20.0	24.9	12.1	11.5	11.3	8.7	4.2	1.8	34.7
Honolulu, HI	4.5	14.3	20.5	13.0	12.7	13.7	11.5	6.0	3.6	42.9
Houston, TX	6.6	19.7	25.1	14.3	11.6	10.7	7.3	3.4	1.3	34.2
Huntsville, AL	5.6	17.7	24.2	12.0	11.2	13.1	9.0	5.2	2.2	36.9
Indianapolis, IN	6.6	20.2	24.0	13.4	11.3	11.8	7.9	3.5	1.3	34.5
Jacksonville, FL	6.0	18.2	22.3	12.9	12.2	13.1	9.3	4.2	1.6	37.4
Kansas City, MO	6.2	18.5	25.0	13.6	11.4	11.9	8.2	3.7	1.5	35.1
Lafayette, LA	5.6	17.9	23.5	12.4	10.9	13.0	10.2	4.6	2.0	37.3
Las Cruces, NM	5.8	20.1	23.5	11.9	10.0	11.2	10.0	5.4	2.1	35.5
Las Vegas, NV	5.7	20.0	20.0	13.5	13.1	12.1	9.4	4.7	1.5	38.0
Lexington, KY	5.7	19.2	24.7	13.3	11.4	11.2	8.6	4.0	1.6	35.2
Lincoln, NE	6.0	20.5	24.9	12.9	10.4	10.8	8.8	3.9	1.7	34.0
Little Rock, AR	6.0	18.7	22.1	13.5	11.8	12.2	9.7	4.3	1.8	37.2
Los Angeles, CA	4.9	17.0	25.6	14.6	12.9	11.5	8.0	3.9	1.7	36.5
Louisville, KY	5.9	19.2	18.9	12.8	12.8	13.4	10.0	4.8	1.9	39.5

Table continued on following page.

Appendix A: Comparative Statistics

City	Under Age 5	Age 5–19	Age 20–34	Age 35–44	Age 45–54	Age 55–64	Age 65–74	Age 75–84	Age 85+	Median Age
Madison, WI	5.0	16.4	33.7	12.6	9.4	9.6	8.1	3.5	1.6	32.0
Manchester, NH	5.3	15.7	26.0	12.6	12.1	13.4	9.0	3.9	2.0	37.0
Miami, FL	4.8	13.6	24.0	15.0	13.5	12.4	8.8	5.5	2.5	39.7
Midland, TX	7.9	21.7	23.5	14.4	10.3	11.0	6.7	3.0	1.5	33.3
Milwaukee, WI	6.8	21.9	25.6	12.6	10.8	10.8	7.3	2.9	1.3	32.1
Minneapolis, MN	5.6	16.1	32.8	14.7	10.3	9.7	7.1	2.6	1.0	32.6
Nashville, TN	6.1	16.6	29.5	14.1	10.7	10.8	7.5	3.3	1.3	33.8
New Haven, CT	5.6	20.8	30.4	12.8	10.0	9.4	6.6	3.1	1.2	31.0
New Orleans, LA	5.5	17.5	24.9	14.0	11.1	12.3	9.4	3.9	1.5	36.2
New York, NY	5.4	16.7	24.8	13.9	12.2	12.0	8.7	4.4	1.9	36.8
Oklahoma City, OK	6.7	20.7	22.7	13.9	11.2	11.4	8.3	3.8	1.5	34.9
Omaha, NE	6.6	20.7	23.1	13.0	11.0	11.7	8.4	3.8	1.6	34.7
Orlando, FL	5.7	17.6	27.2	15.6	12.4	10.1	6.8	3.2	1.3	34.7
Philadelphia, PA	5.5	17.6	27.2	12.9	10.9	11.6	8.5	4.0	1.7	34.8
Phoenix, AZ	6.3	21.6	22.9	13.7	12.4	11.3	7.5	3.2	1.1	34.5
Pittsburgh, PA	4.4	14.5	34.3	11.5	8.8	11.1	9.1	4.2	2.0	33.0
Portland, OR	4.5	14.6	25.8	17.2	13.1	10.8	8.9	3.7	1.4	37.6
Providence, RI	5.6	21.3	29.4	12.4	10.4	9.8	6.6	3.0	1.4	30.9
Provo, UT	7.1	21.4	44.5	8.3	6.1	5.4	3.8	2.2	1.1	23.8
Raleigh, NC	5.5	18.5	28.0	14.0	12.1	10.1	7.0	3.3	1.4	33.7
Reno, NV	5.5	18.0	24.5	12.7	11.3	11.9	9.9	4.6	1.5	36.3
Richmond, VA	5.5	15.8	33.4	12.0	9.3	10.8	8.2	3.4	1.5	32.4
Rochester, MN	6.5	18.6	23.3	13.4	10.5	11.9	8.5	5.0	2.3	36.0
Sacramento, CA	5.9	18.8	24.6	14.1	11.5	11.2	8.5	3.7	1.6	35.4
St. Louis, MO	5.3	15.1	28.8	13.6	10.9	12.8	8.7	3.4	1.4	35.4
Salem, OR	5.9	20.3	21.7	13.6	11.5	11.2	9.6	4.5	1.8	36.3
Salt Lake City, UT	5.1	16.7	33.3	14.1	10.3	9.2	7.0	2.9	1.3	32.1
San Antonio, TX	6.1	20.6	23.4	13.0	11.8	11.4	8.2	3.9	1.6	34.9
San Diego, CA	5.0	16.8	26.7	14.2	11.9	11.3	8.3	4.0	1.7	35.8
San Francisco, CA	4.0	10.5	29.3	15.8	12.5	11.4	9.2	4.6	2.4	38.2
San Jose, CA	5.3	18.5	22.2	14.7	13.9	12.2	7.7	4.0	1.6	37.6
Santa Rosa, CA	5.1	18.5	19.4	13.7	12.1	12.5	10.9	5.4	2.5	39.9
Savannah, GA	5.8	18.4	28.0	12.2	10.2	11.2	8.6	4.0	1.6	33.5
Seattle, WA	4.4	12.6	33.1	16.0	11.8	9.7	7.7	3.3	1.5	35.0
Sioux Falls, SD	7.0	19.8	22.7	13.8	10.7	11.4	8.7	4.0	1.8	35.3
Springfield, IL	5.8	17.6	19.4	12.2	11.6	14.1	11.5	5.5	2.4	40.7
Tampa, FL	5.4	18.7	24.6	13.6	12.4	11.9	8.0	3.8	1.5	35.8
Tucson, AZ	5.3	18.2	24.8	12.0	10.9	12.1	9.9	4.8	1.9	36.2
Tulsa, OK	6.5	19.8	22.5	12.9	11.1	11.8	9.0	4.3	2.0	35.8
Tuscaloosa, AL	5.1	20.8	34.3	10.0	8.8	9.0	7.2	3.3	1.5	27.1
Virginia Beach, VA	5.8	18.6	22.4	13.3	11.8	12.9	9.1	4.4	1.7	37.1
Washington, DC	5.4	13.9	32.9	15.2	10.0	9.9	7.4	3.6	1.5	33.9
Wichita, KS	6.3	21.0	21.7	12.4	11.1	12.4	9.1	4.1	1.8	35.7
Wilmington, NC	4.3	15.1	27.2	11.8	11.0	12.1	10.8	5.7	2.3	37.8
Winston-Salem, NC	5.8	20.5	22.0	12.2	11.6	12.1	9.1	4.5	2.0	36.2
Worcester, MA	5.4	18.9	26.8	12.1	11.5	11.9	7.9	3.7	1.9	34.3
U.S.	5.6	19.2	20.2	12.7	12.4	13.1	10.0	4.9	1.9	38.8

Source: U.S. Census Bureau, 2020 Census

Appendix A: Comparative Statistics

Age: Metro Area

Metro Area	Under Age 5	Age 5–19	Age 20–34	Age 35–44	Age 45–54	Age 55–64	Age 65–74	Age 75–84	Age 85+	Median Age
Albuquerque, NM	5.1	19.2	19.8	12.6	11.7	13.4	11.0	5.2	1.8	39.4
Allentown, PA	5.0	18.5	18.2	11.8	12.9	14.6	11.0	5.6	2.5	41.9
Anchorage, AK	6.5	20.4	22.2	13.7	11.8	12.7	8.6	3.1	0.9	35.5
Ann Arbor, MI	4.7	17.5	28.4	11.6	11.3	11.6	9.1	4.1	1.6	34.5
Athens, GA	5.3	18.8	28.8	11.6	10.9	10.5	8.6	4.2	1.3	32.5
Atlanta, GA	5.7	20.6	20.9	13.7	13.8	12.1	8.3	3.7	1.2	36.9
Austin, TX	5.9	20.0	24.8	15.3	12.4	10.3	7.3	3.1	1.1	34.7
Baltimore, MD	5.6	18.8	20.5	13.0	12.4	13.6	9.6	4.7	1.9	38.6
Boise City, ID	5.9	21.8	19.7	13.4	11.9	11.7	9.5	4.6	1.6	36.9
Boston, MA	4.9	17.2	22.6	12.5	12.6	13.5	9.8	4.8	2.1	39.0
Boulder, CO	4.2	19.0	23.5	12.7	12.7	12.5	9.7	4.2	1.6	37.6
Brownsville, TX	6.5	25.3	19.3	12.0	11.9	10.6	8.6	4.3	1.6	34.0
Cape Coral, FL	4.3	15.4	15.4	10.1	11.0	14.7	16.4	9.7	3.0	49.7
Cedar Rapids, IA	5.9	19.9	19.1	12.8	11.9	13.2	9.7	5.1	2.2	38.8
Charleston, SC	5.8	18.6	21.4	13.5	11.8	12.6	10.0	4.6	1.5	37.8
Charlotte, NC	5.8	20.2	20.0	13.6	13.7	12.3	8.8	4.2	1.4	37.8
Chicago, IL	5.5	19.3	20.8	13.4	12.9	12.9	9.0	4.3	1.8	38.2
Cincinnati, OH	5.9	20.1	19.8	12.4	12.3	13.4	9.7	4.5	1.8	38.2
Clarksville, TN	7.9	21.3	25.4	12.4	10.7	10.6	7.3	3.3	1.1	31.8
Cleveland, OH	5.2	17.7	18.8	11.7	12.4	14.6	11.3	5.6	2.5	41.7
College Station, TX	5.9	22.0	32.3	10.5	8.8	9.1	6.8	3.3	1.3	27.5
Colorado Springs, CO	6.0	20.0	23.1	12.9	11.4	12.4	8.8	3.9	1.4	35.6
Columbia, MO	5.7	20.6	26.7	12.0	10.2	10.9	8.4	3.9	1.5	32.8
Columbia, SC	5.4	20.2	20.1	12.4	12.4	13.2	10.2	4.6	1.6	38.4
Columbus, OH	6.2	19.8	22.2	13.4	12.3	12.0	8.6	3.9	1.5	36.2
Dallas, TX	6.2	21.8	21.4	14.1	13.0	11.4	7.4	3.4	1.1	35.3
Davenport, IA	5.7	19.5	17.9	12.4	11.8	13.6	11.0	5.6	2.3	40.3
Denver, CO	5.5	18.8	23.0	14.7	12.6	11.7	8.5	3.7	1.4	36.6
Des Moines, IA	6.5	20.8	20.2	13.8	12.0	11.9	8.7	4.1	1.7	36.6
Durham, NC	5.2	18.4	23.1	12.7	12.1	12.3	9.9	4.6	1.6	37.4
Edison, NJ	5.4	18.0	21.5	13.3	12.8	13.0	9.2	4.7	2.1	38.7
El Paso, TX	6.1	22.6	22.4	12.1	11.8	11.5	8.0	3.9	1.7	34.2
Fargo, ND	6.7	19.9	25.7	13.7	10.4	10.7	7.7	3.5	1.7	33.5
Fort Collins, CO	4.6	18.5	23.6	12.9	11.0	12.4	10.5	4.8	1.8	37.4
Fort Wayne, IN	6.7	21.3	19.9	12.4	11.7	12.4	9.4	4.4	1.8	36.6
Fort Worth, TX	6.2	21.8	21.4	14.1	13.0	11.4	7.4	3.4	1.1	35.3
Grand Rapids, MI	6.1	20.6	21.8	12.5	11.5	12.5	8.9	4.3	1.8	36.2
Greeley, CO	6.9	22.6	21.3	13.9	11.6	11.1	8.0	3.4	1.2	34.5
Green Bay, WI	5.8	19.8	18.8	12.6	12.2	14.0	10.1	4.8	1.8	39.3
Greensboro, NC	5.3	19.6	19.9	11.7	12.9	13.2	10.2	5.1	1.9	39.4
Honolulu, HI	5.4	17.3	21.1	12.6	12.2	12.9	10.4	5.4	2.8	39.8
Houston, TX	6.5	22.1	21.0	14.3	12.7	11.4	7.7	3.3	1.1	35.3
Huntsville, AL	5.6	19.2	20.4	12.6	12.8	13.9	9.1	4.7	1.7	38.7
Indianapolis, IN	6.2	20.7	20.2	13.5	12.5	12.5	8.8	4.1	1.5	37.0
Jacksonville, FL	5.6	18.9	19.5	12.8	12.6	13.6	10.4	4.8	1.7	39.6
Kansas City, MO	6.1	20.2	19.9	13.4	12.1	12.8	9.3	4.4	1.7	37.7
Lafayette, LA	6.3	20.5	19.3	12.9	11.7	13.5	9.6	4.5	1.6	37.8
Las Cruces, NM	5.8	21.3	21.6	11.4	10.6	12.2	10.2	5.2	1.9	36.0
Las Vegas, NV	5.7	19.4	20.6	13.9	13.1	12.1	9.5	4.6	1.3	38.0
Lexington, KY	5.9	19.7	22.2	13.2	12.1	12.1	9.2	4.2	1.6	36.5
Lincoln, NE	6.0	20.9	23.4	12.9	10.6	11.4	9.1	4.1	1.7	34.8
Little Rock, AR	5.9	19.9	20.2	13.1	12.0	12.7	10.0	4.7	1.6	38.0
Los Angeles, CA	5.0	18.3	22.5	13.7	13.3	12.4	8.6	4.4	1.9	37.9
Louisville, KY	5.8	18.9	19.5	12.9	12.6	13.6	10.2	4.7	1.8	39.3

Table continued on following page.

Appendix A: Comparative Statistics   A-31

Metro Area	Under Age 5	Age 5–19	Age 20–34	Age 35–44	Age 45–54	Age 55–64	Age 65–74	Age 75–84	Age 85+	Median Age
Madison, WI	5.3	18.3	23.6	13.3	11.5	12.3	9.6	4.2	1.8	36.9
Manchester, NH	5.0	17.5	20.0	12.3	13.5	15.2	10.0	4.7	1.9	40.9
Miami, FL	4.8	17.1	18.7	13.0	13.8	13.7	10.2	6.0	2.6	42.1
Midland, TX	7.8	22.3	22.9	14.3	10.7	11.2	6.7	2.9	1.3	33.3
Milwaukee, WI	5.8	19.6	19.9	12.6	12.0	13.5	9.7	4.6	2.1	38.5
Minneapolis, MN	6.1	19.8	20.5	13.7	12.3	13.0	8.9	4.1	1.7	37.5
Nashville, TN	6.0	19.6	22.1	13.9	12.5	12.1	8.6	3.9	1.3	36.4
New Haven, CT	4.9	18.1	20.3	11.9	12.6	14.1	10.4	5.3	2.5	40.4
New Orleans, LA	5.7	18.9	20.3	13.3	11.9	13.4	10.3	4.6	1.7	38.6
New York, NY	5.4	18.0	21.5	13.3	12.8	13.0	9.2	4.7	2.1	38.7
Oklahoma City, OK	6.2	21.0	21.6	13.4	11.3	12.0	8.9	4.2	1.6	35.8
Omaha, NE	6.6	21.5	20.4	13.4	11.5	12.2	8.8	4.0	1.6	36.0
Orlando, FL	5.2	19.5	21.2	13.5	12.9	12.2	9.2	4.6	1.7	37.9
Philadelphia, PA	5.3	18.7	20.7	12.6	12.4	13.7	9.8	4.8	2.1	39.1
Phoenix, AZ	5.7	20.5	20.5	12.8	12.1	11.9	9.8	5.1	1.7	37.5
Pittsburgh, PA	4.9	16.3	19.3	11.8	12.1	14.9	12.0	5.9	2.8	42.9
Portland, OR	5.2	18.3	21.0	14.8	12.8	12.0	9.8	4.4	1.6	38.6
Providence, RI	4.8	17.9	20.0	12.1	12.8	14.5	10.6	5.2	2.4	40.8
Provo, UT	8.9	27.9	26.5	12.8	8.9	6.9	4.9	2.5	0.9	25.9
Raleigh, NC	5.8	21.0	20.5	14.3	13.8	11.7	8.0	3.6	1.2	36.8
Reno, NV	5.4	18.5	21.4	12.3	11.8	13.1	10.9	5.0	1.5	38.5
Richmond, VA	5.5	18.9	20.8	12.7	12.3	13.3	10.1	4.6	1.8	38.6
Rochester, MN	6.2	19.8	19.3	13.2	11.2	13.4	9.4	5.3	2.3	38.4
Sacramento, CA	5.6	19.8	20.3	13.2	12.1	12.7	9.8	4.8	2.0	38.2
St. Louis, MO	5.6	18.9	19.4	12.6	12.1	14.1	10.3	5.0	2.1	39.7
Salem, OR	5.9	20.8	20.0	12.7	11.3	11.9	10.4	5.1	1.9	37.4
Salt Lake City, UT	6.7	22.8	23.7	14.7	11.1	9.7	7.0	3.1	1.1	32.8
San Antonio, TX	6.1	21.4	21.0	13.2	12.2	11.8	8.7	4.1	1.5	36.0
San Diego, CA	5.3	18.5	23.2	13.4	12.2	12.2	9.0	4.3	1.9	37.1
San Francisco, CA	5.0	16.8	21.7	14.7	13.3	12.4	9.3	4.7	2.0	39.1
San Jose, CA	5.3	18.4	22.4	14.6	13.6	12.0	7.7	4.2	1.9	37.5
Santa Rosa, CA	4.6	17.3	18.2	12.9	12.2	14.2	12.7	5.8	2.3	42.6
Savannah, GA	5.9	19.7	22.5	13.0	11.7	12.2	9.3	4.3	1.5	36.3
Seattle, WA	5.7	17.9	22.7	14.9	12.7	12.1	8.5	3.9	1.5	37.2
Sioux Falls, SD	7.0	20.9	20.5	13.8	11.1	11.9	8.8	4.0	1.7	36.0
Springfield, IL	5.6	18.9	17.6	12.5	12.1	14.5	11.4	5.3	2.1	41.2
Tampa, FL	4.8	17.1	18.3	12.3	12.8	14.2	11.8	6.2	2.3	42.7
Tucson, AZ	4.9	17.8	19.8	11.5	10.9	13.1	12.7	6.8	2.4	41.2
Tulsa, OK	6.2	20.6	19.6	12.8	11.8	12.7	9.7	4.9	1.8	37.6
Tuscaloosa, AL	5.8	20.1	24.7	11.9	11.1	11.8	9.0	4.1	1.5	34.5
Virginia Beach, VA	5.8	18.8	22.2	12.5	11.5	13.4	9.5	4.6	1.7	37.3
Washington, DC	5.8	19.4	21.5	14.3	13.2	12.3	8.2	3.9	1.4	37.2
Wichita, KS	6.2	21.6	19.9	12.5	11.2	12.9	9.5	4.4	1.9	36.7
Wilmington, NC	4.8	16.9	20.5	12.7	12.6	13.3	11.7	5.7	2.0	41.1
Winston-Salem, NC	5.3	19.2	18.2	11.6	13.2	14.0	10.8	5.6	2.1	41.1
Worcester, MA	5.0	18.5	19.8	12.3	13.4	14.6	9.9	4.6	2.0	40.3
U.S.	5.6	19.2	20.2	12.7	12.4	13.1	10.0	4.9	1.9	38.8

Note: Figures cover the Metropolitan Statistical Area (MSA)
Source: U.S. Census Bureau, 2020 Census

Appendix A: Comparative Statistics

Ancestry: City

City	German	Irish	English	American	Italian	Polish	French[1]	Scottish	Dutch
Albuquerque, NM	9.2	7.6	7.8	3.3	3.2	1.4	1.8	1.4	0.9
Allentown, PA	9.8	4.7	2.0	2.7	4.2	1.8	0.7	0.4	0.8
Anchorage, AK	13.8	9.4	8.5	3.6	3.2	2.0	2.3	1.9	1.3
Ann Arbor, MI	17.0	10.4	10.1	2.7	4.9	6.0	2.7	2.6	2.4
Athens, GA	8.4	8.2	9.8	3.5	3.4	1.5	2.0	2.8	0.8
Atlanta, GA	6.8	5.9	8.1	4.8	2.9	1.4	1.8	1.5	0.5
Austin, TX	10.9	8.3	8.7	2.9	3.0	1.8	2.4	2.1	0.7
Baltimore, MD	6.1	5.7	3.3	2.8	3.1	2.3	0.9	0.7	0.3
Boise City, ID	16.9	12.1	18.1	4.4	4.2	1.9	2.2	3.2	1.7
Boston, MA	4.8	13.1	4.9	2.2	7.2	2.1	1.8	1.1	0.4
Boulder, CO	16.2	11.5	11.4	2.4	6.0	3.6	2.4	3.3	1.3
Brownsville, TX	0.9	0.5	0.6	1.7	0.4	0.1	0.4	0.1	0.2
Cape Coral, FL	14.2	11.5	7.8	12.3	9.6	3.4	2.0	1.5	0.9
Cedar Rapids, IA	29.0	13.5	9.0	3.6	1.7	1.3	1.9	1.7	1.6
Charleston, SC	10.8	10.5	11.4	21.1	4.2	2.2	2.5	2.3	0.7
Charlotte, NC	8.0	6.9	7.0	4.8	3.4	1.5	1.3	1.7	0.5
Chicago, IL	7.3	7.3	2.8	2.1	3.9	5.2	0.9	0.7	0.5
Cincinnati, OH	17.3	9.4	6.2	3.5	3.8	1.6	1.4	1.1	0.9
Clarksville, TN	12.2	8.6	7.1	6.1	4.2	1.0	1.4	1.6	1.1
Cleveland, OH	9.5	8.5	3.2	2.2	4.6	3.9	0.9	0.6	0.5
College Station, TX	15.9	8.4	8.8	3.3	3.5	1.8	2.9	1.7	0.8
Colorado Springs, CO	17.7	10.6	11.4	4.2	4.7	2.2	2.7	2.7	1.4
Columbia, MO	24.6	12.0	11.0	4.4	3.6	2.2	1.9	2.3	1.2
Columbia, SC	9.6	6.9	7.7	5.5	3.3	1.1	1.9	1.9	0.6
Columbus, OH	15.2	10.2	6.9	4.0	4.9	2.1	1.3	1.6	0.8
Dallas, TX	5.1	4.2	5.1	4.2	1.7	0.8	1.2	1.1	0.4
Davenport, IA	27.7	15.3	7.5	3.4	2.2	2.0	1.5	1.6	1.6
Denver, CO	13.9	10.1	9.0	2.6	5.0	2.7	2.1	2.1	1.1
Des Moines, IA	19.1	11.9	8.2	3.1	3.6	1.2	1.5	1.2	2.3
Durham, NC	8.1	6.5	9.4	3.7	3.3	1.7	1.6	1.6	0.6
Edison, NJ	4.4	5.8	1.6	1.7	7.8	3.3	1.0	0.5	0.2
El Paso, TX	3.8	2.5	1.9	2.2	1.3	0.5	0.7	0.4	0.2
Fargo, ND	35.0	8.2	5.0	2.5	1.0	2.1	3.5	1.2	1.0
Fort Collins, CO	23.4	12.9	13.0	3.6	5.8	3.0	3.2	3.3	1.8
Fort Wayne, IN	23.1	9.4	7.8	5.5	2.3	2.2	2.7	1.6	1.1
Fort Worth, TX	7.2	6.1	6.5	4.2	1.8	1.0	1.3	1.5	0.7
Grand Rapids, MI	14.1	8.0	6.4	2.5	3.0	6.3	1.9	1.6	13.0
Greeley, CO	16.6	8.4	7.5	3.1	2.7	1.6	1.6	1.9	1.0
Green Bay, WI	28.7	8.5	4.3	4.1	2.1	8.0	3.6	1.0	2.6
Greensboro, NC	6.5	5.5	8.6	4.4	2.4	1.0	1.2	1.6	0.5
Honolulu, HI	4.4	3.1	3.2	1.4	1.7	0.8	0.8	0.6	0.2
Houston, TX	4.8	3.5	4.3	3.4	1.6	0.9	1.4	0.9	0.4
Huntsville, AL	9.4	8.9	10.6	10.2	2.3	1.2	1.8	1.9	0.9
Indianapolis, IN	12.8	8.2	7.0	4.9	2.0	1.5	1.6	1.5	0.9
Jacksonville, FL	7.5	7.6	6.5	5.7	3.7	1.4	1.3	1.5	0.6
Kansas City, MO	15.2	10.1	8.1	4.1	3.6	1.7	1.7	1.4	0.8
Lafayette, LA	8.0	5.4	5.9	5.9	3.6	0.3	16.2	1.0	0.4
Las Cruces, NM	7.0	5.8	6.4	2.6	1.9	1.0	1.2	1.1	0.8
Las Vegas, NV	8.5	7.3	6.2	3.2	5.2	1.8	1.6	1.3	0.7
Lexington, KY	13.1	11.0	12.1	8.2	3.1	1.6	1.6	2.6	1.1
Lincoln, NE	31.5	11.5	8.9	3.3	2.0	2.4	1.8	1.4	1.6
Little Rock, AR	7.3	6.2	8.8	5.2	1.4	0.9	1.5	1.6	0.4
Los Angeles, CA	3.8	3.6	3.1	3.9	2.7	1.4	1.1	0.7	0.4
Louisville, KY	15.2	11.5	9.3	6.5	2.6	1.1	1.7	1.6	0.9
Madison, WI	29.4	12.0	8.8	2.0	4.0	5.5	2.4	1.8	1.8
Manchester, NH	6.2	19.3	9.5	2.9	8.8	3.8	11.4	2.7	0.3

Table continued on following page.

Appendix A: Comparative Statistics

City	German	Irish	English	American	Italian	Polish	French[1]	Scottish	Dutch
Miami, FL	1.8	1.3	1.0	2.7	2.5	0.7	0.9	0.2	0.2
Midland, TX	5.8	5.2	6.0	4.7	1.0	0.5	1.5	1.4	0.3
Milwaukee, WI	15.1	5.6	2.1	1.3	2.5	5.9	1.2	0.4	0.6
Minneapolis, MN	20.9	10.5	6.5	1.9	2.6	3.9	2.7	1.4	1.3
Nashville, TN	8.4	7.8	8.7	6.8	2.6	1.4	1.6	1.9	0.7
New Haven, CT	3.9	6.2	3.2	2.0	8.2	2.0	1.2	0.5	0.5
New Orleans, LA	6.1	5.7	4.9	2.2	3.7	0.9	5.2	1.0	0.4
New York, NY	2.9	4.4	1.9	3.8	6.1	2.3	0.8	0.5	0.3
Oklahoma City, OK	10.0	7.8	7.7	5.7	1.8	0.7	1.3	1.6	0.9
Omaha, NE	24.7	13.0	7.8	3.0	4.0	3.5	1.9	1.6	1.4
Orlando, FL	6.2	5.7	5.7	5.6	4.7	1.6	1.5	1.0	0.6
Philadelphia, PA	6.7	9.9	2.8	2.5	6.9	3.1	0.8	0.6	0.3
Phoenix, AZ	9.8	7.4	6.3	2.8	3.8	1.8	1.6	1.2	0.8
Pittsburgh, PA	17.9	13.8	5.4	3.0	12.1	6.7	1.4	1.3	0.5
Portland, OR	15.3	11.2	11.9	4.5	4.5	2.3	2.8	2.9	1.7
Providence, RI	3.7	8.0	3.9	2.1	6.9	1.4	2.9	0.8	0.3
Provo, UT	9.9	5.2	25.3	2.6	1.8	0.7	1.4	4.1	1.7
Raleigh, NC	9.0	8.1	10.4	8.4	3.9	2.0	1.7	2.3	0.9
Reno, NV	12.0	10.6	10.5	4.2	5.7	1.9	2.4	2.0	1.2
Richmond, VA	7.3	7.0	8.9	4.5	3.5	1.4	1.5	1.9	0.5
Rochester, MN	28.7	10.2	6.7	3.1	1.5	2.9	1.8	1.3	1.6
Sacramento, CA	6.6	5.9	5.5	1.8	3.5	1.0	1.5	1.1	0.6
St. Louis, MO	15.7	9.7	5.4	4.4	4.0	1.7	2.3	1.2	0.8
Salem, OR	16.9	9.3	11.1	3.6	2.9	1.4	2.7	2.5	1.8
Salt Lake City, UT	10.9	6.9	17.7	3.2	4.1	1.4	2.1	3.5	1.8
San Antonio, TX	7.0	4.3	4.0	3.2	1.8	1.0	1.4	0.8	0.3
San Diego, CA	8.3	7.1	6.2	2.3	4.2	1.8	1.7	1.4	0.7
San Francisco, CA	6.9	7.6	5.5	2.5	4.6	1.8	2.1	1.3	0.7
San Jose, CA	4.6	4.0	3.8	1.8	3.3	0.8	1.1	0.8	0.5
Santa Rosa, CA	11.1	9.8	9.6	2.5	6.6	1.6	2.8	1.7	1.1
Savannah, GA	6.5	7.6	5.4	4.0	3.1	1.5	1.6	1.3	0.6
Seattle, WA	14.4	11.0	11.1	2.3	4.5	2.6	3.0	2.8	1.3
Sioux Falls, SD	33.6	10.9	6.5	4.2	1.6	1.5	1.8	0.9	6.1
Springfield, IL	18.9	11.4	9.6	4.1	4.5	2.0	1.9	1.8	1.1
Tampa, FL	8.7	7.5	6.7	6.5	6.2	2.0	1.8	1.4	0.7
Tucson, AZ	11.1	8.1	7.4	2.8	3.5	1.9	1.8	1.5	0.8
Tulsa, OK	10.8	8.7	9.3	5.4	2.0	0.9	1.9	2.0	0.8
Tuscaloosa, AL	5.2	6.1	6.4	5.7	1.9	0.7	1.3	2.1	0.5
Virginia Beach, VA	11.3	10.7	10.1	7.8	5.6	2.1	2.2	2.2	0.8
Washington, DC	7.5	7.3	6.1	2.8	4.3	2.2	1.6	1.4	0.7
Wichita, KS	19.0	9.6	9.7	4.8	1.6	0.9	2.0	1.6	1.2
Wilmington, NC	10.2	9.4	11.7	4.7	5.3	2.0	1.8	2.7	0.8
Winston-Salem, NC	8.7	6.4	8.5	4.8	2.4	0.9	1.2	1.9	0.7
Worcester, MA	3.0	14.0	4.6	3.7	8.9	4.2	5.7	1.0	0.3
U.S.	12.8	9.6	8.1	5.7	5.0	2.7	2.2	1.6	1.1

Note: Figures are the percentage of the total population reporting a particular ancestry. The nine most commonly reported ancestries in the U.S. are shown. Figures include multiple ancestries (e.g. if a person reported being Irish and Italian, they were included in both columns); (1) Excludes Basque
Source: U.S. Census Bureau, 2017-2021 American Community Survey 5-Year Estimates

Appendix A: Comparative Statistics

Ancestry: Metro Area

Metro Area	German	Irish	English	American	Italian	Polish	French[1]	Scottish	Dutch
Albuquerque, NM	9.2	7.2	7.7	3.9	3.1	1.3	1.7	1.5	0.7
Allentown, PA	22.8	12.8	6.1	4.9	11.8	4.9	1.4	1.0	1.8
Anchorage, AK	14.7	9.9	8.8	4.0	3.0	2.0	2.4	2.0	1.4
Ann Arbor, MI	18.3	10.6	10.8	5.9	4.6	6.3	2.9	2.7	2.0
Athens, GA	8.4	10.1	11.7	6.7	2.9	1.1	1.8	2.6	1.0
Atlanta, GA	6.5	6.4	8.0	8.0	2.6	1.2	1.3	1.6	0.6
Austin, TX	12.3	8.1	9.1	3.7	2.8	1.6	2.3	2.1	0.8
Baltimore, MD	14.3	11.3	8.0	4.6	5.9	3.8	1.4	1.5	0.6
Boise City, ID	16.4	10.2	17.6	4.9	3.5	1.4	2.4	2.9	1.9
Boston, MA	5.8	20.3	9.7	3.3	12.4	3.1	4.2	2.1	0.5
Boulder, CO	18.4	11.9	13.4	3.0	5.4	3.2	2.7	3.0	1.7
Brownsville, TX	1.9	1.1	1.8	1.9	0.5	0.2	0.5	0.3	0.1
Cape Coral, FL	13.5	10.7	8.4	12.5	7.8	3.1	2.1	1.7	1.1
Cedar Rapids, IA	32.6	14.2	9.1	4.1	1.7	1.1	2.2	1.9	2.0
Charleston, SC	10.1	9.5	10.6	11.8	3.9	1.8	2.1	2.3	0.6
Charlotte, NC	10.7	8.5	8.9	8.8	3.9	1.8	1.5	2.1	0.8
Chicago, IL	13.7	10.5	4.5	2.5	6.4	8.3	1.3	0.9	1.1
Cincinnati, OH	26.1	13.2	10.0	6.2	4.0	1.6	1.8	1.8	1.0
Clarksville, TN	11.8	8.8	8.3	7.4	3.2	1.1	1.4	1.7	1.0
Cleveland, OH	18.7	13.4	7.7	4.2	9.4	7.4	1.5	1.4	0.8
College Station, TX	13.5	7.6	7.6	3.8	2.8	1.8	2.4	1.6	0.7
Colorado Springs, CO	17.8	10.6	10.9	4.4	4.5	2.3	2.6	2.6	1.4
Columbia, MO	25.0	11.7	11.6	6.2	2.9	1.7	2.1	2.1	1.3
Columbia, SC	9.5	7.1	8.3	7.5	2.3	1.3	1.4	1.8	0.6
Columbus, OH	20.7	12.7	9.6	5.7	5.2	2.3	1.7	2.1	1.1
Dallas, TX	8.2	6.5	7.6	5.9	2.1	1.0	1.5	1.5	0.6
Davenport, IA	25.9	13.5	8.2	4.0	2.3	2.1	1.7	1.4	1.8
Denver, CO	17.1	10.7	10.5	3.3	5.0	2.4	2.4	2.2	1.4
Des Moines, IA	26.2	13.0	10.1	4.0	3.1	1.4	1.7	1.5	3.6
Durham, NC	9.3	8.0	11.1	5.4	3.5	1.8	1.7	2.1	0.7
Edison, NJ	6.0	8.9	2.9	4.0	11.6	3.7	0.9	0.6	0.5
El Paso, TX	3.5	2.3	1.8	2.2	1.2	0.5	0.6	0.4	0.2
Fargo, ND	35.4	7.8	4.8	2.5	1.1	2.2	3.1	1.1	1.1
Fort Collins, CO	25.2	13.1	14.1	4.1	5.2	2.8	3.2	3.4	2.1
Fort Wayne, IN	26.4	9.5	8.3	6.4	2.5	2.1	3.1	1.6	1.1
Fort Worth, TX	8.2	6.5	7.6	5.9	2.1	1.0	1.5	1.5	0.6
Grand Rapids, MI	18.8	9.5	8.9	3.4	3.0	6.3	2.5	1.7	18.0
Greeley, CO	20.5	10.1	9.7	4.1	3.7	1.9	1.9	1.8	1.4
Green Bay, WI	35.4	9.6	4.8	3.8	2.1	9.5	3.9	0.8	4.1
Greensboro, NC	8.5	7.0	9.4	7.3	2.4	1.1	1.3	2.1	0.8
Honolulu, HI	5.2	3.9	3.7	1.3	1.9	0.8	1.1	0.8	0.4
Houston, TX	7.3	5.0	5.8	3.8	2.0	1.1	1.9	1.1	0.6
Huntsville, AL	8.9	9.5	11.1	11.7	2.2	1.3	1.6	1.9	0.8
Indianapolis, IN	16.6	9.6	9.5	8.1	2.5	1.7	1.7	1.7	1.2
Jacksonville, FL	9.3	9.4	8.9	7.9	4.3	1.8	1.7	2.0	0.7
Kansas City, MO	19.9	12.3	11.1	4.9	3.2	1.6	2.1	1.9	1.2
Lafayette, LA	6.3	4.3	4.2	6.4	2.6	0.4	16.5	0.6	0.3
Las Cruces, NM	6.5	4.7	5.3	2.5	1.6	0.7	1.1	1.1	0.7
Las Vegas, NV	8.2	6.9	6.3	3.0	4.9	1.8	1.5	1.2	0.6
Lexington, KY	12.7	11.3	12.6	11.4	2.8	1.4	1.6	2.5	1.1
Lincoln, NE	32.9	11.3	8.7	3.6	1.9	2.3	1.8	1.3	1.8
Little Rock, AR	8.9	8.8	9.6	7.1	1.5	0.8	1.5	1.8	0.7
Los Angeles, CA	5.1	4.3	4.1	3.5	2.9	1.2	1.2	0.8	0.5
Louisville, KY	17.3	12.5	10.8	8.1	2.5	1.2	1.9	1.9	1.0
Madison, WI	35.2	12.9	9.1	2.7	3.6	5.1	2.5	1.6	1.7
Manchester, NH	8.0	20.7	13.9	3.3	9.8	4.0	11.2	3.3	0.7

Table continued on following page.

Metro Area	German	Irish	English	American	Italian	Polish	French[1]	Scottish	Dutch
Miami, FL	4.3	4.2	2.9	5.9	4.9	1.8	1.2	0.6	0.4
Midland, TX	6.0	5.0	5.7	5.0	1.2	0.5	1.4	1.2	0.2
Milwaukee, WI	31.9	9.5	4.6	2.1	4.2	10.3	2.2	0.9	1.2
Minneapolis, MN	28.1	10.9	6.3	3.0	2.6	4.1	3.2	1.2	1.4
Nashville, TN	9.9	9.3	11.1	10.2	2.7	1.3	1.7	2.1	0.8
New Haven, CT	7.5	14.2	7.1	2.9	19.9	5.4	3.0	1.0	0.5
New Orleans, LA	9.6	7.9	5.5	4.8	7.3	0.7	11.0	1.0	0.4
New York, NY	6.0	8.9	2.9	4.0	11.6	3.7	0.9	0.6	0.5
Oklahoma City, OK	11.6	8.9	9.1	7.0	1.8	0.8	1.5	1.8	1.0
Omaha, NE	28.3	13.1	9.1	3.5	3.9	3.7	1.9	1.5	1.6
Orlando, FL	8.1	7.2	6.5	8.2	5.1	1.8	1.7	1.2	0.7
Philadelphia, PA	14.1	17.4	7.4	3.2	12.4	4.7	1.2	1.2	0.7
Phoenix, AZ	12.5	8.6	8.6	3.8	4.4	2.3	1.9	1.6	1.0
Pittsburgh, PA	25.1	17.0	8.6	3.3	15.2	8.1	1.6	1.9	1.0
Portland, OR	16.4	10.5	11.7	4.6	3.7	1.8	2.7	2.7	1.7
Providence, RI	4.5	17.2	10.7	3.2	13.1	3.4	8.6	1.5	0.4
Provo, UT	10.0	4.9	29.5	4.2	2.2	0.5	1.6	4.3	1.5
Raleigh, NC	9.9	9.1	11.6	8.2	4.6	2.1	1.8	2.4	0.8
Reno, NV	12.5	10.6	10.9	3.8	6.2	1.8	2.6	2.0	1.2
Richmond, VA	9.0	7.9	11.7	6.7	3.8	1.5	1.5	1.9	0.7
Rochester, MN	34.2	11.0	6.8	3.4	1.3	2.8	1.9	1.2	1.9
Sacramento, CA	10.1	7.9	8.7	2.6	4.7	1.2	1.9	1.6	0.9
St. Louis, MO	26.1	12.9	8.6	5.4	4.6	2.3	3.0	1.5	1.0
Salem, OR	16.9	9.0	10.6	3.7	2.8	1.2	2.6	2.3	1.8
Salt Lake City, UT	9.7	5.7	21.7	4.0	2.9	0.9	1.9	3.6	1.7
San Antonio, TX	10.0	5.7	5.8	3.6	2.1	1.4	1.7	1.2	0.4
San Diego, CA	8.9	7.4	6.7	2.7	4.1	1.7	1.8	1.4	0.8
San Francisco, CA	7.3	7.0	6.2	2.3	4.4	1.4	1.8	1.4	0.7
San Jose, CA	5.8	4.7	4.7	2.0	3.7	1.1	1.3	0.9	0.6
Santa Rosa, CA	12.8	12.2	10.9	2.5	8.3	1.7	3.1	2.5	1.2
Savannah, GA	9.1	9.9	8.7	7.4	3.5	1.4	1.7	1.7	0.6
Seattle, WA	13.8	9.4	10.1	3.0	3.5	1.8	2.6	2.5	1.3
Sioux Falls, SD	35.2	10.4	6.1	5.2	1.4	1.4	1.8	0.9	6.4
Springfield, IL	21.5	12.5	10.9	5.1	4.8	1.9	2.2	1.9	1.3
Tampa, FL	11.6	10.3	8.5	8.6	7.3	2.9	2.4	1.7	0.9
Tucson, AZ	13.1	8.9	9.1	3.3	3.9	2.3	2.1	1.9	1.0
Tulsa, OK	12.6	10.2	9.9	5.6	1.9	0.9	2.0	2.0	1.1
Tuscaloosa, AL	5.0	6.5	6.9	10.9	1.5	0.4	0.9	1.9	0.5
Virginia Beach, VA	9.5	8.8	9.8	8.5	4.0	1.7	1.8	1.7	0.7
Washington, DC	9.0	8.4	7.5	4.0	4.2	2.1	1.5	1.5	0.7
Wichita, KS	21.4	9.9	10.0	5.7	1.7	0.9	2.0	1.8	1.3
Wilmington, NC	11.3	10.8	12.1	5.8	5.6	2.3	1.8	3.0	0.8
Winston-Salem, NC	11.3	8.1	11.0	8.5	2.3	1.1	1.2	2.2	0.8
Worcester, MA	5.5	17.6	9.3	5.5	11.8	5.6	9.5	2.0	0.5
U.S.	12.8	9.6	8.1	5.7	5.0	2.7	2.2	1.6	1.1

Note: Figures are the percentage of the total population reporting a particular ancestry. The nine most commonly reported ancestries in the U.S. are shown. Figures include multiple ancestries (e.g. if a person reported being Irish and Italian, they were included in both columns); Figures cover the Metropolitan Statistical Area; (1) Excludes Basque
Source: U.S. Census Bureau, 2017-2021 American Community Survey 5-Year Estimates

Foreign-born Population: City

City	Any Foreign Country	Asia	Mexico	Europe	Caribbean	Central America[1]	South America	Africa	Canada
Albuquerque, NM	10.2	2.5	5.1	0.9	0.4	0.1	0.4	0.5	0.1
Allentown, PA	20.4	3.1	1.0	0.8	11.5	0.8	2.0	1.3	0.1
Anchorage, AK	11.0	6.1	0.7	1.0	0.6	0.2	0.5	0.6	0.4
Ann Arbor, MI	18.6	12.3	0.5	2.9	0.1	0.1	0.7	1.2	0.8
Athens, GA	9.5	2.9	2.4	0.9	0.3	1.0	1.0	1.0	0.2
Atlanta, GA	8.3	3.4	0.7	1.4	0.8	0.2	0.8	0.8	0.3
Austin, TX	18.5	6.3	6.3	1.5	0.6	1.7	0.8	0.9	0.3
Baltimore, MD	8.1	2.2	0.3	0.9	1.3	1.0	0.4	1.9	0.1
Boise City, ID	6.5	2.8	1.1	1.2	0.1	0.0	0.3	0.5	0.5
Boston, MA	28.1	7.6	0.4	3.1	8.6	2.5	2.3	3.0	0.4
Boulder, CO	10.6	4.4	0.9	3.0	0.2	0.5	0.7	0.3	0.5
Brownsville, TX	27.1	0.5	25.5	0.2	0.0	0.7	0.1	0.0	0.1
Cape Coral, FL	17.4	1.5	0.6	2.4	8.3	0.9	3.2	0.1	0.5
Cedar Rapids, IA	6.8	2.6	0.7	0.5	0.1	0.2	0.2	2.3	0.1
Charleston, SC	5.0	1.5	0.6	1.3	0.4	0.1	0.6	0.3	0.1
Charlotte, NC	17.3	5.3	2.5	1.3	1.2	3.1	1.5	2.1	0.2
Chicago, IL	20.2	5.1	8.1	3.4	0.3	0.9	1.1	1.0	0.2
Cincinnati, OH	6.6	1.9	0.4	0.9	0.2	0.8	0.3	2.0	0.1
Clarksville, TN	6.3	2.0	1.3	0.8	0.5	0.7	0.4	0.4	0.2
Cleveland, OH	6.0	2.4	0.4	1.1	0.6	0.4	0.3	0.7	0.1
College Station, TX	12.3	7.3	1.5	0.9	0.2	0.3	1.1	0.8	0.2
Colorado Springs, CO	7.5	2.2	2.0	1.5	0.3	0.4	0.4	0.4	0.4
Columbia, MO	8.4	5.1	0.6	0.9	0.1	0.2	0.3	1.0	0.1
Columbia, SC	4.8	2.1	0.3	0.6	0.6	0.2	0.4	0.5	0.1
Columbus, OH	13.3	5.0	1.1	0.9	0.5	0.8	0.4	4.7	0.1
Dallas, TX	23.8	2.8	13.9	0.8	0.4	2.9	0.7	2.1	0.2
Davenport, IA	4.5	1.6	1.8	0.4	0.2	0.1	0.0	0.2	0.1
Denver, CO	14.2	2.8	6.6	1.4	0.3	0.6	0.7	1.4	0.3
Des Moines, IA	13.8	5.2	3.6	0.8	0.1	1.1	0.1	2.8	0.1
Durham, NC	14.6	4.4	2.8	1.4	0.6	2.7	0.7	1.5	0.3
Edison, NJ	46.1	37.1	0.5	2.2	1.8	0.6	1.8	1.8	0.3
El Paso, TX	22.8	1.0	20.2	0.5	0.2	0.3	0.2	0.3	0.0
Fargo, ND	9.9	3.7	0.1	0.5	0.1	0.1	0.2	4.8	0.5
Fort Collins, CO	7.3	2.9	1.4	1.4	0.1	0.3	0.6	0.3	0.2
Fort Wayne, IN	8.6	4.3	2.0	0.6	0.1	0.6	0.2	0.6	0.1
Fort Worth, TX	16.7	3.7	9.2	0.6	0.3	0.8	0.6	1.3	0.2
Grand Rapids, MI	10.8	2.4	3.2	1.0	0.7	1.4	0.2	1.7	0.2
Greeley, CO	12.2	0.8	8.3	0.5	0.1	1.1	0.2	1.2	0.1
Green Bay, WI	9.2	2.0	5.2	0.4	0.2	0.4	0.3	0.6	0.1
Greensboro, NC	12.1	4.1	1.8	1.2	0.7	0.5	0.7	2.9	0.2
Honolulu, HI	27.5	22.9	0.2	0.9	0.2	0.1	0.2	0.2	0.2
Houston, TX	28.9	5.9	10.6	1.1	1.0	6.5	1.6	2.0	0.2
Huntsville, AL	6.4	1.9	1.5	0.8	0.3	0.5	0.3	0.7	0.1
Indianapolis, IN	10.0	3.0	2.8	0.5	0.5	0.9	0.4	1.9	0.1
Jacksonville, FL	12.0	4.2	0.6	1.9	2.2	0.8	1.4	0.6	0.2
Kansas City, MO	8.0	2.3	2.2	0.5	0.6	0.6	0.3	1.3	0.1
Lafayette, LA	5.5	2.3	0.4	0.7	0.2	1.1	0.6	0.1	0.1
Las Cruces, NM	11.0	2.3	7.0	0.8	0.1	0.1	0.2	0.4	0.1
Las Vegas, NV	20.8	5.3	8.8	1.6	1.1	2.4	0.8	0.4	0.4
Lexington, KY	10.1	3.8	2.0	1.1	0.3	0.7	0.5	1.5	0.2
Lincoln, NE	9.1	4.9	1.3	1.0	0.4	0.5	0.3	0.8	0.1
Little Rock, AR	7.1	2.6	1.7	0.5	0.1	1.1	0.4	0.4	0.1
Los Angeles, CA	36.2	10.9	12.0	2.4	0.3	8.4	1.1	0.7	0.4
Louisville, KY	8.6	2.6	0.8	0.9	2.0	0.5	0.3	1.4	0.2

Table continued on following page.

City	Percent of Population Born in								
	Any Foreign Country	Asia	Mexico	Europe	Caribbean	Central America[1]	South America	Africa	Canada
Madison, WI	12.0	6.2	1.4	1.6	0.2	0.3	1.0	1.0	0.3
Manchester, NH	14.6	4.3	0.5	2.7	1.7	1.4	1.0	2.1	1.0
Miami, FL	58.1	1.4	1.1	1.9	31.0	11.9	10.3	0.3	0.2
Midland, TX	15.1	2.1	9.0	0.2	1.0	0.5	0.5	1.3	0.5
Milwaukee, WI	10.1	2.8	4.9	0.7	0.4	0.3	0.2	0.8	0.1
Minneapolis, MN	14.8	3.7	1.8	1.2	0.3	0.4	1.5	5.8	0.3
Nashville, TN	13.7	4.0	2.8	0.9	0.3	2.0	0.3	3.0	0.3
New Haven, CT	17.4	4.2	2.7	2.4	2.6	1.3	2.3	1.5	0.3
New Orleans, LA	5.4	1.9	0.3	0.7	0.4	1.3	0.4	0.2	0.2
New York, NY	36.3	10.8	1.8	5.2	9.9	1.4	4.9	1.7	0.3
Oklahoma City, OK	11.6	3.2	5.3	0.5	0.2	1.2	0.4	0.6	0.2
Omaha, NE	10.8	3.3	3.4	0.7	0.1	1.2	0.4	1.5	0.2
Orlando, FL	22.8	2.8	0.6	2.0	6.7	1.1	8.8	0.5	0.3
Philadelphia, PA	14.3	5.5	0.5	2.1	2.9	0.7	0.9	1.6	0.1
Phoenix, AZ	19.2	3.2	11.7	1.4	0.4	0.9	0.4	0.8	0.4
Pittsburgh, PA	9.0	4.5	0.3	1.8	0.4	0.1	0.5	1.0	0.3
Portland, OR	13.1	6.0	1.9	2.5	0.2	0.4	0.3	0.9	0.5
Providence, RI	30.7	3.8	0.3	2.5	13.9	5.4	1.2	3.1	0.4
Provo, UT	11.3	1.9	4.3	0.4	0.4	0.9	2.4	0.4	0.4
Raleigh, NC	13.0	3.9	2.4	1.2	0.9	1.2	0.8	2.3	0.2
Reno, NV	15.6	5.4	5.1	1.4	0.2	1.7	0.4	0.6	0.4
Richmond, VA	7.5	1.6	0.6	0.8	0.6	2.7	0.4	0.7	0.1
Rochester, MN	13.6	5.4	1.0	1.7	0.1	0.2	0.5	4.5	0.2
Sacramento, CA	20.9	10.3	5.8	1.4	0.1	0.7	0.4	0.5	0.2
St. Louis, MO	6.8	2.8	0.7	1.2	0.2	0.3	0.2	1.3	0.1
Salem, OR	11.3	2.4	5.8	1.1	0.1	0.4	0.2	0.2	0.2
Salt Lake City, UT	15.3	4.1	4.9	1.9	0.2	0.7	1.3	1.0	0.4
San Antonio, TX	14.2	2.5	8.9	0.5	0.3	0.9	0.5	0.4	0.1
San Diego, CA	25.1	11.8	8.2	2.2	0.2	0.5	0.9	0.9	0.4
San Francisco, CA	34.1	22.0	2.4	4.5	0.2	2.4	1.1	0.5	0.6
San Jose, CA	40.7	26.4	8.6	2.3	0.1	1.2	0.7	0.8	0.3
Santa Rosa, CA	21.1	4.6	11.9	1.9	0.0	1.1	0.3	0.6	0.4
Savannah, GA	6.1	2.5	0.8	0.8	0.5	0.5	0.5	0.3	0.2
Seattle, WA	19.3	11.0	1.3	2.6	0.1	0.4	0.5	2.0	1.0
Sioux Falls, SD	8.7	2.1	0.5	1.1	0.1	1.1	0.1	3.4	0.1
Springfield, IL	4.4	2.3	0.5	0.5	0.1	0.1	0.2	0.6	0.0
Tampa, FL	18.1	3.8	1.1	1.8	7.1	1.2	2.3	0.5	0.3
Tucson, AZ	14.2	2.3	8.8	1.0	0.1	0.3	0.4	0.9	0.2
Tulsa, OK	11.0	2.6	5.2	0.6	0.2	1.0	0.5	0.6	0.1
Tuscaloosa, AL	4.5	2.3	1.0	0.4	0.1	0.3	0.1	0.2	0.1
Virginia Beach, VA	9.3	4.9	0.4	1.4	0.5	0.6	0.8	0.4	0.2
Washington, DC	13.5	3.0	0.6	2.4	1.2	2.4	1.5	2.1	0.3
Wichita, KS	9.9	3.7	4.2	0.5	0.1	0.5	0.3	0.5	0.1
Wilmington, NC	4.7	1.2	1.1	1.0	0.2	0.4	0.4	0.1	0.2
Winston-Salem, NC	10.2	2.2	4.1	0.6	0.5	1.5	0.7	0.7	0.1
Worcester, MA	21.9	6.1	0.3	3.6	3.0	1.3	2.5	4.9	0.1
U.S.	13.6	4.2	3.3	1.5	1.4	1.1	1.1	0.8	0.2

Note: (1) Excludes Mexico
Source: U.S. Census Bureau, 2017-2021 American Community Survey 5-Year Estimates

Foreign-born Population: Metro Area

Metro Area	Any Foreign Country	Asia	Mexico	Europe	Caribbean	Central America[1]	South America	Africa	Canada
Albuquerque, NM	8.9	1.9	4.9	0.8	0.3	0.2	0.3	0.4	0.1
Allentown, PA	9.7	2.7	0.4	1.4	2.8	0.5	1.1	0.6	0.1
Anchorage, AK	9.0	4.8	0.6	1.1	0.4	0.2	0.4	0.4	0.4
Ann Arbor, MI	12.5	7.3	0.6	2.3	0.1	0.2	0.5	0.9	0.6
Athens, GA	7.4	2.5	1.7	0.7	0.2	0.8	0.7	0.6	0.2
Atlanta, GA	14.1	4.7	2.3	1.1	1.6	1.2	1.2	1.7	0.2
Austin, TX	15.2	4.8	5.8	1.2	0.4	1.2	0.7	0.7	0.3
Baltimore, MD	10.5	4.3	0.4	1.3	0.8	1.1	0.5	1.9	0.1
Boise City, ID	6.5	1.5	2.7	1.0	0.0	0.2	0.4	0.3	0.3
Boston, MA	19.3	6.3	0.2	3.2	3.6	1.6	2.2	1.7	0.4
Boulder, CO	9.9	3.4	2.3	2.3	0.1	0.3	0.6	0.3	0.5
Brownsville, TX	22.8	0.6	20.8	0.2	0.1	0.7	0.1	0.0	0.1
Cape Coral, FL	17.1	1.3	2.3	2.0	6.3	1.9	2.2	0.1	0.9
Cedar Rapids, IA	4.3	1.8	0.4	0.3	0.1	0.1	0.1	1.2	0.1
Charleston, SC	5.8	1.5	1.0	1.1	0.3	0.6	0.7	0.2	0.2
Charlotte, NC	10.5	3.1	2.0	1.1	0.7	1.5	1.0	1.0	0.2
Chicago, IL	17.7	5.3	6.3	3.7	0.2	0.5	0.7	0.7	0.2
Cincinnati, OH	5.1	2.2	0.5	0.7	0.1	0.4	0.2	0.8	0.1
Clarksville, TN	4.9	1.5	0.9	0.6	0.3	0.4	0.3	0.6	0.2
Cleveland, OH	6.0	2.2	0.4	2.2	0.2	0.2	0.2	0.4	0.2
College Station, TX	11.5	3.8	5.0	0.7	0.2	0.5	0.7	0.5	0.1
Colorado Springs, CO	6.7	1.9	1.6	1.5	0.4	0.3	0.4	0.3	0.3
Columbia, MO	5.7	3.3	0.5	0.7	0.1	0.2	0.2	0.7	0.1
Columbia, SC	5.3	1.8	1.0	0.7	0.4	0.6	0.3	0.3	0.1
Columbus, OH	8.8	3.7	0.7	0.8	0.3	0.4	0.3	2.4	0.1
Dallas, TX	18.7	5.7	7.8	0.8	0.3	1.6	0.7	1.6	0.2
Davenport, IA	5.3	1.7	1.7	0.5	0.1	0.1	0.1	0.9	0.1
Denver, CO	12.0	3.3	4.6	1.4	0.2	0.5	0.6	1.1	0.3
Des Moines, IA	8.1	3.2	1.5	1.0	0.1	0.5	0.2	1.5	0.1
Durham, NC	11.8	3.6	2.7	1.4	0.4	1.8	0.6	1.0	0.3
Edison, NJ	29.4	8.7	1.4	4.3	6.9	1.9	4.5	1.4	0.2
El Paso, TX	23.7	0.9	21.3	0.4	0.2	0.3	0.2	0.2	0.0
Fargo, ND	7.0	2.8	0.1	0.5	0.1	0.0	0.1	3.0	0.4
Fort Collins, CO	5.8	1.8	1.4	1.2	0.1	0.2	0.5	0.3	0.2
Fort Wayne, IN	6.7	3.3	1.5	0.6	0.1	0.4	0.2	0.4	0.1
Fort Worth, TX	18.7	5.7	7.8	0.8	0.3	1.6	0.7	1.6	0.2
Grand Rapids, MI	6.6	2.1	1.6	0.9	0.4	0.5	0.2	0.7	0.2
Greeley, CO	8.9	0.8	6.0	0.5	0.1	0.7	0.2	0.5	0.1
Green Bay, WI	4.9	1.6	2.1	0.4	0.1	0.3	0.1	0.2	0.1
Greensboro, NC	9.1	3.0	2.4	0.8	0.4	0.5	0.5	1.4	0.1
Honolulu, HI	19.5	15.7	0.2	0.7	0.2	0.1	0.2	0.2	0.2
Houston, TX	23.5	6.0	8.4	1.1	0.8	3.8	1.6	1.5	0.3
Huntsville, AL	5.2	1.9	1.0	0.7	0.2	0.4	0.3	0.4	0.1
Indianapolis, IN	7.3	2.7	1.6	0.6	0.2	0.5	0.4	1.2	0.1
Jacksonville, FL	9.8	3.3	0.5	1.8	1.6	0.7	1.2	0.4	0.2
Kansas City, MO	6.8	2.3	2.0	0.5	0.2	0.6	0.2	0.8	0.1
Lafayette, LA	3.3	1.3	0.5	0.3	0.2	0.7	0.2	0.1	0.1
Las Cruces, NM	16.0	1.4	13.3	0.6	0.1	0.1	0.1	0.2	0.1
Las Vegas, NV	22.0	7.3	7.8	1.5	1.2	2.0	0.9	0.8	0.4
Lexington, KY	7.6	2.6	1.7	1.0	0.2	0.5	0.3	1.1	0.2
Lincoln, NE	8.0	4.2	1.1	0.9	0.3	0.4	0.2	0.7	0.1
Little Rock, AR	4.2	1.4	1.2	0.4	0.1	0.6	0.2	0.2	0.1
Los Angeles, CA	32.5	12.7	11.5	1.7	0.3	4.3	1.0	0.6	0.3
Louisville, KY	6.4	2.0	0.9	0.7	1.1	0.4	0.2	0.9	0.1

Table continued on following page.

Appendix A: Comparative Statistics

Metro Area	Any Foreign Country	Asia	Mexico	Europe	Caribbean	Central America[1]	South America	Africa	Canada
Madison, WI	7.6	3.5	1.2	1.0	0.1	0.2	0.6	0.6	0.2
Manchester, NH	10.0	3.4	0.3	1.9	1.3	0.5	0.8	0.8	0.9
Miami, FL	41.2	2.2	1.2	2.3	20.9	4.2	9.5	0.4	0.6
Midland, TX	13.7	1.9	8.5	0.3	0.8	0.4	0.4	1.0	0.4
Milwaukee, WI	7.5	2.8	2.3	1.2	0.2	0.2	0.3	0.4	0.1
Minneapolis, MN	10.7	4.1	1.1	1.0	0.1	0.4	0.6	3.0	0.2
Nashville, TN	8.5	2.6	1.9	0.7	0.3	1.1	0.4	1.3	0.2
New Haven, CT	13.4	3.2	1.1	2.9	2.1	0.6	2.1	1.0	0.3
New Orleans, LA	7.6	2.1	0.5	0.5	0.9	2.7	0.4	0.3	0.1
New York, NY	29.4	8.7	1.4	4.3	6.9	1.9	4.5	1.4	0.2
Oklahoma City, OK	7.9	2.3	3.3	0.4	0.1	0.8	0.3	0.5	0.2
Omaha, NE	7.6	2.5	2.4	0.6	0.1	0.7	0.3	1.0	0.1
Orlando, FL	19.3	3.0	1.0	1.7	5.6	1.1	6.0	0.6	0.3
Philadelphia, PA	11.2	4.6	0.8	1.9	1.4	0.5	0.7	1.2	0.2
Phoenix, AZ	14.0	3.2	7.0	1.3	0.3	0.6	0.4	0.6	0.6
Pittsburgh, PA	4.1	2.0	0.1	0.9	0.2	0.1	0.2	0.3	0.1
Portland, OR	12.7	5.1	2.9	2.4	0.2	0.5	0.3	0.6	0.4
Providence, RI	13.9	2.3	0.3	4.1	2.6	1.6	1.2	1.6	0.2
Provo, UT	7.2	1.0	2.5	0.5	0.2	0.6	1.6	0.2	0.3
Raleigh, NC	12.2	4.7	2.4	1.3	0.6	0.9	0.6	1.2	0.3
Reno, NV	14.0	4.0	5.7	1.2	0.2	1.4	0.4	0.4	0.4
Richmond, VA	8.1	3.1	0.6	1.0	0.4	1.6	0.5	0.7	0.1
Rochester, MN	8.5	3.2	0.7	1.1	0.1	0.2	0.4	2.4	0.2
Sacramento, CA	18.6	9.1	4.3	2.7	0.1	0.7	0.4	0.4	0.3
St. Louis, MO	4.8	2.2	0.5	1.1	0.1	0.2	0.2	0.5	0.1
Salem, OR	11.5	1.5	7.2	1.1	0.1	0.5	0.3	0.1	0.2
Salt Lake City, UT	12.4	3.1	4.3	1.3	0.1	0.6	1.5	0.6	0.3
San Antonio, TX	11.7	2.1	7.1	0.6	0.3	0.7	0.4	0.3	0.1
San Diego, CA	22.7	8.8	9.6	1.8	0.2	0.6	0.7	0.6	0.4
San Francisco, CA	30.7	17.8	4.7	2.8	0.2	2.5	1.1	0.9	0.5
San Jose, CA	39.3	26.2	6.7	3.1	0.1	1.0	0.8	0.7	0.5
Santa Rosa, CA	16.3	3.1	8.9	1.9	0.1	0.9	0.4	0.3	0.4
Savannah, GA	6.0	1.9	1.2	1.0	0.6	0.3	0.4	0.3	0.2
Seattle, WA	19.5	10.4	2.3	2.8	0.2	0.6	0.6	1.6	0.7
Sioux Falls, SD	6.5	1.5	0.5	0.9	0.1	0.8	0.1	2.4	0.1
Springfield, IL	2.9	1.5	0.3	0.4	0.1	0.0	0.2	0.3	0.0
Tampa, FL	14.4	2.8	1.3	2.2	4.0	0.8	2.2	0.5	0.6
Tucson, AZ	12.2	2.2	7.0	1.2	0.2	0.3	0.3	0.6	0.3
Tulsa, OK	6.7	1.9	2.8	0.5	0.1	0.5	0.3	0.3	0.1
Tuscaloosa, AL	3.3	1.2	1.1	0.3	0.1	0.4	0.1	0.1	0.1
Virginia Beach, VA	6.6	2.8	0.4	1.1	0.6	0.7	0.4	0.4	0.1
Washington, DC	22.9	8.2	0.8	1.8	1.1	4.8	2.3	3.6	0.2
Wichita, KS	7.3	2.7	2.9	0.5	0.1	0.4	0.2	0.4	0.1
Wilmington, NC	4.6	1.0	1.0	0.9	0.1	0.6	0.4	0.2	0.2
Winston-Salem, NC	7.0	1.4	2.7	0.6	0.3	0.9	0.5	0.3	0.1
Worcester, MA	12.0	3.7	0.3	2.3	1.1	0.6	2.0	1.6	0.4
U.S.	13.6	4.2	3.3	1.5	1.4	1.1	1.1	0.8	0.2

Note: Figures cover the Metropolitan Statistical Area—see Appendix B for areas included; (1) Excludes Mexico
Source: U.S. Census Bureau, 2017-2021 American Community Survey 5-Year Estimates

Marital Status: City

City	Never Married	Now Married[1]	Separated	Widowed	Divorced
Albuquerque, NM	38.2	40.1	1.4	5.5	14.8
Allentown, PA	46.7	34.6	3.9	5.0	9.8
Anchorage, AK	33.6	48.9	1.9	3.6	12.0
Ann Arbor, MI	56.5	34.4	0.4	2.4	6.3
Athens, GA	53.8	31.8	1.7	3.7	9.0
Atlanta, GA	55.1	29.0	1.8	4.0	10.1
Austin, TX	43.0	41.9	1.4	3.0	10.6
Baltimore, MD	52.3	27.2	3.1	6.0	11.4
Boise City, ID	34.8	47.0	1.0	4.4	12.9
Boston, MA	55.7	30.9	2.5	3.6	7.3
Boulder, CO	56.1	31.2	0.7	2.5	9.5
Brownsville, TX	34.2	47.6	4.3	6.2	7.8
Cape Coral, FL	24.4	53.3	1.2	7.3	13.8
Cedar Rapids, IA	35.5	45.7	1.0	5.6	12.2
Charleston, SC	40.3	43.3	1.6	5.1	9.8
Charlotte, NC	41.4	42.0	2.4	3.9	10.3
Chicago, IL	48.9	35.5	2.3	5.0	8.3
Cincinnati, OH	52.6	29.1	2.2	4.5	11.7
Clarksville, TN	30.2	50.3	2.1	3.9	13.6
Cleveland, OH	53.1	24.0	2.9	5.9	14.1
College Station, TX	59.4	31.9	0.8	2.4	5.5
Colorado Springs, CO	30.9	50.2	1.6	4.5	12.9
Columbia, MO	47.8	39.2	1.3	3.1	8.7
Columbia, SC	55.7	29.6	2.3	4.0	8.4
Columbus, OH	45.4	36.7	2.1	4.2	11.6
Dallas, TX	42.3	40.2	2.9	4.3	10.3
Davenport, IA	36.9	43.5	1.3	5.6	12.7
Denver, CO	43.4	39.6	1.6	3.5	11.8
Des Moines, IA	39.5	39.8	2.1	5.5	13.0
Durham, NC	43.1	40.7	2.2	4.1	9.9
Edison, NJ	26.3	61.4	0.8	5.3	6.1
El Paso, TX	34.9	44.8	3.6	5.7	11.1
Fargo, ND	43.0	43.4	1.0	3.9	8.6
Fort Collins, CO	46.6	40.9	0.7	3.3	8.5
Fort Wayne, IN	36.1	44.2	1.5	5.9	12.3
Fort Worth, TX	35.5	46.7	2.2	4.4	11.1
Grand Rapids, MI	45.3	38.1	1.2	4.9	10.5
Greeley, CO	35.4	46.5	1.9	4.8	11.4
Green Bay, WI	37.4	42.2	1.2	5.2	14.0
Greensboro, NC	43.8	36.8	2.6	5.9	11.0
Honolulu, HI	37.5	44.7	1.1	6.7	10.0
Houston, TX	41.1	41.2	3.0	4.5	10.2
Huntsville, AL	36.1	43.6	2.1	5.9	12.4
Indianapolis, IN	41.8	39.4	1.7	4.8	12.3
Jacksonville, FL	36.0	42.4	2.1	5.5	14.0
Kansas City, MO	39.3	40.6	2.0	4.8	13.3
Lafayette, LA	40.6	41.4	2.1	6.0	9.9
Las Cruces, NM	41.9	39.4	1.7	4.7	12.4
Las Vegas, NV	35.6	43.7	2.0	5.2	13.5
Lexington, KY	38.6	43.4	1.5	4.6	11.8
Lincoln, NE	39.7	45.3	0.9	4.0	10.1
Little Rock, AR	38.2	40.4	1.8	5.6	14.1
Los Angeles, CA	46.1	38.9	2.5	4.4	8.1
Louisville, KY	36.9	42.0	2.1	6.3	12.7
Madison, WI	50.3	37.2	0.7	3.3	8.5
Manchester, NH	39.2	39.2	1.8	5.4	14.3

Table continued on following page.

Appendix A: Comparative Statistics   A-41

City	Never Married	Now Married[1]	Separated	Widowed	Divorced
Miami, FL	39.7	37.3	3.5	6.0	13.6
Midland, TX	28.6	55.1	1.9	4.5	9.9
Milwaukee, WI	54.4	29.4	1.9	4.4	9.9
Minneapolis, MN	51.2	34.3	1.4	3.0	10.1
Nashville, TN	41.5	40.4	1.9	4.6	11.6
New Haven, CT	59.1	25.5	2.4	3.9	9.1
New Orleans, LA	49.7	29.4	2.6	5.5	12.8
New York, NY	43.8	39.9	2.9	5.3	8.1
Oklahoma City, OK	33.3	46.6	2.1	5.3	12.7
Omaha, NE	37.2	45.6	1.4	4.8	11.1
Orlando, FL	43.2	37.8	2.4	3.9	12.7
Philadelphia, PA	50.5	31.5	3.0	5.7	9.2
Phoenix, AZ	39.1	42.5	2.1	4.0	12.2
Pittsburgh, PA	53.1	30.4	1.9	5.4	9.2
Portland, OR	41.6	41.1	1.3	3.6	12.4
Providence, RI	53.6	31.9	2.0	4.2	8.4
Provo, UT	48.8	43.8	0.9	2.2	4.3
Raleigh, NC	43.2	40.0	2.1	3.8	11.0
Reno, NV	36.5	42.1	1.9	4.9	14.8
Richmond, VA	51.2	29.4	2.8	5.2	11.4
Rochester, MN	33.3	51.7	1.2	4.7	9.2
Sacramento, CA	40.5	41.1	2.6	4.8	11.2
St. Louis, MO	48.8	30.7	2.9	5.2	12.3
Salem, OR	34.6	45.1	1.6	5.2	13.4
Salt Lake City, UT	44.4	40.3	1.3	3.1	10.8
San Antonio, TX	38.3	41.7	2.8	5.1	12.0
San Diego, CA	40.1	44.8	1.6	4.0	9.5
San Francisco, CA	46.0	40.1	1.4	4.5	8.0
San Jose, CA	36.2	50.3	1.5	4.2	7.8
Santa Rosa, CA	33.8	46.4	2.0	5.4	12.3
Savannah, GA	47.5	32.1	2.6	5.6	12.2
Seattle, WA	45.5	40.3	1.2	3.0	10.0
Sioux Falls, SD	34.5	48.6	1.2	4.3	11.4
Springfield, IL	37.6	39.5	1.6	6.2	15.1
Tampa, FL	40.3	39.1	2.5	5.0	13.1
Tucson, AZ	42.0	36.7	2.2	5.2	13.9
Tulsa, OK	35.0	42.4	2.4	5.7	14.4
Tuscaloosa, AL	52.3	32.6	1.8	4.0	9.4
Virginia Beach, VA	30.9	50.8	2.1	5.1	11.2
Washington, DC	55.8	30.9	1.7	3.5	8.2
Wichita, KS	33.7	45.6	1.9	5.0	13.8
Wilmington, NC	41.6	39.1	2.2	5.3	11.7
Winston-Salem, NC	41.9	39.1	2.6	5.4	11.0
Worcester, MA	47.8	34.0	2.0	4.9	11.3
U.S.	33.8	48.0	1.8	5.6	10.8

Note: Figures are percentages and cover the population 15 years of age and older; (1) Excludes separated
Source: U.S. Census Bureau, 2017-2021 American Community Survey 5-Year Estimates

Appendix A: Comparative Statistics

Marital Status: Metro Area

Metro Area	Never Married	Now Married[1]	Separated	Widowed	Divorced
Albuquerque, NM	35.6	43.5	1.4	5.5	14.1
Allentown, PA	32.7	49.3	1.9	6.2	9.9
Anchorage, AK	32.2	50.5	1.8	3.8	11.8
Ann Arbor, MI	43.1	44.4	0.7	3.6	8.1
Athens, GA	43.0	41.5	1.6	4.4	9.5
Atlanta, GA	35.7	47.6	1.8	4.4	10.6
Austin, TX	35.5	49.4	1.4	3.5	10.3
Baltimore, MD	36.0	46.3	1.9	5.7	10.0
Boise City, ID	29.1	53.3	1.1	4.3	12.2
Boston, MA	37.3	47.6	1.6	4.9	8.7
Boulder, CO	38.5	45.5	0.9	3.7	11.4
Brownsville, TX	33.6	48.2	3.5	6.3	8.4
Cape Coral, FL	25.9	51.9	1.5	7.9	12.8
Cedar Rapids, IA	30.6	51.3	1.1	5.5	11.5
Charleston, SC	33.8	48.5	2.1	5.3	10.3
Charlotte, NC	33.1	49.3	2.3	5.0	10.3
Chicago, IL	37.2	47.0	1.6	5.2	8.9
Cincinnati, OH	32.8	48.7	1.5	5.6	11.4
Clarksville, TN	29.6	51.1	1.9	4.9	12.5
Cleveland, OH	35.8	44.4	1.5	6.3	11.9
College Station, TX	45.5	40.1	1.8	4.1	8.5
Colorado Springs, CO	29.5	53.3	1.4	4.0	11.7
Columbia, MO	40.0	44.8	1.3	4.0	9.8
Columbia, SC	36.3	45.0	2.6	5.6	10.6
Columbus, OH	34.8	47.6	1.7	4.8	11.1
Dallas, TX	32.8	50.8	1.9	4.2	10.3
Davenport, IA	30.5	49.9	1.4	6.2	12.0
Denver, CO	33.6	49.8	1.4	3.8	11.5
Des Moines, IA	30.9	51.7	1.2	4.9	11.2
Durham, NC	37.3	46.1	2.0	4.8	9.8
Edison, NJ	38.1	46.1	2.2	5.5	8.1
El Paso, TX	34.9	45.8	3.5	5.4	10.4
Fargo, ND	37.5	49.1	0.9	4.0	8.5
Fort Collins, CO	34.5	51.3	0.8	4.0	9.4
Fort Wayne, IN	31.5	50.0	1.3	5.6	11.6
Fort Worth, TX	32.8	50.8	1.9	4.2	10.3
Grand Rapids, MI	32.2	52.1	0.9	4.5	10.3
Greeley, CO	28.7	55.2	1.4	4.0	10.7
Green Bay, WI	30.6	52.2	0.7	5.1	11.4
Greensboro, NC	34.1	45.5	2.8	6.2	11.4
Honolulu, HI	34.4	49.7	1.2	6.0	8.7
Houston, TX	33.8	50.2	2.3	4.3	9.4
Huntsville, AL	29.9	51.5	1.6	5.5	11.4
Indianapolis, IN	33.0	49.2	1.3	4.9	11.5
Jacksonville, FL	31.7	47.7	1.8	5.6	13.2
Kansas City, MO	30.8	50.5	1.5	5.0	12.1
Lafayette, LA	33.8	47.9	2.1	5.6	10.6
Las Cruces, NM	38.8	43.7	2.0	4.9	10.7
Las Vegas, NV	35.2	44.3	2.1	5.0	13.4
Lexington, KY	34.1	47.0	1.5	5.1	12.3
Lincoln, NE	37.3	48.1	0.8	4.1	9.7
Little Rock, AR	30.6	48.1	1.9	5.8	13.6
Los Angeles, CA	40.3	44.5	2.0	4.7	8.4
Louisville, KY	31.9	47.5	1.8	6.0	12.9
Madison, WI	37.1	48.2	0.8	4.1	9.9
Manchester, NH	31.3	50.2	1.2	5.1	12.1

Table continued on following page.

Metro Area	Never Married	Now Married[1]	Separated	Widowed	Divorced
Miami, FL	34.1	44.4	2.5	6.2	12.9
Midland, TX	27.9	55.4	1.7	4.5	10.5
Milwaukee, WI	37.4	46.2	1.1	5.1	10.1
Minneapolis, MN	33.7	51.0	1.0	4.1	10.1
Nashville, TN	32.6	50.0	1.5	4.9	11.0
New Haven, CT	38.2	43.7	1.6	5.7	10.8
New Orleans, LA	37.8	41.7	2.3	6.0	12.1
New York, NY	38.1	46.1	2.2	5.5	8.1
Oklahoma City, OK	31.4	49.2	1.8	5.4	12.3
Omaha, NE	32.2	51.3	1.2	4.7	10.7
Orlando, FL	35.2	46.2	2.0	5.0	11.6
Philadelphia, PA	37.3	45.8	2.0	5.7	9.2
Phoenix, AZ	33.7	48.2	1.6	4.8	11.7
Pittsburgh, PA	32.6	48.7	1.7	6.9	10.1
Portland, OR	32.8	49.6	1.3	4.3	12.0
Providence, RI	36.5	45.0	1.5	5.9	11.1
Provo, UT	33.0	58.1	0.8	2.5	5.5
Raleigh, NC	32.2	51.9	2.0	4.2	9.7
Reno, NV	32.4	47.4	1.7	4.9	13.7
Richmond, VA	34.7	46.7	2.3	5.6	10.7
Rochester, MN	29.0	56.0	0.9	4.7	9.3
Sacramento, CA	33.9	48.6	2.0	4.9	10.6
St. Louis, MO	32.2	48.7	1.7	5.9	11.4
Salem, OR	31.8	48.7	1.7	5.3	12.6
Salt Lake City, UT	32.7	52.3	1.4	3.6	10.1
San Antonio, TX	34.0	47.6	2.4	4.9	11.1
San Diego, CA	36.2	47.9	1.6	4.4	9.8
San Francisco, CA	36.6	48.6	1.4	4.6	8.7
San Jose, CA	34.4	52.7	1.4	4.1	7.4
Santa Rosa, CA	32.3	48.7	1.5	5.1	12.5
Savannah, GA	35.7	45.2	2.3	5.3	11.7
Seattle, WA	33.2	50.7	1.3	4.0	10.8
Sioux Falls, SD	30.6	53.2	1.0	4.4	10.8
Springfield, IL	32.4	46.6	1.3	6.1	13.6
Tampa, FL	31.3	46.5	1.9	6.8	13.5
Tucson, AZ	34.3	45.5	1.7	5.6	12.9
Tulsa, OK	29.1	49.8	1.9	6.1	13.0
Tuscaloosa, AL	39.5	43.1	1.7	5.4	10.3
Virginia Beach, VA	33.6	47.7	2.4	5.5	10.8
Washington, DC	36.2	49.2	1.7	4.2	8.7
Wichita, KS	30.3	50.2	1.4	5.4	12.7
Wilmington, NC	33.0	48.2	2.2	5.7	11.0
Winston-Salem, NC	31.0	48.9	2.4	6.4	11.3
Worcester, MA	34.4	47.7	1.5	5.4	11.0
U.S.	33.8	48.0	1.8	5.6	10.8

Note: Figures are percentages and cover the population 15 years of age and older; Figures cover the Metropolitan Statistical Area;
(1) Excludes separated
Source: U.S. Census Bureau, 2017-2021 American Community Survey 5-Year Estimates

Disability by Age: City

City	All Ages	Under 18 Years Old	18 to 64 Years Old	65 Years and Over
Albuquerque, NM	14.2	4.3	12.3	35.3
Allentown, PA	16.0	9.9	15.3	33.5
Anchorage, AK	11.1	3.8	10.0	33.3
Ann Arbor, MI	7.1	4.2	4.9	24.0
Athens, GA	11.8	6.1	9.6	35.6
Atlanta, GA	11.4	4.7	9.3	35.0
Austin, TX	8.7	4.1	7.4	28.5
Baltimore, MD	15.9	6.0	14.1	39.0
Boise City, ID	11.3	4.2	9.4	29.7
Boston, MA	11.8	6.3	8.7	38.3
Boulder, CO	6.6	2.9	4.7	23.1
Brownsville, TX	10.6	4.2	7.8	40.6
Cape Coral, FL	13.4	3.8	9.7	29.3
Cedar Rapids, IA	10.0	3.1	8.1	27.2
Charleston, SC	9.3	2.9	6.2	30.5
Charlotte, NC	7.8	2.6	6.5	27.9
Chicago, IL	10.9	3.3	8.8	34.8
Cincinnati, OH	12.8	5.2	11.8	32.0
Clarksville, TN	15.7	6.1	16.4	43.8
Cleveland, OH	19.5	8.4	18.5	41.9
College Station, TX	6.8	5.1	5.3	27.8
Colorado Springs, CO	13.1	5.2	12.1	30.9
Columbia, MO	11.4	4.6	9.8	33.9
Columbia, SC	12.8	5.1	10.7	38.5
Columbus, OH	11.6	5.2	10.3	34.5
Dallas, TX	10.5	4.5	9.0	34.3
Davenport, IA	13.1	5.2	11.3	31.6
Denver, CO	9.7	3.5	7.6	32.3
Des Moines, IA	13.7	5.3	12.8	35.6
Durham, NC	9.6	3.0	7.6	31.7
Edison, NJ	7.6	4.2	4.5	26.9
El Paso, TX	13.6	5.2	11.1	42.1
Fargo, ND	10.2	5.1	7.7	32.0
Fort Collins, CO	8.4	2.7	6.8	28.0
Fort Wayne, IN	13.9	5.5	12.8	34.2
Fort Worth, TX	9.7	3.4	8.6	34.4
Grand Rapids, MI	11.7	3.9	11.0	30.4
Greeley, CO	11.9	3.4	11.1	33.5
Green Bay, WI	13.8	6.7	12.2	34.9
Greensboro, NC	11.1	4.9	8.9	32.1
Honolulu, HI	11.5	3.1	6.9	32.4
Houston, TX	9.9	3.9	8.0	34.7
Huntsville, AL	13.5	4.4	11.3	33.7
Indianapolis, IN	13.5	5.3	12.4	35.5
Jacksonville, FL	13.1	4.8	11.3	35.3
Kansas City, MO	12.5	3.9	11.1	34.2
Lafayette, LA	12.1	2.8	9.7	34.5
Las Cruces, NM	15.9	7.9	13.6	38.0
Las Vegas, NV	12.5	4.0	10.4	34.8
Lexington, KY	12.5	4.9	10.8	33.2
Lincoln, NE	10.7	4.4	8.9	30.0
Little Rock, AR	13.2	4.7	11.6	34.5
Los Angeles, CA	10.3	3.1	7.5	36.6
Louisville, KY	14.3	4.5	12.8	35.6
Madison, WI	8.3	4.4	6.4	25.0

Table continued on following page.

City	All Ages	Under 18 Years Old	18 to 64 Years Old	65 Years and Over
Manchester, NH	13.9	6.6	11.8	34.7
Miami, FL	11.9	4.5	7.6	37.2
Midland, TX	9.8	2.7	8.1	41.1
Milwaukee, WI	12.5	5.0	11.6	36.6
Minneapolis, MN	11.0	4.9	9.8	32.2
Nashville, TN	11.2	4.6	9.1	34.5
New Haven, CT	10.3	4.2	8.8	33.4
New Orleans, LA	13.7	4.7	11.8	34.0
New York, NY	10.9	3.6	8.0	33.9
Oklahoma City, OK	13.1	4.3	11.9	36.6
Omaha, NE	10.9	3.6	9.6	30.9
Orlando, FL	9.6	4.9	7.7	32.0
Philadelphia, PA	16.9	7.0	15.0	42.0
Phoenix, AZ	10.8	4.2	9.7	32.9
Pittsburgh, PA	14.3	7.7	11.3	35.4
Portland, OR	12.1	4.8	9.9	33.4
Providence, RI	13.6	5.9	12.4	36.4
Provo, UT	9.6	4.9	8.1	41.8
Raleigh, NC	9.0	4.2	7.2	30.1
Reno, NV	11.2	3.2	9.0	31.1
Richmond, VA	14.2	6.5	12.1	35.7
Rochester, MN	10.3	4.2	7.9	30.7
Sacramento, CA	11.8	3.3	9.6	36.7
St. Louis, MO	15.4	6.2	13.3	38.5
Salem, OR	15.2	6.3	13.9	35.5
Salt Lake City, UT	11.0	4.0	9.4	32.6
San Antonio, TX	15.0	6.3	13.2	41.6
San Diego, CA	9.2	3.3	6.5	31.3
San Francisco, CA	10.1	2.6	6.3	33.5
San Jose, CA	8.9	3.1	6.0	33.1
Santa Rosa, CA	11.7	3.2	9.5	29.7
Savannah, GA	15.7	6.4	13.1	42.3
Seattle, WA	9.3	2.5	7.2	30.6
Sioux Falls, SD	10.1	3.4	9.0	28.9
Springfield, IL	14.7	6.2	13.0	31.2
Tampa, FL	12.1	3.7	9.6	38.9
Tucson, AZ	15.0	5.8	12.8	37.5
Tulsa, OK	14.2	4.7	13.1	34.6
Tuscaloosa, AL	9.9	2.9	8.3	28.0
Virginia Beach, VA	11.5	4.3	9.4	31.3
Washington, DC	11.2	4.4	9.2	33.7
Wichita, KS	14.8	5.7	13.7	35.4
Wilmington, NC	13.0	5.1	10.0	32.0
Winston-Salem, NC	11.3	3.5	9.9	30.6
Worcester, MA	14.3	4.7	12.9	37.3
U.S.	12.6	4.4	10.3	33.4

Note: Figures show percent of the civilian noninstitutionalized population that reported having a disability. Disability status is determined from from six types of difficulty: vision, hearing, cognitive, ambulatory, self-care, and independent living. For children under 5 years old, hearing and vision difficulty are used to determine disability status. For children between the ages of 5 and 14, disability status is determined from hearing, vision, cognitive, ambulatory, and self-care difficulties. For people aged 15 years and older, they are considered to have a disability if they have difficulty with any one of the six difficulty types.
Source: U.S. Census Bureau, 2017-2021 American Community Survey 5-Year Estimates

Disability by Age: Metro Area

Metro Area	All Ages	Under 18 Years Old	18 to 64 Years Old	65 Years and Over
Albuquerque, NM	15.1	4.2	13.2	36.3
Allentown, PA	12.7	5.5	10.2	30.3
Anchorage, AK	11.7	3.8	10.7	33.9
Ann Arbor, MI	9.7	3.8	7.7	27.2
Athens, GA	12.5	5.6	10.2	34.4
Atlanta, GA	10.3	4.0	8.6	31.5
Austin, TX	9.3	3.8	7.8	29.4
Baltimore, MD	11.8	4.6	9.7	30.8
Boise City, ID	12.1	4.4	10.6	31.6
Boston, MA	10.5	4.2	7.8	30.2
Boulder, CO	8.4	3.3	6.1	25.5
Brownsville, TX	12.2	5.6	9.5	39.0
Cape Coral, FL	13.6	3.9	9.8	26.9
Cedar Rapids, IA	10.3	4.1	8.1	27.2
Charleston, SC	11.6	3.9	9.2	32.1
Charlotte, NC	10.4	3.5	8.5	31.5
Chicago, IL	10.1	3.3	7.9	30.3
Cincinnati, OH	12.4	5.0	10.6	31.8
Clarksville, TN	16.7	7.1	16.3	42.9
Cleveland, OH	14.0	5.0	11.6	32.6
College Station, TX	9.9	5.5	7.6	33.3
Colorado Springs, CO	12.5	5.1	11.5	30.8
Columbia, MO	12.8	4.9	11.1	33.8
Columbia, SC	14.2	4.7	12.3	36.3
Columbus, OH	11.9	5.0	10.1	32.7
Dallas, TX	9.5	3.8	8.0	32.1
Davenport, IA	12.7	5.2	10.4	30.1
Denver, CO	9.7	3.5	7.8	29.8
Des Moines, IA	10.5	3.7	9.0	30.4
Durham, NC	11.0	3.4	8.6	30.7
Edison, NJ	10.1	3.3	7.3	30.5
El Paso, TX	13.3	5.4	10.9	43.0
Fargo, ND	9.8	4.0	7.8	31.7
Fort Collins, CO	10.0	2.7	7.7	28.8
Fort Wayne, IN	12.4	4.7	11.0	32.0
Fort Worth, TX	9.5	3.8	8.0	32.1
Grand Rapids, MI	10.9	3.8	9.4	29.8
Greeley, CO	10.7	3.6	9.1	34.7
Green Bay, WI	11.3	4.5	9.7	27.7
Greensboro, NC	13.1	4.9	10.9	32.7
Honolulu, HI	11.2	3.0	7.5	33.0
Houston, TX	9.6	3.8	7.9	32.6
Huntsville, AL	13.1	4.0	11.1	35.4
Indianapolis, IN	12.3	4.8	10.8	32.9
Jacksonville, FL	13.0	4.6	10.9	33.2
Kansas City, MO	11.7	4.0	9.9	32.2
Lafayette, LA	14.1	4.9	12.4	37.8
Las Cruces, NM	15.2	6.6	13.4	35.7
Las Vegas, NV	12.1	4.0	9.9	33.9
Lexington, KY	13.5	5.2	11.8	34.2
Lincoln, NE	10.7	4.1	8.8	30.4
Little Rock, AR	15.6	5.8	13.8	38.4
Los Angeles, CA	9.8	3.2	7.0	33.0
Louisville, KY	13.9	4.4	12.1	35.1
Madison, WI	8.9	4.2	6.9	24.6

Table continued on following page.

Metro Area	All Ages	Under 18 Years Old	18 to 64 Years Old	65 Years and Over
Manchester, NH	11.6	4.7	9.5	29.8
Miami, FL	10.8	3.7	7.2	31.1
Midland, TX	9.9	2.6	8.2	41.3
Milwaukee, WI	11.0	3.9	8.9	29.8
Minneapolis, MN	10.0	3.9	8.2	28.5
Nashville, TN	11.6	4.0	9.7	33.6
New Haven, CT	11.6	3.7	9.2	29.9
New Orleans, LA	14.9	5.4	12.7	36.4
New York, NY	10.1	3.3	7.3	30.5
Oklahoma City, OK	14.0	4.5	12.4	38.4
Omaha, NE	11.0	3.6	9.5	31.4
Orlando, FL	12.3	5.7	9.6	33.8
Philadelphia, PA	12.7	5.1	10.5	32.2
Phoenix, AZ	11.8	4.3	9.7	31.4
Pittsburgh, PA	14.4	5.7	11.3	32.5
Portland, OR	12.1	4.1	10.0	32.3
Providence, RI	13.7	5.4	11.5	31.9
Provo, UT	8.3	3.6	8.0	31.9
Raleigh, NC	9.7	3.9	7.9	30.4
Reno, NV	11.7	4.0	9.2	30.9
Richmond, VA	12.8	5.3	10.5	32.1
Rochester, MN	10.0	3.8	7.6	28.6
Sacramento, CA	11.5	3.4	9.0	33.7
St. Louis, MO	13.0	4.7	10.8	32.4
Salem, OR	14.9	5.3	13.0	36.5
Salt Lake City, UT	9.5	3.9	8.4	30.0
San Antonio, TX	14.1	5.9	12.3	38.7
San Diego, CA	10.0	3.3	7.4	31.7
San Francisco, CA	9.6	3.1	6.7	30.0
San Jose, CA	8.3	2.7	5.5	30.7
Santa Rosa, CA	11.6	3.4	8.8	28.4
Savannah, GA	14.2	4.9	12.5	36.6
Seattle, WA	10.8	3.9	8.7	32.8
Sioux Falls, SD	9.9	3.2	8.7	28.5
Springfield, IL	13.7	6.2	11.6	30.4
Tampa, FL	14.1	5.0	10.8	33.6
Tucson, AZ	14.9	5.3	12.1	33.4
Tulsa, OK	14.7	4.8	13.1	37.4
Tuscaloosa, AL	14.3	4.5	12.5	37.4
Virginia Beach, VA	13.3	5.3	11.3	33.7
Washington, DC	8.8	3.3	6.8	28.2
Wichita, KS	14.5	5.8	12.9	35.7
Wilmington, NC	12.9	4.5	10.6	30.3
Winston-Salem, NC	13.5	4.2	11.2	33.6
Worcester, MA	12.4	4.3	10.5	31.6
U.S.	12.6	4.4	10.3	33.4

Note: Figures show percent of the civilian noninstitutionalized population that reported having a disability. Disability status is determined from from six types of difficulty: vision, hearing, cognitive, ambulatory, self-care, and independent living. For children under 5 years old, hearing and vision difficulty are used to determine disability status. For children between the ages of 5 and 14, disability status is determined from hearing, vision, cognitive, ambulatory, and self-care difficulties. For people aged 15 years and older, they are considered to have a disability if they have difficulty with any one of the six difficulty types; Figures cover the Metropolitan Statistical Area
Source: U.S. Census Bureau, 2017-2021 American Community Survey 5-Year Estimates

Appendix A: Comparative Statistics

Religious Groups by Family

Area[1]	Catholic	Baptist	Methodist	LDS[2]	Pentecostal	Lutheran	Islam	Adventist	Other
Albuquerque, NM	32.6	3.2	0.9	2.7	1.7	0.4	0.7	1.5	10.8
Allentown, PA	18.6	0.4	2.3	0.4	0.6	5.4	0.7	1.2	11.0
Anchorage, AK	4.9	3.4	1.0	5.1	1.7	1.5	0.1	1.7	16.3
Ann Arbor, MI	9.7	2.0	2.4	0.8	1.5	2.3	2.2	0.9	10.0
Athens, GA	6.4	12.8	5.7	1.0	2.4	0.3	0.2	1.3	7.9
Atlanta, GA	10.7	14.7	6.7	0.8	2.0	0.4	1.9	1.9	12.4
Austin, TX	18.8	6.5	2.2	1.3	0.7	1.1	1.0	1.0	9.9
Baltimore, MD	12.4	3.2	4.4	0.6	1.2	1.4	3.3	1.2	11.7
Boise City, ID	13.0	0.8	2.5	15.0	1.6	0.8	0.3	1.7	10.0
Boston, MA	37.0	1.0	0.7	0.5	0.7	0.2	2.2	0.9	7.1
Boulder, CO	16.0	0.3	0.7	0.7	0.5	1.7	0.4	0.9	15.2
Brownsville, TX	36.8	2.8	0.7	1.2	1.0	0.2	0.1	2.5	9.4
Cape Coral, FL	18.8	2.5	1.7	0.6	3.0	0.7	0.2	2.0	12.2
Cedar Rapids, IA	16.8	1.0	5.3	1.0	1.3	8.1	1.3	0.6	9.6
Charleston, SC	11.5	7.7	8.0	0.8	1.9	0.7	0.2	1.0	12.8
Charlotte, NC	12.1	13.9	7.0	0.7	2.2	1.1	1.7	1.4	15.9
Chicago, IL	28.6	3.4	1.4	0.3	1.5	2.1	4.7	1.1	9.2
Cincinnati, OH	17.0	5.7	2.3	0.6	1.5	0.8	1.1	0.7	21.8
Clarksville, TN	4.6	23.2	4.4	1.4	3.2	0.5	0.1	0.8	12.4
Cleveland, OH	26.1	4.3	2.3	0.4	1.5	1.8	1.1	1.3	16.8
College Station, TX	17.2	10.6	4.3	1.7	0.5	1.1	0.6	0.5	6.8
Colorado Springs, CO	16.4	2.6	1.3	3.0	1.0	1.2	0.1	1.0	16.2
Columbia, MO	7.1	9.0	3.5	1.7	1.1	1.6	1.4	1.2	12.4
Columbia, SC	6.6	15.1	8.5	1.2	3.8	2.3	0.3	1.3	15.4
Columbus, OH	11.7	3.4	3.0	0.8	1.9	1.7	2.1	0.9	17.5
Dallas, TX	14.2	14.3	4.7	1.4	2.2	0.5	1.8	1.3	13.8
Davenport, IA	13.2	3.2	3.6	0.8	1.5	6.6	0.7	0.8	6.7
Denver, CO	16.1	1.5	1.0	2.1	0.6	1.4	0.3	1.1	10.4
Des Moines, IA	12.1	1.8	4.0	0.9	2.5	6.6	1.6	0.8	8.7
Durham, NC	8.5	12.3	6.5	0.9	1.3	0.3	1.5	1.1	13.7
Edison, NJ	32.5	1.7	1.2	0.3	0.9	0.5	4.5	1.4	10.6
El Paso, TX	47.9	2.5	0.4	1.2	1.1	0.2	0.1	2.1	6.9
Fargo, ND	14.2	0.2	1.0	0.6	1.3	24.0	<0.1	0.6	8.1
Fort Collins, CO	9.9	1.2	1.3	4.0	2.7	2.5	<0.1	1.2	12.1
Fort Wayne, IN	13.1	8.1	3.9	0.4	1.1	7.1	1.0	0.9	17.6
Fort Worth, TX	14.2	14.3	4.7	1.4	2.2	0.5	1.8	1.3	13.8
Grand Rapids, MI	13.1	1.3	1.8	0.4	1.3	1.8	0.8	1.2	19.9
Greeley, CO	14.1	0.5	0.9	2.9	1.1	1.2	<0.1	1.1	6.1
Green Bay, WI	31.8	0.3	1.4	0.5	1.1	10.8	0.4	0.9	7.0
Greensboro, NC	7.9	10.0	8.0	0.7	2.8	0.4	1.5	1.4	17.8
Honolulu, HI	18.0	1.4	0.5	4.1	2.6	0.2	<0.1	1.9	9.8
Houston, TX	18.3	13.1	3.7	1.2	1.6	0.7	1.7	1.5	13.1
Huntsville, AL	7.5	23.6	6.6	1.4	1.2	0.4	0.8	2.7	17.5
Indianapolis, IN	11.5	6.2	3.3	0.7	1.3	1.1	1.1	1.0	17.4
Jacksonville, FL	13.0	14.5	3.0	1.0	1.4	0.4	0.6	1.3	20.5
Kansas City, MO	11.3	9.1	5.0	1.6	2.7	1.7	1.0	1.0	12.1
Lafayette, LA	44.3	9.3	2.0	0.4	1.8	0.1	0.1	0.8	7.0
Las Cruces, NM	19.3	4.1	1.6	2.5	2.5	0.4	0.6	2.2	4.2
Las Vegas, NV	26.2	1.9	0.3	5.8	1.5	0.6	0.3	1.3	5.5
Lexington, KY	5.8	14.9	5.5	1.2	1.6	0.3	0.5	1.2	16.6
Lincoln, NE	13.2	1.0	5.7	1.2	3.1	9.1	0.1	1.8	10.0
Little Rock, AR	4.9	23.5	6.2	0.8	3.7	0.4	0.4	1.0	13.6
Los Angeles, CA	31.1	2.6	0.8	1.5	2.4	0.4	1.4	1.5	9.1
Louisville, KY	11.9	14.5	3.2	0.8	0.9	0.5	1.0	1.0	12.4
Madison, WI	14.4	0.5	2.0	0.7	0.2	9.2	1.2	0.7	8.4
Manchester, NH	16.3	0.6	0.6	0.6	0.3	0.3	0.1	0.8	8.1

Table continued on following page.

Area[1]	Catholic	Baptist	Methodist	LDS[2]	Pentecostal	Lutheran	Islam	Adventist	Other
Miami, FL	23.8	5.1	0.9	0.5	1.3	0.3	0.8	2.4	11.1
Midland, TX	15.4	25.5	2.5	2.0	1.2	0.3	0.4	1.3	16.5
Milwaukee, WI	24.5	3.0	1.0	0.4	2.8	9.1	2.8	0.9	10.7
Minneapolis, MN	19.8	0.8	1.4	0.5	2.5	10.7	2.9	0.7	7.4
Nashville, TN	6.2	16.4	4.8	0.9	1.6	0.4	0.8	1.3	19.4
New Haven, CT	29.9	1.4	1.2	0.4	1.2	0.4	0.9	1.2	9.9
New Orleans, LA	42.1	9.3	2.5	0.5	2.1	0.5	1.4	1.0	8.0
New York, NY	32.5	1.7	1.2	0.3	0.9	0.5	4.5	1.4	10.6
Oklahoma City, OK	10.0	16.6	6.2	1.3	3.9	0.6	0.6	0.9	21.4
Omaha, NE	19.9	2.8	2.8	1.6	1.0	6.1	0.2	1.0	9.0
Orlando, FL	17.6	5.7	2.1	0.9	2.7	0.6	1.3	2.8	14.6
Philadelphia, PA	26.8	3.3	2.4	0.3	1.0	1.2	2.6	1.0	10.5
Phoenix, AZ	22.9	1.7	0.6	6.2	1.5	1.0	1.9	1.5	9.3
Pittsburgh, PA	30.6	1.9	4.3	0.4	1.3	2.5	0.6	0.6	12.5
Portland, OR	11.8	0.8	0.6	3.3	1.4	1.1	0.2	2.0	14.4
Providence, RI	37.9	0.9	0.6	0.3	0.6	0.3	0.5	0.9	6.1
Provo, UT	4.9	0.1	<0.1	82.6	0.1	<0.1	0.3	0.3	0.4
Raleigh, NC	12.4	9.8	5.4	1.2	1.9	0.7	3.2	1.5	12.8
Reno, NV	24.4	1.4	0.5	4.0	0.9	0.5	0.3	1.4	5.3
Richmond, VA	12.3	14.2	4.8	0.9	3.2	0.5	2.1	1.2	14.8
Rochester, MN	15.6	0.4	2.8	1.5	1.9	19.3	1.0	0.7	10.1
Sacramento, CA	17.1	1.9	1.1	3.1	2.2	0.6	1.9	1.9	8.2
St. Louis, MO	21.2	8.6	2.9	0.7	1.4	3.2	1.3	0.8	11.1
Salem, OR	19.5	0.5	0.6	3.8	2.9	1.2	n/a	2.5	10.7
Salt Lake City, UT	9.0	0.6	0.2	52.0	0.7	0.2	1.6	0.7	2.6
San Antonio, TX	27.3	6.4	2.1	1.4	1.6	1.1	0.5	1.5	11.0
San Diego, CA	22.9	1.5	0.6	2.1	1.0	0.6	1.5	1.9	9.4
San Francisco, CA	21.5	2.2	0.9	1.5	1.4	0.4	2.0	1.0	7.7
San Jose, CA	27.2	1.2	0.6	1.4	0.9	0.4	2.0	1.3	11.4
Santa Rosa, CA	23.5	1.1	0.5	1.4	0.5	0.5	0.2	1.8	6.9
Savannah, GA	5.5	11.9	4.8	0.8	1.5	1.1	0.2	1.4	12.3
Seattle, WA	11.0	1.0	0.7	2.6	2.8	1.2	0.6	1.4	19.8
Sioux Falls, SD	13.1	0.7	2.9	0.7	1.7	16.4	0.1	0.6	20.3
Springfield, IL	15.2	4.7	4.3	0.5	1.5	4.7	0.5	0.8	14.6
Tampa, FL	23.1	6.3	2.9	0.5	1.9	0.6	0.7	1.8	12.1
Tucson, AZ	18.9	1.9	0.6	2.8	1.3	1.1	1.0	1.4	9.7
Tulsa, OK	5.6	15.5	7.7	1.2	2.5	0.5	0.5	1.2	22.2
Tuscaloosa, AL	2.6	25.1	6.2	0.6	1.5	0.1	0.3	0.7	13.3
Virginia Beach, VA	8.3	9.5	4.8	0.7	2.0	0.5	1.0	0.9	16.1
Washington, DC	16.1	6.0	4.1	1.1	1.3	0.8	3.3	1.5	12.6
Wichita, KS	12.7	23.5	4.5	1.5	1.4	1.3	0.1	1.1	15.0
Wilmington, NC	13.2	9.9	8.1	1.0	1.0	0.7	0.7	1.4	12.6
Winston-Salem, NC	9.3	12.8	11.4	0.5	1.0	0.6	0.8	1.4	22.5
Worcester, MA	30.1	0.8	0.8	0.3	1.0	0.4	0.6	1.4	7.1
U.S.	18.7	7.3	3.0	2.0	1.8	1.7	1.3	1.3	11.6

Note: Figures are the number of adherents as a percentage of the total population; (1) Figures cover the Metropolitan Statistical Area; (2) Church of Jesus Christ of Latter-day Saints
Source: 2020 U.S. Religion Census, Association of Statisticians of American Religious Bodies; The Association of Religion Data Archives (ARDA)

Religious Groups by Tradition

Area	Catholic	Evangelical Protestant	Mainline Protestant	Black Protestant	Islam	Judaism	Hinduism	Orthodox	Buddhism
Albuquerque, NM	32.6	13.4	2.2	0.5	0.7	0.2	0.2	0.1	0.6
Allentown, PA	18.6	6.2	11.9	0.2	0.7	0.5	0.6	0.4	0.1
Anchorage, AK	4.9	19.2	2.4	0.9	0.1	0.1	0.1	0.5	1.3
Ann Arbor, MI	9.7	8.1	5.6	2.5	2.2	0.8	0.5	0.4	0.3
Athens, GA	6.4	19.1	7.2	2.6	0.2	0.2	0.2	0.1	<0.1
Atlanta, GA	10.7	22.3	7.4	5.3	1.9	0.5	0.7	0.3	0.2
Austin, TX	18.8	13.5	4.0	1.7	1.0	0.2	0.6	0.2	0.3
Baltimore, MD	12.4	10.6	5.9	3.3	3.3	1.7	0.1	0.5	0.1
Boise City, ID	13.0	11.9	3.9	<0.1	0.3	0.1	0.2	0.1	0.1
Boston, MA	37.0	3.4	3.2	0.3	2.2	1.1	0.3	0.9	0.4
Boulder, CO	16.0	12.7	3.4	n/a	0.4	0.7	0.5	0.2	1.0
Brownsville, TX	36.8	13.1	1.2	0.1	0.1	n/a	n/a	n/a	n/a
Cape Coral, FL	18.8	16.4	3.0	0.6	0.2	0.2	0.2	0.1	0.1
Cedar Rapids, IA	16.8	11.9	12.2	0.4	1.3	0.1	0.7	0.1	<0.1
Charleston, SC	11.5	17.1	6.8	6.6	0.2	0.4	<0.1	0.2	n/a
Charlotte, NC	12.1	26.4	9.5	3.4	1.7	0.2	0.2	0.4	0.1
Chicago, IL	28.6	8.2	3.7	3.6	4.7	0.7	0.4	0.7	0.4
Cincinnati, OH	17.0	24.9	4.1	2.0	1.1	0.4	0.3	0.3	0.1
Clarksville, TN	4.6	35.7	4.8	3.4	0.1	n/a	n/a	0.1	n/a
Cleveland, OH	26.1	15.1	5.6	3.5	1.1	1.3	0.3	0.8	0.2
College Station, TX	17.2	16.1	5.3	1.8	0.6	n/a	0.1	0.1	n/a
Colorado Springs, CO	16.4	18.3	2.9	0.9	0.1	<0.1	<0.1	0.1	0.3
Columbia, MO	7.1	19.4	6.3	1.9	1.4	0.2	0.1	0.1	<0.1
Columbia, SC	6.6	27.9	10.7	5.6	0.3	0.2	0.4	0.1	0.3
Columbus, OH	11.7	18.1	6.8	1.5	2.1	0.4	0.4	0.5	0.2
Dallas, TX	14.2	25.4	5.9	3.3	1.8	0.3	0.5	0.3	0.2
Davenport, IA	13.2	8.5	10.6	1.9	0.7	0.1	0.2	0.1	n/a
Denver, CO	16.1	9.6	2.8	0.6	0.3	0.4	0.5	0.4	0.5
Des Moines, IA	12.1	10.3	12.2	1.0	1.6	<0.1	0.2	0.1	0.1
Durham, NC	8.5	20.0	8.8	4.3	1.5	0.5	0.1	0.3	0.1
Edison, NJ	32.5	4.4	3.0	1.5	4.5	4.4	1.0	0.8	0.3
El Paso, TX	47.9	9.9	0.6	0.4	0.1	0.2	<0.1	<0.1	0.2
Fargo, ND	14.2	11.1	23.4	n/a	<0.1	<0.1	n/a	0.1	n/a
Fort Collins, CO	9.9	15.6	3.3	0.4	<0.1	n/a	0.1	0.1	0.1
Fort Wayne, IN	13.1	24.7	6.1	6.5	1.0	0.1	0.1	0.2	0.4
Fort Worth, TX	14.2	25.4	5.9	3.3	1.8	0.3	0.5	0.3	0.2
Grand Rapids, MI	13.1	17.6	7.4	1.0	0.8	0.1	0.2	0.2	<0.1
Greeley, CO	14.1	7.8	2.1	<0.1	<0.1	n/a	n/a	<0.1	0.2
Green Bay, WI	31.8	14.6	6.2	<0.1	0.4	n/a	n/a	<0.1	<0.1
Greensboro, NC	7.9	24.9	10.1	3.5	1.5	0.3	0.3	0.1	0.1
Honolulu, HI	18.0	8.1	2.3	0.2	<0.1	0.1	0.2	<0.1	4.0
Houston, TX	18.3	23.8	4.7	2.3	1.7	0.3	0.7	0.3	0.3
Huntsville, AL	7.5	34.8	8.2	7.2	0.8	0.1	0.9	0.1	0.1
Indianapolis, IN	11.5	16.8	7.6	4.2	1.1	0.4	0.2	0.3	0.1
Jacksonville, FL	13.0	29.8	3.5	5.6	0.6	0.3	0.3	0.3	0.2
Kansas City, MO	11.3	19.1	7.1	3.6	1.0	0.3	0.4	0.1	0.2
Lafayette, LA	44.3	12.6	2.4	5.0	0.1	n/a	<0.1	<0.1	0.1
Las Cruces, NM	19.3	9.8	2.4	0.2	0.6	0.1	0.2	<0.1	n/a
Las Vegas, NV	26.2	6.6	1.0	0.5	0.3	0.3	0.2	0.6	0.7
Lexington, KY	5.8	26.9	8.1	3.5	0.5	0.3	0.1	0.2	<0.1
Lincoln, NE	13.2	16.6	12.9	0.3	0.1	0.1	0.1	0.1	0.1
Little Rock, AR	4.9	32.1	6.6	8.5	0.4	0.1	<0.1	0.1	0.1
Los Angeles, CA	31.1	9.3	1.5	1.7	1.4	0.8	0.4	0.9	0.9
Louisville, KY	11.9	21.1	5.0	4.6	1.0	0.2	0.4	0.2	0.2
Madison, WI	14.4	8.0	10.6	0.2	1.2	0.4	0.1	0.1	0.9

Table continued on following page.

Area	Catholic	Evangelical Protestant	Mainline Protestant	Black Protestant	Islam	Judaism	Hinduism	Orthodox	Buddhism
Manchester, NH	16.3	5.8	2.7	n/a	0.1	0.3	<0.1	0.9	n/a
Miami, FL	23.8	13.7	1.6	2.2	0.8	1.2	0.3	0.2	0.3
Midland, TX	15.4	35.5	3.0	7.6	0.4	n/a	0.2	n/a	n/a
Milwaukee, WI	24.5	16.3	5.4	3.3	2.8	0.4	0.4	0.5	0.4
Minneapolis, MN	19.8	10.6	10.3	0.5	2.9	0.6	0.2	0.3	0.3
Nashville, TN	6.2	30.1	6.0	5.2	0.8	0.2	0.4	1.1	0.2
New Haven, CT	29.9	6.4	4.4	1.4	0.9	1.0	0.3	0.5	0.4
New Orleans, LA	42.1	13.5	3.0	4.9	1.4	0.4	0.3	0.1	0.3
New York, NY	32.5	4.4	3.0	1.5	4.5	4.4	1.0	0.8	0.3
Oklahoma City, OK	10.0	38.7	7.1	2.2	0.6	0.1	0.4	0.1	0.4
Omaha, NE	19.9	10.8	7.9	1.5	0.2	0.3	1.0	0.2	0.2
Orlando, FL	17.6	20.6	2.5	2.7	1.3	0.2	0.5	0.3	0.3
Philadelphia, PA	26.8	7.3	6.6	2.2	2.6	1.1	0.6	0.4	0.4
Phoenix, AZ	22.9	11.0	1.6	0.3	1.9	0.3	0.5	0.4	0.2
Pittsburgh, PA	30.6	8.8	10.1	1.3	0.6	0.6	1.2	0.6	0.1
Portland, OR	11.8	14.6	2.3	0.4	0.2	0.3	0.7	0.3	0.4
Providence, RI	37.9	4.0	3.2	0.1	0.5	0.6	0.1	0.5	0.2
Provo, UT	4.9	0.4	<0.1	n/a	0.3	n/a	0.1	n/a	n/a
Raleigh, NC	12.4	19.3	7.4	2.8	3.2	0.2	0.4	0.3	0.4
Reno, NV	24.4	6.8	1.3	0.2	0.3	0.1	0.1	0.1	0.2
Richmond, VA	12.3	23.1	9.3	3.1	2.1	0.3	1.3	0.4	0.2
Rochester, MN	15.6	15.0	19.1	n/a	1.0	0.1	0.1	0.2	0.2
Sacramento, CA	17.1	10.4	1.4	1.1	1.9	0.2	0.4	0.3	0.5
St. Louis, MO	21.2	16.1	5.7	3.9	1.3	0.6	0.2	0.2	0.3
Salem, OR	19.5	14.4	2.0	0.2	n/a	0.1	<0.1	<0.1	<0.1
Salt Lake City, UT	9.0	2.4	0.7	0.1	1.6	0.1	0.3	0.4	0.3
San Antonio, TX	27.3	17.7	3.1	0.8	0.5	0.2	0.1	0.1	0.3
San Diego, CA	22.9	9.5	1.5	0.6	1.5	0.4	0.3	0.4	0.7
San Francisco, CA	21.5	5.2	2.2	1.8	2.0	0.7	1.1	0.7	1.1
San Jose, CA	27.2	8.4	1.4	0.3	2.0	0.6	2.4	0.6	1.2
Santa Rosa, CA	23.5	5.3	1.5	<0.1	0.2	0.4	0.3	0.4	1.7
Savannah, GA	5.5	19.0	5.7	5.9	0.2	0.7	0.5	0.1	n/a
Seattle, WA	11.0	19.5	2.7	0.6	0.6	0.4	0.4	0.6	1.6
Sioux Falls, SD	13.1	21.0	20.2	0.1	0.1	n/a	n/a	0.8	<0.1
Springfield, IL	15.2	19.0	7.7	2.4	0.5	0.2	0.3	0.1	<0.1
Tampa, FL	23.1	16.9	3.8	1.7	0.7	0.4	0.3	0.8	0.4
Tucson, AZ	18.9	10.4	2.4	0.6	1.0	0.4	0.4	0.2	0.3
Tulsa, OK	5.6	37.8	8.6	1.7	0.5	0.2	0.1	0.1	<0.1
Tuscaloosa, AL	2.6	34.3	4.6	7.3	0.3	0.1	n/a	n/a	n/a
Virginia Beach, VA	8.3	21.3	6.9	3.7	1.0	0.3	0.2	0.3	0.3
Washington, DC	16.1	12.3	6.5	3.3	3.3	1.0	0.9	0.9	0.5
Wichita, KS	12.7	19.4	23.2	2.6	0.1	<0.1	0.1	0.2	0.5
Wilmington, NC	13.2	17.9	9.3	4.6	0.7	0.3	0.1	0.3	n/a
Winston-Salem, NC	9.3	31.4	13.6	3.4	0.8	n/a	<0.1	0.3	0.1
Worcester, MA	30.1	4.9	3.6	0.2	0.6	0.4	0.3	1.0	0.4
U.S.	18.7	16.5	5.2	2.3	1.3	0.6	0.4	0.4	0.3

Note: Figures are the number of adherents as a percentage of the total population; (1) Figures cover the Metropolitan Statistical Area
Source: 2020 U.S. Religion Census, Association of Statisticians of American Religious Bodies; The Association of Religion Data Archives (ARDA)

Gross Metropolitan Product

MSA[1]	2020	2021	2022	2023	Rank[2]
Albuquerque, NM	45.1	50.3	56.1	58.2	70
Allentown, PA	46.7	51.6	56.6	59.9	67
Anchorage, AK	25.8	28.3	31.3	32.6	112
Ann Arbor, MI	25.8	28.1	30.4	32.1	113
Athens, GA	10.5	11.5	12.8	13.4	213
Atlanta, GA	425.4	465.1	507.9	540.7	11
Austin, TX	168.4	192.3	215.9	231.0	22
Baltimore, MD	205.8	219.9	238.6	255.0	19
Boise City, ID	37.9	42.9	46.9	50.4	80
Boston, MA	480.3	526.5	569.8	601.7	8
Boulder, CO	29.7	32.7	35.9	38.1	101
Brownsville, TX	11.9	13.1	14.8	15.6	195
Cape Coral, FL	34.5	38.8	42.7	45.6	85
Cedar Rapids, IA	18.5	20.7	21.9	23.3	147
Charleston, SC	45.6	50.4	55.3	59.2	69
Charlotte, NC	184.0	204.1	222.9	238.2	21
Chicago, IL	693.0	757.2	819.9	861.2	3
Cincinnati, OH	152.1	165.2	178.8	190.5	27
Clarksville, TN	12.3	13.7	14.8	15.6	191
Cleveland, OH	133.6	144.9	157.7	167.2	35
College Station, TX	13.6	14.9	16.6	17.4	185
Colorado Springs, CO	39.5	43.7	47.3	49.9	78
Columbia, MO	10.4	11.6	12.5	13.3	211
Columbia, SC	44.4	48.2	51.8	55.2	74
Columbus, OH	137.3	151.0	164.2	175.3	33
Dallas, TX	538.4	608.8	686.1	722.1	5
Davenport, IA	22.1	24.6	26.3	27.6	126
Denver, CO	223.1	246.9	271.0	286.2	18
Des Moines, IA	55.0	63.3	67.6	71.4	57
Durham, NC	51.6	57.3	61.8	65.6	60
Edison, NJ	1,844.7	1,993.2	2,157.6	2,278.7	1
El Paso, TX	34.1	37.5	40.5	42.6	89
Fargo, ND	15.7	18.0	19.9	20.6	160
Fort Collins, CO	21.6	23.7	25.7	27.3	130
Fort Wayne, IN	24.3	27.3	29.8	31.6	114
Fort Worth, TX	538.4	608.8	686.1	722.1	5
Grand Rapids, MI	61.4	67.8	73.0	78.0	55
Greeley, CO	16.7	17.9	20.0	22.3	162
Green Bay, WI	20.5	22.2	24.3	26.0	139
Greensboro, NC	42.0	46.1	49.5	51.7	75
Honolulu, HI	62.1	66.8	74.3	80.2	56
Houston, TX	488.1	543.0	619.8	654.0	7
Huntsville, AL	30.9	33.5	36.5	39.2	98
Indianapolis, IN	146.9	163.9	178.6	190.0	28
Jacksonville, FL	91.0	100.3	109.1	115.5	42
Kansas City, MO	142.5	154.3	165.9	176.9	32
Lafayette, LA	20.6	22.6	24.8	26.2	135
Las Cruces, NM	7.6	8.5	9.6	10.0	258
Las Vegas, NV	119.4	134.8	151.1	164.0	36
Lexington, KY	29.8	32.5	35.1	36.8	103
Lincoln, NE	21.2	23.8	25.4	26.9	129
Little Rock, AR	38.6	42.3	45.8	48.0	81
Los Angeles, CA	1,007.0	1,129.4	1,226.9	1,295.5	2
Louisville, KY	75.6	83.6	90.5	94.4	47
Madison, WI	51.5	56.1	60.8	64.9	63
Manchester, NH	28.8	32.2	34.1	35.6	104

Table continued on following page.

MSA[1]	2020	2021	2022	2023	Rank[2]
Miami, FL	365.0	402.9	442.8	471.0	12
Midland, TX	21.8	25.3	30.1	33.9	121
Milwaukee, WI	102.4	110.1	119.2	126.3	38
Minneapolis, MN	270.7	298.9	324.7	344.9	15
Nashville, TN	136.6	157.4	173.7	184.5	31
New Haven, CT	53.0	57.1	61.7	64.7	61
New Orleans, LA	76.4	82.6	91.2	96.5	48
New York, NY	1,844.7	1,993.2	2,157.6	2,278.7	1
Oklahoma City, OK	74.4	81.6	92.9	98.2	49
Omaha, NE	69.1	77.9	83.2	88.2	50
Orlando, FL	144.1	160.5	180.2	194.2	30
Philadelphia, PA	439.1	478.2	521.7	553.7	9
Phoenix, AZ	281.0	310.1	336.3	358.7	14
Pittsburgh, PA	153.4	165.5	178.3	189.7	26
Portland, OR	168.4	184.1	201.8	214.4	25
Providence, RI	87.9	95.6	104.0	109.3	45
Provo, UT	31.9	36.5	40.2	43.1	91
Raleigh, NC	95.3	106.6	117.3	125.7	39
Reno, NV	31.8	35.9	39.3	41.9	92
Richmond, VA	91.2	97.3	104.5	110.5	44
Rochester, MN	14.2	15.8	17.1	18.1	178
Sacramento, CA	145.4	161.7	176.8	188.8	29
St. Louis, MO	171.5	187.7	201.8	212.8	23
Salem, OR	19.2	21.0	22.9	24.2	144
Salt Lake City, UT	103.9	114.9	124.5	132.3	37
San Antonio, TX	132.1	146.4	161.1	169.2	34
San Diego, CA	240.4	269.0	294.4	313.2	17
San Francisco, CA	588.3	652.7	713.1	748.9	4
San Jose, CA	360.5	400.1	431.2	450.9	13
Santa Rosa, CA	31.2	35.6	39.1	41.5	93
Savannah, GA	22.0	25.3	27.7	28.7	122
Seattle, WA	426.9	470.6	509.3	539.7	10
Sioux Falls, SD	23.4	26.6	28.7	30.6	118
Springfield, IL	11.7	13.1	13.8	14.6	196
Tampa, FL	169.3	187.4	205.4	217.8	24
Tucson, AZ	45.2	49.1	53.1	56.2	72
Tulsa, OK	53.7	58.3	65.1	68.5	59
Tuscaloosa, AL	11.4	12.2	13.2	13.9	205
Virginia Beach, VA	95.3	102.4	109.4	116.0	41
Washington, DC	560.7	600.8	647.6	688.6	6
Wichita, KS	36.7	40.2	44.0	47.1	83
Wilmington, NC	16.0	18.0	19.3	20.3	161
Winston-Salem, NC	34.0	37.6	40.9	43.7	88
Worcester, MA	50.9	55.1	59.3	62.5	64

Note: Figures are in billions of dollars; (1) Metropolitan Statistical Area; (2) Rank is based on 2021 data and ranges from 1 to 381.
Source: The U.S. Conference of Mayors, U.S. Metro Economies: U.S. Metros Compared to Global and State Economies,, June 2022

Appendix A: Comparative Statistics

Economic Growth

MSA[1]	2018-20 (%)	2021 (%)	2022 (%)	2023	Rank[2]
Albuquerque, NM	-0.4	5.6	4.6	3.6	167
Allentown, PA	-0.3	5.9	3.6	2.6	159
Anchorage, AK	-2.4	0.4	2.3	2.9	323
Ann Arbor, MI	-0.4	5.0	2.9	2.6	164
Athens, GA	-2.1	5.6	6.1	1.6	288
Atlanta, GA	-0.1	5.9	3.3	3.1	151
Austin, TX	3.2	10.1	5.9	3.8	13
Baltimore, MD	-2.0	3.2	2.7	3.5	284
Boise City, ID	2.0	7.4	3.2	4.2	35
Boston, MA	-0.1	6.7	3.2	2.4	146
Boulder, CO	1.5	5.6	3.5	3.8	49
Brownsville, TX	1.3	6.2	4.4	2.9	56
Cape Coral, FL	-0.4	8.7	5.0	2.9	165
Cedar Rapids, IA	-2.3	4.9	-0.2	3.5	310
Charleston, SC	0.4	6.3	3.8	3.8	106
Charlotte, NC	0.5	6.6	3.2	3.6	103
Chicago, IL	-2.4	5.5	2.6	1.8	324
Cincinnati, OH	0.0	4.2	2.4	3.3	145
Clarksville, TN	0.7	7.1	3.0	1.6	91
Cleveland, OH	-1.3	4.3	3.1	2.7	238
College Station, TX	1.1	5.1	4.2	2.8	61
Colorado Springs, CO	1.6	6.0	2.1	3.0	47
Columbia, MO	2.1	5.6	2.9	3.3	29
Columbia, SC	0.1	4.4	1.7	3.2	137
Columbus, OH	0.1	5.8	3.1	3.5	136
Dallas, TX	0.8	8.3	5.3	3.2	84
Davenport, IA	-0.6	5.6	1.2	1.8	184
Denver, CO	0.8	6.2	3.5	3.1	82
Des Moines, IA	1.7	8.2	0.9	2.7	46
Durham, NC	2.7	6.7	2.5	2.9	19
Edison, NJ	-1.5	5.6	3.3	2.4	250
El Paso, TX	2.0	5.5	2.3	1.9	36
Fargo, ND	-0.4	6.0	-0.2	1.2	170
Fort Collins, CO	2.2	5.3	2.6	4.0	27
Fort Wayne, IN	-2.0	8.3	3.1	2.7	285
Fort Worth, TX	0.8	8.3	5.3	3.2	84
Grand Rapids, MI	-2.1	6.3	1.8	3.7	294
Greeley, CO	-4.3	3.2	5.5	9.1	366
Green Bay, WI	-2.5	3.7	3.7	3.9	326
Greensboro, NC	-2.2	5.4	1.5	1.4	302
Honolulu, HI	-5.4	3.6	5.2	4.6	376
Houston, TX	-1.6	4.9	4.4	4.7	254
Huntsville, AL	1.8	4.9	3.4	3.9	42
Indianapolis, IN	-0.2	7.3	3.2	3.1	155
Jacksonville, FL	2.1	6.1	3.1	2.6	30
Kansas City, MO	0.0	4.0	1.7	3.5	140
Lafayette, LA	-3.7	4.2	2.6	3.3	356
Las Cruces, NM	-1.8	6.3	7.3	3.2	273
Las Vegas, NV	-3.4	7.7	5.7	5.1	349
Lexington, KY	-1.6	4.1	1.8	1.6	261
Lincoln, NE	0.1	5.0	0.9	2.8	131
Little Rock, AR	-0.6	5.2	2.2	1.9	182
Los Angeles, CA	-1.6	8.8	3.3	2.6	256
Louisville, KY	-0.4	5.8	2.2	1.2	169
Madison, WI	0.1	4.4	2.7	3.7	132
Manchester, NH	0.9	8.3	1.2	1.0	78

Table continued on following page.

MSA[1]	2018-20 (%)	2021 (%)	2022 (%)	2023	Rank[2]
Miami, FL	-1.4	6.4	4.2	3.1	245
Midland, TX	3.5	15.8	10.1	12.3	12
Milwaukee, WI	-1.8	3.1	2.5	2.8	271
Minneapolis, MN	-1.9	5.9	2.8	3.0	276
Nashville, TN	-1.2	10.6	4.4	3.0	228
New Haven, CT	-0.9	4.6	2.8	1.7	206
New Orleans, LA	-2.2	2.6	1.8	3.3	304
New York, NY	-1.5	5.6	3.3	2.4	250
Oklahoma City, OK	-2.2	2.3	4.2	4.8	307
Omaha, NE	0.2	5.3	0.8	3.0	127
Orlando, FL	-1.2	7.5	6.4	4.4	229
Philadelphia, PA	-1.2	4.9	3.3	2.8	235
Phoenix, AZ	1.9	5.8	2.7	3.4	39
Pittsburgh, PA	-1.6	3.8	1.9	3.1	257
Portland, OR	-0.6	5.8	4.2	2.9	179
Providence, RI	-1.1	5.6	3.4	1.9	224
Provo, UT	5.1	10.9	6.1	4.3	3
Raleigh, NC	-0.1	7.7	4.4	4.0	148
Reno, NV	2.1	7.5	2.8	3.2	31
Richmond, VA	-0.3	3.0	1.7	2.3	160
Rochester, MN	-0.9	6.6	2.9	2.5	209
Sacramento, CA	0.0	7.4	3.6	3.6	142
St. Louis, MO	-1.2	5.3	1.6	2.0	232
Salem, OR	0.3	5.6	4.2	2.6	119
Salt Lake City, UT	1.9	6.1	2.7	3.1	38
San Antonio, TX	0.8	6.2	3.7	2.4	88
San Diego, CA	-0.5	8.2	3.9	3.3	174
San Francisco, CA	1.2	7.1	4.0	1.9	60
San Jose, CA	5.2	8.6	3.3	1.6	2
Santa Rosa, CA	-1.8	9.7	5.0	3.1	269
Savannah, GA	-1.6	10.3	4.8	0.1	262
Seattle, WA	2.2	7.2	3.3	2.6	26
Sioux Falls, SD	0.4	7.1	1.9	3.7	111
Springfield, IL	-3.3	9.4	0.6	2.6	346
Tampa, FL	1.0	7.2	4.1	2.8	72
Tucson, AZ	-1.3	4.0	2.1	2.5	240
Tulsa, OK	-1.7	1.1	3.1	3.5	266
Tuscaloosa, AL	0.9	3.1	3.9	2.4	80
Virginia Beach, VA	-1.4	3.5	1.1	2.5	247
Washington, DC	-0.7	4.0	2.5	3.0	192
Wichita, KS	-2.0	4.3	2.9	4.1	286
Wilmington, NC	1.5	8.5	1.8	1.3	52
Winston-Salem, NC	-4.0	6.0	2.8	3.6	358
Worcester, MA	-0.9	5.3	2.5	2.4	204
U.S.	-0.6	5.7	3.1	2.9	—

Note: Figures are real gross metropolitan product (GMP) growth rates and represent annual average percent change;
(1) Metropolitan Statistical Area; (2) Rank is based on 2020 2-year average annual percent change and ranges from 1 to 381
Source: The U.S. Conference of Mayors, U.S. Metro Economies: U.S. Metros Compared to Global and State Economies,, June 2022

Metropolitan Area Exports

MSA[1]	2016	2017	2018	2019	2020	2021	Rank[2]
Albuquerque, NM	999.7	624.2	771.5	1,629.7	1,265.3	2,215.0	101
Allentown, PA	3,657.2	3,639.4	3,423.2	3,796.3	3,207.4	4,088.7	68
Anchorage, AK	1,215.4	1,675.9	1,510.8	1,348.0	990.9	n/a	n/a
Ann Arbor, MI	1,207.9	1,447.4	1,538.7	1,432.7	1,183.1	1,230.7	141
Athens, GA	332.1	297.7	378.1	442.1	338.7	448.1	223
Atlanta, GA	20,480.1	21,748.0	24,091.6	25,800.8	25,791.0	28,116.4	16
Austin, TX	10,682.7	12,451.5	12,929.9	12,509.0	13,041.5	15,621.9	25
Baltimore, MD	5,288.6	4,674.3	6,039.2	7,081.8	6,084.6	8,200.6	43
Boise City, ID	3,021.7	2,483.3	2,771.7	2,062.8	1,632.9	1,937.1	110
Boston, MA	21,168.0	23,116.2	24,450.1	23,505.8	23,233.8	32,084.2	12
Boulder, CO	956.3	1,012.0	1,044.1	1,014.9	1,110.4	1,078.0	152
Brownsville, TX	5,016.7	n/a	6,293.0	4,741.8	n/a	6,953.0	47
Cape Coral, FL	540.3	592.3	668.0	694.9	654.8	797.5	183
Cedar Rapids, IA	945.0	1,071.6	1,025.0	1,028.4	832.0	980.0	160
Charleston, SC	9,508.1	8,845.2	10,943.2	16,337.9	6,110.5	3,381.6	77
Charlotte, NC	11,944.1	13,122.5	14,083.2	13,892.4	8,225.6	10,554.3	33
Chicago, IL	43,932.7	46,140.2	47,287.8	42,438.8	41,279.4	54,498.1	4
Cincinnati, OH	26,326.2	28,581.8	27,396.3	28,778.3	21,002.2	23,198.7	19
Clarksville, TN	376.1	360.2	435.5	341.8	246.8	288.7	268
Cleveland, OH	8,752.9	8,944.9	9,382.9	8,829.9	7,415.8	8,560.4	41
College Station, TX	113.2	145.4	153.0	160.5	114.9	110.3	346
Colorado Springs, CO	786.9	819.7	850.6	864.2	979.2	866.9	175
Columbia, MO	213.7	224.0	238.6	291.4	256.2	335.4	255
Columbia, SC	2,007.7	2,123.9	2,083.8	2,184.6	2,058.8	2,100.2	104
Columbus, OH	5,675.4	5,962.2	7,529.5	7,296.6	6,304.8	6,557.9	51
Dallas, TX	27,187.8	30,269.1	36,260.9	39,474.0	35,642.0	43,189.0	6
Davenport, IA	4,497.6	5,442.7	6,761.9	6,066.3	5,097.5	6,341.0	52
Denver, CO	3,649.3	3,954.7	4,544.3	4,555.6	4,604.4	4,670.8	62
Des Moines, IA	1,052.2	1,141.2	1,293.7	1,437.8	1,414.0	1,706.6	118
Durham, NC	2,937.4	3,128.4	3,945.8	4,452.9	3,359.3	3,326.4	78
Edison, NJ	89,649.5	93,693.7	97,692.4	87,365.7	75,745.4	103,930.9	2
El Paso, TX	26,452.8	25,814.1	30,052.0	32,749.6	27,154.4	32,397.9	11
Fargo, ND	474.5	519.5	553.5	515.0	438.3	539.4	210
Fort Collins, CO	993.8	1,034.1	1,021.8	1,060.0	1,092.5	1,132.5	146
Fort Wayne, IN	1,322.2	1,422.8	1,593.3	1,438.5	1,144.6	1,592.7	123
Fort Worth, TX	27,187.8	30,269.1	36,260.9	39,474.0	35,642.0	43,189.0	6
Grand Rapids, MI	5,168.5	5,385.8	5,420.9	5,214.1	4,488.3	5,171.7	57
Greeley, CO	1,539.6	1,492.8	1,366.5	1,439.2	1,480.4	2,022.6	109
Green Bay, WI	1,044.0	1,054.8	1,044.3	928.2	736.4	765.6	185
Greensboro, NC	3,730.4	3,537.9	3,053.5	2,561.8	2,007.3	2,356.2	97
Honolulu, HI	330.3	393.6	438.9	308.6	169.0	164.3	319
Houston, TX	84,105.5	95,760.3	120,714.3	129,656.0	104,538.2	140,750.4	1
Huntsville, AL	1,827.3	1,889.2	1,608.7	1,534.2	1,263.0	1,579.5	124
Indianapolis, IN	9,655.4	10,544.2	11,069.9	11,148.7	11,100.4	12,740.4	30
Jacksonville, FL	2,159.0	2,141.7	2,406.7	2,975.5	2,473.3	2,683.7	90
Kansas City, MO	6,709.8	7,015.0	7,316.9	7,652.6	7,862.7	9,177.6	38
Lafayette, LA	1,335.2	954.8	1,001.7	1,086.2	946.2	895.7	167
Las Cruces, NM	1,568.6	1,390.2	1,467.5	n/a	2,149.5	2,408.2	95
Las Vegas, NV	2,312.3	2,710.6	2,240.6	2,430.8	1,705.9	1,866.2	115
Lexington, KY	2,069.6	2,119.8	2,148.0	2,093.8	1,586.3	1,880.0	113
Lincoln, NE	796.9	860.9	885.6	807.0	726.3	872.6	171
Little Rock, AR	1,871.0	2,146.1	1,607.4	1,642.5	n/a	1,370.6	132
Los Angeles, CA	61,245.7	63,752.9	64,814.6	61,041.1	50,185.4	58,588.4	3
Louisville, KY	7,793.3	8,925.9	8,987.0	9,105.5	8,360.3	10,262.8	35
Madison, WI	2,204.8	2,187.7	2,460.2	2,337.6	2,450.5	2,756.3	89
Manchester, NH	1,465.2	1,714.7	1,651.4	1,587.1	1,704.9	2,077.6	106

Table continued on following page.

MSA[1]	2016	2017	2018	2019	2020	2021	Rank[2]
Miami, FL	32,734.5	34,780.5	35,650.2	35,498.9	29,112.1	36,011.3	7
Midland, TX	69.6	69.4	63.6	63.7	57.7	49.9	372
Milwaukee, WI	7,256.2	7,279.1	7,337.6	6,896.3	6,624.0	7,282.8	46
Minneapolis, MN	18,329.2	19,070.9	20,016.2	18,633.0	17,109.5	21,098.8	21
Nashville, TN	9,460.1	10,164.3	8,723.7	7,940.7	6,569.9	8,256.1	42
New Haven, CT	1,819.8	1,876.3	2,082.3	2,133.8	2,330.5	2,667.5	91
New Orleans, LA	29,518.8	31,648.5	36,570.4	34,109.6	31,088.4	35,773.5	8
New York, NY	89,649.5	93,693.7	97,692.4	87,365.7	75,745.4	103,930.9	2
Oklahoma City, OK	1,260.0	1,278.8	1,489.4	1,434.5	1,326.6	1,773.2	116
Omaha, NE	3,509.7	3,756.2	4,371.6	3,725.7	3,852.5	4,595.1	64
Orlando, FL	3,363.9	3,196.7	3,131.7	3,363.9	2,849.8	3,313.6	79
Philadelphia, PA	21,359.9	21,689.7	23,663.2	24,721.3	23,022.1	28,724.4	15
Phoenix, AZ	12,838.2	13,223.1	13,614.9	15,136.6	11,073.9	14,165.1	27
Pittsburgh, PA	7,971.0	9,322.7	9,824.2	9,672.9	7,545.1	9,469.6	36
Portland, OR	20,256.8	20,788.8	21,442.9	23,761.9	27,824.7	33,787.5	10
Providence, RI	6,595.7	7,125.4	6,236.6	7,424.8	6,685.2	6,708.2	49
Provo, UT	1,894.8	2,065.3	1,788.1	1,783.7	1,888.5	2,053.8	108
Raleigh, NC	2,620.4	2,865.8	3,193.2	3,546.8	3,372.0	3,962.7	71
Reno, NV	2,382.1	2,517.3	2,631.7	2,598.3	4,553.3	4,503.0	66
Richmond, VA	3,525.7	3,663.7	3,535.0	3,203.2	2,719.1	3,010.7	84
Rochester, MN	398.0	495.3	537.6	390.1	194.0	224.9	292
Sacramento, CA	7,032.1	6,552.6	6,222.8	5,449.2	4,980.9	5,682.3	54
St. Louis, MO	8,346.5	9,662.9	10,866.8	10,711.1	9,089.4	10,486.1	34
Salem, OR	358.2	339.0	410.2	405.7	350.5	372.0	244
Salt Lake City, UT	8,653.7	7,916.9	9,748.6	13,273.9	13,565.5	13,469.1	28
San Antonio, TX	5,621.2	9,184.1	11,678.1	11,668.0	10,987.9	13,086.4	29
San Diego, CA	18,086.6	18,637.1	20,156.8	19,774.1	18,999.7	23,687.8	18
San Francisco, CA	24,506.3	29,103.8	27,417.0	28,003.8	23,864.5	29,972.0	13
San Jose, CA	21,716.8	21,464.7	22,224.2	20,909.4	19,534.5	22,293.6	20
Santa Rosa, CA	1,194.3	1,168.2	1,231.7	1,234.5	1,131.4	1,301.8	137
Savannah, GA	4,263.4	4,472.0	5,407.8	4,925.5	4,557.0	5,520.5	55
Seattle, WA	61,881.0	59,007.0	59,742.9	41,249.0	23,851.0	28,866.7	14
Sioux Falls, SD	334.3	386.8	400.0	431.5	524.9	547.3	207
Springfield, IL	88.3	107.5	91.2	99.8	90.5	98.9	351
Tampa, FL	5,702.9	6,256.0	4,966.7	6,219.7	5,082.2	5,754.7	53
Tucson, AZ	2,563.9	2,683.9	2,824.8	2,943.7	2,640.7	2,846.1	87
Tulsa, OK	2,363.0	2,564.7	3,351.7	3,399.2	2,567.8	3,064.8	81
Tuscaloosa, AL	n/a	n/a	n/a	n/a	5,175.0	6,675.5	50
Virginia Beach, VA	3,291.1	3,307.2	3,950.6	3,642.4	4,284.3	4,566.3	65
Washington, DC	13,582.4	12,736.1	13,602.7	14,563.8	13,537.3	12,210.8	31
Wichita, KS	3,054.9	3,299.2	3,817.0	3,494.7	2,882.1	3,615.3	74
Wilmington, NC	598.7	759.8	634.4	526.4	553.6	497.8	218
Winston-Salem, NC	1,234.6	1,131.7	1,107.5	1,209.1	913.1	918.2	164
Worcester, MA	3,093.5	2,929.6	2,573.6	2,221.5	2,026.4	2,624.6	92

Note: Figures are in millions of dollars; (1) Metropolitan Statistical Area; (2) Rank is based on 2021 data and ranges from 1 to 388
Source: U.S. Department of Commerce, International Trade Administration, Office of Trade and Economic Analysis, Industry and Analysis, Exports by Metropolitan Area, extracted March 16, 2023

Building Permits: City

City	Single-Family 2021	Single-Family 2022	Pct. Chg.	Multi-Family 2021	Multi-Family 2022	Pct. Chg.	Total 2021	Total 2022	Pct. Chg.
Albuquerque, NM	773	707	-8.5	894	902	0.9	1,667	1,609	-3.5
Allentown, PA	0	27	—	0	0	0.0	0	27	—
Anchorage, AK	840	124	-85.2	293	31	-89.4	1,133	155	-86.3
Ann Arbor, MI	175	135	-22.9	52	4	-92.3	227	139	-38.8
Athens, GA	180	227	26.1	986	1,548	57.0	1,166	1,775	52.2
Atlanta, GA	855	1,775	107.6	1,558	10,078	546.9	2,413	11,853	391.2
Austin, TX	4,180	3,344	-20.0	14,542	15,102	3.9	18,722	18,446	-1.5
Baltimore, MD	191	118	-38.2	1,366	1,539	12.7	1,557	1,657	6.4
Boise City, ID	856	392	-54.2	1,165	1,210	3.9	2,021	1,602	-20.7
Boston, MA	53	53	0.0	3,459	3,882	12.2	3,512	3,935	12.0
Boulder, CO	41	35	-14.6	253	269	6.3	294	304	3.4
Brownsville, TX	883	817	-7.5	246	353	43.5	1,129	1,170	3.6
Cape Coral, FL	4,279	3,813	-10.9	1,133	922	-18.6	5,412	4,735	-12.5
Cedar Rapids, IA	158	129	-18.4	280	225	-19.6	438	354	-19.2
Charleston, SC	1,091	942	-13.7	378	459	21.4	1,469	1,401	-4.6
Charlotte, NC	n/a	n/a	n/a	n/a	n/a	n/a	n/a	n/a	n/a
Chicago, IL	414	412	-0.5	4,927	6,712	36.2	5,341	7,124	33.4
Cincinnati, OH	206	104	-49.5	932	689	-26.1	1,138	793	-30.3
Clarksville, TN	1,452	973	-33.0	1,813	2,160	19.1	3,265	3,133	-4.0
Cleveland, OH	104	158	51.9	27	363	1,244.4	131	521	297.7
College Station, TX	674	592	-12.2	318	97	-69.5	992	689	-30.5
Colorado Springs, CO	n/a	n/a	n/a	n/a	n/a	n/a	n/a	n/a	n/a
Columbia, MO	487	303	-37.8	189	135	-28.6	676	438	-35.2
Columbia, SC	804	772	-4.0	896	1,359	51.7	1,700	2,131	25.4
Columbus, OH	913	642	-29.7	3,555	5,535	55.7	4,468	6,177	38.2
Dallas, TX	2,245	2,349	4.6	7,769	7,880	1.4	10,014	10,229	2.1
Davenport, IA	84	160	90.5	0	0	0.0	84	160	90.5
Denver, CO	1,550	1,323	-14.6	8,450	6,973	-17.5	10,000	8,296	-17.0
Des Moines, IA	248	256	3.2	380	284	-25.3	628	540	-14.0
Durham, NC	1,960	1,595	-18.6	1,361	2,771	103.6	3,321	4,366	31.5
Edison, NJ	105	104	-1.0	250	17	-93.2	355	121	-65.9
El Paso, TX	1,961	1,649	-15.9	272	319	17.3	2,233	1,968	-11.9
Fargo, ND	410	413	0.7	736	820	11.4	1,146	1,233	7.6
Fort Collins, CO	381	287	-24.7	458	515	12.4	839	802	-4.4
Fort Wayne, IN	n/a	n/a	n/a	n/a	n/a	n/a	n/a	n/a	n/a
Fort Worth, TX	7,236	7,421	2.6	4,338	4,557	5.0	11,574	11,978	3.5
Grand Rapids, MI	43	23	-46.5	243	211	-13.2	286	234	-18.2
Greeley, CO	315	345	9.5	600	1,725	187.5	915	2,070	126.2
Green Bay, WI	58	37	-36.2	2	0	-100.0	60	37	-38.3
Greensboro, NC	529	467	-11.7	1,363	676	-50.4	1,892	1,143	-39.6
Honolulu, HI	n/a	n/a	n/a	n/a	n/a	n/a	n/a	n/a	n/a
Houston, TX	7,146	6,800	-4.8	8,103	8,945	10.4	15,249	15,745	3.3
Huntsville, AL	1,483	1,083	-27.0	1,328	47	-96.5	2,811	1,130	-59.8
Indianapolis, IN	1,221	1,099	-10.0	968	1,011	4.4	2,189	2,110	-3.6
Jacksonville, FL	6,191	5,484	-11.4	3,778	5,862	55.2	9,969	11,346	13.8
Kansas City, MO	890	746	-16.2	1,448	1,241	-14.3	2,338	1,987	-15.0
Lafayette, LA	n/a	n/a	n/a	n/a	n/a	n/a	n/a	n/a	n/a
Las Cruces, NM	763	685	-10.2	99	26	-73.7	862	711	-17.5
Las Vegas, NV	2,700	3,001	11.1	1,048	1,024	-2.3	3,748	4,025	7.4
Lexington, KY	792	686	-13.4	863	1,045	21.1	1,655	1,731	4.6
Lincoln, NE	1,093	943	-13.7	1,227	2,179	77.6	2,320	3,122	34.6
Little Rock, AR	666	377	-43.4	460	644	40.0	1,126	1,021	-9.3
Los Angeles, CA	2,475	3,182	28.6	11,613	13,525	16.5	14,088	16,707	18.6
Louisville, KY	1,382	1,151	-16.7	466	1,637	251.3	1,848	2,788	50.9

Table continued on following page.

City	Single-Family 2021	Single-Family 2022	Pct. Chg.	Multi-Family 2021	Multi-Family 2022	Pct. Chg.	Total 2021	Total 2022	Pct. Chg.
Madison, WI	327	314	-4.0	3,299	2,046	-38.0	3,626	2,360	-34.9
Manchester, NH	126	132	4.8	8	6	-25.0	134	138	3.0
Miami, FL	102	127	24.5	6,153	4,231	-31.2	6,255	4,358	-30.3
Midland, TX	858	593	-30.9	0	0	0.0	858	593	-30.9
Milwaukee, WI	28	42	50.0	176	134	-23.9	204	176	-13.7
Minneapolis, MN	63	55	-12.7	3,119	3,626	16.3	3,182	3,681	15.7
Nashville, TN	3,932	3,977	1.1	12,205	10,818	-11.4	16,137	14,795	-8.3
New Haven, CT	13	10	-23.1	286	491	71.7	299	501	67.6
New Orleans, LA	716	615	-14.1	860	1,007	17.1	1,576	1,622	2.9
New York, NY	151	61	-59.6	19,772	21,429	8.4	19,923	21,490	7.9
Oklahoma City, OK	4,127	3,298	-20.1	140	260	85.7	4,267	3,558	-16.6
Omaha, NE	1,620	1,217	-24.9	1,547	2,552	65.0	3,167	3,769	19.0
Orlando, FL	990	1,286	29.9	2,734	2,229	-18.5	3,724	3,515	-5.6
Philadelphia, PA	1,553	478	-69.2	23,704	2,745	-88.4	25,257	3,223	-87.2
Phoenix, AZ	4,922	3,982	-19.1	6,570	10,616	61.6	11,492	14,598	27.0
Pittsburgh, PA	198	115	-41.9	617	1,913	210.0	815	2,028	148.8
Portland, OR	474	489	3.2	2,554	1,708	-33.1	3,028	2,197	-27.4
Providence, RI	1	28	2,700.0	53	271	411.3	54	299	453.7
Provo, UT	98	134	36.7	617	327	-47.0	715	461	-35.5
Raleigh, NC	1,354	1,875	38.5	5,133	6,760	31.7	6,487	8,635	33.1
Reno, NV	1,414	1,158	-18.1	2,539	2,535	-0.2	3,953	3,693	-6.6
Richmond, VA	502	457	-9.0	565	2,192	288.0	1,067	2,649	148.3
Rochester, MN	251	234	-6.8	374	847	126.5	625	1,081	73.0
Sacramento, CA	1,004	905	-9.9	2,079	1,149	-44.7	3,083	2,054	-33.4
St. Louis, MO	146	122	-16.4	809	1,054	30.3	955	1,176	23.1
Salem, OR	447	318	-28.9	399	851	113.3	846	1,169	38.2
Salt Lake City, UT	172	144	-16.3	3,519	3,489	-0.9	3,691	3,633	-1.6
San Antonio, TX	6,567	4,686	-28.6	4,591	9,496	106.8	11,158	14,182	27.1
San Diego, CA	539	506	-6.1	4,249	3,916	-7.8	4,788	4,422	-7.6
San Francisco, CA	33	38	15.2	2,486	2,006	-19.3	2,519	2,044	-18.9
San Jose, CA	299	553	84.9	359	1,450	303.9	658	2,003	204.4
Santa Rosa, CA	420	286	-31.9	1,031	911	-11.6	1,451	1,197	-17.5
Savannah, GA	487	408	-16.2	5	24	380.0	492	432	-12.2
Seattle, WA	264	418	58.3	11,716	8,572	-26.8	11,980	8,990	-25.0
Sioux Falls, SD	1,313	1,036	-21.1	1,819	3,429	88.5	3,132	4,465	42.6
Springfield, IL	137	55	-59.9	87	10	-88.5	224	65	-71.0
Tampa, FL	1,312	1,058	-19.4	1,093	3,753	243.4	2,405	4,811	100.0
Tucson, AZ	1,134	918	-19.0	959	962	0.3	2,093	1,880	-10.2
Tulsa, OK	652	452	-30.7	165	369	123.6	817	821	0.5
Tuscaloosa, AL	401	299	-25.4	725	329	-54.6	1,126	628	-44.2
Virginia Beach, VA	335	231	-31.0	128	966	654.7	463	1,197	158.5
Washington, DC	376	409	8.8	4,364	7,296	67.2	4,740	7,705	62.6
Wichita, KS	760	787	3.6	368	276	-25.0	1,128	1,063	-5.8
Wilmington, NC	n/a	n/a	n/a	n/a	n/a	n/a	n/a	n/a	n/a
Winston-Salem, NC	1,087	1,291	18.8	0	0	0.0	1,087	1,291	18.8
Worcester, MA	66	94	42.4	112	718	541.1	178	812	356.2
U.S.	1,115,400	975,600	-12.5	621,600	689,500	10.9	1,737,000	1,665,100	-4.1

Note: Figures represent new, privately-owned housing units authorized (unadjusted data); All permit data are based on estimates with imputation
Source: U.S. Census Bureau, Manufacturing, Mining, and Construction Statistics, Building Permits, 2021, 2022

Appendix A: Comparative Statistics

Building Permits: Metro Area

Metro Area	Single-Family 2021	Single-Family 2022	Pct. Chg.	Multi-Family 2021	Multi-Family 2022	Pct. Chg.	Total 2021	Total 2022	Pct. Chg.
Albuquerque, NM	2,535	2,002	-21.0	1,486	1,055	-29.0	4,021	3,057	-24.0
Allentown, PA	1,716	1,586	-7.6	890	723	-18.8	2,606	2,309	-11.4
Anchorage, AK	877	166	-81.1	306	47	-84.6	1,183	213	-82.0
Ann Arbor, MI	795	580	-27.0	121	49	-59.5	916	629	-31.3
Athens, GA	856	771	-9.9	992	1,574	58.7	1,848	2,345	26.9
Atlanta, GA	31,560	26,623	-15.6	7,906	21,484	171.7	39,466	48,107	21.9
Austin, TX	24,486	19,717	-19.5	26,421	22,647	-14.3	50,907	42,364	-16.8
Baltimore, MD	4,783	2,832	-40.8	3,051	3,756	23.1	7,834	6,588	-15.9
Boise City, ID	8,342	5,925	-29.0	3,854	4,550	18.1	12,196	10,475	-14.1
Boston, MA	4,820	3,985	-17.3	11,782	10,469	-11.1	16,602	14,454	-12.9
Boulder, CO	343	661	92.7	894	981	9.7	1,237	1,642	32.7
Brownsville, TX	1,573	1,940	23.3	479	569	18.8	2,052	2,509	22.3
Cape Coral, FL	11,020	9,145	-17.0	2,374	4,476	88.5	13,394	13,621	1.7
Cedar Rapids, IA	546	453	-17.0	352	494	40.3	898	947	5.5
Charleston, SC	5,913	6,329	7.0	2,369	2,994	26.4	8,282	9,323	12.6
Charlotte, NC	20,830	19,029	-8.6	9,296	8,183	-12.0	30,126	27,212	-9.7
Chicago, IL	10,071	8,563	-15.0	8,440	9,073	7.5	18,511	17,636	-4.7
Cincinnati, OH	5,358	4,126	-23.0	3,071	2,084	-32.1	8,429	6,210	-26.3
Clarksville, TN	2,217	1,501	-32.3	1,895	2,592	36.8	4,112	4,093	-0.5
Cleveland, OH	2,949	2,915	-1.2	391	820	109.7	3,340	3,735	11.8
College Station, TX	1,765	1,545	-12.5	535	230	-57.0	2,300	1,775	-22.8
Colorado Springs, CO	5,074	3,646	-28.1	4,261	5,198	22.0	9,335	8,844	-5.3
Columbia, MO	838	628	-25.1	191	151	-20.9	1,029	779	-24.3
Columbia, SC	5,853	4,101	-29.9	1,028	1,703	65.7	6,881	5,804	-15.7
Columbus, OH	6,844	5,623	-17.8	5,218	6,472	24.0	12,062	12,095	0.3
Dallas, TX	51,996	43,645	-16.1	26,709	34,249	28.2	78,705	77,894	-1.0
Davenport, IA	436	416	-4.6	193	181	-6.2	629	597	-5.1
Denver, CO	13,113	10,108	-22.9	16,893	13,368	-20.9	30,006	23,476	-21.8
Des Moines, IA	4,888	3,646	-25.4	2,081	2,476	19.0	6,969	6,122	-12.2
Durham, NC	3,735	3,170	-15.1	2,165	3,222	48.8	5,900	6,392	8.3
Edison, NJ	12,947	12,089	-6.6	43,714	46,323	6.0	56,661	58,412	3.1
El Paso, TX	2,655	2,147	-19.1	334	319	-4.5	2,989	2,466	-17.5
Fargo, ND	1,229	1,123	-8.6	1,060	1,191	12.4	2,289	2,314	1.1
Fort Collins, CO	2,149	1,385	-35.6	1,072	1,187	10.7	3,221	2,572	-20.1
Fort Wayne, IN	1,799	1,453	-19.2	179	882	392.7	1,978	2,335	18.0
Fort Worth, TX	51,996	43,645	-16.1	26,709	34,249	28.2	78,705	77,894	-1.0
Grand Rapids, MI	2,811	2,488	-11.5	894	1,710	91.3	3,705	4,198	13.3
Greeley, CO	3,814	3,203	-16.0	1,454	2,940	102.2	5,268	6,143	16.6
Green Bay, WI	830	627	-24.5	578	622	7.6	1,408	1,249	-11.3
Greensboro, NC	2,593	2,161	-16.7	1,371	832	-39.3	3,964	2,993	-24.5
Honolulu, HI	938	652	-30.5	500	1,901	280.2	1,438	2,553	77.5
Houston, TX	52,719	47,701	-9.5	16,544	28,027	69.4	69,263	75,728	9.3
Huntsville, AL	4,230	3,617	-14.5	1,942	418	-78.5	6,172	4,035	-34.6
Indianapolis, IN	10,159	8,578	-15.6	3,292	4,915	49.3	13,451	13,493	0.3
Jacksonville, FL	16,536	14,410	-12.9	6,202	8,759	41.2	22,738	23,169	1.9
Kansas City, MO	7,051	5,204	-26.2	4,203	6,015	43.1	11,254	11,219	-0.3
Lafayette, LA	3,040	2,051	-32.5	4	20	400.0	3,044	2,071	-32.0
Las Cruces, NM	1,239	1,079	-12.9	99	26	-73.7	1,338	1,105	-17.4
Las Vegas, NV	12,156	9,199	-24.3	4,151	3,867	-6.8	16,307	13,066	-19.9
Lexington, KY	1,760	1,460	-17.0	1,183	1,249	5.6	2,943	2,709	-8.0
Lincoln, NE	1,378	1,132	-17.9	1,229	2,217	80.4	2,607	3,349	28.5
Little Rock, AR	2,505	1,863	-25.6	1,130	1,475	30.5	3,635	3,338	-8.2
Los Angeles, CA	11,090	11,184	0.8	20,061	21,326	6.3	31,151	32,510	4.4
Louisville, KY	4,136	3,345	-19.1	1,372	2,111	53.9	5,508	5,456	-0.9

Table continued on following page.

Metro Area	Single-Family 2021	Single-Family 2022	Pct. Chg.	Multi-Family 2021	Multi-Family 2022	Pct. Chg.	Total 2021	Total 2022	Pct. Chg.
Madison, WI	1,737	1,530	-11.9	5,457	4,049	-25.8	7,194	5,579	-22.4
Manchester, NH	683	623	-8.8	659	224	-66.0	1,342	847	-36.9
Miami, FL	8,316	6,970	-16.2	16,997	13,051	-23.2	25,313	20,021	-20.9
Midland, TX	872	594	-31.9	0	0	0.0	872	594	-31.9
Milwaukee, WI	1,779	1,557	-12.5	1,150	1,609	39.9	2,929	3,166	8.1
Minneapolis, MN	11,734	9,114	-22.3	14,343	14,611	1.9	26,077	23,725	-9.0
Nashville, TN	17,422	15,388	-11.7	14,769	12,804	-13.3	32,191	28,192	-12.4
New Haven, CT	497	493	-0.8	486	770	58.4	983	1,263	28.5
New Orleans, LA	4,018	3,101	-22.8	1,264	1,065	-15.7	5,282	4,166	-21.1
New York, NY	12,947	12,089	-6.6	43,714	46,323	6.0	56,661	58,412	3.1
Oklahoma City, OK	7,637	5,971	-21.8	443	940	112.2	8,080	6,911	-14.5
Omaha, NE	3,677	2,651	-27.9	2,705	3,469	28.2	6,382	6,120	-4.1
Orlando, FL	17,795	16,213	-8.9	12,823	12,470	-2.8	30,618	28,683	-6.3
Philadelphia, PA	8,868	8,532	-3.8	27,439	5,881	-78.6	36,307	14,413	-60.3
Phoenix, AZ	34,347	26,857	-21.8	16,234	20,410	25.7	50,581	47,267	-6.6
Pittsburgh, PA	3,891	3,184	-18.2	1,332	2,481	86.3	5,223	5,665	8.5
Portland, OR	8,008	6,029	-24.7	7,015	6,949	-0.9	15,023	12,978	-13.6
Providence, RI	1,788	1,559	-12.8	470	563	19.8	2,258	2,122	-6.0
Provo, UT	7,562	5,153	-31.9	3,613	3,134	-13.3	11,175	8,287	-25.8
Raleigh, NC	14,227	12,488	-12.2	7,422	9,080	22.3	21,649	21,568	-0.4
Reno, NV	2,717	2,184	-19.6	2,620	3,628	38.5	5,337	5,812	8.9
Richmond, VA	5,946	4,503	-24.3	3,601	5,911	64.1	9,547	10,414	9.1
Rochester, MN	721	641	-11.1	414	1,080	160.9	1,135	1,721	51.6
Sacramento, CA	9,390	8,170	-13.0	3,044	2,630	-13.6	12,434	10,800	-13.1
St. Louis, MO	5,716	4,743	-17.0	2,610	4,388	68.1	8,326	9,131	9.7
Salem, OR	1,368	874	-36.1	786	1,943	147.2	2,154	2,817	30.8
Salt Lake City, UT	5,338	3,992	-25.2	6,304	6,110	-3.1	11,642	10,102	-13.2
San Antonio, TX	13,945	10,226	-26.7	8,319	14,113	69.6	22,264	24,339	9.3
San Diego, CA	3,227	3,517	9.0	6,821	5,829	-14.5	10,048	9,346	-7.0
San Francisco, CA	4,301	3,370	-21.6	9,305	7,834	-15.8	13,606	11,204	-17.7
San Jose, CA	2,400	3,899	62.5	2,129	4,308	102.3	4,529	8,207	81.2
Santa Rosa, CA	1,227	954	-22.2	1,391	1,310	-5.8	2,618	2,264	-13.5
Savannah, GA	2,752	2,228	-19.0	475	966	103.4	3,227	3,194	-1.0
Seattle, WA	8,828	7,029	-20.4	21,915	19,632	-10.4	30,743	26,661	-13.3
Sioux Falls, SD	1,893	1,626	-14.1	2,093	3,928	87.7	3,986	5,554	39.3
Springfield, IL	239	146	-38.9	93	64	-31.2	332	210	-36.7
Tampa, FL	19,305	15,678	-18.8	5,526	14,291	158.6	24,831	29,969	20.7
Tucson, AZ	5,116	3,735	-27.0	1,168	1,979	69.4	6,284	5,714	-9.1
Tulsa, OK	4,354	3,843	-11.7	566	1,280	126.1	4,920	5,123	4.1
Tuscaloosa, AL	771	714	-7.4	725	329	-54.6	1,496	1,043	-30.3
Virginia Beach, VA	4,712	3,680	-21.9	2,665	2,633	-1.2	7,377	6,313	-14.4
Washington, DC	13,729	11,657	-15.1	13,685	20,736	51.5	27,414	32,393	18.2
Wichita, KS	1,618	1,586	-2.0	766	1,264	65.0	2,384	2,850	19.5
Wilmington, NC	2,671	2,489	-6.8	1,747	1,932	10.6	4,418	4,421	0.1
Winston-Salem, NC	3,887	3,983	2.5	319	67	-79.0	4,206	4,050	-3.7
Worcester, MA	1,177	1,172	-0.4	876	1,080	23.3	2,053	2,252	9.7
U.S.	1,115,400	975,600	-12.5	621,600	689,500	10.9	1,737,000	1,665,100	-4.1

Note: Figures cover the Metropolitan Statistical Area; Figures represent new, privately-owned housing units authorized (unadjusted data); All permit data are based on estimates with imputation
Source: U.S. Census Bureau, Manufacturing, Mining, and Construction Statistics, Building Permits, 2021, 2022

Appendix A: Comparative Statistics

Housing Vacancy Rates

MSA[1]	Gross Vacancy Rate[2] (%) 2020	2021	2022	Year-Round Vacancy Rate[3] (%) 2020	2021	2022	Rental Vacancy Rate[4] (%) 2020	2021	2022	Homeowner Vacancy Rate[5] (%) 2020	2021	2022
Albuquerque, NM	5.1	5.3	5.3	4.9	5.1	5.1	5.4	6.4	5.5	1.4	0.5	1.0
Allentown, PA	4.9	5.2	8.7	4.8	4.3	8.0	3.9	4.0	6.1	0.7	0.1	1.2
Anchorage, AK	n/a	n/a	n/a	n/a	n/a	n/a	n/a	n/a	n/a	n/a	n/a	n/a
Ann Arbor, MI	n/a	n/a	n/a	n/a	n/a	n/a	n/a	n/a	n/a	n/a	n/a	n/a
Athens, GA	n/a	n/a	n/a	n/a	n/a	n/a	n/a	n/a	n/a	n/a	n/a	n/a
Atlanta, GA	5.8	6.1	5.9	5.4	5.7	5.7	6.4	5.2	6.7	0.8	1.0	0.8
Austin, TX	7.0	6.5	5.5	6.8	6.2	4.9	6.6	8.5	5.6	2.0	1.3	0.6
Baltimore, MD	7.2	6.8	5.9	7.0	6.6	5.7	7.0	6.1	5.3	1.0	1.0	0.5
Boise City, ID	n/a	n/a	n/a	n/a	n/a	n/a	n/a	n/a	n/a	n/a	n/a	n/a
Boston, MA	6.8	7.4	6.2	5.6	6.2	5.4	4.7	4.5	2.5	0.4	0.5	0.7
Boulder, CO	n/a	n/a	n/a	n/a	n/a	n/a	n/a	n/a	n/a	n/a	n/a	n/a
Brownsville, TX	n/a	n/a	n/a	n/a	n/a	n/a	n/a	n/a	n/a	n/a	n/a	n/a
Cape Coral, FL	35.1	36.4	38.2	15.8	13.0	16.9	15.5	10.7	11.6	1.9	2.4	3.9
Cedar Rapids, IA	n/a	n/a	n/a	n/a	n/a	n/a	n/a	n/a	n/a	n/a	n/a	n/a
Charleston, SC	18.1	12.9	10.6	16.5	10.5	7.5	27.7	15.4	8.8	2.3	1.3	0.4
Charlotte, NC	6.6	7.7	7.4	6.3	7.4	7.0	5.6	6.8	5.9	1.0	1.3	0.7
Chicago, IL	7.4	8.7	7.3	7.2	8.6	7.1	7.4	8.0	6.1	1.2	1.3	1.1
Cincinnati, OH	6.6	7.9	6.8	6.2	7.3	6.3	7.9	7.2	6.3	0.7	0.5	0.3
Clarksville, TN	n/a	n/a	n/a	n/a	n/a	n/a	n/a	n/a	n/a	n/a	n/a	n/a
Cleveland, OH	9.3	7.7	7.0	8.8	7.5	6.8	5.5	3.6	3.2	0.7	0.4	1.0
College Station, TX	n/a	n/a	n/a	n/a	n/a	n/a	n/a	n/a	n/a	n/a	n/a	n/a
Colorado Springs, CO	n/a	n/a	n/a	n/a	n/a	n/a	n/a	n/a	n/a	n/a	n/a	n/a
Columbia, MO	n/a	n/a	n/a	n/a	n/a	n/a	n/a	n/a	n/a	n/a	n/a	n/a
Columbia, SC	7.2	7.6	12.0	7.1	7.6	12.0	4.5	4.7	6.1	0.7	1.1	0.6
Columbus, OH	4.7	6.8	5.6	4.5	6.6	5.4	5.9	6.5	3.8	0.3	0.8	0.8
Dallas, TX	6.4	6.6	6.6	6.4	6.5	6.3	7.2	7.0	6.8	0.7	0.7	0.7
Davenport, IA	n/a	n/a	n/a	n/a	n/a	n/a	n/a	n/a	n/a	n/a	n/a	n/a
Denver, CO	5.8	6.5	5.8	5.1	5.3	5.2	4.8	4.6	5.1	0.5	1.0	0.3
Des Moines, IA	n/a	n/a	n/a	n/a	n/a	n/a	n/a	n/a	n/a	n/a	n/a	n/a
Durham, NC	n/a	n/a	n/a	n/a	n/a	n/a	n/a	n/a	n/a	n/a	n/a	n/a
Edison, NJ	9.1	9.8	8.2	7.8	8.7	7.0	4.5	5.2	3.5	1.3	1.2	1.0
El Paso, TX	n/a	n/a	n/a	n/a	n/a	n/a	n/a	n/a	n/a	n/a	n/a	n/a
Fargo, ND	n/a	n/a	n/a	n/a	n/a	n/a	n/a	n/a	n/a	n/a	n/a	n/a
Fort Collins, CO	n/a	n/a	n/a	n/a	n/a	n/a	n/a	n/a	n/a	n/a	n/a	n/a
Fort Wayne, IN	n/a	n/a	n/a	n/a	n/a	n/a	n/a	n/a	n/a	n/a	n/a	n/a
Fort Worth, TX	6.4	6.6	6.6	6.4	6.5	6.3	7.2	7.0	6.8	0.7	0.7	0.7
Grand Rapids, MI	7.1	7.0	4.9	4.7	4.2	3.0	4.6	3.4	2.4	1.1	0.7	0.1
Greeley, CO	n/a	n/a	n/a	n/a	n/a	n/a	n/a	n/a	n/a	n/a	n/a	n/a
Green Bay, WI	n/a	n/a	n/a	n/a	n/a	n/a	n/a	n/a	n/a	n/a	n/a	n/a
Greensboro, NC	8.3	5.9	8.7	8.2	5.9	8.7	7.2	2.7	10.2	0.7	0.5	0.7
Honolulu, HI	10.0	10.6	10.6	9.6	10.1	10.0	5.5	5.1	5.7	1.0	0.6	0.6
Houston, TX	6.8	7.2	6.9	6.3	6.6	6.3	9.7	8.8	8.9	1.1	0.8	0.6
Huntsville, AL	n/a	n/a	n/a	n/a	n/a	n/a	n/a	n/a	n/a	n/a	n/a	n/a
Indianapolis, IN	7.3	6.2	7.7	7.0	6.1	7.2	10.4	8.2	11.0	0.8	0.7	1.0
Jacksonville, FL	9.5	8.3	8.9	9.3	7.6	7.7	7.5	5.6	6.2	1.5	0.4	1.7
Kansas City, MO	9.1	8.3	7.1	9.1	8.2	7.1	9.4	8.9	7.8	0.7	1.2	0.6
Lafayette, LA	n/a	n/a	n/a	n/a	n/a	n/a	n/a	n/a	n/a	n/a	n/a	n/a
Las Cruces, NM	n/a	n/a	n/a	n/a	n/a	n/a	n/a	n/a	n/a	n/a	n/a	n/a
Las Vegas, NV	7.8	7.7	9.2	7.1	7.1	8.3	5.0	3.7	5.7	1.1	0.9	0.9
Lexington, KY	n/a	n/a	n/a	n/a	n/a	n/a	n/a	n/a	n/a	n/a	n/a	n/a
Lincoln, NE	n/a	n/a	n/a	n/a	n/a	n/a	n/a	n/a	n/a	n/a	n/a	n/a
Little Rock, AR	9.4	11.4	9.4	9.1	11.2	9.2	9.1	10.0	11.4	1.3	1.2	0.7
Los Angeles, CA	5.5	6.4	5.9	4.8	5.9	5.5	3.6	4.6	4.1	0.6	0.7	0.5
Louisville, KY	6.9	8.3	5.7	6.9	8.3	5.7	6.4	8.5	5.3	1.4	0.7	0.5

Table continued on following page.

Appendix A: Comparative Statistics   A-63

MSA[1]	Gross Vacancy Rate[2] (%) 2020	2021	2022	Year-Round Vacancy Rate[3] (%) 2020	2021	2022	Rental Vacancy Rate[4] (%) 2020	2021	2022	Homeowner Vacancy Rate[5] (%) 2020	2021	2022
Madison, WI	n/a	n/a	n/a	n/a	n/a	n/a	n/a	n/a	n/a	n/a	n/a	n/a
Manchester, NH	n/a	n/a	n/a	n/a	n/a	n/a	n/a	n/a	n/a	n/a	n/a	n/a
Miami, FL	12.6	12.2	12.6	6.8	6.8	7.5	5.4	5.5	6.3	1.4	1.0	1.1
Midland, TX	n/a	n/a	n/a	n/a	n/a	n/a	n/a	n/a	n/a	n/a	n/a	n/a
Milwaukee, WI	6.6	5.2	5.2	6.3	5.1	5.1	4.6	2.2	5.9	0.6	0.5	0.1
Minneapolis, MN	4.7	5.3	4.8	3.7	4.6	4.5	4.0	4.9	6.7	0.5	0.6	0.8
Nashville, TN	6.5	7.1	7.6	6.1	6.8	7.1	7.3	7.9	6.4	0.7	1.0	0.9
New Haven, CT	9.4	7.9	6.8	8.4	7.2	6.4	7.8	5.4	2.6	0.2	0.5	1.1
New Orleans, LA	10.7	12.6	13.4	9.8	11.1	11.5	6.1	7.2	6.6	1.3	1.0	1.6
New York, NY	9.1	9.8	8.2	7.8	8.7	7.0	4.5	5.2	3.5	1.3	1.2	1.0
Oklahoma City, OK	7.5	6.1	8.6	7.3	6.0	8.5	6.4	5.7	10.6	0.9	0.8	0.9
Omaha, NE	5.6	6.0	5.4	5.3	5.7	5.0	6.5	5.1	4.2	0.5	0.7	0.8
Orlando, FL	12.9	9.5	9.6	9.8	7.5	7.4	8.6	7.5	6.5	1.2	0.5	1.4
Philadelphia, PA	6.0	6.1	5.5	5.8	5.9	5.4	5.4	4.8	4.2	0.7	0.5	1.0
Phoenix, AZ	8.9	9.0	10.9	5.3	5.6	6.7	4.9	4.9	6.4	0.7	0.6	0.9
Pittsburgh, PA	11.5	11.4	11.5	11.3	10.8	11.0	9.3	9.4	8.3	1.0	0.4	0.7
Portland, OR	5.5	6.0	5.4	4.9	5.6	5.1	4.3	5.2	4.0	0.8	0.9	1.2
Providence, RI	8.7	7.9	9.5	6.6	5.8	7.6	3.5	2.7	4.5	0.8	0.7	0.4
Provo, UT	n/a	n/a	n/a	n/a	n/a	n/a	n/a	n/a	n/a	n/a	n/a	n/a
Raleigh, NC	4.6	6.3	7.4	4.5	6.3	7.3	2.3	2.9	7.1	0.4	1.1	0.5
Reno, NV	n/a	n/a	n/a	n/a	n/a	n/a	n/a	n/a	n/a	n/a	n/a	n/a
Richmond, VA	6.0	5.8	6.1	6.0	5.8	6.1	2.7	1.8	3.0	0.9	1.0	0.7
Rochester, MN	n/a	n/a	n/a	n/a	n/a	n/a	n/a	n/a	n/a	n/a	n/a	n/a
Sacramento, CA	6.1	6.7	6.3	5.8	6.5	6.1	4.2	3.6	2.3	1.0	0.7	0.6
St. Louis, MO	6.4	7.0	7.2	6.3	7.0	7.1	5.3	6.5	6.8	0.7	0.5	1.4
Salem, OR	n/a	n/a	n/a	n/a	n/a	n/a	n/a	n/a	n/a	n/a	n/a	n/a
Salt Lake City, UT	5.7	4.1	5.1	5.6	3.9	4.5	6.2	4.1	4.6	0.3	0.8	0.6
San Antonio, TX	7.4	7.6	7.5	6.7	6.9	7.1	7.2	8.4	8.1	1.0	1.1	0.9
San Diego, CA	6.0	6.9	6.9	5.6	6.7	6.6	3.9	3.1	3.6	0.8	0.7	0.6
San Francisco, CA	6.4	7.6	7.9	6.2	7.3	7.7	5.3	6.5	5.4	0.5	1.1	1.3
San Jose, CA	4.7	5.9	5.8	4.7	5.6	5.8	4.4	6.6	4.7	n/a	0.4	0.4
Santa Rosa, CA	n/a	n/a	n/a	n/a	n/a	n/a	n/a	n/a	n/a	n/a	n/a	n/a
Savannah, GA	n/a	n/a	n/a	n/a	n/a	n/a	n/a	n/a	n/a	n/a	n/a	n/a
Seattle, WA	4.7	6.2	5.7	4.5	5.5	5.2	3.6	5.3	4.9	0.6	0.7	0.7
Sioux Falls, SD	n/a	n/a	n/a	n/a	n/a	n/a	n/a	n/a	n/a	n/a	n/a	n/a
Springfield, IL	n/a	n/a	n/a	n/a	n/a	n/a	n/a	n/a	n/a	n/a	n/a	n/a
Tampa, FL	13.0	14.2	13.3	10.1	10.5	9.9	8.9	7.3	8.1	1.5	1.0	1.2
Tucson, AZ	12.1	10.0	13.5	7.7	6.9	10.3	8.6	5.0	8.0	0.5	0.6	1.4
Tulsa, OK	9.4	11.0	8.9	8.8	10.0	8.5	8.6	5.3	5.6	0.8	1.5	0.7
Tuscaloosa, AL	n/a	n/a	n/a	n/a	n/a	n/a	n/a	n/a	n/a	n/a	n/a	n/a
Virginia Beach, VA	7.9	7.7	8.1	7.0	6.9	7.3	5.5	5.5	6.3	0.6	0.6	1.0
Washington, DC	6.5	5.5	5.2	6.2	5.3	5.0	5.5	5.9	5.3	0.7	0.5	0.6
Wichita, KS	n/a	n/a	n/a	n/a	n/a	n/a	n/a	n/a	n/a	n/a	n/a	n/a
Wilmington, NC	n/a	n/a	n/a	n/a	n/a	n/a	n/a	n/a	n/a	n/a	n/a	n/a
Winston-Salem, NC	n/a	n/a	n/a	n/a	n/a	n/a	n/a	n/a	n/a	n/a	n/a	n/a
Worcester, MA	4.8	5.5	4.5	4.6	4.9	4.0	1.3	2.2	1.6	0.4	0.7	0.4
U.S.	10.6	10.8	10.5	8.2	8.4	8.2	6.3	6.1	5.8	1.0	0.9	0.8

Note: (1) Metropolitan Statistical Area; (2) The percentage of the total housing inventory that is vacant; (3) The percentage of the housing inventory (excluding seasonal units) that is year-round vacant; (4) The percentage of rental inventory that is vacant for rent; (5) The percentage of homeowner inventory that is vacant for sale; n/a not available.
Source: U.S. Census Bureau, Housing Vacancies and Homeownership Annual Statistics: 2020, 2021, 2022

Appendix A: Comparative Statistics

Bankruptcy Filings

City	Area Covered	Business Filings 2021	Business Filings 2022	% Chg.	Nonbusiness Filings 2021	Nonbusiness Filings 2022	% Chg.
Albuquerque, NM	Bernalillo County	21	15	-28.6	560	383	-31.6
Allentown, PA	Lehigh County	5	7	40.0	346	283	-18.2
Anchorage, AK	Anchorage Borough	12	4	-66.7	116	77	-33.6
Ann Arbor, MI	Washtenaw County	8	24	200.0	352	350	-0.6
Athens, GA	Clarke County	10	4	-60.0	162	212	30.9
Atlanta, GA	Fulton County	87	124	42.5	2,072	2,323	12.1
Austin, TX	Travis County	113	76	-32.7	443	372	-16.0
Baltimore, MD	Baltimore City	18	17	-5.6	1,323	1,167	-11.8
Boise City, ID	Ada County	13	16	23.1	393	326	-17.0
Boston, MA	Suffolk County	23	42	82.6	224	221	-1.3
Boulder, CO	Boulder County	13	27	107.7	216	160	-25.9
Brownsville, TX	Cameron County	0	4	n/a	171	195	14.0
Cape Coral, FL	Lee County	39	31	-20.5	928	711	-23.4
Cedar Rapids, IA	Linn County	6	10	66.7	193	166	-14.0
Charleston, SC	Charleston County	8	5	-37.5	176	228	29.5
Charlotte, NC	Mecklenburg County	56	21	-62.5	460	459	-0.2
Chicago, IL	Cook County	270	237	-12.2	10,430	10,849	4.0
Cincinnati, OH	Hamilton County	28	25	-10.7	1,500	1,164	-22.4
Clarksville, TN	Montgomery County	11	6	-45.5	333	352	5.7
Cleveland, OH	Cuyahoga County	48	53	10.4	3,240	2,994	-7.6
College Station, TX	Brazos County	8	4	-50.0	66	47	-28.8
Colorado Springs, CO	El Paso County	22	19	-13.6	728	609	-16.3
Columbia, MO	Boone County	1	5	400.0	193	171	-11.4
Columbia, SC	Richland County	8	13	62.5	348	424	21.8
Columbus, OH	Franklin County	128	38	-70.3	2,223	2,029	-8.7
Dallas, TX	Dallas County	186	237	27.4	1,797	1,984	10.4
Davenport, IA	Scott County	5	9	80.0	163	140	-14.1
Denver, CO	Denver County	72	37	-48.6	764	590	-22.8
Des Moines, IA	Polk County	22	17	-22.7	550	474	-13.8
Durham, NC	Durham County	10	5	-50.0	175	143	-18.3
Edison, NJ	Middlesex County	45	30	-33.3	843	746	-11.5
El Paso, TX	El Paso County	46	41	-10.9	961	1,092	13.6
Fargo, ND	Cass County	4	2	-50.0	131	100	-23.7
Fort Collins, CO	Larimer County	14	14	0.0	306	283	-7.5
Fort Wayne, IN	Allen County	6	13	116.7	872	767	-12.0
Fort Worth, TX	Tarrant County	151	200	32.5	2,277	2,447	7.5
Grand Rapids, MI	Kent County	8	10	25.0	469	439	-6.4
Greeley, CO	Weld County	9	16	77.8	447	400	-10.5
Green Bay, WI	Brown County	2	7	250.0	388	290	-25.3
Greensboro, NC	Guilford County	23	8	-65.2	369	336	-8.9
Honolulu, HI	Honolulu County	28	35	25.0	830	671	-19.2
Houston, TX	Harris County	269	213	-20.8	2,310	2,541	10.0
Huntsville, AL	Madison County	18	12	-33.3	894	806	-9.8
Indianapolis, IN	Marion County	45	37	-17.8	2,705	2,399	-11.3
Jacksonville, FL	Duval County	58	38	-34.5	1,336	1,226	-8.2
Kansas City, MO	Jackson County	22	16	-27.3	1,027	1,037	1.0
Lafayette, LA	Lafayette Parish	17	29	70.6	263	296	12.5
Las Cruces, NM	Dona Ana County	8	4	-50.0	187	178	-4.8
Las Vegas, NV	Clark County	181	163	-9.9	5,825	4,525	-22.3
Lexington, KY	Fayette County	8	7	-12.5	450	410	-8.9
Lincoln, NE	Lancaster County	6	14	133.3	430	304	-29.3
Little Rock, AR	Pulaski County	23	19	-17.4	1,157	1,352	16.9
Los Angeles, CA	Los Angeles County	672	626	-6.8	11,316	8,314	-26.5
Louisville, KY	Jefferson County	19	20	5.3	1,918	1,883	-1.8
Madison, WI	Dane County	26	10	-61.5	436	383	-12.2

Table continued on following page.

Appendix A: Comparative Statistics

City	Area Covered	Business Filings 2021	Business Filings 2022	% Chg.	Nonbusiness Filings 2021	Nonbusiness Filings 2022	% Chg.
Manchester, NH	Hillsborough County	19	11	-42.1	253	204	-19.4
Miami, FL	Miami-Dade County	201	224	11.4	6,432	5,081	-21.0
Midland, TX	Midland County	18	7	-61.1	64	73	14.1
Milwaukee, WI	Milwaukee County	20	20	0.0	3,237	2,957	-8.6
Minneapolis, MN	Hennepin County	52	55	5.8	1,240	1,200	-3.2
Nashville, TN	Davidson County	37	32	-13.5	959	989	3.1
New Haven, CT	New Haven County	14	12	-14.3	864	719	-16.8
New Orleans, LA	Orleans Parish	31	11	-64.5	263	287	9.1
New York, NY	Bronx County	23	27	17.4	1,219	862	-29.3
New York, NY	Kings County	108	212	96.3	1,238	1,062	-14.2
New York, NY	New York County	398	240	-39.7	721	595	-17.5
New York, NY	Queens County	82	126	53.7	1,447	1,478	2.1
New York, NY	Richmond County	24	25	4.2	310	352	13.5
Oklahoma City, OK	Oklahoma County	52	50	-3.8	1,424	1,199	-15.8
Omaha, NE	Douglas County	20	21	5.0	807	628	-22.2
Orlando, FL	Orange County	100	127	27.0	1,909	1,588	-16.8
Philadelphia, PA	Philadelphia County	31	28	-9.7	741	952	28.5
Phoenix, AZ	Maricopa County	223	172	-22.9	6,402	5,811	-9.2
Pittsburgh, PA	Allegheny County	79	72	-8.9	1,266	1,135	-10.3
Portland, OR	Multnomah County	33	17	-48.5	802	749	-6.6
Providence, RI	Providence County	16	21	31.3	638	507	-20.5
Provo, UT	Utah County	22	19	-13.6	814	790	-2.9
Raleigh, NC	Wake County	53	50	-5.7	614	536	-12.7
Reno, NV	Washoe County	25	26	4.0	592	467	-21.1
Richmond, VA	Richmond city	21	6	-71.4	590	511	-13.4
Rochester, MN	Olmsted County	0	1	n/a	90	119	32.2
Sacramento, CA	Sacramento County	80	61	-23.8	1,731	1,275	-26.3
St. Louis, MO	Saint Louis City	12	15	25.0	1,395	1,247	-10.6
Salem, OR	Marion County	7	4	-42.9	489	439	-10.2
Salt Lake City, UT	Salt Lake County	27	23	-14.8	2,389	2,147	-10.1
San Antonio, TX	Bexar County	143	84	-41.3	1,102	1,028	-6.7
San Diego, CA	San Diego County	194	158	-18.6	4,533	3,136	-30.8
San Francisco, CA	San Francisco County	65	55	-15.4	334	342	2.4
San Jose, CA	Santa Clara County	80	77	-3.8	868	655	-24.5
Santa Rosa, CA	Sonoma County	23	29	26.1	329	278	-15.5
Savannah, GA	Chatham County	9	7	-22.2	546	591	8.2
Seattle, WA	King County	56	55	-1.8	1,094	979	-10.5
Sioux Falls, SD	Minnehaha County	7	6	-14.3	221	201	-9.0
Springfield, IL	Sangamon County	6	5	-16.7	221	186	-15.8
Tampa, FL	Hillsborough County	87	94	8.0	2,061	1,686	-18.2
Tucson, AZ	Pima County	21	22	4.8	1,379	1,310	-5.0
Tulsa, OK	Tulsa County	30	51	70.0	874	758	-13.3
Tuscaloosa, AL	Tuscaloosa County	4	9	125.0	679	821	20.9
Virginia Beach, VA	Virginia Beach City	11	15	36.4	788	711	-9.8
Washington, DC	District of Columbia	36	36	0.0	264	200	-24.2
Wichita, KS	Sedgwick County	20	14	-30.0	760	658	-13.4
Wilmington, NC	New Hanover County	12	6	-50.0	144	138	-4.2
Winston-Salem, NC	Forsyth County	10	6	-40.0	240	240	0.0
Worcester, MA	Worcester County	24	26	8.3	569	550	-3.3
U.S.	U.S.	14,347	13,481	-6.0	399,269	374,240	-6.3

Note: Business filings include Chapter 7, Chapter 9, Chapter 11, Chapter 12, Chapter 13, Chapter 15, and Section 304; Nonbusiness filings include Chapter 7, Chapter 11, and Chapter 13

Source: Administrative Office of the U.S. Courts, Business and Nonbusiness Bankruptcy, County Cases Commenced by Chapter of the Bankruptcy Code, During the 12-Month Period Ending December 31, 2021 and Business and Nonbusiness Bankruptcy, County Cases Commenced by Chapter of the Bankruptcy Code, During the 12-Month Period Ending December 31, 2022

Income: City

City	Per Capita ($)	Median Household ($)	Average Household ($)
Albuquerque, NM	33,494	56,366	76,833
Allentown, PA	22,976	47,703	61,780
Anchorage, AK	43,125	88,871	113,873
Ann Arbor, MI	47,883	73,276	107,368
Athens, GA	27,194	43,466	65,960
Atlanta, GA	54,466	69,164	118,074
Austin, TX	48,550	78,965	111,233
Baltimore, MD	34,378	54,124	79,399
Boise City, ID	40,056	68,373	93,693
Boston, MA	50,344	81,744	120,939
Boulder, CO	52,057	74,902	123,606
Brownsville, TX	18,207	43,174	58,147
Cape Coral, FL	34,586	65,282	84,169
Cedar Rapids, IA	35,566	63,170	82,815
Charleston, SC	50,240	76,556	111,903
Charlotte, NC	43,080	68,367	104,228
Chicago, IL	41,821	65,781	100,347
Cincinnati, OH	34,060	45,235	73,412
Clarksville, TN	27,437	58,838	71,824
Cleveland, OH	23,415	33,678	49,942
College Station, TX	28,705	50,089	76,307
Colorado Springs, CO	37,979	71,957	93,740
Columbia, MO	32,784	57,463	80,898
Columbia, SC	32,954	48,791	79,637
Columbus, OH	32,481	58,575	75,482
Dallas, TX	37,719	58,231	92,785
Davenport, IA	32,431	56,315	76,281
Denver, CO	50,642	78,177	111,981
Des Moines, IA	31,276	58,444	74,131
Durham, NC	39,496	66,623	91,960
Edison, NJ	47,410	110,896	136,606
El Paso, TX	25,165	51,325	69,692
Fargo, ND	37,522	60,243	82,974
Fort Collins, CO	38,949	72,932	96,301
Fort Wayne, IN	29,268	53,978	70,654
Fort Worth, TX	32,569	67,927	90,141
Grand Rapids, MI	29,060	55,385	72,017
Greeley, CO	28,480	60,601	78,033
Green Bay, WI	29,822	55,221	70,879
Greensboro, NC	31,812	51,667	76,282
Honolulu, HI	41,571	76,495	105,724
Houston, TX	35,578	56,019	90,511
Huntsville, AL	38,838	60,959	87,475
Indianapolis, IN	31,538	54,321	75,792
Jacksonville, FL	32,654	58,263	79,817
Kansas City, MO	35,352	60,042	81,577
Lafayette, LA	35,348	55,329	82,752
Las Cruces, NM	26,290	47,722	64,425
Las Vegas, NV	33,363	61,356	86,008
Lexington, KY	37,475	61,526	88,901
Lincoln, NE	33,955	62,566	83,225
Little Rock, AR	39,141	56,928	89,748
Los Angeles, CA	39,378	69,778	106,931
Louisville, KY	34,195	58,357	81,393
Madison, WI	42,693	70,466	94,746
Manchester, NH	36,440	66,929	83,913

Table continued on following page.

City	Per Capita ($)	Median Household ($)	Average Household ($)
Miami, FL	34,295	47,860	79,886
Midland, TX	44,218	87,900	115,425
Milwaukee, WI	25,564	45,318	61,529
Minneapolis, MN	43,925	70,099	99,741
Nashville, TN	39,509	65,565	92,866
New Haven, CT	29,348	48,973	73,450
New Orleans, LA	34,036	45,594	76,715
New York, NY	43,952	70,663	113,315
Oklahoma City, OK	33,162	59,679	81,931
Omaha, NE	36,749	65,359	90,389
Orlando, FL	36,596	58,968	88,128
Philadelphia, PA	32,344	52,649	77,454
Phoenix, AZ	33,718	64,927	90,481
Pittsburgh, PA	37,655	54,306	80,248
Portland, OR	47,289	78,476	106,948
Providence, RI	31,757	55,787	83,046
Provo, UT	23,440	53,572	76,163
Raleigh, NC	42,632	72,996	102,100
Reno, NV	39,104	67,557	93,306
Richmond, VA	38,132	54,795	82,939
Rochester, MN	43,827	79,159	106,381
Sacramento, CA	35,793	71,074	93,320
St. Louis, MO	33,326	48,751	68,681
Salem, OR	31,610	62,185	82,450
Salt Lake City, UT	42,081	65,880	97,628
San Antonio, TX	28,579	55,084	74,154
San Diego, CA	46,460	89,457	121,230
San Francisco, CA	77,267	126,187	178,742
San Jose, CA	53,574	125,075	162,521
Santa Rosa, CA	41,880	84,823	108,164
Savannah, GA	27,952	49,832	69,653
Seattle, WA	68,836	105,391	144,955
Sioux Falls, SD	36,430	66,761	87,676
Springfield, IL	35,851	57,596	79,460
Tampa, FL	40,962	59,893	97,942
Tucson, AZ	26,373	48,058	63,665
Tulsa, OK	33,492	52,438	79,727
Tuscaloosa, AL	27,789	44,880	69,736
Virginia Beach, VA	41,803	81,810	105,521
Washington, DC	63,793	93,547	138,421
Wichita, KS	31,558	56,374	77,762
Wilmington, NC	38,890	54,066	83,853
Winston-Salem, NC	30,859	50,204	75,459
Worcester, MA	30,855	56,746	76,859
U.S.	37,638	69,021	97,196

Source: U.S. Census Bureau, 2017-2021 American Community Survey 5-Year Estimates

Income: Metro Area

Metro Area	Per Capita ($)	Median Household ($)	Average Household ($)
Albuquerque, NM	32,622	58,335	78,771
Allentown, PA	37,945	73,091	96,205
Anchorage, AK	41,201	86,252	109,817
Ann Arbor, MI	45,500	79,198	110,102
Athens, GA	31,392	52,958	80,272
Atlanta, GA	39,267	75,267	104,478
Austin, TX	44,830	85,398	114,103
Baltimore, MD	45,226	87,513	115,291
Boise City, ID	35,114	69,801	92,742
Boston, MA	53,033	99,039	135,411
Boulder, CO	52,401	92,466	128,190
Brownsville, TX	19,371	43,057	60,107
Cape Coral, FL	37,550	63,235	89,228
Cedar Rapids, IA	37,291	70,210	90,560
Charleston, SC	39,923	70,275	98,682
Charlotte, NC	38,783	69,559	98,559
Chicago, IL	42,097	78,790	109,339
Cincinnati, OH	37,846	70,308	94,687
Clarksville, TN	28,243	57,963	74,308
Cleveland, OH	36,907	61,320	85,864
College Station, TX	30,182	53,541	78,104
Colorado Springs, CO	37,650	75,641	97,647
Columbia, MO	33,131	61,901	82,741
Columbia, SC	32,508	58,992	79,903
Columbus, OH	38,167	71,020	95,315
Dallas, TX	38,609	76,916	105,647
Davenport, IA	34,859	63,282	83,352
Denver, CO	47,026	88,512	117,250
Des Moines, IA	39,333	75,134	97,364
Durham, NC	40,502	68,913	99,164
Edison, NJ	47,591	86,445	127,555
El Paso, TX	23,934	50,849	68,522
Fargo, ND	38,367	68,560	91,642
Fort Collins, CO	42,596	80,664	104,442
Fort Wayne, IN	32,207	62,031	80,675
Fort Worth, TX	38,609	76,916	105,647
Grand Rapids, MI	34,581	70,347	91,126
Greeley, CO	35,707	80,843	99,568
Green Bay, WI	35,678	68,952	87,144
Greensboro, NC	31,655	55,544	77,839
Honolulu, HI	40,339	92,600	118,470
Houston, TX	36,821	72,551	103,497
Huntsville, AL	38,800	71,057	94,763
Indianapolis, IN	36,867	67,330	92,858
Jacksonville, FL	36,316	66,664	91,361
Kansas City, MO	39,175	73,299	96,817
Lafayette, LA	30,758	55,539	77,448
Las Cruces, NM	24,645	47,151	65,405
Las Vegas, NV	33,461	64,210	87,879
Lexington, KY	36,123	63,360	88,439
Lincoln, NE	35,055	65,508	87,123
Little Rock, AR	33,523	58,441	81,542
Los Angeles, CA	39,895	81,652	115,584
Louisville, KY	35,613	64,533	87,361
Madison, WI	43,359	77,519	100,891
Manchester, NH	45,238	86,930	111,733

Table continued on following page.

Metro Area	Per Capita ($)	Median Household ($)	Average Household ($)
Miami, FL	36,174	62,870	94,059
Midland, TX	43,287	87,812	114,916
Milwaukee, WI	38,930	67,448	92,423
Minneapolis, MN	45,301	87,397	114,491
Nashville, TN	39,269	72,537	99,987
New Haven, CT	41,192	75,043	102,367
New Orleans, LA	33,792	57,656	83,052
New York, NY	47,591	86,445	127,555
Oklahoma City, OK	34,136	63,351	85,884
Omaha, NE	38,289	73,757	97,122
Orlando, FL	32,999	65,086	89,689
Philadelphia, PA	43,195	79,070	109,757
Phoenix, AZ	36,842	72,211	97,412
Pittsburgh, PA	39,416	65,894	90,001
Portland, OR	42,946	82,901	108,110
Providence, RI	39,267	74,422	97,540
Provo, UT	29,817	82,742	105,296
Raleigh, NC	42,554	83,581	110,195
Reno, NV	40,299	74,216	100,824
Richmond, VA	40,254	74,592	100,389
Rochester, MN	42,841	80,865	106,479
Sacramento, CA	39,510	81,264	107,069
St. Louis, MO	39,168	69,635	94,953
Salem, OR	31,447	65,881	85,642
Salt Lake City, UT	36,688	82,506	105,669
San Antonio, TX	32,580	65,355	88,127
San Diego, CA	42,696	88,240	118,474
San Francisco, CA	62,070	118,547	165,749
San Jose, CA	64,169	138,370	187,324
Santa Rosa, CA	47,580	91,607	121,206
Savannah, GA	34,908	64,703	89,172
Seattle, WA	51,872	97,675	130,964
Sioux Falls, SD	37,200	72,547	92,236
Springfield, IL	37,961	66,999	87,390
Tampa, FL	35,879	61,121	86,382
Tucson, AZ	33,016	59,215	80,772
Tulsa, OK	33,647	60,866	84,069
Tuscaloosa, AL	28,204	54,449	72,452
Virginia Beach, VA	37,548	71,612	93,415
Washington, DC	54,663	111,252	145,303
Wichita, KS	32,124	61,445	81,209
Wilmington, NC	38,607	63,036	89,355
Winston-Salem, NC	31,238	55,454	76,451
Worcester, MA	40,750	80,333	104,366
U.S.	37,638	69,021	97,196

Note: Figures cover the Metropolitan Statistical Area (MSA)
Source: U.S. Census Bureau, 2017-2021 American Community Survey 5-Year Estimates

Household Income Distribution: City

City	Under $15,000	$15,000 -$24,999	$25,000 -$34,999	$35,000 -$49,999	$50,000 -$74,999	$75,000 -$99,999	$100,000 -$149,999	$150,000 and up
Albuquerque, NM	13.1	8.9	9.8	12.9	18.0	11.6	14.8	10.9
Allentown, PA	13.0	12.4	10.9	16.1	19.7	11.2	10.9	5.7
Anchorage, AK	5.5	5.1	5.5	9.0	17.1	14.1	20.2	23.6
Ann Arbor, MI	14.5	6.2	6.2	8.9	15.2	11.2	15.7	22.2
Athens, GA	17.8	12.2	12.4	12.8	15.4	9.2	11.3	8.8
Atlanta, GA	14.2	8.1	7.3	9.4	14.5	11.0	13.5	22.0
Austin, TX	8.3	5.5	6.7	10.4	16.8	12.6	17.7	22.1
Baltimore, MD	16.6	9.1	8.9	12.2	17.1	10.8	12.7	12.8
Boise City, ID	7.6	7.6	8.6	12.4	18.5	13.9	15.7	15.7
Boston, MA	14.9	7.2	5.5	7.7	11.9	10.5	16.1	26.2
Boulder, CO	13.1	7.8	6.7	8.9	13.6	9.5	13.8	26.6
Brownsville, TX	18.6	13.1	10.0	13.0	18.2	10.7	10.6	5.9
Cape Coral, FL	7.6	6.2	8.7	13.7	20.5	15.4	17.2	10.6
Cedar Rapids, IA	7.1	8.5	9.5	13.6	19.9	14.8	14.9	11.7
Charleston, SC	9.1	6.5	6.2	11.3	15.8	12.3	18.6	20.3
Charlotte, NC	7.8	6.7	8.5	12.7	18.3	12.5	15.8	17.7
Chicago, IL	13.1	8.7	8.2	10.2	14.9	11.7	14.7	18.6
Cincinnati, OH	18.0	11.9	10.5	12.6	15.3	10.1	10.6	11.0
Clarksville, TN	9.6	6.8	9.9	15.2	20.6	15.3	15.5	7.2
Cleveland, OH	25.4	13.8	12.4	13.8	14.7	8.7	7.0	4.4
College Station, TX	19.7	10.2	8.8	11.2	15.3	10.0	12.3	12.4
Colorado Springs, CO	7.8	6.6	7.6	12.0	18.0	14.2	17.3	16.4
Columbia, MO	12.8	9.6	9.8	12.6	17.3	11.5	13.2	13.2
Columbia, SC	18.9	10.2	9.7	12.6	14.8	10.5	11.2	12.1
Columbus, OH	10.8	8.4	9.5	13.6	19.5	13.5	15.3	9.5
Dallas, TX	11.3	8.6	9.6	13.7	18.4	11.3	12.1	14.8
Davenport, IA	10.9	9.1	9.0	13.6	20.8	12.8	14.6	9.2
Denver, CO	8.6	6.1	6.4	10.3	16.9	12.4	17.0	22.2
Des Moines, IA	10.0	8.9	9.4	14.7	20.2	14.3	13.6	8.9
Durham, NC	8.9	6.8	9.7	12.2	17.2	13.1	15.7	16.4
Edison, NJ	4.6	3.4	3.5	7.2	13.3	12.4	21.8	34.0
El Paso, TX	13.8	11.4	10.6	13.3	18.8	10.7	12.7	8.8
Fargo, ND	9.8	9.1	9.7	12.9	18.4	13.0	15.5	11.7
Fort Collins, CO	9.6	6.7	7.5	11.0	16.5	13.0	17.2	18.5
Fort Wayne, IN	10.4	10.4	10.8	14.8	19.8	13.2	13.1	7.5
Fort Worth, TX	8.7	7.0	8.7	11.6	18.6	13.5	17.2	14.6
Grand Rapids, MI	12.5	9.8	8.1	14.1	19.0	14.1	14.3	8.0
Greeley, CO	10.3	8.2	9.7	13.9	16.1	13.7	17.9	10.3
Green Bay, WI	10.1	9.4	10.0	15.0	21.7	13.0	13.6	7.3
Greensboro, NC	12.2	9.7	10.9	15.7	17.5	11.3	12.7	9.9
Honolulu, HI	9.1	6.3	6.1	11.0	16.5	13.2	17.1	20.6
Houston, TX	11.9	9.5	10.6	13.1	17.1	10.7	12.1	14.9
Huntsville, AL	11.5	9.2	10.1	12.3	15.2	11.4	14.4	15.9
Indianapolis, IN	12.1	9.6	9.9	14.5	18.8	11.9	12.9	10.4
Jacksonville, FL	10.9	8.4	9.6	13.8	18.9	13.2	14.3	10.9
Kansas City, MO	11.4	8.8	9.6	12.7	17.2	12.7	15.2	12.3
Lafayette, LA	16.0	8.5	9.7	11.5	15.4	11.4	13.3	14.2
Las Cruces, NM	17.5	12.3	10.4	12.2	17.4	9.8	13.1	7.4
Las Vegas, NV	11.6	8.1	8.7	12.9	17.3	13.1	15.2	13.0
Lexington, KY	10.6	8.9	9.5	12.1	17.6	12.3	14.9	14.1
Lincoln, NE	8.4	7.9	9.8	13.0	20.2	12.4	16.1	12.0
Little Rock, AR	11.5	10.1	10.4	13.4	16.2	11.5	12.3	14.4
Los Angeles, CA	11.6	7.8	7.8	10.4	15.1	11.7	15.4	20.1
Louisville, KY	11.2	8.8	9.5	13.3	18.5	12.3	14.3	11.9

Table continued on following page.

| City | Percent of Households Earning ||||||||
	Under $15,000	$15,000 -$24,999	$25,000 -$34,999	$35,000 -$49,999	$50,000 -$74,999	$75,000 -$99,999	$100,000 -$149,999	$150,000 and up
Madison, WI	10.0	6.8	7.5	11.0	17.5	14.1	16.9	16.0
Manchester, NH	8.0	7.7	7.3	13.7	19.8	14.0	17.0	12.5
Miami, FL	17.7	11.8	10.1	11.8	16.1	9.4	11.1	12.0
Midland, TX	8.0	5.8	6.5	8.5	14.7	12.5	19.6	24.4
Milwaukee, WI	16.5	11.5	11.7	14.6	17.8	11.6	10.5	5.8
Minneapolis, MN	11.3	7.1	7.5	11.0	16.1	12.6	15.9	18.5
Nashville, TN	9.1	7.1	8.2	12.9	19.1	13.2	15.6	14.8
New Haven, CT	18.5	11.0	9.8	11.2	17.2	10.3	11.4	10.6
New Orleans, LA	21.3	11.3	9.5	10.4	15.0	9.4	10.8	12.3
New York, NY	13.2	8.0	7.3	9.6	14.0	11.0	15.0	21.9
Oklahoma City, OK	10.7	7.7	9.6	13.9	18.7	12.8	14.6	12.1
Omaha, NE	9.5	7.3	8.4	12.5	18.9	13.7	15.5	14.1
Orlando, FL	11.2	9.3	8.7	13.6	17.9	11.7	13.0	14.5
Philadelphia, PA	17.1	9.8	9.2	12.0	16.4	11.3	12.4	11.7
Phoenix, AZ	8.4	7.6	8.8	13.5	18.2	13.5	15.3	14.8
Pittsburgh, PA	16.3	9.8	9.6	11.2	16.1	11.7	12.6	12.8
Portland, OR	9.8	6.3	6.7	9.7	15.7	12.6	17.5	21.8
Providence, RI	15.7	10.6	8.8	11.3	17.4	11.9	12.0	12.4
Provo, UT	11.4	10.2	11.3	14.1	19.1	12.7	10.7	10.5
Raleigh, NC	7.5	6.5	8.7	12.1	16.7	12.9	17.0	18.8
Reno, NV	8.6	7.7	8.6	11.5	18.1	13.4	16.7	15.3
Richmond, VA	14.1	9.6	9.4	13.7	17.4	11.3	11.7	12.7
Rochester, MN	6.9	6.3	5.8	10.4	18.0	13.9	18.8	19.9
Sacramento, CA	10.5	6.9	7.2	10.4	17.3	13.8	17.2	16.7
St. Louis, MO	17.0	10.3	10.7	12.9	17.5	10.5	12.1	8.9
Salem, OR	9.9	8.3	8.7	12.8	19.4	13.0	16.6	11.3
Salt Lake City, UT	11.2	6.9	8.6	10.9	18.1	13.1	15.0	16.2
San Antonio, TX	12.2	9.5	10.3	13.6	19.1	12.0	13.3	10.0
San Diego, CA	7.3	5.4	5.9	8.6	15.2	12.6	19.0	26.0
San Francisco, CA	9.2	4.9	4.5	6.0	9.1	8.3	14.9	43.2
San Jose, CA	5.2	4.2	4.2	6.3	10.9	9.9	17.7	41.6
Santa Rosa, CA	7.3	4.9	6.0	10.1	15.6	13.8	20.2	22.1
Savannah, GA	14.7	11.5	10.4	13.6	18.3	11.2	11.7	8.6
Seattle, WA	7.8	4.5	4.7	7.5	12.8	10.6	17.9	34.1
Sioux Falls, SD	7.3	7.4	9.7	12.4	19.1	15.0	17.1	11.9
Springfield, IL	13.8	9.1	9.7	11.9	16.0	13.3	15.0	11.2
Tampa, FL	12.9	8.5	9.4	12.0	15.8	10.8	13.3	17.3
Tucson, AZ	13.9	11.4	11.3	15.2	18.1	12.0	11.7	6.4
Tulsa, OK	12.7	9.8	11.0	14.2	17.7	11.5	11.7	11.5
Tuscaloosa, AL	19.5	10.8	10.9	11.9	15.4	8.7	12.8	10.0
Virginia Beach, VA	5.6	4.5	6.3	10.5	18.8	14.6	20.9	18.8
Washington, DC	11.9	5.1	5.5	6.8	12.2	11.3	15.9	31.3
Wichita, KS	10.8	9.3	10.3	14.0	18.9	12.8	13.6	10.3
Wilmington, NC	14.8	9.7	8.2	13.5	18.5	10.4	12.5	12.5
Winston-Salem, NC	13.8	10.6	11.2	14.2	16.4	12.3	11.7	9.8
Worcester, MA	15.5	9.8	8.5	12.0	15.8	11.7	14.8	11.8
U.S.	9.4	7.8	8.2	11.4	16.8	12.8	16.3	17.3

Source: U.S. Census Bureau, 2017-2021 American Community Survey 5-Year Estimates

Household Income Distribution: Metro Area

Metro Area	Under $15,000	$15,000 -$24,999	$25,000 -$34,999	$35,000 -$49,999	$50,000 -$74,999	$75,000 -$99,999	$100,000 -$149,999	$150,000 and up
Albuquerque, NM	12.0	8.9	9.3	13.0	18.0	12.3	15.0	11.5
Allentown, PA	7.3	7.6	7.6	11.8	17.0	13.7	17.9	17.2
Anchorage, AK	6.1	5.5	5.7	9.0	17.1	14.1	20.1	22.4
Ann Arbor, MI	9.7	6.0	6.9	9.7	15.5	12.5	17.4	22.3
Athens, GA	14.0	10.2	11.1	12.3	15.9	10.2	13.7	12.5
Atlanta, GA	7.6	6.5	7.5	11.1	17.2	13.3	17.3	19.5
Austin, TX	6.8	5.1	6.3	9.7	16.1	13.6	19.1	23.4
Baltimore, MD	8.0	5.5	5.9	9.3	14.8	12.5	18.8	25.1
Boise City, ID	7.0	7.1	7.6	12.0	20.4	14.6	17.3	14.2
Boston, MA	8.1	5.6	5.2	7.6	12.5	11.4	18.2	31.3
Boulder, CO	7.9	5.7	5.5	8.3	13.7	12.1	18.2	28.5
Brownsville, TX	16.8	13.4	11.5	12.9	17.9	10.7	10.6	6.3
Cape Coral, FL	9.1	7.9	9.2	13.2	19.0	13.8	14.9	12.8
Cedar Rapids, IA	6.6	7.4	8.5	12.1	19.2	14.9	17.0	14.4
Charleston, SC	8.4	7.7	7.8	11.6	17.3	13.4	17.1	16.7
Charlotte, NC	7.9	7.3	8.3	12.1	17.7	13.1	16.4	17.2
Chicago, IL	8.7	6.6	7.1	9.9	15.6	12.8	17.9	21.5
Cincinnati, OH	9.2	7.6	8.0	11.1	17.0	13.3	17.5	16.3
Clarksville, TN	10.8	7.6	10.3	14.0	19.6	14.5	14.8	8.5
Cleveland, OH	11.6	8.6	9.0	12.5	17.2	12.7	15.0	13.5
College Station, TX	16.0	9.6	8.9	12.5	17.0	11.2	13.1	11.7
Colorado Springs, CO	6.9	6.2	6.9	11.5	18.1	14.1	18.4	17.9
Columbia, MO	10.8	8.5	9.5	12.3	18.3	13.3	14.8	12.5
Columbia, SC	12.0	8.3	9.4	12.8	18.2	13.1	14.4	11.8
Columbus, OH	8.1	7.0	7.9	11.6	17.9	13.3	17.6	16.6
Dallas, TX	7.1	6.0	7.4	11.1	17.3	13.3	17.9	20.0
Davenport, IA	9.6	8.2	8.7	12.4	18.8	13.7	16.5	12.0
Denver, CO	6.2	4.8	5.7	9.5	16.3	13.2	19.9	24.5
Des Moines, IA	6.4	6.3	7.4	11.8	18.1	14.1	19.0	16.9
Durham, NC	9.2	7.1	9.1	11.5	16.4	12.4	15.6	18.8
Edison, NJ	9.7	6.6	6.3	8.6	13.3	11.2	16.7	27.5
El Paso, TX	13.8	11.2	10.7	13.5	19.0	10.9	12.5	8.3
Fargo, ND	8.7	7.9	7.9	11.8	17.3	13.8	17.9	14.7
Fort Collins, CO	7.9	6.2	6.6	10.0	16.0	14.2	18.8	20.3
Fort Wayne, IN	8.2	8.9	9.5	13.5	19.5	14.9	15.3	10.3
Fort Worth, TX	7.1	6.0	7.4	11.1	17.3	13.3	17.9	20.0
Grand Rapids, MI	7.1	7.4	7.5	12.3	19.2	14.8	17.9	13.9
Greeley, CO	6.6	5.7	7.3	10.2	16.7	14.3	22.2	16.9
Green Bay, WI	7.0	7.1	8.7	12.3	19.2	15.2	18.3	12.1
Greensboro, NC	11.3	9.5	10.3	14.5	17.9	12.1	13.8	10.5
Honolulu, HI	6.5	4.5	5.4	9.0	14.7	13.5	20.0	26.3
Houston, TX	8.4	7.1	8.2	11.0	16.6	12.3	16.5	19.8
Huntsville, AL	8.8	8.0	8.2	11.7	15.4	12.8	16.9	18.2
Indianapolis, IN	8.6	7.4	8.3	12.1	18.4	13.4	16.2	15.6
Jacksonville, FL	9.0	7.1	8.6	12.5	18.3	13.7	15.8	15.0
Kansas City, MO	7.5	6.9	8.1	11.4	17.1	13.9	18.1	17.0
Lafayette, LA	13.7	10.4	10.0	11.9	15.8	12.9	14.4	11.1
Las Cruces, NM	16.8	12.7	10.8	12.2	17.7	9.5	12.9	7.3
Las Vegas, NV	9.7	7.7	8.8	12.8	18.2	13.4	15.7	13.6
Lexington, KY	10.0	8.2	9.3	12.4	17.6	12.9	16.1	13.4
Lincoln, NE	7.8	7.5	9.4	12.6	19.7	12.8	17.1	13.1
Little Rock, AR	11.0	9.2	10.1	13.3	17.5	12.4	14.9	11.6
Los Angeles, CA	9.0	6.4	6.8	9.5	14.8	12.3	17.4	23.8
Louisville, KY	9.2	7.9	8.9	12.9	18.3	13.2	16.0	13.6

Table continued on following page.

Appendix A: Comparative Statistics   A-73

Metro Area	Under $15,000	$15,000 -$24,999	$25,000 -$34,999	$35,000 -$49,999	$50,000 -$74,999	$75,000 -$99,999	$100,000 -$149,999	$150,000 and up
Madison, WI	6.9	6.0	6.7	11.1	17.7	14.3	18.9	18.3
Manchester, NH	5.4	5.5	6.2	10.2	15.7	13.2	20.1	23.7
Miami, FL	10.8	8.5	9.0	12.2	17.2	12.2	14.6	15.5
Midland, TX	7.6	5.8	7.1	8.8	14.1	12.8	19.2	24.6
Milwaukee, WI	9.4	7.8	8.5	11.8	17.1	13.2	16.7	15.5
Minneapolis, MN	6.1	5.2	6.1	9.7	16.0	13.7	20.2	23.2
Nashville, TN	7.4	6.5	7.4	12.1	18.2	13.9	17.5	16.9
New Haven, CT	9.4	7.6	6.9	10.1	15.8	12.5	17.1	20.4
New Orleans, LA	14.1	9.6	9.1	11.5	16.5	11.7	14.0	13.5
New York, NY	9.7	6.6	6.3	8.6	13.3	11.2	16.7	27.5
Oklahoma City, OK	9.4	7.9	9.1	13.0	18.6	13.4	15.6	12.8
Omaha, NE	7.6	6.5	7.7	11.3	17.7	14.2	18.5	16.4
Orlando, FL	8.3	7.9	9.0	12.9	18.5	13.6	15.8	14.0
Philadelphia, PA	9.3	6.7	7.1	9.7	15.1	12.5	17.3	22.5
Phoenix, AZ	7.4	6.6	7.7	12.0	18.1	13.9	17.7	16.7
Pittsburgh, PA	9.7	8.4	8.7	11.8	17.0	12.9	16.5	14.9
Portland, OR	7.2	5.7	6.3	10.0	16.3	13.6	19.5	21.5
Providence, RI	9.7	7.9	7.3	10.1	15.2	13.2	18.2	18.3
Provo, UT	5.1	5.0	6.4	10.4	17.9	15.7	20.8	18.6
Raleigh, NC	6.3	6.0	7.0	10.4	15.8	12.8	19.5	22.3
Reno, NV	7.2	6.7	7.8	10.8	18.0	14.0	18.3	17.2
Richmond, VA	7.9	6.7	7.2	11.2	17.2	13.1	18.3	18.3
Rochester, MN	6.2	6.0	6.4	10.1	17.8	14.0	20.1	19.5
Sacramento, CA	8.3	6.1	6.7	9.5	15.9	13.2	18.3	22.1
St. Louis, MO	8.6	7.4	8.1	11.8	17.5	13.5	16.9	16.3
Salem, OR	8.5	7.8	8.7	12.3	18.9	13.8	17.5	12.3
Salt Lake City, UT	6.0	4.8	6.3	10.2	17.9	14.8	20.6	19.3
San Antonio, TX	9.6	7.9	8.9	12.0	18.2	13.0	16.1	14.4
San Diego, CA	6.9	5.7	6.3	9.1	15.0	12.6	18.9	25.5
San Francisco, CA	6.7	4.3	4.5	6.4	10.8	10.0	17.1	40.0
San Jose, CA	4.9	3.6	3.7	5.5	9.9	9.2	16.8	46.6
Santa Rosa, CA	6.5	5.0	5.9	9.0	14.3	13.4	19.6	26.3
Savannah, GA	9.4	7.9	8.6	12.0	18.6	14.1	15.9	13.5
Seattle, WA	5.9	4.6	5.1	8.2	14.7	12.5	19.8	29.2
Sioux Falls, SD	6.2	6.7	8.7	11.8	18.7	15.7	18.9	13.3
Springfield, IL	10.4	7.9	8.4	11.5	16.2	14.1	18.0	13.7
Tampa, FL	9.9	8.6	9.5	13.2	18.0	12.7	14.6	13.7
Tucson, AZ	10.8	9.2	9.6	13.4	17.3	13.1	14.9	11.7
Tulsa, OK	9.6	8.5	9.9	13.1	18.6	12.8	15.3	12.2
Tuscaloosa, AL	14.3	9.9	10.2	12.1	17.3	12.0	14.5	9.6
Virginia Beach, VA	8.0	7.0	7.6	11.3	18.3	13.9	18.4	15.5
Washington, DC	5.7	3.7	4.4	6.8	12.6	12.0	19.6	35.4
Wichita, KS	9.2	8.6	9.1	13.4	19.6	13.4	15.5	11.0
Wilmington, NC	11.0	8.7	7.8	12.4	18.0	12.0	16.0	14.0
Winston-Salem, NC	11.0	10.0	10.7	13.7	18.1	13.1	13.3	10.1
Worcester, MA	8.6	6.8	7.0	9.6	15.3	12.5	18.5	21.8
U.S.	9.4	7.8	8.2	11.4	16.8	12.8	16.3	17.3

Note: Figures cover the Metropolitan Statistical Area (MSA)
Source: Source: U.S. Census Bureau, 2017-2021 American Community Survey 5-Year Estimates

Poverty Rate: City

City	All Ages	Under 18 Years Old	18 to 64 Years Old	65 Years and Over
Albuquerque, NM	16.2	21.0	15.7	11.7
Allentown, PA	23.3	34.9	19.6	16.6
Anchorage, AK	9.1	11.1	8.8	6.8
Ann Arbor, MI	22.5	10.8	27.7	6.3
Athens, GA	26.6	25.8	29.5	11.1
Atlanta, GA	18.5	27.1	16.5	16.9
Austin, TX	12.5	15.9	11.7	11.3
Baltimore, MD	20.3	27.9	18.2	18.6
Boise City, ID	11.6	13.8	11.6	8.6
Boston, MA	17.6	23.7	15.6	21.0
Boulder, CO	20.9	8.6	25.6	6.4
Brownsville, TX	26.5	36.4	21.2	28.2
Cape Coral, FL	9.9	15.4	8.7	8.8
Cedar Rapids, IA	11.2	15.5	10.9	6.4
Charleston, SC	12.0	14.6	12.6	6.4
Charlotte, NC	11.6	17.3	10.1	8.7
Chicago, IL	17.1	24.2	15.1	15.9
Cincinnati, OH	24.7	37.4	22.3	14.7
Clarksville, TN	13.2	16.9	12.4	7.2
Cleveland, OH	31.4	45.7	28.3	22.8
College Station, TX	28.2	13.2	34.3	5.9
Colorado Springs, CO	10.9	13.7	10.7	7.5
Columbia, MO	19.9	14.9	23.7	6.1
Columbia, SC	24.3	31.3	23.5	16.7
Columbus, OH	18.4	27.1	16.5	11.6
Dallas, TX	17.7	26.9	14.7	14.7
Davenport, IA	15.8	24.7	14.1	9.8
Denver, CO	11.6	16.0	10.4	11.3
Des Moines, IA	15.3	22.6	13.6	9.8
Durham, NC	13.5	19.6	12.5	8.9
Edison, NJ	5.8	7.1	5.1	6.6
El Paso, TX	18.3	25.3	15.1	19.1
Fargo, ND	12.9	14.1	14.1	4.8
Fort Collins, CO	15.7	8.9	18.7	7.3
Fort Wayne, IN	15.5	23.9	13.7	8.3
Fort Worth, TX	13.4	19.1	11.3	10.7
Grand Rapids, MI	18.6	25.6	17.1	13.9
Greeley, CO	15.3	20.5	14.5	9.1
Green Bay, WI	15.4	21.5	14.2	10.3
Greensboro, NC	17.4	24.3	15.9	13.0
Honolulu, HI	11.0	13.3	10.4	10.8
Houston, TX	19.5	29.7	16.3	15.1
Huntsville, AL	14.6	21.8	13.9	8.3
Indianapolis, IN	16.4	23.3	14.9	10.5
Jacksonville, FL	14.9	21.1	13.0	12.7
Kansas City, MO	15.0	22.2	13.4	10.1
Lafayette, LA	19.5	29.0	17.8	12.9
Las Cruces, NM	21.8	26.9	22.4	11.5
Las Vegas, NV	14.9	20.8	13.6	11.3
Lexington, KY	15.7	18.6	16.5	7.6
Lincoln, NE	13.0	13.5	14.4	6.1
Little Rock, AR	15.6	22.9	14.2	9.2
Los Angeles, CA	16.6	22.9	14.7	16.3
Louisville, KY	15.2	22.6	14.0	9.4
Madison, WI	16.6	13.0	19.2	7.1

Table continued on following page.

City	All Ages	Under 18 Years Old	18 to 64 Years Old	65 Years and Over
Manchester, NH	12.5	22.1	10.7	8.6
Miami, FL	20.9	27.8	16.6	30.9
Midland, TX	10.6	13.5	9.1	11.8
Milwaukee, WI	24.1	33.4	21.6	15.9
Minneapolis, MN	17.0	21.2	16.3	13.6
Nashville, TN	14.5	22.7	12.7	10.4
New Haven, CT	24.6	31.4	23.3	17.4
New Orleans, LA	23.8	33.8	21.5	20.6
New York, NY	17.0	23.2	14.7	17.8
Oklahoma City, OK	14.9	21.5	13.6	8.4
Omaha, NE	12.1	15.7	11.4	8.4
Orlando, FL	15.5	21.5	13.7	14.5
Philadelphia, PA	22.8	31.9	20.6	18.9
Phoenix, AZ	15.4	22.7	13.3	10.5
Pittsburgh, PA	19.7	28.8	19.0	14.0
Portland, OR	12.6	13.5	12.7	10.6
Providence, RI	21.5	30.3	18.8	19.5
Provo, UT	24.6	17.7	28.2	10.0
Raleigh, NC	12.1	15.8	11.8	7.2
Reno, NV	12.6	13.6	12.4	11.8
Richmond, VA	19.8	30.2	18.3	13.5
Rochester, MN	8.7	9.6	8.9	6.4
Sacramento, CA	14.8	18.5	14.1	12.1
St. Louis, MO	19.6	27.3	18.3	15.4
Salem, OR	14.7	18.0	14.5	10.2
Salt Lake City, UT	14.7	15.4	15.2	10.3
San Antonio, TX	17.6	25.8	15.3	13.6
San Diego, CA	11.6	13.9	11.3	9.4
San Francisco, CA	10.3	10.1	9.4	14.4
San Jose, CA	7.7	8.2	7.1	9.5
Santa Rosa, CA	9.8	12.9	9.0	9.0
Savannah, GA	19.8	29.7	18.1	12.1
Seattle, WA	10.0	9.5	9.9	11.2
Sioux Falls, SD	9.5	10.6	9.6	6.8
Springfield, IL	18.5	28.2	17.6	9.2
Tampa, FL	17.2	23.7	14.6	19.3
Tucson, AZ	19.8	25.3	19.7	12.5
Tulsa, OK	18.0	26.8	16.7	8.8
Tuscaloosa, AL	22.6	21.7	24.5	14.8
Virginia Beach, VA	7.8	10.5	7.6	4.8
Washington, DC	15.4	22.8	13.7	13.9
Wichita, KS	15.2	20.8	14.5	8.5
Wilmington, NC	18.8	25.3	19.8	8.7
Winston-Salem, NC	19.0	30.1	16.9	9.5
Worcester, MA	19.3	24.8	18.1	16.6
U.S.	12.6	17.0	11.8	9.6

Note: Figures are percentage of people whose income during the past 12 months was below the poverty level;
Source: U.S. Census Bureau, 2017-2021 American Community Survey 5-Year Estimates

Poverty Rate: Metro Area

Metro Area	All Ages	Under 18 Years Old	18 to 64 Years Old	65 Years and Over
Albuquerque, NM	15.3	19.5	14.9	11.3
Allentown, PA	10.4	15.9	9.4	7.3
Anchorage, AK	9.6	11.5	9.2	7.4
Ann Arbor, MI	13.4	11.1	15.8	5.8
Athens, GA	20.1	20.5	22.3	9.5
Atlanta, GA	11.1	15.5	9.9	8.5
Austin, TX	10.2	12.0	9.9	8.3
Baltimore, MD	9.8	12.7	9.0	8.8
Boise City, ID	9.9	11.2	9.9	7.6
Boston, MA	9.0	10.3	8.4	9.5
Boulder, CO	11.0	7.1	13.2	6.4
Brownsville, TX	26.3	37.9	21.2	21.8
Cape Coral, FL	12.0	18.7	11.5	9.0
Cedar Rapids, IA	9.5	12.0	9.4	6.5
Charleston, SC	12.1	18.2	10.9	8.1
Charlotte, NC	10.7	14.9	9.7	8.4
Chicago, IL	11.1	15.1	10.1	9.4
Cincinnati, OH	11.6	15.5	10.9	8.1
Clarksville, TN	13.5	17.0	12.6	9.2
Cleveland, OH	13.7	19.6	12.8	9.7
College Station, TX	22.3	20.5	25.3	8.6
Colorado Springs, CO	9.5	12.0	9.2	6.6
Columbia, MO	16.2	14.6	18.7	6.8
Columbia, SC	14.9	19.9	14.2	10.6
Columbus, OH	12.3	17.0	11.5	7.7
Dallas, TX	10.9	15.4	9.4	8.9
Davenport, IA	12.6	18.5	11.8	7.6
Denver, CO	8.1	10.2	7.6	7.1
Des Moines, IA	9.0	11.5	8.6	6.6
Durham, NC	13.2	17.8	12.9	8.2
Edison, NJ	12.3	16.6	10.8	12.1
El Paso, TX	19.3	26.5	15.9	20.0
Fargo, ND	11.3	12.1	12.2	5.5
Fort Collins, CO	11.1	8.8	13.0	6.6
Fort Wayne, IN	12.1	17.9	10.9	6.9
Fort Worth, TX	10.9	15.4	9.4	8.9
Grand Rapids, MI	9.8	11.7	9.5	7.8
Greeley, CO	9.7	12.1	9.0	7.7
Green Bay, WI	9.4	12.0	9.0	7.1
Greensboro, NC	15.1	21.5	14.0	10.3
Honolulu, HI	8.6	11.0	7.9	8.0
Houston, TX	13.3	18.9	11.5	10.5
Huntsville, AL	11.0	15.0	10.1	8.9
Indianapolis, IN	11.1	15.0	10.2	7.7
Jacksonville, FL	12.3	17.2	11.3	9.3
Kansas City, MO	9.8	13.5	9.0	7.0
Lafayette, LA	18.5	26.6	16.6	12.9
Las Cruces, NM	23.2	30.9	22.2	14.7
Las Vegas, NV	13.6	19.0	12.5	9.8
Lexington, KY	14.1	17.2	14.4	8.3
Lincoln, NE	11.8	11.9	13.1	5.9
Little Rock, AR	14.0	18.8	13.4	9.1
Los Angeles, CA	12.9	17.2	11.6	12.4
Louisville, KY	12.0	17.0	11.1	8.2
Madison, WI	10.1	9.0	11.5	5.8

Table continued on following page.

Metro Area	All Ages	Under 18 Years Old	18 to 64 Years Old	65 Years and Over
Manchester, NH	7.2	9.8	6.5	6.2
Miami, FL	13.6	18.0	11.6	15.6
Midland, TX	11.2	15.9	8.9	11.2
Milwaukee, WI	12.6	17.7	11.6	9.0
Minneapolis, MN	8.1	10.1	7.7	6.8
Nashville, TN	10.9	14.6	10.2	8.3
New Haven, CT	11.5	15.8	11.1	7.9
New Orleans, LA	17.3	24.6	15.7	13.3
New York, NY	12.3	16.6	10.8	12.1
Oklahoma City, OK	13.6	18.6	12.9	7.8
Omaha, NE	9.3	11.2	9.0	7.1
Orlando, FL	12.6	17.1	11.7	9.9
Philadelphia, PA	11.7	16.0	10.9	9.2
Phoenix, AZ	12.0	16.9	11.0	8.3
Pittsburgh, PA	10.7	14.2	10.3	8.3
Portland, OR	9.9	11.3	9.8	8.2
Providence, RI	11.2	15.2	10.3	9.6
Provo, UT	9.3	7.9	10.7	5.2
Raleigh, NC	9.3	12.1	8.7	6.9
Reno, NV	11.0	12.8	10.6	9.9
Richmond, VA	10.2	14.1	9.4	7.7
Rochester, MN	7.4	8.6	7.4	6.0
Sacramento, CA	12.2	14.9	12.0	8.8
St. Louis, MO	10.5	14.4	9.9	7.7
Salem, OR	13.1	16.8	12.8	8.8
Salt Lake City, UT	8.2	9.2	8.0	6.5
San Antonio, TX	13.8	19.4	12.1	10.7
San Diego, CA	10.7	13.2	10.3	8.9
San Francisco, CA	8.4	9.1	8.1	9.1
San Jose, CA	6.7	6.8	6.3	8.2
Santa Rosa, CA	8.7	10.3	8.6	7.4
Savannah, GA	12.5	17.5	11.5	8.6
Seattle, WA	8.3	9.7	7.9	7.8
Sioux Falls, SD	7.9	8.5	8.0	6.3
Springfield, IL	13.6	20.0	13.2	7.3
Tampa, FL	12.9	17.4	12.1	10.9
Tucson, AZ	15.1	20.2	15.5	8.6
Tulsa, OK	13.4	19.0	12.6	7.6
Tuscaloosa, AL	17.5	22.8	17.0	11.8
Virginia Beach, VA	10.9	16.1	9.8	7.6
Washington, DC	7.7	9.9	7.0	7.1
Wichita, KS	12.6	16.7	12.0	7.6
Wilmington, NC	13.4	16.6	14.2	7.0
Winston-Salem, NC	15.1	23.7	13.6	9.0
Worcester, MA	10.0	12.0	9.6	8.8
U.S.	12.6	17.0	11.8	9.6

Note: Figures are percentage of people whose income during the past 12 months was below the poverty level; Figures cover the Metropolitan Statistical Area
Source: U.S. Census Bureau, 2017-2021 American Community Survey 5-Year Estimates

Employment by Industry

Metro Area[1]	(A)	(B)	(C)	(D)	(E)	(F)	(G)	(H)	(I)	(J)	(K)	(L)	(M)	(N)
Albuquerque, NM	6.2	n/a	16.6	5.0	19.4	1.4	10.6	4.2	n/a	2.9	16.6	10.5	3.7	2.8
Allentown, PA	3.4	n/a	20.9	3.3	10.0	1.3	8.6	10.5	n/a	3.7	13.2	10.4	11.0	3.7
Anchorage, AK	6.2	5.1	18.4	4.5	19.2	1.9	10.8	1.3	1.1	3.6	11.3	11.5	8.5	2.8
Ann Arbor, MI	2.0	n/a	13.1	3.1	38.2	2.6	7.0	5.5	n/a	2.6	13.6	7.2	2.2	3.0
Athens, GA	n/a	n/a	n/a	n/a	27.8	n/a	11.5	n/a	n/a	n/a	9.0	11.1	n/a	n/a
Atlanta, GA	4.7	4.6	13.1	6.7	11.3	3.8	9.8	5.9	0.1	3.5	19.4	10.1	6.5	5.3
Austin, TX	5.9	n/a	11.2	6.0	14.3	4.1	11.2	5.5	n/a	3.8	21.6	9.2	2.8	4.5
Baltimore, MD	6.0	n/a	19.1	5.5	16.0	1.1	8.6	4.2	n/a	3.4	17.7	9.0	5.8	3.7
Boise City, ID	8.4	n/a	14.8	5.8	13.2	1.2	10.1	7.6	n/a	3.4	15.4	10.6	4.4	5.0
Boston, MA[4]	3.9	n/a	22.9	8.3	10.3	3.6	9.0	4.0	n/a	3.4	21.9	7.2	2.5	3.0
Boulder, CO	2.9	n/a	12.7	3.5	19.4	4.0	9.5	10.8	n/a	4.0	20.6	8.0	1.1	3.6
Brownsville, TX	2.3	n/a	30.2	3.2	18.6	0.4	11.0	4.6	n/a	2.2	10.7	11.5	3.4	2.0
Cape Coral, FL	12.5	n/a	11.7	5.0	14.6	1.1	14.9	2.6	n/a	3.7	14.5	14.3	2.4	2.8
Cedar Rapids, IA	6.0	n/a	15.3	7.4	11.5	2.1	8.2	13.9	n/a	3.5	10.8	10.3	6.9	4.1
Charleston, SC	5.4	n/a	11.7	4.9	16.7	2.2	12.5	7.6	n/a	3.9	16.2	10.9	5.1	3.0
Charlotte, NC	5.6	n/a	10.4	9.1	12.2	2.0	10.6	8.3	n/a	3.7	16.9	10.5	6.0	4.8
Chicago, IL[2]	3.5	3.4	16.2	7.2	10.5	1.9	9.5	7.3	<0.1	4.1	19.2	8.9	6.6	5.0
Cincinnati, OH	4.5	n/a	14.7	6.8	11.2	1.2	10.4	10.4	n/a	3.5	16.2	9.4	6.4	5.1
Clarksville, TN	4.3	n/a	13.2	3.4	19.4	1.2	12.1	12.0	n/a	3.4	10.2	14.2	3.4	n/a
Cleveland, OH	3.7	n/a	19.4	7.0	12.3	1.5	9.0	11.4	n/a	3.6	14.4	9.1	3.6	5.0
College Station, TX	5.7	n/a	11.3	3.2	34.3	1.1	13.9	4.4	n/a	2.6	9.5	10.0	1.9	2.1
Colorado Springs, CO	5.9	n/a	13.8	5.8	17.7	1.6	12.1	3.7	n/a	6.8	17.0	10.3	3.3	2.0
Columbia, MO	n/a	n/a	n/a	n/a	28.2	n/a	n/a	n/a	n/a	n/a	n/a	10.5	n/a	n/a
Columbia, SC	4.0	n/a	12.8	8.6	19.9	1.2	9.2	7.6	n/a	4.1	13.7	10.8	4.2	3.8
Columbus, OH	4.2	n/a	14.1	7.3	16.0	1.6	9.1	6.4	n/a	3.8	16.5	9.0	8.5	3.6
Dallas, TX[2]	5.3	n/a	11.4	9.7	10.9	2.8	9.2	6.5	n/a	3.0	20.6	8.9	5.9	5.9
Davenport, IA	n/a	n/a	n/a	n/a	n/a	n/a	n/a	n/a	n/a	n/a	n/a	n/a	n/a	n/a
Denver, CO	6.9	n/a	12.2	7.3	12.7	3.3	10.6	4.5	n/a	4.1	19.6	8.9	5.0	4.9
Des Moines, IA	5.9	n/a	14.3	14.3	12.3	1.6	8.7	5.9	n/a	3.3	13.5	10.6	4.5	5.0
Durham, NC	2.9	n/a	21.9	4.8	18.9	1.8	7.7	8.5	n/a	3.4	17.5	7.1	2.5	2.8
Edison, NJ[2]	3.6	n/a	22.7	9.0	12.4	3.9	8.9	2.6	n/a	4.0	16.5	8.3	4.3	3.7
El Paso, TX	5.1	n/a	14.5	3.9	20.7	1.8	11.7	5.5	n/a	2.7	12.2	12.1	6.4	3.6
Fargo, ND	6.0	n/a	19.2	7.5	13.5	1.8	9.6	7.9	n/a	3.3	10.0	10.0	5.0	6.1
Fort Collins, CO	6.8	n/a	10.9	4.0	24.0	1.5	11.9	8.3	n/a	3.6	11.9	11.4	2.4	3.2
Fort Wayne, IN	5.2	n/a	18.4	5.5	9.4	0.8	9.0	16.4	n/a	5.0	9.7	10.7	5.1	4.8
Fort Worth, TX[2]	6.6	n/a	12.8	6.4	11.9	0.9	10.5	9.3	n/a	3.4	13.4	10.7	9.0	4.9
Grand Rapids, MI	4.7	n/a	16.5	4.8	8.6	1.2	8.2	20.0	n/a	3.9	13.8	8.7	3.5	6.0
Greeley, CO	15.1	n/a	9.9	4.1	16.5	0.5	9.3	12.3	n/a	3.2	10.5	10.6	4.2	4.0
Green Bay, WI	4.7	n/a	15.3	6.2	11.5	0.8	8.9	17.7	n/a	4.5	10.6	9.9	5.1	5.0
Greensboro, NC	4.8	n/a	14.6	4.6	11.9	1.1	9.9	13.8	n/a	3.4	12.6	11.2	6.3	5.8
Honolulu, HI	6.2	n/a	14.5	4.7	21.0	1.6	15.3	2.1	n/a	4.4	12.2	9.7	5.4	3.0
Houston, TX	8.8	6.7	13.2	5.5	13.4	1.0	10.3	6.9	2.0	3.5	16.6	9.8	5.9	5.2
Huntsville, AL	3.9	n/a	8.5	3.1	20.4	1.0	8.2	12.0	n/a	3.3	25.5	10.1	1.7	2.4
Indianapolis, IN	5.3	5.2	14.9	6.6	12.1	1.1	9.0	8.3	0.1	3.9	16.6	9.0	8.3	4.8
Jacksonville, FL	6.4	6.3	15.2	9.4	10.0	1.7	11.2	4.5	0.1	3.4	16.3	10.9	7.4	3.7
Kansas City, MO	5.1	n/a	14.5	7.0	12.9	1.5	9.7	7.6	n/a	4.0	17.1	9.8	6.3	4.6
Lafayette, LA	10.5	5.4	17.2	5.5	12.8	0.9	10.6	8.1	5.2	3.5	10.4	12.9	3.2	4.4
Las Cruces, NM	4.7	n/a	22.7	3.1	26.7	0.8	11.4	4.4	n/a	2.1	9.1	9.9	3.2	1.9
Las Vegas, NV	7.3	7.3	10.8	5.4	10.0	1.2	25.9	2.6	<0.1	2.9	14.8	10.4	6.4	2.4
Lexington, KY	4.8	n/a	13.0	4.0	19.0	1.0	11.1	10.8	n/a	4.4	13.2	10.2	4.5	3.8
Lincoln, NE	5.5	n/a	15.7	5.6	22.1	1.9	9.4	7.7	n/a	3.9	10.3	9.8	5.8	2.2
Little Rock, AR	4.9	n/a	16.2	6.4	17.9	1.5	8.6	5.1	n/a	6.6	12.3	10.2	5.8	4.6
Los Angeles, CA[2]	3.2	3.2	19.4	4.7	12.3	5.0	11.4	6.9	<0.1	3.4	14.9	9.2	5.1	4.4
Louisville, KY	4.3	n/a	14.7	6.8	10.5	1.3	9.3	12.4	n/a	3.7	12.9	9.4	10.2	4.6
Madison, WI	4.8	n/a	12.3	5.8	21.7	4.6	7.9	9.3	n/a	5.0	12.6	9.5	2.8	3.7
Manchester, NH[3]	5.0	n/a	22.7	6.5	10.3	2.2	8.4	6.9	n/a	4.1	16.2	10.8	3.0	3.9

Table continued on following page.

Appendix A: Comparative Statistics   A-79

Metro Area[1]	(A)	(B)	(C)	(D)	(E)	(F)	(G)	(H)	(I)	(J)	(K)	(L)	(M)	(N)
Miami, FL[2]	4.0	4.0	16.4	7.1	10.9	1.9	11.1	3.4	<0.1	3.7	16.4	11.6	7.5	6.0
Midland, TX	33.3	n/a	6.6	4.5	8.4	1.0	9.8	4.2	n/a	3.5	9.8	8.3	4.9	5.7
Milwaukee, WI	4.0	3.9	20.3	6.0	9.6	1.4	8.4	13.5	0.1	5.2	13.9	8.9	4.2	4.6
Minneapolis, MN	4.1	n/a	18.0	7.6	12.5	1.5	8.9	10.5	n/a	3.6	15.4	9.3	4.3	4.3
Nashville, TN	5.2	n/a	14.6	6.7	10.9	2.8	11.0	7.5	n/a	4.1	17.3	9.2	6.6	4.2
New Haven, CT[3]	3.7	n/a	29.2	3.9	11.9	1.3	8.7	7.8	n/a	3.5	10.4	9.0	6.7	3.9
New Orleans, LA	5.6	5.1	19.0	5.1	12.1	1.6	14.0	5.3	0.6	4.0	13.5	10.6	5.3	3.9
New York, NY[2]	3.6	n/a	22.7	9.0	12.4	3.9	8.9	2.6	n/a	4.0	16.5	8.3	4.3	3.7
Oklahoma City, OK	6.6	4.9	15.4	5.4	18.8	0.9	11.2	5.2	1.6	4.2	13.3	10.4	5.2	3.4
Omaha, NE	6.3	n/a	16.3	8.3	13.3	2.0	9.7	6.9	n/a	3.8	14.2	10.5	5.3	3.3
Orlando, FL	6.0	6.0	12.6	6.3	8.9	1.9	19.4	3.7	<0.1	3.1	19.3	10.8	4.5	3.6
Philadelphia, PA[2]	2.5	n/a	31.6	6.5	12.7	2.0	9.1	3.3	n/a	4.0	14.5	7.4	4.2	2.4
Phoenix, AZ	6.6	6.4	15.9	9.3	10.2	1.8	10.1	6.4	0.1	3.1	17.0	10.5	5.1	4.0
Pittsburgh, PA	5.4	4.7	21.2	6.5	9.7	1.9	9.6	7.2	0.7	4.0	16.6	10.1	4.4	3.6
Portland, OR	6.7	6.6	15.0	6.2	12.2	2.3	9.4	10.2	0.1	3.4	16.2	9.7	4.3	4.6
Providence, RI[3]	4.8	4.8	20.8	6.4	12.8	1.2	10.6	8.6	<0.1	4.4	12.7	10.9	3.4	3.4
Provo, UT	10.0	n/a	19.8	4.2	11.7	4.7	8.6	7.7	n/a	2.3	15.0	11.7	1.8	2.5
Raleigh, NC	6.6	n/a	13.0	5.7	13.8	3.6	10.4	4.7	n/a	4.0	20.4	10.2	3.5	4.1
Reno, NV	8.4	8.3	11.1	4.4	12.1	1.4	14.4	10.8	0.1	2.4	12.7	9.3	9.4	3.9
Richmond, VA	5.8	n/a	14.1	8.0	16.2	0.9	9.2	4.6	n/a	4.5	17.7	9.6	5.4	4.0
Rochester, MN	4.0	n/a	43.3	2.4	10.5	0.9	8.5	7.9	n/a	3.0	5.4	9.9	2.1	2.1
Sacramento, CA	6.8	6.8	16.9	4.9	22.7	1.0	10.3	3.7	<0.1	3.5	14.0	9.6	4.0	2.6
Salem, OR	7.6	7.3	17.8	3.8	24.5	0.9	8.8	6.7	0.3	3.0	9.5	11.0	4.1	2.3
Salt Lake City, UT	7.0	n/a	11.5	7.6	13.6	3.2	8.3	7.8	n/a	2.8	17.8	9.9	5.8	4.5
San Antonio, TX	5.9	5.3	14.9	8.9	15.6	1.7	12.2	5.1	0.6	3.5	14.0	10.9	4.1	3.3
San Diego, CA	5.7	5.6	15.0	4.8	15.9	1.4	12.8	7.6	<0.1	3.6	18.6	9.1	2.7	2.8
San Francisco, CA[2]	3.4	3.4	13.1	7.4	10.9	10.6	10.2	3.3	<0.1	3.2	26.3	5.7	4.1	1.9
San Jose, CA	4.8	4.7	16.3	3.3	8.3	9.1	8.5	15.4	<0.1	2.1	21.7	6.4	1.8	2.4
Santa Rosa, CA	7.9	7.8	17.3	4.0	12.7	1.3	12.4	11.5	0.1	3.6	12.2	11.4	2.3	3.5
Savannah, GA	4.7	n/a	14.1	3.5	11.8	0.8	13.7	9.8	n/a	4.0	12.6	12.0	9.5	3.5
Seattle, WA[2]	6.1	6.0	12.9	5.0	11.7	7.9	8.7	8.1	<0.1	3.3	20.0	8.1	4.2	4.1
Sioux Falls, SD	5.8	n/a	21.6	9.1	9.1	1.5	9.5	8.7	n/a	3.9	9.8	11.8	3.8	5.5
Springfield, IL	3.4	n/a	19.2	5.6	24.1	2.0	9.6	3.3	n/a	5.5	11.4	10.9	2.3	2.9
St. Louis, MO	5.0	n/a	18.6	6.9	10.9	2.0	10.0	8.3	n/a	3.8	15.5	9.6	4.7	4.8
Tampa, FL	6.2	6.2	15.2	9.1	10.2	1.9	10.8	4.9	<0.1	3.3	19.3	11.3	3.6	4.1
Tucson, AZ	5.4	4.9	16.8	4.8	19.3	1.3	11.2	7.2	0.5	3.5	12.8	10.6	5.2	2.0
Tulsa, OK	6.1	5.3	16.0	5.2	12.7	1.2	10.1	10.7	0.8	4.5	13.8	11.0	5.2	3.7
Tuscaloosa, AL	5.7	n/a	8.5	3.5	25.7	0.7	10.3	16.8	n/a	4.1	9.3	10.4	3.1	1.9
Virginia Beach, VA	5.2	n/a	14.8	5.0	19.7	1.2	11.1	7.4	n/a	4.2	14.7	10.4	4.0	2.4
Washington, DC[2]	4.8	n/a	12.9	4.4	22.2	2.5	9.2	1.4	n/a	6.2	24.3	7.6	2.7	1.9
Wichita, KS	5.7	n/a	14.9	3.9	14.3	1.2	10.8	16.8	n/a	3.7	11.3	10.3	4.0	3.1
Wilmington, NC	7.4	n/a	17.0	5.1	12.6	2.0	14.8	4.2	n/a	4.2	13.1	12.7	3.3	3.5
Winston-Salem, NC	4.3	n/a	20.1	5.0	11.3	0.7	10.5	12.6	n/a	3.5	12.9	11.6	4.5	3.1
Worcester, MA[3]	4.1	n/a	23.5	4.8	15.7	0.9	8.3	9.2	n/a	3.6	11.1	10.2	5.3	3.2
U.S.	5.4	5.0	16.1	5.9	14.5	2.0	10.3	8.4	0.4	3.7	14.7	10.2	4.9	3.9

Note: All figures are percentages covering non-farm employment as of December 2022 and are not seasonally adjusted;
(1) Figures cover the Metropolitan Statistical Area (MSA) except where noted. See Appendix B for areas included; (2) Metropolitan Division; (3) New England City and Town Area; (4) New England City and Town Area Division; (A) Construction, Mining, and Logging (some areas report Construction separate from Mining and Logging); (B) Construction; (C) Private Education and Health Services; (D) Financial Activities; (E) Government; (F) Information; (G) Leisure and Hospitality; (H) Manufacturing; (I) Mining and Logging; (J) Other Services; (K) Professional and Business Services; (L) Retail Trade; (M) Transportation and Utilities; (N) Wholesale Trade; n/a not available
Source: Bureau of Labor Statistics, Current Employment Statistics, Employment, Hours, and Earnings, December 2022

Appendix A: Comparative Statistics

Labor Force, Employment and Job Growth: City

City	Civilian Labor Force Dec. 2021	Dec. 2022	% Chg.	Workers Employed Dec. 2021	Dec. 2022	% Chg.
Albuquerque, NM	286,208	278,969	-2.5	272,867	270,719	-0.7
Allentown, PA	55,657	56,449	1.4	52,269	54,138	3.5
Anchorage, AK	154,601	155,471	0.5	148,017	150,605	1.7
Ann Arbor, MI	63,522	64,736	1.9	62,006	63,139	1.8
Athens, GA	60,379	61,240	1.4	58,643	59,627	1.6
Atlanta, GA	271,164	274,219	1.1	261,888	265,951	1.5
Austin, TX	626,475	642,058	2.4	609,403	625,541	2.6
Baltimore, MD	280,450	278,592	-0.6	262,676	266,256	1.3
Boise City, ID	135,152	140,433	3.9	132,075	137,857	4.3
Boston, MA	394,417	392,029	-0.6	379,015	380,790	0.4
Boulder, CO	66,246	67,538	1.9	64,727	66,197	2.2
Brownsville, TX	78,951	79,589	0.8	73,562	74,739	1.6
Cape Coral, FL	96,606	100,709	4.2	93,922	97,833	4.1
Cedar Rapids, IA	69,935	70,822	1.2	66,849	68,200	2.0
Charleston, SC	75,129	76,762	2.1	73,011	74,897	2.5
Charlotte, NC	498,644	513,354	2.9	481,757	496,911	3.1
Chicago, IL	1,370,152	1,365,082	-0.3	1,301,665	1,299,230	-0.1
Cincinnati, OH	147,147	145,962	-0.8	141,899	140,924	-0.6
Clarksville, TN	64,581	62,625	-3.0	62,259	60,449	-2.9
Cleveland, OH	154,230	153,656	-0.3	144,455	146,635	1.5
College Station, TX	63,443	64,403	1.5	61,598	62,625	1.6
Colorado Springs, CO	243,995	246,112	0.8	234,766	238,820	1.7
Columbia, MO	68,593	68,729	0.2	67,043	67,523	0.7
Columbia, SC	56,736	55,816	-1.6	54,797	54,043	-1.3
Columbus, OH	484,399	482,990	-0.2	469,341	467,547	-0.3
Dallas, TX	707,758	735,922	3.9	679,409	711,095	4.6
Davenport, IA	50,142	51,938	3.5	47,788	49,912	4.4
Denver, CO	428,646	439,359	2.5	411,447	426,400	3.6
Des Moines, IA	109,744	111,230	1.3	104,975	107,148	2.0
Durham, NC	155,641	159,589	2.5	151,405	155,264	2.5
Edison, NJ	55,370	56,778	2.5	53,727	55,594	3.4
El Paso, TX	302,469	303,815	0.4	288,907	292,314	1.1
Fargo, ND	72,514	72,188	-0.4	70,902	70,818	-0.1
Fort Collins, CO	100,891	102,741	1.8	98,235	100,394	2.2
Fort Wayne, IN	126,450	130,964	3.5	124,397	127,828	2.7
Fort Worth, TX	462,444	475,802	2.8	444,256	459,728	3.4
Grand Rapids, MI	101,134	105,118	3.9	96,771	100,836	4.2
Greeley, CO	51,681	51,829	0.2	49,366	50,105	1.5
Green Bay, WI	53,463	52,666	-1.4	52,235	51,500	-1.4
Greensboro, NC	143,008	144,251	0.8	137,220	138,826	1.1
Honolulu, HI	459,370	457,096	-0.5	440,467	441,407	0.2
Houston, TX	1,138,573	1,173,802	3.0	1,085,474	1,128,659	3.9
Huntsville, AL	102,295	104,297	1.9	100,086	102,254	2.1
Indianapolis, IN	450,127	464,032	3.0	441,617	452,513	2.4
Jacksonville, FL	470,543	493,413	4.8	456,509	481,988	5.5
Kansas City, MO	257,158	258,850	0.6	247,609	252,172	1.8
Lafayette, LA	59,534	60,606	1.8	57,818	58,830	1.7
Las Cruces, NM	48,477	48,211	-0.5	46,260	46,735	1.0
Las Vegas, NV	301,290	316,801	5.1	286,123	299,424	4.6
Lexington, KY	175,989	174,916	-0.6	170,668	170,430	-0.1
Lincoln, NE	161,763	164,641	1.7	159,144	161,093	1.2
Little Rock, AR	95,576	95,929	0.3	92,287	93,043	0.8
Los Angeles, CA	2,047,789	2,027,026	-1.0	1,931,445	1,935,875	0.2
Louisville, KY	400,329	398,800	-0.3	384,379	387,119	0.7
Madison, WI	162,642	161,298	-0.8	160,375	158,871	-0.9

Table continued on following page.

Appendix A: Comparative Statistics

City	Civilian Labor Force Dec. 2021	Civilian Labor Force Dec. 2022	% Chg.	Workers Employed Dec. 2021	Workers Employed Dec. 2022	% Chg.
Manchester, NH	63,249	66,044	4.4	61,619	64,357	4.4
Miami, FL	227,422	231,754	1.9	220,939	228,420	3.3
Midland, TX	83,370	84,916	1.8	80,102	82,715	3.2
Milwaukee, WI	272,797	266,036	-2.4	262,401	257,421	-1.9
Minneapolis, MN	241,913	246,063	1.7	235,948	240,094	1.7
Nashville, TN	413,734	407,521	-1.5	402,245	397,879	-1.0
New Haven, CT	65,615	66,515	1.3	62,503	64,310	2.8
New Orleans, LA	175,708	180,265	2.5	166,032	172,381	3.8
New York, NY	4,085,159	4,113,259	0.6	3,782,405	3,907,975	3.3
Oklahoma City, OK	327,538	333,291	1.7	320,689	324,655	1.2
Omaha, NE	250,414	253,695	1.3	244,895	246,725	0.7
Orlando, FL	168,524	173,274	2.8	162,788	169,122	3.8
Philadelphia, PA	712,569	723,233	1.5	667,785	690,464	3.4
Phoenix, AZ	865,943	889,029	2.6	842,267	864,868	2.6
Pittsburgh, PA	148,500	152,028	2.3	142,551	147,423	3.4
Portland, OR	387,410	393,179	1.4	373,537	376,724	0.8
Providence, RI	88,878	88,200	-0.7	85,136	85,603	0.5
Provo, UT	70,289	73,861	5.0	69,267	72,590	4.8
Raleigh, NC	255,398	264,381	3.5	247,896	256,967	3.6
Reno, NV	134,416	141,155	5.0	131,188	136,416	3.9
Richmond, VA	115,165	116,068	0.7	110,750	112,086	1.2
Rochester, MN	67,368	68,064	1.0	65,967	66,601	0.9
Sacramento, CA	237,842	239,915	0.8	226,017	231,146	2.2
Salem, OR	84,706	83,973	-0.8	81,711	80,171	-1.8
Salt Lake City, UT	121,702	125,773	3.3	119,545	123,299	3.1
San Antonio, TX	735,449	751,540	2.1	707,860	727,368	2.7
San Diego, CA	711,954	721,000	1.2	684,180	701,197	2.4
San Francisco, CA	560,450	578,421	3.2	543,659	566,695	4.2
San Jose, CA	546,462	558,687	2.2	529,424	546,728	3.2
Santa Rosa, CA	85,496	86,918	1.6	82,307	84,605	2.7
Savannah, GA	69,179	68,684	-0.7	66,698	66,661	0.0
Seattle, WA	483,713	490,565	1.4	471,546	477,991	1.3
Sioux Falls, SD	109,388	111,832	2.2	106,662	109,520	2.6
Springfield, IL	55,434	55,938	0.9	53,040	53,888	1.6
St. Louis, MO	150,418	149,690	-0.4	143,212	145,026	1.2
Tampa, FL	211,042	219,467	3.9	205,058	214,586	4.6
Tucson, AZ	257,903	262,655	1.8	249,443	254,180	1.9
Tulsa, OK	194,312	199,027	2.4	189,673	193,469	2.0
Tuscaloosa, AL	46,912	47,393	1.0	45,459	46,256	1.7
Virginia Beach, VA	222,270	227,788	2.4	216,500	221,941	2.5
Washington, DC	378,144	386,520	2.2	358,132	370,787	3.5
Wichita, KS	190,708	192,293	0.8	184,998	186,223	0.6
Wilmington, NC	65,317	66,641	2.0	63,471	64,589	1.7
Winston-Salem, NC	116,216	117,459	1.0	112,011	113,308	1.1
Worcester, MA	93,362	90,627	-2.9	88,807	87,239	-1.7
U.S.	161,696,000	164,224,000	1.6	155,732,000	158,872,000	2.0

Note: Data is not seasonally adjusted and covers workers 16 years of age and older
Source: Bureau of Labor Statistics, Local Area Unemployment Statistics

Appendix A: Comparative Statistics

Labor Force, Employment and Job Growth: Metro Area

Metro Area[1]	Civilian Labor Force Dec. 2021	Dec. 2022	% Chg.	Workers Employed Dec. 2021	Dec. 2022	% Chg.
Albuquerque, NM	445,726	434,352	-2.5	424,396	421,074	-0.7
Allentown, PA	447,351	458,516	2.5	428,287	443,287	3.5
Anchorage, AK	205,827	206,845	0.4	196,305	199,569	1.6
Ann Arbor, MI	192,598	196,315	1.9	187,000	190,417	1.8
Athens, GA	102,226	103,727	1.4	99,578	101,194	1.6
Atlanta, GA	3,175,581	3,216,104	1.2	3,085,734	3,133,430	1.5
Austin, TX	1,339,834	1,372,624	2.4	1,301,083	1,335,791	2.6
Baltimore, MD	1,501,247	1,502,740	0.1	1,434,164	1,455,751	1.5
Boise City, ID	400,832	416,686	3.9	390,861	407,819	4.3
Boston, MA[4]	1,673,210	1,666,434	-0.4	1,614,446	1,622,005	0.4
Boulder, CO	198,590	201,887	1.6	193,073	197,458	2.2
Brownsville, TX	175,175	176,374	0.6	163,657	166,276	1.6
Cape Coral, FL	362,039	377,849	4.3	352,239	366,908	4.1
Cedar Rapids, IA	140,768	142,727	1.3	135,170	137,743	1.9
Charleston, SC	400,171	408,735	2.1	388,529	398,569	2.5
Charlotte, NC	1,377,149	1,414,791	2.7	1,332,923	1,371,461	2.8
Chicago, IL[2]	3,826,621	3,838,545	0.3	3,671,983	3,676,358	0.1
Cincinnati, OH	1,123,242	1,116,215	-0.6	1,088,875	1,082,108	-0.6
Clarksville, TN	120,311	117,511	-2.3	115,795	113,311	-2.1
Cleveland, OH	1,006,515	1,010,141	0.3	963,990	975,650	1.2
College Station, TX	138,941	140,832	1.3	134,636	136,870	1.6
Colorado Springs, CO	364,630	367,853	0.8	350,819	356,889	1.7
Columbia, MO	100,630	100,708	0.0	98,278	98,981	0.7
Columbia, SC	399,511	392,721	-1.7	387,182	381,702	-1.4
Columbus, OH	1,121,138	1,118,600	-0.2	1,088,089	1,084,246	-0.3
Dallas, TX[2]	2,825,024	2,943,498	4.1	2,723,620	2,851,201	4.6
Davenport, IA	185,485	190,708	2.8	177,815	183,615	3.2
Denver, CO	1,691,446	1,735,541	2.6	1,629,015	1,687,640	3.6
Des Moines, IA	362,322	367,598	1.4	350,192	357,259	2.0
Durham, NC	311,304	319,367	2.5	303,354	310,936	2.5
Edison, NJ[2]	6,978,612	7,057,593	1.1	6,599,840	6,759,099	2.4
El Paso, TX	365,233	366,661	0.3	347,953	352,057	1.1
Fargo, ND	143,613	142,810	-0.5	140,498	140,046	-0.3
Fort Collins, CO	208,863	212,087	1.5	202,604	207,057	2.2
Fort Wayne, IN	213,153	220,727	3.5	210,157	215,921	2.7
Fort Worth, TX[2]	1,345,295	1,384,350	2.9	1,295,323	1,340,078	3.4
Grand Rapids, MI	563,869	586,790	4.0	545,813	568,603	4.1
Greeley, CO	167,574	168,716	0.6	161,228	163,640	1.5
Green Bay, WI	173,797	170,959	-1.6	170,171	167,408	-1.6
Greensboro, NC	360,317	364,357	1.1	347,114	351,304	1.2
Honolulu, HI	459,370	457,096	-0.5	440,467	441,407	0.2
Houston, TX	3,460,832	3,565,905	3.0	3,294,015	3,425,418	3.9
Huntsville, AL	239,285	244,014	1.9	234,543	239,596	2.1
Indianapolis, IN	1,076,300	1,110,642	3.1	1,060,871	1,086,712	2.4
Jacksonville, FL	806,862	847,564	5.0	785,663	829,550	5.5
Kansas City, MO	1,138,286	1,149,586	0.9	1,105,453	1,121,442	1.4
Lafayette, LA	211,602	215,089	1.6	204,894	208,467	1.7
Las Cruces, NM	99,600	99,107	-0.5	94,429	95,399	1.0
Las Vegas, NV	1,093,227	1,149,504	5.1	1,039,029	1,087,331	4.6
Lexington, KY	275,622	274,006	-0.5	267,238	266,822	-0.1
Lincoln, NE	188,166	191,439	1.7	185,143	187,374	1.2
Little Rock, AR	350,674	353,640	0.8	341,122	343,843	0.8
Los Angeles, CA[2]	5,001,852	4,965,511	-0.7	4,701,620	4,747,043	0.9
Louisville, KY	672,926	678,057	0.7	650,589	659,926	1.4
Madison, WI	400,355	395,887	-1.1	393,718	389,430	-1.0

Table continued on following page.

Metro Area[1]	Civilian Labor Force Dec. 2021	Civilian Labor Force Dec. 2022	% Chg.	Workers Employed Dec. 2021	Workers Employed Dec. 2022	% Chg.
Manchester, NH[3]	118,844	124,173	4.4	116,140	121,300	4.4
Miami, FL[2]	1,345,385	1,397,307	3.8	1,304,718	1,369,536	4.9
Midland, TX	103,649	105,497	1.7	99,519	102,761	3.2
Milwaukee, WI	817,582	799,375	-2.2	796,196	780,437	-1.9
Minneapolis, MN	1,991,752	2,028,489	1.8	1,943,478	1,975,295	1.6
Nashville, TN	1,124,910	1,111,047	-1.2	1,096,732	1,085,200	-1.0
New Haven, CT[3]	327,755	334,058	1.9	315,344	324,400	2.8
New Orleans, LA	582,640	600,820	3.1	558,375	579,744	3.8
New York, NY[2]	6,978,612	7,057,593	1.1	6,599,840	6,759,099	2.4
Oklahoma City, OK	699,178	711,592	1.7	685,472	694,168	1.2
Omaha, NE	502,000	508,654	1.3	490,956	495,693	0.9
Orlando, FL	1,366,646	1,407,116	2.9	1,323,163	1,374,399	3.8
Philadelphia, PA[2]	1,004,235	1,021,788	1.7	946,859	979,293	3.4
Phoenix, AZ	2,518,007	2,590,356	2.8	2,453,226	2,520,303	2.7
Pittsburgh, PA	1,147,805	1,177,164	2.5	1,096,709	1,134,155	3.4
Portland, OR	1,369,607	1,391,563	1.6	1,322,133	1,334,787	0.9
Providence, RI[3]	706,157	698,803	-1.0	679,845	680,282	0.0
Provo, UT	345,721	363,397	5.1	340,264	356,597	4.8
Raleigh, NC	737,649	764,883	3.6	718,092	744,560	3.6
Reno, NV	249,159	261,626	5.0	243,158	252,847	3.9
Richmond, VA	664,206	670,336	0.9	643,038	650,950	1.2
Rochester, MN	126,103	127,371	1.0	123,345	124,243	0.7
Sacramento, CA	1,102,380	1,115,511	1.1	1,055,002	1,078,900	2.2
Salem, OR	210,043	208,341	-0.8	202,733	198,916	-1.8
Salt Lake City, UT	699,196	722,471	3.3	686,309	707,898	3.1
San Antonio, TX	1,217,217	1,244,094	2.2	1,171,224	1,203,295	2.7
San Diego, CA	1,570,184	1,588,968	1.2	1,505,925	1,543,381	2.4
San Francisco, CA[2]	1,003,772	1,035,986	3.2	974,872	1,015,702	4.1
San Jose, CA	1,067,389	1,093,480	2.4	1,036,363	1,070,252	3.2
Santa Rosa, CA	243,938	248,408	1.8	235,525	242,101	2.7
Savannah, GA	199,752	198,853	-0.4	194,065	193,933	0.0
Seattle, WA[2]	1,724,262	1,779,111	3.1	1,675,402	1,725,495	2.9
Sioux Falls, SD	159,168	162,847	2.3	155,392	159,650	2.7
Springfield, IL	103,907	105,050	1.1	99,703	101,310	1.6
St. Louis, MO	1,460,514	1,459,027	-0.1	1,407,703	1,422,207	1.0
Tampa, FL	1,596,468	1,661,495	4.0	1,552,983	1,625,105	4.6
Tucson, AZ	482,383	492,280	2.0	468,330	477,224	1.9
Tulsa, OK	479,679	491,520	2.4	468,777	478,458	2.0
Tuscaloosa, AL	114,876	116,118	1.0	111,656	113,579	1.7
Virginia Beach, VA	821,309	840,432	2.3	795,009	815,342	2.5
Washington, DC[2]	2,676,340	2,681,074	0.1	2,582,644	2,604,564	0.8
Wichita, KS	317,498	320,744	1.0	309,104	311,289	0.7
Wilmington, NC	154,267	157,407	2.0	150,051	152,775	1.8
Winston-Salem, NC	322,524	326,477	1.2	312,552	316,261	1.1
Worcester, MA[3]	358,980	351,150	-2.1	344,046	339,514	-1.3
U.S.	161,696,000	164,224,000	1.6	155,732,000	158,872,000	2.0

Note: Data is not seasonally adjusted and covers workers 16 years of age and older; (1) Figures cover the Metropolitan Statistical Area (MSA) except where noted. See Appendix B for areas included; (2) Metropolitan Division; (3) New England City and Town Area; (4) New England City and Town Area Division
Source: Bureau of Labor Statistics, Local Area Unemployment Statistics

Unemployment Rate: City

City	\multicolumn{12}{c}{2022}
	Jan.	Feb.	Mar.	Apr.	May	Jun.	Jul.	Aug.	Sep.	Oct.	Nov.	Dec.
Albuquerque, NM	4.9	4.3	4.0	3.9	3.7	4.4	4.1	4.0	4.0	3.6	3.2	3.0
Allentown, PA	7.3	6.5	6.1	6.0	5.8	6.2	6.2	6.5	5.0	4.6	4.6	4.1
Anchorage, AK	4.8	4.4	4.0	3.9	3.7	3.8	3.6	2.9	2.9	3.1	3.3	3.1
Ann Arbor, MI	2.7	3.1	2.5	2.5	3.0	3.4	3.3	2.9	2.7	2.7	2.5	2.5
Athens, GA	3.2	3.2	3.2	2.3	2.7	3.5	2.9	3.2	2.5	3.1	2.7	2.6
Atlanta, GA	4.0	3.8	3.9	2.9	3.1	3.7	3.4	3.5	3.1	3.4	3.2	3.0
Austin, TX	3.2	3.2	2.6	2.4	2.6	2.9	2.9	2.9	2.7	2.7	2.6	2.6
Baltimore, MD	6.3	6.1	5.8	4.9	5.1	6.1	5.6	5.9	5.1	5.6	5.0	4.4
Boise City, ID	2.8	2.7	2.5	2.0	2.0	2.4	2.2	2.3	2.3	2.4	2.3	1.8
Boston, MA	4.4	3.5	3.2	3.0	3.2	3.5	3.6	3.5	3.0	2.9	2.7	2.9
Boulder, CO	2.6	2.7	2.3	2.1	2.2	2.8	3.0	2.4	2.3	2.6	2.7	2.0
Brownsville, TX	7.9	7.4	6.1	6.0	6.1	7.1	6.9	6.4	5.9	5.5	5.7	6.1
Cape Coral, FL	3.4	2.9	2.6	2.3	2.4	2.8	2.7	2.6	2.5	4.2	3.6	2.9
Cedar Rapids, IA	4.9	3.9	3.6	2.7	2.9	3.4	3.7	3.8	3.3	3.4	3.7	3.7
Charleston, SC	3.1	3.5	2.9	2.1	2.5	2.8	2.6	2.6	2.4	2.8	2.2	2.4
Charlotte, NC	4.0	3.8	3.7	3.5	3.5	3.9	3.6	3.9	3.3	3.8	3.7	3.2
Chicago, IL	5.8	5.5	5.0	4.7	4.9	5.7	5.8	5.9	5.6	5.2	5.3	4.8
Cincinnati, OH	4.6	4.2	3.8	3.5	3.5	4.6	4.8	4.8	3.9	4.2	3.3	3.5
Clarksville, TN	4.0	3.6	3.4	3.5	3.9	4.8	4.6	4.1	3.6	4.1	3.9	3.5
Cleveland, OH	7.7	8.0	8.2	7.5	7.2	7.7	6.5	6.0	5.9	6.4	5.8	4.6
College Station, TX	3.5	3.4	2.7	2.6	2.8	3.6	3.3	3.3	3.0	3.0	3.2	2.8
Colorado Springs, CO	4.1	4.2	3.6	3.2	3.1	3.4	3.8	3.6	3.5	3.7	3.5	3.0
Columbia, MO	3.0	2.2	2.4	1.7	2.4	1.9	2.4	2.5	1.5	1.9	1.9	1.8
Columbia, SC	3.7	4.3	3.5	2.9	3.9	4.0	3.9	3.7	3.4	4.2	3.3	3.2
Columbus, OH	3.9	3.8	3.4	3.1	3.1	3.9	3.8	4.0	3.4	3.7	2.9	3.2
Dallas, TX	4.5	4.4	3.6	3.4	3.5	4.0	4.0	3.9	3.6	3.6	3.5	3.4
Davenport, IA	5.5	4.4	4.1	3.1	3.2	4.0	4.0	3.9	3.3	3.4	3.8	3.9
Denver, CO	4.3	4.3	3.9	3.4	3.3	3.4	3.6	3.6	3.5	3.7	3.4	2.9
Des Moines, IA	5.7	4.7	4.3	3.0	2.8	3.0	3.2	3.3	2.8	2.9	3.2	3.7
Durham, NC	3.2	3.0	3.0	2.9	3.1	3.5	3.1	3.3	2.7	3.4	3.2	2.7
Edison, NJ	3.3	3.0	2.9	2.5	2.5	2.8	2.7	2.6	2.0	2.1	2.1	2.1
El Paso, TX	5.1	5.0	4.1	4.0	4.2	4.7	4.5	4.4	4.1	4.1	4.1	3.8
Fargo, ND	2.7	2.5	2.7	2.1	1.8	2.2	1.7	1.8	1.4	1.5	1.6	1.9
Fort Collins, CO	3.0	3.2	2.7	2.4	2.4	2.8	2.9	2.7	2.6	2.8	2.8	2.3
Fort Wayne, IN	2.5	2.7	2.8	2.5	2.6	3.3	3.6	3.1	2.3	2.9	2.9	2.4
Fort Worth, TX	4.5	4.4	3.6	3.4	3.6	4.2	4.2	4.0	3.7	3.6	3.5	3.4
Grand Rapids, MI	5.0	5.0	4.3	4.2	4.6	5.2	5.0	4.6	4.3	4.2	4.0	4.1
Greeley, CO	4.9	5.0	4.4	3.7	3.5	3.9	4.5	3.9	3.8	3.9	3.7	3.3
Green Bay, WI	3.1	3.1	3.1	2.9	2.8	3.4	3.2	3.4	3.3	2.9	2.5	2.2
Greensboro, NC	4.6	4.5	4.4	4.3	4.3	4.8	4.6	4.8	4.0	4.5	4.4	3.8
Honolulu, HI	3.7	3.5	3.2	3.3	3.4	3.9	3.5	3.4	3.3	3.4	3.8	3.4
Houston, TX	5.3	5.2	4.3	4.1	4.2	4.7	4.8	4.6	4.2	4.1	4.0	3.8
Huntsville, AL	2.8	2.6	2.1	1.7	2.1	3.0	2.8	2.6	2.3	2.3	2.1	2.0
Indianapolis, IN	2.7	3.0	3.0	2.5	2.8	3.5	3.8	3.4	2.4	2.9	3.0	2.5
Jacksonville, FL	3.6	3.2	2.7	2.5	2.6	3.3	3.2	3.1	2.7	2.8	2.7	2.3
Kansas City, MO	4.3	4.3	4.1	3.1	3.2	2.6	3.4	3.4	2.2	2.7	2.7	2.6
Lafayette, LA	3.6	3.1	3.1	2.9	3.1	3.9	3.8	3.2	3.0	2.7	2.6	2.9
Las Cruces, NM	4.8	3.9	3.6	3.5	3.4	4.9	4.7	4.6	4.5	3.8	3.4	3.1
Las Vegas, NV	5.9	5.4	5.2	5.2	5.4	5.8	5.7	5.8	5.4	5.8	5.7	5.5
Lexington, KY	3.3	3.0	3.1	2.8	2.9	3.5	3.3	3.0	2.8	3.3	3.1	2.6
Lincoln, NE	2.3	2.1	2.2	1.8	1.9	2.4	2.3	2.1	1.9	2.1	2.1	2.2
Little Rock, AR	4.3	4.2	3.7	3.8	3.6	4.1	4.6	3.9	3.9	3.3	3.2	3.0
Los Angeles, CA	6.3	5.5	5.0	4.9	4.6	5.3	5.2	5.1	4.6	4.6	4.6	4.5
Louisville, KY	4.7	3.9	4.7	3.1	4.1	3.8	4.1	3.4	3.0	3.5	3.3	2.9
Madison, WI	1.9	2.0	2.0	1.9	2.2	2.8	2.5	2.4	2.6	2.2	2.0	1.5

Table continued on following page.

Appendix A: Comparative Statistics A-85

City	2022 Jan.	Feb.	Mar.	Apr.	May	Jun.	Jul.	Aug.	Sep.	Oct.	Nov.	Dec.
Manchester, NH	3.6	2.6	2.5	2.3	1.9	2.0	2.0	2.4	2.4	2.7	2.7	2.6
Miami, FL	3.0	2.6	2.8	2.4	2.2	2.0	2.2	2.2	1.9	1.7	1.5	1.4
Midland, TX	4.3	4.3	3.4	3.2	3.2	3.6	3.5	3.3	3.0	3.0	2.8	2.6
Milwaukee, WI	4.8	5.1	5.0	5.0	4.9	5.4	5.5	5.5	4.8	4.6	4.1	3.2
Minneapolis, MN	3.0	2.2	2.4	1.5	1.7	2.4	2.2	2.3	2.0	1.9	2.0	2.4
Nashville, TN	3.3	2.9	2.7	2.7	2.9	3.5	3.2	2.9	2.5	2.8	2.7	2.4
New Haven, CT	5.5	5.4	4.4	4.1	4.8	5.0	5.6	5.4	4.7	4.7	4.0	3.3
New Orleans, LA	6.5	6.0	5.9	5.5	5.5	6.5	6.6	5.5	4.8	4.1	4.0	4.4
New York, NY	7.8	7.2	6.3	5.7	5.4	5.5	5.4	5.2	4.5	5.0	5.0	5.0
Oklahoma City, OK	2.9	3.0	2.9	2.7	2.8	3.4	3.0	3.3	3.2	3.4	2.9	2.6
Omaha, NE	2.9	2.8	2.7	2.3	2.3	2.9	3.1	2.7	2.4	2.6	2.5	2.7
Orlando, FL	3.9	3.6	3.1	2.9	2.9	3.3	3.1	3.1	2.7	2.8	2.7	2.4
Philadelphia, PA	7.7	6.8	6.3	6.0	5.7	6.2	6.2	6.4	4.9	4.7	4.8	4.5
Phoenix, AZ	3.4	3.3	2.5	2.8	3.0	3.4	3.4	3.5	3.6	3.5	3.0	2.7
Pittsburgh, PA	4.9	4.1	4.0	3.8	3.9	4.3	4.4	4.4	3.2	3.1	3.0	3.0
Portland, OR	4.5	3.9	3.9	3.4	3.0	3.5	3.7	4.1	3.8	3.8	4.1	4.2
Providence, RI	5.5	5.3	3.7	3.3	3.5	3.5	4.0	5.0	4.3	4.1	4.3	2.9
Provo, UT	1.8	1.5	1.6	1.7	2.0	2.4	1.8	1.8	1.6	1.8	1.8	1.7
Raleigh, NC	3.3	3.3	3.2	3.1	3.3	3.6	3.4	3.5	3.0	3.5	3.4	2.8
Reno, NV	3.1	2.8	2.5	2.7	2.9	3.3	3.2	3.5	3.1	3.6	3.5	3.4
Richmond, VA	4.6	4.1	3.7	3.5	3.9	3.8	3.7	4.1	3.4	3.5	3.9	3.4
Rochester, MN	2.6	2.0	2.1	1.2	1.3	1.9	1.7	1.8	1.6	1.5	1.6	2.1
Sacramento, CA	5.7	4.9	4.3	3.7	3.3	3.8	3.8	4.1	3.8	3.9	4.2	3.7
Salem, OR	4.4	4.0	4.0	3.7	3.1	3.8	4.2	4.5	4.1	4.2	4.3	4.5
Salt Lake City, UT	2.4	2.1	2.0	2.1	2.1	2.3	2.1	2.1	1.9	2.1	2.0	2.0
San Antonio, TX	4.3	4.2	3.5	3.3	3.5	4.0	3.9	3.8	3.5	3.5	3.4	3.2
San Diego, CA	4.5	3.9	3.3	2.9	2.6	3.0	2.9	3.2	2.9	3.0	3.2	2.7
San Francisco, CA	3.5	3.0	2.5	2.2	1.9	2.2	2.1	2.3	2.1	2.2	2.3	2.0
San Jose, CA	3.5	3.1	2.6	2.3	2.0	2.4	2.3	2.5	2.2	2.3	2.5	2.1
Santa Rosa, CA	4.3	3.8	3.3	2.7	2.4	2.8	2.7	2.9	2.7	2.8	3.1	2.7
Savannah, GA	4.2	4.0	4.1	3.1	3.2	3.8	3.3	3.5	3.0	3.4	3.1	2.9
Seattle, WA	3.0	2.5	2.1	1.6	1.9	2.4	2.6	2.8	2.6	2.6	2.7	2.6
Sioux Falls, SD	2.6	2.8	2.4	2.0	1.9	2.1	1.7	2.0	1.6	1.9	1.8	2.1
Springfield, IL	5.3	5.0	4.6	4.9	5.2	4.6	4.8	4.9	4.3	4.5	4.3	3.7
St. Louis, MO	5.4	5.0	4.9	3.6	3.8	3.3	4.1	4.1	2.5	3.0	3.2	3.1
Tampa, FL	3.5	3.0	2.6	2.3	2.4	2.9	2.8	2.8	2.6	2.7	2.6	2.2
Tucson, AZ	4.0	3.9	3.1	3.4	3.6	4.2	4.2	4.3	4.3	4.2	3.6	3.2
Tulsa, OK	3.2	3.3	3.2	3.0	3.1	3.7	3.4	3.7	3.6	3.7	3.2	2.8
Tuscaloosa, AL	3.6	3.4	2.6	2.4	2.9	4.1	4.0	3.4	2.9	3.1	2.7	2.4
Virginia Beach, VA	3.2	2.7	2.6	2.4	2.9	2.9	2.8	3.0	2.5	2.7	2.9	2.6
Washington, DC	6.3	5.6	5.1	4.2	4.3	4.9	4.7	4.6	4.1	4.3	4.1	4.1
Wichita, KS	3.7	3.6	3.6	2.8	3.2	3.5	4.1	3.8	3.1	3.2	3.1	3.2
Wilmington, NC	3.4	3.4	3.2	3.3	3.5	3.9	3.5	3.7	3.1	3.6	3.6	3.1
Winston-Salem, NC	4.1	4.0	3.9	3.8	4.0	4.5	4.3	4.4	3.8	4.3	4.1	3.5
Worcester, MA	5.5	4.6	4.1	3.9	4.2	4.6	4.6	4.6	4.0	3.7	3.5	3.7
U.S.	4.4	4.1	3.8	3.3	3.4	3.8	3.8	3.8	3.3	3.4	3.4	3.3

Note: Data is not seasonally adjusted and covers workers 16 years of age and older; All figures are percentages
Source: Bureau of Labor Statistics, Local Area Unemployment Statistics

Unemployment Rate: Metro Area

Metro Area[1]	2022											
	Jan.	Feb.	Mar.	Apr.	May	Jun.	Jul.	Aug.	Sep.	Oct.	Nov.	Dec.
Albuquerque, NM	5.1	4.4	4.1	4.0	3.8	4.6	4.3	4.1	4.2	3.7	3.3	3.1
Allentown, PA	5.5	4.8	4.5	4.1	3.9	4.4	4.5	4.5	3.3	3.2	3.3	3.3
Anchorage, AK	5.3	4.9	4.5	4.3	4.0	4.2	3.9	3.2	3.2	3.3	3.6	3.5
Ann Arbor, MI	3.3	3.7	3.1	3.0	3.6	4.1	4.0	3.5	3.3	3.3	3.1	3.0
Athens, GA	2.9	2.9	2.9	2.1	2.5	3.1	2.6	2.9	2.3	2.9	2.5	2.4
Atlanta, GA	3.3	3.2	3.2	2.4	2.6	3.2	2.8	3.0	2.5	2.9	2.7	2.6
Austin, TX	3.3	3.3	2.7	2.5	2.7	3.1	3.1	3.0	2.8	2.8	2.8	2.7
Baltimore, MD	4.2	4.3	4.2	3.3	3.6	4.6	4.1	4.3	3.7	4.0	3.5	3.1
Boise City, ID	3.1	3.0	2.8	2.4	2.2	2.7	2.6	2.7	2.5	2.6	2.5	2.1
Boston, MA[4]	4.2	3.4	3.1	2.8	2.9	3.1	3.0	3.0	2.7	2.7	2.5	2.7
Boulder, CO	3.1	3.2	2.8	2.4	2.4	2.8	2.9	2.6	2.5	2.8	2.6	2.2
Brownsville, TX	7.6	7.3	6.1	5.9	6.0	6.9	6.8	6.4	5.8	5.6	5.7	5.7
Cape Coral, FL	3.4	2.9	2.5	2.2	2.4	2.9	2.8	2.7	2.6	4.0	3.6	2.9
Cedar Rapids, IA	4.9	4.0	3.7	2.6	2.6	3.0	3.2	3.4	2.9	3.0	3.3	3.5
Charleston, SC	3.2	3.6	2.9	2.3	2.8	3.0	2.7	2.8	2.7	3.1	2.2	2.5
Charlotte, NC	3.7	3.7	3.5	3.2	3.4	3.8	3.4	3.6	3.1	3.7	3.5	3.1
Chicago, IL[2]	5.2	5.0	4.4	4.3	4.5	5.3	5.1	5.2	4.6	4.5	4.4	4.2
Cincinnati, OH	3.9	3.8	3.5	3.0	3.0	3.9	3.9	3.8	3.3	3.6	3.0	3.1
Clarksville, TN	4.1	3.7	3.6	3.6	4.0	4.7	4.5	4.1	3.6	4.0	3.9	3.6
Cleveland, OH	5.6	6.0	5.6	4.8	4.9	5.3	4.9	4.5	4.1	3.9	3.6	3.4
College Station, TX	3.7	3.5	2.9	2.7	2.9	3.6	3.5	3.5	3.1	3.1	3.1	2.8
Colorado Springs, CO	4.1	4.2	3.8	3.3	3.3	3.5	3.9	3.6	3.5	3.8	3.6	3.0
Columbia, MO	3.0	2.3	2.6	1.7	2.3	1.8	2.3	2.4	1.4	1.9	1.8	1.7
Columbia, SC	3.5	3.8	3.1	2.5	3.0	3.3	3.1	3.1	2.9	3.4	2.6	2.8
Columbus, OH	3.8	3.7	3.3	2.9	2.9	3.8	3.7	3.8	3.3	3.5	2.7	3.1
Dallas, TX[2]	4.1	4.0	3.3	3.1	3.3	3.8	3.7	3.6	3.4	3.3	3.2	3.1
Davenport, IA	5.3	4.6	4.4	3.7	3.8	3.7	3.8	3.8	3.4	3.5	3.7	3.7
Denver, CO	4.0	4.0	3.6	3.2	3.1	3.3	3.5	3.3	3.2	3.5	3.3	2.8
Des Moines, IA	4.2	3.4	3.2	2.1	2.2	2.5	2.6	2.7	2.3	2.5	2.8	2.8
Durham, NC	3.0	2.9	2.8	2.8	3.0	3.4	3.1	3.2	2.7	3.3	3.2	2.6
Edison, NJ[2]	6.1	5.6	5.1	4.7	4.6	4.9	5.3	5.4	4.1	4.1	4.2	4.2
El Paso, TX	5.4	5.3	4.3	4.2	4.3	4.9	4.8	4.6	4.4	4.3	4.2	4.0
Fargo, ND	2.8	2.4	2.7	1.9	1.6	2.1	1.7	1.7	1.4	1.4	1.5	1.9
Fort Collins, CO	3.4	3.5	3.1	2.7	2.6	2.9	3.0	2.8	2.7	2.9	2.8	2.4
Fort Wayne, IN	2.2	2.4	2.6	2.2	2.3	3.0	3.2	2.8	2.0	2.7	2.6	2.2
Fort Worth, TX[2]	4.2	4.2	3.4	3.2	3.4	3.9	3.9	3.8	3.5	3.4	3.4	3.2
Grand Rapids, MI	3.7	3.8	3.3	3.1	3.4	3.9	3.8	3.4	3.2	3.1	3.0	3.1
Greeley, CO	4.2	4.3	3.9	3.4	3.3	3.6	3.8	3.6	3.4	3.7	3.5	3.0
Green Bay, WI	2.8	3.0	3.0	2.7	2.6	3.2	3.0	3.0	2.9	2.6	2.4	2.1
Greensboro, NC	4.2	4.1	4.0	3.8	4.0	4.5	4.2	4.4	3.7	4.3	4.1	3.6
Honolulu, HI	3.7	3.5	3.2	3.3	3.4	3.9	3.5	3.4	3.3	3.4	3.8	3.4
Houston, TX	5.5	5.3	4.4	4.1	4.3	4.8	4.8	4.6	4.2	4.1	4.0	3.9
Huntsville, AL	2.6	2.4	1.9	1.6	1.9	2.7	2.6	2.3	2.1	2.2	2.0	1.8
Indianapolis, IN	2.2	2.5	2.5	2.0	2.4	3.0	3.3	2.8	2.1	2.6	2.6	2.2
Jacksonville, FL	3.2	2.9	2.5	2.2	2.3	2.9	2.8	2.8	2.5	2.5	2.5	2.1
Kansas City, MO	3.4	3.7	3.3	2.4	2.7	2.6	3.2	3.1	2.2	2.6	2.5	2.4
Lafayette, LA	3.8	3.4	3.4	3.1	3.2	4.1	4.0	3.3	3.2	2.8	2.7	3.1
Las Cruces, NM	5.7	5.1	4.8	4.8	4.4	5.3	5.0	4.6	4.8	4.2	4.0	3.7
Las Vegas, NV	5.8	5.3	5.0	5.0	5.2	5.7	5.6	5.7	5.3	5.6	5.6	5.4
Lexington, KY	3.4	3.1	3.1	2.8	2.9	3.5	3.3	3.0	2.8	3.3	3.1	2.6
Lincoln, NE	2.3	2.1	2.1	1.8	1.9	2.4	2.3	2.1	1.9	2.0	2.1	2.1
Little Rock, AR	3.8	3.8	3.3	3.2	3.2	3.7	4.0	3.5	3.5	2.8	2.9	2.8
Los Angeles, CA[2]	6.5	5.8	5.2	4.8	4.5	4.9	4.9	4.7	4.3	4.5	4.5	4.4
Louisville, KY	4.1	3.5	4.3	2.8	3.7	3.5	3.8	3.1	2.7	3.3	3.1	2.7
Madison, WI	2.3	2.5	2.4	2.1	2.2	2.8	2.5	2.5	2.6	2.2	2.0	1.6

Table continued on following page.

Metro Area[1]	2022 Jan.	Feb.	Mar.	Apr.	May	Jun.	Jul.	Aug.	Sep.	Oct.	Nov.	Dec.
Manchester, NH[3]	3.3	2.3	2.3	2.1	1.8	1.9	1.9	2.2	2.3	2.5	2.4	2.3
Miami, FL[2]	3.2	2.9	3.0	2.6	2.5	2.6	2.8	2.9	2.6	2.4	2.1	2.0
Midland, TX	4.4	4.3	3.5	3.2	3.3	3.6	3.5	3.3	3.0	2.9	2.8	2.6
Milwaukee, WI	3.4	3.7	3.6	3.5	3.4	4.0	4.0	3.9	3.6	3.3	3.0	2.4
Minneapolis, MN	3.0	2.4	2.6	1.5	1.6	2.2	2.0	2.2	1.9	1.7	1.9	2.6
Nashville, TN	2.9	2.7	2.4	2.5	2.8	3.4	3.1	2.7	2.4	2.7	2.6	2.3
New Haven, CT[3]	4.6	4.6	3.9	3.5	3.8	3.9	4.2	4.1	3.7	3.7	3.3	2.9
New Orleans, LA	4.9	4.5	4.4	4.1	4.1	5.1	5.0	4.1	3.8	3.3	3.1	3.5
New York, NY[2]	6.1	5.6	5.1	4.7	4.6	4.9	5.3	5.4	4.1	4.1	4.2	4.2
Oklahoma City, OK	2.8	2.9	2.7	2.6	2.7	3.2	2.9	3.1	3.1	3.3	2.8	2.4
Omaha, NE	2.9	2.7	2.6	2.1	2.1	2.7	2.7	2.5	2.2	2.4	2.4	2.5
Orlando, FL	3.8	3.4	2.9	2.6	2.7	3.2	3.0	2.9	2.7	2.8	2.7	2.3
Philadelphia, PA[2]	7.0	6.2	5.7	5.5	5.2	5.7	5.7	5.9	4.5	4.3	4.4	4.2
Phoenix, AZ	3.2	3.1	2.4	2.7	2.9	3.4	3.3	3.4	3.5	3.5	3.0	2.7
Pittsburgh, PA	5.8	5.1	4.6	4.2	4.0	4.6	4.7	4.8	3.4	3.3	3.5	3.7
Portland, OR	4.4	3.9	3.9	3.4	3.1	3.5	3.6	4.0	3.7	3.7	3.9	4.1
Providence, RI[3]	4.9	4.7	3.4	3.0	2.9	3.0	3.3	4.0	3.4	3.3	3.4	2.7
Provo, UT	2.0	1.8	1.8	1.8	2.0	2.3	1.8	1.9	1.7	1.9	1.9	1.9
Raleigh, NC	3.1	3.0	2.9	2.9	3.1	3.4	3.1	3.3	2.8	3.3	3.2	2.7
Reno, NV	3.2	2.8	2.6	2.7	2.9	3.3	3.2	3.5	3.1	3.5	3.5	3.4
Richmond, VA	3.7	3.2	2.9	2.8	3.2	3.2	3.1	3.4	2.8	3.0	3.2	2.9
Rochester, MN	3.0	2.3	2.4	1.3	1.3	1.9	1.7	1.8	1.5	1.4	1.6	2.5
Sacramento, CA	5.0	4.4	3.7	3.3	2.9	3.4	3.3	3.6	3.3	3.4	3.7	3.3
Salem, OR	4.5	3.9	3.9	3.6	3.1	3.7	4.0	4.4	4.0	4.2	4.3	4.5
Salt Lake City, UT	2.4	2.2	2.1	2.1	2.2	2.4	2.1	2.1	1.9	2.1	2.0	2.0
San Antonio, TX	4.3	4.2	3.5	3.3	3.5	4.0	4.0	3.8	3.5	3.5	3.4	3.3
San Diego, CA	4.7	4.0	3.4	3.0	2.7	3.2	3.1	3.4	3.1	3.2	3.3	2.9
San Francisco, CA[2]	3.3	2.9	2.4	2.1	1.8	2.1	2.1	2.3	2.1	2.1	2.3	2.0
San Jose, CA	3.4	3.0	2.5	2.2	1.9	2.3	2.2	2.4	2.2	2.2	2.4	2.1
Santa Rosa, CA	4.0	3.5	3.0	2.6	2.3	2.7	2.6	2.8	2.6	2.6	2.9	2.5
Savannah, GA	3.3	3.2	3.2	2.4	2.6	3.1	2.7	2.9	2.5	2.9	2.6	2.5
Seattle, WA[2]	3.3	2.8	2.6	2.3	2.6	3.0	3.3	3.3	3.3	3.4	2.9	3.0
Sioux Falls, SD	2.5	2.7	2.3	1.9	1.9	2.1	1.7	2.0	1.5	1.8	1.7	2.0
Springfield, IL	5.1	4.8	4.5	4.6	4.7	4.2	4.3	4.3	3.8	3.9	3.9	3.6
St. Louis, MO	4.3	3.7	3.7	2.9	3.2	2.8	3.2	3.3	2.3	2.7	2.7	2.5
Tampa, FL	3.3	2.9	2.5	2.3	2.4	2.9	2.7	2.7	2.5	2.6	2.6	2.2
Tucson, AZ	3.6	3.6	2.8	3.1	3.3	3.9	3.9	4.0	4.1	4.0	3.4	3.1
Tulsa, OK	3.1	3.3	3.1	2.9	3.0	3.6	3.3	3.4	3.4	3.5	3.0	2.7
Tuscaloosa, AL	3.5	3.2	2.5	2.1	2.5	3.6	3.4	3.0	2.6	2.7	2.4	2.2
Virginia Beach, VA	3.9	3.4	3.1	3.0	3.4	3.4	3.3	3.6	3.0	3.2	3.4	3.0
Washington, DC[2]	4.0	3.6	3.5	3.0	3.3	3.6	3.4	3.6	3.0	3.2	3.1	2.9
Wichita, KS	3.4	3.3	3.3	2.6	3.0	3.2	3.8	3.5	2.9	3.0	2.9	2.9
Wilmington, NC	3.3	3.2	3.1	3.0	3.3	3.7	3.3	3.5	3.0	3.6	3.4	2.9
Winston-Salem, NC	3.6	3.5	3.4	3.3	3.6	4.0	3.6	3.8	3.3	3.8	3.7	3.1
Worcester, MA[3]	5.0	4.4	3.9	3.4	3.5	3.7	3.7	3.8	3.3	3.2	3.0	3.3
U.S.	4.4	4.1	3.8	3.3	3.4	3.8	3.8	3.8	3.3	3.4	3.4	3.3

Note: Data is not seasonally adjusted and covers workers 16 years of age and older; All figures are percentages; (1) Figures cover the Metropolitan Statistical Area (MSA) except where noted. See Appendix B for areas included; (2) Metropolitan Division; (3) New England City and Town Area; (4) New England City and Town Area Division
Source: Bureau of Labor Statistics, Local Area Unemployment Statistics

Average Hourly Wages: Occupations A – C

Metro Area[1]	Accountants/ Auditors	Automotive Mechanics	Book-keepers	Carpenters	Cashiers	Computer Programmers	Computer Systems Analysts
Albuquerque, NM	35.62	21.48	20.91	23.25	13.53	39.45	44.30
Allentown, PA	38.74	23.90	21.73	26.50	12.78	48.46	45.52
Anchorage, AK	38.08	28.88	25.34	35.06	16.27	47.28	47.93
Ann Arbor, MI	41.17	24.91	22.53	27.04	13.30	46.31	50.46
Athens, GA	35.00	22.03	20.51	23.47	11.77	29.81	35.56
Atlanta, GA	42.89	23.34	23.13	24.77	12.29	47.05	50.28
Austin, TX	41.33	25.45	22.37	24.23	13.85	46.80	48.67
Baltimore, MD	42.20	24.80	24.11	26.91	14.41	50.01	51.61
Boise City, ID	34.92	22.86	21.24	21.41	13.64	37.89	44.85
Boston, MA[2]	46.85	25.85	27.28	34.31	16.21	55.26	57.55
Boulder, CO	46.88	27.50	24.94	27.55	16.30	71.67	61.71
Brownsville, TX	31.30	20.87	17.66	18.88	11.54	n/a	40.71
Cape Coral, FL	37.19	23.44	21.35	21.78	12.98	43.01	46.18
Cedar Rapids, IA	36.04	23.48	22.67	24.39	13.19	42.82	43.29
Charleston, SC	38.80	22.64	20.63	23.50	12.44	n/a	51.58
Charlotte, NC	45.21	24.42	22.12	22.36	12.80	54.86	52.23
Chicago, IL	42.15	25.15	25.13	35.45	14.91	43.54	49.11
Cincinnati, OH	38.18	21.73	22.50	26.23	12.78	44.15	50.79
Clarksville, TN	32.20	21.35	19.54	21.38	11.96	n/a	39.23
Cleveland, OH	39.26	22.70	22.17	27.47	12.94	40.92	48.16
College Station, TX	36.77	21.75	19.34	20.12	12.47	36.69	39.40
Colorado Springs, CO	36.34	25.04	21.56	25.51	14.94	56.28	53.00
Columbia, MO	32.30	21.77	20.39	25.95	12.91	37.12	38.74
Columbia, SC	31.51	22.42	19.63	22.23	11.56	46.56	41.41
Columbus, OH	38.54	23.63	22.84	26.80	12.98	44.12	48.82
Dallas, TX	43.06	24.09	22.81	23.70	13.14	46.27	54.07
Davenport, IA	34.44	23.03	21.58	25.54	13.39	41.58	42.03
Denver, CO	43.21	26.75	24.91	26.47	16.03	59.06	58.10
Des Moines, IA	36.71	23.68	23.50	25.01	13.40	44.45	45.98
Durham, NC	42.03	24.33	23.51	22.09	12.86	51.67	48.44
Edison, NJ	54.94	26.81	26.44	37.06	16.55	57.97	60.54
El Paso, TX	33.19	19.58	18.00	18.84	11.04	32.89	38.82
Fargo, ND	33.62	23.74	21.80	24.78	14.30	43.53	46.07
Fort Collins, CO	40.07	25.91	23.02	25.81	15.48	47.61	50.60
Fort Wayne, IN	35.91	21.07	20.51	24.46	12.43	41.88	40.51
Fort Worth, TX	43.06	24.09	22.81	23.70	13.14	46.27	54.07
Grand Rapids, MI	36.05	23.88	21.43	25.03	13.24	43.23	45.05
Greeley, CO	40.39	26.16	22.81	25.71	14.89	42.19	47.48
Green Bay, WI	35.84	24.15	21.27	27.33	13.29	48.63	44.13
Greensboro, NC	39.53	23.26	20.74	21.12	11.95	47.79	44.56
Honolulu, HI	35.01	25.53	23.01	40.03	15.19	40.35	44.09
Houston, TX	45.35	24.26	22.16	23.53	12.84	44.09	53.59
Huntsville, AL	38.65	23.32	19.18	21.60	12.06	48.90	59.97
Indianapolis, IN	38.48	24.17	21.02	26.70	12.72	55.30	46.41
Jacksonville, FL	37.78	21.66	22.39	21.96	12.81	45.61	47.46
Kansas City, MO	37.26	22.90	22.32	28.49	13.42	32.32	43.98
Lafayette, LA	33.20	21.50	19.60	21.95	10.71	46.32	40.06
Las Cruces, NM	31.08	19.52	19.12	19.82	12.79	32.88	40.51
Las Vegas, NV	32.32	23.93	22.52	31.29	12.95	46.77	45.39
Lexington, KY	34.78	19.88	21.74	24.79	12.65	41.29	41.63
Lincoln, NE	33.19	25.66	21.09	22.21	12.89	42.91	38.01
Little Rock, AR	34.54	21.76	20.43	20.73	12.61	39.86	36.35
Los Angeles, CA	44.41	27.03	25.38	32.48	16.40	52.39	56.78
Louisville, KY	37.30	20.62	21.86	24.50	12.91	39.53	43.77
Madison, WI	37.27	24.24	22.60	27.63	14.13	56.02	44.74

Table continued on following page.

Appendix A: Comparative Statistics

Metro Area[1]	Accountants/ Auditors	Automotive Mechanics	Book-keepers	Carpenters	Cashiers	Computer Programmers	Computer Systems Analysts
Manchester, NH[2]	38.41	25.34	23.03	25.30	13.47	37.37	55.74
Miami, FL	40.21	23.98	22.09	23.23	13.04	57.52	49.49
Midland, TX	45.27	22.73	23.16	24.74	13.53	46.24	60.82
Milwaukee, WI	38.84	25.28	22.52	27.42	13.47	48.26	47.82
Minneapolis, MN	41.61	26.35	24.93	31.05	14.83	56.92	51.73
Nashville, TN	37.26	23.62	22.19	23.17	13.16	55.27	45.76
New Haven, CT[2]	40.18	25.11	25.93	29.63	14.82	46.28	50.48
New Orleans, LA	35.71	22.89	21.05	23.83	11.45	n/a	42.24
New York, NY	54.94	26.81	26.44	37.06	16.55	57.97	60.54
Oklahoma City, OK	37.21	22.78	20.87	21.48	12.66	43.42	43.52
Omaha, NE	36.79	24.01	22.22	22.88	13.40	45.89	44.58
Orlando, FL	39.04	22.82	21.76	22.25	13.41	44.68	49.23
Philadelphia, PA	41.83	25.23	23.94	30.34	13.39	48.86	51.32
Phoenix, AZ	40.79	24.61	23.11	24.95	14.93	42.27	50.03
Pittsburgh, PA	36.77	22.54	21.77	27.30	12.18	44.53	44.54
Portland, OR	40.08	26.62	24.24	30.98	16.34	54.65	56.22
Providence, RI[2]	44.90	22.35	24.22	29.76	14.61	43.32	51.67
Provo, UT	36.53	24.47	21.59	22.45	13.70	50.42	42.69
Raleigh, NC	40.68	23.79	21.92	22.09	12.55	51.36	48.99
Reno, NV	36.36	26.22	23.68	30.24	13.43	47.35	51.99
Richmond, VA	39.80	24.06	22.01	22.95	13.04	46.05	49.01
Rochester, MN	39.00	23.13	22.86	28.86	14.39	43.06	50.23
Sacramento, CA	41.27	28.35	25.70	32.41	16.67	54.48	52.53
Salem, OR	37.81	26.17	23.29	27.37	15.07	43.99	48.05
Salt Lake City, UT	38.26	24.06	23.32	24.89	13.79	48.36	47.68
San Antonio, TX	40.79	22.70	21.14	21.56	13.19	42.04	48.72
San Diego, CA	43.86	27.06	25.51	32.52	16.54	61.76	55.08
San Francisco, CA	54.83	31.95	30.30	38.33	18.96	64.89	70.44
San Jose, CA	55.92	37.42	29.94	37.76	19.15	70.63	79.75
Santa Rosa, CA	44.48	28.50	27.43	37.66	17.71	51.79	53.46
Savannah, GA	37.20	21.80	21.94	22.17	12.01	40.03	51.98
Seattle, WA	45.25	28.69	26.09	35.16	17.95	64.30	62.53
Sioux Falls, SD	36.65	24.92	19.54	20.96	13.46	31.23	41.70
Springfield, IL	37.41	23.85	22.33	28.27	13.91	43.32	48.50
St. Louis, MO	37.46	23.04	23.29	29.99	13.92	39.08	49.69
Tampa, FL	39.60	22.77	21.91	22.26	12.70	42.78	47.41
Tucson, AZ	34.99	23.11	21.61	21.37	14.27	39.03	51.23
Tulsa, OK	39.68	22.38	20.66	21.83	12.73	44.62	44.82
Tuscaloosa, AL	35.59	21.58	19.16	21.27	11.34	40.66	45.86
Virginia Beach, VA	36.48	23.14	20.67	23.04	12.50	45.16	49.26
Washington, DC	48.98	27.98	26.17	28.25	15.21	59.90	58.64
Wichita, KS	36.01	21.40	19.47	23.61	12.22	33.61	40.07
Wilmington, NC	37.58	21.31	19.94	21.32	11.98	51.25	42.16
Winston-Salem, NC	38.18	21.78	20.62	20.32	11.93	48.29	46.37
Worcester, MA[2]	42.78	26.08	24.24	29.55	15.32	49.03	50.87

Notes: (1) Figures cover the Metropolitan Statistical Area (MSA) except where noted. See Appendix B for areas included; (2) New England City and Town Area; n/a not available
Source: Bureau of Labor Statistics, May 2022 Metro Area Occupational Employment and Wage Estimates

Appendix A: Comparative Statistics

Average Hourly Wages: Occupations C – E

Metro Area	Comp. User Support Specialists	Construction Laborers	Cooks, Restaurant	Customer Service Reps.	Dentists	Electricians	Engineers, Electrical
Albuquerque, NM	25.04	17.98	15.25	17.46	92.90	27.76	63.45
Allentown, PA	29.17	23.73	15.53	19.08	76.30	35.65	52.01
Anchorage, AK	31.03	26.21	18.32	20.61	86.58	38.38	51.77
Ann Arbor, MI	26.14	23.76	16.10	19.39	76.15	34.45	48.28
Athens, GA	23.39	17.59	14.12	16.00	83.95	25.40	51.99
Atlanta, GA	30.05	19.06	14.12	19.35	n/a	27.76	56.29
Austin, TX	28.69	19.04	15.59	19.39	85.63	27.12	62.22
Baltimore, MD	28.42	20.10	16.72	20.48	78.23	31.44	56.06
Boise City, ID	26.11	19.73	15.37	18.74	71.88	26.06	55.65
Boston, MA[2]	35.38	31.95	19.78	24.00	89.08	39.81	61.23
Boulder, CO	37.04	20.81	18.99	21.92	77.69	28.91	61.37
Brownsville, TX	21.36	14.98	12.36	16.29	n/a	21.42	44.90
Cape Coral, FL	27.26	18.06	16.07	18.46	77.81	23.54	48.44
Cedar Rapids, IA	27.05	22.70	14.19	20.25	95.40	28.53	47.69
Charleston, SC	26.98	18.51	15.93	18.41	87.52	25.86	46.55
Charlotte, NC	30.39	18.19	15.26	19.72	98.68	25.03	49.35
Chicago, IL	29.52	32.85	17.06	21.26	67.54	42.79	50.03
Cincinnati, OH	25.81	24.39	15.01	19.74	86.77	28.47	48.44
Clarksville, TN	22.21	17.54	13.67	17.08	n/a	25.15	45.92
Cleveland, OH	26.60	26.17	15.16	20.42	78.04	29.88	46.94
College Station, TX	22.57	17.19	13.51	16.40	n/a	25.15	44.21
Colorado Springs, CO	31.65	20.22	17.67	19.52	88.61	27.65	54.86
Columbia, MO	26.05	25.63	14.43	17.49	80.29	27.19	40.87
Columbia, SC	26.44	18.07	14.25	17.29	76.98	25.73	41.58
Columbus, OH	26.03	26.04	15.34	20.25	69.07	29.48	53.22
Dallas, TX	28.45	18.68	15.57	19.64	76.46	26.46	50.66
Davenport, IA	27.11	23.89	14.54	19.17	75.24	30.25	46.40
Denver, CO	33.31	20.88	18.61	21.35	73.17	29.06	53.05
Des Moines, IA	27.24	22.43	14.73	21.45	80.98	30.12	48.91
Durham, NC	31.57	18.55	15.87	19.93	106.19	27.22	56.69
Edison, NJ	35.55	30.93	19.55	23.75	89.01	41.22	53.37
El Paso, TX	20.96	15.44	12.46	15.69	78.62	21.95	40.61
Fargo, ND	27.94	22.00	15.80	19.82	80.70	29.07	47.71
Fort Collins, CO	30.99	20.70	17.57	19.06	n/a	28.15	54.42
Fort Wayne, IN	25.05	22.43	14.31	19.63	81.34	29.66	48.26
Fort Worth, TX	28.45	18.68	15.57	19.64	76.46	26.46	50.66
Grand Rapids, MI	27.43	21.17	15.94	19.17	88.95	27.51	43.36
Greeley, CO	33.01	20.70	17.40	18.44	65.47	27.92	50.58
Green Bay, WI	29.31	22.68	15.04	20.32	81.73	30.20	43.80
Greensboro, NC	25.86	17.39	14.20	18.33	85.11	24.46	46.74
Honolulu, HI	29.83	32.93	19.44	20.16	n/a	43.15	50.24
Houston, TX	27.70	18.56	14.67	18.59	74.27	27.69	55.91
Huntsville, AL	24.38	16.49	14.48	17.51	87.97	25.26	53.71
Indianapolis, IN	25.93	23.51	14.76	20.25	98.07	31.79	46.72
Jacksonville, FL	27.33	18.20	15.75	19.12	82.64	24.62	48.04
Kansas City, MO	28.08	22.55	15.09	19.33	85.61	32.19	49.54
Lafayette, LA	26.07	17.53	12.87	16.84	63.45	25.23	43.20
Las Cruces, NM	22.91	17.03	14.13	15.26	76.28	25.44	44.62
Las Vegas, NV	25.53	21.97	17.17	18.68	n/a	33.87	42.86
Lexington, KY	25.84	20.07	14.54	17.87	n/a	25.25	44.15
Lincoln, NE	25.23	19.61	15.58	17.91	73.53	25.71	47.33
Little Rock, AR	22.91	17.13	14.00	18.06	85.98	21.91	46.55
Los Angeles, CA	33.66	25.96	18.92	22.21	n/a	37.09	65.13
Louisville, KY	26.08	21.24	14.55	19.09	87.22	28.92	45.08
Madison, WI	29.94	23.76	16.05	20.72	83.83	34.25	46.88

Table continued on following page.

Appendix A: Comparative Statistics   A-91

Metro Area	Comp. User Support Specialists	Construction Laborers	Cooks, Restaurant	Customer Service Reps.	Dentists	Electricians	Engineers, Electrical
Manchester, NH[2]	30.81	20.40	17.24	20.95	139.57	28.40	53.87
Miami, FL	27.62	18.58	16.91	19.16	80.27	25.35	47.59
Midland, TX	29.09	19.01	15.29	19.91	n/a	29.47	42.56
Milwaukee, WI	27.77	24.14	15.78	21.30	86.72	36.15	46.03
Minneapolis, MN	30.92	27.61	17.93	22.61	93.89	37.09	50.35
Nashville, TN	25.45	19.33	15.20	18.93	89.30	28.19	47.79
New Haven, CT[2]	31.79	25.19	17.29	21.99	95.87	33.24	50.00
New Orleans, LA	25.14	18.62	13.82	17.57	88.12	27.99	51.29
New York, NY	35.55	30.93	19.55	23.75	89.01	41.22	53.37
Oklahoma City, OK	26.61	19.08	14.94	18.11	84.37	27.58	47.89
Omaha, NE	26.48	20.49	15.05	18.92	78.54	27.41	47.76
Orlando, FL	26.77	17.79	17.07	18.69	91.27	24.05	50.65
Philadelphia, PA	31.04	26.48	16.51	21.24	93.37	38.35	53.63
Phoenix, AZ	29.29	21.22	18.08	19.49	87.37	25.61	49.97
Pittsburgh, PA	29.16	24.33	14.67	19.68	68.86	34.15	49.62
Portland, OR	30.08	25.00	18.56	21.22	91.21	41.15	51.53
Providence, RI[2]	29.79	26.46	17.00	21.03	97.31	30.94	54.51
Provo, UT	28.02	21.54	15.72	18.34	65.12	26.76	56.26
Raleigh, NC	31.64	18.40	15.45	19.52	107.63	24.71	52.39
Reno, NV	26.75	25.44	17.06	19.43	56.35	32.25	48.35
Richmond, VA	28.49	17.43	15.43	18.72	79.72	27.27	50.41
Rochester, MN	31.25	25.20	16.86	20.61	83.58	33.41	51.22
Sacramento, CA	44.86	26.69	18.68	22.15	81.12	35.93	59.48
Salem, OR	29.88	23.00	17.44	19.55	94.78	37.27	52.49
Salt Lake City, UT	30.53	20.17	16.82	20.02	64.38	28.08	58.74
San Antonio, TX	26.07	18.15	14.44	18.47	90.08	25.79	50.10
San Diego, CA	31.80	26.98	18.75	22.23	70.37	33.63	61.94
San Francisco, CA	40.10	31.48	20.39	25.95	98.09	46.31	77.67
San Jose, CA	39.13	30.35	21.53	26.29	103.12	47.71	n/a
Santa Rosa, CA	34.14	28.67	19.90	23.15	79.52	36.36	60.81
Savannah, GA	26.01	17.96	15.06	16.30	n/a	25.68	56.50
Seattle, WA	36.00	28.67	21.69	24.71	84.44	44.45	60.98
Sioux Falls, SD	21.59	18.01	15.46	18.54	69.39	26.54	46.30
Springfield, IL	26.48	30.22	16.03	19.00	72.48	35.32	47.34
St. Louis, MO	30.84	27.50	15.55	20.00	n/a	33.40	50.08
Tampa, FL	29.20	18.14	15.73	18.73	77.98	24.40	49.32
Tucson, AZ	27.18	19.78	16.51	17.76	87.60	24.71	56.86
Tulsa, OK	26.87	19.26	14.72	18.17	83.90	27.67	48.62
Tuscaloosa, AL	29.58	15.23	14.27	17.16	93.58	25.75	55.16
Virginia Beach, VA	26.21	17.52	14.70	17.30	78.65	27.29	47.22
Washington, DC	33.96	21.29	18.00	22.02	85.40	34.04	59.45
Wichita, KS	27.25	18.13	13.72	17.53	76.11	28.57	43.15
Wilmington, NC	25.96	18.29	14.56	18.04	76.66	23.28	48.09
Winston-Salem, NC	26.98	17.33	14.50	18.08	91.37	23.79	49.50
Worcester, MA[2]	31.83	28.53	18.32	21.98	n/a	37.55	57.13

Notes: (1) Figures cover the Metropolitan Statistical Area (MSA) except where noted. See Appendix B for areas included;
(2) New England City and Town Area; n/a not available
Source: Bureau of Labor Statistics, May 2022 Metro Area Occupational Employment and Wage Estimates

Average Hourly Wages: Occupations F – J

Metro Area	Fast Food and Counter Workers	Financial Managers	First-Line Supervisors/ of Office Workers	General and Operations Managers	Hair-dressers/ Cosme-tologists	Home Health and Personal Care Aides	Janitors/ Cleaners
Albuquerque, NM	12.75	59.44	27.81	58.98	13.60	13.30	14.36
Allentown, PA	12.66	74.84	31.48	58.15	16.54	13.96	16.71
Anchorage, AK	14.73	72.72	32.44	54.98	15.13	17.28	16.95
Ann Arbor, MI	13.66	71.39	31.10	62.22	19.87	14.08	17.50
Athens, GA	11.00	67.23	27.18	47.82	17.24	12.56	14.99
Atlanta, GA	11.65	83.96	31.25	59.75	18.59	12.95	15.06
Austin, TX	12.48	81.29	32.79	56.28	16.04	12.07	14.63
Baltimore, MD	14.31	76.62	32.11	55.22	19.90	15.32	16.24
Boise City, ID	11.97	56.23	27.15	38.95	15.45	13.80	14.80
Boston, MA[2]	16.22	88.25	36.88	74.45	23.51	17.13	19.76
Boulder, CO	16.24	90.26	34.38	77.36	23.64	17.40	18.80
Brownsville, TX	10.12	59.69	25.20	41.63	12.81	10.33	12.36
Cape Coral, FL	12.56	69.72	30.29	51.54	18.15	15.99	14.30
Cedar Rapids, IA	12.59	60.69	29.72	45.54	15.24	16.20	15.98
Charleston, SC	11.69	65.85	29.33	52.71	16.62	13.41	13.93
Charlotte, NC	12.43	84.45	30.59	64.62	18.90	12.92	14.10
Chicago, IL	14.28	78.05	33.78	63.64	21.49	15.66	17.40
Cincinnati, OH	12.33	74.98	31.83	54.62	19.64	13.84	15.79
Clarksville, TN	11.02	59.25	27.42	46.82	16.59	12.82	13.88
Cleveland, OH	12.12	74.24	31.50	57.05	17.94	13.45	16.17
College Station, TX	10.89	65.41	26.24	47.87	13.68	11.46	13.57
Colorado Springs, CO	14.73	83.92	31.26	65.50	23.17	16.66	16.75
Columbia, MO	12.77	n/a	27.71	47.42	18.61	13.29	15.66
Columbia, SC	10.98	59.98	30.75	48.46	15.32	12.35	13.42
Columbus, OH	12.65	71.54	32.35	57.91	20.68	13.75	16.00
Dallas, TX	12.14	79.36	31.46	56.66	16.24	11.66	14.42
Davenport, IA	12.80	60.84	29.38	47.04	16.42	14.44	16.52
Denver, CO	15.81	94.94	34.80	75.18	21.59	16.85	17.70
Des Moines, IA	13.07	72.01	31.64	49.19	16.70	15.41	15.75
Durham, NC	13.08	84.49	31.92	70.01	22.31	13.24	16.43
Edison, NJ	16.08	110.67	38.32	83.82	20.85	17.10	20.14
El Paso, TX	10.10	62.87	24.90	40.58	13.11	9.83	12.05
Fargo, ND	13.47	68.39	30.87	48.98	16.61	16.62	16.77
Fort Collins, CO	14.91	86.90	31.88	63.72	26.75	16.84	17.15
Fort Wayne, IN	11.84	56.74	29.78	57.29	15.67	13.51	15.11
Fort Worth, TX	12.14	79.36	31.46	56.66	16.24	11.66	14.42
Grand Rapids, MI	13.09	65.10	29.78	55.04	18.45	14.38	15.34
Greeley, CO	14.57	83.73	32.68	64.82	19.24	16.62	17.37
Green Bay, WI	11.72	67.97	32.04	64.87	16.41	14.33	15.45
Greensboro, NC	11.81	73.43	28.58	57.79	18.33	12.20	13.36
Honolulu, HI	13.92	65.00	29.47	57.59	15.94	15.75	16.29
Houston, TX	11.74	84.66	31.01	56.99	13.81	11.18	13.63
Huntsville, AL	11.05	69.15	28.19	67.02	18.45	12.03	13.17
Indianapolis, IN	12.43	70.85	32.23	62.85	15.39	14.07	15.71
Jacksonville, FL	12.07	73.04	31.15	55.91	16.72	13.54	14.39
Kansas City, MO	13.01	74.13	31.26	52.71	19.13	13.99	16.10
Lafayette, LA	10.23	58.26	26.05	58.46	12.89	9.92	12.05
Las Cruces, NM	12.21	46.68	25.64	50.87	13.04	12.29	13.56
Las Vegas, NV	12.19	58.11	29.10	60.12	13.20	15.34	15.69
Lexington, KY	11.82	65.06	29.85	45.50	13.22	14.88	14.75
Lincoln, NE	12.48	61.87	26.83	47.07	17.83	14.17	14.69
Little Rock, AR	12.41	56.25	26.41	41.68	13.73	12.92	13.43
Los Angeles, CA	16.43	87.66	34.56	67.77	22.18	15.68	18.46
Louisville, KY	11.98	70.09	32.22	48.89	14.19	15.29	14.97

Table continued on following page.

Metro Area	Fast Food and Counter Workers	Financial Managers	First-Line Supervisors/ of Office Workers	General and Operations Managers	Hair-dressers/ Cosme-tologists	Home Health and Personal Care Aides	Janitors/ Cleaners
Madison, WI	12.42	72.88	33.73	65.92	17.32	14.89	16.04
Manchester, NH[2]	13.09	72.83	33.58	67.22	16.38	15.63	17.06
Miami, FL	12.93	81.34	31.90	56.01	15.37	13.24	14.03
Midland, TX	12.27	94.45	32.60	59.45	14.46	12.12	14.35
Milwaukee, WI	12.08	74.52	33.87	68.48	18.97	13.83	15.71
Minneapolis, MN	14.79	76.74	34.96	56.37	20.87	15.64	17.94
Nashville, TN	12.17	72.46	32.48	67.20	19.75	13.96	15.14
New Haven, CT[2]	14.76	71.48	34.08	70.00	18.17	16.48	18.12
New Orleans, LA	12.70	67.00	26.71	61.48	14.26	11.09	12.91
New York, NY	16.08	110.67	38.32	83.82	20.85	17.10	20.14
Oklahoma City, OK	11.19	64.38	30.11	48.66	17.09	12.14	13.56
Omaha, NE	12.76	65.55	28.58	47.42	21.04	14.54	15.19
Orlando, FL	12.49	77.76	30.12	55.62	17.02	13.54	13.87
Philadelphia, PA	13.26	78.78	33.31	68.82	17.70	14.31	17.24
Phoenix, AZ	15.53	76.99	30.64	54.46	20.15	15.17	15.82
Pittsburgh, PA	11.65	73.72	29.71	55.74	16.69	13.88	16.22
Portland, OR	15.88	75.43	32.27	56.83	18.86	17.48	18.11
Providence, RI[2]	14.82	81.58	34.07	65.29	15.61	17.07	17.99
Provo, UT	12.33	68.82	29.37	47.51	18.44	15.63	13.80
Raleigh, NC	12.10	74.45	29.75	64.48	21.68	13.39	14.13
Reno, NV	12.62	59.63	29.96	61.79	16.20	17.81	15.57
Richmond, VA	12.47	80.46	31.31	59.05	18.60	13.05	14.79
Rochester, MN	14.09	65.15	31.71	51.56	19.51	15.54	18.28
Sacramento, CA	16.46	79.36	35.50	67.53	21.69	15.29	18.34
Salem, OR	14.60	64.50	30.14	46.82	18.25	17.28	17.05
Salt Lake City, UT	13.19	69.34	30.21	53.16	19.62	16.45	14.30
San Antonio, TX	11.50	73.39	30.02	50.98	14.16	10.89	14.02
San Diego, CA	16.37	83.73	33.77	n/a	21.87	16.23	18.06
San Francisco, CA	18.38	107.34	40.24	80.86	23.34	16.61	21.39
San Jose, CA	18.80	103.92	41.82	90.32	20.99	17.24	20.64
Santa Rosa, CA	17.13	81.95	34.88	64.13	21.59	16.52	22.75
Savannah, GA	11.64	71.42	27.26	51.37	16.53	12.70	14.18
Seattle, WA	17.49	87.94	37.50	72.41	23.93	18.81	20.41
Sioux Falls, SD	13.18	76.40	28.08	71.87	19.15	15.27	15.35
Springfield, IL	13.61	64.09	30.02	52.04	18.76	14.39	16.63
St. Louis, MO	13.40	72.89	31.51	54.93	18.85	13.32	16.09
Tampa, FL	12.44	76.40	30.65	53.47	17.46	13.80	13.88
Tucson, AZ	14.40	62.10	27.35	44.86	19.75	14.57	15.53
Tulsa, OK	11.21	72.14	29.35	51.65	16.50	12.65	14.02
Tuscaloosa, AL	11.34	62.63	28.60	55.95	17.32	11.32	14.40
Virginia Beach, VA	12.47	72.27	28.99	54.70	17.34	12.57	14.20
Washington, DC	15.12	87.75	35.74	72.97	22.54	15.70	17.34
Wichita, KS	11.16	70.00	28.52	46.78	16.45	12.10	14.45
Wilmington, NC	11.32	74.45	26.02	53.42	19.04	12.45	13.87
Winston-Salem, NC	12.15	74.71	27.78	58.23	18.87	12.67	13.23
Worcester, MA[2]	15.52	71.84	32.65	61.97	21.83	16.77	18.83

Notes: (1) Figures cover the Metropolitan Statistical Area (MSA) except where noted. See Appendix B for areas included; (2) New England City and Town Area; n/a not available
Source: Bureau of Labor Statistics, May 2022 Metro Area Occupational Employment and Wage Estimates

Appendix A: Comparative Statistics

Average Hourly Wages: Occupations L – N

Metro Area	Landscapers	Lawyers	Maids/House-keepers	Maintenance/Repairers	Marketing Managers	Network Admin.	Nurses, Licensed Practical
Albuquerque, NM	16.24	54.41	13.69	20.91	61.49	44.73	28.50
Allentown, PA	17.57	64.68	14.89	24.13	66.34	41.40	26.64
Anchorage, AK	21.00	58.26	15.86	24.49	52.64	42.70	31.62
Ann Arbor, MI	17.82	60.75	15.15	22.11	66.72	43.40	28.93
Athens, GA	15.97	n/a	12.50	19.81	54.36	36.48	24.20
Atlanta, GA	17.07	84.73	13.58	21.53	73.79	50.54	26.03
Austin, TX	16.91	72.31	13.88	20.40	70.73	46.20	27.17
Baltimore, MD	18.68	77.46	14.74	23.34	69.41	52.41	28.83
Boise City, ID	17.90	48.56	15.14	20.73	51.10	39.68	27.38
Boston, MA[2]	21.78	97.55	19.01	27.11	80.96	52.37	33.67
Boulder, CO	21.69	n/a	17.31	27.19	85.56	48.32	29.85
Brownsville, TX	12.90	56.07	10.80	15.45	56.84	36.42	22.93
Cape Coral, FL	16.34	58.21	14.40	20.21	65.93	42.44	25.89
Cedar Rapids, IA	16.78	57.59	13.71	22.16	61.42	41.95	25.54
Charleston, SC	16.99	53.48	13.47	21.41	52.80	46.31	25.74
Charlotte, NC	17.24	78.03	13.43	22.36	71.03	44.85	26.52
Chicago, IL	18.93	78.47	17.07	26.11	70.74	44.98	30.01
Cincinnati, OH	16.69	64.18	13.58	23.48	69.92	46.45	25.99
Clarksville, TN	16.66	51.48	11.75	22.30	50.21	34.09	22.40
Cleveland, OH	17.23	64.28	14.02	23.06	69.27	45.69	26.09
College Station, TX	15.78	75.98	12.68	18.38	57.23	37.16	23.08
Colorado Springs, CO	n/a	53.62	16.06	22.51	79.04	47.29	27.54
Columbia, MO	15.24	58.60	13.42	20.64	52.19	38.68	23.50
Columbia, SC	15.84	53.72	12.62	20.68	59.00	43.75	25.20
Columbus, OH	17.46	65.26	13.91	23.16	69.18	47.97	26.41
Dallas, TX	16.86	87.42	13.78	21.23	67.66	45.36	26.59
Davenport, IA	16.43	56.57	13.68	22.09	60.27	40.41	25.09
Denver, CO	20.25	84.07	16.80	25.27	86.32	50.59	30.30
Des Moines, IA	17.60	59.08	14.22	22.01	64.50	44.01	25.09
Durham, NC	17.41	73.85	14.21	23.68	75.77	48.52	26.52
Edison, NJ	20.81	92.92	21.40	26.67	93.41	55.75	30.31
El Paso, TX	13.79	65.20	11.07	16.87	49.29	37.25	22.95
Fargo, ND	19.28	61.05	14.33	22.10	61.40	39.32	25.14
Fort Collins, CO	19.43	88.05	16.17	22.69	87.40	43.41	28.74
Fort Wayne, IN	16.18	62.54	13.34	23.13	56.84	37.68	25.80
Fort Worth, TX	16.86	87.42	13.78	21.23	67.66	45.36	26.59
Grand Rapids, MI	17.18	64.19	14.27	21.10	64.10	41.89	27.34
Greeley, CO	20.33	67.70	16.09	25.25	80.70	41.55	29.06
Green Bay, WI	17.41	72.57	14.43	22.47	75.00	42.60	23.59
Greensboro, NC	15.69	66.92	13.04	21.27	64.13	41.11	25.19
Honolulu, HI	19.21	50.95	23.06	25.25	59.72	44.72	27.07
Houston, TX	16.29	84.79	14.27	20.87	71.45	47.28	26.65
Huntsville, AL	15.92	69.72	11.97	20.71	68.35	45.60	22.75
Indianapolis, IN	17.19	74.02	14.20	23.30	65.78	42.49	27.80
Jacksonville, FL	16.00	62.74	13.79	20.57	72.46	43.58	24.97
Kansas City, MO	17.47	70.16	14.27	22.59	68.75	42.01	26.30
Lafayette, LA	14.42	53.24	10.93	18.12	47.53	41.24	21.48
Las Cruces, NM	15.38	53.03	12.60	18.02	n/a	41.48	27.19
Las Vegas, NV	17.85	82.94	17.87	23.05	51.14	49.43	30.50
Lexington, KY	15.64	51.22	12.88	22.07	55.36	38.28	24.21
Lincoln, NE	16.86	56.01	13.97	21.04	49.76	40.83	24.46
Little Rock, AR	15.21	50.96	12.84	18.37	51.80	38.74	23.12
Los Angeles, CA	19.81	93.69	18.69	24.86	81.73	49.56	32.95
Louisville, KY	16.00	52.07	13.67	23.69	68.37	40.49	25.32
Madison, WI	18.73	66.28	14.97	22.80	70.25	43.19	25.83

Table continued on following page.

Appendix A: Comparative Statistics   A-95

Metro Area	Landscapers	Lawyers	Maids/House-keepers	Maintenance/Repairers	Marketing Managers	Network Admin.	Nurses, Licensed Practical
Manchester, NH[2]	19.05	69.50	15.17	23.02	70.51	42.70	31.39
Miami, FL	16.61	69.69	14.17	20.30	73.31	45.42	26.47
Midland, TX	16.75	87.92	13.55	20.19	76.35	46.75	26.25
Milwaukee, WI	17.75	80.34	14.73	22.70	68.47	46.07	26.39
Minneapolis, MN	19.96	83.25	17.58	25.64	78.99	46.85	27.70
Nashville, TN	17.05	73.05	13.44	21.40	76.32	44.89	23.71
New Haven, CT[2]	20.86	73.87	15.86	24.69	71.85	45.08	30.20
New Orleans, LA	14.72	68.27	12.41	20.69	61.89	39.84	24.25
New York, NY	20.81	92.92	21.40	26.67	93.41	55.75	30.31
Oklahoma City, OK	16.15	53.26	12.31	18.75	64.04	41.84	23.45
Omaha, NE	17.69	59.74	14.69	22.11	58.09	44.11	25.44
Orlando, FL	16.23	70.07	14.29	20.33	76.95	43.75	26.40
Philadelphia, PA	18.71	76.88	15.47	23.49	71.68	47.15	28.52
Phoenix, AZ	17.31	72.30	16.08	22.41	68.83	45.37	30.07
Pittsburgh, PA	16.84	66.28	14.29	22.49	60.70	45.38	25.74
Portland, OR	20.88	73.57	17.60	24.55	66.94	48.17	33.26
Providence, RI[2]	20.58	74.38	16.14	24.78	79.73	51.47	31.28
Provo, UT	18.30	72.07	14.71	21.46	62.12	43.16	25.28
Raleigh, NC	17.40	67.47	14.15	22.67	71.21	45.26	26.69
Reno, NV	18.37	72.00	16.74	23.76	64.64	55.57	32.19
Richmond, VA	16.43	80.05	13.35	22.55	72.33	48.67	25.75
Rochester, MN	18.74	57.71	15.90	23.54	62.16	48.04	25.78
Sacramento, CA	20.30	79.67	20.36	24.95	77.80	43.18	34.27
Salem, OR	19.59	67.46	16.44	22.28	52.32	46.22	30.83
Salt Lake City, UT	18.82	65.12	16.12	23.79	65.16	45.48	29.02
San Antonio, TX	15.69	68.81	13.15	19.50	60.00	41.81	25.93
San Diego, CA	19.61	89.63	18.37	24.59	84.68	49.31	32.57
San Francisco, CA	23.72	115.06	22.92	29.95	100.73	61.21	38.69
San Jose, CA	24.14	128.77	22.48	30.88	113.98	72.84	38.75
Santa Rosa, CA	21.42	88.92	20.35	26.12	75.37	46.00	36.88
Savannah, GA	15.94	n/a	11.85	20.32	68.95	44.17	24.10
Seattle, WA	23.52	83.85	18.50	27.19	82.15	53.30	35.34
Sioux Falls, SD	16.41	60.68	13.76	20.54	66.13	35.57	22.26
Springfield, IL	18.70	61.68	16.39	23.40	62.68	36.92	25.11
St. Louis, MO	17.58	68.34	14.77	24.01	64.07	45.06	26.06
Tampa, FL	15.63	66.40	13.55	19.72	72.41	44.44	25.31
Tucson, AZ	16.04	61.60	14.58	20.08	58.86	41.53	29.01
Tulsa, OK	15.90	60.61	12.45	19.66	69.45	41.63	24.26
Tuscaloosa, AL	15.89	55.63	11.48	18.71	54.09	37.32	21.53
Virginia Beach, VA	16.35	61.10	13.16	21.28	70.40	44.66	24.37
Washington, DC	19.67	101.85	17.03	25.65	84.53	55.96	29.10
Wichita, KS	15.78	54.07	12.87	19.99	63.35	40.60	23.92
Wilmington, NC	16.23	61.99	12.83	19.80	67.91	39.92	25.28
Winston-Salem, NC	16.17	81.73	13.42	21.32	72.60	42.13	25.36
Worcester, MA[2]	20.03	69.75	17.11	24.75	73.90	47.65	30.85

Notes: (1) Figures cover the Metropolitan Statistical Area (MSA) except where noted. See Appendix B for areas included; (2) New England City and Town Area; n/a not available
Source: Bureau of Labor Statistics, May 2022 Metro Area Occupational Employment and Wage Estimates

Average Hourly Wages: Occupations N – P

Metro Area	Nurses, Registered	Nursing Assistants	Office Clerks	Physical Therapists	Physicians	Plumbers	Police Officers
Albuquerque, NM	41.94	16.74	16.26	44.66	129.51	25.36	27.99
Allentown, PA	39.14	17.79	20.19	48.05	n/a	32.16	36.38
Anchorage, AK	49.59	20.50	22.26	49.64	112.03	43.11	47.16
Ann Arbor, MI	41.54	18.36	19.11	46.21	120.10	33.25	34.05
Athens, GA	38.59	14.53	19.23	49.24	106.67	26.88	24.49
Atlanta, GA	43.40	17.12	19.42	46.86	123.80	28.56	26.02
Austin, TX	41.69	16.17	19.06	47.33	136.94	28.42	35.58
Baltimore, MD	43.03	17.71	19.28	45.91	120.21	28.83	34.65
Boise City, ID	39.06	17.88	17.66	43.44	148.73	28.88	30.67
Boston, MA[2]	51.44	20.42	23.38	46.36	106.88	39.70	36.32
Boulder, CO	44.57	19.72	25.81	48.20	142.09	32.34	40.88
Brownsville, TX	35.07	13.19	14.88	45.71	116.21	20.29	26.68
Cape Coral, FL	38.04	16.24	19.43	43.77	177.87	24.29	31.19
Cedar Rapids, IA	33.68	17.02	19.34	40.86	125.70	32.41	31.90
Charleston, SC	36.96	17.18	17.46	41.79	141.24	24.76	25.12
Charlotte, NC	38.24	15.93	18.96	46.12	133.48	25.11	28.24
Chicago, IL	40.99	18.37	21.22	48.81	100.40	43.17	41.59
Cincinnati, OH	38.82	16.53	19.80	45.46	108.34	31.67	33.83
Clarksville, TN	34.52	14.53	16.20	42.52	143.21	24.18	23.65
Cleveland, OH	38.95	17.21	20.05	47.43	79.22	31.97	34.02
College Station, TX	37.59	14.34	15.70	46.21	n/a	24.11	31.36
Colorado Springs, CO	39.78	18.31	23.24	45.18	n/a	28.01	37.67
Columbia, MO	34.00	15.71	18.99	41.76	132.62	28.50	24.89
Columbia, SC	35.37	15.81	16.30	41.97	142.61	22.81	24.96
Columbus, OH	38.80	16.67	20.13	48.56	102.84	31.99	37.43
Dallas, TX	42.24	16.34	18.59	50.76	118.86	26.94	35.82
Davenport, IA	32.77	16.26	18.58	41.53	n/a	32.66	32.09
Denver, CO	42.21	19.35	24.74	47.13	156.83	31.18	41.85
Des Moines, IA	34.16	17.50	19.96	41.72	105.11	31.79	34.32
Durham, NC	n/a	16.82	19.49	40.71	n/a	26.00	25.40
Edison, NJ	50.41	21.50	21.90	53.25	128.42	42.38	42.43
El Paso, TX	36.36	13.69	15.17	45.54	105.87	22.73	30.10
Fargo, ND	36.60	17.94	22.07	40.35	105.75	29.18	34.03
Fort Collins, CO	40.85	18.30	23.55	42.61	n/a	29.30	43.64
Fort Wayne, IN	35.21	15.77	18.98	44.25	n/a	33.18	31.73
Fort Worth, TX	42.24	16.34	18.59	50.76	118.86	26.94	35.82
Grand Rapids, MI	36.98	17.03	20.33	42.66	126.06	30.06	31.96
Greeley, CO	41.14	17.60	23.36	47.67	n/a	26.96	36.95
Green Bay, WI	37.41	17.41	19.40	44.40	177.48	33.56	34.37
Greensboro, NC	38.59	14.93	17.77	45.22	n/a	23.39	24.52
Honolulu, HI	55.38	19.29	20.72	49.00	132.28	37.07	43.41
Houston, TX	42.73	16.18	18.74	52.20	138.31	28.24	32.31
Huntsville, AL	31.99	14.59	13.92	46.53	139.48	24.93	25.54
Indianapolis, IN	38.68	16.97	20.15	45.55	161.40	33.28	32.70
Jacksonville, FL	37.74	15.99	19.42	44.49	132.91	23.81	27.88
Kansas City, MO	36.82	17.33	20.48	44.96	104.46	31.93	29.20
Lafayette, LA	35.91	12.92	13.92	44.44	140.81	25.47	22.67
Las Cruces, NM	37.30	14.84	15.58	40.75	135.79	22.92	27.37
Las Vegas, NV	46.96	19.90	19.84	51.20	126.98	31.07	36.94
Lexington, KY	37.36	16.43	17.56	40.93	146.74	29.90	24.95
Lincoln, NE	35.52	16.53	16.75	44.49	131.40	25.79	33.34
Little Rock, AR	34.48	15.09	17.64	44.50	90.44	22.44	23.08
Los Angeles, CA	60.26	20.49	21.66	52.02	113.43	34.45	50.13
Louisville, KY	39.08	16.62	18.11	43.91	144.45	29.23	25.96
Madison, WI	41.46	18.71	20.66	43.49	152.61	35.91	35.34

Table continued on following page.

Appendix A: Comparative Statistics

Metro Area	Nurses, Registered	Nursing Assistants	Office Clerks	Physical Therapists	Physicians	Plumbers	Police Officers
Manchester, NH[2]	39.38	18.40	22.10	43.45	n/a	28.32	30.78
Miami, FL	39.33	16.17	19.87	42.11	102.65	24.64	43.87
Midland, TX	39.34	16.60	20.43	50.09	124.58	26.81	34.27
Milwaukee, WI	39.44	17.93	19.83	45.40	104.93	35.62	35.72
Minneapolis, MN	44.32	22.36	22.34	43.60	145.35	39.07	39.69
Nashville, TN	37.13	16.08	17.70	44.33	131.73	26.77	26.07
New Haven, CT[2]	46.18	18.43	21.09	48.79	130.80	34.63	36.86
New Orleans, LA	38.18	14.49	14.52	46.62	151.73	27.73	23.68
New York, NY	50.41	21.50	21.90	53.25	128.42	42.38	42.43
Oklahoma City, OK	37.19	14.90	16.78	44.06	126.14	24.68	33.22
Omaha, NE	36.18	17.53	18.19	43.62	142.86	32.29	34.43
Orlando, FL	38.04	16.41	18.94	45.58	133.16	23.14	29.83
Philadelphia, PA	42.23	18.17	21.08	48.69	n/a	34.76	37.93
Phoenix, AZ	42.03	18.44	21.73	48.80	98.99	28.48	35.65
Pittsburgh, PA	36.65	17.51	19.95	45.42	59.50	34.72	36.66
Portland, OR	53.66	21.15	21.40	46.36	111.11	40.51	40.50
Providence, RI[2]	42.39	18.87	21.07	45.70	100.09	32.22	34.35
Provo, UT	34.96	15.59	18.82	43.16	82.30	25.73	28.90
Raleigh, NC	37.82	16.03	19.56	42.43	140.14	24.57	26.56
Reno, NV	44.85	19.69	21.19	49.42	142.69	32.67	35.21
Richmond, VA	39.75	15.79	18.79	46.28	79.68	25.66	29.03
Rochester, MN	43.30	19.09	21.24	41.61	143.61	37.05	34.21
Sacramento, CA	69.82	21.17	21.97	58.89	145.43	33.87	48.52
Salem, OR	46.17	21.59	20.38	45.54	158.13	34.34	37.37
Salt Lake City, UT	38.16	16.66	19.23	45.74	120.76	30.62	32.06
San Antonio, TX	39.92	15.47	18.02	45.42	145.35	24.88	31.55
San Diego, CA	56.65	20.39	21.38	52.92	125.61	34.09	47.51
San Francisco, CA	79.21	25.13	26.29	60.61	114.31	44.23	57.43
San Jose, CA	76.94	24.81	25.56	64.33	124.09	46.57	62.36
Santa Rosa, CA	72.67	20.99	22.86	60.31	112.97	36.74	49.57
Savannah, GA	40.41	14.89	18.02	45.44	100.61	28.19	25.28
Seattle, WA	50.74	21.40	24.29	50.43	120.27	41.46	48.78
Sioux Falls, SD	30.18	15.47	15.70	41.62	n/a	25.38	31.52
Springfield, IL	37.80	17.22	20.11	46.06	146.21	38.31	34.84
St. Louis, MO	36.14	16.41	20.76	44.14	142.81	35.55	29.89
Tampa, FL	38.42	16.72	19.64	46.29	132.49	23.00	33.26
Tucson, AZ	40.19	17.25	20.55	44.89	n/a	25.56	30.75
Tulsa, OK	38.32	15.05	17.16	43.95	78.82	26.43	26.48
Tuscaloosa, AL	30.81	14.13	13.87	48.68	105.13	23.92	27.48
Virginia Beach, VA	38.20	15.13	18.11	45.34	n/a	26.56	27.70
Washington, DC	44.61	18.33	22.52	49.52	101.91	30.71	37.25
Wichita, KS	33.08	15.61	14.16	43.47	100.53	27.23	25.83
Wilmington, NC	36.27	14.86	17.25	41.09	112.33	22.57	23.49
Winston-Salem, NC	38.57	15.34	17.36	47.28	n/a	22.79	24.14
Worcester, MA[2]	47.38	18.71	21.03	44.80	108.84	40.47	30.41

Notes: (1) Figures cover the Metropolitan Statistical Area (MSA) except where noted. See Appendix B for areas included;
(2) New England City and Town Area; n/a not available
Source: Bureau of Labor Statistics, May 2022 Metro Area Occupational Employment and Wage Estimates

Average Hourly Wages: Occupations P – S

Metro Area	Postal Mail Carriers	R.E. Sales Agents	Retail Sales-persons	Sales Reps., Technical/Scientific	Secretaries, Exc. Leg./Med./Exec.	Security Guards	Surgeons
Albuquerque, NM	26.30	22.73	15.08	37.39	20.16	15.37	n/a
Allentown, PA	27.45	27.37	16.75	51.14	20.39	17.28	n/a
Anchorage, AK	25.73	34.80	18.27	36.27	20.62	20.74	n/a
Ann Arbor, MI	27.10	33.57	16.77	128.93	22.52	18.34	n/a
Athens, GA	25.97	21.38	14.84	41.34	17.79	19.33	n/a
Atlanta, GA	26.65	28.00	15.55	52.79	19.44	16.02	212.04
Austin, TX	27.22	39.51	16.52	44.57	21.45	17.41	n/a
Baltimore, MD	27.22	32.50	15.99	50.13	21.48	20.09	162.71
Boise City, ID	27.00	21.80	16.72	41.57	18.67	16.67	n/a
Boston, MA[2]	28.27	38.33	18.39	54.97	25.44	19.80	148.22
Boulder, CO	28.10	49.41	18.86	n/a	22.19	21.46	n/a
Brownsville, TX	26.80	24.87	14.27	n/a	16.45	15.55	n/a
Cape Coral, FL	26.49	24.97	15.73	53.67	18.53	14.53	n/a
Cedar Rapids, IA	27.18	30.06	15.63	51.91	20.40	17.15	n/a
Charleston, SC	26.88	29.27	15.26	37.04	19.15	14.67	n/a
Charlotte, NC	27.50	27.29	15.72	54.96	20.17	14.89	276.15
Chicago, IL	27.84	21.56	17.49	56.01	23.34	17.98	136.81
Cincinnati, OH	28.15	27.69	16.23	51.86	20.51	17.09	184.17
Clarksville, TN	25.40	28.07	15.47	32.81	18.04	18.30	n/a
Cleveland, OH	27.79	20.71	16.56	52.20	20.38	17.47	n/a
College Station, TX	26.30	31.28	14.39	39.76	18.70	14.38	n/a
Colorado Springs, CO	26.35	34.84	17.44	46.25	19.90	17.50	n/a
Columbia, MO	26.18	20.94	14.99	n/a	18.33	16.33	n/a
Columbia, SC	25.68	28.52	14.63	40.39	18.64	13.48	n/a
Columbus, OH	27.37	21.29	16.00	58.13	20.96	17.83	n/a
Dallas, TX	27.30	38.08	16.19	43.31	20.33	16.99	142.82
Davenport, IA	26.31	33.24	15.72	50.09	19.78	18.10	n/a
Denver, CO	28.16	40.40	19.03	54.91	22.11	19.02	146.05
Des Moines, IA	27.78	34.49	15.88	54.80	21.22	17.63	n/a
Durham, NC	27.82	26.02	15.72	58.46	21.42	18.04	n/a
Edison, NJ	27.72	47.01	19.51	63.64	23.24	19.89	149.60
El Paso, TX	26.59	27.97	14.09	n/a	16.30	15.14	n/a
Fargo, ND	27.52	29.08	17.14	54.63	20.53	16.86	n/a
Fort Collins, CO	27.22	33.68	17.51	46.18	21.02	16.93	n/a
Fort Wayne, IN	26.91	27.25	14.91	51.06	18.31	17.67	n/a
Fort Worth, TX	27.30	38.08	16.19	43.31	20.33	16.99	142.82
Grand Rapids, MI	27.01	27.56	16.20	52.99	20.23	14.75	121.07
Greeley, CO	26.49	52.77	18.12	47.78	20.32	16.95	n/a
Green Bay, WI	27.20	29.62	16.28	34.34	20.34	16.22	n/a
Greensboro, NC	27.21	26.84	15.24	42.34	19.33	14.54	n/a
Honolulu, HI	26.72	26.75	17.85	54.70	23.30	17.09	205.79
Houston, TX	26.87	38.86	16.04	46.77	20.43	15.78	162.09
Huntsville, AL	26.36	41.38	14.54	38.34	20.21	15.35	n/a
Indianapolis, IN	27.71	32.61	15.60	52.85	20.15	16.75	185.56
Jacksonville, FL	27.22	29.37	15.49	46.55	19.30	15.13	n/a
Kansas City, MO	27.63	26.48	16.44	53.53	19.21	18.98	119.29
Lafayette, LA	26.29	17.52	13.84	40.17	17.91	13.48	n/a
Las Cruces, NM	25.66	22.91	13.98	n/a	18.37	15.27	n/a
Las Vegas, NV	26.97	38.35	16.82	41.45	21.22	15.06	n/a
Lexington, KY	27.17	27.67	15.76	45.14	20.09	14.57	n/a
Lincoln, NE	27.48	19.09	15.39	43.72	19.78	14.91	n/a
Little Rock, AR	26.80	n/a	14.90	44.97	18.48	15.34	n/a
Los Angeles, CA	28.35	35.65	18.93	52.61	24.22	18.19	n/a
Louisville, KY	27.28	22.31	15.89	49.19	19.91	16.60	194.02
Madison, WI	27.00	33.85	16.03	36.52	21.15	17.01	n/a

Table continued on following page.

Appendix A: Comparative Statistics   A-99

Metro Area	Postal Mail Carriers	R.E. Sales Agents	Retail Salespersons	Sales Reps., Technical/ Scientific	Secretaries, Exc. Leg./ Med./Exec.	Security Guards	Surgeons
Manchester, NH[2]	27.77	30.34	16.93	41.73	20.73	18.41	n/a
Miami, FL	27.09	26.19	16.30	50.86	20.66	16.16	92.08
Midland, TX	25.08	48.44	16.59	48.08	20.58	17.08	n/a
Milwaukee, WI	27.42	24.00	16.36	39.18	20.72	16.44	n/a
Minneapolis, MN	27.77	n/a	17.68	47.57	23.29	18.79	176.40
Nashville, TN	27.31	19.02	16.18	40.84	20.51	15.94	135.32
New Haven, CT[2]	26.76	29.22	18.46	45.89	26.88	18.52	n/a
New Orleans, LA	26.86	24.99	14.66	40.90	18.95	15.17	n/a
New York, NY	27.72	47.01	19.51	63.64	23.24	19.89	149.60
Oklahoma City, OK	27.22	n/a	15.14	39.45	18.26	15.95	n/a
Omaha, NE	27.42	29.75	16.07	41.32	19.89	17.42	158.30
Orlando, FL	26.72	26.11	15.51	46.62	18.93	15.30	n/a
Philadelphia, PA	27.23	27.12	16.66	57.64	21.81	18.05	196.21
Phoenix, AZ	27.93	29.19	17.07	46.98	21.31	17.03	n/a
Pittsburgh, PA	26.80	30.60	15.60	50.53	19.68	16.59	n/a
Portland, OR	27.17	28.64	19.03	56.64	24.16	18.14	n/a
Providence, RI[2]	27.29	35.48	17.17	39.71	22.88	17.75	n/a
Provo, UT	27.30	27.88	16.90	43.62	19.25	15.75	n/a
Raleigh, NC	27.38	27.61	16.28	55.59	20.25	15.48	n/a
Reno, NV	27.69	24.89	17.26	42.94	22.47	16.07	n/a
Richmond, VA	26.92	35.50	15.56	47.20	19.90	17.63	n/a
Rochester, MN	27.15	n/a	16.90	35.30	21.71	17.79	156.35
Sacramento, CA	28.15	32.19	19.11	58.98	23.74	18.43	n/a
Salem, OR	26.44	29.11	17.64	53.51	22.97	18.21	n/a
Salt Lake City, UT	28.08	26.96	18.75	57.43	20.26	17.09	219.11
San Antonio, TX	26.74	32.87	15.92	41.27	19.44	15.80	n/a
San Diego, CA	27.48	41.65	18.69	57.24	23.50	18.37	n/a
San Francisco, CA	29.20	39.87	21.47	60.73	28.82	21.09	75.20
San Jose, CA	29.08	36.25	21.34	78.03	28.34	21.24	n/a
Santa Rosa, CA	27.31	39.25	19.94	53.84	25.29	19.11	n/a
Savannah, GA	26.97	23.15	14.40	40.36	18.89	15.54	n/a
Seattle, WA	28.57	34.93	19.75	74.86	26.09	20.72	97.57
Sioux Falls, SD	27.07	n/a	18.12	57.97	17.76	16.09	n/a
Springfield, IL	26.37	26.10	16.08	39.68	20.55	17.77	n/a
St. Louis, MO	27.22	23.21	17.00	48.57	19.80	17.68	n/a
Tampa, FL	26.91	27.94	16.01	45.68	18.84	15.00	191.11
Tucson, AZ	27.62	27.03	16.59	48.00	19.49	15.65	n/a
Tulsa, OK	27.22	40.04	15.59	38.20	18.07	15.18	n/a
Tuscaloosa, AL	27.01	29.05	14.09	n/a	19.12	15.31	n/a
Virginia Beach, VA	26.24	33.80	15.11	45.63	20.00	16.42	n/a
Washington, DC	27.72	36.03	17.61	62.98	24.44	23.65	186.07
Wichita, KS	26.65	27.02	15.34	51.87	17.74	15.50	n/a
Wilmington, NC	26.03	28.16	15.41	60.83	19.24	15.17	n/a
Winston-Salem, NC	27.50	33.61	14.59	44.22	19.35	16.60	n/a
Worcester, MA[2]	27.11	n/a	17.84	55.25	23.77	18.53	n/a

Notes: (1) Figures cover the Metropolitan Statistical Area (MSA) except where noted. See Appendix B for areas included; (2) New England City and Town Area; n/a not available
Source: Bureau of Labor Statistics, May 2022 Metro Area Occupational Employment and Wage Estimates

Appendix A: Comparative Statistics

Average Hourly Wages: Occupations T – W

Metro Area	Teacher Assistants[3]	Teachers, Secondary School[3]	Telemarketers	Truck Drivers, Heavy	Truck Drivers, Light	Waiters/ Waitresses
Albuquerque, NM	14.88	28.99	20.16	22.67	20.43	16.14
Allentown, PA	16.36	35.24	14.10	27.04	22.74	15.35
Anchorage, AK	17.44	36.14	n/a	27.93	26.04	13.47
Ann Arbor, MI	15.21	35.99	n/a	24.45	23.48	17.37
Athens, GA	11.12	31.25	n/a	26.85	22.03	13.09
Atlanta, GA	14.07	34.25	15.50	26.24	21.28	14.52
Austin, TX	15.16	30.16	16.31	23.73	22.03	13.42
Baltimore, MD	19.37	34.31	18.80	26.63	22.04	17.63
Boise City, ID	14.04	27.88	17.64	25.05	24.37	14.76
Boston, MA[2]	20.14	40.58	19.82	27.78	23.55	19.76
Boulder, CO	18.12	35.67	17.68	26.67	24.66	20.98
Brownsville, TX	13.50	26.50	n/a	22.21	18.91	10.94
Cape Coral, FL	14.90	33.25	16.95	22.84	20.22	15.70
Cedar Rapids, IA	14.26	28.59	n/a	25.17	19.97	13.27
Charleston, SC	12.32	27.85	n/a	25.58	19.54	11.64
Charlotte, NC	13.20	26.35	16.09	25.66	19.89	13.70
Chicago, IL	16.89	37.13	15.52	27.99	24.27	15.53
Cincinnati, OH	16.00	33.81	14.72	26.16	21.77	14.51
Clarksville, TN	14.59	26.06	n/a	22.96	19.13	11.97
Cleveland, OH	16.13	35.16	14.85	25.57	20.45	14.38
College Station, TX	13.43	25.97	n/a	22.43	22.97	12.47
Colorado Springs, CO	15.06	26.75	19.45	24.71	22.21	19.75
Columbia, MO	14.65	n/a	n/a	24.11	22.20	15.51
Columbia, SC	12.00	26.34	10.78	23.99	19.35	10.82
Columbus, OH	16.49	34.42	15.65	26.61	22.93	15.07
Dallas, TX	14.09	30.46	18.24	24.73	22.27	13.17
Davenport, IA	15.10	31.35	14.97	26.12	20.97	13.22
Denver, CO	17.40	32.50	20.16	27.32	23.68	18.48
Des Moines, IA	14.28	32.05	15.86	26.85	21.17	13.46
Durham, NC	13.63	26.62	15.07	24.94	19.89	14.16
Edison, NJ	18.07	45.24	20.35	29.43	23.63	23.01
El Paso, TX	12.23	27.72	14.74	20.95	18.70	11.05
Fargo, ND	16.83	28.97	n/a	27.94	23.00	14.71
Fort Collins, CO	16.36	28.98	18.28	25.19	22.91	19.93
Fort Wayne, IN	13.32	27.57	15.78	25.45	20.20	13.17
Fort Worth, TX	14.09	30.46	18.24	24.73	22.27	13.17
Grand Rapids, MI	15.09	31.35	15.93	24.69	20.89	17.53
Greeley, CO	16.03	27.26	n/a	26.14	23.11	18.76
Green Bay, WI	15.77	29.64	n/a	25.81	21.30	15.02
Greensboro, NC	12.50	24.32	18.68	24.84	18.97	12.88
Honolulu, HI	16.06	29.35	16.92	26.64	21.01	16.89
Houston, TX	13.73	30.64	17.46	24.72	22.19	13.02
Huntsville, AL	10.75	28.00	n/a	23.90	20.20	11.55
Indianapolis, IN	14.25	30.46	17.62	26.92	23.09	13.35
Jacksonville, FL	14.72	31.72	15.08	24.87	21.39	15.33
Kansas City, MO	15.24	28.68	20.21	26.24	22.59	15.86
Lafayette, LA	11.25	24.62	n/a	21.71	17.50	11.88
Las Cruces, NM	14.06	33.00	n/a	21.52	17.37	15.04
Las Vegas, NV	16.36	30.96	15.02	24.98	20.79	13.18
Lexington, KY	16.94	29.65	n/a	26.48	21.58	14.02
Lincoln, NE	12.27	28.33	13.08	35.10	21.50	14.17
Little Rock, AR	14.46	25.70	n/a	26.45	22.85	13.89
Los Angeles, CA	20.58	43.33	18.39	26.10	22.77	18.08
Louisville, KY	15.01	30.29	15.36	27.04	23.90	13.48
Madison, WI	16.63	29.79	n/a	25.52	20.60	15.98

Table continued on following page.

Metro Area	Teacher Assistants[3]	Teachers, Secondary School[3]	Telemarketers	Truck Drivers, Heavy	Truck Drivers, Light	Waiters/ Waitresses
Manchester, NH[2]	16.19	33.56	15.33	25.70	20.52	16.61
Miami, FL	14.59	31.87	16.79	24.62	21.37	16.13
Midland, TX	13.37	30.50	n/a	25.69	20.91	12.89
Milwaukee, WI	16.86	33.03	16.38	26.40	21.54	15.68
Minneapolis, MN	18.50	31.91	22.98	28.77	23.50	13.34
Nashville, TN	13.61	26.44	n/a	26.23	21.56	11.99
New Haven, CT[2]	18.30	36.32	23.10	26.23	21.59	19.08
New Orleans, LA	14.50	27.00	n/a	24.66	19.53	12.15
New York, NY	18.07	45.24	20.35	29.43	23.63	23.01
Oklahoma City, OK	11.92	27.00	18.98	24.66	20.54	12.33
Omaha, NE	13.94	28.50	13.51	32.23	21.83	15.36
Orlando, FL	13.42	26.07	14.29	24.63	21.37	16.41
Philadelphia, PA	16.04	35.76	16.16	27.40	22.39	15.81
Phoenix, AZ	15.19	30.07	17.98	25.42	22.85	22.24
Pittsburgh, PA	15.05	39.73	16.91	25.67	20.10	14.85
Portland, OR	19.64	41.94	19.08	28.25	22.77	18.37
Providence, RI[2]	17.68	36.31	16.60	27.14	22.45	16.64
Provo, UT	13.34	31.61	17.82	25.28	20.06	17.18
Raleigh, NC	12.44	25.67	15.51	24.80	19.06	14.41
Reno, NV	18.08	36.23	n/a	26.51	21.26	13.12
Richmond, VA	14.32	37.47	n/a	24.27	20.61	16.35
Rochester, MN	17.00	31.98	n/a	26.90	21.79	12.51
Sacramento, CA	19.35	41.56	18.78	26.24	23.03	17.51
Salem, OR	19.13	39.59	16.13	26.69	21.33	16.15
Salt Lake City, UT	14.52	33.46	15.85	26.89	21.89	17.80
San Antonio, TX	14.17	29.61	17.04	22.61	20.69	13.14
San Diego, CA	19.50	47.51	17.68	25.83	22.99	17.49
San Francisco, CA	22.38	44.23	22.03	30.83	25.29	18.52
San Jose, CA	22.29	46.64	20.56	29.99	24.72	19.37
Santa Rosa, CA	20.52	43.10	n/a	27.66	24.22	18.13
Savannah, GA	15.18	29.79	n/a	24.85	20.20	13.87
Seattle, WA	22.89	44.03	20.78	30.34	24.18	23.47
Sioux Falls, SD	12.99	24.57	n/a	26.46	21.01	13.23
Springfield, IL	15.04	30.36	n/a	24.23	23.13	14.77
St. Louis, MO	15.52	29.12	18.25	26.27	22.92	16.19
Tampa, FL	14.33	32.73	14.35	23.41	20.06	15.84
Tucson, AZ	14.47	23.84	n/a	23.82	21.31	20.77
Tulsa, OK	12.67	28.15	18.01	24.99	19.91	11.71
Tuscaloosa, AL	10.07	26.64	n/a	24.19	20.50	10.78
Virginia Beach, VA	16.04	31.98	17.71	23.13	19.47	15.39
Washington, DC	19.39	40.33	20.08	27.54	23.67	19.91
Wichita, KS	14.41	28.44	n/a	23.66	20.17	14.48
Wilmington, NC	12.82	25.18	15.79	22.70	20.42	13.33
Winston-Salem, NC	11.63	25.01	n/a	24.69	18.96	12.01
Worcester, MA[2]	19.32	38.25	19.51	26.93	22.55	18.31

Notes: (1) Figures cover the Metropolitan Statistical Area (MSA) except where noted. See Appendix B for areas included; (2) New England City and Town Area; (3) Hourly wages were calculated from annual wage data assuming a 40 hour work week; n/a not available
Source: Bureau of Labor Statistics, May 2022 Metro Area Occupational Employment and Wage Estimates

Means of Transportation to Work: City

City	Car/Truck/Van Drove Alone	Car/Truck/Van Car-pooled	Public Transportation Bus	Public Transportation Subway	Public Transportation Railroad	Bicycle	Walked	Other Means	Worked at Home
Albuquerque, NM	76.6	8.9	1.3	0.0	0.1	0.8	1.9	1.1	9.4
Allentown, PA	67.4	15.5	3.7	0.0	0.0	0.1	4.4	1.9	6.9
Anchorage, AK	73.7	12.1	1.4	0.0	0.0	0.9	2.6	2.1	7.1
Ann Arbor, MI	48.5	4.9	7.9	0.2	0.0	3.1	15.5	0.6	19.1
Athens, GA	72.0	8.0	2.7	0.0	0.0	1.4	4.8	1.0	10.2
Atlanta, GA	59.8	4.8	4.8	3.6	0.2	1.0	4.4	2.8	18.6
Austin, TX	66.2	7.7	2.5	0.1	0.1	1.0	2.6	1.4	18.4
Baltimore, MD	58.2	7.8	11.8	1.2	1.1	0.8	5.9	2.7	10.8
Boise City, ID	73.8	6.9	0.5	0.0	0.0	2.5	2.9	1.6	11.7
Boston, MA	36.1	5.5	10.6	15.5	1.1	2.0	14.4	2.6	12.3
Boulder, CO	45.8	4.3	6.5	0.0	0.0	8.8	9.1	1.3	24.3
Brownsville, TX	80.7	10.2	0.7	0.0	0.0	0.1	1.3	1.2	5.7
Cape Coral, FL	79.3	7.8	0.1	0.0	0.0	0.2	0.9	1.9	9.8
Cedar Rapids, IA	80.2	7.6	0.4	0.0	0.0	0.5	2.0	1.0	8.5
Charleston, SC	74.5	6.2	0.8	0.0	0.0	1.8	3.8	1.3	11.6
Charlotte, NC	68.8	8.6	1.9	0.3	0.1	0.1	1.8	1.8	16.7
Chicago, IL	47.4	7.5	11.1	10.7	1.4	1.5	5.8	2.2	12.3
Cincinnati, OH	69.0	8.5	6.1	0.0	0.0	0.3	5.5	1.4	9.2
Clarksville, TN	84.5	7.7	0.7	0.0	0.0	0.0	1.2	1.4	4.5
Cleveland, OH	68.6	9.9	7.3	0.4	0.1	0.5	4.7	1.7	6.9
College Station, TX	74.7	8.8	2.1	0.0	0.0	1.8	2.6	0.9	9.0
Colorado Springs, CO	74.7	9.8	0.7	0.0	0.0	0.5	1.7	1.1	11.4
Columbia, MO	75.0	9.0	0.9	0.0	0.0	1.2	6.4	0.7	6.8
Columbia, SC	63.8	5.7	1.5	0.0	0.0	0.4	20.3	1.6	6.7
Columbus, OH	75.0	7.2	2.5	0.0	0.0	0.4	2.7	1.1	11.0
Dallas, TX	72.3	11.2	2.3	0.3	0.2	0.2	2.2	1.6	9.7
Davenport, IA	83.4	6.5	0.6	0.0	0.0	0.2	2.3	0.7	6.3
Denver, CO	62.7	6.8	3.5	0.6	0.4	2.0	4.4	2.3	17.2
Des Moines, IA	75.4	10.6	1.4	0.1	0.0	0.5	2.4	1.4	8.2
Durham, NC	70.7	8.0	2.6	0.0	0.0	0.5	2.2	1.3	14.6
Edison, NJ	64.0	8.1	0.7	0.5	9.9	0.1	1.1	1.3	14.1
El Paso, TX	79.1	10.2	1.4	0.0	0.0	0.1	1.1	2.4	5.7
Fargo, ND	79.5	7.8	1.2	0.0	0.0	0.5	3.5	1.9	5.5
Fort Collins, CO	66.7	6.3	1.8	0.0	0.0	4.4	4.3	1.1	15.5
Fort Wayne, IN	80.9	9.6	1.0	0.0	0.0	0.5	1.5	0.8	5.8
Fort Worth, TX	77.3	11.0	0.5	0.0	0.1	0.2	1.3	1.0	8.6
Grand Rapids, MI	71.5	10.0	3.3	0.0	0.0	0.9	4.4	1.0	8.8
Greeley, CO	76.0	12.4	0.5	0.0	0.0	0.5	3.1	0.7	6.8
Green Bay, WI	77.7	10.7	1.1	0.0	0.0	0.2	2.3	1.1	6.9
Greensboro, NC	78.2	7.7	2.3	0.0	0.0	0.2	2.3	1.0	8.3
Honolulu, HI	57.7	13.1	9.4	0.0	0.0	1.6	8.2	3.6	6.4
Houston, TX	73.7	9.8	3.4	0.1	0.0	0.4	1.9	2.4	8.3
Huntsville, AL	81.8	6.2	0.4	0.0	0.0	0.2	1.2	0.8	9.4
Indianapolis, IN	77.6	9.3	1.6	0.0	0.0	0.4	1.9	0.9	8.4
Jacksonville, FL	77.3	8.7	1.4	0.0	0.0	0.3	1.4	2.0	8.8
Kansas City, MO	77.2	7.4	2.2	0.0	0.0	0.2	1.7	1.5	9.8
Lafayette, LA	83.4	4.8	0.8	0.0	0.0	0.5	2.4	1.0	7.0
Las Cruces, NM	74.3	13.2	0.5	0.0	0.0	1.6	1.7	1.4	7.4
Las Vegas, NV	75.5	9.8	2.8	0.0	0.0	0.2	1.3	2.9	7.4
Lexington, KY	77.0	8.1	1.7	0.0	0.0	0.6	3.5	1.1	8.2
Lincoln, NE	78.2	9.1	1.0	0.0	0.0	0.8	3.3	0.7	7.0
Little Rock, AR	78.5	9.7	0.7	0.0	0.0	0.2	1.8	1.5	7.7
Los Angeles, CA	65.2	8.9	6.6	0.8	0.1	0.7	3.2	2.1	12.4
Louisville, KY	76.6	8.4	2.6	0.0	0.0	0.3	1.9	1.6	8.5

Table continued on following page.

City	Car/Truck/Van Drove Alone	Car-pooled	Bus	Subway	Railroad	Bicycle	Walked	Other Means	Worked at Home
Madison, WI	60.5	6.6	7.0	0.0	0.1	3.6	8.9	1.3	12.1
Manchester, NH	77.8	8.9	0.5	0.0	0.0	0.2	2.6	1.2	8.8
Miami, FL	65.9	7.7	6.1	1.1	0.1	0.8	4.8	3.5	10.1
Midland, TX	82.4	10.4	0.2	0.0	0.0	0.3	0.6	0.7	5.5
Milwaukee, WI	71.2	9.5	5.8	0.0	0.0	0.6	4.1	1.0	7.7
Minneapolis, MN	56.4	6.3	8.6	0.6	0.2	2.9	6.6	2.6	15.8
Nashville, TN	72.8	9.1	1.6	0.0	0.1	0.2	2.2	1.3	12.7
New Haven, CT	58.6	8.0	7.5	0.1	1.1	2.1	11.6	1.9	9.1
New Orleans, LA	65.6	8.9	4.6	0.1	0.0	2.6	5.4	2.9	9.9
New York, NY	22.4	4.4	9.7	38.4	1.2	1.4	9.5	2.5	10.7
Oklahoma City, OK	80.0	9.7	0.4	0.0	0.0	0.2	1.6	1.4	6.8
Omaha, NE	77.2	8.9	1.3	0.0	0.0	0.2	2.1	1.0	9.3
Orlando, FL	75.2	8.1	2.3	0.0	0.0	0.6	1.4	2.7	9.7
Philadelphia, PA	48.3	7.8	13.5	5.2	2.2	2.0	7.6	2.7	10.8
Phoenix, AZ	70.8	11.5	2.1	0.0	0.0	0.5	1.5	1.9	11.5
Pittsburgh, PA	52.1	6.6	14.5	0.3	0.0	1.2	9.7	1.8	13.9
Portland, OR	53.8	7.4	7.2	0.5	0.2	4.7	5.1	3.2	18.0
Providence, RI	64.0	11.3	3.3	0.1	1.0	0.9	7.3	1.7	10.4
Provo, UT	59.2	11.2	3.2	0.1	0.9	2.0	11.8	1.0	10.5
Raleigh, NC	70.9	7.1	1.7	0.0	0.0	0.2	1.4	1.4	17.2
Reno, NV	71.1	12.0	2.7	0.0	0.0	0.7	2.8	2.5	8.3
Richmond, VA	67.8	8.5	4.2	0.1	0.0	1.8	4.5	1.6	11.5
Rochester, MN	67.8	11.9	5.4	0.0	0.0	0.8	4.2	1.2	8.8
Sacramento, CA	68.9	9.6	1.7	0.2	0.3	1.6	2.9	2.2	12.6
St. Louis, MO	69.9	6.6	5.8	0.4	0.1	0.9	4.4	1.4	10.5
Salem, OR	71.7	9.5	2.2	0.0	0.0	1.4	3.4	1.2	10.5
Salt Lake City, UT	63.1	8.8	3.8	0.3	0.6	2.1	4.8	3.2	13.2
San Antonio, TX	74.6	11.8	2.1	0.0	0.0	0.2	1.8	1.6	8.0
San Diego, CA	68.9	8.2	2.8	0.1	0.1	0.7	3.2	2.0	14.0
San Francisco, CA	29.4	6.5	17.8	7.0	1.3	3.3	11.0	5.6	18.0
San Jose, CA	69.2	10.5	2.0	0.3	0.9	0.6	1.9	1.8	13.0
Santa Rosa, CA	76.1	10.3	1.4	0.1	0.1	0.8	1.8	1.4	7.9
Savannah, GA	71.7	10.7	3.1	0.0	0.0	1.2	4.2	1.8	7.3
Seattle, WA	40.5	6.1	15.4	1.0	0.1	2.8	9.7	2.9	21.4
Sioux Falls, SD	81.7	7.8	0.6	0.0	0.0	0.3	2.1	0.7	6.8
Springfield, IL	79.6	6.4	1.6	0.1	0.0	0.5	1.6	1.7	8.7
Tampa, FL	71.9	8.2	1.9	0.0	0.0	0.8	2.1	1.9	13.2
Tucson, AZ	71.3	10.4	2.6	0.0	0.0	1.9	2.9	1.7	9.2
Tulsa, OK	78.4	9.9	0.6	0.0	0.0	0.2	1.8	1.9	7.2
Tuscaloosa, AL	80.0	9.7	1.4	0.0	0.0	0.5	1.8	1.0	5.6
Virginia Beach, VA	79.1	7.6	0.7	0.0	0.0	0.4	2.1	1.6	8.4
Washington, DC	30.7	4.7	10.0	16.7	0.2	3.7	11.3	2.7	19.8
Wichita, KS	81.4	9.8	0.6	0.0	0.0	0.4	1.2	1.4	5.1
Wilmington, NC	75.4	7.5	0.7	0.0	0.0	0.6	2.5	0.8	12.6
Winston-Salem, NC	77.7	8.9	1.3	0.0	0.0	0.3	2.1	1.2	8.5
Worcester, MA	68.3	11.4	1.9	0.2	0.6	0.2	6.2	2.9	8.3
U.S.	73.2	8.6	2.0	1.6	0.5	0.5	2.5	1.5	9.7

Note: Figures are percentages and cover workers 16 years of age and older
Source: U.S. Census Bureau, 2017-2021 American Community Survey 5-Year Estimates

Means of Transportation to Work: Metro Area

Metro Area	Drove Alone	Car-pooled	Bus	Subway	Railroad	Bicycle	Walked	Other Means	Worked at Home
Albuquerque, NM	76.8	9.4	1.0	0.0	0.1	0.6	1.7	1.1	9.4
Allentown, PA	78.4	7.9	1.2	0.1	0.1	0.1	2.3	1.2	8.7
Anchorage, AK	73.7	11.5	1.2	0.0	0.0	0.8	2.4	3.0	7.4
Ann Arbor, MI	66.1	6.5	4.1	0.1	0.0	1.3	6.9	0.8	14.2
Athens, GA	75.1	8.0	1.6	0.0	0.0	0.8	3.4	1.2	9.9
Atlanta, GA	72.7	8.7	1.5	0.7	0.1	0.2	1.2	1.7	13.2
Austin, TX	69.7	8.4	1.3	0.0	0.1	0.6	1.8	1.3	16.8
Baltimore, MD	72.5	7.4	3.4	0.7	0.7	0.2	2.3	1.5	11.2
Boise City, ID	76.4	7.9	0.2	0.0	0.0	1.1	1.9	1.3	11.0
Boston, MA	62.2	6.6	3.2	5.5	1.8	0.9	5.0	1.7	13.0
Boulder, CO	60.1	6.6	3.9	0.0	0.0	3.6	4.0	1.1	20.8
Brownsville, TX	81.3	9.1	0.4	0.0	0.0	0.1	1.6	1.2	6.3
Cape Coral, FL	76.3	9.6	0.5	0.0	0.0	0.7	1.0	2.3	9.6
Cedar Rapids, IA	80.3	7.0	0.3	0.0	0.0	0.3	1.8	0.8	9.4
Charleston, SC	79.1	7.6	0.6	0.0	0.0	0.6	1.8	1.2	9.1
Charlotte, NC	74.7	8.4	0.9	0.1	0.0	0.1	1.3	1.3	13.1
Chicago, IL	66.7	7.6	3.7	3.6	2.6	0.6	2.8	1.5	10.9
Cincinnati, OH	78.8	7.7	1.4	0.0	0.0	0.2	1.9	0.9	9.1
Clarksville, TN	82.2	8.6	0.5	0.0	0.0	0.2	2.9	1.3	4.3
Cleveland, OH	77.9	7.4	2.1	0.1	0.0	0.3	2.1	1.2	8.8
College Station, TX	78.2	9.5	1.1	0.0	0.0	1.1	1.7	1.2	7.2
Colorado Springs, CO	73.8	9.6	0.5	0.0	0.0	0.3	3.2	1.0	11.4
Columbia, MO	77.1	9.6	0.6	0.0	0.0	0.8	4.4	0.8	6.7
Columbia, SC	78.7	8.1	0.6	0.0	0.0	0.1	4.2	1.6	6.7
Columbus, OH	77.1	6.7	1.3	0.0	0.0	0.3	2.0	1.0	11.6
Dallas, TX	75.8	9.5	0.6	0.1	0.2	0.1	1.2	1.3	11.1
Davenport, IA	83.9	6.8	0.7	0.0	0.0	0.2	2.2	0.7	5.6
Denver, CO	69.8	7.5	2.2	0.3	0.2	0.8	2.1	1.7	15.4
Des Moines, IA	78.3	7.6	0.6	0.0	0.0	0.2	1.7	1.1	10.5
Durham, NC	70.8	7.7	2.6	0.0	0.0	0.6	2.3	1.3	14.5
Edison, NJ	47.4	6.1	6.7	17.4	3.1	0.7	5.5	2.3	10.6
El Paso, TX	78.6	10.6	1.1	0.0	0.0	0.1	1.4	2.3	5.8
Fargo, ND	79.8	8.0	0.9	0.0	0.0	0.4	2.6	1.4	6.9
Fort Collins, CO	70.7	6.4	1.1	0.1	0.0	2.4	2.8	1.1	15.4
Fort Wayne, IN	82.1	8.7	0.7	0.0	0.0	0.4	1.3	0.7	6.2
Fort Worth, TX	75.8	9.5	0.6	0.1	0.2	0.1	1.2	1.3	11.1
Grand Rapids, MI	79.0	8.5	1.2	0.0	0.0	0.4	2.2	0.7	7.9
Greeley, CO	76.7	10.4	0.4	0.0	0.0	0.2	1.9	0.8	9.5
Green Bay, WI	81.4	7.6	0.5	0.0	0.0	0.1	1.8	0.8	7.8
Greensboro, NC	79.8	8.8	1.1	0.0	0.0	0.2	1.5	1.1	7.5
Honolulu, HI	65.4	13.2	6.3	0.0	0.0	0.9	5.2	2.5	6.4
Houston, TX	77.1	9.3	1.7	0.0	0.0	0.3	1.2	1.6	8.7
Huntsville, AL	83.6	5.8	0.2	0.0	0.0	0.1	0.7	1.0	8.6
Indianapolis, IN	78.7	8.2	0.7	0.0	0.0	0.2	1.4	0.9	9.8
Jacksonville, FL	76.8	8.2	0.9	0.0	0.0	0.4	1.3	1.9	10.5
Kansas City, MO	79.0	7.3	0.7	0.0	0.0	0.1	1.1	1.0	10.6
Lafayette, LA	83.9	6.7	0.3	0.0	0.0	0.2	1.9	1.2	5.8
Las Cruces, NM	76.4	12.3	0.4	0.0	0.0	0.9	1.7	1.3	7.1
Las Vegas, NV	75.8	10.1	2.6	0.0	0.0	0.2	1.3	2.5	7.4
Lexington, KY	78.2	8.4	1.1	0.0	0.0	0.4	2.9	1.0	8.0
Lincoln, NE	78.5	8.9	0.8	0.0	0.0	0.8	3.2	0.7	7.2
Little Rock, AR	81.6	9.4	0.4	0.0	0.0	0.1	1.1	1.1	6.3
Los Angeles, CA	70.9	9.3	3.4	0.4	0.2	0.6	2.3	1.8	11.2
Louisville, KY	78.9	8.2	1.5	0.0	0.0	0.2	1.4	1.1	8.7

Table continued on following page.

Appendix A: Comparative Statistics

Metro Area	Car/Truck/Van Drove Alone	Car/Truck/Van Car-pooled	Public Transportation Bus	Public Transportation Subway	Public Transportation Railroad	Bicycle	Walked	Other Means	Worked at Home
Madison, WI	71.0	6.5	3.3	0.0	0.0	1.8	4.9	1.0	11.5
Manchester, NH	77.6	7.2	0.6	0.1	0.1	0.2	1.8	0.9	11.5
Miami, FL	75.1	9.1	2.1	0.3	0.1	0.5	1.5	2.1	9.2
Midland, TX	82.7	9.9	0.1	0.0	0.0	0.2	1.2	0.7	5.1
Milwaukee, WI	77.4	7.1	2.4	0.0	0.0	0.4	2.3	0.8	9.5
Minneapolis, MN	72.1	7.4	3.2	0.1	0.1	0.6	2.1	1.3	13.1
Nashville, TN	76.7	8.6	0.7	0.0	0.1	0.1	1.2	1.1	11.6
New Haven, CT	74.9	8.1	2.3	0.1	0.7	0.4	3.4	1.3	8.7
New Orleans, LA	76.2	9.6	1.7	0.0	0.0	0.9	2.4	1.7	7.4
New York, NY	47.4	6.1	6.7	17.4	3.1	0.7	5.5	2.3	10.6
Oklahoma City, OK	80.6	9.1	0.3	0.0	0.0	0.3	1.6	1.2	7.0
Omaha, NE	79.5	8.0	0.7	0.0	0.0	0.1	1.7	1.0	9.0
Orlando, FL	75.8	9.4	1.1	0.0	0.1	0.4	1.1	1.9	10.2
Philadelphia, PA	68.2	7.1	4.2	1.7	1.7	0.6	3.2	1.5	11.7
Phoenix, AZ	71.6	10.3	1.3	0.0	0.0	0.6	1.4	1.8	13.0
Pittsburgh, PA	73.0	7.4	4.2	0.2	0.0	0.2	3.0	1.3	10.8
Portland, OR	66.2	8.4	3.6	0.4	0.2	1.7	3.1	2.0	14.4
Providence, RI	77.8	8.3	1.2	0.1	0.7	0.2	2.7	1.0	7.8
Provo, UT	70.1	10.3	1.0	0.1	0.7	0.7	3.3	1.0	12.8
Raleigh, NC	72.9	7.4	0.7	0.0	0.0	0.1	1.1	1.0	16.8
Reno, NV	73.1	12.0	2.0	0.0	0.0	0.5	2.0	2.0	8.3
Richmond, VA	76.2	7.7	1.2	0.0	0.1	0.4	1.4	1.1	11.9
Rochester, MN	71.2	11.0	3.4	0.0	0.0	0.5	3.5	1.0	9.4
Sacramento, CA	72.1	8.8	1.3	0.1	0.2	1.1	1.6	1.7	13.1
St. Louis, MO	79.2	6.7	1.4	0.2	0.1	0.2	1.6	1.0	9.8
Salem, OR	74.3	10.1	1.3	0.0	0.0	0.8	2.6	1.1	9.8
Salt Lake City, UT	71.0	10.3	1.5	0.2	0.4	0.6	1.9	1.7	12.5
San Antonio, TX	75.6	10.7	1.3	0.0	0.0	0.2	1.6	1.4	9.1
San Diego, CA	71.6	8.4	2.0	0.1	0.1	0.5	2.9	2.0	12.5
San Francisco, CA	53.4	8.6	6.1	5.7	1.2	1.6	4.3	2.8	16.3
San Jose, CA	67.1	9.4	1.8	0.3	1.0	1.4	2.1	1.6	15.3
Santa Rosa, CA	72.8	10.0	1.2	0.1	0.2	0.6	2.3	1.5	11.3
Savannah, GA	79.8	8.6	1.3	0.0	0.0	0.6	1.9	1.7	6.2
Seattle, WA	62.4	9.1	6.7	0.3	0.4	0.9	3.6	1.6	14.9
Sioux Falls, SD	81.7	7.6	0.5	0.0	0.0	0.3	1.9	0.6	7.4
Springfield, IL	81.6	6.4	0.9	0.1	0.0	0.4	1.4	1.3	8.0
Tampa, FL	74.8	8.2	1.0	0.0	0.0	0.5	1.3	1.6	12.4
Tucson, AZ	73.4	9.7	1.7	0.0	0.0	1.2	2.1	1.7	10.3
Tulsa, OK	80.7	9.1	0.3	0.0	0.0	0.1	1.3	1.3	7.1
Tuscaloosa, AL	82.3	10.3	0.8	0.0	0.0	0.2	0.9	0.6	5.0
Virginia Beach, VA	78.3	7.9	1.3	0.0	0.0	0.3	3.1	1.6	7.5
Washington, DC	60.7	8.5	3.6	5.8	0.6	0.7	2.9	1.7	15.4
Wichita, KS	82.2	8.7	0.4	0.0	0.0	0.3	1.5	1.3	5.6
Wilmington, NC	77.5	8.0	0.3	0.0	0.0	0.4	1.4	0.6	11.8
Winston-Salem, NC	80.7	8.8	0.6	0.0	0.0	0.1	1.3	0.9	7.6
Worcester, MA	76.2	7.6	0.7	0.2	0.7	0.2	2.6	1.7	10.2
U.S.	73.2	8.6	2.0	1.6	0.5	0.5	2.5	1.5	9.7

Note: Figures are percentages and cover workers 16 years of age and older; (1) Figures cover the Metropolitan Statistical Area
Source: U.S. Census Bureau, 2017-2021 American Community Survey 5-Year Estimates

Travel Time to Work: City

City	Less Than 10 Minutes	10 to 19 Minutes	20 to 29 Minutes	30 to 44 Minutes	45 to 59 Minutes	60 to 89 Minutes	90 Minutes or More
Albuquerque, NM	11.0	35.9	27.8	18.1	3.1	2.5	1.6
Allentown, PA	10.6	33.2	30.0	15.2	4.3	4.6	2.1
Anchorage, AK	16.1	44.4	23.4	11.2	2.1	1.2	1.6
Ann Arbor, MI	13.9	45.7	18.6	14.0	5.0	2.4	0.5
Athens, GA	18.0	45.8	16.6	9.8	3.5	3.5	2.8
Atlanta, GA	6.9	29.5	25.6	21.8	7.3	5.4	3.5
Austin, TX	9.7	32.0	24.5	21.7	6.9	3.7	1.5
Baltimore, MD	6.7	23.6	23.3	25.6	8.7	7.4	4.7
Boise City, ID	13.6	44.5	26.2	11.4	1.6	1.5	1.2
Boston, MA	6.9	20.4	19.6	29.8	12.1	9.1	2.1
Boulder, CO	19.7	44.5	16.1	9.5	5.8	3.2	1.2
Brownsville, TX	8.7	42.9	28.9	14.3	2.5	1.7	1.0
Cape Coral, FL	8.0	25.3	22.2	27.4	9.4	5.4	2.3
Cedar Rapids, IA	20.0	48.9	17.0	9.2	1.9	1.5	1.5
Charleston, SC	11.4	30.7	26.6	20.6	7.6	1.6	1.4
Charlotte, NC	8.6	29.6	26.7	23.2	6.5	3.3	2.1
Chicago, IL	4.7	16.4	18.4	30.5	15.1	11.9	3.1
Cincinnati, OH	11.4	33.0	26.8	19.1	4.3	3.2	2.1
Clarksville, TN	10.3	33.0	25.3	14.1	6.8	8.5	2.2
Cleveland, OH	10.2	34.0	27.0	20.0	3.9	3.0	2.1
College Station, TX	17.6	55.5	17.1	6.2	0.5	2.0	1.1
Colorado Springs, CO	11.5	35.9	28.0	15.9	3.3	2.9	2.5
Columbia, MO	20.0	54.4	13.7	7.3	2.5	1.0	1.1
Columbia, SC	29.8	36.0	19.0	10.0	2.1	1.8	1.4
Columbus, OH	10.3	34.2	30.4	18.7	3.2	1.9	1.3
Dallas, TX	8.2	26.9	23.3	25.8	8.0	5.9	1.9
Davenport, IA	16.5	47.5	22.0	8.2	3.1	1.8	1.0
Denver, CO	7.9	29.0	24.7	26.0	7.2	3.7	1.4
Des Moines, IA	13.5	43.1	26.6	12.3	2.2	1.3	1.1
Durham, NC	9.2	38.4	25.5	17.9	4.8	2.7	1.4
Edison, NJ	7.6	22.0	18.1	17.8	12.2	12.6	9.6
El Paso, TX	9.5	33.5	28.5	19.7	4.7	2.2	1.8
Fargo, ND	20.6	56.3	15.2	3.6	1.4	1.9	0.9
Fort Collins, CO	15.4	43.8	20.6	10.0	5.4	3.3	1.5
Fort Wayne, IN	12.8	38.2	28.0	13.5	3.0	2.6	1.8
Fort Worth, TX	7.7	29.0	22.9	23.9	8.7	5.8	2.0
Grand Rapids, MI	14.5	44.0	23.5	11.6	3.7	2.0	0.8
Greeley, CO	15.9	37.3	15.3	14.4	5.9	9.2	1.9
Green Bay, WI	18.2	48.6	19.5	8.5	2.8	1.3	1.1
Greensboro, NC	12.5	40.0	23.6	15.9	3.2	3.0	2.0
Honolulu, HI	8.7	38.2	22.6	20.6	5.0	3.6	1.2
Houston, TX	7.2	25.5	23.0	27.7	8.9	5.9	1.8
Huntsville, AL	13.1	41.0	26.2	15.5	2.5	1.0	0.8
Indianapolis, IN	9.5	30.4	28.8	22.7	4.3	2.4	1.8
Jacksonville, FL	8.7	28.5	27.2	25.4	6.0	2.8	1.4
Kansas City, MO	11.6	33.4	27.9	20.3	4.0	1.7	1.2
Lafayette, LA	15.8	44.0	19.3	11.9	2.8	3.6	2.6
Las Cruces, NM	16.2	49.2	16.2	9.5	3.5	4.8	0.7
Las Vegas, NV	7.3	24.0	30.6	27.4	6.2	2.7	1.9
Lexington, KY	13.2	39.5	26.2	13.9	2.9	2.4	1.8
Lincoln, NE	16.7	44.7	22.8	9.9	2.6	2.1	1.2
Little Rock, AR	15.4	45.3	23.6	11.0	2.3	1.5	0.9
Los Angeles, CA	5.9	22.2	19.3	28.5	10.5	10.1	3.6
Louisville, KY	9.6	32.6	31.4	19.1	3.9	2.0	1.4
Madison, WI	14.9	39.6	24.8	15.1	3.0	1.8	0.8

Table continued on following page.

City	Less Than 10 Minutes	10 to 19 Minutes	20 to 29 Minutes	30 to 44 Minutes	45 to 59 Minutes	60 to 89 Minutes	90 Minutes or More
Manchester, NH	12.6	35.5	23.4	14.6	6.4	5.1	2.4
Miami, FL	6.0	21.8	24.7	30.5	9.1	6.6	1.4
Midland, TX	14.2	47.3	18.9	12.0	2.9	2.4	2.4
Milwaukee, WI	10.4	36.6	26.1	19.1	3.5	2.7	1.7
Minneapolis, MN	7.9	32.6	30.2	20.9	4.5	2.7	1.1
Nashville, TN	9.1	29.0	26.6	23.2	7.0	3.6	1.5
New Haven, CT	13.2	40.4	21.6	13.6	4.5	4.2	2.5
New Orleans, LA	11.0	34.8	24.2	19.5	5.0	3.5	2.0
New York, NY	4.0	12.3	13.5	27.1	16.3	19.2	7.6
Oklahoma City, OK	10.5	36.0	29.0	18.2	3.5	1.4	1.4
Omaha, NE	14.5	41.2	26.7	12.4	2.5	1.9	0.9
Orlando, FL	7.2	25.4	27.6	26.6	7.2	3.9	2.2
Philadelphia, PA	6.1	19.2	20.2	28.1	12.9	9.5	4.0
Phoenix, AZ	8.6	26.6	26.6	24.5	7.4	4.5	1.8
Pittsburgh, PA	9.4	32.3	26.6	21.8	4.6	3.6	1.7
Portland, OR	8.3	28.2	26.8	24.0	7.1	4.1	1.5
Providence, RI	10.3	40.4	19.4	15.3	6.2	5.5	2.8
Provo, UT	21.4	44.2	16.8	9.8	3.5	3.1	1.2
Raleigh, NC	9.3	32.4	27.0	20.8	5.7	3.0	1.8
Reno, NV	15.6	40.3	22.8	12.5	4.7	2.7	1.4
Richmond, VA	11.4	37.4	27.3	16.8	2.9	2.7	1.5
Rochester, MN	17.7	55.5	14.1	6.5	2.8	2.2	1.2
Sacramento, CA	8.4	31.3	24.9	22.4	5.6	4.2	3.1
St. Louis, MO	9.2	35.2	26.5	19.7	4.3	2.9	2.1
Salem, OR	13.0	41.0	19.7	12.7	6.0	6.0	1.6
Salt Lake City, UT	14.1	45.1	21.4	12.6	3.5	2.2	1.2
San Antonio, TX	9.4	31.4	26.3	21.8	6.0	3.4	1.7
San Diego, CA	7.7	32.9	27.5	20.9	5.7	3.6	1.7
San Francisco, CA	4.5	19.3	21.4	29.5	11.6	10.1	3.7
San Jose, CA	5.6	24.6	23.2	26.1	10.1	7.5	3.0
Santa Rosa, CA	12.6	40.1	21.3	14.4	4.3	4.0	3.3
Savannah, GA	15.7	39.1	22.8	13.3	4.8	2.8	1.5
Seattle, WA	7.3	24.0	24.1	27.6	10.6	5.0	1.5
Sioux Falls, SD	16.7	51.6	22.0	5.8	1.7	1.2	1.0
Springfield, IL	17.4	53.1	17.9	6.3	1.8	2.3	1.3
Tampa, FL	11.1	30.2	22.5	23.4	6.8	4.3	1.8
Tucson, AZ	11.8	34.9	25.4	19.6	4.7	2.0	1.6
Tulsa, OK	14.2	44.9	26.3	10.1	1.9	1.4	1.2
Tuscaloosa, AL	16.8	46.6	21.7	7.6	3.1	3.1	1.1
Virginia Beach, VA	10.1	30.9	27.9	22.0	5.3	2.5	1.4
Washington, DC	5.3	19.0	22.3	33.1	11.6	6.6	2.1
Wichita, KS	14.3	44.9	26.7	9.9	1.6	1.4	1.2
Wilmington, NC	16.1	47.0	21.7	9.5	2.5	1.7	1.5
Winston-Salem, NC	14.0	40.3	22.6	14.3	4.6	2.6	1.7
Worcester, MA	13.4	34.6	19.5	17.8	5.9	6.3	2.5
U.S.	12.4	28.5	21.0	20.9	8.2	6.2	2.9

Note: Figures are percentages and include workers 16 years old and over
Source: U.S. Census Bureau, 2017-2021 American Community Survey 5-Year Estimates

Travel Time to Work: Metro Area

Metro Area	Less Than 10 Minutes	10 to 19 Minutes	20 to 29 Minutes	30 to 44 Minutes	45 to 59 Minutes	60 to 89 Minutes	90 Minutes or More
Albuquerque, NM	10.7	31.5	26.0	20.7	5.7	3.5	1.8
Allentown, PA	12.6	27.7	23.5	18.5	7.3	6.6	3.8
Anchorage, AK	15.0	40.4	21.8	11.4	4.5	4.1	2.7
Ann Arbor, MI	11.5	32.6	24.5	19.1	7.3	3.8	1.1
Athens, GA	14.2	38.2	21.9	13.5	5.2	4.0	3.0
Atlanta, GA	6.9	22.5	19.9	25.2	12.2	9.6	3.5
Austin, TX	9.3	26.6	22.1	23.8	10.1	6.3	1.9
Baltimore, MD	8.0	23.3	21.0	24.7	11.0	8.3	3.7
Boise City, ID	12.8	33.4	25.0	19.7	5.5	2.2	1.4
Boston, MA	9.1	22.7	18.6	24.4	11.7	10.1	3.3
Boulder, CO	14.5	33.4	20.5	17.6	7.6	4.8	1.6
Brownsville, TX	12.8	40.5	25.7	15.0	3.4	1.6	1.0
Cape Coral, FL	8.6	25.3	22.8	26.0	9.8	5.2	2.3
Cedar Rapids, IA	18.8	40.1	20.6	12.8	4.3	2.0	1.5
Charleston, SC	8.8	26.0	24.1	25.1	9.5	4.8	1.7
Charlotte, NC	9.8	27.8	22.6	23.3	9.3	5.1	2.1
Chicago, IL	8.5	21.9	19.0	25.3	12.2	10.0	3.1
Cincinnati, OH	10.9	28.2	25.2	23.1	7.5	3.5	1.6
Clarksville, TN	14.8	31.0	22.4	16.1	6.5	6.5	2.7
Cleveland, OH	11.6	28.2	25.9	23.2	6.7	2.9	1.6
College Station, TX	16.1	49.4	18.4	10.4	2.3	2.1	1.4
Colorado Springs, CO	11.5	32.8	26.9	18.0	4.7	3.6	2.5
Columbia, MO	17.3	44.2	19.4	11.9	3.8	1.7	1.7
Columbia, SC	12.6	28.8	24.1	22.2	6.9	3.3	2.2
Columbus, OH	11.4	29.5	26.7	21.7	6.1	3.1	1.5
Dallas, TX	8.6	25.2	21.7	25.6	10.3	6.7	2.0
Davenport, IA	18.3	36.1	24.9	13.1	3.9	2.4	1.3
Denver, CO	8.4	25.1	23.0	26.5	9.6	5.5	1.9
Des Moines, IA	15.0	35.0	27.5	16.1	3.7	1.5	1.1
Durham, NC	9.8	31.4	24.8	21.0	7.3	4.2	1.5
Edison, NJ	7.0	18.5	16.3	24.0	12.7	14.7	6.8
El Paso, TX	10.3	31.9	27.4	21.0	5.2	2.3	1.9
Fargo, ND	17.8	52.1	18.3	6.0	2.4	1.9	1.4
Fort Collins, CO	13.5	35.4	21.8	15.9	6.3	4.9	2.2
Fort Wayne, IN	13.0	35.3	28.4	15.7	3.4	2.4	1.8
Fort Worth, TX	8.6	25.2	21.7	25.6	10.3	6.7	2.0
Grand Rapids, MI	14.8	35.3	24.7	16.1	5.0	2.6	1.5
Greeley, CO	11.6	26.7	18.8	22.8	9.8	8.1	2.3
Green Bay, WI	17.9	40.4	21.9	13.0	3.6	1.7	1.4
Greensboro, NC	12.8	34.6	24.4	18.6	4.8	3.0	1.9
Honolulu, HI	9.8	26.1	19.9	24.9	9.4	7.3	2.6
Houston, TX	7.6	23.2	20.4	26.7	11.6	8.2	2.3
Huntsville, AL	10.1	31.7	27.7	22.1	5.2	1.9	1.2
Indianapolis, IN	11.4	27.7	23.9	24.5	7.4	3.4	1.7
Jacksonville, FL	9.1	26.1	24.3	26.1	8.6	4.2	1.6
Kansas City, MO	12.3	30.6	25.5	21.6	6.3	2.5	1.3
Lafayette, LA	13.3	33.5	20.9	18.5	5.9	3.8	4.0
Las Cruces, NM	13.9	40.3	20.0	14.2	5.2	4.8	1.7
Las Vegas, NV	7.8	27.5	29.4	25.4	5.4	2.6	1.9
Lexington, KY	14.5	35.6	24.5	16.8	4.3	2.6	1.7
Lincoln, NE	16.9	41.6	23.5	11.6	3.0	2.2	1.3
Little Rock, AR	13.0	32.7	22.6	20.4	7.0	2.9	1.4
Los Angeles, CA	7.1	24.8	19.9	25.4	9.9	9.3	3.5
Louisville, KY	9.7	30.1	28.8	22.0	5.7	2.4	1.5
Madison, WI	15.9	32.2	24.8	18.2	5.3	2.5	1.1

Table continued on following page.

Metro Area	Less Than 10 Minutes	10 to 19 Minutes	20 to 29 Minutes	30 to 44 Minutes	45 to 59 Minutes	60 to 89 Minutes	90 Minutes or More
Manchester, NH	10.9	29.7	21.2	19.5	8.7	6.7	3.4
Miami, FL	6.6	22.6	22.7	27.7	10.2	7.6	2.6
Midland, TX	14.7	42.7	21.0	13.5	3.3	2.5	2.2
Milwaukee, WI	12.1	32.1	25.7	21.2	5.0	2.5	1.4
Minneapolis, MN	10.6	28.0	25.2	23.2	7.7	4.0	1.4
Nashville, TN	9.4	26.2	21.5	23.5	10.9	6.5	2.0
New Haven, CT	11.7	31.6	23.1	19.7	6.3	4.6	3.0
New Orleans, LA	10.9	30.8	21.8	20.7	8.0	5.5	2.4
New York, NY	7.0	18.5	16.3	24.0	12.7	14.7	6.8
Oklahoma City, OK	11.9	32.3	25.4	20.6	5.7	2.5	1.6
Omaha, NE	14.1	36.1	27.3	16.0	3.6	1.9	1.1
Orlando, FL	7.2	22.9	22.3	28.1	11.2	6.0	2.4
Philadelphia, PA	9.6	23.9	20.6	24.0	11.1	7.8	3.1
Phoenix, AZ	9.9	26.1	24.0	23.6	8.9	5.6	1.9
Pittsburgh, PA	11.8	27.0	21.3	22.9	9.1	5.8	2.1
Portland, OR	10.8	27.5	23.0	22.7	8.9	5.1	2.0
Providence, RI	11.7	30.4	21.3	19.8	7.8	6.2	2.8
Provo, UT	17.1	34.7	20.2	16.5	6.2	3.9	1.5
Raleigh, NC	8.6	26.7	24.4	24.4	9.1	4.9	1.9
Reno, NV	13.0	35.6	24.5	17.2	5.2	2.9	1.6
Richmond, VA	9.3	28.8	26.7	23.5	6.6	3.1	2.1
Rochester, MN	18.1	41.7	18.6	12.6	4.3	2.9	1.9
Sacramento, CA	9.9	28.3	22.4	23.1	7.9	4.7	3.7
St. Louis, MO	11.0	27.3	24.4	24.0	7.9	3.8	1.7
Salem, OR	13.7	32.6	20.9	16.9	7.6	6.3	2.0
Salt Lake City, UT	10.8	33.5	26.9	19.2	5.5	3.0	1.2
San Antonio, TX	9.2	27.8	24.1	23.2	8.7	4.8	2.2
San Diego, CA	8.1	29.4	24.5	23.5	7.5	5.0	2.1
San Francisco, CA	7.0	22.9	17.8	23.6	11.9	12.0	4.9
San Jose, CA	7.0	26.5	23.0	24.3	9.1	7.0	3.1
Santa Rosa, CA	14.0	32.4	20.4	17.1	6.4	6.0	3.8
Savannah, GA	11.0	29.3	24.8	21.8	8.2	3.6	1.5
Seattle, WA	8.2	22.3	21.1	25.2	11.2	8.6	3.4
Sioux Falls, SD	16.8	43.8	24.1	10.0	2.6	1.4	1.2
Springfield, IL	15.0	43.3	23.5	11.8	2.5	2.1	1.8
Tampa, FL	9.6	26.9	21.0	23.7	10.2	6.3	2.3
Tucson, AZ	10.6	29.4	24.7	24.1	7.0	2.4	1.7
Tulsa, OK	13.3	33.7	26.9	18.0	4.6	2.1	1.4
Tuscaloosa, AL	11.1	33.8	23.3	17.4	6.7	5.7	2.0
Virginia Beach, VA	11.1	31.1	23.5	21.4	7.1	4.0	1.7
Washington, DC	6.1	19.3	18.2	26.2	13.7	12.1	4.3
Wichita, KS	16.1	37.2	26.2	15.1	2.7	1.5	1.3
Wilmington, NC	12.7	38.0	22.6	16.0	5.7	2.8	2.1
Winston-Salem, NC	12.5	32.5	24.3	19.3	6.1	3.2	2.2
Worcester, MA	12.3	26.0	18.5	20.6	10.4	8.5	3.8
U.S.	12.4	28.5	21.0	20.9	8.2	6.2	2.9

Note: Figures are percentages and include workers 16 years old and over; Figures cover the Metropolitan Statistical Area
Source: U.S. Census Bureau, 2017-2021 American Community Survey 5-Year Estimates

2020 Presidential Election Results

City	Area Covered	Biden	Trump	Jorgensen	Hawkins	Other
Albuquerque, NM	Bernalillo County	61.0	36.6	1.5	0.5	0.4
Allentown, PA	Lehigh County	53.1	45.5	1.2	0.1	0.2
Anchorage, AK	State of Alaska	42.8	52.8	2.5	0.0	1.9
Ann Arbor, MI	Washtenaw County	72.4	25.9	0.9	0.3	0.4
Athens, GA	Clarke County	70.1	28.1	1.6	0.1	0.1
Atlanta, GA	Fulton County	72.6	26.2	1.2	0.0	0.0
Austin, TX	Travis County	71.4	26.4	1.5	0.3	0.4
Baltimore, MD	Baltimore City	87.3	10.7	0.7	0.6	0.7
Boise City, ID	Ada County	46.1	50.0	2.0	0.1	1.8
Boston, MA	Suffolk County	80.6	17.5	0.9	0.5	0.5
Boulder, CO	Boulder County	77.2	20.6	1.2	0.3	0.6
Brownsville, TX	Cameron County	56.0	42.9	0.6	0.3	0.1
Cape Coral, FL	Lee County	39.9	59.1	0.5	0.1	0.3
Cedar Rapids, IA	Linn County	55.6	41.9	1.6	0.3	0.7
Charleston, SC	Charleston County	55.5	42.6	1.5	0.3	0.1
Charlotte, NC	Mecklenburg County	66.7	31.6	1.0	0.3	0.5
Chicago, IL	Cook County	74.2	24.0	0.8	0.5	0.5
Cincinnati, OH	Hamilton County	57.1	41.3	1.2	0.3	0.0
Clarksville, TN	Montgomery County	42.3	55.0	1.9	0.2	0.7
Cleveland, OH	Cuyahoga County	66.4	32.3	0.7	0.3	0.3
College Station, TX	Brazos County	41.4	55.7	2.1	0.3	0.4
Colorado Springs, CO	El Paso County	42.7	53.5	2.4	0.3	1.0
Columbia, MO	Boone County	54.8	42.3	2.2	0.3	0.4
Columbia, SC	Richland County	68.4	30.1	1.0	0.4	0.1
Columbus, OH	Franklin County	64.7	33.4	1.2	0.3	0.4
Dallas, TX	Dallas County	64.9	33.3	1.0	0.4	0.4
Davenport, IA	Scott County	50.7	47.2	1.2	0.2	0.7
Denver, CO	Denver County	79.6	18.2	1.2	0.3	0.7
Des Moines, IA	Polk County	56.5	41.3	1.3	0.2	0.7
Durham, NC	Durham County	80.4	18.0	0.8	0.3	0.4
Edison, NJ	Middlesex County	60.2	38.2	0.7	0.3	0.6
El Paso, TX	El Paso County	66.7	31.6	1.0	0.5	0.2
Fargo, ND	Cass County	46.8	49.5	2.9	0.0	0.7
Fort Collins, CO	Larimer County	56.2	40.8	1.8	0.3	0.9
Fort Wayne, IN	Allen County	43.2	54.3	2.2	0.0	0.3
Fort Worth, TX	Tarrant County	49.3	49.1	1.2	0.3	0.0
Grand Rapids, MI	Kent County	51.9	45.8	1.5	0.3	0.5
Greeley, CO	Weld County	39.6	57.6	1.7	0.2	0.9
Green Bay, WI	Brown County	45.5	52.7	1.3	0.0	0.5
Greensboro, NC	Guilford County	60.8	37.7	0.8	0.2	0.4
Honolulu, HI	Honolulu County	62.5	35.7	0.9	0.6	0.4
Houston, TX	Harris County	55.9	42.7	1.0	0.3	0.0
Huntsville, AL	Madison County	44.8	52.8	1.9	0.0	0.5
Indianapolis, IN	Marion County	63.3	34.3	1.8	0.1	0.4
Jacksonville, FL	Duval County	51.1	47.3	1.0	0.2	0.5
Kansas City, MO	Jackson County	59.8	37.9	1.4	0.4	0.5
Lafayette, LA	Lafayette Parish	34.7	63.3	1.3	0.0	0.7
Las Cruces, NM	Dona Ana County	58.0	39.7	1.4	0.5	0.4
Las Vegas, NV	Clark County	53.7	44.3	0.9	0.0	1.1
Lexington, KY	Fayette County	59.2	38.5	1.6	0.1	0.6
Lincoln, NE	Lancaster County	52.3	44.6	2.4	0.0	0.7
Little Rock, AR	Pulaski County	60.0	37.5	1.0	0.3	1.3
Los Angeles, CA	Los Angeles County	71.0	26.9	0.8	0.5	0.8
Louisville, KY	Jefferson County	58.9	38.8	1.2	0.1	1.0
Madison, WI	Dane County	75.5	22.9	1.1	0.1	0.6
Manchester, NH	Hillsborough County	52.8	45.2	1.7	0.0	0.3

Table continued on following page.

City	Area Covered	Biden	Trump	Jorgensen	Hawkins	Other
Miami, FL	Miami-Dade County	53.3	46.0	0.3	0.1	0.3
Midland, TX	Midland County	20.9	77.3	1.3	0.2	0.2
Milwaukee, WI	Milwaukee County	69.1	29.3	0.9	0.0	0.7
Minneapolis, MN	Hennepin County	70.5	27.2	1.0	0.3	1.0
Nashville, TN	Davidson County	64.5	32.4	1.1	0.2	1.8
New Haven, CT	New Haven County	58.0	40.6	0.9	0.4	0.0
New Orleans, LA	Orleans Parish	83.1	15.0	0.9	0.0	1.0
New York, NY	Bronx County	83.3	15.9	0.2	0.3	0.3
New York, NY	Kings County	76.8	22.1	0.3	0.4	0.4
New York, NY	New York County	86.4	12.2	0.5	0.4	0.5
New York, NY	Queens County	72.0	26.9	0.3	0.4	0.4
New York, NY	Richmond County	42.0	56.9	0.4	0.3	0.4
Oklahoma City, OK	Oklahoma County	48.1	49.2	1.8	0.0	0.9
Omaha, NE	Douglas County	54.4	43.1	2.0	0.0	0.6
Orlando, FL	Orange County	60.9	37.8	0.7	0.2	0.4
Philadelphia, PA	Philadelphia County	81.2	17.9	0.7	0.1	0.2
Phoenix, AZ	Maricopa County	50.1	48.0	1.5	0.0	0.3
Pittsburgh, PA	Allegheny County	59.4	39.0	1.2	0.0	0.4
Portland, OR	Multnomah County	79.2	17.9	1.2	0.6	1.0
Providence, RI	Providence County	60.5	37.6	0.8	0.0	1.0
Provo, UT	Utah County	26.3	66.7	3.6	0.3	3.1
Raleigh, NC	Wake County	62.3	35.8	1.2	0.3	0.5
Reno, NV	Washoe County	50.8	46.3	1.4	0.0	1.5
Richmond, VA	Richmond City	82.9	14.9	1.5	0.0	0.6
Rochester, MN	Olmsted County	54.2	43.4	1.2	0.3	0.9
Sacramento, CA	Sacramento County	61.4	36.1	1.4	0.5	0.7
St. Louis, MO	St. Louis City	81.9	16.0	1.1	0.4	0.5
Salem, OR	Marion County	48.9	47.7	2.0	0.5	0.9
Salt Lake City, UT	Salt Lake County	53.0	42.1	2.2	0.4	2.2
San Antonio, TX	Bexar County	58.2	40.1	1.1	0.4	0.2
San Diego, CA	San Diego County	60.2	37.5	1.3	0.5	0.5
San Francisco, CA	San Francisco County	85.3	12.7	0.7	0.6	0.7
San Jose, CA	Santa Clara County	72.6	25.2	1.1	0.5	0.6
Santa Rosa, CA	Sonoma County	74.5	23.0	1.3	0.6	0.6
Savannah, GA	Chatham County	58.6	39.9	1.4	0.0	0.0
Seattle, WA	King County	75.0	22.2	1.5	0.5	0.8
Sioux Falls, SD	Minnehaha County	43.8	53.3	2.8	0.0	0.0
Springfield, IL	Sangamon County	46.5	50.9	1.4	0.6	0.6
Tampa, FL	Hillsborough County	52.7	45.8	0.8	0.2	0.5
Tucson, AZ	Pima County	58.4	39.8	1.5	0.0	0.3
Tulsa, OK	Tulsa County	40.9	56.5	1.8	0.0	0.8
Tuscaloosa, AL	Tuscaloosa County	41.9	56.7	1.0	0.0	0.4
Virginia Beach, VA	Virginia Beach City	51.6	46.2	1.8	0.0	0.4
Washington, DC	District of Columbia	92.1	5.4	0.6	0.5	1.4
Wichita, KS	Sedgwick County	42.6	54.4	2.4	0.0	0.5
Wilmington, NC	New Hanover County	50.2	48.0	1.2	0.3	0.4
Winston-Salem, NC	Forsyth County	56.2	42.3	0.9	0.2	0.4
Worcester, MA	Worcester County	57.6	39.7	1.7	0.6	0.4
U.S.	U.S.	51.3	46.8	1.2	0.3	0.5

Note: Results are percentages and may not add to 100% due to rounding
Source: Dave Leip's Atlas of U.S. Presidential Elections

House Price Index (HPI)

Metro Area[1]	National Ranking[3]	Quarterly Change (%)	One-Year Change (%)	Five-Year Change (%)	Since 1991Q1 (%)
Albuquerque, NM	67	0.95	14.03	58.76	256.02
Allentown, PA	104	-0.97	12.09	52.30	165.53
Anchorage, AK	215	-0.36	8.00	27.30	235.38
Ann Arbor, MI	210	-4.46	8.26	40.08	220.18
Athens, GA	33	0.64	16.98	76.16	301.70
Atlanta, GA	40	-0.35	16.14	73.42	274.52
Austin, TX	222	-5.35	7.56	75.92	618.91
Baltimore, MD	199	0.91	8.63	34.77	214.03
Boise City, ID	256	-6.44	1.06	96.45	501.63
Boston, MA[2]	195	-1.14	8.90	44.63	310.81
Boulder, CO	150	-1.96	10.66	47.80	588.29
Brownsville, TX	n/a	n/a	n/a	n/a	n/a
Cape Coral, FL	6	-0.47	20.91	83.64	358.39
Cedar Rapids, IA	243	-4.60	5.29	30.92	170.24
Charleston, SC	29	-0.34	17.51	66.55	441.52
Charlotte, NC	19	0.48	18.66	78.79	310.41
Chicago, IL[2]	205	-1.86	8.51	31.58	168.46
Cincinnati, OH	96	-0.52	12.38	55.37	199.65
Clarksville, TN	n/a	n/a	n/a	n/a	n/a
Cleveland, OH	189	-1.76	9.23	49.32	153.83
College Station, TX	n/a	n/a	n/a	n/a	n/a
Colorado Springs, CO	231	-3.83	6.63	67.59	425.90
Columbia, MO	148	1.10	10.69	48.19	225.68
Columbia, SC	23	1.44	18.32	59.58	209.37
Columbus, OH	94	-1.27	12.41	59.08	243.03
Dallas, TX[2]	43	-1.44	15.77	61.60	325.13
Davenport, IA	220	0.26	7.72	30.21	202.26
Denver, CO	216	-2.41	7.96	52.15	548.72
Des Moines, IA	108	0.29	12.00	40.34	223.17
Durham, NC	45	-3.85	15.68	66.89	294.13
Edison, NJ[2]	212	-0.09	8.22	34.61	258.57
El Paso, TX	21	2.05	18.42	54.29	201.64
Fargo, ND	133	0.78	11.14	32.39	270.20
Fort Collins, CO	141	-2.34	10.88	51.04	508.13
Fort Wayne, IN	68	1.56	14.01	67.52	186.04
Fort Worth, TX[2]	53	-1.47	15.09	66.00	306.95
Grand Rapids, MI	116	n/a	11.72	62.74	262.62
Greeley, CO	207	-3.14	8.35	53.74	462.73
Green Bay, WI	25	3.83	17.89	59.68	250.27
Greensboro, NC	26	0.70	17.71	64.64	188.62
Honolulu, HI	122	-5.39	11.51	33.52	222.93
Houston, TX	81	0.53	13.01	46.44	300.24
Huntsville, AL	109	-1.12	11.99	73.58	211.74
Indianapolis, IN	99	-1.53	12.29	62.22	209.62
Jacksonville, FL	35	-1.80	16.79	76.35	371.41
Kansas City, MO	102	-0.14	12.17	58.36	257.00
Lafayette, LA	179	-0.60	9.73	25.29	232.27
Las Cruces, NM	n/a	n/a	n/a	n/a	n/a
Las Vegas, NV	157	-3.37	10.38	70.87	260.78
Lexington, KY	72	0.70	13.70	53.19	235.38
Lincoln, NE	107	0.03	12.01	49.08	257.46
Little Rock, AR	119	0.21	11.59	41.21	196.34
Los Angeles, CA[2]	200	-1.90	8.62	46.01	298.97
Louisville, KY	147	1.02	10.70	47.57	251.74
Madison, WI	121	-1.67	11.52	45.50	303.94

Table continued on following page.

Appendix A: Comparative Statistics   A-113

Metro Area[1]	National Ranking[3]	Quarterly Change (%)	One-Year Change (%)	Five-Year Change (%)	Since 1991Q1 (%)
Manchester, NH	126	-0.32	11.34	59.79	253.04
Miami, FL[2]	4	2.23	21.62	75.85	539.14
Midland, TX	n/a	n/a	n/a	n/a	n/a
Milwaukee, WI	134	-1.54	11.11	45.94	239.44
Minneapolis, MN	239	-1.83	6.08	41.05	273.41
Nashville, TN	34	-1.19	16.94	75.36	429.41
New Haven, CT	113	0.91	11.80	48.13	135.81
New Orleans, LA	202	0.06	8.58	36.52	291.68
New York, NY[2]	212	-0.09	8.22	34.61	258.57
Oklahoma City, OK	97	0.36	12.37	49.27	260.86
Omaha, NE	161	-0.79	10.26	51.61	252.12
Orlando, FL	13	0.53	19.76	74.99	330.12
Philadelphia, PA[2]	187	1.72	9.32	47.35	257.72
Phoenix, AZ	144	-4.25	10.82	83.46	453.06
Pittsburgh, PA	224	-1.54	7.43	42.48	223.87
Portland, OR	247	-2.87	4.63	43.13	493.76
Providence, RI	153	-0.93	10.48	54.47	232.15
Provo, UT	206	-3.27	8.39	75.92	514.28
Raleigh, NC	57	-2.71	14.97	69.49	298.33
Reno, NV	244	-1.71	5.01	60.21	333.43
Richmond, VA	79	-0.25	13.11	53.64	254.70
Rochester, MN	234	-3.55	6.25	42.75	234.69
Sacramento, CA	253	-3.63	3.17	45.83	234.41
St. Louis, MO	190	-0.80	9.10	40.60	193.95
Salem, OR	204	-1.19	8.51	62.82	461.52
Salt Lake City, UT	197	-2.92	8.70	74.37	596.70
San Antonio, TX	50	0.79	15.27	62.24	345.76
San Diego, CA	181	-2.11	9.62	51.34	344.82
San Francisco, CA[2]	177	3.28	9.77	19.08	360.06
San Jose, CA	101	1.47	12.23	31.21	389.33
Santa Rosa, CA	250	-4.80	3.50	26.56	276.48
Savannah, GA	12	1.20	19.86	70.81	361.13
Seattle, WA[2]	236	-3.59	6.21	48.84	436.06
Sioux Falls, SD	92	-1.20	12.49	55.67	315.04
Springfield, IL	158	-0.16	10.38	29.11	125.30
Tampa, FL	10	-0.71	19.98	91.22	438.13
Tucson, AZ	73	-1.74	13.68	74.77	329.80
Tulsa, OK	58	0.72	14.67	52.24	236.95
Tuscaloosa, AL	n/a	n/a	n/a	n/a	n/a
Virginia Beach, VA	131	0.74	11.17	43.79	243.78
Washington, DC[2]	238	-1.35	6.16	35.79	253.98
Wichita, KS	151	-1.84	10.63	47.99	197.78
Wilmington, NC	18	-1.23	18.70	72.00	356.80
Winston-Salem, NC	37	0.94	16.66	66.13	201.85
Worcester, MA	184	-1.36	9.48	52.36	218.67
U.S.[4]	—	0.34	8.41	58.44	289.08

Note: The HPI is a weighted repeat sales index. It measures average price changes in repeat sales or refinancings on the same properties. This information is obtained by reviewing repeat mortgage transactions on single-family properties whose mortgages have been purchased or securitized by Fannie Mae or Freddie Mac since January 1975; all figures are for the period ended December 31, 2022; (1) figures cover the Metropolitan Statistical Area (MSA) unless noted otherwise; (2) Metropolitan Division; (3) Rankings are based on annual percentage change, for all MSAs containing at least 15,000 transactions over the last 10 years and ranges from 1 to 257; (4) figures based on a weighted division average; (a) Not ranked because of increased index variability due to smaller sample size; n/a not available
Source: Federal Housing Finance Agency, Change in FHFA Metropolitan Area House Price Indexes, 2022Q4

Home Value: City

City	Under $100,000	$100,000 -$199,999	$200,000 -$299,999	$300,000 -$399,999	$400,000 -$499,999	$500,000 -$999,999	$1,000,000 or more	Median ($)
Albuquerque, NM	8.2	36.2	31.9	13.0	5.9	4.2	0.6	214,600
Allentown, PA	19.9	58.7	14.0	3.6	1.8	1.4	0.5	145,700
Anchorage, AK	6.7	10.2	25.3	28.2	13.9	14.3	1.4	327,500
Ann Arbor, MI	2.4	10.8	20.5	24.6	18.8	19.9	3.0	366,600
Athens, GA	16.0	34.3	25.3	10.4	5.8	6.9	1.2	199,300
Atlanta, GA	8.9	17.3	17.4	13.6	10.3	23.2	9.3	346,600
Austin, TX	3.6	8.4	20.6	21.5	15.3	24.7	6.0	381,400
Baltimore, MD	21.5	35.5	21.4	10.3	4.3	5.9	1.0	175,300
Boise City, ID	5.2	12.8	27.2	22.0	13.5	17.2	2.3	322,300
Boston, MA	2.6	1.0	5.5	11.1	15.0	48.4	16.5	610,400
Boulder, CO	5.2	3.5	3.6	5.3	6.9	44.1	31.4	790,100
Brownsville, TX	53.5	34.4	9.1	1.4	0.6	0.8	0.1	95,700
Cape Coral, FL	3.4	25.6	35.3	19.8	6.7	8.1	1.2	255,700
Cedar Rapids, IA	18.6	53.5	19.0	5.4	1.7	1.5	0.3	149,000
Charleston, SC	3.1	7.6	23.0	23.5	11.5	23.2	8.1	369,500
Charlotte, NC	7.8	27.5	23.8	14.8	8.8	13.3	4.0	258,000
Chicago, IL	8.5	22.4	24.5	16.5	9.6	14.2	4.3	277,600
Cincinnati, OH	24.5	35.2	17.3	9.2	4.7	7.2	1.8	162,300
Clarksville, TN	13.0	51.0	25.3	6.3	1.6	2.6	0.3	172,700
Cleveland, OH	67.7	23.2	4.6	2.2	0.7	1.3	0.2	74,700
College Station, TX	2.2	18.2	39.2	25.7	7.6	6.3	0.7	269,100
Colorado Springs, CO	4.6	11.0	28.1	26.0	14.7	14.1	1.4	324,100
Columbia, MO	8.9	35.8	29.2	14.1	6.5	5.1	0.5	215,300
Columbia, SC	17.9	34.1	18.9	9.7	5.5	11.7	2.2	193,100
Columbus, OH	19.2	40.1	25.2	9.3	2.9	2.8	0.5	174,400
Dallas, TX	17.6	27.3	15.3	11.0	8.6	14.8	5.5	230,000
Davenport, IA	28.0	44.6	17.1	7.5	1.1	1.4	0.3	138,000
Denver, CO	2.3	4.6	12.8	20.0	17.5	34.9	7.9	459,100
Des Moines, IA	20.9	53.8	17.0	4.6	1.5	1.9	0.3	149,700
Durham, NC	5.0	24.8	31.4	20.4	8.2	9.0	1.1	264,100
Edison, NJ	3.9	3.9	14.5	26.0	20.3	29.1	2.3	408,100
El Paso, TX	25.7	52.3	14.1	4.5	1.7	1.4	0.3	137,600
Fargo, ND	7.4	30.1	36.2	16.5	4.6	4.4	0.7	232,900
Fort Collins, CO	4.0	2.8	10.0	24.0	29.5	27.3	2.4	431,300
Fort Wayne, IN	32.7	46.5	14.2	4.0	1.2	1.1	0.2	130,700
Fort Worth, TX	15.9	29.7	31.6	12.1	4.7	4.8	1.2	212,300
Grand Rapids, MI	16.4	49.8	24.0	6.0	2.0	1.4	0.3	168,700
Greeley, CO	9.3	8.9	33.0	31.0	10.6	6.8	0.3	296,300
Green Bay, WI	17.2	57.2	16.1	5.1	2.4	1.8	0.2	151,000
Greensboro, NC	19.7	40.5	20.3	9.3	4.4	4.8	1.0	169,100
Honolulu, HI	1.6	1.6	5.5	11.7	10.7	41.2	27.6	726,000
Houston, TX	19.1	30.8	17.1	11.0	6.7	11.3	4.0	200,700
Huntsville, AL	21.0	30.5	21.8	12.5	6.6	6.4	1.1	194,500
Indianapolis, IN	23.7	43.7	17.7	7.2	3.1	3.9	0.7	156,300
Jacksonville, FL	17.0	32.0	28.0	12.0	4.8	4.9	1.4	203,400
Kansas City, MO	23.0	34.6	21.2	11.4	4.1	4.8	0.8	175,400
Lafayette, LA	13.7	33.6	25.7	11.7	7.0	6.7	1.6	209,100
Las Cruces, NM	17.4	49.1	21.5	7.7	1.5	2.5	0.3	167,800
Las Vegas, NV	4.3	14.0	31.2	23.5	11.7	13.1	2.2	302,100
Lexington, KY	9.0	36.1	25.2	14.5	6.4	7.6	1.2	216,800
Lincoln, NE	9.6	42.9	27.9	11.1	4.5	3.2	0.7	193,800
Little Rock, AR	22.0	33.4	17.9	11.1	5.5	8.4	1.6	179,500
Los Angeles, CA	2.2	1.3	2.4	6.2	11.3	50.1	26.6	705,900
Louisville, KY	17.5	40.5	20.3	10.8	5.0	5.1	0.9	174,400
Madison, WI	3.4	18.6	35.0	22.5	10.9	8.3	1.3	277,800

Table continued on following page.

City	Under $100,000	$100,000 -$199,999	$200,000 -$299,999	$300,000 -$399,999	$400,000 -$499,999	$500,000 -$999,999	$1,000,000 or more	Median ($)
Manchester, NH	4.7	21.9	39.9	23.6	6.6	3.1	0.1	258,100
Miami, FL	4.5	9.8	20.4	22.1	14.7	20.0	8.4	369,100
Midland, TX	11.2	22.4	32.5	17.2	6.3	8.8	1.5	250,300
Milwaukee, WI	30.6	48.6	14.1	3.3	1.2	1.8	0.5	135,600
Minneapolis, MN	4.2	19.5	31.1	20.3	9.7	12.6	2.5	284,400
Nashville, TN	4.4	18.9	29.1	21.3	9.6	13.3	3.3	291,400
New Haven, CT	11.0	36.4	29.4	10.5	5.4	5.7	1.6	207,600
New Orleans, LA	9.7	28.7	20.4	13.4	8.3	15.2	4.2	255,500
New York, NY	4.3	3.6	5.5	8.2	10.8	44.7	22.9	660,700
Oklahoma City, OK	23.1	38.5	21.4	8.2	3.8	3.8	1.2	168,900
Omaha, NE	15.7	42.7	23.3	9.7	4.0	3.9	0.7	177,700
Orlando, FL	7.5	23.3	22.9	20.6	10.8	12.3	2.6	283,700
Philadelphia, PA	21.6	33.0	22.8	10.0	4.6	6.6	1.4	184,100
Phoenix, AZ	7.3	19.8	28.5	18.6	9.6	13.8	2.4	277,700
Pittsburgh, PA	33.7	31.4	13.9	7.9	4.8	7.2	1.1	147,600
Portland, OR	2.6	2.8	9.9	21.8	20.5	38.3	4.1	462,800
Providence, RI	4.9	27.5	34.7	14.0	4.1	11.6	3.2	248,900
Provo, UT	5.3	9.2	27.9	26.4	12.3	16.1	2.7	328,500
Raleigh, NC	4.0	21.6	28.3	18.3	11.0	14.2	2.7	285,400
Reno, NV	5.9	5.9	14.6	25.8	20.2	24.1	3.5	391,500
Richmond, VA	9.5	26.4	21.0	16.5	8.6	14.2	3.8	263,000
Rochester, MN	5.8	30.7	30.8	16.9	8.6	6.8	0.5	236,400
Sacramento, CA	4.0	5.0	19.4	25.1	19.3	24.0	3.0	385,500
St. Louis, MO	29.9	36.3	17.8	8.4	3.4	3.4	0.9	153,200
Salem, OR	7.5	13.6	32.7	26.7	11.1	7.9	0.5	289,500
Salt Lake City, UT	3.8	10.8	19.8	19.3	14.6	26.2	5.3	380,200
San Antonio, TX	24.0	38.4	21.9	8.7	3.3	3.1	0.6	167,700
San Diego, CA	2.6	1.4	3.1	8.1	13.7	51.4	19.8	664,000
San Francisco, CA	1.5	0.8	1.0	1.9	1.6	26.1	67.1	1,194,500
San Jose, CA	2.3	2.5	2.0	1.6	2.6	40.3	48.6	986,700
Santa Rosa, CA	4.1	2.6	4.0	7.3	13.6	60.0	8.4	598,700
Savannah, GA	19.1	41.2	21.4	6.7	4.4	5.9	1.3	170,500
Seattle, WA	1.1	0.6	2.7	6.3	8.6	55.3	25.4	767,500
Sioux Falls, SD	10.1	32.4	31.9	12.6	6.1	5.6	1.3	218,600
Springfield, IL	34.4	38.8	15.9	6.3	2.4	1.9	0.4	132,900
Tampa, FL	9.0	22.7	22.8	14.6	9.9	14.9	6.1	277,700
Tucson, AZ	17.8	41.3	26.3	8.4	3.0	2.4	0.7	177,800
Tulsa, OK	28.0	36.9	15.4	8.2	4.4	5.5	1.5	151,500
Tuscaloosa, AL	14.2	37.7	19.5	11.1	6.0	10.0	1.6	194,500
Virginia Beach, VA	3.8	15.6	32.0	21.6	11.7	12.8	2.6	295,900
Washington, DC	1.8	2.2	7.5	12.3	12.7	42.1	21.4	635,900
Wichita, KS	31.2	39.6	17.3	6.7	2.2	2.7	0.3	145,300
Wilmington, NC	5.9	23.6	25.8	19.2	8.2	13.7	3.7	279,900
Winston-Salem, NC	22.4	44.2	16.7	7.0	3.5	5.6	0.6	158,600
Worcester, MA	4.7	20.1	40.8	22.2	6.8	4.6	0.9	259,800
U.S.	16.2	24.2	20.1	13.6	8.3	13.6	4.1	244,900

Note: Figures are percentages except for median and cover owner-occupied housing units.
Source: U.S. Census Bureau, 2017-2021 American Community Survey 5-Year Estimates

Home Value: Metro Area

MSA[1]	Under $100,000	$100,000 -$199,999	$200,000 -$299,999	$300,000 -$399,999	$400,000 -$499,999	$500,000 -$999,999	$1,000,000 or more	Median ($)
Albuquerque, NM	11.7	34.6	28.4	12.3	5.9	5.9	1.1	210,700
Allentown, PA	9.9	31.5	28.8	17.1	7.2	5.1	0.6	227,900
Anchorage, AK	6.7	12.7	28.8	26.2	12.5	12.0	1.1	306,700
Ann Arbor, MI	9.2	18.2	24.0	19.4	12.7	14.5	1.9	293,800
Athens, GA	16.8	30.0	23.5	12.5	7.6	8.0	1.7	211,500
Atlanta, GA	8.9	26.9	25.0	16.1	9.3	11.7	2.0	252,100
Austin, TX	6.2	12.5	25.9	20.6	12.6	18.1	4.1	326,400
Baltimore, MD	6.7	15.8	23.5	20.6	12.8	18.2	2.4	319,500
Boise City, ID	6.9	15.9	25.8	21.3	13.1	14.9	2.1	306,300
Boston, MA	2.5	3.6	10.6	18.0	17.3	38.5	9.4	487,600
Boulder, CO	4.1	2.1	5.7	13.1	16.3	44.3	14.5	575,700
Brownsville, TX	53.6	31.8	8.9	2.9	1.1	1.4	0.2	94,200
Cape Coral, FL	12.0	23.6	27.5	16.4	7.3	10.5	2.8	248,300
Cedar Rapids, IA	17.2	44.7	22.6	8.4	3.7	3.0	0.5	165,500
Charleston, SC	10.8	21.0	24.9	16.5	8.1	14.0	4.6	270,700
Charlotte, NC	13.0	27.8	23.7	15.3	8.0	10.0	2.3	237,300
Chicago, IL	8.6	25.3	26.7	17.5	8.5	10.9	2.5	258,500
Cincinnati, OH	16.4	37.7	23.2	11.6	4.9	5.4	0.9	187,000
Clarksville, TN	19.0	41.2	23.4	9.2	2.9	3.7	0.7	174,300
Cleveland, OH	23.8	37.8	20.5	9.2	4.1	3.9	0.6	164,400
College Station, TX	20.3	25.9	24.8	14.8	5.2	7.7	1.3	213,600
Colorado Springs, CO	4.6	10.9	26.6	25.1	14.8	16.3	1.6	331,300
Columbia, MO	14.6	36.8	24.4	12.8	5.2	5.2	1.0	195,600
Columbia, SC	22.5	38.6	19.7	9.2	4.2	4.9	1.0	167,800
Columbus, OH	14.2	32.0	25.3	14.2	6.8	6.6	0.9	213,600
Dallas, TX	10.9	24.1	26.2	17.0	9.3	10.2	2.4	255,600
Davenport, IA	27.9	41.0	17.1	8.3	2.8	2.6	0.4	145,200
Denver, CO	3.2	3.4	11.5	22.5	21.7	32.8	4.9	443,400
Des Moines, IA	12.8	35.7	26.8	13.6	5.6	5.0	0.6	205,200
Durham, NC	10.6	23.8	24.0	17.7	9.2	12.7	1.9	264,400
Edison, NJ	3.5	5.2	11.1	16.7	16.1	36.2	11.2	483,500
El Paso, TX	29.8	49.6	13.5	4.1	1.4	1.2	0.3	131,200
Fargo, ND	8.0	29.3	32.7	16.9	6.0	6.3	0.8	235,600
Fort Collins, CO	4.9	3.0	11.4	25.9	23.2	28.1	3.4	420,200
Fort Wayne, IN	26.2	42.9	18.0	6.8	2.7	2.8	0.5	150,600
Fort Worth, TX	10.9	24.1	26.2	17.0	9.3	10.2	2.4	255,600
Grand Rapids, MI	14.0	34.9	27.4	12.2	5.7	4.7	1.1	203,500
Greeley, CO	7.1	7.0	21.1	28.5	17.5	17.3	1.5	352,000
Green Bay, WI	12.8	41.4	26.0	10.9	4.6	3.6	0.7	188,800
Greensboro, NC	22.8	39.9	19.0	9.0	4.4	4.2	0.7	162,700
Honolulu, HI	1.6	1.6	3.6	8.3	9.7	53.8	21.5	726,800
Houston, TX	13.5	30.4	25.4	13.7	6.5	8.0	2.5	221,400
Huntsville, AL	17.1	33.2	24.5	12.5	6.2	5.8	0.7	199,000
Indianapolis, IN	17.1	37.2	22.1	11.7	5.5	5.6	0.9	186,700
Jacksonville, FL	13.2	26.5	26.7	15.0	7.8	8.5	2.2	235,300
Kansas City, MO	15.2	31.5	24.6	14.0	6.8	6.8	1.1	211,900
Lafayette, LA	28.0	34.1	21.1	9.0	3.7	3.3	0.7	167,400
Las Cruces, NM	26.6	38.7	19.7	7.3	3.9	3.4	0.4	162,200
Las Vegas, NV	5.6	12.8	29.4	25.2	12.4	12.3	2.3	308,800
Lexington, KY	10.9	37.5	24.2	13.2	6.0	7.1	1.2	206,000
Lincoln, NE	9.4	39.9	27.0	12.5	5.5	4.7	0.9	202,300
Little Rock, AR	23.2	39.9	20.4	8.5	3.2	4.0	0.8	164,200
Los Angeles, CA	3.2	1.7	3.2	7.0	11.9	52.3	20.7	671,700
Louisville, KY	15.4	37.8	23.3	12.0	5.0	5.4	0.9	189,900
Madison, WI	5.1	20.5	30.8	21.7	10.9	9.4	1.6	277,400

Table continued on following page.

MSA[1]	Under $100,000	$100,000 -$199,999	$200,000 -$299,999	$300,000 -$399,999	$400,000 -$499,999	$500,000 -$999,999	$1,000,000 or more	Median ($)
Manchester, NH	4.2	13.5	30.7	27.5	12.9	10.7	0.5	306,000
Miami, FL	8.7	15.9	21.8	20.7	12.8	15.2	4.9	317,800
Midland, TX	16.5	20.8	29.5	16.1	6.9	8.7	1.4	243,400
Milwaukee, WI	10.6	29.0	27.8	16.4	7.5	7.4	1.2	235,100
Minneapolis, MN	4.6	17.1	32.2	21.8	11.2	11.4	1.7	287,600
Nashville, TN	6.6	19.5	27.4	19.2	9.9	14.1	3.2	286,800
New Haven, CT	6.4	25.9	29.4	18.7	10.0	8.3	1.2	259,400
New Orleans, LA	11.5	34.6	25.7	13.3	5.8	7.5	1.7	214,300
New York, NY	3.5	5.2	11.1	16.7	16.1	36.2	11.2	483,500
Oklahoma City, OK	21.7	39.2	20.6	9.0	4.1	4.1	1.2	169,300
Omaha, NE	13.4	38.4	24.8	12.5	5.4	4.7	0.8	195,000
Orlando, FL	10.4	20.5	30.9	19.9	8.1	8.3	1.9	260,800
Philadelphia, PA	9.6	21.9	25.7	18.4	10.4	12.1	1.8	270,400
Phoenix, AZ	8.3	15.9	27.3	20.3	11.4	13.9	2.9	294,700
Pittsburgh, PA	25.5	34.6	19.9	9.9	4.5	4.9	0.7	167,500
Portland, OR	4.2	3.7	12.4	25.2	21.3	29.7	3.5	421,300
Providence, RI	3.5	12.7	31.4	24.1	12.7	13.5	2.1	309,600
Provo, UT	3.1	6.2	22.3	28.1	17.5	20.2	2.6	365,500
Raleigh, NC	7.0	20.0	25.5	20.2	12.4	13.2	1.7	289,700
Reno, NV	5.5	6.4	16.4	25.0	18.1	22.9	5.9	387,400
Richmond, VA	6.4	24.3	29.8	18.4	9.3	10.4	1.5	262,900
Rochester, MN	9.2	29.8	26.8	16.1	8.6	8.3	1.2	234,700
Sacramento, CA	4.1	3.6	11.7	22.0	20.6	33.7	4.4	441,800
St. Louis, MO	20.0	33.1	22.7	12.1	5.2	5.7	1.2	189,600
Salem, OR	8.1	12.8	29.6	24.3	12.1	12.1	1.0	298,400
Salt Lake City, UT	3.8	8.2	22.9	24.5	16.6	21.1	2.9	361,600
San Antonio, TX	18.7	31.5	24.5	12.0	5.8	6.2	1.3	199,200
San Diego, CA	4.2	2.2	3.5	7.9	14.3	52.3	15.7	627,200
San Francisco, CA	2.0	1.4	1.7	3.8	5.9	40.7	44.4	933,300
San Jose, CA	2.1	2.0	1.7	1.6	2.3	32.2	58.0	1,113,700
Santa Rosa, CA	3.9	2.9	2.9	5.1	9.9	58.1	17.2	665,800
Savannah, GA	14.2	32.9	25.4	11.2	5.1	9.1	2.1	210,400
Seattle, WA	3.3	3.2	9.5	16.3	15.8	39.3	12.5	518,000
Sioux Falls, SD	11.0	31.1	29.9	14.0	6.4	6.5	1.2	221,500
Springfield, IL	29.8	38.6	19.5	7.3	2.4	2.0	0.4	148,000
Tampa, FL	16.4	25.3	26.4	14.8	6.9	8.1	2.0	229,400
Tucson, AZ	15.0	29.7	26.3	13.5	6.8	7.4	1.3	217,700
Tulsa, OK	24.2	39.1	19.5	8.6	3.5	4.1	0.9	163,100
Tuscaloosa, AL	24.9	35.9	20.8	9.4	3.6	4.6	0.8	171,100
Virginia Beach, VA	6.5	23.8	31.1	18.5	9.8	9.0	1.3	261,800
Washington, DC	2.4	4.9	14.2	19.7	16.6	34.4	7.8	453,100
Wichita, KS	28.6	40.0	18.4	7.4	2.6	2.6	0.4	151,900
Wilmington, NC	9.2	24.0	25.8	18.0	8.9	11.6	2.4	262,500
Winston-Salem, NC	20.7	42.5	19.5	8.7	3.7	4.4	0.5	165,000
Worcester, MA	3.6	16.4	30.3	22.9	12.3	13.1	1.3	298,900
U.S.	16.2	24.2	20.1	13.6	8.3	13.6	4.1	244,900

Note: (1) Figures cover the Metropolitan Statistical Area (MSA); Figures are percentages except for median and cover owner-occupied housing units.
Source: U.S. Census Bureau, 2017-2021 American Community Survey 5-Year Estimates

Homeownership Rate

Metro Area	2015	2016	2017	2018	2019	2020	2021	2022
Albuquerque, NM	64.3	66.9	67.0	67.9	70.0	69.5	66.5	67.3
Allentown, PA	69.2	68.9	73.1	72.1	67.8	68.8	70.4	73.1
Anchorage, AK	n/a	n/a	n/a	n/a	n/a	n/a	n/a	n/a
Ann Arbor, MI	n/a	n/a	n/a	n/a	n/a	n/a	n/a	n/a
Athens, GA	n/a	n/a	n/a	n/a	n/a	n/a	n/a	n/a
Atlanta, GA	61.7	61.5	62.4	64.0	64.2	66.4	64.2	64.4
Austin, TX	57.5	56.5	55.6	56.1	59.0	65.4	62.2	62.4
Baltimore, MD	65.3	68.5	67.5	63.5	66.5	70.7	67.5	70.4
Boise City, ID	n/a	n/a	n/a	n/a	n/a	n/a	n/a	n/a
Boston, MA	59.3	58.9	58.8	61.0	60.9	61.2	60.7	59.4
Boulder, CO	n/a	n/a	n/a	n/a	n/a	n/a	n/a	n/a
Brownsville, TX	n/a	n/a	n/a	n/a	n/a	n/a	n/a	n/a
Cape Coral, FL	62.9	66.5	65.5	75.1	72.0	77.4	76.1	70.8
Cedar Rapids, IA	n/a	n/a	n/a	n/a	n/a	n/a	n/a	n/a
Charleston, SC	65.8	62.1	67.7	68.8	70.7	75.5	73.2	71.9
Charlotte, NC	62.3	66.2	64.6	67.9	72.3	73.3	70.0	68.7
Chicago, IL	64.3	64.5	64.1	64.6	63.4	66.0	67.5	66.8
Cincinnati, OH	65.9	64.9	65.7	67.3	67.4	71.1	72.1	67.1
Clarksville, TN	n/a	n/a	n/a	n/a	n/a	n/a	n/a	n/a
Cleveland, OH	68.4	64.8	66.6	66.7	64.4	66.3	64.7	63.0
College Station, TX	n/a	n/a	n/a	n/a	n/a	n/a	n/a	n/a
Colorado Springs, CO	n/a	n/a	n/a	n/a	n/a	n/a	n/a	n/a
Columbia, MO	n/a	n/a	n/a	n/a	n/a	n/a	n/a	n/a
Columbia, SC	66.1	63.9	70.7	69.3	65.9	69.7	69.4	70.9
Columbus, OH	59.0	57.5	57.9	64.8	65.7	65.6	64.6	61.5
Dallas, TX	57.8	59.7	61.8	62.0	60.6	64.7	61.8	60.4
Davenport, IA	n/a	n/a	n/a	n/a	n/a	n/a	n/a	n/a
Denver, CO	61.6	61.6	59.3	60.1	63.5	62.9	62.8	64.6
Des Moines, IA	n/a	n/a	n/a	n/a	n/a	n/a	n/a	n/a
Durham, NC	n/a	n/a	n/a	n/a	n/a	n/a	n/a	n/a
Edison, NJ	49.9	50.4	49.9	49.7	50.4	50.9	50.7	50.5
El Paso, TX	n/a	n/a	n/a	n/a	n/a	n/a	n/a	n/a
Fargo, ND	n/a	n/a	n/a	n/a	n/a	n/a	n/a	n/a
Fort Collins, CO	n/a	n/a	n/a	n/a	n/a	n/a	n/a	n/a
Fort Wayne, IN	n/a	n/a	n/a	n/a	n/a	n/a	n/a	n/a
Fort Worth, TX	57.8	59.7	61.8	62.0	60.6	64.7	61.8	60.4
Grand Rapids, MI	75.8	76.2	71.7	73.0	75.2	71.8	65.0	68.1
Greeley, CO	n/a	n/a	n/a	n/a	n/a	n/a	n/a	n/a
Green Bay, WI	n/a	n/a	n/a	n/a	n/a	n/a	n/a	n/a
Greensboro, NC	65.4	62.9	61.9	63.2	61.7	65.8	61.9	70.0
Honolulu, HI	59.6	57.9	53.8	57.7	59.0	56.9	55.9	57.7
Houston, TX	60.3	59.0	58.9	60.1	61.3	65.3	64.1	63.7
Huntsville, AL	n/a	n/a	n/a	n/a	n/a	n/a	n/a	n/a
Indianapolis, IN	64.6	63.9	63.9	64.3	66.2	70.0	70.1	68.8
Jacksonville, FL	62.5	61.8	65.2	61.4	63.1	64.8	68.1	70.6
Kansas City, MO	65.0	62.4	62.4	64.3	65.0	66.7	63.8	63.8
Lafayette, LA	n/a	n/a	n/a	n/a	n/a	n/a	n/a	n/a
Las Cruces, NM	n/a	n/a	n/a	n/a	n/a	n/a	n/a	n/a
Las Vegas, NV	52.1	51.3	54.4	58.1	56.0	57.3	57.7	58.7
Lexington, KY	n/a	n/a	n/a	n/a	n/a	n/a	n/a	n/a
Lincoln, NE	n/a	n/a	n/a	n/a	n/a	n/a	n/a	n/a
Little Rock, AR	65.8	64.9	61.0	62.2	65.0	67.7	64.6	64.4
Los Angeles, CA	49.1	47.1	49.1	49.5	48.2	48.5	47.9	48.3
Louisville, KY	67.7	67.6	71.7	67.9	64.9	69.3	71.4	71.7
Madison, WI	n/a	n/a	n/a	n/a	n/a	n/a	n/a	n/a
Manchester, NH	n/a	n/a	n/a	n/a	n/a	n/a	n/a	n/a

Table continued on following page.

Metro Area	2015	2016	2017	2018	2019	2020	2021	2022
Miami, FL	58.6	58.4	57.9	59.9	60.4	60.6	59.4	58.3
Midland, TX	n/a	n/a	n/a	n/a	n/a	n/a	n/a	n/a
Milwaukee, WI	57.0	60.4	63.9	62.3	56.9	58.5	56.8	57.3
Minneapolis, MN	67.9	69.1	70.1	67.8	70.2	73.0	75.0	73.0
Nashville, TN	67.4	65.0	69.4	68.3	69.8	69.8	65.7	70.4
New Haven, CT	64.6	59.4	58.7	65.0	65.1	63.4	61.0	63.3
New Orleans, LA	62.8	59.3	61.7	62.6	61.1	66.3	66.2	66.3
New York, NY	49.9	50.4	49.9	49.7	50.4	50.9	50.7	50.5
Oklahoma City, OK	61.4	63.1	64.7	64.6	64.3	68.3	61.9	64.8
Omaha, NE	69.6	69.2	65.5	67.8	66.9	68.6	68.6	67.9
Orlando, FL	58.4	58.5	59.5	58.5	56.1	64.2	63.0	62.1
Philadelphia, PA	67.0	64.7	65.6	67.4	67.4	69.2	69.8	68.2
Phoenix, AZ	61.0	62.6	64.0	65.3	65.9	67.9	65.2	68.0
Pittsburgh, PA	71.0	72.2	72.7	71.7	71.5	69.8	69.1	72.7
Portland, OR	58.9	61.8	61.1	59.2	60.0	62.5	64.1	65.2
Providence, RI	60.0	57.5	58.6	61.3	63.5	64.8	64.1	66.3
Provo, UT	n/a	n/a	n/a	n/a	n/a	n/a	n/a	n/a
Raleigh, NC	67.4	65.9	68.2	64.9	63.0	68.2	62.7	65.1
Reno, NV	n/a	n/a	n/a	n/a	n/a	n/a	n/a	n/a
Richmond, VA	67.4	61.7	63.1	62.9	66.4	66.5	64.9	66.3
Rochester, MN	n/a	n/a	n/a	n/a	n/a	n/a	n/a	n/a
Sacramento, CA	60.8	60.5	60.1	64.1	61.6	63.4	63.2	63.5
St. Louis, MO	68.7	66.4	65.6	65.8	68.1	71.1	73.8	69.9
Salem, OR	n/a	n/a	n/a	n/a	n/a	n/a	n/a	n/a
Salt Lake City, UT	69.1	69.2	68.1	69.5	69.2	68.0	64.1	66.6
San Antonio, TX	66.0	61.6	62.5	64.4	62.6	64.2	62.7	62.9
San Diego, CA	51.8	53.3	56.0	56.1	56.7	57.8	52.6	51.6
San Francisco, CA	56.3	55.8	55.7	55.6	52.8	53.0	54.7	56.4
San Jose, CA	50.7	49.9	50.4	50.4	52.4	52.6	48.4	53.1
Santa Rosa, CA	n/a	n/a	n/a	n/a	n/a	n/a	n/a	n/a
Savannah, GA	n/a	n/a	n/a	n/a	n/a	n/a	n/a	n/a
Seattle, WA	59.5	57.7	59.5	62.5	61.5	59.4	58.0	62.7
Sioux Falls, SD	n/a	n/a	n/a	n/a	n/a	n/a	n/a	n/a
Springfield, IL	n/a	n/a	n/a	n/a	n/a	n/a	n/a	n/a
Tampa, FL	64.9	62.9	60.4	64.9	68.0	72.2	68.3	68.4
Tucson, AZ	61.4	56.0	60.1	63.8	60.1	67.1	63.5	71.6
Tulsa, OK	65.2	65.4	66.8	68.3	70.5	70.1	63.8	63.7
Tuscaloosa, AL	n/a	n/a	n/a	n/a	n/a	n/a	n/a	n/a
Virginia Beach, VA	59.4	59.6	65.3	62.8	63.0	65.8	64.4	61.4
Washington, DC	64.6	63.1	63.3	62.9	64.7	67.9	65.8	66.2
Wichita, KS	n/a	n/a	n/a	n/a	n/a	n/a	n/a	n/a
Wilmington, NC	n/a	n/a	n/a	n/a	n/a	n/a	n/a	n/a
Winston-Salem, NC	n/a	n/a	n/a	n/a	n/a	n/a	n/a	n/a
Worcester, MA	64.2	65.5	64.9	63.4	62.7	65.9	68.7	64.8
U.S.	63.7	63.4	63.9	64.4	64.6	66.6	65.5	65.8

Note: Figures are percentages and cover the Metropolitan Statistical Area; n/a not available
Source: U.S. Census Bureau, Housing Vacancies and Homeownership Annual Statistics: 2015-2022

Year Housing Structure Built: City

City	2020 or Later	2010-2019	2000-2009	1990-1999	1980-1989	1970-1979	1960-1969	1950-1959	1940-1949	Before 1940	Median Year
Albuquerque, NM	0.2	5.7	16.1	14.9	15.1	19.1	9.8	11.8	4.3	3.1	1981
Allentown, PA	0.1	2.3	4.6	3.4	5.3	10.8	11.5	15.0	7.2	39.7	1952
Anchorage, AK	<0.1	4.7	11.9	11.9	25.8	28.0	10.2	5.8	1.2	0.5	1982
Ann Arbor, MI	0.2	5.0	5.8	11.7	11.3	16.9	18.0	11.1	5.0	15.0	1971
Athens, GA	0.1	5.7	17.6	18.6	15.8	15.8	12.5	6.6	2.2	5.1	1985
Atlanta, GA	0.4	12.7	22.0	10.2	7.6	7.7	11.0	10.6	5.7	12.1	1984
Austin, TX	0.2	17.5	17.1	14.7	18.6	15.0	7.7	4.5	2.1	2.6	1990
Baltimore, MD	<0.1	3.4	3.6	3.9	4.3	5.7	8.6	15.8	11.9	42.8	1946
Boise City, ID	0.1	9.0	11.0	22.5	15.8	17.1	7.8	6.8	3.9	6.2	1985
Boston, MA	0.2	7.2	6.6	4.4	5.6	7.5	7.6	7.3	5.4	48.2	1943
Boulder, CO	0.1	7.9	7.7	12.0	16.7	19.6	17.7	9.0	1.7	7.7	1977
Brownsville, TX	0.2	12.9	22.9	18.0	14.8	15.5	6.2	4.4	2.8	2.3	1992
Cape Coral, FL	0.1	8.4	34.8	17.6	21.6	11.7	4.6	0.8	0.2	0.1	1996
Cedar Rapids, IA	0.1	7.7	11.5	10.5	7.1	14.6	14.8	12.8	4.1	16.8	1971
Charleston, SC	0.3	18.9	20.0	10.6	12.0	8.8	8.5	5.5	3.4	11.9	1990
Charlotte, NC	0.2	13.2	21.5	19.3	14.4	11.2	8.7	6.3	2.5	2.7	1992
Chicago, IL	<0.1	3.8	8.0	5.1	4.8	7.7	9.6	11.8	8.8	40.3	1951
Cincinnati, OH	0.1	3.3	3.7	4.2	6.0	9.4	12.2	11.5	8.4	41.4	1950
Clarksville, TN	0.2	15.6	22.2	20.2	12.9	12.0	7.2	4.8	2.8	2.1	1994
Cleveland, OH	0.1	2.9	3.5	3.4	2.8	5.5	7.8	12.7	11.2	50.0	<1940
College Station, TX	0.6	20.8	20.7	20.0	16.6	14.8	3.5	2.0	0.4	0.6	1996
Colorado Springs, CO	0.3	9.5	14.7	15.4	18.9	17.2	9.4	7.0	2.0	5.5	1985
Columbia, MO	0.1	15.5	20.0	18.1	11.8	12.1	10.5	4.4	2.3	5.3	1992
Columbia, SC	0.2	9.3	15.2	11.3	10.2	10.2	10.2	13.9	10.1	9.5	1976
Columbus, OH	0.1	8.0	11.7	15.1	12.9	14.3	11.5	10.4	4.3	11.8	1978
Dallas, TX	0.2	9.8	10.5	10.8	16.4	16.5	12.5	13.2	4.9	5.2	1979
Davenport, IA	<0.1	3.9	8.5	8.7	6.8	15.2	12.5	10.9	5.6	27.8	1965
Denver, CO	0.3	12.8	11.1	6.7	7.6	12.7	10.6	14.2	5.8	18.2	1971
Des Moines, IA	0.1	5.5	6.7	7.0	6.4	13.6	10.0	14.9	7.8	28.0	1960
Durham, NC	0.4	17.0	17.9	16.6	14.6	10.4	8.1	5.7	3.3	5.9	1991
Edison, NJ	0.1	2.5	5.7	9.8	24.2	11.6	18.6	17.8	4.0	5.5	1973
El Paso, TX	0.1	12.1	14.1	12.9	14.4	16.3	10.5	11.1	3.7	4.8	1982
Fargo, ND	0.3	18.3	14.2	15.1	13.1	14.2	6.1	8.0	2.3	8.3	1988
Fort Collins, CO	0.3	13.1	18.0	21.0	15.0	16.8	6.7	3.0	1.5	4.6	1991
Fort Wayne, IN	0.1	2.2	6.7	13.6	11.5	17.5	14.9	12.8	6.5	14.2	1971
Fort Worth, TX	0.3	14.8	21.3	12.3	13.5	9.4	7.7	10.2	4.9	5.7	1989
Grand Rapids, MI	<0.1	3.8	4.9	6.3	6.6	8.5	9.0	14.9	8.9	37.1	1953
Greeley, CO	0.1	9.4	17.2	16.7	10.2	21.2	9.4	6.4	2.2	7.2	1984
Green Bay, WI	0.1	2.3	7.0	10.4	12.0	18.6	12.9	15.6	6.5	14.7	1970
Greensboro, NC	0.1	8.0	15.0	16.8	16.5	13.3	11.3	10.2	3.7	5.1	1984
Honolulu, HI	0.1	6.0	6.8	8.2	9.8	26.1	21.0	11.9	5.2	5.0	1973
Houston, TX	0.2	11.8	12.7	9.8	14.6	19.6	13.0	10.0	4.2	4.2	1980
Huntsville, AL	0.2	13.6	12.4	11.0	15.8	12.8	20.6	8.6	2.4	2.6	1982
Indianapolis, IN	0.1	5.0	9.2	12.5	11.5	12.9	13.6	12.8	6.2	16.3	1971
Jacksonville, FL	0.6	8.4	18.1	14.7	15.6	12.4	9.9	10.8	4.5	5.0	1985
Kansas City, MO	0.2	6.9	9.8	9.2	8.9	11.8	12.5	13.4	5.9	21.3	1968
Lafayette, LA	<0.1	10.1	10.7	10.1	19.5	22.0	12.8	9.0	3.2	2.5	1980
Las Cruces, NM	0.3	10.7	19.9	15.0	16.9	15.5	8.1	8.9	2.1	2.6	1988
Las Vegas, NV	0.2	7.1	21.8	31.0	16.3	10.1	7.6	4.2	1.1	0.5	1993
Lexington, KY	0.2	8.4	14.2	16.5	13.2	15.2	13.5	8.9	2.9	7.1	1982
Lincoln, NE	0.1	10.3	13.1	14.2	10.4	15.4	9.4	10.7	3.4	13.0	1979
Little Rock, AR	0.0	8.0	11.4	12.3	13.7	18.5	13.8	9.4	5.1	7.8	1978
Los Angeles, CA	0.1	4.8	5.5	6.0	10.6	13.4	13.6	16.8	9.3	19.7	1963
Louisville, KY	0.2	6.6	11.0	11.1	6.9	12.4	13.6	14.6	7.2	16.5	1969
Madison, WI	0.1	10.1	13.5	12.8	9.8	13.7	11.8	9.4	4.5	14.2	1977

Table continued on following page.

City	2020 or Later	2010 -2019	2000 -2009	1990 -1999	1980 -1989	1970 -1979	1960 -1969	1950 -1959	1940 -1949	Before 1940	Median Year
Manchester, NH	0.3	2.5	6.2	8.3	16.3	11.9	8.1	10.1	7.2	29.1	1965
Miami, FL	0.2	11.5	18.0	6.6	7.5	12.8	10.0	14.4	9.9	9.1	1975
Midland, TX	0.2	18.2	8.1	13.4	18.0	11.7	8.9	17.8	2.6	1.2	1984
Milwaukee, WI	0.1	2.6	3.5	3.3	4.1	8.7	11.4	19.5	10.4	36.5	1952
Minneapolis, MN	<0.1	7.3	6.3	4.0	6.8	8.2	7.5	9.0	6.9	43.9	1949
Nashville, TN	0.8	13.4	13.8	12.3	14.5	13.5	11.6	9.7	4.0	6.4	1983
New Haven, CT	0.0	3.8	4.6	3.1	6.8	9.5	11.2	10.3	7.4	43.2	1949
New Orleans, LA	0.1	4.4	6.9	3.3	7.6	13.9	10.9	12.1	7.3	33.4	1958
New York, NY	<0.1	4.1	5.4	3.8	4.9	7.0	12.5	12.9	9.5	39.9	1950
Oklahoma City, OK	0.3	12.0	13.4	9.9	14.2	15.9	11.5	10.0	5.0	7.9	1980
Omaha, NE	0.1	5.1	8.3	12.4	10.9	15.1	14.4	10.9	4.6	18.3	1971
Orlando, FL	0.2	13.7	20.3	14.7	15.6	14.5	7.2	8.3	2.8	2.8	1989
Philadelphia, PA	0.1	3.6	3.0	3.2	4.0	7.4	11.1	15.7	11.2	40.7	1948
Phoenix, AZ	0.2	6.4	16.3	15.4	17.5	19.4	11.0	9.6	2.4	1.9	1983
Pittsburgh, PA	0.1	3.9	3.0	3.6	4.4	6.6	8.3	13.2	8.3	48.8	1941
Portland, OR	0.2	8.9	9.9	7.9	6.8	10.8	8.6	11.4	7.8	27.7	1964
Providence, RI	0.1	1.2	4.6	4.6	5.7	7.9	5.4	7.1	5.7	57.7	<1940
Provo, UT	0.4	6.9	10.7	18.8	14.4	18.5	9.9	7.8	5.0	7.6	1981
Raleigh, NC	0.3	14.6	23.4	18.5	16.8	9.9	7.6	4.2	1.6	3.1	1994
Reno, NV	1.0	9.8	19.0	17.3	13.8	18.0	8.8	6.1	3.1	3.1	1988
Richmond, VA	0.1	6.5	5.3	5.8	7.1	9.9	11.8	14.7	9.1	29.6	1958
Rochester, MN	0.4	12.3	18.0	14.4	12.0	12.5	10.0	8.8	3.4	8.1	1986
Sacramento, CA	0.1	4.6	14.5	8.7	15.6	14.2	11.4	12.3	7.3	11.3	1975
St. Louis, MO	<0.1	2.4	4.0	3.0	3.2	4.4	6.5	10.2	8.1	58.2	<1940
Salem, OR	0.2	6.9	12.5	16.8	9.7	19.9	9.5	10.6	4.9	9.0	1978
Salt Lake City, UT	0.2	8.1	6.8	6.4	7.6	11.3	9.8	12.8	9.2	27.8	1960
San Antonio, TX	0.2	10.2	14.9	12.9	16.2	14.4	10.3	9.9	5.5	5.4	1983
San Diego, CA	0.2	5.7	10.2	11.0	17.5	20.7	12.5	11.5	4.1	6.7	1977
San Francisco, CA	0.1	5.4	6.3	4.2	5.4	7.2	7.9	8.6	8.8	46.2	1944
San Jose, CA	0.2	6.4	9.2	10.1	12.5	24.3	18.0	11.1	2.8	5.3	1975
Santa Rosa, CA	0.5	4.6	12.5	13.2	17.9	21.1	12.0	8.1	4.7	5.5	1979
Savannah, GA	0.1	9.6	9.7	6.5	10.9	11.5	12.2	14.5	8.0	17.0	1969
Seattle, WA	0.1	14.7	11.9	8.3	7.6	7.7	8.3	9.1	8.0	24.2	1971
Sioux Falls, SD	0.3	17.8	17.9	14.7	9.7	12.1	7.0	8.3	3.1	9.1	1990
Springfield, IL	<0.1	3.0	8.6	13.0	8.8	17.4	12.6	10.8	6.0	19.7	1971
Tampa, FL	0.3	10.8	17.3	12.5	11.9	11.3	9.3	13.0	5.1	8.6	1982
Tucson, AZ	0.1	3.4	12.6	13.3	17.2	20.5	11.0	13.9	4.6	3.4	1978
Tulsa, OK	0.1	4.6	6.2	9.2	13.4	20.6	14.4	16.5	6.4	8.7	1972
Tuscaloosa, AL	0.1	16.7	16.7	14.4	11.6	14.9	9.8	8.3	3.9	3.6	1988
Virginia Beach, VA	0.1	6.4	11.1	14.1	27.1	20.4	12.4	6.1	1.2	1.1	1983
Washington, DC	0.2	10.3	7.9	3.1	4.7	6.8	11.1	12.1	10.8	32.9	1955
Wichita, KS	0.1	5.9	9.9	12.2	12.3	13.1	9.8	18.6	8.0	10.2	1973
Wilmington, NC	0.1	10.8	15.0	17.3	15.3	12.9	6.7	6.8	5.5	9.6	1986
Winston-Salem, NC	0.1	6.4	13.2	13.0	14.3	16.4	11.8	12.2	4.9	7.7	1978
Worcester, MA	0.0	2.1	4.6	5.2	10.1	7.9	7.8	11.6	7.5	43.3	1949
U.S.	0.2	7.3	13.6	13.6	13.2	14.8	10.3	10.0	4.7	12.2	1979

Note: Figures are percentages except for median year
Source: U.S. Census Bureau, 2017-2021 American Community Survey 5-Year Estimates

Year Housing Structure Built: Metro Area

Metro Area	2020 or Later	2010-2019	2000-2009	1990-1999	1980-1989	1970-1979	1960-1969	1950-1959	1940-1949	Before 1940	Median Year
Albuquerque, NM	0.2	5.9	17.2	17.3	16.8	17.8	8.7	9.3	3.6	3.2	1984
Allentown, PA	0.1	4.0	11.4	10.3	11.0	12.0	9.5	10.9	5.2	25.7	1969
Anchorage, AK	0.1	6.4	17.2	13.3	25.0	23.5	8.3	4.7	1.0	0.5	1985
Ann Arbor, MI	0.2	4.8	12.8	17.0	11.2	16.0	12.4	9.7	4.5	11.5	1977
Athens, GA	0.2	7.5	17.8	20.4	16.4	15.2	10.0	5.3	1.9	5.2	1988
Atlanta, GA	0.3	9.4	23.6	20.8	17.1	12.4	7.3	4.5	1.7	2.8	1992
Austin, TX	0.6	22.4	22.8	16.7	15.5	10.6	4.9	3.0	1.5	2.1	1997
Baltimore, MD	0.1	6.0	9.4	13.4	13.4	12.9	10.4	12.8	6.2	15.4	1974
Boise City, ID	0.5	14.3	23.2	20.7	9.8	14.1	5.2	4.3	2.8	5.2	1994
Boston, MA	0.1	5.8	7.5	7.4	10.4	10.8	10.1	10.7	5.0	32.2	1962
Boulder, CO	0.2	9.4	11.7	19.4	16.4	19.7	10.6	4.8	1.3	6.3	1984
Brownsville, TX	0.2	11.0	22.2	17.0	17.9	16.0	5.7	5.3	2.6	2.1	1990
Cape Coral, FL	0.2	8.9	29.7	17.4	21.0	14.4	5.2	2.2	0.4	0.6	1994
Cedar Rapids, IA	0.1	8.3	13.7	12.7	7.2	13.8	12.3	10.4	3.5	18.0	1974
Charleston, SC	0.3	16.4	20.8	15.5	15.4	13.0	7.7	4.8	2.4	3.7	1992
Charlotte, NC	0.2	13.6	22.6	18.9	12.9	10.8	7.7	6.3	2.9	4.1	1993
Chicago, IL	0.1	3.6	11.4	11.2	9.1	14.1	11.5	12.7	5.9	20.5	1969
Cincinnati, OH	0.1	5.3	12.0	13.8	10.7	13.8	10.5	11.6	4.8	17.3	1974
Clarksville, TN	0.4	13.8	19.7	20.2	12.2	13.9	7.9	6.0	2.9	3.0	1992
Cleveland, OH	0.1	3.4	6.8	8.9	6.9	12.4	13.6	17.7	7.6	22.5	1962
College Station, TX	0.6	17.0	18.8	18.0	16.6	14.4	6.0	4.3	2.1	2.3	1992
Colorado Springs, CO	0.3	10.7	17.8	16.4	17.6	16.2	8.1	6.2	1.6	5.1	1987
Columbia, MO	<0.1	12.1	18.1	17.6	13.2	14.8	9.6	4.7	2.6	7.2	1988
Columbia, SC	0.3	11.3	18.6	18.3	13.7	14.9	9.2	6.7	3.2	3.7	1989
Columbus, OH	0.2	8.0	14.2	15.9	11.6	13.8	10.7	9.8	3.7	12.2	1980
Dallas, TX	0.4	14.0	19.1	15.6	17.3	13.3	8.3	7.1	2.4	2.6	1989
Davenport, IA	0.1	4.6	7.9	8.5	6.8	15.9	12.8	12.1	7.2	24.2	1965
Denver, CO	0.3	10.7	16.0	14.8	13.8	17.2	9.0	9.0	2.6	6.5	1984
Des Moines, IA	0.3	14.1	15.7	12.5	8.0	13.3	7.9	8.8	3.9	15.4	1981
Durham, NC	0.5	13.4	17.9	18.2	15.3	12.0	8.4	6.1	2.9	5.3	1990
Edison, NJ	0.1	4.1	6.5	6.2	7.8	9.7	13.5	15.6	8.5	28.1	1959
El Paso, TX	0.2	14.0	15.8	14.1	14.5	15.2	9.2	9.4	3.3	4.3	1986
Fargo, ND	0.4	17.5	17.3	13.6	10.2	15.0	6.8	7.8	2.5	8.9	1989
Fort Collins, CO	0.4	14.9	18.1	19.1	12.4	17.9	6.6	3.3	1.8	5.6	1991
Fort Wayne, IN	0.2	5.9	11.5	14.3	10.4	15.3	12.4	11.0	5.4	13.7	1975
Fort Worth, TX	0.4	14.0	19.1	15.6	17.3	13.3	8.3	7.1	2.4	2.6	1989
Grand Rapids, MI	0.2	6.9	12.6	15.8	11.3	13.6	9.3	10.0	5.1	15.2	1978
Greeley, CO	0.7	16.2	26.7	15.4	7.2	14.6	5.6	3.9	1.9	7.7	1996
Green Bay, WI	<0.1	7.5	13.4	16.3	11.6	15.4	9.8	9.5	4.3	12.3	1979
Greensboro, NC	0.1	7.3	15.8	17.9	14.5	14.4	10.4	9.5	4.1	6.0	1984
Honolulu, HI	0.1	6.7	9.7	11.8	12.4	24.3	17.9	10.1	3.8	3.1	1976
Houston, TX	0.4	15.6	20.3	13.9	15.3	15.8	8.1	5.9	2.4	2.4	1990
Huntsville, AL	0.2	14.6	18.9	16.7	16.1	10.6	13.0	5.9	1.9	2.1	1990
Indianapolis, IN	0.2	8.8	14.9	16.3	10.3	12.1	10.6	10.1	4.5	12.3	1980
Jacksonville, FL	0.7	11.2	21.2	15.9	16.4	12.0	7.7	7.7	3.2	4.0	1989
Kansas City, MO	0.2	7.1	13.3	14.1	12.0	14.7	11.7	11.0	4.3	11.7	1978
Lafayette, LA	0.2	12.8	14.8	12.9	15.8	15.9	10.3	9.0	3.7	4.5	1984
Las Cruces, NM	0.2	11.0	17.9	19.3	18.3	15.3	7.0	6.3	1.9	2.7	1989
Las Vegas, NV	0.3	10.0	29.1	27.6	14.2	10.6	4.9	2.1	0.7	0.4	1996
Lexington, KY	0.2	8.7	16.1	17.4	13.4	14.8	11.1	7.7	3.0	7.6	1984
Lincoln, NE	0.1	10.1	13.5	14.2	10.1	15.6	9.6	9.8	3.3	13.7	1979
Little Rock, AR	0.3	12.0	17.4	16.6	14.0	15.9	10.0	6.8	3.2	3.8	1987
Los Angeles, CA	0.1	4.2	6.1	7.7	12.4	16.1	15.5	18.2	8.0	11.7	1968
Louisville, KY	0.2	6.7	12.8	13.8	9.2	14.8	12.1	12.2	5.9	12.3	1975
Madison, WI	0.2	9.4	15.4	15.5	10.7	14.3	9.5	7.6	3.5	13.9	1981

Table continued on following page.

Appendix A: Comparative Statistics   A-123

Metro Area	2020 or Later	2010 -2019	2000 -2009	1990 -1999	1980 -1989	1970 -1979	1960 -1969	1950 -1959	1940 -1949	Before 1940	Median Year
Manchester, NH	0.1	4.2	9.7	10.9	20.4	15.6	9.5	7.0	3.8	18.8	1977
Miami, FL	0.2	6.0	12.7	14.6	19.2	21.0	11.9	9.8	2.7	2.1	1981
Midland, TX	0.2	19.5	11.0	14.2	17.8	10.9	7.8	14.6	2.6	1.4	1987
Milwaukee, WI	0.1	4.2	8.2	10.9	7.8	12.9	11.5	15.7	6.9	21.8	1965
Minneapolis, MN	0.2	7.0	13.5	13.9	14.2	14.3	9.8	9.5	3.7	13.8	1979
Nashville, TN	0.6	15.4	18.5	16.8	13.5	12.5	8.8	6.4	2.8	4.5	1991
New Haven, CT	<0.1	2.5	5.8	7.4	12.6	13.6	12.2	14.8	7.1	23.9	1963
New Orleans, LA	0.2	5.1	12.1	10.0	13.3	19.0	12.9	9.7	4.6	13.0	1975
New York, NY	0.1	4.1	6.5	6.2	7.8	9.7	13.5	15.6	8.5	28.1	1959
Oklahoma City, OK	0.3	11.8	14.7	11.0	14.3	16.8	11.4	9.2	4.6	5.9	1981
Omaha, NE	0.3	9.0	14.4	12.5	9.8	14.1	11.7	8.4	3.5	16.3	1977
Orlando, FL	0.3	12.7	22.2	19.4	19.4	12.6	5.8	5.1	1.2	1.5	1992
Philadelphia, PA	0.1	4.3	7.9	9.4	9.8	12.0	12.0	15.3	7.2	22.0	1965
Phoenix, AZ	0.3	9.8	24.5	19.4	16.8	15.4	6.9	4.8	1.2	0.9	1992
Pittsburgh, PA	0.1	4.0	6.2	7.6	7.7	12.0	11.4	16.5	8.6	25.9	1959
Portland, OR	0.3	9.2	14.0	17.3	11.3	16.7	8.2	6.9	4.5	11.7	1982
Providence, RI	0.1	2.7	6.1	8.1	11.2	12.1	10.7	11.5	6.0	31.4	1961
Provo, UT	0.4	19.6	24.2	17.6	8.9	12.7	4.7	5.0	2.7	4.2	1997
Raleigh, NC	0.5	17.9	23.9	21.6	14.6	8.6	5.4	3.4	1.4	2.7	1996
Reno, NV	0.7	8.8	20.1	18.8	14.8	18.9	8.6	4.7	2.3	2.3	1989
Richmond, VA	0.2	8.7	14.2	15.0	15.6	14.5	9.6	8.8	4.3	9.0	1982
Rochester, MN	0.3	9.6	17.9	14.4	10.8	13.2	9.0	7.6	3.4	13.8	1983
Sacramento, CA	0.2	5.3	16.9	14.9	16.7	18.0	10.6	9.7	3.4	4.2	1982
St. Louis, MO	0.2	5.3	11.4	12.1	11.1	13.0	12.6	12.6	5.5	16.2	1972
Salem, OR	0.2	6.5	13.4	17.3	9.7	22.3	10.3	8.0	4.0	8.4	1979
Salt Lake City, UT	0.2	12.6	14.8	15.1	11.9	17.4	8.6	8.3	3.5	7.5	1984
San Antonio, TX	0.5	16.2	19.2	13.9	14.5	12.4	8.0	7.2	3.8	4.3	1990
San Diego, CA	0.2	5.1	11.8	12.2	18.6	22.2	11.9	10.5	3.4	4.2	1979
San Francisco, CA	0.1	4.6	7.6	8.1	10.9	14.7	13.1	13.6	7.7	19.7	1967
San Jose, CA	0.2	7.5	8.9	10.0	12.1	21.3	17.6	13.9	3.5	5.0	1975
Santa Rosa, CA	0.3	4.0	10.3	13.7	18.2	20.6	11.6	8.9	4.4	8.0	1978
Savannah, GA	0.3	13.3	19.8	14.7	13.2	11.2	7.6	7.8	4.2	8.0	1989
Seattle, WA	0.2	10.6	14.7	15.2	14.1	13.4	10.8	7.1	4.2	9.7	1983
Sioux Falls, SD	0.2	16.0	18.0	14.9	8.7	12.7	6.7	7.4	3.2	12.2	1989
Springfield, IL	<0.1	4.3	10.0	13.2	8.7	17.3	11.7	11.0	6.0	17.8	1972
Tampa, FL	0.3	8.2	15.8	14.0	19.9	19.9	9.1	8.3	2.0	2.6	1984
Tucson, AZ	0.2	6.2	18.1	17.3	17.7	19.1	8.4	8.2	2.8	2.0	1985
Tulsa, OK	0.3	9.1	13.7	12.1	14.1	18.8	10.5	10.5	4.3	6.7	1980
Tuscaloosa, AL	0.1	12.4	18.5	18.3	13.5	14.7	9.0	6.6	3.2	3.6	1989
Virginia Beach, VA	0.2	8.0	12.6	14.8	18.4	15.2	11.6	9.3	4.2	5.7	1982
Washington, DC	0.2	9.0	14.0	14.0	15.4	13.5	11.8	8.9	4.9	8.3	1982
Wichita, KS	0.1	6.7	11.8	13.5	12.4	13.1	8.8	16.4	6.5	10.7	1976
Wilmington, NC	0.3	12.4	20.4	20.9	15.1	12.0	5.6	4.6	3.4	5.3	1992
Winston-Salem, NC	0.1	6.8	15.2	16.6	14.8	16.6	10.2	9.2	4.1	6.2	1982
Worcester, MA	0.1	3.8	8.7	9.5	12.4	11.3	8.9	11.0	5.6	28.9	1965
U.S.	0.2	7.3	13.6	13.6	13.2	14.8	10.3	10.0	4.7	12.2	1979

Note: Figures are percentages except for median year; Figures cover the Metropolitan Statistical Area
Source: U.S. Census Bureau, 2017-2021 American Community Survey 5-Year Estimates

Gross Monthly Rent: City

City	Under $500	$500-$999	$1,000-$1,499	$1,500-$1,999	$2,000-$2,499	$2,500-$2,999	$3,000 and up	Median ($)
Albuquerque, NM	7.3	49.4	31.5	9.8	1.1	0.5	0.5	932
Allentown, PA	7.6	31.1	44.6	14.9	1.3	0.3	0.3	1,100
Anchorage, AK	4.8	20.1	34.7	23.1	11.6	4.0	1.8	1,350
Ann Arbor, MI	3.9	17.0	37.0	24.4	9.7	3.5	4.4	1,382
Athens, GA	5.4	52.2	29.1	9.4	2.2	0.8	0.8	939
Atlanta, GA	11.0	18.0	31.3	25.2	9.2	2.9	2.4	1,342
Austin, TX	2.8	10.6	43.9	26.9	10.3	3.0	2.6	1,415
Baltimore, MD	14.9	22.2	37.2	17.6	5.5	1.5	1.1	1,146
Boise City, ID	4.2	34.8	42.3	15.3	1.9	0.7	0.8	1,103
Boston, MA	14.1	10.7	13.3	20.9	17.7	9.6	13.6	1,783
Boulder, CO	3.1	6.2	29.1	27.4	16.5	6.4	11.3	1,711
Brownsville, TX	20.5	54.9	19.9	3.9	0.7	0.2	0.0	794
Cape Coral, FL	1.2	11.9	40.8	37.8	5.8	0.9	1.5	1,456
Cedar Rapids, IA	12.8	56.9	24.8	3.1	0.6	0.2	1.7	836
Charleston, SC	5.1	13.9	39.7	27.1	8.4	2.8	3.0	1,400
Charlotte, NC	3.4	19.6	48.2	21.7	4.5	1.5	1.2	1,260
Chicago, IL	8.6	25.4	32.7	17.7	8.6	3.9	3.2	1,209
Cincinnati, OH	15.9	52.7	21.5	6.4	2.1	0.7	0.7	814
Clarksville, TN	4.2	44.4	38.0	10.4	2.6	0.3	0.1	1,016
Cleveland, OH	20.3	53.7	19.1	4.7	1.3	0.6	0.4	774
College Station, TX	2.2	44.2	33.0	14.9	3.9	1.4	0.5	1,042
Colorado Springs, CO	3.3	21.7	39.4	25.1	6.5	2.8	1.2	1,300
Columbia, MO	5.7	52.3	30.3	6.6	4.2	0.8	0.1	935
Columbia, SC	10.3	38.9	37.0	11.2	2.0	0.3	0.3	1,007
Columbus, OH	5.2	37.8	43.6	10.1	2.3	0.4	0.6	1,061
Dallas, TX	3.5	28.7	42.6	16.5	5.2	1.7	1.8	1,178
Davenport, IA	9.4	61.7	21.9	4.3	0.7	0.5	1.5	815
Denver, CO	7.1	10.5	32.7	27.6	14.0	5.1	3.0	1,495
Des Moines, IA	7.8	52.1	31.7	6.4	1.7	0.2	0.2	916
Durham, NC	6.7	26.5	44.8	17.4	3.1	0.4	1.1	1,157
Edison, NJ	3.2	3.3	26.6	39.0	22.8	4.0	1.1	1,716
El Paso, TX	12.3	48.4	31.0	6.7	1.2	0.3	0.2	910
Fargo, ND	5.7	65.4	21.2	5.3	1.9	0.3	0.2	841
Fort Collins, CO	2.0	17.4	34.7	28.6	13.4	2.2	1.7	1,443
Fort Wayne, IN	9.5	63.9	22.8	3.0	0.4	0.2	0.2	823
Fort Worth, TX	3.7	28.4	40.5	19.2	5.9	1.4	0.9	1,187
Grand Rapids, MI	10.7	38.1	37.4	9.2	3.4	0.8	0.4	1,013
Greeley, CO	9.1	29.7	37.4	16.2	6.0	1.1	0.5	1,134
Green Bay, WI	9.1	66.5	22.1	1.8	0.2	0.0	0.2	805
Greensboro, NC	5.7	53.2	33.2	5.9	1.2	0.3	0.6	944
Honolulu, HI	6.7	10.1	27.5	24.0	13.2	7.9	10.7	1,620
Houston, TX	3.4	34.1	38.9	15.8	4.4	1.5	1.8	1,136
Huntsville, AL	7.5	52.1	31.9	6.8	0.7	0.5	0.5	912
Indianapolis, IN	6.0	49.3	34.3	7.9	1.7	0.4	0.4	962
Jacksonville, FL	5.4	29.0	43.7	17.5	3.6	0.5	0.4	1,146
Kansas City, MO	7.2	39.0	38.6	11.6	2.4	0.7	0.5	1,040
Lafayette, LA	6.9	50.5	32.1	8.7	1.0	0.2	0.6	948
Las Cruces, NM	13.0	56.6	25.0	4.0	1.0	0.1	0.4	824
Las Vegas, NV	4.0	25.7	42.9	20.6	4.9	1.0	0.9	1,219
Lexington, KY	6.4	47.7	34.5	8.1	2.3	0.5	0.4	967
Lincoln, NE	6.2	53.4	30.1	7.6	1.4	0.3	1.1	920
Little Rock, AR	7.8	49.3	33.3	6.7	1.4	0.7	0.8	940
Los Angeles, CA	4.9	11.1	27.1	24.6	15.1	8.1	9.2	1,641
Louisville, KY	11.4	47.2	32.6	6.8	1.2	0.2	0.6	931
Madison, WI	4.2	25.0	44.1	17.9	5.5	1.6	1.7	1,212

Table continued on following page.

City	Under $500	$500 -$999	$1,000 -$1,499	$1,500 -$1,999	$2,000 -$2,499	$2,500 -$2,999	$3,000 and up	Median ($)
Manchester, NH	7.0	21.3	43.4	20.8	5.4	1.4	0.8	1,220
Miami, FL	9.1	17.6	31.5	20.1	11.7	5.0	4.9	1,361
Midland, TX	2.8	19.5	44.3	19.5	9.2	3.6	1.1	1,273
Milwaukee, WI	7.7	55.0	28.4	6.3	1.6	0.6	0.4	910
Minneapolis, MN	10.9	27.0	33.1	17.8	7.4	2.0	1.9	1,159
Nashville, TN	7.4	20.6	41.1	20.6	6.9	1.9	1.5	1,250
New Haven, CT	13.5	14.2	40.8	20.6	7.4	2.4	1.1	1,267
New Orleans, LA	10.9	31.7	36.8	13.8	4.6	1.2	0.8	1,079
New York, NY	9.5	12.4	24.4	23.3	13.3	6.6	10.5	1,579
Oklahoma City, OK	6.5	51.2	32.1	7.8	1.6	0.4	0.4	933
Omaha, NE	5.4	44.7	36.8	10.2	1.6	0.4	0.9	999
Orlando, FL	3.4	15.1	45.7	26.9	6.3	1.6	1.1	1,346
Philadelphia, PA	9.3	27.7	38.4	15.3	5.5	2.0	1.8	1,149
Phoenix, AZ	3.8	28.5	43.3	18.5	4.2	0.9	0.8	1,175
Pittsburgh, PA	13.0	33.7	31.0	13.9	5.5	2.0	0.9	1,043
Portland, OR	5.6	14.2	37.6	25.6	10.8	3.9	2.3	1,406
Providence, RI	19.3	21.5	38.2	14.8	3.7	1.3	1.2	1,098
Provo, UT	9.1	44.7	29.6	11.4	4.1	0.5	0.6	973
Raleigh, NC	3.2	19.5	52.4	19.0	4.3	0.9	0.9	1,237
Reno, NV	5.7	27.4	37.5	21.1	6.4	1.0	1.0	1,213
Richmond, VA	11.2	26.1	41.7	16.2	3.6	0.6	0.7	1,132
Rochester, MN	7.8	34.8	32.6	17.7	3.4	1.3	2.4	1,120
Sacramento, CA	5.5	16.1	33.0	30.1	11.3	2.5	1.6	1,434
St. Louis, MO	10.6	54.3	26.8	6.1	1.7	0.3	0.2	873
Salem, OR	6.3	30.7	43.7	15.2	2.8	0.6	0.7	1,125
Salt Lake City, UT	8.0	30.3	36.6	17.7	5.4	1.2	0.8	1,141
San Antonio, TX	6.2	34.8	41.6	13.5	2.6	0.7	0.6	1,090
San Diego, CA	2.7	6.1	19.8	27.8	21.3	11.6	10.7	1,885
San Francisco, CA	8.6	10.0	13.7	14.1	13.3	11.6	28.5	2,130
San Jose, CA	3.7	5.6	9.3	17.0	19.6	18.0	26.7	2,366
Santa Rosa, CA	4.9	5.3	21.2	27.5	21.2	11.7	8.1	1,837
Savannah, GA	8.6	29.0	45.1	13.3	2.8	0.5	0.7	1,116
Seattle, WA	5.4	6.3	21.6	27.9	19.6	9.7	9.6	1,801
Sioux Falls, SD	6.2	58.7	27.7	5.7	0.6	0.4	0.8	892
Springfield, IL	10.6	58.7	23.8	4.8	0.9	0.8	0.4	852
Tampa, FL	7.4	21.2	39.2	19.4	8.2	2.4	2.1	1,249
Tucson, AZ	6.0	53.6	30.2	8.0	1.2	0.5	0.6	907
Tulsa, OK	8.9	54.8	28.8	4.8	1.3	0.5	0.9	882
Tuscaloosa, AL	11.0	51.3	28.3	5.9	2.0	0.6	0.9	907
Virginia Beach, VA	2.3	9.1	45.2	30.5	8.6	2.5	1.8	1,433
Washington, DC	9.2	10.4	22.3	22.4	15.2	9.2	11.3	1,681
Wichita, KS	8.1	60.2	26.3	3.9	0.8	0.2	0.5	856
Wilmington, NC	10.1	31.3	40.1	15.0	2.5	0.5	0.6	1,093
Winston-Salem, NC	8.8	57.2	26.5	5.3	1.3	0.3	0.6	871
Worcester, MA	13.8	21.1	41.4	18.7	3.6	0.7	0.7	1,179
U.S.	8.1	30.5	30.8	16.8	7.3	3.1	3.5	1,163

Note: Figures are percentages except for Median; Gross rent is the contract rent plus the estimated average monthly cost of utilities (electricity, gas, and water and sewer) and fuels (oil, coal, kerosene, wood, etc.) if these are paid by the renter (or paid for the renter by someone else).
Source: U.S. Census Bureau, 2017-2021 American Community Survey 5-Year Estimates

Gross Monthly Rent: Metro Area

MSA[1]	Under $500	$500 -$999	$1,000 -$1,499	$1,500 -$1,999	$2,000 -$2,499	$2,500 -2,999	$3,000 and up	Median ($)
Albuquerque, NM	7.2	47.4	32.9	10.2	1.3	0.4	0.5	952
Allentown, PA	8.9	28.4	39.4	17.7	3.9	0.9	0.9	1,141
Anchorage, AK	5.1	21.7	34.9	22.4	10.8	3.5	1.5	1,314
Ann Arbor, MI	5.1	24.0	40.6	18.9	6.1	2.2	3.1	1,218
Athens, GA	5.6	51.9	28.9	9.1	2.7	0.9	0.8	939
Atlanta, GA	4.3	19.1	43.9	23.8	6.2	1.5	1.2	1,294
Austin, TX	2.6	12.4	43.5	26.5	9.9	2.7	2.4	1,398
Baltimore, MD	8.2	14.4	35.1	26.4	11.0	3.0	2.0	1,387
Boise City, ID	6.5	32.7	40.5	16.2	2.6	0.8	0.7	1,107
Boston, MA	10.9	10.8	20.5	24.5	16.4	8.4	8.6	1,659
Boulder, CO	3.5	7.0	27.3	31.3	15.9	6.9	8.0	1,694
Brownsville, TX	18.4	59.0	18.3	3.2	0.7	0.2	0.2	785
Cape Coral, FL	3.6	19.1	45.6	21.7	5.9	1.8	2.4	1,307
Cedar Rapids, IA	13.4	57.1	23.0	4.2	0.8	0.1	1.4	806
Charleston, SC	4.6	20.9	43.3	20.1	6.9	2.0	2.1	1,274
Charlotte, NC	4.8	31.3	41.3	16.7	3.6	1.2	1.0	1,147
Chicago, IL	6.9	25.3	36.0	18.6	7.6	2.9	2.5	1,209
Cincinnati, OH	10.6	49.6	28.4	7.8	2.1	0.7	0.8	906
Clarksville, TN	7.7	45.9	35.8	8.3	1.9	0.2	0.1	967
Cleveland, OH	11.5	52.2	27.1	6.5	1.4	0.5	0.8	880
College Station, TX	5.0	44.7	32.9	12.3	3.1	1.2	0.7	1,003
Colorado Springs, CO	3.3	20.8	36.2	28.6	7.6	2.6	1.1	1,349
Columbia, MO	7.4	52.9	29.9	5.6	3.5	0.6	0.2	917
Columbia, SC	7.1	43.7	35.6	9.8	2.7	0.5	0.5	993
Columbus, OH	6.0	38.6	41.3	10.3	2.4	0.7	0.6	1,049
Dallas, TX	2.6	22.1	43.0	21.2	7.7	1.9	1.5	1,264
Davenport, IA	12.9	58.7	21.1	4.7	1.2	0.4	1.1	808
Denver, CO	4.5	9.6	32.5	31.5	14.2	5.0	2.7	1,554
Des Moines, IA	6.8	46.8	34.7	8.9	2.0	0.3	0.6	972
Durham, NC	6.6	30.7	41.7	15.5	3.6	0.7	1.3	1,127
Edison, NJ	8.4	11.4	26.5	24.9	13.4	6.3	9.1	1,573
El Paso, TX	12.0	48.6	30.8	7.0	1.2	0.2	0.2	908
Fargo, ND	6.6	60.9	22.5	7.6	1.6	0.4	0.3	855
Fort Collins, CO	2.8	17.7	34.1	28.7	12.2	2.9	1.7	1,433
Fort Wayne, IN	8.9	62.4	23.7	4.1	0.6	0.2	0.2	839
Fort Worth, TX	2.6	22.1	43.0	21.2	7.7	1.9	1.5	1,264
Grand Rapids, MI	8.4	45.1	34.9	7.7	2.5	0.9	0.6	973
Greeley, CO	7.1	26.4	33.6	21.2	7.5	2.6	1.6	1,234
Green Bay, WI	6.8	64.8	24.4	2.9	0.3	0.3	0.4	851
Greensboro, NC	9.0	55.6	28.9	4.6	1.1	0.3	0.6	900
Honolulu, HI	5.4	8.4	20.9	20.8	15.0	12.0	17.6	1,870
Houston, TX	3.3	29.1	39.7	19.2	5.7	1.5	1.6	1,189
Huntsville, AL	8.0	51.8	30.9	7.1	1.1	0.6	0.5	912
Indianapolis, IN	5.7	46.0	35.5	9.7	2.0	0.5	0.6	987
Jacksonville, FL	4.9	27.9	41.7	18.9	4.6	1.0	1.0	1,175
Kansas City, MO	6.5	38.5	38.5	11.8	3.0	0.8	0.9	1,052
Lafayette, LA	13.8	54.5	25.3	4.8	1.1	0.1	0.4	853
Las Cruces, NM	16.4	55.8	22.5	3.8	1.2	0.1	0.3	785
Las Vegas, NV	2.3	24.0	42.7	23.4	5.6	1.2	0.8	1,257
Lexington, KY	7.5	50.4	32.5	7.0	1.8	0.4	0.3	934
Lincoln, NE	6.5	53.2	30.0	7.4	1.5	0.3	1.1	918
Little Rock, AR	8.1	55.9	29.1	5.3	0.9	0.4	0.4	893
Los Angeles, CA	3.8	8.7	24.8	26.8	17.5	8.9	9.5	1,737
Louisville, KY	11.0	47.2	33.5	6.2	1.3	0.2	0.6	934
Madison, WI	4.5	31.5	41.8	15.7	4.3	1.1	1.2	1,143

Table continued on following page.

MSA[1]	Under $500	$500 -$999	$1,000 -$1,499	$1,500 -$1,999	$2,000 -$2,499	$2,500 -2,999	$3,000 and up	Median ($)
Manchester, NH	6.7	18.6	40.2	24.7	6.8	1.9	1.1	1,305
Miami, FL	4.5	11.5	34.6	28.5	12.9	4.5	3.6	1,492
Midland, TX	4.2	19.9	43.6	19.0	9.0	3.3	1.0	1,271
Milwaukee, WI	6.9	48.0	32.3	9.1	2.4	0.7	0.5	963
Minneapolis, MN	8.1	24.0	37.9	20.4	6.3	1.7	1.6	1,207
Nashville, TN	6.7	25.1	39.7	20.0	5.7	1.6	1.2	1,211
New Haven, CT	10.6	19.5	41.4	19.9	5.6	1.6	1.4	1,223
New Orleans, LA	8.0	35.7	39.3	12.2	3.5	0.7	0.6	1,064
New York, NY	8.4	11.4	26.5	24.9	13.4	6.3	9.1	1,573
Oklahoma City, OK	6.8	50.2	32.3	8.0	1.6	0.5	0.6	937
Omaha, NE	6.4	43.7	36.5	10.2	1.7	0.5	1.2	1,000
Orlando, FL	2.7	16.2	43.2	27.2	7.5	1.9	1.2	1,363
Philadelphia, PA	7.2	22.3	40.2	19.2	6.7	2.3	2.0	1,230
Phoenix, AZ	3.0	23.1	41.3	22.9	6.3	1.7	1.7	1,268
Pittsburgh, PA	14.0	47.0	26.4	7.9	2.9	0.9	0.9	892
Portland, OR	4.1	12.6	38.8	28.4	10.8	3.2	2.0	1,434
Providence, RI	14.9	29.3	35.5	14.2	4.1	1.0	0.9	1,066
Provo, UT	4.6	31.0	36.2	20.0	6.2	1.0	1.1	1,193
Raleigh, NC	4.4	22.5	46.4	19.1	5.2	1.2	1.2	1,230
Reno, NV	4.8	26.6	36.7	22.2	6.7	1.5	1.5	1,250
Richmond, VA	6.6	23.4	45.3	18.7	3.9	0.9	1.2	1,202
Rochester, MN	10.2	39.0	30.7	14.7	2.8	1.0	1.8	1,013
Sacramento, CA	4.3	14.1	34.2	27.8	13.3	3.9	2.5	1,465
St. Louis, MO	7.9	47.8	33.0	7.6	2.1	0.6	1.1	952
Salem, OR	5.9	30.4	45.3	14.0	2.9	1.0	0.5	1,128
Salt Lake City, UT	4.6	21.7	43.4	22.2	6.0	1.1	0.9	1,253
San Antonio, TX	5.6	32.5	41.5	15.3	3.5	0.9	0.7	1,122
San Diego, CA	2.9	5.9	21.1	29.4	19.7	10.6	10.4	1,842
San Francisco, CA	5.6	7.0	13.2	18.3	19.2	14.0	22.8	2,155
San Jose, CA	3.0	4.7	7.8	14.7	19.4	18.5	31.9	2,511
Santa Rosa, CA	4.8	7.8	19.2	25.6	21.0	11.3	10.3	1,856
Savannah, GA	5.5	26.3	47.1	16.1	3.7	0.6	0.6	1,161
Seattle, WA	4.3	8.4	25.0	30.5	17.7	7.5	6.6	1,701
Sioux Falls, SD	7.0	57.8	27.5	5.8	0.8	0.3	0.7	889
Springfield, IL	10.4	57.4	25.5	4.8	0.8	0.6	0.5	857
Tampa, FL	4.1	24.2	42.4	19.8	6.2	1.8	1.5	1,230
Tucson, AZ	5.5	46.8	33.6	10.3	1.9	0.8	1.1	976
Tulsa, OK	8.7	51.9	30.3	6.3	1.6	0.4	0.8	909
Tuscaloosa, AL	14.9	50.5	27.1	4.8	1.5	0.6	0.5	879
Virginia Beach, VA	6.1	22.2	42.3	21.1	5.5	1.5	1.3	1,227
Washington, DC	4.3	6.4	20.9	32.5	19.2	8.6	8.1	1,783
Wichita, KS	8.8	57.8	26.3	5.4	0.9	0.4	0.5	868
Wilmington, NC	8.0	29.7	41.7	15.1	3.2	1.5	0.8	1,118
Winston-Salem, NC	11.0	59.4	23.7	4.3	1.0	0.2	0.4	834
Worcester, MA	13.2	26.4	37.7	15.9	4.7	1.2	1.0	1,126
U.S.	8.1	30.5	30.8	16.8	7.3	3.1	3.5	1,163

Note: (1) Figures cover the Metropolitan Statistical Area (MSA); Figures are percentages except for Median; Gross rent is the contract rent plus the estimated average monthly cost of utilities (electricity, gas, and water and sewer) and fuels (oil, coal, kerosene, wood, etc.) if these are paid by the renter (or paid for the renter by someone else).
Source: U.S. Census Bureau, 2017-2021 American Community Survey 5-Year Estimates

Highest Level of Education: City

City	Less than H.S.	H.S. Diploma	Some College, No Deg.	Associate Degree	Bachelors Degree	Masters Degree	Profess. School Degree	Doctorate Degree
Albuquerque, NM	9.1	21.8	22.7	9.1	20.4	11.5	2.9	2.6
Allentown, PA	19.4	36.5	19.3	7.5	11.5	3.8	1.1	0.8
Anchorage, AK	5.8	23.7	25.0	8.6	22.8	9.8	2.8	1.3
Ann Arbor, MI	2.2	7.6	8.9	4.0	30.5	26.8	8.3	11.6
Athens, GA	10.3	19.2	17.0	6.4	23.4	14.8	2.7	6.1
Atlanta, GA	7.9	17.5	13.6	5.4	31.6	15.8	5.6	2.7
Austin, TX	9.4	14.4	15.7	5.4	34.2	14.9	3.5	2.6
Baltimore, MD	13.7	28.1	18.8	5.2	17.2	11.3	3.2	2.5
Boise City, ID	4.8	20.4	22.8	8.3	28.0	10.8	2.8	2.0
Boston, MA	11.8	18.5	12.9	4.7	27.8	15.7	5.1	3.6
Boulder, CO	3.1	5.9	10.6	3.6	37.1	25.0	5.7	9.0
Brownsville, TX	32.0	24.2	16.0	7.3	14.6	4.7	0.9	0.3
Cape Coral, FL	7.1	37.1	23.0	9.2	15.6	5.3	1.5	1.3
Cedar Rapids, IA	6.2	25.7	22.8	12.5	22.7	7.2	2.0	0.8
Charleston, SC	4.2	16.8	16.1	7.3	34.5	13.6	4.8	2.9
Charlotte, NC	10.3	16.9	19.2	7.9	29.5	12.2	2.9	1.2
Chicago, IL	13.7	21.9	17.0	5.7	24.1	12.2	3.6	1.8
Cincinnati, OH	11.4	24.0	17.6	7.4	23.0	11.0	3.4	2.2
Clarksville, TN	6.4	26.9	26.3	11.6	18.7	8.2	0.8	1.1
Cleveland, OH	17.4	33.3	22.8	7.4	11.4	5.2	1.7	0.8
College Station, TX	5.2	13.1	17.0	6.7	30.3	15.4	2.1	10.3
Colorado Springs, CO	6.1	19.1	24.0	10.7	24.3	12.0	2.3	1.7
Columbia, MO	4.5	17.5	17.6	6.6	28.4	15.5	4.6	5.3
Columbia, SC	9.5	19.3	18.8	7.7	25.1	11.7	4.5	3.3
Columbus, OH	9.7	24.8	20.3	7.4	24.3	10.0	2.1	1.6
Dallas, TX	20.4	21.8	17.4	4.8	22.1	9.0	3.2	1.3
Davenport, IA	7.9	31.4	22.0	11.7	17.9	6.6	1.6	0.9
Denver, CO	10.0	16.0	16.0	5.6	32.0	13.9	4.5	2.1
Des Moines, IA	12.9	29.6	20.2	9.2	19.3	6.2	1.8	0.8
Durham, NC	9.4	16.2	14.7	6.9	27.7	15.8	4.3	5.0
Edison, NJ	7.9	18.1	11.9	5.8	30.1	21.4	2.6	2.3
El Paso, TX	18.6	23.1	22.7	8.8	17.7	6.6	1.4	1.0
Fargo, ND	5.2	19.3	20.3	13.6	28.1	9.9	1.8	2.0
Fort Collins, CO	3.0	14.4	17.3	8.6	32.8	17.5	2.5	3.8
Fort Wayne, IN	11.1	28.9	21.9	10.1	19.0	7.1	1.1	0.8
Fort Worth, TX	16.5	24.5	20.8	7.2	20.6	7.8	1.6	1.1
Grand Rapids, MI	11.3	22.2	20.1	7.6	25.6	9.7	2.2	1.4
Greeley, CO	16.4	26.0	22.8	8.8	15.9	7.7	1.4	1.2
Green Bay, WI	12.2	31.3	19.7	11.7	18.3	5.0	0.9	0.8
Greensboro, NC	9.8	21.3	20.4	9.0	24.5	10.7	2.4	1.9
Honolulu, HI	9.6	23.1	18.1	10.8	24.0	9.1	3.1	2.1
Houston, TX	20.5	21.6	17.2	6.0	20.9	9.1	3.0	1.8
Huntsville, AL	8.9	17.6	20.9	7.9	26.7	13.7	1.9	2.5
Indianapolis, IN	13.3	27.3	18.8	7.6	21.1	8.2	2.3	1.2
Jacksonville, FL	9.7	28.7	21.5	9.9	20.3	7.2	1.6	1.0
Kansas City, MO	9.0	24.9	22.2	7.4	23.0	9.8	2.6	1.2
Lafayette, LA	9.7	26.2	19.5	5.2	24.9	8.7	3.9	1.9
Las Cruces, NM	12.5	19.8	22.0	9.3	20.5	11.7	2.2	2.0
Las Vegas, NV	14.6	27.4	24.0	8.0	16.7	6.4	1.9	0.9
Lexington, KY	7.6	18.9	20.0	7.9	25.9	12.2	4.2	3.4
Lincoln, NE	7.1	20.7	20.9	11.2	25.3	9.8	2.2	2.8
Little Rock, AR	8.1	21.7	19.8	6.4	25.3	11.8	4.3	2.8
Los Angeles, CA	21.6	18.8	17.2	6.3	23.7	8.1	3.0	1.5
Louisville, KY	9.8	28.2	22.1	8.3	18.9	9.0	2.1	1.5
Madison, WI	4.4	14.2	15.4	7.5	32.5	15.9	4.2	5.9

Table continued on following page.

City	Less than H.S.	H.S. Diploma	Some College, No Deg.	Associate Degree	Bachelors Degree	Masters Degree	Profess. School Degree	Doctorate Degree
Manchester, NH	11.4	28.8	18.8	9.1	21.5	8.0	1.5	1.0
Miami, FL	20.8	25.8	12.6	7.8	19.8	8.2	3.9	1.1
Midland, TX	15.5	23.4	22.1	8.1	22.5	6.4	1.4	0.6
Milwaukee, WI	15.1	30.9	21.1	7.4	16.3	6.7	1.4	1.0
Minneapolis, MN	9.3	14.2	16.4	7.4	31.7	14.5	3.9	2.5
Nashville, TN	10.0	21.5	18.4	6.2	27.5	10.7	3.2	2.6
New Haven, CT	14.6	30.2	14.2	4.6	16.3	11.9	4.0	4.3
New Orleans, LA	11.8	22.4	21.6	5.0	21.9	10.4	4.5	2.2
New York, NY	16.8	23.6	13.5	6.5	22.9	11.8	3.3	1.6
Oklahoma City, OK	12.5	24.6	22.5	8.1	20.5	8.0	2.6	1.2
Omaha, NE	9.7	21.7	22.0	7.8	24.9	9.1	3.1	1.6
Orlando, FL	8.4	23.2	16.8	11.5	25.0	10.3	3.1	1.7
Philadelphia, PA	13.4	31.4	16.7	6.0	18.4	9.3	3.0	1.8
Phoenix, AZ	16.5	22.9	22.1	8.0	19.1	8.2	2.1	1.2
Pittsburgh, PA	6.5	24.7	14.9	8.2	23.5	13.7	4.6	3.9
Portland, OR	6.7	15.1	19.4	6.9	31.2	13.9	4.3	2.4
Providence, RI	16.5	30.6	14.6	5.1	17.4	9.5	3.5	2.9
Provo, UT	7.3	14.4	25.3	8.6	31.6	8.7	1.6	2.4
Raleigh, NC	7.7	15.7	16.9	7.3	32.7	13.7	3.5	2.5
Reno, NV	10.2	22.7	23.3	8.3	21.6	9.2	2.5	2.3
Richmond, VA	12.3	20.4	19.2	5.0	25.1	12.1	3.7	2.2
Rochester, MN	5.6	18.6	15.8	11.3	26.6	13.1	5.2	3.6
Sacramento, CA	13.6	20.3	22.6	8.4	22.2	8.4	3.2	1.4
St. Louis, MO	10.8	24.4	20.3	6.5	21.3	11.3	3.2	2.2
Salem, OR	11.6	23.2	25.8	9.4	18.4	8.4	1.8	1.4
Salt Lake City, UT	8.9	16.6	17.9	6.7	28.3	13.4	4.6	3.5
San Antonio, TX	16.7	25.5	22.5	8.0	16.9	7.2	2.0	1.2
San Diego, CA	10.7	15.4	18.6	7.7	27.9	12.8	3.6	3.4
San Francisco, CA	11.2	11.4	12.7	5.2	35.4	16.0	5.1	3.0
San Jose, CA	14.5	16.3	16.2	7.6	26.0	14.5	2.2	2.8
Santa Rosa, CA	14.5	18.0	23.2	10.0	21.3	8.7	3.0	1.3
Savannah, GA	11.2	26.9	24.6	6.8	19.3	7.9	2.1	1.2
Seattle, WA	4.5	9.7	13.9	6.0	37.3	19.4	5.3	3.9
Sioux Falls, SD	6.7	24.6	20.5	12.2	24.3	8.3	2.4	1.0
Springfield, IL	8.7	26.6	22.1	8.2	20.2	9.6	3.5	1.2
Tampa, FL	11.6	23.4	15.3	7.9	24.8	10.6	4.4	2.0
Tucson, AZ	13.7	22.8	25.7	8.9	17.5	8.2	1.4	1.8
Tulsa, OK	12.1	25.3	22.1	8.0	20.7	7.7	2.7	1.3
Tuscaloosa, AL	9.9	27.1	18.6	6.8	20.5	11.0	2.1	4.0
Virginia Beach, VA	5.5	20.8	24.1	11.0	24.3	10.7	2.3	1.4
Washington, DC	7.8	15.5	12.4	3.0	25.5	21.9	9.7	4.3
Wichita, KS	11.8	26.2	23.4	8.1	19.3	8.4	1.7	1.1
Wilmington, NC	6.5	19.7	20.0	10.3	28.3	10.2	3.2	1.8
Winston-Salem, NC	12.0	24.9	20.7	7.7	20.3	9.2	2.8	2.2
Worcester, MA	14.2	28.3	17.1	8.2	19.2	8.8	2.0	2.3
U.S.	11.1	26.5	20.0	8.7	20.6	9.3	2.2	1.5

Note: Figures cover persons age 25 and over
Source: U.S. Census Bureau, 2017-2021 American Community Survey 5-Year Estimates

Highest Level of Education: Metro Area

Metro Area	Less than H.S.	H.S. Diploma	Some College, No Deg.	Associate Degree	Bachelors Degree	Masters Degree	Profess. School Degree	Doctorate Degree
Albuquerque, NM	10.0	23.8	23.2	9.2	18.6	10.5	2.4	2.2
Allentown, PA	9.1	33.6	16.6	9.4	19.5	8.7	1.6	1.4
Anchorage, AK	6.0	26.2	25.5	9.1	20.9	8.8	2.4	1.2
Ann Arbor, MI	4.3	14.6	17.0	6.9	26.9	19.0	5.0	6.2
Athens, GA	10.6	22.7	17.6	7.4	20.8	13.0	3.2	4.7
Atlanta, GA	9.5	23.3	18.9	7.8	24.9	11.1	2.6	1.6
Austin, TX	9.0	18.2	18.9	6.5	30.1	12.7	2.6	2.0
Baltimore, MD	8.4	24.1	18.9	6.9	22.7	13.7	3.0	2.3
Boise City, ID	7.9	24.1	24.9	9.2	22.6	8.1	1.9	1.3
Boston, MA	7.9	21.2	14.1	7.1	26.9	15.8	3.6	3.5
Boulder, CO	4.5	11.1	15.0	6.6	34.5	19.1	3.9	5.3
Brownsville, TX	30.5	26.1	17.1	7.4	13.2	4.4	0.9	0.5
Cape Coral, FL	10.2	30.8	20.5	9.4	17.8	7.5	2.3	1.4
Cedar Rapids, IA	5.2	28.0	21.3	13.4	22.1	7.4	1.7	0.9
Charleston, SC	8.5	24.3	19.7	9.5	24.0	10.0	2.6	1.4
Charlotte, NC	10.1	22.9	20.5	9.4	24.5	9.7	2.0	0.9
Chicago, IL	10.5	23.4	19.0	7.3	23.8	11.6	2.8	1.5
Cincinnati, OH	8.2	29.3	18.7	8.4	21.9	9.8	2.1	1.5
Clarksville, TN	8.6	28.9	25.1	11.0	17.0	7.4	1.2	0.9
Cleveland, OH	8.6	28.5	21.3	8.8	19.8	9.2	2.5	1.3
College Station, TX	12.1	23.4	19.3	6.7	21.6	9.8	2.0	5.1
Colorado Springs, CO	5.4	19.8	24.4	10.9	23.9	12.0	1.9	1.6
Columbia, MO	5.9	23.1	18.3	7.5	25.4	12.6	3.3	3.8
Columbia, SC	9.4	26.0	21.5	9.5	20.5	9.2	2.1	1.8
Columbus, OH	7.9	26.7	19.4	7.6	24.0	10.4	2.5	1.5
Dallas, TX	13.4	22.0	20.6	7.3	23.8	9.8	1.9	1.2
Davenport, IA	8.2	29.9	22.9	11.1	17.8	7.7	1.5	0.9
Denver, CO	8.1	19.2	18.9	7.6	29.1	12.5	2.8	1.8
Des Moines, IA	6.6	25.6	19.5	10.7	25.8	8.4	2.1	1.3
Durham, NC	9.9	19.0	15.8	7.9	24.4	14.1	4.1	4.8
Edison, NJ	12.7	24.0	14.4	6.8	24.2	12.7	3.4	1.7
El Paso, TX	20.4	23.8	22.3	9.0	16.5	6.0	1.3	0.8
Fargo, ND	4.8	19.7	21.1	14.1	27.8	8.9	1.8	1.7
Fort Collins, CO	3.7	17.4	20.4	9.1	29.5	14.4	2.4	3.1
Fort Wayne, IN	9.8	29.0	21.0	11.0	19.8	7.1	1.5	1.0
Fort Worth, TX	13.4	22.0	20.6	7.3	23.8	9.8	1.9	1.2
Grand Rapids, MI	7.7	26.7	21.6	9.5	22.5	9.1	1.8	1.2
Greeley, CO	11.9	25.4	23.8	9.5	19.3	7.8	1.3	1.1
Green Bay, WI	7.5	31.5	19.1	12.8	20.5	6.3	1.4	0.8
Greensboro, NC	11.8	26.7	21.4	9.7	19.8	7.9	1.5	1.3
Honolulu, HI	7.3	25.6	19.8	11.1	23.2	8.9	2.5	1.6
Houston, TX	15.6	22.7	20.2	7.4	21.6	8.8	2.2	1.5
Huntsville, AL	9.2	20.9	21.0	8.0	25.2	12.4	1.5	1.8
Indianapolis, IN	9.4	27.3	18.9	8.0	23.2	9.4	2.3	1.3
Jacksonville, FL	8.6	27.5	21.0	9.9	21.6	8.4	2.0	1.1
Kansas City, MO	7.3	25.1	21.6	8.0	23.8	10.6	2.4	1.3
Lafayette, LA	14.0	36.5	18.4	6.5	17.0	5.1	1.7	0.8
Las Cruces, NM	19.3	21.5	20.9	8.3	17.5	9.2	1.7	1.7
Las Vegas, NV	13.6	28.0	24.3	8.3	17.1	6.2	1.7	0.9
Lexington, KY	8.3	23.8	20.5	8.3	22.4	10.8	3.4	2.5
Lincoln, NE	6.6	21.4	20.7	11.7	25.1	9.8	2.1	2.6
Little Rock, AR	8.4	29.1	22.2	8.3	19.9	8.6	2.2	1.4
Los Angeles, CA	18.4	19.6	18.8	7.2	23.2	8.6	2.7	1.5
Louisville, KY	9.1	29.3	21.7	8.7	18.9	8.8	2.1	1.4
Madison, WI	4.3	20.6	17.5	9.8	28.8	12.3	3.1	3.5

Table continued on following page.

Appendix A: Comparative Statistics

Metro Area	Less than H.S.	H.S. Diploma	Some College, No Deg.	Associate Degree	Bachelors Degree	Masters Degree	Profess. School Degree	Doctorate Degree
Manchester, NH	7.1	25.6	17.7	9.9	25.0	11.4	1.7	1.6
Miami, FL	13.5	25.8	16.9	9.6	21.1	8.6	3.2	1.3
Midland, TX	15.6	24.5	23.1	8.2	20.0	6.8	1.2	0.5
Milwaukee, WI	7.9	26.1	19.7	8.9	24.3	9.4	2.3	1.5
Minneapolis, MN	6.0	20.5	19.4	10.6	28.3	10.9	2.6	1.7
Nashville, TN	9.0	25.7	19.6	7.3	24.9	9.4	2.3	1.8
New Haven, CT	9.7	29.6	16.7	7.3	19.4	11.9	3.2	2.2
New Orleans, LA	11.9	26.9	22.4	6.5	20.0	8.0	2.9	1.3
New York, NY	12.7	24.0	14.4	6.8	24.2	12.7	3.4	1.7
Oklahoma City, OK	10.2	26.4	22.9	8.1	20.7	8.1	2.2	1.4
Omaha, NE	7.7	23.1	22.0	9.4	24.3	9.6	2.4	1.4
Orlando, FL	9.9	25.4	19.4	11.6	21.9	8.6	2.0	1.1
Philadelphia, PA	8.4	27.9	16.5	7.3	23.3	11.5	2.9	2.0
Phoenix, AZ	11.3	22.8	23.8	9.0	20.9	9.0	2.0	1.3
Pittsburgh, PA	5.5	31.4	16.0	10.5	22.2	10.3	2.3	1.7
Portland, OR	7.2	20.1	22.9	8.9	25.5	10.8	2.7	2.0
Providence, RI	12.0	28.7	17.5	8.6	20.2	9.4	2.0	1.6
Provo, UT	4.9	17.2	25.6	10.4	29.0	9.4	1.7	1.7
Raleigh, NC	7.4	17.3	17.7	9.0	30.1	13.6	2.6	2.3
Reno, NV	11.4	23.8	23.9	8.6	19.8	8.5	2.2	1.8
Richmond, VA	8.9	24.6	19.9	7.6	23.7	11.0	2.5	1.7
Rochester, MN	5.3	23.2	17.8	12.6	23.9	10.6	4.1	2.4
Sacramento, CA	10.2	20.8	24.1	9.9	22.3	8.3	2.8	1.5
St. Louis, MO	7.2	25.7	21.7	9.2	21.5	10.9	2.2	1.6
Salem, OR	13.2	25.1	26.3	9.7	16.7	6.8	1.3	1.0
Salt Lake City, UT	8.2	22.8	23.5	9.2	23.4	9.3	2.2	1.5
San Antonio, TX	13.6	25.2	22.7	8.2	19.0	8.2	1.9	1.2
San Diego, CA	11.7	18.2	21.5	8.4	24.5	10.5	2.9	2.3
San Francisco, CA	10.3	15.1	16.5	6.7	29.9	14.5	3.9	3.1
San Jose, CA	11.0	14.1	14.7	6.9	27.5	18.7	2.8	4.4
Santa Rosa, CA	10.8	18.3	24.2	9.5	23.2	9.2	3.3	1.5
Savannah, GA	9.3	26.5	22.9	7.8	20.7	9.0	2.4	1.5
Seattle, WA	6.8	19.1	20.3	9.4	27.1	12.5	2.7	2.0
Sioux Falls, SD	6.3	25.7	20.2	13.0	24.1	7.8	2.0	1.0
Springfield, IL	7.1	28.0	22.7	8.8	20.3	9.4	2.6	1.1
Tampa, FL	9.6	28.1	20.0	9.8	20.8	8.2	2.2	1.2
Tucson, AZ	10.6	21.4	24.6	9.0	19.7	10.2	2.2	2.2
Tulsa, OK	10.0	28.8	23.3	9.2	19.2	6.7	1.8	1.0
Tuscaloosa, AL	11.5	31.7	20.2	8.8	16.6	7.6	1.2	2.4
Virginia Beach, VA	7.6	24.7	23.8	10.1	20.6	9.8	1.9	1.4
Washington, DC	8.5	17.7	15.5	6.0	26.4	18.2	4.6	3.3
Wichita, KS	9.8	26.5	23.8	8.8	20.1	8.5	1.5	1.0
Wilmington, NC	7.2	20.8	21.3	10.9	26.2	9.4	2.8	1.5
Winston-Salem, NC	12.0	29.1	21.8	9.6	17.7	6.7	1.7	1.3
Worcester, MA	8.7	27.8	17.9	9.2	21.5	11.4	1.8	1.8
U.S.	11.1	26.5	20.0	8.7	20.6	9.3	2.2	1.5

Note: Figures cover persons age 25 and over; Figures cover the Metropolitan Statistical Area
Source: U.S. Census Bureau, 2017-2021 American Community Survey 5-Year Estimates

School Enrollment by Grade and Control: City

City	Preschool (%) Public	Preschool (%) Private	Kindergarten (%) Public	Kindergarten (%) Private	Grades 1 - 4 (%) Public	Grades 1 - 4 (%) Private	Grades 5 - 8 (%) Public	Grades 5 - 8 (%) Private	Grades 9 - 12 (%) Public	Grades 9 - 12 (%) Private
Albuquerque, NM	57.2	42.8	86.7	13.3	86.7	13.3	90.7	9.3	91.7	8.3
Allentown, PA	80.2	19.8	86.2	13.8	87.7	12.3	90.5	9.5	89.0	11.0
Anchorage, AK	50.1	49.9	91.5	8.5	87.5	12.5	89.0	11.0	92.0	8.0
Ann Arbor, MI	34.0	66.0	86.6	13.4	88.7	11.3	87.6	12.4	94.0	6.0
Athens, GA	61.1	38.9	96.2	3.8	91.8	8.2	88.7	11.3	91.8	8.2
Atlanta, GA	50.7	49.3	75.7	24.3	85.9	14.1	78.5	21.5	79.9	20.1
Austin, TX	52.0	48.0	87.1	12.9	88.8	11.2	87.9	12.1	90.9	9.1
Baltimore, MD	69.2	30.8	83.5	16.5	84.0	16.0	85.0	15.0	85.3	14.7
Boise City, ID	32.0	68.0	77.1	22.9	89.8	10.2	91.7	8.3	88.4	11.6
Boston, MA	51.0	49.0	87.0	13.0	84.7	15.3	86.1	13.9	88.8	11.2
Boulder, CO	50.4	49.6	88.4	11.6	88.7	11.3	90.1	9.9	89.7	10.3
Brownsville, TX	95.8	4.2	92.3	7.7	95.6	4.4	94.7	5.3	97.5	2.5
Cape Coral, FL	73.5	26.5	96.9	3.1	88.6	11.4	94.2	5.8	90.2	9.8
Cedar Rapids, IA	69.1	30.9	85.6	14.4	88.0	12.0	91.4	8.6	87.2	12.8
Charleston, SC	42.4	57.6	81.0	19.0	83.5	16.5	83.8	16.2	76.6	23.4
Charlotte, NC	48.9	51.1	86.9	13.1	89.2	10.8	85.8	14.2	89.3	10.7
Chicago, IL	54.2	45.8	80.2	19.8	82.7	17.3	84.1	15.9	86.0	14.0
Cincinnati, OH	64.4	35.6	70.7	29.3	76.8	23.2	78.9	21.1	80.3	19.7
Clarksville, TN	61.1	38.9	85.7	14.3	93.4	6.6	92.1	7.9	87.1	12.9
Cleveland, OH	71.3	28.7	80.0	20.0	81.4	18.6	78.8	21.2	78.0	22.0
College Station, TX	51.4	48.6	86.9	13.1	91.0	9.0	93.9	6.1	88.3	11.7
Colorado Springs, CO	56.0	44.0	89.3	10.7	88.6	11.4	89.0	11.0	91.0	9.0
Columbia, MO	42.1	57.9	84.4	15.6	86.5	13.5	85.4	14.6	91.4	8.6
Columbia, SC	50.6	49.4	75.0	25.0	88.4	11.6	86.6	13.4	91.7	8.3
Columbus, OH	63.4	36.6	78.5	21.5	84.4	15.6	84.8	15.2	86.2	13.8
Dallas, TX	71.3	28.7	91.0	9.0	91.3	8.7	91.4	8.6	90.6	9.4
Davenport, IA	59.7	40.3	83.7	16.3	85.5	14.5	86.6	13.4	94.0	6.0
Denver, CO	57.4	42.6	85.2	14.8	90.6	9.4	89.6	10.4	91.8	8.2
Des Moines, IA	73.4	26.6	90.8	9.2	89.8	10.2	89.4	10.6	92.0	8.0
Durham, NC	53.6	46.4	84.7	15.3	89.3	10.7	84.4	15.6	88.5	11.5
Edison, NJ	18.4	81.6	71.4	28.6	88.2	11.8	89.7	10.3	91.9	8.1
El Paso, TX	88.6	11.4	92.5	7.5	94.3	5.7	94.0	6.0	95.8	4.2
Fargo, ND	43.0	57.0	92.4	7.6	92.6	7.4	90.6	9.4	94.5	5.5
Fort Collins, CO	44.8	55.2	89.3	10.7	93.6	6.4	93.0	7.0	93.8	6.2
Fort Wayne, IN	50.8	49.2	76.9	23.1	79.4	20.6	82.2	17.8	79.9	20.1
Fort Worth, TX	62.1	37.9	83.6	16.4	90.6	9.4	90.1	9.9	92.2	7.8
Grand Rapids, MI	66.8	33.2	74.2	25.8	78.3	21.7	82.3	17.7	82.3	17.7
Greeley, CO	72.4	27.6	92.8	7.2	94.1	5.9	92.8	7.2	94.4	5.6
Green Bay, WI	70.8	29.2	87.5	12.5	87.8	12.2	84.9	15.1	91.3	8.7
Greensboro, NC	55.5	44.5	90.0	10.0	93.3	6.7	91.0	9.0	89.1	10.9
Honolulu, HI	40.2	59.8	73.5	26.5	79.4	20.6	75.4	24.6	71.9	28.1
Houston, TX	64.5	35.5	89.1	10.9	93.1	6.9	92.0	8.0	92.5	7.5
Huntsville, AL	58.2	41.8	85.2	14.8	81.8	18.2	78.4	21.6	82.1	17.9
Indianapolis, IN	58.5	41.5	86.4	13.6	83.9	16.1	84.2	15.8	87.5	12.5
Jacksonville, FL	54.4	45.6	85.0	15.0	83.7	16.3	80.4	19.6	84.8	15.2
Kansas City, MO	55.9	44.1	86.9	13.1	87.6	12.4	88.5	11.5	83.8	16.2
Lafayette, LA	63.6	36.4	67.4	32.6	70.2	29.8	72.4	27.6	79.5	20.5
Las Cruces, NM	84.8	15.2	91.5	8.5	92.9	7.1	96.6	3.4	96.2	3.8
Las Vegas, NV	63.4	36.6	88.2	11.8	90.3	9.7	91.1	8.9	92.5	7.5
Lexington, KY	37.3	62.7	84.6	15.4	83.2	16.8	83.9	16.1	85.4	14.6
Lincoln, NE	50.3	49.7	73.0	27.0	83.5	16.5	83.1	16.9	87.0	13.0
Little Rock, AR	67.9	32.1	88.9	11.1	78.3	21.7	79.1	20.9	76.2	23.8
Los Angeles, CA	57.1	42.9	85.7	14.3	88.0	12.0	87.6	12.4	89.1	10.9
Louisville, KY	51.6	48.4	80.2	19.8	82.9	17.1	82.3	17.7	78.3	21.7
Madison, WI	51.2	48.8	87.9	12.1	88.7	11.3	88.1	11.9	90.6	9.4

Table continued on following page.

City	Preschool (%) Public	Preschool (%) Private	Kindergarten (%) Public	Kindergarten (%) Private	Grades 1 - 4 (%) Public	Grades 1 - 4 (%) Private	Grades 5 - 8 (%) Public	Grades 5 - 8 (%) Private	Grades 9 - 12 (%) Public	Grades 9 - 12 (%) Private
Manchester, NH	58.7	41.3	86.5	13.5	89.0	11.0	93.0	7.0	92.0	8.0
Miami, FL	58.9	41.1	85.5	14.5	85.8	14.2	84.2	15.8	90.8	9.2
Midland, TX	70.6	29.4	83.7	16.3	83.1	16.9	77.6	22.4	83.9	16.1
Milwaukee, WI	74.3	25.7	77.9	22.1	75.8	24.2	74.5	25.5	81.4	18.6
Minneapolis, MN	55.0	45.0	85.0	15.0	87.3	12.7	88.9	11.1	90.7	9.3
Nashville, TN	48.4	51.6	84.0	16.0	84.6	15.4	80.0	20.0	81.9	18.1
New Haven, CT	80.4	19.6	89.7	10.3	95.2	4.8	93.4	6.6	92.5	7.5
New Orleans, LA	49.2	50.8	78.4	21.6	81.5	18.5	81.9	18.1	80.2	19.8
New York, NY	63.8	36.2	79.0	21.0	81.8	18.2	80.9	19.1	80.3	19.7
Oklahoma City, OK	70.9	29.1	87.6	12.4	89.5	10.5	88.2	11.8	88.1	11.9
Omaha, NE	52.7	47.3	81.2	18.8	82.9	17.1	83.3	16.7	83.2	16.8
Orlando, FL	62.9	37.1	84.3	15.7	88.0	12.0	87.0	13.0	86.7	13.3
Philadelphia, PA	54.6	45.4	78.1	21.9	79.2	20.8	80.8	19.2	79.4	20.6
Phoenix, AZ	61.2	38.8	86.5	13.5	90.6	9.4	91.6	8.4	93.1	6.9
Pittsburgh, PA	50.4	49.6	76.4	23.6	76.9	23.1	76.5	23.5	79.5	20.5
Portland, OR	37.9	62.1	84.9	15.1	87.2	12.8	88.2	11.8	87.1	12.9
Providence, RI	56.9	43.1	80.9	19.1	88.4	11.6	84.5	15.5	89.6	10.4
Provo, UT	63.9	36.1	91.4	8.6	92.1	7.9	95.5	4.5	90.2	9.8
Raleigh, NC	37.3	62.7	87.2	12.8	85.6	14.4	87.7	12.3	87.7	12.3
Reno, NV	59.8	40.2	92.4	7.6	94.3	5.7	92.0	8.0	93.1	6.9
Richmond, VA	50.9	49.1	89.3	10.7	85.0	15.0	84.6	15.4	83.6	16.4
Rochester, MN	52.1	47.9	90.2	9.8	90.8	9.2	88.0	12.0	89.3	10.7
Sacramento, CA	65.0	35.0	91.0	9.0	93.1	6.9	91.5	8.5	90.9	9.1
St. Louis, MO	56.8	43.2	73.9	26.1	82.9	17.1	78.8	21.2	80.6	19.4
Salem, OR	61.3	38.7	87.8	12.2	90.0	10.0	93.3	6.7	96.5	3.5
Salt Lake City, UT	42.5	57.5	86.4	13.6	88.6	11.4	91.0	9.0	94.8	5.2
San Antonio, TX	74.0	26.0	89.7	10.3	92.1	7.9	92.3	7.7	91.5	8.5
San Diego, CA	46.8	53.2	89.4	10.6	90.4	9.6	91.7	8.3	91.2	8.8
San Francisco, CA	34.0	66.0	67.4	32.6	71.0	29.0	66.6	33.4	75.5	24.5
San Jose, CA	43.4	56.6	81.8	18.2	87.0	13.0	87.6	12.4	85.9	14.1
Santa Rosa, CA	53.7	46.3	86.2	13.8	92.9	7.1	89.1	10.9	93.8	6.2
Savannah, GA	77.0	23.0	89.0	11.0	91.9	8.1	91.5	8.5	88.5	11.5
Seattle, WA	36.3	63.7	79.0	21.0	79.2	20.8	73.5	26.5	77.3	22.7
Sioux Falls, SD	53.8	46.2	92.3	7.7	86.4	13.6	88.8	11.2	84.6	15.4
Springfield, IL	53.6	46.4	80.8	19.2	80.5	19.5	86.1	13.9	86.8	13.2
Tampa, FL	51.4	48.6	81.9	18.1	87.9	12.1	83.5	16.5	82.2	17.8
Tucson, AZ	70.3	29.7	84.3	15.7	86.8	13.2	88.9	11.1	93.6	6.4
Tulsa, OK	63.6	36.4	82.4	17.6	85.0	15.0	83.0	17.0	81.8	18.2
Tuscaloosa, AL	78.7	21.3	94.7	5.3	84.3	15.7	96.4	3.6	94.9	5.1
Virginia Beach, VA	35.4	64.6	75.9	24.1	90.1	9.9	90.1	9.9	92.2	7.8
Washington, DC	74.2	25.8	90.9	9.1	88.6	11.4	82.4	17.6	80.7	19.3
Wichita, KS	62.8	37.2	84.4	15.6	86.4	13.6	83.7	16.3	84.5	15.5
Wilmington, NC	62.4	37.6	84.8	15.2	75.5	24.5	74.3	25.7	88.8	11.2
Winston-Salem, NC	56.5	43.5	90.6	9.4	91.7	8.3	91.4	8.6	91.9	8.1
Worcester, MA	54.7	45.3	96.0	4.0	93.5	6.5	92.0	8.0	88.1	11.9
U.S.	58.8	41.2	86.3	13.7	88.3	11.7	88.6	11.4	89.4	10.6

Note: Figures shown cover persons 3 years old and over
Source: U.S. Census Bureau, 2017-2021 American Community Survey 5-Year Estimates

School Enrollment by Grade and Control: Metro Area

Metro Area	Preschool (%) Public	Preschool (%) Private	Kindergarten (%) Public	Kindergarten (%) Private	Grades 1 - 4 (%) Public	Grades 1 - 4 (%) Private	Grades 5 - 8 (%) Public	Grades 5 - 8 (%) Private	Grades 9 - 12 (%) Public	Grades 9 - 12 (%) Private
Albuquerque, NM	57.8	42.2	84.8	15.2	86.4	13.6	89.8	10.2	90.8	9.2
Allentown, PA	52.6	47.4	86.9	13.1	89.7	10.3	91.2	8.8	91.3	8.7
Anchorage, AK	51.6	48.4	90.9	9.1	87.2	12.8	88.1	11.9	90.9	9.1
Ann Arbor, MI	49.9	50.1	89.4	10.6	87.1	12.9	88.1	11.9	93.0	7.0
Athens, GA	64.9	35.1	93.2	6.8	89.6	10.4	87.0	13.0	88.4	11.6
Atlanta, GA	54.8	45.2	85.7	14.3	89.8	10.2	88.2	11.8	89.0	11.0
Austin, TX	49.5	50.5	89.5	10.5	90.6	9.4	89.8	10.2	91.7	8.3
Baltimore, MD	47.8	52.2	82.9	17.1	85.3	14.7	84.6	15.4	83.2	16.8
Boise City, ID	35.5	64.5	84.5	15.5	87.8	12.2	90.3	9.7	89.0	11.0
Boston, MA	45.1	54.9	88.5	11.5	91.0	9.0	89.6	10.4	86.5	13.5
Boulder, CO	50.1	49.9	84.8	15.2	90.1	9.9	90.4	9.6	94.6	5.4
Brownsville, TX	95.5	4.5	95.8	4.2	97.0	3.0	96.5	3.5	96.7	3.3
Cape Coral, FL	60.7	39.3	89.9	10.1	90.4	9.6	90.7	9.3	90.5	9.5
Cedar Rapids, IA	69.0	31.0	86.7	13.3	89.3	10.7	90.5	9.5	91.0	9.0
Charleston, SC	46.6	53.4	83.0	17.0	86.2	13.8	88.5	11.5	88.5	11.5
Charlotte, NC	50.3	49.7	87.4	12.6	89.5	10.5	87.5	12.5	89.9	10.1
Chicago, IL	56.6	43.4	84.4	15.6	88.3	11.7	88.6	11.4	90.3	9.7
Cincinnati, OH	53.2	46.8	79.7	20.3	82.8	17.2	83.5	16.5	82.3	17.7
Clarksville, TN	62.6	37.4	88.2	11.8	86.8	13.2	88.6	11.4	87.0	13.0
Cleveland, OH	52.8	47.2	79.0	21.0	81.1	18.9	82.0	18.0	82.4	17.6
College Station, TX	59.9	40.1	86.3	13.7	91.4	8.6	92.1	7.9	92.3	7.7
Colorado Springs, CO	58.9	41.1	87.2	12.8	88.7	11.3	90.1	9.9	90.8	9.2
Columbia, MO	52.3	47.7	87.6	12.4	85.9	14.1	87.6	12.4	91.3	8.7
Columbia, SC	58.5	41.5	90.7	9.3	92.0	8.0	92.7	7.3	92.9	7.1
Columbus, OH	57.3	42.7	82.1	17.9	87.4	12.6	87.9	12.1	88.7	11.3
Dallas, TX	59.0	41.0	88.8	11.2	91.3	8.7	91.6	8.4	91.9	8.1
Davenport, IA	68.6	31.4	88.3	11.7	91.0	9.0	92.0	8.0	92.1	7.9
Denver, CO	58.0	42.0	88.1	11.9	90.8	9.2	90.9	9.1	91.5	8.5
Des Moines, IA	67.2	32.8	90.4	9.6	91.9	8.1	90.5	9.5	92.2	7.8
Durham, NC	47.9	52.1	81.8	18.2	88.9	11.1	86.0	14.0	90.4	9.6
Edison, NJ	56.6	43.4	81.6	18.4	84.6	15.4	84.8	15.2	84.1	15.9
El Paso, TX	88.3	11.7	93.1	6.9	94.3	5.7	94.7	5.3	96.3	3.7
Fargo, ND	59.7	40.3	91.9	8.1	91.0	9.0	91.1	8.9	91.6	8.4
Fort Collins, CO	45.2	54.8	88.9	11.1	88.9	11.1	86.8	13.2	88.3	11.7
Fort Wayne, IN	46.6	53.4	75.5	24.5	76.6	23.4	77.4	22.6	80.7	19.3
Fort Worth, TX	59.0	41.0	88.8	11.2	91.3	8.7	91.6	8.4	91.9	8.1
Grand Rapids, MI	61.5	38.5	81.4	18.6	82.3	17.7	85.8	14.2	85.3	14.7
Greeley, CO	71.5	28.5	91.2	8.8	92.1	7.9	91.7	8.3	94.2	5.8
Green Bay, WI	67.1	32.9	86.7	13.3	88.4	11.6	86.7	13.3	91.8	8.2
Greensboro, NC	55.7	44.3	86.7	13.3	88.5	11.5	88.1	11.9	88.2	11.8
Honolulu, HI	38.4	61.6	78.3	21.7	82.6	17.4	79.3	20.7	75.9	24.1
Houston, TX	56.6	43.4	88.9	11.1	92.0	8.0	92.4	7.6	92.5	7.5
Huntsville, AL	57.2	42.8	80.7	19.3	82.7	17.3	81.5	18.5	81.8	18.2
Indianapolis, IN	52.2	47.8	87.2	12.8	86.8	13.2	87.0	13.0	88.4	11.6
Jacksonville, FL	54.8	45.2	86.3	13.7	84.9	15.1	83.2	16.8	87.2	12.8
Kansas City, MO	59.2	40.8	88.2	11.8	88.3	11.7	89.5	10.5	88.8	11.2
Lafayette, LA	66.3	33.7	78.7	21.3	80.8	19.2	78.8	21.2	78.7	21.3
Las Cruces, NM	83.3	16.7	92.7	7.3	90.3	9.7	96.5	3.5	94.7	5.3
Las Vegas, NV	60.9	39.1	88.6	11.4	91.5	8.5	92.4	7.6	92.7	7.3
Lexington, KY	44.3	55.7	82.5	17.5	85.0	15.0	84.0	16.0	86.6	13.4
Lincoln, NE	49.5	50.5	74.6	25.4	81.6	18.4	83.9	16.1	87.2	12.8
Little Rock, AR	70.5	29.5	90.1	9.9	87.0	13.0	86.6	13.4	86.4	13.6
Los Angeles, CA	55.8	44.2	86.9	13.1	90.0	10.0	90.1	9.9	91.1	8.9
Louisville, KY	52.4	47.6	81.8	18.2	82.3	17.7	82.4	17.6	80.7	19.3
Madison, WI	67.4	32.6	88.0	12.0	89.6	10.4	90.2	9.8	94.3	5.7

Table continued on following page.

Metro Area	Preschool (%) Public	Preschool (%) Private	Kindergarten (%) Public	Kindergarten (%) Private	Grades 1 - 4 (%) Public	Grades 1 - 4 (%) Private	Grades 5 - 8 (%) Public	Grades 5 - 8 (%) Private	Grades 9 - 12 (%) Public	Grades 9 - 12 (%) Private
Manchester, NH	49.7	50.3	81.7	18.3	87.4	12.6	87.8	12.2	88.9	11.1
Miami, FL	51.1	48.9	82.4	17.6	85.2	14.8	85.6	14.4	86.1	13.9
Midland, TX	75.7	24.3	79.8	20.2	83.8	16.2	82.0	18.0	85.2	14.8
Milwaukee, WI	58.0	42.0	78.8	21.2	79.9	20.1	79.6	20.4	85.4	14.6
Minneapolis, MN	61.4	38.6	87.3	12.7	89.0	11.0	89.6	10.4	91.6	8.4
Nashville, TN	50.2	49.8	85.0	15.0	85.7	14.3	84.7	15.3	83.3	16.7
New Haven, CT	65.6	34.4	93.4	6.6	92.1	7.9	90.4	9.6	88.9	11.1
New Orleans, LA	54.1	45.9	76.7	23.3	77.8	22.2	77.5	22.5	74.9	25.1
New York, NY	56.6	43.4	81.6	18.4	84.6	15.4	84.8	15.2	84.1	15.9
Oklahoma City, OK	71.5	28.5	87.9	12.1	89.2	10.8	88.8	11.2	89.1	10.9
Omaha, NE	57.9	42.1	83.0	17.0	85.1	14.9	85.4	14.6	85.4	14.6
Orlando, FL	50.4	49.6	81.5	18.5	84.1	15.9	85.5	14.5	87.5	12.5
Philadelphia, PA	46.2	53.8	81.2	18.8	84.8	15.2	84.6	15.4	83.3	16.7
Phoenix, AZ	61.7	38.3	86.0	14.0	89.6	10.4	91.1	8.9	92.7	7.3
Pittsburgh, PA	50.8	49.2	82.7	17.3	88.7	11.3	89.0	11.0	89.6	10.4
Portland, OR	41.3	58.7	85.1	14.9	87.5	12.5	89.1	10.9	90.2	9.8
Providence, RI	56.5	43.5	88.3	11.7	90.4	9.6	89.4	10.6	88.4	11.6
Provo, UT	54.2	45.8	89.1	10.9	91.5	8.5	93.7	6.3	94.4	5.6
Raleigh, NC	33.6	66.4	84.1	15.9	86.7	13.3	86.5	13.5	88.1	11.9
Reno, NV	54.1	45.9	89.2	10.8	93.0	7.0	92.3	7.7	92.1	7.9
Richmond, VA	44.8	55.2	87.7	12.3	88.8	11.2	89.4	10.6	90.2	9.8
Rochester, MN	63.8	36.2	91.4	8.6	90.6	9.4	89.8	10.2	91.2	8.8
Sacramento, CA	59.9	40.1	90.0	10.0	91.7	8.3	91.9	8.1	91.7	8.3
St. Louis, MO	53.6	46.4	80.8	19.2	83.8	16.2	82.7	17.3	85.1	14.9
Salem, OR	59.7	40.3	86.9	13.1	89.6	10.4	91.7	8.3	93.9	6.1
Salt Lake City, UT	55.1	44.9	86.9	13.1	90.6	9.4	93.7	6.3	93.7	6.3
San Antonio, TX	67.2	32.8	89.3	10.7	91.6	8.4	91.2	8.8	91.1	8.9
San Diego, CA	49.0	51.0	89.7	10.3	90.8	9.2	91.8	8.2	92.3	7.7
San Francisco, CA	40.5	59.5	83.1	16.9	85.1	14.9	84.7	15.3	86.2	13.8
San Jose, CA	36.0	64.0	78.9	21.1	85.4	14.6	86.0	14.0	85.9	14.1
Santa Rosa, CA	48.2	51.8	87.3	12.7	92.4	7.6	89.8	10.2	92.0	8.0
Savannah, GA	53.9	46.1	81.7	18.3	85.0	15.0	88.0	12.0	85.4	14.6
Seattle, WA	42.0	58.0	82.0	18.0	86.4	13.6	86.9	13.1	90.2	9.8
Sioux Falls, SD	56.2	43.8	91.6	8.4	87.3	12.7	90.0	10.0	87.1	12.9
Springfield, IL	58.6	41.4	85.1	14.9	85.1	14.9	89.7	10.3	90.4	9.6
Tampa, FL	54.7	45.3	82.3	17.7	84.8	15.2	85.9	14.1	87.4	12.6
Tucson, AZ	67.5	32.5	85.8	14.2	87.9	12.1	88.9	11.1	91.0	9.0
Tulsa, OK	66.3	33.7	85.2	14.8	86.1	13.9	86.5	13.5	85.9	14.1
Tuscaloosa, AL	71.4	28.6	87.3	12.7	86.8	13.2	89.9	10.1	88.1	11.9
Virginia Beach, VA	50.5	49.5	79.9	20.1	88.8	11.2	90.0	10.0	90.1	9.9
Washington, DC	45.8	54.2	84.0	16.0	87.7	12.3	87.4	12.6	88.2	11.8
Wichita, KS	64.9	35.1	83.7	16.3	86.6	13.4	86.2	13.8	87.4	12.6
Wilmington, NC	48.0	52.0	81.2	18.8	83.4	16.6	82.0	18.0	88.8	11.2
Winston-Salem, NC	52.2	47.8	88.5	11.5	90.0	10.0	89.8	10.2	88.4	11.6
Worcester, MA	59.0	41.0	91.1	8.9	92.2	7.8	90.6	9.4	90.5	9.5
U.S.	58.8	41.2	86.3	13.7	88.3	11.7	88.6	11.4	89.4	10.6

Note: Figures shown cover persons 3 years old and over; Figures cover the Metropolitan Statistical Area
Source: U.S. Census Bureau, 2017-2021 American Community Survey 5-Year Estimates

Educational Attainment by Race: City

City	High School Graduate or Higher (%)					Bachelor's Degree or Higher (%)				
	Total	White	Black	Asian	Hisp.[1]	Total	White	Black	Asian	Hisp.[1]
Albuquerque, NM	90.9	93.0	94.3	87.7	84.8	37.4	41.1	36.2	54.1	24.3
Allentown, PA	80.6	84.7	83.6	80.4	70.5	17.3	21.5	11.2	42.3	7.7
Anchorage, AK	94.2	96.4	93.2	88.4	85.6	36.8	44.0	21.6	26.4	24.5
Ann Arbor, MI	97.8	98.5	93.2	98.0	92.7	77.2	79.5	36.4	85.6	69.9
Athens, GA	89.7	94.3	83.2	92.5	67.4	47.1	59.0	23.3	72.4	27.0
Atlanta, GA	92.1	98.3	86.3	96.7	84.0	55.6	79.9	29.9	86.1	48.0
Austin, TX	90.6	93.2	89.5	92.7	76.2	55.1	59.5	31.6	76.5	30.9
Baltimore, MD	86.3	91.5	84.1	90.2	72.2	34.2	59.7	18.7	71.6	32.9
Boise City, ID	95.2	96.2	78.5	90.0	82.7	43.7	43.9	31.0	57.7	26.7
Boston, MA	88.2	94.7	85.2	80.6	72.7	52.1	68.7	25.0	57.1	25.7
Boulder, CO	96.9	98.2	89.2	95.5	81.4	76.8	78.0	34.2	84.3	51.2
Brownsville, TX	68.0	67.8	78.7	92.7	66.5	20.5	20.4	37.3	61.2	19.3
Cape Coral, FL	92.9	94.0	84.8	87.3	88.5	23.6	23.9	22.7	44.4	16.4
Cedar Rapids, IA	93.8	95.3	83.0	86.2	82.8	32.8	33.6	17.8	51.5	22.4
Charleston, SC	95.8	97.8	89.2	98.6	86.5	55.7	63.7	24.3	66.2	41.3
Charlotte, NC	89.7	94.7	91.2	84.3	60.8	45.7	59.2	30.8	61.5	19.1
Chicago, IL	86.3	90.8	86.4	87.6	70.9	41.7	55.5	23.5	64.1	18.5
Cincinnati, OH	88.6	92.9	83.1	94.7	76.9	39.6	54.9	16.8	80.3	33.3
Clarksville, TN	93.6	94.2	94.0	87.4	87.1	28.7	30.6	25.3	37.3	17.2
Cleveland, OH	82.6	85.7	81.1	75.3	71.4	19.2	27.6	11.2	46.9	9.2
College Station, TX	94.8	95.9	91.0	94.2	87.1	58.0	58.7	31.9	78.7	41.2
Colorado Springs, CO	93.9	95.5	93.8	85.8	82.6	40.2	43.4	28.1	42.7	20.4
Columbia, MO	95.5	96.6	92.6	94.7	89.1	53.8	56.5	29.4	68.9	47.1
Columbia, SC	90.5	96.2	83.5	95.7	87.6	44.7	63.4	21.6	76.0	35.4
Columbus, OH	90.3	93.0	87.0	86.5	73.5	37.9	44.5	20.1	60.7	24.1
Dallas, TX	79.6	80.5	88.4	87.4	55.4	35.6	44.3	22.3	66.0	13.5
Davenport, IA	92.1	93.9	87.7	71.8	78.3	27.1	29.1	13.6	35.3	15.4
Denver, CO	90.0	93.6	89.8	85.6	69.6	52.5	60.7	27.7	56.5	19.4
Des Moines, IA	87.1	91.9	82.1	58.6	60.2	28.1	31.1	16.4	21.8	10.1
Durham, NC	90.6	93.8	90.0	93.0	54.7	52.8	65.7	35.4	77.8	19.8
Edison, NJ	92.1	94.0	95.0	92.0	86.3	56.4	38.6	43.0	76.2	25.0
El Paso, TX	81.4	84.1	96.1	88.5	77.8	26.7	28.7	32.3	56.8	22.7
Fargo, ND	94.8	96.7	79.3	82.7	91.6	41.8	43.5	19.0	57.2	16.4
Fort Collins, CO	97.0	97.6	91.7	93.4	87.4	56.6	58.0	36.7	73.4	33.1
Fort Wayne, IN	88.9	93.5	85.4	47.6	63.7	28.0	31.6	15.3	21.6	11.6
Fort Worth, TX	83.5	88.1	89.1	80.9	63.5	31.0	37.5	22.7	44.5	14.4
Grand Rapids, MI	88.7	92.6	86.4	80.6	57.7	38.8	46.0	20.4	44.7	13.3
Greeley, CO	83.6	86.1	69.8	81.6	64.7	26.1	28.3	21.9	50.3	9.1
Green Bay, WI	87.8	90.7	76.5	75.1	57.7	25.1	27.0	16.9	26.0	9.3
Greensboro, NC	90.2	93.9	89.3	77.0	68.0	39.5	50.5	26.7	47.0	19.3
Honolulu, HI	90.4	97.9	94.5	87.4	93.9	38.4	54.2	31.3	37.9	31.6
Houston, TX	79.5	82.2	89.1	87.1	59.6	34.7	42.7	25.0	62.3	15.5
Huntsville, AL	91.1	93.8	86.8	88.8	72.3	44.8	51.8	29.4	56.2	29.2
Indianapolis, IN	86.7	89.7	85.3	70.5	60.6	32.9	38.4	20.9	44.3	15.8
Jacksonville, FL	90.3	92.0	88.2	87.8	83.9	30.2	33.0	21.3	49.4	27.0
Kansas City, MO	91.0	93.9	88.6	86.1	71.3	36.5	45.2	16.9	48.4	19.0
Lafayette, LA	90.3	95.1	80.3	92.2	72.5	39.4	49.1	15.2	63.9	33.0
Las Cruces, NM	87.5	90.4	83.9	85.3	83.2	36.4	38.7	47.4	63.0	24.8
Las Vegas, NV	85.4	89.5	88.3	91.9	66.0	25.9	29.4	18.8	43.3	11.6
Lexington, KY	92.4	94.8	88.9	89.4	64.1	45.6	49.7	23.7	69.0	25.3
Lincoln, NE	92.9	95.0	87.1	79.8	69.0	40.1	41.7	26.6	43.7	19.9
Little Rock, AR	91.9	94.1	90.0	87.5	67.6	44.1	57.8	25.7	61.9	13.0
Los Angeles, CA	78.4	84.6	89.3	90.9	58.3	36.2	44.9	29.3	56.8	14.0
Louisville, KY	90.2	91.8	88.2	80.0	77.1	31.6	35.2	18.8	50.7	24.4
Madison, WI	95.6	97.2	88.8	92.4	79.2	58.5	60.9	24.7	70.9	40.0

Table continued on following page.

City	High School Graduate or Higher (%)					Bachelor's Degree or Higher (%)				
	Total	White	Black	Asian	Hisp.[1]	Total	White	Black	Asian	Hisp.[1]
Manchester, NH	88.6	90.4	78.2	81.0	67.1	31.9	32.9	17.6	40.8	13.0
Miami, FL	79.2	80.7	75.7	96.5	76.5	33.1	37.3	15.6	68.9	29.6
Midland, TX	84.5	88.0	88.2	72.1	71.2	30.9	35.0	16.2	45.8	15.5
Milwaukee, WI	84.9	90.5	84.9	74.8	64.4	25.5	37.6	13.5	32.7	10.8
Minneapolis, MN	90.7	96.7	74.7	84.7	66.1	52.6	63.7	17.2	57.3	25.6
Nashville, TN	90.0	92.2	89.3	80.3	59.3	43.9	50.7	28.8	52.3	17.2
New Haven, CT	85.4	87.2	87.3	94.8	71.6	36.5	49.2	22.5	78.5	14.5
New Orleans, LA	88.2	96.4	83.7	76.7	80.9	39.1	65.3	21.0	47.9	40.4
New York, NY	83.2	90.5	84.7	76.8	70.8	39.6	54.6	25.3	44.0	20.1
Oklahoma City, OK	87.5	89.5	91.2	80.6	57.6	32.3	35.4	24.3	42.3	10.4
Omaha, NE	90.3	93.1	87.9	72.2	60.3	38.7	42.8	17.7	49.8	13.8
Orlando, FL	91.6	94.7	84.5	92.5	90.2	40.1	48.5	20.6	54.5	32.2
Philadelphia, PA	86.6	91.8	86.9	73.2	71.9	32.5	46.4	19.3	41.4	18.1
Phoenix, AZ	83.5	87.0	89.8	86.8	65.5	30.6	33.8	25.9	60.2	12.0
Pittsburgh, PA	93.5	95.0	89.1	92.5	87.3	45.7	51.2	19.8	77.7	49.3
Portland, OR	93.3	95.7	89.2	79.9	79.1	51.9	56.1	26.6	43.6	34.5
Providence, RI	83.5	88.8	85.7	84.1	73.3	33.3	41.9	27.0	50.4	12.3
Provo, UT	92.7	94.5	95.3	84.4	73.5	44.3	46.4	17.0	47.4	19.3
Raleigh, NC	92.3	96.3	91.6	89.4	62.6	52.4	64.4	32.6	61.7	23.0
Reno, NV	89.8	93.9	90.8	92.4	66.3	35.5	38.3	31.1	49.5	13.5
Richmond, VA	87.7	94.7	81.5	88.6	58.3	43.1	68.0	14.8	70.7	22.5
Rochester, MN	94.4	96.8	70.6	88.5	76.7	48.7	49.9	19.9	61.8	33.6
Sacramento, CA	86.4	91.5	91.3	81.6	75.4	35.1	42.6	24.8	39.3	21.6
St. Louis, MO	89.2	94.4	83.1	87.1	79.1	38.0	53.9	16.6	57.9	36.7
Salem, OR	88.4	92.3	95.0	84.5	61.8	30.0	32.6	27.1	44.4	11.1
Salt Lake City, UT	91.1	95.3	84.5	83.1	69.3	49.8	54.8	32.1	57.8	21.2
San Antonio, TX	83.3	84.8	91.5	86.1	76.7	27.3	28.9	25.7	55.7	18.0
San Diego, CA	89.3	91.8	91.2	89.2	73.4	47.6	52.0	28.3	55.1	22.6
San Francisco, CA	88.8	97.3	87.3	80.4	79.2	59.5	75.4	31.5	48.9	38.1
San Jose, CA	85.5	90.9	91.4	87.6	69.6	45.4	48.2	38.3	57.5	16.6
Santa Rosa, CA	85.5	92.6	83.5	86.8	62.4	34.3	40.0	27.4	48.4	14.4
Savannah, GA	88.8	94.8	84.1	78.6	84.0	30.5	45.4	16.3	50.7	31.9
Seattle, WA	95.5	98.2	89.8	90.1	85.7	65.9	70.7	32.9	66.9	46.5
Sioux Falls, SD	93.3	95.3	83.9	74.3	73.5	36.0	37.9	20.0	44.2	17.9
Springfield, IL	91.3	93.6	80.0	94.0	86.8	34.4	37.2	14.3	69.9	43.3
Tampa, FL	88.4	91.9	84.1	87.7	78.2	41.8	49.8	18.7	65.4	26.7
Tucson, AZ	86.3	89.9	84.2	87.3	75.0	28.9	32.7	20.8	51.6	15.5
Tulsa, OK	87.9	90.8	89.6	74.0	59.8	32.4	37.6	17.8	37.0	11.5
Tuscaloosa, AL	90.1	95.5	85.9	91.4	66.5	37.6	57.4	15.7	67.5	20.2
Virginia Beach, VA	94.5	96.0	92.5	89.5	87.4	38.6	41.7	29.3	40.9	30.1
Washington, DC	92.2	98.6	88.0	94.4	78.6	61.4	90.8	31.1	82.4	52.8
Wichita, KS	88.2	91.6	87.8	73.7	63.9	30.5	33.6	17.7	35.1	13.3
Wilmington, NC	93.5	95.6	87.4	84.0	78.0	43.6	49.0	20.9	60.7	32.3
Winston-Salem, NC	88.0	90.7	88.1	89.9	58.9	34.6	43.0	20.9	70.4	15.1
Worcester, MA	85.8	88.9	89.5	74.9	69.5	32.2	33.9	31.7	41.7	13.9
U.S.	88.9	91.4	87.2	87.6	71.2	33.7	35.5	23.3	55.6	18.4

Note: Figures shown cover persons 25 years old and over; (1) People of Hispanic origin can be of any race
Source: U.S. Census Bureau, 2017-2021 American Community Survey 5-Year Estimates

Educational Attainment by Race: Metro Area

Metro Area	High School Graduate or Higher (%)					Bachelor's Degree or Higher (%)				
	Total	White	Black	Asian	Hisp.[1]	Total	White	Black	Asian	Hisp.[1]
Albuquerque, NM	90.0	92.1	92.0	89.6	83.8	33.7	37.5	34.4	54.4	21.7
Allentown, PA	90.9	92.5	87.6	89.0	77.5	31.2	32.2	21.7	61.7	15.7
Anchorage, AK	94.0	95.8	92.9	88.2	86.4	33.3	38.1	21.8	26.1	24.3
Ann Arbor, MI	95.7	96.8	90.8	95.7	87.2	57.2	58.9	29.1	82.1	46.1
Athens, GA	89.4	92.3	82.2	89.7	69.1	41.7	46.6	21.7	67.5	30.6
Atlanta, GA	90.5	92.5	91.5	87.7	67.2	40.4	44.6	32.6	59.7	22.9
Austin, TX	91.0	93.4	92.3	92.8	77.1	47.4	50.3	33.1	73.7	26.1
Baltimore, MD	91.6	93.9	89.0	89.1	76.2	41.8	46.4	28.4	63.1	32.4
Boise City, ID	92.1	94.1	80.8	88.2	70.7	33.9	35.1	25.3	52.0	16.6
Boston, MA	92.1	95.1	86.2	86.6	73.7	49.7	52.5	29.6	64.1	24.9
Boulder, CO	95.5	97.0	86.9	92.5	75.8	62.9	64.6	30.4	70.8	31.3
Brownsville, TX	69.5	70.7	82.1	89.3	66.1	19.0	18.7	26.6	59.8	16.2
Cape Coral, FL	89.8	92.0	81.0	91.5	74.4	29.0	30.9	16.7	50.0	14.7
Cedar Rapids, IA	94.8	95.7	83.9	87.6	79.9	32.1	32.5	18.5	49.3	23.6
Charleston, SC	91.5	94.6	85.7	89.7	70.2	38.0	45.2	18.5	50.8	23.0
Charlotte, NC	89.9	92.2	89.9	86.7	65.7	37.1	40.0	28.1	60.8	20.5
Chicago, IL	89.5	92.9	88.7	91.1	70.5	39.7	44.4	24.5	66.5	16.8
Cincinnati, OH	91.8	92.7	87.3	89.4	77.4	35.4	36.4	21.6	65.9	29.4
Clarksville, TN	91.4	91.9	90.6	87.5	85.7	26.5	27.3	23.3	42.7	18.7
Cleveland, OH	91.4	93.3	86.1	86.8	77.9	32.7	36.2	16.8	63.5	17.6
College Station, TX	87.9	89.3	87.7	94.5	67.8	38.6	40.7	18.3	76.8	17.3
Colorado Springs, CO	94.6	95.8	95.1	87.2	84.7	39.4	41.9	29.6	42.2	21.4
Columbia, MO	94.1	94.7	91.6	94.2	88.0	45.1	46.2	25.5	67.1	38.5
Columbia, SC	90.6	92.8	88.1	92.3	70.0	33.6	37.9	24.7	62.2	23.1
Columbus, OH	92.1	93.6	87.6	88.4	76.8	38.4	40.3	22.7	64.1	27.4
Dallas, TX	86.6	88.9	91.8	88.8	63.9	36.8	38.9	30.0	62.8	16.2
Davenport, IA	91.8	93.9	80.3	78.7	75.3	27.9	29.0	11.8	51.7	16.9
Denver, CO	91.9	94.5	90.4	84.9	74.1	46.2	50.1	29.2	53.1	19.6
Des Moines, IA	93.4	95.6	84.8	71.0	68.2	37.6	39.0	20.7	37.1	15.8
Durham, NC	90.1	93.0	87.9	92.8	56.5	47.4	54.2	30.3	77.1	21.3
Edison, NJ	87.3	92.2	86.3	84.1	73.1	42.0	49.1	26.8	56.0	21.3
El Paso, TX	79.6	82.4	96.1	89.2	76.0	24.6	26.5	32.2	54.0	20.8
Fargo, ND	95.2	96.5	78.9	85.9	86.7	40.3	41.5	20.4	55.6	21.7
Fort Collins, CO	96.3	96.9	94.2	93.2	84.3	49.4	50.0	33.0	66.7	28.5
Fort Wayne, IN	90.2	93.3	86.0	55.8	66.3	29.3	31.4	16.4	30.4	12.5
Fort Worth, TX	86.6	88.9	91.8	88.8	63.9	36.8	38.9	30.0	62.8	16.2
Grand Rapids, MI	92.3	94.3	87.7	75.5	69.4	34.5	36.4	20.6	40.5	16.2
Greeley, CO	88.1	90.1	79.6	89.1	67.8	29.5	31.3	31.0	41.1	10.1
Green Bay, WI	92.5	94.3	76.4	83.4	61.7	29.1	29.8	19.0	47.3	13.4
Greensboro, NC	88.2	90.3	87.8	78.5	61.1	30.5	32.9	24.1	47.0	14.3
Honolulu, HI	92.7	97.6	97.1	90.3	95.1	36.2	50.0	33.8	37.4	28.7
Houston, TX	84.4	86.6	91.8	87.3	66.4	34.2	36.5	30.0	56.9	16.7
Huntsville, AL	90.8	92.5	87.5	89.5	74.7	40.9	43.4	32.1	60.6	27.7
Indianapolis, IN	90.6	92.5	86.5	81.0	67.3	36.3	38.5	22.9	55.5	21.3
Jacksonville, FL	91.4	92.8	88.4	89.4	85.5	33.1	35.6	22.0	49.9	27.9
Kansas City, MO	92.7	94.3	89.8	88.2	72.4	38.0	40.9	20.4	56.2	19.1
Lafayette, LA	86.0	88.8	79.2	76.0	70.7	24.6	27.7	13.2	38.0	19.1
Las Cruces, NM	80.7	83.8	84.8	88.6	73.5	30.0	32.5	44.9	60.3	19.8
Las Vegas, NV	86.4	90.0	89.9	90.6	68.4	25.8	28.3	19.8	41.0	11.9
Lexington, KY	91.7	93.3	89.0	89.2	63.6	39.0	40.9	22.8	65.5	22.1
Lincoln, NE	93.4	95.2	87.1	79.5	69.3	39.6	40.9	26.6	43.4	20.1
Little Rock, AR	91.6	92.8	90.2	87.1	70.1	32.1	34.4	24.8	51.1	15.5
Los Angeles, CA	81.6	86.5	90.5	88.8	64.5	36.0	40.8	29.5	54.5	15.1
Louisville, KY	90.9	91.9	88.1	85.5	73.8	31.1	32.7	19.7	57.5	21.6
Madison, WI	95.7	96.8	90.1	90.5	77.2	47.7	48.1	25.2	68.5	30.6

Table continued on following page.

Appendix A: Comparative Statistics

Metro Area	High School Graduate or Higher (%)					Bachelor's Degree or Higher (%)				
	Total	White	Black	Asian	Hisp.[1]	Total	White	Black	Asian	Hisp.[1]
Manchester, NH	92.9	93.8	82.8	89.8	73.6	39.6	39.8	20.5	62.1	19.0
Miami, FL	86.5	88.7	83.6	87.9	81.2	34.1	38.5	21.2	54.3	29.8
Midland, TX	84.4	87.4	89.1	75.0	71.5	28.5	31.3	16.7	51.6	14.1
Milwaukee, WI	92.1	95.2	85.9	86.1	71.0	37.4	42.3	15.1	53.3	16.6
Minneapolis, MN	94.0	96.6	82.8	82.7	73.9	43.5	46.1	23.6	46.0	24.1
Nashville, TN	91.0	92.2	90.0	86.0	64.9	38.4	39.9	30.0	55.3	19.4
New Haven, CT	90.3	92.7	88.2	89.7	74.5	36.6	39.8	23.0	64.1	15.6
New Orleans, LA	88.1	91.7	84.1	80.3	74.7	32.2	39.2	19.9	43.4	22.4
New York, NY	87.3	92.2	86.3	84.1	73.1	42.0	49.1	26.8	56.0	21.3
Oklahoma City, OK	89.8	91.3	91.6	83.3	62.2	32.4	34.4	24.0	47.2	13.2
Omaha, NE	92.3	94.2	88.8	75.9	66.1	37.7	39.7	20.5	49.0	17.3
Orlando, FL	90.1	92.1	85.6	89.2	85.5	33.7	36.3	23.3	52.0	25.7
Philadelphia, PA	91.6	94.4	89.0	84.5	73.0	39.8	44.5	23.0	58.3	20.7
Phoenix, AZ	88.7	91.3	91.7	89.3	71.8	33.1	35.2	28.2	59.7	14.9
Pittsburgh, PA	94.5	95.1	90.8	87.5	88.5	36.6	37.0	21.6	69.2	37.5
Portland, OR	92.8	94.6	90.8	87.6	73.2	41.0	41.6	31.3	54.0	22.1
Providence, RI	88.0	89.8	84.7	86.4	73.3	33.2	34.9	25.8	53.2	15.5
Provo, UT	95.1	95.8	95.1	93.1	79.7	41.9	42.6	34.1	54.0	24.9
Raleigh, NC	92.6	95.1	91.1	92.7	65.6	48.6	52.8	32.3	75.7	21.1
Reno, NV	88.6	92.8	90.7	92.0	64.2	32.3	34.9	28.0	47.1	13.2
Richmond, VA	91.1	94.0	87.4	89.9	68.9	38.9	45.5	22.8	65.6	22.8
Rochester, MN	94.7	96.1	71.8	88.1	77.4	41.0	41.1	19.5	59.6	31.3
Sacramento, CA	89.8	93.2	91.2	84.7	76.7	35.0	36.8	25.5	44.8	20.1
St. Louis, MO	92.8	94.2	87.5	90.8	82.3	36.2	38.6	20.4	68.0	31.3
Salem, OR	86.8	90.9	92.8	81.5	60.7	25.7	28.0	25.2	37.3	10.0
Salt Lake City, UT	91.8	94.9	84.6	86.6	73.5	36.4	38.9	25.4	49.1	17.1
San Antonio, TX	86.4	88.1	92.7	87.8	78.4	30.3	32.0	31.4	53.9	19.4
San Diego, CA	88.3	90.8	91.6	90.0	73.1	40.3	43.2	27.4	53.0	19.6
San Francisco, CA	89.7	95.0	91.3	88.1	73.1	51.4	58.7	31.6	57.6	23.9
San Jose, CA	89.0	92.7	92.4	91.4	71.9	53.4	53.4	41.7	67.5	19.0
Santa Rosa, CA	89.2	94.2	87.2	88.3	66.1	37.1	41.5	32.1	48.5	15.9
Savannah, GA	90.7	93.4	87.0	83.3	84.4	33.6	39.7	21.0	51.4	25.1
Seattle, WA	93.2	95.5	90.8	90.0	75.9	44.3	44.9	27.5	58.3	25.0
Sioux Falls, SD	93.7	95.1	84.5	75.7	73.0	34.8	36.1	19.6	44.4	18.6
Springfield, IL	92.9	94.4	80.8	90.9	89.3	33.4	34.8	15.5	68.2	42.6
Tampa, FL	90.4	91.9	88.7	85.1	81.4	32.4	33.1	25.0	51.8	24.6
Tucson, AZ	89.4	92.5	87.6	87.7	77.9	34.4	38.1	27.6	55.7	18.5
Tulsa, OK	90.0	91.7	90.1	76.7	65.8	28.7	31.1	19.6	34.9	14.0
Tuscaloosa, AL	88.5	91.2	84.9	86.9	64.6	27.8	34.2	15.3	61.0	17.4
Virginia Beach, VA	92.4	94.9	88.7	88.4	84.8	33.8	38.2	23.8	44.2	28.3
Washington, DC	91.5	95.1	92.4	91.3	70.4	52.4	61.3	37.2	66.0	28.0
Wichita, KS	90.2	92.8	87.6	74.2	66.9	31.1	33.0	19.0	35.5	16.4
Wilmington, NC	92.8	94.4	87.9	82.0	78.9	39.9	43.0	22.5	63.9	27.1
Winston-Salem, NC	88.0	89.3	87.7	88.3	60.1	27.4	28.9	21.0	54.6	13.5
Worcester, MA	91.3	92.9	89.3	85.0	73.7	36.4	36.4	34.4	59.8	16.6
U.S.	88.9	91.4	87.2	87.6	71.2	33.7	35.5	23.3	55.6	18.4

Note: Figures shown cover persons 25 years old and over; Figures cover the Metropolitan Statistical Area; (1) People of Hispanic origin can be of any race
Source: U.S. Census Bureau, 2017-2021 American Community Survey 5-Year Estimates

Cost of Living Index

Urban Area	Composite	Groceries	Housing	Utilities	Transp.	Health	Misc.
Albuquerque, NM	93.8	104.8	84.5	87.7	97.2	99.8	96.6
Allentown, PA	104.4	98.4	114.0	103.4	104.8	94.6	100.6
Anchorage, AK	124.5	132.6	140.0	124.0	114.8	144.2	109.7
Ann Arbor, MI	n/a	n/a	n/a	n/a	n/a	n/a	n/a
Athens, GA	n/a	n/a	n/a	n/a	n/a	n/a	n/a
Atlanta, GA	102.8	103.4	103.5	85.1	103.6	107.1	106.0
Austin, TX	99.7	91.2	105.5	95.2	90.7	105.8	101.4
Baltimore, MD	n/a	n/a	n/a	n/a	n/a	n/a	n/a
Boise City, ID	98.7	94.5	97.5	81.9	108.5	103.0	102.8
Boston, MA	151.0	109.3	228.6	120.5	112.0	118.3	129.3
Boulder, CO	n/a	n/a	n/a	n/a	n/a	n/a	n/a
Brownsville, TX	76.6	80.2	58.0	108.2	88.1	80.3	79.6
Cape Coral, FL	100.6	107.8	89.6	98.8	98.7	108.5	106.3
Cedar Rapids, IA	96.2	94.8	83.0	102.1	96.6	107.0	103.9
Charleston, SC	97.2	99.7	93.2	120.4	86.6	97.5	95.9
Charlotte, NC	98.2	101.7	88.8	95.6	90.7	105.1	106.0
Chicago, IL	120.6	101.9	155.7	92.4	125.9	100.0	109.4
Cincinnati, OH	99.7	91.2	105.5	95.2	90.7	105.8	101.4
Clarksville, TN	n/a	n/a	n/a	n/a	n/a	n/a	n/a
Cleveland, OH	96.9	106.0	83.3	96.1	99.4	104.4	102.6
College Station, TX	n/a	n/a	n/a	n/a	n/a	n/a	n/a
Colorado Springs, CO	101.1	95.9	101.3	97.2	97.7	108.6	104.1
Columbia, MO	91.8	95.5	75.0	100.0	92.0	102.6	99.8
Columbia, SC	93.5	103.1	72.7	126.2	87.1	79.9	100.5
Columbus, OH	92.6	98.6	81.2	89.1	95.5	88.5	99.7
Dallas, TX	108.2	100.2	118.8	106.8	96.7	105.4	106.7
Davenport, IA	92.0	99.7	76.9	98.9	105.8	105.3	93.7
Denver, CO	111.3	98.3	139.3	80.5	100.9	103.6	106.6
Des Moines, IA	89.9	95.2	80.2	90.1	99.1	95.4	92.3
Durham, NC[1]	n/a	n/a	n/a	n/a	n/a	n/a	n/a
Edison, NJ[2]	120.6	108.7	149.3	105.8	107.8	102.5	112.4
El Paso, TX	87.7	102.3	73.7	85.7	99.0	99.3	89.0
Fargo, ND	98.6	111.5	77.6	90.5	100.4	120.1	108.9
Fort Collins, CO	n/a	n/a	n/a	n/a	n/a	n/a	n/a
Fort Wayne, IN	86.9	86.7	62.3	95.7	99.5	101.5	98.6
Fort Worth, TX	94.9	92.4	88.4	107.2	96.9	101.5	96.2
Grand Rapids, MI	94.1	92.8	87.4	98.5	104.1	92.3	96.3
Greeley, CO	n/a	n/a	n/a	n/a	n/a	n/a	n/a
Green Bay, WI	91.1	91.0	77.9	97.4	97.7	101.8	96.6
Greensboro, NC	n/a	n/a	n/a	n/a	n/a	n/a	n/a
Honolulu, HI	192.9	165.0	332.6	172.3	138.2	118.8	124.2
Houston, TX	95.8	88.4	91.2	105.8	95.2	92.0	100.3
Huntsville, AL	91.3	95.1	66.6	99.0	97.3	96.4	104.7
Indianapolis, IN	92.4	94.1	78.4	105.4	97.9	90.6	98.0
Jacksonville, FL	91.7	98.4	88.0	97.7	86.0	83.7	92.7
Kansas City, MO	95.8	102.4	82.6	100.6	92.6	105.9	101.7
Lafayette, LA	88.9	101.8	72.0	88.0	104.7	88.0	93.3
Las Cruces, NM	n/a	n/a	n/a	n/a	n/a	n/a	n/a
Las Vegas, NV	103.6	95.8	118.3	98.6	114.0	100.2	94.2
Lexington, KY	92.7	89.9	83.7	95.6	96.7	78.9	100.7
Lincoln, NE	93.0	95.6	78.7	90.2	93.4	105.8	102.2
Little Rock, AR	96.0	95.1	88.1	97.4	94.7	89.6	103.2
Los Angeles, CA	146.7	116.3	230.6	106.2	134.8	110.8	112.0
Louisville, KY	94.1	91.8	79.8	94.6	98.1	105.2	103.7
Madison, WI	107.0	107.6	108.6	99.8	104.4	124.0	106.0
Manchester, NH	108.9	102.2	109.6	117.9	104.1	116.0	108.9

Table continued on following page.

Urban Area	Composite	Groceries	Housing	Utilities	Transp.	Health	Misc.
Miami, FL	115.0	110.5	144.3	102.0	101.5	100.6	102.7
Midland, TX	102.1	93.6	91.5	106.6	104.1	96.5	112.6
Milwaukee, WI	96.7	93.4	100.5	94.8	99.8	115.9	92.4
Minneapolis, MN	106.6	103.6	102.9	97.5	104.4	105.6	113.9
Nashville, TN	98.9	99.5	98.5	97.0	97.9	92.4	100.4
New Haven, CT	122.3	111.0	128.5	136.7	110.6	115.8	121.9
New Orleans, LA	105.0	102.6	125.5	81.5	101.3	115.1	96.1
New York, NY[3]	181.6	128.4	339.0	121.4	113.7	107.1	123.1
Oklahoma City, OK	86.0	93.3	69.6	95.3	86.2	95.0	92.1
Omaha, NE	92.3	96.8	83.6	99.4	98.3	96.4	93.3
Orlando, FL	92.1	100.7	85.1	97.2	89.3	88.3	94.1
Philadelphia, PA	110.9	118.7	116.5	105.6	116.1	101.8	104.8
Phoenix, AZ	99.3	99.7	103.8	109.5	107.2	90.1	91.9
Pittsburgh, PA	103.1	111.9	105.7	116.1	114.0	93.1	92.6
Portland, OR	134.7	112.4	186.4	87.1	131.0	115.6	119.4
Providence, RI	119.2	106.7	132.8	126.4	112.1	109.3	114.6
Provo, UT	98.2	93.0	96.1	84.7	100.7	94.5	105.4
Raleigh, NC	95.4	92.7	89.0	98.3	90.9	103.8	100.9
Reno, NV	114.1	118.7	125.8	85.9	126.3	113.9	107.6
Richmond, VA	94.2	89.0	86.0	97.6	86.9	106.7	102.1
Rochester, MN	n/a	n/a	n/a	n/a	n/a	n/a	n/a
Sacramento, CA	118.4	120.2	134.2	102.9	139.0	113.6	104.8
Saint Louis, MO	n/a	n/a	n/a	n/a	n/a	n/a	n/a
Salem, OR	n/a	n/a	n/a	n/a	n/a	n/a	n/a
Salt Lake City, UT	103.6	108.0	106.7	87.8	103.6	105.7	103.6
San Antonio, TX	89.5	88.0	82.2	87.6	89.1	87.2	96.5
San Diego, CA	142.1	116.1	216.3	123.2	129.2	107.3	107.3
San Francisco, CA	197.9	131.3	368.9	123.0	145.3	129.6	133.4
San Jose, CA	n/a	n/a	n/a	n/a	n/a	n/a	n/a
Santa Rosa, CA	n/a	n/a	n/a	n/a	n/a	n/a	n/a
Savannah, GA	89.5	95.7	66.2	96.0	94.9	106.1	100.0
Seattle, WA	157.5	129.1	227.6	108.0	137.8	128.6	136.2
Sioux Falls, SD	92.5	96.3	86.3	84.7	91.9	107.7	96.3
Springfield, IL	n/a	n/a	n/a	n/a	n/a	n/a	n/a
Tampa, FL	91.2	104.8	79.2	85.9	99.4	98.3	93.7
Tucson, AZ	97.5	100.5	87.9	99.9	101.1	98.7	102.0
Tulsa, OK	86.0	96.2	62.7	99.5	84.4	91.6	96.1
Tuscaloosa, AL	n/a	n/a	n/a	n/a	n/a	n/a	n/a
Virginia Beach, VA[4]	94.1	92.7	89.1	97.4	92.2	90.4	98.7
Washington, DC	159.9	116.0	277.1	117.9	110.6	95.8	118.1
Wichita, KS	91.1	94.3	69.6	99.3	95.3	96.1	102.5
Wilmington, NC	n/a	n/a	n/a	n/a	n/a	n/a	n/a
Winston-Salem, NC	90.8	101.4	66.7	94.6	92.0	119.5	100.5
Worcester, MA	n/a	n/a	n/a	n/a	n/a	n/a	n/a
U.S.	100.0	100.0	100.0	100.0	100.0	100.0	100.0

Note: The Cost of Living Index measures regional differences in the cost of consumer goods and services, excluding taxes and non-consumer expenditures, for professional and managerial households in the top income quintile. It is based on more than 50,000 prices covering almost 60 different items for which prices are collected three times a year by chambers of commerce, economic development organizations or university applied economic centers in each participating urban area. The numbers shown should be read as a percentage above or below the national average of 100. For example, a value of 115.4 in the groceries column indicates that grocery prices are 15.4% higher than the national average. Small differences in the index numbers should not be interpreted as significant. In cases where data is not available for the city, data for the metro area or for a neighboring city has been provided and noted as follows: (1) Chapel Hill NC; (2) Middlesex-Monmouth NJ; (3) Brooklyn, NY; (4) Hampton Roads-SE Virginia

Source: The Council for Community and Economic Research, Cost of Living Index, 2022

Grocery Prices

Urban Area	T-Bone Steak ($/pound)	Frying Chicken ($/pound)	Whole Milk ($/half gal.)	Eggs ($/dozen)	Orange Juice ($/64 oz.)	Coffee ($/11.5 oz.)
Albuquerque, NM	11.88	1.01	2.29	2.30	3.89	5.52
Allentown, PA	15.80	1.61	2.56	2.11	3.74	3.90
Anchorage, AK	16.43	2.25	2.85	2.16	4.61	6.29
Ann Arbor, MI	n/a	n/a	n/a	n/a	n/a	n/a
Athens, GA	n/a	n/a	n/a	n/a	n/a	n/a
Atlanta, GA	12.23	1.21	1.94	1.87	3.63	4.51
Austin, TX	11.44	1.08	2.14	2.18	3.36	4.26
Baltimore, MD	15.04	1.96	2.45	2.54	4.38	5.31
Boise City, ID	13.59	1.60	2.21	1.69	3.58	5.27
Boston, MA	n/a	n/a	n/a	n/a	n/a	n/a
Boulder, CO	n/a	n/a	n/a	n/a	n/a	n/a
Brownsville, TX	10.74	1.02	2.10	2.06	3.34	3.77
Cape Coral, FL	14.43	2.34	2.55	1.83	4.28	4.04
Cedar Rapids, IA	14.03	1.66	2.19	2.32	3.68	5.08
Charleston, SC	12.23	1.63	2.11	2.00	4.07	4.90
Charlotte, NC	13.63	1.23	2.11	2.12	3.68	5.31
Chicago, IL	n/a	n/a	n/a	n/a	n/a	n/a
Cincinnati, OH	13.66	2.66	2.15	1.68	3.92	6.05
Clarksville, TN	n/a	n/a	n/a	n/a	n/a	n/a
Cleveland, OH	16.00	2.16	1.86	2.08	3.91	4.91
College Station, TX	n/a	n/a	n/a	n/a	n/a	n/a
Colorado Springs, CO	14.09	1.35	2.17	2.04	3.53	5.14
Columbia, MO	12.00	1.39	3.08	2.51	3.99	5.68
Columbia, SC	12.03	1.56	2.36	2.02	3.66	4.95
Columbus, OH	14.20	1.44	1.93	1.99	4.00	5.76
Dallas, TX	12.76	1.26	2.34	2.12	3.60	4.62
Davenport, IA	13.66	2.17	2.57	2.18	3.81	5.91
Denver, CO	13.30	1.65	2.07	2.07	3.66	4.97
Des Moines, IA	11.66	2.33	2.79	2.40	3.41	5.05
Durham, NC[1]	13.15	1.77	1.97	2.14	4.23	5.04
Edison, NJ[2]	n/a	n/a	n/a	n/a	n/a	n/a
El Paso, TX	14.35	2.08	2.19	2.14	3.96	5.58
Fargo, ND	n/a	n/a	n/a	n/a	n/a	n/a
Fort Collins, CO	n/a	n/a	n/a	n/a	n/a	n/a
Fort Wayne, IN	12.91	1.22	2.46	1.84	3.53	4.98
Fort Worth, TX	13.46	1.51	2.16	2.25	3.40	4.73
Grand Rapids, MI	15.24	1.48	1.92	2.07	3.33	3.68
Greeley, CO	n/a	n/a	n/a	n/a	n/a	n/a
Green Bay, WI	15.09	1.55	2.25	1.74	3.86	4.01
Greensboro, NC	n/a	n/a	n/a	n/a	n/a	n/a
Honolulu, HI	18.12	2.74	4.32	4.32	5.31	8.59
Houston, TX	11.65	1.42	2.10	2.00	3.76	4.58
Huntsville, AL	14.42	1.54	2.22	2.04	3.86	5.03
Indianapolis, IN	14.69	1.70	2.12	1.99	3.50	4.75
Jacksonville, FL	13.82	1.79	2.26	2.53	3.59	4.86
Kansas City, MO	13.21	1.90	2.42	2.03	3.44	4.53
Lafayette, LA	12.53	1.49	2.57	3.19	3.66	5.04
Las Cruces, NM	13.28	1.47	2.51	2.47	3.97	5.37
Las Vegas, NV	14.35	1.87	2.51	2.43	4.05	5.47
Lexington, KY	13.65	1.26	2.02	1.80	3.65	4.54
Lincoln, NE	13.05	1.58	2.23	1.79	3.20	4.97
Little Rock, AR	12.30	1.41	2.12	2.08	3.74	3.90
Los Angeles, CA	14.79	1.77	2.76	3.66	4.20	6.21
Louisville, KY	14.49	1.35	1.51	1.48	3.61	4.28
Madison, WI	16.50	1.80	2.27	1.88	3.60	5.26

Table continued on following page.

Appendix A: Comparative Statistics   A-143

Urban Area	T-Bone Steak ($/pound)	Frying Chicken ($/pound)	Whole Milk ($/half gal.)	Eggs ($/dozen)	Orange Juice ($/64 oz.)	Coffee ($/11.5 oz.)
Manchester, NH	16.69	1.85	2.66	2.57	4.36	5.25
Miami, FL	11.37	1.69	3.62	2.72	4.62	5.14
Midland, TX	12.66	1.09	2.11	2.23	3.77	4.78
Milwaukee, WI	15.29	1.57	2.52	2.18	3.77	4.12
Minneapolis, MN	14.32	1.95	2.28	1.83	3.78	4.69
Nashville, TN	14.63	1.68	2.33	1.83	3.95	4.92
New Haven, CT	13.03	1.44	2.84	2.53	3.81	4.79
New Orleans, LA	15.23	1.37	2.57	2.32	3.68	4.26
New York, NY[3]	16.18	1.70	2.88	2.77	4.42	4.89
Oklahoma City, OK	12.72	1.51	2.34	2.04	3.32	4.72
Omaha, NE	15.11	1.71	2.00	1.72	3.59	5.20
Orlando, FL	13.49	1.37	2.67	2.44	3.89	3.89
Philadelphia, PA	16.43	1.91	2.57	2.47	4.19	5.67
Phoenix, AZ	14.66	1.65	2.06	2.51	4.00	5.82
Pittsburgh, PA	16.67	2.16	2.50	1.93	3.90	5.33
Portland, OR	12.15	1.28	2.88	2.75	4.10	6.48
Providence, RI	15.73	1.68	2.42	2.52	3.90	3.94
Provo, UT	14.23	1.44	2.04	2.18	4.02	5.39
Raleigh, NC	11.98	1.14	1.99	1.71	4.00	3.54
Reno, NV	13.35	1.68	2.82	2.46	3.75	5.69
Richmond, VA	12.49	1.38	2.09	1.44	3.87	4.49
Rochester, MN	n/a	n/a	n/a	n/a	n/a	n/a
Sacramento, CA	12.12	1.51	3.08	3.34	4.02	5.25
Saint Louis, MO	17.61	1.85	1.97	2.17	3.66	4.65
Salem, OR	n/a	n/a	n/a	n/a	n/a	n/a
Salt Lake City, UT	13.19	1.85	2.28	2.25	4.46	5.46
San Antonio, TX	11.06	1.05	2.20	1.86	3.41	4.07
San Diego, CA	14.80	1.85	2.70	3.71	4.32	5.91
San Francisco, CA	18.36	1.95	3.38	3.83	4.48	7.00
San Jose, CA	n/a	n/a	n/a	n/a	n/a	n/a
Santa Rosa, CA	n/a	n/a	n/a	n/a	n/a	n/a
Savannah, GA	13.73	1.29	2.24	1.99	3.42	4.55
Seattle, WA	17.83	2.43	2.97	2.23	4.41	6.55
Sioux Falls, SD	12.85	1.47	2.61	2.26	3.63	5.53
Springfield, IL	14.11	2.05	1.85	1.54	3.88	4.88
Tampa, FL	12.92	1.93	2.78	2.83	4.18	4.31
Tucson, AZ	12.19	1.47	2.37	2.22	4.03	5.97
Tulsa, OK	13.52	1.46	2.57	1.97	3.57	4.66
Tuscaloosa, AL	n/a	n/a	n/a	n/a	n/a	n/a
Virginia Beach, VA[4]	12.02	1.45	2.24	1.64	3.95	3.93
Washington, DC	13.41	1.21	2.91	2.62	4.08	5.36
Wichita, KS	13.71	1.63	2.05	1.95	4.15	4.95
Wilmington, NC	n/a	n/a	n/a	n/a	n/a	n/a
Winston-Salem, NC	13.05	1.11	2.31	2.28	3.98	4.30
Worcester, MA	n/a	n/a	n/a	n/a	n/a	n/a
Average*	13.81	1.59	2.43	2.25	3.85	4.95
Minimum*	10.17	0.90	1.51	1.30	2.90	3.46
Maximum*	19.35	3.30	4.32	4.32	5.31	8.59

Note: **T-Bone Steak** (price per pound); **Frying Chicken** (price per pound, whole fryer); **Whole Milk** (half gallon carton); **Eggs** (price per dozen, Grade A, large); **Orange Juice** (64 oz. Tropicana or Florida Natural); **Coffee** (11.5 oz. can, vacuum-packed, Maxwell House, Hills Bros, or Folgers); (*) Average, minimum, and maximum values for all 286 areas in the Cost of Living Index report; n/a not available; In cases where data is not available for the city, data for the metro area or for a neighboring city has been provided and noted as follows: (1) Chapel Hill NC; (2) Middlesex-Monmouth NJ; (3) Brooklyn, NY; (4) Hampton Roads-SE Virginia
Source: The Council for Community and Economic Research, Cost of Living Index, 2022

Appendix A: Comparative Statistics

Housing and Utility Costs

Urban Area	New Home Price ($)	Apartment Rent ($/month)	All Electric ($/month)	Part Electric ($/month)	Other Energy ($/month)	Telephone ($/month)
Albuquerque, NM	383,227	1,215	-	107.21	43.71	191.37
Allentown, PA	485,339	1,679	-	99.25	82.35	193.11
Anchorage, AK	656,122	1,516	-	102.07	130.31	188.62
Ann Arbor, MI	n/a	n/a	n/a	n/a	n/a	n/a
Athens, GA	n/a	n/a	n/a	n/a	n/a	n/a
Atlanta, GA	489,573	1,551	-	90.61	44.15	188.95
Austin, TX	484,044	1,807	-	101.22	51.85	196.79
Baltimore, MD	440,295	1,868	-	92.51	93.60	196.85
Boise City, ID	576,971	1,640	-	63.81	63.35	174.27
Boston, MA	n/a	n/a	n/a	n/a	n/a	n/a
Boulder, CO	n/a	n/a	n/a	n/a	n/a	n/a
Brownsville, TX	274,631	757	-	139.72	54.99	196.56
Cape Coral, FL	495,794	1,824	182.94	-	-	195.37
Cedar Rapids, IA	339,825	846	-	106.96	45.22	189.46
Charleston, SC	423,780	1,572	224.48	-	-	195.28
Charlotte, NC	377,295	1,498	155.34	-	-	184.19
Chicago, IL	n/a	n/a	n/a	n/a	n/a	n/a
Cincinnati, OH	368,833	1,083	-	76.34	81.75	184.60
Clarksville, TN	n/a	n/a	n/a	n/a	n/a	n/a
Cleveland, OH	347,809	1,302	-	89.55	82.10	188.12
College Station, TX	n/a	n/a	n/a	n/a	n/a	n/a
Colorado Springs, CO	497,622	1,512	-	104.56	85.71	186.39
Columbia, MO	442,644	861	-	96.49	65.29	194.74
Columbia, SC	322,903	1,107	-	112.85	167.25	190.68
Columbus, OH	366,506	1,200	-	88.37	72.63	184.15
Dallas, TX	439,403	1,563	-	136.69	79.10	196.79
Davenport, IA	285,682	1,014	-	88.01	57.06	198.79
Denver, CO	639,886	1,841	-	58.60	78.48	190.08
Des Moines, IA	337,128	741	-	79.63	53.25	188.32
Durham, NC[1]	582,565	1,411	-	85.31	62.68	176.30
Edison, NJ[2]	n/a	n/a	n/a	n/a	n/a	n/a
El Paso, TX	292,519	1,130	-	93.81	47.74	200.02
Fargo, ND	n/a	n/a	n/a	n/a	n/a	n/a
Fort Collins, CO	n/a	n/a	n/a	n/a	n/a	n/a
Fort Wayne, IN	296,241	1,083	-	105.04	65.35	191.60
Fort Worth, TX	372,205	1,327	-	137.89	75.49	199.27
Grand Rapids, MI	384,672	1,273	-	105.38	79.74	190.37
Greeley, CO	n/a	n/a	n/a	n/a	n/a	n/a
Green Bay, WI	382,340	881	-	83.06	80.95	186.93
Greensboro, NC	n/a	n/a	n/a	n/a	n/a	n/a
Honolulu, HI	1,605,915	3,589	309.47	-	-	182.54
Houston, TX	378,106	1,292	-	123.18	45.33	195.79
Huntsville, AL	350,811	1,023	173.74	-	-	186.08
Indianapolis, IN	340,588	1,325	-	111.24	89.87	188.71
Jacksonville, FL	385,800	1,507	187.84	-	-	196.12
Kansas City, MO	439,207	1,471	-	98.92	78.39	198.58
Lafayette, LA	284,856	1,063	-	89.62	58.12	186.23
Las Cruces, NM	364,513	926	-	95.18	40.12	192.31
Las Vegas, NV	491,447	1,600	-	121.78	57.89	196.21
Lexington, KY	351,975	982	-	90.87	109.72	189.80
Lincoln, NE	359,724	1,066	-	63.75	64.03	199.14
Little Rock, AR	395,450	946	-	81.77	91.69	204.44
Los Angeles, CA	1,098,874	3,182	-	123.99	84.34	192.21
Louisville, KY	338,400	1,315	-	90.92	105.78	184.63
Madison, WI	475,954	1,205	-	114.02	94.46	183.66

Table continued on following page.

Appendix A: Comparative Statistics

Urban Area	New Home Price ($)	Apartment Rent ($/month)	All Electric ($/month)	Part Electric ($/month)	Other Energy ($/month)	Telephone ($/month)
Manchester, NH	441,922	2,064	-	107.51	118.35	184.25
Miami, FL	584,754	2,690	192.68	-	-	195.67
Midland, TX	366,614	927	-	121.06	40.30	195.66
Milwaukee, WI	432,791	1,481	-	104.40	98.25	186.18
Minneapolis, MN	404,076	1,318	-	102.55	74.40	188.30
Nashville, TN	483,320	1,465	-	90.92	51.95	190.02
New Haven, CT	434,014	2,127	-	166.18	115.11	186.44
New Orleans, LA	654,349	1,851	-	71.40	46.62	187.68
New York, NY[3]	1,349,755	3,727	-	106.15	87.34	195.04
Oklahoma City, OK	333,325	860	-	90.04	66.60	195.02
Omaha, NE	350,853	1,290	-	92.74	60.25	198.80
Orlando, FL	448,493	1,766	154.33	-	-	192.14
Philadelphia, PA	430,067	1,542	-	105.62	103.27	196.34
Phoenix, AZ	497,561	2,083	187.70	-	-	185.99
Pittsburgh, PA	418,872	1,281	-	118.68	149.99	194.84
Portland, OR	661,664	2,636	-	80.74	76.64	181.33
Providence, RI	462,061	2,085	-	132.22	119.10	193.25
Provo, UT	532,268	1,449	-	67.96	72.66	194.35
Raleigh, NC	400,445	1,614	-	112.40	74.47	184.19
Reno, NV	576,610	1,515	-	97.93	44.46	185.65
Richmond, VA	383,637	1,334	-	95.49	99.23	182.67
Rochester, MN	n/a	n/a	n/a	n/a	n/a	n/a
Sacramento, CA	582,334	2,402	-	152.89	43.30	189.21
Saint Louis, MO	339,758	981	-	80.89	68.47	201.40
Salem, OR	n/a	n/a	n/a	n/a	n/a	n/a
Salt Lake City, UT	575,689	1,609	-	77.74	74.42	194.94
San Antonio, TX	327,632	1,388	-	99.94	37.03	198.89
San Diego, CA	1,001,748	3,057	-	145.75	74.47	183.97
San Francisco, CA	1,502,557	3,585	-	172.31	95.33	201.38
San Jose, CA	n/a	n/a	n/a	n/a	n/a	n/a
Santa Rosa, CA	n/a	n/a	n/a	n/a	n/a	n/a
Savannah, GA	297,041	1,176	158.44	-	-	186.50
Seattle, WA	940,665	3,031	188.83	-	-	198.78
Sioux Falls, SD	450,933	1,111	-	84.19	47.87	182.72
Springfield, IL	408,667	1,152	-	91.51	94.77	185.67
Tampa, FL	414,223	1,528	167.09	-	-	192.89
Tucson, AZ	481,931	1,410	-	103.78	69.05	186.26
Tulsa, OK	313,413	852	-	90.90	68.43	190.79
Tuscaloosa, AL	n/a	n/a	n/a	n/a	n/a	n/a
Virginia Beach, VA[4]	395,804	1,258	-	98.78	95.60	184.73
Washington, DC	1,156,418	3,220	-	117.06	100.23	188.98
Wichita, KS	314,516	978	-	93.16	71.97	198.70
Wilmington, NC	n/a	n/a	n/a	n/a	n/a	n/a
Winston-Salem, NC	319,961	1,290	157.68	-	-	180.76
Worcester, MA	n/a	n/a	n/a	n/a	n/a	n/a
Average*	450,913	1,371	176.41	99.93	76.96	190.22
Minimum*	229,283	546	100.84	31.56	27.15	174.27
Maximum*	2,434,977	4,569	356.86	249.59	272.24	208.31

Note: **New Home Price** *(2,400 sf living area, 8,000 sf lot, in urban area with full utilities);* **Apartment Rent** *(950 sf 2 bedroom/1.5 or 2 bath, unfurnished, excluding all utilities except water);* **All Electric** *(average monthly cost for an all-electric home);* **Part Electric** *(average monthly cost for a part-electric home);* **Other Energy** *(average monthly cost for natural gas, fuel oil, coal, wood, and any other forms of energy except electricity);* **Telephone** *(price includes the base monthly rate plus taxes and fees for three lines of mobile phone service); (*) Average, minimum, and maximum values for all 286 areas in the Cost of Living Index report; n/a not available; In cases where data is not available for the city, data for the metro area or for a neighboring city has been provided and noted as follows: (1) Chapel Hill NC; (2) Middlesex-Monmouth NJ; (3) Brooklyn, NY; (4) Hampton Roads-SE Virginia*
Source: The Council for Community and Economic Research, Cost of Living Index, 2022

Health Care, Transportation, and Other Costs

Urban Area	Doctor ($/visit)	Dentist ($/visit)	Optometrist ($/visit)	Gasoline ($/gallon)	Beauty Salon ($/visit)	Men's Shirt ($)
Albuquerque, NM	114.36	105.38	123.65	3.81	45.00	29.72
Allentown, PA	107.20	115.92	108.43	4.12	53.07	35.54
Anchorage, AK	228.37	152.08	252.89	4.49	55.00	34.08
Ann Arbor, MI	n/a	n/a	n/a	n/a	n/a	n/a
Athens, GA	n/a	n/a	n/a	n/a	n/a	n/a
Atlanta, GA	115.86	132.58	128.60	3.87	51.09	40.24
Austin, TX	122.17	119.14	118.78	3.47	52.91	34.72
Baltimore, MD	80.00	115.58	87.78	3.67	56.91	27.22
Boise City, ID	140.88	86.46	138.00	4.43	39.00	43.44
Boston, MA	n/a	n/a	n/a	n/a	n/a	n/a
Boulder, CO	n/a	n/a	n/a	n/a	n/a	n/a
Brownsville, TX	90.00	91.61	73.32	3.46	23.67	13.19
Cape Coral, FL	127.67	112.88	96.64	3.86	50.60	29.74
Cedar Rapids, IA	139.68	101.88	94.68	3.84	34.39	26.11
Charleston, SC	146.94	92.17	71.32	3.61	59.17	37.27
Charlotte, NC	140.33	135.13	125.78	3.68	31.70	49.35
Chicago, IL	n/a	n/a	n/a	n/a	n/a	n/a
Cincinnati, OH	142.44	100.47	107.60	4.01	43.10	45.33
Clarksville, TN	n/a	n/a	n/a	n/a	n/a	n/a
Cleveland, OH	113.00	109.47	94.21	3.86	35.71	41.99
College Station, TX	n/a	n/a	n/a	n/a	n/a	n/a
Colorado Springs, CO	134.96	108.29	123.36	3.96	47.60	44.38
Columbia, MO	125.84	92.11	110.19	3.84	43.33	29.87
Columbia, SC	124.17	82.50	53.00	3.26	42.36	37.12
Columbus, OH	118.38	87.19	61.70	3.77	42.53	38.24
Dallas, TX	141.13	129.77	139.62	3.39	64.32	38.33
Davenport, IA	136.67	84.83	102.07	3.46	34.89	37.75
Denver, CO	106.00	118.21	115.00	3.72	47.09	35.52
Des Moines, IA	131.59	90.21	119.28	3.34	39.44	39.61
Durham, NC[1]	143.27	113.91	132.86	3.70	53.11	22.22
Edison, NJ[2]	n/a	n/a	n/a	n/a	n/a	n/a
El Paso, TX	146.74	84.59	98.23	3.61	28.33	30.52
Fargo, ND	n/a	n/a	n/a	n/a	n/a	n/a
Fort Collins, CO	n/a	n/a	n/a	n/a	n/a	n/a
Fort Wayne, IN	140.00	105.42	88.55	3.70	34.67	39.66
Fort Worth, TX	92.61	96.41	111.17	3.58	55.08	32.87
Grand Rapids, MI	104.35	109.29	109.72	4.13	36.00	26.03
Greeley, CO	n/a	n/a	n/a	n/a	n/a	n/a
Green Bay, WI	152.75	98.67	75.78	3.45	27.46	26.90
Greensboro, NC	n/a	n/a	n/a	n/a	n/a	n/a
Honolulu, HI	168.32	97.93	209.95	5.03	75.67	53.63
Houston, TX	99.00	115.42	103.21	3.53	64.48	26.78
Huntsville, AL	124.50	99.17	88.78	3.55	49.33	33.22
Indianapolis, IN	97.22	99.33	68.63	3.65	39.23	42.46
Jacksonville, FL	90.43	93.90	72.66	3.68	63.00	25.84
Kansas City, MO	90.64	101.00	89.60	3.40	33.07	36.41
Lafayette, LA	109.56	100.77	100.99	3.43	43.28	30.76
Las Cruces, NM	114.46	118.68	146.98	3.89	41.11	36.87
Las Vegas, NV	108.58	98.81	101.71	4.55	46.52	20.35
Lexington, KY	97.28	98.17	80.03	3.78	58.71	52.93
Lincoln, NE	157.42	104.71	103.26	3.64	38.48	50.37
Little Rock, AR	116.78	58.25	94.06	3.52	52.55	37.55
Los Angeles, CA	130.00	128.20	132.27	5.54	82.67	36.49
Louisville, KY	82.50	87.22	61.89	4.13	84.44	45.50
Madison, WI	207.78	115.45	65.67	3.59	54.45	43.08

Table continued on following page.

Appendix A: Comparative Statistics   A-147

Urban Area	Doctor ($/visit)	Dentist ($/visit)	Optometrist ($/visit)	Gasoline ($/gallon)	Beauty Salon ($/visit)	Men's Shirt ($)
Manchester, NH	175.70	152.18	115.00	4.03	59.17	41.12
Miami, FL	109.83	94.65	100.82	3.81	80.15	24.94
Midland, TX	118.20	107.50	108.50	3.51	45.00	25.17
Milwaukee, WI	181.86	123.58	75.00	3.66	37.70	33.64
Minneapolis, MN	161.06	88.15	100.90	3.94	37.88	35.74
Nashville, TN	106.23	100.08	86.77	3.57	41.35	27.39
New Haven, CT	146.79	125.96	131.33	4.04	46.14	28.74
New Orleans, LA	168.89	125.56	105.55	3.92	42.78	39.00
New York, NY[3]	124.61	125.08	113.20	4.34	68.52	42.89
Oklahoma City, OK	111.16	120.92	115.53	3.36	43.00	21.10
Omaha, NE	140.67	89.91	120.78	3.75	30.74	28.27
Orlando, FL	98.00	108.72	79.50	3.83	60.44	45.42
Philadelphia, PA	136.17	96.17	118.67	4.19	63.11	34.67
Phoenix, AZ	99.00	99.00	117.08	4.30	50.83	19.04
Pittsburgh, PA	98.25	112.80	96.58	3.99	37.03	20.62
Portland, OR	142.04	113.83	122.48	4.72	56.61	32.88
Providence, RI	143.54	117.33	120.06	3.98	51.00	34.08
Provo, UT	105.44	95.74	116.76	4.24	40.94	46.89
Raleigh, NC	121.09	115.41	113.39	3.86	50.42	26.62
Reno, NV	124.83	110.67	109.50	4.63	36.67	21.59
Richmond, VA	145.32	104.74	115.73	3.61	49.08	29.41
Rochester, MN	n/a	n/a	n/a	n/a	n/a	n/a
Sacramento, CA	176.26	109.67	149.00	5.48	57.08	33.30
Saint Louis, MO	86.89	101.96	85.05	3.81	39.83	21.57
Salem, OR	n/a	n/a	n/a	n/a	n/a	n/a
Salt Lake City, UT	114.47	93.33	109.59	4.14	39.28	46.00
San Antonio, TX	123.35	111.47	125.52	3.43	58.84	35.83
San Diego, CA	116.25	118.33	126.18	5.50	66.33	36.49
San Francisco, CA	174.07	148.07	154.96	5.42	85.61	50.77
San Jose, CA	n/a	n/a	n/a	n/a	n/a	n/a
Santa Rosa, CA	n/a	n/a	n/a	n/a	n/a	n/a
Savannah, GA	119.64	141.34	89.22	3.40	37.92	35.96
Seattle, WA	176.92	144.83	170.85	4.95	65.43	43.45
Sioux Falls, SD	164.33	103.08	126.50	3.57	33.33	24.13
Springfield, IL	120.00	103.33	123.00	3.95	28.33	17.09
Tampa, FL	100.17	104.90	106.73	3.80	31.35	28.97
Tucson, AZ	140.00	101.33	108.10	4.09	39.50	37.99
Tulsa, OK	126.65	101.50	105.72	3.23	43.68	29.27
Tuscaloosa, AL	n/a	n/a	n/a	n/a	n/a	n/a
Virginia Beach, VA[4]	88.07	115.80	111.36	3.72	40.74	32.74
Washington, DC	129.71	105.20	75.00	3.98	81.00	37.83
Wichita, KS	106.36	92.39	162.06	3.75	41.30	51.01
Wilmington, NC	n/a	n/a	n/a	n/a	n/a	n/a
Winston-Salem, NC	142.38	133.67	132.58	3.71	45.00	35.83
Worcester, MA	n/a	n/a	n/a	n/a	n/a	n/a
Average*	124.91	107.77	117.66	3.86	43.31	34.21
Minimum*	36.61	58.25	51.79	2.90	22.18	13.05
Maximum*	250.21	162.58	371.96	5.54	85.61	63.54

Note: **Doctor** (general practitioners routine exam of an established patient); **Dentist** (adult teeth cleaning and periodic oral examination); **Optometrist** (full vision eye exam for established adult patient); **Gasoline** (one gallon regular unleaded, national brand, including all taxes, cash price at self-service pump if available); **Beauty Salon** (woman's shampoo, trim, and blow-dry); **Men's Shirt** (cotton/polyester dress shirt, pinpoint weave, long sleeves); (*) Average, minimum, and maximum values for all 286 areas in the Cost of Living Index report; n/a not available; In cases where data is not available for the city, data for the metro area or for a neighboring city has been provided and noted as follows: (1) Chapel Hill NC; (2) Middlesex-Monmouth NJ; (3) Brooklyn, NY; (4) Hampton Roads-SE Virginia

Source: The Council for Community and Economic Research, Cost of Living Index, 2022

Appendix A: Comparative Statistics

Number of Medical Professionals

City	Area Covered	MDs[1]	DOs[1,2]	Dentists	Podiatrists	Chiropractors	Optometrists
Albuquerque, NM	Bernalillo County	472.2	22.0	87.6	8.9	25.1	16.3
Allentown, PA	Lehigh County	359.4	84.6	88.1	12.5	28.8	20.8
Anchorage, AK	Anchorage Borough	383.0	45.1	130.5	5.6	64.2	31.2
Ann Arbor, MI	Washtenaw County	1,319.8	42.2	198.4	7.9	26.8	18.4
Athens, GA	Clarke County	326.1	16.3	52.1	4.7	22.5	15.5
Atlanta, GA	Fulton County	536.7	14.7	74.5	5.3	58.4	19.8
Austin, TX	Travis County	327.2	18.8	74.5	4.5	35.0	17.9
Baltimore, MD	Baltimore City	1,113.1	23.8	82.9	8.3	14.9	16.0
Boise City, ID	Ada County	283.7	33.7	81.1	3.9	53.3	20.7
Boston, MA	Suffolk County	1,576.4	17.2	235.9	9.9	15.7	36.8
Boulder, CO	Boulder County	361.2	31.7	107.7	6.1	82.8	27.9
Brownsville, TX	Cameron County	140.1	7.1	31.4	3.1	7.8	6.6
Cape Coral, FL	Lee County	203.1	31.1	53.7	8.1	27.9	13.2
Cedar Rapids, IA	Linn County	182.0	23.5	74.3	7.9	58.5	17.5
Charleston, SC	Charleston County	831.9	31.3	113.3	5.8	52.1	24.5
Charlotte, NC	Mecklenburg County	343.0	16.9	72.0	3.7	35.2	14.5
Chicago, IL	Cook County	434.1	22.5	95.4	12.6	29.2	21.1
Cincinnati, OH	Hamilton County	614.9	25.9	76.1	10.2	20.5	22.8
Clarksville, TN	Montgomery County	97.7	16.3	43.0	2.2	12.3	11.8
Cleveland, OH	Cuyahoga County	715.5	51.1	110.1	18.9	19.1	17.3
College Station, TX	Brazos County	270.8	16.2	55.3	3.4	17.7	16.5
Colorado Springs, CO	El Paso County	207.1	31.6	104.2	5.3	45.4	25.1
Columbia, MO	Boone County	808.6	57.6	71.6	5.4	38.2	28.5
Columbia, SC	Richland County	357.2	15.4	93.7	7.2	22.5	19.8
Columbus, OH	Franklin County	442.5	62.5	93.6	7.6	25.4	28.6
Dallas, TX	Dallas County	357.1	21.3	93.4	4.3	37.6	14.7
Davenport, IA	Scott County	240.7	53.3	81.0	4.6	184.3	17.2
Denver, CO	Denver County	611.2	31.8	81.0	6.5	39.4	16.9
Des Moines, IA	Polk County	215.9	99.2	77.3	11.3	59.4	21.7
Durham, NC	Durham County	1,130.5	16.3	75.4	4.3	19.9	14.1
Edison, NJ	Middlesex County	377.3	20.2	88.4	9.9	24.9	20.0
El Paso, TX	El Paso County	204.1	13.3	47.4	3.9	9.1	10.4
Fargo, ND	Cass County	404.1	21.1	82.5	4.3	75.6	32.7
Fort Collins, CO	Larimer County	251.3	31.4	83.6	6.1	56.8	21.2
Fort Wayne, IN	Allen County	263.0	29.3	66.9	5.9	23.4	26.0
Fort Worth, TX	Tarrant County	190.1	33.9	62.9	4.5	29.2	16.6
Grand Rapids, MI	Kent County	358.3	69.8	76.9	5.0	39.2	25.4
Greeley, CO	Weld County	126.4	18.1	46.2	2.1	23.2	12.9
Green Bay, WI	Brown County	253.8	27.9	80.9	3.0	49.7	18.5
Greensboro, NC	Guilford County	257.0	14.8	60.5	4.8	14.4	10.3
Honolulu, HI	Honolulu County	351.4	16.2	97.1	3.6	20.4	24.8
Houston, TX	Harris County	348.8	12.3	73.7	4.9	23.1	21.2
Huntsville, AL	Madison County	274.6	13.3	51.6	3.3	23.5	19.0
Indianapolis, IN	Marion County	451.2	21.7	92.0	6.4	16.8	20.9
Jacksonville, FL	Duval County	341.1	22.8	79.5	7.1	25.9	15.9
Kansas City, MO	Jackson County	314.4	59.1	91.9	6.4	47.6	20.2
Lafayette, LA	Lafayette Parish	377.7	11.6	71.7	3.7	32.8	14.3
Las Cruces, NM	Dona Ana County	166.0	13.6	59.1	6.3	18.5	8.6
Las Vegas, NV	Clark County	182.9	36.0	65.4	4.5	20.5	14.1
Lexington, KY	Fayette County	764.3	38.2	146.7	7.8	24.5	26.4
Lincoln, NE	Lancaster County	223.6	13.0	102.6	5.5	47.1	21.3
Little Rock, AR	Pulaski County	743.0	15.3	77.7	4.8	22.1	21.9
Los Angeles, CA	Los Angeles County	315.0	14.6	94.2	6.5	30.7	19.7
Louisville, KY	Jefferson County	480.0	18.7	104.9	8.1	27.8	16.6
Madison, WI	Dane County	615.0	20.6	73.4	4.8	45.0	20.9
Manchester, NH	Hillsborough County	240.8	24.4	82.8	5.7	26.2	21.9

Table continued on following page.

Appendix A: Comparative Statistics   A-149

City	Area Covered	MDs[1]	DOs[1,2]	Dentists	Podiatrists	Chiropractors	Optometrists
Miami, FL	Miami-Dade County	375.0	18.6	75.2	10.2	19.4	15.6
Midland, TX	Midland County	157.4	7.6	63.7	2.4	13.1	12.5
Milwaukee, WI	Milwaukee County	388.3	22.2	88.0	7.1	21.1	11.5
Minneapolis, MN	Hennepin County	532.0	24.0	103.5	5.2	77.1	21.6
Nashville, TN	Davidson County	647.1	14.1	81.0	5.3	26.8	17.5
New Haven, CT	New Haven County	577.3	10.3	77.7	9.6	27.2	16.6
New Orleans, LA	Orleans Parish	887.3	24.0	81.2	4.2	10.1	8.2
New York, NY	New York City	471.8	16.8	87.4	13.4	16.3	18.2
Oklahoma City, OK	Oklahoma County	423.1	43.0	109.1	5.3	28.9	20.5
Omaha, NE	Douglas County	547.3	26.0	101.4	5.0	42.2	21.7
Orlando, FL	Orange County	323.9	23.6	51.7	3.8	28.7	13.2
Philadelphia, PA	Philadelphia County	587.8	43.6	81.6	16.8	15.4	19.0
Phoenix, AZ	Maricopa County	255.3	33.2	71.1	7.0	33.9	16.7
Pittsburgh, PA	Allegheny County	640.1	44.3	97.1	9.2	44.0	20.7
Portland, OR	Multnomah County	646.7	32.2	101.6	5.1	76.3	24.8
Providence, RI	Providence County	489.8	17.1	58.3	9.7	21.1	21.6
Provo, UT	Utah County	119.4	20.8	59.3	4.7	26.4	11.7
Raleigh, NC	Wake County	289.4	12.4	72.7	3.7	28.3	16.8
Reno, NV	Washoe County	298.1	20.5	69.5	3.9	29.0	23.9
Richmond, VA	Richmond City	777.8	27.8	150.5	11.9	7.5	16.8
Rochester, MN	Olmsted County	2,470.7	46.0	125.4	6.7	44.1	22.6
Sacramento, CA	Sacramento County	329.3	16.6	80.7	4.6	21.8	18.4
St. Louis, MO	St. Louis City	1,222.5	35.3	63.1	4.8	21.1	19.4
Salem, OR	Marion County	182.0	15.0	84.4	5.8	34.0	16.4
Salt Lake City, UT	Salt Lake County	387.4	18.7	79.5	6.4	28.2	14.1
San Antonio, TX	Bexar County	329.0	18.9	94.2	5.4	17.2	18.9
San Diego, CA	San Diego County	346.3	19.7	96.3	4.7	35.5	20.4
San Francisco, CA	San Francisco County	834.7	13.1	171.0	11.8	43.1	31.8
San Jose, CA	Santa Clara County	445.9	12.0	124.2	6.9	45.0	28.8
Santa Rosa, CA	Sonoma County	284.4	19.0	96.7	7.4	43.0	18.3
Savannah, GA	Chatham County	352.3	19.0	68.5	6.7	20.2	13.8
Seattle, WA	King County	502.8	16.6	113.5	6.3	47.7	22.8
Sioux Falls, SD	Minnehaha County	369.1	23.8	56.1	5.5	58.1	19.0
Springfield, IL	Sangamon County	644.3	24.0	86.3	5.6	39.0	21.6
Tampa, FL	Hillsborough County	366.3	31.8	61.6	6.0	27.7	15.0
Tucson, AZ	Pima County	372.3	24.5	67.2	5.9	19.2	17.0
Tulsa, OK	Tulsa County	264.3	111.5	70.3	4.3	38.8	23.6
Tuscaloosa, AL	Tuscaloosa County	223.2	9.2	44.9	4.0	18.9	15.9
Virginia Beach, VA	Virginia Beach City	259.3	14.6	80.6	6.6	26.2	17.3
Washington, DC	District of Columbia	817.4	19.0	128.8	9.6	10.4	14.0
Wichita, KS	Sedgwick County	252.9	34.0	69.1	1.9	43.3	29.0
Wilmington, NC	New Hanover County	359.2	30.5	82.1	8.7	36.7	24.9
Winston-Salem, NC	Forsyth County	680.1	29.8	65.6	6.0	17.6	18.4
Worcester, MA	Worcester County	360.6	19.0	75.4	6.6	19.8	18.9
U.S.	U.S.	289.3	23.5	72.5	6.2	28.7	17.4

Note: All figures are rates per 100,000 population; Data as of 2021 unless noted; (1) Data as of 2020 and includes all active, non-federal physicians; (2) Doctor of Osteopathic Medicine
Source: U.S. Department of Health and Human Services, Health Resources and Services Administration, Bureau of Health Professions, Area Resource File (ARF) 2021-2022

Health Insurance Coverage: City

City	With Health Insurance	With Private Health Insurance	With Public Health Insurance	Without Health Insurance	Population Under Age 19 Without Health Insurance
Albuquerque, NM	92.1	60.6	44.2	7.9	4.3
Allentown, PA	88.6	46.4	50.2	11.4	4.7
Anchorage, AK	89.5	69.7	32.7	10.5	7.6
Ann Arbor, MI	97.4	87.5	20.3	2.6	1.3
Athens, GA	87.5	70.8	25.1	12.5	9.1
Atlanta, GA	89.4	70.1	27.0	10.6	6.2
Austin, TX	87.2	74.3	20.3	12.8	7.9
Baltimore, MD	94.1	59.3	45.9	5.9	3.4
Boise City, ID	92.1	75.5	28.2	7.9	4.2
Boston, MA	96.6	68.6	35.9	3.4	1.7
Boulder, CO	96.0	83.6	21.0	4.0	1.1
Brownsville, TX	69.2	37.3	35.7	30.8	18.5
Cape Coral, FL	87.2	64.4	38.6	12.8	10.1
Cedar Rapids, IA	95.2	73.2	34.4	4.8	2.2
Charleston, SC	93.2	79.8	25.0	6.8	2.4
Charlotte, NC	87.2	68.2	26.4	12.8	7.7
Chicago, IL	90.2	61.6	35.5	9.8	3.6
Cincinnati, OH	92.7	60.4	40.5	7.3	5.2
Clarksville, TN	91.5	71.6	34.9	8.5	3.5
Cleveland, OH	92.5	44.5	56.6	7.5	3.3
College Station, TX	91.3	84.1	14.3	8.7	5.6
Colorado Springs, CO	92.1	69.2	36.4	7.9	4.6
Columbia, MO	92.5	80.0	22.1	7.5	3.8
Columbia, SC	91.4	70.7	30.7	8.6	3.4
Columbus, OH	90.7	63.4	34.7	9.3	5.6
Dallas, TX	76.5	53.3	29.3	23.5	16.0
Davenport, IA	93.3	66.2	39.9	6.7	4.9
Denver, CO	90.4	66.9	31.3	9.6	5.5
Des Moines, IA	93.7	63.7	42.0	6.3	2.2
Durham, NC	88.1	69.6	27.9	11.9	7.7
Edison, NJ	95.2	80.5	23.8	4.8	1.9
El Paso, TX	80.0	54.6	33.9	20.0	10.2
Fargo, ND	93.8	79.9	25.1	6.2	3.8
Fort Collins, CO	93.9	78.5	23.9	6.1	5.1
Fort Wayne, IN	90.8	64.6	37.0	9.2	6.2
Fort Worth, TX	81.2	61.1	26.9	18.8	12.5
Grand Rapids, MI	91.6	63.6	37.7	8.4	4.9
Greeley, CO	90.2	60.8	40.2	9.8	5.1
Green Bay, WI	91.7	64.2	36.7	8.3	5.5
Greensboro, NC	90.3	66.3	34.1	9.7	4.1
Honolulu, HI	96.0	76.9	36.2	4.0	1.9
Houston, TX	76.2	51.7	30.5	23.8	14.5
Huntsville, AL	90.1	72.6	33.3	9.9	3.9
Indianapolis, IN	90.2	62.4	37.4	9.8	6.3
Jacksonville, FL	87.9	64.4	34.2	12.1	6.9
Kansas City, MO	88.2	68.9	28.9	11.8	6.9
Lafayette, LA	91.5	64.4	38.6	8.5	4.0
Las Cruces, NM	92.0	54.9	50.8	8.0	2.2
Las Vegas, NV	87.1	60.7	36.0	12.9	8.6
Lexington, KY	93.2	70.9	33.1	6.8	3.1
Lincoln, NE	92.6	77.1	26.4	7.4	4.9
Little Rock, AR	91.3	63.9	38.7	8.7	4.4
Los Angeles, CA	89.3	55.1	40.8	10.7	3.8
Louisville, KY	94.4	66.2	41.2	5.6	3.4
Madison, WI	96.0	82.9	23.3	4.0	2.4

Table continued on following page.

Appendix A: Comparative Statistics   A-151

City	With Health Insurance	With Private Health Insurance	With Public Health Insurance	Without Health Insurance	Population Under Age 19 Without Health Insurance
Manchester, NH	90.9	65.9	35.1	9.1	3.8
Miami, FL	81.0	49.9	34.5	19.0	8.1
Midland, TX	83.5	69.9	20.7	16.5	14.2
Milwaukee, WI	90.6	54.1	44.8	9.4	3.5
Minneapolis, MN	93.9	68.8	33.0	6.1	3.1
Nashville, TN	87.6	68.7	29.3	12.4	8.2
New Haven, CT	92.2	51.9	46.3	7.8	3.1
New Orleans, LA	91.2	54.1	45.3	8.8	5.0
New York, NY	93.1	58.8	43.6	6.9	2.4
Oklahoma City, OK	85.6	64.7	32.3	14.4	7.5
Omaha, NE	89.7	70.8	28.7	10.3	7.0
Orlando, FL	84.9	64.3	27.5	15.1	8.9
Philadelphia, PA	92.6	57.7	45.8	7.4	4.1
Phoenix, AZ	85.5	57.9	35.0	14.5	10.0
Pittsburgh, PA	94.5	73.0	33.7	5.5	3.9
Portland, OR	93.9	72.1	31.8	6.1	2.3
Providence, RI	93.2	55.8	45.4	6.8	3.9
Provo, UT	89.3	78.1	17.5	10.7	10.8
Raleigh, NC	89.6	74.3	24.5	10.4	6.1
Reno, NV	90.0	69.1	30.5	10.0	8.4
Richmond, VA	89.3	63.7	35.5	10.7	6.9
Rochester, MN	96.2	79.1	30.9	3.8	2.0
Sacramento, CA	94.3	64.2	40.8	5.7	2.4
St. Louis, MO	89.5	62.6	35.2	10.5	4.3
Salem, OR	92.9	64.7	41.5	7.1	2.1
Salt Lake City, UT	88.9	74.0	22.7	11.1	9.9
San Antonio, TX	82.8	58.9	33.4	17.2	9.2
San Diego, CA	92.8	71.1	31.1	7.2	3.7
San Francisco, CA	96.4	76.2	29.5	3.6	1.9
San Jose, CA	94.9	72.9	29.9	5.1	2.1
Santa Rosa, CA	92.4	68.5	36.9	7.6	5.5
Savannah, GA	84.3	58.4	35.4	15.7	7.7
Seattle, WA	95.6	80.7	23.5	4.4	1.5
Sioux Falls, SD	92.0	77.5	26.1	8.0	5.2
Springfield, IL	95.7	69.7	41.8	4.3	1.4
Tampa, FL	88.9	63.5	33.0	11.1	5.1
Tucson, AZ	88.7	57.2	42.3	11.3	7.6
Tulsa, OK	83.3	58.7	35.8	16.7	8.7
Tuscaloosa, AL	92.1	70.9	32.9	7.9	2.3
Virginia Beach, VA	92.9	79.8	27.6	7.1	4.3
Washington, DC	96.6	71.9	34.7	3.4	2.2
Wichita, KS	87.8	65.8	33.6	12.2	5.8
Wilmington, NC	88.9	70.3	32.6	11.1	6.5
Winston-Salem, NC	87.7	62.3	36.6	12.3	4.5
Worcester, MA	97.0	61.1	46.4	3.0	1.5
U.S.	91.2	67.8	35.4	8.8	5.3

Note: Figures are percentages that cover the civilian noninstitutionalized population
Source: U.S. Census Bureau, 2017-2021 American Community Survey 5-Year Estimates

Health Insurance Coverage: Metro Area

Metro Area	With Health Insurance	With Private Health Insurance	With Public Health Insurance	Without Health Insurance	Population Under Age 19 Without Health Insurance
Albuquerque, NM	92.0	60.1	45.5	8.0	4.7
Allentown, PA	94.6	72.8	35.7	5.4	2.9
Anchorage, AK	88.6	68.1	33.5	11.4	9.0
Ann Arbor, MI	96.6	82.5	27.2	3.4	1.8
Athens, GA	88.1	70.2	27.8	11.9	7.0
Atlanta, GA	87.4	69.4	27.2	12.6	7.9
Austin, TX	87.7	75.1	21.7	12.3	8.1
Baltimore, MD	95.2	75.1	33.7	4.8	3.2
Boise City, ID	90.5	72.3	30.7	9.5	5.4
Boston, MA	97.0	76.8	32.6	3.0	1.6
Boulder, CO	95.4	79.9	26.0	4.6	2.3
Brownsville, TX	71.5	38.4	38.3	28.5	17.1
Cape Coral, FL	86.9	61.9	43.5	13.1	9.8
Cedar Rapids, IA	96.2	75.9	33.5	3.8	1.8
Charleston, SC	89.7	71.5	31.4	10.3	6.7
Charlotte, NC	89.7	70.1	29.6	10.3	5.5
Chicago, IL	92.4	70.5	31.6	7.6	3.3
Cincinnati, OH	94.6	72.7	33.0	5.4	3.5
Clarksville, TN	91.6	69.8	36.8	8.4	5.6
Cleveland, OH	94.6	68.7	38.7	5.4	3.4
College Station, TX	87.5	73.3	23.8	12.5	8.4
Colorado Springs, CO	92.7	71.3	35.4	7.3	4.7
Columbia, MO	92.4	78.6	25.0	7.6	4.7
Columbia, SC	90.4	69.8	34.4	9.6	4.5
Columbus, OH	93.0	71.1	31.8	7.0	4.5
Dallas, TX	83.4	66.4	24.5	16.6	11.7
Davenport, IA	94.5	71.5	37.8	5.5	3.5
Denver, CO	92.2	72.6	29.1	7.8	4.7
Des Moines, IA	95.7	76.3	31.8	4.3	2.2
Durham, NC	90.0	71.8	30.0	10.0	5.7
Edison, NJ	93.2	67.3	36.5	6.8	3.0
El Paso, TX	78.7	52.8	33.7	21.3	10.9
Fargo, ND	94.5	80.8	25.2	5.5	4.4
Fort Collins, CO	94.0	76.6	28.9	6.0	4.4
Fort Wayne, IN	91.9	69.8	33.3	8.1	6.1
Fort Worth, TX	83.4	66.4	24.5	16.6	11.7
Grand Rapids, MI	95.0	76.1	31.3	5.0	3.0
Greeley, CO	91.2	68.7	32.3	8.8	4.7
Green Bay, WI	94.9	74.8	31.6	5.1	3.7
Greensboro, NC	89.9	64.9	36.0	10.1	4.5
Honolulu, HI	96.5	79.2	34.3	3.5	2.3
Houston, TX	81.3	61.6	26.6	18.7	12.3
Huntsville, AL	91.9	77.2	29.5	8.1	3.1
Indianapolis, IN	92.4	71.4	31.8	7.6	5.2
Jacksonville, FL	89.3	68.7	33.1	10.7	6.7
Kansas City, MO	90.9	74.8	27.2	9.1	5.6
Lafayette, LA	91.9	61.3	41.3	8.1	3.5
Las Cruces, NM	89.4	48.3	52.6	10.6	4.8
Las Vegas, NV	88.1	63.3	34.7	11.9	8.0
Lexington, KY	93.9	71.2	34.6	6.1	3.4
Lincoln, NE	93.1	78.1	26.2	6.9	4.7
Little Rock, AR	92.3	66.2	39.1	7.7	4.3
Los Angeles, CA	91.4	61.2	37.6	8.6	3.6
Louisville, KY	94.6	70.7	37.3	5.4	3.5
Madison, WI	96.1	83.0	25.6	3.9	2.4

Table continued on following page.

Metro Area	With Health Insurance	With Private Health Insurance	With Public Health Insurance	Without Health Insurance	Population Under Age 19 Without Health Insurance
Manchester, NH	93.8	77.2	28.7	6.2	3.4
Miami, FL	85.3	59.9	33.0	14.7	8.3
Midland, TX	84.0	69.8	21.3	16.0	13.0
Milwaukee, WI	94.3	71.8	34.1	5.7	2.8
Minneapolis, MN	95.7	77.9	29.9	4.3	2.8
Nashville, TN	90.5	72.7	28.4	9.5	5.7
New Haven, CT	94.9	66.9	39.6	5.1	2.5
New Orleans, LA	91.2	58.8	42.8	8.8	4.5
New York, NY	93.2	67.3	36.5	6.8	3.0
Oklahoma City, OK	87.4	68.4	31.5	12.6	6.9
Omaha, NE	92.3	75.4	27.6	7.7	5.0
Orlando, FL	87.8	65.8	31.3	12.2	6.8
Philadelphia, PA	94.7	73.0	34.8	5.3	3.2
Phoenix, AZ	89.2	65.8	34.2	10.8	8.6
Pittsburgh, PA	96.3	76.2	36.5	3.7	1.9
Portland, OR	93.9	73.0	32.9	6.1	3.1
Providence, RI	96.0	70.2	39.4	4.0	2.2
Provo, UT	92.2	82.4	17.0	7.8	6.2
Raleigh, NC	90.9	75.9	25.2	9.1	5.2
Reno, NV	90.2	69.8	31.2	9.8	7.8
Richmond, VA	92.5	74.5	31.1	7.5	4.7
Rochester, MN	95.7	79.6	30.8	4.3	3.3
Sacramento, CA	95.1	70.1	38.0	4.9	2.6
St. Louis, MO	93.7	74.5	30.5	6.3	3.4
Salem, OR	92.2	63.8	41.9	7.8	3.1
Salt Lake City, UT	90.2	77.7	20.2	9.8	8.2
San Antonio, TX	85.0	64.7	31.2	15.0	8.9
San Diego, CA	92.5	69.4	33.6	7.5	3.9
San Francisco, CA	95.9	76.0	30.5	4.1	2.3
San Jose, CA	95.8	77.5	26.7	4.2	1.9
Santa Rosa, CA	94.1	72.5	36.2	5.9	3.5
Savannah, GA	87.2	68.1	30.9	12.8	6.3
Seattle, WA	94.3	75.8	29.2	5.7	2.6
Sioux Falls, SD	92.8	79.1	25.2	7.2	4.7
Springfield, IL	96.2	74.4	37.3	3.8	1.4
Tampa, FL	88.3	63.7	36.4	11.7	6.2
Tucson, AZ	91.1	62.9	42.4	8.9	6.9
Tulsa, OK	86.3	65.3	33.3	13.7	7.7
Tuscaloosa, AL	92.6	70.5	34.5	7.4	2.6
Virginia Beach, VA	92.3	74.5	32.6	7.7	4.4
Washington, DC	92.7	77.8	26.4	7.3	4.5
Wichita, KS	89.8	70.6	31.6	10.2	5.2
Wilmington, NC	89.7	72.8	32.3	10.3	7.2
Winston-Salem, NC	89.0	65.0	36.4	11.0	4.8
Worcester, MA	97.4	73.0	37.5	2.6	1.3
U.S.	91.2	67.8	35.4	8.8	5.3

Note: Figures are percentages that cover the civilian noninstitutionalized population; Figures cover the Metropolitan Statistical Area (MSA)—see Appendix B for areas included
Source: U.S. Census Bureau, 2017-2021 American Community Survey 5-Year Estimates

Crime Rate: City

City	Total Crime	Murder	Rape	Robbery	Aggrav. Assault	Burglary	Larceny -Theft	Motor Vehicle Theft
Albuquerque, NM	6,355.7	14.2	78.5	256.0	994.9	902.9	3,225.8	883.3
Allentown, PA[1]	2,669.6	5.7	52.5	139.5	188.7	427.6	1,656.1	199.4
Anchorage, AK	4,659.4	6.3	194.8	194.8	816.4	504.2	2,541.7	401.2
Ann Arbor, MI	1,563.2	0.8	40.6	31.5	170.7	126.8	1,125.6	67.1
Athens, GA	3,463.9	3.1	81.9	79.6	345.7	465.9	2,213.8	273.9
Atlanta, GA[2]	5,423.2	17.7	49.4	221.5	480.1	621.2	3,366.4	666.8
Austin, TX	4,098.2	4.4	47.8	110.1	304.7	477.3	2,747.3	406.6
Baltimore, MD[1]	6,169.9	58.3	54.2	813.1	933.1	906.5	2,745.1	659.5
Boise City, ID	1,933.2	1.7	73.5	23.8	193.8	207.2	1,312.6	120.7
Boston, MA	2,490.8	8.3	26.4	131.8	457.9	243.5	1,439.4	183.6
Boulder, CO	4,092.0	1.9	29.1	67.5	223.3	613.5	2,808.7	348.0
Brownsville, TX	2,250.2	3.8	45.2	83.3	269.6	219.5	1,563.0	65.9
Cape Coral, FL	1,195.5	0.5	9.0	10.0	108.3	152.9	848.1	66.7
Cedar Rapids, IA	3,488.4	8.2	11.9	75.9	225.6	619.4	2,132.8	414.7
Charleston, SC	2,771.1	12.2	38.7	71.6	343.2	233.6	1,747.4	324.5
Charlotte, NC	4,076.6	12.4	25.6	184.0	614.4	449.9	2,478.9	311.4
Chicago, IL	n/a	28.6	50.0	292.1	616.2	320.9	n/a	373.2
Cincinnati, OH	4,576.3	30.2	70.6	246.1	546.1	762.0	2,427.1	494.2
Clarksville, TN	2,852.9	9.3	52.1	48.4	500.1	273.6	1,715.6	253.8
Cleveland, OH	5,727.5	42.2	103.7	420.2	1,090.7	973.8	2,321.2	775.7
College Station, TX	2,082.2	1.7	45.5	22.3	110.1	265.7	1,463.2	173.8
Colorado Springs, CO	3,976.6	7.4	82.5	77.5	429.6	533.5	2,344.8	501.4
Columbia, MO	3,106.6	10.4	71.3	46.5	314.0	323.6	1,985.1	355.7
Columbia, SC	5,227.8	14.4	65.3	156.3	516.0	552.4	3,442.2	481.1
Columbus, OH	3,686.0	19.1	89.5	197.1	249.9	609.1	2,180.6	340.7
Dallas, TX	4,291.0	17.3	41.7	241.5	544.2	727.6	1,955.6	763.1
Davenport, IA	4,661.8	9.8	65.8	133.6	527.5	895.8	2,568.6	460.7
Denver, CO	5,506.6	13.1	90.8	165.1	588.9	708.0	2,800.8	1,139.9
Des Moines, IA	4,606.3	15.3	55.3	114.3	519.8	894.1	2,347.1	660.5
Durham, NC	4,596.6	12.6	43.9	219.7	582.6	668.9	2,730.2	338.7
Edison, NJ	1,242.2	1.0	9.0	31.1	62.3	131.5	889.7	117.5
El Paso, TX	1,557.6	4.1	38.1	42.2	231.9	123.6	1,057.2	60.6
Fargo, ND	3,929.0	5.5	84.3	48.1	322.2	800.5	2,302.1	366.4
Fort Collins, CO[1]	2,389.9	0.6	24.0	21.1	171.5	204.8	1,834.5	133.4
Fort Wayne, IN	2,659.5	14.3	35.6	90.0	272.9	240.6	1,818.8	187.3
Fort Worth, TX	3,274.2	11.8	48.0	93.3	387.9	366.9	1,988.9	377.4
Grand Rapids, MI	2,666.0	13.8	59.7	94.8	544.2	228.6	1,437.9	286.9
Greeley, CO	2,888.6	8.1	48.0	70.6	298.6	333.9	1,774.6	354.7
Green Bay, WI	2,056.4	5.7	67.8	43.0	410.9	196.8	1,222.2	109.9
Greensboro, NC	4,513.0	19.7	31.7	193.7	656.6	737.6	2,501.9	371.8
Honolulu, HI	n/a	n/a	n/a	n/a	n/a	n/a	n/a	n/a
Houston, TX	5,435.1	17.0	48.5	373.2	817.5	672.9	2,875.9	630.0
Huntsville, AL	n/a	n/a	n/a	n/a	n/a	n/a	n/a	n/a
Indianapolis, IN	4,440.6	24.3	64.3	243.2	538.9	580.6	2,376.9	612.5
Jacksonville, FL	3,569.3	15.2	49.5	100.8	532.3	419.3	2,129.5	322.6
Kansas City, MO	5,705.4	35.2	76.5	257.3	1,216.8	615.2	2,595.1	909.2
Lafayette, LA	5,081.3	11.1	13.4	116.0	421.5	843.9	3,352.6	322.9
Las Cruces, NM[1]	4,077.5	9.7	61.8	55.1	370.0	631.8	2,652.6	296.6
Las Vegas, NV	2,738.2	5.7	63.1	100.8	358.1	416.8	1,390.7	403.0
Lexington, KY	3,191.6	8.6	54.6	102.8	154.1	445.0	2,108.3	318.2
Lincoln, NE[1]	3,133.7	1.7	110.9	57.0	213.3	339.4	2,255.4	155.9
Little Rock, AR	6,707.0	24.8	99.1	190.2	1,535.8	772.4	3,572.3	512.4
Los Angeles, CA	2,869.9	8.8	49.6	200.3	463.3	344.3	1,274.6	529.1
Louisville, KY[1]	4,578.4	13.9	29.8	149.2	494.0	638.9	2,670.2	582.4

Table continued on following page.

Appendix A: Comparative Statistics   A-155

City	Total Crime	Violent Crime Rate				Property Crime Rate		
		Murder	Rape	Robbery	Aggrav. Assault	Burglary	Larceny-Theft	Motor Vehicle Theft
Madison, WI	3,099.3	3.8	28.2	62.8	225.7	497.5	2,034.7	246.6
Manchester, NH	2,858.0	4.4	64.6	97.3	426.5	253.9	1,854.6	156.6
Miami, FL	3,305.4	12.8	19.7	128.1	394.9	305.2	2,104.0	340.7
Midland, TX	2,436.7	6.6	53.8	33.2	271.0	268.4	1,494.1	309.6
Milwaukee, WI	4,325.4	32.4	73.2	326.8	1,164.5	578.5	1,388.2	761.8
Minneapolis, MN	5,713.0	18.2	83.0	409.5	644.2	899.8	2,747.1	911.3
Nashville, TN	5,228.7	16.4	56.0	253.2	830.1	544.3	3,086.9	441.9
New Haven, CT	4,218.8	16.1	22.3	257.9	411.4	419.8	2,507.3	584.0
New Orleans, LA	5,863.9	51.0	180.8	280.9	811.6	506.4	3,138.3	894.9
New York, NY	2,136.3	5.6	27.1	158.8	386.2	167.5	1,279.4	111.5
Oklahoma City, OK	4,621.5	9.5	84.2	123.1	509.1	881.3	2,444.3	569.9
Omaha, NE	3,805.8	7.7	73.1	96.6	453.9	316.7	2,227.2	630.7
Orlando, FL	4,663.8	10.6	57.6	172.8	619.4	408.4	3,003.8	391.3
Philadelphia, PA[2]	4,005.6	22.1	69.0	331.6	486.0	409.4	2,329.5	357.9
Phoenix, AZ	3,788.0	10.9	62.5	191.8	533.2	433.4	2,121.4	434.7
Pittsburgh, PA[2]	3,594.8	18.8	40.0	230.0	289.9	443.2	2,331.9	241.0
Portland, OR	5,261.6	8.0	39.5	121.7	353.4	567.0	3,211.0	960.9
Providence, RI	2,900.8	9.5	36.7	101.9	338.0	335.2	1,776.7	302.9
Provo, UT[1]	1,623.0	0.9	37.5	11.1	65.7	139.1	1,259.5	109.2
Raleigh, NC	2,412.8	4.4	34.2	97.0	256.5	270.0	1,468.3	282.4
Reno, NV	2,710.2	6.6	108.4	110.4	338.0	426.4	1,345.1	375.4
Richmond, VA	3,269.8	28.3	8.6	117.4	194.6	330.4	2,328.7	261.8
Rochester, MN	2,172.3	4.2	61.5	36.6	147.1	275.9	1,519.1	128.0
Sacramento, CA	3,428.4	8.1	24.1	169.3	481.8	546.0	1,715.2	483.8
Saint Louis, MO	7,846.6	88.1	78.4	416.2	1,433.5	855.2	3,895.8	1,079.3
Salem, OR	4,187.2	1.1	15.9	83.8	294.4	383.8	2,780.4	627.9
Salt Lake City, UT	8,274.5	8.4	137.0	240.9	536.1	764.1	5,503.8	1,084.1
San Antonio, TX	4,362.2	8.3	75.5	137.5	514.2	503.4	2,679.8	443.7
San Diego, CA	2,060.6	3.9	33.7	84.0	247.3	231.2	1,116.0	344.5
San Francisco, CA	4,938.4	5.4	22.5	270.9	245.3	845.4	2,872.2	676.8
San Jose, CA	2,741.2	3.9	55.0	115.1	251.0	392.9	1,237.2	686.2
Santa Rosa, CA	2,120.0	2.3	62.2	76.3	375.3	306.3	1,059.7	237.9
Savannah, GA[2]	2,865.5	11.6	35.1	110.2	248.5	364.9	1,824.4	270.8
Seattle, WA	5,498.9	6.7	39.0	190.7	389.9	1,351.5	2,884.6	636.5
Sioux Falls, SD	3,729.0	6.9	51.8	54.4	484.6	365.1	2,273.0	493.1
Springfield, IL	n/a	9.7	88.7	171.2	676.8	822.6	n/a	223.0
Tampa, FL	1,885.4	10.1	24.8	79.8	405.5	227.1	980.2	157.8
Tucson, AZ	4,319.0	11.1	84.1	177.7	425.3	381.0	2,898.7	341.2
Tulsa, OK	6,244.2	17.9	94.0	184.3	836.5	1,095.8	3,045.0	970.7
Tuscaloosa, AL[2]	4,843.6	4.9	46.2	137.6	316.4	739.9	3,289.0	309.5
Virginia Beach, VA	1,610.5	3.8	13.3	27.5	54.1	110.7	1,262.7	138.4
Washington, DC	4,389.2	27.8	43.1	309.8	577.3	275.4	2,683.2	472.8
Wichita, KS[1]	6,462.8	9.0	94.1	118.2	919.8	686.3	4,044.6	590.9
Wilmington, NC	3,175.8	17.5	52.5	113.7	445.2	473.0	1,915.8	158.2
Winston-Salem, NC	n/a	n/a	n/a	n/a	n/a	n/a	n/a	n/a
Worcester, MA	2,631.3	5.4	21.6	113.6	491.8	360.8	1,396.3	241.8
U.S.	2,356.7	6.5	38.4	73.9	279.7	314.2	1,398.0	246.0

Note: Figures are crimes per 100,000 population in 2020 except where noted; n/a not available; (1) 2019 data; (2) 2018 data; Due to the transition to the National Incident-Based Reporting System (NIBRS), limited city and metro area data was released for 2021
Source: FBI Uniform Crime Reports, 2018, 2019, 2020

Crime Rate: Suburbs

Suburbs[1]	Total Crime	Murder	Rape	Robbery	Aggrav. Assault	Burglary	Larceny -Theft	Motor Vehicle Theft
Albuquerque, NM	2,025.9	1.9	34.6	40.4	405.3	354.2	870.1	319.4
Allentown, PA	n/a	n/a	n/a	n/a	n/a	n/a	n/a	n/a
Anchorage, AK	3,312.3	0.0	63.6	42.4	445.2	233.2	2,247.1	280.9
Ann Arbor, MI	1,734.3	3.2	74.1	38.7	378.3	167.6	942.7	129.7
Athens, GA	1,270.6	2.3	20.5	11.4	171.1	219.0	735.7	110.6
Atlanta, GA[3]	2,666.3	4.6	24.0	82.5	168.8	373.2	1,770.4	242.7
Austin, TX	1,578.6	2.3	40.3	25.2	129.8	227.0	1,028.7	125.3
Baltimore, MD[2]	2,213.3	3.9	31.8	88.1	260.3	217.8	1,485.2	126.1
Boise City, ID	1,206.5	1.9	52.0	6.9	189.1	178.4	674.0	104.3
Boston, MA	1,043.0	1.2	21.0	22.6	147.3	96.5	677.6	76.8
Boulder, CO	2,552.6	0.9	66.0	30.7	181.8	304.8	1,686.2	282.2
Brownsville, TX	2,358.5	2.5	38.8	39.2	248.9	317.7	1,598.9	112.6
Cape Coral, FL	1,333.2	5.3	37.6	48.3	222.8	148.9	761.7	108.6
Cedar Rapids, IA	1,291.6	0.7	39.3	10.0	135.0	318.6	660.1	127.9
Charleston, SC	2,958.7	11.2	35.6	81.5	313.9	324.5	1,914.7	277.3
Charlotte, NC	n/a	n/a	n/a	n/a	n/a	n/a	n/a	n/a
Chicago, IL	n/a	n/a	n/a	n/a	n/a	n/a	n/a	n/a
Cincinnati, OH	1,469.5	1.9	27.0	24.3	78.3	177.6	1,049.2	111.1
Clarksville, TN	1,659.2	4.0	32.5	25.9	161.9	300.0	988.2	146.7
Cleveland, OH	1,328.9	3.0	20.9	35.0	104.7	154.4	907.3	103.7
College Station, TX	2,209.2	5.4	86.2	41.4	262.1	349.1	1,310.7	154.2
Colorado Springs, CO	1,620.4	4.1	66.6	24.3	191.2	193.8	966.8	173.6
Columbia, MO	1,789.7	2.3	52.8	19.9	179.4	218.1	1,128.2	188.8
Columbia, SC	3,572.6	8.2	37.6	61.2	415.2	504.0	2,183.1	363.3
Columbus, OH	1,664.0	1.5	28.2	27.2	77.2	205.1	1,223.7	101.1
Dallas, TX	n/a	n/a	n/a	n/a	n/a	n/a	n/a	n/a
Davenport, IA	n/a	5.8	57.2	48.2	268.5	345.6	n/a	174.3
Denver, CO	3,233.8	3.8	57.7	70.7	238.2	357.6	1,904.0	601.8
Des Moines, IA	1,384.2	2.2	25.9	9.9	141.1	218.8	859.4	126.9
Durham, NC	1,768.6	4.6	17.6	32.3	169.1	319.6	1,113.7	111.7
Edison, NJ	n/a	n/a	n/a	n/a	n/a	n/a	n/a	n/a
El Paso, TX	1,026.7	3.1	36.2	20.0	217.8	121.7	554.9	73.0
Fargo, ND	2,397.0	5.8	53.5	17.3	159.7	489.9	1,455.9	214.9
Fort Collins, CO[2]	1,855.9	1.1	44.9	14.6	189.3	184.4	1,296.7	124.9
Fort Wayne, IN	988.4	1.4	22.3	16.7	146.5	136.7	579.0	85.8
Fort Worth, TX	n/a	n/a	n/a	n/a	n/a	n/a	n/a	n/a
Grand Rapids, MI	1,390.3	2.5	70.8	21.3	172.1	149.8	837.9	135.8
Greeley, CO	2,286.0	3.2	56.2	25.4	188.9	212.4	1,410.9	389.1
Green Bay, WI	816.1	0.9	22.7	3.2	54.1	122.4	580.0	32.8
Greensboro, NC	2,458.1	7.5	28.3	53.6	282.3	415.1	1,477.5	193.7
Honolulu, HI	n/a	n/a	n/a	n/a	n/a	n/a	n/a	n/a
Houston, TX	2,188.3	5.4	42.8	68.3	212.3	270.6	1,338.7	250.2
Huntsville, AL	n/a	n/a	n/a	n/a	n/a	n/a	n/a	n/a
Indianapolis, IN	n/a	n/a	n/a	n/a	n/a	n/a	n/a	n/a
Jacksonville, FL	1,375.4	2.4	28.0	23.8	169.5	172.0	880.2	99.5
Kansas City, MO	n/a	n/a	n/a	n/a	n/a	n/a	n/a	n/a
Lafayette, LA	2,189.8	7.4	23.9	35.5	344.1	400.2	1,210.2	168.4
Las Cruces, NM[2]	1,781.8	1.7	52.3	10.5	546.8	362.8	699.5	108.1
Las Vegas, NV	1,944.4	5.0	31.6	99.0	209.5	261.9	1,057.0	280.4
Lexington, KY	2,178.6	1.5	29.6	28.6	75.6	317.7	1,508.9	216.6
Lincoln, NE[2]	1,017.1	0.0	77.9	0.0	41.1	119.0	705.4	73.6
Little Rock, AR	3,185.5	8.9	56.1	52.4	493.6	457.2	1,830.0	287.2
Los Angeles, CA	2,435.2	4.2	28.0	102.7	228.4	355.9	1,303.4	412.7
Louisville, KY[2]	1,847.8	1.9	21.7	30.8	98.0	230.7	1,263.0	201.7

Table continued on following page.

Appendix A: Comparative Statistics

Suburbs[1]	Total Crime	Violent Crime Rate				Property Crime Rate		
		Murder	Rape	Robbery	Aggrav. Assault	Burglary	Larceny-Theft	Motor Vehicle Theft
Madison, WI	1,304.6	1.7	21.3	17.4	85.0	157.7	930.9	90.6
Manchester, NH	801.4	0.0	34.0	8.8	36.6	64.3	609.1	48.6
Miami, FL	2,551.6	7.0	31.8	85.7	280.9	220.2	1,689.2	236.7
Midland, TX	2,973.5	8.2	30.0	13.6	360.1	349.2	1,606.8	605.6
Milwaukee, WI	1,624.3	1.5	20.3	29.8	78.2	114.7	1,274.1	105.6
Minneapolis, MN	n/a	n/a	n/a	n/a	n/a	n/a	n/a	n/a
Nashville, TN	1,755.3	3.0	29.0	27.7	266.9	199.9	1,090.1	138.6
New Haven, CT	2,076.3	4.2	20.2	61.1	82.9	193.7	1,413.6	300.7
New Orleans, LA	2,268.4	8.6	24.1	45.2	233.6	244.1	1,581.0	131.9
New York, NY	n/a	n/a	n/a	n/a	n/a	n/a	n/a	n/a
Oklahoma City, OK	2,313.8	6.3	37.1	28.2	177.5	392.7	1,432.3	239.8
Omaha, NE	1,602.2	1.5	37.1	23.2	163.9	191.7	977.7	207.1
Orlando, FL	1,994.4	5.4	40.1	59.7	267.8	251.1	1,217.2	153.1
Philadelphia, PA[3]	1,935.5	7.6	16.3	96.8	235.8	202.8	1,235.3	140.9
Phoenix, AZ	2,118.2	3.8	35.2	43.8	211.2	276.5	1,380.4	167.3
Pittsburgh, PA[3]	1,402.7	3.5	23.7	33.2	168.7	159.1	958.5	55.9
Portland, OR	n/a	n/a	41.7	37.9	150.0	262.3	1,381.0	296.2
Providence, RI	1,264.5	1.7	40.2	29.7	189.1	149.7	749.5	104.7
Provo, UT[2]	1,312.0	1.1	30.2	7.2	46.1	131.5	1,018.1	77.8
Raleigh, NC	1,376.5	2.8	12.2	21.8	100.3	201.3	956.0	82.2
Reno, NV	1,808.3	4.5	59.7	39.2	243.4	304.1	959.0	198.4
Richmond, VA	1,784.2	5.9	23.2	30.9	126.7	136.3	1,342.0	119.3
Rochester, MN	824.5	1.0	36.1	2.9	75.1	191.3	456.7	61.5
Sacramento, CA	2,102.6	3.8	27.9	64.5	196.3	323.1	1,274.4	212.6
Saint Louis, MO	n/a	5.6	29.6	39.0	241.8	262.7	n/a	283.8
Salem, OR	2,400.4	1.9	29.2	29.6	123.4	258.0	1,578.0	380.3
Salt Lake City, UT	3,411.8	4.1	53.4	45.4	176.7	364.6	2,327.6	439.9
San Antonio, TX	1,759.0	3.9	36.2	22.5	151.5	297.8	1,074.4	172.6
San Diego, CA	1,655.8	3.1	25.4	69.7	229.9	210.0	887.9	229.9
San Francisco, CA	3,106.9	5.3	33.9	157.3	219.7	345.9	1,757.2	587.6
San Jose, CA	2,331.9	1.7	27.1	56.1	116.6	343.6	1,474.4	312.3
Santa Rosa, CA	1,554.3	1.9	41.1	41.8	329.5	232.8	807.9	99.2
Savannah, GA[3]	3,497.3	5.3	37.2	67.1	245.2	497.1	2,366.1	279.1
Seattle, WA	3,022.6	4.0	29.2	70.5	168.3	442.6	1,893.4	414.8
Sioux Falls, SD	1,410.7	2.3	31.5	8.2	172.8	462.4	597.9	135.5
Springfield, IL	n/a	1.1	36.1	21.9	259.1	349.8	n/a	122.4
Tampa, FL	1,648.1	3.1	34.5	42.4	204.3	176.5	1,068.6	118.6
Tucson, AZ	2,196.1	4.9	16.1	37.5	172.4	257.0	1,582.6	125.6
Tulsa, OK	2,005.9	3.6	31.0	21.9	174.2	380.7	1,150.1	244.3
Tuscaloosa, AL[3]	2,503.0	3.3	28.5	41.7	249.6	518.3	1,449.1	212.5
Virginia Beach, VA	2,536.3	12.5	30.6	67.3	327.6	197.9	1,701.5	198.8
Washington, DC	n/a	n/a	n/a	n/a	n/a	n/a	n/a	n/a
Wichita, KS[2]	n/a	1.6	42.3	14.5	156.8	271.8	n/a	129.8
Wilmington, NC	1,803.5	2.3	27.7	24.3	135.2	300.9	1,220.4	92.7
Winston-Salem, NC	n/a	n/a	n/a	n/a	n/a	n/a	n/a	n/a
Worcester, MA	922.7	0.4	32.3	16.3	166.2	115.4	522.3	69.7
U.S.	2,356.7	6.5	38.4	73.9	279.7	314.2	1,398.0	246.0

Note: Figures are crimes per 100,000 population in 2020 except where noted; n/a not available; (1) All areas within the metro area that are located outside the city limits; (2) 2019 data; (3) 2018 data; Due to the transition to the National Incident-Based Reporting System (NIBRS), limited city and metro area data was released for 2021
Source: FBI Uniform Crime Reports, 2018, 2019, 2020

Appendix A: Comparative Statistics

Crime Rate: Metro Area

Metro Area[1]	Total Crime	Murder	Rape	Robbery	Aggrav. Assault	Burglary	Larceny -Theft	Motor Vehicle Theft
Albuquerque, NM	4,660.5	9.4	61.3	171.6	764.1	688.1	2,303.5	662.5
Allentown, PA[3]	n/a	n/a	n/a	n/a	n/a	n/a	n/a	n/a
Anchorage, AK	4,576.1	5.9	186.7	185.4	793.4	487.5	2,523.4	393.8
Ann Arbor, MI	1,678.4	2.4	63.2	36.3	310.4	154.3	1,002.5	109.3
Athens, GA	2,572.9	2.8	57.0	51.9	274.8	365.6	1,613.3	207.6
Atlanta, GA[4]	2,895.7	5.7	26.1	94.1	194.7	393.9	1,903.2	278.0
Austin, TX	2,682.2	3.2	43.6	62.4	206.4	336.6	1,781.5	248.5
Baltimore, MD[3]	3,057.2	15.5	36.6	242.7	403.8	364.7	1,753.9	239.9
Boise City, ID	1,424.4	1.8	58.5	11.9	190.5	187.0	865.5	109.2
Boston, MA[2]	1,249.7	2.2	21.8	38.2	191.6	117.5	786.3	92.1
Boulder, CO	3,053.3	1.2	54.0	42.7	195.3	405.2	2,051.3	303.6
Brownsville, TX	2,311.6	3.1	41.6	58.3	257.9	275.1	1,583.3	92.3
Cape Coral, FL	1,298.3	4.1	30.4	38.6	193.8	149.9	783.6	98.0
Cedar Rapids, IA	2,367.4	4.4	25.9	42.3	179.4	465.9	1,381.3	268.3
Charleston, SC	2,926.8	11.3	36.1	79.8	318.9	309.0	1,886.2	285.4
Charlotte, NC	n/a	n/a	n/a	n/a	n/a	n/a	n/a	n/a
Chicago, IL[2]	n/a	n/a	n/a	n/a	n/a	n/a	n/a	n/a
Cincinnati, OH	1,894.4	5.7	33.0	54.6	142.3	257.5	1,237.7	163.5
Clarksville, TN	2,276.1	6.7	42.6	37.5	336.7	286.4	1,364.1	202.0
Cleveland, OH	2,145.2	10.3	36.2	106.5	287.7	306.5	1,169.7	228.4
College Station, TX	2,152.0	3.7	67.9	32.8	193.6	311.5	1,379.4	163.0
Colorado Springs, CO	3,139.6	6.2	76.8	58.6	344.9	412.8	1,855.2	384.9
Columbia, MO	2,572.2	7.1	63.8	35.7	259.4	280.8	1,637.3	288.0
Columbia, SC	3,830.0	9.2	41.9	76.0	430.9	511.5	2,378.9	381.6
Columbus, OH	2,523.0	9.0	54.3	99.3	150.6	376.7	1,630.2	202.9
Dallas, TX[2]	n/a	n/a	n/a	n/a	n/a	n/a	n/a	n/a
Davenport, IA	n/a	6.9	59.6	71.2	338.3	493.9	n/a	251.4
Denver, CO	3,793.1	6.1	65.8	93.9	324.5	443.9	2,124.7	734.2
Des Moines, IA	2,362.1	6.2	34.8	41.6	256.0	423.8	1,310.9	288.8
Durham, NC	3,000.9	8.1	29.1	113.9	349.3	471.8	1,818.1	210.6
Edison, NJ[2]	n/a	n/a	n/a	n/a	n/a	n/a	n/a	n/a
El Paso, TX	1,457.0	3.9	37.7	38.0	229.2	123.2	962.0	62.9
Fargo, ND	3,180.0	5.6	69.3	33.0	242.8	648.6	1,888.3	292.3
Fort Collins, CO[3]	2,112.3	0.8	34.8	17.7	180.7	194.2	1,555.0	129.0
Fort Wayne, IN	2,083.1	9.9	31.0	64.7	229.3	204.7	1,391.1	152.3
Fort Worth, TX[2]	n/a	n/a	n/a	n/a	n/a	n/a	n/a	n/a
Grand Rapids, MI	1,628.8	4.6	68.8	35.1	241.6	164.6	950.1	164.0
Greeley, CO	2,487.0	4.8	53.4	40.4	225.5	253.0	1,532.2	377.6
Green Bay, WI	1,216.1	2.5	37.3	16.0	169.2	146.4	787.1	57.6
Greensboro, NC	3,250.8	12.2	29.6	107.7	426.7	539.5	1,872.7	262.4
Honolulu, HI[3]	n/a	n/a	n/a	n/a	n/a	n/a	n/a	n/a
Houston, TX	3,249.2	9.2	44.7	167.9	410.0	402.1	1,841.0	374.3
Huntsville, AL	n/a	n/a	n/a	n/a	n/a	n/a	n/a	n/a
Indianapolis, IN	n/a	n/a	n/a	n/a	n/a	n/a	n/a	n/a
Jacksonville, FL	2,653.0	9.9	40.5	68.6	380.8	316.0	1,607.7	229.4
Kansas City, MO	n/a	n/a	n/a	n/a	n/a	n/a	n/a	n/a
Lafayette, LA	2,937.4	8.4	21.2	56.3	364.1	514.9	1,764.1	208.4
Las Cruces, NM[3]	2,871.0	5.5	56.8	31.6	462.9	490.4	1,626.2	197.5
Las Vegas, NV	2,525.2	5.5	54.6	100.3	318.2	375.2	1,301.2	370.1
Lexington, KY	2,811.4	5.9	45.2	75.0	124.6	397.2	1,883.4	280.1
Lincoln, NE[3]	2,843.7	1.5	106.4	49.2	189.7	309.2	2,043.0	144.7
Little Rock, AR	4,117.3	13.1	67.5	88.9	769.4	540.6	2,291.0	346.8
Los Angeles, CA[2]	2,567.7	5.6	34.6	132.5	300.0	352.3	1,294.6	448.2
Louisville, KY[3]	3,300.8	8.3	26.0	93.8	308.7	447.9	2,011.8	404.3

Table continued on following page.

Appendix A: Comparative Statistics

Metro Area[1]	Total Crime	Murder	Rape	Robbery	Aggrav. Assault	Burglary	Larceny -Theft	Motor Vehicle Theft
Madison, WI	2,007.2	2.5	24.0	35.2	140.1	290.7	1,363.0	151.7
Manchester, NH	1,355.7	1.2	42.2	32.7	141.6	115.4	944.8	77.7
Miami, FL[2]	2,609.4	7.5	30.9	88.9	289.6	226.7	1,721.0	244.7
Midland, TX	2,541.9	6.9	49.1	29.4	288.5	284.2	1,516.1	367.5
Milwaukee, WI	2,634.0	13.1	40.0	140.8	484.3	288.1	1,316.8	350.9
Minneapolis, MN	n/a	n/a	n/a	n/a	n/a	n/a	n/a	n/a
Nashville, TN	2,968.8	7.7	38.4	106.5	463.7	320.3	1,787.7	244.5
New Haven, CT	2,425.5	6.1	20.5	93.2	136.5	230.5	1,591.8	346.9
New Orleans, LA	3,378.9	21.7	72.5	118.0	412.2	325.1	2,061.9	367.5
New York, NY[2]	n/a	n/a	n/a	n/a	n/a	n/a	n/a	n/a
Oklahoma City, OK	3,387.0	7.8	59.0	72.3	331.7	619.9	1,902.9	393.3
Omaha, NE	2,710.6	4.6	55.2	60.1	309.8	254.6	1,606.2	420.2
Orlando, FL	2,288.9	5.9	42.0	72.2	306.6	268.4	1,414.3	179.4
Philadelphia, PA[2,4]	3,462.1	18.3	55.2	270.0	420.3	355.2	2,042.3	300.9
Phoenix, AZ	2,681.7	6.2	44.4	93.8	319.9	329.5	1,630.4	257.5
Pittsburgh, PA[4]	1,687.7	5.5	25.8	58.8	184.5	196.1	1,137.0	80.0
Portland, OR	n/a	n/a	41.1	60.0	203.7	342.7	1,864.0	471.6
Providence, RI	1,445.8	2.5	39.8	37.7	205.6	170.2	863.3	126.6
Provo, UT[3]	1,368.4	1.1	31.6	7.9	49.6	132.9	1,061.8	83.5
Raleigh, NC	1,727.9	3.3	19.7	47.3	153.3	224.6	1,129.7	150.1
Reno, NV	2,291.8	5.6	85.8	77.4	294.1	369.6	1,165.9	293.3
Richmond, VA	2,050.3	9.9	20.6	46.4	138.8	171.1	1,518.7	144.8
Rochester, MN	1,552.4	2.7	49.8	21.1	114.0	237.0	1,030.4	97.4
Sacramento, CA	2,393.6	4.8	27.0	87.5	259.0	372.0	1,371.2	272.1
Saint Louis, MO	n/a	14.3	34.8	79.2	368.7	325.8	n/a	368.6
Salem, OR	3,123.1	1.6	23.8	51.5	192.6	308.9	2,064.3	480.4
Salt Lake City, UT	4,200.7	4.8	67.0	77.1	235.0	429.5	2,842.9	544.4
San Antonio, TX	3,339.5	6.6	60.1	92.3	371.7	422.6	2,049.1	337.2
San Diego, CA	1,830.5	3.4	29.0	75.8	237.4	219.1	986.3	279.3
San Francisco, CA[2]	3,448.3	5.3	31.8	178.5	224.5	439.0	1,965.0	604.2
San Jose, CA	2,543.9	2.8	41.6	86.7	186.2	369.1	1,351.5	506.0
Santa Rosa, CA	1,758.4	2.0	48.7	54.2	346.0	259.4	898.8	149.2
Savannah, GA[4]	3,107.5	9.2	35.9	93.7	247.2	415.6	2,032.0	274.0
Seattle, WA[2]	3,496.7	4.5	31.1	93.5	210.7	616.6	2,083.1	457.2
Sioux Falls, SD	3,001.8	5.5	45.4	39.9	386.8	395.6	1,747.6	381.0
Springfield, IL	n/a	5.8	65.2	104.7	490.8	612.0	n/a	178.2
Tampa, FL	1,678.0	4.0	33.3	47.1	229.7	182.8	1,057.5	123.6
Tucson, AZ	3,298.3	8.1	51.4	110.3	303.7	321.4	2,265.9	237.5
Tulsa, OK	3,701.1	9.3	56.2	86.8	439.1	666.7	1,908.0	534.9
Tuscaloosa, AL[4]	3,445.1	4.0	35.6	80.3	276.5	607.5	2,189.7	251.6
Virginia Beach, VA	2,301.0	10.3	26.2	57.2	258.1	175.7	1,590.0	183.5
Washington, DC[2]	n/a	n/a	n/a	n/a	n/a	n/a	n/a	n/a
Wichita, KS[3]	n/a	6.1	74.0	77.9	623.3	525.2	n/a	411.7
Wilmington, NC	2,373.9	8.6	38.0	61.5	264.0	372.4	1,509.5	120.0
Winston-Salem, NC	n/a	n/a	n/a	n/a	n/a	n/a	n/a	n/a
Worcester, MA	1,285.0	1.5	30.1	36.9	235.2	167.5	707.6	106.2
U.S.	2,356.7	6.5	38.4	73.9	279.7	314.2	1,398.0	246.0

Note: Figures are crimes per 100,000 population in 2020 except where noted; n/a not available; (1) Figures cover the Metropolitan Statistical Area except where noted; (2) Metropolitan Division (MD); (3) 2019 data; (4) 2018 data; Due to the transition to the National Incident-Based Reporting System (NIBRS), limited city and metro area data was released for 2021
Source: FBI Uniform Crime Reports, 2018, 2019, 2020

Temperature & Precipitation: Yearly Averages and Extremes

City	Extreme Low (°F)	Average Low (°F)	Average Temp. (°F)	Average High (°F)	Extreme High (°F)	Average Precip. (in.)	Average Snow (in.)
Albuquerque, NM	-17	43	57	70	105	8.5	11
Allentown, PA	-12	42	52	61	105	44.2	32
Anchorage, AK	-34	29	36	43	85	15.7	71
Ann Arbor, MI	-21	39	49	58	104	32.4	41
Athens, GA	-8	52	62	72	105	49.8	2
Atlanta, GA	-8	52	62	72	105	49.8	2
Austin, TX	-2	58	69	79	109	31.1	1
Baltimore, MD	-7	45	56	65	105	41.2	21
Boise City, ID	-25	39	51	63	111	11.8	22
Boston, MA	-12	44	52	59	102	42.9	41
Boulder, CO	-25	37	51	64	103	15.5	63
Brownsville, TX	16	65	74	83	106	25.8	Trace
Cape Coral, FL	26	65	75	84	103	53.9	0
Cedar Rapids, IA	-34	36	47	57	105	34.4	33
Charleston, SC	6	55	66	76	104	52.1	1
Charlotte, NC	-5	50	61	71	104	42.8	6
Chicago, IL	-27	40	49	59	104	35.4	39
Cincinnati, OH	-25	44	54	64	103	40.9	23
Clarksville, TN	-17	49	60	70	107	47.4	11
Cleveland, OH	-19	41	50	59	104	37.1	55
College Station, TX	-2	58	69	79	109	31.1	1
Colorado Springs, CO	-24	36	49	62	99	17.0	48
Columbia, MO	-20	44	54	64	111	40.6	25
Columbia, SC	-1	51	64	75	107	48.3	2
Columbus, OH	-19	42	52	62	104	37.9	28
Dallas, TX	-2	56	67	77	112	33.9	3
Davenport, IA	-24	40	50	60	108	31.8	33
Denver, CO	-25	37	51	64	103	15.5	63
Des Moines, IA	-24	40	50	60	108	31.8	33
Durham, NC	-9	48	60	71	105	42.0	8
Edison, NJ	-8	46	55	63	105	43.5	27
El Paso, TX	-8	50	64	78	114	8.6	6
Fargo, ND	-36	31	41	52	106	19.6	40
Fort Collins, CO	-25	37	51	64	103	15.5	63
Fort Wayne, IN	-22	40	50	60	106	35.9	33
Fort Worth, TX	-1	55	66	76	113	32.3	3
Grand Rapids, MI	-22	38	48	57	102	34.7	73
Greeley, CO	-25	37	51	64	103	15.5	63
Green Bay, WI	-31	34	44	54	99	28.3	46
Greensboro, NC	-8	47	58	69	103	42.5	10
Honolulu, HI	52	70	77	84	94	22.4	0
Houston, TX	7	58	69	79	107	46.9	Trace
Huntsville, AL	-11	50	61	71	104	56.8	4
Indianapolis, IN	-23	42	53	62	104	40.2	25
Jacksonville, FL	7	58	69	79	103	52.0	0
Kansas City, MO	-23	44	54	64	109	38.1	21
Lafayette, LA	8	57	68	78	103	58.5	Trace
Las Cruces, NM	-8	50	64	78	114	8.6	6
Las Vegas, NV	8	53	67	80	116	4.0	1
Lexington, KY	-21	45	55	65	103	45.1	17
Lincoln, NE	-33	39	51	62	108	29.1	27
Little Rock, AR	-5	51	62	73	112	50.7	5
Los Angeles, CA	27	55	63	70	110	11.3	Trace
Louisville, KY	-20	46	57	67	105	43.9	17
Madison, WI	-37	35	46	57	104	31.1	42

Table continued on following page.

City	Extreme Low (°F)	Average Low (°F)	Average Temp. (°F)	Average High (°F)	Extreme High (°F)	Average Precip. (in.)	Average Snow (in.)
Manchester, NH	-33	34	46	57	102	36.9	63
Miami, FL	30	69	76	83	98	57.1	0
Midland, TX	-11	50	64	77	116	14.6	4
Milwaukee, WI	-26	38	47	55	103	32.0	49
Minneapolis, MN	-34	35	45	54	105	27.1	52
Nashville, TN	-17	49	60	70	107	47.4	11
New Haven, CT	-7	44	52	60	103	41.4	25
New Orleans, LA	11	59	69	78	102	60.6	Trace
New York, NY	-2	47	55	62	104	47.0	23
Oklahoma City, OK	-8	49	60	71	110	32.8	10
Omaha, NE	-23	40	51	62	110	30.1	29
Orlando, FL	19	62	72	82	100	47.7	Trace
Philadelphia, PA	-7	45	55	64	104	41.4	22
Phoenix, AZ	17	59	72	86	122	7.3	Trace
Pittsburgh, PA	-18	41	51	60	103	37.1	43
Portland, OR	-3	45	54	62	107	37.5	7
Providence, RI	-13	42	51	60	104	45.3	35
Provo, UT	-22	40	52	64	107	15.6	63
Raleigh, NC	-9	48	60	71	105	42.0	8
Reno, NV	-16	33	50	67	105	7.2	24
Richmond, VA	-8	48	58	69	105	43.0	13
Rochester, MN	-40	34	44	54	102	29.4	47
Sacramento, CA	18	48	61	73	115	17.3	Trace
Saint Louis, MO	-18	46	56	66	115	36.8	20
Salem, OR	-12	41	52	63	108	40.2	7
Salt Lake City, UT	-22	40	52	64	107	15.6	63
San Antonio, TX	0	58	69	80	108	29.6	4
San Diego, CA	29	57	64	71	111	9.5	Trace
San Francisco, CA	24	49	57	65	106	19.3	Trace
San Jose, CA	21	50	59	68	105	13.5	Trace
Santa Rosa, CA	23	42	57	71	109	29.0	n/a
Savannah, GA	3	56	67	77	105	50.3	Trace
Seattle, WA	0	44	52	59	99	38.4	13
Sioux Falls, SD	-36	35	46	57	110	24.6	38
Springfield, IL	-24	44	54	63	112	34.9	21
Tampa, FL	18	63	73	82	99	46.7	Trace
Tucson, AZ	16	55	69	82	117	11.6	2
Tulsa, OK	-8	50	61	71	112	38.9	10
Tuscaloosa, AL	-6	51	63	74	106	53.5	2
Virginia Beach, VA	-3	51	60	69	104	44.8	8
Washington, DC	-5	49	58	67	104	39.5	18
Wichita, KS	-21	45	57	68	113	29.3	17
Wilmington, NC	0	53	64	74	104	55.0	2
Winston-Salem, NC	-8	47	58	69	103	42.5	10
Worcester, MA	-13	38	47	56	99	47.6	62

Source: National Climatic Data Center, International Station Meteorological Climate Summary, 9/96; NOAA

Weather Conditions

City	Temperature 10°F & below	Temperature 32°F & below	Temperature 90°F & above	Daytime Sky Clear	Daytime Sky Partly cloudy	Daytime Sky Cloudy	Precipitation 0.01 inch or more precip.	Precipitation 1.0 inch or more snow/ice	Thunder-storms
Albuquerque, NM	4	114	65	140	161	64	60	9	38
Allentown, PA	n/a	123	15	77	148	140	123	20	31
Anchorage, AK	n/a	194	n/a	50	115	200	113	49	2
Ann Arbor, MI	n/a	136	12	74	134	157	135	38	32
Athens, GA	1	49	38	98	147	120	116	3	48
Atlanta, GA	1	49	38	98	147	120	116	3	48
Austin, TX	<1	20	111	105	148	112	83	1	41
Baltimore, MD	6	97	31	91	143	131	113	13	27
Boise City, ID	n/a	124	45	106	133	126	91	22	14
Boston, MA	n/a	97	12	88	127	150	253	48	18
Boulder, CO	24	155	33	99	177	89	90	38	39
Brownsville, TX	n/a	n/a	116	86	180	99	72	0	27
Cape Coral, FL	n/a	n/a	115	93	220	52	110	0	92
Cedar Rapids, IA	n/a	156	16	89	132	144	109	28	42
Charleston, SC	<1	33	53	89	162	114	114	1	59
Charlotte, NC	1	65	44	98	142	125	113	3	41
Chicago, IL	n/a	132	17	83	136	146	125	31	38
Cincinnati, OH	14	107	23	80	126	159	127	25	39
Clarksville, TN	5	76	51	98	135	132	119	8	54
Cleveland, OH	n/a	123	12	63	127	175	157	48	34
College Station, TX	<1	20	111	105	148	112	83	1	41
Colorado Springs, CO	21	161	18	108	157	100	98	33	49
Columbia, MO	17	108	36	99	127	139	110	17	52
Columbia, SC	<1	58	77	97	149	119	110	1	53
Columbus, OH	n/a	118	19	72	137	156	136	29	40
Dallas, TX	1	34	102	108	160	97	78	2	49
Davenport, IA	n/a	137	26	99	129	137	106	25	46
Denver, CO	24	155	33	99	177	89	90	38	39
Des Moines, IA	n/a	137	26	99	129	137	106	25	46
Durham, NC	n/a	n/a	39	98	143	124	110	3	42
Edison, NJ	n/a	90	24	80	146	139	122	16	46
El Paso, TX	1	59	106	147	164	54	49	3	35
Fargo, ND	n/a	180	15	81	145	139	100	38	31
Fort Collins, CO	24	155	33	99	177	89	90	38	39
Fort Wayne, IN	n/a	131	16	75	140	150	131	31	39
Fort Worth, TX	1	40	100	123	136	106	79	3	47
Grand Rapids, MI	n/a	146	11	67	119	179	142	57	34
Greeley, CO	24	155	33	99	177	89	90	38	39
Green Bay, WI	n/a	163	7	86	125	154	120	40	33
Greensboro, NC	3	85	32	94	143	128	113	5	43
Honolulu, HI	n/a	n/a	23	25	286	54	98	0	7
Houston, TX	n/a	n/a	96	83	168	114	101	1	62
Huntsville, AL	2	66	49	70	118	177	116	2	54
Indianapolis, IN	19	119	19	83	128	154	127	24	43
Jacksonville, FL	<1	16	83	86	181	98	114	1	65
Kansas City, MO	22	110	39	112	134	119	103	17	51
Lafayette, LA	<1	21	86	99	150	116	113	<1	73
Las Cruces, NM	1	59	106	147	164	54	49	3	35
Las Vegas, NV	<1	37	134	185	132	48	27	2	13
Lexington, KY	11	96	22	86	136	143	129	17	44
Lincoln, NE	n/a	145	40	108	135	122	94	19	46
Little Rock, AR	1	57	73	110	142	113	104	4	57
Los Angeles, CA	0	<1	5	131	125	109	34	0	1
Louisville, KY	8	90	35	82	143	140	125	15	45

Table continued on following page.

City	Temperature 10°F & below	Temperature 32°F & below	Temperature 90°F & above	Daytime Sky Clear	Daytime Sky Partly cloudy	Daytime Sky Cloudy	Precipitation 0.01 inch or more precip.	Precipitation 1.0 inch or more snow/ice	Thunder-storms
Madison, WI	n/a	161	14	88	119	158	118	38	40
Manchester, NH	n/a	171	12	87	131	147	125	32	19
Miami, FL	n/a	n/a	55	48	263	54	128	0	74
Midland, TX	1	62	102	144	138	83	52	3	38
Milwaukee, WI	n/a	141	10	90	118	157	126	38	35
Minneapolis, MN	n/a	156	16	93	125	147	113	41	37
Nashville, TN	5	76	51	98	135	132	119	8	54
New Haven, CT	n/a	n/a	7	80	146	139	118	17	22
New Orleans, LA	0	13	70	90	169	106	114	1	69
New York, NY	n/a	n/a	18	85	166	114	120	11	20
Oklahoma City, OK	5	79	70	124	131	110	80	8	50
Omaha, NE	n/a	139	35	100	142	123	97	20	46
Orlando, FL	n/a	n/a	90	76	208	81	115	0	80
Philadelphia, PA	5	94	23	81	146	138	117	14	27
Phoenix, AZ	0	10	167	186	125	54	37	<1	23
Pittsburgh, PA	n/a	121	8	62	137	166	154	42	35
Portland, OR	n/a	37	11	67	116	182	152	4	7
Providence, RI	n/a	117	9	85	134	146	123	21	21
Provo, UT	n/a	128	56	94	152	119	92	38	38
Raleigh, NC	n/a	n/a	39	98	143	124	110	3	42
Reno, NV	14	178	50	143	139	83	50	17	14
Richmond, VA	3	79	41	90	147	128	115	7	43
Rochester, MN	n/a	165	9	87	126	152	114	40	41
Sacramento, CA	0	21	73	175	111	79	58	<1	2
Saint Louis, MO	13	100	43	97	138	130	109	14	46
Salem, OR	n/a	66	16	78	118	169	146	6	5
Salt Lake City, UT	n/a	128	56	94	152	119	92	38	38
San Antonio, TX	n/a	n/a	112	97	153	115	81	1	36
San Diego, CA	0	<1	4	115	126	124	40	0	5
San Francisco, CA	0	6	4	136	130	99	63	<1	5
San Jose, CA	0	5	5	106	180	79	57	<1	6
Santa Rosa, CA	n/a	43	30	n/a	365	n/a	n/a	n/a	2
Savannah, GA	<1	29	70	97	155	113	111	<1	63
Seattle, WA	n/a	38	3	57	121	187	157	8	8
Sioux Falls, SD	n/a	n/a	n/a	95	136	134	n/a	n/a	n/a
Springfield, IL	19	111	34	96	126	143	111	18	49
Tampa, FL	n/a	n/a	85	81	204	80	107	<1	87
Tucson, AZ	0	18	140	177	119	69	54	2	42
Tulsa, OK	6	78	74	117	141	107	88	8	50
Tuscaloosa, AL	1	57	59	91	161	113	119	1	57
Virginia Beach, VA	<1	53	33	89	149	127	115	5	38
Washington, DC	2	71	34	84	144	137	112	9	30
Wichita, KS	13	110	63	117	132	116	87	13	54
Wilmington, NC	<1	42	46	96	150	119	115	1	47
Winston-Salem, NC	3	85	32	94	143	128	113	5	43
Worcester, MA	n/a	141	4	81	144	140	131	32	23

Note: Figures are average number of days per year
Source: National Climatic Data Center, International Station Meteorological Climate Summary, 9/96; NOAA

Air Quality Index

MSA[1] (Days[2])	Good	Moderate	Unhealthy for Sensitive Groups	Unhealthy	Very Unhealthy	Maximum	Median
Albuquerque, NM (365)	23.6	70.7	5.2	0.5	0.0	166	62
Allentown, PA (365)	69.9	29.0	0.8	0.3	0.0	153	43
Anchorage, AK (365)	80.3	18.6	0.8	0.3	0.0	160	25
Ann Arbor, MI (365)	76.2	23.8	0.0	0.0	0.0	100	40
Athens, GA (365)	71.8	27.9	0.3	0.0	0.0	107	41
Atlanta, GA (365)	57.3	40.5	2.2	0.0	0.0	150	47
Austin, TX (365)	68.2	31.5	0.3	0.0	0.0	101	43
Baltimore, MD (365)	68.8	27.1	4.1	0.0	0.0	140	45
Boise City, ID (365)	55.1	39.5	4.4	1.1	0.0	168	49
Boston, MA (365)	77.0	21.6	1.1	0.3	0.0	153	40
Boulder, CO (365)	55.9	34.5	8.8	0.8	0.0	159	48
Brownsville, TX (365)	64.4	35.6	0.0	0.0	0.0	99	43
Cape Coral, FL (365)	91.0	9.0	0.0	0.0	0.0	97	36
Cedar Rapids, IA (365)	64.4	34.5	1.1	0.0	0.0	123	44
Charleston, SC (365)	79.5	20.5	0.0	0.0	0.0	93	40
Charlotte, NC (365)	64.4	34.8	0.8	0.0	0.0	128	46
Chicago, IL (365)	34.2	58.1	7.1	0.5	0.0	169	58
Cincinnati, OH (365)	45.8	52.1	2.2	0.0	0.0	140	52
Clarksville, TN (365)	70.4	29.3	0.3	0.0	0.0	138	43
Cleveland, OH (365)	47.4	50.4	2.2	0.0	0.0	122	52
College Station, TX (356)	87.6	12.4	0.0	0.0	0.0	84	30
Colorado Springs, CO (365)	64.7	27.7	7.7	0.0	0.0	140	47
Columbia, MO (245)	95.1	4.9	0.0	0.0	0.0	77	37
Columbia, SC (365)	74.0	25.5	0.5	0.0	0.0	102	41
Columbus, OH (365)	71.2	28.8	0.0	0.0	0.0	100	43
Dallas, TX (365)	54.0	37.5	7.4	0.8	0.3	209	49
Davenport, IA (365)	56.2	43.0	0.8	0.0	0.0	112	49
Denver, CO (365)	30.1	51.5	13.7	4.7	0.0	177	61
Des Moines, IA (365)	77.8	21.9	0.3	0.0	0.0	110	40
Durham, NC (365)	81.6	18.4	0.0	0.0	0.0	90	40
Edison, NJ (365)	54.8	39.5	4.9	0.8	0.0	154	49
El Paso, TX (365)	38.6	56.2	5.2	0.0	0.0	150	54
Fargo, ND (363)	76.6	18.7	2.2	2.5	0.0	192	37
Fort Collins, CO (365)	54.0	36.4	8.8	0.8	0.0	156	50
Fort Wayne, IN (365)	70.7	29.3	0.0	0.0	0.0	100	41
Fort Worth, TX (365)	54.0	37.5	7.4	0.8	0.3	209	49
Grand Rapids, MI (365)	62.2	36.4	1.4	0.0	0.0	143	44
Greeley, CO (365)	54.5	36.2	9.0	0.3	0.0	154	49
Green Bay, WI (365)	73.4	25.2	1.4	0.0	0.0	125	40
Greensboro, NC (365)	75.9	24.1	0.0	0.0	0.0	100	42
Honolulu, HI (365)	99.7	0.3	0.0	0.0	0.0	52	26
Houston, TX (365)	38.6	53.2	5.8	2.5	0.0	179	54
Huntsville, AL (357)	75.4	24.1	0.6	0.0	0.0	105	41
Indianapolis, IN (365)	42.2	55.9	1.9	0.0	0.0	114	53
Jacksonville, FL (365)	73.4	26.6	0.0	0.0	0.0	93	43
Kansas City, MO (365)	52.9	43.6	3.6	0.0	0.0	147	50
Lafayette, LA (365)	81.6	18.4	0.0	0.0	0.0	87	38
Las Cruces, NM (365)	38.4	53.2	5.5	2.2	0.3	665	55
Las Vegas, NV (365)	32.6	58.1	8.5	0.8	0.0	174	59
Lexington, KY (363)	77.4	22.0	0.6	0.0	0.0	108	40
Lincoln, NE (276)	93.1	6.9	0.0	0.0	0.0	84	35
Little Rock, AR (365)	58.4	41.1	0.5	0.0	0.0	112	47
Los Angeles, CA (365)	10.7	62.5	19.5	7.1	0.3	281	77
Louisville, KY (365)	60.8	37.3	1.9	0.0	0.0	143	46

Table continued on following page.

Appendix A: Comparative Statistics

MSA[1] (Days[2])	Good	Moderate	Unhealthy for Sensitive Groups	Unhealthy	Very Unhealthy	Maximum	Median
Madison, WI (365)	67.1	32.6	0.3	0.0	0.0	101	42
Manchester, NH (365)	91.8	7.7	0.5	0.0	0.0	144	36
Miami, FL (365)	70.4	28.8	0.8	0.0	0.0	135	44
Midland, TX (n/a)	n/a	n/a	n/a	n/a	n/a	n/a	n/a
Milwaukee, WI (365)	57.3	39.5	3.3	0.0	0.0	129	47
Minneapolis, MN (365)	63.0	34.8	1.4	0.8	0.0	182	44
Nashville, TN (365)	60.5	38.1	1.4	0.0	0.0	133	46
New Haven, CT (365)	77.0	19.2	3.3	0.5	0.0	159	40
New Orleans, LA (365)	76.4	22.7	0.8	0.0	0.0	108	42
New York, NY (365)	54.8	39.5	4.9	0.8	0.0	154	49
Oklahoma City, OK (365)	48.2	49.0	2.7	0.0	0.0	140	51
Omaha, NE (365)	72.9	25.8	1.4	0.0	0.0	150	42
Orlando, FL (365)	82.7	17.3	0.0	0.0	0.0	97	39
Philadelphia, PA (365)	49.9	46.0	3.6	0.5	0.0	152	51
Phoenix, AZ (365)	3.0	32.1	28.2	16.7	20.0	272	123
Pittsburgh, PA (365)	44.9	52.6	2.2	0.3	0.0	153	53
Portland, OR (365)	79.7	20.0	0.0	0.3	0.0	161	37
Providence, RI (365)	76.2	22.7	1.1	0.0	0.0	147	41
Provo, UT (365)	60.0	35.3	4.7	0.0	0.0	144	46
Raleigh, NC (365)	71.0	29.0	0.0	0.0	0.0	97	43
Reno, NV (365)	54.2	36.2	4.4	4.4	0.8	291	49
Richmond, VA (365)	76.4	22.7	0.8	0.0	0.0	112	42
Rochester, MN (361)	83.4	16.1	0.6	0.0	0.0	125	36
Sacramento, CA (365)	37.8	46.3	10.4	3.3	1.4	448	62
St. Louis, MO (365)	38.1	57.8	3.6	0.5	0.0	187	55
Salem, OR (363)	87.1	12.9	0.0	0.0	0.0	93	33
Salt Lake City, UT (365)	47.4	39.5	10.7	2.5	0.0	177	52
San Antonio, TX (365)	54.5	42.2	3.3	0.0	0.0	147	48
San Diego, CA (365)	26.8	68.8	4.4	0.0	0.0	133	64
San Francisco, CA (365)	58.1	39.2	2.5	0.3	0.0	151	46
San Jose, CA (365)	60.5	37.5	1.9	0.0	0.0	147	46
Santa Rosa, CA (365)	87.9	12.1	0.0	0.0	0.0	88	33
Savannah, GA (363)	75.8	24.0	0.3	0.0	0.0	103	41
Seattle, WA (365)	72.1	26.0	1.4	0.5	0.0	177	43
Sioux Falls, SD (349)	81.7	16.9	0.9	0.6	0.0	182	36
Springfield, IL (362)	80.7	19.3	0.0	0.0	0.0	97	38
Tampa, FL (365)	72.9	26.8	0.3	0.0	0.0	129	44
Tucson, AZ (365)	39.2	57.0	3.6	0.0	0.0	315	53
Tulsa, OK (365)	60.3	37.0	2.2	0.5	0.0	163	47
Tuscaloosa, AL (281)	94.3	5.7	0.0	0.0	0.0	90	31
Virginia Beach, VA (365)	85.8	14.2	0.0	0.0	0.0	94	38
Washington, DC (365)	61.6	35.6	2.5	0.3	0.0	153	46
Wichita, KS (365)	59.7	38.9	1.4	0.0	0.0	147	47
Wilmington, NC (360)	89.4	10.6	0.0	0.0	0.0	93	34
Winston-Salem, NC (365)	67.4	31.8	0.8	0.0	0.0	124	44
Worcester, MA (365)	81.6	17.5	0.8	0.0	0.0	140	39

Note: The Air Quality Index (AQI) is an index for reporting daily air quality. EPA calculates the AQI for five major air pollutants regulated by the Clean Air Act: ground-level ozone, particle pollution (also known as particulate matter), carbon monoxide, sulfur dioxide, and nitrogen dioxide. The AQI runs from 0 to 500. The higher the AQI value, the greater the level of air pollution and the greater the health concern. There are six AQI categories: "Good" The AQI is between 0 and 50. Air quality is considered satisfactory; "Moderate" The AQI is between 51 and 100. Air quality is acceptable; "Unhealthy for Sensitive Groups" When AQI values are between 101 and 150, members of sensitive groups may experience health effects; "Unhealthy" When AQI values are between 151 and 200 everyone may begin to experience health effects; "Very Unhealthy" AQI values between 201 and 300 trigger a health alert; "Hazardous" AQI values over 300 trigger health warnings of emergency conditions; (1) Data covers the Metropolitan Statistical Area; (2) Number of days with AQI data in 2021
Source: U.S. Environmental Protection Agency, Air Quality Index Report, 2021

Air Quality Index Pollutants

MSA[1] (Days[2])	Carbon Monoxide	Nitrogen Dioxide	Ozone	Sulfur Dioxide	Particulate Matter 2.5	Particulate Matter 10
Albuquerque, NM (365)	0.0	0.0	49.6	(3)	16.7	33.7
Allentown, PA (365)	0.0	1.6	48.8	(3)	49.6	0.0
Anchorage, AK (365)	0.0	0.0	0.0	(3)	68.5	31.5
Ann Arbor, MI (365)	0.0	0.0	62.5	(3)	37.5	0.0
Athens, GA (365)	0.0	0.0	32.9	(3)	67.1	0.0
Atlanta, GA (365)	0.0	3.6	40.8	(3)	55.6	0.0
Austin, TX (365)	0.0	1.6	50.7	(3)	46.6	1.1
Baltimore, MD (365)	0.0	7.4	60.5	(3)	32.1	0.0
Boise City, ID (365)	0.0	0.8	44.9	(3)	51.2	3.0
Boston, MA (365)	0.0	3.3	53.4	(3)	43.0	0.3
Boulder, CO (365)	0.0	0.0	74.8	(3)	24.7	0.5
Brownsville, TX (365)	0.0	0.0	31.2	(3)	68.8	0.0
Cape Coral, FL (365)	0.0	0.0	66.0	(3)	32.9	1.1
Cedar Rapids, IA (365)	0.0	0.0	35.1	(3)	64.7	0.3
Charleston, SC (365)	0.0	0.0	41.4	(3)	58.6	0.0
Charlotte, NC (365)	0.0	0.3	59.2	(3)	40.5	0.0
Chicago, IL (365)	0.0	4.9	34.2	(3)	51.0	9.9
Cincinnati, OH (365)	0.0	3.0	28.8	(3)	64.1	4.1
Clarksville, TN (365)	0.0	0.0	47.4	(3)	52.6	0.0
Cleveland, OH (365)	0.0	1.4	35.9	(3)	60.8	1.9
College Station, TX (356)	0.0	0.0	0.0	(3)	100.0	0.0
Colorado Springs, CO (365)	0.0	0.0	95.1	(3)	4.9	0.0
Columbia, MO (245)	0.0	0.0	100.0	(3)	0.0	0.0
Columbia, SC (365)	0.0	0.0	51.8	(3)	48.2	0.0
Columbus, OH (365)	0.0	2.7	44.7	(3)	52.6	0.0
Dallas, TX (365)	0.0	3.3	61.4	(3)	35.3	0.0
Davenport, IA (365)	0.0	0.0	33.4	(3)	46.8	19.7
Denver, CO (365)	0.0	18.6	63.6	(3)	11.2	6.6
Des Moines, IA (365)	0.0	3.6	43.3	(3)	51.8	1.4
Durham, NC (365)	0.0	0.0	51.8	(3)	48.2	0.0
Edison, NJ (365)	0.0	12.3	41.4	(3)	46.3	0.0
El Paso, TX (365)	0.0	5.8	53.2	(3)	35.9	5.2
Fargo, ND (363)	0.0	1.4	54.5	(3)	44.1	0.0
Fort Collins, CO (365)	0.0	0.0	91.0	(3)	9.0	0.0
Fort Wayne, IN (365)	0.0	0.0	51.0	(3)	49.0	0.0
Fort Worth, TX (365)	0.0	3.3	61.4	(3)	35.3	0.0
Grand Rapids, MI (365)	0.0	1.9	50.1	(3)	47.9	0.0
Greeley, CO (365)	0.0	0.3	78.6	(3)	21.1	0.0
Green Bay, WI (365)	0.0	0.0	48.8	(3)	51.2	0.0
Greensboro, NC (365)	0.0	0.0	52.9	(3)	46.3	0.8
Honolulu, HI (365)	0.3	0.8	83.8	(3)	11.5	3.6
Houston, TX (365)	0.0	0.8	38.9	(3)	55.3	4.9
Huntsville, AL (357)	0.0	0.0	33.3	(3)	63.0	3.6
Indianapolis, IN (365)	0.0	2.2	25.5	(3)	72.3	0.0
Jacksonville, FL (365)	0.0	0.0	36.4	(3)	63.6	0.0
Kansas City, MO (365)	0.0	0.3	38.6	(3)	50.1	11.0
Lafayette, LA (365)	0.0	0.0	61.9	(3)	38.1	0.0
Las Cruces, NM (365)	0.0	2.5	58.1	(3)	6.3	33.2
Las Vegas, NV (365)	0.0	1.6	66.6	(3)	24.9	6.8
Lexington, KY (363)	0.0	5.5	38.3	(3)	55.9	0.3
Lincoln, NE (276)	0.0	0.0	78.6	(3)	21.4	0.0
Little Rock, AR (365)	0.0	1.6	27.9	(3)	70.4	0.0
Los Angeles, CA (365)	0.0	6.6	46.0	(3)	45.2	2.2
Louisville, KY (365)	0.0	2.2	39.5	(3)	58.4	0.0

Table continued on following page.

Appendix A: Comparative Statistics

	Percent of Days when AQI Pollutant was...					
MSA[1] (Days[2])	Carbon Monoxide	Nitrogen Dioxide	Ozone	Sulfur Dioxide	Particulate Matter 2.5	Particulate Matter 10
Madison, WI (365)	0.0	0.0	39.2	(3)	60.8	0.0
Manchester, NH (365)	0.0	0.0	92.1	(3)	7.9	0.0
Miami, FL (365)	0.0	6.8	33.7	(3)	59.5	0.0
Midland, TX (n/a)	n/a	n/a	n/a	(3)	n/a	n/a
Milwaukee, WI (365)	0.0	1.4	52.3	(3)	43.6	2.7
Minneapolis, MN (365)	0.0	3.3	47.7	(3)	41.1	7.9
Nashville, TN (365)	0.0	5.2	33.4	(3)	61.4	0.0
New Haven, CT (365)	0.0	5.2	55.9	(3)	37.5	1.4
New Orleans, LA (365)	0.0	0.0	48.2	(3)	51.5	0.3
New York, NY (365)	0.0	12.3	41.4	(3)	46.3	0.0
Oklahoma City, OK (365)	0.0	3.0	41.6	(3)	54.8	0.5
Omaha, NE (365)	0.0	0.0	53.4	(3)	38.4	8.2
Orlando, FL (365)	0.0	0.0	66.0	(3)	33.2	0.8
Philadelphia, PA (365)	0.0	6.0	39.7	(3)	54.0	0.3
Phoenix, AZ (365)	0.0	0.0	75.3	(3)	6.3	18.4
Pittsburgh, PA (365)	0.0	0.3	32.6	(3)	67.1	0.0
Portland, OR (365)	0.0	0.5	61.1	(3)	38.4	0.0
Providence, RI (365)	0.0	2.2	63.0	(3)	34.8	0.0
Provo, UT (365)	0.0	3.3	78.9	(3)	16.4	1.4
Raleigh, NC (365)	0.0	0.5	53.7	(3)	45.8	0.0
Reno, NV (365)	0.0	1.4	72.6	(3)	24.9	1.1
Richmond, VA (365)	0.0	6.3	51.8	(3)	41.9	0.0
Rochester, MN (361)	0.0	0.0	61.5	(3)	38.5	0.0
Sacramento, CA (365)	0.0	0.0	66.0	(3)	33.4	0.5
St. Louis, MO (365)	0.0	0.5	25.8	(3)	70.1	3.6
Salem, OR (363)	0.0	0.0	39.7	(3)	60.3	0.0
Salt Lake City, UT (365)	0.0	7.9	64.4	(3)	24.1	3.6
San Antonio, TX (365)	0.0	0.3	44.9	(3)	54.2	0.5
San Diego, CA (365)	0.0	1.1	59.5	(3)	38.6	0.8
San Francisco, CA (365)	0.0	1.1	47.9	(3)	51.0	0.0
San Jose, CA (365)	0.0	0.0	54.8	(3)	44.1	1.1
Santa Rosa, CA (365)	0.0	0.0	59.5	(3)	37.5	3.0
Savannah, GA (363)	0.0	0.0	24.5	(3)	75.5	0.0
Seattle, WA (365)	0.0	2.2	62.2	(3)	35.6	0.0
Sioux Falls, SD (349)	0.0	4.6	65.9	(3)	22.3	7.2
Springfield, IL (362)	0.0	0.0	43.1	(3)	56.9	0.0
Tampa, FL (365)	0.0	0.0	51.2	(3)	48.2	0.5
Tucson, AZ (365)	0.0	0.0	54.8	(3)	15.9	29.3
Tulsa, OK (365)	0.0	0.0	52.9	(3)	46.3	0.8
Tuscaloosa, AL (281)	0.0	0.0	72.6	(3)	27.4	0.0
Virginia Beach, VA (365)	0.0	6.8	49.6	(3)	43.6	0.0
Washington, DC (365)	0.0	8.5	52.1	(3)	39.5	0.0
Wichita, KS (365)	0.0	0.5	42.7	(3)	48.8	7.9
Wilmington, NC (360)	0.0	0.0	46.7	(3)	53.3	0.0
Winston-Salem, NC (365)	0.0	1.6	46.6	(3)	51.8	0.0
Worcester, MA (365)	0.0	2.5	58.1	(3)	39.2	0.3

Note: The Air Quality Index (AQI) is an index for reporting daily air quality. EPA calculates the AQI for five major air pollutants regulated by the Clean Air Act: ground-level ozone, particle pollution (also known as particulate matter), carbon monoxide, sulfur dioxide, and nitrogen dioxide. The AQI runs from 0 to 500. The higher the AQI value, the greater the level of air pollution and the greater the health concern; (1) Data covers the Metropolitan Statistical Area—see Appendix B for areas included; (2) Number of days with AQI data in 2021; (3) Sulfur dioxide is no longer included in this table (as of December 8, 2021) because SO_2 concentrations tend to be very localized and not necessarily representative of broad geographical areas like counties and CBSAs.
Source: U.S. Environmental Protection Agency, Air Quality Index Report, 2021

Air Quality Trends: Ozone

MSA[1]	1990	1995	2000	2005	2010	2015	2018	2019	2020	2021
Albuquerque, NM	0.072	0.070	0.072	0.073	0.066	0.066	0.074	0.067	0.071	0.071
Allentown, PA	0.093	0.091	0.091	0.086	0.080	0.070	0.067	0.064	0.063	0.063
Anchorage, AK	n/a	n/a	n/a	n/a	n/a	n/a	n/a	n/a	n/a	n/a
Ann Arbor, MI	0.025	0.034	0.035	0.023	0.034	0.064	0.072	0.058	0.067	0.063
Athens, GA	n/a	n/a	n/a	n/a	n/a	n/a	n/a	n/a	n/a	n/a
Atlanta, GA	0.088	0.089	0.089	0.077	0.067	0.069	0.068	0.070	0.059	0.064
Austin, TX	0.088	0.089	0.088	0.082	0.074	0.073	0.072	0.065	0.066	0.066
Baltimore, MD	0.100	0.103	0.088	0.089	0.084	0.073	0.071	0.070	0.064	0.071
Boise City, ID	n/a	n/a	n/a	n/a	n/a	n/a	n/a	n/a	n/a	n/a
Boston, MA	0.078	0.085	0.067	0.075	0.066	0.065	0.061	0.052	0.053	0.059
Boulder, CO	n/a	n/a	n/a	n/a	n/a	n/a	n/a	n/a	n/a	n/a
Brownsville, TX	n/a	n/a	n/a	n/a	n/a	n/a	n/a	n/a	n/a	n/a
Cape Coral, FL	0.069	0.066	0.073	0.071	0.065	0.058	0.065	0.062	0.061	0.055
Cedar Rapids, IA	n/a	n/a	n/a	n/a	n/a	n/a	n/a	n/a	n/a	n/a
Charleston, SC	0.068	0.071	0.078	0.073	0.067	0.054	0.058	0.064	0.059	0.062
Charlotte, NC	0.094	0.091	0.099	0.089	0.082	0.071	0.070	0.073	0.060	0.067
Chicago, IL	0.074	0.094	0.073	0.084	0.070	0.066	0.073	0.069	0.076	0.071
Cincinnati, OH	0.083	0.082	0.074	0.075	0.069	0.069	0.073	0.067	0.067	0.065
Clarksville, TN	n/a	n/a	n/a	n/a	n/a	n/a	n/a	n/a	n/a	n/a
Cleveland, OH	0.084	0.090	0.079	0.084	0.074	0.069	0.072	0.067	0.069	0.066
College Station, TX	n/a	n/a	n/a	n/a	n/a	n/a	n/a	n/a	n/a	n/a
Colorado Springs, CO	n/a	n/a	n/a	n/a	n/a	n/a	n/a	n/a	n/a	n/a
Columbia, MO	n/a	n/a	n/a	n/a	n/a	n/a	n/a	n/a	n/a	n/a
Columbia, SC	0.091	0.079	0.089	0.082	0.069	0.058	0.059	0.063	0.053	0.061
Columbus, OH	0.090	0.091	0.085	0.084	0.073	0.066	0.062	0.060	0.062	0.061
Dallas, TX	0.094	0.103	0.096	0.096	0.079	0.078	0.079	0.070	0.070	0.076
Davenport, IA	0.065	0.072	0.064	0.065	0.057	0.060	0.067	0.066	0.063	0.066
Denver, CO	0.077	0.070	0.069	0.072	0.070	0.073	0.071	0.068	0.079	0.080
Des Moines, IA	n/a	n/a	n/a	n/a	n/a	n/a	n/a	n/a	n/a	n/a
Durham, NC	0.078	0.080	0.082	0.079	0.074	0.061	0.063	0.063	0.051	0.063
Edison, NJ	0.101	0.105	0.089	0.090	0.080	0.074	0.073	0.067	0.064	0.069
El Paso, TX	0.080	0.078	0.082	0.074	0.072	0.071	0.077	0.074	0.076	0.071
Fargo, ND	n/a	n/a	n/a	n/a	n/a	n/a	n/a	n/a	n/a	n/a
Fort Collins, CO	0.066	0.072	0.074	0.075	0.072	0.070	0.073	0.065	0.070	0.077
Fort Wayne, IN	0.086	0.094	0.086	0.081	0.067	0.061	0.071	0.063	0.064	0.062
Fort Worth, TX	0.094	0.103	0.096	0.096	0.079	0.078	0.079	0.070	0.070	0.076
Grand Rapids, MI	0.098	0.092	0.073	0.084	0.069	0.066	0.070	0.063	0.074	0.067
Greeley, CO	0.076	0.072	0.069	0.078	0.073	0.073	0.073	0.065	0.072	0.076
Green Bay, WI	n/a	n/a	n/a	n/a	n/a	n/a	n/a	n/a	n/a	n/a
Greensboro, NC	0.097	0.089	0.089	0.082	0.076	0.064	0.067	0.064	0.057	0.066
Honolulu, HI	0.034	0.049	0.044	0.042	0.046	0.048	0.046	0.053	0.044	0.045
Houston, TX	0.119	0.114	0.102	0.087	0.079	0.083	0.073	0.074	0.067	0.072
Huntsville, AL	0.079	0.080	0.088	0.075	0.071	0.063	0.065	0.063	0.057	0.061
Indianapolis, IN	0.085	0.095	0.081	0.081	0.070	0.065	0.076	0.066	0.065	0.067
Jacksonville, FL	0.080	0.068	0.072	0.076	0.068	0.060	0.060	0.062	0.057	0.061
Kansas City, MO	0.075	0.095	0.087	0.082	0.067	0.063	0.072	0.061	0.064	0.067
Lafayette, LA	n/a	n/a	n/a	n/a	n/a	n/a	n/a	n/a	n/a	n/a
Las Cruces, NM	0.073	0.075	0.075	0.070	0.060	0.070	0.072	0.068	0.071	0.079
Las Vegas, NV	n/a	n/a	n/a	n/a	n/a	n/a	n/a	n/a	n/a	n/a
Lexington, KY	0.078	0.088	0.077	0.078	0.070	0.069	0.063	0.059	0.060	0.064
Lincoln, NE	0.057	0.060	0.057	0.056	0.050	0.061	0.062	0.056	0.054	0.059
Little Rock, AR	0.080	0.086	0.090	0.083	0.072	0.063	0.066	0.059	0.062	0.066
Los Angeles, CA	0.128	0.109	0.090	0.086	0.074	0.082	0.082	0.080	0.096	0.076
Louisville, KY	0.082	0.091	0.087	0.083	0.076	0.071	0.069	0.064	0.063	0.064
Madison, WI	0.077	0.084	0.072	0.079	0.062	0.064	0.066	0.059	0.070	0.066
Manchester, NH	0.085	0.088	0.070	0.082	0.067	0.061	0.066	0.054	0.055	0.061

Table continued on following page.

Appendix A: Comparative Statistics

MSA[1]	1990	1995	2000	2005	2010	2015	2018	2019	2020	2021
Miami, FL	0.068	0.072	0.075	0.065	0.064	0.061	0.064	0.058	0.058	0.057
Midland, TX	n/a	n/a	n/a	n/a	n/a	n/a	n/a	n/a	n/a	n/a
Milwaukee, WI	0.095	0.106	0.082	0.092	0.079	0.069	0.073	0.066	0.074	0.072
Minneapolis, MN	0.068	0.084	0.065	0.074	0.066	0.061	0.065	0.059	0.060	0.067
Nashville, TN	0.089	0.092	0.084	0.078	0.073	0.065	0.068	0.064	0.061	0.064
New Haven, CT	0.121	0.117	0.087	0.092	0.079	0.081	0.077	0.084	0.080	0.083
New Orleans, LA	0.082	0.088	0.091	0.079	0.074	0.067	0.065	0.062	0.061	0.060
New York, NY	0.101	0.105	0.089	0.090	0.080	0.074	0.073	0.067	0.064	0.069
Oklahoma City, OK	0.080	0.087	0.083	0.077	0.071	0.067	0.072	0.065	0.066	0.068
Omaha, NE	0.054	0.075	0.063	0.069	0.058	0.055	0.063	0.050	0.055	0.055
Orlando, FL	0.081	0.075	0.080	0.083	0.069	0.060	0.062	0.062	0.059	0.061
Philadelphia, PA	0.102	0.109	0.099	0.091	0.083	0.074	0.075	0.067	0.065	0.068
Phoenix, AZ	0.080	0.086	0.082	0.077	0.075	0.072	0.073	0.071	0.079	0.079
Pittsburgh, PA	0.080	0.100	0.084	0.083	0.077	0.070	0.070	0.062	0.066	0.066
Portland, OR	0.081	0.065	0.059	0.059	0.056	0.064	0.062	0.058	0.058	0.058
Providence, RI	0.106	0.107	0.087	0.090	0.072	0.070	0.074	0.064	0.065	0.067
Provo, UT	n/a	n/a	n/a	n/a	n/a	n/a	n/a	n/a	n/a	n/a
Raleigh, NC	0.093	0.081	0.087	0.082	0.071	0.065	0.063	0.064	0.054	0.062
Reno, NV	0.074	0.069	0.067	0.069	0.068	0.071	0.077	0.063	0.073	0.078
Richmond, VA	0.083	0.089	0.080	0.082	0.079	0.062	0.062	0.061	0.054	0.061
Rochester, MN	n/a	n/a	n/a	n/a	n/a	n/a	n/a	n/a	n/a	n/a
Sacramento, CA	0.087	0.092	0.085	0.084	0.072	0.073	0.074	0.067	0.072	0.073
St. Louis, MO	0.077	0.084	0.074	0.078	0.069	0.067	0.072	0.066	0.066	0.067
Salem, OR	n/a	n/a	n/a	n/a	n/a	n/a	n/a	n/a	n/a	n/a
Salt Lake City, UT	n/a	n/a	n/a	n/a	n/a	n/a	n/a	n/a	n/a	n/a
San Antonio, TX	0.090	0.095	0.078	0.084	0.072	0.079	0.072	0.075	0.069	0.070
San Diego, CA	0.110	0.085	0.079	0.074	0.073	0.068	0.069	0.069	0.078	0.068
San Francisco, CA	0.062	0.077	0.060	0.060	0.063	0.064	0.056	0.062	0.062	0.064
San Jose, CA	0.078	0.084	0.065	0.063	0.072	0.067	0.059	0.061	0.066	0.067
Santa Rosa, CA	0.063	0.071	0.061	0.050	0.053	0.059	0.055	0.052	0.052	0.052
Savannah, GA	n/a	n/a	n/a	n/a	n/a	n/a	n/a	n/a	n/a	n/a
Seattle, WA	0.082	0.062	0.056	0.053	0.053	0.059	0.067	0.052	0.052	0.052
Sioux Falls, SD	n/a	n/a	n/a	n/a	n/a	n/a	n/a	n/a	n/a	n/a
Springfield, IL	n/a	n/a	n/a	n/a	n/a	n/a	n/a	n/a	n/a	n/a
Tampa, FL	0.080	0.075	0.081	0.075	0.067	0.062	0.065	0.065	0.063	0.060
Tucson, AZ	0.073	0.078	0.074	0.075	0.068	0.065	0.069	0.065	0.070	0.068
Tulsa, OK	0.086	0.091	0.081	0.072	0.069	0.061	0.067	0.062	0.061	0.063
Tuscaloosa, AL	n/a	n/a	n/a	n/a	n/a	n/a	n/a	n/a	n/a	n/a
Virginia Beach, VA	0.085	0.084	0.083	0.078	0.074	0.061	0.061	0.059	0.053	0.057
Washington, DC	0.075	0.083	0.073	0.069	0.069	0.067	0.068	0.064	0.057	0.066
Wichita, KS	0.077	0.069	0.080	0.074	0.075	0.064	0.064	0.062	0.059	0.061
Wilmington, NC	0.082	0.079	0.080	0.075	0.062	0.057	0.062	0.059	0.054	0.062
Winston-Salem, NC	0.084	0.086	0.089	0.080	0.078	0.065	0.064	0.062	0.058	0.062
Worcester, MA	0.097	0.096	0.076	0.085	0.070	0.063	0.065	0.060	0.063	0.063
U.S.	0.087	0.089	0.081	0.080	0.072	0.067	0.069	0.065	0.065	0.067

Note: (1) Data covers the Metropolitan Statistical Area; n/a not available. The values shown are the composite ozone concentration averages among trend sites based on the highest fourth daily maximum 8-hour concentration in parts per million. These trends are based on sites having an adequate record of monitoring data during the trend period. Data from exceptional events are included.
Source: U.S. Environmental Protection Agency, Air Quality Monitoring Information, "Air Quality Trends by City, 1990-2021"

Maximum Air Pollutant Concentrations: Particulate Matter, Ozone, CO and Lead

Metro Aea	PM 10 (ug/m³)	PM 2.5 Wtd AM (ug/m³)	PM 2.5 24-Hr (ug/m³)	Ozone (ppm)	Carbon Monoxide (ppm)	Lead (ug/m³)
Albuquerque, NM	221	11.3	28	0.076	1	n/a
Allentown, PA	44	9.9	27	0.069	n/a	0.06
Anchorage, AK	97	6	21	n/a	2	n/a
Ann Arbor, MI	n/a	8.8	18	0.066	n/a	n/a
Athens, GA	n/a	10.1	25	0.06	n/a	n/a
Atlanta, GA	44	9.7	22	0.07	2	n/a
Austin, TX	91	9.4	21	0.066	1	n/a
Baltimore, MD	27	8.9	21	0.075	1	n/a
Boise City, ID	113	9.2	37	0.075	1	n/a
Boston, MA	50	8.3	18	0.067	1	n/a
Boulder, CO	51	10	54	0.082	n/a	n/a
Brownsville, TX	n/a	9.2	24	0.056	n/a	n/a
Cape Coral, FL	54	7.3	17	0.055	n/a	n/a
Cedar Rapids, IA	57	8.8	24	0.064	n/a	n/a
Charleston, SC	40	9.5	20	0.059	n/a	n/a
Charlotte, NC	39	9.3	21	0.067	1	n/a
Chicago, IL	166	10.8	27	0.079	1	0.03
Cincinnati, OH	178	12.1	27	0.07	2	n/a
Clarksville, TN	n/a	10.4	27	0.06	n/a	n/a
Cleveland, OH	89	12.6	29	0.072	2	0.01
College Station, TX	n/a	8	21	n/a	n/a	n/a
Colorado Springs, CO	39	6	21	0.078	1	n/a
Columbia, MO	n/a	n/a	n/a	0.058	n/a	n/a
Columbia, SC	42	9	22	0.064	1	n/a
Columbus, OH	32	9.9	24	0.064	1	n/a
Dallas, TX	56	9.6	23	0.085	1	0.02
Davenport, IA	137	9.4	26	0.066	1	n/a
Denver, CO	96	10.3	41	0.089	2	n/a
Des Moines, IA	54	8.3	23	0.061	n/a	n/a
Durham, NC	40	8	18	0.063	n/a	n/a
Edison, NJ	40	9.8	26	0.079	2	n/a
El Paso, TX	153	9.2	37	0.073	3	n/a
Fargo, ND	n/a	11	60	0.063	n/a	n/a
Fort Collins, CO	n/a	8.5	29	0.085	1	n/a
Fort Wayne, IN	n/a	9	21	0.065	n/a	n/a
Fort Worth, TX	56	9.6	23	0.085	1	0.02
Grand Rapids, MI	42	10.1	26	0.069	1	n/a
Greeley, CO	n/a	9.8	31	0.083	1	n/a
Green Bay, WI	n/a	8.7	26	0.068	n/a	n/a
Greensboro, NC	35	7.7	18	0.066	n/a	n/a
Honolulu, HI	34	3.3	6	0.047	2	n/a
Houston, TX	103	11.4	24	0.083	2	n/a
Huntsville, AL	36	7.5	17	0.061	n/a	n/a
Indianapolis, IN	55	12.6	32	0.067	2	n/a
Jacksonville, FL	54	8.8	18	0.061	1	n/a
Kansas City, MO	103	11.2	31	0.071	1	n/a
Lafayette, LA	56	7.6	16	0.063	n/a	n/a
Las Cruces, NM	439	9.3	26	0.086	n/a	n/a
Las Vegas, NV	176	9.9	33	0.076	2	n/a
Lexington, KY	27	9.6	23	0.064	n/a	n/a
Lincoln, NE	n/a	7.1	21	0.059	n/a	n/a
Little Rock, AR	32	9.7	25	0.067	1	n/a
Los Angeles, CA	113	13.4	48	0.097	3	0.06
Louisville, KY	46	11.2	28	0.073	1	n/a
Madison, WI	49	9.5	27	0.066	n/a	n/a

Table continued on following page.

Metro Area	PM 10 (ug/m³)	PM 2.5 Wtd AM (ug/m³)	PM 2.5 24-Hr (ug/m³)	Ozone (ppm)	Carbon Monoxide (ppm)	Lead (ug/m³)
Manchester, NH	n/a	4.5	13	0.062	1	n/a
Miami, FL	73	9.5	26	0.058	1	n/a
Midland, TX	n/a	n/a	n/a	n/a	n/a	n/a
Milwaukee, WI	70	10.2	27	0.073	1	n/a
Minneapolis, MN	115	8.8	30	0.07	2	0.08
Nashville, TN	50	9.4	24	0.066	2	n/a
New Haven, CT	68	8.8	22	0.083	1	n/a
New Orleans, LA	45	7.6	17	0.063	1	0.05
New York, NY	40	9.8	26	0.079	2	n/a
Oklahoma City, OK	64	11.2	28	0.07	1	n/a
Omaha, NE	70	8.9	26	0.066	1	0.09
Orlando, FL	51	7.6	15	0.062	1	n/a
Philadelphia, PA	60	10.1	25	0.077	1	0
Phoenix, AZ	225	12.7	36	0.083	3	n/a
Pittsburgh, PA	81	11.8	30	0.068	4	0
Portland, OR	29	6.4	16	0.062	1	n/a
Providence, RI	29	9.3	21	0.069	1	n/a
Provo, UT	100	7.7	31	0.077	1	n/a
Raleigh, NC	56	9.2	22	0.066	1	n/a
Reno, NV	284	12.4	105	0.08	2	n/a
Richmond, VA	40	8.3	19	0.066	1	n/a
Rochester, MN	n/a	n/a	n/a	0.067	n/a	n/a
Sacramento, CA	406	11.3	57	0.085	1	n/a
St. Louis, MO	161	10	23	0.073	1	0.06
Salem, OR	n/a	n/a	n/a	0.063	n/a	n/a
Salt Lake City, UT	103	10.3	43	0.087	1	n/a
San Antonio, TX	87	8.9	22	0.078	1	n/a
San Diego, CA	119	11.2	24	0.078	1	0.02
San Francisco, CA	35	9.1	23	0.074	2	n/a
San Jose, CA	76	10.9	25	0.074	1	n/a
Santa Rosa, CA	53	n/a	n/a	0.055	1	n/a
Savannah, GA	n/a	10.1	22	0.058	n/a	n/a
Seattle, WA	22	7.1	22	0.078	1	n/a
Sioux Falls, SD	110	n/a	n/a	0.065	1	n/a
Springfield, IL	n/a	8.7	22	0.057	n/a	n/a
Tampa, FL	61	8.5	18	0.063	1	0.08
Tucson, AZ	249	6.6	14	0.068	1	n/a
Tulsa, OK	99	10.1	29	0.068	1	n/a
Tuscaloosa, AL	n/a	7.8	20	0.053	n/a	n/a
Virginia Beach, VA	44	7.2	16	0.061	1	n/a
Washington, DC	47	9.6	21	0.072	2	n/a
Wichita, KS	89	11.3	31	0.067	n/a	n/a
Wilmington, NC	41	4.8	13	0.062	n/a	n/a
Winston-Salem, NC	41	9.2	41	0.066	n/a	n/a
Worcester, MA	31	9.1	19	0.068	1	n/a
NAAQS[1]	150	15.0	35	0.075	9	0.15

Note: Data from exceptional events are included; Data covers the Metropolitan Statistical Area; (1) National Ambient Air Quality Standards; ppm = parts per million; ug/m³ = micrograms per cubic meter; n/a not available
Concentrations: Particulate Matter 10 (coarse particulate)—highest second maximum 24-hour concentration; Particulate Matter 2.5 Wtd AM (fine particulate)—highest weighted annual mean concentration; Particulate Matter 2.5 24-Hour (fine particulate)—highest 98th percentile 24-hour concentration; Ozone—highest fourth daily maximum 8-hour concentration; Carbon Monoxide—highest second maximum non-overlapping 8-hour concentration; Lead—maximum running 3-month average
Source: U.S. Environmental Protection Agency, Air Quality Monitoring Information, "Air Quality Statistics by City, 2021"

Maximum Air Pollutant Concentrations: Nitrogen Dioxide and Sulfur Dioxide

Metro Area	Nitrogen Dioxide AM (ppb)	Nitrogen Dioxide 1-Hr (ppb)	Sulfur Dioxide AM (ppb)	Sulfur Dioxide 1-Hr (ppb)	Sulfur Dioxide 24-Hr (ppb)
Albuquerque, NM	8	44	n/a	3	n/a
Allentown, PA	10	42	n/a	6	n/a
Anchorage, AK	n/a	n/a	n/a	n/a	n/a
Ann Arbor, MI	n/a	n/a	n/a	n/a	n/a
Athens, GA	n/a	n/a	n/a	n/a	n/a
Atlanta, GA	17	50	n/a	4	n/a
Austin, TX	13	44	n/a	3	n/a
Baltimore, MD	16	51	n/a	16	n/a
Boise City, ID	10	45	n/a	2	n/a
Boston, MA	12	45	n/a	9	n/a
Boulder, CO	n/a	n/a	n/a	n/a	n/a
Brownsville, TX	n/a	n/a	n/a	n/a	n/a
Cape Coral, FL	n/a	n/a	n/a	n/a	n/a
Cedar Rapids, IA	n/a	n/a	n/a	40	n/a
Charleston, SC	n/a	n/a	n/a	9	n/a
Charlotte, NC	7	37	n/a	2	n/a
Chicago, IL	17	54	n/a	73	n/a
Cincinnati, OH	16	49	n/a	28	n/a
Clarksville, TN	n/a	n/a	n/a	n/a	n/a
Cleveland, OH	9	38	n/a	39	n/a
College Station, TX	n/a	n/a	n/a	11	n/a
Colorado Springs, CO	n/a	n/a	n/a	10	n/a
Columbia, MO	n/a	n/a	n/a	n/a	n/a
Columbia, SC	n/a	n/a	n/a	1	n/a
Columbus, OH	10	47	n/a	2	n/a
Dallas, TX	13	48	n/a	8	n/a
Davenport, IA	n/a	n/a	n/a	4	n/a
Denver, CO	26	71	n/a	7	n/a
Des Moines, IA	6	34	n/a	n/a	n/a
Durham, NC	n/a	n/a	n/a	1	n/a
Edison, NJ	19	65	n/a	17	n/a
El Paso, TX	14	57	n/a	n/a	n/a
Fargo, ND	4	31	n/a	n/a	n/a
Fort Collins, CO	n/a	n/a	n/a	n/a	n/a
Fort Wayne, IN	n/a	n/a	n/a	n/a	n/a
Fort Worth, TX	13	48	n/a	8	n/a
Grand Rapids, MI	8	39	n/a	4	n/a
Greeley, CO	6	42	n/a	n/a	n/a
Green Bay, WI	n/a	n/a	n/a	5	n/a
Greensboro, NC	n/a	n/a	n/a	n/a	n/a
Honolulu, HI	3	22	n/a	44	n/a
Houston, TX	12	49	n/a	16	n/a
Huntsville, AL	n/a	n/a	n/a	n/a	n/a
Indianapolis, IN	12	40	n/a	3	n/a
Jacksonville, FL	11	41	n/a	39	n/a
Kansas City, MO	10	44	n/a	9	n/a
Lafayette, LA	n/a	n/a	n/a	n/a	n/a
Las Cruces, NM	8	48	n/a	n/a	n/a
Las Vegas, NV	22	53	n/a	3	n/a
Lexington, KY	6	n/a	n/a	5	n/a
Lincoln, NE	n/a	n/a	n/a	n/a	n/a
Little Rock, AR	7	38	n/a	6	n/a
Los Angeles, CA	25	76	n/a	4	n/a
Louisville, KY	15	50	n/a	13	n/a
Madison, WI	n/a	n/a	n/a	2	n/a

Table continued on following page.

Metro Area	Nitrogen Dioxide AM (ppb)	Nitrogen Dioxide 1-Hr (ppb)	Sulfur Dioxide AM (ppb)	Sulfur Dioxide 1-Hr (ppb)	Sulfur Dioxide 24-Hr (ppb)
Manchester, NH	n/a	n/a	n/a	1	n/a
Miami, FL	13	49	n/a	2	n/a
Midland, TX	n/a	n/a	n/a	n/a	n/a
Milwaukee, WI	13	42	n/a	n/a	n/a
Minneapolis, MN	8	38	n/a	14	n/a
Nashville, TN	13	52	n/a	4	n/a
New Haven, CT	12	48	n/a	3	n/a
New Orleans, LA	9	37	n/a	56	n/a
New York, NY	19	65	n/a	17	n/a
Oklahoma City, OK	13	47	n/a	1	n/a
Omaha, NE	n/a	n/a	n/a	48	n/a
Orlando, FL	n/a	n/a	n/a	n/a	n/a
Philadelphia, PA	14	54	n/a	6	n/a
Phoenix, AZ	26	59	n/a	7	n/a
Pittsburgh, PA	10	36	n/a	54	n/a
Portland, OR	9	31	n/a	3	n/a
Providence, RI	16	36	n/a	3	n/a
Provo, UT	9	42	n/a	n/a	n/a
Raleigh, NC	8	31	n/a	2	n/a
Reno, NV	12	47	n/a	3	n/a
Richmond, VA	13	48	n/a	3	n/a
Rochester, MN	n/a	n/a	n/a	n/a	n/a
Sacramento, CA	7	41	n/a	n/a	n/a
St. Louis, MO	10	46	n/a	34	n/a
Salem, OR	n/a	n/a	n/a	n/a	n/a
Salt Lake City, UT	16	51	n/a	7	n/a
San Antonio, TX	7	32	n/a	3	n/a
San Diego, CA	13	54	n/a	1	n/a
San Francisco, CA	12	40	n/a	11	n/a
San Jose, CA	12	39	n/a	2	n/a
Santa Rosa, CA	3	20	n/a	n/a	n/a
Savannah, GA	n/a	n/a	n/a	50	n/a
Seattle, WA	16	49	n/a	3	n/a
Sioux Falls, SD	n/a	n/a	n/a	n/a	n/a
Springfield, IL	n/a	n/a	n/a	n/a	n/a
Tampa, FL	9	37	n/a	29	n/a
Tucson, AZ	8	38	n/a	1	n/a
Tulsa, OK	7	38	n/a	5	n/a
Tuscaloosa, AL	n/a	n/a	n/a	n/a	n/a
Virginia Beach, VA	7	40	n/a	3	n/a
Washington, DC	15	50	n/a	3	n/a
Wichita, KS	7	39	n/a	4	n/a
Wilmington, NC	n/a	n/a	n/a	n/a	n/a
Winston-Salem, NC	6	32	n/a	4	n/a
Worcester, MA	9	44	n/a	2	n/a
NAAQS[1]	53	100	30	75	140

Note: Data from exceptional events are included; Data covers the Metropolitan Statistical Area; (1) National Ambient Air Quality Standards; ppb = parts per billion; n/a not available
Concentrations: Nitrogen Dioxide AM—highest arithmetic mean concentration; Nitrogen Dioxide 1-Hr—highest 98th percentile 1-hour daily maximum concentration; Sulfur Dioxide AM—highest annual mean concentration; Sulfur Dioxide 1-Hr—highest 99th percentile 1-hour daily maximum concentration; Sulfur Dioxide 24-Hr—highest second maximum 24-hour concentration
Source: U.S. Environmental Protection Agency, Air Quality Monitoring Information, "Air Quality Statistics by City, 2021"

Appendix B: Metropolitan Area Definitions

Metropolitan Statistical Areas (MSA), Metropolitan Divisions (MD), New England City and Town Areas (NECTA), and New England City and Town Area Divisions (NECTAD)

Note: In March 2020, the Office of Management and Budget (OMB) announced changes to metropolitan and micropolitan statistical area definitions. Both current and historical definitions (December 2009) are shown below. If the change only affected the name of the metro area, the counties included were not repeated.

Albuquerque, NM MSA
Bernalillo, Sandoval, Torrance, and Valencia Counties

Allentown-Bethlehem-Easton, PA-NJ MSA
Carbon, Lehigh, and Northampton Counties, PA; Warren County, NJ

Anchorage, AK MSA
Anchorage Municipality and Matanuska-Susitna Borough

Ann Arbor, MI MSA
Washtenaw County

Athens-Clarke County, GA MSA
Clarke, Madison, Oconee, and Oglethorpe Counties

Atlanta-Sandy Springs-Roswell, GA MSA
Barrow, Bartow, Butts, Carroll, Cherokee, Clayton, Cobb, Coweta, Dawson, DeKalb, Douglas, Fayette, Forsyth, Fulton, Gwinnett, Haralson, Heard, Henry, Jasper, Lamar, Meriwether, Morgan, Newton, Paulding, Pickens, Pike, Rockdale, Spalding, and Walton Counties
Previously Atlanta-Sandy Springs-Marietta, GA MSA
Barrow, Bartow, Butts, Carroll, Cherokee, Clayton, Cobb, Coweta, Dawson, DeKalb, Douglas, Fayette, Forsyth, Fulton, Gwinnett, Haralson, Heard, Henry, Jasper, Lamar, Meriwether, Newton, Paulding, Pickens, Pike, Rockdale, Spalding, and Walton Counties

Austin-Round Rock, TX MSA
Previously Austin-Round Rock-San Marcos, TX MSA
Bastrop, Caldwell, Hays, Travis, and Williamson Counties

Baltimore-Columbia-Towson, MD MSA
Previously Baltimore-Towson, MD MSA
Baltimore city; Anne Arundel, Baltimore, Carroll, Harford, Howard, and Queen Anne's Counties

Boise City, ID MSA
Previously Boise City-Nampa, ID MSA
Ada, Boise, Canyon, Gem, and Owyhee Counties

Boston, MA

Boston-Cambridge-Newton, MA-NH MSA
Previously Boston-Cambridge-Quincy, MA-NH MSA
Essex, Middlesex, Norfolk, Plymouth, and Suffolk Counties, MA; Rockingham and Strafford Counties, NH

Boston, MA MD
Previously Boston-Quincy, MA MD
Norfolk, Plymouth, and Suffolk Counties

Boston-Cambridge-Nashua, MA-NH NECTA
Includes 157 cities and towns in Massachusetts and 34 cities and towns in New Hampshire
Previously Boston-Cambridge-Quincy, MA-NH NECTA
Includes 155 cities and towns in Massachusetts and 38 cities and towns in New Hampshire

Boston-Cambridge-Newton, MA NECTA Division
Includes 92 cities and towns in Massachusetts
Previously Boston-Cambridge-Quincy, MA NECTA Division
Includes 97 cities and towns in Massachusetts

Boulder, CO MSA
Boulder County

Brownsville-Harlingen, TX MSA
Cameron County

Cape Coral-Fort Myers, FL MSA
Lee County

Cedar Rapids, IA, MSA
Benton, Jones, and Linn Counties

Charleston-North Charleston, SC MSA
Previously Charleston-North Charleston-Summerville, SC MSA
Berkeley, Charleston, and Dorchester Counties

Charlotte-Concord-Gastonia, NC-SC MSA
Cabarrus, Gaston, Iredell, Lincoln, Mecklenburg, Rowan, and Union Counties, NC; Chester, Lancaster, and York Counties, SC
Previously Charlotte-Gastonia-Rock Hill, NC-SC MSA
Anson, Cabarrus, Gaston, Mecklenburg, and Union Counties, NC; York County, SC

Chicago, IL

Chicago-Naperville-Elgin, IL-IN-WI MSA
Previous name: Chicago-Joliet-Naperville, IL-IN-WI MSA
Cook, DeKalb, DuPage, Grundy, Kane, Kendall, Lake, McHenry, and Will Counties, IL; Jasper, Lake, Newton, and Porter Counties, IN; Kenosha County, WI

Chicago-Naperville-Arlington Heights, IL MD
Cook, DuPage, Grundy, Kendall, McHenry, and Will Counties
Previous name: Chicago-Joliet-Naperville, IL MD
Cook, DeKalb, DuPage, Grundy, Kane, Kendall, McHenry, and Will Counties

Elgin, IL MD
DeKalb and Kane Counties
Previously part of the Chicago-Joliet-Naperville, IL MD

Gary, IN MD
Jasper, Lake, Newton, and Porter Counties

Lake County-Kenosha County, IL-WI MD
Lake County, IL; Kenosha County, WI

Cincinnati, OH-KY-IN MSA
Brown, Butler, Clermont, Hamilton, and Warren Counties, OH; Boone, Bracken, Campbell, Gallatin, Grant, Kenton, and Pendleton County, KY; Dearborn, Franklin, Ohio, and Union Counties, IN
Previously Cincinnati-Middletown, OH-KY-IN MSA
Brown, Butler, Clermont, Hamilton, and Warren Counties, OH; Boone, Bracken, Campbell, Gallatin, Grant, Kenton, and Pendleton County, KY; Dearborn, Franklin, and Ohio Counties, IN

Clarksville, TN-KY MSA
Montgomery and Stewart Counties, TN; Christian and Trigg Counties, KY

Cleveland-Elyria-Mentor, OH MSA
Cuyahoga, Geauga, Lake, Lorain, and Medina Counties

College Station-Bryan, TX MSA
Brazos, Burleson and Robertson Counties

Colorado Springs, CO MSA
El Paso and Teller Counties

Columbia, MO MSA
Boone and Howard Counties

Columbia, SC MSA
Calhoun, Fairfield, Kershaw, Lexington, Richland and Saluda Counties

Columbus, OH MSA
Delaware, Fairfield, Franklin, Licking, Madison, Morrow, Pickaway, and Union Counties

Dallas, TX

Dallas-Fort Worth-Arlington, TX MSA
Collin, Dallas, Denton, Ellis, Hunt, Johnson, Kaufman, Parker, Rockwall, Tarrant, and Wise Counties

Dallas-Plano-Irving, TX MD
Collin, Dallas, Denton, Ellis, Hunt, Kaufman, and Rockwall Counties

Davenport-Moline-Rock Island, IA-IL MSA
Henry, Mercer, and Rock Island Counties, IA; Scott County

Denver-Aurora-Lakewood, CO MSA
Previously Denver-Aurora-Broomfield, CO MSA
Adams, Arapahoe, Broomfield, Clear Creek, Denver, Douglas, Elbert, Gilpin, Jefferson, and Park Counties

Des Moines-West Des Moines, IA MSA
Dallas, Guthrie, Madison, Polk, and Warren Counties

Durham-Chapel Hill, NC MSA
Chatham, Durham, Orange, and Person Counties

Edison, NJ
See New York, NY (New York-Jersey City-White Plains, NY-NJ MD)

El Paso, TX MSA
El Paso County

Fargo, ND-MN MSA
Cass County, ND; Clay County, MN

Fort Collins, CO MSA
Previously Fort Collins-Loveland, CO MSA
Larimer County

Fort Wayne, IN MSA
Allen, Wells, and Whitley Counties

Fort Worth, TX

Dallas-Fort Worth-Arlington, TX MSA
Collin, Dallas, Denton, Ellis, Hunt, Johnson, Kaufman, Parker, Rockwall, Tarrant, and Wise Counties

Fort Worth-Arlington, TX MD
Hood, Johnson, Parker, Somervell, Tarrant, and Wise Counties

Grand Rapids-Wyoming, MI MSA
Barry, Kent, Montcalm, and Ottawa Counties
Previously Grand Rapids-Wyoming, MI MSA
Barry, Ionia, Kent, and Newaygo Counties

Greeley, CO MSA
Weld County

Green Bay, WI MSA
Brown, Kewaunee, and Oconto Counties

Greensboro-High Point, NC MSA
Guilford, Randolph, and Rockingham Counties

Honolulu, HI MSA
Honolulu County

Houston-The Woodlands-Sugar Land-Baytown, TX MSA
Austin, Brazoria, Chambers, Fort Bend, Galveston, Harris, Liberty, Montgomery, and Waller Counties
Previously Houston-Sugar Land-Baytown, TX MSA
Austin, Brazoria, Chambers, Fort Bend, Galveston, Harris, Liberty, Montgomery, San Jacinto, and Waller Counties

Huntsville, AL MSA
Limestone and Madison Counties

Indianapolis-Carmel, IN MSA
Boone, Brown, Hamilton, Hancock, Hendricks, Johnson, Marion, Morgan, Putnam, and Shelby Counties

Jacksonville, FL MSA
Baker, Clay, Duval, Nassau, and St. Johns Counties

Kansas City, MO-KS MSA
Franklin, Johnson, Leavenworth, Linn, Miami, and Wyandotte Counties, KS; Bates, Caldwell, Cass, Clay, Clinton, Jackson, Lafayette, Platte, and Ray Counties, MO

Lafayette, LA MSA
Acadia, Iberia, Lafayette, St. Martin, and Vermilion Parishes

Las Cruces, NM MSA
Doña Ana County
Previously Las Cruces, NM MSA
Doña Ana and San Miguel Counties

Las Vegas-Henderson-Paradise, NV MSA
Previously Las Vegas-Paradise, NV MSA
Clark County

Lexington-Fayette, KY MSA
Bourbon, Clark, Fayette, Jessamine, Scott, and Woodford Counties

Lincoln, NE MSA
Lancaster and Seward Counties

Little Rock-North Little Rock-Conway, AR MSA
Faulkner, Grant, Lonoke, Perry, Pulaski, and Saline Counties

Los Angeles, CA

Los Angeles-Long Beach-Anaheim, CA MSA
Previously Los Angeles-Long Beach-Santa Ana, CA MSA
Los Angeles and Orange Counties

Los Angeles-Long Beach-Glendale, CA MD
Los Angeles County

Anaheim-Santa Ana-Irvine, CA MD
Previously Santa Ana-Anaheim-Irvine, CA MD
Orange County

Louisville/Jefferson, KY-IN MSA
Clark, Floyd, Harrison, Scott, and Washington Counties, IN; Bullitt, Henry, Jefferson, Oldham, Shelby, Spencer, and Trimble Counties, KY

Madison, WI MSA
Columbia, Dane, and Iowa Counties

Manchester, NH

Manchester-Nashua, NH MSA
Hillsborough County

Manchester, NH NECTA
Includes 11 cities and towns in New Hampshire
Previously Manchester, NH NECTA
Includes 9 cities and towns in New Hampshire

Miami, FL

Miami-Fort Lauderdale-West Palm Beach, FL MSA
Previously Miami-Fort Lauderdale-Pompano Beach, FL MSA
Broward, Miami-Dade, and Palm Beach Counties

Miami-Miami Beach-Kendall, FL MD
Miami-Dade County

Midland, TX MSA
Martin, and Midland Counties

Milwaukee-Waukesha-West Allis, WI MSA
Milwaukee, Ozaukee, Washington, and Waukesha Counties

Minneapolis-St. Paul-Bloomington, MN-WI MSA
Anoka, Carver, Chisago, Dakota, Hennepin, Isanti, Le Sueur, Mille Lacs, Ramsey, Scott, Sherburne, Sibley, Washington, and Wright Counties, MN; Pierce and St. Croix Counties, WI

Nashville-Davidson-Murfreesboro-Franklin, TN MSA
Cannon, Cheatham, Davidson, Dickson, Hickman, Macon, Robertson, Rutherford, Smith, Sumner, Trousdale, Williamson, and Wilson Counties

New Haven-Milford, CT MSA
New Haven County

New Orleans-Metarie-Kenner, LA MSA
Jefferson, Orleans, Plaquemines, St. Bernard, St. Charles, St. James, St. John the Baptist, and St. Tammany Parish
Previously New Orleans-Metarie-Kenner, LA MSA
Jefferson, Orleans, Plaquemines, St. Bernard, St. Charles, St. John the Baptist, and St. Tammany Parish

New York, NY

New York-Newark-Jersey City, NY-NJ-PA MSA
Bergen, Essex, Hudson, Hunterdon, Middlesex, Monmouth, Morris, Ocean, Passaic, Somerset, Sussex, and Union Counties, NJ; Bronx, Dutchess, Kings, Nassau, New York, Orange, Putnam, Queens, Richmond, Rockland, Suffolk, and Westchester Counties, NY; Pike County, PA
Previous name: New York-Northern New Jersey-Long Island, NY-NJ-PA MSA
Bergen, Essex, Hudson, Hunterdon, Middlesex, Monmouth, Morris, Ocean, Passaic, Somerset, Sussex, and Union Counties, NJ; Bronx, Kings, Nassau, New York, Putnam, Queens, Richmond, Rockland, Suffolk, and Westchester Counties, NY; Pike County, PA

Dutchess County-Putnam County, NY MD
Dutchess and Putnam Counties
Dutchess County was previously part of the Poughkeepsie-Newburgh-Middletown, NY MSA. Putnam County was previously part of the New York-Wayne-White Plains, NY-NJ MD

Nassau-Suffolk, NY MD
Nassau and Suffolk Counties

New York-Jersey City-White Plains, NY-NJ MD
Bergen, Hudson, Middlesex, Monmouth, Ocean, and Passaic Counties, NJ; Bronx, Kings, New York, Orange, Queens, Richmond, Rockland, and Westchester Counties, NY
Previous name: New York-Wayne-White Plains, NY-NJ MD
Bergen, Hudson, and Passaic Counties, NJ; Bronx, Kings, New York, Putnam, Queens, Richmond, Rockland, and Westchester Counties, NY

Newark, NJ-PA MD
Essex, Hunterdon, Morris, Somerset, Sussex, and Union Counties, NJ; Pike County, PA
Previous name: Newark-Union, NJ-PA MD
Essex, Hunterdon, Morris, Sussex, and Union Counties, NJ; Pike County, PA

Oklahoma City, OK MSA
Canadian, Cleveland, Grady, Lincoln, Logan, McClain, and Oklahoma Counties

Omaha-Council Bluffs, NE-IA MSA
Harrison, Mills, and Pottawattamie Counties, IA; Cass, Douglas, Sarpy, Saunders, and Washington Counties, NE

Orlando-Kissimmee-Sanford, FL MSA
Lake, Orange, Osceola, and Seminole Counties

Philadelphia, PA

Philadelphia-Camden-Wilmington, PA-NJ-DE-MD MSA
New Castle County, DE; Cecil County, MD; Burlington, Camden, Gloucester, and Salem Counties, NJ; Bucks, Chester, Delaware, Montgomery, and Philadelphia Counties, PA

Camden, NJ MD
Burlington, Camden, and Gloucester Counties

Montgomery County-Bucks County-Chester County, PA MD
Bucks, Chester, and Montgomery Counties
Previously part of the Philadelphia, PA MD

Philadelphia, PA MD
Delaware and Philadelphia Counties
Previous name: Philadelphia, PA MD
Bucks, Chester, Delaware, Montgomery, and Philadelphia Counties

Wilmington, DE-MD-NJ MD
New Castle County, DE; Cecil County, MD; Salem County, NJ

Phoenix-Mesa-Scottsdale, AZ MSA
Previously Phoenix-Mesa-Glendale, AZ MSA
Maricopa and Pinal Counties

Pittsburgh, PA MSA
Allegheny, Armstrong, Beaver, Butler, Fayette, Washington, and Westmoreland Counties

Portland-Vancouver-Hillsboro, OR-WA MSA
Clackamas, Columbia, Multnomah, Washington, and Yamhill Counties, OR; Clark and Skamania Counties, WA

Providence, RI

Providence-New Bedford-Fall River, RI-MA MSA
Previously Providence-New Bedford-Fall River, RI-MA MSA
Bristol County, MA; Bristol, Kent, Newport, Providence, and Washington Counties, RI

Providence-Warwick, RI-MA NECTA
Includes 12 cities and towns in Massachusetts and 36 cities and towns in Rhode Island
Previously Providence-Fall River-Warwick, RI-MA NECTA
Includes 12 cities and towns in Massachusetts and 37 cities and towns in Rhode Island

Provo-Orem, UT MSA
Juab and Utah Counties

Raleigh, NC MSA
Previously Raleigh-Cary, NC MSA
Franklin, Johnston, and Wake Counties

Appendix B: Metropolitan Area Definitions

Reno, NV MSA
Previously Reno-Sparks, NV MSA
Storey and Washoe Counties

Richmond, VA MSA
Amelia, Caroline, Charles City, Chesterfield, Dinwiddie, Goochland, Hanover, Henrico, King William, New Kent, Powhatan, Prince George, and Sussex Counties; Colonial Heights, Hopewell, Petersburg, and Richmond Cities

Rochester, MN MSA
Dodge, Fillmore, Olmsted, and Wabasha Counties

Sacramento—Roseville—Arden-Arcade, CA MSA
El Dorado, Placer, Sacramento, and Yolo Counties

Saint Louis, MO-IL MSA
Bond, Calhoun, Clinton, Jersey, Macoupin, Madison, Monroe, and St. Clair Counties, IL; St. Louis city; Franklin, Jefferson, Lincoln, St. Charles, St. Louis, and Warren Counties, MO
Previously Saint Louis, MO-IL MSA
Bond, Calhoun, Clinton, Jersey, Macoupin, Madison, Monroe, and St. Clair Counties, IL; St. Louis city; Crawford (part), Franklin, Jefferson, Lincoln, St. Charles, St. Louis, Warren, and Washington Counties, MO

Salem, OR MSA
Marion and Polk Counties

Salt Lake City, UT MSA
Salt Lake and Tooele Counties

San Antonio-New Braunfels, TX MSA
Atascosa, Bandera, Bexar, Comal, Guadalupe, Kendall, Medina, and Wilson Counties

San Diego-Carlsbad, CA MSA
Previously San Diego-Carlsbad-San Marcos, CA MSA
San Diego County

San Francisco, CA

San Francisco-Oakland-Hayward, CA MSA
Previously San Francisco-Oakland- Fremont, CA MSA
Alameda, Contra Costa, Marin, San Francisco, and San Mateo Counties

San Francisco-Redwood City-South San Francisco, CA MD
San Francisco and San Mateo Counties

Previously San Francisco-San Mateo-Redwood City, CA MD
Marin, San Francisco, and San Mateo Counties

San Jose-Sunnyvale-Santa Clara, CA MSA
San Benito and Santa Clara Counties

Santa Rosa, CA MSA
Previously Santa Rosa-Petaluma, CA MSA
Sonoma County

Savannah, GA MSA
Bryan, Chatham, and Effingham Counties

Seattle, WA

Seattle-Tacoma-Bellevue, WA MSA
King, Pierce, and Snohomish Counties

Seattle-Bellevue-Everett, WA MD
King and Snohomish Counties

Sioux Falls, SD MSA
Lincoln, McCook, Minnehaha, and Turner Counties

Springfield, IL MSA
Menard and Sangamon Counties

Tampa-St. Petersburg-Clearwater, FL MSA
Hernando, Hillsborough, Pasco, and Pinellas Counties

Tucson, AZ MSA
Pima County

Tulsa, OK MSA
Creek, Okmulgee, Osage, Pawnee, Rogers, Tulsa, and Wagoner Counties

Tuscaloosa, AL MSA
Hale, Pickens, and Tuscaloosa Counties

Virginia Beach-Norfolk-Newport News, VA-NC MSA
Currituck County, NC; Chesapeake, Hampton, Newport News, Norfolk, Poquoson, Portsmouth, Suffolk, Virginia Beach and Williamsburg cities, VA; Gloucester, Isle of Wight, James City, Mathews, Surry, and York Counties, VA

Washington, DC

Washington-Arlington-Alexandria, DC-VA-MD-WV MSA
District of Columbia; Calvert, Charles, Frederick, Montgomery, and Prince George's Counties, MD; Alexandria, Fairfax, Falls Church, Fredericksburg, Manassas Park, and Manassas cities, VA; Arlington, Clarke, Culpepper, Fairfax, Fauquier, Loudoun, Prince William, Rappahannock, Spotsylvania, Stafford, and Warren Counties, VA; Jefferson County, WV
Previously Washington-Arlington-Alexandria, DC-VA-MD-WV MSA
District of Columbia; Calvert, Charles, Frederick, Montgomery, and Prince George's Counties, MD; Alexandria, Fairfax, Falls Church, Fredericksburg, Manassas Park, and Manassas cities, VA; Arlington, Clarke, Fairfax, Fauquier, Loudoun, Prince William, Spotsylvania, Stafford, and Warren Counties, VA; Jefferson County, WV

Washington-Arlington-Alexandria, DC-VA-MD-WV MD
District of Columbia; Calvert, Charles, and Prince George's Counties, MD; Alexandria, Fairfax, Falls Church, Fredericksburg, Manassas Park, and Manassas cities, VA; Arlington, Clarke, Culpepper, Fairfax, Fauquier, Loudoun, Prince William, Rappahannock, Spotsylvania, Stafford, and Warren Counties, VA; Jefferson County, WV
Previously Washington-Arlington-Alexandria, DC-VA-MD-WV MD
District of Columbia; Calvert, Charles, and Prince George's Counties, MD; Alexandria, Fairfax, Falls Church, Fredericksburg, Manassas Park, and Manassas cities, VA; Arlington, Clarke, Fairfax, Fauquier, Loudoun, Prince William, Spotsylvania, Stafford, and Warren Counties, VA; Jefferson County, WV

Wichita, KS MSA
Butler, Harvey, Kingman, Sedgwick, and Sumner Counties

Wilmington, NC MSA
New Hanover and Pender Counties
Previously Wilmington, NC MSA
Brunswick, New Hanover and Pender Counties

Winston-Salem, NC MSA
Davidson, Davie, Forsyth, Stokes, and Yadkin Counties

Worcester, MA

Worcester, MA-CT MSA
Windham County, CT; Worcester County, MA
Previously Worcester, MA MSA
Worcester County

Worcester, MA-CT NECTA
Includes 40 cities and towns in Massachusetts and 8 cities and towns in Connecticut
Previously Worcester, MA-CT NECTA
Includes 37 cities and towns in Massachusetts and 3 cities and towns in Connecticut

Appendix C: Government Type and Primary County

This appendix includes the government structure of each place included in this book. It also includes the county or county equivalent in which each place is located. If a place spans more than one county, the county in which the majority of the population resides is shown.

Albuquerque, NM
Government Type: City
County: Bernalillo

Allentown, PA
Government Type: City
County: Lehigh

Anchorage, AK
Government Type: Municipality
Borough: Anchorage

Ann Arbor, MI
Government Type: City
County: Washtenaw

Athens, GA
Government Type: Consolidated city-county
County: Clarke

Atlanta, GA
Government Type: City
County: Fulton

Austin, TX
Government Type: City
County: Travis

Baltimore, MD
Government Type: Independent city

Baton Rouge, LA
Government Type: Consolidated city-parish
Parish: East Baton Rouge

Boise City, ID
Government Type: City
County: Ada

Boston, MA
Government Type: City
County: Suffolk

Boulder, CO
Government Type: City
County: Boulder

Brownsville, TX
Government Type: City
County: Cameron

Cape Coral, FL
Government Type: City
County: Lee

Cedar Rapids, IA
Government Type: City
County: Linn

Charleston, SC
Government Type: City
County: Charleston

Charlotte, NC
Government Type: City
County: Mecklenburg

Chicago, IL
Government Type: City
County: Cook

Cincinnati, OH
Government Type: City
County: Hamilton

Clarksville, TN
Government Type: City
County: Montgomery

Cleveland, OH
Government Type: City
County: Cuyahoga

College Station, TX
Government Type: City
County: Brazos

Colorado Springs, CO
Government Type: City
County: El Paso

Columbia, MO
Government Type: City
County: Boone

Columbia, SC
Government Type: City
County: Richland

Columbus, OH
Government Type: City
County: Franklin

Dallas, TX
Government Type: City
County: Dallas

Davenport, IA
Government Type: City
County: Scott

Denver, CO
Government Type: City
County: Denver

Des Moines, IA
Government Type: City
County: Polk

Durham, NC
Government Type: City
County: Durham

Edison, NJ
Government Type: Township
County: Middlesex

El Paso, TX
Government Type: City
County: El Paso

Fargo, ND
Government Type: City
County: Cass

Fort Collins, CO
Government Type: City
County: Larimer

Fort Wayne, IN
Government Type: City
County: Allen

Fort Worth, TX
Government Type: City
County: Tarrant

Grand Rapids, MI
Government Type: City
County: Kent

Greeley, CO
Government Type: City
County: Weld

Green Bay, WI
Government Type: City
County: Brown

Greensboro, NC
Government Type: City
County: Guilford

Honolulu, HI
Government Type: Census Designated Place (CDP)
County: Honolulu

Houston, TX
Government Type: City
County: Harris

Huntsville, AL
Government Type: City
County: Madison

Indianapolis, IN
Government Type: City
County: Marion

Jacksonville, FL
Government Type: City
County: Duval

Kansas City, MO
Government Type: City
County: Jackson

Lafayette, LA
Government Type: City
Parish: Lafayette

Appendix C: Government Type and Primary County

Las Cruces, NM
Government Type: City
County: Doña Ana

Las Vegas, NV
Government Type: City
County: Clark

Lexington, KY
Government Type: Consolidated city-county
County: Fayette

Lincoln, NE
Government Type: City
County: Lancaster

Little Rock, AR
Government Type: City
County: Pulaski

Los Angeles, CA
Government Type: City
County: Los Angeles

Louisville, KY
Government Type: Consolidated city-county
County: Jefferson

Madison, WI
Government Type: City
County: Dane

Manchester, NH
Government Type: City
County: Hillsborough

Memphis, TN
Government Type: City
County: Shelby

Miami, FL
Government Type: City
County: Miami-Dade

Midland, TX
Government Type: City
County: Midland

Milwaukee, WI
Government Type: City
County: Milwaukee

Minneapolis, MN
Government Type: City
County: Hennepin

Nashville, TN
Government Type: Consolidated city-county
County: Davidson

New Haven, CT
Government Type: City
County: New Haven

New Orleans, LA
Government Type: City
Parish: Orleans

New York, NY
Government Type: City
Counties: Bronx; Kings; New York; Queens; Staten Island

Oklahoma City, OK
Government Type: City
County: Oklahoma

Omaha, NE
Government Type: City
County: Douglas

Orlando, FL
Government Type: City
County: Orange

Philadelphia, PA
Government Type: City
County: Philadelphia

Phoenix, AZ
Government Type: City
County: Maricopa

Pittsburgh, PA
Government Type: City
County: Allegheny

Portland, OR
Government Type: City
County: Multnomah

Providence, RI
Government Type: City
County: Providence

Provo, UT
Government Type: City
County: Utah

Raleigh, NC
Government Type: City
County: Wake

Reno, NV
Government Type: City
County: Washoe

Richmond, VA
Government Type: Independent city

Riverside, CA
Government Type: City
County: Riverside

Rochester, MN
Government Type: City
County: Olmsted

Rochester, NY
Government Type: City
County: Monroe

Sacramento, CA
Government Type: City
County: Sacramento

Saint Louis, MO
Government Type: Independent city

Salem, OR
Government Type: City
County: Marion

Salt Lake City, UT
Government Type: City
County: Salt Lake

San Antonio, TX
Government Type: City
County: Bexar

San Diego, CA
Government Type: City
County: San Diego

San Francisco, CA
Government Type: City
County: San Francisco

San Jose, CA
Government Type: City
County: Santa Clara

Santa Rosa, CA
Government Type: City
County: Sonoma

Savannah, GA
Government Type: City
County: Chatham

Seattle, WA
Government Type: City
County: King

Sioux Falls, SD
Government Type: City
County: Minnehaha

Springfield, IL
Government Type: City
County: Sangamon

Tampa, FL
Government Type: City
County: Hillsborough

Tucson, AZ
Government Type: City
County: Pima

Tulsa, OK
Government Type: City
County: Tulsa

Tuscaloosa, AL
Government Type: City
County: Tuscaloosa

Virginia Beach, VA
Government Type: Independent city

Washington, DC
Government Type: City
County: District of Columbia

Wichita, KS
Government Type: City
County: Sedgwick

Wilmington, NC
Government Type: City
County: New Hanover

Winston-Salem, NC
Government Type: City
County: Forsyth

Worcester, MA
Government Type: City
County: Worcester

Appendix D: Chambers of Commerce

Albuquerque, NM
Albuquerque Chamber of Commerce
P.O. Box 25100
Albuquerque, NM 87125
Phone: (505) 764-3700
Fax: (505) 764-3714
www.abqchamber.com

Albuquerque Economic Development Dept
851 University Blvd SE, Suite 203
Albuquerque, NM 87106
Phone: (505) 246-6200
Fax: (505) 246-6219
www.cabq.gov/econdev

Allentown, PA
Greater Lehigh Valley Chamber of Commerce
Allentown Office
840 Hamilton Street, Suite 205
Allentown, PA 18101
Phone: (610) 751-4929
Fax: (610) 437-4907
www.lehighvalleychamber.org

Anchorage, AK
Anchorage Chamber of Commerce
1016 W Sixth Avenue
Suite 303
Anchorage, AK 99501
Phone: (907) 272-2401
Fax: (907) 272-4117
www.anchoragechamber.org

Anchorage Economic Development Department
900 W 5th Avenue
Suite 300
Anchorage, AK 99501
Phone: (907) 258-3700
Fax: (907) 258-6646
aedcweb.com

Ann Arbor, MI
Ann Arbor Area Chamber of Commerce
115 West Huron
3rd Floor
Ann Arbor, MI 48104
Phone: (734) 665-4433
Fax: (734) 665-4191
www.annarborchamber.org

Ann Arbor Economic Development Department
201 S Division
Suite 430
Ann Arbor, MI 48104
Phone: (734) 761-9317
www.annarborspark.org

Athens, GA
Athens Area Chamber of Commerce
246 W Hancock Avenue
Athens, GA 30601
Phone: (706) 549-6800
Fax: (706) 549-5636
www.aacoc.org

Athens-Clarke County Economic Development Department
246 W. Hancock Avenue
Athens, GA 30601
Phone: (706) 613-3233
Fax: (706) 613-3812
www.athensbusiness.org

Atlanta, GA
Metro Atlanta Chamber of Commerce
235 Andrew Young International Blvd NW
Atlanta, GA 30303
Phone: (404) 880-9000
Fax: (404) 586-8464
www.metroatlantachamber.com

Austin, TX
Greater Austin Chamber of Commerce
210 Barton Springs Road
Suite 400
Austin, TX 78704
Phone: (512) 478-9383
Fax: (512) 478-6389
www.austin-chamber.org

Baltimore, MD
Baltimore City Chamber of Commerce
P.O. Box 43121
Baltimore, MD 21236
443-860-2020
baltimorecitychamber.org

Baltimore County Chamber of Commerce
102 W. Pennsylvania Avenue
Suite 305
Towson, MD, 21204
Phone: (410) 825-6200
Fax: (410) 821-9901
www.baltcountychamber.com

Boise City, ID
Boise Metro Chamber of Commerce
250 S 5th Street
Suite 800
Boise City, ID 83701
Phone: (208) 472-5200
Fax: (208) 472-5201
www.boisechamber.org

Boston, MA
Greater Boston Chamber of Commerce
265 Franklin Street
12th Floor
Boston, MA 02110
Phone: (617) 227-4500
Fax: (617) 227-7505
www.bostonchamber.com

Boulder, CO
Boulder Chamber of Commerce
2440 Pearl Street
Boulder, CO 80302
Phone: (303) 442-1044
Fax: (303) 938-8837
www.boulderchamber.com

City of Boulder Economic Vitality Program
P.O. Box 791
Boulder, CO 80306
Phone: (303) 441-3090
www.bouldercolorado.gov

Brownsville, TX
Brownsville Chamber of Commerce
1600 University Blvd.
Brownsville, TX 78520
Phone: (956) 542-4341
brownsvillechamber.com

Cape Coral, FL
Chamber of Commerce of Cape Coral
2051 Cape Coral Parkway East
Cape Coral, FL 33904
Phone: (239) 549-6900
Fax: (239) 549-9609
www.capecoralchamber.com

Cedar Rapids, IA
Cedar Rapids Chamber of Commerce
424 First Avenue NE
Cedar Rapids, IA 52401
Phone: (319) 398-5317
Fax: (319) 398-5228
www.cedarrapids.org

Cedar Rapids Economic Development
50 Second Avenue Bridge, Sixth Floor
Cedar Rapids, IA 52401-1256
Phone: (319) 286-5041
Fax: (319) 286-5141
www.cedar-rapids.org

Charleston, SC
Charleston Metro Chamber of Commerce
P.O. Box 975
Charleston, SC 29402
Phone: (843) 577-2510
www.charlestonchamber.net

Charlotte, NC
Charlotte Chamber of Commerce
330 S Tryon Street
P.O. Box 32785
Charlotte, NC 28232
Phone: (704) 378-1300
Fax: (704) 374-1903
www.charlottechamber.com

Charlotte Regional Partnership
1001 Morehead Square Drive, Suite 200
Charlotte, NC 28203
Phone: (704) 347-8942
Fax: (704) 347-8981
www.charlotteusa.com

Chicago, IL
Chicagoland Chamber of Commerce
200 E Randolph Street
Suite 2200
Chicago, IL 60601-6436
Phone: (312) 494-6700
Fax: (312) 861-0660
www.chicagolandchamber.org

City of Chicago Department of Planning
and Development
City Hall, Room 1000
121 North La Salle Street
Chicago, IL 60602
Phone: (312) 744-4190
Fax: (312) 744-2271
www.cityofchicago.org/city/en/depts/dcd.html

Cincinnati, OH
Cincinnati USA Regional Chamber
3 East 4th Street, Suite 200
Cincinnati, Ohio 45202
Phone: (513) 579-3111
www.cincinnatichamber.com

Clarksville, TN
Clarksville Area Chamber of Commerce
25 Jefferson Street, Suite 300
Clarksville, TN 37040
Phone: (931) 647-2331
www.clarksvillechamber.com

Cleveland, OH
Greater Cleveland Partnership
1240 Huron Rd. E, Suite 300
Cleveland, OH 44115
Phone: (216) 621-3300
www.gcpartnership.com

College Station, TX
Bryan-College Station Chamber of
Commerce
4001 East 29th St, Suite 175
Bryan, TX 77802
Phone: (979) 260-5200
www.bcschamber.org

Colorado Springs, CO
Colorado Springs Chamber and EDC
102 South Tejon Street
Suite 430
Colorado Springs, CO 80903
Phone: (719) 471-8183
coloradospringschamberedc.com

Columbia, MO
Columbia Chamber of Commerce
300 South Providence Rd.
P.O. Box 1016
Columbia, MO 65205-1016
Phone: (573) 874-1132
Fax: (573) 443-3986
www.columbiamochamber.com

Columbia, SC
The Columbia Chamber
930 Richland Street
Columbia, SC 29201
Phone: (803) 733-1110
Fax: (803) 733-1113
www.columbiachamber.com

Columbus, OH
Greater Columbus Chamber
37 North High Street
Columbus, OH 43215
Phone: (614) 221-1321
Fax: (614) 221-1408
www.columbus.org

Dallas, TX
City of Dallas Economic Development
Department
1500 Marilla Street
5C South
Dallas, TX 75201
Phone: (214) 670-1685
Fax: (214) 670-0158
www.dallas-edd.org

Greater Dallas Chamber of Commerce
700 North Pearl Street
Suite1200
Dallas, TX 75201
Phone: (214) 746-6600
Fax: (214) 746-6799
www.dallaschamber.org

Davenport, IA
Quad Cities Chamber
331 W. 3rd Street
Suite 100
Davenport, IA 52801
Phone: (563) 322-1706
quadcitieschamber.com

Denver, CO
Denver Metro Chamber of Commerce
1445 Market Street
Denver, CO 80202
Phone: (303) 534-8500
Fax: (303) 534-3200
www.denverchamber.org

Downtown Denver Partnership
511 16th Street
Suite 200
Denver, CO 80202
Phone: (303) 534-6161
Fax: (303) 534-2803
www.downtowndenver.com

Des Moines, IA
Des Moines Downtown Chamber
301 Grand Ave
Des Moines, IA 50309
Phone: (515) 309-3229
desmoinesdowntownchamber.com

Greater Des Moines Partnership
700 Locust Street
Suite 100
Des Moines, IA 50309
Phone: (515) 286-4950
Fax: (515) 286-4974
www.desmoinesmetro.com

Durham, NC
Durham Chamber of Commerce
P.O. Box 3829
Durham, NC 27702
Phone: (919) 682-2133
Fax: (919) 688-8351
www.durhamchamber.org

North Carolina Institute of Minority
Economic Development
114 W Parish Street
Durham, NC 27701
Phone: (919) 956-8889
Fax: (919) 688-7668
www.ncimed.com

Edison, NJ
Edison Chamber of Commerce
939 Amboy Avenue
Edison, NJ 08837
Phone: (732) 738-9482
www.edisonchamber.com

El Paso, TX
City of El Paso Department of Economic
Development
2 Civic Center Plaza
El Paso, TX 79901
Phone: (915) 541-4000
Fax: (915) 541-1316
www.elpasotexas.gov

Greater El Paso Chamber of Commerce
10 Civic Center Plaza
El Paso, TX 79901
Phone: (915) 534-0500
Fax: (915) 534-0510
www.elpaso.org

Fargo, ND
Chamber of Commerce of Fargo Moorhead
202 First Avenue North
Fargo, ND 56560
Phone: (218) 233-1100
Fax: (218) 233-1200
www.fmchamber.com

Greater Fargo-Moorhead Economic
Development Corporation
51 Broadway, Suite 500
Fargo, ND 58102
Phone: (701) 364-1900
Fax: (701) 293-7819
www.gfmedc.com

Fort Collins, CO
Fort Collins Chamber of Commerce
225 South Meldrum
Fort Collins, CO 80521
Phone: (970) 482-3746
Fax: (970) 482-3774
fortcollinschamber.com

Fort Wayne, IN
City of Fort Wayne Economic Development
1 Main St
1 Main Street
Fort Wayne, IN 46802
Phone: (260) 427-1111
Fax: (260) 427-1375
www.cityoffortwayne.org

Greater Fort Wayne Chamber of Commerce
826 Ewing Street
Fort Wayne, IN 46802
Phone: (260) 424-1435
Fax: (260) 426-7232
www.fwchamber.org

Fort Worth, TX
City of Fort Worth Economic Development
City Hall
900 Monroe Street
Suite 301
Fort Worth, TX 76102
Phone: (817) 392-6103
Fax: (817) 392-2431
www.fortworthgov.org

Appendix D: Chambers of Commerce   A-183

Fort Worth Chamber of Commerce
777 Taylor Street, Suite 900
Fort Worth, TX 76102-4997
Phone: (817) 336-2491
Fax: (817) 877-4034
www.fortworthchamber.com

Grand Rapids, MI
Grands Rapids Area Chamber of Commerce
111 Pearl Street N.W.
Grand Rapids, MI 49503
Phone: (616) 771-0300
Fax: (616) 771-0318
www.grandrapids.org

Greeley, CO
Greeley Area Chamber of Commerce
902 7th Avenue
Greeley, CO 80631
Phone: (970) 352-3566
www.greeleychamber.com

Green Bay, WI
Economic Development
100 N Jefferson Street
Room 202
Green Bay, WI 54301
Phone: (920) 448-3397
Fax: (920) 448-3063
www.ci.green-bay.wi.us

Green Bay Area Chamber of Commerce
300 N. Broadway
Suite 3A
Green Bay, WI 54305-1660
Phone: (920) 437-8704
Fax: (920) 593-3468
www.titletown.org

Greensboro, NC
Greensboro Chamber of Commerce
111 W. February One Place
Greensboro, NC 27401
Phone: (336) 387-8301
greensboro.org

Honolulu, HI
The Chamber of Commerce of Hawaii
1132 Bishop Street
Suite 402
Honolulu, HI 96813
Phone: (808) 545-4300
Fax: (808) 545-4369
www.cochawaii.com

Houston, TX
Greater Houston Partnership
1200 Smith Street, Suite 700
Houston, TX 77002-4400
Phone: (713) 844-3600
Fax: (713) 844-0200
www.houston.org

Huntsville, AL
Chamber of Commerce of
Huntsville/Madison County
225 Church Street
Huntsville, AL 35801
Phone: (256) 535-2000
Fax: (256) 535-2015
www.huntsvillealabamausa.com

Indianapolis, IN
Greater Indianapolis Chamber of Commerce
111 Monument Circle, Suite 1950
Indianapolis, IN 46204
Phone: (317) 464-2222
Fax: (317) 464-2217
www.indychamber.com

The Indy Partnership
111 Monument Circle, Suite 1800
Indianapolis, IN 46204
Phone: (317) 236-6262
Fax: (317) 236-6275
indypartnership.com

Jacksonville, FL
Jacksonville Chamber of Commerce
3 Independent Drive
Jacksonville, FL 32202
Phone: (904) 366-6600
Fax: (904) 632-0617
www.myjaxchamber.com

Kansas City, MO
Greater Kansas City Chamber of Commerce
2600 Commerce Tower
911 Main Street
Kansas City, MO 64105
Phone: (816) 221-2424
Fax: (816) 221-7440
www.kcchamber.com

Kansas City Area Development Council
2600 Commerce Tower
911 Main Street
Kansas City, MO 64105
Phone: (816) 221-2121
Fax: (816) 842-2865
www.thinkkc.com

Lafayette, LA
Greater Lafayette Chamber of Commerce
804 East Saint Mary Blvd.
Lafayette, LA 70503
Phone: (337) 233-2705
Fax: (337) 234-8671
www.lafchamber.org

Las Cruces, NM
Greater Las Cruces Chamber of Commerce
505 S Main Street, Suite 134
Las Cruces, NM 88001
Phone: (575) 524-1968
Fax: (575) 527-5546
www.lascruces.org

Las Vegas, NV
Las Vegas Chamber of Commerce
6671 Las Vegas Blvd South
Suite 300
Las Vegas, NV 89119
Phone: (702) 735-1616
Fax: (702) 735-0406
www.lvchamber.org

Las Vegas Office of Business Development
400 Stewart Avenue
City Hall
Las Vegas, NV 89101
Phone: (702) 229-6011
Fax: (702) 385-3128
www.lasvegasnevada.gov

Lexington, KY
Greater Lexington Chamber of Commerce
330 East Main Street
Suite 100
Lexington, KY 40507
Phone: (859) 254-4447
Fax: (859) 233-3304
www.commercelexington.com

Lexington Downtown Development
Authority
101 East Vine Street
Suite 500
Lexington, KY 40507
Phone: (859) 425-2296
Fax: (859) 425-2292
www.lexingtondda.com

Lincoln, NE
Lincoln Chamber of Commerce
1135 M Street
Suite 200
Lincoln, NE 68508
Phone: (402) 436-2350
Fax: (402) 436-2360
www.lcoc.com

Little Rock, AR
Little Rock Regional Chamber
One Chamber Plaza
Little Rock, AR 72201
Phone: (501) 374-2001
Fax: (501) 374-6018
www.littlerockchamber.com

Los Angeles, CA
Los Angeles Area Chamber of Commerce
350 South Bixel Street
Los Angeles, CA 90017
Phone: (213) 580-7500
Fax: (213) 580-7511
www.lachamber.org

Los Angeles County Economic
Development Corporation
444 South Flower Street
34th Floor
Los Angeles, CA 90071
Phone: (213) 622-4300
Fax: (213) 622-7100
www.laedc.org

Louisville, KY
The Greater Louisville Chamber of
Commerce
614 West Main Street
Suite 6000
Louisville, KY 40202
Phone: (502) 625-0000
Fax: (502) 625-0010
www.greaterlouisville.com

Madison, WI
Greater Madison Chamber of Commerce
615 East Washington Avenue
P.O. Box 71
Madison, WI 53701-0071
Phone: (608) 256-8348
Fax: (608) 256-0333
www.greatermadisonchamber.com

Manchester, NH
Greater Manchester Chamber of Commerce
889 Elm Street
Manchester, NH 03101
Phone: (603) 666-6600
Fax: (603) 626-0910
www.manchester-chamber.org

Manchester Economic Development Office
One City Hall Plaza
Manchester, NH 03101
Phone: (603) 624-6505
Fax: (603) 624-6308
www.yourmanchesternh.com

Miami, FL
Greater Miami Chamber of Commerce
1601 Biscayne Boulevard
Miami, FL 33132-1260
Phone: (305) 350-7700
Fax: (305) 374-6902
www.miamichamber.com

The Beacon Council
80 Southwest 8th Street, Suite 2400
Miami, FL 33130
Phone: (305) 579-1300
Fax: (305) 375-0271
www.beaconcouncil.com

Midland, TX
Midland Chamber of Commerce
109 N. Main
Midland, TX 79701
Phone: (432) 683-3381
Fax: (432) 686-3556
www.midlandtxchamber.com

Milwaukee, WI
Greater Milwaukee Chamber of Commerce
6815 W. Capitol Drive
Suite 300
Milwaukee, WI 53216
Phone: (414) 465-2422
www.gmcofc.org

Metropolitan Milwaukee Association of Commerce
756 N. Milwaukee Street
Suite 400
Milwaukee, WI 53202
Phone: (414) 287-4100
Fax: (414) 271-7753
www.mmac.org

Minneapolis, MN
Minneapolis Regional Chamber
81 South Ninth Street, Suite 200
Minneapolis, MN 55402
Phone: (612) 370-9100
Fax: (612) 370-9195
www.minneapolischamber.org

Minneapolis Community Development Agency
Crown Roller Mill
105 5th Avenue South
Suite 200
Minneapolis, MN 55401
Phone: (612) 673-5095
Fax: (612) 673-5100
www.ci.minneapolis.mn.us

Nashville, TN
Nashville Area Chamber of Commerce
211 Commerce Street, Suite 100
Nashville, TN 37201
Phone: (615) 743-3000
Fax: (615) 256-3074
www.nashvillechamber.com

Tennessee Valley Authority Economic Development
400 West Summit Hill Drive
Knoxville TN 37902
Phone: (865) 632-2101
www.tvaed.com

New Haven, CT
Greater New Haven Chamber of Commerce
900 Chapel Street, 10th Floor
New Haven, CT 06510
Phone: (203) 787-6735
www.gnhcc.com

New Orleans, LA
New Orleans Chamber of Commerce
1515 Poydras Street
Suite 1010
New Orleans, LA 70112
Phone: (504) 799-4260
Fax: (504) 799-4259
www.neworleanschamber.org

New York, NY
New York City Economic Development Corporation
110 William Street
New York, NY 10038
Phone: (212) 619-5000
www.nycedc.com

The Partnership for New York City
One Battery Park Plaza
5th Floor
New York, NY 10004
Phone: (212) 493-7400
Fax: (212) 344-3344
www.pfnyc.org

Oklahoma City, OK
Greater Oklahoma City Chamber of Commerce
123 Park Avenue
Oklahoma City, OK 73102
Phone: (405) 297-8900
Fax: (405) 297-8916
www.okcchamber.com

Omaha, NE
Omaha Chamber of Commerce
1301 Harney Street
Omaha, NE 68102
Phone: (402) 346-5000
Fax: (402) 346-7050
www.omahachamber.org

Orlando, FL
Metro Orlando Economic Development Commission of Mid-Florida
301 East Pine Street, Suite 900
Orlando, FL 32801
Phone: (407) 422-7159
Fax: (407) 425.6428
www.orlandoedc.com

Orlando Regional Chamber of Commerce
75 South Ivanhoe Boulevard
P.O. Box 1234
Orlando, FL 32802
Phone: (407) 425-1234
Fax: (407) 839-5020
www.orlando.org

Philadelphia, PA
Greater Philadelphia Chamber of Commerce
200 South Broad Street
Suite 700
Philadelphia, PA 19102
Phone: (215) 545-1234
Fax: (215) 790-3600
www.greaterphilachamber.com

Phoenix, AZ
Greater Phoenix Chamber of Commerce
201 North Central Avenue
27th Floor
Phoenix, AZ 85073
Phone: (602) 495-2195
Fax: (602) 495-8913
www.phoenixchamber.com

Greater Phoenix Economic Council
2 North Central Avenue
Suite 2500
Phoenix, AZ 85004
Phone: (602) 256-7700
Fax: (602) 256-7744
www.gpec.org

Pittsburgh, PA
Allegheny County Industrial Development Authority
425 6th Avenue
Suite 800
Pittsburgh, PA 15219
Phone: (412) 350-1067
Fax: (412) 642-2217
www.alleghenycounty.us

Greater Pittsburgh Chamber of Commerce
425 6th Avenue
12th Floor
Pittsburgh, PA 15219
Phone: (412) 392-4500
Fax: (412) 392-4520
www.alleghenyconference.org

Portland, OR
Portland Business Alliance
200 SW Market Street
Suite 1770
Portland, OR 97201
Phone: (503) 224-8684
Fax: (503) 323-9186
www.portlandalliance.com

Providence, RI
Greater Providence Chamber of Commerce
30 Exchange Terrace
Fourth Floor
Providence, RI 02903
Phone: (401) 521-5000
Fax: (401) 351-2090
www.provchamber.com

Rhode Island Economic Development Corporation
Providence City Hall
25 Dorrance Street
Providence, RI 02903
Phone: (401) 421-7740
Fax: (401) 751-0203
www.providenceri.com

Provo, UT
Provo-Orem Chamber of Commerce
51 South University Avenue, Suite 215
Provo, UT 84601
Phone: (801) 851-2555
Fax: (801) 851-2557
www.thechamber.org

Raleigh, NC
Greater Raleigh Chamber of Commerce
800 South Salisbury Street
Raleigh, NC 27601-2978
Phone: (919) 664-7000
Fax: (919) 664-7099
www.raleighchamber.org

Reno, NV
Greater Reno-Sparks Chamber of Commerce
1 East First Street, 16th Floor
Reno, NV 89505
Phone: (775) 337-3030
Fax: (775) 337-3038
www.reno-sparkschamber.org

The Chamber Reno-Sparks-Northern Nevada
449 S. Virginia Street, 2nd Floor
Reno, NV 89501
Phone: (775) 636-9550
www.thechambernv.org

Richmond, VA
Greater Richmond Chamber
600 East Main Street
Suite 700
Richmond, VA 23219
Phone: (804) 648-1234
www.grcc.com

Greater Richmond Partnership
901 East Byrd Street
Suite 801
Richmond, VA 23219-4070
Phone: (804) 643-3227
Fax: (804) 343-7167
www.grpva.com

Rochester, MN
Rochester Area Chamber of Commerce
220 South Broadway
Suite 100
Rochester, MN 55904
Phone: (507) 288-1122
Fax: (507) 282-8960
www.rochestermnchamber.com

Sacramento, CA
Sacramento Metro Chamber
One Capitol Mall
Suite 700
Sacramento, CA 95814
Phone: (916) 552-6800
metrochamber.org

Saint Louis, MO
St. Louis Regional Chamber
One Metropolitan Square, Suite 1300
St. Louis, MO 63102
Phone: (314) 231-5555
www.stlregionalchamber.com

Salem, OR
Salem Chamber
1110 Commercial Street NE
Salem, OR 97301
Phone: (503) 581-1466
salemchamber.org

Salt Lake City, UT
Salt Lake Chamber
175 E. University Blvd. (400 S), Suite 600
Salt Lake City, UT 84111
Phone: (801) 364-3631
www.slchamber.com

San Antonio, TX
The Greater San Antonio Chamber of Commerce
602 E. Commerce Street
San Antonio, TX 78205
Phone: (210) 229-2100
Fax: (210) 229-1600
www.sachamber.org

San Antonio Economic Development Department
P.O. Box 839966
San Antonio, TX 78283-3966
Phone: (210) 207-8080
Fax: (210) 207-8151
www.sanantonio.gov/edd

San Diego, CA
San Diego Economic Development Corp.
401 B Street
Suite 1100
San Diego, CA 92101
Phone: (619) 234-8484
Fax: (619) 234-1935
www.sandiegobusiness.org

San Diego Regional Chamber of Commerce
402 West Broadway
Suite 1000
San Diego, CA 92101-3585
Phone: (619) 544-1300
Fax: (619) 744-7481
www.sdchamber.org

San Francisco, CA
San Francisco Chamber of Commerce
235 Montgomery Street
12th Floor
San Francisco, CA 94104
Phone: (415) 392-4520
Fax: (415) 392-0485
www.sfchamber.com

San Jose, CA
Office of Economic Development
60 South Market Street
Suite 470
San Jose, CA 95113
Phone: (408) 277-5880
Fax: (408) 277-3615
www.sba.gov

The Silicon Valley Organization
101 W Santa Clara Street
San Jose, CA 95113
Phone: (408) 291-5250
www.thesvo.com

Santa Rosa, CA
Santa Rosa Chamber of Commerce
1260 North Dutton Avenue
Suite 272
Santa Rosa, CA 95401
Phone: (707) 545-1414
www.santarosachamber.com

Savannah, GA
Economic Development Authority
131 Hutchinson Island Road
4th Floor
Savannah, GA 31421
Phone: (912) 447-8450
Fax: (912) 447-8455
www.seda.org

Savannah Chamber of Commerce
101 E. Bay Street
Savannah, GA 31402
Phone: (912) 644-6400
Fax: (912) 644-6499
www.savannahchamber.com

Seattle, WA
Greater Seattle Chamber of Commerce
1301 Fifth Avenue
Suite 2500
Seattle, WA 98101
Phone: (206) 389-7200
Fax: (206) 389-7288
www.seattlechamber.com

Sioux Falls, SD
Sioux Falls Area Chamber of Commerce
200 N. Phillips Avenue
Suite 102
Sioux Falls, SD 57104
Phone: (605) 336-1620
Fax: (605) 336-6499
www.siouxfallschamber.com

Springfield, IL
The Greater Springfield Chamber of Commerce
1011 S. Second Street
Springfield, IL 62704
Phone: (217) 525-1173
Fax: (217) 525-8768
www.gscc.org

Tampa, FL
Greater Tampa Chamber of Commerce
P.O. Box 420
Tampa, FL 33601-0420
Phone: (813) 276-9401
Fax: (813) 229-7855
www.tampachamber.com

Tucson, AZ
Tucson Metro Chamber
212 E. Broadway Blvd
Tucson, AZ 85701
Phone: (520) 792-1212
tucsonchamber.org

Tulsa, OK
Tulsa Regional Chamber
One West Third Street
Suite 100
Tulsa, OK 74103
Phone: (918) 585-1201
www.tulsachamber.com

Tuscaloosa, AL
The Chamber of Commerce of West Alabama
2201 Jack Warner Parkway
Building C
Tuscaloosa, AL 35401
Phone: (205) 758-7588
tuscaloosachamber.com

Virginia Beach, VA
Hampton Roads Chamber of Commerce
500 East Main Street, Suite 700
Virginia Beach, VA 23510
Phone: (757) 664-2531
www.hamptonroadschamber.com

Washington, DC
District of Columbia Chamber of Commerce
1213 K Street NW
Washington, DC 20005
Phone: (202) 347-7201
Fax: (202) 638-6762
www.dcchamber.org

District of Columbia Office of Planning and Economic Development
J.A. Wilson Building
1350 Pennsylvania Ave NW, Suite 317
Washington, DC 20004
Phone: (202) 727-6365
Fax: (202) 727-6703
www.dcbiz.dc.gov

Wichita, KS
Wichita Regional Chamber of Commerce
350 W Douglas Avennue
Wichita, KS 67202
Phone: (316) 265-7771
www.wichitachamber.org

Wilmington, NC
Wilmington Chamber of Commerce
One Estell Lee Place
Wilmington, NC 28401
Phone: (910) 762-2611
www.wilmingtonchamber.org

Winston-Salem, NC
Winston-Salem Chamber of Commerce
411 West Fourth Street
Suite 211
Winston-Salem, NC 27101
Phone: (336) 728-9200
www.winstonsalem.com

Worcester, MA
Worcester Regional Chamber of Commerce
311 Main Street, Suite 200
Worcester, MA 01608
Phone: (508) 753-2924
worcesterchamber.org

Appendix E: State Departments of Labor

Alabama
Alabama Department of Labor
P.O. Box 303500
Montgomery, AL 36130-3500
Phone: (334) 242-3072
www.labor.alabama.gov

Alaska
Dept of Labor and Workforce Devel.
P.O. Box 11149
Juneau, AK 99822-2249
Phone: (907) 465-2700
www.labor.state.ak.us

Arizona
Industrial Commission or Arizona
800 West Washington Street
Phoenix, AZ 85007
Phone: (602) 542-4411
www.azica.gov

Arkansas
Department of Labor
10421 West Markham
Little Rock, AR 72205
Phone: (501) 682-4500
www.labor.ar.gov

California
Labor and Workforce Development
445 Golden Gate Ave., 10th Floor
San Francisco, CA 94102
Phone: (916) 263-1811
www.labor.ca.gov

Colorado
Dept of Labor and Employment
633 17th St., 2nd Floor
Denver, CO 80202-3660
Phone: (888) 390-7936
cdle.colorado.gov

Connecticut
Department of Labor
200 Folly Brook Blvd.
Wethersfield, CT 06109-1114
Phone: (860) 263-6000
www.ctdol.state.ct.us

Delaware
Department of Labor
4425 N. Market St., 4th Floor
Wilmington, DE 19802
Phone: (302) 451-3423
dol.delaware.gov

District of Columbia
Department of Employment Services
614 New York Ave., NE, Suite 300
Washington, DC 20002
Phone: (202) 671-1900
does.dc.gov

Florida
Florida Department of Economic Opportunity
The Caldwell Building
107 East Madison St. Suite 100
Tallahassee, FL 32399-4120
Phone: (800) 342-3450
www.floridajobs.org

Georgia
Department of Labor
Sussex Place, Room 600
148 Andrew Young Intl Blvd., NE
Atlanta, GA 30303
Phone: (404) 656-3011
dol.georgia.gov

Hawaii
Dept of Labor & Industrial Relations
830 Punchbowl Street
Honolulu, HI 96813
Phone: (808) 586-8842
labor.hawaii.gov

Idaho
Department of Labor
317 W. Main St.
Boise, ID 83735-0001
Phone: (208) 332-3579
www.labor.idaho.gov

Illinois
Department of Labor
160 N. LaSalle Street, 13th Floor
Suite C-1300
Chicago, IL 60601
Phone: (312) 793-2800
www.illinois.gov/idol

Indiana
Indiana Department of Labor
402 West Washington Street, Room W195
Indianapolis, IN 46204
Phone: (317) 232-2655
www.in.gov/dol

Iowa
Iowa Workforce Development
1000 East Grand Avenue
Des Moines, IA 50319-0209
Phone: (515) 242-5870
www.iowadivisionoflabor.gov

Kansas
Department of Labor
401 S.W. Topeka Blvd.
Topeka, KS 66603-3182
Phone: (785) 296-5000
www.dol.ks.gov

Kentucky
Department of Labor
1047 U.S. Hwy 127 South, Suite 4
Frankfort, KY 40601-4381
Phone: (502) 564-3070
www.labor.ky.gov

Louisiana
Louisiana Workforce Commission
1001 N. 23rd Street
Baton Rouge, LA 70804-9094
Phone: (225) 342-3111
www.laworks.net

Maine
Department of Labor
45 Commerce Street
Augusta, ME 04330
Phone: (207) 623-7900
www.state.me.us/labor

Maryland
Department of Labor, Licensing & Regulation
500 N. Calvert Street
Suite 401
Baltimore, MD 21202
Phone: (410) 767-2357
www.dllr.state.md.us

Massachusetts
Dept of Labor & Workforce Development
One Ashburton Place
Room 2112
Boston, MA 02108
Phone: (617) 626-7100
www.mass.gov/lwd

Michigan
Department of Licensing and Regulatory Affairs
611 W. Ottawa
P.O. Box 30004
Lansing, MI 48909
Phone: (517) 373-1820
www.michigan.gov/lara

Minnesota
Dept of Labor and Industry
443 Lafayette Road North
Saint Paul, MN 55155
Phone: (651) 284-5070
www.doli.state.mn.us

Mississippi
Dept of Employment Security
P.O. Box 1699
Jackson, MS 39215-1699
Phone: (601) 321-6000
www.mdes.ms.gov

Missouri
Labor and Industrial Relations
P.O. Box 599
3315 W. Truman Boulevard
Jefferson City, MO 65102-0599
Phone: (573) 751-7500
labor.mo.gov

Montana
Dept of Labor and Industry
P.O. Box 1728
Helena, MT 59624-1728
Phone: (406) 444-9091
www.dli.mt.gov

Appendix E: State Departments of Labor

Nebraska
Department of Labor
550 S 16th Street
Lincoln, NE 68508
Phone: (402) 471-9000
dol.nebraska.gov

Nevada
Dept of Business and Industry
3300 W. Sahara Ave, Suite 425
Las Vegas, NV 89102
Phone: (702) 486-2750
business.nv.gov

New Hampshire
Department of Labor
State Office Park South
95 Pleasant Street
Concord, NH 03301
Phone: (603) 271-3176
www.nh.gov/labor

New Jersey
Department of Labor & Workforce Devel.
John Fitch Plaza, 13th Floor, Suite D
Trenton, NJ 08625-0110
Phone: (609) 777-3200
lwd.dol.state.nj.us/labor

New Mexico
Department of Workforce Solutions
401 Broadway, NE
Albuquerque, NM 87103-1928
Phone: (505) 841-8450
www.dws.state.nm.us

New York
Department of Labor
State Office Bldg. # 12
W.A. Harriman Campus
Albany, NY 12240
Phone: (518) 457-9000
www.labor.ny.gov

North Carolina
Department of Labor
4 West Edenton Street
Raleigh, NC 27601-1092
Phone: (919) 733-7166
www.labor.nc.gov

North Dakota
North Dakota Department of Labor and Human Rights
State Capitol Building
600 East Boulevard, Dept 406
Bismark, ND 58505-0340
Phone: (701) 328-2660
www.nd.gov/labor

Ohio
Department of Commerce
77 South High Street, 22nd Floor
Columbus, OH 43215
Phone: (614) 644-2239
www.com.state.oh.us

Oklahoma
Department of Labor
4001 N. Lincoln Blvd.
Oklahoma City, OK 73105-5212
Phone: (405) 528-1500
www.ok.gov/odol

Oregon
Bureau of Labor and Industries
800 NE Oregon St., #32
Portland, OR 97232
Phone: (971) 673-0761
www.oregon.gov/boli

Pennsylvania
Dept of Labor and Industry
1700 Labor and Industry Bldg
7th and Forster Streets
Harrisburg, PA 17120
Phone: (717) 787-5279
www.dli.pa.gov

Rhode Island
Department of Labor and Training
1511 Pontiac Avenue
Cranston, RI 02920
Phone: (401) 462-8000
www.dlt.state.ri.us

South Carolina
Dept of Labor, Licensing & Regulations
P.O. Box 11329
Columbia, SC 29211-1329
Phone: (803) 896-4300
www.llr.state.sc.us

South Dakota
Department of Labor & Regulation
700 Governors Drive
Pierre, SD 57501-2291
Phone: (605) 773-3682
dlr.sd.gov

Tennessee
Dept of Labor & Workforce Development
Andrew Johnson Tower
710 James Robertson Pkwy
Nashville, TN 37243-0655
Phone: (615) 741-6642
www.tn.gov/workforce

Texas
Texas Workforce Commission
101 East 15th St.
Austin, TX 78778
Phone: (512) 475-2670
www.twc.state.tx.us

Utah
Utah Labor Commission
160 East 300 South, 3rd Floor
Salt Lake City, UT 84114-6600
Phone: (801) 530-6800
laborcommission.utah.gov

Vermont
Department of Labor
5 Green Mountain Drive
P.O. Box 488
Montpelier, VT 05601-0488
Phone: (802) 828-4000
labor.vermont.gov

Virginia
Dept of Labor and Industry
Powers-Taylor Building
13 S. 13th Street
Richmond, VA 23219
Phone: (804) 371-2327
www.doli.virginia.gov

Washington
Dept of Labor and Industries
P.O. Box 44001
Olympia, WA 98504-4001
Phone: (360) 902-4200
www.lni.wa.gov

West Virginia
Division of Labor
749 B Building 6
Capitol Complex
Charleston, WV 25305
Phone: (304) 558-7890
labor.wv.gov

Wisconsin
Dept of Workforce Development
201 E. Washington Ave., #A400
P.O. Box 7946
Madison, WI 53707-7946
Phone: (608) 266-6861
dwd.wisconsin.gov

Wyoming
Department of Workforce Services
1510 East Pershing Blvd.
Cheyenne, WY 82002
Phone: (307) 777-7261
www.wyomingworkforce.org

Titles from Grey House

Visit www.GreyHouse.com for Product Information, Table of Contents, and Sample Pages.

Opinions Throughout History
Opinions Throughout History: Church & State
Opinions Throughout History: Conspiracy Theories
Opinions Throughout History: The Death Penalty
Opinions Throughout History: Diseases & Epidemics
Opinions Throughout History: Drug Use & Abuse
Opinions Throughout History: The Environment
Opinions Throughout History: Free Speech & Censorship
Opinions Throughout History: Gender: Roles & Rights
Opinions Throughout History: Globalization
Opinions Throughout History: Guns in America
Opinions Throughout History: Immigration
Opinions Throughout History: Law Enforcement in America
Opinions Throughout History: Mental Health
Opinions Throughout History: Nat'l Security vs. Civil & Privacy Rights
Opinions Throughout History: Presidential Authority
Opinions Throughout History: Robotics & Artificial Intelligence
Opinions Throughout History: Social Media Issues
Opinions Throughout History: The Supreme Court
Opinions Throughout History: Voters' Rights
Opinions Throughout History: War & the Military
Opinions Throughout History: Workers Rights & Wages

This is Who We Were
This is Who We Were: Colonial America (1492-1775)
This is Who We Were: 1880-1899
This is Who We Were: In the 1900s
This is Who We Were: In the 1910s
This is Who We Were: In the 1920s
This is Who We Were: A Companion to the 1940 Census
This is Who We Were: In the 1940s (1940-1949)
This is Who We Were: In the 1950s
This is Who We Were: In the 1960s
This is Who We Were: In the 1970s
This is Who We Were: In the 1980s
This is Who We Were: In the 1990s
This is Who We Were: In the 2000s
This is Who We Were: In the 2010s

Working Americans
Working Americans—Vol. 1: The Working Class
Working Americans—Vol. 2: The Middle Class
Working Americans—Vol. 3: The Upper Class
Working Americans—Vol. 4: Children
Working Americans—Vol. 5: At War
Working Americans—Vol. 6: Working Women
Working Americans—Vol. 7: Social Movements
Working Americans—Vol. 8: Immigrants
Working Americans—Vol. 9: Revolutionary War to the Civil War
Working Americans—Vol. 10: Sports & Recreation
Working Americans—Vol. 11: Inventors & Entrepreneurs
Working Americans—Vol. 12: Our History through Music
Working Americans—Vol. 13: Education & Educators
Working Americans—Vol. 14: African Americans
Working Americans—Vol. 15: Politics & Politicians
Working Americans—Vol. 16: Farming & Ranching
Working Americans—Vol. 17: Teens in America
Working Americans—Vol. 18: Health Care Workers
Working Americans—Vol. 19: The Performing Arts

Grey House Health & Wellness Guides
Addiction Handbook & Resource Guide
The Autism Spectrum Handbook & Resource Guide
Autoimmune Disorders Handbook & Resource Guide
Cardiovascular Disease Handbook & Resource Guide
Dementia Handbook & Resource Guide
Depression Handbook & Resource Guide
Diabetes Handbook & Resource Guide
Nutrition, Obesity & Eating Disorders Handbook & Resource Guide

Consumer Health
Complete Mental Health Resource Guide
Complete Resource Guide for Pediatric Disorders
Complete Resource Guide for People with Chronic Illness
Complete Resource Guide for People with Disabilities
Older Americans Information Resource
Parenting: Styles & Strategies
Teens: Growing Up, Skills & Strategies

General Reference
American Environmental Leaders
Constitutional Amendments
Encyclopedia of African-American Writing
Encyclopedia of Invasions & Conquests
Encyclopedia of Prisoners of War & Internment
Encyclopedia of the Continental Congresses
Encyclopedia of the United States Cabinet
Encyclopedia of War Journalism
The Environmental Debate
Financial Literacy Starter Kit
From Suffrage to the Senate
The Gun Debate: Gun Rights & Gun Control in the U.S.
Historical Warrior Peoples & Modern Fighting Groups
Human Rights and the United States
Political Corruption in America
Privacy Rights in the Digital Age
The Religious Right and American Politics
Speakers of the House of Representatives, 1789-2021
US Land & Natural Resources Policy
The Value of a Dollar 1600-1865 Colonial to Civil War
The Value of a Dollar 1860-2019

Business Information
Business Information Resources
Complete Broadcasting Industry Guide: TV, Radio, Cable & Streaming
Directory of Mail Order Catalogs
Environmental Resource Handbook
Food & Beverage Market Place
The Grey House Guide to Homeland Security Resources
The Grey House Performing Arts Industry Guide
Guide to Healthcare Group Purchasing Organizations
Guide to U.S. HMOs and PPOs
Guide to Venture Capital & Private Equity Firms
Hudson's Washington News Media Contacts Guide
New York State Directory
Sports Market Place

Grey House Imprints

Visit www.GreyHouse.com for Product Information, Table of Contents, and Sample Pages.

Grey House Titles, continued

Education
Complete Learning Disabilities Resource Guide
Digital Literacy: Skills & Strategies
Educators Resource Guide
The Comparative Guide to Elem. & Secondary Schools
Special Education: Policy & Curriculum Development

Statistics & Demographics
America's Top-Rated Cities
America's Top-Rated Smaller Cities
The Comparative Guide to American Suburbs
Profiles of America
Profiles of California
Profiles of Florida
Profiles of Illinois
Profiles of Indiana
Profiles of Massachusetts
Profiles of Michigan
Profiles of New Jersey
Profiles of New York
Profiles of North Carolina & South Carolina
Profiles of Ohio
Profiles of Pennsylvania
Profiles of Texas
Profiles of Virginia
Profiles of Wisconsin

Canadian Resources
Associations Canada
Canadian Almanac & Directory
Canadian Environmental Resource Guide
Canadian Parliamentary Guide
Canadian Venture Capital & Private Equity Firms
Canadian Who's Who
Cannabis Canada
Careers & Employment Canada
Financial Post: Directory of Directors
Financial Services Canada
FP Bonds: Corporate
FP Bonds: Government
FP Equities: Preferreds & Derivatives
FP Survey: Industrials
FP Survey: Mines & Energy
FP Survey: Predecessor & Defunct
Health Guide Canada
Libraries Canada

Weiss Financial Ratings
Financial Literacy Basics
Financial Literacy: How to Become an Investor
Financial Literacy: Planning for the Future
Weiss Ratings Consumer Guides
Weiss Ratings Guide to Banks
Weiss Ratings Guide to Credit Unions
Weiss Ratings Guide to Health Insurers
Weiss Ratings Guide to Life & Annuity Insurers
Weiss Ratings Guide to Property & Casualty Insurers
Weiss Ratings Investment Research Guide to Bond & Money Market Mutual Funds
Weiss Ratings Investment Research Guide to Exchange-Traded Funds
Weiss Ratings Investment Research Guide to Stock Mutual Funds
Weiss Ratings Investment Research Guide to Stocks

Books in Print Series
American Book Publishing Record® Annual
American Book Publishing Record® Monthly
Books In Print®
Books In Print® Supplement
Books Out Loud™
Bowker's Complete Video Directory™
Children's Books In Print®
El-Hi Textbooks & Serials In Print®
Forthcoming Books®
Law Books & Serials In Print™
Medical & Health Care Books In Print™
Publishers, Distributors & Wholesalers of the US™
Subject Guide to Books In Print®
Subject Guide to Children's Books In Print®

Grey House Publishing | Salem Press | H.W. Wilson | 4919 Route, 22 PO Box 56, Amenia NY 12501-0056

Titles from Salem Press

Visit www.SalemPress.com for Product Information, Table of Contents, and Sample Pages.

LITERATURE

Critical Insights: Authors

- Louisa May Alcott
- Sherman Alexie
- Isabel Allende
- Maya Angelou
- Isaac Asimov
- Margaret Atwood
- Jane Austen
- James Baldwin
- Saul Bellow
- Roberto Bolano
- Ray Bradbury
- The Brontë Sisters
- Gwendolyn Brooks
- Albert Camus
- Raymond Carver
- Willa Cather
- Geoffrey Chaucer
- John Cheever
- Joseph Conrad
- Charles Dickens
- Emily Dickinson
- Frederick Douglass
- T. S. Eliot
- George Eliot
- Harlan Ellison
- Ralph Waldo Emerson
- Louise Erdrich
- William Faulkner
- F. Scott Fitzgerald
- Gustave Flaubert
- Horton Foote
- Benjamin Franklin
- Robert Frost
- Neil Gaiman
- Gabriel Garcia Marquez
- Thomas Hardy
- Nathaniel Hawthorne
- Robert A. Heinlein
- Lillian Hellman
- Ernest Hemingway
- Langston Hughes
- Zora Neale Hurston
- Henry James
- Thomas Jefferson
- James Joyce
- Jamaica Kincaid
- Stephen King
- Martin Luther King, Jr.
- Barbara Kingsolver
- Abraham Lincoln
- C.S. Lewis
- Mario Vargas Llosa
- Jack London
- James McBride
- Cormac McCarthy
- Herman Melville
- Arthur Miller
- Toni Morrison
- Alice Munro
- Tim O'Brien
- Flannery O'Connor
- Eugene O'Neill
- George Orwell
- Sylvia Plath
- Edgar Allan Poe
- Philip Roth
- Salman Rushdie
- J.D. Salinger
- Mary Shelley
- John Steinbeck
- Amy Tan
- Leo Tolstoy
- Mark Twain
- John Updike
- Kurt Vonnegut
- Alice Walker
- David Foster Wallace
- Edith Wharton
- Walt Whitman
- Oscar Wilde
- Tennessee Williams
- Virginia Woolf
- Richard Wright
- Malcolm X

Critical Insights: Works

- Absalom, Absalom!
- Adventures of Huckleberry Finn
- The Adventures of Tom Sawyer
- Aeneid
- All Quiet on the Western Front
- All the Pretty Horses
- Animal Farm
- Anna Karenina
- The Awakening
- The Bell Jar
- Beloved
- Billy Budd, Sailor
- The Book Thief
- Brave New World
- The Canterbury Tales
- Catch-22
- The Catcher in the Rye
- The Color Purple
- The Crucible
- Death of a Salesman
- The Diary of a Young Girl
- Dracula
- Fahrenheit 451
- The Grapes of Wrath
- Great Expectations
- The Great Gatsby
- Hamlet
- The Handmaid's Tale
- Harry Potter Series
- Heart of Darkness
- The Hobbit
- The House on Mango Street
- How the Garcia Girls Lost Their Accents
- The Hunger Games Trilogy
- I Know Why the Caged Bird Sings
- In Cold Blood
- The Inferno
- Invisible Man
- Jane Eyre
- The Joy Luck Club
- Julius Caesar
- King Lear
- The Kite Runner
- Life of Pi
- Little Women
- Lolita
- Lord of the Flies
- The Lord of the Rings
- Macbeth
- The Merchant of Venice
- The Metamorphosis
- Midnight's Children
- A Midsummer Night's Dream
- Moby-Dick
- Mrs. Dalloway
- Nineteen Eighty-Four
- The Odyssey
- Of Mice and Men
- The Old Man and the Sea
- On the Road
- One Flew Over the Cuckoo's Nest
- One Hundred Years of Solitude
- Othello
- The Outsiders
- Paradise Lost
- The Pearl
- The Plague
- The Poetry of Baudelaire
- The Poetry of Edgar Allan Poe
- A Portrait of the Artist as a Young Man
- Pride and Prejudice
- A Raisin in the Sun
- The Red Badge of Courage
- Romeo and Juliet
- The Scarlet Letter
- Sense and Sensibility
- Short Fiction of Flannery O'Connor
- Slaughterhouse-Five
- The Sound and the Fury
- A Streetcar Named Desire
- The Sun Also Rises
- A Tale of Two Cities
- The Tales of Edgar Allan Poe
- Their Eyes Were Watching God
- Things Fall Apart
- To Kill a Mockingbird
- War and Peace
- The Woman Warrior

Critical Insights: Themes

- The American Comic Book
- American Creative Non-Fiction
- The American Dream
- American Multicultural Identity
- American Road Literature
- American Short Story
- American Sports Fiction
- The American Thriller
- American Writers in Exile
- Censored & Banned Literature
- Civil Rights Literature, Past & Present
- Coming of Age
- Conspiracies
- Contemporary Canadian Fiction
- Contemporary Immigrant Short Fiction
- Contemporary Latin American Fiction
- Contemporary Speculative Fiction

Grey House Publishing | Salem Press | H.W. Wilson | 4919 Route, 22 PO Box 56, Amenia NY 12501-0056

Titles from Salem Press

Visit www.SalemPress.com for Product Information, Table of Contents, and Sample Pages.

Crime and Detective Fiction
Crisis of Faith
Cultural Encounters
Dystopia
Family
The Fantastic
Feminism Flash Fiction
Gender, Sex and Sexuality
Good & Evil
The Graphic Novel
Greed
Harlem Renaissance
The Hero's Quest
Historical Fiction
Holocaust Literature
The Immigrant Experience
Inequality
LGBTQ Literature
Literature in Times of Crisis
Literature of Protest
Love
Magical Realism
Midwestern Literature
Modern Japanese Literature
Nature & the Environment
Paranoia, Fear & Alienation
Patriotism
Political Fiction
Postcolonial Literature
Power & Corruption
Pulp Fiction of the '20s and '30s
Rebellion
Russia's Golden Age
Satire
The Slave Narrative
Social Justice and American Literature
Southern Gothic Literature
Southwestern Literature
Survival
Technology & Humanity
Truth & Lies
Violence in Literature
Virginia Woolf & 20th Century Women Writers
War

Critical Insights: Film
Bonnie & Clyde
Casablanca
Alfred Hitchcock
Stanley Kubrick

Critical Approaches to Literature
Critical Approaches to Literature: Feminist
Critical Approaches to Literature: Moral
Critical Approaches to Literature: Multicultural
Critical Approaches to Literature: Psychological

Literary Classics
Recommended Reading: 600 Classics Reviewed

Novels into Film
Novels into Film: Adaptations & Interpretation
Novels into Film: Adaptations & Interpretation, Volume 2

Critical Surveys of Literature
Critical Survey of American Literature
Critical Survey of Drama
Critical Survey of Long Fiction
Critical Survey of Mystery and Detective Fiction
Critical Survey of Poetry
Critical Survey of Poetry: Contemporary Poets
Critical Survey of Science Fiction & Fantasy Literature
Critical Survey of Shakespeare's Plays
Critical Survey of Shakespeare's Sonnets
Critical Survey of Short Fiction
Critical Survey of World Literature
Critical Survey of Young Adult Literature

Critical Surveys of Graphic Novels
Heroes & Superheroes
History, Theme, and Technique
Independents & Underground Classics
Manga

Critical Surveys of Mythology & Folklore
Creation Myths
Deadly Battles & Warring Enemies
Gods & Goddesses
Heroes and Heroines
Love, Sexuality, and Desire
World Mythology

Cyclopedia of Literary Characters & Places
Cyclopedia of Literary Characters
Cyclopedia of Literary Places

Introduction to Literary Context
American Poetry of the 20th Century
American Post-Modernist Novels
American Short Fiction
English Literature
Plays
World Literature

Magill's Literary Annual
Magill's Literary Annual, 2023
Magill's Literary Annual, 2022
Magill's Literary Annual, 2021
Magill's Literary Annual (Backlist Issues 2020-1977)

Masterplots
Masterplots, Fourth Edition
Masterplots, 2010-2018 Supplement

Notable Writers
Notable African American Writers
Notable American Women Writers
Notable Mystery & Detective Fiction Writers
Notable Writers of the American West & the Native American Experience
Notable Writers of LGBTQ+ Literature

Grey House Publishing | Salem Press | H.W. Wilson | 4919 Route, 22 PO Box 56, Amenia NY 12501-0056

Titles from Salem Press

Visit www.SalemPress.com for Product Information, Table of Contents, and Sample Pages.

HISTORY

The Decades
The 1910s in America
The Twenties in America
The Thirties in America
The Forties in America
The Fifties in America
The Sixties in America
The Seventies in America
The Eighties in America
The Nineties in America
The 2000s in America
The 2010s in America

Defining Documents in American History
Defining Documents: The 1900s
Defining Documents: The 1910s
Defining Documents: The 1920s
Defining Documents: The 1930s
Defining Documents: The 1950s
Defining Documents: The 1960s
Defining Documents: The 1970s
Defining Documents: The 1980s
Defining Documents: American Citizenship
Defining Documents: The American Economy
Defining Documents: The American Revolution
Defining Documents: The American West
Defining Documents: Business Ethics
Defining Documents: Capital Punishment
Defining Documents: Civil Rights
Defining Documents: Civil War
Defining Documents: The Constitution
Defining Documents: The Cold War
Defining Documents: Dissent & Protest
Defining Documents: Domestic Terrorism & Extremism
Defining Documents: Drug Policy
Defining Documents: The Emergence of Modern America
Defining Documents: Environment & Conservation
Defining Documents: Espionage & Intrigue
Defining Documents: Exploration and Colonial America
Defining Documents: The First Amendment
Defining Documents: The Free Press
Defining Documents: The Great Depression
Defining Documents: The Great Migration
Defining Documents: The Gun Debate
Defining Documents: Immigration & Immigrant Communities
Defining Documents: The Legacy of 9/11
Defining Documents: LGBTQ+
Defining Documents: Manifest Destiny and the New Nation
Defining Documents: Native Americans
Defining Documents: Political Campaigns, Candidates & Discourse
Defining Documents: Postwar 1940s
Defining Documents: Prison Reform
Defining Documents: Secrets, Leaks & Scandals
Defining Documents: Slavery
Defining Documents: Supreme Court Decisions
Defining Documents: Reconstruction Era
Defining Documents: The Vietnam War
Defining Documents: U.S. Involvement in the Middle East
Defining Documents: Workers' Rights
Defining Documents: World War I
Defining Documents: World War II

Defining Documents in World History
Defining Documents: The 17th Century
Defining Documents: The 18th Century
Defining Documents: The 19th Century
Defining Documents: The 20th Century (1900-1950)
Defining Documents: The Ancient World
Defining Documents: Asia
Defining Documents: Genocide & the Holocaust
Defining Documents: Human Rights
Defining Documents: The Middle Ages
Defining Documents: The Middle East
Defining Documents: Nationalism & Populism
Defining Documents: The Nuclear Age
Defining Documents: Pandemics, Plagues & Public Health
Defining Documents: Renaissance & Early Modern Era
Defining Documents: Revolutions
Defining Documents: Women's Rights

Great Events from History
Great Events from History: American History, Exploration to the Colonial Era, 1492-1775
Great Events from History: The Ancient World
Great Events from History: The Middle Ages
Great Events from History: The Renaissance & Early Modern Era
Great Events from History: The 17th Century
Great Events from History: The 18th Century
Great Events from History: The 19th Century
Great Events from History: The 20th Century, 1901-1940
Great Events from History: The 20th Century, 1941-1970
Great Events from History: The 20th Century, 1971-2000
Great Events from History: Modern Scandals
Great Events from History: African American History
Great Events from History: The 21st Century, 2000-2016
Great Events from History: LGBTQ Events
Great Events from History: Human Rights
Great Events from History: Women's History

Great Lives from History
Great Athletes
Great Athletes of the Twenty-First Century
Great Lives from History: The 17th Century
Great Lives from History: The 18th Century
Great Lives from History: The 19th Century
Great Lives from History: The 20th Century
Great Lives from History: The 21st Century, 2000-2017
Great Lives from History: African Americans
Great Lives from History: The Ancient World
Great Lives from History: American Heroes
Great Lives from History: American Women
Great Lives from History: Asian and Pacific Islander Americans
Great Lives from History: Autocrats & Dictators
Great Lives from History: The Incredibly Wealthy
Great Lives from History: Inventors & Inventions
Great Lives from History: Jewish Americans
Great Lives from History: Latinos
Great Lives from History: The Middle Ages
Great Lives from History: The Renaissance & Early Modern Era
Great Lives from History: Scientists and Science

Grey House Publishing | Salem Press | H.W. Wilson | 4919 Route, 22 PO Box 56, Amenia NY 12501-0056

Titles from Salem Press

Visit www.SalemPress.com for Product Information, Table of Contents, and Sample Pages.

History & Government
American First Ladies
American Presidents
The 50 States
The Ancient World: Extraordinary People in Extraordinary Societies
The Bill of Rights
The Criminal Justice System
The U.S. Supreme Court

Innovators
Computer Technology Innovators
Fashion Innovators
Human Rights Innovators
Internet Innovators
Music Innovators
Musicians and Composers of the 20th Century
World Political Innovators

SOCIAL SCIENCES
Civil Rights Movements: Past & Present
Countries, Peoples and Cultures
Countries: Their Wars & Conflicts: A World Survey
Education Today: Issues, Policies & Practices
Encyclopedia of American Immigration
Ethics: Questions & Morality of Human Actions
Issues in U.S. Immigration
Principles of Sociology: Group Relationships & Behavior
Principles of Sociology: Personal Relationships & Behavior
Principles of Sociology: Societal Issues & Behavior
Racial & Ethnic Relations in America
Weapons, Warfare & Military Technology
World Geography

HEALTH
Addictions, Substance Abuse & Alcoholism
Adolescent Health & Wellness
Aging
Cancer
Community & Family Health Issues
Integrative, Alternative & Complementary Medicine
Genetics and Inherited Conditions
Infectious Diseases and Conditions
Magill's Medical Guide
Nutrition
Parenting: Styles & Strategies
Psychology & Behavioral Health
Teens: Growing Up, Skills & Strategies
Women's Health

Principles of Health
Principles of Health: Allergies & Immune Disorders
Principles of Health: Anxiety & Stress
Principles of Health: Depression
Principles of Health: Diabetes
Principles of Health: Nursing
Principles of Health: Obesity
Principles of Health: Occupational Therapy & Physical Therapy
Principles of Health: Pain Management
Principles of Health: Prescription Drug Abuse

SCIENCE
Ancient Creatures
Applied Science
Applied Science: Engineering & Mathematics
Applied Science: Science & Medicine
Applied Science: Technology
Biomes and Ecosystems
Digital Literacy: Skills & Strategies
Earth Science: Earth Materials and Resources
Earth Science: Earth's Surface and History
Earth Science: Earth's Weather, Water and Atmosphere
Earth Science: Physics and Chemistry of the Earth
Encyclopedia of Climate Change
Encyclopedia of Energy
Encyclopedia of Environmental Issues
Encyclopedia of Global Resources
Encyclopedia of Mathematics and Society
Forensic Science
Notable Natural Disasters
The Solar System
USA in Space

Principles of Science
Principles of Aeronautics
Principles of Anatomy
Principles of Astronomy
Principles of Behavioral Science
Principles of Biology
Principles of Biotechnology
Principles of Botany
Principles of Chemistry
Principles of Climatology
Principles of Computer-aided Design
Principles of Computer Science
Principles of Digital Arts & Multimedia
Principles of Ecology
Principles of Energy
Principles of Fire Science
Principles of Forestry & Conservation
Principles of Geology
Principles of Information Technology
Principles of Marine Science
Principles of Mathematics
Principles of Mechanics
Principles of Microbiology
Principles of Modern Agriculture
Principles of Pharmacology
Principles of Physical Science
Principles of Physics
Principles of Programming & Coding
Principles of Robotics & Artificial Intelligence
Principles of Scientific Research
Principles of Sports Medicine & Exercise Science
Principles of Sustainability
Principles of Zoology

Grey House Publishing | Salem Press | H.W. Wilson | 4919 Route, 22 PO Box 56, Amenia NY 12501-0056

Titles from Salem Press

Visit www.SalemPress.com for Product Information, Table of Contents, and Sample Pages.

CAREERS

Careers: Paths to Entrepreneurship
Careers in Archaeology & Museum Services
Careers in Artificial Intelligence
Careers in the Arts: Fine, Performing & Visual
Careers in the Automotive Industry
Careers in Biology
Careers in Biotechnology
Careers in Building Construction
Careers in Business
Careers in Chemistry
Careers in Communications & Media
Careers in Cybersecurity
Careers in Education & Training
Careers in Engineering
Careers in Environment & Conservation
Careers in Financial Services
Careers in Fish & Wildlife
Careers in Forensic Science
Careers in Gaming
Careers in Green Energy
Careers in Healthcare
Careers in Hospitality & Tourism
Careers in Human Services
Careers in Information Technology
Careers in Law, Criminal Justice & Emergency Services
Careers in the Music Industry
Careers in Manufacturing & Production
Careers in Nursing
Careers in Physics
Careers in Protective Services
Careers in Psychology & Behavioral Health
Careers in Public Administration
Careers in Sales, Insurance & Real Estate
Careers in Science & Engineering
Careers in Social Media
Careers in Sports & Fitness
Careers in Sports Medicine & Training
Careers in Technical Services & Equipment Repair
Careers in Transportation
Careers in Writing & Editing
Careers Outdoors
Careers Overseas
Careers Working with Infants & Children
Careers Working with Animals

BUSINESS

Principles of Business: Accounting
Principles of Business: Economics
Principles of Business: Entrepreneurship
Principles of Business: Finance
Principles of Business: Globalization
Principles of Business: Leadership
Principles of Business: Management
Principles of Business: Marketing

Grey House Publishing | Salem Press | H.W. Wilson | 4919 Route, 22 PO Box 56, Amenia NY 12501-0056

Titles from H.W. Wilson

Visit www.HWWilsonInPrint.com for Product Information, Table of Contents, and Sample Pages.

The Reference Shelf

Affordable Housing
Aging in America
Alternative Facts, Post-Truth and the Information War
The American Dream
Artificial Intelligence
The Business of Food
Campaign Trends & Election Law
College Sports
Democracy Evolving
The Digital Age
Embracing New Paradigms in Education
Food Insecurity & Hunger in the United States
Future of U.S. Economic Relations: Mexico, Cuba, & Venezuela
Gene Editing & Genetic Engineering
Global Climate Change
Guns in America
Hacktivism
Hate Crimes
Immigration
Income Inequality
Internet Abuses & Privacy Rights
Internet Law
LGBTQ in the 21st Century
Marijuana Reform
Mental Health Awareness
Money in Politics
National Debate Topic 2014/2015: The Ocean
National Debate Topic 2015/2016: Surveillance
National Debate Topic 2016/2017: US/China Relations
National Debate Topic 2017/2018: Education Reform
National Debate Topic 2018/2019: Immigration
National Debate Topic 2019/2021: Arms Sales
National Debate Topic 2020/2021: Criminal Justice Reform
National Debate Topic 2021/2022: Water Resources
National Debate Topic 2022/2023: Emerging Technologies & International Security
National Debate Topic 2023/2024: Economic Inequality
New Frontiers in Space
Policing in 2020
Pollution
Prescription Drug Abuse
Propaganda and Misinformation
Racial Tension in a Postracial Age
Reality Television
Renewable Energy
Representative American Speeches, Annual Editions
Rethinking Work
Revisiting Gender
The South China Sea Conflict
Sports in America
The Supreme Court
The Transformation of American Cities
The Two Koreas
UFOs
Vaccinations
Voting Rights
Whistleblowers

Core Collections

Children's Core Collection
Fiction Core Collection
Graphic Novels Core Collection
Middle & Junior High School Core
Public Library Core Collection: Nonfiction
Senior High Core Collection
Young Adult Fiction Core Collection

Current Biography

Current Biography Cumulative Index 1946-2021
Current Biography Monthly Magazine
Current Biography Yearbook

Readers' Guide to Periodical Literature

Abridged Readers' Guide to Periodical Literature
Readers' Guide to Periodical Literature

Indexes

Index to Legal Periodicals & Books
Short Story Index
Book Review Digest

Sears List

Sears List of Subject Headings
Sears List of Subject Headings, Online Database
Sears: Lista de Encabezamientos de Materia

History

American Game Changers: Invention, Innovation & Transformation
American Reformers
Speeches of the American Presidents

Facts About Series

Facts About the 20th Century
Facts About American Immigration
Facts About China
Facts About the Presidents
Facts About the World's Languages

Nobel Prize Winners

Nobel Prize Winners: 1901-1986
Nobel Prize Winners: 1987-1991
Nobel Prize Winners: 1992-1996
Nobel Prize Winners: 1997-2001
Nobel Prize Winners: 2002-2018

Famous First Facts

Famous First Facts
Famous First Facts About American Politics
Famous First Facts About Sports
Famous First Facts About the Environment
Famous First Facts: International Edition

American Book of Days

The American Book of Days
The International Book of Days

Grey House Publishing | Salem Press | H.W. Wilson | 4919 Route, 22 PO Box 56, Amenia NY 12501-0056